Ireland

Altitude in metres		Motorway		Railway
2000		National Primary Road		International Border
1000		National Secondary Road		County Border
0		Regional Road	□ **BELFAST**	Capital City
Neighbouring Country	N65	Route Number	○ **Galway**	County Town

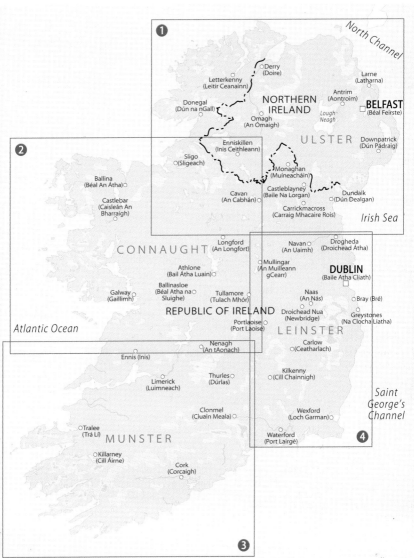

①

North Channel

Derry (Doire)

Letterkenny (Leitir Ceanainn)

Larne (Latharna)

Donegal (Dún na nGall)

Antrim (Aontroim)

BELFAST (Béal Feirste)

NORTHERN IRELAND

Omagh (An Ómaigh)

Lough Neagh

ULSTER

Downpatrick (Dún Pádraig)

②

Enniskillen (Inis Ceithleann)

Sligo (Sligeach)

Monaghan (Muineacháin)

Ballina (Béal An Átha)

Castleblayney (Baile Na Lorgan)

Dundalk (Dún Dealgan)

Castlebar (Caisleán An Bharraigh)

Cavan (An Cabhán)

Carrickmacross (Carraig Mhacaire Rois)

Irish Sea

Longford (An Longfort)

CONNAUGHT

Navan (An Uaimh)

Drogheda (Droichead Átha)

Athlone (Bail Átha Luain)

Mullingar (An Muilleann gCearr)

DUBLIN (Baile Átha Cliath)

Ballinasloe (Béal Atha na Sluighe)

Tullamore (Tulach Mhór)

Naas (An Nás)

Bray (Bré)

Galway (Gaillimh)

REPUBLIC OF IRELAND

Droichead Nua (Newbridge)

Greystones (Na Clocha Liatha)

Portlaoise (Port Laoise)

LEINSTER

Atlantic Ocean

Nenagh (An tAonach)

Carlow (Ceatharlach)

Ennis (Inis)

④

Limerick (Luimneach)

Thurles (Dúrlas)

Kilkenny (Cill Chainnigh)

Saint George's Channel

Clonmel (Cluain Meala)

Wexford (Loch Garman)

Tralee (Trá Lí)

MUNSTER

Waterford (Port Lairgé)

Killarney (Cill Áirne)

Cork (Corcaigh)

③

Celtic Sea

N

0 miles 20
0 km 20

© Crown Copyright

Ireland Handbook

Published by Footprint Handbooks
6 Riverside Court
Lower Bristol Road
Bath BA2 3DZ. England
T +44 (0)1225 469141
F +44 (0)1225 469461
Email discover@footprintbooks.com
Web www.footprintbooks.com
ISBN 1 900949 55 5
CIP DATA: A catalogue record for this
book is available from the British Library

In USA, published by
Passport Books, a division of
NTC/Contemporary Publishing Group
4255 West Touhy Avenue, Lincolnwood
(Chicago), Illinois 60712-1975, USA
T 847 679 5500 F 847 679 2494
Email NTCPUB2@AOL.COM
ISBN   0-658-00369-0
Library of Congress Catalog Card
Number on file

© Footprint Handbooks Ltd 2000
First edition

® Footprint Handbooks and the
Footprint mark are a registered
trademark of Footprint Handbooks Ltd.

The maps for the Republic of Ireland are
based on Ordnance Survey Ireland and
used by permission of the Government
Permit No 7019 © Government of Ireland.

The maps of Northern Ireland are based
on Ordnance Survey of Northern Ireland
material with permission of the
Controller of Her Majesty's Stationery
Office © Crown Copyright. Permit
number 1371. Ordnance Survey of
Northern Ireland, Colby House,
Stranmillis Court, Belfast BT9 5BJ,
T 02890 255755, F 02890 255700, Email
osni@nics.gov.uk. OSNI have large and
small scale products available in both
digital and/or paper format.

Credits

Series editors
Patrick Dawson and Rachel Fielding
Editorial
Editors: Bookcraft and Stephanie Lambe
Maps: Bookcraft and Sarah Sorenson
Production
Pre-press Manager: Jo Morgan
Typesetting: Bookcraft and
Emma Bryers
Maps: Bookcraft, Kevin Feeney,
Robert Lunn and Claire Benison
Proof reading: Bookcraft

Design
Mytton Williams

Photography & drawings
Front cover: The Travel Library
Back cover: Tony Stone Images
Inside colour section: Art Directors and
Trip Photo Library, Tony Stone Images,
Impact Photos, The Travel Library, Robert
Harding Picture Library
Illustrations: Sahra Carter
(also see Acknowledgements)

Printed and bound
in Italy by LEGOPRINT

Ireland

Footprint

Sean Sheehan and Patricia Levy

*You can leave Killarney behind you, walk …
up and up until everything touristed and
ticketed is below in the deep valley, until you
feel the colour of the mountains, soaking into
your eyes, your hair, the fragile fabric of skin,
until the silence of the high places has seeped
into your soul.*

Benedict Kiely: 'Land Without Stars' in
Capucchin Annual, 1945/6

Handbook

Ireland

DONEGAL

°Derry

DERRY

ANTRIM

TYRONE

°Omagh

BELFAST□

°Donegal

NORTHERN IRELAND

DOWN

FERMANAGH

Armagh °

Downpatrick°

°Sligo

°Enniskillen

ARMAGH

°Monaghan

SLIGO

LEITRIM

°Cavan

MONAGHAN

Dundalk°

°Carrick-on
-Shannon

CAVAN

LOUTH

MAYO

°Castlebar

ROSCOMMON

°Longford

Roscommon°

LONGFORD

°Navan

MEATH

WESTMEATH

°Mullingar

GALWAY

DUBLIN□

°Galway

OFFALY

°Tullamore

KILDARE DUBLIN

Naas°

Portlaoise°

WICKLOW

CLARE

LAOIS

Wicklow°

Ennis°

REPUBLIC OF IRELAND

°Carlow

CARLOW

°Limerick

°Kilkenny

TIPPERARY

KILKENNY

LIMERICK

°Tipperary

WEXFORD

Wexford°

°Tralee

Waterford°

KERRY

WATERFORD

CORK

Cork°

N

0 miles   20

0 km   20

Contents

1

Republic of Ireland

3

4

5

6

7

8

9

Right: the 200 metre-high limestone and shale cliffs of Moher, County Clare.

A foot in the door

Highlights

A Celtic soul? Ireland is often portrayed as a charming laboratory time capsule of pre-industrial Europe and its people as either a beguiling race of quaint and gullible country folk, fondly imbued with an affectionate lack of logic, or as irrational individuals with a disingenuous blarney. The truth is more complicated but Ireland has leapfrogged over the industrial age into a high-tech, postmodern economy, and the country is far from being a social or cultural backwater. Indeed, the very vibrancy of the people and their society is what attracts so many visitors. But Ireland remains bewitchingly different from mainstream Europe and continues, with good reason, to fascinate travellers seeking an alternative to packaged holidays and predictable tourist attractions. The image of Ireland as the last home of the Celtic soul is a fanciful one but it plays on the awareness that Ireland beckons to travellers of the 21st century. This small island perched on the fringe of Europe is felt to be home to an anarchical and poetic spirit, one profoundly at odds with the Anglo-Saxon temperament. And even though much of the unconscious beauty of Ireland's past has vanished – donkey carts loaded with turf and thatched cottages belong more to postcards than to real life – the living and talking Irish people of today have created an engaging lifestyle that will rub off on most visitors sooner or later.

Dublin The Republic of Ireland's capital city is a cracking place. James Joyce captured its unique identity some 80 years ago and you can still overhear pub conversations that sound like dialogue from one of his books. Dublin street life is vibrant, so play the *flâneur* and enjoy what comes along. The Georgian architecture, Dublin Castle, Trinity College, the Book of Kells and Christ Church Cathedral are steeped in centuries of history but the city also buzzes with a youthful modernity which is best soaked up in a comedy club or a pub gig. The country's major art galleries, museums and shops are in Dublin, rubbing shoulders with chic new restaurants and cafés for all and sundry. Love it and leave it: the Wicklow countryside is a bus ride away to the south and Newgrange, the most remarkable prehistoric sight in Europe, can be visited on a day trip.

West coast A wander around the west coast takes in spectacular coastal routes, remote offshore islands, Gaeltacht areas where Irish is spoken, village pubs, castles and fading country houses, traditional music, *craic*, unbelievable long-distance walks, and landscapes and seascapes that will astonish your senses and subdue your soul. Heady stuff, indeed, but not idle boasts. Mind you, the capricious weather can dampen your spirits as well as your wet gear and much depends on knowing where not to go. Driving around the Ring of Kerry is a waste of time, Killarney town is the pits and Inishmór, the largest of the fabled Aran islands, must now have the playwright Synge howling in his grave. But seek out a quiet backwater in west Cork, walk the western end of the Dingle Way, experience the sheer buzz of Galway City or explore the wilderness of west Mayo, and the best of what Ireland has to offer will open up before you.

Northern counties Just for a minute forget the term Northern Ireland, it's a political and not a geographical concept, and remember that County Donegal is also part of Ulster. Seen in this way the northern counties offer the traveller an engrossing amalgam of landscape and culture. Donegal is so ruggedly beautiful, so visually stunning, that we are half tempted to play down its appeal in case too many visitors go there and spoil it. The neighbouring city of Derry is remarkably charming and relaxed, a cool city indeed, and with one of the most enlightening museums anywhere in the country. The coastal route that passes the Giant's Causeway and runs down past the Antrim mountains is a succession of delightful surprises and the Mourne mountains and south Armagh are just waiting to be discovered by a new generation of travellers.

Left: the famous basalt columns of the Giant's Causeway in County Antrim. Victorian tourists would sometimes take away pieces as adornments for their houses.

Below: the limestone of the late 18th-century Custom House in Dublin which survived a burning by Republicans in 1921, and has now been fully restored.

Above: moody blues of an island landscape in lonely, wild Donegal on the northwest coast.
Left: Joyce, who was more "interested in the Dublin street names than in the riddle of the universe", knew Ormond Quay well.

Next page: riding through the shallows, Connemara, Galway. "Like breathing champagne", remarked a visitor of the air of Connemara, "silvery, level, water-striped and overflowing with light" said Limerick's Kate O'Brien.

12

Right: country
landscape in summer,
Lough Corrib, County
Galway.
Below: the passive
waters of County
Tyrone's Lough Muck:
an unlovely name for
a lovely part of
Northern Ireland.

Centre: 5000 years
old and steady as a
rock, the Poulnabrone
Dolmen glows in the
evening sunshine
when the crowds
have gone home,
Burren, County Clare.

Right: a monastery
at Glendalough,
County Wicklow, was
founded in the 6th
century by St Kevin;
the round towers
date from the
10th century.

Irish countryside

Uncrowded and unpolluted space is Ireland's great gift when looking for a beach to **Outdoor life** surf from or build sandcastles on, a river to fish, roads to cycle on, hills to climb or long-distance trails to tramp along. Throw in other watersports, birdwatching, mountain climbing, rock climbing or horse riding and you'll see how Ireland as a whole offers freely to all what has to be jealously pocketed when found in other parts of Europe. Travellers will find their own favourite haunts but walkers and climbers can happily wear out their footware in Kerry and Cork, Connemara and Clare, anglers die for north Cork and Tipperary, surfing beaches are dotted around from Portrush in the north to Wexford in the southeast and Achill in the west.

Forget the history books, heritage centres and the stately homes, and just take a **Living history** wander through any village. Ireland's history is still a living, breathing part of the landscape. It is impossible to cover much ground at all in Ireland without bumping into an historic site of some kind. The big ones have been packaged just like everywhere else but all over the country, in fields, at the side of the road, even in people's gardens, ancient raths, stone circles, dolmens, beehive huts, ancient churches, castles and Iron-Age mines sit contentedly, largely ignored by the people who gladly share their space without much thought of their significance. On the Dingle Peninsula it is almost impossible to distinguish the thousand-year-old beehive huts from the modern ones since the design is still in use for storage sheds or animal shelters. Dig even deeper into the Irish countryside and you will find elderly people who still remember stories passed down through their families for generations – stories going back to the Famine and before. Travel through the northern counties and you'll see a new history chapter being written before your eyes as some communities reassert their long-repressed culture while others readjust to a new era.

Only when the car is abandoned and a townscape is what you see departing over **Green bliss** your shoulder does Ireland's rich natural diversity come into its own. Waymarked long-distance walks cover nearly all the scenic locations: the Ulster Way in the north, the Wicklow Way south of Dublin, the Beara Way in the southwest, the Burren Way along the cliffs of Moher, the Bangor Trail in wild Mayo - these are just some of our favourites but there are many more. With a little planning it is possible to walk for a single day or cross the entire country on foot, rarely passing a vehicle. But the real beauty of Ireland is that it has what other European countries have lost - a variety of wildlife and habitats unspoiled by industrialization or even the heritage industry. The Burren is an amazing place, a limestone upland area with alpine plants uncommon in the British Isles, underground river systems and wild cliff edges supporting a diverse bird life. The desolate and unpopulated bogland of northwest Mayo is unique, despairing when the rain sets in but profound and strangely disturbing at other times. The offshore islands of the southwest are home to a mind-boggling number and variety of sea and migrant birds, as well as plants which are becoming increasingly rare in other places. Around Killarney, that nadir of tourist traps, a strange flora and fauna can be found nestling beside the tea shops and tour buses. A number of plants and insects, unknown in Britain, flourish here, while at Derrynane the near-extinct Kerry lily has its last ecological niche.

14

Right: Ireland's most famous exile, James Joyce, is now everywhere: on banknotes, in museums, and on Ireland's streets. Earl Street North, Dublin.

Below: during the summer months you are never far from music and dance festivals of one kind or another; this one is in Letterkenny in County Donegal.

Above: musicians in Shannonbridge, County Offaly. This is the real thing: unrehearsed, sometimes unsolicited, music off the cuff. *Right*: there is no shortage of pubs with music in Westport, County Mayo, and this one is owned by a musician – Matt Molloy of The Chieftains. *Next page*: 'Kelt, Briton, Roman, Saxon, Dane and Scot, time and this island tied a crazy knot'. John Hewitt's burden of history is lifted in the autumn tranquility at Glen Erriff in County Mayo.

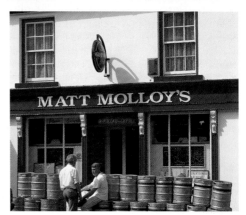

Cultural Ireland

Music

The music scene in Ireland is diverse, starting with an alarmingly unhealthy interest in awful country-and-western sounds but quickly ascending through rock bands like U2, as well as the more modern The Frames, DC and The Divine Comedy, and hitting a high with good old-fashioned traditional music from The Dubliners and the brilliant noise and musical poetry of post-Pogues Shane MacGowan and The Popes. Seek out traditional folk sessions in pubs where musicians who may be complete strangers to one another, and without a score sheet in sight, entertain themselves and anyone else who happens to be around. Doolin in County Clare is one of the places renowned for traditional music, but any town worth its tourist salt will have something on.

A literary state of mind

Lovers of literature will find associations with their favourite writers all over Ireland. A Joycean walk through the streets of the Dublin would take in major sites, obscure byways and an excursion south to Sandycove. Echoes of Gerard Manley Hopkins, Oscar Wilde, Sean O'Casey, Brendan Behan and Flann O'Brien resound in the city's pubs, parks and houses. The counties of Sligo and Galway have essential associations with W.B. Yeats, Derry with Seamus Heaney, Carrickfergus with MacNeice, County Down with the Brontë family, Monaghan with Kavanagh, west Cork with Swift, the list goes on and on.

Literary festivals and summer schools are dotted around the country during the summer months, open to all and refreshingly non-academic. Totally free is the literary state of mind that finds expression in everyday talk. People choose their words with care, savouring the good turn of phrase and recycling the best ones. Irish English has its own rhythms and patterns, less harsh than British or American English with their sharply defined meanings and questions that require a yes or no answer. Best of all is the *craic* that you can hear in the pub when a few well-oiled friends of 30 years start the 'slagging', a heartless form of teasing where anything goes. The trick is not to show you are offended by the slagging or the other person has won!

Crafts and arts

Anyone returning from a tour bus trip around Ireland could be forgiven for thinking that its chief cultural artefacts are stuffed leprechauns and tea towels with crass rhymes printed on them. But Ireland is an amazing source of small cottage industries, all producing attractive, individually designed artefacts that have found a market worldwide. While there are big factories like the famous one at Waterford making glass crystal, or the lesser known concern in Belleek creating Parian ware china, some of the best discoveries are in the tiny craft centres scattered around in places like Donegal or Enniskillen, or the larger workshops south of Kilkenny City. They are quite genuine places where craftspeople make their own designs on the premises. Some individuals have an international reputation, such as Louis Mulcahy, whose pottery at the end of the Dingle Peninsula ships his wares all over the world.

Lifestyle

Sure, internet cafés are popping up like mushrooms and cars get wheel-clamped in the capital, but at a deeper and more pleasurable level the pace of life and the instincts of many Irish people remain traditional and deeply appealing. There is a surface egalitarianism that works a disarming magic and helps make Ireland a country to explore in a quietly personal way. There is a quirkiness in the people and the landscape that is both enjoyable and fulfilling: a day of glorious sunshine is followed by a couple of days or more of misty rain; people have the time for aimless conversations but there are also glorious and unique opportunities to get away from the human and commercial world to appreciate a wild but benign nature. In the ambivalent dawn of the 21st century, a visit to Ireland must be compelling for travellers sensitive to the depressing march of an increasingly cohesive Western civilization.

Essentials

2

Essentials

Planning your trip

Where to go

Ireland is a fairly small country, about 310 miles (500 km) north to south and a little over 186 miles (300 km) west to east, and although it is not difficult to get around (see **Getting around**, page 48) there is plenty to see, and some choices have to be made about where not to go, or at least where not to dawdle. Some of the decisive factors are how long you have for your trip, what your mode of transport will be, your interests and inclinations, and whether this is a first-time trip or not. The level of your budget is a factor, but not a critical one, because costs are fairly uniform, although accommodation is pricier in Dublin than anywhere else in the country, and the wider range of options for spending money in the capital should be borne in mind. The more you travel, the higher the transport costs, and with single tickets on buses and trains often costing almost as much as return tickets this factor may be worth considering.

Length of trip If your stay is from three to six days there is little point in tearing around the country, so think about which airport to arrive at. First-time travellers will probably want to see Dublin, and international travellers may have little choice but to land there, but Cork airport is well serviced from London, as is Belfast, and with a new affordable service between London and Derry the north west of the country is more accessible than it was. With a hired car waiting at Shannon airport, the west coast is half a day's drive away (see **Getting there**, page 32, for details). With a short stay a choice probably has to be made between a city-based vacation or a short burst of rural bliss.

For a stay of a week or more it is quite feasible to take in Dublin, a few excursions such as Glendalough and Newgrange, and spend some time on the western seaboard visiting The Burren, Kerry or Galway City. With two weeks or more, depending on mode of transport, the visitor can pick and choose two, three or more locations and explore them in some depth. There would be time to skip from one end of the country to the other and briefly explore several places in between or, alternatively, focus on just one or two locations and have time for a leisurely walking or cycling trip. With a month or more it should be possible to visit most regions in the country that match your interests, and have time to slow down and get to know some places in real depth.

Modes of transport The **Getting around** section (page 48) covers the transport options in detail, but bear in mind that internal flights are limited in choice and usefulness and that the use or non-use of a car or motorcycle is likely to be a determining factor in deciding where to go. With vehicular transport the length of stay will be the only major factor limiting your choices, but reliance on public transport will necessitate a fair degree of planning if you wish to get out of the cities and big towns and optimise your time. If you're planning a walking holiday or are focused on other particular activities, such as mountain climbing or wind surfing, public transport is generally adequate, and for walking trips the use of a car can be a hindrance because there is always the need to get back to the vehicle.

Scenery & beaches The obvious destination for visitors interested in getting away from urban life and appreciating wild scenery and beaches is the west coast and County Donegal. From the Inishowen peninsula, just north of Derry, to Roaringwater Bay in West Cork, the coastline follows an almost uninterrupted margin of stunning seascapes and glorious countryside. Patches worth skipping are the stretches between the towns of Donegal and Sligo, between Rossaveal and south of Galway City, and the coastline between Ennis and Tralee; just about everywhere other than those stretches covers the best of Counties Donegal and Mayo, Connemara, The Burren and County Clare, and the peninsulas of Kerry and West Cork. This still leaves out some marvellous areas in the

Essentials

rest of the country, chief amongst which are the Antrim coastline, the Mourne Mountains in Down, and the Wicklow Mountains south of Dublin.

Ireland's islands A favourite for devotees of **nature, wildlife and solitude** are the offshore islands that pepper Ireland's coasts. The most famous are the Aran Islands in County Galway, and although fame has turned the largest of the three islands into a tourist ghetto in July and August the other two, Inishmaan and Inisheer, are always worth visiting, and the main island of Inishmór is still rewarding in off-season months. Achill Island off the west coast of Mayo is reached by a causeway and is large enough to accommodate its popularity, and Mayo also has the lesser-known and far smaller Clare Island, which is ideal for getting away from it all. The main island of the Blaskets in Kerry is glorious in spring and autumn; no accommodation and no restaurants here so if you bring a tent you'll have the place to yourself once the last boat has departed. The Skelligs, also in Kerry, are justly famous for their bird life, but it is not possible to stay overnight. County Cork has Dursey Island, reached by a cable car, off the Beara Peninsula, and like the Blaskets there is no accommodation or restaurants. Further south, reached from Baltimore, are Clear Island and Sherkin Island; both popular in the summer but never overbearingly so. The Saltee Islands in County Wexford, like Clear Island, are noted for bird life. The islands of Rathlin and Tory, off the north coast of Ireland, are easily reached and bask in the glory of not being well known and spoiled by tourism.

Activity trips Destinations for activity trips vary but **walking** and **cycling** are the most readily available and easy to arrange activities across the length and breadth of the country, though opportunities for a diverse range of **sports** are well distributed across Ireland. For details of these and other special interests see the **Special interest travel** section (p. 23). This also covers where to go for **surfing** and **scuba diving**.

Museums, galleries & stately homes Museums, galleries and stately homes are dotted around Ireland and the trick is to know which ones to skip. Dublin has major museums and galleries which should not be missed, and Derry, Strokestown in Roscommon, Enniscorthy in County Wexford, and Limerick all have excellent museums which are worth special journeys, and Glebe House and Gallery in County Donegal can probably be added to the 'essential visit' list. As a general rule, beware of places proclaiming themselves as heritage or interpretation centres. A few are awful and a waste of money, many are just plain mediocre and only suitable for a wet afternoon, some are well thought out and genuinely educational. The *Céide Fields Interpretative Centre* in north Mayo, *The Blasket Centre* on the Dingle Peninsula, and the *Cobh Heritage Centre* outside Cork are all outstandingly informative and will not disappoint.

The stately homes of the Anglo-Irish aristocracy that are open to the public are alluring places, but very often a disappointing anti-climax. Mount Stewart House in Down and Westport House in Mayo are notable failures, but *Strokestown House* in Roscommon is absolutely superb, and *Castle Coole* in Fermanagh is a wheeze.

Castles & sites of archaeological interest Castles and sites of archaeological interest are to be found everywhere, and it would be hard to think of a town in Ireland that didn't have something of interest in its vicinity. *Dublin Castle* in the capital and *Newgrange* in County Meath, the most famous of Ireland's passage graves, within striking distance of Dublin, should not be missed; *Kilkenny Castle* and the *Rock of Cashel* are equally compelling, while Cork and Kerry are choc-a-bloc with stone circles and other sites of prehistoric interest.

Cultural events For mainstream cultural events such as theatre and classical music, Dublin has the famous Abbey as well as the Gaiety, Olympia and Gate Theatres and the Dublin Theatre Festival which takes place in October. Theatres in the cities of Cork, Galway and Sligo usually feature an interesting programme, and Tralee is home to the

National Folk Theatre. The National Concert Hall and events organised by the Royal Dublin Society feature performances of classical music in the capital. Some religious sites are of major cultural interest: these include Clonmacnois in County Offaly, Glendalough in County Wicklow, Mellifont Abbey, and the High Crosses at Monasterboice in County Louth.

In Ireland socialising and partying are art forms in their own right, with a tendency to be confined within pub culture. Dublin would seem the obvious destination, but there is a hopeless shortage of pubs for the actual population (see the box on page 57) and this makes them terribly overcrowded. There is also the small problem that licensing laws tend to be enforced in the city centre. For serious socialising into the early hours of the morning head for small village pubs or just about anywhere off the beaten track. At night and during the summer, some of the off-shore islands like Clare Island or Achill, Sherkin or Inishbofin, can be so lively that it's best not to say anything more on the subject. **Festivals** are great occasions for partying because licensing hours are sometimes officially extended; the summer festival in Galway City is enormously popular with young people, while Killorglin's Puck Fair in Kerry attracts an older crowd. There are countless other festivals taking place throughout the summer in most regions of Ireland, and not all of them are of the partying kind. Visit the Irish Writers' Centre website (http://www.iol.ie/~iwc/) or the Dingle Music website (http://www.iol.ie/-dingmus/) for some inspiration.

Socialising & partying

Essentials

When to go

There is no easy answer to this question. The weather is notoriously changeable and you can have a week of mild, dry days in February or a week of depressing drizzle in August. These are exceptions, however, and extremes of wind, rain or sunshine are rare; the climate is generally mild, thanks to the benign influence of the Gulf Stream. July and August are definitely the busiest months in terms of visitor numbers, and a trip in early spring or late autumn has a lot to recommend it. Dublin is busy throughout the year, and accommodation in the capital always needs advance planning.

Some important festivals take place at fixed times of the year, so this may be a factor determining when to visit Ireland. The Galway Arts Festival takes place in late July/early August, and this is a popular time for many summer festivals across the country. Cork's International Jazz Festival takes off in October, as does Wexford's two-week Opera Festival, and these and other events are mentioned under their relevant towns and cities in the text.

In Northern Ireland the 'marching season' reaches a climax in July and, currently at least, this is a time to avoid parts of Belfast and towns like Portadown and Kilkeel. As a general rule, consider avoiding loyalist towns in July (in-your-face Union Jack flags clearly demarcate these areas) because, if nothing else, travel plans may be scuppered by having so many streets and roads blocked off to vehicular traffic.

Ireland's climate (a quip with some truth is that Ireland doesn't have a climate, just weather) is equable, with fairly uniform temperatures across the country as a whole: summer temperatures average between 15°C to 20°C while winter temperatures average between 5°C and 10°C. The coldest months are January and February, but temperatures usually stay above 3°C, it rarely snows, and in the southwest heavy frost is unusual. July and August are the warmest months, with exceptional days at this time of the year climbing into the very high 20°Cs. Across a whole year about six hours of daylight is the average, but in July and August it is still light at 2300 while in winter it can start getting dark at 1600.

Climate

They say in Galway that if you can see the Aran Islands it's going to rain, and if you can't see them then it's already raining

Average rainfall in low-lying areas is between 800 and 1,200 mm, while in mountainous areas it may exceed 2,000 mm. The southeast is the driest part of the country, with less than 750 mm. But pay no heed to the statistics, because rain is endemic to Ireland and only its unpredictability is certain. When people say it's a "soft day" this can mean anything from light drizzle to continuous rain. Winter on the western seaboard can be exhilarating, to put it mildly, when an Atlantic storm that has been brewing up for thousands of miles across the ocean finally hits land in the shape of western Ireland. Hurricane-force storms are not unknown, 15m-high waves lash the rocks, and cuts to the power supply are predictable.

Once you are in Ireland, detailed national and sea area forecasts are available on RTE Radio 1 (89FM) at 0602, 0755, 1253 and 2355.

What to take

The two essentials are a state of mind that won't get you down if it rains and wet weather gear for the times when it does rain. Health insurance is advisable for non-EU travellers (see **Health**, page 60) and a basic first aid kit should include pills for possible hangovers and/or stomach upsets. Walkers should be prepared for blisters and small cuts, and a compass is advisable for walks in mountainous areas. A sleeping bag and/or a sheet with a pillow cover is a very good idea for stays in hostels. Other useful items, depending on circumstances, might include an adapter plug for electrical appliances, a small torch and sunglasses.

Tours and tour operators

Popular regions of Ireland, such as Killarney, the Burren, the Aran Islands and Connemara, are well served by local tour companies, and from Dublin local tours run to Newgrange, the Wicklow mountains and further afield. *Iarnród Éireann,* the national railway, organises a variety of guided one-day tours to Connemara, Cork, Kerry, Dingle, Burren, Leitrim, Wexford, Waterford, Kilkenny, and Antrim and Donegal. For full details contact *Railtours Ireland*, 58 Lower Gardiner St, Dublin 1, T01-8560045.

The following companies offer a variety of tours and holidays, including all or some of accommodation, activity holidays including angling, city and rural breaks, cycling, golf and walking, car hire, air tickets, donkey rambles, river cruising, horse-drawn gypsy caravans and self-catering.

Tour operators in mainland Britain offering holidays in Ireland *Aer Lingus Holidays*, T020-88994747 and 0645-737747; *Cresta Holidays*, Tabley Court, Victoria St. Altrincham, Cheshire WA14 IEZ, T0161-9269999; *Enjoy Ireland Holidays*, Suite 425, Glenfield Park II, Blackburn, Lancashire BBI 5QH. T01254-692899, F01254-693075; *Flanagan & Sons*, 115 Radford Rd, Coventry, T0500-026385; *Gerry Feeney Travel*, 8 Centre Way, High Rd, Ilford IGI IND, T020-85145141; *Irish Ferries Holidays*, Reliance House, Water St, Liverpool, L2 8TP, T0990-171717, F0151-2551123; *Leisure Breaks & Golf*, 33 Dovedale Rd, Liverpool LI8 5EP, T0151-7345200; *Rural Cottages Holidays*, St Anne's Court, 59 North St, Belfast BT1 1NB; *Slattery's*, 162 Kentish Town Rd, London NW5 2AG, T0800-515900, F020-74821206, ireland@slattery.com *Stena Line Holidays*, Charter House, Park St, Ashford, Kent TN24 8EX, T0990-747474; *Swansea Cork Ferries*, King's Dock, Swansea, West Glamorgan, Wales, T01792-456116.

Tour operators in the USA *Adventures Abroad*, T1-800-6653998, http://www. adventures-abroad.com; *CIE International Tours*, T1-800-2486832, http://www. cietours.com; *Collette Tours*, T1-800-2488986; *Destinations Ireland*, T1-800-8321848, info@digbtravel.com, http://www.digbtravel.com/tours; *Distinctive Journeys*, T1-

800-9222060; *Irish American International Tours*, T1-800-6330505; *Kenny Tours*, T1-800-6481492; *Saga Holidays*, T1-800-3430273.

Tour operators in Australia *Adventure World*, 73 Walker St, North Sydney, T02-99567766; *Eblana Travel*, 4th Level, 67 Castlereagh St, Sydney, T02-92328144.

Special interest travel

Walking is the least expensive and most ecologically sound activity worth pursuing in Ireland, and there are now nearly 30 waymarked trails covering over 1,492 miles (2,300 km) as well as countless local walking routes in scenic areas. Worth consulting are some of the specialist walking guidebooks that cover the whole country but, unless walking is going to be your sole activity for a fair length of time, they are a less worthwhile investment than some of the smaller books that focus on popular walking areas and which are ideal for one-day walks if staying a while in a particular region (see **Further Reading**, page 60, and on the web http://www.obrien.ie for one of the main publishers). Bord Fáilte (the Irish Tourist Board) sells an inexpensive *Walking Ireland* booklet that describes each of the waymarked Ways and gives contact details for further information, accommodation, travel and maps.

Walking
The Northern Ireland Tourist Board dispense a useful booklet detailing 14 walks on the Ulster Way, accompanied with maps and sources of information

Essentials

Detailed information about some of the more popular long-distance walks, such as the Kerry Way, the Beara Way, the Dingle Way and the Sheep's Head Way, are included in this book, and shorter details are given of some of the others (see box on page 23). To complete all or part of the best waymarked trails all that is really needed are the relevant *Ordnance Survey Discovery Maps* at a scale of 1:50,000 (2.5 in to 1 mile/2 cm to 1 km); they show the routes of the Ways. *EastWest Mapping*, Ballyredmond, Enniscorthy, County Wexford (T&F054-77835) also publishes 1:50,000 scale maps of particular Ways. It is worth checking with the *Ordnance Survey Service*, Phoenix Park, Dublin 8 (T01-8206100; F01-8204156) or *Ordnance Survey of Northern Ireland*, Colby House, Stranmillis Court, Belfast BT9 5BJ (T028-90661244) to see which is the latest update available and whether the route of the Way is included. Tourist offices in Dublin, Belfast, Cork and Galway, as well as smaller local tourist offices in the relevant areas, also sell mostly inexpensive guides covering a particular Way, such as those published by EastWest Mapping, and these can be a useful supplement to the Ordnance Survey maps. The Ordnance Survey maps are available in the big bookshops in Dublin, as well as the *Government Publications Sales Office Bookshop*, Sun Alliance House, Molesworth St, Dublin 2 (T01-6613111), and are often available in local bookshops and tourist offices around the country. For walks requiring overnight stays it is essential to have accommodation booked in advance.

Organized walking holidays, usually including airport transfers and luggage transport between accommodation stops, are available through various companies, including *Irish Ways*, The Old Rectory, Ballycanew, Gorey, County Wexford, T055-27479, F055-27655/27479, irishways@iol.ie and *Go Ireland*, Killorglin, County Kerry, T066-62094; freephone 0800-371203 (from the UK), 800-5551864 (from the USA), and 0130-829468 (from Germany), F066-62098, goireland@fexco.ie http://www.goireland.fexco.ie. Another company which, like Go Ireland, specializes in the western counties is *South West Walks*, 40 Ashe Street, Tralee, County Kerry, T066-28733, F066-28762, sww@iol.ie http://www.limerick.ireland.com/activity-holidays/ See also http://www.hikethoseheights.com for hillwalking in Cork and Kerry from Kinsale.

For specialist walking holidays in the Burren contact *Burren Walking Holidays*, Carrigann Hotel, Lisdoonvarna, County Clare, T065-74036, F065-74567; and *Fertile Rock Study Tours*, Station Road, Lahinch, County Clare, T&F065-81168. For hikes on the Iveragh peninsula, including guided trips to Ireland's highest mountain, contact *Wilderness Tours*, Climber's Inn, Glencar, County Kerry, T066-60101, F066-60104, climbers@iol.ie http://www.iol.ie/~climbers.

Essentials

Walking the Way

To give some idea of the walking possibilities here are brief details of some of the best Ways:

Wicklow Way Ireland's first long-distance trail is 82 miles (132 km) in length and starts in south Dublin and finishes in Clonegal in the east of county Carlow. The entire Way would take at least 10 days but it is easy to choose a shorter section and variety of terrain is a feature of the Way; longest one-day stage is 14 miles (22 km). Map guides are available (see page 186) and Ordnance Survey Maps Nos 50, 56 and 62 cover the entire route.

Kerry Way Through and around the Iveragh peninsula and infinitely more enjoyable than driving around the Ring of Kerry. Total length is 134 miles (214 km) and the longest stage is 15 miles (24 km). Some sections are more enjoyable than others (see page 364); map guides are available in Killarney or Kenmare and Ordnance Survey Maps Nos 78, 83, 84 and 85 show the route.

Beara Way Spectacular in places (see page 329) as it weaves its way around the Beara peninsula in Kerry connecting Kenmare, Glengarriff and Castletownbere, with Dursey Island thrown in for good measure. Total distance is 120 miles (196 km); longest stage is 14 miles (23 km). Ordnance Survey Maps Nos 78, 84 and 85.

Dingle Way Another circular route, this time around the Dingle peninsula, with the western end of the Way far more fulfilling than the east (see page 385). Total length 95 miles (153 km) and longest stage is 15 miles (24 km). Ordnance Survey Maps Nos 70 and 71.

Sheep's Head Way Starts and ends in Bantry in West Cork with some spectacular views of Bantry Bay and Dunmanus Bay along the way (see page 321). Total length is 55 miles (88 km) and longest stage is 10 miles (16 km). Ordnance Survey Maps Nos 85 and 88, and a local map and guide is available.

Burren Way Only 22 miles (35 km) but covering the jagged terrain of this unique landscape noted for its geological features, archaeological remains, special flora and the magnificent Cliffs of Moher. Longest stage is 12.5 miles (20 km) and Ordnance Survey Maps No 51 covers the route.

Western Way Starts at Oughterard in County Galway, and follows the shore of Lough Corrib and then through mountain ranges and down into the narrow valley of Killary Harbour. This leg is 31 miles (50 km)

British tour operators who also cover walking holidays include **Enjoy Ireland Holidays**, suite 425, Glenfield Park 2, Blackburn BB1 5HQ. T01254-692899, F01254-693075; **PAB Travel**, T0121-3777080. In the USA, **Backroads**, T1-800/GO-ACTIVE, 4622848, http://www.backroads.com specializes in walking and cycling holidays.

For walking holidays in Northern Ireland contact **Enjoy Holidays** above, Murphy's Travel, 12 Belvoir Close, Belfast BT8 4PL, T028-90693232, **Celtic Journeys Walking Holidays**, 111 Whitepark Rd, Ballycastle, BT54 6LR, T028-20769651, or **Wrightlines**, Old Mill, Banbridge, T028-40662126 for self-guided walking holidays in the Mournes.

Walking World Ireland is a monthly magazine that carries detailed maps and commentary on walks all over the country.; it is available from newsagents or on subscription from 288 Harold's Cross Road, Dublin 6 (T01-4923030; F01-4923089).

Cycling There are very few motorways in Ireland so nearly all the roads can be cycled. There is a vast network of quiet country roads, and distances between towns and villages are never prohibitively long. Bicycles can brought to Ireland by air or boat, but check with your airline or ferry company for their policy and prices. Within Ireland, north or south, it is possible to carry bicycles on buses, and on nearly all train routes (but not the DART system around Dublin); prices vary, so always check.

Bicycles can be hired on a daily or weekly basis in most towns across Ireland: the daily rate varies from IR£7 to IR£10; weekly rates are around IR£35, plus a returnable in total. The second leg runs from Killary Harbour across county Mayo to the Ox Mountains near the Sligo border. Superb variety of terrains, including the unique boglands of Mayo. Total length of this second leg is 110 miles (177 km) and Ordnance Survey Maps Nos 23, 24, 30, 37 and 38 are required to cover the whole route. Local map guides available.

Grand Canal Way Perfect for the beginner, being flat all the way as it follows the canal; the starting point is reached by bus from Dublin to Lucan or Milltown. Total distance is 71 miles (114 km) and the longest stage is 18 miles (29 km).

Royal Canal Way A walk along the towpath of the Royal Canal from Dublin for 48 miles (77 km), eventually linking up with the River Shannon at Clondra in County Longford. The longest stage is 15.5 miles (25.5 km) and Ordnance Survey Maps Nos 12, 13 and 16 are needed. Information on this Way and the Grand Canal Way from **Waterways Service**, Department of Arts, Heritage, Gaeltacht and the Islands, 51 St Stephens's Green, Dublin 2 (T01-6613111).

Ballyhoura Way A 50-mile (80 km) walk between Limerick Junction, just north of Tipperary town, and St. John's Bridge (nearest town is Kanturk in north Cork). The longest stage is 15 miles (24 km) and although parts of the Way are through boring forestry plantations this is compensated by the route over Castle Philip and through the Ballyhoura Country Park. Ordnance Survey Maps Nos 65, 66, 73 and 74.

Lough Derg Way Lough Derg is one of the main lakes on the River Shannon, and the best part of the walk is along the eastern shores of the lake. Total distance is only 32 miles (52 km) and the longest stage is 11 miles (18 km). Contact **Shannon Development**, Shannon Town Centre, Shannon, County Clare, T061-361555, who also have information on other walks in the region.

Ulster Way The total length is around 560 miles (900 km), so choices have to be made. Sections following the north Antrim coast, the Glens of Antrim, and the Mourne mountains (called the Mourne Trail) are the best, plus the 69-mile (111 km) Donegal section. Advance planning is necessary: The Northern Ireland Tourist Board has information on sections and Paddy Dillon's book (see page 65) should be consulted.

deposit. **Raleigh Ireland** have dealers around the country, some of whom participate in a scheme for collecting and delivering from different agents, and their head office is at Raleigh House, Kylemore Rd, Dublin 10 (T01-6261333). **Irish Cycle Hire**, Mayoralty St, Drogheda, Co Louth, T041-41067 and 1-800-298100, F041-35369, is a smaller outfit who also allow collection and delivery from different agents around the country. There are also countless independent operators who operate on a local basis and details are given under the particular town. **The Federation of Irish Cyclists** can be contacted at 619 North Circular road, Dublin 1. T01-8551522. **Shannon Development**, Shannon Town Centre, Shannon, County Clare, T061-361555, have useful free leaflets detailing cycling tours in the region. The Northern Ireland Tourist Board issue a very useful **Information Guide to Cycling** with maps for suggested routes, details of bike hire places, and operators offering package holidays.

Organised cycling holidays are operated by a number of companies who include all or some services like bike hire, airport transfers, luggage storage and transport, booked accommodation, tours for groups or individuals, plus maps and route descriptions. For an idea of prices, **Irish Cycling Safaris** (see below) cost IR£330 per person per week and covers seven nights hotel/guesthouse accommodation, bicycle rental, tour guide and luggage van.

Essentials

 A genealogical trip

If you are planning a genealogical fieldtrip it helps enormously to carry out some preliminary research before reaching Ireland. Try to establish the county and townland from which your ancestors departed plus full names, maiden as well as married ones, and dates of birth, marriage and death. Sources worth exploring in your own country include birth, marriage and death records, census returns, immigration and naturalization papers, and ships' passenger lists. For general information and details of local centres within Ireland contact the **Genealogical Office**, 2 Kildare St, Dublin 2, T01-603-0200, or **The General Register Office**, Oxford House, 49 Chichester St, Belfast BT1 4HL, T028-90252000. Central records prior to 1922 are held in Dublin but the Belfast General Register Office will arrange for searches to be made of births, marriages or deaths in Northern Ireland before 1922. **The Public Record Office of Northern Ireland**, 66 Balmoral Ave, Belfast BT9 6NY, T028-90251318, F028-90255999, does not conduct research but visitors can make their own searches there.

There are various research companies that will carry out research for a fee and one of the more well-established companies is **Hibernian Research Company**, PO Box 3097, Dublin 6, T01-4966522, F01-4973011. Bord Fáilte have a booklet, **Tracing your Ancestors in Ireland**, which is packed with contact addresses.

Contacts *Go Ireland* in Britain and *Backroads* in the USA (see under Walking, page 24). *Celtic Cycling* (specializing in the southeast), Lorum Old Rectory, Bagenalstown, County Carlow, T0503-75282, F0503-75455, cycling@indigo.ie *Celtic Trails*, 28 Upper Fitzwilliam St, Dublin 2. T01-6619546, F01-6619547, celtictrails@compuserve. com, http://www.celtictrails.com *Classic Adventures*, in the USA, T1-800/7778090. *Irish Cycling Safaris*, Belfield House, UCD, Dublin 4. T01-2600749, F01-7061168, ics@kerna.ie http://www.kerna.ie/ics/ *Kingfisher Cycle Trail*, Tourist Information Centre, Wellington Road, Enniskillen, County Fermanagh BT74 7EF. T028-66320121, F028-66325511 *McCycle Tours*, 2 Brookesborough Rd, Maguiresbridge, County Fermanagh, BT94 4LR. T028-6621749 *Shannon Cycle Centre*, Clonlohan, Newmarket-on-Fergus, County Clare. T061-361280, F061-360686, bikeirl@iol.ie http://www.iol.ie/~bikeirl/ *South East Cycle Tours* (specialising in the south-east), 1 Mary Street, Enniscorthy, County Wexford, T&F054-33255, seastcyc@iol.ie *Wrightlines*, The Old Mill, Ballydown, Banbridge, County Down BT32 5JN. T028-40662126.

Water sports Ireland has some magnificent beaches, and while most are safe for **swimming** there are some that can be dangerous. Most of these are mentioned in the text but it is always worth checking, especially if no one else is in the water. **Windsurfing** is growing in popularity. A list of recognised windsurfing schools in the Republic is available from the *Irish Sailing Association*, 3 Park Rd, Dun Laoghaire, Dublin, T01-2800239, F01-2807558, isa@iol.ie http://www.sailing.org/isa/

Surfing beaches in the west of Ireland include Achill Island, Easkey in county Sligo, and Spanish Point and Lahinch in Clare. Further south, there is Castlegregory on the north side of the Dingle Peninsula, Inch on the south side, Caherdaniel on the Iveragh Peninsula and Barley Cove on the Mizen Peninsula. In the southeast, Rosslare Strand in County Wexford, and Dunmore East, Tramore, Ballinacourty and Dungarvan in County Waterford are all noted for their surfing beaches. In the north, Portrush on the north Antrim coast is the main surfing centre and here, as in most of the other areas (but not Barley Cove), it is possible to hire equipment and garner local information. *The Irish Surfing Association* is based at Tirchonaill St, Donegal, T073-21053.

Scuba diving   Dive centres in Ireland are listed below. While all of them have bottles and all but two of them (Baltimore Diving and Dry Suit Repairs) hire out equipment, it is advisable to contact them first. *Subsea* is Ireland's diving magazine and an annual subscription for four issues is IR£12; available from the *Irish Underwater Council*, 78A Patrick St, Dun Laoghaire, Co Dublin, T01-2844601, F01-2844602, scubairl@indigo.ie http://www.indigo.ie/scuba-irl **Diving centres** *Aquaventures Ltd*, The Stone House, Baltimore, Co Cork, T028-20511, F028-20511 *Ballinskellig Watersports*, Dungegan, Ballinskelligs, Co Kerry, T066-9479182 *Baltimore Diving & Watersports*, Baltimore, West Cork, T028-20300, F028-20300, http://scuba/baltimore/diving.htm *Bantry Bay Divers*, Main St, Glengarriff, Co Cork, T027-51310, F027-51310 *Clew Bay Adventures*, Quay Cottage, Westport Harbour, Co Mayo, T098-26412 or 25412, F098-28120 *Cuan na Farraige*, Aughoose, Pullathomas, Ballina, Co Mayo, T097-87800, F097-87800 *Dry Suit Repairs*, 199 Newvale Cottages, Library Road, Shankill, Co Dublin, T01-2721255, Cnoc Ard Yard, Oysterhaven, Co Cork, T021-770748 or 088-2752428, F021-770748 *D.V. Diving*, 138 Mountstewart Rd, Newtownards, Co Down BT22 2E5, T01247-464671, dvdivingw@ dial.pipex.com *Kinsale Dive Centre*, Castlepark Marina Centre, Kinsale, Co Cork, T021-774959, F021-774958, maritime@indigo.ie *Malinmore Adventure Centre*, Glencolmcille, Co Donegal, T073-30311, F073-30123, http://homepage.tinet.ie/ ~nmv *North Irish Lodge*, Self Catering Cottages and Dive Shop, 161 Low Rd, Islandmagee, Co Antrim, BT40 3RF, T028-93382246 or UK T0411-190130, F080-1960382246 *Oceantec*, 10 Marine Terrace, Dun Laoghaire, T01-2801083, F01-2843885 *Schull Watersport Centre Ltd*, The Pier, Schull, Co Cork, T028-28554, F028-28554 *Scubadive West*, Lettergesh, Renvyle, Co Galway, T095-43922, F095-43923 *Skellig Aquatics* Caherdaniel, Co Kerry, T066-9475277, F066- 9475277 *Valentia Island Seasports*, Knightstown, Valentia Island, Co Kerry, T066- 9476204 and 087-2420714, F066-9476367 *Wexford Diving Centre* (Sundancer II), Riverstown, Murrinstorm, Co Wexford, T053-39373 and 087-2259580, F053- 39373.

Sailing   Contact the *Irish Sailing Association* (ISA), 3 Park Rd, Dun Laoghaire, Dublin, T01-2800239, F01-2807558, isa@iol.ie http://www.sailing.org/isa/ They provide literature on visitor moorings as well as information on ISA-approved sailing programmes in dinghies, keel boats, catamarans and powerboats.

Canoeing   Contact the *Irish Canoe Union*, House of Sports, Long Mile Rd, Walkinstown, Dublin 12, T01-4509838. Canoeing trips are run by *Shannon Adventure Canoeing Holidays*, The Marina, Banagher, Co Offaly, T&F0509-51411, and *Tiglin Adventure Centre*, Ashford, Co Wicklow, T0404-40169.

Water skiing   Contact the *Irish Water-Ski Federation*, 29 Hermitage Rd, Lucan, Co Dublin, T01-6240526.

Ireland's reputation as Europe's last unspoilt fishing location is built on its unpolluted **Fishing** waters, a plenitude of fish-bearing rivers, miles of coastline and hundreds of game fishing lakes. There are superb opportunities for game and coarse angling, as well as sea angling. In the Republic, salmon and trout fisheries are either privately owned or managed by the state or angling clubs and organizations. Permits are required, the cost of which varies from IR£5 to IR£50 per day depending on the location. A state national licence is also required for salmon and sea trout fishing: a 21 day licence costs IR£10, a daily license is IR£3. These are obtainable at local tackle shops, from the *Western Regional Fisheries Board*, The Weir Lodge, Earl's Island, Galway, T091-563118, F091-566335, wrfb@iol.ie or from one of the other regional boards in Ballyshannon, T072-51435, Ballina, T096-22788, Limerick, T061-55171, Macroom, T026-41222, or Clonmel, T052-23624. Licences are not needed for brown trout, rainbow trout, coarse fishing or sea angling.

Essentials

In Northern Ireland a rod licence is required, costing about £10 for 8 days. For the Foyle area this is obtainable from the *Foyle Fisheries Commission*, 8 Victoria Rd, Derry BT47 2AB, T01504-42100; for other regions from the *Fisheries Conservancy Board*, 1 Mahon Rd, Portadown, Craigavon, County Armagh, T01762-334666. A permit is also required, costing £8 for one day or £32.50 for 8 days, obtainable from the *Department of Agriculture*, Dundonald House, Upper Newtownlands Rd, Belfast BT4 3SB, T028-90520100.

Bord Fáilte publish a useful *Angling in Ireland* booklet with practical information about accommodation and charter-boat operators, and separate booklets on sea angling and coarse angling. Gill & Macmillan publish three guides, *Game Angling*, *Coarse Angling* and *Sea Angling*, which cover the best places for angling in the Republic. The regional Fisheries Boards are also worth contacting for information and literature on their areas: *Western Regional Fisheries Board*, The Weir Lodge, Earl's Island, Galway. T091-563118, F091-566335, wrfb@iol.ie *The North-Western Regional Fisheries Board*, Ard na Rí House, Abbey St, Ballina, County Mayo. T096-22788, F096-70543, nwrfb@iol.ie; *The Shannon Regional Fisheries Board*, Thomond Weir, Limerick. T061-455171, F096-326533. *Ireland West Tourism*, Áras Fáilte, Galway, T091-563081, F091-565201, dispense a useful brochure, *The Coarse Angler's Paradise*, covering Counties Galway, Mayo and Roscommon and including practical information on suitable accommodation. *Game Angling Ireland West* is a similar brochure available from the Fishery Boards. *The Great Fishing Houses of Ireland*, PO Box 6375, Dublin 4, T01-6688278, F01-6605566, issues a booklet with details of hotels specializing in fishing holidays. These include the Pontoon Bridge Hotel (see page 492) which runs courses for beginners as well as catering to old hands.

Many of the general tour operators, see above, organize specialist fishing packages and in the USA there is also *Fishing International*, T1-800/9504242.

Golf There are more golf courses per head of population in Ireland than anywhere else in Europe, ranging from lush parkland courses in the east to rugged and challenging links courses on the western coastline. Contact Bord Fáilte and the Northern Ireland Tourist Board for general literature and information on specialist golfing packages. http://www.golfing-ireland.com is worth looking at and South East Tourism in Waterford dispense a useful *Golfers' Guide* with practical information on local golf courses and accommodation. Green fees range enormously: at Hotel Carrigart in County Donegal residents can play for free on a links course, while at Mount Juliet in County Kilkenny (designed by Jack Nicklaus) residents can expect to pay IR£45 and non-residents IR£70. Average fees are in the IR£10 to IR£20 range.

Equestrian The possibilities range from a small farm with horses to hire by the hour to top-notch riding establishments offering post-to-post trail riding, instruction in show jumping, dressage and polocrosse. Contact Bord Fáilte and the Northern Ireland Tourist Board for literature and information. *Equestrian Holidays Ireland* issue a booklet with details of riding establishments in Ireland; contact them at Whispering Pines, Crosshaven, County Cork, T021-831950, F021-831679, info@ehi.ie www.ehi.ie Other contacts are *The Association of Irish Riding Establishments*, 11 Moore Park, Newbridge, Co Kildare, T045-431584, F045-435103; *The Association of Irish Riding Clubs*, 8 Main St, Bray, Co Wicklow, T01-2860196; *The Irish Pony Club*, Clashwilliam, Gowran, Co Kilkenny, T056-26186, F056-26443, http://www.@-maginet.com/ponyclub/ The southeast is especially resourceful in this area and a guide to *Equestrian Activity in Ireland's South East* is available from tourist offices in that region.

At Colmcille in Co Donegal there are Irish language courses for adults as well as cultural **Culture**
activity holidays with separate week-long programmes in bodhrán and flute playing,
Donegal dances, marine painting, archaeology, Celtic pottery, tapestry weaving and
some other pursuits. For a brochure write to *Oideas Gael*, Gleann Cholm Cille, Co Dhún na
nGall, T073-30248, F073-30348, oideasgael@iol.ie http://oideas-gael.com

There are various summer schools that can provide a focus for cultural, and
especially language and literary interests. For details of the *James Joyce Summer
School* that lasts a week and takes place in Dublin each July write to Helen Gallagher,
Newman House, St Stephen's Green, Dublin, T01-7068480. For the *Yeats International
Summer School* in Sligo each July, another annual week-long event, write to Sheila
McCabe, Hawk's Well Theatre, Sligo, T071-42693, F071-42780. For the *Synge and
Parnell Summer Schools* in Co Wicklow see page 188.

Finding out more

A great deal of tourist information is available from the tourist boards and their
websites. If contacting Bord Fáilte (The Irish Tourist Board) or the Northern Ireland
Tourist Board, be as specific as possible, because they have far too much literature to
send out everything to everybody.

Bord Fáilte is the official Irish tourist organisation. Their main address in Ireland is PO **Bord Fáilte**
Box 273, Dublin 8, T01-6024000, F01-6024100, user@irishtouristboard.ie In other
countries Bord Fáilte's offices are, in Britain: 150 New Bond St, London WIY OAQ, T020-
74933201/75180800, F020-74939065, info@irishtouristboard.co.uk There is also All-
Ireland information at the Britain Visitor Centre, 1 Regent St, London SW1Y 4XT. T0870-
1555250. In the USA: 345 Park Ave, New York, NY 10154, T0212-4180800, F0212-
3719052. In Canada: 120 Eglinton Ave, East Suite 500, Toronto M4P IE2, T0416-4873335,
F0416-3223129/ 4870803. In Australia: 5th Level, 36 Carrington St, Sydney NSW
2000, T02-92996177, F02-92996323, ib@next.com.au In New Zealand: Dingwall
Building, 87 Queen St, Auckland 1, T09-3793708. In Holland: Het Nationaal Bureau
voor Toerisme, Spuistraat 104, 1012 VA Amsterdam, T020-6223101, F020-6208089,
info@irishtouristboard.nl In Germany: Irische Fremdenverkehrszentrale, Unter-
mainanlage 7, D60329 Frankfurt/Main, T069-92318550, F069-92318588, info@
irishtouristboard.de In France: Office du Tourisme Irlandais, 33 Rue de Miromesnil,
75008 Paris, T01-53431212, F01-47420164, info@irlande-tourisme.fr

The *Northern Ireland Tourist Board*'s head office is at 59 North St, Belfast BT1 1NB, **Northern**
T028-90231221, F028-90240960. In Britain its address is 24 Haymarket, London SW1Y **Ireland Tourist**
4DG, T020-77669920, F020-77669929; there is also All-Ireland Information at the **Board**
Britain Visitor Centre (see above); in the USA: 551 Fifth Ave, Suite 701, New York, NY
10176, T0212-9220101, F0212-9220099; in Canada: 111 Avenue Rd, Suite 450, Toronto,
Ontario M5R 3J8, T0416-9256368, F0416-9612175; in Australia and New Zealand the
NITB shares offices with Bord Fáilte (see above). In Germany the NITB is at
Taunusstrasse 52-60, 60329 Frankfurt, T69-234504, F069-233480; and in France at 3
rue de Pontoise, 78100 St Germain-en-Laye, T01-39219380, F01-39219390.

You will find a growing number of informative websites about Ireland on the World **Websites**
Wide Web. Among the most useful are *Bord Fáilte*'s site at http://www.ireland.travel.ie
and the *Northern Ireland Tourist Board*'s at http://www.ni-tourism.com For cultural
life go to www.bess.tcd.ie/ireland.htm, and for Irish cuisine www.irishfood.com is a
well-designed site. Jobs in Ireland can be found at http://www.exp.ie, and the
Republic of Ireland government website is at http://www.irlgov.ie A site devoted to
Irish goods is http://www.shopirish.com, while the *US Irish Network* has a site at
http://www.usairish.net

Essentials

Consulates and Embassies

Irish

Great Britain, 17 Grosvenor Place, London SW1X 7HR, T020-72459033, F020-72456910, http://www.irlgov.ie/iveagh
USA (Washington), 2234 Massachusetts Ave NW, Washington, DC 20008. T202-4623939
USA (New York), 345 Park Ave, 17th Floor, New York, NY 10154. T212-3192555
USA (San Francisco), 44 Montgomery St, Suite 3830, San Francisco, CA 94104. T415-3924214
USA (Boston), 535 Boylston St, Boston, MA 02116. T617-2679330
USA (Chicago), 400 N Michigan Ave, Chicago, IL 60611. T312-3371868

Australia, 20 Arkana St, Yarralumla, Canberra, ACT 2600. T02-62733022
New Zealand, 2nd Floor, Dingwall Building, Queen St, Auckland. T09-3022867

British

Ireland, 29 Merrion Rd, Dublin 4. T01-2053700, F01-2053885
USA, 3100 Massachusetts Ave NW, Washington DC 20008. T202-5886500
Australia, Commonwealth Ave, Yarralumla, Canberra, ACT 2600. T02-62571982
New Zealand, 44 Hill St, Wellington. T04-4726049

Before you travel

Getting in

Passports All visitors to either the Republic or Northern Ireland require a valid passport, except British nationals. Holders of UK passports not born in Great Britain or Northern Ireland should bring their passport, and even British nationals should consider bringing theirs because some form of valid ID is required for changing travellers' cheques and perhaps also for cases of emergency medical treatment.

Visas EU nationals can stay in the Republic indefinitely without a visa; travellers from the USA, Canada, Australia and New Zealand can stay for three months without a visa, and this can usually be extended by making an application at the local main Garda Síochána (police) station. In Dublin, go to the *Aliens Registration Office*, Harcourt St, T01-4755555. Nationals of other countries should contact the Irish Embassy for details about visa regulations.

EU nationals can stay in Northern Ireland without a visa; citizens of the USA, Canada, Australia and New Zealand can stay for up to six months without a visa, though evidence of a return ticket and sufficient funds may be required. For an extension of the six-month rule write in advance to the Undersecretary of State, Home Office, 40 Wellesley Rd, Croydon CR92BY England. Nationals of other countries should contact the British Consular office for details about visa regulations.

Customs There are no customs restrictions affecting travel within the EU, and there are no longer any duty free allowances. Pets can be taken freely between Britain, Northern Ireland and the Republic, but strict quarantine regulations are in force for pets from any other part of the world. USA visitors can take home $400 worth of goods per person, Canadians $500.

Vaccinations None are compulsory or even necessary unless arriving from an infected area. See also the **Health** section (page 60).

Money

In the Republic the currency is based around the Irish pound, called the *punt*, with IR£20, IR£10 and IR£5 notes most commonly used. IR£50 and IR£100 notes are rumoured to exist but are rarely seen; the bulk of them have probably been stashed away by corrupt politicians. The currency is decimal-based and coins come in the form of IR£1, 50p, 20p, 10p, 5p, 2p and 1p.

Currency
See inside front cover for further details of exchange rates.

In Northern Ireland, British currency is used, with the same denomination notes and coins as in Ireland, plus a £2 coin. However, notes are also issued by Northern Ireland banks and, while these are interchangeable with the standard British notes within Northern Ireland, they are *not* generally accepted in mainland Britain other than through banks.

Until the euro comes into circulation in both the Republic and Northern Ireland (in 2002 for the Republic and a date still to be decided for Britain), the currencies of the Republic and Northern Ireland are not interchangeable, and at the current rate of exchange one pound sterling is worth around IR£1.30.

European Monetary Union (EMU) currency comes into use on 1 January 2002 in the Republic of Ireland, and from 1 July 2002 it will be the only legal currency in the Republic and other EMU countries. The new currency, the euro, consists of 100 cents . Notes will be 5, 10, 20 50, 100, 200 and 500; coins will be 1, 2, 5, 10, 20 and 50 cents and 1 euro.

Visa and Mastercard/Access credit cards are widely accepted in the Republic and Northern Ireland and, if you have a personal identification number (PIN), cash withdrawals can be made using them from automatic teller machines (ATMs) which are found in all towns. International money systems, like Cirrus and Plus, are linked to ATMs. Check with your bank or credit card company regarding which ATMs and banks you can use and what charges might be applicable.

Credit cards

UK travellers can use cashcards to withdraw money direct from accounts in the Republic and Northern Ireland, but check with your bank or building society regarding which banks or building societies to use and what charges may be applicable.

American Express and Diners' Club cards, especially the latter, are not as readily accepted as credit cards.

Using travellers' cheques is the safest way to carry money and all the main brands, Thomas Cook, Visa and American Express, are readily accepted at banks across the whole of Ireland. If travelling between the Republic and Northern Ireland it makes sense to have them issued in sterling, but US dollar cheques are just as readily accepted. As always, keep a record of the cheque numbers separate from the cheques themselves so as to facilitate a refund should they get lost or stolen. Travellers' cheques are rarely directly accepted in lieu of cash. A commission charge is made when cashing traveller cheques, but this may be avoided by cashing American Express or Thomas Cook cheques at their own offices in Dublin (see page 147) or Belfast (page 613). Eurocheques can also be cashed across Ireland but a Eurocheque card is needed.

Travellers' cheques

The best exchange rates are available at banks; the worst are across the counter in hotels. Bureaux de change, found at airports and ferry terminals, city centres and some key tourist areas like Killarney, are useful when banks are closed, but the rate will not be as good. In the Republic banks generally open Monday-Friday 1000-1600, but in many towns they may close between 1230 and 1330. On Thursdays banks often stay open until 1700 or sometimes 1900. In Northern Ireland normal banking hours are 0930-1630 (0930-1700 on Thursdays), and often also Saturday morning in cities.

Changing money

Essentials

Value Added Tax Visitors from non-EU countries leaving the Republic within two months of a purchase (three months in Northern Ireland) can obtain a refund of the Value Added Tax (VAT) added to the price of most goods. The shop has to be a participant in the Retail Export Scheme, and there will usually be a display at the entrance or on the counter to this effect, but shops have different ways of operating the scheme so enquire before making a purchase. The scheme does not apply to hotel bills and other services.

Money transfers If the need arises you can telephone, or perhaps fax, your home bank and arrange for money to be transferred to a local bank in Ireland where you can collect it after showing your passport. Before you leave home, ensure you have the necessary bank details. American Express cardholders can arrange for money to be sent to Ireland; check out the details before you leave home. It may also be worth checking with Western Union about details of their money transfer facilities.

Getting there

Air

From Britain The only consistently available and reasonably-priced tickets are the so-called **Apex** (Advanced Purchase Excursion) tickets which have various conditions attached to them, the most important being that your return date is fixed and no refunds are available. Currently, the cheapest Apex fares between London and Dublin are around £80, between London and Cork around £90, between London and Belfast around £80. In order to secure these prices it is advisable to book as far ahead as possible, especially at peak times like summer, Easter and Christmas, and do not be unduly surprised to discover that the cheapest seats have gone. Outside of peak times there are often special offers that represent very good value, like two return tickets for the price of one.

Bicycles are normally carried free of charge as part of the normal baggage allowance, but Ryanair charge £15 extra each way. Always check before you purchase a ticket.

Student/Youth fares are always worth asking about, though different airlines have different rules and regulations. An International Student Identity Card (ISIC) is usually required. It is advisable to check through a specialist agency like STA Travel, 86 Old Brompton Rd, London SW7 3LH, T020-73616161, who also have offices in a number of other cities across Britain. Another company worth trying is Usit Campus, 52 Grosvenor Gardens, London SW1W OAG, T020-77303402, who also have regional offices in cities and at universities in Britain. *Usit Now* is the Irish youth and student travel organisation. Its head office is 19 Aston Quay, Dublin 2, T01-6798833; other offices are listed in relevant directories.

Specialist travel agents A good agent to try, with a freephone number, is *Ireland Direct* at 0500-026385. Specialist companies in London include *Pat Carroll Travel*, T020-76259669; *Gerry Feeney Travel*, T020-85145141; and *Tara Travel*, T020-76258601. In Liverpool try *Towns Travel,* T0151-7331476; in Manchester *Curry Travel*, T0161-2251133; in the West Midlands *Claddagh Travel*, T0121-3824803, and in Scotland *Sibbald Travel*, T0131-6679172 or *Going Places*, T0141-2215715.

From Britain to the Republic It takes about an hour to fly between London and Dublin; about 90 minutes to Cork or Shannon. The main destinations in the Republic are Dublin, Cork and Shannon, but it is also possible to fly to Knock, Kerry, Waterford and Galway.

From Britain to Northern Ireland It takes about an hour and a half to fly between London and Belfast, a bit longer to Derry. The airports are Belfast International, Belfast City and City of Derry and while most departures are from London (Heathrow, Stansted and Gatwick), Manchester and

Airlines operating between British mainland airports and the Republic

Birmingham → Cork	Aer Lingus, Jersey European
Birmingham → Dublin	Aer Lingus, Ryanair
Birmingham → Knock	Aer Lingus
Birmingham → Shannon	Aer Lingus, Jersey European
Blackpool → Dublin	Comed
Bournemouth → Dublin	Ryanair
Bristol → Dublin	Aer Lingus, Ryanair
Bristol → Cork	British Airways
Cardiff → Dublin	Manx Airlines, Ryanair
East Midlands → Dublin	British Midland
Edinburgh → Dublin	Aer Lingus
Exeter → Cork	Jersey European
Exeter → Dublin	Jersey European
Exeter → Shannon	Jersey European
Guernsey → Cork	Jersey European
Guernsey → Dublin	Jersey European
Glasgow → Cork	Jersey European
Glasgow → Dublin	Aer Lingus
Glasgow Prestwick → Dublin	Ryanair
Isle of Man → Cork	Jersey European
Isle of Man → Dublin	Manx Airlines
Jersey → Cork	Jersey European, Manx Airlines
Jersey → Dublin	Aer Lingus, Jersey European, Manx Airlines
Leeds Bradford → Dublin	Aer Lingus, Ryanair
Liverpool → Dublin	Ryanair
London City → Dublin	Jersey European/Cityjet
London Gatwick → Cork	British Airways
London Gatwick → Dublin	British Airways, Ryanair
London Gatwick → Shannon	Aer Lingus
London Heathrow → Cork	Aer Lingus
London Heathrow → Dublin	Aer Lingus, British Midland
London Heathrow → Shannon	Aer Lingus
London Luton → Dublin	Ryanair
London Stansted → Cork	Ryanair
London Stansted → Dublin	Aer Lingus, Ryanair
London Stansted → Kerry	Ryanair
London Stansted → Knock	Ryanair
London Stansted → Shannon	Virgin Express
London Stansted → Waterford	British Airways
Manchester → Cork	British Airways
Manchester → Dublin	Aer Lingus, Luxair, Ryanair
Manchester → Knock	British Airways
Manchester → Shannon	British Airways
Manchester → Waterford	British Airways
Newcastle → Dublin	Aer Lingus
Sheffield → Cork	Celtic Airways (commence Spring 2000)
Sheffield → Dublin	British Airways
Southampton → Dublin	British Airways
Teesside → Dublin	Ryanair

Essentials

Airlines operating between British mainland airports and Northern Ireland

Aberdeen → Belfast International	British Airways
Birmingham → Belfast City	Jersey European
Birmingham → Belfast International	British Airways
Blackpool → Belfast City	Comed, Jersey European
Bristol → Belfast City	Jersey European
Cardiff → Belfast City	British Airways
Cardiff → Belfast International	British Airways
East Midlands → Belfast International	British Midland
Edinburgh → Belfast City	British Airways
Edinburgh → Belfast International	British Airways
Exeter → Belfast City	Jersey European
Glasgow → Belfast City	British Airways
Glasgow → Belfast International	British Airways
Glasgow → City of Derry	British Airways
Glasgow Prestwick → Belfast City	Gill Airways
Guernsey → Belfast City	Jersey European
Isle of Man → Belfast City	Comed, Jersey European
Jersey → Belfast City	Jersey European
Jersey → Belfast International	British Midland
Leeds Bradford → Belfast City	Jersey European
Liverpool → Belfast City	British Airways
Liverpool → Belfast International	Easyjet
London Gatwick → Belfast City	Jersey European
London Heathrow → Belfast International	British Airways, British Midland
London Luton → Belfast International	Easyjet
London Stansted → Belfast City	Jersey European
London Stansted → City of Derry	Ryanair
Manchester → Belfast City	British Airways
Manchester → Belfast International	British Airways
Manchester → City of Derry	British Airways
Newcastle Upon Tyne → Belfast City	Gill Airways
Newcastle Upon Tyne → Belfast International	British Airways, Gill Airways
Sheffield → Belfast City	British Airways
Southampton → Belfast City	British Airways
Teeside → Belfast International	Gill Airways

Birmingham, it is also possible to fly from Aberdeen, Blackpool, Bristol, Cardiff, East Midlands, Edinburgh, Exeter, Glasgow, Guernsey, Isle of Man, Jersey, Leeds/Bradford, Luton, Liverpool, Newcastle and Southampton.

The main carriers are British Airways, British Airways Express, British Midland and Ryanair. The other airlines are Gill Airways and Jersey European Airways.

Between the Republic & NI Air South West operate daily flights between Cork and Belfast City airport.

Airline details *AB Airlines*, International Call Centre, Engineering Block, Belfast International Airport, BT29 4AA. T0800-4588111, reservations@abairlines.com http@//www.abairlines.com *Air South West*, Terminal Building, Cork Airport, Cork, Ireland. T021-316900 (reservations 0345-446447) *Aer Lingus*, 83 Staines Rd, Hounslow, Middlesex TW3 3JB. T020-88994747 (London), 0645-737747 (outside London) *Air Kilroe/GillAirways*, New Aviation House, Newcastle Airport, Newcastle Upon Tyne, NE13 8BT. T0191-

Airlines operating between major European cities and Ireland

Amsterdam	Aer Lingus
Barcelona	Iberia, AB Airlines
Berlin	AB Airlines
Brussels	Aer Lingus, Sabena, Ryanair
Cologne	Lufthansa
Copenhagen	Aer Lingus
Dusseldorf	Aer Lingus
Frankfurt	Aer Lingus, Lufthansa
Lisbon	TAP
Madrid	Aer Lingus, Iberia
Milan	Aer Lingus, Alitalia
Moscow	Aeroflot
Nice	AB Airlines
Munich	Lufthansa
Paris	Aer Lingus, Air France, Cityjet, Ryanair
Rome	Aer Lingus, Alitalia
Zurich	Aer Lingus, Crossair

Essentials

2146666 **British Airways**, 156 Regent St, London W1R 6LB. T0645-737747 British Midland, Donington Hall, Castle Donington, Derby DE7 2SB. T0345-554554 **CityFlyer Express**, Lain Stewart Centre, Beehive Ring Rd, Gatwick RH6 0PB. T0345-222111 **CityJet**, London City Airport, The Royal Docks, London E16 2PX. T0345-445588 **Gill Airways**, New Aviation House, Newcastle Airport, Newcastle upon Tyne NE13 8BT. T0191-2146666 **Jersey European Airways**, Exeter Airport, Exeter, Devon EX5 2BD. T0990-676676 **Luxair**, Room 2003, Heathrow Terminal 2, Hounslow, Middlesex TW6 1HL. T020-87454254 **Manx Airlines**, Ronaldsway Airport, Ballasalla, Isle of Man IM9 2JE. T0345-256256 **Ryanair,** Enterprise House, Stansted Airport, Essex CM24 1QW. T051-569569 **Suckling Airways**, Cambridge Airport, Cambridge CB5 8RT **Virgin Airways**, Virgin House, Shannon Airport, Co Clare, Ireland. T0800-891199.

Ryanair now has online booking where real bargains can be had. Look them up at www.ryanair.com.

There are numerous direct and indirect flights to Ireland from European cities. Students under the age of 30 with valid ID and travellers under the age of 26 with a European Youth Card (EYC) are eligible for discounted fares. The above box shows the airlines that offer flights to Ireland from European cities:

From Europe

There are direct Aer Lingus flights to Dublin and Shannon from New York and Boston, and Apex fares average between $360 and $545. Aeroflot (Shannon only), Continental Airlines and Delta Airlines also fly to Shannon and Dublin.

From North America

Flights from the West Coast cost considerably more, starting around $600 and climbing to over $1000 in the summer months, with a significant difference between weekday and weekend prices. It may be a better deal to fly to London and take an Apex flight from there to Ireland. There are also direct flights to Belfast from New York, costing between $350 and $550 depending on the time of year. As with flights from Britain, there are occasional special offers at times of the year when the demand for seats dips. Airlines and some travel agents are listed below and the weekend sections of papers like the *New York Times* and *San Francisco Chronicle* are worth checking out. Student fares are available through agents like STA Travel in New York and Travel Cuts in Toronto.

There are no direct flights to Ireland from Canada, but Air Canada fly to Dublin, Shannon and Belfast via London from Montréal, Toronto and Vancouver. The least expensive flights from Montréal or Toronto to the Republic entail fixed dates that cannot be changed. Prices average around Can$1000, but can cost from Can$100 to

Can$200 more or less depending on the season. As with flights from the US West Coast, it is worth checking out the cost of flying to London and having a separate Apex ticket from there to Ireland.

Airlines and agents offering flights from North America *Air Canada*, T1-800-7763000 *Aer Lingus*, T1-800-2236537 *Aeroflot*, T1-800-8678774 *Airtech*, 588 Broadway, Suite 204, New York, NY 10017. T1-800-5758324, http://www.airtech.com *American Airlines*, T1-800-4337300 *British Airways*, T1-800-2479297; Canada T1-800-6681059 *Continental Airlines* T1-800-2310856 *Council Travel*, 205 E 42nd St, New .York, NY 10017. T1-800-2268624 *Delta Airlines*, T1-800-2414141 *Educational Travel Centre*, 438 N Francis St, Madison, WI 53703. T1-800-7475551 *High Adventure Travel*, 353 Sacramento St, Suite 600, San Francisco, CA 94111. T1-800-3500612 *STA Travel*, 10 Downing St, New York, NY 10014. T1-800-7770112 *Travel Cuts*, 187 College St, Toronto, ON M5T 1P7. T1-800-6672887 *United Airlines*, T1-800-5382929 *Virgin Atlantic Airways*, T1-800-8628621.

From Australia & New Zealand There are no direct flights from Australia or New Zealand, so the usual route is to fly to London and then on to Ireland. Various airlines offer indirect tickets to Ireland this way and ones to check out include not only Aer Lingus and British Airways, but also KLM, Singapore Airlines and Malaysia Airlines. The single most important factor determining the price of a ticket is the season and peak times. Between May and August expect to pay at least A$2500 for a discounted return ticket. From around the second half of January to early March the same route could cost A$2000 or less. From New Zealand expect to pay around NZ$2600.

Before making a decision check out other major airlines that fly to London, because very often it does not cost a lot to have a London-Dublin ticket added to your Apex-type main fare.

Airlines and agents offering flights from Australia and New Zealand *Aer Lingus*, World Aviation Systems, 64 York St, Sydney, T02-93219123; 6th Floor, 229 Queen St, Auckland, T09-3794455 *Air New Zealand*, Queen St, Auckland, T09-3662424; 5 Elizabeth St, Sydney, T02-92234666 *British Airways*, 64 Castlereagh St, Sydney, T02-92583300; 154 Queen St, Auckland, T09-3568690 *KLM*, Level 6, 5 Elizabeth St, Sydney, T02-92316333 *Malaysia Airlines*, 16 Spring St, Sydney, T02-93643535; 12th Floor, The Swanson Centre, Swanson St, Auckland, T09-3732741 *Qantas*, 70 Hunter St, Sydney, T02-99514294; Qantas House, 154 Queen St, Auckland, T0800-808767 *Singapore Airlines*, 17-19 Bridge St, Sydney, T02-93500121; Lower Ground Floor, West Plaza Building, Customs & Albert Sts, Auckland, T0800-808909 *STA Travel*, 855 George St, Sydney, T1-800-637444 *Traveller's Centre*, 10 High St, Auckland, T09-3090458 (and branches throughout both countries) *Thomas Cook*, 175 Pitt St, Sydney, T02-92296611; 159 Queen St, Auckland, T09-3793924 *UTAG Travel Agents*, 122 Walker St, North Sydney (and branches throughout the country) T02-99568399.

Ferry

From Britain The box on the next page covers the routes and sailing times of passage to Ireland by car and passenger ferries. Car hire in the Republic (see page 51) is more expensive than in Britain or the USA and so, if you are planning to use a car, a journey by ferry can be worthwhile. Bear in mind, too, that the cost of a ferry fare for a car and passengers may compare favourably with two, three or more individual air fares for the same journey.

Fares vary depending on the time of year, type of vessel and sometimes the time of sailing. For example, on Stena Line's Holyhead to Dun Laoghaire route there is a choice between the 99-minute crossing on the jet-propelled *Stena HSS* and the 3 hour and 45 minute crossing on the regular ferry (that sails from Dublin Port rather than from Dun

Ferry crossings and operators between the British mainland and Ireland

Cairnryan → Larne	P&O Ferries	2 hrs 15 mins
		Jerliner 60 mins
Campbeltown → Ballycastle	Argyll & Antrim Steam Packet Co	2 hrs 45 mins
Fishguard → Rosslare	Stena Line	Stena Lynx 99 mins
		Superferry 3 hrs 30 mins
Holyhead → Dun Laoghaire	Stena Line	Stena HSS 99 mins
Holyhead → Dublin (Ferryport)	Stena Line	Superferry 3 hrs 45 mins
Holyhead → Dublin (Ferryport)	Irish Ferries	Cruise Ferry 3 hrs 15 mins
Holyhead → Dublin (Ferryport)	Irish Ferries	under 2 hrs
Isle of Man → Dublin	Isle of Man Steam Packet Co	Seacat 2 hrs 45 mins
Liverpool → Belfast	Norse Irish Ferries	11 hrs
Liverpool → Dublin	Sea Containers Ferries Scotland Ltd;	
	Merchant Ferries	Super Seacat 3 hrs 55 mins
Pembroke → Rosslare	Irish Ferries	Cruise Ferry 4 hrs
Stranraer → Belfast	Stena Line	90 mins
Swansea → Cork	Swansea/Cork Ferries	10 hrs

Laoghaire). A single fare on the *Stena HSS* in the middle of July currently costs £249 for a car and up to 4 passengers, plus £139 to £199 for a caravan or trailer, £22 for a motorcycle, £35 for a foot passenger with or without a bicycle. The same journey between 12 April and 27 May costs £139 for a car and up to four passengers, plus £49 to £89 for a caravan or trailer, IR£10 for a motorcycle, £30 for a passenger with or without a bicycle. Fares at other times of the year fall between these quoted rates. Members of a Youth Hostel/Hostelling International organisation (see page 46) receive a 20% discount on foot passenger fares on Irish Ferries and Stena Line.

Bear in mind extra costs like the price of meals and drinks on board and a possible need for overnight stays in Britain and/or Ireland in order to make unhelpful departure or arrival times. On many of the routes, especially the 10-hour Swansea-Cork ferry, there are extra charges for cabin accommodation, although you can bring a sleeping bag and try to find a quiet corner for a night's sleep. Some companies, like Irish Ferries, insist on travel insurance, and unless you can quote an existing policy that covers you (an annual world or Europe travel policy for instance) there will be an extra charge for this as well.

Travelling as a foot passenger on a combined coach/ferry or train/ferry ticket can be good value although obviously it takes far longer than a flight. Holders of ISIC cards should ask about student reductions, whether travelling as a driver or foot passenger, although discounts are not available on all the routes. Cheapest travel of all for a foot passenger is to try and hitch a ride at the ferry terminal, because in a car with fewer than four passengers there would be no extra charge.

There are some big ships sailing to Ireland. The *Stena HSS* is the size of a football pitch, accommodates up to 1,500 passengers and, with four gas turbines producing 100,000 horsepower, belts along with a top speed of over 50 mph.

Ferry operators *Argyll & Antrim Steam Packet Co*, T0990-523523 *Irish Ferries*, T08705-171717 *Isle of Man Steam Packet Co*, T 0990-523523 *Merchant Ferries*, T01524-855018 *Norse Irish Ferries*, T01232-779090 *P&O* T0990-980666 *Sea Containers Ferries Scotland Ltd*, T0990-523523 *Stena Line*, T0990-707070 *Swansea/Cork Ferries*, T01792- 456116, T0800-7838004.

Irish Ferries run three routes from northern France to Rosslare in Co Wexford, and two **From Europe** routes to Cork. The fastest, over 18 hours, is from Cherbourg to Rosslare; the route from Le Havre to Rosslare takes 22 hours. The fare for both routes with four passengers and a car in the summer months approaches £400. Between May and September there is a ferry service between Le Havre and Cork, taking over 20 hours, and between May and August a Roscoff to Cork ferry also operates, taking 15 hours.

Train/coach

Train/ferry The cost of combined train and ferry tickets depends on the time of year and departure times. A return fare from London to Dublin ranges from around £45 to £65, from Manchester from around £35. A return fare from London to Belfast, via Dublin, ranges from £55 to around £85. Combined train and ferry tickets can be booked through a travel agent or from a mainline railway station. *Stena Line*, T0990-455455, also offer competitive rail/ferry packages. Travellers under the age of 26 with a Young Person's Railcard, currently £18 a year, can get one-third off standard rail fares. Contact the *National Rail Enquiry Service*, T0345-484950, for details. For details of **European rail passes** that can be used to get to and travel throughout Ireland, contact CIE T1-800-CIE-TOUR or 973-2923899 or Rail Europe T1-800-4387245 in the USA and T1-800-5552748 in Canada.

Coach/ferry This is the least expensive but also the most time-consuming method of getting to Ireland. The largest operator of scheduled coach services to Ireland is *Slattery's*, with daily services to Dublin, Galway, Cork, Tralee, Waterford, Limerick and many other towns. Coaches depart from London, Bristol, Birmingham, Reading, Liverpool, Manchester and Leeds. An adult return from London to Dublin at peak times is £39 by day, £49 by night.

National Express Eurolines run regular day and night services between London and Dublin, via Birmingham, taking an average of 12 hours, depending on the ferry crossing. The cost of a return ticket ranges from £29 to £39, day service, and £39 to £49 overnight. Combined tickets from other cities across Britain are available. Tickets using other ferry crossings are also available, as are combined tickets to other parts of Ireland using the *Bus Éireann* network. Enquiries and ticket purchases may be made in person from any National Express station or their agents, or by phone (contact details are given below). Reductions are available to passengers under 26 and to senior citizens.

Ulsterbus operates a coach/ferry service between London and Belfast via Birmingham, from Birmingham via Manchester, and from Edinburgh via Glasgow using the Stranraer ferry. The return fare from London is around £50 and takes 12 hours; from Edinburgh the coast is IR£36 and takes 7 hours. Tickets can be purchased through *National Express*.

Contacts *National Express Eurolines*, 52 Grosvenor Gardens, Victoria, London SW1W 0AU, T0990-808080 (National Express call number), 0990-143219 (credit/debit card bookings), F020-77308721, http://www.eurolines.co.uk *Slattery's*, 162 Kentish Town Rd, London NW5 2AG. T0800-515900/020-74851438, ireland@slatterys.com *Ulster Bus Enquiry Service*, Europa Buscentre, Belfast BT12 5AH. TT028-90337002.

Touching down

Airport information The main airports at Dublin, Shannon, Cork and Belfast all have money exchange facilities, car hire desks, taxis and public transport to and from the city. For detailed information on the airports see page 143 for Dublin, page 393 for Shannon, page 590 for Belfast and page 291 for Cork. Information about the smaller regional airports at Derry, Galway and Waterford is given under their relevant sections.

Airport taxes are added on to the price of your air or ferry ticket at the time of **Airport tax**
purchase.

Tourist Boards The airports at Dublin, Shannon and Belfast all have tourist **Tourist**
information offices which include an accommodation booking service. Local tourist **information**
information offices are found in cities and towns all across Ireland and, while they are
nearly always staffed by helpful and considerate people, some are better organised
and more oriented to the independent traveller than others. In the Republic, most
tourist offices are run by the national tourist organisation, called Bord Fáilte, though
you will also come across some that have been set up and funded on a local basis, and
this includes Dublin Tourism as well as village-based offices. Non-Bord Fáilte offices
will not usually arrange to book accommodation for you outside of their local area.
The Northern Ireland Tourist Board (NITB) runs all the tourist offices in Northern
Ireland; you will see the brown signs pointing to them in town centres.

   Normal hours for most tourist offices are 0900-1700 Monday to Friday, 0900-1300
on Saturday. In larger towns and major tourist areas, during high season, the closing
hours are often extended and they may open all day Saturday and Sunday. But also be
prepared to find a tourist office closed on a Saturday, Sunday or a public holiday
anywhere and at any time of the year. Outside of the summer months, opening hours
can be frustratingly idiosyncratic.

There is no shortage of good quality maps of Ireland. For a single, large-scale road map **Maps & guides**
of the whole country try the No 405 Michelin 1:400,000 or the AA 1:350,000 map. For
more detail of a large area your best bet are the four maps that make up the *Ordnance
Survey Holiday Maps* series (North, West, East and South), at a scale of 1:250,000. For
more detail of a particular area, and essential for walking, it is impossible to beat the

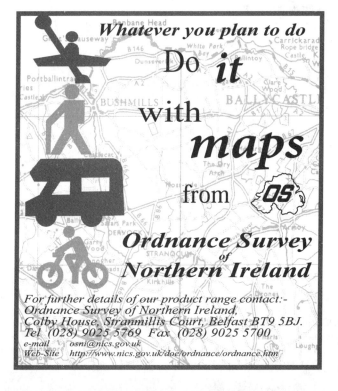
Essentials

Basic information

Business hours

Normal business hours are 0900 to 1700, Monday to Friday; shops open 0900-1730 or 1800, Monday to Saturday; the large stores in Dublin stay open late on Thursday and Friday. In small towns, shops and even businesses may close for an hour over lunchtime and for the whole of one afternoon each week.

Directory enquiries

T11811 in the Republic, T192 in Northern Ireland.

Electricity

230V AC in the Republic and 240V AC in Northern Ireland. Plugs are the 3-pin flat sort, and 2-pin round wall sockets are also found. British electrical appliances will work everywhere, North American ones will require a transformer and a plug adaptor, and Australian and New Zealand appliances just a plug adaptor.

Emergency services

T999 or T112

IDD codes

The international direct dialing code (IDD) code for the Republic is 353 and for Northern Ireland is 44.

Official time

Ireland is on Greenwich Mean Time (GMT), so when it is 1800 in Dublin or Belfast it's 1300 in New York, 0900 in San Francisco, and 0400 in Sydney. However, daylight saving time changes mean that clocks are advanced by one hour between mid-March and the end of October.

Weights & measures

Confusion reigns because metrication has been adopted but not enforced. Distances are measured in both miles and kilometres; drinks in pubs come in pints, in shops they come in litres; food is weighed and sold in both pounds and kilograms, petrol comes in litres.

To convert: miles to kilometres multiply by 1.61; kilometres to miles multiply by 0.62; pounds to kilograms multiply by 0.45; kilograms to pounds multiply by 2.20.

Ordnance Survey Discovery Series at a scale of 1:50,000 (2.5in to 1 mile/2cm to 1 km). Avoid the seriously out-of-date Ordnance Survey 1:25,000 (half an inch to one mile) series of maps which are still being sold.

Contacts *Stanfords*, 12-14 Long Acre, London WC2, T020-78361321, can supply all these maps by mail. In the USA, *Rand McNally*, T1-800-3330136, can do the same.

For guide books about Ireland see page 60.

Concessionary cards A *Heritage Card*, purchased in the Republic for IR£15, gives unlimited free admission to all the parks, monuments, gardens, inland waterways and cultural institutions under the management of *Dúchas*, the national heritage department of the Irish government. The card can be bought at the first site you visit or from their main office at 51 St Stephen's Green, Dublin 2, T01-6613111. Dúchas sites are indicated as such in this guide.

In Northern Ireland *The National Trust* is a similar kind of organization but their card costs £28, or £13 if you are under 25. It covers the whole of Britain and Northern Ireland, and does not represent value for money if you are only visiting Northern Ireland.

Student & youth travellers Some form of identity card confirming your student or youth status is required for any discounts available on travel to and within Ireland, entry charges to museums and sundry other benefits and discounts. As a general rule, before paying for any form of travel or for any entrance fee or ticket ask whether a student or youth discount is available.

Admission prices quoted in this book are for adults and do not take into account the discounts that are commonly available to students and children. The most commonly recognised form of ID is an International Student Identity Card (ISIC), available to anyone in full-time education and obtainable from *STA, Council Travel* or *Travel Cuts* offices in your country . It costs £5 in Britain and Northern Ireland, IR£7 in the Republic, and US$20 in the US. In Ireland the card is obtainable through USIT offices.

The Go-25 Card, if you are 25 or under, performs much the same function as an ISIC card and is obtainable through Council Travel in the US or STA in Australia and New Zealand. Holders of ISIC cards, once in Ireland, can pay IR£8 and obtain a Travelsave Stamp from USIT offices. This allows for discounts on some bus fares and a 50% discount on rail fares.

Improvements continue to be made, but generally speaking Ireland is still lagging behind some countries in its provisions for disabled travellers. However, with advance planning and all the available information at your disposal a visit can still be an enjoyable experience. Contact both Bord Fáilte and NITB for their specialist literature, and in the Republic the *National Rehabilitation Board* (NRB) is well worth contacting for their guides to accommodation, tourist facilities, restaurants and pubs. They also produce a detailed guide to Dublin which contains good general information and advice as well as listings which include a list of wheelchair accessible public toilets. Some of these toilets require a special key, available from the NRB. *The Restaurant Association of Ireland* will send you their free *Dining in Ireland* booklet which identifies wheelchair-accessible restaurants and *Iarnród Éireann* (Irish Rail) will send their free *Guide for Mobility Impaired Passengers*. Contact *Dublin Bus Customer Service* for their No 3 route through the city with wheelchair access and see page 144 for other information pertaining to Dublin. Travellers from Britain using a car should contact the *Disabled Drivers Association. Irish Ferries* and *Stena Line* have discounts for disabled travellers, but it is advisable to check their details *before* booking passage because the date of travel will make a difference. In the USA, *Directions Unlimited* specialize in vacations for disabled travellers.

Disabled travellers

Contacts *Bord Fáilte,* see page 29 *Directions Unlimited,* 720 N Bedford Rd, Bedford Hills, NY 10507, T1-800-5355343 *Disabled Drivers Association*, Ashwellthorpe, Norwich, NR16 1EX, T01508-489449 *Disability Action*, 2 Annadale Ave, Belfast BT7 3JH, T028-9049 *Dublin Bus Customer Service*, 59 Upper O'Connell St, Dublin 1, T01-8734222 *Iarnród Éireann*, Travel Centre, Connolly Station, Amiens ST, Dublin1, T01-7032369 *Irish Wheelchair Association*, Blackheath Drive, Clontarf, Dublin 3, T01-8338241/8335366 *National Rehabilitation Board*, 25 Clyde Rd, Dublin 4, T01-6080400 *Northern Ireland Tourist Board*, see page 29 *Restaurants Association of Ireland,* 11 Bridge Court, Dublin 8, T01-6779901.

Contact information for gay and lesbian travellers is given below, but apart from Dublin, Cork and Belfast (and these in descending order) there is little understanding of gay life, and society is generally blinkered if not intolerant. In rural areas especially, there is widespread ignorance, and overt gay behaviour is not advisable. Dublin (see page 138) has gay accommodation, pubs and clubs.

Gay & lesbian travellers

Contacts *Dublin Lesbian Line*, T01-8729911 (Thursday 1900-2100) *Gay Switchboard Dublin*, Carmichael House, North Great Brunswick St, Dublin 7, T01-8721055 (Sunday-Friday 1530-1800 and 2000-1200) *Lesbian Line Belfast* T028-90238668 (Thursday 1930-2200) *Northern Ireland Gay Rights Association (NIGRA)*, Cathedral Building, Lower Donegall St, Belfast, T028-90664111 *Outhouse*, Gay & Lesbian Community & Resource Centre, 6 South William St, Dublin 2, T01-6706377.

Rules, customs and etiquette

Conduct By and large the Republic is a laid-back place with a healthy disregard for authority and nit-picking rules. Social customs and etiquette are much the same as the average European, North American or Australasian visitor would expect although, as noted above, attitudes to gay life need to be taken into account. A dress code in a restaurant is rare indeed and even in the most expensive establishments smart but casual attire is generally acceptable. Class divisions certainly exist in Ireland, and in Dublin, Belfast and certain other cities this is painfully obvious, but in the Republic it can often be difficult to demarcate social class in terms of behaviour, dress or language.

Northern Ireland is socially very conservative. Racist attitudes, especially as regards black travellers, are common across Ireland as a whole, and the best that can be said is that more often than not it is rooted in plain ignorance rather than deliberate malice. The recent arrival of refugees from eastern Europe has exposed a very ugly strain of virulent racism behind the very discreet charm of the Irish bourgeoisie.

Prohibitions There is nothing in Ireland that is unusually illegal, and the law is pretty much as one would expect it to be in a modern European country. Travellers caught importing illegal drugs will be prosecuted according to the law, up to and including imprisonment, but punishments do reflect the nature of the drug in question. In the Republic, possession of cannabis for personal use carries a fine of IR£300, for other drugs IR£1,000 or 12 months in jail before a District Court and an unlimited fine and/or prison up to 7 years if tried before a judge and jury, and the *garda* (police) can detain anyone for up to 7 days without charge on suspicion of a drug offence. The legal age for drinking alcohol is 18, and in city pubs customers may be asked to prove their age. There are strict laws regarding driving while under the influence of alcohol and the traditional tolerance towards drink and driving in rural areas in the Republic is fast disappearing.

Religion In theory the Republic is overwhelmingly Roman Catholic, but times are changing and in the cities church attendance is not as high as one might expect. In rural areas going to church is a social obligation for the majority of people and should not be mistaken for devotional piety, although that exists in large doses as well. In Northern Ireland religious affiliation is all too often a marker for political and social differences, and visitors are well advised to tread carefully in this area.

Safety The general level of personal safety in Ireland is high for both male and female travellers, *Northern Ireland has some of the lowest crime statistics to be found anywhere in Europe and, generally speaking, Belfast is a far safer city for the visitor than Dublin* especially in the countryside, but do not be lulled into a false sense of security. Crimes, minor and major, do occur and common sense should always govern your behaviour. Parts of Dublin are highly prone to street crime, largely fuelled by drug addiction, and this includes the city centre. Northern Ireland is remarkably safe for the traveller, both in the cities and in the countryside. Unless the present peace accord explodes into violence once more, there is no more need to take precautions about personal safety, or where to park your car, than you would anywhere else in Europe. As always, exercise your common sense. Women travellers tend to find Ireland an easier place in which to travel around, alone or in company, than other countries of Europe, and old-fashioned chauvinism is relatively easy to deal with. It is not uncommon to see women hitchhiking alone, but they usually live locally and expect a hitch from another local.

Tipping When it comes to tipping there are no hard and fast rules. Upmarket hotels and restaurants will usually have a service charge (10-15%) added to the bill, but if paying by plastic a space will still be left on the receipt for a tip. As a general rule, a tip of 10% is the norm if you do decide to tip. In bars certainly, and even pub restaurants, tipping is not generally necessary or even expected. For porters in hotels or elsewhere think in terms of a 50p tip for each piece of luggage.

Where to stay

The choice of accommodation ranges from top-notch luxury hotels and historic country houses to dormitory beds in a hostel or free camping in a farmer's field. In between there are medium-range hotels, one-star hotels, guest houses, farm houses, self-catering, the ubiquitous bed and breakfast (B&B) in a private home, and camping and caravan parks. Prices quoted in this book refer to the price of a double room in high season, so usually expect to pay less at other times of the year, though the more expensive establishments are less likely to have variable rates. Single person supplements are common and sometimes exorbitant. Rates for families with children vary depending on the number of children and their ages, and the rate is often negotiable. Most rooms in hotels and guesthouses, and in a growing number of B&Bs, have a tea and coffee making facility.

See inside front cover for hotel price codes.

Breakfast is usually included in the price of accommodation, but some of the more expensive hotels and most hostels charge extra for this. Travellers who are vegetarian, or just diet-conscious, often have good reason to feel aggrieved about the inadequate alternatives to the hearty fry-up that is served as the standard breakfast in most establishments. A recent development has been the growth of small hotels charging a flat rate for a room, usually up to three adults or two adults and two children, and not including breakfast. Usually called a travel lodge or an inn, they can be very good value if a cholesterol-laden breakfast is not something you want to feel obliged to eat.

Always confirm the price of your accommodation when making a reservation and, whenever possible, always try to make a reservation. In Dublin this is essential whatever the time of year, and in popular tourist areas the summer months and holidays weekends can sometimes see most of the reasonably-priced accommodation fully booked. This is particularly true at the time of popular festivals (see page 59).

Gulliver is a computer data base system that includes a booking system for a wide range of accommodation (hotels, B&Bs, farmhouses, guesthouses, hostels, self catering) across the whole of Ireland through call-free numbers. The cost of a booking is IR£3, and IR£1 for each subsequent booking, and there is also a non-refundable IR£10 deposit taken on your credit card; with self-catering accommodation it is also possible to pay by cheque.

The Gulliver System

Telephone reservations can be made Monday-Friday, 0800-2000, and Saturday and Sunday 0800-1900. Freephone + 800-66866866 (+ denotes the international access code in the country where the call is made), thus within Europe (including Northern Ireland) T00800-66866866, and within the USA T011-800-66866866. Within Ireland the final 66 is not used, so T1800-668668.

There is a tempting choice to choose from across Ireland, nearly all of which are to be found in the Republic. Many of the country houses belong to the *Blue Book Group* while castles as well as some country houses belong to *The Green Book of Ireland* group. *The Hidden Ireland* is an interesting collection of buildings of character and architectural interest offering accommodation and sometimes meals. All three groups have glossy illustrated brochures, but bear in mind that places pay to be part of the group and their inclusion does not guarantee quality of accommodation.

Country houses, castles & heritage houses

Contacts *Blue Book Group*, Ardbraccan Glebe, Navan, Co Meath, T046-23416, F046-23292, bluebook@iol.ie http://www.irelands~blue~book.ie *The Green Book of Ireland*, 12 Lower Hatch St, Dublin 2, T01-6762555, F01-6762995, ireland@greenbook.ie http://www.iol.ie/green-book-of-ireland *The Hidden Ireland*, 37 Lower Baggot St, Dublin2, T01-6627166, F01-6627144, reservations@hidden-ireland.com http://www.hidden-ireland.com

Essentials

Hotels Hotels are graded from 5-star to 1-star, and for IR£3 Bord Fáilte retail a *Be Our Guest* illustrated guide to all the hotels and guesthouses in the Republic registered with them. NITB have a similar, non-illustrated, *Where to Stay* guide for £4.99 that includes hotels. Two main groups that middle-range hotels belong to are listed below and they can be contacted for their illustrated brochures. Depending on supply and demand, room rates are a lot more negotiable than many people realise, and if you can think of a reason for asking for a discount – more than one night's stay, only one night's stay, booking a dinner, commercial traveller's rate, off-season rate, weekend rate, mid-week rate – it is often worth negotiating.

Contacts *Manor House Hotels* (typically in the **A** range) 1 Sandyford Office Park, Foxrock, Dublin 18, T01-2958900, F01-2958900, cmv@indigo.ie http://www.iol.ie/hotels *Coast & Country Village Inn* (typically in the **B** range) 1 Sandyford Office Park, Foxrock, Dublin 18, T01-2958900, F01-2958900, cmv@indigo.ie http://www.iol.ie/hotels

Guesthouses The difference between a guesthouse and a small, family-run hotel is often hard to fathom as the demarcation criteria that Bord Fáilte employs is fairly meaningless to most travellers. Guesthouses can provide better value than many hotels because they are invariably family-run, and can often offer a more satisfying degree of pampering by your host. The higher-grade ones will have direct dial telephones in the rooms, a private car park, a lounge and sometimes a bar, and often a more interesting choice for breakfast than many hotels.

Contacts *Friendly Homes of Ireland* (IR£1), Tourism Resources, PO Box 2281, Dublin 4, http://www.tourismresources.ie contains details of a fairly mixed group of guesthouses and small hotels. *Premier Guesthouses* 4 Whitefriars, Aungier St, Dublin 2, T01-4751813, F01-4755321, info@premier-guesthouse.ie htttp://www.premier-guesthouse.ie

B&Bs If you stay in Bed & Breakfasts more than just occasionally you will soon discover what a surprising variety of people, decors, and styles of welcome and service lay behind those innocuous B&B boards that pop up everywhere outside farms and houses. The most typical is an owner-occupied bungalow with two or three rooms set aside for guests, which are increasingly likely to have their own toilet and shower room. Prices are usually between IR£13 and IR£22 per person sharing, and the less expensive ones are likely to have shared bathroom facilities. Similar prices in sterling apply to the North.

The best B&Bs are professionally run, clean, friendly and helpful. Evening meals are sometimes available, though they tend to be expensive (IR£14-IR£18) considering the lack of choice and the milieu, while afternoon tea can be a delight if fresh breads and scones are served. The least satisfying B&Bs tend to be those where you are made too conscious of being in someone's home.

B&Bs can be booked through tourist offices on payment of a 10% booking deposit (which is what the tourist board charges the establishment) plus a IR£1 fee for a local booking (IR£2 non-local) or IR£3 per credit card booking (in the Republic only). At the height of the season in popular tourist areas like Dublin, Killarney or Galway this can be well worth the money, because a number of calls may have to be made. Bord Fáilte sell an illustrated guide (IR£2.50) to all the B&Bs registered with them, as well as a separate illustrated (IR£2) *Irish Farmhouse B&B* guide which at least allows you to see which ones are modern bungalows and which traditional buildings. The NITB's *Where to Stay* guide (£4.99) includes B&Bs.

A number of B&Bs choose not to register with Bord Fáilte and opt instead for the Family Homes of Ireland group. They tend to be a little less expensive, and the group's illustrated booklet (IR£3) is available from *Family Homes of Ireland*, Oughterard, County Galway, T091-552000, F091-552666, bandb@family-homes.ie http://www.family-homes.ie.

Houses, and apartments to a far lesser extent, are usually rented on a weekly basis, though outside of the summer months it is also possible to book a place for shorter periods, like a long weekend or 4 or 5 days over Easter. **Self-catering**

Bord Fáilte's *Self Catering* guide costs IR£5 and is packed with over 3,000 premises, and the NITB's *Where to Stay* guide includes self-catering. Tour operators like Stena Line Holidays, Enjoy Ireland Holidays or Slatterys (see page 22) also arrange self-catering deals and *Family Homes of Ireland*, (see above) have an illustrated booklet (IR£2) with some very good-value choices. *Self-Catering Ireland Ltd*, Tourist Office, Kilrane, Rosslare, Co Wexford, T053-33999, F053-33808, info@selfcatering-ireland.com is typical of the companies specialising in this field, and they will post out their free brochure on request.

Self-catering tends to be more economically viable if part of a small group because the rent is fixed and beds for six or more people are more common than one-room apartments. Prices range enormously depending on the location and time of year. A house in Cork or Kerry in August could cost from IR£300-IR£600 a week, less than half that outside of the peak season or in a less popular region like county Monaghan or Roscommon.

Hostels in Ireland fall into two basic categories: independent ones, and the more traditional ones that belong to Hostelling International (HI), though they are still called Youth Hostels despite the fact that people of any age can use them. The traditional hostels have a membership scheme; the independent ones do not. Hostels can represent the best value for money when it comes to accommodation in Ireland. They also provide great opportunities to meet fellow travellers, chat and exchange information in an informal atmosphere. **Hostels**

Essentials

Essentials

Independent There are two hostel associations in Ireland which do not require membership. The
hostels largest is the *Independent Holiday Hostels* (IHH), approved by Bord Fáilte, and a list
and map giving full details of all their 150 member hostels is available from their
Dublin office. They operate a book ahead system, and for a nominal fee a bed at the
next hostel will be guaranteed. The other association is the *Independent Hostel
Owners* (IHO), the original independent hostel group and still outside Bord Fáilte's
domain, and a map and list of their 130 member hostels is available from their
Donegal office. There are also some totally independent hostels that don't belong to
either IHH or IHO, but this does not mean they are of a lower standard. There is also the
Celtic Budget Accommodation group, consisting mainly of IHH and IHO hostels, that
cater specifically to small and large groups of travellers.

The overnight fee outside of Dublin is around IR£7 and this gives you a bed in a
dormitory, varying in size from two beds to well over a dozen, and use of the hostel's
facilities which at their most basic include an equipped kitchen, a common room with
usually a television, hot showers (a very few hostels charge 50p for a shower), and
telephone. Some hostels will provide free pick-up from the nearest town or village,
some include a free continental breakfast and provide evening meals at reasonable
prices, and some will have camping space with use of all or some hostel facilities.
Better-equipped ones have laundry facilities, bicycles for hire and other amenities. It
helps to travel with a sleeping sheet or sleeping bag, though some hostels include
fresh linen and all will rent you sheets; duvets or blankets are freely provided. There is
usually no curfew at independent hostels and you can stay indoors all day if you wish.

Most hostels will also have private rooms, usually for two people (though singles
are available in some) or for a family with young children. Outside of Dublin, the price
averages about IR£10 per person and this represents a very viable alternative to B&Bs
if you are going to make use of the kitchen and prepare your own meals. At peak times,
when some hostels get overcrowded, a private room does provide some private space
and also minimises the problem of being kept awake by inebriated hostellers
returning early in the morning.

The Backpackers Press publishes annually *The Independent Hostel Guide: UK and
Ireland*. This includes detailed descriptions and opinions of some 40 hostels in Ireland,
nearly all IHH and IHO but some completely independent ones as well, and is available
for £3.95 (including postage) from their England address. Also available by mail from
England is *Ireland – All the Hostels* (£3) which carries details of all the hostels in Ireland,
including the totally independent ones, plus short reviews of 200 of what are
considered the best hostels.

Traditional Traditional hostels, now under the general umbrella of Hostelling International, are, in
hostels the Republic, part of *An Óige*, the official Irish Youth Hostel Association, and the
equivalent organisation in the North is the *Youth Hostel Association of Northern
Ireland* (YHANI). You can become a member for IR£7.50 at any of their hostels in
Ireland or join through a Youth Hostel/Hostelling International in your own country.
An Óige members receive a 20% discount on ferry passenger rates on Irish Ferries,
Stena Line (and boats to the Aran Islands and Inishbofin) and there are discounts on
car hire, some tours, some shops and a host of historical and cultural attractions.
Various touring holidays, including cycling, walking and historical ones, can also be
booked through An Óige. For £75, YANI offer seven days unlimited travel on buses and
trains in Northern Ireland, vouchers for six nights of accommodation in their hostels
and timetables.

So while it helps to be a member, anyone can still usually book a bed for the night,
and the rates are usually a pound or more cheaper than the independent hostels;
under 18s receive an even better rate. Hostel facilities can match those of independent
hostels but some tend to be a little spartan. Some hostels have private rooms and
some have outstanding locations and/or fine and spacious buildings. A free booking-

ahead service is available at the hostels and many provide breakfast, packed lunches and evening meal. A disadvantage is that some close for part of the day, usually the afternoon, and some will have a curfew hour before which time you have to return.

Contacts *An Óige*, 67 Mountjoy St, Dublin 7, T01-8304555, F01-8305808, mailbox@anoige.ie http://www.irelandyha.org *Celtic Budget Accommodation*, 13 South Leinster St, Dublin 2, T01-6621991, F01-6785011, info@celtic-accommodation.ie http://www.celtic-accommodation.ie *Hostelling International-American Youth Hostels*, 773 15th St NW, Suite 840, PO Box 37613, Washington DC 20005. T1-800-4446111 *IHH Office*, 57 Lower Gardiner Street, Dublin 1, T01-8364700, F01-8364710, ihh@oil.ie http://www.iol.ie.hostel *IHO Information Office*, Dooey Hostel, Glencolmcille, Co Donegal, T073-30130, F073-30339, www.eroicapub.com/ihi *Ireland – All the Hostels*, Flat 2A, 72 Woodstock Rd, Moseley, Birmingham B13 9BN, England *The Backpackers Press*, 2 Rockview Cottages, Matlock Bath, Derbyshire, DE4 3PG, England. T&F01629-580427 *Youth Hostel Association (YHA) England & Wales*, 8 St Stephen's Hill, St Albans, Herts AL1 2DY, England T01727-845047, F01727-844126, yhacustomerservices@compuserve.com *Youth Hostel Association of Northern Ireland*, 22-32 Donegall Rd, Belfast BT12 5JN, T028-90324733, F028-90439699.

Camping &   Camping for free is a lot easier in Ireland than many other countries, but you should
caravanning   always take the trouble of finding the landowner and asking their permission. If you camp in a field near the farmhouse you should be able to access an outdoor water supply. Some farmers, in touristy areas mainly, may charge a small amount for camping in their fields.

A number of independent hostels have an area set aside for camping, and usually the charge includes the use of hostel facilities.

Organized camping and caravan parks vary a lot in the level of services they provide, and this is reflected in the rates they charge, from IR£3.50 to IR£9 for a small tent. Most places will also have different rates for campers on foot, on a motorcycle, in a car or a motor home. *The Irish Caravan & Camping Council* publish an annual illustrated guide, *Caravan & Camping Ireland*, available from PO Box 4443, Dublin 2. F098-28237, info@camping-ireland.ie http://www.camping-ireland.ie This does not include all the camping sites in Ireland, and in tourist areas there are quite a few independent operators. For Northern Ireland, NRIB's *Where to Stay* guide covers all the camping and caravan parks.

You won't find the Irish using them, but horse-drawn gypsy-style caravans can be hired through tour operators like *Slattery's* or *Enjoy Ireland Holidays* (see page 22) – prices start from IR£186 per person for one week.

Getting around

Rail

Fares &   Trains in the Republic are run by *Iarnród Éireann* (Irish Rail), and while there are a
timetables   number of routes the system is by no means comprehensive and is very much based around routes in and out of Dublin. Many parts of the west and the north are without trains. Fares can be expensive: an off-peak Dublin-Galway single is IR£15, a lot more at weekends, a month return ticket is IR£35, and bicycles are extra (from IR£2 to IR£6). Iarnród Éireann's timetable costs 50p but does not include fare information. In the North, free booklets contain train and bus information for different areas, and are available from stations.

Students (see page 40) can obtain 50% discounts and non-students should consider the various train, and train and bus, passes available. A IR£60 *Explorer Rail Pass* allows five days travel out of 15 consecutive days and includes DART (page 146); for IR£75 the *Rover Rail Pass* is similar but includes Northern Ireland trains. A IR£90 *Explorer Rail/Bus Pass* allows eight days of travel out of 15 consecutive days; for IR£105 the *Emerald Bus/Rail Pass* is similar but includes Northern Ireland trains. An Emerald Pass for 15 days travel out of 30 consecutive days is IR£180. A *Freedom of Northern Ireland Pass* allows for 7 days unlimited travel on all rail and bus services for £35 and unlimited travel for one day is £10. A *Sunday Rambler* gives unlimited bus travel on a Sunday for £5. These passes are available from main train and bus stations. See page 46 for a deal with Hostelling International.

Discounts & passes

Rail passes that cover Europe are worth considering if Ireland is part of your itinerary. *Eurail Youthpass* is for travellers under 26 and starts at US$376 for 15 consecutive days; 1-month and 2-month versions are also available. A version for over-26s costs US$538. Perhaps more useful is the *Eurail Flexipass* which covers 10 or 15 days of travel in a 2-month period: for under-26s for 10 days the cost is US$444, over 26 and it costs US$634. These can be purchased in North America, Australia and New Zealand, through some travel agents catering for students as well as some tour operators, or contact *Rail Europe*, T1-800-4387245 in the USA (T1-800-5552748 in Canada), or *CIT*, 263 Clarence St, Sydney,

Overseas passes

Essentials

Railway routes

© Crown Copyright

T02-92671255, or one of their branches across Australia. Internal train and bus passes can also be purchased in advance in Australia and New Zealand.

Contacts Tickets and passes can be bought at *Iarnród Éireann* Travel Centres, 35 Lower Abbey St, Dublin, T01-7031821, or 65 Patrick St, Cork, T504888, as well as main railway stations. Credit card bookings on T01-7034070 or T021-504888. Iarnród Éireann head office is at Connolly Station, Dublin 1, T01-8363333/7032355. Timetable information on T8366222, http://www.irishrail.ie *Northern Ireland Railways* can be contacted at Central Station, Belfast, T028-90899400, but for general enquiries T028-90899411 or 90434424.

Bus

Fares & timetables *Bus Éireann* operates most of the buses in the Republic, but in some areas, like Donegal, private bus companies are an important supplement and no more expensive. *Ulsterbus* run the buses in the North. Bus Éireann offer various deals that improve on the cost of standard single/return tickets: day return tickets, family tickets covering a monthly return, and midweek returns (Tuesday to Thursday) for the price of a single. A midweek return from Dublin to Waterford is IR£7, to Sligo or Galway IR£10, Donegal or Belfast IR£11, Cork IR£13, Killarney IR£15. A 'day break' return to Wicklow from Dublin, for example, is IR£4.40, to Drogheda IR£4.80, to Kilkenny or Wexford IR£7, to Derry IR£14. Bicycles are IR£5 single, whatever the journey, but space is limited and cannot be taken for granted. 'Day breaks' are also available from Cork and to Blarney, for example, it is IR£1.65, Kinsale IR£3.80, to Glengarriff IR£9, to Killarney IR£12.

If you are going to be using buses a lot it is worth buying the IR£1 Bus Éireann national timetable (fare information is not provided). Missing a bus, and they do run on time, can mean a long wait or even an overnight stay. Ulsterbus provide a free booklet detailing the express services between the main towns as well as booklets covering local area bus and train timetables. In the Republic few towns have a bus station as such, so you need to find out where they stop because there are no prominent signs; the relevant timetable is usually, but not always, displayed nearby. Large towns in the North have bus stations near the centre of town.

Discounts & passes Students with a Travelsave stamp (see page 40) on their ID receive deductions on bus fares in the Republic, while in the North an ISIC card will suffice. A *Rambler Pass* covers 2/8/15 days travel out of 8/15/30 consecutive days for IR£28/68/98. A *Rover Bus Pass* is similar but includes Northern Ireland and costs IR£36/85/130. In the North a *Day Tracker Pass* gives unlimited travel on trains on a Sunday for £3. See the Rail section above for combined bus and train passes and see page 46 for a deal with Hostelling International.

Contacts For general *Bus Éireann* information: *Busáras*, Store St, Dublin 1, T01-8366111/8302222, buse@cie.iol.ie http://www.buseireann.ie For *Dublin Bus*, T01-8734222, http://www.dublinbus.ie For *Ulsterbus*, T028-90333000 or T028-90315655, feedback@translink.co.uk.

Car

Drivers should carry a current licence and non-UK drivers will also need an international driving permit which is readily purchasable through motoring organisations in your country. If you are bringing your own car, bring the registration/ownership documents and check with your insurance company that your policy covers driving in Ireland. If you belong to a motoring organization like the AA, RAC or AAC, check with them before you depart because there is usually a reciprocal agreement with the Irish AA in relation to their 24-hour emergency breakdown service.

Driving is **on the left** and the national speed limit on main roads is 55 mph/88 kmph. In towns and built-up areas the normal speed limit is 30 mph/50 kmph but be guided by posted signs. Front seat occupants must wear seat belts, and motorcyclists and their passengers must wear helmets. Unleaded petrol is around 56p-60p per litre. Disc parking, purchasable in newsagents and displayed inside your car, applies to an increasing number of towns.

Driving in the Republic

Driving is **on the left** and the national speed limit on motorways/freeways is 70 mph/110 kmph and 60 mph/100 kmph on other main roads. In towns and built-up areas the normal speed limit is 30-40 mph/50-60 kmph, but be guided by posted signs. Front seat occupants must wear seat belts and motorcyclists and their passengers must wear helmets. Unleaded petrol is around 70p per litre.

Driving in Northern Ireland

Major car hire companies have desks at airports, ferry terminals and cities across Ireland. Car rental in the Republic is expensive, around IR£200-300 a week, and it is worth checking out advanced car hire booking or combined fly/drive or ferry/drive tickets when working out your travel to Ireland. Tourist areas have their own local car hire companies and these can often be a little cheaper. If a car hire deal is quoted at a rate that is significantly less than others check that it includes a collision damage waiver, for if this is not included the hirer will be responsible for the first IR£500-1000 of damage to the car. Car hire to people under the age of 23 is unlikely; over 21 is sometimes possible. Car hire in Northern Ireland follows more or less the same rules as in the Republic but it will cost less. If you are planning to drive between the North and the Republic, starting in either direction, check that this is allowed for under the contract.

Car rental

There is always a risk in hitching, whatever your sex, so it can never be recommended as a safe way to travel; this applies to Ireland as it does to anywhere else in the world. Having said that, hitching in the Republic is fairly common, and you will often see single people and couples outside towns and cities patiently waiting for an obliging driver. It will often take some time, but sooner or later someone usually stops and it can often lead to interesting and informative conversations. Hitching in Northern Ireland is a lot less common, especially for single males, but getting lifts from the Republic into Northern Ireland does not present any special problems.

Hitching

Bicycle

The weather notwithstanding, cycling around Ireland is definitely one of the most enjoyable and meaningful ways to explore Ireland. Cycling allows you to experience the countryside in a way that cannot be compared to seeing it through the window of a car. Country roads, compared to Britain certainly, are less crowded with traffic and the experience can easily become the highlight of any visit to Ireland. An alternative to relying on a bicycle for the whole duration of your trip is to hire one for a few days, or for a week or more; see page 24 for more information.

Keeping in touch

See the directories in the Dublin (page 147) and Belfast (page 614) chapters for details of embassies that you can turn to in the event of a problem.

Points of contact

Essentials

Essentials

The Gaeltacht

Gaeltacht is the name for areas where Irish is still spoken. When Ireland became independent in 1922 the Irish language was still the everyday language of communication in parts of Cork, Kerry, Waterford, Galway, Mayo and Donegal, and it is the more rural parts of these counties that constitute the Gaeltacht. This does not mean English is not understood or spoken as well, but in Gaeltacht areas you will have an opportunity to hear Irish being spoken and used on a daily basis.

The Irish language, and its offshoots of Scottish Gaelic and Manx, is the Irish branch of the Celtic languages that include Welsh, Cornish and Breton. The number of people speaking Irish in Ireland today is somewhere in the region of 80,000 but you are more likely to hear it spoken on RTE radio where occasional programmes and daily news bulletins are broadcast in Irish. There is also an Irish-language radio station broadcast from Connemara, Radio na Gaeltachta, and a national Irish-language television station, **TG4.**

Language English is spoken by everyone in Ireland, and this is the only language you need to know. There are regional accents and if you travel around for any length of time you will begin to appreciate the distinct differences in sound between, say, the English spoken in Dublin and the English spoken in Cork and Kerry. Stay for long enough in the southwest and you might begin to detect the differences between English in Cork and the English spoken in Kerry. The accent in the north of Ireland is different again and it can take a few hours, or even days, to pick it up. There are colloquial and slang expressions peculiar to the English spoken in Ireland, as there are in all cultures that use English, but they are never a barrier to communication and simply add to the pleasure of everyday communication. It often does seem to be the case that the Irish use the English language in a particularly rich and idiosyncratic way and if you keep your ears tuned you will soon collect some creative (and scatological) expressions.

Some everyday words commonly appear in Irish and it helps to be familiar with them:

Mná	*me-naw*	women
Fir	*fear*	men
Gardai	*gar-dee*	police
Oifig an Phoist	*ifig-on-pwist*	post office

See the glossary on page 709 for Irish words that are commonly found in place names. If you want to impress or just show off you can occasionally use fairly common Irish words like 'slán agat' (*slawn-aguth*), meaning goodbye, or 'go raibh maith agat' (*go-rev-moh-aguth*), meaning thank you. 'Fáilte' (*fawl-cha*) means welcome.

Postal services Postal services across Ireland are efficient and reliable, with a range of services that include recorded or registered mail. A standard letter or postcard to any EU country, and this includes mail between the Republic and Northern Ireland, is 30p (up to 20g) and should bear an air mail sticker (there is no surface mail). In the Republic letters going outside the EU cost from 45p; in Northern Ireland from 44p.

Most post offices in the Republic and Northern Ireland are open 0900-1730, Monday to Friday, and 0900-1300 on Saturday. In rural areas and small towns the post office may close for one afternoon during the week, often on a Wednesday. For postal enquiries in the North T0345-740740.

Fax & email **Fax** If you need to send or receive a fax the first place to try is your place of accommodation, as all hotels, nearly all hostels and some B&Bs will have a fax machine which you will often be able to use for the cost of the call. The next best place to try is

What's the story?

English spoken in Ireland has some delightful inflections and idioms and this list is a mere smattering. Keep your ears open and many more will be heard.

Yoke anything vaguely functional, from an ancient screwdriver to a satellite space station

Craic a good time, good conversation, 'that's the craic' means 'that's the news'; pronounced 'crack'

Eejit gentle (sometimes not-so-gentle) term of contempt for a complete fool

Good luck idiomatic expression of farewell, heard in some parts of the west

Wee small amount

What's the story? what's the news? A polite request for idle gossip

Knacker term of abuse for someone felt to be objectionable

Culchie a country yokel

Sláinte cheers

Sambo a sandwich

Feck a deletable expletive, mispronounced deliberately

the nearest post office or public library, and if they don't have one they might be able to suggest the nearest place that does. In Northern Ireland, if you have a credit card, faxes can be sent over the phone on T0800-190190 , with a basic charge of £5.25 plus 18p per page of text (58 lines of text, including the address), dictated over the phone, rising to a maximum of £7.

Email Some libraries have an email service available to the public, and Internet cafés are to be found not only in Dublin and Belfast but in a growing number of other cities, towns and even some villages.

Republic Public payphones are easy to find and come in two versions: coin-operated or cardphone-operated. Sometimes the two types are found next to each other in separate booths and sometimes there will only be the one kind available (and, increasingly, this will be the card-operated version). Phonecards, bought at newsagents and post offices, are more convenient to use, especially for long-distance or international calls. Phone cards are sold in denominations of IR£2, IR£3.50, IR£8 and IR£16. All calls, whether local, long-distance or international, are cheapest after 1800 or on a Saturday or Sunday. Local calls from payphones during the day cost 20p for 3 minutes, though payphones in pubs and other places may cost 30p.

Using telephones
See inside front cover for dialling codes for phoning out of and within Ireland.

Making an international call from the Republic T00+country code+area code (without the 0)+number. So, for example, to phone the UK number 020-71231234, T00-44-20-71231234. To call Northern Ireland, however, T80+ area code (without the 0)+number.

Northern Ireland Public payphones, as in the Republic, are either operated with coins or cards (called phonecards), and sometimes the same payphone will accept either. In towns, and rural areas especially, coin-operated payphones are less common than card-operated ones.

Making an international call from Northern Ireland The procedure is the same as in the Republic: T00+country code+area code (without the 0)+number. So, for example, to phone the US number 01-212-1231234, T00-1-212-1231234. The same applies to phoning the Republic, so to reach the Dublin number 01-6024000 you would dial T00-353-1-6024000.

Using mobile phones Only digital phones with GSM subscriptions and a roaming agreement will work in Ireland. Check with your supplier before you leave.

Changes to telephone numbers in Northern Ireland

From June 1999 the Northern Ireland area code changed to 028, so that where previously there were different area codes for different areas (Belfast was 01232, Derry was 01504) there is now only the one area code, which is 028. Also from June 1999, all local 5- and 6-digit numbers became 8 digits long, and it is these 8-digit numbers that appear in this book. However, the old area codes and the old 5- or 6- digit numbers (which do not appear in this guide) will continue to be usable until 16 September 2000. So if you have an old number from some source other than this book you can use it until 16 September 2000, but not after that date.

Operator services

In the Republic

Emergency services	T999 or T112
Operator	T10

In the Republic and Northern Ireland

Irish (Republic and NI) enquiries	T11811
International directory enquiries	T11818
International operator services	T114
Telegram	T196

In Northern Ireland

Emergency services	T999
Operator	T100
Directory enquiries	T192
International directory enquiries	T153
International operator services	T155
Telegrams	T0800-190190

Media

Newspapers **Republic** The quality daily newspaper is *The Irish Times*, but during the week its slim size hardly makes it worth the price of 85p; Saturday's edition is better in this respect. Of the other dailies, the *Irish Independent* is lighter in tone while *The Examiner* makes for more interesting reading. The *Star* is a fairly useless tabloid, but if you really want gutter-press journalism take a look at the Irish edition of *The Sun*. All the English daily and Sunday newspapers are readily available on the day of publication, and in Dublin city centre, foreign newspapers are also available. Irish Sunday newspapers don't amount to much; the *Sunday World* is sensationalist and the *Sunday Tribune* is probably the best read. Counties produce their own local papers, and Dublin and Cork have evening papers, mainly of local interest.

Northern Ireland Apart from the British dailies there is the *Irish News*, read predominantly by the nationalist community and usually a good read, and the tabloid *News Letter* which presents a staunchly loyalist view of events. The *Belfast Telegraph* is an evening paper and mainly of local interest only. *An Phoblacht* (Republican News) is a Sinn Féin weekly paper.

Magazines International magazines like *Time* and *Newsweek* can be found in most towns across Ireland, and there is also a host of Irish-produced magazines catering to special interests and hobbies. The *Phoenix* is a satirical magazine along the lines of Britain's

Private Eye and there is never any shortage of political and business scandals fuelling its contents. *Magill* is also worth reading when it uncovers a juicy story of yet more political shenanigans. *Hot Press* carries listings of musical gigs and other cultural events and its features on music, politics and much else is often interesting.

Television

RTE (Radio Telefís Éireann) runs RTE 1 and Network 2, 2 national stations in the Republic. RTE 1 broadcasts the more interesting news programmes and shows of cultural and historical interest. Network 2 has the occasionally riveting programme but the usual diet is a mix of chat shows, cheap films and serials. There is also an Irish-language channel (see page 52). Around Dublin and other parts of the eastern half of the country, some British channels can be picked up. In Northern Ireland there are the British television channels, and the Republic's channels can also be received. Cable or satellite television is usually found in hotels and guesthouses, but too often only the basic package is subscribed to and the film channels are not available.

Radio

In the **Republic** three radio channels are also run by RTE: Radio 1, a generally good mix of news and cultural programmes; 2FM for pop music; and Radio na Gaeltachta, which is an Irish-language channel. There is also Lyric FM, a classical music channel. Today FM 100-104 provides some competition to RTE and is best listened to in the evening. There is also a host of independent close to RTE and is best listened to in the evening. There is also a host of independent local stations. In **Northern Ireland** there is the full gamut of British radio stations and some local channels.

Food and drink

Restaurants
See inside front cover for restaurant price grades.

The much-heralded wave of new Irish cooking does indeed have a lot going for it, and anyone returning to Ireland after an absence of a few years will be in for gastronomic treats. The best restaurants use local produce to serve up an array of traditional and modern dishes, and when it is done well the results are truly terrific and often good value for money. Sometimes a restaurant tries too hard to be international; Parmesan shavings and goat's cheese on a menu does not guarantee an interesting meal. Hotel restaurants sometimes use rich sauces to disguise overcooked food.

Seafood is often the highlight of menus in coastal counties, but do not assume that because a restaurant is near the sea its fish is absolutely fresh. It is not unknown for fresh fish to be landed, hauled up to Dublin, and sold through a national wholesaler before being delivered to a restaurant close to where it was first landed. It is always worth asking how fresh the fish is, and more times than not you will receive an honest answer. Locally-sourced beef and lamb is another speciality to look out for, and a good steak or leg of lamb from Kerry should not disappoint. Vegetarian restaurants are thin on the ground, and we have drawn attention to every half-decent one we could find. Most menus include a 'vegetarian dish of the day', but if it turns out to be lasagne then forget it, for in our experience that is one sure sign of a restaurateur's indifference.

County Cork (but this does *not* include Kinsale) is currently enjoying a well-deserved reputation for some of the best food in the country, and other counties in the west are beginning to catch up. Northern Ireland, with a few individual exceptions, is generally awful as regards eating out, and while Dublin, Wicklow and Wexford have some excellent restaurants, the capital city has its fair share of trendy and expensive dross. For a combination of value for money and a sense of occasion, excellent meals can be enjoyed in some of the country houses dotted around the country, and most of them welcome non-residents (and vegetarians) as long as a reservation is made in advance. Expect to pay around IR£25-30 for a three-course meal, excluding wine or other drinks.

Restaurants offering Chinese food, and Indian to a lesser extent, are fairly common in the cities and a number of towns, but apart from noted places in Dublin and Belfast the food is fairly hideous; most offer a take-away service that is slightly better value.

Pubs

The pub is very much the centre of social life in Ireland, indeed for males it sometimes seems to be the only centre of social life, and a visit to Ireland without experiencing a few would be to miss out on an essential aspect of cultural life. It is not obligatory to consume only alcohol, but asking for tea or coffee at 2300 in a crowded bar is pushing it a bit. The pub is a great place to meet other travellers, and if you visit some of the popular bars in tourist towns like Clifden, Westport, Kinsale or Killarney they will probably be the only other customers that you will meet. To mix with locals and enjoy a good conversation it is often necessary to seek out the quieter places to which the regulars retreat in the summer months. Pubs with sessions of traditional music are never hard to find in tourist areas, but usually nothing starts to happen until at least 2100.

Pub summer hours (mid-April-early October) in the Republic are 1030-2230 (2300 in winter), Monday to Saturday, and 1230-1400 and 1600 to 2300 on Sunday. Opening hours in the North are 1100 to 2300, Monday to Saturday, 1230-2200 on Sunday.

Italian restaurants also often offer good value, and many towns will have places serving pasta and pizza dishes, while the cities have Italian restaurants in their own right. There are also some interesting Japanese restaurants dotted around Ireland; these are all described in the text.

The price range for a restaurant is given in the text, but remember that this is an indication of the average price for main dishes. Expect to pay around IR£25 for a good three-course evening meal, excluding drinks, and around IR£12-IR£15 for a good lunch.

Pub food The quality of the food varies enormously, but pubs are nearly always your best bet when looking for an informal and affordable meal at lunch or dinner time. Many pubs serve food from 1200 to 2100 and some will have separate dining areas. The standard price for a pub lunch is around IR£5, and while there is a tendency to rely on the standard meat/fish with potatoes/chips and vegetables, pubs in tourist areas can be relied on to offer alternatives. Home-made soups may not be filling enough for everyone, but they are often tasty, and salads and open seafood sandwiches are worth considering. Unless you ask for brown, expect tasteless white bread.

Bars in hotels, especially at lunchtime, offer comfortable seating most of the time, and competition from pubs ensures that their prices are similar. There is absolutely no obligation to consume alcohol as tea, coffee and soft drinks are also available. Pub food in the North is generally disappointing: the idea of a meal without meat seems quite foreign, overcooked vegetables and unimaginative presentations the norm. Champ, potatoes mashed with spring onions, is a tasty speciality in the North, and there are some superb soda breads.

Picnic food When the weather is fine, a picnic lunch is a satisfying and economical way to enjoy a meal, and every town has a supermarket or two, the larger ones with a delicatessen section, and often a good bakery where fresh delicious breads and scones are usually available. Local cheeses are always worth seeking out, and such is their popularity that you will often find them far from their origins. If a town has a river there will usually be bankside benches or somewhere suitable to lay out your food, and while planned parks are not so common most towns are not far from the countryside.

Drinks Ireland is not in the top 10 list of alcohol-consuming countries of the world, but it ranks second, after the Czech Republic, in the list of beer-drinking countries, at 250 pints/142 litres per year per head of the population. (The UK ranks seventh position at

Where to go for a drink – not Dublin!

Unbelievable but true: Dublin is short of pubs. The capital has 29% of the population but only 9% of its pubs, an anomaly due to an antiquated system that makes it well nigh impossible to open new licensed premises (pub licences in the capital change hands for half a million punts). A 1902 law, strenuously upheld by the Catholic Church and the Licensed Vintners Association, puts the brake on new licenses being created other than for exceptional circumstances. Unfortunately, exceptional circumstances do not include population shifts and the result is that an area like Tallaght in Dublin has the record for the fewest number of pubs per head in the whole of Ireland. In the 1960s, when Tallaght was a village of 400 souls, there were eight pubs; it is now a working class suburb of nearly 90,000 people and the number of pubs is ten. A tragedy for people living there, but visitors can leave the capital and head for just about anywhere else – where the situation is just a little different …

180 pints/102 litres and the USA is ranked 13th.) **Guinness** is the world-renowned Irish drink, and it is no idle boast that the best pint of Guinness is served in Ireland, Dublin to be exact, and if you have tasted draught Guinness in an ordinary pub in Britain this will soon become apparent. Guinness with oysters is a classic lunchtime dish, and on some menus you will see the famous black stuff featured in dishes. There are alternative stouts, and both Beamish and Murphy's should be sampled; they are not only cheaper, but fine drinks in their own right. A variety of lagers, draught and bottled, is also readily available in all pubs. A pint of beer costs around IR£1.90 to IR£2.30 and unless you ask for "a glass (ie a half pint) of Guinness", or whatever your drink is, a pint will automatically be served.

Irish ***whiskeys*** taste quite different to Scotch – superior in our opinion – and there are quite a few you can try in order to be convinced. A hot whiskey comes with cloves and lemon and is a heart-warming drink on a cold day. Any spirit served in a pub is a substantially larger measure than its counterpart in Britain or North America.

Wine in pubs is most likely to come in the form of a ¼-bottle, and costs around IR£2.50. It is not that usual to order a whole bottle of wine in a pub and while it is possible there is often not much of a choice. Some restaurants have a BYO (Bring Your Own) policy and a reasonable choice of wines is available in most supermarkets. Expect to pay at least IR£5 for the cheapest, and usually not very palatable, wine and from around IR£8 and upwards for a half-decent bottle. In the cities it is possible to purchase reliable wines for between IR£5 and IR£10; consult a copy of *The Best of Wine in Ireland* which good supermarkets and wine shops should have manacled to the counter or shelf.

Non-alcoholic drinks come in the form of a limited choice of bottled beers and outrageously-priced soft and fizzy drinks. A cup or pot of tea is available in nearly all pubs and coffee is served with milk.

Shopping

Visitors from Britain or North America will not find any spectacular shopping bargains in Ireland, but that does not mean there aren't lots of interesting and well priced purchases to be considered. As a general rule, the best buys are in the form of Irish-produced craft and art products like clothing, pottery and jewellery, and tourist areas all have large shops conveniently filled with a wide choice of possibilities. In these shops you will find everything from tacky leprechaun-shaped telephones to expensive hand-knitted garments, and if you are travelling around Ireland they are a good place to start in order to get some idea of prices, because you will usually come across similar stock in another tourist town.

What to buy

Essentials

👉 *For peat's sake have a whiskey*

There are a number of differences in the distilling process that account for the distinct taste of Irish whiskey as opposed to Scotch whisky (but they don't account for the spelling), and the peaty smokiness of Scotch is often contrasted with the smoothness of Irish. This seems odd to some tipplers who appreciate the spiky aromatics found in some Irish whiskeys and, besides, there is an Irish single malt called Connemara that is sweeter and more peaty than most Scotches. Millar's and Inishowen are blended whiskeys distilled by the same company, and they also turn out an unpeated single malt called Tyrconnell. Bushmills whiskey, smooth and creamy indeed, is distilled in County Antrim (see page 570), while Jameson comes from Midleton near Cork (see page 296). Near-relations of Jameson are Power's and Paddy, and the lighter Tullamore Dew.

Aran sweaters, named after the County Galway islands where the women traditionally knitted them, are world famous, and while nowadays they are largely machine-made they are still attractive and distinctive. If you prefer something less chunky and white there is a choice of shawls, skirts, blouses, and jackets for both sexes, in a variety of materials from thick tweeds to fine linens.

Irish pottery can be exquisitely beautiful, and is available to suit most budgets both in terms of quality and quantity. It mostly takes a practical form in the shape of plates, mugs, bowls, table lamps, clocks and candlesticks, but decorative items, like the Belleek pottery that comes as brooches and little pots of flowers, are also available, and some of the more expensive pottery is best reserved for display anyway. A similar mix of the practical and decorative is found in Irish crystal, of which the Waterford variety is famous around the world.

The craft shops that sell pottery often have small but enticing collections of Irish jewellery which are often fashioned around Celtic designs; look out also for the distinctive Claddagh rings that originated in Connaught and are composed of a crowned heart nestling between a pair of hands, or jewellery worked in the form of Ogham script. You can often have a necklace made with your own name on it in Ogham.

Irish memorabilia takes myriad forms if looking merely for souvenirs or small gifts, including penny whistles with sheet music, shillelagh walking sticks which are traditionally made of blackthorn or oak, carved pieces of Connemara marble, and CDs of traditional music ranging from John McCormack to Shane McGowan.

Where to buy Individual shops worth mentioning are found under the Shopping section for particular towns and cities. Many travellers to Ireland will first arrive in Dublin, and if this is where you will also depart from then it makes sense for serious shoppers to conduct a reconnaissance trip around the major shops (see page 138), taking note of the merchandise and their prices, before returning to make purchases after having travelled elsewhere in the country. Some of the best crafts and arts are found in small workshop premises outside of the capital.

For Aran sweaters and other quality garments, some of the best clothing stores are to be found in the counties of Galway and Donegal, and to a lesser extent Wicklow. The city of Limerick is associated with Irish lace products. Small and large pottery shops are dotted all around Ireland but for real quality head for Kerry, particularly the Dingle Peninsula, and West Cork. The little village of Belleek in Fermanagh, easily reached from Donegal, is famous for its bone china. Wexford also has some good pottery shops and in and around the city of Kilkenny there are noted workshops. Outside of Dublin, Kilkenny has a claim to be the single best shopping city in Ireland, and there are quality examples of most crafts and arts as well as some top-notch jewellery and pottery workshops to the south of the city. For crystal there is the internationally-

Major festivals and events (2000 dates)

March 17	St Patrick's Day Festivals
March 23-28	Irish Masters Snooker
April 15-25	Dublin Film Festival
May 27-31	Kilkenny's Cat Laughs Comedy Festival
June 1-6	Listowel Writers' Week
June 10-20	Music Festival in Great Irish Houses
July 15-25	Galway International Arts Festival
July 31-August 6	Galway Races
August 10-12	Puck Fair, Killorglin
August 13-22	Kilkenny Arts Week
August 19	Clifden Connemara Pony Show
August 20-26	Rose of Tralee International Festival
September 10-12	Clarenbridge Oyster Festival
September 12	All Ireland Hurling Finals
September 18-23	Listowel Races
September 21-24	Galway Oyster Festival
September 26	All Ireland Football Finals
September 18-October 3	Waterford International Festival of Light Opera
October 4-16	Dublin Theatre Festival
October 7-10	Kinsale Gourmet Festival
October 10-17	Cork International Film Festival
October 19-November 5	Wexford Opera Festival
October 22-25	Cork Jazz Festival
October 30	Dublin Marathon
October 29-mid Nov	Belfast Festival at Queen's

Essentials

Public Holidays

Republic	**Northern Ireland**
January 1 New Year's Day	January 1 New Year's Day
March 17, St Patrick's Day	March 17, St Patrick's Day
Easter Monday	Easter Monday
First Monday in May	First Monday in May
First Monday in June	Last Monday in May
First Monday in August	July 12, Orange Day
Last Monday in October	Last Monday in August
December 25	December 25
December 26	December 26

renowned Waterford factory with its comprehensive display of items for sale, but in the city of Waterford itself it is possible to purchase less expensive crystal products and there are other areas in the country that produce their own modest examples of this craft.

Shopping on the Internet A growing number of Irish shopping outlets are adding an Internet-based mail order service to their offerings. Among those worth a visit are http://www.iol.ie/gnorman-photography (a gallery with outlets in Dublin and Kinsale); http://www.houseofnames.ie (House of Names, with heraldic shops in Dublin and Killarney); http://www. celticrhythm.com (Soundz of Muzic in Kenmare); and http://www.heritagecrystal.com (Heritage Crystal in Waterford).

Holidays and festivals

A *Calendar of Events*, a useful joint publication by Bord Fáilte and the NITB, has an awesome list of festivals held up and down the country along with dates, contact names and telephone numbers. It also lists the Irish racing calendar. Don't be too taken in by this, however, because tourist boards always feel overly obliged to present their countries as festive places brimming with carnival spirit. St Patrick's Day has never been a particularly festive occasion; those events that are now held on in or around the 17th March are nearly all recent inventions, and publicans and other merchants have recently seen the value of manufacturing and hosting local festivals at sundry times of the year. There are some notable exceptions with venerable histories and/or real carnival spirit, as well as some excellent annual cultural events, and these, plus some of the more successful recent inventions, are listed above. The dates refer to 2000 and may change slightly from one year to the next, so always check in advance and enquire from the tourist boards about literature specific to individual events. See also the box on the previous page.

Health

There are no alarming facts or fears to take into account when travelling within Ireland. The water is safe to drink, no inoculations are required or necessary, and there is a generally excellent health service; to cap it all there are no snakes and little danger of sunburn.

What to take
Make sure you are covered for emergency medical treatment in Ireland. Visitors from *EU countries* are entitled to free medical treatment but to facilitate this bring with you a Form E111 from your country (available from post offices in Britain). British visitors can receive emergency treatment and medicines without ever having to show this form, but it is still advisable to bring it because in some circumstances it could make a difference. British visitors to the North require no documents and will receive treatment as they would in Britain. Visitors from *non-EU countries* are charged for all medical treatment except out-patient treatment at accident and emergency units of public hospitals. *Medical insurance* is therefore highly advisable for those citizens.

Travel insurance is worth considering for all visitors to Ireland, especially for those arriving from outside Britain. A good policy will cover loss or theft of luggage, including money, and it will also cover medical expenses including emergency expatriation

A *first aid kit* is useful and should include pills for possible hangovers and/or stomach upsets as well as any an adequate supply of any prescribed or essential drugs or medicines. Walkers should be prepared for blisters and small cuts and a compass is advisable for walks in mountainous areas.

Further reading

All books are paperback unless stated as hardback (HB).

Art, architecture & gardens
Courtney Davis *Celtic Illumination: The Irish School* Thames & Hudson, 1998; illustrations and sensitive text describing Celtic manuscripts from the 7th century to the 12th. **Sean Rothery** *The Buildings of Ireland* Lilliput Press, 1997; delicate ink drawings accompany each of the 194 buildings selected by the author as fine examples of buildings dotted around towns and dating from early Christian times to

the 20th century. **Dorothy Walker** *Modern Art in Ireland* Lilliput Press, 1997 (HB); the best illustrated guide to Irish art from the 1940s, when artists began to challenge the nationalist and academic notions of orthodoxy in paintings, to the contemporary. Foreword by Seamus Heaney. **Brian P Kennedy** *Irish Painting* Town House & Country House, 1993 (HB); starts about 1640 with an unknown artist and ends with a 1953 Jack B Yeats painting, all in colour, plus biographies. **Jeremy Williams** *Architecture in Ireland 1837-1921* Irish Academic Press, 1994 (HB); comprehensive gazetteer detailing the architecture of post-Georgian Ireland county by county and building by building; opinionated and knowledgeable. **Olda FitzGerald** *Irish Gardens* Conran Octopus, 1999 (HB); **Melanie Eclare** *Glorious Gardens of Ireland*, Kyle Cathie, 1999 (HB) £30 and £25 respectively but gorgeous colour photographs that will have you green with envy. **Seán O'Reilly** *Irish Houses and Gardens* Aurum Press, 1998 (HB); collection of archival *Country Life* articles with many rare photographs of grand interiors.

Frank McCourt *Angela's Ashes* Flamingo, 1997; although the winner of the 1997 **Autobiography** Pulitzer Prize for Non-Fiction, this book merges with the novel form to tell the bittersweet memoir of the writer growing up in New York and Ireland in the 1930s and '40s. **Nuala O'Faolain** *Are You Somebody?* New Island Books, 1996; growing up in Dublin under an alcoholic mother and a scoundrel father; this is a great classic already. **Aidan Higgins** *Donkey's Years* Minerva, 1995; the perfect companion piece to McCourt's grim humour, set in the same period of time but a different part of the country, Kildare, and a profoundly different social class, the young Higgins having a privileged upbringing – materially, at least. But McCourt and Higgins have a lot in common as their memories remorselessly expose a terribly pained Irish childhood. **Gerry Adams** *Falls Memories*, Brandon, 1993; nostalgic and humourous memories of growing up in the Falls Rd. **Bobby Sands** *Bobby Sands Writings from Prison*, Mercier, 1998; secretly written and smuggled out from Long Kesh, a painful account of a man's attempt to preserve his identity in prose and poetry.

Fintan Vallely & Charlie Piggott *Blooming Meadows*, Town House & Country **Culture** House, 1998; the musical lives of over a score of musicians like Brendan Begley, Mary Begin, Paddy Keenan, Ann Mulqueen, and Sharon Shannon. Strictly for lovers of traditional Irish music, **Fintan Vallely** *Companion to Irish Traditional Music*, Cork University Press, 1998, (HB); accompanied by a CD, a good reference for the enthusiast. **Pat Levy** *Culture Shock! Ireland*, Graphic Arts Center Publishing, 2000; full of insights (well, we would say that wouldn't we?) into the lifestyle and mentality of contemporary Ireland. **M Daly, M Hearn and P Pearson** *Dublin's Victorian Houses*, A & A Farmer, 1998; much more than the title suggests and a lovely way in to Victorian Dublin. **Dorothy Harrison Therman** *Stories from Tory Island*, Town House & Country House, 1989; transcriptions of conversations with the Antrim islanders; foreword by Derek Hill. **J M Synge** *The Aran Islands*, Oxford; the 1907 travelogue sparkles with the writer's affection for the place though tales told around turf fires about children taken by the fairies are now ancient history. **Fintan O'Toole** *The Lie of the Land*, Verso, 1997; journalistic essays covering the decline of the Church, emigration, the Haughey era and other aspects of Irish life in the '90s. **Helen Brennan** *The Story of Irish Dance*, Brandon, 1999; from medieval times to contemporary set dancing; far too sympathetic to *Riverdance* but a useful study nonetheless. **Margaret Johnson** *The Irish Heritage Cookbook*, Wolfhound Press, 1999; onion and Murphy's Stout soup followed by chicken with cabbage and bacon, plus another 200 recipes of traditional and not-so-traditional meals. **Terry Eagleton** *The Truth About The Irish*, New Island Books, 1999; a laugh a minute, literally, in this alphabet of Irish mores. Worth reading for the entry on B&Bs alone.

Essentials

Literature

The individual books listed here make up a very partial and subjective selection of mostly modern writers

General Ulick O'Connor *Celtic Dawn*, Town House & Country House, 1985; a portrait of the Irish literary renaissance, told with warm affection. **Terry Eagleton** *Crazy John and the Bishop and Other Essays on Irish Culture*, Cork University Press, 1998; not exactly light reading but thoroughly stimulating collection of innovative essays on Irish culture from the 18th century onwards. **Declan Kiberd** *Inventing Ireland: The Literature of the Modern Nation*, Cape, 1995; Wilde, Yeats, Joyce and Beckett – by way of lesser-known writers like Sommerville & Ross, Elizabethan Bowen and others. Refreshing and stimulating look at the colonial and post-colonial writers of Ireland. **Gerald Dawe and Jonathan Williams**, editors, *Krino*, Gill & Macmillan, 1996; anthology of prose, poetry, reviews, essays and interviews from the magazine of contemporary Irish literature. **Robert Welch**, editor, *The Oxford Companion to Irish Literature*, Oxford, 1996; perfect general purpose reference guide to Ireland's literary heritage. **P J Kavanagh** *Voices in Ireland*, John Murray, London, 1994; this traveller's literary companion is an excellent paperback, divided into geographical regions, to stuff into the luggage.

Literature Roddy Doyle *A Star Called Henry*, Cape, 1999, (HB); a long way from *The Commitments* but an interesting development after the disappointing *Paddy Clarke Ha Ha Ha*. A novel that reflects on heroism and the Easter 1916 hullabaloo. Paperback edition should soon follow. **John McGahern** *Amongst Women*, Faber, 1990; perhaps the most resonant of McGahern's works, blending the personal and the political in a masterful and disturbing way. **John Trolan** *Any Other Time*, Brandon, 2000; set in the underworld of junkie Dublin, this is the antidote to Bord Fáilte's capital. **Tom Phelan** *Derrycloney*, (Brandon, 1999) A captivating tale of an Irish rural townland in the 1940s. **Dermot Bolger** *Ladies Night at Finbar's Hotel*, edited by New Island Books, 1999; the female follow up to the *Finbar's Hotel* anthology, a comic literary 'whodunit' with the authorship of the seven chapters left to the reader to discover. **Seamus Deane** *Reading in the Dark*, Vintage, 1997; set in Derry in the 1950s and '60s and reaching into a personal and political heart of darkness. **Patricia Craig**, editor, *The Belfast Anthology*, Blackstaff, 1999, (HB); where else would Gerry Adams, Graham Greene, Philip Larkin and Van Morrison rub shoulders? Material from the 17th century to the present: memoirs, poetry, fiction, travel writing, history and letters. **Éilís Ní Dhuibhne** *The Dancers Dancing*, Blackstaff Press, 1999; a group of girls attending a summer school in county Donegal provide a setting for this exploration of sex, politics, and Irishness. **Liam O'Flaherty** *The Informer*, Wolfhound Press; written in 1925 and set against the background of 1920s Ireland, this is O'Flaherty's best work. **Somerville and Ross** *The Real Charlotte*, Quartet Books, 1977; the female cousins' most accomplished work, a haunting microcosm of the Anglo-Irish world. **Gabrielle Warnock** *The Silk Weaver*, London, 1998; an historical novel set in 18th-century Dublin. **Flann O'Brien** *The Third Policeman*, Grafton; written in 1940, this brilliantly subversive and enormously comic novel deconstructs the deadening conventionality of Irish life under deValera. **John B Keane** *Three Plays*, Mercier Press, 1990; text of *Sive*, *the Field* and *Big Maggie* by the Kerry playwright who is finally being recognised. **Laurence Sterne** *Tristram Shandy*, Vintage; this outrageously post-modernist novel first came out in 1759. Read it for a long, literary laugh. **James Joyce** *Ulysses*, Vintage, first published 1922; the first couple of chapters put most would-be readers off ever finishing the novel. Persevere, make use of a recorded reading (see CDs below), and listen to the voices of Dublin that have never been so astonishingly recreated in written form before or since. *Finnegans Wake* is another kettle of fish but recorded readings will open a window on this extraordinary work **Robert Nicholson** *The Ulysses Guide*, Methuen, 1988; the best practical *Ulysses* guide, it follows the eighteen episodes on their original locations accompanied by clear maps, detailed directions and summaries of each episode. Suitable for the newcomer or the seasoned Joycean. **Samuel Beckett** *Waiting for Godot*, Faber; though first performed in French in 1953, recent productions by Dublin's Gate Theatre have revealed the Irish syntax that lies behind the English translation by Beckett himself.

Poetry Seamus Heaney *Opened Ground*, Faber, 1998; to date, this is the closest Heaney comes to presenting his *oeuvre*, containing selections from *Wintering Out* (1972), *Stations* and *North* (1975), *Field Work* (1979), *Station Island* (1983), *The Haw Lantern* (1987), *Seeing Things* (1990) and *The Spirit Level* (1996). Enough here to last a lifetime. **Seamus Heaney** *North*, Faber, 1975; Heaney's most controversial set of poems as he sets about confronting brute facts like colonialism, the British army and the social divisions of his country. His mythologising instinct comes face to face with violence and the poetry reaches new heights. **Patricia Boyle Haberstroh**, editor, *Women Creating Women: Contemporary Irish Women Poets*, Attic Press, Cork, 1996; studies of the finest women poets writing in Ireland today: Eavan Boland, Eiléan Ní Chuilleanáin, Medbh McGuckian and Nuala Ní Dhomhnaill.

General Jonathan Barden *A History of Ulster*, Belfast, 1992; easily the best history of the northern province, even-handed throughout and in a style that makes it a pleasure to read. Find a place for it in your luggage. **T Bartlett & K Jeffrey**, editor, *A Military History of Ireland* Cambridge, 1996; military history but without the militarism. Scholarly, but highly readable, collection of 19 essays covering a thousand years of Irish history. Illustrated. **John O'Beirne Ranelagh** *A Short History of Ireland*, Cambridge, 1983; updated to 1998, a useful one-volume account of Irish history. **Sean Duffy**, editor, *Atlas of Irish History* Gill & Macmillan, 1997; a visual and highly satisfying summary of the sweep of Irish history and politics up to modern times. **Margaret Ward**, editor, *In Their Own Voice: Women and Irish Nationalism*, Attic Press, 1995; anthology of women's accounts of the struggle for Irish independence. **Charles Townshend** *Ireland: The 20th Century*, Arnold, 1998; detailed but readable account of modern Ireland from the origins of Sinn Féin onwards. **James Lydon** *The Making of Ireland*, Routledge, 1998; one of the best general histories of the country from ancient times onwards. **S J Connolly**, editor *The Oxford Companion to Irish History*, Oxford, 1998; comprehensive and indispensible reference guide for Irish history.

Pre-history Michael J O'Kelly *Early Ireland*, Cambridge University Press, 1989; covering much the same ground as Harbison's book but with a more scholarly tone. **Simon James** *Exploring the World of the Celts*, Thames & Hudson, 1993, (HB); well-illustrated survey of Celtic history and culture. **Peter Harbison** *Pre-Christian Ireland*, Thames & Hudson, 1998; comprehensive and readable synthesis of early Ireland and its archaeology. **Simon James** *The Atlantic Celts*, British Museum Press, 1999; controversial but convincing thesis, delivering a big blow to New Age Celtists, that the false idea of an insular Celtic identity was engendered by the rise of nationalism in the 18th century. **John Matthews** *The Celtic Seers' Source Book*, Blandford Cassell, 1999 (HB); if you really want to explore the visions, magic, legacy and teachings of the ancient Celts then dip into this book, though be warned this is not for the faint-hearted. Also available by Matthews, in paperback, are *The Bardic Source Book* and *The Druid Source Book*.

Specialist Bernard O'Mahoney & Mick McGovern *A Soldier of the Queen*, (Brandon, 2000) The revealing and shocking life of an ordinary soldier serving in Northern Ireland at the height of the Dirty War. *Blood in the Streets* Guildhall Press, 1972 and 1998; a chilling account of what happened in Derry on Bloody Sunday in 1972. **Tom Reilly** *Cromwell An Honourable Enemy*, Brandon, 1999; who said Cromwell was the scourge of the Irish? A daring reassessment of the the most reviled figure in Irish history. **Francis J Costello** *Enduring the Most*, Brandon Books, 1995; the story of Terrence MacSwiney's 73-day hunger strike in 1920. **Margaret Ward** *Hanna*

Sheehy Skeffington: A Life, Attic Press, 1997; valuable biography of the feminist socialist who became an important figure in Sinn Féin at the turn of the century. *Hazel: A Life of Lady Lavery*, Lilliput Press, 1996; the astonishing story of how a girl from boomtown Chicago became the confidant of Michael Collins, Kevin O'Higgins and many other notables of the times. **Peter Taylor** *Loyalists*, Bloomsbury, 1999; based on a series of interviews with leading loyalist paramilitaries; a frigtening book. **K Theodore Hoppen** *Ireland Since 1800*, Longman, 1989; pithy and full of concise insights into Irish history from Daniel O'Connell to church scandals in the 1980s. **Peter Taylor** *Provos*, Bloomsbury, 1997; the most informative and balanced account of the IRA to be published. **John McGurk** *The Elizabethan Conquest of Ireland*, Manchester, 1997; fascinating for its details and its focus on the social impact of the Nine Years' War. **Thomas Keneally** *The Great Shame*, Chatto & Windus, 1998; the author of *Schindler's Ark* turns his masterly narrative art on the story of Irish emigration. **Dáire and Nicholas Furlong**, editor, *The Women of 1798*, (Four Courts Press, Dublin, 1998) Long-overdue account of the role of women in the tumultous events of 1798. **Thomas Bartlett** *Theobold Wolfe Tone*, Dundalgan Press, 1997; concise but engaging biography of Wolfe Tone, one of the most attractive of the many revolutionary figures produced by Irish history.

The Anglo-Irish **Mark Bence-Jones** *Life in an Irish Country House*, Constable, 1996; over 20 chapters, each focusing on a particular house and the life lived therein. *Mary Carberry's West Cork Journals, 1898-1901*, Lilliput Press, 1998, (HB); encounters with local life and customs and the writer's winning indifference to the grander aspects of an Anglo-Irish Ascendancy makes this a fascinating read. *Seventy Years Young* Lilliput Press, 1991; Anglo-Irish memoirs of Elizabeth, Countess of Fingall, who married at the age of 17 into the Ascendancy and ended up working for the United Irishwomen. **Peter Somerville-Large** *The Irish Country House*, Sinclair-Stevenson, 1995 (HB); well-illustrated and lively social history of the Ascendancy class in Ireland **David Thomson** *Woodbrook*, Vintage, 1991; a memoir of Anglo-Irish life in Sligo in the 1930s and a moving love-story. Lyrical and hauntingly sad.

Ecology & **FHA Aalen and Kevin Whelan**, editors, *Atlas of the Irish Rural Landscape*, edited by
natural history Cork University Press, 1997 (HB); definitive and stupendous account of the Irish landscape. **David Cabot** *Ireland*, HarperCollins, 1999 (HB); expensive (£35) but comprehensive and well-nigh indispensable account of the natural history of Ireland, focusing on the diverse habitats and with over 200 illustrations. **David Cabot** *Irish Birds* Collins; there is more than one guide for bird-watchers in Ireland but this affordable and practical book is one of the best. **Terry Carruthers** *Kerry: A Natural History*, Collins Press, 1998 (HB); colour-illustrated account of Kerry's flora, fauna, marine and freshwater life, agriculture and conservation issues. (Did you know that the introduced Japanese sika deer are hooked on goose droppings and that Kerry is the only county with all the Irish species of insect-eating plants?) **Robert Lloyd Praeger** *The Way That I Went*, Collins Press, 1998; one of Ireland's greatest naturalists (1865-1953) and of all his works, (*The Botanist in Ireland* (1934), *Natural History of Ireland* (1950), *Irish Landscape* (1953) and others), this topographical classic is his most memorable.

Walking guides **David Marshall** *Best Walks in Ireland*, Constable, London, 1996; five in the North and 15 in the Republic, graded in difficulty from an easy day's stroll to an ambitious and demanding climb up a mountain. Good maps, clear instructions and anecdotes along the way. **Michael Fewer** *The Way-Marked Trails of Ireland*, Gill & Macmillan, 1996; a reliable guide to the best way-marked trails in the Republic, with maps and practical information on where to stay and eat. **Sandra Bardwell, Pat Levy and Gareth McCormack** *Walking in Ireland*, Lonely Planet, 1999; practical guide to walks across the length and breadth of Ireland. **Kevin Corcoran** *West of Ireland Walks/West Cork Walks/Kerry Walks*, O'Brien Press, Dublin; superb little books with maps and ecological anecdotes of the politically correct kind along the way. **Paddy Dillon** *The Ulster Way*, O'Brien Press, 1999; the complete Ulster Way written by a noted author of many walking guides **J B Malone** *The Complete Wicklow Way*, O'Brien Press, 1999; an updated edition of a guide to this long-distance walk.

Iain Zaczek *Ancient Ireland*, Collins & Brown, 1998. (HB); the text is so-so but the photographs by David Lyons capture the other-worldly appeal of an island that tangibly evokes an ancient past. **Simon Marsden and Duncan McLaren** *In Ruins*, Little, Brown and Company, 1997. (HB); evocative photographs and informative text. **Peter Somerville-Large and Jason Hawkes** *Ireland From the Air*, Weidenfeld & Nicholson, London, (HB); arresting aerial images of the country with intelligent text. **Mathias Oppersdorff** *People of the Road*, Syracuse University Press, 1997; a set of photographs of Travellers taken between the 1960s and the '90s, capturing just how at odds with contemporary Ireland they remain. **Myrtle Hill & Vivienne Pollock** *Women of Ireland*, Blackstaff, 1999; every picture tells a story of women's working life between 1880 and 1920; a coffee table book for people who don't have coffee tables. *Ireland*, Michael O' Mara Books, 1999 (HB); you won't remember the text but the photographs should stir up memories long after you have left Ireland.

Colour illustrated books

Essentials

Film Ireland FilmBase, Irish Film Centre, 6 Eustace Street, Dublin 2. F01-6796717, www.iftn.ie Film reviews, interviews, research articles. Bi-monthly. IR£1.95. Annual subscription IR£16. *History Ireland* P.O. Box 695, Dublin 8. F01-4533234, historyireland@connect.ie A refreshing range of articles from the obvious to the marginal. IR£15 for the four annual issues. *Irish Studies Review* Carfax Publishing, PO Box 25, Abingdon, Oxfordshire, OX14 3UE. F01235-401550. A scholarly but broad-based journal covering history and the arts. Three issues a year £20.

Journals

Dear Harp of My Country, The Irish Melodies of Thomas Moore Wolfhound Press, Dublin; this book comes with two CDs of Moore's *Irish Melodies* sung by James Flannery. *Finnegans Wake*, read by Jim Norton with Marcella Riordan, Naxos Audio Books; 4 CDs or 4 cassettes include a booklet containing the abridged spoken text. The only way to make a start with this notoriously difficult but highly musical work. Recordings of other Joyce works are available through the same company. *The Croppy Boy*, Ger Busher Gold Sun Records, Camelot, Coolcotts Lane, Wexford, Ireland, 1998. Music and drama rendering a stirring narrative of the 1798 insurgence in County Wexford; an engaging alternative to the hefty tomes that academics have devoted to the subject. *The Croppy's Complaint* Craft Recordings, 11 Merton Avenue, South Circular Rd, Dublin 8. Music and song covering the 1798 rebellion. **Elizabeth Bowen** *The Last September*, (Audio Books, Bath, BA2 3AX). Bowen's Anglo-Irish comedy of manners set in the troublesome 1920s. Recorded on cassettes but CD versions can't be far away. Other Irish classics, including Brian Moore and Edna O'Brien, are also available through the same company; check their website at http://www.chivers.co.uk *Fellowship of Freedom* National Library of Ireland, Dublin; the context, causes and campaigns of the United Irishmen and their uprising. *The National Gallery of Ireland* National Gallery of Ireland, Dublin; one hundred of the best paintings, easy to install and use. *Ulysses*, read by Jim Norton with Marcella Riordan, Naxos Audio Books; these four CDs or four cassettes (and still abridged) should help you realise what all the acclaim is about.

CDs

Top 10

The following are highly subjective and selective lists culled from the very many places in Ireland we have enjoyed. There are, of course, numerous equally delightful places to stay and eat omitted here which you will come across in your wanderings through the book and country.

Hotels

1 **Merrion Hotel**, Upper Merrion St, Dublin, T6030600 (page 123)
2 **Park Hotel,** Kenmare, County Kerry, T41200 (page 362)
3 **Sheen Falls Lodge**, Kenmare, County Kerry, T41600 (page 362)
4 **St Helen's Hotel**, Stillorgan Rd, Dublin, T2186000 (page 123)
5 **Belfast Hilton**, 4 Lanyon Place, Belfast, T90277000 (page 604)
6 **Stephen's Hall,** Earlsfort Centre, Lower Leeson St, Dublin, T6610585 (page 123)
7 **Buswell's**, Molesworth St, Dublin, T6146500 (page 122)
8 **Brooks**, Drury St, Dublin, T6704000 (page 122)
9 **Waterford Castle**, The Island, Waterford, County Waterford, T878203 (page 249)
10 **Harvey's Point Country Hotel**, Lough Eske, Donegal, County Donegal, T22208 (page 519)

Country houses

1 **Currarevagh House**, Oughterard, County Galway, T552312 (page 446)
2 **Enniscoe House**, Castlehill, near Crossmolina, Ballina, T31112, F31773 (page 487)
3 **The Old Rectory Country House**, Wicklow Town, County Wicklow, T67048 (page 197)
4 **Gregan's Castle Hotel**, Corkscrew Hill, County Clare, T707705 (page 410)
5 **Ballyrafter House Hotel**, Lismore, County Waterford, T54002 (page 259)
6 **St John's Country House**, Fahan, County Donegal, T60289 (page 546)
7 **Hunter's Hotel**, WicklowTown, County Wicklow, T40106 (page 197)
8 **Caragh Lodge**, Caragh, T9769115, (page 347)
9 **Coopershill House**, T071-65108, Sligo (page 507)
10 **Rosleague Manor**, Letterfrack, County Galway, T41101 (page 455)

Guesthouses/Bed & Breakfasts

1 **Clare Island Lighthouse**, Clare Island, County Mayo, T45120 (page 478)
2 **Pax House**, Upper St John St, Dingle, County Kerry, T9151518 (page 375)
3 **The Moorings**, T772376, F772675, Scilly (page 303)
4 **Old Presbytery**, Cork St, Kinsale, County Cork, T772027 (page 303)
5 **Maddybenny Farm**, 18 Maddybenny Park, Portrush, County Antrim, T70823394 (page 568)
6 **The Quay House**, Beach Rd, Clifden, County Galway, T21360 (page 451)
7 **Fuschia House**, Muckross Rd, Killarney, County Kerry, T33743 (page 339)
8 **Milltown House**, Dingle, County Kerry, T9151372 (page 375)
9 **McMenamin's Townhouse**, Auburn Terrace, Redmond Rd, Wexford, County Wexford, T24609 (page 202)
10 **The Narrows**, Shore Rd, Portaferry, County Down, T42728148 (page 622)

Hostels

1 **Whitepark Bay Hostel**, Ballycastle, County Antrim, T20731745 (page 573)
2 **Bunrower House Hostel**, Ross Rd, Killarney, County Kerry, T33914 (page 341)
3 **Old Monastery Hostel**, Letterfrack, County Galway, T41132, (page 455)
4 **Ballintaggart Hostel**, Dingle, County Kerry, T9151454 (page 376)
5 **Viking House**, Coffee House Lane, The Quay, Waterford, County Waterford, T853827 (page 250)
6 **Dublin International Hostel**, 61 Mountjoy St, Dublin, T8301766 (page 126)
7 **Aghadoe House**, Killarney, County Kerry, T31240 (page 341)
8 **Glendalough Hostel**, Glendalough, County Wicklow, T01-8301766 (page 188)
9 **Wild Haven Hostel**, Achill Island, County Mayo, T45392 (page 483)
10 **Valentia Island Hostel**, Kingston, T9476141 (page 354)

Restaurants over IR£25 a head

1 **The Commons**, Newman House, 85-6 St Stephen's Green, Dublin,T4752597 (page 127)
2 **Ramore**, Portrush, County Antrim, T70824313 (page 569)
3 **Sea View House Restaurant**, Bantry, County Cork, T50073 (page 324)
4 **Chez Youen**, Baltimore, County Cork, T20136 (page 316)
5 **Arbutus Lodge**, Cork, County Cork, T4501237 (page 289)
6 **Ardagh Hotel and Restaurant**, Ballyconneely Rd, Clifden, Country Galway, T21384 (page 451)
7 **The Beginish**, Green St, Dingle, County Kerry, T9151588 (page 376)
8 **Le Panto**, St Helen's Hotel, Stillorgan Rd, Dublin, T2186000 (page 130)
9 **Deane's**, 38 Howard St, Belfast, T90560000 (page 608)
10 **Gregan's Castle Hotel**, Corkscrew Hill, County Clare, T707705 (page 410)

Good value places to eat

1 **Michael's**, 71 St Patrick's St, Cork, County Cork, T4277716 (page 289)
2 **La Jolie Brise**, Baltimore, County Cork, T20600 (page 315)
3 **Lettercollum House**, Timoleague, County Cork, T46251 (page 306)
4 **The Old Dublin Restaurant**, 91 Francis St, Dublin, T4542028 (page 130)
5 **Dwyer's Restaurant**, 5 Mary St, Waterford, County Waterford, T877478 (page 250)
6 **Nick's Warehouse**, Belfast, T90439690 (page 608)
7 **Eamonn O'Reilly's One Pico Restaurant**, 1 Upper Camden St, Dublin, T4780307 (page 130)
8 **Larchwood House Restaurant**, Pearsons Bridge, Bantry, T66181, West Cork (page 324)
9 **Crawford Gallery Café**, Emmett Pl, Cork, Country Cork, T4274415 (page 289)
10 **Sheedy's Orchid Restaurant**, Lisdoonvarna, County Clare (page 403)

Pubs

1 **O'Connor's Pub**, Fisherstreet, Doolin, County Clare (page 403)
2 **Mansworth's**, Midleton St, Cobh, County Cork, T811965 (page 295)
3 **The Smugglers Creek**, Rossnowlagh, County Donegal (page 516)
4 **Fisherman's Bar**, Valentia Island, County Kerry, T9477103 (page 354)
5 **Crown Liquor Saloon**, Great Victoria St, Belfast (page 597)
6 **The Gravediggers**, 1 Prospect Square, Dublin (page 134)
7 **Henry Downes**, 10 Thomas St, Waterford, County Waterford (page 251)
8 **House of McDonnell**, Ballycastle, County Antrim (page 575)
9 **Doheny & Nesbitt**, 5 Baggott St, Dublin (page 132)
10 **Fitzpatricks**, Kilcrohane, County Cork (page 321)

Sites and sights

1 **Cliffs of Moher**, County Clare (page 405)
2 **Skellig Michael**, County Kerry (page 353)
3 **The Giant's Causeway**, County Antrim (page 571)
4 **Dún Aenghus**, Inishmore, Aran Islands (page 436)
5 **Gallarus Oratory**, Dingle Peninsula, County Kerry (page 383)
6 **High Cross**, Monasterboice, County Louth (page 169)
7 **Christ Church Cathedral**, Christ Church Place, Dublin (page 111)
8 **Poulnabrone Dolmen**, Ballyvaughan, County Clare (page 410)
9 **The Burren**, Ballyvaughan, County Clare (page 408)
10 **Newgrange**, County Meath (page 160)

Beaches

1 **Keem**, Achill Island, County Mayo (page 482)
2 **Keel**, Achill Island, County Mayo (page 482)
3 **Inch Beach**, Clonakility, County Cork (page 307)
4 **Dog's Bay**, Roundstone, Connemara, County Galway (page 449)
5 **Inishbofin**, Inishbofin Island, County Galway (page 453)
6 **Clogherhead**, County Louth (page 169)
7 **Portacloy**, County Mayo (page 486)
8 **Barley Cove**, County Cork (page 320)
9 **Stradbally and Castelgregory**, County Waterford (page 254)
10 **Portstewart Strand**, County Derry (page 565)

Museums/Heritage centres

1 **The Queenstown Story**, Heritage Centre, Cobh, County Cobh,
T813591 (page 294)
2 **Strokestown House**, Strokestown, County Roscommon, T33013 (page 463)
3 **National Museum**, Kildare Street & Merrion Row, Dublin, T6777444 (page 101)
4 **O'Doherty Tower**, Union Hall Place, Derry, County Derry, T71372411 (page 559)
5 **National 1798 Visitor Centre**, Enniscorthy, County Wexford, T37596 (page 210)
6 **The Hunt Collection**, Custom House, Rutland Street, Limerick, County Limerick,
T312833 (page 273)
7 **Ulster-American Folk Park**, Omagh, County Tyrone, T82243292 (page 650)
8 **Ulster Folk & Transport Museum**, Belfast, T90428428 (page 603)
9 **Blasket Interpretative Centre**, County Kerry, T9156444 (page 380)
10 **Bunratty Folk Park** , Ennis, County Clare, T061-36078 (page 396)

Walks

1 **Blasket Island**, County Kerry (page 381)
2 **Clare Island**, County Mayo (page 477)
3 **Sheep's Head Way**, Sheep's Head Peninsula, County Cork (page 321)
4 **The first two days of the Kerry Way**, County Kerry (page 364)
5 **Days 1, 4 and 5 of the Dingle Way**, County Kerry (page 385)
6 **Insihboffin Island**, County Galway (page 453)
7 **Knockmealdowns Mountains**, County Waterford (page 258)
8 **Millstreet to Shrone on the Blackwater Way**, County Waterford
(see page 258)
9 **Around Abbey Hill near Ballyvaughan**, County Clare (see page 409)
10 **Slievemore**, Achill Island, County Mayo (page 482)

Places for kids

1 **Dingle Harbour and Fungie the dolphin**, Dingle, County Kerry (page 374)
2 **Watersports at Portrush**, Country Antrim (page 567)
3 **Kerry the Kingdom**, 40 English Street, Tralee, County Kerry (page 369)
4 **St Patrick's Trian**, Armagh, County Armagh, T521801 (page 637)
5 **Carrick-a-rede Rope Bridge**, Antrim, County Antrim, T20731159 (page 573)
6 **Aillwee Caves**, County Clare, T7077036 (page 409)
7 **Downpatrick Steam Railway**, Market Street, Downpatrick, County Down,
T615779 (page 625)
8 **Boat ride to Sherkin Island and cart ride to the beach**, County Cork
(page 316)
9 **Dolphinwatch**, The Square, Carrigaholt, County Clare, T9058156 (page 414)
10 **Dingle Oceanworld**, Dingle, County Kerry, T9152111 (page 375)

Essentials

Castles

1 **King John Castle**, Limerick (page 268)
2 **Trim** (page 161)
3 **Kilkenny** (page 217)
4 **Three Castles Head** (page 316)
5 **Dublin Castle** (page 109)
6 **Donegal Castle** (page 513)
7 **Ennis Castle** (page 392)
8 **Cahir Castle** (page 259)
9 **Dunluce** (page 567)
10 **Blarney** (page 288)

Gardens

1 **Creagh**, West Cork (page 309)
2 **Illnacullin**, Glengarriff (page 321)
3 **Derreen Garden**, Kerry (page 358)
4 **Powerscourt Gardens**, County Wicklow (page 184)
5 **Timoleague Castle Gardens**, West Cork (page 302)
6 **Glenveagh Castle Gardens**, County Donegal (page 539)
7 **War Memorial Gardens**, Dublin (page 90)
8 **National Botanic Gardens**, Dublin (page 95)
9 **Tropical Ravine**, Belfast (page 597)
10 **Tollymore Forest Park**, County Down (page 628)

Irish Memories

1 The smell of a turf fire drifting across a village in the west of Ireland
2 The everyday poetry of Dubliners at talk
3 Walking on the small islands off the west coast, identifying seabirds and wild flowers
4 Waiting interminably to be served somewhere and realising that no-one feels stressed by it except you – the pressure of non-pressure
5 Catching a mackerel off the rocks in west Cork or Kerry
6 Sensing the confidence and fun of Derry on a Saturday evening
7 Feeling like a tourist, eating oysters with a glass of Guinness on a summer's evening
8 Listening to the cattle auction at the Skibbereeb mart
9 Listening to a good Irish music session in an unreconstructed village pub
10 Soaking up the atmosphere with a pizza on the quayside at Baltimore

Dublin

In Dublin's fair city,
Where the girls are so pretty,
I first set my eyes on sweet Molly Malone.

Anonymous: *Cockles and Mussels*

Dublin

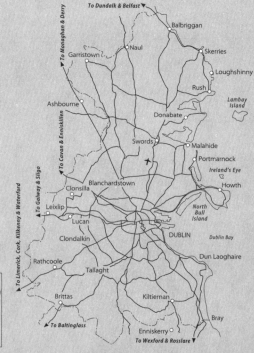

What lends such charm to Dublin, one of Europe's finest capital cities, is that it avoided the excesses of the high rise architecture of the post war years. Now enjoying a cultural and economic renaissance, its Georgian tenements have emerged from almost two centuries of neglect to make the city an open and airy place, dominated by the river which divides and at the same time gives a unity to this compact and vibrant metropolis.

   Dublin is young and self-confident but is also cloaked in a time-worn habit. It has one of the youngest populations in Europe and you can see them every day, incessantly chatting in the mushrooming cafés or always-busy pubs. But, as the Irish will tell you, there is a dialectic at work in the passing of time. While Viking and medieval remains pop out of buildings sites and the bullet scars of the Easter Rising and the civil war can still be seen on the walls of the GPO there are other less attractive vestiges of the past. Aging 1960s housing estates ring the city where a dispossessed class lurks behind the new wealth and politicians bicker over how best to develop a twenty-first century transport system. After a few days in Dublin you'll know your way around but you'll be only scratching the surface. Dublin's friendliness and ebullience encourages people to stay and because it takes time to savour its deadly sense of humour Dublin is a city to return to again and again.

Dublin

★ *Try to find time for*

    Taking a healthy, historical walk around the Phoenix Park

    Visiting the dead famous in Prospect Cemetery, Glasnevin

    Marvelling at the hoards of gold in the National Museum

    Admiring the floor tiles in Christ Church Cathedral

    Pottering about in Mother Redcap's market

    Smelling the gorse flowers in May on Howth Hill

    Listening to the buskers in Grafton Street

    People-watching in St Stephen's Green

    Enjoying the craic in Temple Bar

Ins and outs

Getting there

Population: 900,000
Area code: 01
Colour map 4,
grid A2 & 3
For more detailed
information, see
Transport page143

Whether you arrive in the city by plane, ferry, car or train, access to the centre is fairly simple. From the airport, 8 miles (12 km) north of the centre, there are frequent buses into the city, while taxis also ply the route with surcharges for the pickup and extra luggage. From Dun Laoghaire ferry terminal there is the DART train service, which takes about 40 minutes into town, as well as several buses, which take considerably longer, while a bus meets the Dublin ferries as they arrive at the terminal in Alexandra Rd. Trains arrive at two destinations in Dublin – Connolly St Station for trains from the north, and Heuston Station for trains from the south. Connolly is easy walking distance from the centre of town, while from Heuston there are cabs and a very heavily used bus service.

Getting around

Dublin is a small city and most sights are easily within walking distance of the centre. The river marks the boundary between the north and the south of the city and if you think in terms of O'Connell Street and Parnell Square to its north and Grafton Street and St Stephen's Green to its south, you will find that most tourist spots, markets, shops, hotels and restaurants are close at hand to one of these areas. The two canals mark the nothern and southern beginnings of the suburbs. Most of the sights lie between them, so you can parcel up your visits into north of the river and south of the river, as they are presented here. The city is fairly walker-friendly, although you will see Dubliners taking off across busy main roads with a completely cavalier attitude to the flashing green man – and you will find yourself doing the same before long, since waiting at crossings seems to take much longer here than anywhere else in Europe. As long as you keep the north-of-the-river and south-of-the-river divide in your head it is difficult to get lost

Dublin

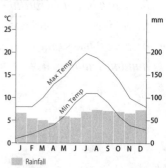

Rainfall

in Dublin, and half the fun of discovering the city is in wandering through the streets, punctuating your travels with rest stops in the many pubs.

The main tourist office in Dublin is in the beautiful St Andrew's Church (1866), Suffolk St, T850230330, now owned by **Dublin Tourism**. Open summer Monday-Saturday, 0830-2000, Sunday 1030-1400; winter, Monday-Saturday, 0900-1700. Services include a bureau de change, car rental, accommodation and ticket booking service, café and book shop. Outside the tourist office is a 24-hr touch screen accommodation booking unit, where for a 10% credit card deposit you can book hotels, B&Bs, etc. The tourist office gets very crowded; queuing is by ticket number. There is another Dublin Tourism branch in Exclusively Irish, 14 O'Connell St, daily 1000-1330, 1400-1730, closed bank holidays. There are also small branches at Dun Laoghaire ferry terminal, daily 0800-1300, closed 25th, 26th December, 1st January and at Dublin Airport, daily 0800-2200, closed 25th, 26th December, 1st January: both these places have the 24-hr touch screen terminal.

Tourist information

The head offices of **Bord Fáilte** are in Wilton Terrace, T6765871, near Baggot Bridge, and there is a very small shop and a tourist information desk in the foyer. There is a USIT (Union of Students in Ireland) office at 19-21 Aston Quay, O'Connell Bridge, T6798833.

History

Dublin's history has been a turbulent one. Celts gave way to Norsemen, who were driven out by Gaelic-speaking Irishmen, who in turn folded under the assault of the Normans. The English, in one form or another, held the city through many attempts to wrest it back into Irish hands, from the 1798 uprising to the 1916 Easter Rishing. Finally Irish again in 1922, the city went into economic decline, from which it has recently been reborn, like a post-modern phoenix, all designer bars and on-line businesses.

There have been human settlements in Dublin since at least mesolithic times and there are several neolithic sites in and around the city. Bronze Age settlements also existed, one giving the city its present Irish name of *Baile Atha Cliath* (pronounced 'ballia or kleeyah': Town of the Hurdle Ford). This was a point where four ancient routes crossed the river, and is thought to be where the Father Matthew Bridge now stands. In CE140 Ptolemy drew up a map of Ireland showing a settlement – which he called 'Eblana' – in the Dublin area. St Patrick's Cathedral is said to stand on the site of a well that St Patrick once used to baptize converts during the fifth century.

Early settlement

The people who really got the place moving were the Vikings, who arrived as raiders at first but who had started to settle by the ninth century. A Viking settlement existed around Islandbridge, where a Viking cemetery has been excavated. These early settlers were driven out by local chieftains around 900, but the Viking town of Dyfflin, a corruption of the Irish name, *dubh linn*, probably established itself around 917 under Ivar the Boneless. The modern name for the city is taken from the place where the first settlement was built, beside a *dubh linn* or black pool, which was next to where Dublin castle now stands. The present helicopter pad was once an intersection of two rivers, the Liffey and the Poddle, now reduced to a stagnant pool under the foundations of the castle. The Viking town was surrounded first by an earth embankment and then stone walls. A main road ran along where Castle Street is today and smaller streets ran down to the river. When Fishamble Street was excavated in

The Vikings

the 1970s many Viking artefacts were found beside the remains of a stone wall. Around 1000 the Vikings built a *thingmote*, a huge earth mound where they held meetings; College Green now stands there.

In 997 coins were being minted and in 1030 a wooden church was erected on the site of what is now Christ Church Cathedral. The settlement had around 5,000 citizens and was the first urban settlement in Ireland. The Viking influence extended north and south along the coast, and west as far as Leixlip; they traded and carried out raids on other Irish settlements. The Vikings gradually intermarried, learned Gaelic and converted to Christianity, and it is probable that the Battle of Clontarf in 1014, generally considered to be the moment when Viking power in Ireland was broken, had Vikings on both sides of the battlefield.

The Normans The Anglo-Norman invasion began in 1169 and Dublin was taken in 1170 by an army led by Richard FitzGilbert de Clare, Earl of Pembroke, better known to history as Strongbow. The Vikings still did not leave but shifted to Oxmantown on the north bank of the Liffey. By the 14th century they had become completely assimilated into the Anglo-Norman Gaelic society. Meanwhile, Dublin had two stone cathedrals and had become a city. It was the fifth largest port in Ireland and the largest trader in wine. There were 50 trade guilds in the city and great monasteries, villages in themselves, operated around its outskirts.

Dublin

Related maps:
A. *Dublin: north city centre, page 80;*
B. *Dublin: south city centre, page 98*

The 14th century was not so fruitful for the city. It was beset by plague, fires and invasions. The population declined and the Pale was set up, fortified by ditches and small castles and stretching from Drogheda to Dalkey, in order to keep out the Irish. By the 15th century Dublin was just another town like several others along the coast of Wicklow and County Dublin.

In the 16th century the Reformation freed the lands of the religious orders around the city and a wave of building began. Trinity College was built on land formerly owned by a religious order, and other monastic buildings were dismantled for use as building materials. Population growth began again and by the end of the 17th century, despite the troubles of Cromwell's time and another outbreak of plague in 1649, the city's population stood at about 60,000.

Reformation & restoration

During the Restoration, building began on sites outside the old city walls, which were by now in a sad state of repair. In the 18th century the first Georgian planned streets were constructed, to the northeast and southeast of the city. Grand public buildings were constructed as well as elaborate town houses, which expressed the confidence of the Anglo-Irish in their ownership of the city. Dublin became the second city of the British Empire, and each Anglo-Irish family kept a town house in one of the Georgian mansions, where they lived during the winter months. The Dublin of this time would have been recognizable today – Phoenix Park was in place, the Royal Hospital stood south of the river to the west of town, the Royal Barracks were under construction, the Custom House was built in its present location, and the estates of Georgian houses to the north and south of the city were already built. The city became the national centre for trade and commerce as well as the seat of government. A Viceroy held court for at least part of each year at Dublin Castle.

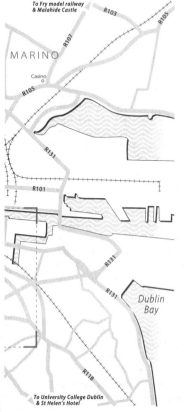

The decline set in after the 1798 uprising: Britain saw Ireland as an unstable colony and passed the Act of Union, dissolving the Irish parliament. The effect on Dublin was enormous. With no parliament sitting, the landowners left for their country estates. Houses stood vacant and industries that had serviced their owners went into decline. Then, 46 years later, the Famine brought thousands of sick and homeless into the city. The great Georgian mansions became tenements.

Dublin's decline

The decline continued into the 19th century. Wealthy families continued to move out of the city and, beyond a few churches and a new water supply, few improvements were made. Half the city's families lived in one-room slums in the old Georgian houses and the infant mortality rate soared. Most of the working classes were employed as casual labourers and experienced long periods of unemployment. By the turn of the century Belfast had replaced Dublin as the industrial heartland of Ireland and events such as the Great Lockout of 1913 (which started when Dublin employers compelled workers to withdraw from the Transport and General Workers Union or face dismissal, and climaxed with 20,000 workers on strike or locked out of their factories), and the 1916 Easter Rising (when about 1,200 republicans seized key buildings in Dublin and declared a provisional government for the Republic of Ireland) burdened the city even further.

Modern times The Irish Free State began a series of planned housing developments, creating the suburbs of modern Dublin. Buses and then private car ownership made life in the suburbs comfortable. The city centre remained much as it had been in Georgian times, with a few big public developments such as the Busáras building and the Dublin Corporation buildings, erected amid much controversy in the 1970s. Those Georgian streets that survived clearances and building of soon-to-be problem housing blocks mouldered quietly. Then, unobtrusively, in the 1990s Dublin began to revive, first with the development of the Temple Bar area, and then as businesses found cheap property and a well-educated workforce desperate for employment. Now, the Celtic Tiger, as the economic boom in Ireland has been called, has finally put an end to two centuries of decline for Dublin. Today it is near impossible to walk down a city street without seeing planning application notices; the Georgian terraces are being rebuilt, some with considerable care; the high-rise horrors of the 1960s are confined to some council estates in the suburbs; and mobile-phone transmitters scar the skylines.

Sights north of the river

Most of the city's tourist spots are located in the southern half of the city, but the north has much to offer and fewer crowds; there is also a more genuine, earthy feel to it, being less geared up to the tourist market. The recent developments at Smithfield have given the area a very classy new hotel, bar, restaurant and Ceol, a traditional music venue and museum where you can while away an afternoon and enjoy good traditional music and dancing. O'Connell Street and Gardiner Street, with its many hostels and B&Bs, are here, as are the bus station and Connelly (train) Station. In the O'Connell Street area, with its strong historical and literary associations, you can see one of Ireland's finest Catholic churches tucked modestly away in a side street; Parnell Square and the Rotunda Hospital; some of the earliest Georgian buildings in the city; the excellent Hugh Lane gallery with its fine collection of modern art; and the Four Courts, scene of some of the worst of the fighting during the civil war. Further from the centre is Phoenix Park, home to some historical monuments and herds of deer; Glasnevin cemetery, home to some famous dead people; and the Botanic Gardens with its lovely old Victorian glasshouses and a good collection of unusual plants.

O'Connell Street and around

Now quite tacky in appearance, with fast food joints and minimarkets lining the route, O'Connell Street was, in its heyday, one of the finest and widest boulevards in Europe. Looking up above the neon, the skyline of the once grand road, with its corner turrets and other architectural details, can still be made out. A street was first built here in the early 18th century by Henry Moore, the

Dublin's Viking Adventure

Malahide Castle

Fry Model Railway

Something to write home about

James Joyce Museum

Shaw Birthplace

Dublin Writers Museum

Dear Sarah

We're having an amazing time, Dublin is even more than we expected. Our first stop was **Malahide Castle** - a magnificent place with splendid rooms and antique furnishings. In the grounds we found the **Fry Model Railway**, it's like a small boy's wildest dream and your Father couldn't get enough of it. Back in town we went to **Dublin's Viking Adventure**. We didn't just meet live vikings, we smelt them as well ! It was just like being in Dublin a thousand years ago.

The history here is something else, it's certainly the land of scholars (though we're not sure about the saints yet). We started our literary round-up at the **Shaw Birthplace** (where 'GBS' was born) - a real Victorian experience. Our next stop was the **Dublin Writers Museum**, in a gorgeous old Georgian house all gilt and plasterwork, full of literary memorabilia. It's astonishing how many great writers were Irish, and all with such fascinating lives ! Of course the best of the lot has the **James Joyce Museum** all to himself in a great spot by the sea in Sandycove. I was so thrilled to be there where Ulysses begins that I made your Father promise to read it - tonight !

We had planned to come home at the weekend but we're having such a great time we might just stay another week.

Bye for now,
Lots of love -
Mum & Dad

For further information please contact:
Tel:+353 1 846 2184 Fax:+353 1 846 2537
enterprises@dublintourism.ie
www.visitdublin.com

Dublin Tourism Enterprises

Dublin

Plans are well under way to transform O'Connell St. Traffic lanes will be reduced, trams will trundle passengers up and down, and something very iconic will be erected in the centre of the street, post-Nelson's Pillar (see page 83) as Ireland's answer to the Eiffel tower.

Earl of Drogheda, and was named after him, as were several of the side streets – Henry Street, Moore Street, Off (originally Of) Street and Earl Street. It was a narrower road when first built but was subsequently altered to form a square with a central garden area in 1749, when the area was acquired by Luke Gardiner. He was a Georgian Mr Big: banker, property developer and holder of the government post of deputy vice-treasurer, which he used to channel money into his own investments, including the building of large tracts of Georgian Dublin. Later still the square was extended down towards the river, renamed Sackville Street after a 19th century Viceroy, and connected to the south bank by Carlysle Bridge, the narrower precursor of O'Connell Bridge. The road finally took its current name in 1924 from the Great Liberator, Daniel O'Connell.

Custom House Before you begin the stroll down O'Connell Street, a small diversion along Eden Quay and Custom House Quay brings you to the Custom House. Best viewed from Moss Street on the other side of the river, where its vast scale and stunning skyline can be best appreciated, the Custom House has had a long and chequered history. Custom houses were always placed on rivers in order

Dublin: north city centre

Related map:
A. Dublin: south city centre, page 98

0 yards 200
0 metres 200

■ **Sleeping**	7 Dublin International	13 Ormonde
1 Abbey Hostel	Youth Hostel	
2 Abraham House Hostel	8 Gresham	● **Eating & drinking**
3 Barry's	9 Globetrotters & The	1 101 Talbot
4 Cardijn House Hostel	Townhouse	2 Beshoff's
5 Celts Hostel	10 Isaac's Hotel & Hostel	3 Kylemore Café
6 Charles Stuart Parnell	11 Jacob's Inn	4 Slattery's Bar
Hostel	12 Marlborough Hostel	5 Zanzibar

The Easter Rising in Dublin

In 1916 a group of Republicans, led by James Connolly, Padraig Pearse, Joseph Mary Plunkett and Thomas McDonagh, seized the GPO and several other sites in Dubin in the vain hope that their stand would prompt other Republicans throughout the country to follow their lead and take up arms in the cause of Irish independence. In Dublin the Post Office was an unofficial focal point for the city and was the first place to be taken by Pearse and Connolly, with a complement of 1,200 supporters. The proclamation of the Irish Republic was read from the front steps of the building. Other contingents took St Stephen's Green and the College of Surgeons, and City Hall which was designated a field hospital.

The life of the city went on around the fighting with many non-combatants suffering. Francis Sheehy Skeffington, a pacifist, was arrested while trying to prevent looting and was shot under the orders of Captain Bowen-Colthurst, an English officer who was later found to be insane. Those in the post office resisted for five days before withdrawing their troops and surrendering. Countess Markievicz, not knowing about the surrender, held out for another day at the Royal College of Surgeons, but she too surrendered her troops and, like the other leaders, was sentenced to death, reprieved only for fear of the international outcry sure to follow the execution of a woman. If the city wasn't roused to open rebellion by the sight of the republicans being shelled in the Post Office, both it and the world were outraged at the summary executions that took place afterwards, Connolly strapped to a chair since he was too badly injured to stand.

Dublin

to collect customs duties on boats arriving in Ireland. In the case of Dublin the building had been in the heart of the medieval city on Essex Quay, but as the city developed eastwards, a new building was planned to the east of the quay. As you might expect, all those merchants and businessmen who operated in the old city area objected strongly to the move, since it would shift the balance of the city more firmly eastwards, and result in a loss of business for them. The men who planned this radical shift in the city offered the job to a London architect called James Gandon, who turned down offers of work in St Petersburg and came to Dublin instead in 1781. The city's merchants, determined to put up a struggle, hired gangs to attack the builders, and Gandon took to wearing a sword when he visited the site. Eight years later, still beset by opposition, the building was burned, but no major damage was done. Later, in 1833, another fire did considerable damage, but the real trouble came in 1921: by this time the building was being used as local government offices, and it became the target of nationalists. It burned for days, the stones cracked, and metal fittings melted in the heat. The building has undergone restoration work twice in the twentieth century. In 1991, the bicentenary of its opening, the building was reopened with a visitor's centre with exhibitions on the various notables who have had offices there, as well as James Gandon himself who remained in Dublin and was responsible for much of its Georgian architecture. The building itself is built in the neo-classical style and has outstanding skyline sculptures by Edward Smyth. Following the 1921 damage, the peristyle that supports the dome was rebuilt in local stone rather than the imported Portland stone of the original, and has darkened in colour and doesn't quite match the rest of the building. In its original form the building had chimneys. ■ *Directly across the river from Tara St station, T8787660. IR£1.00. March to November, Monday-Friday 1000-1700, Saturday and Sunday 1400-1700; November to March, Wednesday-Friday 1000-1700, Sunday 1400-1700.*

Abbey Theatre

The Abbey Theatre, one of the most famous theatres in the world, is unfortunately one of the city's least distinguished structures, architecturally at least.

A brief walk along Abbey Street Lower brings you to the Abbey Theatre. This is a national monument of a kind. It opened in 1904, and was a radical place in its time. It was founded by the Gaelic Revival movement, notably Lady Gregory and Yeats. Revolutionary plays were produced there, such as Synge's *Playboy of the Western World*, in which the protagonist murders his father and the use of the word 'shift' (referring to women's underwear) caused riots in the streets. In 1926 O'Casey's *The Plough and the Stars* ended in open fighting between the actors and the audience when the Irish flag was taken, dramatically speaking, into a public house where prostitutes were drinking. Most of the time the Abbey presented Yeats' plays to a minuscule audience, the actors declaiming the lines in the style that Yeats attributed to Homer – no one moved when they spoke their lines and all was spoken in a 'Homeric' monotone. When asked how he knew how Homer would have said the lines, Yeats replied, 'the ability of the man [ie Yeats himself] justifies the assumption.' The theatre went into a decline in the middle years of the 20th century and was burned to the ground in 1951, the site then becoming for a time that of the city morgue. It reopened in 1966 as the Abbey Theatre, having spent the previous decade in the huge Queen's Theatre where it earned a reputation for safe, audience-attracting productions, but also pioneered the work of Ireland's newest playwrights such as Brian Friel whose 1962 *The Enemy Within* was first performed by the Abbey Company. The new theatre has two incarnations, the Peacock where more experimental work is performed and the Abbey itself where newly commissioned works by Irish playwrights take turns with well established actors in more conventional and well known productions.

O'Connell Street statues

Back at the head of O'Connell Street stands a statue of O'Connell himself. The statue took 30 years to erect, 214 committee meetings and two design competitions, and offended innumerable architects whose designs were rejected. One rejected design had the Liberator entwined in the arms of a young woman (tasteless in the light of his known infidelities), while another had him sitting on a stove! The present one has the Liberator clutching a cloak and surrounded by winged victories, some of which bear bullet marks from 1916.

In 1916 large tracts of the street were destroyed by the British, as they shelled the republicans who were occupying the **General Post Office**, led by Padraig Pearse (see box on page 81). The GPO was part of the last wave of Georgian public building between 1815 and 1818. In front of it stood Nelson's Column (see box on page 83), and along the portico stood (and their replacements still stand) three figures: Mercury, Hibernia and Fidelity. The building was gutted by fire and shelling in 1916 and was rebuilt in 1929, after suffering further damage in 1922 during the Civil War. Inside is a statue depicting the death of Cuchulain ('coo-cu-len' or 'coo-hu-len'), a mythical Irish hero. The figure is fighting to the last breath and commemorates the deaths of the men who bravely made a hopeless stand for a cause that they believed in. The analogy between Cuchulain and the leaders of the Uprising doesn't bear too much scrutiny though, since Cuchulain murdered his best friend, slept around indiscriminately and seemed to spend his entire mythological life fighting for the sheer hell of it. The front façade of the building is scarred with bullet holes from the two battles.

Opposite the GPO is **Clery's**, a famous Dublin department store, previously the Dublin Drapery Store. In 1913, the year of the Great Lockout, the building also housed the Imperial Hotel. James Larkin, a labour leader wanted for sedition, got into the hotel disguised as a priest and made a rousing speech to his supporters from its balcony. He went on to become a member of the Dáil and a union leader, and a statue of him stands in the central island of O'Connell

The day Lord Nelson lost his head

Outside the GPO stood Nelson's Pillar, erected in 1808 (several decades before the London version). The Doric column it stood on was hollow with an internal staircase allowing visitors to climb to the top and look out over the city. In 1966, to commemorate the 50th anniversary of the Easter Rising, Sean Treacy, an IRA activist, allegedly stole a key to the entrance, got inside and planted explosives. The resulting explosion quite neatly took the statue and the top of the column off with no damage to surrounding buildings. Someone, realizing the commercial value of such an act, appropriated the head and it went on the market soon after. Later, the Irish army was called in to demolish the rest of the column and did extensive damage to the surrounding buildings in doing so. For a time two heads of the statue were circulating but the genuine one is now in the Dublin Civic Museum in South William St. Like the Berlin Wall, more ordinary remains of the pillar went on sale all over Ireland and England.

Sean Treacy allegedly went on to break colleagues out of prison twice, using on one occasion a helicopter and on another an earth mover with a reinforced steel frame. He retired from active service and returned to his profession as a steel erector. He was killed in July 1998 when an unsupported ditch he was working in collapsed on him.

The destruction of Nelson's Pillar was the last in a long Irish tradition of blowing up imperial monuments. William III on horseback was blown off his pediment in College Green in 1928, George II and his horse copped it in the 1940s and George I also bit the dust. Queen Victoria, who stood outside Leinster House till the 1940s, was dismantled for safe-keeping and is now an asylum-seeker in Australia. William III was melted down and used to patch sewer pipes. Another Protestant, Wolfe Tone, was hit in 1989, this time by the Ulster Volunteer Force, who must have objected to his aligning himself with the cause of Irish freedom. He was collected up and rebuilt and still stands on St Stephen's Green. For some reason no one has taken exception to the statue of Prince Albert that lurks outside the Natural History Museum, or, come to that, the enormous memorial to Wellington in Phoenix Park.

Street, still 'giving out' to his public. In place of Nelson in the central aisle of the street is a new, apolitical creature, Anna Livia, Joyce's embodiment of the river Liffey; she is better known to her admirers as the floosie in the jacuzzi, or better still the whore (pronounced 'hoower' by Dubliners) in the shower (pronounced 'shoower').

Other notable statuary in the street includes the 19th century Nationalist leader Parnell at the north end, Sir John Grey, who organized a new water supply for the city in the 19th century, and Father Theobald Matthew, who founded the Total Abstinence Movement. James Joyce, uncharacteristically dishevelled, stands in North Earl Street.

Near to O'Connell Street is the Pro Cathedral in Marlborough Street, which is accessed via Cathedral Street.

The Pro Cathedral

In this case, Pro isn't a diminutive for Protestant. It means 'almost but not quite' – since the city already has two cathedrals, another would be a bit excessive. Both the others are still recognized by Rome as cathedrals and so before St Mary's got the official title, one of the other two would have to be disestablished. So this one, which is far better attended, is only a Pro. The 19th century saw a great boom in church building all over Ireland as a response to the relaxation of the laws against Catholics (the Penal Laws) and the increasing wealth of Catholic families. This example was tactfully built in a side street, its position not living up to the grandeur of its design. The neo-classical school looked

Dublin

The Hugh Lane Collection

In the 19th century Charlemont House became an expensive burden to Lord Charlemont's heirs and it was sold to the government. It became the register office for a time, and part of it still fulfils this function, but in 1933 it became home to an art collection formerly owned by Sir Hugh Lane, a nephew of Lady Gregory. In 1905 he bequeathed his extensive collection to the state on the understanding that a suitable exhibition place would be found for it. It was given a temporary home in Clonmell House in Harcourt Street, but when the government dithered about finding a permanent exhibition site Lane changed

his will and left it to Britain. He changed his mind again and made a codicil to his will bequeathing the collection once more to Ireland. Unfortunately, in 1915 he took a trip to America on the Lusitania before signing the codicil and, along with 1,194 others, lost his life to a German U-boat. The collection went to Britain and for 44 years remained in dispute. In the meantime, in 1933, the Municipal Gallery of Modern Art was opened without the core collection. In 1959 the British and Irish governments finally decided to split the collection between them and every five years they swap paintings.

back to the simplicity of form of Greek architecture and the interior Doric columns reflect that. The exterior portico was added later but is in keeping with the building's austere, simple lines. Inside, the place is a bit cluttered with memorials to dead notables but the crypt is good for a browse and there is a restful sense of space.

From the cathedral a brief walk up O'Connell Street brings you to Parnell Square.

Parnell Square

This is Dublin's oldest city square, formerly 'The Barley Fields', and acquired by Dr Bartholomew Mosse in 1748. He laid out the fields as a pleasure garden, which he used to raise funds for a lying-in hospital to be built at the southern end of the gardens. The hospital was built after 1748 and was Europe's first maternity hospital, a function that it still fulfils. In 1764 the Rotunda of the **Assembly Rooms** (now the Ambassador Cinema) was built, again to raise money for the hospital. The hospital, still called **The Rotunda**, has a particularly interesting chapel with very elaborate plasterwork, which can be found above the main entrance of the hospital. ■ *Buses to Parnell Square: Nos 10, 11, 11A, 11B, 19, 19A, 22, 22A and 36. Connolly Station is a 10-minute walk.*

Dublin Writers Museum Around the gardens and the hospital a city square sprang up in a fairly haphazard fashion: originally called Rutland Square after the then viceroy. The east side was the first to be developed and the palatial houses were bought up by low-level dignitaries such as Lord Wicklow, who bought No 4 for £3,500: a vast sum in those days. No 11 was once home to the Earls of Ormond, and Oliver St John Gogarty, Buck Mulligan of *Ulysses* fame and friend to Michael Collins, was born at No 5. At Nos 18 and 19 are the Irish Writers' Centre and the Dublin Writers Museum, which includes memorabilia and rare copies of the works of famous Irish writers including Swift, Sheridan, Oscar Wilde, GB Shaw, Yeats, Beckett, and Seamus Heaney. ■ *T8722077. June to August, Monday-Friday 1000-1800, Saturday 1000-1700; September to May, Monday-Saturday 1000-1700; All year, Sunday and public holidays 1100-1700. IR£2.95. Bookshop and coffee shop open museum hours. Restaurant (see 'Eating – North of the city' on page 130). Tours in French, German, Spanish and Japanese.*

Around 1762 Charlemont House was built on the west side of the square by Scottish architect Sir William Chambers for Lord Charlemont (owner of the **Casino at Marino** on the Malahide Road, see page 148). The house is currently the Hugh Lane Municipal Gallery, a collection of 20th century Irish and international art. It includes works by Corot, Manet, Monet, Renoir, Augustus John and Ireland's own Jack Yeats, as well as many others (see box on page 84). The stained glass room contains *The Eve of St Agnes*, the best-known work of Harry Clarke, one of Ireland's foremost artists, concentrating on the medium of stained glass. His style is strange, almost surreal, slightly reminiscent of Beardsley. His works were commissioned all over the world and you can see more of them in Dublin: in the National Gallery of Ireland (*The Song of the Mad Prince*), and oddly enough in Bewleys Café in Grafton Street. ■ *22, Parnell Square North, T8741903, hughlane@iol.ie Free. April to August, Tuesday-Wednesday 0930-1800,Thursday 0930-2000; September to March, Thursday 0930-1800; all year, Friday-Saturday 0930-1700, Sunday 1100-1700. Closed Mondays. Shop and restaurant open during gallery hours. Sunday lunchtime concerts and public lectures during winter.*

Hugh Lane Municipal Gallery

Top 5 Irish Paintings in the Gallery: The Dockers, Maurice MacGonigal (1900); Lakeside Cottages, Paul Henry (1876-1958); The Little Seamstress, Payrick Tuohy (1894-1930); Towards Night and Day, Frank O'Meara (1853-88); Mrs Lavery Sketching, John Lavery (1856-1941).

In the gardens at the heart of the square is the Garden of Remembrance, established in 1966 to mark the 50th anniversary of the Easter Rising (see box on page 81) and commemorating all those who have given their lives in the cause of Irish freedom. The site was chosen because it was here that the Irish Volunteers were held overnight, in the open, before being taken to Kilmainham Gaol. A statue called 'The Children of Lir', by Oisín Kelly, was added in 1971. The legend of the children of Lir tells us that they were the children of the sea god whose second wife turned them into swans in a fit of jealousy, doomed to swim the shores of Ireland for 900 years. At the end of that time they staggered ashore and died of extreme old age. The connection from this to the martyrs to Irish freedom isn't too clear since the children didn't seem to suffer in any particular cause. Perhaps it's just the general sense of doom that appeals. Anyway, it's a remarkable piece of artistry.

Garden of Remembrance

At the north end of the square on the corner of Frederick Street is the **Abbey Presbyterian Church**, more commonly known as Findlater's Church, built in 1864 with cash put up by a local businessman, Findlater. Its spire stands out on Dublin's skyline and it is open during the summer.

Abbey Presbyterian Church

From the northwest corner of the Square a brief walk along Granby Row brings you to the National Wax Museum.

This is the usual collection of chamber of horrors, pop stars and national political and literary figures. It also has a dodgy life-size depiction of Leonardo's *Last Supper* and a fairyland, where children can have fun. Good for children and people who like to see what the figures of Irish history look like in wobbly 3D rather than oils or bronze. ■ *T8726340. Monday-Saturday 1000-1730, Sundays 1200-1730. IR£3.50. Bus nos 11, 13, 16, 22, 22A.*

National Wax Museum

Around Mountjoy Square

Another north Dublin Georgian square, built between 1792 and 1818 and named after Lord Mountjoy, who instigated it, this was once a very fashionable part of the city. The houses vary in style and grandeur: some were built as an estate to be let out, while others were commissioned by various bigwigs. In the 19th century the square gradually fell into decay, but has recently become a bijou area again, and most of the houses are being fairly faithfully restored. The gardens in the middle were once the sole territory of the square's residents, who strolled there protected from the horses and carriages that must have used Gardiner Street as a thoroughfare. The square features in James Joyce's *Ulysses* as the scene of the incident in which Bloom bumps into David Sheehy MP, a genuine resident of the square in 1904 and the father of Hannah Sheehy Skeffington, the feminist and wife of Francis, who was killed during the 1916 Easter Rising (see box on page 81).

St George's Heading west from Mountjoy Square along Great Denmark Street and Temple
Church Street brings you to St George's Church, now deconsecrated and renamed the Temple Theatre. It was built between 1802 and 1813 as an Anglican church (in 1806 the Duke of Wellington was married here) and was designed by Francis Johnston. If Londoners find it vaguely familiar it is because its spire is based on St Martin's-in-the-Fields. The architect lived nearby in Eccles Street and donated the bells himself: they had been in his garden, and the neighbours complained when he rang them. Johnston was an Irishman from Armagh whose observatory he designed, as well as the GPO and the Chapel Royal in Dublin Castle. Nearby are three places associated with James Joyce: the Joyce Centre, Belvedere College and Eccles St, which are described in the **Joyce's Dublin** section (see page 118).

Gaelic Athletic If you're in the area of Mountjoy Square and are a sports enthusiast, the GAA
Association Museum in the newly built New Stand in Croke Park is a brisk step away.
Museum Highly sponsored and seriously interactive, the museum has displays on the various Gaelic games and the history of the association. While you are at the museum you might want to take a moment to reflect on the day in 1920 when, in reprisal for the murders of 11 English Intelligence officers, British tanks opened fire on a crowd watching a football match here, killing 14 people and wounding 60 others. ■ *Main entrance in Clonliffe Road, T8558176. Daily May to September 1000-1700; October to April closed Mondays. Only pre-booked groups on match days. IR£3. Bus Nos 3, 11, 11A, 16, 16A, 123 from O'Connell St. 15 minutes walk from Connolly Station.*

The Four Courts and around

An architectural To approach from Mountjoy Square, you could take a walk along Gardiner
walk Place and Temple Street (described in the *Ulysses* Walk, page 118) up to Dorset
Street, and follow it back towards the river, passing by the Black Church lurking in the centre of St Mary's Place. A Dublin belief was that if you walked twice around this church the devil would appear. The church, made of black calp stone, is no longer open. As Dorset Street passes into Bolton Street you are walking through some pretty run-down parts of the city, but this area is due for bigger things, with the development of Smithfield 'village' nearer to the river. A side detour down Henrietta Street, once the classiest area of Dublin, brings you to the King's Inns, designed by Gandon and completed in 1817. The garden in the centre was once part of the Royal Canal and, like the Custom House and the Four Courts, this building was designed to be seen from across the water. You can't go inside, but the exterior and garden are worth a peek. Turning left out of Bolton Street into Church Street brings you back to the river, six blocks west of O'Connell Street and in the newest touristified part of the city.

The Four Courts The Four Courts of Chancery, King's Bench, Exchequer and Common Pleas are James Gandon's second Dublin masterpiece. Where the Custom House is delicate, with a central dome sitting primly at the top, these buildings are massive and imposing, and the dome broods over the city. Gandon took an existing building (the current east wing) and made a duplicate wing to the west. Great Corinthian columns mark the front of the building, and the whole edifice is linked up by arcades, screens and two triumphal arches. Gandon faced the same problems with this building as he had with the Custom House: everyone wanted their twopennorth of say in how it got built. It cost £200,000 and took 16 years to build. In the Civil War it was occupied by the anti-treaty forces and eventually bombarded: the Public Records Office and all the priceless historical records inside were destroyed. Renovation began soon after and the Four Courts reopened in 1931. They are currently open to the public when the courts are sitting.

Just round the corner in Church Street is St Michan's Church, founded in 1095 by the Vikings who had left the city for Oxmantown. None of the original building remains, although the tower is 15th century. The rest was rebuilt several times: in the 17th and 19th centuries and later after the damage done in the civil war. Its chief claim to fame is the bodies in its vaults, hundreds of years old, preserved by the peculiar conditions there. Among them are the bodies of the Sheares brothers, executed for their part in the 1798 uprising. In the graveyard are two more 1798 rebels, Oliver Bond and the Reverend William Jackson. Inside the church itself is an organ, one of the oldest still in use in Ireland, used by

St Michan's Church

Handel for the first performance of his *Messiah*. Also on show are a penitent's stool and some beautiful woodcarvings around the organ case. ■ *T8724154. 31st March to 31st October, Monday-Friday 1000-1245, 1400-16.45, Saturday 1000-1245; 1st November to 30th March, Monday-Friday 1200-1500, Saturday 1000-1300. IR£1.50. Guided tours of the crypt are available.*

Old Jameson Distillery A few minutes away from St Michan's in Bow Street is the Old Jameson Distillery, now dedicated to the history of whiskey production. It's a pleasant enough trip, taking in the old copper stills, bottling line, fermentation vessels and all the other paraphernalia of whiskey manufacture, with a museum, theatre and shop as well as a 1920s-style bar and of course a whiskey-tasting session at the end of the tour. ■ *T8725566. Daily, 0930-1730. IR£3.50. Tours last 50 minutes. Bus Nos 67, 67A, 68, 69, 70, 90.*

Ceol & the Chimney
The comedian, Ed Byrne, explains in his show how he's been travelling the world apologising for Riverdance: 'the reason it tours the world is because it was asked to leave Ireland'.

Part of the Chief O'Neill complex, all built on the site of the original Jameson distillery, Ceol is a very interactive, modern exhibition about traditional music. School groups storm through noisily, but if you care to take the time there is much to engage you in this place, from the artwork, videos of musicians complaining about or praising the modern interest in traditional Irish music, a dance floor where you can try some set dancing, and a musical floor where you can play the uillean pipes by walking around the room. One room shows videos of Irish dancing set beside Riverdance material, where you can see just how untraditional Riverdance is with its low cut dresses and miniskirts, bare male chests and leather pants. Outside the entrance is the Chimney, 175 ft high with a glass walled lift to take you to the top, from where the city is spread out beneath you. The original street has been recobbled and should return to being an open air market when it is finished, although the horse fair may never find its way back to this newly-gentrified area. ■ *Smithfield, T8173820. Monday-Saturday 0930-1830. Sunday 1030-1830. Closed Christmas Day and Good Friday. IR£3.95. Cafe/bar, gift shop.*

The Phoenix Park and around

It is easy to put on a good pair of walking shoes and make a whole day of the Phoenix Park. It is the largest enclosed public park in Europe at 1,752 acres and includes Dublin Zoo, a police museum, the visitor centre, an early 17th-century fortified house, monuments to assorted public figures, the homes of the Irish president and American ambassador, several lakes, deer, a thriving wildlife community, a neolithic cromlech and an interesting ruin of a magazine fort to wander around. Dubliners use this park for all sorts of activities, from practising their golf swings to model aeroplane flying, hurling matches and just sitting about in the sunshine.

History Before the Reformation the land belonged to the Knights Hospitallers of St John of Jerusalem. With the confiscation of all the church lands, its ownership fell to the crown. In 1662 the Duke of Ormond became Lord Lieutenant of Ireland, and thought it would be great craic to enclose the land and make a deerpark for Charles II to use when he popped over. At this time the park extended across the river and took in Chapelizod to the west, Islandbridge and the land on which now stands the National Museum of Modern Art. When the Royal Hospital at Kilmainham was built, most of the land south of the river was converted from parklands.

The park opened to the public in 1747, during the great period of Protestant ascendancy when the descendants of the Norman invaders of earlier years finally felt established enough to lay out some cash on building a fine city. The Lord Lieutenant of the time, Lord Chesterfield, began building the lodges that are still dotted around the park. He was responsible for the Phoenix Column, a sad excuse for a phoenix, which stands near the centre of the park. The name Phoenix has nothing to do with mythical winged creatures but is a corruption of the Irish *fionn uisce*, meaning pure water and referring to a spring that once existed in the park. The main boulevard that runs southeast to northwest across the park was laid out in 1834. A shuttle bus runs around part of the park from the main gates to the Visitor Centre, stopping at the zoo, the visitor centre and the papal cross.

A walk in the Phoenix Park

The following is a suggested walk around the Phoenix Park, taking in the sights and getting a feel of the size of the place. Actually pottering about each sight will make the walk take most of the day. Take a picnic or plan to stop for a pub lunch in Chapelizod (see page 91).

From the main gates head northwest for a few paces along the main boulevard **To the zoo** and then turn off right into the **People's Flower Garden,** laid out in 1865 by the Earl of Carlisle. To your right is a Georgian building, recently renovated, which is now the main headquarters of the Irish army but was once a military hospital, designed by Gandon. Meeting the road you come across a statue of Sean Heuston, one of the leaders of the 1916 uprising, after whom the railway station and nearby bridge are named. Across the road is the **Hollow in the Park** where a Victorian bandstand is still used on Sunday afternoons when an army band plays here. Crossing the hollow, follow Zoo Road around to the zoo entrance where you can drop in on the animals. This is the second oldest zoo in Europe and has a petting zoo and monkey islands, and is set in 30 acres. It is said that the MGM lion's roar was recorded from a lion bred in Dublin zoo.
■ *T6671425. Monday-Saturday 0930-1800, Sunday 1030-1800. IR£5.90. Daily tours, restaurant, gift shop. Bus Nos 10 from O'Connell Street; 25, 26 from Middle Abbey Street.*

The Phoenix Park

The Phoenix Park Murders

In 1882 Chief Secretary Frederick Cavendish and Under-Secretary Thomas Burke were murdered just outside the gates of the Vice Regal Lodge by members of a group called the Invincibles. The assassinations came at a crisis point in Irish history: the previous three years had seen the Land War, in which increasingly militant tenants had revolted against unfair rents and evictions; Gladstone's government had just signed the Kilmainham Treaty with Parnell, brought in laws to protect tenants in Ireland, and was about to disband much of the machinery of coercion being used against tenants; the steam had gone out of the tenants' movement, which upset militant nationalists such as the Invincibles, who saw the movement as a means of achieving Irish independence. As they intended, the murders threw the whole issue up in the air again, prevented the disbanding of Gladstone's coercive measures and brought Parnell to a very low point in his career.

The assassins were hunted down with vigour and one of them, James Carey, gave evidence against the others in exchange for his own freedom. Five men were hanged for the murders and eight others imprisoned. Carey was released but was later murdered by a former comrade, Patrick Donnell. The episode didn't end there. In 1887 the Times *began publishing a series of articles about Parnell, claiming that he had connections with Irish terrorism. A set of letters were published, allegedly written by Parnell, connecting him with the murders in Phoenix Park. The resulting government inquiry into Parnell's affairs revealed that the letters were a forgery, bringing the reputation of the* Times *into question, as well as that of the government that had taken the* Times' *articles seriously.*

A final little irony is that, while the murdered men are commemorated by a small plaque in Phoenix Park, a large monument in Glasnevin Cemetery commemorates the hanged murderers.

Gough Monument & Wellington Testimonial

Heading towards the Wellington Testimonial (the extremely large obelisk that dominates the park) you pass a place still marked in street atlases as the Gough Monument. This was a bronze equestrian statue commemorating the deeds of Hugh Viscount Gough, who fought with Wellington at Waterloo. This statue attracted the same animosity as Nelson's Pillar (see box on page 83). First the Viscount's head and arm were cut off and thrown in the Liffey, then the horse's right leg went, and finally he was blown apart altogether.

Approaching the Wellington Testimonial, the sheer scale of the thing is what strikes the eye. It was begun in 1817, and the £22,000 intended for its construction was used up on the first 98 feet (30 metres). Wellington fell from grace at around this time and the monument was not completed. In 1861 work on it began again, with the addition of the bronze plaques celebrating Waterloo, the defeat of the Indian Mutiny and, strangely with regard to someone who opposed Catholic emancipation, civil and religious liberty. But the project was never completed according to the original plan. The lions intended for the statue's feet were never made, and the plinths that had been set out to hold them were taken down. Even so, it is the largest obelisk in Europe.

War Memorial Park

Heading south out of the park and crossing Sarah Bridge, turn right following signs to the War Memorial Park. This little park is dedicated to the memory of the 49,400 Irish people who died in the First World War. Follow the path past the university rowing club and along the river for a few metres as far as a little pavilion and then head south into the memorial gardens. They were designed by Sir Edwin Lutyens and laid out by Gertrude Jekyll. The gardeners will give a guided tour on request and you can ask to go inside the bookrooms, where the names of all those who died are recorded. ■ *T6613111, 6770236. Monday-Friday 0800-dusk, Saturday-Sunday 1000-dusk. Free. Phone in advance for tour and access to bookroom.*

Return to the river bank, where the Liffey is looking very rural, and follow it westwards though a gate and along the river bank. This brings you out to St Laurence Road, which you should follow to the Chapelizod Bridge.

The village of Chapelizod has an ancient pedigree. Its name is probably a corruption of 'Chapel of Isolde', daughter of the king of Ireland and loved by Tristram. The land was confiscated from the Knights Templar by Henry II during the Norman invasion, and remained part of the Royal Demesne until the 14th century. In the 17th century it was reacquired by Charles II who built a king's house here. William of Orange stayed in the house after the Battle of the Boyne. Earlier, Huguenot refugees from La Rochelle came here and set up linen-weaving shops, which, by the middle of the 19th century, had expanded to become a major industry. **Chapelizod**

At the turn of the century a whiskey company was set up here. One of its investors was John Joyce, father of the writer. He worked as secretary while the company still functioned, but was bankrupted when it failed. James Joyce spent some of his childhood here: he used it as a setting for part of *Finnegan's Wake*, and a character in one of his short stories in *Dubliners* lived here. The village might be a good spot to stop for lunch. The *Village Pub* does soup and sandwiches at lunchtime.

From the village head back into Phoenix Park by turning left out of the *Village Pub*, and following the sign marked 'Cromlech' into Park Lane and through a metal gate. Turn left into the park and follow the tarmac path up to a road. Here you are in the part of the park called the Furry Glen, an area of natural woodland with a pond. Passing to the left of the pond, follow it round to another road where there is a little interpretive centre and some picnic benches and toilets. This might make a good alternative spot for lunch. If the interpretive centre is open, you can check out its displays about the wildlife of the park. **Furry Glen & Fifteen Acres**

Return to the pond and descend to the right bank, following the pond for a while and then climbing some steps up to the left. This brings you out into the Fifteen Acres, where there are sports pitches marked out and a model aircraft flying area. Ahead looms the Wellington Testimonial, which you should head towards. Here you should be able to see one of the herds of deer. There are several different species, some of them the descendants of the animals installed by the Duke of Ormond in the 17th century. Male and female deer keep to separate herds, only coming together at mating time. They are tame and will ignore you as you approach.

Head for the single building, which is a keeper's lodge, part of the park layout by Burton in the mid-19th century. Behind this is the signposted **cromlech**: this is a wedge tomb and it may look inconspicuous, but it was found to contain two male skeletons, one of which dates back to 3,500BCE, 1,000 years before the Great Pyramids were built. The site must have been re-used many times and contained ashes and bone fragments as well as Bronze-Age food vessels, shell necklaces, and a flint knife. There is more information and a model of the interior in the Visitor's Centre. From the cromlech head back to the open land and head towards Wellington again. You will pass by the grounds of the Cheshire Home and St Mary's Hospital. The buildings are well worth a look at: they were designed in 1766 and once held the Royal Hibernian Military School.

Magazine fort Head across open ground, with Wellington at about 11 o'clock, towards a grey building on a little hill. This is the infamous magazine fort, built in 1735 in what general opinion considered to be the silliest place possible. Dean Swift wrote about it:

> *Behold! A proof of Irish sense;*
> *How Irish wit is seen!*
> *When nothing's left*
> *That's worth defence*
> *We build a magazine.*

In the middle of a public park and with nothing of any value to protect except itself it does seem a little odd to have built it. Munitions were stored there for many years, and of course invited attack by people needing weapons. In 1916 it was raided, guns were stolen for the Uprising and what couldn't be carried was burned; in 1939 the IRA took 40 lorryloads of ammunition. Today it awaits restoration as perhaps a new tourist location. You can walk around the outside and gaze in at the Georgian buildings inside. It offers excellent views of the park, the city and the river.

Papal Cross From the northwest side of the fort follow the line of the tarmac road towards the Papal Cross. In September 1970 the pope stood here in front of an estimated 1.25 million people and said mass. 1,500 temporary toilets were in place, 2,400 communion bowls were used, 2,000 Eucharistic ministers were helping out, 40 miles of rope organized everyone, 40 tons of steel were used in the building, 600 *gardai* kept order (a remarkably small number!) and 12,000 stewards moved the crowds along. A thousand million people watched the event on TV. In September 1998 the beleaguered President Clinton and his wife landed here by helicopter, to be quickly shunted off to the American Embassy nearby. Jokes about cigars and little black dresses abounded.

Visitor's Centre From the Papal Cross return to the road and head north towards the **Phoenix Monument**. The US embassy, which you pass on the left, dates back to 1776, and used to be the residence of the British Chief Secretary for Ireland. After 1927 it became an American diplomatic residence. It is not open to the public. At the Phoenix Monument follow the signs to **Ashtown Castle** and the Visitor's Centre. The Visitor's Centre is mildly interesting and contains those tableaux of wax models with dodgy wigs that start to talk as you walk past. The contents of the cromlech (known as the **Knockmary Cromlech**) are on display, as well as lots of photos of the pope's visit. ■ *T6770095. November to mid-March, Saturday-Sunday 0930-1630; March to June, daily 0930-1730; June to September, daily 1000-1800; October, daily 0930-1700. IR£2.00. Access to castle is by guided tour only. Coffee shop and restaurant. Bus Nos 37, 38 from Lower Abbey St; 39 from Middle Abbey St. Buses go to the Ashtown Gate, from where there is a 20-minute walk into the park. Bus 10 to Infirmary Road, then the park shuttle bus. Tickets for the tour of Áras an Uachtaráin, home of the Irish President (see page 93), can be obtained here on Saturdays only.*

Ashtown Castle The castle is more interesting and a guided tour lasts about 20 minutes. It was discovered in 1978 when the 18th century building that surrounded it, the Papal Nuncio's residence, was knocked down. That building, Ashtown Lodge, had originally been the residence of the British Under Secretary and was built around the older shell in 1782. It is typical of the 1970s that such an old building should have been demolished but lucky that in the process the older building wasn't lost. Dendochronology (dating wooden objects by counting the tree rings) suggests that the castle is early 17th century, and records show that it was owned by John Connell, an ancestor of Daniel O'Connell, in 1641. His estate consisted of 200 acres and so probably took up a lot of the modern parkland . It was bought by the Duke of Ormond in 1663.

From the castle you have seen most of the major sights of the park. There is still a large area of the northwest corner to explore, so if you like to walk some more head southwest out of the Visitor Centre along Furze Road, which brings you through Oldtown Wood and then back along Ordnance Survey Road to the main road. Head out of the park back to the main gate.

On the way you pass Áras an Uachtaráin, the home of the Irish President, for- **Áras an** merly the Vice Regal Lodge, home of the Lord Lieutenant of Ireland. Queen **Uachtaráin** Victoria stayed here four times, one of them during the Famine, of which her letters make no mention. Between 1876 and 1879, while the Duke of Marlborough was the Lord Lieutenant, his grandson Winston Churchill lived in a small lodge near this house and played in the park. ■ *T6709155. Saturday 0940-1620. Admission is free. Tickets are issued at the Visitor's Centre (see page 92) on Saturdays only. No advance booking is possible. Tour includes a film at the Visitor's Centre, return transport, tour of the exhibition centre and the main state reception rooms. No bags, buggies, cameras, mobile phones or smoking are allowed in Áras an Uachtaráin and there are no public toilets. Bus No 10 to Infirmary Road then the park shuttle bus to the Visitor's Centre.*

Close by the park in Benburb St is the oldest and largest military barracks in **Collins Barracks** Europe, designed by Thomas Burgh in 1701 to house 5,000 men. It was finally decommissioned in 1969. The surrounding streets held its jail, church and married quarters; the jail held many famous prisoners, including Wolfe Tone, the leader of the United Irishmen. In the churchyard behind the barracks are buried the bodies of the leaders of the 1916 uprising and a simple commemorative wall is inscribed with the words of their Declaration. The barracks now house the part of the National Museum dedicated to decorative arts, with some odd displays such as various museum-workers' favourite pieces, a collection of fascinating rural furniture, displays on disappearing rural crafts, and lots more. There are interactive computer displays and some knowledgeable tours. It lacks a history of the building itself and the events that have taken place there, but it is early days and that will hopefully come in phase two of the museum's development. ■ *T6777444. Tuesday-Saturday 1000-1700, Sunday 1400-1700. Free. Café and bookshop open museum hours; guided tours. Bus Nos 90, 25, 25A, 66, 67.*

Glasnevin

It is possible to find your way from the Phoenix Park or Collins Barracks up Prussia Street or further east up Church Street to Constitution Hill and so along the suburban Phibsborough Road to Glasnevin, an area in the north of the city where you can visit the Prospect Cemetery and the Botanic Gardens. The distance is about three miles, however, and might be better done on a bus from the city centre.

It's not often you see a cemetery on a list of sightseeing places, but this one is **Prospect** seriously worth a visit for many reasons. First, within its walls are interred the **Cemetery** bodies of probably hundreds of people who have played significant parts in the history, art, literature and religious life of Ireland and beyond, and standing beside their graves gives their stories an immediacy that a dull paragraph in a history book never does. Secondly, it is a stunning piece of social history, written in the architecture and design of the thousands of tombstones, revealing the pretensions, passions, wealth and poverty of the people who are buried there. Whoever said that death doesn't distinguish between rich and poor? Thirdly, it is a timely reminder to seize the day. The sheer numbers of dead people here are overwhelming: 1,200,000 and rising. You can stand in the centre of the graveyard and look over a sea of tombstones, packed in tight like sardines, the more bijou areas packed the tightest. ■ *Daylight hours. Guided tours Wednesday and Friday afternoons, T8301133; also May to September, Sunday 1130, T8321312; book in advance. Bus Nos 40, 40A, 40B from Parnell Street.*

History   The cemetery opened in 1832 after a long campaign to make religious funerals for Catholics possible. Until the final repeal of the Penal Laws Catholics had practised their religion in a sort of underhand way, tolerated as long as they kept a low profile. Most cemeteries were officially Protestant and, while Catholics were still buried in them, no Catholic prayers were allowed at the graveside. In the 19th century began the great church-building spree, and along with this came the opening of the Prospect Cemetery, officially non-denominational, but sponsored by Daniel O'Connell's Catholic Association.

The cemetery, and much of the surrounding city, is dominated by the central round tower dedicated to **Daniel O'Connell**. To the left of the main entrance are the clerical graves, a tight, cold-looking bunch of great stones dedicated to assorted bishops, and dominated by the rococo mausoleum to **Cardinal McCabe**, archbishop of Dublin from 1879 to 1885, remembered chiefly for his opposition to Parnell's Land League and the 'no rent' manifesto, which Parnell issued from Kilmainham Jail in 1881. Heading north past the stately trees you come to **Parnell's monument**, a massive granite boulder from his home in County Wicklow. 200,000 people attended his funeral.

Returning towards the main wall and one of the watchtowers set in it, you can follow the perimeter path around the cemetery and turn right at the watchtower. This brings you to the plots of the various Religious Orders. In the Jesuit plot is buried the poet **Gerard Manley Hopkins** (1844-89). An Englishman with no Irish connections at all, he was sent by the Order to work as a teacher of Classics at University College Dublin, and seems to have had a lonely and unfulfilled life there. On his death, five years after arriving in Dublin, he was just a Jesuit priest; a complete volume of his poetry was not published until 30 years later.

Joyce enthusiasts might like to continue along the road, and then turn right into the Dublin West section to find the **Joyce family plot**, which lies northeast of Parnell's plot. Its actual reference number is XF 6.5 and you might have a little scrambling about to do to find it. Joyce's father is buried there. Also in this section is a monument raised to, but not the actual burying place of, Zozimus (Michael Moran), an infamous street poet and beggar who died in 1846, and who is actually buried in the pauper's section. As you cross this area of the graveyard you will notice that it is currently in use, and you can study some of the modern designs in grave ornamentation, a number of which are repeated several times over.

Nearby you can see the cremation garden, a brightly coloured wall where the ashes of those cremated in the cemetery are buried, and close by this again is the **1916 memorial**, dedicated to those who led the Easter Rising. The Cathleen mentioned in the epitaph is in fact Cathleen Ni Houlihan, a fictional creature immortalised by W B Yeats and Lady Gregory, who represents the nation of Ireland, the embodiment of the true and faithful woman ravaged by her enemies. The image doesn't sit too well with modern women, who tend to feel that Cathleen should have spent a little less time being true and faithful and a bit more fighting her own battles.

Returning towards the O'Connell Tower on the left is **Eamon De Valera's plot**, and rounding the O'Connell Tower brings you to the **Republican plot** where many famous names are lined up including Maude Gonne McBride, Constance Markievicz and Cathal Brugha, while nearby is the grave of James Larkin, the labour leader.

From the Republican plot head southeast through some very old and ornate tombstones, one a set of linked hands held together by a chain, another a carved marble scroll hanging at the side of a grave. In this area, almost opposite one another are the graves of **Brendan Behan**, the playwright, and **Hannah Sheehy Skeffington**, the feminist.

Returning first southwest, to the outer path of the cemetery, and then west, back towards the main building, brings you to the monument to **Michael Collins**, in rather splendid but lonely isolation in a big plot all to himself. Nearby among the ordinary graves is the burial place of Kitty Kiernan, his fiancée.

The cemetery is much larger than this brief outline suggests. To the north are the older graves, tumbling and unattended, with regular sprays of herbicide keeping the area brown and dreary-looking. Another bare section holds the paupers' graves where victims of the many epidemics that hit Dublin are buried. Yet another area is given over to the graves of children who died soon after birth. The towers around the cemetery walls date back to the early days of the cemetery, when it was illegal to use bodies for medical research, and grave robbers often raided the cemetery.

National Botanic Gardens

The gardens, close by the cemetery, comprise 20 hectares of plants, both indigenous collections and more exotic creatures. They were founded in 1795 and are worth the visit just to admire the great 19th-century glasshouses. There are more than 20,000 species of plant here, including several that were developed at Glasnevin. It is one of Glasnevin's collectors that the British Isles has to thank for the stands of pampas grass that grace suburban gardens, although we can't blame him for the pink ones that came later. ■ *T8374388. Free. Gardens: summer, Monday-Saturday 0900-1800, Sunday 1100-1800; winter, Monday-Saturday 1000-1630, Sunday 1100-1630. Glasshouses: summer, Monday-Friday 0900-1715, Saturday 0900-1745; winter, Monday to Saturday 1000-1615, Sunday 1400-1615. Closed Christmas Day. Guided tours by arrangement.*

The Royal Canal

Built well after the heyday of the canals, and in competition with the older and better-established Grand Canal, this one was a commercial flop from the start. Legend says it was built as an act of spite when one of the directors of the Grand Canal quit in a huff and decided to go into competition. The canal went out of use in the 1960s and almost disappeared, but the towpath has been reclaimed as a waymarked long-distance walk. A pleasant introduction to the long-distance walks of Ireland can be had here. The canal is a little seedy as it passes through the inner city (it is not advisable to walk here in the evening), but from Ashtown Bridge, near to the Phoenix Park, it is very pleasant and rural. A day's meander along it will bring you to Maynooth, passing through Leixlip on the way. Alternatively, you could travel by train to Maynooth (the train follows the canal) and walk back, hopping on and off trains as the mood takes you.

Sights south of the river

This is the real heart of tourist Dublin, with Trinity College and its famous contents, Temple Bar (with its art galleries, shops and restaurants), Dublin Castle, St Stephen's Green, the cathedrals, and much more. The big sights get very crowded during the summer months, with the real crowds around the Book of Kells, so if you want a good browse without having to shuffle past, make your visit early or mid-week.

Trinity College

Founded in 1592 by Queen Elizabeth, who hoped that it would prevent the young Protestant intellectuals of the Pale going to Europe and discovering Roman Catholicism, the college stands in College Green at the junction of Westmoreland, Dame and Grafton Streets, on ground confiscated from the Augustinian priory, which lay just outside the city walls. Its past students include playwrights Congreve, Wilde, Synge, Beckett, the poet Goldsmith, novelists Swift and Bram Stoker, revolutionaries Wolfe Tone and Robert Emmet, and philosopher George Berkeley (after whom Berkeley and Berkeley College in the US are named), and many more. The university opened its doors to Catholics in 1793, but few Catholics attended because of an edict against it by the Catholic Church. Women were admitted in 1903. ■ *Walking tours of the university meet at the main gate and the price includes the cost of entry to the Long Room where the Book of Kells is kept.*

Other examples of Chambers' work in Ireland are the Casino at Marino (see page 148) and Charlemont House (now the Hugh Lane Gallery) in Parnell Sq (see page 84).

Entering Trinity College from the exhaust-driven hurly burly of College Green, especially in the early morning before the crowds arrive, you discover a little time capsule of smooth lawns, cobble stones, statuary and formal buildings, looking more like Oxford's dreaming spires than many of the Oxford colleges do. Midday in July is another matter. Almost none of the present buildings dates back further than the great building spree of the 18th century. Walking through the main gate, built in 1752-9, you see to your right and left two symmetrical buildings, the chapel and the theatre, both designed by the Scottish architect, Sir William Chambers, in the 1770s, and in front the three squares are dominated by the tower, or campanile (1852, Sir Charles Lanyon). Beside the campanile is a Henry Moore statue, 'Reclining Connected Forms'. The chapel, originally Anglican, is now non-denominational; its points of interest are original plasterwork, painted windows and Ionic columns. Beside

Trinity College

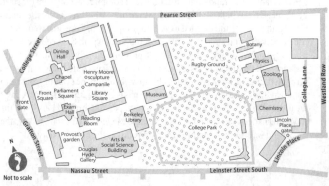

Not to scale

it is the Dining Hall, designed and built in 1743, rebuilt in 1758 because of structural problems and destroyed by fire in 1984 and restored in its original form. It contains portraits of university VIPs. Over to your far right, behind the theatre and open to the public by appointment only, is the Provost's house, built in 1759 from a copy of a copy of a mansion designed by Palladio. It has been lived in continually since that time by the various Provosts of the university. On the north side of Library Square is the Graduates' Memorial Building (1898) and on the left is the finest building on the campus, the Old Library, built between 1712 and 1732. Trinity Library's collection began in 1601 and several famous libraries have been bequeathed to it. Since 1801 the library has had the right to a copy of every book published in the UK, and its total collection now exceeds two million books.

The crowds around here indicate the presence of the Book of Kells in the col- **The Book of** onnades. This was probably made around CE800, which makes it one of the **Kells** oldest books in the world. It is thought to have been created by the monks of St Colmcille's monastery on the island of Iona, off the Scottish coast, and brought to the monastery at Kells in County Meath for safekeeping from the Viking raids on that island. Its beauty lies in the full page illustrations, the minuscule creatures drawn on every page, and the wonderful illustrated capital letters that adorn this version of the Four Gospels. In his Voices of Ireland, P J Kavanagh quotes from a technical account explaining where the monks found their colours: 'reds from red lead and kermes, made from the pregnant body of a Mediterranean insect (kermoccus vermilio) … mauves and maroons from a Mediterranean plant (crozophora tinctoria) … shades of blue from lapis lazuli … brought via merchants of many nationalities from mines in the Badakshan district of Afghanistan in the foothills of the Himalayas!' It now consists of 680 pages, 30 of the opening and ending folios being lost during its turbulent history. It was stolen from Kells and buried, and then rediscovered in 1007; later the shrine it was kept in was taken by a particularly philistine Viking, who saw no value to the pages but just wanted the valuable metal casket. In 1953 it was rebound into four volumes, and two are usually on display, with the pages turned regularly, so you can go several times if you want to see more of it. The library also contains Trinity's collection of the oldest of its books, including the 807 Book of Armagh and the late seventh century Book of Durrow (an illustrated version of the Four Gospels, older and less beautiful than the Book of Kells), an original copy of the 1916 Proclamation of Independence, and a harp dating back to around 1400. ■ *All year, Monday-Saturday 0930-1700; October-May, Sunday 1200-1630. IR£3.50. Closed for ten days over the Christmas/New Year period.*

Across Fellowes Square from the Old Library is the second hive of tourist activ- **The Arts Block** ity, the Arts Block built in 1980 to a design by Paul Koralec. Inside is the Douglas Hyde Gallery, a collection of conceptual and avant garde art. ■ *All year, Monday-Thursday 1100-1800, Friday 1100-1645. Free.*

In the same building is the **Dublin Experience**, a 45-minute audio-visual description of Dublin from Viking times to the present. ■ *T6082320. 18th May-4th October, daily 1000-1700. IR£3.00.*

On the top floor is the **Weingreen Museum of Biblical Antiquities**, full of antiquities from the ancient world. ■ *Appointment to view necessary.*

The west end of Fellowes Square is dominated by the Berkeley Library (1967, **Berkeley Library** Paul Koralek) which is much admired by architects and is said to be the finest **& Museum** example of architecture of that period in Ireland. Beyond it is the Museum **Building**

Dublin

Building (1854, Sir Thomas Deane, Son and Woodward), now the Engineering Department. The building came at the later end of the 19th century when the Victorian love affair with the Gothic form was at its height. It is designed along lines that John Ruskin thought proper: the stonework is chosen for its decorative effect as well as its suitability as a building material: structural polychromy, or the streaky-bacon look. Inside, the columns and balustrades are made of different-coloured marbles, and the domed ceilings are covered in coloured tiles. The stonework around the exterior is abundantly carved – the masons, the O'Shea brothers from Cork and Mr Rowe of Lambeth, were allowed to carve the stone at will in the manner of the medieval churches. Inside the main doors are the skeletons of two Giant Irish Elk, and upstairs is a small geological museum.
■ *T6081477 Appointment to view necessary.*

The Bank of Ireland With its sweeping niched walls, Ionic porticos and piazza, enclosed by projecting pavilions, this building is altogether far too grand to house a humble bank. It is in fact the old Houses of Parliament, dissolved by the Act of Union in 1801.

Dublin: south city centre

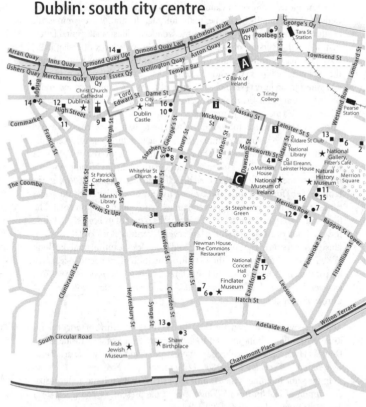

Related maps:
A. Temple Bar area, page 108
B. Dublin: north city centre, page 80
C. South of Temple Bar, page 107

N

0 yards   200
0 metres   200

■ **Sleeping**
1 Abbey Hostel
2 Alexander
3 Avalon House
4 Buswell's
5 Conrad
6 Davenport
7 Harcourt

8 Holiday Inn
9 Jury's Christchurch Inn
10 Lansdowne
11 Merrion
12 Molesworth Court Suites
13 Mont Clare
14 Ormonde
15 Schoolhouse

16 Shelbourne Side Door
17 Stephen's Hall & Morel's Bistro
18 The Hibernian

● **Eating & drinking**
1 Baggott Inn
2 Bewleys

It was designed by Sir Edward Lovett Pearce in the Palladian style, which returned to the classical forms of the ancient Greeks. The style was taken up in England in the 17th century by Inigo Jones and spread to Ireland via Pearce and Richard Castle (see page 457).

The building was constructed between 1729 and 1739, at a time when Parliament basically represented the interests of the Protestant Anglo-Irish. Of the members, 234 were elected by a single patron, while the other 66 were elected on a narrow property-owning male franchise. Two houses met, the commons and the lords, at various times annually, every other year or every two years. For a time, during the period known as 'Grattan's Parliament' (see page 99), it became fiercely independent of England, although never going so far as to suggest Catholics might be represented by its members. In 1801 it meekly voted itself out of existence, fearing independence and the Catholics far more than control from London.

The building you see at the busy intersection in front of Trinity College is not entirely the original design of Lovett. The two Corinthian porticos and niched walls to the east and west are later additions by Gandon and Richard Parke. The observer of the 1740s would have seen a wide open space between the classic Palladian façade of Trinity and the corresponding Ionic portico and projecting pavilions of the two houses of parliament.

In 1790 the original octagonal House of Commons was destroyed by fire and rebuilt as a circular chamber, and then in 1804 it was destroyed to make way for a boardroom and offices for its new owners, the Bank of Ireland. But the Lords remains intact, complete with the mace from the House of Commons and original oak panelling fireplaces. Also kept in the room are 1730s tapestries depicting the Battle of the Boyne in 1690 and the Siege of Derry in 1689, which this parliament would have considered great victories. In the Bank of Ireland Arts Centre is **The Story of Banking Museum**, with exhibitions on the wonderful things banks have done for the country over the centuries. Outside the bank is the statue of Henry Grattan (1746-1820), who supported the independence of the Irish Parliament but who opposed the repeal of the Penal Laws for the bulk of his career as an MP in Ireland. He finally changed his tune in 1793 in favour of Catholic emancipation, but supported the move allowing the king to have the final say in the appointment of Catholic bishops, thus ensuring

3 Bleeding Horse
4 Brazen Head
5 Break for the Border
6 Chocolate Bar
7 Doheny & Nesbitt's
8 Govinda's
9 John Mulligan's Bar
10 Juice
11 Mother Redcap's Tavern & Market
12 O'Donoghue's
13 One Pico
14 O'Shea's Merchant
15 Patrick Gilbaud
16 Yamamori

👉 *William Dargan*

A truly self-made Victorian man, William Dargan was the son of a Carlow farmer, sent to England to get his education, and trained as a surveyor. He worked with Thomas Telford, the great Victorian road-builder, and then brought his roadmaking skills back to Ireland, setting up himself as a road-builder. He built Ireland's first railway, the Dublin to Kingstown line, in 1831 and went on to build 600 more miles of railway, the Ulster Canal and large areas of the Belfast docks. In 1853, inspired by the success of a similar exhibition in Cork in the previous year, he put up the cash for the Great Exhibition of Irish industry in the grounds of Leinster House in a temporary building. The exhibition was a financial failure, despite being visited by Queen Victoria four times in one week. Because Irish industry was a tiny creature, and few foreign visitors were tempted over, the exhibition became rather a display of arts and crafts and antiques and it was this that inspired the creation of the National Gallery. Victoria definitely took to Dargan, actually visiting him at home and offering him a baronetcy, but he declined the offer. After the financial loss of the exhibition Dargan's fortunes went into a decline as he invested unwisely, and he finally died having been unable to pay his debts. His widow got a fairly healthy pension from the civil list.

that only loyal clergy controlled the Catholic masses. ■ *Bank: T6776801. Monday-Wednesday and Friday 1000-1600, Thursday 1000-1700. Free. Tours of the Lords: Tuesday 1030, 1130, 1345 (except bank holidays). Museum: Tuesday-Friday 1000-1600. IR£1.50.*

Merrion Square and around

Just south of Trinity College and tightly packed with museums and other places to visit, the area between Merrion Square, the Georgian heartland of Dublin, and the main gate of Trinity is Dublin's tourist centre, with more stuffed leprechauns and t-shirts claiming to have Irish roots than any other part of Ireland (with the exception perhaps of Killarney, home of the amusing printed tea towel). Starting from the corner of Leinster Street and Kildare Street a whole day could be spent wandering around. First, though, look at the building on the corner of the two streets, the Kildare Street Club as was, now the **Heraldic Museum and Genealogical Office**. Built in 1861 by Deane and Son, the same firm that built the Engineering building in Trinity College, this red brick and limestone building has fancy carved animals around its window-sills; one of them, a bunch of monkeys playing billiards, is said to be the stonemasons' comment on the wealthy men inside. If you like heraldry this is just the place for you, with lots of exhibits of all kinds of examples of coats of arms; also, this is a good place to start if you are tracing your Irish roots. ■ *2 Kildare Street, T6614877. Monday-Friday 1000-1430. Free.*

Kildare Street Heading up Kildare Street to the next big stop, Leinster House, you pass on your left two interesting buildings. Firstly, there is the **Royal College of Physicians**, built in 1864 and home to the finest medical historical library in Ireland with books dating back to the 16th century and original plasterwork inside. It is not open to the general public, but medical history fanatics can persuade the Secretary to admit them. Beside it is the **National Library**, which is open to the public, designed in 1884-90 by the architects of the streaky bacon look, Deane and Son, as part of the complex of the **National Library and Museum**. These rather ponderous buildings with a profusion of detailed ornamentation and colonnaded porticoes are cramped even further by the railings that now divide up what was once an open courtyard. The entrance to the library often holds exhibitions, and the reading-room is certainly worth a look, especially for fans of the novel *Ulysses*. ■ *Kildare Street. Monday 1000-1700, Tuesday-Wednesday and Friday 1000-1700, Thursday and Saturday 1000-1300. Free. Bus Nos 7, 7A, 8 from Burgh Quay, 10, 11, 13 from O'Connell Street. Pearse Street DART station.*

When Parnell Square in north Dublin became a little too nouveau riche around 1745, James Fitzgerald, the Earl of Kildare, decided to move out to the country, and had a house built south of the river. The chattering classes said he was mad, but before long his peers were fighting each other to move south before all the space was taken. The house was designed by Richard Castle, the architect of the Rotunda Hospital, and had two entrances: the one facing Kildare Street, which you are looking at now, was designed to look like a typical Palladian townhouse; the other entrance, which faced on to fields, was built in a country-house style. When Kildare became the Earl of Leinster he changed the name of his house to suit his title. His son, Edward, was a radical who fought in the American War of Independence and grew to admire the French Revolution. He would have become a leading figure in the United Irishmen's insurrection in 1798 if he had not been arrested and mortally wounded before the rebellion took place. Seventeen years later his son sold the house to the Royal Dublin Society, which turned it into a museum and built the two buildings on either side, as well as the School of Art and the National Gallery at the Merrion Square side of the estate. In 1908 a giant statue of Queen Victoria was stuck out in the open courtyard, with another of the Prince Consort round the back. Albert survives but ironically Victoria is in Australia, which is where lots of Dublin's citizens ended up. The building is now home to the two Houses of Parliament, *Oireachtas na hÉireann* in Irish. The lower house, the *Dáil*, is housed in a Victorian lecture theatre out the back, while the upper house, the *Seanad*, meets in the very classy north wing saloon. ■ *Kildare Street, Dublin 2, T6183066. All year, Monday-Friday by prior arrangement only.*

Leinster House
One way of visiting the Dáil is to persuade a TD (Teachta Dála) to take you in with them (if you can find one).

The museum is full of the most wonderful things from Bronze-Age gold hoards to a display about ancient Egyptian embalming techniques and an informative if male-oriented study called *The Road to Independence*.

The National Museum

But before you even enter the galleries, stop to admire the entrance lobby with its beautiful mosaic floor portraying the signs of the zodiac and the domed roof, which is 62 feet (18.9 metres) high. The exterior of the building has its own grand Victorian beauty, and has been undergoing a massive refurbishment programme designed to clean up and repair the worst damage and weathering of the last hundred years or so.

The first exhibition you come to is called **Prehistoric Ireland** and should be followed in an anticlockwise direction. It has displays on food gathering, burial customs and religion. The centrepiece of this collection is the main hall, full of gleaming gold hoards from the Bronze Age. Judging from the extent of it, our ancestors must have been a mistrustful (and forgetful) lot. Virtually none of it was excavated by archaeologists – it turned up behind ploughs, in railway cuttings and peat bogs. Ranging from scrap gold to intricate brooches, torques and tiaras, it fills the main hall and is the finest exhibition of prehistoric gold in Europe. The dating of these gold pieces ranges from 2200BCE to 700BCE.

The **Treasury** contains gold and other items made by the Celts who arrived in Ireland around 300BCE. Among the pieces on display, look out for the Ardagh Chalice, the **Tara Brooch** and the Loughnashade trumpet.

Top 10 Irish Paintings in the National Gallery

Sackville Street, Dublin, *Michael Angelo Hayes (1820-77)*	**Achill Horses,** *Mainie Jellet (1897-1944)*
William Butler Yeats, *John Butler Yeats (1839-1922)*	**The Custom House,** Dublin, *James Malton (1760-1803)*
Helleili and Hildebrand, *Frederic William Burton (1816-1900)*	**A View of Dublin from Chapelizod,** *William Ashford (1746-1824)*
A View of Powerscourt Waterfall, *George Barret (1728-84)*	**A Thunderstorm: the Frightened Wagoner,** *James Arthur O'Connor (1792-1841)*
The Marriage of Strongbow and Aoife, *Daniel Maclise (1806-70)*	**An Ejected Family,** *Erskine Nicol (1825-1904)*

If you can tear your eyes away from the glimmer and put off your plans for buying a metal detector, the rest of the museum is just as fascinating. Still on the ground floor are some relics of Early Christian and Celtic Ireland, and one of the highlights of the museum is the *sheela na gig* (a pagan fertility symbol; see page 394) discovered in Clonmel, County Tipperary, joyously clutching her genitals and most probably horrifying generations of good Catholics.

Upstairs are exhibitions on Viking and medieval Dublin, and the museum's collections of Ancient Egyptian artefacts.

In the exhibition called **The Road to Independence** the many Irish women who risked their lives as doctors, workers and fighters have been sadly ignored, with the exception of one or two big names. The exhibition charts the course of the early years of the twentieth century in Ireland, and death masks and bullet-ridden uniforms figure largely, as well as a bunch of banners and medals donated by those involved. A huge screen shows some interesting archive material. ■ *Kildare Street and Merrion Row, T6777444. Tuesday-Saturday 1000-1700, Sunday 1400-1700. Closed Mondays. Free. Shop selling replicas, café. Regular tours of the exhibits, IR£1. Bus Nos 7, 7A, 8 from Burgh Quay, 10, 11, 13 from O'Connell Street. Pearse Street DART station.*

The Natural History Museum Round the corner, in Merrion Street Upper, is another of the Victorian buildings established by the Royal Dublin Society, the Natural History Museum. It is a very Victorian zoological collection, well kept up but dead just the same. There are stuffed things, skeletons (including three giant elk, extinct for 10,000 years), a butterfly collection as well as cases of pinned insects, and collections of African and Asian creatures, many of whom met their fate at the hands of intrepid Victorian explorers. Opposite the museum at No 24 is the house where the Duke of Wellington, who gave his name to the famous boot, was born, now the Merrion Hotel. ■ *Merrion Street. T6777444. Tuesday-Saturday 1000-1700, Sunday 1400-1700. Free. Bus Nos 7, 7A, 8 from Burgh Quay. Pearse Street DART station.*

The National Gallery In 1853, while the National Library and National Museum were still under construction, William Dargan, a railway magnate, organized the Great Industrial Exhibition in the grounds of Leinster House and dedicated the proceeds to the creation of the gallery, or would have, if there had been any proceeds but it's the thought that counts! The gallery got under way with the purchase of 15 paintings in Rome in 1856. Help came later from GB Shaw, who donated the royalties from *Pygmalion* (1916) to the gallery's coffers. The gallery opened in 1864 with the Dargan Wing, added the Milltown Rooms in 1899-1903 and the Modern Wing in 1964-8.

The Gallery has a worthy collection of art with the Italian school in the Milltown Rooms represented by Titian, Tintoretto, Mantegna, Fra Angelico and Caravaggio (*The Taking of Christ* was discovered in Leeson Street hanging on a wall in a dark corner of the Jesuits' study hall). There are sound collections of Flemish and Dutch paintings in the North Wing (including three works by Rembrandt and a Vermeer), a French collection (also in the Milltown Rooms on the first floor covering 1,000 years of paintings, including a Picasso), and a Spanish collection that includes El Greco and Velasquez. There is also a British collection in the ground floor of the north wing, and a fine Irish collection on the ground floor of the Milltown Rooms, with a room dedicated to Jack Yeats.

From this side of Leinster House you can see the country villa front as well as the many pieces of statuary in the grounds. Dargan is there, while the obelisk in the centre is a testament to Michael Collins, Arthur Griffith and Kevin O'Higgins, generally considered to be the founding fathers of the Free State. At 59 feet (18 metres) it doesn't match Wellington's in Phoenix Park but illustrates the maxim that biggest isn't always best. ■ *Merrion Square West, T6615133. Monday-Saturday 1000-1730 (2030 on Thursday), Sunday 1400-1700. Bus No 10 to Merrion Row and Pembroke Street; bus Nos 5, 6, 7A, 8 to Merrion Square North and Clare Street; bus nos 44, 47, 47B, 48A, 62 to Merrion Square West. Pearse Street DART Station is five minutes away on foot.*

Merrion Square Surrounding a central park is a near-perfect Georgian Square with doors, fanlights, door furniture, boot scrapers, door flaps, and coal hole covers intact. It was begun in 1762 as a rough square of houses with a park in the middle; the park was originally owned by the Church and was donated to the corporation of Dublin by Bishop Dermot Ryan, after whom it was named. At the west end of the park is the Rutland Fountain, designed by a pupil of James Gandon and erected in 1791. It was used by many local slum dwellers for years as their main

National Gallery

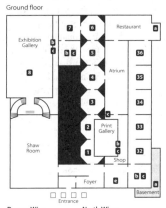

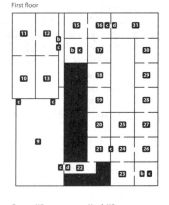

Dargan Wing	North Wing
Shaw Room	32 Portrait Gallery
8 Yeats Museum	33–36 British Painting
	Atrium
Mezzanine level	Restaurant
Exhibition Gallery	Gallery Shop
	Lecture Theatre
Milltown Rooms	*Mezzanine level*
1–6 Irish Painting	Print Gallery
7 Multimedia Gallery	

Dargan Wing	North Wing
9 Baroque Room	23–31 Icons and Dutch,
	Flemish, Italian,
Upper level	Spanish Painting
10–13 French Painting	
	a Toilets
Milltown Rooms	b Lift
15–16 French Painting	c Stairs
17–21 Italian Painting	d Wheelchair access
	e Cloakroom

water supply. During the Famine a soup kitchen operated in the park, feeding some of the thousands of peasants who came into the city.

You will notice many plaques on the houses marking the homes of Dublin's well-to-do and downright famous. At No 1 lived Oscar Wilde and his remarkable father who, as the plaque tells us, was an 'aural and ophthalmic surgeon, archaeologist, ethnologist, antiquarian, biographer, statistician, naturalist, topographer, historian, folklorist': he must have been a hard act to follow. In the park opposite this house is a statue of Oscar Wilde, gloriously decorated with semiprecious stones – blue pearl granite trousers, jacket of jade, shoes of granite – reclining on a white quartz rock and holding a green carnation to his breast (and nicknamed by the populace 'The Quare in the Square'). Daniel O'Connell lived for a time at 58, WB Yeats lived at 82, Joseph Sheridan Le Fanu (author of the vampire novel *Carmilla*) at 70, the poet Æ (George Russell) worked at 84 and scientist Erwin Schrödinger (winner of the Nobel Prize) lived at 65. No 39 was the British Embassy until 1972, when it was burnt down after Bloody Sunday, when British troops opened fire on a demonstration in Derry on 30th January killing 14 people.

The Irish Architectural Archive is at 73, tracing the history of Dublin's buildings from 1560 to modern times, while at the south corner of the square, at **29 Fitzwilliam Street**, is a restored and authentically furnished Georgian town house, owned by the Electricity Supply Board who demolished the rest of the row of houses to build an office block. It's a sort of 'Upstairs Downstairs' effort, showing what life was like for the swanky family who lived in the upper floors and the servants who inhabited the basement. Crockery, furniture and clothes are all originals and borrowed from the National Museum. ■ *29 Lower Fitzwilliam Street. T7026165, F7027796. Tuesday-Saturday 1000-1700, closed Sunday and Monday and two weeks prior to Christmas. IR£2.50. Tea room and gift shop. Bus Nos 7, 8, 10, 45 from city centre. Pearse Street DART station.*

Around Merrion Square The streets around Merrion Square contain many beautiful Georgian mansions, and if you have a mind to you can make an interesting stroll down Merrion Street Upper and Ely Place where more plaques tell of the assorted illuminati who lived in them. Travelling east down Mount Street Upper brings you first of all to **St Stephen's Church**, built in 1825 and renamed 'the pepper canister' because of its shape. A little further on you meet the **Grand Canal**, a contemporary of the grand Georgian mansions, whose construction began in 1755. By 1803 it stretched 340 miles and linked the Shannon with the port of Dublin. Bustling with horses and barges 200 years ago, the canal is now part of a quiet suburb with tree-lined banks and a waymarked walking trail.

South of Merrion Square is Fitzwilliam Square, another undisturbed Georgian relic, the last of the great 18th century building sprees, built in earnest between 1791 and 1825; some of the houses, however, predate the square and were built in the first decade of the 18th century. More doorknockers, fanlights, bootscrapers and cast-iron balconies make good photo opportunities. At No 18 Jack Yeats, the artist and brother of the poet, had a studio for a time, and the civil engineer William Dargan lived at No 2.

St Stephen's Green and around

> *Dublin can be heaven with coffee at eleven*
> *And a stroll in Stephen's Green.*
> 'Anon'

For centuries the 'in' place to be, St Stephen's Green has had many incarnations since the city moved out to meet it. In the 17th century it was an expanse of open ground where people grazed their cattle and public executions took place. In the 1660s the land surrounding the green was sold off for building, and the green itself was partially fenced. The 27 acres (10.9 hectares) were laid out as a public park, with seats and tree-lined walks, but it was closed to public access in 1814, the annual fee for keyholders being one guinea. In 1877 a bill, brought by Lord Ardilaun, opened the park to the public again, and at his expense it was renovated into something like what you see today.

St Stephen's Green is a pleasant enough little park, great for lunch on a sunny day with occasional music in the bandstand and lots of memorabilia. The main entrance at the corner of Grafton Street commemorates the Royal Dublin Fusiliers who died in the Boer War, and is modelled on the Arch of Titus in Rome. At the opposite entrance is a statue called the Three Fates, given to the Irish government by Germany in thanks for their help to the German people after World War II. Wolfe Tone is commemorated at the northwest corner of the park, opposite Merrion Row. Local wags are said by the tourist office to have renamed the granite obelisks 'Tonehenge'. There is a bust of Countess Markievicz who led the taking of the nearby Royal College of Surgeons in 1916, and who, incidentally, was the first woman ever to be elected to a British parliament. When she was released from prison she went to Westminster to look at her name on her coat peg, but never took her seat.

Much of the surrounding Georgian architecture has been lost to the developers, but there are still lots of things to see. Worth a quick look is the **Shelbourne Hotel**, built in 1867 and packed to the ceiling with celebrities and wannabes, and famous for, among other things, employing Aloys Hitler, half brother to Adolf, as a wine waiter. Gold-card holders might want to pop in for afternoon tea. Beside the Shelbourne Hotel is the Huguenot cemetery established in the late 17th century after the influx of refugees from France.

On the south side of the square, and still intact at Nos 80-81, is Richard Castle's first design for a house (1730), built for the bishop of Cork and bought in the 19th century by Lord Iveagh, father to Ardilaun of the Guinness family. It is currently the Department of Foreign Affairs.

A little way south of the green in Earlsfort Terrace is the 1978 **National Concert Hall**, built in what was previously University College Dublin, and before that part of the International Exhibition held in Dublin in 1865. Behind it are **Iveagh Gardens**, formerly the Winter Gardens, and an excellent quiet spot for a picnic lunch. Nearby in Upper Hatch Street is **The Findlater Museum**, set in the Harcourt Street Vaults and recording the history of the wealthy merchant family who built the Abbey Presbyterian Church in Parnell Square. ■ *10 Upper Hatch Street. Monday-Friday 0900-1800, Saturday 1030-1730.*

On the south side of St Stephen's Green are the two renovated Georgian houses known as Newman House. No 85 is the earlier of the two buildings, designed by Castle for Hugh Montgomery, MP for County Fermanagh, but later bought by Richard Whaley (known as 'Burnchapel' due to his propensity for burning down Catholic churches in Wicklow, and father of the even more notorious Buck Whaley, founder of the Hell Fire Club, nicknamed 'Jerusalem' after walking to the said city for a bet). Whaley the elder built the house next door in a similar but grander style. The buildings were bought in 1865 by the Catholic University of Ireland under John Henry Newman, a convert from the Anglican church. Gerard Manley Hopkins spent a lonely five years in the attic at No 86, and his room has been restored to its original state. James Joyce, Padraig

The poet, James Stephens, watched the 1916 rebels building a barricade in St Stephen's Green from outside the Shelbourne Hotel. A man tried to reclaim his cart from the barricade and he ignored orders to desist and 'a rifle spat at him, and in two undulating movements the man sank on himself and sagged to the ground'.

Newman House
If you have to choose one Georgian house to visit, make it this one rather than Number 29: it has more history, and the Jesuit additions to the plasterwork are good fun.

Dublin

Pearse (one of the leaders of the 1916 Easter Rising) and Eamon De Valera studied here, and it was for their benefit no doubt that the naked female figures on the ceilings were clothed, to give them a more modest appearance. In the recent renovations, which began in 1989, one of the Jesuit alterations has been left for our edification.

Guided tours of the two buildings include visits to Hopkins' room in the attic, the Apollo Room in No 85 with its stunning stucco work by the Lafranchini brothers, the saloon, where Georgian gentry would once have entertained beneath even more elaborate ceiling sculptures. In No 86 the saloon was turned into a chapel by the Jesuits (it is here that the beclothing of Juno and her nymphs took place). No 86 is given over to the building's other various incarnations with the lecture theatre used by Joyce both as a student and later as a visiting writer, and the Bishop's Room where the university committee met. (The Catholic University later became University College and moved to Belfield.) In the basement is the very fashionable *Commons* restaurant. Next door is the Catholic University Church, built in 1855 and designed by the Professor of Art at the university, John Pollen It is very marbled inside. ■ *85-6 St Stephen's Green, T7067422, F7067211. June, July and August only, Tuesday-Friday 1200-1700, Saturday 1400-1700, Sunday 100-1400. Closed Mondays. IR£2. 10,11,13,14,14A, 15A, 15B.*

The Shaw birthplace A five-minute walk along Harcourt Street brings you to the house where GB Shaw, the playwright, grew up, set out as it might have been in his Victorian childhood of genteel poverty. It was from this house that his mother left his father and went to live in London with her singing teacher. By age 16 George Bernard was living in London with her, studying during the day and writing unsuccessful novels in the evening. He refused to accept his Nobel Prize for Literature, but must have had a great love of one part of Dublin at least, since he endowed the National Gallery so generously. Interesting as a little island of Victoriana in a sea of Georgiana. ■ *33 Synge Street, Dublin 8, T4750854, F8722231. May to October only, Monday-Saturday 1000-1700, Sunday and public holidays 1100-1700. Bus Nos 16, 19, 22.*

Grafton Street Adjoining St Stephen's Green is the major shopping area of Grafton Street. Much improved since it was pedestrianized, this bustling area has partly succumbed to the high-street chainstore syndrome of so many other city shopping areas, but still retains some of the charm that James Joyce describes in *Ulysses*. There are any number of buskers: brass quartets, digeridoo players, Mexican salsa bands, those strange characters that pretend to be statues and robots, and blokes with guitars churning out Lennon and McCartney numbers. Stalls sell fresh flowers, ethnic jewellery and t-shirts, and music blares from shop doorways. From side streets, cafés pour out on to the pavement in summer, and grubby kids hurtle up and down, dodging the mechanical road-sweeping machine and pursued by harassed *gardai*.

Dublin Civic Museum Five minutes from Stephen's Green's northern corner with Grafton Street is this little museum, occupying the building originally erected by the Society of Artists in 1765. It is a strange mishmash of artefacts to do with the city, including one of the original Proclamations of Independence, a series of 18th century aquatints of the city, a giant pair of shoes, and Nelson's head, blown off his shoulders in the IRA attack on Nelson's Pillar in 1966 (see box on page 83). ■ *58, South William St. Tuesday-Saturday 1000-1800, Sunday 1100-1400. Closed Monday. Free. Bus nos 10, 11, 13 from O'Connell St.*

Opposite is Powerscourt House, built in 1771 and another example of Georgian architecture that you can peer into. It is used as offices but is open to the public.

Temple Bar and around

Nowadays a vibrant, seething mixture of tourist ghetto and alternative living, the network of narrow lanes that criss-cross between the river, Dame Street, Trinity and Fishamble Street is known as Temple Bar, after its 17th century developer, Sir William Temple. What he owned was then well outside the city boundaries, which stopped at Parliament Street to the east; it was open marshland sloping down to a shallow, wide, unnavigable river. Temple reclaimed the land, built quays out into the river (thereby making it navigable by large ships), and laid out the modern street system. The area turned into warehouses and factories where the produce from the many ships that could now moor here was processed. Time wasn't kind to the area, however: ships got bigger and could no longer navigate so far upstream. The docklands moved downriver with the Custom House and, after a century or so as a shopping and manufacturing centre, the area went into a decline.

In the 1960s the whole area was bought up by the state in order to turn it into a bus depot, and in the interim the old warehouses and shops were let out on a short-term basis. Vegetarian cafés, alternative clothes and bookshops, second-hand dealers and, more recently, Internet cafés found niches in the area, and it became a kind of Bohemia. When the bus-depot scheme went out of fashion in the 1980s the government saw the possibilities of the area and made IR£200 million in public and private money available to develop the area. The investment has taken most of the avant-garde edge off the place, and the fake cobbles and olde worlde lampposts don't do a lot for it either, but it is a place that jumps in the evenings and if some of the restaurants are a little pricey and pretentious there are lots of others to choose from.

South of Temple Bar

3	Café en Seine
4	Cedar Tree
5	Chilli Club
6	Dame Tavern
7	Davy Byrne's Pub
8	Fitzer's Café
9	Gotham Café
10	International Bar
11	La Cave
12	QV2
13	Shalimar Indian
14	Stag's Head
15	Trocadero

■ **Sleeping**
1 Brooke's
2 Central

● **Eating & drinking**
1 Bailey Bar
2 Bewleys Oriental Café

The **Irish Film Centre** shows art house films in a very post-modern conversion of an old Quaker Meeting House; the Temple Bar Information Centre in Eustace Street provides fairly up-to-date maps of the area (places come and go here quite quickly) and information about what's on; and the **Gallery of Photography** in Meeting House Square has nice views over the area from its roof. You should also look out for **Designyard** in Essex Street, with its very modern jewellery designs, and **Temple Bar Gallery and Studios** at 5-9 Temple Bar. The area also boasts the **Temple Bar Music Centre**, just off Temple Lane, where there are recording studios and a music venue, and **The Ark Cultural Centre**, focussing on productions for children with a child-sized theatre that can be opened out into Meeting House

Square. For other good places to visit in the area see the 'Essentials' section beginning on page 121.

Despite all this renovation and redevelopment there are a few remnants of this part of the city still intact. In Anglesea Street is the Stock Exchange (1878, Millar & Symes), still doing the same job with the addition of some computer screens. It is open to the public during trading hours. At Nos 28 and 10 are two late 19th-century Queen Anne revival shopfronts. In Crampton Row are Crampton Buildings, built for the Dublin Artisan Dwelling Company in 1891 and intended for poor families. On the corner of Parliament Street is Sunlight Chambers (1901) built for Lever Brothers, with multicoloured terracotta reliefs displaying the benefits of soap, which seem mostly to be providing work for women to do. Also on Parliament Street, a Georgian road-widening development, is Read's Cutlers at No 4, Dublin's oldest business, trading under the same name since 1760: until very recently they still made swords for the Irish army. They still charpen knives but now you must take them into the café/bar next door. Another relic of a past age is Merchant's Arch, part of a Merchant's Hall built in 1822. It leads out to the Ha'penny Bridge, a cast-iron footbridge built in 1816 and named for the toll levied on it until 1916. An interesting piece of contemporary history is the Green Building in Eustace Street, which is made from recycled materials. It has its own solar and wind generator and recycles all its own water. It is not open to the public.

Dublin's Viking Adventure

Also lurking in Temple Bar, and a good outing for children, is Dublin's Viking Adventure, in the 1815 Franciscan church of Ss Michael and John (the oldest Catholic church in Ireland until 1990 when it was deconsecrated). The site is also famous for the Smock Alley Theatre, built here in 1661 and the workplace of Peg Woffington, Edmund Keane, both famous actors, and George Farquhar, the playwright. Nowadays it's a re-creation of Viking Dublin, complete with people dressed up in Viking gear, reconstructions of huts and wall divisions, and artefacts that were dug up around Fishamble Street and Wood Quay when it was rebuilt. ■ *T6796040. March to October 1000-1300, 1400-1630. Closed Sunday, Monday. IR£4.75. Viking feast nightly IR£35. Craft shop. Bus Nos 51, 51A, 51B, 79, 90 from Aston Quay.*

Temple Bar area

■ **Sleeping**	7 River House & Danger Doyle's	3 Auld Dubliner Pub
1 Aston	8 Temple Bar House	4 Auriga
2 Bloom's		5 Bad Ass Café
3 Clarence	● **Eating & drinking**	6 Bad Bob's Bar
4 Harding's	1 Abrakebabra	7 Bewleys
5 Kinlay House	2 Alamo	8 Botticelli
6 Oliver St John Gogerty		9 Central Percs

Dublin Castle and around

From Temple Bar, a suicide dash across Dame Street brings you to Dublin Castle.

Taking part in one of the guided tours of Dublin Castle, the only way to get a **Dublin Castle** look inside, it is difficult to surmise from the hand-tufted carpets and 18th century plasterwork that this was once Dublin's biggest stronghold, built in 1204 to defend the city against the native Irish. Built into the city walls and protected on two sides by the Liffey and the now defunct Poddle, the castle had a central circular keep surrounded by a curtain wall with massive towers and a portcullis barring the entrance in Castle Street. It must have looked the part too, because apart from a Fitzgerald attack in 1534 and an aborted attempt at seizing it in 1641, the castle saw very little action. The most exciting thing to take place here must have been the night during the Black and Tan war, at its height between 1920 and 1921, when Michael Collins broke into the records office to find out what information the British had on him. In 1922 the castle was officially handed over to him as Commander in Chief of the Irish Army.

What Collins took charge of was a very different building to the one King John commissioned. The original 13th century castle had given way to more domestic functions as the stone walls and towers were gradually replaced by Viceregal living quarters. In 1684, a fire necessitated the complete reconstruction of the building, and in the Georgian building spree of the 18th century the modern building came into being.

The tour covers the still-used state apartments. Notable is the inlaid table given to Queen Victoria by a prison inmate who built it out of matchsticks or something, only to have her royal majesty leave it here because some of the inlaid designs were a bit saucy for her tastes. In St Patrick's Hall the ceiling is worth getting a crick in your neck to admire. The paintings are by Vincent Waldré and one depicts an allegory of George III receiving the homage of the Irish kings. In it, Irish noblewomen are depicted wearing breast-baring garments, which hasn't gone down well with generations of Catholic matrons visiting their heritage.

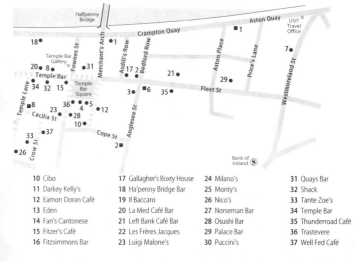

10 Cibo	17 Gallagher's Boxty House	24 Milano's	31 Quays Bar
11 Darkey Kelly's	18 Ha'penny Bridge Bar	25 Monty's	32 Shack
12 Eamon Doran Café	19 Il Baccaro	26 Nico's	33 Tante Zoe's
13 Eden	20 La Med Café Bar	27 Norseman Bar	34 Temple Bar
14 Fan's Cantonese	21 Left Bank Café Bar	28 Osushi Bar	35 Thunderroad Café
15 Fitzer's Café	22 Les Frères Jacques	29 Palace Bar	36 Trastevere
16 Fitzsimmons Bar	23 Luigi Malone's	30 Puccini's	37 Well Fed Café

Never in the real line of fire, the castle has, however, been home to some well-known enemies of the state in its time, from Donal McMurrough, 13th century king of Leinster, to James Connolly, who was held here (in one of the first rooms you pass through during the tour) in 1916 prior to being taken to Kimainham for execution. Ironically, the same building was used to incarcerate many of the antitreaty side during the civil war.

The tour gets more interesting as it passes out of the state rooms and into the upper yard, where you can see the statue of Justice over the gateway, unblindfolded and with her back to the city she should have been defending. Until she was mended in the 1980s, her scales of justice regularly tipped when it rained and they filled with water. A fitting comment on British justice in Ireland.

From here you visit the undercroft, excavated when the modern conference centre was being built. Here you can see the remains of Viking fortifications, and part of the old medieval city wall and the moat. You are free to visit the Chapel Royal and admire the designs of Francis Johnston, he of Armagh, GPO and St George's Church (now the Temple Theatre) fame.

Chester Beatty Library By the time you read this you should also be able to visit the Chester Beatty Library at the castle. It is a collection of ancient manuscripts, including 270 copies of the Koran as well as ancient copies of the Bible, Japanese manuscripts and copies of Tibetan tankas. ■ *Dame Street, Dublin 2, T6777129, F6797831. Monday-Friday 1000-1700, Saturday, Sunday and bank holidays 1400-1700. IR2.50. Guided tours only, lasting approximately 40 minutes. Last admission one hour before closing. Coffee shop and restaurant. Bus Nos 50, 54A, 56, 77 from Eden Quay.*

City Hall Turning left out of the main gates of the castle you come to City Hall, built by Thomas Cooley in 1769-79. He won the commission in a public competition, came to Ireland to oversee the building and stayed for the rest of his life, building the precursor to the Four Courts, and several public buildings in Armagh. The building was originally designed to be a Royal Exchange, with a two-storey domed hall where business was carried out. It is now open to the public and contains lots of Royal charters and other knick-knacks.

The Christ Church Cathedral

Travelling west along Lord Edward Street through busy city traffic, crocodiles of tour groups and largely 19th-century architecture, you come to Christ Church Cathedral. The church is a gratifying mixture of Victorian fantasy Gothic, Norman doorways, Romanesque arches and wonderful fake medieval floor tiles, all perfumed by that Church of Ireland polish and damp hymnbook smell that never seems to find its way into Catholic churches; well worth the IR£1 you are expected to donate at the door. Also at the door are leaflets which give a useful guided tour of the building.

Christ Church Cathedral

First built in wood in 1038 – according to legend by Sitric Silkbeard, king of the Viking settlers, whose city lay between the church site and the river – it has been rebuilt several times, notably between 1172 and 1240 by Archbishop (later Saint) Laurence O'Toole and Richard (Strongbow) Fitz Gilbert, the Norman conqueror of Ireland. The south nave's wall and roof collapsed in 1562 since the foundations were, and still are, built on peat bog, but this was quickly restored. The Victorians did a Gothic hatchet job on the place, knocking down the 14th century 'Long Choir' and Chapel of St Mary and stone cladding the place. The man who put up the cash for the restoration, distiller Henry Roe, was bankrupted by the project and the architect, George Edmund Street, died before his Gothic extravaganza was completed. The flying bridge and buttresses are pure Victorian fantasy and the rood screen has met continuous opposition since it was installed, with its depiction of Christ as a lamb with a flag in its mouth. But credit where it's due: the building was in a state of collapse in 1871 when work began, with the crypt in use as a series of taverns and the nave a market place.

Inside the church there is much to see. Walking anticlockwise around the building you come to the tomb of Strongbow, the Norman conqueror of Ireland and the man who contributed so much to building the cathedral. This is actually a 16th century replica of the tomb, which perished in the collapse of 1562; since the tomb had become the business centre of the ancient city it had to be replaced. It is possible that the small figure beside the tomb is part of the original.

The south transept is one of the few remaining parts of the 13th century building and contains the 18th century tomb of the 19th Earl of Kildare. Opening off the south transept is the chapel of Saint Laurence O'Toole, co-builder of the cathedral. In the southeast corner of the church is the peace chapel of Saint Laud, a 5th century French bishop. In here is a reliquary said to contain the heart of Archbishop O'Toole. On the floor are medieval tiles, rediscovered

Dublin

Christ Church Cathedral

after John Redmill, DipArch, RBA

N

0 yards   10

0 metres   10

site of Long Choir

1 Entrance
2 Musicians' corner
3 Baptistry
4 Tomb of Strongbow
5 Civic pew
6 Brass mediaeval lectern
7 Sedilia
8 Screen showing cross of Cong, lamb & flag
9 South transept
10 Peace chapel of St Laud
11 Lady chapel
12 Chapel of St Edmund
13 Chapter House
14 Mediaeval stone carvings
15 Cathedral shop
16 Quire
17 Entrance to crypt
18 Ruins of 13th century chapter house

during the Victorian renovations and copied throughout the building. There are 63 different patterns. If you are here at midday you might like to join in the prayers for world peace that take place here daily.

In the centre of the church is the choir, where the archbishop's throne rests alongside Victorian stalls where the choir and canons sit during services. From here you can see that the north wall of the nave is 50 centimetres out of kilter.

The crypt is a long underground chamber, untouched by the Victorian renovations and supported by rough stone pillars, which bear the entire weight of the building. It is the only crypt in Britain or Ireland that runs the length of the building, and contains a collection of all the old bits and pieces left over after renovations or shifted here from other parts of the city, including statues of Charles I and II. Look out for the 17th century stocks and the mummified cat and mouse discovered in the old organ pipes when the organ was replaced recently.

Outside are the remains of the 13th-century chapter house, and set into the wall of the church, a 12th-century Romanesque doorway. ■ *Christ Church Place, Dublin 8, T6778099, F6798991. Daily 1000-1700 except Christmas Day. IR£1 Donation. Bus Nos 78a from Aston Quay, 50 from Eden Quay.*

Dublinia The flying Gothic bridge over Winetavern Street links the cathedral with the 19th century synod hall, now Dublinia, an audio-visual attempt to recreate the sights and sounds of medieval Dublin, including finds from various excavations in the city and life-size recreations of local scenes: a merchant's kitchen, a cobbler's shop and the quayside, which once was a centre for medieval wine bars and keg makers, the bars even finding their way into the church itself. You can see some interesting views of the city from the top of St Michael's tower, part of the 13th century church that once stood here, incorporated into the synod hall by its architect, George Street. ■ *St Michael's Hill, Christ Church, Dublin 8, T6794611, F6797116. 1st April to 30th September 1000-1700 daily; 1st October to 31st March, Monday-Saturday 1100-1600, Sundays and Bank Holidays 1000-1600. Closed 24th-26th December. IR£3.95. Bus No 50 from Eden Quay, 78A from Aston Quay.*

The Liberties The name 'Liberties' refers back to medieval Ireland, when the areas outside Dublin's city walls were ruled by local earls and the citizens paid no taxes to the Norman rulers. The areas south and west of Dublin made up a series of very small liberties, each one ruled by a local chieftain and inhabited by Gaelic-speaking peasant farmers. For some reason the name has stuck to this area of Dublin south of the High Street to the Coombe, with St Patrick's Cathedral at its eastern border, although in the 13th century it was possible to travel along the coast from Wexford to Antrim passing only through liberties.

In recent times the area looks a little seedy, with the beautiful old Iveagh Trust housing estate growing more run down by the minute, but it's only a matter of time before someone realizes it is better to renovate the houses than lose them altogether, and the upwardly mobile move in.

After the French persecution of the Protestant Huguenots began in the late 17th century serious numbers of French refugees came to the area to join a tiny community that had existed there since the early part of the century. They set up silk- and linen-weaving industries and the area became known for its cloth markets. Like the Huguenot communities in other parts of the island, the area became culturally distinct, and there are still families who can trace their descent from French Protestant families living in the area.

If Christ Church became the Norman cathedral, St Patrick's was the people's cathedral. It is reputed to be on the site of a church set up by St Patrick himself. It is one of the earliest Christian sites in the city and a pre-Norman church probably stood here in the fifth century, making it considerably older than Christ Church. St Patrick is said to have baptized converts from a well in the church grounds. The site is, like Christ Church, on marshy ground with the River Poddle flowing beneath it. A stone church was built here in 1192 only 20 years after the other major expenditure on Christ Church and less than a mile away. The two cathedrals began to vie for glory, and after a dispute between the dean of Christ Church and Henry, the dean of St Patrick's, Henry claimed cathedral status for St Patrick's, and began a major rebuilding programme in the early 13th century. The pope stuck his oar in around 1300 and declared that Christ Church was the supreme church, but this didn't end the unholy rivalry between the two cathedrals. In 1320 a papal university was set up at St Patrick's to improve its status, but foundered 170 years later. The 14th century wasn't good for St Patrick's: the spire was blown down in a storm in 1316 and two fires followed. The damage spurred on extensive rebuilding programmes, the last of which involved the rebuilding of the west tower, leaving it slightly out of alignment with the rest of the building, which you can clearly see from Patrick Street.

The Reformation saw St Patrick's demoted back to church status, while Christ Church flourished as the state representation of religious power. The parallel between the two rival churches continued though: cathedral status was grabbed back in 1554 but in the same year the ceiling collapsed, to be followed less than 10 years later by a similar collapse in Christ Church. Both churches went into a decline after Cromwell's depredations in the city in the 17th century and by the 19th century both were crumbling, St Patrick's in particular reduced to a series of small churches made from the individual chapels. Strangely, the parallel continues: both churches were taken on by very wealthy merchants dealing in alcohol, Christ Church by the distiller, Roe, and St Patrick's by one of the Guinness family. Both did quite remarkable hatchet jobs, Guinness with the aid of Sir Thomas Drew, the architect.

Despite its ugly exterior, St Patrick's, the national cathedral of the Church of Ireland, is the more interesting of the two cathedrals, with much more of the medieval interior intact. It was of course the workplace (and burial ground) of the 18th-century writer, satirist and dean, Jonathan Swift for many years, and

St Patrick's Cathedral
A few statistics: the largest church in Ireland; the largest ringing peal of bells in Ireland; Ireland's first university; no crypt owing to the marshy ground.

The German writer, Heinrich Böll was not impressed by his visit to St Patrick's: 'At Swift's tomb my heart had caught a chill, so clean was St Patrick's Cathedral, so empty of people and so full of patriotic marble figures; so deep under the cold stone did the desperate Dean seem to lie, Stella beside him.'

St Patrick's Cathedral

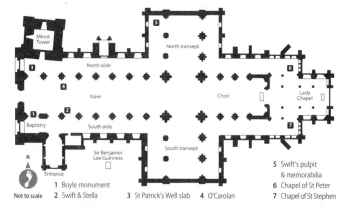

North transept
Minot Tower
North aisle
Nave
Choir
Lady Chapel
Baptistry
South aisle
South transept
Sir Benjamin Lee Guinness
N
Entrance
Not to scale

1 Boyle monument
2 Swift & Stella
3 St Patrick's Well slab
4 O'Carolan
5 Swift's pulpit & memorabilia
6 Chapel of St Peter
7 Chapel of St Stephen

memorabilia of his deanship is plentiful, including a death mask: not the cheeriest of mementoes. The steps down to the entrance indicate how far the street level has risen since medieval times. Inside the baptistry by the main entrance is an enormous wooden monument to the Boyle family, the 17th-century Earls of Cork, which once decorated the east end of the choir, where the entire congregation had to look at it, and seemingly to bow before it, every time they prayed. This wasn't popular with the clerics of the time and it was removed to this more humble spot. The man who organized the removal, Strafford (the British viceroy of Dublin), lived, or rather died, to regret it since he made an enemy of Boyle, who was a leading figure in Strafford's later impeachment and execution. The monument is an exercise in pomposity, with several generations of the entire family depicted around the centrepiece of Richard Boyle and his wife. The carved small boy is said to be his son, Robert Boyle who was to become the great physicist, giving us all the Charles/Boyle gas law to learn in school.

Leaving aside 17th-century aggrandizement, an anticlockwise stroll around the church brings you into the south aisle where Dean Swift and his friend Esther Johnson are interred. In the south transept is an old door with a hole cut in it, which was said to have been made in 1492 when a fight broke out in the cathedral between the Earls of Ormond and Kildare and their cronies over who should take precedence at a service. Ormond, losing the argument, ran into the south transept, then walled off as the chapter house. The deadlock was broken when the two men agreed to shake hands and the hole was cut in the door, giving rise to the expression 'chancing one's arm'. True or not, it makes a good story.

The Lady Chapel, at the east end of the church, is the original 13th-century building and for 150 years from 1666 it was given to the Huguenot community of the Liberties. Moving on round to the north aisle, you'll find the banners of the Royal Irish regiments followed by assorted memorials to dead rich people and generals and also, unusually, one to Turlogh O'Carolan, a poor and powerless composer and harpist. In the northwest corner is a very old cross-engraved stone said to date back to the time of St Patrick, which once marked the site of the well at which he baptized converts.

Outside the church the 19th-century changes are more obvious with the obligatory Gothic flying buttresses, the porch through which you entered and a corresponding porch on the north side as well as the main doors and windows at the west end of the church. ■ *St Patrick's Close, Dublin 8, T4754817, F4546374. Monday-Friday 0900-1800, Saturday 0900-1700 (1600 November to March) Sunday 1000-1630. IR£2.00. Choir sings at Matins (0940) and Evensong (1735) daily except Saturday and Wednesday. Christians of all denominations are welcome at all services. Bus Nos 50, 54A, 56A from Eden Quay.*

Around the cathedral Next to St Patrick's Cathedral is **St Patrick's Park**, laid out at the end of the 19th century so as to give a better aspect to the cathedral. It was part of a massive redevelopment scheme funded by the Guinness family, who demolished vast tracts of slum dwellings and erected in their place the Iveagh Baths and model flats, now either awaiting demolition in their turn or gone already, they are well worth a peek for their art nouveau design and terracotta panels. Get there quick before they are demolished. The play centre they built to house the slum children is now a technical school. This was one of the few redevelopment schemes of its time that actually rehoused the people whose homes were cleared. The park has assorted bits of memorabilia as well as the actual holy well reputedly used by Paddy himself.

Outside the church a quick stroll down St Patrick's Close brings you to **Marsh's Library**, built in 1701 by William Robinson, the architect of the Royal

Hospital at Kilmainham (see page 115), for Archbishop Narcissus Marsh. It was a public library and the interior is little changed from when it was first built. Between the ancient oak shelves are cages where readers were locked in to prevent them from walking away with precious books. The collection includes about 25,000 books from the 16th to 18th centuries. Swift used the place regularly and a look in the visitor's book will show that James Joyce also used it. The library holds exhibitions of ancient works and is still open to scholars. ■ *St Patrick's Close, Dublin 8, T4543511. All year, closed Wednesdays and Sundays. Monday-Tuesday, Thursday-Friday 1000-1245, 1400-1700, Saturday 1030-1245. IR£1 donation. Bus Nos 50, 54A, 56A from Eden Quay.*

Kilmainham

A quick bus ride west brings you past the massively depressing Guinness brewery to Kilmainham, where there are two places well worth the trip and a brief and pleasant walk apart.

The **Royal Hospital** at Kilmainham, now the Irish Museum of Modern Art, built between 1680 and 1684, designed by William Robinson, the Surveyor General of Ireland, and based on Les Invalides in Paris, is the first great building in the Classical style to have been erected in Ireland. It was designed as a retirement home for old soldiers, in a rectangle with an interior courtyard and a loggia with open arches on three sides. The Great Hall in the centre of the north side is now used for concerts and has assorted royalty displayed on its panelled walls. To the right is the chapel with carved wooden pediments over the doors, thought to have been executed by James Tarbery, a Huguenot settler from the city. The building became a police barracks in 1922, and went into a serious decline after that. Fortunately it was the subject of one of Dublin's first restoration programmes in 1981, and since 1991 it has been the Museum of Modern Art. The building itself, rather like Collins Barracks, tends to overpower its function as a museum and one tends to feel it is lacking an exhibition on its history, and possibly a pensioner's bedroom, but that may yet come. It is possible to pre-book heritage tours, and there are regular lectures on the history of the building. The art collection is interesting enough, dedicated to the avant garde with lots of much more engaging temporary exhibitions. The bookshop in the gallery has an excellent collection of books on art and architecture. ■ *Military Road, Kilmainham, Dublin 8, T6129900, F6129999, info@modernart.ie Museum: Tuesday-Saturday 1000-1730, Sunday, bank holidays 1200-1530, closed Mondays. Chapel: Sundays 1400-1500. Free. Guided tours Wednesday, Friday 1430, Sunday 1215. Heritage tours can be arranged two days in advance. Coffee shop and bookshop open museum hours. Bus Nos 79 from Aston Quay, 90 from Heuston, Tara Street, and Connolly stations.*

Irish Museum of Modern Art

Leaving the hospital by the west exit you pass by the formal gardens, which are being restored to their 17th century design on the north side of the building and follow a pleasant footpath across some open, ancient land to the 19th century Gothic Richmond Tower gateway, removed to this spot from the Liffey Quays in 1844. As you approach the gate you pass by **Bully's Acre**, a graveyard dating back at least a thousand years. The son and grandson of Brian Boru, the Gaelic high king who defeated the Danes, are said to have been buried here after the battle of Clontarf in 1014. Through the gates and across the South Circular Road, passing the *Patriot's Inn*, which has been the site of a tavern since 1793, you come to Inchicore Road and the next, rather sombre, sight.

Dublin

Kilmainham Gaol

Give yourself an hour for the tour and at least half an hour more for the museum.

Built in 1792, 17 years after the American revolution, three years after the French Revolution and open just in time to take in the survivors of the 30,000 rebels who died in the Uprising of 1798, this building saw hundreds of men suffer and die for their belief in independence in 1798, 1803, 1848, 1867, 1916 and 1922. Most of the big names in Republican history spent time in here and some of them died here. The last man to walk out was, ironically enough, De Valera, at the end of the civil war in 1923, whereupon the gaol was abandoned as it stood. Forty years later a voluntary group of history buffs decided to restore it, the work was completed by the state and Kilmainham was opened to the public. There is a museum of early 20th-century political history as well as prison memorabilia where you can wait for a guided tour. Exhibits in the museum include a painting by Constance Markievicz called the Good Shepherd, depicting herself as the metaphorical shepherd, the calling card of William Marwood, one of the prison's hangmen, and an original Land League banner from the first meeting in Mayo of 1879. Visiting the rest of the prison is by tour only. It takes you around the dungeons, tiny cells, the chapel where Joseph Plunkett was married three hours before his execution and the grim yard where Connolly, Plunkett and 15 other leaders of the 1916 Uprising were executed. ■ *Inchicore Road, Dublin 8, T4535984, F4532037. April to September, daily 0930-1645; October to March, Monday-Friday 0930-1600, Sunday 1000-1645, closed Saturday. IR£3. Access is by tour only. Last tour is one hour before closing. Bus Nos 51, 79 from Aston Quay, 51A from Lower Abbey Street.*

Other South Dublin sights

Whitefriar Street Carmelite Church

Whitefriar Street Carmelite Church is a Victorian building standing on the site of a much earlier priory. It is famous because it contains the remains of St Valentine, which for some unaccountable reason were given to Father Spratt by Pope Gregory XVI. Up until then the remains had been resting peacefully in the cemetery of St Hippolytus in Rome. Strangely, in 1999 the Franciscan friars of the Gorbals in Glasgow announced that they had had Valentine's bones in a shoebox on top of a wardrobe in St Francis' Church since 1868 and had finally decided to put them on show in the new pastoral centre at Blessed John Duns Scotus in that city. Let us hope the dispute doesn't turn nasty.

There is also a well dedicated to St Albert, which is believed to have curative properties. The life-size Madonna is of oak and is thought to pre-date the Reformation, one of the few pieces of statuary in Dublin that does. ■ *56 Aungier Street. Monday, Wednesday, Thursday, Friday 0800-1830, Saturday 0800-1900, Tuesday 0800-2130, bank holidays 0930-1300. Bus Nos 16, 16A, 19, 19A, 22, 22A from O'Connell Street.*

The Guinness Hop Store

The Guinness Hop Store offers a free pint of the black stuff with every entrance ticket. This takes you around old vats and pipework and a display of advertising posters. Not much about the Guinnesses: real patriarchal Victorian liberals who deserve more for what they did for the people of Dublin. ■ *St James's Gate, Dublin 8, T4536700. IR£4. April 1 to September 30, Monday-Saturday 0930, last admission 1700. Sunday, Bank Holidays 1030, last admission 1630. October 1 to March 31, Monday-Saturday 0930, last admission 1600. Sunday, Bank Holidays 1200, last admission 1600.*

The Irish Jewish Museum is in the Portobello area of Dublin, north of the canal. Features documents, the original synagogue and a Jewish kitchen from around 1900. ■ *3-4 Walworth Road, Portobello, Dublin 8, T4531797. May to September, Sunday, Tuesday Thursday 1100-1530; October to April Sunday only or by appointment, 1030-1500. Donation. Bus 16, 16A, 19, 19A, 22, 22A.*

The Irish Jewish Museum

In Haddington Road, south of the canal, is the National Print Museum, in the chapel of the old military garrison. It has a genuinely interesting and some-times quite beautiful display of printing technology, from hand-assembly print blocks to early computers, a display about book-binding as well as audio-visual displays on the history of the print, all set in very historic surroundings. The barracks were the first to be handed over to the Irish in 1922 and this was also the place where Erskine Childers was executed by the Free State govern-ment. ■ *Garrison Chapel, Beggars Bush, Dublin 4, T6603770, F6673545, npmuseum@iol.ie May to September, Monday-Friday 1000-1230, 1430-1700, Saturday, Sunday, bank holidays 1200-1700; October to April, Tuesday, Thurs-day, Saturday, Sunday 1400-1700. IR£2.50. Coffee shop. Guided tours and audio visual show. DART Lansdown Road, Bus Nos 5, 7, 7A, 8, 45.*

National Print Museum

This museum is in Rathmines, with a display of dolls, prams and other toys some dating back to the 17th century. It is a private collection and only open on Sunday afternoons. ■ *20 Palmerston Park, Rathmines, T4973223, Sunday 1400-1730. IR£1. Bus No 13.*

Museum of Childhood

Dedicated to the memory of the man who led the Easter Rising, this Georgian mansion was once the bilingual school that he ran along quite radical lines. Displays in the building show his teaching methods and beliefs. Pearse joined the relatively apolitical Gaelic League as a teenager because of his cultural interests rather than any political convictions, but rapidly became convinced that the British would never grant Home Rule while there was Unionist oppo-sition. He gradually came to believe that slavery, as he saw it, was worse than death and that a blood sacrifice was needed to move the fight for independence on. His most famous words are: 'Ireland unfree shall never be at peace'. He certainly got that right. Even if you don't like his politics, the school is worth a visit for the gardens it is set in. ■ *St Enda's, Grange Road, Rathfarnham, Dublin 16, T4934208. November to January, daily 1000-1600; February to April, daily 1000-1700; May-August, daily 1000-1730; September to October, daily 1000-1700. Closed daily 1300-1400. Free. Guided tours on request. Last admission 45 minutes before closing. Audio-visual show, self-guided nature trail, Nature Study centre, tearoom open in summer months and at weekends in February to April and October. Bus No 16 from city centre.*

The Pearse Museum

A semi-fortified house, this is believed to have been built in 1583 by Arch-bishop Adam Loftus, a Yorkshireman. The castle is undergoing renovations and visitors are shown around the works as they progress, getting a different glimpse of structures and alterations at each visit. Some interiors are 18th century and attributed to Sir William Chambers and James Stuart. ■ *Rathfarnham Road, Rathfarnham, Dublin 16. T499462. April 1000-1700 Sundays only; Easter weekend Saturday-Monday 1000-1700; May, daily 1000-1700; June-September, daily 1000-1800; October, daily 1000-1700; T6613111 for winter opening hours. IR£1.50. Last admission one hour before closing. Access by guided tour only. Tearoom.*

Rathfarnham Castle

Dublin

Dublin

Joyce's Dublin

Generally agreed to be the greatest 20th-century novel in the English language, *Ulysses* is set in a single day, 16th June 1904, the day when Joyce first walked out with Nora Barnacle, the woman with whom he shared the rest of his life. The novel traces the wanderings around the city of Leopold Bloom, mirroring the wanderings of Odysseus on his journey home to Ithaca. Stephen Dedalus, Bloom's Telemachus or figurative son, joins him for part of the day. Joyce took the job of getting Bloom's journey technically correct very seriously, consulting railway and bus timetables, getting relatives and friends to time journeys, check entrance-ways and so on. While many of the shops and pubs he lists have disappeared, several still stand and you can join in the annual fun on Bloomsday and spend near enough 24 hours wandering in Bloom's footsteps around the city. This is a more potted version of his day, taking in some Joyce memorabilia.

Joyce's Dublin

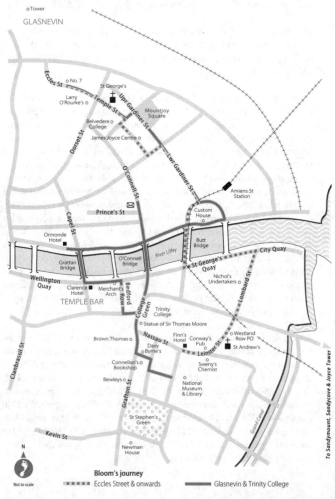

No 7 Eccles Street no longer exists. It was knocked down in 1980 to make way for an extension to the Mater Hospital, but a plaque marks the spot where Bloom would have lived if he had existed. It is possible to cross the road and examine the door flap on No 78, which is similar to the one Joyce describes closing behind Bloom. Records show that on 16th June No 7 stood unoccupied, but Joyce knew the house since his friend JF Byrne, whom he immortalized as Cranly in *A Portrait of the Artist as a Young Man*, lived there.

Eccles Street & onwards

Bloom goes off right into Dorset Street to an imaginary butcher's shop, pausing at Larry O'Rourke's bar (now the *Snug*) to smell the odour of beer. After his breakfast he wanders into town down Hardwicke Place, past St George's Church (now the Temple Theatre). At the junction of Denmark Place you could detour from Bloom's journey and visit first of all Belvedere College, where Joyce attended school between 1893 and 1898. Joyce's father became bankrupt after putting most of his money into a distillery in Chapelizod, which went bust, and Joyce's time in north Dublin was one of genteel poverty and midnight flits to avoid the debt collectors. He and his brother attended Belvedere, a fee-paying school, because the fees were waived in favour of two such promising young men. Belvedere had the same problems as the Catholic University in St Stephen's Green – here the Jesuits thought the plaster Venus on one of the ceilings improper for the eyes of young men and had her removed.

Directly opposite Belvedere House is North Great George Street, a row of once very dilapidated Georgian terraces now a bijou area once again. At No 35 is the James Joyce Centre, a beautiful building in its own right but home to lots of Joyce memorabilia, including the door to 7 Eccles Street, lots of family portraits from the days before the family were impoverished, first editions and foreign-language editions of his works, and a library whose facilities are open to visitors as well as an audio-visual presentation about Joyce's Dublin. One of the living people whom Joyce put into his novel, Mr Dennis J Maginni, a dancing instructor, actually lived here. ■ *35 North Great George Street, T8788547, F8788488, joycecen@iol.ie All year, Monday-Saturday 0930-1700, Sundays 1230-1700. Closed 24th, 25th December. IR£2.75. Coffee shop, book and gift shop. Bus Nos 3, 10, 11, 11A, 13, 16, 16A, 19, 19A, 22, 22A to top of O'Connell Street then signposted from Parnell Monument.*

James Joyce Centre

Back on the *Ulysses* trail, Bloom heads into town along Gardiner Street, now very different with modern apartment blocks where once Georgian terraces stood. He passes under the railway bridge at the bottom of the street and crosses Butt Bridge, walks along St George's and City Quay and along Lombard Street and Westland Row. In Lombard Street Bloom notices Nichol's Undertakers, which is still there, its appearance barely changed since 1904. In Westland Row he stops at the Post Office, now part of the DART station, and collects a secret letter, which he takes round to the back of the railway arch in Cumberland Street – still much the same as Bloom would have seen it. His next port of call is **St Andrew's Church** in Westland Row, All Hallows in the novel, and watches the sleepy congregation. This scene parallels the lotus-eaters story in the Odyssey, the link being the axiom that religion is the opium of the people.

To Leinster Street

He travels along Westland Row past Conway's pub, still doing the same trade but now called **Fitzsimon's**, and calls in at **Sweny's chemist**, still there doing business, with the same shop front and sign 96 years later! Bloom buys lemon soap in the chemist, and it is still sold there: as Bloom says, 'Chemists rarely move'. The next section of Bloom's journey takes him past the back gate of Trinity, shifted about 10 yards along the road in 1997 but still the same

Dublin

stones, past *Finn's Hotel*, where Nora Barnacle worked, and to some public baths in Leinster Street, now gone.

Glasnevin &
Trinity College

After the visit to the baths Bloom goes to Sandymount to join a funeral procession along O'Connell Street to Glasnevin cemetery, and from there back to O'Connell Street, where the next place mentioned is the GPO, with Nelson's Pillar in front of it. Bloom goes to his place of work in Prince's Street, where the side exit to **Eason's** is now. From there he crosses O'Connell Bridge, having passed Lemon's sweetshop, now a sportswear shop. This section of Bloom's route is marked out by a series of brass plaques set in the pavement.

On O'Connell Bridge he pauses to watch a Guinness brewery barge go past, buys a bun from a stallholder and throws it to the seabirds over the river. In College Green Bloom passes the statue to Thomas Moore, the poet, famous for *The Meeting of the Waters,* and is amused that this man should stand in effigy above a public toilet. For Bloom, the Protestant University of Trinity College has a 'surly front'. He passes the Provost's House, still keeping the same function, and sees the city marshall, brother to Parnell, and Æ (George Russell, the poet). He passes down Grafton Street, then as now 'gay with housed awnings'. **Brown Thomas**, the department store, still in Grafton street but now on the other side, is noted. Bloom turns into Duke Street and famously pops into **Davy Byrne's**, 'the moral pub', for a Gorgonzola sandwich and a glass of burgundy. *Davy Byrne's* is still in business and serves the Gorgonzola every 16th June.

National Library
to Temple Bar

After this Bloom heads towards the National Library, turning right into Dawson Street, passing Long John's (*Graham O'Sullivan's* delicatessen nowadays) and Connellan's bookshop Tea Time Express now gone at No 13 Dawson Street. On the way Bloom ducks into the National Museum to avoid his wife's lover, Blazes Boylan, and lingers in the vestibule checking to 'certify the presence or absence of posterior rectal orifices in the case of the Hellenic female divinities'. From here he goes on to the library – the two buildings were once linked by an open courtyard, rather than fenced apart as they are now. In the library he passes between Buck Mulligan and Stephen Dedalus, who are arguing.

Bloom leaves the library and heads to Temple Bar for the second-hand bookshops – he wants to buy his wife a paperback novel to read. He walks along Bedford Row, passes through Merchant's Arch and on to Wellington Quay. By this time it is about half past three. From here he walks along Wellington Quay, past the **Clarence** (now owned by U2) to the **Ormond Hotel** (still in business and making the most of its role in the novel). His day continues until well into the early hours of the next morning, when he and Stephen Dedalus return past the Custom House, back up Gardiner Street to Eccles Street.

James Joyce
Museum

At Sandycove, set in the Martello Tower, where Joyce lived for a time, is the James Joyce Museum. The collection includes letters and first editions of his books as well as his waistcoat, guitar and piano, photographs and a reconstruction of the room he shared with Oliver St John Gogarty (Buck Mulligan) and an Anglo-Irishman called Trench (Haines in *Ulysses*). He fled the tower after Trench had a nightmare that he was killing a black panther and fired his gun at it. Gogarty took the gun and fired the rest of the bullets over Joyce's head at some pans. Trench, Gogarty and the nightmare all appear in *Ulysses*. In the novel, Stephen carries the burden of paying the rent while Mulligan sponges off him but in reality Joyce was the sponger – Gogarty paid the rent. Joyce afficionados might also like to visit Joyce's home in Bray (page 186, Wicklow), Nora Barnacle's house in Galway (page 420), the Victoria Hotel in Cork City (page 283) and the newsagent's in Mullingar (page 175) where Bloom's daughter fictionally worked. ■ *The Joyce Tower, Sandycove, County Dublin, T2809265, F2809265. April to October, Monday-Saturday 1000-1700, Sunday and public holidays 1400-1800. Closed 1300-1400. IR£2.50. Small bookshop. Sandycove DART station, Bus No 8 from Burgh Quay.*

Essentials

Sleeping

Dublin's accommodation is growing like Topsy, from 5-star luxury hotels to comfortable if crowded hostels, and yet as fast as new places go up the rooms fill up; at weekends it is often difficult to get rooms even in winter. Once you have planned a holiday that includes Dublin, book your accommodation straight away. If arriving in town without accommodation, your best bet is to go to one of the tourist offices and ask them to book a room, which they will do for a fee of IR£1. There are offices at the airport, at the ferry terminal at Dun Laoghaire and in St Andrew's Church in Suffolk St.

Generally the most expensive and upmarket hotels are south of the river, while the north is dominated by hostels and B&Bs. There are lots of quite small friendly hotels and not so many of the big chains, although this is changing rapidly. A good idea at weekends, if peace and quiet is important, might be to go for one of the out-of-town hotels at Howth or Dun Laoghaire. At the more expensive hotels breakfast is extra, and the price of a single occupancy is very much the same as a double.

Hotels
■ *on maps*
Price codes:
see inside front cover

North Dublin LL *The Gresham*, O'Connell St, Dublin 1, T8746881, F8787175, ryan@indigo.ie Business centre, car parking, hotel shop, non-smoking rooms, 24-hour room service. Its 304 rooms are spacious and interesting, it claims to have the highest ratio of porters to rooms in Ireland, and the Toddy Bar has 63 different brands of whiskey. The *Gresham* first opened its doors to paying guests in 1817, charging 3 shillings (15p!) a night. Close to the GPO, it was destroyed by the shelling of the British in 1916 and withstood the Beatles in the 1960s. The closing scene of 'The Dead' in Joyce's *Ulysses* is set in one of the hotel rooms. **L** *Ashling*, Parkgate St, Dublin 8, T6772324, F6793783, info@ashlinghotel.ie Recently extended and modernized with 100 well-appointed rooms, triple rooms and suites, this hotel is close to Heuston Station and the Phoenix Park in the west of the city. Great views of the river and Guinness Brewery. A good deal for its price, which includes breakfast, is affordable for a single person and has special packages. Two pleasant, café-style restaurants. **L-LL** *Morrison Hotel*, 15, Ormond Quay, Dublin 1, T6684321. Part of the gentrification of north Dublin, this classy new hotel sits unobtrusively on the bank of the river. Modern, jazzy décor, themed in black and white, refreshingly un-Irish. **L** *Chief O'Neill's Hotel*, Smithfield Village, T8173838, F8173839, reservations@chiefoneills.com Toll free USA & Canada 1800 44Utell. New, modernist hotel, all frosted green glass and trendy lighting, and bedrooms that strive, successfully, to be different. Café/bar downstairs, in the centre of the newly renovated Smithfield village. Breakfast is extra. If you are fed up with anonymous, all-too-similar hotels, stay here. **AL** *Ormonde Hotel*, 7-11 Upper Ormond Quay, Dublin 7, T8721811, F8721909. Newly renovated hotel, which features in *Ulysses*, centrally located. Restaurant. **A** *Barry's Hotel*, 1-2 Great Denmark St, Dublin 1, T8746943, F8746508. Georgian building, close to O'Connell St, most rooms en suite. Restaurant. **A** *Hotel Isaacs*, Store St, Dublin 1, T8550067, F8365390. hotisaac@indigo.ie Relatively new, in a converted wine warehouse. Restaurant (*Il Vignardo*: Italian food). **A** *Jury's Custom House Inn*, Custom House Quay, Dublin 1, T6075000, F8290400, info@jurys.com freephone/toll-free reservations from UK T1800-8433311. Same basis as the Christ Church branch but bigger.

Dublin

South Dublin LL *Alexander Hotel*, Fenian St, Dublin 2, T6073700, F6615663, alexanderhotel@tinet.ie The modern Alexander Hotel, tucked away around the corner from the north side of Merrion Sq, has a contemporary style that delivers comfort and a touch of luxury. The *Davenport* and *Mont Clare* hotels, both in Merrion Sq, are sister hotels, and you can use all three hotels' bars and restaurants under one account. **LL** *Brooks*, Drury St, Dublin 2, T6704000, F6704455. Designer hotel with a real touch of class, located in the heart of Dublin. Everything about the place is stylish in the best sense of the word, from a restful library to an innovative basement restaurant. No car-park, but a multi-storey car-park is opposite the hotel and special rates are available. **LL** *Buswell's*, Molesworth St, Dublin 2, T6146500, F6762090. Non-smoking rooms. Carvery and fine dining restaurants. This small, 60-room hotel has a long history. Its Georgian buildings have been a hotel of sorts since it was built, first as Gallagher's and then since the 1920s as Buswell's. Close to the government buildings, this was the place where the Mace was kept until the Act of Union in 1801. It also boasts the first lift in Ireland, although the one you will be using now is not the original. Much of the original plasterwork is listed, and while the hotel has been extended it still retains all its originality and charm. Truman's restaurant has an excellent reputation. **LL** *The Clarence*, 6-8 Wellington Quay, Dublin 2, T6709000, F6707800, clarence@indigo.ie Restaurant. Elderly hotel taken over by U2 and given a new look in modern décor. Each room individually styled, not always successfully. Penthouse suite has glorious views and rooftop Jacuzzi and a price tag of IR£1,400 a night. David Bowie stayed there for several weeks. **LL** *The Conrad*, Earlsfort Terrace, Dublin 2, T6765555, F6765420, info@conrad-international.ie Brasserie restaurant and fine dining. Centrally located and multi-award-winning, this 191-room, 9-suite hotel has all that you would expect from this high-profile chain of hotels: from luxuriously appointed, spacious rooms to fluffy bathtowels and designer soaps. Decidedly

business-orientated, it has extensive business-centre facilities. **LL** *The Hibernian Hotel*, Eastmoreland Place, Ballsbridge, T6687666, F660265. Elegant Victorian building, 40 bedrooms individually decorated, fresh flowers, antiques and oil paintings, good service, restaurant, library, board room. **LL** *Merrion Hotel*, Upper Merrion St, T6030600, F6030700, info@merrionhotel.ie The ultimate in understated luxury in the middle of the city. Four converted Georgian houses, one of which was the birthplace of Wellington, plus a new block in the same style surround pretty formal gardens. Big comfortable rooms, two restaurants, pool and fitness centre plus a fairly astounding collection of artwork scattered around the beautiful Georgian interiors. **LL** *Radisson SAS St Helen's Hotel*, Stillorgan Rd, Co Dublin, T2186000, F2186010, Web www.radisson.com. Grand old Georgian mansion, beautifully converted into a modern luxury hotel, quite unlike the usual Radisson style. The house belonged to Viscount Hugh Gough (1779-1869) who served at Waterloo and crushed the Chinese during the Opium War, and later had his statue dismembered in Phoenix Park (see page 92), and is well out of town but on the 46A bus route. Two restaurants, large gardens, fitness room, billiard room, a superb drawing room in the grand old style and an airy bar. **LL** *The Shelbourne*, 27 St Stephen's Green, Dublin 2, T6766471, F6616006. 1- or 2-bedroom suites, presidential suite, over 160 individually decorated rooms, extensively refurbished, the more expensive rooms overlooking the Green. Babysitting, bars, beauty salon, shop. Very stylish hotel full of self-important people taking morning coffee and afternoon tea in the Lord Mayor's Lounge. Open as a hotel since 1864 and a Dublin landmark. **LL** *Stephen's Hall*, Earlsfort Centre, Lower Leeson St, Dublin 2, T6610585, F6610606, Californian-style bistro restaurant (*Morel's*, page 127). This all-suite hotel is certainly the best value for money at this end of the market with large spacious rooms, open fireplaces, workstations with computers, fully equipped kitchens, dining and lounge areas, and a shopping service. More orientated to long-stay business visitors, this is nevertheless centrally located and perfect for a holiday visit, especially for families. The penthouse suites have excellent rooftop balconies and views. Some non-smoking rooms. **LL** *The Towers*, Lansdowne Rd, Dublin 4, T6670033, F6605324, info@jurys.com (Freephone from UK T1800-8433311). 100 large bedrooms with walk-in wardrobes, work area, etc. Restaurants, indoor pool. Very classy place, adjacent to the main *Jury's Hotel*.

L *Aston Hotel*, 7-9 Aston Quay, Dublin 2, T6779300, F6779007, aston@indigo.ie Big, comfortable double and triple rooms in very central location. Great views over the river but a little noisy especially at weekends. Restaurant. **L** *Bloom's*, 6 Anglesea St, Dublin 2, T6715622, F6715997. Small hotel with 86 rooms all well designed, centrally located in Temple Bar. Nightclub doesn't bother guests, popular bar for lunches. Restaurant and café. **L** *Central Hotel*, Exchequer St, Dublin 2, T6797303, F6797303,

Dublin

restaurant. Centrally located in a quiet street, this Victorian Hotel is part of the *Best Western* chain. **L** *School House Hotel*, 2-8 Northumberland Rd, T6675014, F6675015. Beside the canal on the southern outskirts of the city centre, this prettily renovated old schoolhouse offers a high standard of accommodation, restaurant in a classroom, and a blackboard in the lobby with lines to remember to memorise. Small and friendly and close to town.

AL *Plaza Hotel*, Belgard Rd, Tallaght, T 4624200, F4624600. 6 miles west of the city this is a modern, spacious hotel with two good restaurants and cafe. Good value, especially if you prefer to stay out of town, breakfast not included. Look out for Marilyn Monroe's shoes in the Di Maggio sports bar and restaurant. The Playhouse Nightclub. **AL** *Holiday Inn*, 99-107 Pearse St, Dublin 2, T6703666, F6703636. 10-minute walk from the city, located at the working-class end of Pearse St. Nearly 100 rooms and the benefit of a gym and sauna. Car parking is IR£10 a day. The bar, the *Esther Keogh*, is popular with locals and has live music at weekends, ranging from jazz to karaoke. **AL** *Lansdowne Hotel*, 27 Pembroke Rd, Dublin 4, T6682522, F6682309. Small hotel with 40 bedrooms, a little way out of the centre in a quiet location. Beer garden, good bargain at this price range. Restaurant (*Druids*). **AL** *River House Hotel*, 23-24 Eustace St, Temple Bar, Dublin 2, T6707655, F6707650, 101473.1007@compuserve.com 28 small but adequately furnished, comfortable rooms in this small family-run hotel in the heart of Temple Bar. Double and triple rooms. Restaurant open till 2100.

A *Harding Hotel*, Copper Alley, Fishamble St, Christ Church, Dublin 2, T6796500, F6796504, harding@usit.ie Spacious double and triple rooms, fully equipped and comfortable, in a quiet area of the city centre beside Temple Bar. A small hotel, only 53 rooms, which has been built with a good eye for design, incorporating the medieval Copper Alley into the building. Bar food and restaurant. **A** *Jury's Christ Church Inn*, Christ Church Place, Dublin 8, T4540000, F4540012, info@jurys.com toll-free reservations from UK T1800-8433311. Based on a single room rate for 3 adults, or 2 adults and 2 children, this is excellent value with fair-sized, comfortable rooms, centrally located, bath and shower en suite, nice pub with traditional music, secure car-park.

Guesthouses & B&Bs These vary from small five-room B&B places to near hotels with suites. All guesthouses have en-suite rooms, direct dial phones and TV, as well as secure parking. They generally tend to not have restaurants but offer dinner to guests. B&Bs are always in private homes with a few rooms for guests, either with or without en suite bathrooms. Meals are taken with the family, and breakfast always extends to the full Irish. Most B&Bs are a good way out of the city and involve bus or DART rides into town.

North Dublin **A** *Clifden Guesthouse*, 32 Gardiner Place, Dublin 1, T8746364, F8746122. Single, twin and family rooms. Secure car-park. **A** *The Townhouse*, 47-8 Lower Gardiner St, Dublin 1, T8788808, F8788787, gtrotter@indigo.ie Doubles and triple rooms at very competitive prices, some with kitchenette, all en suite and with tea- and coffee-making facilities, TV. Rates include continental breakfast. **B** *Anchor Guest House*, 49 Lower Gardiner St, Dublin 1, T8786913, F8788038, gtcoyne@gpo.iol.ie **B** *Carmel House*, 16 Upper Gardiner St, Dublin 1, T8741639, F8786803. Very small guesthouse, secure parking. **B** *Glen Guesthouse*, 84 Lower Gardiner St, Dublin 1, T8551374. Small, central, reasonable rates, recently restored. **B** *Harvey's Guesthouse*, 11 Upper Gardiner St, Dublin 1, T8748384, F8745510. **B** *Marian Guesthouse*, 21 Upper Gardiner St, Dublin 1, T8744129. Guesthouse standard, B&B prices. Good value, close to town.

Dublin

South Dublin B *Ardagh House B&B*, Mrs K Lee, 6 St Anne's Rd South, South Circular Rd, Dublin 8, T4536615. Single room and double rooms, some en suite, bus service into town. **B** *Ariel House*, 52 Lansdowne Rd, Ballsbridge, Dublin 4, T6685512, F6685845. Listed Victorian house, close to DART. **B** *Carmel Chambers B&B*, 25 Anglesea Rd, Ballsbridge, Dublin 4, T/F6687346. Close to DART, 1 en suite, single, double and triple rooms. **B** *Haddington Lodge B&B*, 49 Haddington Rd, Ballsbridge, Dublin 4, T6600974. Good value for 2 people sharing, TV in rooms, all en suite. **B** *Oak Lodge B&B*, Teresa Muldoon, 4 Pembroke Park, Ballsbridge, Dublin 4, T/F6681721. Close to DART, single room, some en suite, TV in rooms, 50% reduction for children.**B** *St Dunstans B&B*, Mai Bird, 25A Oakley Rd, Ranelagh, Dublin 6. A little out of town but good bus services, no en-suite rooms, TV, tea- and coffee-making facilities in rooms, reasonable rates.

Hostels These are a booming industry in Dublin. Many have all the facilities of a hotel, with single and double rooms, but at much lower prices and with self-catering kitchens thrown in. Dorm beds are usually readily available at most hostels, but the good-value singles and doubles, and even four-bed rooms, are booked up months in advance.

North Dublin C *Abraham House*, 82-3 Lower Gardiner St, Dublin 1, T8550600, F8550598. Very reasonable single and double rooms, though not a lot of comfort. Self-catering kitchen, free car park, launderette, breakfast included in price. Fills up very quickly so book early. **C** *Charles Stewart Hostel*, 5-6 Parnell Square, Dublin 1, T8780350, F8368178, cstuart@iol.ie Very modern, new hostel in original Georgian house where Oliver St John Gogarty was born. Singles and doubles put you into a higher price bracket but all are en suite with TV, tea- and coffee-making facilities, which explains the higher prices for these rooms. Secure parking overnight, self-catering kitchen, games room. Price includes breakfast. **C** *Durban House*, 69 Lower Gardiner St, Dublin 1, T8364668. A guest house with dormitory rooms in the basement. Café-style dining-room. **C** *Isaac's Hostel*, 2-5 Frenchman's Lane, Dublin 1, T8556215, F8556524, restaurant. Very popular place with multi-bed dorms, singles, doubles and family rooms. No access even to private rooms for periods of the day, but no night-time curfew. Fines for leaving bags in rooms after 1100. Self-catering kitchen. Jazz on Sundays. **C** *Jacob's Inn*, 21-8 Talbot Place, Dublin 1, T8555660, F8555664. Family and dormitory rooms are good value, single and double rooms put you into a much higher price bracket. Very new, trendy café-style restaurant, self-catering kitchen.

D *The Abbey Hostel*, 29 Bachelor's Walk, Dublin 1, T8780700, F8780719, info@abbey-hostel.ie Very newly built hostel accommodation in central location by O'Connell Bridge. Double rooms available if you don't mind paying near hotel rates, all rooms en suite, barbecue area,

Dublin

TV room, no curfew so it could get noisy at weekends but very up-to-date security. **D** *An Óige Dublin International*, 61 Mountjoy St, Dublin 7, T8301766, F8301600, restaurant. Multi-bed, double and single rooms, some en suite in this massively renovated old convent. Pool rooms, huge kitchen, secure parking, brilliant dining-room in old chapel, TV room, supplement for non-members. **D** *Backpackers Ireland Citi Hostel*, 61-2 Lower Gardiner St, T8550035. Good-value private rooms. **D** *Backpackers Ireland Euro Hostel*, 80-1 Lower Gardiner St, T8364900. Good-value private rooms, secure parking. **D** *Cardijn House*, 15 Talbot St, Dublin 1, T8788484, F8788091. Vaguely Christian, tiny, ageist hostel, good-value twin rooms, breakfast included, self-catering kitchens. **D** *Celts House*, 32 Blessington St, Dublin 7, T/F8300657. Small hostel with private rooms, family and multi-bed rooms. Meals available. **D** *Globetrotters*, 46-8 Lower Gardiner St, T8735893, F8788787, gtrotter@indigo.ie The dormitory end of *The Townhouse* (see 'Guesthouses', page 124). **D** *Marlborough Hostel*, 81-2 Marlborough St, Dublin 1, T8747629, F8745172, marlboro@internet-ireland.ie Good-value, relaxed small hostel. Twin rooms particularly reasonable value, self-catering kitchen, TV room.

South Dublin C *The Oliver St John Gogarty*, 18-21 Anglesea St, T6711822, F8745172. Aimed at the posh end of the hostel trade, this place lies in the epicentre of the stag-night world. Private rooms put you into a higher price range. Restaurant. **D** *Ashfield House*, 19-20 D'Olier St, Dublin 2, T6797734, F6790852, ashfield@indigo.ie Multi-bed, single and double rooms. Doubles are good value. **D** *Avalon House*, 55 Aungier St, Dublin 2, T4750001, F4750303. Singles and doubles at very good rates as well as family rooms and mixed dormitory rooms. Some en suite, toilets also mixed. Problems with noisy guests and very overcrowded when full, as it is from Easter onwards. Price includes breakfast. No lounge area. Café/restaurant open unreliable hours. **D** *The Brewery Hostel*, 22-3 Thomas St, Dublin 8, T4538600, F4538616, brewery@indigo.ie All rooms en suite, good-value single and double rooms, self-catering kitchen. **D** *Kinlay House*, 2-12 Lord Edward St, Dublin 2, T6796644, F6797437, kindub@usit.ie Singles, twins at very reasonable prices and mixed multi-bed rooms, some en suite, mixed washrooms and toilets, breakfast and linen included. Nice kitchens and dining area, recently renovated. Very central, good security, but the usual noise problem at weekends. **D** *Temple Bar House*, 1 Cecilia St, Temple Bar, Dublin 2, T6716277, F6716591, templeba@barnacles.iol.ie Self-catering kitchen, nice modern lounge area, big windows, some double rooms at still reasonable rates, all rooms en suite, bedlinen included in price, good security.

Self-catering These tend to be arranged on a weekly basis but, depending on the season and place, shorter periods can be arranged.

North Dublin *Jacobs Apartments*, Jacobs Inn, 21-8 Talbot Place, T8555660, F8555664, jacob@indigo.ie Apartments with 1 or 2 bedrooms, living-room and kitchen area. Short-term and long-term lets.

South Dublin *Molesworth Court Suites*, 35 Schoolhouse Lane, Dublin 2, T6764799, F6764982. Apartments sleeping up to 6 people a night. Can be rented on a nightly basis. *The Oliver St John Gogarty*, 18-21 Anglesea St, Dublin 2, T6711822, F8745172. Classy 1-, 2- and 3-bedroom apartments in the heart of Temple Bar can be booked by the night. *Trident Holiday Homes*, 24 Lansdowne Rd, Ballsbridge, Dublin 4, T6683534. 2 miles from city centre in quiet suburban area. Rented weekly. Close to DART.

University accommodation Lots of student accommodation is rented out during the long vacation. Single rooms or apartments can be rented by the week or day. Mostly self-catering with good bus services and parking, these can be a good bargain for a family or small group.

North Dublin C *Dublin City University*, Glasnevin, Dublin 9, T7045736, F7045777. 9 June to 20 September. All single rooms shared kitchen and bathrooms. Rooms on campus with access to sports facilities, cafeteria, bars, shops. 15 mins by car from city centre.

South Dublin C-B *Trinity College*, Dublin 2 T6081177. 16th June to 3rd October. Single rooms, some en suite. Bar, kitchens, laundry, sports facilities, car-park. Breakfast included. **C** *UCD Village*, Belfield, Dublin 4, T2697111. 16th June to 14th Sept. Single rooms or self-catering apartments for up to 4 people, nightly or weekly. Bar, cafeteria, coffee shop.

The nearest camping and caravan site to Dublin is a 35-minute drive away at Clondalkin: **Camping sites** *Camac Valley Tourist Caravan and Campling Park*, Naas Rd, Clondalkin, Dublin 22, T4640644, F4640643. 163 pitches, no hire caravans, and a good range of facilities including a TV lounge, good for those rainy days. 2 people plus tents around IR£8. No dogs in July and August. *Shankill Caravan and Camping Park*, Shankill, Co Dublin, 12 miles south of the city, T2820011, F2820108. Smaller, close to the DART, the Stena Line ferry and Bray, with caravans to hire. 2 people and tent IR£6. No dogs in mobile homes.

Eating

While many of Temple Bar's restaurants (see page 128) are fun, fashionable and rela- **Around** tively inexpensive places to enjoy a meal, the area from St Stephen's Green to Merrion **Stephen's** Square is where the real money tends to eat. Don't even look at the menus if you are **Green &** on a tight budget, but for seriously fine dining, or just splashing out on a treat, this is **Merrion Square** where many of the capital's best restaurants are to be found. Reservations are advisable at all times, often essential.

Expensive *The Alexandra Restaurant*, Conrad Hotel, Earlsfort Terrace, T6765555. ● *on maps* Serves imaginative food in an old-fashioned, bourgeois-style restaurant. Appetizers, *Price codes:* costing from IR£3-10, range from lobster ravioli with lemon grass and coconut to foie *see inside front cover* gras with a figs and turnip marmalade dip. There is a superb choice of main fish and meat courses, mostly around IR£18, and an exciting dessert menu. Monday-Saturday, 1830-2230, live piano music after 2000. *The Commons*, Newman House, 85-6 St Stephen's Green, T4752597. Situated downstairs in the beautiful old Jesuit university building, it serves a wonderful combination of classical and nouvelle Irish cuisine, surrounded by a collection of Joyce-inspired paintings. Open for a IR£22 lunch, Monday-Friday, when the place is very business-orientated; Monday-Saturday for dinner, with the weekends noticeably less formal; when the summer days are long be sure to enjoy pre-dinner drinks outside on the terrace. Dinner around IR£40. *L'Ecrivain*, 109 Lower Baggot St, T6611919, F6610617. Small and intimate, serving classic French and Irish dishes, but given an interesting touch. Open for dinner Monday-Saturday, lunch Monday-Friday. Dinner around IR£40. *The Grey Door*, 22-3 Upper Pembroke St, T6763286, F6763287. An award-winning restaurant focusing on the best of Irish cooking in the elegant surroundings of a Georgian townhouse. Even vegetarians can eat here without feeling they have no choices. Dinner 7 days, lunch Monday-Friday. Expect to pay IR£40 plus for dinner. *Restaurant Patrick Guilbaud*, 21 Upper Merrion St, T6764192, F6610052. Owner of countless awards and a Michelin star, with a reputation as Dublin's best modern French restaurant. To eat here you pay a lot but you get what you pay for, as do the many seriously famous people who patronize the place. Make sure your plastic is working.

Affordable *Morel's* in the basement of Stephen's Hall Hotel, 14-17 Lower Leeson St, T6622480. Another lively bistroish kind of place to eat. It has a relaxed atmosphere and buzzes pleasantly. Cuisine is definitely Californian with some superb combinations. Try the white chocolate with cherry and pepper sauce. It's wonderful. Dinner around IR£20. *The Side Door*, Shelbourne Hotel, 27 St Stephen's Green, T6766471. Nothing like the hotel it is based in. Loud colours, a fun menu and afford-able prices make for an entertaining evening. Dinner around IR£18. There are several *Fitzers* restaurants around the city, all very different and popular. At 51 Dawson St, T6771155, the mood is Mediterranean with outside tables (with portable heaters just in case it gets too cold) and a Californian/Mediterranean menu. At the National Gal-lery, T6614496, the mood is a little more formal but with a similar menu, open Museum hours, which means lunch only.

Temple Bar Thank goodness the new bus station scheme was abandoned, otherwise where would you eat in Dublin? Temple Bar is a little Mecca of eating places, some preten-tiously overpriced, others good basic value for money and some in between but there's almost no end to the list of eateries in this area. For the money-conscious, check out the early-bird menus that a lot of places do here; around 1800, a smaller menu is offered at very good prices.

The impishly named Tea Room at the Clarence Hotel, 6-8 Wellington Quay, T6707766, has the reputation of serving up some of the most imaginative dishes in the capital. Try the cider-flavoured crème brûlée with an apple and raisin won ton for a pudding to remember.

Expensive *Les Frères Jacques*, 74 Dame St, T6794555, F6794725. A French restaurant specializing in classic seafood dishes. Dinner will set you back over IR£20 a head. Closed Sundays and bank holidays. *Café Auriga*, 6 Temple Bar Square, T6718228, F6712596. A very fashionable and attractive place to eat with an interesting glass roof and wide views over Temple Bar and the city. Its menu is Californian, in that there are some strange but successful combinations of food on it, including ostrich. It is open Tuesday-Saturday, evenings only, from 1730. Meals work out at around IR£20 a head. *Eden*, Meeting House Square, T6705327, F6703330. A very post-modern sort of place with tables outside in the square and really cool people inside. Food is pricey but worth it with quite classic dishes as well as the unusual, such as quesilladas or grilled vegetable stacks, a welcome relief for vegetarians from the ubiquitous vegetable lasagne. Open 7 days for dinner, Monday-Friday for lunch. Two courses will cost you about IR£15. Other ethnic cuisines are also well represented in Temple Bar. *Tante Zoé's*, 1 Crow St, T6794407, serves Cajun and Creole cooking, specializing in blackened dishes. Open 7 days for lunch and dinner. Can get expensive. Reservations recommended.

Affordable *Fitzers*, Temple Bar Square, T6790440, F6790445. Now a Dublin institu-tion with very different branches around the city. This one is very laid-back: jazz accompanies the food, which is trendy European in style, with an enormous menu running to steaks and burgers as well as more sophisticated fare . Open 7 days 1200-2330. Dinner can cost IR£10-15. *Fan's*, 60 Dame St, T6794263, F6790128. Open 7 days 0900-2330, offering Cantonese cuisine. *Osushi*, 12 Fownes St, T6776111. A tiny place opposite Luigi Malone's, serving, as you might guess, sushi, as well as sashimi, tem-pura, ramen and, oddly, Thai curries at less than IR£10 for an evening meal. Open for lunch and dinner Monday-Saturday; Sundays for dinner only. *Thunder Road Café*, Fleet St, is loud and sassy and does Hard Rock stuff at about IR£17 for dinner. *Trastevere*, Temple Bar Square, T6708343, is another ultra-cool place with big win-dows on to the square and tables outside. An interesting menu extends far beyond the usual pizzas and pasta choices; open from 1230 till late so you can spend the after-noon there, people-watching, and dinner will cost you less than IR£15. *Gallagher's Boxty House*, 20-21 Temple Bar, T6772762, sells the eponymous filled potato pan-cakes. It has a nice old-fashioned country-kitchen feel to it, with newspapers for the clients to read and bookcases with real books in them. *The Shack*, 24 East Essex St, T6790043, F6790394, is another busy country kitchen, with a long menu: Irish stew, enchiladas, seabass cooked in sambuca and fennel, and good vegetarian choices; main courses around IR£9. 1200-2300. *The Alamo*, T6776546, next door to Gallaghers, has been serving good, reasonably priced Mexican food for several years.

The Indian subcontinent is well represented in Temple Bar, primarily at *Monty's of Kathmandu*, 28 Eustace St, T6704911. Don't let the photos of Tarantino put you off – this is excellent Nepalese cooking. Set lunch is superb value and there is an early-bird menu.

Nico's, 53 Dame St, T6773062, is a popular Italian restaurant, serving quite traditional dishes with a strong Irish influence and live music, open for lunch Monday to Friday and dinner Monday to Saturday. Main courses cost around IR£12. Irish-Italian food is very popular in Temple Bar, with *Puccini's* at 33-4 Essex St, T6704860, a very spacious pleasant place doing pizzas and seafood at reasonable prices. Open Tuesday-Sunday 1700-2300. At 3 Temple Bar is *Botticelli*, T6727289, a cosy, tiny place doing reasonably priced pizzas open from 1000, 7 days. *Milano*, 19 Essex St East, T6703384, is in fact the English *Pizza Express* with a similar menu and style. Dinner costs about IR£14.

Cheap Also basically Italian but definitely for the young and lovers of loud music is *Bad Ass Café*, 9-11 Crowne Alley, T6712596. It sells burgers and pizzas in a bright red-and-white environment and claims to have employed Sinéad O'Connor as a waitress once. A couple of doors down is the smaller, quieter *Cibo*, T6717288, which does pizzas, salads and burgers with an early-bird menu at a very good IR£6.95.

Very popular indeed is the new *Luigi Malone's* (Italian-Irish and a sense of humour) in Fownes St, T6792723, which claims to have food and drink from the four corners of the globe. It has a vast menu, comes recommended by lots of Dubliners and has a Happy Hour 1700-2130.

This is the best of Temple Bar food, but there is plenty more. Most of the pubs do Irish stew, or carvery lunches, or sandwiches. There are lots of places to snack including the *Cyberia Café* in Temple Lane, where you can slurp coffee, eat a bagel or two and surf the net at the same time, or *Central Percs* at 10 East Essex St does filled baguettes and sandwiches. *Quays Bar* in Temple Bar Square does soup and sandwiches. For masochists there is an *Abrakebabra*, selling things in pitta breads amid loud music in Merchant's Arch.

Exclusively **vegetarian** places are a bit short on the ground – not really a Dublin tradition yet – but at *Well Fed Café*, 6 Crow St, there is wholefood aplenty in a long-established cooperative that doesn't take credit cards. Can life get any better?

Expensive Slightly less rarefied are the restaurants around Grafton St, although *QV2*, 14-15 St Andrew's St, T6773363, is a very modish place serving European-style food, with a regularly changing menu of seafood, poultry and lamb. Booking necessary at weekends. Dinner around IR£20 plus. *The Cedar Tree* at No 11, T6772121, serves Lebanese food to a mixed clientele. It has some pleasant vegetarian choices and is open till midnight Monday to Saturday. Dinner can cost IR£18 but there are much cheaper options. The *Trocadero*, or 'Troc' as the locals call it, at No 3, is a very down-to-earth but fashionable place to be. Open till past midnight Monday to Saturday. Dinner around IR£25. It is said that the menu hasn't changed in 20 years, but Dubliners who know about these things swear that it's a place where diners can rely on an excellent meal. In South Anne St to the east of Grafton Street are several interesting places.

Around Grafton St

Affordable/cheap *La Cave*, at number 28, quite ancient by Dublin standards, is a small basement bistro and wine bar with lots of posters, open till late and an interesting menu of French dishes. Good vegetarian choices. Dinner around IR£17. At No 8 is the *Gotham Café* which does a grand pizza and some inventive Californian-cum-Italian choices. Very young. Dinner IR£10. At 1, Anne's Lane, South Anne St, T6773721, is *The Chilli Club*, one of Dublin's first ethnic restaurants serving traditional Thai food with lots of coconut and great satays. Dinner around IR£15. In Grafton St itself are lots

Dublin

of fast-food places, as well as *Bewleys*, open till 0530 on Friday and Saturday nights and 0100 every other night. Long lost in the tearoom with cream cakes market they are moving into all-night food places, and are really getting better. At Stephen's St Lower, T4780300, is *Break for the Border*, a huge place, unmissable because of the statuary outside, which does Mexican cowboy food at fairly reasonable rates. OK if you like lots of noise.

Around South Great George St **Expensive** Eamonn O'Reilly's *One Pico Restaurant*, 1 Upper Camden St, Dublin 2, T4780307, is a 5-minute walk away from the centre and well worth the effort. Set in an old convent, its cosy streetside dining room is often full, popularity due to excellent dishes in the modern Irish style; so expect clever turns with fish, like tuna sashimi for starters or salmon teriyaki, mildly curried scallops or cod tempura for a main course. IR£20 plus for dinner, IR£15 for three courses at lunchtime.

Some Dublin restaurants are not easy to pigeonhole, and *The Old Dublin Restaurant*, 91 Francis St, T4542028, is one of the best examples of this rare breed. Using 3 rooms of what was a house of tenement apartments until 1981, the restaurant has a relaxed living-room style that has seasoned with age. The food is delightfully influenced by Scandinavian and Russian cuisine and the wine list is impressive. Lunch, Monday to Friday, is around IR£14 and an early evening set dinner, ordered between 1830-1930, is IR£12. Regular set dinner is IR£21 and main à la carte dishes, from turbot with a caviare sauce to a sirloin steak with pepper sauce, are around IR£16.

Affordable Running parallel with Grafton St, two roads westwards, is South Great George St, where another cluster of good food places has accumulated. Best of all if you are a vegetarian is *Juice*, T4757856, at number 73-78, which serves interesting meals in a quiet atmosphere. Inexpensive set lunches and good value early bird menu. IR9-10 main courses. Open late at weekends. A little further along at No 17, T6710738, is *Shalimar*, serving good authentic Indian food with perhaps no big surprises, but lots of choice for vegetarians. Dinner around IR£16. Further along, at 4 Aungier St, is the wacky *Govinda's*, T4750309, open from 1100-2100 Monday to Saturday, where you can have vegetarian food to the sound of old George Harrison records. Great prices, good lunch specials. At 71-2 South Great Georges St, T4755001, is *Yamamori*, the 'in place' to be, judging by the queues outside waiting for a table. It serves noodle dishes, as well as soups and sushi at very reasonable prices.

Cheap For good lunches, the area is awash with places. The Powerscourt Shopping Centre has floors of lunch-orientated cafés, with *Blazing Salads* being the most popular, judging by the size of the queues.

South of the canal **Expensive** *Le Panto* at the Radisson SAS St Helen's Hotel, Stillorgan Rd, Co Dublin, T2186000 has style. Set in the private library of the original owner of the house, with big open fire, lots of space, fine views out of the windows and a very relaxed atmosphere. Dinner around IR£35 plus. A very understated menu produces little essays in food preparation which are as much fun to look at and investigate as eat; a healthy Irish balance between haute and nouvelle.

Less expensive is *Satchel's* at the School House Hotel, 2-8 Northumberland Rd, T6675014, set in original old schoolroom lined with books, with lots of space and a relaxed atmosphere. A small menu, a bit too animal based for vegetarian tastes, modern Irish in style with some creative sauces and an Asian influence. Taped music doesn't interfere. Dinner less than IR£20.

North of the river **Expensive** *Chapter One*, at 18-19 Parnell Square in the Dublin Writer's Museum, T8732266, is very upmarket, serving classical cuisine in an elegant Georgian house. Dinner at around IR£25 plus. *The Aberdeen*, T8746881, in the *Gresham Hotel*, is pleasant, candle-lit, expensive, a little bit like the dining room in the Titanic but without the iceberg, and needs a reservation. RTE's first broadcast was made from here before it became a restaurant. Superb lunches.

Affordable For **vegetarians** there is *101 Talbot*, at 100-102 Talbot St, T8745011, which does wholefood dishes as well as carnivore food. Reasonable prices. Open 1800-2300 daily. Still in O'Connell St is the very popular *Toddy's*, the bar at the Gresham Hotel which serves very good bar food at out of the city prices all day until late and a carvery lunch which might work out at around IR£11 for three courses. Vegetarian choices.

Cheap Not so many choices on this side of the river unless you like fast food. O'Connell St has most of them, plus shops selling sandwiches to take out if it's lunch you're after. *The Kylemore*, 1-2 O'Connell St, serves cafeteria-style food out of hot plates. *Beshoff*, a few doors further up at No 6, is one of a chain of fish-and-chip shops offering very reasonable fish and chips amidst pleasant but scruffy Edwardian décor, and at comfortable prices. Open from late morning to 2100 Monday-Wednesday, 2300 Thursday to Saturday. At No 61 is *Flanagan's*, a pizza and steak place that does very reasonable food for reasonable prices.

Affordable Here a whole slew of new options will be available in 2000. The hotel café bar, also called *Chief O'Neill's*, has a very reasonably priced menu including Irish stew and *colcannon* but with vegetarian options and lots of sandwiches and snacks served till 2200, if you don't mind the loud taped music, occasionally interspersed with some good live traditional musicians. Only just opened in late 1999 but promising stylish Irish oriental cuisine is *Kelly and Ping*, in the forecourt in front of the Old Jameson Distillery while inside the distillery is the longer established *Stillroom*, T8072355, serving a carvery lunch and snacks outside of the lunch hour in peaceful surroundings. **Smithfield**

Pubs and music

'Good puzzle would be to cross Dublin without passing a pub,' thinks Leopold Bloom as he wanders about the city. Probably an impossible puzzle, since Dublin has even more pubs than it has places to eat. There are pubs for every taste, from real Victoriana to fake, from basic 1950s plywood to expensive fantasias such as *Zanzibar* or *Café en Seine*, high-tech, early morning, musical, literary, sporty, the list is endless. The pubs of Dublin are not all wonderful places, the craic inside isn't necessarily better than anywhere else in the world, and a drunk is a drunk wherever they are but, that said, Dublin has some curious places where you can drink, eat, people-watch, listen to some good music, chat to strangers and eavesdrop on other people's lives. Opening hours are almost continental, 1100-2330 in summer, with perhaps a short closure in the afternoon, and quieter pubs tolerate children at least to early evening.

At night in summer the heart of Temple Bar turns into a huge street party with people overflowing from the pubs on to the street, more people in sidewalk cafés, pavement artists, musicians busking, policemen chasing pickpockets, and a general feeling of bonhomie. The overall feeling is young and inebriated, but if you want a more sedate night in Temple Bar the periphery, especially the pubs in Dame St, are a little quieter. There has been a general agreement among the Temple Bar publicans to bar stag and hen nights, although whether this will actually work in the light of the vast profits to be made from these shindigs is another matter. If they do stick to the ban the street party will be a far more enjoyable experience. The following list is by no means comprehensive. **Temple Bar**

The Auld Dubliner, 17 Anglesea St, recently spruced up a little, is one of the area's oldest residents and not too badly tuned into tourists. It has traditional music on Sunday mornings and Tuesday nights and part of its lunchtime menu is coddle. *Bad Bob's*, in East Essex St, is seriously dedicated to live music of various sorts and drinking, with a Happy Hour 1600-1930 when cocktails are half-price. *Il Baccaro* is a pleasant, quiet wine bar in Meeting House Square, all brick ceilings and foreign posters. *The Crane Bar* at 34 Essex St is very popular, filling up and spilling over into the street early on in the evening. *Danger Doyle's*, 24 Eustace St, is also young, very loud and very popular, with bar food until 1900 and a club taking over after hours. It has live traditional Irish music Wednesday evenings and Saturday afternoons. *Fitzsimmons* in Temple Bar may well go out of business if the stag/hen ban carries on. Its chief clientele, at weekends at least, are young, drunk and British. Big-screen football matches, carvery lunches, chart music. Traditional music Mon-Thur, Sat+Sun afternoons. *The Temple Bar*, 44 Temple Bar, is an unmissable red on the outside, and heaving inside at all hours of the day. Live traditional music every day and an extensive bar menu. *Eamon Doran's* has live music of various sorts during the evening and turns into an indie and house disco after midnight. *The Ha'penny Bridge*, 42 Wellington Quay, is a lively traditional pub with lots of locals and comedy nights. For film buffs *The Irish Film Centre Bar* is modernistic with lots of beech and aluminium, and you can check out what movies or live music are playing there. Close to the Temple Bar pub is *The Norseman*, 27 Essex St East, has a clientele of arty types and theatre-goers, many of whom end up on the street in the general crowd. No renovation for this place – its mahogany bar is the genuine Victorian article. Very cool place to be. Lots of traditional music sessions and a comedy club on Thursdays at 2100. *The Octagon Bar* in the Clarence Hotel is a grand place to sit, with big comfy seating and good cocktails. Opposite The Auld Dubliner, and very popular with the weekend visitor crowd, is the *Oliver St John Gogarty*, 57 Fleet St, with strange things made into bar furniture, stone floors and quieter snug areas. Traditional music on Saturdays and no cover charge. Restaurant upstairs and bar food. Near by is *The Palace Bar*, 21 Fleet St, unrenovated, quieter and popular with journalists. Off Dame St the *Stag's Head*, 1 Dame Court, *Molly Malone's Tavern* and the *Dame Tavern* provide another street party on summer evenings. The Stag's Head was built in 1770 and became the pub you see today in Victorian times. Good pub food. Other places worth checking out for music are *The Left Bank* in Fleet St and *Quays*, 11 Temple Bar. *La Med*, 22 East Essex St, is a Mediterranean restaurant as well as a café bar, with jazz in the evenings.

South of the river

Around the city centre *The Bailey*, 2 Duke St, a busy office workers' pub, serving good pub food and lively in the evenings. It has been a pub since 1837 and has a stunning list of famous clientele, all now sadly dead: not the fault of the pub of course. The front door of 7 Eccles St, which was here, is now in the James Joyce Centre. Close by, *Davy Byrne's*, 21 Duke St, heaves by day and night. There are remnants of its famous and literary past with sketches by Cecil Ffrench Salkheld, an amazing old mirror, good pub food at lunchtime, but not the Gorgonzola sandwiches that Leopold Bloom ate here in *Ulysses*. *The Baggot Inn*, 143 Lower Baggot St, has lots of live rock music while *Doheny & Nesbitt*, 5 Baggott St, sounds more like a funeral directors', but is in fact a very popular pub, its frontage intact after 130 years, an authentic Victorian interior and cosy partitioned sections to drink in. Quiet during the day, very busy at night.

Around Camden Street The *Bleeding Horse*, 24 Camden St Upper, has a prime location at a major road junction. Big dark timbers and high ceilings, and all genuinely 19th century, although a pub has stood here since Cromwell's time. Also in Camden St is *Flannery's*, a kind of café-bar pub, with a working model railway running around it. At No 71 is *Devitt's Bar*, with live music every night and bar food. On the way to

Camden St are two young, fashionable, crowded and interesting bars, both in South Great George St, *The Globe* at No 11 and *Hogan's* at No 35. At No 51 is a traditional Irish pub called *The Long Hall*, which is well worth a visit. Close by is *The International* at 23 Wicklow St, where there is always something going on, whether it's the comedy club upstairs, live music or a play. Lovely old interior, quiet in the afternoons.

Lower Bridge Street The *Brazen Head*, 20 Lower Bridge St, is Dublin's oldest inn, chartered in 1688 but in existence as an inn of one sort or another since the 12th century. The present building was erected in 1754. It's well worth a visit (but not at weekends when it is oversubscribed) for its moody historical low-beamed rooms, live traditional music nightly (except Thursday when the live music is jazz and blues), the graffiti scratched into one of the landing window-panes and Robert Emmet's desk. Carvery lunch and hot specials. Among many famous names to have drunk here, the United Irishmen (not all of them mind, just the leaders) planned their rebellion here. Also in Lower Bridge St is *O'Shea's Merchant*, at No 12, where you can try your hand at traditional dancing to live music on weekday nights.

Café bars *Café en Seine*, 40 Dawson St, is one of the very new, hip places to be in Dublin. It is a café bar rather than a pub, and you could easily spend a night here without alcohol passing your lips, although you'd be buzzing all night from your caffeine intake. It's a huge place, really quite well done with vast arched ceilings, comfortable cushioned seating and little balconied areas. Another super-trendy place is *The Chocolate Bar*, Upper Hatch St, in a converted railway station with fantasy décor, and a chocolate theme to the food and cocktails it serves. In the same super-trendy café-bar mode is *Zanzibar*, in Lower Ormond Quay, open 1600-0200 at weekends, and normal pub hours on weekdays. It's a bit of a *Café en Seine* clone except that the theme is Middle Eastern exotic rather than French left bank. Bar food.

In Poolbeg St, way over behind Tara St Station, is *Mulligan's*, licensed in 1782. JF Kennedy drank here when he worked in Dublin in 1945. Newspaper people are reputed to drink in the 3 bars. Legend has it that the best Guinness in town is here.

Music bars At 15 Merrion Row is *O'Donoghue's*, famous because The Dubliners played and drank here, where there are lots of impromptu music sessions in the unreconstructed and pleasant old pub. A nice mix of real people and tourists. Other good south Dublin pubs for traditional music are: *The Harcourt Hotel*, 60 Harcourt St, gigline 1850664455, with traditional music sessions on weeknights in summer. *The Mean Fiddler*, 16 Wexford St, has traditional music as well as rock bands, and a late bar. *Mother Redcap's*, Back Lane, The Liberties is a new old pub with bricks and fireplaces and live music most nights.

G F Handel, 165-6 Capel St, is a good music pub, generally young and modern rather **North of** than traditional, with jazz on Sundays. Also in Capel St is the biggest music pub in the **the river** city, *Slattery's* at No 129. Check the papers, since music varies from traditional to jazz and ballads and more. In Chancery St, near the Four Courts, is *Hughes' Bar* at No 19, with court cases during the day but live music and set dancing in the evenings. *Lanigan's*, the *Clifton Court Hotel*, O'Connell Bridge is genuinely old, with turf fires, live music every night, and a tourist menu, whatever that is. To the west of the city are *Keatings* in Jeruis St, Dublin 1, which has traditional music 7 nights a week, while at 12 Lower Bridge St is *O'Shea's Merchant Pub*, also 7 nights of music from 2130. *Ryan's*, 28 Parkgate St, is a beautifully unrestored 1890s pub with a locked snug that you must ask for a seat in, wonderful unreconstructed toilets, and good bar food. The *Hole in the Wall*, Blackhorse Ave, is so named after the hole broken into the wall of the next-door park for soldiers to buy their beer through, in the days when the army was stationed in the park. The pub claims to be the longest in Ireland, and does pub food and live countryish music sessions. Finally, if you are visiting Glasnevin cemetery you should pay a visit to *Kavanagh's*, known locally as *The Gravediggers*, 1 Prospect Square, where the gravediggers had a special hole through which they could buy beer as they dug the graves. Built in 1833 and untouched, this is the closest you'll get to a real, untrendified Dublin pub.

Entertainment

Clubbing It is possible to drink somewhere in Dublin, if you have a mind, 24 hours a day. When the pubs close at 2330 in summer the clubs, usually in the basement or upstairs of the same building, open and the fun continues. Most clubs serve drinks until 0200 and don't close until 0300. Then it's off to one of the early-morning pubs in one of the markets. Clubs usually charge an entrance fee, which varies according to the day of the week or the visiting DJs. They often have a dress code and an age limit. Most venues host very different events on different nights, so you should check in the listings of *The Event Guide* before setting off to the club of your choice. Clubs go in and out of fashion rapidly, and this week's cool spot is next week's bore of the week and the week after's empty building. The following list is alphabetical and not comprehensive.

Boomerang is based in the Temple Bar Hotel, Fleet St, open Thursday-Sunday 2200-0230. What will become of it when stag nights are banned is anyone's guess. IR£5-6. Young and alcohol-dedicated. *Break for the Border* in Lower Stephen St, 2230-0230, Thursday-Sunday, is a bit of a cattle market for young Dubliners, but a good place to drink yourself to oblivion. By day it's a country-music joint, while late on it is a popular hits and oldies disco. Over 23s.

Club M is in Bloom's Hotel in Anglesea St, open Tuesday-Sunday, 2300 till late. Laser lights, VIP room and busy at weekends. Open 2 or 3 nights a week only is *Columbia* at Sir John Rogerson's Quay. Thursdays is special for women, with giveaway magazines and makeup samples. IR£7. *The Court* in Harcourt St, Tuesday-Sunday, plays chart hits and oldies.

The *Da Club*, 2 Johnson's Place, is small but good fun. Live music, comedy, disco music. 2230-0200 Monday-Sunday. *Digges Downstairs*, in the basement of the *Drury Court Hotel*, 28-30 Lower Stephen St, is a drinking rather than dancing club. Table service, fine wines. *Eamon Doran's*, 3A Crown Alley (see also 'Pubs in Temple Bar', page 131) 2400-0200, 7 nights, does assorted DJ-driven sessions. *The Fleet Club*, Fleet St, Temple Bar is open Fridays and Saturdays with disco music.

At the *Gaiety Theatre* there are a variety of activities on Fridays and Saturdays from movies to cabaret, live jazz or soul and salsa discos. Friday in particular is salsa night, 2300-0300, IR£6. There is no cover charge at *Hogan's* (see page 132) where the basement opens 2200 till late, while the bar becomes a quieter place to chat. *Howl at the Moon*, in Lower Mount St, is open all week from 2300 till late. It features disco music, a bar and tarot readings. IR£5 weekends, cheaper weekdays. *Kitchen*, East Essex St, 2330-0230 daily is where the really cool people go. U2 own it and occasionally visit. IR£4-6. *Klub Zuzu* is another Temple Bar place, in the basement of *Danger Doyle's* pub (see 'Pubs in Temple Bar' on page 131) with soundproofing to keep the noise in and expensive decorations. *Lillie's Bordello*, Adam Court, Grafton St is where the even more cool people go. Very fussy bouncers at the door, dress code.

Major Tom's in South King St is another 7 nights a week, open till 0200, free-admission place. *POD*, Harcourt St, 2300-0230, Wednesday-Sunday, is the club part of the *Chocolate Bar*, seriously well designed with rather self-consciously gorgeous clubbers. *Renards*, in South Frederick St, is a live jazz and blues supper club from Monday to Wednesday, 2100-0200. For the rest of the week it opens 2300-0300 as a pretty exclusive club with a well-heeled slightly older crowd. Pool room upstairs, fussy

Welcome to the
Home *of* Baileys®

ICON, the Home of Baileys® in Ireland is a unique entertainment, food, drink and shopping experience... a haven of sheer indulgence!

Experience the essence of Ireland past and present in a spectacular audio visual show... ÉRIU . Admission to the show £4 (€5.08) includes a complimentary glass of Baileys®.

Meet up with friends and be spoilt for choice in any one of our three full bars where the atmosphere is always on tap!

Enjoy superb Irish and European Cuisine at The Restaurant , the Mill , the Street or the Servery .

A 4,000 sq. foot shopping extravaganza awaits in the new Baileys® and Kilkenny stores.

Daily ICON shuttle service available to and from ICON from the City Centre.

ICON is open 363 days a year, 10am until late, Sundays from 12pm. Shops open until 8.00pm. ICON at The Baileys® Centre, Leopardstown Road, Foxrock, Dublin 18. Tel (00 353 1) 289 1000 Web: www.baileys.com E-mail: info@iconireland.com

doormen. *Rí Rá*, South Great George St, the basement of the Globe pub, is open 2300-0300 daily, is young, lively with techno and dance music.

Comedy clubs Dublin has several venues for comedy clubs including one 400-seater purpose-built place, but as well as those listed here there are often one-offs in the clubs and pubs around town, so you should keep an eye out in the *Event Guide,* free in most hotels, hostels, etc, or watch for posters around town. *Murphy's Laughter Lounge* is very obvious at Eden Quay and has shows most nights in summer and weekends in winter. Tickets cost around IR£10 depending on who's on. The *International Bar*, 23 Wicklow St, has comedy shows Mondays, Wednesdays and Thursdays from around 2100. Entrance is around IR£4. *The Ha'penny Bridge*, Wellington Quay, has comedy shows on Wednesdays and Thursdays at 2100. IR£3. *Milano*, in Dawson St, T6707744, has a Sunday-night effort, which involves a meal and comedy show with a cover charge of IR£1 plus your meal. Reservations advisable.

Cinemas *Ambassador*, O'Connell St, T8727000. 1 screen housed in an 18th century building, part of the Rotunda Hospital. *Classic*, Harold's Cross, Dublin 6, T4923699. 2 screens, shows *The Rocky Horror Picture Show* late on Fridays. *Irish Film Centre*, 6, Eustace St, T6793477. Weekly membership IR£1 allows you to buy tickets for yourself and 3 guests. Tickets around IR£4. This is the best venue for catching an interesting film. *IMAX*, Parnell Square, Dublin 1, T8174222. Big-screen, stomach-churning movies of roller-coasters and people falling out of aeroplanes. IR£4.95. *Savoy*, O'Connell St, T8748487. 5 screens, all the big releases. *Screen*, D'Olier St, T6714988. 3 screens show a mix of arty and commercial films. *Virgin Cinemas*, Parnell Centre, Parnell St, Dublin 1, T8728400. 9 screens.

Theatres Dublin has had a theatre festival for 40 years, taking place in the middle weeks of October when theatre groups from all over the world visit with major productions, as well as lots of fringe events (organized from 47 Nassau St, T6778439, dubfest@iol.ie http://indigo.ie/~fmk/fringe/   http://www.iftn.ie/dublinfestival). The programme is available from August and bookings for the big events should be made as soon as possible (as well of course as accommodation arrangements). Fringe events are inexpensive and can't be booked in advance.

The *Abbey Theatre*, 26, Lower Abbey St, Dublin 1, T4569569. One of the most famous theatres in the world, this was rebuilt in the 1960s in the 1960s in a fairly brutalist style. The main theatre tends to put on audience attracting productions, often with big names while the Peacock is more experimental, offering works by young and relatively unknown playwrights. *Andrew's Lane Studio and Theatre*, 9-13 Andrew's Lane, T6795270. Commercial productions from foreign touring companies and provincial companies. *The Crypt Arts Centre*, Dublin Castle, Dame St, T6713387. Intimate place in the crypt of the church used by smaller, avant garde companies. *The Dublin Writer's Museum*, Parnell Square, T8722077. Productions of classic Irish theatre. *Gaiety Theatre*, South King St, T6771717. Where every possible variety of theatre and musical production turns up sooner or later. *The Gate*, 1 Cavendish Row, T8744045. Dublin's other famous theatre, workplace of Orson Welles, and where James Mason put on Oscar Wilde's *Salome* when it was banned in Britain. A little more conservative and less avant-garde now, but a beautiful theatre with no balconies or pillars or boxes for the wealthy. *The New Theatre*, 43 East Essex St, T6703361. *Olympia Theatre*, 72 Dame St, T6777744. Old music-hall theatre with lots of variety in its shows. *The Peacock*, 26 Lower Abbey St, Dublin 1, T4569569. The experimental wing of the *Abbey*. *Project@the Mint*, Henry Place, off Henry St, Dublin 1, T6712321. Experimental dance, drama and performing arts. *Samuel Beckett Centre*, Trinity College, T6082461. *Tivoli*, 135-8 Francis St, Dublin 1, T4544472. Theatre, musicals, and much more.

Wren boys

This is a purely Irish tradition disappearing back into the mists of time; it is certainly older than Christianity in Ireland. A pagan goddess, Cliodhna, was said to lure young men to their sexual damnation with her banshee-like howling and often appeared as a wren. The wren boys must have got it into their heads to kill all the wrens they could find in order to put this terrible danger to rest. Quite why they chose to do it on St Stephen's Day (26th December) is anyone's guess but probably has something to do with the death of the old year and all that. Anyway, wren boys carried their dead wrens about in the torn-off branch of a tree and visited each house with a rhyme and lots of banging of pots and pans to drive out whatever it was worried them. In living memory it was a tradition akin to carol singing with the wren boys in their straw masks singing at each house for a beer or food. Nowadays, little gangs of kids go about banging on doors and singing a bit in exchange for cash. If you are lucky you might see real enactments of some wren boy dancing and singing with straw masks and costumes as opposed to Darth Vader outfits and last year's Hallowe'en masks.

Dublin

Festivals

Festival time is a good time to be in Dublin, although of course room rates and air fares rise mysteriously to coincide with them. For the big festivals it is important to book everything early because air fares, particularly, rise as the event approaches and places to stay fill up alarmingly quickly, as do the big events at the film and theatre festivals. In February the year kicks off with the *Film Festival*, usually at the end of the month. Festival movies are shown at all the major city movie-houses as well as lots of suburban ones. Book early: T6792937, F6792939, dff@iol.ie http://www.iol.ie/dff/

March 17th March is *St Patrick's Day* and anyone expecting green beer, etc, should try to be in Dublin: it is altogether a pretty quiet affair everywhere else. There is a parade with floats, bands, and costumes starting at midday and travelling from Christ Church to O'Connell St; possibly also a fun-fair. A 2-day traditional music festival is held in Temple Bar at the weekend nearest to Paddy's Day. Free music all over Temple Bar, in the pubs and in Meeting House Square. There is also a two-day dog show at Cloghran, County Dublin.

June Not much after that until 16th June when for, several days, *Bloomsday* is celebrated. There are readings, lectures, performances and lots of dressing up and drinking. Book early for the big lectures: T8788547, http://www.joycecen.com On the 3rd Sunday in June is *National Concert Hall Day* when the National Concert Hall opens its doors to the public with free concerts all day in the Hall and Iveagh Gardens. T4751666.

July The 3rd weekend in July sees the *Guinness Blues Festival*, where pubs, mostly in Temple Bar, host free performances of all kinds of blues music. Some of the late shows have a cover charge. No advance booking, so get there early.

August In the first week in August is the Kerrygold Horse Show, at the RDS in Ballsbridge. Thursday is Ladies' Day, when everyone puts on silly hats, and Friday is the Aga Khan cup. It's a very big international event so again book early. Tickets IR£6-12. T6680866.

October In the 2nd week of October is the *Theatre Festival*. Book well in advance: T6774839, http://www.istm.ie/dublinfestival.   The last Monday in October is the *City Marathon*, which attracts thousands of competitors and even more spectators: T6764647, http://www.internet-Ireland.ie/Dublin-Marathon

December On Christmas Eve there is a vigil in St Mary's Pro-Cathedral and on St Stephen's Day, 26th December, gangs of strangely dressed youths, Wren Boys, are occasionally seen going around the city singing at front doors for money (see box on page 137).

Gay Dublin

Homosexuality was decriminalized in Ireland in 1990 as a result of cases taken to the European Court of Human Rights, and the age of consent lowered to 17, making the Republic a more liberal country than the UK. Despite the Church, Ireland, Dublin in particular, is a tolerant place, and Dublin has an increasingly popular and lively gay scene. The *Irish Gay Community News* is widely available with details of new places and events. The end of June usually sees a gay pride week, while there is the Lesbian and Gay Film festival at the end of July. *Outhouse*, 6 South William St, T6706377, is a community centre that provides a meeting place dedicated to gay and lesbian issues, as well as a café; *LOT* (Lesbians Organizing Together), 5 Capel St, Dublin 1, T8727770, is a small resource centre and library open Monday-Thursday 1000-1800, Friday 1000-1600. *Waterstones*, the *Winding Stair*, and *Books Upstairs* (36 College Green), all have good gay and lesbian sections.

Several clubs have gay and lesbian nights, which tend to shift about, so check in the *IGCN*. Most popular are *Strictly Handbag* at *Rí Rá*, Mondays 2315 onwards; *Powderbubble*, at the *POD*, usually once a month, T4780225 for details; and *Wonderbar* at *Temple Bar Music Centre*, on the 1st and 3rd Saturday of the month, T6709202 for details. Dedicated gay venues are *Incognito*, 1-2 Bow Lane East (off Aungier St) T4783504, a men-only sauna, Monday-Thursday 1300-0500, Friday, Saturday 1300-0900, Sunday 1400-1700; *Out on the Liffey*, 27 Upper Ormond Quay, T8722480, a pub well out of the trendy gay areas; and *Stonewalz*, Griffith College South Circular Rd, Dublin 8, T4549427, a women-only club open alternate Saturdays 2100-0200, bar, pool, DJ.

Other places enjoy a mixed crowd, regardless of sexual orientation. The *George*, the *Globe* and *Hogan's*, all pubs in South Great George St, offer a good time to all, as does *Front Lounge*, 34 Parliament St, Temple Bar.

Shopping

The main area for shopping in Dublin is of course the pedestrianized Grafton St and the myriad of little streets that lie around it. St Stephen's Green Shopping Centre and Powerscourt Shopping Centre are close by. Two blocks away, South Great George St has 3 or 4 charity shops for those who like to buy their stuff and do good at the same time. Temple Bar used to be the place for second-hand clothes but now it tends towards designer galleries, arts and crafts and trendy kitchenware.

North of the river O'Connell St has 1 or 2 big department stores, the nearby Jervis Shopping Centre with department stores and lots of designer clothes shops, the ILAC centre with more shops, and Moore St street market.

To the west of the old city is Francis St where there is a collection of antique shops and, close by, Mother Redcap's Market selling bric-à-brac. There are no big bargains to be had in Dublin although groceries will be noticeably cheaper to British visitors, but Dublin excels in branches of designer and craft shops that would otherwise be scattered around tiny villages all over Ireland. *Louis Mulcahy*, for example, is a potter whose workshop is at the furthest extreme of western Europe at the end of the Dingle peninsula, but there is a *Mulcahy* shop at 51C Dawson St where, if you can't watch them make the pots, you can at least browse and then pop into Bewleys for a drink.

Bookshops Dublin is a booklover's dream with the big chain stores in the main shopping areas and tens of smaller special-interest stores, from religious texts to maps to antiquarian bookstores. Dublin had bookstore/coffee-shops long before they became fashionable in London. *Eason's* in O'Connell St has a vast magazine section, stationery, art supplies and lots of Irish interest books. *Waterstone's*, in Dawson St and the Jervis Centre, has a wider range of literature and special-interest books. Across the road, *Hodges Figgis* has a cultured atmosphere and a stock of books to justify this. *Tower Books*, Wicklow St, has a large selection of popular culture, music and gay literature. *Hughes and Hughes* in St Stephen's Green Shopping Centre has a good range of books, especially children's and Irish interest. There is also a branch at the airport which has a good selection of guides. *Dublin Books*, in Grafton St, is imaginatively stocked, independent and friendly. *Fred Hanna's* in Nassau St is academic in orientation, bigger than it looks from outside, and with a second-hand and antiquarian section. *Forbidden Planet*, 2 Crampton Quay, sells sci-fi and fantasy novels, movie posters, videos and spin-off toys from sci-fi movies. *Books Upstairs*, 36 College Green.

Second-hand *Cathac Books*, 10 Duke St, is an antiquarian bookseller focusing on Irish interest and writers. Has signed first editions of all sorts of people as well as old maps and prints. On Ormond Quay is *The Winding Stair Bookshop and Café*, with lots of good second-hand bargains over two floors, plus a great café overlooking the river.

Already listed are several department stores with individual designer sections, several **Clothes** second-hand clothes stores for the avant garde and lots of Irish craft woollies and things. *BT2* in Grafton St has all the big labels and price tags. Look out for pieces by Paul Costello, John Rocha and Louise Kennedy, who has dressed Mary Robinson and Cherie Blair. In the same street, those more financially challenged can try looking in *A-wear*, which has lots of Irish designer clothes at almost feasible prices. Names to look out for here are Mary Gregory and Quinn & Donnelly. At less stratospheric levels all the British big chains are here: *Next*, *Monsoon*, *Benetton*, *Miss Selfridge*, *Principles*, *Jigsaw* and *River Island* are all in Grafton St. In Temple Lane, Temple Bar is *Lowe Alpine* selling outdoor gear, boots and maps.

You can't go far in Ireland without bumping into a branch of *Blarney Woollen Mills* and **Craft & gift** Dublin is no exception. It's in Nassau St and sells the usual barrage of hand-knit jumpers, **shops** hand-woven clothes and things with leprechauns on. There are some good bargains to be had if you poke around. *Cleo Ltd*, 18 Kildare St, sells 'wearable art', ie handmade clothes, ceramics, wooden bowls and lots of other things, all of Irish origin. The *Crafts Council of Ireland*, in Powerscourt Townhouse Centre has a collection of the best of Irish crafts. In the same centre are several other jewellery, crafts and funny t-shirt shops, as well as antique shops, so give yourself time for a long browse. *Design Yard*, East Essex St, sells very expensive Irish-designed jewellery. No claddagh rings here. *Dublin Woollen Co*, in Lower Ormond Quay, is a cheaper clone of Blarney Woollen Mills. *House of Ireland*, in Nassau St, sells fine china and crystal, woollens and handmade cloth and leather goods, all of Irish origin. The *Irish Celtic Craft Shop* in Lord Edward St sells the entire range of Irish ethnic stuff. The *Kilkenny Shop* in Nassau St has another vast range of very classy woollens, hand-woven clothes, crafts and a great café upstairs for lunch. At 5 Castlegate is *Whichcraft*, with really neat crafts from Ireland and around the world. You should also check out the St Stephen's Green Centre, where there are strange t-shirt shops, lots of ethnic stalls, candle shops and quirky furnishings, although not all necessarily of Irish origin. All around O'Connell St are many tacky places selling t-shirts with leprechauns, bodhráns, mugs and other joke Irish stuff.

Arnott's, 12 Henry St, specializes in clothing, lots of designer concessions. The restau- **Department** rant upstairs gets very busy at lunchtime. *Brown Thomas*, 88-95 Grafton St, has a long **stores** history in Dublin, a mention in *Ulysses*, and is its most upmarket store. *Clery's* dominates O'Connell St with its vast Selfridges-style window displays and enormous range of goods. Reasonable prices, lots of Irish gifts. *Debenhams* has 4-storeys in the Jervis

Centre. *Dunnes* has branches all over town, notably in Henry St and St Stephen's Green shopping centre. It's the Irish *Marks & Sparks*, although a little cheaper. Lots of reasonably fashionable clothes, sportswear, household goods, baby clothes. *Marks & Spencer* itself is in Grafton St, but British people shouldn't expect any bargains. Wait till you get back. *Roches* in Henry St focuses on housewares but has clothing sections too. Good prices.

Markets *Moore St* is Dublin's famous market, used by one and all for their fresh fruit and vegetables and good for listening to Dublin accents, if not actually buying anything. *Mother Redcap's* in Back Lane, near Christ Church sells bric-à-brac, junk, herbal teas, tarot readings, second-hand books and many other uncategorizable objects. On Saturdays, Meeting House Square in Temple Bar hosts an esoteric food market where sun-dried tomatoes, balsamic vinegar and olives nestle beside smoked fish, goat's cheese, strange Mexican health foods and snail-nibbled organic vegetables. Worth seeking out is Blackrock Sunday market where crafts, food, second-hand clothes, electrical goods and much more are on sale. In George's Arcade, between South Great George St and Drury St are second-hand clothes and book shops, candle shops, piercing shops, music stalls, as well as the usual variety of covered-market stalls.

Sport

Dublin can provide the sports-orientated with a full range of sporty things to do and watch, from Ireland's own two field sports – hurling, which dates back maybe 2,000 years, and Gaelic football, which has a slightly briefer pedigree – to the many golf courses that some might say blight the land, go-karting, ice skating, windsurfing, even skiing. Horse-racing is a national preoccupation and Dublin has plenty to offer there too. The public parks have lots of pitches marked out for hurling, football and rugby, which are free to the public as well as basketball courts, also free, and tennis; jogging in the parks is a pleasant and safe experience.

Bowling Ten-pin bowling is dominated by the Leisureplex group. There are alleys all around the suburbs: among others at Malahide Road, Coolock, T8485722; Tallaght, T4599411; and Stillorgan, Co Dublin, T2881656. Bowling greens open to the public are at Moran Park in Dun Laoghaire and Herbert Park in Ballsbridge.

Canoeing *Surfdock*, Grand Canal Dock Yard, South Dock Rd, Ringsend, T6683945, organizes canoeing courses (as well as sailing and windsurfing). There is the annual Liffey Descent in September, when canoeists race the Liffey, cheered on in the Dublin section by supporters who drive from bridge to bridge and hang over yelling encouragement.

Cycling In 1998 the Tour de France, unaccountably, started off in Dublin, and cycling is a seriously popular sport in the country. Cycling around the city is a definite possibility, although there are no cycle paths and very few official bike parks, all the likely places having notices warning of removal. At the *Eamonn Ceannt Park* (see 'Tennis', page 142) there is a cycling track open to the public but the pathways all over Wicklow and in the parks in the city are all possible cycle routes.

Dog racing Held all year at *Harold's Cross*, Dublin 6, T4971081; and *Shelbourne Park*, Lott's Road, Ringsend, Dublin 4, T6683502.

Increasingly popular in Ireland since Jackie Charlton recruited a national team and **Football**
took them through to the quarter-final of the 1990 World Cup, football is played professionally by several teams in Dublin, the best being Shamrock Rovers at *Spawell Leisure Complex*, Dublin 6. The national team consists of players, including two black
people, whose ancestors may once have been Irish (an apocryphal story tells of one
team member telling reporters he loved Ireland's capital, Cardiff).

A kind of invention of the Gaelic Athletic Association, Gaelic football had existed in Ire- **Gaelic football**
land as a form of football played with the hands as well as the feet from about the 17th
century, but no formalized set of rules existed until the GAA invented them in 1885. It
evolved over the next 20 years to become the game that is so popular in Ireland today.
There are 15 players in a team, who play with a ball similar to an English football, but
can use their hands to pass it or score goals. The goal resembles that of rugby with a
score over the bar being worth less than a score below the bar. You can watch amateur games in the Phoenix Park at weekends for free, or check out Croke Park.

Kart City, Old Airport Rd, Dublin 9, T8426322. IR£6-30. Book in advance. **Go-karting**

Most golf clubs are private, and you need to be a member of a union and have a hand- **Golf**
icap to play. Public golf courses are at Sillogue, Elm Green and Stepaside. Information
T8347208. Golf watchers can watch the Murphy's Irish Open at Druids Glen, County
Wicklow, T2694111, F2695368, gui@iol.ie

Somehow, when Ireland entered the motorized age, no one thought to tell Irish peo- **Horse racing**
ple that they should stop loving horses, and so they didn't. In Britain horses and horse- **& riding**
racing are the pursuit of the monied classes. This is not the case in Ireland, where kids
in the council estates keep horses tethered on grass verges and Smithfield market
heaves with horses and owners every month. There are 23 race meetings at
Leopardstown, 6 miles south of the city centre during the year, T2893607, admission
IR£7-13. This is the most popular race-meeting spot with Dubliners, and has been
since it opened in 1888 in what was then named Leperstown. Another good race
course is *Fairyhouse*, 12 miles northwest of Dublin, T8256167, admission IR£6-10. A
special bus service from Dublin (Busaras) is operated on race days, T8734222. There
are no riding schools in the city but there are a few in the outskirts: *Brennanstown
School*, T2863778, is at Kilmacanogue, County Wicklow, beyond Bray and charges
IR£15 an hour.

Europe's oldest field game, played with a curved ash stick and small hard ball. Played **Hurling**
in public parks from August to May. Big game watchers could try for the All Ireland
Football and Hurling Finals in September, held at Croke Park.

Dublin Ice Rink, Dolphin's Barn, South Circular Rd, Dublin 8, T4534153, 1030-1300, **Ice skating**
1430-1700, 1930-2200 daily. IR£3-4.

The season is from August to May; international matches take place at Lansdowne Rd **Rugby**
Stadium, T6689300. There are 14 domestic rugby clubs, which compete over the
course of the season for the Leinster Senior Cup. For domestic matches, you could try
Bective Rangers, Donnybrook, Dublin 4, T2838245; Blackrock College RFC, Stradbrook
Rd, Co Dublin, T2800151; Old Belvedere, Anglesea Rd, Dublin 4, T6603378.

Unlike riding, sailing is a distinctly élitist affair in Ireland. There are schools that offer **Sailing**
courses in sailing, but nowhere to hire boats. The *Irish National Sailing
School*,T2844195, at Dun Laoghaire, offers intensive courses in sailing throughout the
year at IR£110 for adults.

Dublin

Skiing   *Ski Club of Ireland*, Kilternan, T2955658, open September-March. Equipment hire.

Swimming   As we all know since Michelle Smith hit the world's headlines, Ireland has no pool longer than 25m. All the public pools are in the suburbs. Try *St Paul's College*, Raheny, Dublin 5, T8316283, or *St Vincent's CBS Swimming Pool*, Glasnevin, Dublin 9, T8306716.

Tennis   The following parks have tennis courts that can be booked by the public: *Albert College Park*, Glasnevin, Dublin 9, T8373891. *Bushy Park*, Terenure, Dublin 6, T4900320. *Eamonn Ceannt Park*, Crumlin, Dublin 12, T4540799. *Herbert Park*, Ballsbridge, Dublin 4, T6684364. *St Anne's Park*, Raheny, Dublin 5, T8331859.

Windsurfing   *Fingall Windsurfing*, Malahide, T8451979. *Surfdock Windsurfing*, South Docks, T6683945.

Tours

An excellent way to get an insight into the city that tourists often don't have access to is to join one of the many specialist tours daily doing the rounds of the familiar and not-so-familiar sites of historical and cultural interest. These usually run daily and can be joined at the starting point as well as booked ahead. Some of the more unusual ones should be booked, since they may not run if there isn't enough interest. They can be booked at the numbers given, or through Dublin Tourism, Suffolk St.

Active   *Dublin Bike Tours*, T6790899. 1st July-31st October, daily 1000, 1400, 1800. Saturday only, 'Dublin at Dawn' 0600. Meets at *Darkey Kelly's Bar*, Fishamble St. 3 hours including refreshment stops. Looks at historical and contemporary Dublin. Bikes are provided and routes avoid main roads. Child seats available. Arrive 15 minutes before tour starts. IR£12 covers bike hire, tour and insurance.

Ghostly   *The Dublin Ghostbus Tour*, T8734222. 1930 Tuesday, Thursday, Friday, Saturday and Sunday. Tour starts at *Dublin Bus*, 59 Upper O'Connell St, Dublin 1. A bus ride around Dublin's creepier parts, taking in St Kevin's graveyard where bodysnatching took place, haunted houses, an Irish wake, Bram Stoker's house and ends up in the *Legal Eagle* pub telling ghost stories. *Walk Macabre*, T6057769. 1930 daily. Meets at main gates of Stephen's Green. Tour focuses on some of the many horror writers who wrote in Dublin: Le Fanu, Bram Stoker, and others. Actors pop out and tell stories. 1½ hours, IR£6. *The Zozimus Experience*, T6618646. Booking in advance is essential. 1800 nightly by appointment. Lasts 1½ hours. Meets at pedestrian gate to Dublin Castle in Dame St. Tour around creepy events of medieval Dublin, with guide dressed up as the old blind storyteller who once wandered Dublin's streets telling stories.

Historical   *Footsoldiers Revolutionary Dublin*, T6629976. Focuses on the period between 1916 when the Easter Rising took place and 1923 when the civil war ended. Visits Stephen's Green, Trinity College, O'Connell St, Dublin Castle, Crow St and Ha'penny Bridge. Run by Trinity graduates. IR£5. Daily at 1230. *Historical Walking Tours of Dublin*, T8780227, F8783787. May-September, daily 1100, 1200, 1500; October-April, Friday-Sunday 1200. The tours are conducted by history graduates of Trinity College and visit most of the important sites around the old city. Concludes with a look at the current peace process. IR£5.*The 1916 Rebellion Tour*, T6762493. Meets at *The International Bar*, 23 Wicklow St, at 1130 Tuesday to Saturday. Lasts 2½ hours and travels the relevant sites describing and analysing the events that took place. Tour includes a free copy of the *Proclamation of the Republic*. IR£6.

Airline offices in Dublin

Aer Lingus, 40-41 O'Connell St, Dublin 1, T7052222/7053333 (reservations); 7056705 (flight information)

Aeroflot, 15 Dawson St, Dublin 2, T6791453

Air France, 29-30 Dawson St, Dublin 2, T6778899

Alitalia, 4-5 Dawson St, Dublin 2, T6775171

British Airways Express, T1800-626747

British Midland, Nutley, Merrion Rd, Dublin 4, T2838833

Delta Airlines, 24 Merrion Square, Dublin 2, T6768080

Iberia Airlines, 54 Dawson St, Dublin 2, T6779846

Lufthansa, Dublin Airport, T8445544

Manx Airlines, T2601588 (reservations)

Qantas, Dublin Airport, T8747747

Ryanair, 3 Dawson St, Dublin 2, T6774422; 6097800 (reservations); 550500500 (flight information)

SAS, Dublin Airport T8445440

Singapore Airlines, 29 Dawson St, Dublin 2, T6710722

Virgin, 30 Lower Abbey St, Dublin 1, T8733388

Literary *The Jameson Literary Pub Crawl*. T4540228. Easter-3rd October, nightly at 1930, and Sundays 1200; winter, Saturday 1930, Sunday 1200, 1930. Tour starts at *The Duke* pub in Duke Street and crawls its way around pubs associated with Dublin's famous writers. A team of actors perform from their works *in situ*. 2½ hours of Joyce, O'Casey, Behan, Yeats and more. IR£6.

Musical *Musical Pub Crawl*, T4780193. 10th May-25th October, 1930 nightly except Friday, occasional days during winter. Meets at *The Oliver St John Gogarty* bar at the corner of Fleet St and Anglesea St, Temple Bar. Two musicians take you around musical pubs in the city. IR£6. *Rock Trail*, T6795077. Tuesday-Saturday 1230, Sunday 1630. Meets at *Rock Trail Shop*, 13 Trinity St. 2 hours, including a free pint of Guinness and a copy of *Hot Press*. Travels around sites connected with Sinéad O'Connor, U2, the Cranberries, Bob Geldof, Van Morrison and the Dubliners. Ends at U2's wall where you can scribble something. IR£5.

Self-guided You can also hire an audio walking tour of the city from *Audio Tours Ireland Ltd* at 7-9 Aston Quay, T6705266. Cost varies depending on how long you keep the machine.

Out of the city There are several companies that do a wide range of tours in the city and further afield. *Cultúr Beo*, T4599159, does day-long walking and driving tours around Blessington, Glenasmole, Hollywood, and more. Most tours work out at around IR£12. *Mat Gibbon's Tours* T2839973 does full-day coach tours to Newgrange, Powerscourt and Glendalough, and a city tour that takes half a day.

Transport

Air Dublin has one airport, T8444900, 8 miles (12 km) north of the city. For international connections see the Getting There section on page 32. There are internal flights to Belfast, Cork, Derry, Galway, Knock, Shannon, Sligo, Waterford and several other towns, run either by Ryanair – T6097800 for bookings, T1-550500500 for information – or Aer Lingus T7052222, T7053333 (bookings), T7056705 (flight information). Most internal flights take less than an hour but are expensive and often not worth the cost when you take into account checking-in time and getting to and from out-of-town airports. See also the box on page 143.

The airport has 2 places for currency exchange, a branch of the Bank of Ireland and a counter in the arrivals area. In the main arrivals hall is a Dublin Tourism counter, open daily from 0800-2200 (2230 in July and August), which can book accommodation. Next to it is a CIE counter with information on bus transport. Nearby are car-hire counters. At the car-park level is a post office. There are also left-luggage facilities as well as assorted shops, bars and cafés.

Airport buses There is no train service to the airport. An Airlink Express bus runs from the central bus station every 15 minutes and takes about half an hour, IR£3; the same bus can be picked up at Heuston station, IR£3.50. Services are less frequent on Sundays. Local buses Nos 41 and 41A go to the airport from Eden Quay, cost IR£1.50 but take up to an hour. Their bus stop is outside the airport just next to the Airlink Express bus stop. The route from the airport makes several stops in the north of the city, which might be useful if you plan to stay around there.

Bicycle Being fairly flat and comparatively uncongested (as long as you don't try to cycle during the rush hour), Dublin is a pleasant city to cycle around in. There are no bike lanes and all over the city centre are signs warning that chained bicycles will be removed from railings, but cycling would be an excellent way to reach some of the out-of-the-way places and to see the rest of the country. *Rent-a-Bike Ireland* has a branch at 58 Lower Gardiner St, Dublin 1, T8725399. Bikes can be rented here and returned at any other branch of the company in Ireland, including Belfast. They will even organize tours, book accommodation and plan your route. *Raleigh Rent-a-Bike* has several branches in Dublin, the most central being at 27 North Great George's St, Dublin 2, T8788473. Many of the hostels also have bikes to hire.

Bus **Long-distance** *Bus Éireann*, T8366111, operates an extensive system of express buses to all parts of Ireland from the Busáras in Store St. Express buses go to Cork 4 times a day at an adult midweek return fare of IR£13. Journey time includes a 30-min stop and takes about 4½ hours. There are hourly buses to Galway 0800-2100 at a midweek return fare of £IR9, journey time 3½ hours. Up to 7 daily buses to Belfast 0800-1945 at a midweek return fare of IR£11.50, journey time about 3 hours.

Express buses also travel daily to Armagh, Athlone, Ballina, Derry, Donegal, Killarney, Letterkenny, Limerick, Portrush, Portumna, Rosslare, Shannon, Sligo, Waterford, West Clare, Westport and Wexford, and many other towns. Express bus tickets must be bought before you get on the bus. If you intend to do much travelling by bus you might want to consider the Rambler Ticket, which allows you to travel throughout the Bus Éireann network for 3, 8 or 15 days of your choice over a limited period. The 15-day ticket costs IR£98 and is valid for a month, out of which you may choose any 15 days to make as many journeys as you choose, on local buses as well as express buses. Avoid seats at the back if you get at all travel-sick, and if you are travelling alone it is a good idea to get on towards the end of the queue, when you can choose who you sit next to, rather than have someone choose you. Buses fill up and there is not much room for baggage inside the bus: being squashed beside the window next to someone with several shopping bags or worse is no fun at all.

Local The local buses are fairly frequent and cheap. Bus stops are painted green, and a little sign on them says where the stop is, and indicates which buses stop there. There is sometimes a timetable for those particular buses half-way up the pole but this is sometimes vandalized, so don't depend on it. Buses more or less conform to the timetables. You pay the driver on entry and should have the correct fare if you know it. Up to 3 stages costs 55p, 4-7 stages 80p, 8-13 stages IR£1, and 14 or more IR£1.10. If you plan to get about the city a lot by bus there are several concessionary tickets, which will make travel easier and cheaper and which can be bought from some of the bigger newsagents as well as the tourist office in Suffolk St, and the Head Office at 59 Upper O'Connell St, T8720000. Pre-paid tickets can be bought for daily, weekly or

Car hire companies

Argus, 59 Terenure Rd, East Dublin 6, T/F4904444; Dublin Tourism Centre, Suffolk St, Dublin 2, T6057701; Airport, T8444257, http://www.argus-rentacar.com

Avis, 1 Hanover St East, Dublin 2 & Dublin Airport, T6057500

Belgard Self Drive, Tallaght, Dublin 24, T4518444, belgard@itw.ie

Budget, 1 Lower Drumcondra Rd, Dublin 9, T8379611; Airport T8445919

County Car Rentals, Rochestown Avenue,

Dun Laoghaire, T2352030, F2857016

Dan Dooley Rent-a-car, Westland Row, Dublin 2, T6772723

Eurodollar, T8423166

Hertz, 149 Leeson St, Dublin 2, T6602255; Airport T8445156

Murrays Europcar, Baggot St Bridge, Dublin 4, T6681777; Airport T06002400

Thrifty Rent A Car, 14 Duke St, Dublin 2, T6799402; Airport T8444190

Windsor Rent A Car, 33 Bachelor's Walk, O'Connell Bridge, Dublin 1, T1800-515800

Dublin

monthly unlimited travel on the DART, buses and suburban rail lines (IR£4.50 daily). Unlimited bus travel for a day costs IR£3.30. There are 10-journey tickets, but they are for people who make regular journeys, and save very little: a 10-journey ticket for a 55p fare costs IR£5.50. Higher value tickets do save a little. A daily Family Bus Travel Wide ticket costs IR£5.50 and allows unlimited bus travel on buses. For IR£6.50 you can buy a family pass for bus and trains, and for IR£10 per adult a 4-day unlimited off-peak bus and DART travel pass.

There is a range of student offers for which you need a valid ISIC and a Travelsave stamp which you get from 59, O'Connell St Bus services stop at around 2330 but 15 Nitelink buses run every Thursday, Friday and Saturday from the city centre to the various suburbs (T8734222).

Car

Ireland is a nation of car drivers, most people preferring to make the tiniest journey by car rather than walk. That doesn't mean that travelling around Ireland by car is easy. The initial routes out of Dublin are up to international standards but once you are off them, even trunk routes are two-lane affairs, which makes overtaking difficult and journeys are slowed to the pace of the big vehicles on the road. The cost of bringing a car to Ireland from Europe or Britain can be high, especially in peak periods, but it is still cheaper than hiring one. All car-hire companies run out of vehicles at the peak of the summer months so booking in advance is highly recommended. *Avis*, *Hertz*, *Budget Rent-A-Car* and *Eurodollar* have desks at the airport. In the high season daily rates can be between IR£50 and IR£100. It is best to shop around, as rates vary depending on how the season is going. For car hire companies, see page 145.

Dublin

DART Dublin Area Rapid Transit links the coastal suburbs with the city centre and is useful for trips out to the coast. They are clean and fast but get very crowded at peak times. Suburban rail lines run out westwards to Leixlip and Maynooth, stopping at northwestern suburbs on the way. You cannot take bikes on the DART.

Taxis There is no extra charge on taxis to the airport, although they can charge for each piece of baggage, and for a telephone booking, and for unsocial hours, ie between 2000 and 0800. Make sure they either have the meter switched on or, if it's 'broken', tell you how much they are going to charge. It should cost IR£15, so for 4 people sharing would work out about the same as the airport express bus. Some phone cab companies charge a fixed rate for certain journeys such as the airport and will tell you in advance. There are 24-hour taxi ranks at Aston Quay, College Green, Eden Quay, O'Connell St Upper, O'Connell St Lower, Westland Row station, Stephen's Green and Lansdowne Rd. From the airport to town there is an IR£1.30 surcharge.

Taxis tend to congregate at cab ranks rather than cruise around looking for fares. Flagfall is IR£1.90 and then the meter goes up by 10p per ninth of a mile or 40 seconds. If you are out clubbing and want a cab, remember that so does everyone else at 0300 and make for a cab rank or carry a phone cab number. Phone cab companies include: *ABC Taxis*, T2855444; *Access* and *Metro Cabs*, T6683333; *Black Cab Company*, T8722222; *City Cabs*, T8722688; *Co-op Taxis*, T6766666; *Pony Cabs*, T6612233. For complaints or queries contact the *Irish Taxi Federation*, T8364166.

Train Dublin has 2 intercity railway stations: Connolly Station in Amiens St, T8363333, north of the river, serves Belfast, Derry, Sligo, Roslaire; Heuston Station in St John's Road West, T8365421, serves Cork, Galway, Westport, Tralee, Killarney, Limerick, Wexford and Waterford and places in the south and west.

DART and suburban rail network

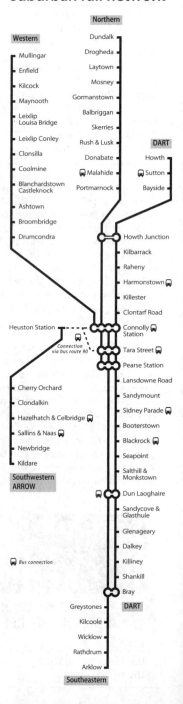

For details of intercity lines and connections contact *Iarnród Éireann* Travel Centre at 35 Abbey St Lower, Monday-Friday 0900-1700, Saturday 0900-1300, T8366222. Train travel is far more expensive, especially for one-way journeys, but swifter and roomier than the intercity bus services.

Directory

Banking hours are Mon-Wed 1000-1600 and Fri 1000-1700. ATM machines are outside most **Banks** banks and you can withdraw up to IR£200 per day, more if you go into the bank. **Bureaux de Change** all banks have a foreign exchange counter, as do post offices and building societies, *Arnott's* in Henry St and *Clery's* in O'Connell St. *American Express Travel Service* is at 116 Grafton St, T1800-709907, while *Thomas Cook* is at No 18 in the same street. **Credit cards** *American Express* T1800-626000. *Visa* T1800 558002. *Mastercard* T1800-557378

Post offices *O'Connell St Post Office*, Mon-Sat 0800-2000, Sun 1030-1800. Poste restante mail **Communications** should be addressed here. *Anne St South Post Office*, Mon-Fri 0900-1730, Sat 0900-1300. Post boxes are green with two slots – 'Dublin only' and 'All other places'. **Telephones** labelled cardphone or coinphone. Some take credit cards. **Internet** *Lazer Home Entertainment Video Library Internet Cafe*, 23, South Great Georges St, Dublin 2, 6790583. Sunday-Wednesday 1000-2200, Thursday-Saturday 1000-2400. IR£4.50 per hour. *Global Internet Cafe*, 8 Lower O'Connell St, Dublin 1, T8780295. Monday-Saturday, 1000-2300, Sunday 1300-2200. IR£1.25 for 15minutes. *Beta Cafe*, Arthouse Multimedia Centre, Curved St, Temple Bar, Dublin 2, T6056837. IR£1 for 15 minutes.

Alliance Française, I Kildare St, Dublin 2, T6761732. *British Council*, Newmount House, 22-4 **Cultural Centres** Mount St Lower, Dublin 2, T6764088. *Goethe Institute*, 37 Merrion Square, Dublin 2, T6611155. *Instituto Cervantes*, 58 Northumberland Rd, Dublin 4, T6682024.

National Rehabilitation Board, 25 Clyde Rd, Ballsbridge, Dublin 4. Also 44 North Gt George's St, **Disabled** T8747503. Wheelchair-accessible taxis can be booked in advance through *Eurocab/Dublin Black* **travellers** *Cab*, T01-8445844, and *National Radio Cabs*, T01-8365555. *Vantastic*, T01-8304926, require a day's notice but can provide a door-to-door service in their adapted vans (also, see page 41).

Australia: 6th floor, Fitzwilliam House, Wilton Terrace, Dublin 2, T6761517. *Canada*: 65-8 St **Embassies &** Stephen's Green, Dublin 2, T4781988. *Denmark*: 121 St Stephen's Green, Dublin 2 T4756404. **consulates** *France*: 36 Ailesbury Rd, Dublin 4,T2601666. *Germany*: 31 Trimleston Ave, Bakerstown, Co Dublin, T2693011. *Italy*: 63 Northumberland Rd, Dublin 4, T6601744. *Japan*: Nutley Building Merrion Centre, Nutley Lane, Dublin 4, T2694244. *Netherlands*: 160 Merrion Rd, Dublin 4, T2693444. *Norway*: 34 Molesworth St, Dublin 2, T6621800. *Portugal*: Knocksinna House, Foxrock, Dublin 18, T2894416. *Spain*: 17A Merlyn Park, Dublin 4, T2691640. *Sweden*: Sun Alliance House, Dawson St, Dublin 4, T6715822. *Switzerland*: 6 Ailesbury Rd, Dublin 4, T2692515. *UK*: 31 Merrion Rd, Dublin 4, T2053700. *USA*: 42 Elgin Rd, Dublin 4, T6688777.

Samaritans, T8727700. *Alcoholics Anonymous*, T4538998/6795967/6796555. *Drug Advisory &* **Help lines** *Treatment Centre*, T6771122. *Astma Line*, T1850-445464

Laundry Shop, 191 Parnell St, Dublin 1. *Launderette*, 110 Dorset St, Lower Dublin 1. *All American* **Laundries** *Launderette*, 40 South Great George's St.

Central Library, ILAC Centre, Henry St, Dublin 1. T8734333. *Dublin Corporation Library*, 138-142 **Libraries** Pearse St, Dublin 2, T6772764.

Dentists *Grafton Street Dental Practice*, Grafton St, Dublin 2, T6719200. *Molesworth Clinic*, 2 **Medical services** Molesworth Place, Dublin 2, T6615544. **Emergency services** dial 999 or 112. Accident and emergency departments at *Adelaide & Meath Hospital*, Tallaght, T4143500; *Beaumont Hospital*, Beaumont Rd, Dublin 9, T8092714. **Late night Pharmacies** *Corrigans*, 80 Malahide Rd, Dublin 3, T8338803. *O'Connell's Late Niight Pharmacies*, Grafton St, T6790467, Westmoreland St, T6778440, Henry St, T8731077. **Women's health** *Rotunda Hospital*, Parnell St, Dublin 1,

T8730700. Maternity hospital. *Well Woman Clinic*, 73 Lower Leeson St, T6610083. The 'morning-after pill' can be prescribed here.

Motoring *Automobile Association* (AA), 23 Suffolk Street, Dublin 2, T6779481. Breakdowns, T1800-677788. *RAC*, breakdowns, T1800-535005. *Alert Towing & Breakdown*, T8555220. *Auto Centre*, T4901600

Places of worship (only main churches listed) **Church of Ireland**: Christ Church Cathedral, Dublin 8, T6778099. **Lutheran**: Adelaide Rd, T6766548. **Methodist**: Abbey St, Dublin 1, T8742810. **Presbyterian**: Abbey Church, Dublin 1, T8742810. **Roman Catholic**: Pro-Cathedral, Marlborough St, Dublin 1.

Police Emergency telephone number for the garda (police), fire or ambulance is 999 or 112. Garda stations in the city centre are found at: Store St, Dublin 1, T8557761. Pearse St, Dublin 2, T6778141. Fitgibbon St, Dublin 1, T8363113. Garda Síochána Dublin metropolitan HQ, Harcourt Square, Dublin 2, T4755555.

Travel agencies *American Express* and *Thomas Cook* are in Grafton St (see 'Banks' above).

Useful addresses *Drugs Advisory and Treatment Centre*, Trinity Court, 30-31 Pearse St, T6771122. *Rape Crisis Centre*, 70 Leeson St Lower, T6614911/1800-7788888.

North of the city

The casino at Marino Not Dublin's equivalent to Monte Carlo, but an 18th century gentleman's retreat, the casino was commissioned by James Cauldfield, the Earl of Charlemont and built by Sir William Chambers. Work began in the late 1750s on this summerhouse in the grounds of Marino House, Charlemont's country estate. The estate was dispersed after the death of Cauldfield, whose extravagant tastes bankrupted him, and the casino was bought by the state in the 1930s in a state of dereliction. It is still under restoration, but is open to the public. It is a whimsical place, full of secret staircases, looking like a Greek temple from the south but in fact a 3-storey building with 16 rooms, the urns on the roof actually being chimney-pots while the hollow Ionic columns serve as house drainpipes. ■ *Marino, Dublin, T8331618. June to September, daily 1930-1830; October, daily 1000-1700; February to April and November, Sunday and Wednesday 1200-1600. Last admission 45 minutes before closing. Access by guided tour only. IR£2. Bus nos 20A, 20B, 27, 27A, 27B, 42, 42C from the city centre near Busáras.*

North Bull Island This island is relatively new territory, having been created since the building of the North Bull Wall in 1820 at the suggestion of Captain Bligh, of Mutiny on the Bounty fame. It is given over to the ubiquitous lumps and bumps of a golf course, but it also happens to be the winter residence of thousands of migratory birds, as well as lots of more common permanent creatures eking out a living dodging golf balls and motor mowers. There is an interpretive centre on the island (1000-1800 daily), which gives an account of its wildlife. ■ *Clontarf, from where North Bull Island can be accessed, is on the northern line of the DART.*

Howth

Colour map 4, grid A3 A quiet little town, popular with yacht-owners and home to a small fleet, Howth (rhymes with 'both') derives its name from the Viking word *hoved*, meaning head, or the name of the wife of an Irish chieftain, Étair (the Irish name is Beann (which means hill) Éadair – but no one knows for sure. It is a pleasant half-hour ride away from central Dublin on the DART. Once the main harbour of Dublin, where mail and visitors for Dublin arrived, Howth fell into disuse when the harbour silted up and by the middle of the 19th century Dun Laoghaire harbour had replaced it.

Getting there Howth is 15 km (9 miles) from central Dublin. It is the last stop on the DART, about 20 minutes from the city centre with hotels in Sutton, one stop before Howth, and also in Howth.

For visitors its finest point has to be the wonderful walks across Howth Head, but there are several other interesting places to visit. **Howth Castle** is not open

Dublin

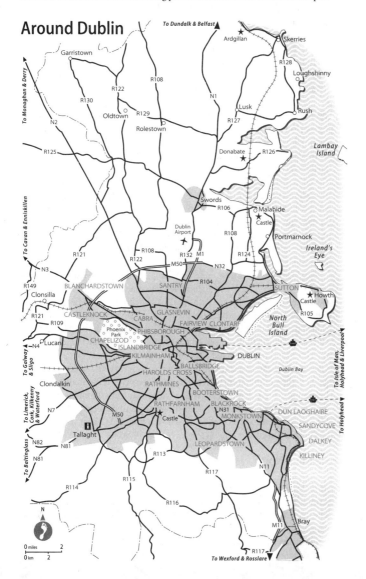

Around Dublin

to the public but its grounds are well worth a walk around, especially in May when the rhododendrons are blooming. The demesne has been owned by the same family, the St Lawrences, since 1177, passed down from father to son for 8 centuries. The castle wasn't built until 1564 and has been altered many times since then, the last renovations being organized by Sir Edwin Lutyens in the early 20th century. In 1575 Grace O'Malley visited the castle on her way home to Galway from visiting Queen Elizabeth in England and called at the castle for food and shelter in the tradition of Brehon law (see page 673). When she was refused entry she managed to kidnap a son of the family, holding him to ransom until the family agreed always to open their doors to strangers in the traditional way. The family are said still to keep a place laid in case she turns up again. Also in the grounds are an ancient dolmen and the ruins of the 16th century Corr Castle. The ruins of **St Mary's Abbey** are in the centre of the village. It was founded in 1042 by the Viking Sitric, founder of Christ Church. Most of the ruins are 15th century.

The National Transport Museum is basically a collection of vehicles, including the tram that ran up Howth Hill for the first 50 years of this century. The museum is just inside the gates to the castle. ■ *June to August, daily 1000-1800; August to June, weekends only 1400-1700. IR£1.50.*

A pleasant afternoon's **walk** can be had around the peninsula and across the hill of Howth. (Joyce fans should not miss this opportunity to visit the location of the climactic moment at the end of *Ulysses*, when Molly Bloom recalls in her semi-sleep her magic moment with Leopold Bloom.) From the DART station go directly across the road to a gap in the wall, which used to be the entrance to the tram station. Follow the steps and then the footpath uphill and behind some houses to a suburban street, Grace O'Malley Park. Turn right, follow the road a little way, still climbing the hill and then turn right between some houses, into a street called Balkil Park and through a fence into the open land of the hill. Head south and uphill across the open land, heading towards a mobile-phone transmitter aerial. From here there are excellent views of the peninsula.

Head downhill and west, following a line of white painted stones, to get a view of the golf course and then make your way through heather-covered slopes, but always keeping to pathways, to Carrickbrack Road. Turn right and follow the road for a few hundred metres until a sign appears on the seaward side of the road indicating a dangerous cliff edge. Follow the path towards the cliffs and you will find yourself on the cliff walk around Howth Head. Follow the cliff round to the left and a two-hour walk brings you back past amazing views of beaches and seabirds to the village, passing on your way footpaths that go up to the summit, from where there are more views. It was in the area at the beginning of this cliff walk that Erskine Childers landed a shipment of machine guns to help the nationalists in their struggle against the new Irish Free State. He was captured and executed by his erstwhile friends. His boat, *The Asgard*, is at Kilmainham goal.

Heading North

Malahide   *Mullach Íde* in Gaelic, this is a coastal town north of Howth and is pretty much a suburb of the city, although it retains some of its seaside village atmosphere. The main reason for visiting is Malahide Castle, set in its own demesne of 1,250 acres with the Fry Model Railway in the grounds, the Talbot Botanic Gardens beside it and a great children's playground.

The **castle** is a three-storey 12th-century fortified house open to the public and owned for almost 800 years by one family, the Talbots, with a brief interlude during Cromwell's invasion of Ireland. It was bought by Dublin County Council in 1975 and opened to the public. Many of the original furnishings and paintings of the family are on show. The castle was extended over the years and one addition is the 16th century Oak Room, with amazing carvings of events from the Old Testament pictured in oak on the walls. It still has its original medieval hall, the only one of its kind in Ireland. One sad legend associated with the house is that on the morning of the Battle of the Boyne, 14 first cousins of the Talbot clan had breakfast here and all died later that day on the battlefield. Beside the castle is a 14th-century abbey, roofless but containing a tomb thought to be that of Maud Plunkett, 'maid, wife and widow on one day', whose husband, Sir Walter Hussey, was killed on their wedding day by a raiding party. She later married Sir Richard Talbot. The west gable of the building holds a *sheela na gig* (see box on page 394). ■ *Malahide, Co Dublin: T8462184, April to October, Monday-Saturday 1000-1700, Sundays and public holidays 1100-1800; November to March, Monday-Friday 1000-1700, Saturday, Sunday and bank holidays 1400-1700. Restaurant, craft shop. IR£3. Bus No 42 from Beresford Place, Dundalk suburban rail from Connolly or Pearse Stations to Malahide.*

Children young and old will appreciate the Fry Model Railway, in an old corn store in the grounds of the castle. ■ *T8463779. April to September, Monday-Friday 1000-1800, Saturday 1000-1700, Sundays and public holidays 1400-1800; April and May closed Fridays; October to March, Saturday 1400-1700, Sundays and public holidays 1400-1700. IR£2.75.*

Also worth a peek in Malahide is St Doulagh's Church, the oldest church in Ireland in continuous use. Its eastern end is from the 12th century while the tower was added in the 15th century. The church stands on the main Malahide to Dublin road.

Newbridge House, Donabate

One stop on from Malahide on the Dundalk line is Donabate, worth the trip for Newbridge House, an 18th-century manor house built by Richard Castle for Charles Cobb, the Archbishop of Dublin, in 1737 and set in 350 acres of land. The original plasterwork is by Robert West and the rooms are full of original period furniture. Outside is a restored 19th-century courtyard, farm buildings, complete with pettable animals and a fantastic children's playground. ■ *Donabate, Co Dublin, T8436534, F8462537, April to September, Tuesday-Saturday 1000-1700, Sunday and public holidays 1400-1800; October to March, Saturday, Sunday and public holidays 1400-1700. Coffee shop, craft shop, organized tours. IR£2.85. Suburban rail, Bus No 33B from Eden Quay.*

Lusk Church & Heritage Centre

Lusk is an ancient settlement, which had a craft market as early as the eighth century. The church, which is the main reason to visit, has a huge ninth-century tower, eight storeys high, which makes it the highest tower in Ireland. The church is now Lusk Heritage Centre with an exhibition on medieval churches, including the medieval floor tiles found in the church during its renovation in 1976. The original church monuments are intact, including a 1575 table tomb with the figures of Sir Christopher Barnewell and his wife Marion Sharl resting on top, the faces worn but the details of their clothing in excellent condition. ■ *Lusk Heritage Centre, T8437683. Mid-June to mid-September, Friday only 1000-1700. Last admission 45 minutes before closing. IR£1. Bus 33 from Eden Quay (one hour).*

Dublin

Skerries Half ancient fishing village, half commuter town, Skerries (*Na Sceiri*) is said to be the place where St Patrick first set foot on Irish soil. The harbour is pretty and there is an abundance of wildlife, including seals. To the south there is a pleasant cliff walk as far as Loughshinny. For those who prefer a quiet life to the bustle of Dublin this would make an excellent base, although it must be remembered that the last train from Connolly to Skerries leaves at 2210. The village has a lively nightlife. Look out for *Shenannigans*, T8491708, which calls itself an entertainment emporium and provides accommodation.

Essentials

Sleeping **Howth** **L** *The Deer Park Hotel*, Howth, T8322624, F8392405, sales@deerpark. iol.ie Restaurant, swimming pool, golf complex, sauna, TV, tea and coffee making facilities. Set in a pleasant country environment with lots of facilities. **L** *Howth Lodge Hotel*, Howth, T8321010, F8322268. Restaurant. 10 minutes from the village, en suite rooms, some with sea view. Pool, leisure complex, TV, tea- and coffee-making facilities. **L** *Marine Hotel*, Sutton Cross, Dublin 13, T8322688, F8320442. Bustling hotel with good restaurant, *The Meridian*, heated indoor pool, nicely appointed rooms. 5-minute walk from DART. **L** *Sutton Castle Hotel*, Redrock, Sutton, T8322688, F8324476. Near to Howth, set in panoramic grounds close to the shore, *Red Rock Bistro* and carvery. **AL** *Bailey Court Hotel*, Main St, Howth, T8322691, F8323730. *Chervil's Bistro* serves carvery lunch and dinner, close to DART. **AL** *Red Bank Lodge Guesthouse and Restaurant*, 6-7 Church St, Skerries, T8491005, F8491598, redbank@tinet.ie Has an excellent reputation for its seafood. Dinner IR£25. **B** *Hazlewood*, Mrs Rosaleen Hobbs, 2, Thormanby Woods, Thormanby Road, Howth, Dublin 13, T/F8391391. B&B with en-suite rooms, car parking, evening meals. You could try the Rickard family, at *Geann na Smól*, Nashville Rd, T8322936, or Mrs Margaret Campbell, *Highfield*, Thormanby Rd, T8323936. Thormanby Rd and Nashville Rd in Howth have several *B&Bs*.

Eating **Howth** As for places to eat, Howth has a bustling night life and lots of good pubs to eat in as well as a few very good restaurants. *Adrian's*, 8 Abbey St, T8391696, is lively at weekends with its owner/chef doing very creative things with food. Dinner around IR£16. 1230-1400, 1800-2130. *Casa Pasta*, 12 Harbour Rd, T8393823, is very good value with lots of pasta dishes, but plenty more on offer as well as sea views. Dinner around IR£12. *The King Sitric*, East Pier, T8325235, is a fish restaurant with lots of recommendations to its name. Dinner IR£30. At the other end of the market is *Caffé Caira* at 1 East Pier, serving bags of fish and chips to a long queue of customers. Some seating available. There are several good pubs in Harbour Rd, notably *The Pier House* and *The Waterside Inn*. In Main St is *Ye Olde Abbey Tavern*, T8322006, which needs booking in advance at weekends. All have live music ranging from traditional to jazz.

Malahide *Duffy's Bar & Lounge* has traditional music every Thursday after 2100.

Skerries The *Mistral*, Harbour Rd, Skerries, serves seafood and great views, while *Joe May's*, Harbour Rd, Skerries, also serves seafood, with traditional music this time.

South of the city

Travelling southwards from Dublin, the DART follows the coastline as far as Bray, the first interesting stop being at Booterstown where the marsh, right beside the DART station, is home to some interesting birdlife. The next stop is Dun Laoghaire.

Dun Laoghaire

Dun Laoghaire is both a major seaport and a seaside town, with huge Victorian villas lining the seafront looking out at the great passenger ferries trawling their way in and out of the harbour. A fishing village until the middle years of the 18th century, Dun Laoghaire became Kingstown when the first pier was built. The Martello tower at Sandycove was built in the early years of the 19th century and then the two piers of the present harbour were constructed, beginning in 1817 and more or less completed in 1842. The port has never looked back, with the first car ferry making the journey to Holyhead in the early 1960s. At the town hall in Royal Marine Road you can pick up a series of leaflets outlining walks along the coast from Dun Laoghaire to Bray, which are full of historical interest.

Colour map 4, grid A3

From Dublin, the DART trains run on from Dun Laoghaire to Bray, on the border of County Wicklow. Bus Nos 7, 7A, and 8 connect Dun Laoghaire with the city centre while 45A links the city with Bray. For places north and west of Dublin you must return to the city by bus or the DART for a connection. **Getting there**

The **National Maritime Museum** is housed in the Mariner's Church in Haigh Terrace, with exhibits such as a captured longboat from the aborted French invasion at Bantry in 1796, a huge light from the Bailey Lighthouse at Howth and lots more. ■ *T2800969. May to September, daily 1300-1700. IR£1.50.*

Close to the museum in Moran Park and worth a look is a statue called **Christ the King**, which was bought in 1949 but kept in storage until modern Dun Laoghaire felt it was ready to see it. It is by Andrew O'Connor, intended as a memorial to all those who died in the First World War, and is really quite a remarkable piece of work.

Following along the coast, at Sandycove, beside the Joyce Tower, you come to the **Forty Foot Bathing Place**, originally for men only – its sign reads 'Gentlemen's Bathing Place', generally referred to as the 'Forty Foot,' as it is claimed that the name came from the 40th Regiment of Foot which was billeted beside the bathing place and not from the depth of the water. Here gentlemen bathed (and some still do) in the altogether. Legend says a notice pinned up at the Forty Foot Pool once said 'No dogs, no togs'. If you continue along the coast it will bring you to **Dalkey** with its restored Bullock Castle, Dalkey Hill with its tower on the summit and, further on, Killiney Hill with an obelisk erected as part of the famine relief programme.

Like Howth and Skerries, Dun Laoghaire is a nice place to get away from the hustle and bustle of Dublin, especially at weekends. There are good hotels, lots of B&Bs and a hostel to choose from. **L** *Royal Marine Hotel*, Marine Rd, T2801911, F2841600, ryan@indigo.ie By far the classiest hotel in town, with fine views of the incoming boats, an elegant restaurant and pretty landscaped gardens. The rooms are nicely appointed and good value for their size. **AL** *Kingston Hotel*, Adelaide St, T2801810, F2801237. Smaller, but also has pleasant gardens and a restaurant. **B** *Pierre*, Victoria Terr, T2800291, F2843322. Has some elegant rooms overlooking the sea, a pleasant restaurant and is quite famous for its jazz and traditional music in the bar. **B** *Sandycove Guesthouse*, Newtonsmith, Sandycove Seafront, T/F2841600. A little further along the coast, close to the DART and set on the seafront overlooking Dublin Bay. **B** *Mrs Anne Harkin*, 7 Claremont Villas, T/F2805346. B&B. **B** *Glenview House*, Mrs Mary Murphy, Rochestown Avenue, T/F2855043. B&B. **B** *Belmont*, Colette Di Felice, 3 Mulgrave Terrace, T/F2801422. B&B **D** *Old School House Hostel*, Eblana Avenue, has 23 private singles and doubles at IR£12–13.50 per person. **Sleeping**

Dublin

Eating Dun Laoghaire has its fair share of fast-food outlets, mostly along George St. Going upmarket there is *Brasserie Na Mara*, T2806767, close to the DART station and harbour where the innovative, fashionable, mostly seafood menu is good value and where dinner should be less than IR£20 per head. The *Powerscourt Room* in the *Royal Marine Hotel* is a very popular venue, set in a big old Victorian dining-room with huge bay windows looking out to the harbour. Service is pleasant and the atmosphere is relaxed. Fairly traditional menu, but the food is well cooked. Dinner less than IR£20. If it's Indian food you have a hankering for there is a good restaurant, *Lal Qila*, in Convent Rd, off George St Lower. Prices are very reasonable: dinner less than IR£15.

*'A land whose countryside would be
bright with cosy homesteads, whose fields and
villages would be joyous with the sounds of
industry, with the romping of sturdy children,
the contests of athletic youths and the laughter
of comely maidens, whose firesides would be
forums for the wisdom of old age.'*

Eamon de Valera (1882-1975):
Radio Broadcast, St Patrick's Day, 1943

Central North

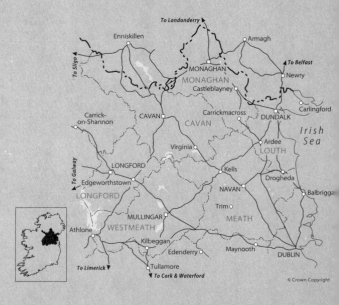

© Crown Copyright

This mixed set of counties has little in common other than the dubious distinction of being either places that visitors tend to pass through on their way to somewhere else, or counties with particular attractions, such as Newgrange or the Cooley peninsula. While this elides their separate histories and identities, it also gives the visitor a valuable chance to discover a part of Ireland for themselves without the preconditioned images and clichés of touristland.

★ *Try to find time for*

Gazing up at the beam-walled roof of the Newgrange passage grave

The Mourne Mountains from the Cooley peninsula

Early morning at Monasterboice

The kitchens at Tullynally Castle

Dinner at Castle Leslie in County Monaghan

County Meath

The rich soil of the Boyne valley that first attracted farmers in the Stone Age has now produced a fresh crop of prosperous farmers, who manage to make Meath's ancient past infinitely more interesting than anything the contemporary scene has to offer. Newgrange is unmissable and can be managed as a day trip from the capital or an excursion while travelling between Dublin and either Drogheda or Sligo. Both Slane and Trim, with modest but interesting sites in their vicinities, suggest themselves as possible bases for an overnight stay.

Newgrange and Knowth

Colour map 4, grid A2   The valley of the Boyne has a cluster of prehistoric tombs and two of them, Newgrange and Knowth, near to the village of Donore, constitute one of the major Stone Age sites in Europe. Along with the Pyramids and Mycenae, they are variations on the passage grave theme, but any profound historical connection between these sites is nebulous given that the Boyne tombs have been dated centuries earlier than those in the Nile valley.

Getting there   Donore is south of the River Boyne on the L21, and the Brú na Bóinne Centre is one mile to the west; signposted from Drogheda, off the N1, and from Slane, off the N2. *Bus Éireann* run a daily IR£7 return service between Dublin and Donore, via Drogheda, leaving the capital, Monday to Saturday, on the hour between 0900 and 1100 and then 1330, 1415 and 1500, and on Sunday at 1045, 1215 and 1415. The last bus back to Dublin is 1605, and 1525 on Sunday.

Newgrange   Newgrange (see page 692) has mythological overtones – the home of the *Tuatha de Danainn*, a subterranean race of supernatural beings dedicated to the goddess Danu – though it was only in 1699 that the central tomb was accidentally discovered. The 62-foot (19-metre) passageway from the entrance to the central cavern slopes upwards, so when light shines through it only reaches about half-way. The builders inserted a **roof box** in the roof above the entrance, so that when the sun rises on the shortest day of the year a pencil of light penetrates all the way to the central chamber. This only occurs around the winter solstice, and even then only for a maximum of 17 minutes in the morning: it is not possible for members of the public to experience this on the solstice itself, but the guided tour simulates the effect to give some idea of just how magical a moment this must have been. For the rest of the year, presumably, the massive carved stone that now rests outside blocked up the doorway.

The **geometric art motifs** that decorate the interior stones give credence to the idea that Newgrange was far more than just a burial place for some important ruling clan. Lozenge and zigzag designs, and especially the double and triple spiral patterns, have never been interpreted to everyone's satisfaction so your guess is as valid as most but what remains undisputed is the sense of awe associated with finely executed stonecarving chiselled by craftspeople over 5,000 years ago.

Standing in the central chamber the most spectacular sight is **the roof**: it is not regular corbelling, but each stone rests on the twin halves of stones underneath, and the whole construction slopes downwards away from the centre. The effect is dizzyingly angular when viewed from below, and, as a feat of engineering that has kept the chamber bone dry for millennia, there is little to match it in the ancient world.

Not as well known as Newgrange, Knowth continues to excite the archaeological world. The large central mound, which most unusually has two passage graves back to back, is surrounded by 18 smaller satellite tombs, each with its own grave. The central mound has yielded a number of surprises, the most remarkable being the twin chambers orientated to the east and west. They are built in two different styles and the eastern one, which has a cruciform chamber, is an astonishing 130 feet (40 metres) long. A wealth of decorated stones has been found in both chambers, almost as many as previously existed from all over passage graves in Ireland. Unlike Newgrange, the guided tour of Knowth does not bring visitors inside.

Knowth
Passage grave: neolithic burial chamber characterized by a circular mound reached via a straight, long passageway, both lined with stones.

Visits to Newgrange and Knowth must now begin at the **Brú na Bóinne Visitor Centre** at Donore, reached via Drogheda or Slane. A shuttle bus takes visitors to Newgrange and Knowth for guided tours, and be warned that in summer there are long delays due to the limited number of people that can enter Newgrange at one time. Try to arrive for opening time and still be prepared for a wait. ■ *Donore. T041-24488. June to mid-September, daily 0900-1900; May and mid to end of September, daily 0900-1830; March to April and October, daily 0930-1730; November to February, daily 0930-1700. IR£2 for Centre. IR£3 for Centre and Newgrange; IR£5 for Centre, Newgrange and Knowth. Dúchas site. Guided tours. Tearoom.*

Some 10 miles (15 kilometres) west of Drogheda, the small town of Slane has a certain Georgian charm, but as Slane Castle is still closed to the public since a disastrous fire nearly a decade ago there is little to do except admire the stone buildings and take a walk up the **Hill of Slane**. The hill is less than a mile above the village to the north and on a fine day, by climbing the steps of the always-open **tower** on the summit that was once part of a Franciscan friary, provides a vantage point for taking in the Boyne valley.

Slane

Less than a mile east of the village is the **Francis Ledwidge Museum** in the house where a poor peasant family brought up a family of eight children, including the poet Francis Ledwidge. A republican and trade unionist, he wrote feelingly in a Keatsian manner and yet went off to fight in France where he died in 1917. ■ *April to September, daily 0900-1300, 1400-1900; October to March, daily, closes 1630. IR£1.*

AL *Conyngham Arms Hotel*, T988444, where Francis Ledwidge supped an occasional pint, is convenient for bar food and a restaurant. For a B&B, there is no avoiding the ubiquitous bungalow. One within walking distance of Newgrange is **B** *Roselawn*, Newgrange, T24711. Also, a couple of miles south of Slane on the N2, **B** *Bondique House*, Cullen, Beauparc, T/F9824823, has rooms with and without private bathrooms.

Around Navan

An ancient and modern crossroads, Navan town today has little to distinguish it, although it suggests itself as a watering hole. The **tourist office** is at hand with local information, and banks, post office and pubs serving food are conveniently located around the shopping centre on Kennedy Street.

Phone code: 046
Colour map 4, grid A2

Athlumney Castle makes a good destination for an easy stroll out of town for a mile or so: head south over the bridge and follow the signs. A 15th-century four-storied tower stands next to a Tudor edifice with its mullioned windows intact. Legend has it that the owner of the place set it alight, rather than see it fall into the hands of the English. Keys to the place can be picked up at the nearby Loreto convent. ■ *Tourist office: Railway Street, T215181. Monday-Saturday 1000-1700, Sunday 1000-1300.*

County Meath

The main attractions around Navan are outside of town on the Dublin road and the chief attraction is the hill of Tara.

Tara What you see is not what you get, and it requires an act of imagination to empathize with the tremendous historical and mythological significance of Tara. What is basically a mound in a meadow is traditionally regarded as the seat of the high kings of Ireland. Whether any one ruler could have had influence over the whole of Ireland before the ninth century is doubtful, but there is no mistaking the symbolic clout accorded to the notion of a kingship of Tara. The origins and functioning of Tara are lost in the prehistory of late neolithic and Bronze Age times, but so entwined is the place with mythology that what you see today was in some sense the capital of ancient Ireland. The god Lug, the Zeus of the Irish pantheon, is associated with Tara, as are the ancient female fertility figures of Eithne and Medb. A seventh-century history of St Patrick relates how he provocatively lit a bonfire on the hill of Slane and was called to account by the king of Tara, whom he managed to convert in the process. The significance of Tara was not lost in the 1641 uprising, it also played a part in the 1798 insurrection, and in 1843 a million supporters of Daniel O'Connell apparently turned up here to hear him speak.

The **Visitor Centre** brings some of all this to life with a 20-minute audio-visual show, *Tara, Meeting Place of Heroes*, and a useful guided tour of the site that includes a chance to peer in at a passage grave dated 2000BCE, which yielded a treasure trove of artefacts. There is also the Rath of the Synods, which was vandalized by British Israelites in 1899, putative excavators searching for the biblical Ark of the Covenant. A few days before their visit some Roman coins were buried for them to find by supporters hoping to encourage their belief that Tara was a biblical site, but excavations in the 1950s revealed genuine Roman finds, indicative of trade with the Roman world of the early centuries CE. ■ *Navan, T25903. Mid-June to mid-September, daily 0930-1830; early May to mid-June and mid-September to October, daily 1000-1700. IR£1.50. Dúchas site. Coffee shop, T25534, near the car-park. Tara is eight miles (12 kilometres) south of Navan off the N3.*

Dunsany Castle From Tara it is a short hop to the village of Dunsany and its eponymous castle where the poet, Francis Ledwidge, found an honourable patron in Lord Dunsany (1878-1957), who introduced the poet's first collection of verse: 'I hope that not too many will be attracted to this book on account of the author being a peasant, lest he come to be praised by the how-interesting school.' He later went on to become a most strange writer in his own right. Shot in the face while attempting to help the British in the Easter Rising, Dunsany also played a part in supporting another local writer, Mary Lavin. Tours of the house, taking in a noted collection of art and assorted artefacts, are conducted but telephone ahead to reserve a place. ■ *T25198. July and August, Monday-Saturday 0900-1300. IR£3.*

While in the area, it is worth the short journey west of Dunsany to admire **Bective Abbey**, one of the earliest Cistercian abbeys in Ireland. Founded in 1147, precious little remains from that era and most of what you see today, including a fine cloister, was constructed in the 15th century.

Trim

Phone code: 046
Colour map 4, grid A2

Trim wouldn't be Trim without its splendid **castle** in the centre of town, which waited until 1995 before film people discovered its potential as a film set and brought in Mel Gibson to re-enact the Scots' assault on the perfidious English at York for the film *Braveheart*. The castle was built by the Norman de Lacy family in the early 13th century and, with the main tower having walls some 11 feet (three metres) thick, was built to withstand anything the Irish might hurl at them. A great curtain wall with D-shaped towers was constructed as a secondary line of defence, but in the English Civil War the castle was twice captured and left in disuse after the Cromwellians departed.

On the other side of the river to the castle stands **Talbot Castle**, an impressive manor house built by the viceroy of Ireland, Sir John Talbot, in 1415. It was built using part of an earlier Augustinian abbey but all that now remains of this is the **Yellow Steeple**, a tall bell tower that was badly damaged by Cromwell's army. Also here is the **Sheep Gate**, a surviving remnant of the 14th-century town walls.

A mile-long walk along the Dublin road from Trim Castle, crossing the river once again, brings you to the signposted ruins of **St Patrick's Church** and its cemetery. Points of interest are the medieval grave stones and the 16th-century tomb of a couple known as the jealous man and woman; the sword that lies between them giving rise to a story of marital discord! There is an assortment of other ruins in the area: contact the Tourist office for information. ■ *Mill Street, T37111*.

Next door to the Tourist office is the **Trim Visitor's Centre**, with an exhibition on the town's medieval history. ■ *T37227. Monday-Saturday 1000-1700. Sunday 1330-1700.*

A *Wellington Court Hotel*, Summerhill Rd, T31516, F36002. Trim's only hotel: a family run place with 18 rooms. **B** *Brogan's Guesthouse*, High St, T31237, brogangh@ iol.ie Has 14 well equipped rooms, private car-parking and a public bar. **B** *Tigh Cathain*, Longwood Rd, T31996, tigh_cathain@hotmail.com This Tudor-style house seems like a quieter place. **D** *Bridge House Holiday Hostel*, Bridge St, T31848, F31635. An IHH place next to the tourist office, open from June to August, and includes 2 private rooms for IR£12 per person. Bed rates include breakfast, and bikes can be hired. For food, take your pick from the pubs or try the *Wellington Court Hotel* for a restaurant meal.

Sleeping & eating

Kells and around

As it is situated on the N3 road between Dublin and Enniskillen, Kells only tends to be visited when travelling that route. Of course, if the famous Book of Kells was actually kept here then life would be very different. As it is, visitors need content themselves with some fine high crosses and a recent memorial to

Phone code: 046
Colour map 4, grid C1

County Meath

Trim Castle

Jim Connell, author of the socialist anthem *The Red Flag*, who was born here in 1852 and wrote the song on a 20-minute train ride from Charing Cross to Lewisham in London in 1889.

Sights The **Church of St Columba**, west of town, is where the monastic settlement stood that received the Book of Kells when it arrived here in 807. The nearby bell tower has a small display devoted to the book, and close to the neighbouring round tower there are three **high crosses** as well as the remains of a fourth. Outside the churchyard, take a left to go up the hill for **St Colmcille's House**, and if it's not open the key can be collected from the brown house, 1 Lower Church View, going up the hill. Not much is known about the building's history but is almost certainly linked to the monastic settlement and retains a sense of the ancient about it.

Walking Ask at the **tourist office** for directions for local walks in the **Loughcrew Mountains** or, for something more organized, contact *Kelltic Walking Tours* ■ *Tourist office: Headford Place, T49336. Kelltic Walking Tours: T40322, keltic@tinet.ie*

Sleeping **A** *Headford Arms Hotel*, T40063, F40587. A pleasantly run hotel in the centre of town: with food available daily until 2200 it makes a convenient resting place. **B** *Avalon*, 5 Headfort Park, T41536. Offers town-house accommodation in a cul-de-sac, and private parking. **D** *Kells Hostel*, T40100, F40680, hostels@iol.ie Part of *Monaghan's* pub on the Cavan road and includes a few private rooms for around IR£10 per person; camping is also possible.

Eating *Jacks Railway Bar & Restaurant*, Athboy Rd, serves food until 2100 daily but can attract coach parties. The *Round Tower* in Farrell St features Irish, Chinese and Thai food from 1500-2200 as well as lunch, and live music on Thursday and Saturday nights. Try the *Westway Bar* in Bective St for lunch.

County Louth

The name of Ireland's smallest county, Louth, doesn't quite trip off the tongue. But hold on a while, for the two main towns of Drogheda and Dundalk are intrinsically interesting and ideal bases for exploring the surrounding countryside. Drogheda, just north of Dublin, is perfect for taking in the Boyne valley and Dundalk is at last coming into its own as a jumping-off point for the Cooley peninsula and the county of Armagh.

Drogheda

Phone code: 041
Colour map 4, grid A2

Scruffy and unpretentious, Drogheda is in the process of re-inventing itself but hopefully it will take a long time before Dublin yuppyland and its new money lowers the tone of this historic and ancient town. The town was founded by the Vikings, then a medieval walled town of consequence, ethnically cleansed by Cromwell in the 17th century and ruled solidly thereafter by Protestants through prosperous times over the following two centuries. The **Drogheda Heritage Centre** has newly opened in the old Church of Ireland in Mary St. A fine example of the town walls can be seen in the grounds of the Centre and it was here that Oliver Cromwell breached the walls to enter the room.

From Wolfe Tone to Samba

When Wolfe Tone came to Drogheda in 1792 he described it as "a small town enclosing four broad streets, and a collection of miserable cottages within ancient walls".

Gaze down on the town from Millmount and you'll see his point, but come in July for the Samba Festival and the Latin rhythms tell you Drogheda has moved on.

Starting from the tourist office and bus station head east towards town and before the bridge turn right up Barrack St for the **Millmount Museum** housed in former barracks built for the British and occupied by anti-Treaty forces in the civil war. Drogheda was fiercely anti-Treaty and some of the artillery used to shell the Four Courts in Dublin was brought up here to shell the rebels. This is a lovely old museum, run by dedicated local people who on a quiet day will find time to explain the arcane iconography of the precious 18th-century guild banners on display. ■ *T9833097. Tuesday-Saturday 1000-1800, Sunday 1430-1700. IR£1.50. Separate admission charge for the Governor's House Exhibition. The Martello Tower at Millmount is now open to the public (same hours as the Museum).*

A walking tour

Back down to the bridge and a pause to admire eastwards the elegant viaduct that carries the Dublin to Belfast trains (original journey time was 17 hours), a superb example of Victorian engineering, with an Irish-designed 1920s, single-track steel girder in the centre replacing the original wrought iron.

Cross the bridge and up Shop Street, turning left into West Street, where the Bank of Ireland utilizes the 1770 Tholsel with its clock tower that chimes every 15 minutes. The building has style, unlike the Gothic enormity of **St Peter's Roman Catholic Church** in West Street, in your face on the right. The church is famous as the final resting place of **St Oliver Plunkett** – well, his head and assorted bits of bone at least – and you will also find the door of his cell from

County Louth

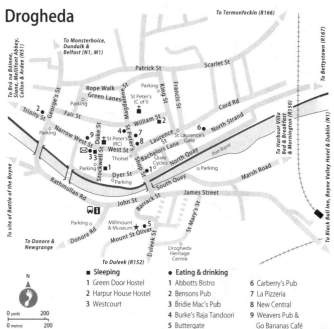

Drogheda

■ Sleeping	● Eating & drinking	
1 Green Door Hostel	1 Abbotts Bistro	6 Carberry's Pub
2 Harpur House Hostel	2 Bensons Pub	7 La Pizzeria
3 Westcourt	3 Bridie Mac's Pub	8 New Central
	4 Burke's Raja Tandoori	9 Weavers Pub &
	5 Buttergate	Go Bananas Café

☞ *The Curse of Cromwell?*

The 1640s was a particularly unstable decade in Ireland, beginning with the rising of 1641 and ending with the fall of Drogheda to Cromwell in 1649. Events were complicated by the outbreak of civil war in England, with royalists in Ireland on the defensive and the insurgents organizing themselves into the Confederate Catholics. A ceasefire was established but this broke down in 1646 and Cromwell arrived in August 1649 with an army of 20,000 men, a navy, and heavy artillery. On the 10th September his handwritten ultimatum was delivered to the governor of Drogheda, a royalist town, promising that an "effusion of blood may be prevented" if surrender was swift. There was to be no surrender, Cromwell's army breached a hole in the city's defensive walls and in the ensuing fighting some

3000 people lost their lives. At Millmount, a converted Viking fort, the leaders were cornered and slain and the town's governor, Aston, was seized upon, for rumour had it that his wooden leg was packed with gold and angry soldiers, finding the leg empty, used it to beat him to death.

In his Cromwell, An Honourable Enemy *(see page 63), Irish historian Tom Reilly argues that there is no primary evidence for the folk tradition of wholesale slaughter at Drogheda. He sees the siege as a military encounter between two English factions struggling for power where there was no more indiscriminate killing than the rules of war allowed for. The folk tradition of Cromwell's infamy arose later in accounts of the siege by people who never took part in it.*

Newgate prison in London, where he was held for eight months before being hung, drawn and quartered on 1st July 1681. Oliver Plunkett (1625-81) was a Catholic Archbishop who was arrested on suspicion of planning a French invasion. The case against him collapsed when witnesses, mostly fellow priests he had managed to antagonize, withdrew, but Plunkett was shipped off to London for a second trial. He was canonized in 1975.

By the church corner, turn right into Duke Street and right again into Fair Street, which leads across Peter Street into William Street where **St Peter's Church of Ireland** stands. Citizens fleeing Cromwell and seeking refuge here were burned to death in its former wooden steeple. There are interesting memorial tablets inside the church and though it may not always be open the graveyard has a fascinating cadaver tombstone dated 1520. The father of Swift's Vanessa, Bartholomew Van Homrigh, who came to Ireland from Amsterdam with William of Orange before the Revolution of 1687, is buried here – Van Homrigh acquired the Freedom of Dublin by 1685, member of Dublin Corporation, and then Alderman (1688). Walk down William Street, turn right into Palace Street and go to the end to stand before the 13th century **St Laurence's Gate**, an impressive reminder of the way most important Irish towns were walled and protected by barbican gates such as this.

Turning right into Laurence Street leads back to Shop Street and the Tholsel.

St Laurences' Gate,
Drogheda

The not-the-12th July Battle of the Boyne

The Battle of the Boyne in July 1690, the one that loyalists in the North are so intent on celebrating, took place at Oldbridge three miles upstream from Drogheda. The battle itself, which saw the retreat of the Jacobites, was not as decisive as the later encounter at Aughrim, but its fame developed from the personal presence of both William and James. The Orange Order, celebrating the event from the 1790s onwards and misunderstanding the workings of the 1752 calendar reform, incorrectly dated it as the 12th July when it fact it took place on 1st July.

To reach a point overlooking the site of the battle, take the N51 Slane Road for 1.8 miles (three kilometres), passing the Obelisk Bridge Information Centre, T9841644, at Oldbridge. This 1869 wrought-iron bridge had an obelisk beside it marking the battle, which was blown up in 1921. A stroll can also be taken along the Towney Hall Nature Walk, just further along.

L *Boyne Valley Hotel*, T9837737, F9839188. Almost a 30-min walk from town on the Dublin Rd, but if arriving on bus from Dublin ask to be dropped off outside. It is a comfortable country house with good facilities. **A-AL** *Westcourt Hotel*, Wall St, T9830965, F9830970. Where Michael Collins and Harry Boland stayed in September 1921 (then the *White House*), this is in the centre of town. *Neptune Beach Hotel*, Bettystown, T9827107, F9827412. Overlooking beach, restaurant, leisure centre. **B** *Boynehaven House*, T9836700. On the Dublin Rd near Bettystown, this is a top-notch B&B with a breakfast menu of 10 courses. **B** *River Boyne House*, Oldbridge, T9836180, is out of town at the Battle of the Boyne site: a quieter place to bed down for the night. **D** *Harper House Tourist Hostel*, William St, T9832736. A completely independent hostel. *The Green Door*, John St, is a new hostel about to open opposite the tourist office.

Sleeping
● *on map*
Price codes:
see inside front cover

The best place for a good meal is the *Buttergate*, Millmount Sq, T9834759, comprising bar area downstairs and spacious restaurant upstairs with window tables overlooking the town. Set meals between IR£14 and IR£20, plus à la carte, which includes a delicious game terrine for IR£4, fish and meat courses for IR£13, and a reasonable wine list. Open daily for lunch also. The next best place is *Abbots Bistro* on Shop St, T9845684, for lunch or dinner (closed Monday). Out of town at Bettystown, *Bacchus*, T982851, has been recommended for the quality of its cuisine. Tuesday-Saturday for dinner, Sunday lunch, and an early bird menu from 1800 for good value. Another good-value meal, 10 mins away by car, is the early bird menu at *The Triple House* in Termonfeckin (see page 167).

The Terrace Café in the *Westcourt Hotel* has a self-service system and choice of places to plonk down your tray of standard carbohydrate bulk for around IR£5. *Bridie Mac's* pub next door is a comfortable alternative for lunch, or cross the road to *Go Bananas* for a choice of sandwiches. *Weavers* next door is popular with locals, especially for Sunday lunch, serving beef, lamb and the like with chips. The cheapest pub lunches are available at *The Old Wall* pub and *The New Central*, 29 Peter St. Also on Peter St, *Burke's Restaurant* is a plain café open daily until 1800 (1600 on Sunday) with a breakfast menu, grills, omelettes, salads and sandwiches all between IR£2.50 and IR£9.50. *Raja Tandoori*, T9844990, close by, has a IR£5 lunch and at night you can bring your own bottle; open until gone midnight at weekends. Opposite, 38 Peter St, *La Pizzeria* has pizza and pasta dishes for around IR£6.

Eating
● *on map*
Price codes:
see inside front cover

When night falls, from a window table at the Buttergate in Drogheda, the Dublin to Belfast train chugging across the Victorian viaduct east of town is a stirring sight.

Carberry's on North Strand is the town's best-known traditional Irish music venue, sessions every Tuesday night and Sunday morning. *The New Central*, 29 Peter St, has music every night and an Irish night on Wednesday. Other good music venues are *McPhails* in Laurence St and *Bensons* in Trinity St.

Entertainment

County Louth

Festivals Samba Festival, T9833946, second week in July.

Shopping The *Millmount Craft Centre* is home to a variety of small shops and studios: Jewellery at *Elaine Hanrahan*, hand-painted silks and fabrics at *Mel Bradley* and *Pauline Holt*, ceramics sculptured without a wheel from *Maureen Finn* and decorative glass from *William Healy*.

Transport **Bicycle hire** from IR£5-7 a day, from *Quay Cycles*, 11a North Quay, T9834526, and *Irish Cycle Hire*, Workspace, Mayoralty, T9841067. **Bus** the station, T9835023, is on Donore Rd south of the river and there are a number of daily connections with Dublin, Dundalk and Belfast as well as services to Athlone, Downpatrick, Galway, Kells, Mullingar, Navan, Newgrange, Newry, and Slane. **Taxis** from T9838439, T9832211, T9837082, T9832244 and T9822666. **Train** the station is east of town, also south of the river, off the Dublin Rd, T988749. Drogheda is on the Dublin-Belfast line and there are at least 7 trains a day in either direction and 4 on Sunday.

Directory Banks, *AIB*, *Ulster Bank*, *TSB* and others are found in West St. **Tourist office** is at the bus station on Donore Rd, T9837070, all year, Mon-Sat, 0900-1730. Sun, 1145-1700, Apr-Nov. There is also one at Millmount, T9845684, Mon-Fri, 1000-1300 and 1400-1700. **Walking tours** every Tue-Sat, IR£1.50, depart from the Donore Rd tourist office at 1020, covering the south side of town, and 1420 for the north side.

Around Drogheda

Drogheda makes a great base for visiting Boyne valley sights such as Newgrange and these are covered in the Meath chapter beginning on page 158. There are other nearby sights within the county of Louth, which can easily be taken in on day trips from Drogheda by bicycle or car.

Mellifont Abbey The first Cistercian abbey in Ireland was founded five miles (eight kilometres) north of Drogheda in 1142 at the behest of St Malachy of Armagh as part of his drive to reform the laid-back monastic life of Irish monks. Mellifont, with hundreds of resident monks, came to preside over dozens of other Cistercian abbeys across the country until they were all suppressed by Henry VIII in 1539. The place was converted into a private mansion and gave refuge to Hugh O'Neill who surrendered here in 1603 after his defeat at Kinsale.

Like the ruins of a Greek temple, there is not a lot to see on the site but with the help of the free ground plan it is possible to trace out the buildings from the excavated foundations. The substantial remains of a 13th-century **lavabo**, an octagonal washing house for the monks, help evoke the architectural elegance that the French brought to monastic design.

It is easy to get misty-eyed imagining pacifist monks tending beehives and chanting dulcet tones about the place, but history presents a less flattering picture. Irish monks affiliated to Mellifont did not take kindly to spot checks by the order; not untypical was a monastery in county Limerick, which barred its doors, laid an ambush and attacked the visitors. It wasn't just the Cistercians who took to fisticuffs; in-fighting by Franciscan monks led to a pitched battle in 1291 with several fatalities. ■ *Tullyallen, T9826459. Mid-June to mid-September, daily, 0930-1830; May to mid-June and mid-September to October, daily, 1000-1700. IR£1.50. Dúchas site. One mile (1.5 kilometres) off the main Drogheda to Collon road. No bus service; car, taxi or bicycle from Drogheda.*

Monasterboice is an old Irish monastery founded by St Buite in the sixth cen- **Monasterboice**
tury, the kind of place that the Cistercians of Mellifont were designed to eclipse. *Colour map 1, grid C5*
Nothing remains of the monastery but there is an elegant **round tower** and one
of the most elaborately decorated **high crosses** to be seen anywhere in Ireland.

Getting there Take the signposted slip road off the N1 at the *Monasterboice Inn* 7
miles (10 km) north of Drogheda. If travelling by bus between Drogheda and Dundalk,
it is usually possible to ask to be dropped off by the pub and still use the ticket to
resume the journey by hailing down a later bus on the same route.

There are two crosses to admire and the best is the first one that you come to on
entering the churchyard: **Muiredach's Cross**, dating from the 10th century. It
is astonishing to find such priceless art plonked here in a quiet countryside setting. On the east side, there are two animals on the base, with the panel above
showing Adam and Eve on the left and Cain and Abel on the right. Above this
there are scenes from the life of David, a panel showing Moses striking a rock
for water, and then a panel of the Adoration of the Magi. Below the central
cross depicting Christ in Majesty there is a graphic scene of St Michael weighing a soul on scales with the devil pulling for all his worth from below. The
scene at the very top is hard to decipher.

The west side has an inscription at the bottom with cats, then a panel showing the arrest of Christ, a panel above depicting the doubting Thomas and then
a scene with the Apostles. The central cross, showing the Crucifixion, is sur-
mounted by a biblical scene featuring Moses.

The other cross, the **West Cross**, has faded badly but there is a notice board
explaining the content of its panels. The round tower is a fine example of its
type but is closed to the public.

Not-so-ancient tombstones fill the churchyard and one, on the east side of
the crumbling old church near Muiredach's Cross, erected by Thomas Cregan
to members of his family is, literally, monumental proof of the Irish diaspora.

The *Monasterboice Inn*, owned by a controversial ex-Minister of Defence in
a 1970s government, serves the same lunch food in the lounge and bar (where
it costs IR£1 less) and there is also an evening menu.

The main N1 road is the speediest way to travel between Drogheda and **Drogheda to**
Dundalk, but apart from accessing Monasterboice along the way the journey is **Dundalk**
purely functional. An inland route is possible via Collon and Mellifont Abbey
and, midway to Dundalk, the rural town of **Ardee** offers itself as a tranquil
backwater for anyone with a lazy itinerary wishing to take in this little-visited
corner of Ireland. There are a couple of crumbling castles, nature walks in
Ardee bog, fishing and other activity possibilities, and a smattering of places to
eat and stay. No tourist office, but the town library has some local information.
B *Setanta*, 7 Castle St, T6853319, setanta@destination-ireland.com offers
B&B in a comfortable, centrally located Georgian town house. For a touch of
luxury **AL** *Red House*, T/F6853523, is a fine country house with pool and tennis court. *The Railway Bar*, Main St, is an attractive, old-style pub with a restaurant at the back serving good food.

If time allows, take the coastal road via Baltray, with its famous golf course,
T9822329, and refreshments at the nearby *The 19th Hole* pub. There is also
lovely **Termonfeckin** with its old castle (key available from neighbouring
bungalow), the pretty good *At An Grianan* garden centre, T9322158, and fine
food at *The Triple House*, T9322616, a converted 200-year-old farmhouse, or,
less expensively, the *Waterside Inn* pub. Follow the coastal road north to
Clogherhead and a superb beach – one of Ireland's least-known safe and

County Louth

sandy beaches – that stretches up to Port and looks across to the Sellafield nuclear plant in England. From Port the road travels scenically inland to reach the coast again at **Annagassan**, which also has a huge, safe, beach, and then it is just a short hop to **Castlebellingham**, where pub and restaurant food and bedrooms await in **AL** *Bellingham Castle Hotel*, T9372176, F9372766.

Dundalk

Phone code: 042
Colour map 1, grid C5

Dundalk is a lively, underestimated town, well worth considering as a base for exploring south Armagh and Monaghan. Once tagged as a border town of ill-repute, the town is justifiably fed up with tired clichés from the past, and for visitors who appreciate a town unsullied by mass tourism smart Dundalk is a place to see and savour.

Walking tour Starting outside the **tourist office** on Jocelyn Street, the **County Museum** is next door in a restored 18th-century warehouse and houses two new floors, one devoted to archaeology and early history and the other to Norman and medieval history. ■ *T9327056. Tuesday-Saturday, 1030-1730, Sunday 1400-1800. IR£2.*

Walk down Jocelyn Street, past the tourist office, to the road junction; don't turn directly right into Castle Street but take the right fork along Roden Place,

County Louth

Dundalk

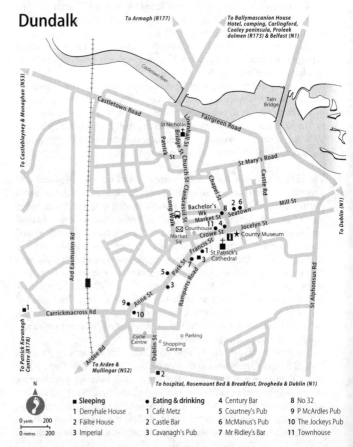

To Armagh (R177)

To Ballymascanion House Hotel, camping, Carlingford, Cooley peninsula, Proleek dolmen (R173) & Belfast (N1)

Castletown River

Tain Bridge

To Castleblayney & Monaghan (N53)

Castletown Road

Fairgreen Road

St Nicholas

Linenhall St
Bridge St
Patrick St
Church St
Clanbrassil St
St Mary's Road
Castle Rd
Mill St
Chapel St

Long Walk

Bachelor's Wk
Market St
Courthouse
Market Sq
Crowe St
Francis St
Seatown
Jocelyn St
County Museum
St Patrick's Cathedral

To Dublin (N1)

Ard Easmuinn Rd

Park St
Rampants Road
Anne St
Carrickmacross Rd

St Alphonsus Rd

To Patrick Kavanagh Centre (R178)

Cycle Centre
Dublin St
Parking
Shopping Centre

To Ardee & Mullingar (N52)
Ardee Rd

To hospital, Rosemount Bed & Breakfast, Drogheda & Dublin (N1)

N

| 0 yards | 200 |
| 0 metres | 200 |

■ **Sleeping**	● **Eating & drinking**	4 Century Bar	8 No 32
1 Derryhale House	1 Café Metz	5 Courtney's Pub	9 P McArdles Pub
2 Fáilte House	2 Castle Bar	6 McManus's Pub	10 The Jockeys Pub
3 Imperial	3 Cavanagh's Pub	7 Mr Ridley's Bar	11 Townhouse

pausing before you do so to admire the art nouveau *Century Pub* on the corner. Built to celebrate the beginning of the twentieth century, original features of its design are retained externally and inside there are more features, such as the fireplace, to admire over a morning drink. Crowe Street leads past the Greek-style **Courthouse**, one of the finest examples of a 19th-century courthouse in Ireland, on the corner with Clanbrassil Street. Doric columns cut from white Portland stone and the granite ashlar blocks of the stern flanking walls of this still-functioning courthouse proclaim a Spartan rather than Athenian sense of justice.

Go up Clanbrassil Street, passing the superb example of Victorian commercial architecture at No 70, to where **St Nicholas' Church** stands on the right just past Yorke Street. A mishmash of architectural styles, the churchyard has the grave of Agnes Galt, sister of the poet Robert Burns, who lived just outside of town for nearly 20 years. Continue along Yorke Street and turn right into Chapel Street to return to the *Century Bar*.

AL *Ballymascanlon House Hotel*, T9371124, F9371598. Out of town on the road to the Cooley peninsula, this is a grand Victorian edifice brought up to date with top-class sports facilities, but retaining an historical link with the Proleek Dolmen from around 3000BCE in its grounds. Recommended. **AL-A** *Derryhale House Hotel*, Carrickmacross Rd, T9335471, F9335471, info@minotel.iol.ie A listed Victorian building within walking distance of town, comfortable and friendly. **B** *Fáilte House*, Dublin Rd, T9335152, reliable B&B, on the corner with Long Ave. **B** *Rosemount*, Dublin Rd, T9335878. South of town, this is generally regarded as one of the best B&B establishments in the area.

Sleeping
■ *on map*
Price codes:
see inside front cover

Camping *Gyles Quay*, T9376262, is a well-provided caravan and mobile home site but has space for 10 tent pitches between April and September. Situated 11 miles (16 km) west of town on the Cooley peninsula.

For IR£22 a degree of elegance accompanies a set dinner at *Ballymascanlon House Hotel's* restaurant, with an unpretentious but responsible wine list based around grape varieties. Both the bar food and the restaurant at the convivial *Derryhale Hotel* on Carrickmacross Rd are reasonably priced, and food from the bar menu can also be enjoyed sitting in the period reception area. Easy to find, opposite St Patrick's Cathedral, the cosy *Townhouse*, T9329898, in a Georgian building with original features, has a four-course Thai set meal for IR£16.50 as well as à la carte such as Thai vegetarian for IR£8, chilli chicken for IR£9 and steaks for IR£15. The trendy *Café Metz*, Francis St, opens for breakfast, IR£7 lunch, and dinner in the IR£15-20 bracket; drop in for a coffee and check out the menu. The retro-style *No 32*, 32 Chapel St, T933113, serves substantial lunches and a varied menu with dishes IR£8-15, such as leek sausages, pork and cider, and decent vegetarian choices. For an excellent carvery head for *The Jockeys*, 47 Anne St, or try pleasant *Courtney's* in Patrick St for light food.

Eating
● *on map*
Price codes:
see inside front cover

Traditional Irish music every Friday at *The Jockeys*, 47 Anne St. On a Thursday try *The Castle Bar* aka *Corbetts*, Seatown, and on Monday and Friday nights music starts at 2100 in *McManus's*, Seatown, with delightful old-style snugs to settle into. For a quieter atmosphere, *P McArdles*, Anne St, attracts a more purist crowd of performers and audience on the first and third Thursday of each month. *Cavanaghs*, Park St, is a big new pub with sessions every Tuesday night. On a Tuesday head out of town for a couple of miles on the Dublin Rd and enjoy traditional music at *Sextons's* pub. Check out a newly opened pub on the Quay, *The Spirit Stone*, T9352697. Very atmospheric, no kirsch, live bands every Friday night. Music of a non-traditional kind comes alive in the *Terrace Bar* of the Ballymascalon Hotel on Saturday night and there is also a live band in the ballroom. Weekend discos in the *Imperial Hotel* and *Mr Ridleys*, both in Park St.

Pubs & music

County Louth

Transport **Bicycle** *Cycle Centre*, 44 Dublin St, T9337159. Bike hire. **Buses** station: Longwalk, T9334075. Services to Armagh, Belfast, Carlingford, Drogheda, Dublin, Enniskillen, Galway, Mullingar, Newry and Sligo. **Taxis** *Classic Cabs*, T9336000; *Top Rank*, T9326555; *Whiteline*, T9326999. **Train** station: Carrick Rd, T9335521. Dundalk is on the Dublin to Belfast line; at least 7 trains a day in either direction, and 4 on Sunday.

Directory **Banks** Clanbrassil St and Park St. **Bureaux de change**: there is a money exchange desk (pounds/punts/dollars only) in the Dundalk Shopping Centre near the bus station. **Communications** Post Office: Clanbrassil St. **Tourist office** Jocelyn St, T9335484. May-Sep, Mon-Sat 0900-1800; Oct-Apr, Mon-Fri, 0930-1730. **Walking tours** history-based, conducted by Hugh Smyth, T9328061, once a week during the evening. Also, self-guided walking brochure from the tourist office.

Cooley Peninsula

Phone code: 042
Colour map 2,
grid B6

Nestled between Dundalk Bay and Carlingford Lough (a true fjord), the Cooley peninsula and the view across to the Mourne Mountains never looks better than on a soft day when a gentle mist shrouds the land. The area's association with a rich vein of Irish mythology then seeps through the landscape evoking the tales of Cú Chulainn who, in just one of his adventures, had to cope with the magic of Morrígan in the triple guise of a red-eared heifer, a she-wolf and then a black eel. More down to earth in every sense of the word is Carlingford, a village that retains its medieval heritage to a remarkable degree yet risks voluntary mutation into a prettified, Kinsale-like consumer den.

Walking in the steps of Cú Chulainn

With a copy of Kinsella's translation of *The Táin* and Ordnance Survey sheet 29 in the Discovery Series a day or a holiday could be spent walking the hills between Carlingford and Omeath. The Táin Trail, a 25-mile (40-kilometre) waymarked walking route, is one possibility (though restricted to asphalt too much of the time) and the tourist office in Carlingford sells *The Táin Way Map Guide*, IR£2.50, with a 1:50,000 scale map. *Rambles*, similarly priced, is a booklet with simple maps that briefly describes nearly a dozen walks that all begin from Carlingford and last from one to six hours. With just the OS map you can devise your own route: start, for example, on the Táin Trail, and head off for the **Windy Gap**, *Bernas Bo Ulad* in the saga, and the setting for a much later love tragedy featuring the tragic death of a Spanish woman who is brought here after being deceived into thinking she has a rich land to inhabit.

A recommended eight-mile (12-kilometre) walk (OS map essential) is a circular route from Ravensdale up the Black Mountain to Clermont Cairn (1675 feet; 510 metres), along the Táin Trail and through Ravensdale Forest to the R174 road. Between May and August a flower guidebook would be useful.

Medieval Carlingford

What makes Carlingford unique is that this medieval town remained largely unchanged throughout the 1960s and 70s, when the rest of Ireland was reinventing and repackaging itself for Nostalgia Inc. It still has the feel of an unmolested little corner of Ireland and there are marvellous medieval remains: the **Mint** in Tholsel Street, with its machicolated and carved limestone windows, **King John's Castle** by the lough, and the Tholsel, a surviving gate. In the **Holy Trinity Heritage Centre**, a mural, video and exhibitions tell the history. ■ *Churchyard Road, T9373454. Mid-March to September, daily 0930-1700.*

The Cattle Raid of Cooley

One of the most ancient tales in Europe's oral tradition, the Táin Bó Cuailnge (Cattle Raid of Cooley) received a written form in the eighth century. It tells of Medb, Queen of Connaught in the west, and her attempt to steal a great bull from the Ulstermen on the Cooley peninsula to rival her husband's fine beast. Only the Homeric Cú Chulainn is free of a debilitating curse and able to mount resistance and the saga recounts in fantastic manner his superhuman exploits and the final duel between the two bulls. The best modern translation of this Celtic saga, complete with a map, is by Thomas Kinsella, The Táin (1969).

A *Beaufort House*, Ghan Rd, Carlingford, T9373879, F9373878. By the water's edge, this guesthouse has rooms with views and runs a seaschool. **A** *Granvue House* Omeath, T9375109, F9375415. A smartly run guesthouse on the shore charging IR£24 per person. **A** *McKevitt's Village Hotel*, Market Sq, Carlingford, T9373116, F9373144. A welcoming place but busy in the summer. **B** *Murphy's*, 9 Dundalk St, Carlingford, T9373735. In the centre of the village. **C-D** *Tain Holiday Village*, Ballyroonan, Omeath, T9375385, F9375417. Just south of the village on the Carlingford Rd, this has great facilities for children and is worth considering if beds are tight. **D** *Carlingford Adventure Centre & Holiday Hostel*, Tholsel St, Carlingford, T9373100, F9373651. An IHH place open from February to November, which includes 1 private room for IR£21.

Sleeping
Carlingford can get very busy, but accommodation is also available at Omeath, which is just up the main road.

The Oystercatcher Bistro, T9373922, is opposite *McKevitt's Hotel* and is keen on seafood. Oysters cooked half a dozen different ways for IR£6.50, or black pudding mousse for a startling change, IR£5. Fish and meat dishes are IR£11-13. *Magee's Bistro*, T9373751, has pizza for starters, chicken fajitas and Creole-style meat dishes.

The long-standing *Jordans*, T9373223, has a 'bistro dinner' for IR£23.50 that starts with stuffed squid with Thai dressing and a choice of meat, fish and one game dish. Also worth checking is the new *Ghan House*, T9373682, whose Sunday brunch has been well spoken of, and the *Kingfisher Bistro*, T9373716, with dishes such as prawn chow mein for IR£12 and Thai-style pork for IR£11.

One place that should not be missed is *Georgina's*, a little walk up Castle Hill, T9373346, a modest little teashop dishing up superb open and regular sandwiches for IR£2.75 and IR£1.60, perfect cakes such as cream gâteaux or cheesecake for IR£1.60, and a takeaway service. *O'Hare's Pub* does oysters and Guinness.

Eating
Everywhere's a bistro in Carlingford and many of them only open for dinner and close on Monday.

The pubs are nothing to write home about but P J O'Hare's, aka **the Anchor Bar**, T9373106, has the old-style grocery/bar division and traditional music on Monday and Saturday nights. For a quiet evening, head out to *Lily Finnegan's Pub* at Whitestown, a couple of miles outside Carlingford, on the Dundalk Rd. Go as far as The Cooley Inn, take a right, pass the church and go through the village. If you hit the beach, you've gone too far.

Pubs & music

Tholsel Crafts, *Irish Secrets*, and *Memories*, with a little café open daily from 1100 to 1800, are three little craft shops squeezed into Tholsel St. *Old Quay Antiques* is next to the tourist office while *Village Antiques* is next to *McKevitt's Hotel*. *Comtemporary Crafts Gallery*, D'arcy McGee Grainstore, houses the best in locally-produced quality crafts.

Shopping

Adventure sports Land and water based activities, bookable through *East Coast Adventure*, T/F9373118. **Sailing** courses and yacht chartering through the *Carlingford Yacht Charter & Seaschool*, T93738789, F9373878. *Deep Sea Angling*, Peader Elmore, T9373239.

Sport

County Louth

Transport **Buses** *Bus Éireann* runs a service, Monday to Saturday, between Dundalk and Newry via Carlingford five times a day. On Sunday, mid-June to September, a service runs once, one way, from Newry to Dundalk via Carlingford.

Directory **Cookery school** *Ghan House*, Carlingford, T/F9373862, ghanhouse@tinet.ie Includes accommodation if necessary. **Tourist office** T9373888, in the middle of the village. Daily 0930-1700.

County Monaghan

Monaghan's characteristic drumlins, hills formed by the retreating Ice Age, stretch from Donegal to Strangford Lough and formed a natural barrier that helped define Ulster from prehistoric times onwards. The main town, bearing the same name as the county, is where most visitors pause and it makes an obvious base for sampling the surrounding countryside. The political border is best forgotten, for in terms of history, culture and geography the county should be explored and enjoyed along with its Ulster neighbours of Fermanagh and Armagh.

Ins & outs Five *Bus Éireann* buses run daily between Dublin and Monaghan via Slane. The routes to Letterkenny and Derry, 5 a day and 2 on Sunday, also stop in Slane, Carrickmacross and Omagh. Three times a day, and twice on Sunday, the Dublin– Dungannon – Coleraine – Portrush service stops in Slane and Monaghan.

The daily Belfast to Galway service connects Monaghan with these towns as well as Armagh, Athlone, Cavan, Clones, Enniskillen, Longford, Roscommon, and Sligo. The Sligo to Dundalk and Dundalk to Cavan routes both come through Monaghan. There is no bus link with Glaslough, but for Iniskeen a local service between Dundalk and Cavan, 4 times a day, Monday to Saturday, stops here before going on to Carrickmacross.

Monaghan town

Phone code: 047
Colour map 1, grid C4

No major sights or sites, but a town to walk around, admiring the Victorian civic edifices that range from an elaborate drinking fountain to a distinguished and very churchified bank building built on a curve in Church Square, and appreciate as a splinter of Ulster divorced from its natural context. 'Men not prone to emotion shed tears', relates a historian, when it was learnt that Monaghan, Cavan and Donegal would be severed from the six counties making up Northern Ireland.

The **Monaghan County Museum** is a useful place to learn something about where you are. Exhibitions start with prehistory, include a rare 15th-century bronze cross, and continue up to the present. ■ *Tuesday-Saturday, 1100-1300 and 1400-1700. Free.*

Sleeping &
eating
A *Lakeside Hotel*, North Rd, T83599. Is indeed by a lake and has 10 rooms and a restaurant. **B** *Ashleigh House*, 37 Dublin St, T81227. Centrally located, has 12 rooms with and without bathrooms. A short walk around the town centre will throw up a few places to eat inexpensively and for a better evening meal, around IR£15, try the Victorian-styled *Andy's*, T82277, opposite the tourist office in Market St or the *Hillgrove Hotel*, Old Armagh Rd, T81288. *The Squealing Pig Bar* at the Diamond has a restaurant serving American-style food.

Directory **Tourist office** Market St, T81122. Jul and Aug, Mon-Sat 0900-1800 and Sun 1000-1400; Mar-Jun and Sep-Dec, Mon-Fri 0900-1300 and 1400-1700, Sat 0900-1300.

Hypocrites

' "Hypocrites, humbug", the priest went on, "coming here Sunday after Sunday – blindfolding the devil in the dark as the saying goes. And the headquarters of all this rascality is a townland called Drumnay." The congregation smiled. Tarry Flynn stooped his head and smiled too, although he was a native of that terrible townland. The calf-dealer at the door cocked his ear more acutely; he too was interested in his townland and pleased when its evil deeds got the air.'

Patrick Kavanagh, Tarry Flynn (1948).

Around Monaghan town and county

Places of interest are scattered about the county like drumlins and your own transport is pretty essential. Glaslough is six miles (nine kilometres) northeast of Monaghan town, Clones is 12 miles (19 kilometres) to the southwest, while Carrickmacross and Iniskeen are tucked away in the east near Dundalk.

Glaslough The pre-Plantation ruling family in Monaghan were the MacMahons, and after the death of Ross MacMahon in 1589 the English partitioned the land amongst members of his family in a classic divide-and-rule ploy designed to extend England's control. Plantation properly got under way the following century and there is no better expression of Protestant hegemony, in what is now the Republic, than in the earnest, saturnine soberness of Glaslough's stone cottages. Whether staying a night or not, try to visit the baroque **LL** *Castle Leslie*, three miles out on the L46 road towards Ballyhaise, T88109, F88256. Dour, Scottish Baronial castles don't come any quirkier than this, and both in the architecture and antiques there is much to admire. Dean and satirist Jonathan Swift stayed here and wrote of the library with its 'rows of books upon shelves, written by Leslies all about themselves'. Dinner, IR£25, is served at 2000 (24 hours notice required) by Victorian-dressed waitresses. **B** *Pillar House Hotel*, near the entrance to the castle, T88125, charges IR£18 per person for bed and breakfast.

Clones The railway station at Clones was the scene of a shoot-out between constables and republicans early in 1922, just after the Treaty was signed, and sparked sectarian attacks by loyalists in Belfast that saw 44 dead. Convivial Clones (pronounced *clo-nez*) today carries no trace of such discord and a rich Protestant legacy is to be seen in the centrally located **St Tiernach's Church**. What remains of St Tiernach's monastery can be seen in Abbey Street near a damaged round tower. More satisfaction may be gained by deciphering the fine **high cross**, which stands in the Diamond.

Some three miles (five kilometres) south of Clones on the Ballyhaise Road, **Hilton Park** has been replanted to reflect the original 18th-century formal garden and **L** accommodation is also available here. ■ *T56007. May to September, daily 1400-1800, IR£2.50.*

Sleeping and eating **B** *Lennard Arms Hotel*, The Diamond, T51350. A modest hotel but proud to portray photographs of the town's most famous son, Barry McGuigan, world featherweight boxing champion. **B** *Creighton Arms*, Fermanagh St, T51055. A couple of pounds more. While both hotels serve food it is worth first checking out *Cúil Darrach* at The Diamond or *The Round Tower Bar* on Cara St.

Transport Bicycles can be hired from *Ulster Canal Stores* on Cara St.

Carrickmacross A one-street town famous for its hand-made lace industry, established in the early 19th century, still surviving and with items for sale in the town centre. The Catholic church has two Harry Clarke windows and for country walks the **Dún a Rí Forest Park** is a couple of miles away on the R179 Kingscourt Road.

To the east, the village of **Iniskeen** celebrates being the birthplace of Patrick Kavanagh (1904-67), Ireland's best poet after Yeats and Heaney, and author of the great *Tarry Flynn*, but hardly known outside the country. The Patrick Kavanagh Centre also has material on local history and a set of paintings illustrating the poet's greatest epic, *The Great Hunger*. ■ *T/F78560. All year, Monday-Friday 1100-1700; June to September, also Sunday and Saturday 1400-1800. IR£1.50. Patrick Kavanagh Weekend, annually, last weekend in November.*

County Cavan

A sister county to Monaghan, historically and geographically, Cavan is more likely to be visited as it is on the main route between Dublin and Donegal. Until the plantations of the early 17th century the land belonged mostly to the O'Reilly clan and they took their revenge in the 1641 rebellion by releasing their prisoners 'turned naked, without respect of age or sex, upon the wild, barren mountains, in the cold age, exposed to all the severity of the winter'. Since partition, when Cavan was cut adrift from Ulster, like Donegal and Monaghan, life has proceeded fairly uneventfully and this is part of the county's appeal. Everything is low key, there are no major places of interest, and time spent here is best devoted to the wilder west Cavan around Ballyconnell.

Ins & outs The Dublin to Donegal service, at least 4 times a day and 3 on Sunday, stops at Cavan, and Ballyconnell on request. Ballyconnell can also be reached on a local bus, Monday to Saturday, that travels between Cavan and Bawnboy. From Cavan itself buses connect with Armagh, Athlone, Belfast, Clones, Dundalk, Enniskillen, Galway, Kells, Killybegs, Longford, Monaghan, Portadown and Roscommon.

Cavan town & around

Phone code: 049
Colour map 1, grid C3

Cavan developed from a Franciscan friary of 1300 and, although nothing of this now remains, the **tourist office** has some information on a few places of minor interest, namely the **Lifeforce Mill**, T4362722, by the Kennypottle River. A tour begins with the making of soda bread and ends with collecting it hot from the oven. The **Cavan Crystal Factory** just outside town is also worth a visit. ■ *Tourist office: Farnham Street, T4331942. Monday-Friday 0900-1700, Saturday 0900-1300. Crystal Factory: Dublin Road, T4331800.*

For an excursion, try the **Killykeen Forest Park**, or the miscellany of folk artefacts at the **Pighouse Folk Museum**, T4337248. At Cornafean, bikes can be hired from *On Yer Bike*, Abbeyset Buildings, Farnham Street, T4331932.

Sleeping & eating **AL** *Farnham Arms Hotel*, Main St. Has 30 beds and is rarely full. **B** *Lisnamadra*, Killeshandra Road, Crossdoney, T4337196, F4337111. Offers pleasant accommodation on a dairy farm 4 miles (7 km) southwest of Cavan, so why stay in town? For quick meals the pubs in town offer much of the sameness, while for something more memorable the *Annalee Restaurant*, Hotel Kilmore, Dublin Rd, T4332288, has a reputation for dishing up local fish and game. Open for lunch and dinner, closed Monday. *Lifeforce Mill* has a coffee shop, serves snacks and wholesome meals. Open between May and September, Tuesday to Sunday 0900-1700.

West Cavan

Phone code: 049

If you're just speeding through between Dublin and Donegal you will miss the most interesting part of the county, though it is only a short detour off the N3 at Belturbet to access **Ballyconnell** on the R200. The **Cavan Way**, a 17-mile (26-kilometre) waymarked walking trail, connects Blacklion with Dowra and could be completed in a day. Accommodation and food is better in Blacklion, so start from Dowra with the help of Ordnance Survey map No 26 and the *Cavan Way Mapguide* available from the tourist office in Cavan. From Blacklion the Way is mostly by road but it ends up as hill walking.

Sleeping and eating L *Slieve Russell Hotel*, T9526444, F9526474. A 'Golf and Country Club', this has all the facilities expected from 4-star accommodation. Enquire about weekend breaks and other offers or pop in for the food. **A-B** *Macnean House and Bistro*, Main St, Blacklion, T072-530220. B&B on the Cavan Way, serves dinner for IR£16. **B** *Hi Way Inn*, Dowra, T078- 43025. B&B handy for those walking the Cavan Way. **B** *Mount View House*, Ballyconnell, T9526456. A B&B departing from the vernacular on a grandiloquent scale **D** *Sandville House Hostel*, T9526297, http://www. homepage.tinet.ie/~sandville   Two miles west of Ballyconnell (telephone for a pick-up), this makes a comfortable base for walking or cycling through the local countryside. Bikes are available, there is no extra charge for double rooms, IR£6 per person, and camping is also possible.

Counties of Longford and Westmeath

When visitors dismiss the midlands of Ireland as boring it is the counties of Longford and Westmeath they usually have in mind. But speak to the anglers who fly in from Britain and head straight for Lanesborough and they wouldn't have it any other way, left alone to pursue their sport with not a tour coach or backpacker in sight. The waterways of Longford – the River Shannon, Lough Ree, the Royal Canal (see page 661) – have boating and other water-based activities that attract families on holidays, but there is precious little else to detain the traveller.

Westmeath is a county of some consequence, though not from the traveller's point of view, benefiting from some of the richest farming land in the country and within commutable distance of Dublin. The main N4 road from the capital to Sligo passes through Mullingar, and while this busy commercial town sums up what is unappealing about Westmeath there are a couple of points of interest worth noting. Other areas of the county worth exploring include the Fore valley in the northeast and Athlone, on the N6 road between Galway and Dublin.

Mullingar and around

Phone code: 044
Colour map 2, grid B6

The county town of Westmeath is not the kind of place to fall in love with but convenient nevertheless for breaking a journey, and with a couple of places of interest around town that might detain you longer than anticipated. Mullingar's one long street changes its name from Austin Friar Street at the Dublin end to Pearse Street and Oliver Plunkett Street in the centre, and finally to Dominick Street and Patrick Street heading out west to Athlone. The Royal Canal (see page 95) does a perimeter loop around town, and Mount Street

Strictly for James Joyce aficionados

Before John Joyce ruined himself through the bottle he had a respectable and well-paid job as a government official, which took him to Mullingar where his son visited him at the turn of the century. It was all grist to the artist's mill, and the Greville Arms Hotel (hence the wax model in the foyer), the Royal Canal and the Columb Barracks find their way into Stephen Hero. The photographer that Bloom's daughter worked for is now Fagan's newsagent on Pearse Street, and the story about Belvedere in Ulysses must have been picked up by Joyce on his visit here.

heads south to Belvedere House and Kilbeggan from the junction of Pearse and Oliver Plunkett Streets. It's hard to get lost.

Ins & outs   Bus Éireann's Dublin to Ballina service goes via Mullingar at least 3 times a day, as does the Dublin to Sligo service. Twice a day, and once on Sunday, the Galway to Newry bus stops in Mullingar and connects the town with Athlone, Navan and Dundalk. Trains from Dublin to Sligo stop in Mullingar, T48274, at least 4 times a day, 3 on Sunday.

Museums   Of the three museums in town, the least interesting is the **Ecclesiastical Museum**, in the aesthetically offensive Cathedral of Christ the King at the top of Mary Street. ■ *T48338. Key from the house on the right inside the gates.*

The **Market House Museum**, in the centre of town near the tourist office, is a worthy example of that endangered species, the unreconstructed heritage centre. Full of artefacts donated by local people, from ancient quernstones to rubber bullets, a visit here would comfortably while away a wet afternoon. Best of all, it may set you off on the trail of Adolphus Cooke (see page 177). ■ *Pearse Street, T48152. July to September, Monday-Saturday 1400-1730. 50p.*

To reach the **Military Museum**, take College Street past the cathedral, cross the canal by the diminutive Carey Bridge and head across the road to a spire. Built as a barracks for the British and now home to the Irish army, the museum has a weird and wonderful collection of uncatalogued items ranging from a weighing chair for recruits to weapons and uniforms. Telephone before your visit. ■ *Columb Barracks, T48391.*

Sleeping   **AL** *Greville Arms Hotel*, Pearse St, Mullingar, T48563, F48052. A busy and popular town centre hotel redeemed by its garden and conservatory. **A-B** *An Tintáin Guest-house*, Main St, Multyfarnham, T71411. **B** *McCormacks*, Old Dublin Rd, Mullingar, T41483. A working farm well geared up to visitors and with various packages. **B** *Woodside*, Dublin Rd, Mullingar, T41636. B&B within walking distance of town, and there are plenty more B&Bs along the main roads going into and out of Mullingar. **D** *Farragh House Holiday Hostel*, Bunrosna, Multyfarnham, T71446. Over 30 dorm beds and 2 private rooms for IR£9 per person. **Camping**   *Lough Derravaragh Caravan & Camping Park*, Multyfarnham, T71500. The *Lough Ennell Caravan & Camping Park*, Tuddenham Carrick, T/F48101, April to September. 4 miles (6 km) south of Mullingar on the road to Kilbeggan and charges IR£8 for two campers with a car. On the shore of Lough Ennell and popular with Irish holiday-makers.

If staying overnight, you could also consider a 5-mile (9 km) journey further out on the N4 to the less frantic village of Multyfarnham where there are pubs with traditional music, good food and accommodation.

Eating   No problem finding places to eat in Mullingar, with a host of busy cafés, restaurants and pubs all easy to find in the town centre. Good food too at the *Greville Arms* and *Austins* at the *Austin Friar Hotel*, Austin Friars St, T45777. For something on a grander scale head for the late 18th-century rectory of *Crookedwood House*, Crookedwood, T72165 (with accommodation in the **L** category) a few miles north on the R394 road. Set dinner is IR£25, plus à la carte, lunch also on Sunday.

Equestrian Centre Athlone Rd, Mullingar, T48331, horsehol@iol.ie Opens daily for **Sport**
lessons and treks. **Fishing** Lanesborough Tourism Co-Op, Main St, Lanesborough,
Co Longford, T/F043-21977.

Banks All located along the name-changing main street. **Communications** Post office: on the **Directory**
Dominick St stretch at the west end of town. **Tourist office** Centrally located on Pearse St at
Market House, T48650. Daily 0930-1300 and 1400-1700.

Around Mullingar

A visit to the Market House Museum will have introduced the eccentric **Adolphus**
Adolphus Cooke who served under Wellington before losing his mind to the **Cooke**
notion that the family turkey was his grandfather reincarnated. When he later
sentenced his dog to death for immoral behaviour, the executioner was
attacked by his dog; this convinced him of another family connection and the
dog was duly pardoned. To find his highly individual tomb, the shape of which
makes sense when you know he was destined to be reincarnated as a bee, take
the N52 to Delvin for eight miles (12 kilometres) and park outside the *Bee Hive
Nite Club*. Inside the arched entrance, cross the field to the old churchyard and
the beehive grave is easily found.

A more conventional attraction is Belvedere House and Gardens, south of **Belvedere**
town on the N52 road to Tullamore. The House is not yet open to the public **House &**
but the gardens are noted for the Jealous Wall, an elaborate folly built by Lord **gardens**
Belvedere to block the sight of a neighbouring house belonging to his younger
brother. If you think this was taking sibling rivalry too far, then pity the plight
of his poor wife who was incarcerated in the house for 31 years because Lord
Belfield suspected another brother of having an affair with her. She died protesting her innocence and the brother was jailed in London for the rest of his
life. ■ *April to October, daily 1200-1600 (1800 at weekends). IR£1.*

Further south at Kilbeggan, Locke's Distillery has produced whiskey for 200 **Locke's**
years and now dispenses a wee drop to visitors as well. ■ *T0506-32134. Daily* **Distillery**
*0900-1800 (1000-1600 in winter). IR£3. Food all day, including a takeaway ser-
vice, and drink at the nearby* Black Kettle *pub.*

Some 12 miles (20 kilometres) north of Mullingar the R394 leads to **Tullynally**
Castlepollard, and then the road to Granard and Tullynally Castle and **Castle &**
Gardens. Owned by the Pakenhams, later the Earls of Longford, since the 17th **gardens**
century, the exterior of this vast Gothic Revival 'castle' is not pleasing to the
eye, but the guided tour reveals a wealth of features and includes an educational glimpse of working life for the army of servants who slaved away in the
kitchen and laundry. ■ *T61159. Castle: mid-June to July, 1400-1800. Gardens:
May to September, 1400-1800. Combined ticket, IR£4; Gardens only, IR£2.*

To the east of Tullynally, reached via the R195 from Castlepollard, the village **Fore**
of Fore is the natural starting point for a walking excursion into the **Fore**
Valley. The village has pubs, but a day out with a picnic from Mullingar is quite
feasible. The valley is home to the Seven Wonders, a group of early Christian
sites associated with St Fechin and illustrated in murals in the *Abbey* village
pub. You'll be hard put to identify all seven but St Fechin's Church, with an
interesting Greek cross on the lintel, is easy to find and from here a path leads
to the neat little Anchorite's Cell (key available from the *Seven Wonders* pub in
the village).

Counties Longford & Westmeath

Athlone

The strong castle of Athlone, commanding a strategically important crossing point of the Shannon, sums up the town's troubled history as a place to be fought over down the centuries. The **tourist office** is conveniently located next to **Athlone Castle & Museum**, with exhibits on the Shannon's flora and fauna and the life of the great tenor John McCormack as well as the castle's history. The top floor of the museum is well worth a visit, a little gem of a folk collection which includes a working gramophone that John McCormack travelled with. Ask for a record to be played while sauntering around the miscellany of other exhibits. Downstairs, check out the two *sheelagh na gig* sculptures (pagan fertility symbols). ■ *Market Square, T929192. Monday-Saturday 1000-1600. IR£2.50.*

Ins & outs The bus and train stations (T73300) are on the other side of the river to the castle. Athlone is a major transport link and there are buses to just about every main town in Ireland. Trains connect the town with Westport, Galway and Dublin.

The road north of Athlone, the N55, heads up the east side of Lough Ree to what numerous brown signs will tell you is **Goldsmith Country**. The poet, playwright and novelist, Oliver Goldsmith (1728-74) was born just north of Glasson in county Longford. The country is pleasantly flat for cyclists and mildly distracting and the village of Glasson is picturesque enough, but there is not a great deal to see or do other than pass through admiring the countryside.

Sleeping The oddly named **AL** *Prince of Wales Hotel*, Church St, T72626, F75658, is in town on the banks of the river and with over 70 rooms is unlikely to be full. **A** *Shamrock Lodge*, less than ten minutes walk from town is better value. **B** *Dun Mhuire House*, Bonavalley, Dublin Rd, T75360. Typical of the countless B&Bs spread out along the approach roads (but it's not a bungalow), this B&B also provides dinner for IR£15.

Eating *Restaurant Le Château*, St Peter's Port, the Docks, T94517, is an old church on the banks of the river down from the castle. Open daily at 1730 for an early bird menu until 1900 at IR£15.50, a set dinner for IR£23 until 2000 plus à la carte.
   Stay in Ireland long enough and you'll lose count of pubs like *Sean's Bar*, T92358, on Main St close to the tourist office, claiming to be the oldest in the land, but at least this pub does have some character, and a beer garden overlooking the Shannon.

Cruises Lough Ree cruises, lasting 90 minutes with a commentary, are conducted daily through *Athlone Cruisers*, T72892, for IR£5. Self-drive cruises can also be arranged through the same company on a weekly or weekend basis. Departures from the Jolly Mariner marina beside the Athlone bypass. *Rosana Cruises*, T73383, conduct river trips in a 'Viking Longboat' from the town centre.

*The mountains were thrown higgledy-
piggledy into the distance where the sea was. The
white dusty road wound round the near flank of
the valley and then fell gracefully away to the one-
arched bridge below. Among the few tufted oaks
beyond the bridge the church lurked. A cluster of
thatched houses crouched about it.*

Bryan MacMahon (1909-)
Evening in Ireland

Counties Wicklow & Wexford

County Wicklow's sobriquet, 'The Garden of Ireland', gives some hint of the beauty that singles out this part of the country. The northern border of Wicklow is only 12 miles (19 kilometres) from Dublin's city centre, which is astonishing to reflect on when walking alone in the heather-coloured Wicklow Mountains. As well as the grandeur of the mountains the county boasts stately homes, archaeological and historical sites, superb beaches and some of the best food in the Republic. The county divides neatly into three areas: the north including the picturesque village of Enniskerry and the seaside town of Bray; Glendalough and West Wicklow including Blessington; and south of Glendalough with the county town of Wicklow, nearby Arklow and the Vale of Avoca, better known to couch potatoes as Ballykissangel.

Dubbed the 'sunny southeast' because of slightly higher average temperatures and lower rainfall than the rest of Ireland, County Wexford, and especially the towns of Wexford and Enniscorthy, has strong historical connections with the 1798 rebellion. The south Wexford coast is most attractively represented by the fishing village of Kilmore Quay and the Hook peninsula, while the east coast has long stretches of sandy beach.

★ *Try to find time for*

1798 Centre, Enniscorthy

Bird watching on the Hook peninsula

Walking the Wexford Coastal Path

Fringe events at the Wexford Opera Festival

A walk up Maulin in County Wicklow

County Wicklow

County Wicklow

North Wicklow and the Wicklow Mountains

Phone code: 01 Discerning Dubliners know well how blessed they are by having the granite hills and purple glens of the Wicklow Mountains almost in their backyard. The R115 road, better known as the **Military Road**, makes its way through Glencree and the Sally Gap before meandering south to Glendalough and it can be joined at Glencree from Enniskerry and Bray. The Military Road was made by the British in the years after the 1798 rebellion, in a determined effort to wipe out the remaining insurgents who were using the inaccessible mountains as their base.

A **suggested tour** of the area starts with the seaside town of Bray before taking the road west to the postcard-pretty village of Enniskerry and – the reason for the village's existence – the Powerscourt Estate. From Enniskerry the road continues west to Glencree, where the Military Road can be picked up. Rather than stay on this road all the way south to Laragh, it is worth heading off to **Roundwood** at the Sally Gap and then going on to Laragh and Glendalough from there. The scenery between the Sally Gap and Roundwood, is quite spectacular and the village of Roundwood itself makes a pleasant place to stop for a meal and a rest.

The Wicklow Way

There are many well-laid-out and exciting walks in the Wicklow Mountains, all eagerly walked by local people and visitors. The best way to see the mountains is by walking the five days of the Wicklow Way, Ireland's first and oldest waymarked walking route (81 miles/131 kilometres). It is well signposted and you are unlikely to travel as much as a day without meeting anyone.

Mapping and information *EastWest Mapping* produces a strip map and booklet about accommodation along the Way, which you could just about get by with, but ideally you should bring with you the Ordnance Survey Discovery Series maps Nos 50, 56 and 62. You must have good walking boots, wet weather gear, food for each day you intend to walk, and, as a minimum for safety equipment, a whistle, compass and first aid kit. If you have only one day, the best in our opinion is Day 2 from Knockree to Glendalough past the Powerscourt Waterfall. Do not walk if it is misty.

Day 1 Day 1 begins in Marlay Park to the south of the city. It quickly leaves suburbia *Wicklow to Knockree* behind as you head up Kilmashogue Lane to Kilmashogue Wood. As you *(13 miles/21 km)* make your way upwards, views open up of the coast and the city that have been left behind. Crossing **Two Rock Mountain**, high up at about 1,476 feet (450 metres), you come to the R116 and Glencullen. Out of the village and on to open moorland again you come eventually to Knockree. There you can break for the evening and perhaps make a trip into Enniskerry for dinner and provisions. ■ *Marlay Park open 1000. Bus No 47B from city centre.*

Day 2 is a lovely walk along a river and then past the waterfall at Powerscourt; you are truly among the Wicklow Mountains, with the Sugarloaf behind you and Maulin stretching beautifully up to the north. Go down to the Dargle River and then along the shoulder of Djouce Mountain to Lough Tay. The day could end at Roundwood, which is a little way off the track. There are a few B&Bs there (see 'Sleeping') Alternatively you can walk on to Glendalough, which is an excellent place to rest for a day or so and explore the walks in the area.

Day 2
Knockree to
Glendalough
(18 miles/29 km)

The Wicklow Way

Day 3 passes through Glenmalure, with glorious views of the valley since the forestry has been felled, passing Lugnaquilla, which is the highest point in the Wicklow Mountains. Crossing Slieve Maan, Carrickashane you arrive at a tarmac road at Iron Bridge, from where you can easily find your way to the village of Aghavannagh.

Day 3
Glendalough to
Aghavannagh
(18 miles/29 km)

County Wicklow

Day 4 is less demanding but still passes through some beautiful scenery. Climbing up Shielstown Hill and down again by a curious route, you do need to keep an eye out for waymarkers along this stretch of the Way. Following a minor road for a time you cross a valley and begin to climb Garryhoe Mountain with wide-open views all around of the Wicklow Hills. You cross another mountain, Coolafunsgoge, along its lower slopes and then begin to catch sight of the next stop – Tinahely, which has shops for provisions.

Day 4
Aghavannagh to
Tinahely (14 miles/
22 km)

Day 5 involves quite a lot of road walking but it will be deserted most of the way. The highlight of the walk is Urelands Hill, where there are wonderful views of Mount Leinster.

Day 5
Tinahely to Clonegal
(18 miles/29 km)

For an organized walk try contacting *Footfalls Walking Holidays*. They conduct group walking tours of from 6 to 10 miles (10-15 km) each day, with luggage, food, accommodation and transport organized as part of the package. Self-guided tours are also available for independent walkers. ■ *Trooperstown, Roundwood, T/F0404-45152, cstacey@iol.ie*

**Organized
walks**

Wicklow festivals

The **Gardens Festival**, mid-**May** to the third week in **June**, has been going for 10 years. As well as the grand gardens like Powerscourt and Mount Usher there are many private gardens that only open to the public during the Festival on selected days. Other events include floral dinners, guided tours, exhibitions and demonstrations. For a festival brochure contact Wicklow County Tourism or the tourist office in Wicklow, Bray or Blessington.

A two-day spring **walking festival** takes place in early **May**; for further details contact the tourist office in Wicklow town or Footfalls Walking Holidays. An autumn walking festival takes place in late **October**, T0404-44696 for information. Rathdrum has its own little festival in early April. Details from Wicklow County Tourism (see page 194).

A Synge Summer School takes place in July; contact Irene Parsons, Whaley Lodge, Ballinaclash, Rathdrum, Co Wicklow, T0404-46131, F0404-46044. A Parnell Summer School takes place in early August; contact Ms Maura Tobin, 78 Heatherview, Greystones, Co Wicklow. Both courses last a week and the cost is around IR£165, excluding accommodation.

Sleeping **B** *Ballincar House*, Mary Malone, Roundwood, T2818168. B&B with rooms from around IR£15 per person sharing. **B** *Orchard House*, T0402-38264. B&B. **B** *Park Lodge Farm*, Clonegal, T055-29149. B&B, evening meal by arrangement. **B** *Rossbane House*, T0402-38100. B&B. **B** *Woodside*, Mrs Nancy O'Brien, Roundwood, T2818185. Rooms from around IR£15 per person sharing in this B&B. **D** *Aghavannagh Hostel*, T0402-36366. An Óige hostel, booking dvisable in advance from Dublin hostel (T01-8301766). **D** *Glendalough Hostel*, Glendalough, T01-8301766 (Dublin hostel). An Óige hostel: advance booking advisable. **D** *Knockree Hostel*, Lacken House, Knockree, T8301766 (Dublin hostel). Advance booking essential at this An Óige hostel.

Enniskerry

The pretty, busy little village owes its existence to the Powerscourt Family who had the nearby estate and the village laid out during the 18th century, when they were lords of all they surveyed. Besides a few cafés and pubs and one of the first Gothic Revival Catholic Churches in Ireland (1843, Patrick Byrne) its chief claim to fame is as a stepping-off point for walks in the area, and of course the nearby Powerscourt Gardens.

Powerscourt gardens & waterfall The Powercourt estate lies just 12 miles (19 kilometres) south of Dublin, in the foothills of the Wicklow mountains. It is a huge estate – the approach road to the house is a mile (nearly 2 kilometres) long and it has the magnificent backdrop of the two Sugarloaf mountains. It also has the imposing presence of Powerscourt House, designed, like Russborough House on the other side of the mountains, by Richard Castle in the first half of the 18th century (see box on page 457).

The house, restored after a serious fire in 1974, is not open to the public but the **formal gardens** are the major highlight of any visit, if only to admire how the natural landscape helps moderate the ostentatiousness of the landscaping. The gardens were laid out in the 18th century but substantially modified in the 19th century; there is a free leaflet available with routes for a one-hour walk and a 40-minute stroll around the various points of interest. Accounts of the

Italian garden often tell the story of how it was designed by Daniel Robertson while he was being wheeled around in a barrow with a bottle of sherry to stimulate the flow of his imagination; it then took 12 years for over 100 labourers to transform his visions into reality. The Japanese gardens attract a lot of attention but numerous manifestations of European high art have also been imported into the landscape: the entrance gate comes from a Bavarian cathedral, classical statutory and urns copied from Versailles are dotted around and there is a fountain imitating that in the Piazza Babberini in Rome.

There is a signposted four-miles (six-kilometre) walk through the estate to the lovely Powerscourt Waterfall. The walk is recommended for the opportunity to admire the landscape and wonder at the sheer size of this estate and the Anglo-Irish ebullience that led to its creation. ■ *Powerscourt Estate, Enniskerry. T2867676. Gardens: March to October, daily 0930-1730. Waterfall: summer, daily 0930-1900; winter, daily 1030-dusk. IR£4 for garden and visitor centre; IR£3 garden only. Guided tour of gardens available. Tea rooms, craft shop, garden centre, picnic area. Bray Bus Tours, T2828602, run a return trip from Bray on Wednesdays and Fridays at 1430 and on Saturdays at 1000. IR£5.*

AL *Enniscree Lodge Hotel*, Cloon, Enniskerry, T2863542, F2866037. Open January-September. Picturesquely situated off the Enniskerry to Glencree road. **A** *Coillte*, 4 Enniskerry Demense, T2766614, F2766618. No evening meal. **B** *Corner House*, Enniskerry, T2860149. No evening meal at this B&B. **B** *Ferndale*, Enniskerry, T2863518, F2863518. B&B. No evening meal. **B** *Powerscourt Arms*, Enniskerry, T2828903. Conveniently located in the centre of the village. **D** *Glencree Hostel*, Stone House, Glencree, T2864037. Another *An Óige* hostel, as popular as that at Knockree and requires advance booking in summer. **D** *Knockree Hostel*, Lacken House, Knockree, T2864036. An Óige hostel, 4 miles (7 km) southwest of Enniskerry and on the Wicklow Way, and reached by taking Bus No 185 from Bray to Shop River.

Camping *Roundwood Caravan & Camping Park*, Roundwood, T2818163. Opens 10th April until late September.

There are a number of little cafés and restaurants serving food in Enniskerry. Try *Poppies*, on the village square, offering snacks and light meals around IR£5. The *Glenwood Inn* serves pub food at lunchtime. An evening meal at the *Enniscree Lodge* is excellent but very expensive; in another village hotel, *Summerhill House*, T2867928, dinner is in the more modest IR£20 bracket. The *Gallery Restaurant*, T6540993, at Powerscourt House, is run by the same family that cooks the food at *Avoca Handweavers* and it is equally satisfying. Outdoor seats on the terrace. The *Roundwood Inn*, Roundwood, T2818107, has a reputation for quality Irish and European cuisine and reservations are usually necessary. Open for lunch and dinner, closed all day Monday and Sunday evening. Bar food is always available and may include a delicious lobster salad and oysters.

Bicycle *Johnny Price's Garage*, Main St, Roundwood, T2818128. Bicycle hire. **Bus** From Dublin: Bus No 44, T8734222, from Hawkins St. **Rail** DART electric trains, T8366222, run from Howth to Bray via Dublin city centre every 15 mins on weekdays and up to every 30 mins at weekends. Bray bus No 85 goes to Enniskerry. **Road** Enniskerry is just over 1 mile (1.6 km) away from the main N11 road that connects Dublin with Waterford.

Sleeping

Eating

Transport

County Wicklow

Bray

Colour map 4,
grid A3 & B2

"They halted, looking
towards the blunt cape
of Bray Head that lay on
the water like the snout
of a sleeping whale."
Ulysses, James Joyce

Once a genteel Victorian resort town and now a rather run-down dormitory town that stirs to life in the summer when hordes of Dubliners and their families come and fill up the boarding houses, play on the stony beach and in the amusement arcades, and pack the pubs at night. On the plus side, there is plenty of accommodation, an excellent little town brochure that the tourist office dispenses and a delightful cliff walk, and with DART transport to Dublin the town could be considered as a place to stay for a day or two as a base for exploring parts of County Wicklow.

James Joyce came to live at 1 Martello Terrace, with his family, when he was six and remained there until 1891. The dining room of this house was the setting for the acrimonious Christmas dinner scene in *A Portrait of the Artist as a Young Man*. Martello Terrace is at the north end of the esplanade, easily reached by walking to the end of Strand Road or down Seapoint Road from the tourist office. ■ *Tuesdays and Thursdays 1400-1630.*

For an **architectural tour** of the town and its fine examples of Georgian and Victorian dwellings, get the tourist office's booklet and set off to explore some of the streets and buildings it describes. An excellent five-mile (eight-kilometre) **cliff walk** threads its way from the south end of the promenade to Greystones and a small detour at the beginning brings you up to Bray Hill with its cracking views. Details of other local walks and climbs are available from the tourist office.

A big attraction in Bray is the **National Sea-Life Centre**, a hi-tech aquarium, on the seafront. The tourist office also houses a **heritage centre** focusing on local history and personalities. Just south of town, near the roundabout on the Greystones road, **Kilruddery House and Gardens** has the largest surviving French-style garden in the country, dating back to the 1680s, with twin canals and a lovely avenue of lime trees. ■ *T2862777. April to September, daily 1300-1700. IR£2.50.*

Kilmacanogue The **Avoca Handweavers** have one of their large craft stores open daily in Kilmacanogue, just a couple of miles south of Bray, and there is also a terrace restaurant that serves excellent food. The store has its own **gardens**, created by a member of the Jameson whiskey family in the 1870s, which contain the only mature specimen of the rare Weeping Monterey Cypress in the world.

National Garden Exhibition Centre Garden-lovers may wish to make another 4 mile (7 km) journey south to the National Garden Exhibition Centre, Kilquade. Stay on the N11 as far as Kilpedder and take the signposted left turning for Kilquade. There are 16 different gardens on three acres (1.2 hectares), with names like the Seaside Garden, the Herb Knot, the Geometric Garden, Acid Garden, and Pythagoras at Play. A timbered pavilion houses a horticultural shop and a tea house serving lunch and snacks. ■ *T2819890. Monday-Saturday 1000-1800, Sunday 1300-1800. IR£2.50. Bray Bus Tours, T2828602, run a return trip on Tuesdays at 1430 and Thursdays at 1000 for IR£5.*

Sleeping **L** *Esplanade*, Esplanade, T2862056, F2866496. Interesting-looking hotel. **L** *Royal Hotel*, Main St, T2862935, F2867373. Next to the tourist office and twice the size of the *Esplanade*. **A** *Strand Hotel*, Esplanade, T2862327. Open June to September. **B** *Churchtown House*, Tagoat, T32555. A Georgian guesthouse just off the N25 on the R736 and five minutes from the harbour by car. Comfortable accommodation and evening meals if notice is given. **B** *Mayfair*, 1 Florence Terrace, T2862219. B&B. **B** *Rosslyn House*, Killarney Rd, T2860993, F2862419. B&B open all year. **B** *Sea Breeze House*, 1 Marine Terrace, T2868337. B&B closes over Christmas.

Bray has no shortage of places providing quick meals but for something more inter-**Eating**
esting try the *Tree of Idleness*, on Strand Rd, T2863498. This Greek-Cypriot restaurant
is famous for its roast, stuffed suckling pig, with plenty of mezze to nibble on and a
dessert trolley laden with Middle Eastern temptations. Main dishes like taramasalata
and moussaka, or saddle of lamb, are around IR£13. Recommended. Surprisingly, the
self-service restaurant at *Avoca Handweavers* produces above-average food that is
well worth considering. Interesting soups and meals with a taste.

South of Bray, in Greystones, *The Hungry Monk*, T2875759, is in the centre of the
village and specializes in fish in the summer and game in winter. For the good food
and candlelit atmosphere expect to pay around IR£25. Open Tuesday-Saturday 1900-
2100, and Sunday 1230-2000.

Golf *Greystones Golf Club*, T2874136. *Old Conna Golf Club*, Bray, T2826055. **Sport**
Woodbrook Golf Club, Bray, T2824799. All 18-hole courses. **Horse-riding** *Brennanstown Riding School*, Hollybrook, Kilmacanogue, Bray, T2863778,
F2829590. Lessons, courses and cross-country rides. **Leisure centre** *International Leisure Bowl*, Bray, T2864455. Indoor bowling, snooker, pool, sports shop and restaurant.

Bicycle *Bray Sports*, 8 Main St, T2863046. Bike hire. *ER Harris*, 87c Greenpark Rd, **Transport**
T2863357. Nike hire. **Bus** Bus No 45, from Hawkins St, and No 84 from Eden Quay run
between Dublin and Bray regularly throughout the day. From Bray, No 85 runs westwards to Enniskerry. *St Kevin's Bus Service*, T2818119, runs between the town hall in
Bray and Dublin twice daily. It is also possible to get off *Bus Éireann*'s Rosslare Harbour
to Dublin service at Bray, T8366111. **Train** DART trains run between Bray, T2363333,
and Dublin about every 15 mins during weekdays and up to every 30 mins at
weekends.

Tourist office Old Court House, Main St, T2866796/2867128. May-Sep, Mon-Fri 0900-1700, Sat **Directory**
1000-1600; Oct-Apr, Mon-Fri 0900-1600, Sat 1000-1600. Closed 1300-1400 throughout the year.

West Wicklow

This area of Wicklow takes in the extremely scenic Glendalough and the
equally pretty area to the west including Blessington, where there is some
excellent walking territory, the grand Russborough House and Baltinglass
Abbey, a 12th-century ruin.

The major draw in west Wicklow is Russborough House, a Palladian mansion with quite an exceptional collection of art, due to a quirk of history. The
road there from Glendalough is a delightful one, rolling across the Wicklow
Mountains and through the Wicklow Gap down to Holywood on the N81.
Russborough House lies directly to the north while at Donard to the south
there is a turning for the sombre Glen of Imaal. Lugnaquilla (3,038 feet/926
metres), the highest mountain in County Wicklow, is nearby.

Glendalough

Glendalough has become enormously popular in recent years and if you arrive on Phone code: 0404
a busy day in summer and only visit the monastic sites, then the natural magic Colour map 4, grid B3
*that attracted St Kevin and his cohorts may escape you. Up to 1,000 people can
turn up on one day and the car parks at Glendalough may both become overfull.
At any time, the flavour of the place is best enjoyed by heading off for a walk in the
area around the Upper Lakes.*

County Wicklow

History In the sixth century an early Christian monk , St Cóemgen (Kevin), a member of the ruling clan of Leinster, established a monastery in a valley setting beside two lakes (*Glean dá Loch*, glen of the two lakes) – at the time he was living in a tree – and the wisdom of his choice is still apparent in the stark beauty of the place. Perhaps the picturesque setting helped attract the growing number of pilgrims and devotees who came after St Kevin, causing new monastic buildings to spring up as Glendalough's reputation as a place of learning spread across Europe in the Dark Ages. Monastic life was not finally extinguished until the early 17th century, having survived several Viking raids and, later, sacking by the English in 1398.

Walking The information centres at the Lower and Upper Lakes dispense a booklet, *Exploring Glendalough* (IR£1.50), with details of two short nature trails and a longer, five-mile (eight-kilometre) route in the Upper Lake area. A half-hour stroll along the north side of the Upper Lake, parallel to the road, is pleasant enough and it leads to old zinc and lead mines. A more vigorous excursion would be to walk along the south side of the Upper Lake and this could be continued to complete a circuit of the entire lake. It takes about six hours to complete the 11-mile (17-kilometre) circuit and it would be advisable to use a local walking guide, such as David Herman's *Hill Walkers Wicklow* (IR£3.75). This also includes a shorter and easier four-hour circuit of Spink mountain to the south of the Upper Lake.

Glendalough The logical place to begin a tour of the sites, with an important cluster of build-
Visitor Centre ings located nearby at the Lower Lake, before taking the 20-minute walk westwards along the designated green road to the sites around the Upper Lake. There is an audio-visual presentation on Irish monasticism, and guided tours of the site leave every half-hour and take an hour. It is not necessary to purchase entry to the Centre in order to walk around the sites. ■ *T45325. June to August, and mid-March to May, daily 0900-1830; September to mid-October, daily 0930-1800; mid-October to mid-March, daily 0930-1700. IR£2. Dúchas site.*

Lower Lake The 10th-century **Round Tower**, with its doorway characteristically placed
monastic sites some 10 feet (three metres) above the ground, is not easy to miss. The nearest ruin to the Visitor Centre is the **cathedral**, begun perhaps as early as the ninth century but added to in the 11th-12th centuries, and with an ornamental east

Glendalough

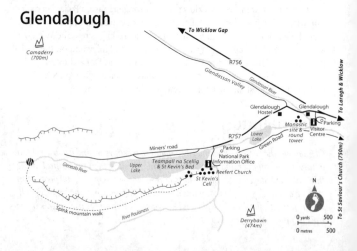

window worthy of appreciation. There are fine examples of 18th-century tombstones around the place. To the south, the **Priest's House** dates originally from the 12th century but a lot of what you see today was restored in 1875-80. The name derives from the practice of burying priests here. The most interesting site is **St Kevin's Church** or **Kitchen**, a fine two-storey oratory that may date back to St Kevin's own times although the belfry is 11th century and the sacristy at the other end was added later. The other main site involves walking eastwards to the other side of the Visitor Centre, but because the 12th-century **St Saviour's** has the finest examples of Irish Romanesque decoration in Glendalough it is worth the detour.

As one approaches the Upper Lake along the green road, **Reefert church** is over to the left and overlooking the lake. It is a straightforward Romanesque structure of the 11th century and while in fairly good condition it cannot match St Saviour's for decorative details. There are steps from the churchyard leading to the Pollanass Waterfall and further to the west are the remains of **St Kevin's Cell**, a small beehive hut associated with the saint. **St Kevin's Bed**, further to the west and above the line of the water, is a cave on a rocky ledge where, legend has it, the holy Kevin dealt with the unwelcome solicitations of a young woman by hurling her into the lake below. Still further west are the very scant remains of **Teampull na Scellig** ('the church of the rock'), thought to be the earliest site in the valley.

Upper Lake monastic sites

AL *Glendalough Hotel*, T45135, F45142. Just beyond the Lower Lake car park, the only hotel in the vicinity and called the *Royal Hotel* when Yeats stayed there in 1932. **A** *Derrybawn House*, T45134, F45109. South of Laragh on the road to Rathdrum. Offers country-house style accommodation. **B** *Dunroamin House*, Laragh, T/F45297. A little outside the village. Closed January. **B** *Gleann Aibhe*, Laragh, T45236. In the village. Open all year. **B** *Valeview*, Laragh, T45292. At the Glendalough end of the village. Recommended for its comfort and location. **D** *Ballinclea Hostel*, Ballinclea, Donard, T045-404657. Old farmhouse. Family rooms available. **D** *Glendaloch Hostel*, T&F45342. An Óige hostel in a terrific location, being only a few hundred metres from the Lower Lake sites. Renovated to a high standard and the private rooms are a good way of minimizing the occasionally hectic atmosphere. **D** *Old Mill Hostel*, off Rathdrum Rd, Laragh, T45156. Private rooms for around IR£15. **D** *Wicklow Way Hostel*, Laragh, T43545/45364. Next to *Lynham's Inn*. Completely independent hostel, which and also has private rooms.

Sleeping

Camping *Moat Farm Caravan & Camping Park*, Donard, T045-404727. Open all year. Convenient for exploring the Vale of Imaal and Lugnaquilla.

The *Glendalough Hotel* is the most convenient place for a meal after visiting the monastic sites. The evening fixed meal, available 1900-2130, is around IR£20 and usually has a choice of fish and meat dishes and the ubiquitous vegetarian lasagne – often a bad omen – may make an appearance. The lunch menu has IR£6 main courses like lamb stew and fried plaice and also offers open and toasted sandwiches and an identical menu serves for bar food. A more elegant dining experience is offered at *Derrybawn House*, T45134, for around IR£18.

Eating

Lynham's Inn, at the main junction in the village of Laragh, is a comfortable low-ceilinged hostelry with a bar food menu and specials on a blackboard. Tables and beer garden outside and in winter a warm inviting fire. Prices from IR£5 for fish and chips to IR£10 for a steak. Around the corner, on the road to Glendalough, the *Wicklow Heather*, T45157, has fairly standard meals of fish, chicken and meat for around IR£7.

Transport **Bicycle** *J Kenny*, Laragh, T45236. Bike hire. **Bus** *Bray Bus Tours*, T01-2828602, run a IR£10 return trip to Glendalough from Bray on Monday and Friday. *Bus Éireann* offer a day tour of Glendalough and Wicklow April to October, T01-836111. Departs from Busáras in Dublin at 1030 and the tourist office at Dun Laoghaire at 1100, for IR£17, but only returns to Dublin. From January to March, and November to December, the tour runs on Wednesday, Saturday and Sunday for IR£14. *Bus Éireann* also run a tour of Russborough House and Powerscourt Gardens (see page 184). *St Kevin's Bus Service*, T01-2818119, daily via Bray to Glendalough (outside the College of Surgeons) off St Stephen's Green in Dublin, 1130 and 1800. From Glendalough 0715 (0945 on Saturday and Sunday) and 1615 (1730 on Sunday). One-way/return fare IR£5/8. *Wicklow Tours Ltd*, T0404-67671, operates a daily mini coach service from Wicklow Town to Glendalough via Rathdrum, June to August. **Car** The car park at the Glendalough Visitor Centre is free, but it costs IR£1.50 to park in the Upper Lake car park.

Directory **Tourist Information** *Glendalough Visitor Centre*, T45325. Also a smaller office, near the Upper Lake, T45425. **Tours** T01-6611348/087-609362. Organized cycling treks in the Glendalough region, May-Oct, Thu-Sun.

Blessington

Russborough House
Phone code: 045
Colour map 4, grid B2

A particularly fine expression of Anglo-Irish confidence from the first half of the 18th century, though only one of a flush of extravagantly elegant houses built around that time. Like Westport House and Powerscourt, it was designed by Richard Castle (see page 457) who was brought to Ireland for just this kind of work. He worked on Russborough House with Francis Blindon, an architect from the west of Ireland. They almost went over the top with the immensely horizontal exterior; it stretches out on both sides from the main granite-built house with colonnades, walls, pillars and pavillions that finally terminate with kitchen and stable quarters. This is the Palladian style at its grandest and paler imitations are dotted around the Irish countryside.

The interior is noted for the plasterwork by the famed Lafranchini brothers and for truly spectacular plasterwork over the staircase by a local artist of the time whose name has been lost to us. The art collection of Russborough owes its richness to the profits of South African diamond mines, when the owner who purchased the house in 1952 inherited the prized paintings of his uncle Sir Alfred Beit, co-founder with Cecil Rhodes of the De Beer Diamond Mining Company. The collection includes Gainsborough, Goya, Rubens, Velázquez and others, and while some may be on loan to the National Gallery of Ireland at any one time there is always a remarkable set of paintings on show. The selection available to Rose Dugdale was especially rich when she burgled 16 of them for the IRA in 1974 (all of which were subsequently recovered undamaged), but there was no political motive to a 1986 larceny and the loot of that heist has still not been fully recovered. The house also has its fair share of fine furniture, tapestries, porcelain, silver and bronzes. ■ *Blessington. T865239. June to August, daily 1030-1730; May and September, Monday-Saturday 1030-1430, Sunday and Bank Holidays 1030-1730; April and October, Sundays and Bank Holidays 1030-1730. IR£3 for 45-minute tour of main rooms and paintings; IR£1.50 for 30-minute tour of bedrooms. Restaurant and shop. 19 miles/ 30 kilometres from Dublin on the N81, two miles (three kilometres) south of Blessington on the N81.*

Sleeping **LL** *Rathsallagh House*, Dunlavin, T403112, F403343. **LL** *Tulfarris House*, Blessington, T867555, F867561. Offers 9-hole golf course, indoor pool, tennis courts and sauna. **AL** *Downshire House*, Blessington, T865199, F865335. Just the place to stay if

Dwyer and McAlister

Michael Dwyer (1771-1826), the 'Chief', was the leader of a guerilla band that roamed the Wicklow Mountains in the aftermath of the 1798 insurrection. In the winter of 1799 he and his band took refuge in a cottage at Derrynamuck where they were surrounded and vastly outnumbered by English soldiers. One of the group, Sam McAlister, drew the fire of the English by running from the cottage, and his death allowed Dwyer to escape and flee barefoot in the snow pursued by a pack of hounds. On this occasion he escaped but finally surrendered at the end of 1803 and was transported to Australia where he spent some time on Norfolk Island and then Van Diemen's Land, both prison islands, before, ironically, ending up as High Constable of Liverpool, Australia in 1815. He was shortly afterwards sacked for drunkenness and became the owner of an inn.

In Derrynamuck, the cottage itself was later destroyed by fire but was finally restored in 1946 and renovated in 1992. ■ Mid-June to mid-September, 1400-1800. IR£2. To reach the cottage take the road from Knockanarrigan to Rathdangan in the Glen of Imaal and it is on the right about a mile from Knockanarrigan.

Russborough House has scratched an itch for aristocratic country-house living and a spot of clay-pigeon shooting. **B** *The Heathers*, Poulaphouca, T864554. B&B. **B** *San Michelle*, Baltinglass Rd, Blessington, T865114. B&B. **D** *Baltyboys Hostel*, Baltyboys, T867266. *An Óige* hostel in a converted old school house overlooking water.

Pubs in Blessington are a good bet for lunchtime food and the *Courtyard Restaurant*, **Eating** T865850, has lunch specials on a daily basis and a dinner menu. Open 1100-2200 but closed Mondays. *O'Connors*, a pub in Main St, has been recommended for its homecooked bar lunches. For an evening dining experience, *Tulfarris House*, T867555 or *Rathsallagh House*, Dunlavin, T403112, can be relied on for traditional hearty fare in Irish classical style, but expect to pay around IR£30.

Adventure centre *Blessington Lakes Adventure Centre*, T865092. A few hundred **Sport** metres south of Blessington on the shores of the Blessington Lakes. Land- and water-based activities, including windsurfing and lake tours on the *MV Blessington*.

Bicycle *Hillcrest Hire*, Main St, Blessington, T865066. Bike hire. **Bus** *Bus Éireann* **Transport** Dublin to Waterford and Dublin to Rosslare Harbour services stop in Blessington. The suburban No 65 bus service from Dublin runs to Blessington.

Tourist office Blessington, T865850. Jun-Aug, Mon-Sat 1000-1800. **Directory**

Baltinglass Abbey

Glendalough and the area around Blessington are the most frequently visited *Phone code: 0508* parts of west Wicklow but the N81 continues south through to County Carlow *Colour map 4, grid B2* and on the Wicklow side of the border lies the small town of Baltinglass. Its abbey is to the north of town on the east bank of the River Slaney. It was founded by Diarmit Mac Murchadha, the king of Leinster, in 1148 for the Cistercians and functioned as a working abbey until the middle of the 16th century. Only fragments of the church and parts of the cloister have survived but points of interest include the Romanesque doorways, the sedilla in the presbytery and details of the decorative stonework. The neo-Gothic bell tower belongs to the early 19th century, as does the granite mausoleum of local landed gentry. ■ *24 hours. Half a mile (800 metres) north of Baltinglass. Free.*

County Wicklow

Sleeping **& eating**	**B** *Germaine's* pub, T81284. B&B. **B** *Stratford House*, T81632. B&B accommodation just outside the town. **D** *Rathcoran House Hostel*, Baltinglass, T81073. Mid-June to August. Includes 5 private rooms at IR£21. For food and drink try *Horan's* in Main Sreet, or *Quinn's*.
Transport	*Bus Éireann* runs a Dublin to Waterford service, which stops in Baltinglass, as does the Dublin to Rosslare Harbour bus.

South Wicklow

If your trip so far has taken you around the beauties of Glendalough and Blessington, the glorious views over Lough Tay and Dan on the Wicklow Way, then a couple more days travel will introduce you to equally pretty views and perhaps your first sighting of a small Irish market town. The Vale of Avoca, especially seen out of season when the tour bus subsides, has a still kind of beauty while Wicklow town is small, with narrow winding streets and traditional ornamental shopfronts that lend character to this modest and engaging place. Further south is Arklow, another ancient and very popular seaside town with a long history and some pretty sights. Throw in a couple of gardens and Brittas Bay and you have a couple of days pleasant sightseeing.

Walking

Wicklow Town
& cliff walk

This walk begins outside Wicklow's historic gaol, from where you walk down to Main Street and turn left and pass the monument to Billy Byrne. Continue along Main Street and past the post office until another monument, the **Halpin Memorial**, is reached. Captain Robert Halpin sailed Brunel's steamship *The Great Eastern* to America, laying the first transatlantic cable from Valentia to Newfoundland. He was born in the town and also died nearby, from a septic toe that was not properly treated.

Turn up Church Street and take the first turning on the right, which leads towards the river. Do not go as far as the bridge but turn to the right and walk along South Quay by the side of the River Vartry. Clovers rare to Ireland, brought from Scandinavia by 12th-century Vikings, are said still to grow along the river. South Quay leads to the shore where the bare ruins of Black Castle stand. It was built in the 12th century by the Norman Fitzgeralds who were granted the land around Wicklow by Strongbow (Richard fitz Gilbert, ex-Earl of Pembroke who fought for Diarmit Mac Murchadha in his efforts to regain the kingship of Leinster around 1170). The castle was destroyed by local clans in 1301. With the ruins behind you, walk along Travilahawk Strand for a cliff walk of two miles (three kilometres) to Wicklow Head's three lighthouses.

Wicklow Town

Phone code: 0404
Colour map 4, grid B3

A settlement of sorts here goes back to CE400, and after the Vikings arrived in the 10th century the town's Norse name, Vikinglough, gradually gave way to Wicklow. Its Irish name is *Cill Mhantáin*, (the church of St Mantan). Wicklow saw most of the action during the 15th and 16th centuries when the English lords were at the mercy of the O'Byrnes, the local clan who raided the place regularly, demanding rents and finally razing the castle in 1580. Soon after, Wicklow became part of the Pale, a safe area dominated by the English gentry who settled all around here in their great houses. The 1798 rebellion passed the little town by although there were several trials of rebels, one of whom, Billy

Byrne, possibly a descendant of the O'Byrnes who caused so much trouble in the 16th century, was the son of a wealthy Catholic family and led the south and central bands of the Wicklow rebels until he was caught and executed at Gallow's Hill in the town. A monument in the town stands in his memory.

Gaol Wicklow's historic gaol was built in 1702, held insurgents from 1798 and other political prisoners awaiting transportation in the years that followed. Exhibitions on three floors focus on the terrible prison conditions that people endured, the 1798 Uprising, the tragedy of the Famine years and the trauma of transportation that carried some 50,000 Irish people to Australia. The gaol also houses a genealogy centre, a shop and a café. ■ *Kilmantin Hill, Wicklow Town, T61599. http://www.wicklow.ie/gaol Daily, 1000-1800. IR£3.50. Tours every 10 minutes. At the southern end of town, beside the courthouse.*

Mount Usher Gardens Mount Usher is regarded as an exemplary garden of the romantic Robinsonian type, with cascades, suspension bridges, and trees and shrubs introduced from many parts of the world. It dates back to 1860 and is laid out along the River Vartry in a style of natural, relaxed informality. In spring the meadows are bursting with flowering bulbs and the autumn colours are sublime. ■ *Ashford, T40205. 14th March to 2nd November, daily 1030-1800. IR£3. Tea room and craft shops. On the N11 road, under four miles (seven kilometres) from Wicklow Town.*

Beaches **Brittas Bay** is one of the best beaches on the east coast of Ireland and especially popular with daytripping Dubliners. The Blue Flag beach is situated midway between Wicklow town and Arklow and stretches for over two miles (three kilometres) with lovely powdery sand, and sand dunes where botanists search for plants. ■ *Bus Éireann's No 2 service from Dublin to Jack White's Cross, then a walk of over a mile (two kilometres).*

Silver Strand is nearer to Wicklow Town and also has a car-park, but it is far smaller and lacks the grandeur and appeal of Brittas Bay.

Sleeping **L** *The Old Rectory Country House and Restaurant*, T67048, F69181, mail@ oldrectory.ie http://www.indigo.ie/~oldrec Open early March to December. An unashamedly floral theme runs through the house and even extends to the restaurant. Comfortable rooms and a choice of Irish, Scottish, American or Swiss breakfast. Go for one of the 2-, 3- or 4- night deals that include dinner. **A** *Bayview Hotel*, The Mall, T67383. Situated in the centre of town and open all year. **B** *Bridge Tavern*, Bridge St, T67718, F61192. Captain Halpin was born here. **B** *Rospark*, Dunbar, T69615. B&B. **B** *Thalassa*, Dunbar Park, T67135. Greek-inspired B&B. **D** *Wicklow Bay Hostel*, Marine House, The Murrough, T69213/61174, F69213. Recommended for its friendliness and spaciousness. Open from March to early November and there are 2 private rooms for IR£20. Bike hire available.

Camping *Avonmore Riverside Caravan and Camping Park*, Rathdrum, T46080.

Eating For an evening meal of distinction, *The Old Rectory*, T67048, is worth a visit to experience the floral cuisine and organic salads that form an integral part of the 6-course gourmet menu for around IR£30. Recommended. On the left near a supermarket and garage, as you come into town on the N11 from Dublin.

Inland, on the Rathnew to Greystones road, the restaurant in *Hunter's Hotel*, T40106, can be recommended for the quality of the food, and a pre-dinner drink in the garden that overlooks the River Vartry makes the perfect start to an evening's fine dining. Expect to pay around IR£25.

County Wicklow

The *Bakery Café & Restaurant*, Church St, is undoubtedly the best place in Wicklow town for a meal. *The Opera House*, Market Square, runs the usual gamut of pizza and pasta dishes for around IR£6. The *Restaurant del Forno*, The Mall Centre, Main St, is open 7 days a week, 1000-2300 and has a bewildering choice of some 170 items on the menu! The *Grand Hotel*, T67337, Abbey St, offers carvery lunches, and pubs doing food include *The Beehive Inn* on the N11 and *The Old Court Inn*, The Square, which serves delicious crab specials.

Pubs & music *O'Connor's* pub has thoroughly enjoyable but irregular sessions of traditional music, especially on Thursday nights. At weekends, *Fitzpatrick's* comes alive with music and *The Leitrim Lounge* is currently a trendy spot with big bands and cabaret acts.

Sport **Adventure centre** *Tiglin Adventure Centre*, at the Devil's Glen near Ashford, T40169, F40701. Specializes in weekend and weekly courses in orienteering, caving, hang gliding, rock climbing and various water sports. **Fishing** *National Disabled Angling Facility*, Aughrim, T0402-36552. 5-acre (2ha) lake stocked with game fish. Equipment for hire. IR£15 per day, IR£9 for 4 hours, IR£5 for 2 hours. Open all year; summer 0800-2000 (to 2200 July and August). **Golf** *Ballincarrig Park*, Brittas Bay, T47195. A 9-hole course. *Blainroe Golf Club*, T68168, just over 3 miles (5 km) south of Wicklow Town on the coast road. *The European Club*, Brittas Bay, T47415. An 18-hole course. *Wicklow Golf Club*, Dunbar, T67379. An 18-hole course. **Horse-riding** *Ballinteskin Farm*, near Wicklow Town, T69441. *Bel Air Riding School*, Ashford, T40109. *Broom Lodge Stables*, Nun's Cross, Ashford, T40404. *Devil's Glen Equestrian Centre*, Ashford, T40637.

Transport **Bicycle** *Wicklow Hire Service*, Wicklow Town, T68149. Bike hire. *T McGrath*, Main St, Rathdrum, T46172. Bike hire. **Bus** *Bus Éireann*, T0902-73300. Service No 133, Dublin to Arklow, calls at Wicklow 9 times daily in each direction, stopping outside the *Grand Hotel*. The Dublin to Rosslare Harbour service stops outside the *Grand Hotel* at 1030. From Rosslare to Dublin there is a drop-off service only at Wicklow. **Train** Station, T67329, at the north end of town, just off the N11 road to Dublin. Trains running between Dublin and Rosslare Harbour stop in Wicklow Town.

Directory **Tourist Office** Fitzwilliam Square, Wicklow Town, T69117. Mon-Sat 0930-1800. *Wicklow County Tourism*, St Manntans House, Kilmantin Hill, Wicklow Town, T66058. Mon-Sat 0930-1700.

Vale of Avoca

Phone code: 0402
Colour map 4, grid B3

The Vale of Avoca is one of those places highlighted on maps as a 'scenic route' and in recent years it has been rendered even more popular thanks to the previously nondescript little village of Avoca being chosen as the location for the *Ballykissangel* television series. The scenic highlight is the **Meeting of the Waters**, where the confluence of the rivers Avonbeg and Avonmore form the River Avoca, immortalized by Thomas Moore in a poem and now marked by a pub, *The Meetings*.

Avoca Village The village of Avoca is reached by a narrow bridge from the main road and the place everyone heads for is the pub, in the hope of nosing themselves into the background of a *Ballykissangel* scene. Another attraction is *Avoca Handweavers*, located in the oldest working mill in Ireland and offering guided tours to see weavers at work. The shop is open daily and has an excellent range of crafts and clothing, and the café is worth visiting in its own right.

Anna Parnell

Born in 1852 at Avondale to an Irish American mother, Anna Parnell learned radical politics at an early age. In the US she supported the anti-slavery movement and women's rights movements and in 1881 she was asked by Michael Davitt to return to Ireland, her family home, to organize the Land League in the absence of her brother, then serving time in Kilmainham Gaol. The Land League was a disparate group ranging from the very radical who were prepared to use any tactics they could, to the conservative, like her brother, who was willing to use parliamentary politics to get what he wanted. They wanted a range of things from the appropriation of the land by the people to the more modest fair rents and security of tenure.

Never having known women in politics before, the men who approved Anna's intervention had no idea of the tiger they were catching by the tail. Possibly they thought she would knit things or have bake sales. She travelled widely across the country, encouraging people to refuse to pay rent to the landlords, organizing meetings, distributing the Land League newspaper, arranging shelter for dispossessed tenants, but above all encouraging women to join the front line in the resistance against evictions. She frightened the rightist elements of the League, most notably her brother who was currently negotiating a deal on a watered-down form of land reform. The now time-honoured epithets emerged in the press – "harpy", "harridan", "fanatic" – and eventually the Ladies Land League was dismantled by Parnell himself who cut off their funds. Anna left Ireland and never spoke to her brother again. She drowned in 1911.

County Wicklow

Charles Stewart Parnell, one of the great Irish nationalist leaders of the 19th century, was born into a Protestant landlord family in Avondale. The house, although it was built in 1770 and designed most likely by James Wyatt, has an interior restored to a mid-Victorian setting. There is also the obligatory video about the life and times of Parnell. The 794-acre (200-hectare) forest park has nature trails, forest walks and an acclaimed arboretum. ■ *Rathdrum. T0404-46111. May to September, daily 1000-1800; October to April, daily 1100-1700. House: IR£2.75; Park in grounds: IR£2. Bus Éireann's 133 service stops a mile (1.6 kilometres) from the house.*

Avondale House & forest park

Busy traffic on the N11 Dublin to Wexford road, which passes down the town's main street, is coming close to destroying the appeal of this once-famous port. During the 1798 Uprising a bloody battle for control of the town saw hundreds of rebels mowed down by the superior guns and artillery of the English. There is a small **maritime museum** in St Mary's Road that traces the eventful history of the town and its port. ■ *Daily 1000-1300 and 1400-1700. IR£2.*

Arklow

Clogga Beach is about four miles (seven kilometres) south of town and is safe for swimming. There is a seasonal **tourist office**, T32484, next to the Ormonde cinema and town hall.

L *Arklow Bay*, Arklow, T32309, F32300. The town's biggest hotel, with nearly 40 rooms. **AL** *Vale View*, Avoca, T35236, F35144. This is the only hotel in Avoca and is open all year. **A** *Bridge Hotel*, Bridge St, Arklow, T31666. Situated next to the bridge beside the River Avoca. **A** *Marine Hotel*, 58 Main St, Arklow, T32436. **A** *Sheepwalk House*, Beech Rd, Avoca, T35189, F35789. A charming Georgian residence overlooking the sea, but no meals are available. Superior self-catering accommodation available in the grounds. **B** *Cedar Lodge*, Wexford Rd, Arklow, T32797. Dormer bungalow just outside town on the N11. **B** *The Old Coach House* , The

Sleeping

Meeting of the Waters, Vale of Avoca, T/F35301. Evening dinner IR£19. Just over a mile (2 km) from the village. **B** *Willowcrest*, Coolgreaney Rd, Arklow, T39118. Split-level house in town. **C** *Riverview House*, Avoca, T35181. Open May to October but no meals available. Shared bathroom facilities. Situated right where the bus stops, on the hillside overlooking the village. **D** *Avonmore House Hostel*, Ferrybank, Arklow, T32825, F33772, avonmorehouse@tinet.ie   1 private room. Bikes for hire. Open early April to early November. **D** *The Old Presbytery*, The Fairgreen, Rathdrum, T46930, F46604. Cleverly-designed modern hostel. 3 private rooms for IR£22. Bicycles for hire.

Camping   *River Valley Caravan & Camping Park*, Redcross Village, T41647. Open from mid-March to late September. On the R754. For self-catering, see *Sheepwalk House*, above.

Eating   In Avoca, *The Avoca Inn*'s décor won't be winning any prizes but the bridge-side location is enviable and the downstairs restaurant, with fairly standard food, overlooks the river. For a quick bite to eat, there is a fish and chip shop opposite. A little south of Avoca, on the main road and virtually impossible to miss, a very old coaching inn and now *The Woodenbridge Hotel*, T35146, is such a stupendous establishment it almost obliges one to stop (as did Eamonn de Valera, Michael Collins and others in their time). Bar food all day and a restaurant.

In Arklow, *The Birthistle* pub is at the Wexford end of the long Main Street and has a good range of starters, and meals around IR£6. In the middle of the same street, *Murphy's* pub is popular with shoppers for its restaurant's large menu of standard dishes, including steaks. Alternatively, pop into *Joanne's* on Main St, which runs a bakery as well as a restaurant, and consider taking a picnic down by the river where there are benches. From the car-park opposite Joanne's there is direct access to the river. *The Ostán Beag*, 33044, is a faded-looking hotel on Main St with an old-fashioned bar and a wide range of food, including lunch specials listed on a pavement blackboard. From 1700, a set dinner is around IR£10.

Pubs & music   In Avoca, the film pilgrim's shrine is *Fitzgerald's*, T35108, impossible to miss as you enter the village across the bridge. *The Meetings*, T35226, a pub and restaurant on the Vale of Avoca road, has an open air ceilidh every Sunday afternoon between April and October and entertainment of one sort or another most days of the weeks in summer. In Arklow, *Christie's* has live entertainment in its garden during the summer and *The Mary B* has some enjoyable informal music sessions. *The Brook House* has music Thursday to Sunday and *The Nineteen Arches* is also worth checking out to see what musical entertainment might be on.

Shopping   At the seaward end of South Quay, *Arklow Pottery*, T39442, was established in 1934 and now specializes in earthenware dinnerware. Guided factory tours, Summer, Monday-Friday. *Noritake Arklow Pottery*, South Quay, Arklow, T31101, opens its factory shop daily. *Wicklow Vale Pottery*, The Old School House, Tinahask, Arklow, T39442, has showrooms and tea room and a range of crystal and Avoca Blue and Wicklow Vale ceramics. Open daily. On Saturday, 1030-1200, there is a *country market* in the Masonic Hall, Arklow. *Fitzgerald's Crafts* in Avoca sell *Ballykissangel* souvenirs and general gifts, but *Avoca Handweavers* is a far more interesting proposition.

Transport   **Bicycle**   Black Cycles, Upper Main St, Arklow, T31898. Bike hire. **Bus**   Bus Éireann's 133 service, T01-8366111, connects Dublin and Arklow via Avoca, The Meetings, Woodenbridge and Arklow. Of the 9 daily buses from Dublin, only 2 stop at Avoca and Arklow; the majority terminate at Wicklow Town. On Sunday, only the 1400 departure from Dublin goes on to Avoca and Arklow. **Trains**   Trains running between Dublin and Rosslare Harbour stop in Rathdrum, T46426, and Arklow, T32519.

County Wexford

Wexford

The compact little town of Wexford, with a fair range of accommodation and restaurants, is an obvious base for a tour of the county. Its closeness to Rosslare and the ferry routes makes it a busy place in the summer months but its soul has not been lost to tourism, helped by the fact that there are no major attractions within the town itself. Satirist Jonathan Swift liked Wexford, advising Stella in 1711 to pay a visit: "Go and drink your waters and make yourself well; and pray walk there." Sound advice.

Phone code: 053
Colour map 4, grid C2

Ins and outs

See the Rosslare section for details of the ferry routes from Britain and France to Rosslare Harbour, 12 miles (20 km) south of Wexford. The bus and train stations are together and link the town with Rosslare Harbour, Dublin, and other cities. The town is small enough to walk around but this also means parking space is limited: a parking-disc system operates. There is a free car park opposite the *Talbot Hotel*. Bicycles can be hired for day trips out of town (see 'Transport' on page 200).

Getting there & around

Background

Wexford was a Viking settlement until Dermot MacMurrough and his Anglo-Norman chums took over in 1169. The Normans built an encircling wall in the 12th century and the town was safe until 1649 when Cromwell (who stayed where Penny's department store on North Main Street now stands) left his usual visiting card in the form of a mass slaughter and the destruction of the churches. In the momentous 1798 rising, Wexford was held by the rebels and a commemorative stone was laid in the town on the 200th anniversary of the event (see page 207). Lady Wilde, poet and mother of Oscar, was born in a rectory in Main Street in 1826 (see box on page 198). A large historical map in the George Street entrance of *White's* hotel conveys a good impression of the old walled town and sites of historical interest.

Sights

More or less in the centre of town where a number of streets meet, this was where bull-baiting took place, but the square also marks the place where Cromwell's massacre occurred (see box on page 200). As such it was the obvious place to erect the Lone Pikeman statue to the insurgents of the 1798 rebellion, and in 1998 a tree was also planted to commemorate the revolutionary event. A stone laid on the pavement behind it is inscribed with the words of the United Irishmen catechism, about the tree of liberty growing in the US (the American War of Independence), blooming in France (the French Revolution) but falling in Ireland (in 1798).

Bull Ring

The **West Gate** is a restored city gate from around 1300 and the best-preserved sections of the original **city walls** can be seen nearby. Also nearby is the 12th-century **Selskar Abbey**, but what you see today is what remained after Cromwell's troops paid a visit in 1649.

Buildings

Radical mother to a radical son

Born in Wexford town, Jane Elgee (1826-1896) was a champion for the romantic nationalists of the Young Ireland movement before she met and married William Wilde in 1851 and settled in what was to become the famous address of 1 Merrion Square, Dublin (see page 100). She became Lady Wilde after her husband was knighted but this did little to dilute her strong republican sentiments and she continued to write nationalist pamphlets. Oscar Wilde was influenced by this political atmosphere and he went on to build and develop libertarian ideas that were probably first suggested by his mother. Lady Wilde shared with her husband a keen interest in folklore and after his death she moved to London where she published his collections of folktales and legends of the Irish countryside. She was fully behind her son's decision to face trial rather than flee the country but by this time she herself had little money and managed on very little until her death in 1896, four years before the demise of Oscar himself.

On Main Street is **St Iberius church**, an elegant 1775 church with a 19th-century façade, offering a guided tour around the interior for IR£1. ■ *Daily 1000-1700.*

Essentials

Sleeping
■ *on map*
Price codes:
see inside front cover

L *Talbot Hotel*, Trinity St, T22566, F23377, talbotwx@tinet.ie   www.talbothotel.ie Modern rooms, a good restaurant, and a leisure centre with pool, gym and sauna, in a family-orientated hotel that dates back to 1905. **L** *White's Hotel*, George St, T22311, F45000, info@whiteshotel. iol.ie Can also offer comfort and style in the centre of town. **AL** *Wexford Lodge*, The Bridge, T23611, F23342. Hotel on the east side of the River Slaney, which it overlooks.

A-B *Auburn House*, 2 Auburn Terrace, Redmond Rd, T/F23605. Guesthouse with large bedrooms, some with views of the river. **A-B** *Westgate House*, Westgate, T/F22167. A guesthouse, close to Selskar Abbey, furnished in period style befitting a house that was a 19th-century hotel, and with its own car-park. **B** *The Blue Door*, 18 George St, T21047. A smart B&B in a Georgian townhouse opposite *White's* hotel. **B** *John's Gate Street House*, John's Gate St, T/F41124. This B&B has 6 bedrooms in a Georgian house in the centre of town. **B** *Kilderry*, St Johns Rd, T/F23848. This B&B has 3 rooms but only opens between June and October. **B** *McMenamin's Townhouse*, Auburn Terrace, Redmond Rd, T46442. **B** *Mount Auburn*, Auburn Terrace, Redmond Rd, T24609. B&B next to Auburn House. **D** *Kirwan House*, 3 Mary St, T21208, F2177, kirwanhostel@tinet.ie

County Wexford

Hostel open all year with 30 beds, and 2 private rooms for IR£20 each. Breakfast included and bike hire available.

Camping *Ferrybank Camping & Caravan Park*, Ferrybank, T42987, F45947. Open Easter to September, and a 5-minute walk from town across the bridge on the R741. Facilities include a heated indoor pool.

Restaurants The *Slaney Restaurant*, Talbot Hotel, Trinity St, T22566, has a set dinner for around IR£20 or à la carte choices of steak, duck or fish around IR£11. Hearty and substantial food with lashings of vegetables so arrive with an appetite. Live classical guitar music and a relaxed style in a formal setting. The daily carvery lunch is around IR£6. *Tim's Tavern*, South Main St, T23861, has pub food and a restaurant entrance in Harper's Lane. A fair range of starters and traditional Irish food like bacon and cabbage and lamb's stew, entitled United Irishmen Stew on the menu, alongside sweet and sour chicken. Such dishes are around IR£9. Sunday lunch accompanied by traditional music. *La Dolce Vita*, Westgate, T23935, is an Italian restaurant with antipasti around IR£4 and main dishes, like brill with pepper sauce, veal and parma ham, venison with juniper berry sauce, around IR£13. *Michael's*, 94 North Main St, is one of the better places for an affordable meal. A large menu with fish, curries, meat dishes for under IR£10. *Lotus House*, 70 South Main St, T24273, and *Emerald Gardens*, 117 South Main St, T24836, are both Chinese restaurants with non-Oriental choices on the menu.

Eating
● *on map*
Price codes:
see inside front cover

Quick bites At 80 South Main St *Kelly's Deli* would suffice for a quick IR£4 meal or a coffee, or there's *Uncle Sam's*, 53 South Main St. At the very end of the street, *Gusto* is a little café serving breakfast and IR£4 lunches like chicken or vegetable curry displayed on a blackboard. *Robertino's*, 19 North Main St, has a bit of everything on the menu: pizza, pasta, burgers, steak, fish, starting around IR£6. *The Book Centre* on North Main St has a useful coffee bar. Further up North Main St, *Greenacres Food Hall* serves light meals and food to take away.

Pubs & music The Viking at the bottom end of South Main St has celtic rock and ballad sessions and young folk also patronize the *Centenary Stores* on Charlotte St, worth a visit on Sunday morning for its traditional Irish music, though every

County Wexford

Wexford

To Enniscorthy & Dublin (N11)

To New Ross & Waterford (N25)

To Gorey (R741)

City wall

Wexford Bridge

Wexford Harbour

To Rosslare (N25)

To Duncannon, Hook Head & Arthurstown Ferry (R733)

0 yards 100
0 metres 100

■ Sleeping
1 Blue Door Bed & Breakfast
2 John's Gate House
3 Kilderry Bed & Breakfast
4 Kirwan House
5 McMenamin's Townhouse
6 Mount Auburn
7 O'Briens Auburn House
8 Talbot
9 Westgate House
10 White's

● Eating & drinking
1 Centenary Stores Bar
2 Dolce Vita
3 Emerald Gardens
4 Greenacres Food Hall
5 Gusto
6 Kelly's Deli
7 Lotus House
8 Michael's
9 Robertino's
10 Tim's Tavern
11 Uncle Sam's
12 Viking Bar
13 Wren's Nest

County Wexford

 Oliver Cromwell before the town of Wexford

For the Commander-in-Chief within the town of Wexford:

Before Wexford, 3rd October 1649
   Sir, Having brought the army belonging to the Parliament of England before this place, to reduce it to obedience, to the end effusion of blood may be prevented and the town and country about it preserved from ruin, I thought fit to summon you to deliver the same to me, in the use of the State

of England. By this offer, I hope it will clearly appear where the guilt will lie, if innocent persons should come to suffer with the nocent. I expect your speedy answer; and rest, Sir,
   Your Servant, O Cromwell.

Cromwell's Roundhead army took Wexford with force and 1,500 defenders were killed in the assault. The market place, now called the Bull Ring, is where a great deal of the killing took place.

night is fairly lively and musical. *The Wren's Nest*, Custom House Quay, has traditional music on Tuesday and Thursday nights. The *Trinity Bar* in the Talbot has music at weekends, attracting an older set of customers, and *Harper's* in *White's* hotel has entertainment most nights.

Entertainment The annual **Wexford Opera Festival** in late October/early November is internationally renowned for the opportunity it presents to see full stagings of lesser-known works, supported by a catholic programme of concerts, recitals and lectures. A healthy fringe programme of drama, art exhibitions, special tours and assorted events is now a regular part of the occasion. Devotees are advised to book as early as possible for the three main operas being performed. Contact Theatre Royal, High St, Wexford, T22400, F24289, info@wexfordopera.com http://www.wexfordopera.com
   The Theatre Royal, High St, T22144, plays host to visiting drama groups. There is also the *Art Centre*, Cornmarket, T23764, open all year and with regular exhibitions.

Shopping Close to Selskar Abbey there are two antique shops: Selskar Abbey Antiques, Selskar Court, is on one corner while *Forum Antiques* (closed Mondays), with a good selection of second-hand books as well as prints and bric-à-brac, is just across the road. *Barker's*, 36 North Main St, has an array of glass and crystal gifts plus pottery. *The Book Centre* on North Main St is a good bookshop for Irish-related literature and *Readers Paradise* on North Main St has lots of second-hand books. Next door, *Wexford Silver* has affordable jewellery.

Sport **Fishing** Fishing licenses and permits from *Murphy's Tackle Shop*, 92 North Main St, T24717.

Transport **Bicycle** Bike hire: *The Bike Shop*, 9 Selskar St, T22514. *Dave Allen Cycles*, 84 South Main St, T22516. *Hayes Cycles*, 108 South Main St, T22462. **Bus** *Bus Éireann*, T33114/33162, arrive and depart from outside the bus station in Redmond Pl. Up to 6 buses a day run from Dublin to Rosslare Harbour stop in Wicklow via Wicklow and Enniscorthy. There is also a service from Rosslare Harbour to Tralee, which stops in Wexford as well as Waterford, and Cork. Other buses connect Wexford with Limerick, Kilmore Quay, Fethard-on-Sea and other parts of the county. **Taxis** *Jim's Cabs*, T47108, have a small office near Dunne's supermarket and the rate for trips around town is IR£2.50. Other taxi companies include *Abbey Cabs*, T41741; *Wexford Taxi Service*, T46666; *Whitty Cabs*, T22221. **Train** The railway station, T22522, is at the north end of town at Redmond Place and up to 3 trains a day stop here on the Dublin to Rosslare Harbour route. Trains also run daily to Wicklow and Enniscorthy.

Directory

Banks The *Bank of Ireland* is on Custom House Quay and money can also be changed at Mulcahy's newsagents on North Main St. **Communications** Post office: Ann St. **Laundry** *My Beautiful Laundrette*, Peter's St, T24317. Has complimentary hot drinks and ironing facilities. Mon-Sat 1000-2100. **Tourist office** Crescent Quay, T23111. Apr-Jun and Sep-Oct, Mon-Sat 0900-1800; Jul and Aug, Mon-Sat 0900-1800 and Sun 1100-1700; Nov-Mar, Mon-Fri 0930-1300 and 1400-1730. **Walking Club** The Wexford Hill Walkers Club meets on various Sundays and visitors welcomed. Contact Senan O' Reilly, T44634, market@indigo.ie

Around Wexford

Irish National Heritage Park
Phone code: 053

Ambitious to say the least, this historical theme park sets out to encapsulate nearly 9,000 years in the country's development: starting with the earliest prehistoric settlements and finishing with the arrival of the Normans in the 12th century. Models of dolmens and other modes of burial, stone monasteries, a High Cross, and *raths* are just some of the displays making up a series of 14 replicated sites dotted around the park. There is of course the inevitable audiovisual show, and for young visitors or anyone with little or no acquaintance with pre-Norman Ireland the Park's guided tours do offer a bird's-eye view of what can be sought out for real in the rest of the country. ■ *T20911, inhp@iol.ie http://www.wexford.ie 7th April to 1st November, daily 0930-1830. IR£5. Restaurant open for breakfast, lunch and snacks throughout the day. Celtic banquets on selected evenings. Located at Ferrycarrig, three miles (five kilometres) from Wexford town just off the N11 road.* Viking Tours, *T21053, are about to provide transport between the Park and Wexford, departing town at noon and returning at 1500, for IR£2.*

North Sloblands

Not the most endearing of names but the white-fronted geese are not bothered because they arrive in their thousands every year from Greenland and stay for the winter. There are hides for bird watching, and a visitor's centre with exhibitions on the various birds that can be spotted here. See the box on page 202 for details of other bird-watching locations in Wexford. ■ *T23129. 16th April to end of September, daily 0900-1800; October to 15th April, daily 1000-1700. Free.*

Rosslare Strand

Not to be confused with Rosslare Harbour (see page 201), Rosslare is five miles (eight kilometres) north of the ferry port and nine miles (15 kilometres) south of Wexford town. It is worth visiting for its long sandy beach and opportunities for water sports.

Close to the beach is the *Oyster Restaurant*, T32439, open from 1700 to 2130 between Easter and November, specializing in local seafood. The *Rosslare Sailboard and Watersports Centre*, T32566, opens from June to August, daily 1000-1800.

Rosslare Harbour

Two major ferry companies, Irish Ferries and Stena Line, operate out of Rosslare Harbour and so for many visitors this is their first or last port of call in Ireland. This is all Rosslare Harbour amounts to and there is no reason to stay any longer than it takes to board or disembark from one of the ferries. Depending on the weather, especially in the winter months, there can however be delays to the sailing schedules and sometimes an overnight stay may be necessary. If you are delayed for a long time at Rosslare harbour, there is a small sandy beach within walking distance.

At the harbour there is a **tourist office**, open to meet scheduled sailings. ■ *T33232. June to September.* There is a second tourist office north of the harbour on the main Wexford road at Kilrane. ■ *T33622. May to September, daily 1100-2000; October to April, Tuesday-Sunday 1400-2000.*

County Wexford

Bird watching and the Saltee Islands

Apart from the North Sloblands (see page 201) there are other local locations suitable for bird watching. Viewing from the shore of Our Lady's Island, nesting terns may be observed in the summer alongside teals, redshanks and godwits. In nearby Tacumshin Lake waterfowl are present in the winter. Brent geese and herons can be seen at Fethard and at nearby Bannow Bay waterfowl also arrive in the winter. Hook Head is always a good place to visit with binoculars and migrant landbirds are the speciality here, but take care clambering over the rocks because there are unmarked blowholes and a danger of freak waves. The last of the now extinct great auks to be found alive in the British Isles was brought past Hook Head in 1834 by local fisherman – so you're unlikely to spot any more of them.

The real draw for anyone with an ornithological interest are the uninhabited Saltee Islands. From late spring to early summer the rocks are alive with puffins, kittiwakes, gannets, razorbills, shearwaters and other sea birds. Boat trips can be arranged in Kilmore Quay, and Declan Bates, T29900/29684, is one of the more established operators.

Sleeping **AL** *Devereux Hotel*, Wexford Rd, T33216, F33301, devhotel@iol.ie Has various deals for stays longer than just 1 night. *Great Southern Hotel*, T33233, F33543, res@rosslare.gsh.ie One of a number of plush hotels overlooking the harbour from a clifftop. A leisure centre with a swimming pool helps while away the hours waiting for a delayed ferry. **AL** *Hotel Rosslare*, T33110, F33386. Close by the *Great Southern* and offers diversions in the form of squash, snooker, sauna, and a comfortable maritime-inspired bar.

A *Ferryport House*, T33933, F33363. Less than 500 yds/m from the harbour, a very smart guesthouse with good facilities. **B** *Ailesbury*, 5 The Moorings, T/F33185. It is possible to get an early breakfast at this B&B, if catching an early ferry. **B** *Alisa Lodge*, T33230, F33581. B&B overlooking the harbour, which is 5 minutes away, and happy to prepare early morning breakfast. **B** *Carragh Lodge*, Station Rd. B&B. Will serve early breakfast for morning ferry departures. **B** *Clover Lawn*, Kilrane, T33413. It is possible to get an early breakfast at this B&B, if catching an early ferry. **B** *Dungara*, Kilrane, T33391. If going for an early ferry, this B&B will serve an early breakfast. **B** *Lyndell*, Kilrane, T33316. B&B 100 yds/m off the N25 and less than a mile (1.6 km) from the harbour. **B** *Marianella*, Kilrane, T33139, is a bungalow on the N25 and equally close to the harbour. **B** *Old Orchard Lodge*, Kilrane, T33468. B&B on a quieter road but just as convenient for the ferries. **D** *Rosslare Harbour Hostel*, T33399, F33624. An *Óige* hostel located on the hill overlooking the ferry port.

Camping *Burrow Holiday Park*, Rosslare, T32190, F32256, burrowpk@iol.ie A 15-minute drive from the ferry port and has 25 pitches for tents. *St Margarets Beach Caravan & Camping Park*, Our Lady's Island, T/F31169, stmarg@indigo.ie Open Easter to end of October, follow the signs for Lady's Island/Carne from Tagoat on the N25. Six miles (9 km) from Rosslare Harbour.

Eating None of the B&Bs does an evening meal so if you are staying overnight there is little choice but to eat in one of the hotels. The average price for a dinner is IR£17, while the Portholes Bar in the *Hotel Rosslare* is the best bet for bar food and serves complete meals in comfortable surroundings.

Transport **Bus** *Bus Éireann*, T33114, run up to 6 buses a day between Dublin and Rosslare Harbour, via Bray, Wicklow, Enniscorthy and Wexford. Up to 3 a day run from the harbour to Tralee, via Wexford, Waterford, Cork and Killarney. In the summer 1 bus a day runs to Galway via Cahir, Limerick and Ennis. **Car** Cars can be rented from a desk in the terminal at Rosslare Harbour. *Dan Dooley* T0800-282189 in UK; T1800-3319301 in USA **Ferry** *Irish Ferries*, T33158, sail daily to and from Pembroke on a 4hr voyage, departing from Rosslare Harbour at 0915, 2130 and from Pembroke at 0315 and 1500. Irish Ferries also run a daily service to and from Cherbourg, departing from Rosslare Harbour at 1800 and 2300 and from Cherbourg at 2000 and 2200. *Stena Line*, T33115, sail daily to and from Fishguard on a 3½hr voyage, departing from Rosslare Harbour at 0900 and 2150, and from Fishguard at 1430 and 0315. *Stena Line* also run a daily service to and from Fishguard on the fast Stena Lynx, which only takes 100 minutes, departing from Rosslare Harbour at 1315 and 1800, and from Fishguard at 1045 and 1530. **Train** The railway station at Rosslare Harbour, T33114, now has the grand name of Rosslare Europort and trains depart at 0720 (0852 on Sunday), 1445 and 1825 for Dublin, via Wexford, Wicklow and Bray. There is also a Monday to Saturday service from the harbour to Waterford, which connects with a service to Limerick.

South Wexford coast

County Wexford

Most travellers head north from Rosslare Harbour to Wexford before heading off north to Dublin or west to Waterford – entirely forgetting the south coast – and on leaving Ireland there is the same tendency to speed by on one's way to the ferry port using the main roads. But the south coast of Wexford, and the Hook Head peninsula in particular, has its modest charms and with the help of the seven-minute ferry journey across Waterford harbour a leisurely meandering journey can be enjoyed between Rosslare Harbour and Waterford.

Phone code: 053

Kilmore Quay

This little fishing village, the departure point for trips to the Saltee Islands, has thatched cottages, a sandy beach and a few accommodation possibilities. Early to middle July is a good time to visit, when a **Seafood Festival** brings the place alive with food tastings and music and dance. ■ *T29922.*

Colour map 4, grid C2

A *Hotel Saltees*, T29601, F29602. The only hotel in town. **A-B** *Quay House*, T29988, F29808. A superior kind of guesthouse with its own dining room that comes a close second to the hotel, and welcomes divers and anglers. **B** *Harbour Lights*, T29881. B&B. **B** *Innish View*, T29674. B&B. **D** *Kilturk Hostel*, T/F29883, opens from May to September and has 5 private rooms for IR£16. Meals are available here, as well as bike hire, and camping is also possible.

Sleeping

The *Coningbeg Seafood Restaurant* in the *Hotel Saltees* is probably the best place to enjoy a good evening meal at around IR£20. There is also *The Silver Fox Seafood Restaurant*, T29888, open for lunch and dinner. There are a couple of pubs doing bar food and worth checking out is *Kehoe's Pub*, T29830, with a dedicated maritime theme, a beer garden to the rear and a satisfying bar menu of seafood and meat dishes.

Eating

Country Crafts, overlooking the harbour, opens daily with a collection of crafts and collectibles and paintings by local artists. *The Willowstrand Bookshop*, T29655, is outside the village at Ballyteigue, on the road to Wexford, is a secondhand bookshop.

Shopping

Kilmore Quay has a few places catering to **fishing** and **diving** enthusiasts: *Kilmore Quay Angling & Diving Centre*, T29988; *Kilmore Quay Boat Charters*, T29704; *Sharkhunter*, T29967; *Wexford Boat charters*, T45888.

Sport

Transport **Bus** *Bus Éireann*, T01-8366111, runs a limited service, on Wednesday and Saturday only, between Wexford and Kilmore Quay. The bus leaves Wexford at 1000 and 1530 on Wednesday, returning at 1035 and 1610. The corresponding times on Saturday are 1100 and 1620, returning at 1135 and 1700.

The Wexford Coastal Path

The Wexford Coastal Path is a signposted long distance walk of 125 miles (200 kilometres) in total, starting at Courtown Harbour near Gorey on the east coast and making its way south to Carnsore Point. It then heads west to follow the south Wexford coast as far as Kilmore Quay, passing lagoons and with fine views of the Saltee Islands off the coast. The Way then diverts inland to pass around Bannow Bay via Wellington Bridge and subsequently goes south again around Hook Head and up the east side to end at Ballyhack.

Mapping and information Ordnance Survey maps, Nos 62, 69, 76, 77 and 82 are needed to cover the whole Way but shorter sections may be enjoyed along the south Wexford coast. Further information from T42211 and Wexford County Council also publish a guide to the Way.

Hook Head peninsula

Phone code: 051
Colour map 4, grid C2

Even if the peninsula weren't steeped in history this would still be the most interesting part of the south Wexford coast to visit. Accommodation is dotted around the place and the area is small enough to make everywhere conveniently close. The roads are straight and flat, ideal for a cycling trip out of Waterford using the ferry from Passage East. For picnic food and general supplies, including a post office and a seasonal tourist information post, head for Wellington Bridge at the top of Bannow Bay on the northeast side of the peninsula.

It was in **Bannow Bay** in May 1169 that a force of mercenaries landed and met up with Dermot MacMurrough (see page 672) before their combined forces captured Wexford. This brought Strongbow and then Henry II to Ireland, thus setting the stage for 800 years of conquest. In the 17th, century when Oliver Cromwell was playing his part in that sorry drama, he noted that Waterford would be taken by "Hook or by Crooke", signifying the two places where an assault could be launched: the Hook peninsula or Crooke on the other side in county Waterford.

Tintern Abbey An austere but impressive Cistercian abbey founded around 1200 and named after the famous Tintern abbey in Wales, from where its first monks came. The founder, William the Earl Marshall, on a particularly rough voyage over to Ireland is said to have promised God he would found a church if he survived the journey (anyone who has made a stormy passage in winter will find this quite believable). Occupied as a private home from the 16th century until the 1960s, the nave, chancel, chapel, cloister and a tower remain. ■ *T562650. Mid-June to late September, daily 0930-1830. IR£1.50. Near the village of Saltmills, off the R734 road. Dúchas site.*

Ballyhack Castle Strategically located on a slope overlooking Waterford estuary, this substantial tower house was built around the middle of the 15th century. Very little is definitely known about its history, and although the official line is that it was probably built by the Knights Hospitallers of St John this is just speculation based on the fact that the Knights Templar did have a presence at this inlet in the estuary. ■ *T389468. June to September, Monday-Friday 1000-1300 and 1400-1800, Saturday and Sunday 1000-1800. IR£1. Situated in Ballyhack village. Dúchas site.*

The second of two Cistercian abbeys on the peninsula, Dunbrody was founded in the late 12th century by an uncle of Strongbow. It has the distinction of being one of the longest Cistercian churches in Ireland (195 feet/59 metres) and the east window is architecturally the most interesting part to have survived the centuries. The adjoining Visitor Centre has a small museum, the ruins of an old castle, a hedge maze, and a craft gallery. ■ *T388603. April to September, daily 1000-1800. IR£1.50. Admission to hedge maze is IR£1.50.*

Dunbrody Abbey

The story goes that this is Europe's oldest lighthouse, monks having lit a beacon here from the fifth century onwards, and that marauding Vikings never visited their customary ransacking on the place because of this. A more permanent lighthouse structure was built by the Normans in the late 12th century and the circular keep that is still visible dates back to this time. There is no public access to this lighthouse, but there are plans to open it as a heritage centre very soon. If tempted to wander over the rocks take note of the sign warning of freak waves.

Hook Head lighthouse

LL-L *Dunbrody Country House Hotel & Restaurant*, Arthurstown, T389600, F389601. A Georgian manor set in 200 acres of parkland, which boasts an award-winning restaurant. On the R733 and close to the Ballyhack ferry. Large bedrooms with pacific views and lavish breakfasts are 2 good reasons for staying here. **A** *Horetown House*, Foulksmills, T565771, F565633, poloxirl@iol.ie One of the more expensive B&B places in the area. **A** *The Horse & Hound Inn*, Ballinaboola, Foulksmills, T428323, F428471. A rather more expensive B&B. **B** *Arthur's Rest*, T/F389192. B&B on the road to Duncannon from Arthurstown. **B** *Glendine House*, Arthurstown, T/F389258. A substantial 1830s building, but there are only 4 rooms for guests in this B&B so reservations are useful. **B** *Marsh Mere Lodge*, Arthurstown, T389186. Pink-coloured guesthouse at the Ballyhack end of town, with 4 rooms. **B** *Naomh Seosamh Hotel*, Fethard, T/F397129. A popular meeting place for divers and general holiday-makers. **D** *Coastguard Station*, Arthurstown, T389411, anoige@iol.ie An Óige hostel.

Sleeping

County Wexford

Hook Head Lighthouse

Camping *Ocean Island Caravan & Camping Park*, Fethard, T397148, F397148. Within walking distance of the sea. *Fethard Caravan & Camping Park*, Fethard, T397123/397230. At the north end of the village.

Self-Catering Places to contact at Duncannon include *Clonsharra*, T389122, and *Eileen Roche*, T389188, F389346. At Fethard there is *Conna*, T397146, and at Hook Head itself there is the *Hookless Holiday Village & Leisure Centre*, T/F397329.

Eating The *Hotel Naomh Seosamh Restaurant* in Fethard, T397129, is open for lunch and dinner and pub food is served in the hotel bar from noon until 2100. There are also other pubs in Fethard serving the usual run of bar food. The *Neptune Restaurant*, Ballyhack, T389284, overlooking the estuary and with the picturesque Ballyhack Castle behind it, has a set dinner for IR£17 and à la carte choices of dishes like venison, lobster and crab pancake, or baked guinea fowl with Baileys sauce for around IR£14.

Courses in the art of Irish cuisine are available at the Neptune Restaurant. Enquire about the recipes of traditional dishes ·

At the Ballyhack end of Arthurstown the *Waterfront Restaurant*, T389534, does lunch and dinner at affordable prices but featuring unexciting dishes like roast beef and 'vegetarian dish of the day'. *Templers Inn*, T397162, on the road from Duncannon to Hook Head, at the junction for Templetown, is a large pub with outdoor tables, serving bar food as well as having a seafood restaurant.   An evening meal at *The Cellar Restaurant*, Horetown House, Foulksmills, T565771, is over IR£20 and the place has a good reputation.

Pubs & music Fethard is the best place for evening entertainment and the *Hotel Naomh Seosamh* has music most nights of the week in the summer, as does *Molloy's*. *Neville's*, opposite the hotel, is the place to go for a quiet drink and a chat. *Droopy's Inn* is very popular, often has music, and local fisherman frequent the place.

Transport **Bus** *Bus Éireann*, T01-8366111, run a service between Waterford (T051-879000) and Wexford, which on Monday and Thursday only travels via Duncannon, Templetown and Fethard. Buses depart Waterford at 0945 and Wexford at 1450.

Enniscorthy

Phone code: 054
Colour map 4, grid C2

The town of Enniscorthy is worth visiting for its 1798 connections, but there is little else to recommend about the place, unless you arrive for one of the festivals (see page 208). Enniscorthy is also home to *Southeast Cycle Tours*, which organizes cycling trips including accommodation and a guide along the way. ■ *1 Mary St, T/F33255, seastcyc@iol.ie*

1798 Visitor Centre This is the highlight of any visit to Enniscorthy and should not be missed; a brilliant example of a visitor centre that achieves the opposite of dumbing down, and which places the 1798 rebellion within both its Irish context and the larger European and American dimensions that gave such it such force and meaning. Allow at least an hour's visit to immerse yourself in the revolutionary mood of late 18th-century Europe, listening to the debate between Edmund Burke and Thomas Paine, and visiting the Chess Room, which graphically depicts the struggle of the times. The Wexford Room focuses on the events in the county itself, a 15-minute film brings to life on a multi-screen the showdown at Vinegar Hill, and the aftermath of the event is chronicled in a look at the growth of democracy in Ireland. The shop includes a good selection of books on 1798, including two recently released CDs (see page 65), which help bring to life this defining moment in Irish history. ■ *T37596. Monday-Saturday 0930-1800, Sunday 1100-1800. Picnic area, café and gift shop.*

1798 and County Wexford

One of the four main centres of action during the insurrection of 1798 (see page 676) was County Wexford. On 27th May the rebels attacked the yeomanry at Oulart, before moving on to capture Enniscorthy. Within three days Wexford town was taken and for the next three weeks it remained the revolutionary capital of the insurgents. Unfortunately, after the failure to take New Ross and Arklow early in June, the rebels chose to encamp on Vinegar Hill and await a showdown with the English military. This decision was not unanimous but calls for rural guerilla tactics were not heeded and the decisive encounter duly took place on 21st June. The Irish survivors were lucky to escape (see page 207) and on the following

day Wexford itself was reclaimed by the English.

Some controversy surrounds the Wexford uprising because in the southeast, where there was a relatively large Protestant presence, a vein of sectarianism manifested itself in acts like the burning to death of 200 Protestants in a barn at Scullabogue and mass executions by the rebels in Wexford town. Notwithstanding this, recent research has confirmed that the Wexford uprising was a remarkably revolutionary act that involved some 20,000 men and women, many of whom were quite aware of the political significance of what they were attempting to achieve.

County Wexford

It was at Vinegar Hill that the rebels encamped in June 1798 to await developments in the tumultuous aftermath of the initial uprising. On the 21st June General Lake, with 400 coaches of ammunition and 20 pieces of artillery, stormed the hill with 10,000 men. However, reinforcements under General Needham arrived too late to complete the encirclement of Vinegar Hill and through a gap, known thereafter as Needham's Gap, the majority of the 20,000 insurgents managed to escape southwards to Wexford, leaving behind 500 dead and many injured. There are great views of the surrounding countryside from the top of the hill, which is reached from town by crossing the bridge, taking the first right turn after *Treacy's Hotel* and following the signs. The sight is 10 minutes away from town in a car.

Vinegar Hill
At Vinegar Hill, in the memorable words of Heaney (Requiem for the Croppies), the rebels faced the English 'shaking scythes at cannon'.

AL *Murphy Floods Hotel*, Main St, T/F33413. Has various package deals for midweek and weekend stays. **AL** *Riverside Park Hotel*, The Promenade, T37800, F37900, riversideparkhotel@tinet.ie A short walk from the town centre and overlooking the River Slaney but hardly merging with the landscape. Two bars and a restaurant, dreadful modern décor. **A-B** *Oakville Lodge*, Ballycarney, T88626. Six miles (9 km) north of town on the N80 road to Bunclody and Carlow, this B&B has seatrout fishing on private waters. **B** *Lemongrove House*, Blackstoops, T36115. A large B&B house with 5 rooms. Less than a mile (1.6 km) north of town at the roundabout on the Dublin/Rosslare N11 road. **B** *Moyhill*, Bellefield, T34739. B&B just off the R702 road to Kiltealy and Kilkenny. **D** *Enniscorthy Holiday Hostel*, Platform 1, Railway Square, T37766, F37769, plat@indigo.ie This hostel was new at the time of research and little is known about it.

Sleeping

A difficult town to find a decent place to eat. For a light meal the most comfortable place is the small and snug *Antique Tavern* at the end of Slaney St that runs down to the river from near the monument in the centre of town. Some meals are available plus sandwiches, toasted or plain, with a large choice of fillings. The *Promenade Bar* in the *Riverside Park Hotel* has a spacious dining area for standard lunch meals at IR£6 and there is also a carvery at lunchtime in the hotel's *Mill House Bar*, for around IR£5. For an evening meal the hotel's *Moorings Restaurant*, T37800, is worth considering; main dishes range from IR£9 for chicken or spinach and ricotta tortellini to IR£14 for fish.

Eating

Along Rafter St, the main street that runs down to the central monument, there are a number of small restaurants and cafés serving inexpensive meals. *Paris Café* is a self-service cafeteria but *Karen's Kitchen* is next door and offers a better choice of meals. *The Baked Potato* serves lunch for IR£5.

Festivals Late June and early July sees the *Strawberry Fair*, nine days of music and craic, T056-21688. The end of August witnesses a lively *Music Festival*, T37950, fleadh@tinet.ie and in early September there is the *Blackstairs Blues Festival*, T053-42211 ext. 285/369.

Shopping Local potteries, dating back to the 17th century, can be visited and their produce purchased. *Carleys Bridge Potteries*, Carleys Bridge, T33512, is on the road to New Ross, while *Kiltrea Bridge Pottery*, T35107, is northwest of town and reached by taking the signposted right turn off the R890 road.

Sport **Greyhound racing** T33172, Monday and Thursday at 2000, IR£3. **Horse-riding** *Boro Hill Equestrian Centre*, Clonroche, T44117.

Transport **Bicycle** *Kennys for Bikes*, Slaney St, T33255. Bikes hire. **Bus** Bus Éireann's Dublin to Rosslare Harbour and Dublin to Waterford services stop in Enniscorthy. On Wednesday only there is a bus to and from New Ross and on Wednesday and Friday there is a service to and from Wexford, T01-8366111. **Train** The Dublin to Rosslare Harbour train service stops in Enniscorthy and the station, T33488, is on the east bank of the river.

Directory **Guided walks** T36800. May-Sep. Depart from town at 1030 and 1430. IR£2.50. **Tourist office** T34699. In the centre of town. Jun-Sep, Mon-Fri, 1000-1800.

Courtown harbour and east coast beaches

Phone code: 055
Colour map 4, grid B3

The R742 road follows the coast for most of the way from Courtown Harbour, near Gorey in the north of the county, south to Wexford town. Courtown and Curracloe have Blue Flag beaches and it was at Curracloe that scenes from Spielberg's *Saving Private Ryan* were filmed. The beach at Courtown is the most commercially developed and the best choice of accommodation is here. The Wexford Coastal Path (see box on page 204) runs close to the coastline for most of the way between Courtown and Wexford. There is a **tourist office** in Gorey. ■ *Main St, Gorey, T34699. June to September, Monday-Friday 1000-1800.*

Sleeping **AL** *Bayview Hotel*, Courtown Harbour, T25307, F25576. Overlooks the marina and there is a squash and tennis centre for guests. **B** *Ardamine House*, Ardamine, Courtown Harbour, T25264, F25548. About a mile (1.6 km) south of Courtown and close to Ardamine beach. **B** *Harbour House Guesthouse*, Courtown Harbour, T/F25117. Just 3mins away from the beach. **B** *Macamore House*, Ounavarra Rd, Courtown, T/F25353. B&B, with the beach 10mins walk away. **D** *The Anchorage*, Poulshane, Courtown Harbour, T25335. A small hostel, about 3 miles (5 km) south of Courtown, with 2 private rooms for IR£14.

Camping *Morriscastle Strand*, Kilmuckridge, T053-30124, camacmorriscastle@ tinet.ie Large and popular with Irish families. *Parklands Holiday Park*, Ardamine, T25202, F25689. A large camping and caravan park.

A reliable place for food is the *Bayview Hotel* in Courtown Harbour and there are also **Eating**
a couple of restaurants in Kilmuckridge as well as in Gorey itself.

New Ross

Given its prominent position by the River Barrow and on the N25 road *Phone code: 051*
between Wexford and Cork, the town of New Ross is frequently passed
through by travellers and just as quickly dismissed for not looking sufficiently
glamorous or twee. But there are fine views of the river from the top of the steep
and narrow streets, which have their own unreconstructed character, and the
ruins of the 13th-century **Church of St Mary** contain some interesting medieval tombs. The failure by the insurgents to capture New Ross in the 1798
uprising was decisive in halting the march of the revolutionaries and thousands died in the battle for the town.

Places of interest in the vicinity include the **John F Kennedy Arboretum**:
the US president's grandfather was born in nearby Dunganstown. ■ *T388171.
Open all year. Summer, daily 1000-2000. IR£2. Dúchas site. Eight miles (12 kilometres) south of New Ross on the R733.*

AL *Creacon Lodge Hotel*, Creacon, T421897, F422560, creacon@iol.ie A comfortable **Sleeping**
place outside of town. **AL** *Brandon House Hotel*, New Ross, T421703, F421567. A 100-
year-old manor house with top class leisure facilities. **B** *Inishross House*, 96 Mary St,
T421335. Has rooms sharing bathroom facilities for IR£32. **D** *MacMurrough Farm
Hostel*, T421383. A couple of miles northeast of town and includes 1 private room for
IR£16.

County Wexford

Brandon House
hotel & leisure centre

One of the first things you notice, when you arrive at Brandon House Hotel is the air of
tranquility throughout this manor house. Soak in the genteel atmosphere of the Library
Bar, the welcoming ambience, and the beautiful gardens overlooking pastoral vistas.

The delightful en suite rooms offer guests a host of amenities designed to ensure you
have a comfortable and relaxing stay.

With its fusion of traditional and modern cuisine, dining at Brandon House Hotel is a
culinary experience to be savoured.

Whether on business or pleasure, Brandon House Hotel's Leisure Centre is at your disposal.
Designed for pampering and energising fun, this is where you can luxuriate in the pool
or relax in the sunbed, tone up in the gym or treat yourself to a massage.

Brandon House Hotel & Leisure Centre
New Ross, Co. Wexford, Ireland

tel: +353 (0) 51 421703   **email:**   **website:**
fax: +353 (0) 51 421567   brandonhouse@tinet.ie   www.brandonhousehotel.ie

Eating The *Galley Cruising Restaurants*, T421950, operating from New Ross between April and November, cruise the River Barrow and include either lunch for IR£13, afternoon tea for IR£6 or an evening trip with dinner for IR£20-24. In New Ross itself the pubs are the best bet for a meal, while for a special night out there is the *Old Rectory Restaurant*, Rosbercon, T421719, situated in a country house hotel.

People who spend most of their natural lives riding iron bicycles over the rocky roadsteads of this parish get their personalities mixed up with the personalities of their bicycles as a result of the interchanging of the atoms of each of them and you would be surprised at the number of people in these parts who nearly are half people and half bicycles.

Flann O'Brien (1911-1966):
The Third Policeman

Central South

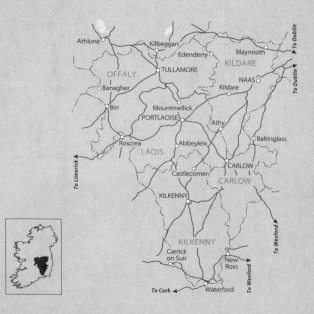

The city of Kilkenny, with its medieval history and flavour, possesses excellent transport links which make it an obvious destination as a base for exploring the lush and picturesque countryside to the south. Cycling is an ideal way to discover the quaint villages that lie dotted along the Nore and Barrow valleys, and for walkers the undemanding South Leinster Way winds its way gently through the county.

Carlow is one of Ireland's least distinguished counties, covering a small area of land surrounding the Rivers Barrow and Slaney. Laois (pronounced 'Leash') is another of Ireland's lesser-known counties, one of those places that travellers can pass through without ever registering the fact. A dull kind of prosperity characterizes the towns, but the Slieve Bloom mountains open up unspoilt Irish countryside.

County Kildare is close enough to the capital to turn parts of it into commuter land, but this also makes it handy for excursions out of Dublin. The north of County Offaly is marked by bogland, the northwest by the twisting River Shannon and the south by the rising hills of the Slieve Bloom range. Though visitors find this region relatively flat, it holds much of interest to those who appreciate places off the well-trodden tourist tracks.

★ *Try to find time for*

St Canice's Cathedral and its tombstones

A quiet drink in Tynan's Bridge pub

Shopping in craft shops in Kilkenny and Bennettsbridge

The Cantwell knight in Kilfane church

A cycling excursion in the Nore valley

Jerpoint Abbey and Kells Priory

County Kilkenny

Kilkenny

Phone code: 056
Colour map 4, grid B1

Most of Ireland's most interesting cities are found close to the sea, a pattern first established by the Vikings, but Kilkenny is a rich exception to the rule and we have the Normans to thank for this. The town developed in importance under their influence, and the medieval legacy of their era is one of the chief delights of a visit to a humming city that integrates tasteful shops and restaurants into time-hallowed streets and preserves a tangible sense of olde-Ireland. The downside to the town's unique blend of the medieval and the cosmopolitan is that Kilkenny features on countless coach tours, and at the height of summer the major attractions and shopping venues are heaving with visitors. In summer accommodation should be booked in advance.

Ins and outs

Getting there The bus and train stations are together. There are direct bus links to Dublin, Cork and Waterford and trains to Dublin (2 hrs away) and Waterford. See **Transport**, page 221 for further details.

Getting around Kilkenny is a small and compact town and the medieval attractions and the castle are within walking distance of the centre. Bicycles and cars can be hired. A disc system governs parking in the city centre, and you can get discs from newsagents and other shops.

History

Kilkenny's known history goes back to early Christian times but it was in the 13th century that the place grew to prominence under the Marshall family, the earls of Pembroke and lords of Leinster. William Marshall (c.1147-1219) married the daughter of Strongbow and spent a lot of time in Ireland consolidating his position and putting Kilkenny on the political map. Wealth to some came from trading in wool, and in medieval times Kilkenny had its own Anglo-Norman parliament that at times made the town the effective capital of Ireland. The most famous legislation arising from its parliament was the notorious Statutes of Kilkenny of 1366, aimed at reversing the growing Gaelicization of the English colony. In the 16th and 17th centuries Kilkenny was the political capital for the great Ormond family, also known as the Butlers because an ancestor who came over with the Normans became chief butler to Prince John. After the rising of 1641, an important gathering of Catholic interests took place here, known as the Confederation of Kilkenny, under a lord related to the Ormonds and the papal nuncio Rinuccini. Papal power wanted the full restoration of Catholicism and excommunicated any party willing to do business with Cromwell. The Protector himself turned up in 1650 and battered the town walls for five days, but although economic power passed to Protestants in the last quarter of the 17th century the town never quite lost its Catholic flavour. Kilkenny prospered through to the 19th century, with an important road link to both Dublin and Cork, and never lost its cultural influence within the country as a whole. In the last quarter of the 20th century this cultural significance

The Statutes of Kilkenny

Terms like apartheid and ethnic cleansing were not around in the 14th century, but clauses in the Statutes of Kilkenny seem to have been directed along those lines. Anglo-Normans residing in the colony of Ireland were required to use only the English language and to have recourse only to English law in settling disputes. Marriage to the native Irish was forbidden in an attempt to preserve the racial purity of the colonizers and non-martial games of Gaelic provenance were also punishable activities. In order to prepare for the military quashing of any outbreaks of native Irish rebellion, the sale of horses or armour to the Irish was outlawed and regular reviews of the colonial forces were instituted. Many of these clauses had been promulgated before but the Statutes were a systematic attempt to reinforce colonial rule and preserve the ruling class from infiltration by the resurgent Irish. They were broadly enforced throughout the 15th century and were not repealed until the early 17th century.

has reasserted itself with Kilkenny emerging as a provincial centre for the arts and, in particular, for the promotion of native craft design.

Sights

Kilkenny Castle The original castle was built in 1192 by William Marshall, Strongbow's son-in-law, but the strategic site commanding the river suggests that a defensive site of some kind existed before the Normans arrived. In the late 14th century ownership passed to the Ormonds and in 1967 the 24th Earl of Ormond sold the castle to the State for a nominal sum, after most of the contents had been auctioned. While the outer walls of the castle are original, substantial rebuilding and renovation work took place in the 1820s and 30s under the supervision of the London architect, William Robertson. So what is seen today as you are led around on the guided tour is very much a 19th-century creation.

Much of the guided tour focuses, naturally enough, on the **Long Picture Gallery** on the first floor. The wooden hammer-beam roof is profusely decorated in Pre-Raphaelite style, undertaken by John Hungerford Pollen in 1861, and while the array of exotic beasts and birds is undeniably a surprise, the images are fading and what can be seen is not artistically brilliant by any means. The walls are lined with countless family portraits. In the basement there is an exhibition of contemporary art in the Butler Gallery and the original kitchen area is now a very good restaurant. ■ *T21450. June to September, daily 1000-1900; April and May, daily 1030-1700; October to March, Tuesday-Saturday 1030-1245 and 1400-1700, Sunday 1100-1245 and 1400-1700, closed Monday. Compulsory one-hour guided tour. IR£3. Café open during summer months. Dúchas site.*

St Canice's Cathedral The largest medieval cathedral in Ireland after St Patrick's in Dublin was built in the 12th and 13th centuries, but suffered enormous damage after the usual bout of vandalism by Cromwell's army. The English took the roof off, stole the bells and the valuable glass, and left only the hinges on the doors 'that Hogs might come, and root, and Dogs gnaw the bones of the dead'. Restoration work means that none of this is now obvious and the architectural form of this Early Gothic church remains sufficiently unaltered to make it the finest example of its kind outside of Dublin. The actual site has an ecclesiastical history that goes as far back as perhaps the sixth century, and this itself suggests the ground may have a pre-Christian significance. The philosopher George

County Kilkenny

Berkeley and satirist Jonathan Swift, at the end of the 17th century, were educated in a school that once stood in the cathedral grounds.

Do not be put off by the symmetrical dullness of the exterior; the inside of St Canice's Cathedral is a rich pot-pourri of funeral monuments and effigies, our favourite being the tombstone near the stall that sells postcards and the like. Its 10-line epitaph records the death of Mary Stoughton, who died in childbirth in 1631. There is no end of fine carved effigies accompanying the tombs of more illustrious folk and while most of them are 16th-century, there are a couple

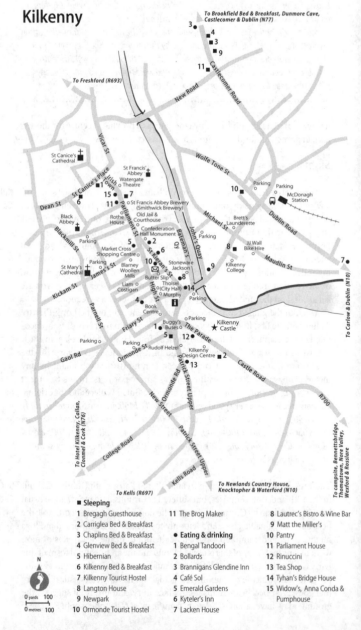

Kilkenny

■ **Sleeping**

1	Bregagh Guesthouse
2	Carriglea Bed & Breakfast
3	Chaplins Bed & Breakfast
4	Glenview Bed & Breakfast
5	Hibernian
6	Kilkenny Bed & Breakfast
7	Kilkenny Tourist Hostel
8	Langton House
9	Newpark
10	Ormonde Tourist Hostel
11	The Brog Maker

● **Eating & drinking**

1	Bengal Tandoori
2	Bollards
3	Brannigans Glendine Inn
4	Café Sol
5	Emerald Gardens
6	Kyteler's Inn
7	Lacken House
8	Lautrec's Bistro & Wine Bar
9	Matt the Miller's
10	Pantry
11	Parliament House
12	Rinuccini
13	Tea Shop
14	Tyhan's Bridge House
15	Widow's, Anna Conda & Pumphouse

N

0 yards   100
0 metres   100

A riverside stroll with Thomas Moore

The grounds of Kilkenny Castle are open all year around and on a fine day they make a delightful place in which to wander and enjoy a picnic. The poet Thomas Moore (1779-1852), famed for his Irish Melodies, *while performing in an amateur theatrical in Kilkenny, found himself acting alongside a 14-year-old girl, Elizabeth Dyke, whom he married two years later in 1811. He was then 32. Two decades later they were still together and returned to Kilkenny to stroll along the river by the castle where they first flirted. He wrote in his diary how they 'recollected the time when we used, in our love-making days, to stroll for hours there together. We did not love half so really then as we do now.'*

dating back to the 13th century. The naturalistic style of the effigies of Margaret and Piers Butler in the south transept makes a dramatic contrast with the inept renderings of various Apostles liberally dotted around, but this is all part of the wonderful variety of sculptures in the church.

The **round tower** that abuts the south apse has the distinction of being accessible to visitors and offers good views from the top, but forego the experience if given to claustrophobia or fear of heights. ■ *T64971. Monday-Saturday 0900-1300 and 1400-1800, Sunday 1400-1800. Free; IR£1 donation requested for Restoration Fund.*

Rothe House

This stone-built Tudor merchant's house is a superb and unique survival of Kilkenny's prosperous era. The Rothes came to Ireland from Yorkshire in the 14th century and by the late 16th century they were sufficiently wealthy to have built for themselves this substantial house in the centre of the town. It is made up of three buildings linked by courtyards and small rooms, and the Kilkenny Archaeological Society, which now owns the place, has used the rooms to display a fairly uninspiring collection of costumes and assorted artefacts. These are laboriously described in a 20-minute video, which is worth missing, but the building itself has been remarkably well restored and contains some fine features. The stonework is original and the Irish oak roof on the second floor has been sensitively restored using the methods and style of the medieval period. Features worth admiring include the octagonal chimneys, the mullioned windows, and the original escutcheon next to the restored oriel window that rests on the original corbel. The reception area, entered through an original arcade and where 400 years ago the merchant owner laid out his wares for prospective buyers, has a collection of new and second-hand books about Ireland for sale. ■ *Parliament Street, T22893. April to October, Monday-Saturday 1030-1700, Sunday 1500-1700; November to March, Monday-Saturday 1300-1700, Sunday 1500-1700. IR£2.*

Other historical sights

Black Abbey, Abbey Street, is a Dominican church, founded in 1225 by William Marshall and dissolved in 1543. It earns the name because the Dominicans were called the Black Friars. Cromwell's army vandalized the place and it remained a ruin until it was again used as a church in the 18th century. Worth admiring are some of the original windows that date back to the 14th century.

The Tholsel, High Street, was built in 1761 by an amateur architect and perhaps this helps account for its aesthetic appeal. A tholsel, or tolsel or tolzey court, is an ancient name for a tollbooth or guildhall and here in Kilkenny it continues – uniquely – to fulfil its historical function as it is now the local office for the collection of rates. It has a projecting arcade and an octagonal clock tower, built on the spot where the unfortunate Petronilla was executed as a witch in 1324 (see page 218).

County Kilkenny

....

Alice Kyteler and Petronilla – the witches of Kilkenny

Ireland largely escaped the great witch hunts of the 16th and 17th centuries, but around the 1320s Alice Kyteler and her maid Petronella de Midia got a foretaste of what was to come. Alice was of Flemish descent and the first of her four husbands was a member of the influential Outlawe family. She was accused by a witch-obsessed English bishop of having sex

with a demon spirit named Robin FitzArt and sacrificing cockerels to the devil. Family members of her subsequent husbands, who saw a chance to weaken the power of the Outlawes, accused her of sorcery in order to favour her first son. She was put on trial and, though she managed to escape to England, her unfortunate maid was put to death.

....

Just past the Tholsel, a little further up the High Street, there is a narrow medieval alley, **Butter Slip**, that takes its name from the custom of selling butter there. Nowadays you can purchase sushi rolls instead in a modern little restaurant housed in the lane, which leads down to Dunne's supermarket.

Continuing back up the High Street, which turns into Parliament St, there is a **monument** marking the location of the Confederation Parliament of 1641 and just past this, opposite Rothe House, the **courthouse and former prison** is where insurgents from the 1798 rebellion were executed. The only way to see some of the cells is by joining Tynan's walking tour of the town (see page 221).

Shee Alms House, home to the tourist office in Rose Inn Street, dates back to the late 16th century, when it was built as an alms house by local bigwig Sir Richard Shee.

St Francis Abbey Brewery Now part of the Guinness empire and producing Smithwicks, Budweiser and Kilkenny Irish beer for home and abroad, the fact that the brewery occupies the site of a Franciscan monastery founded by William Marshall in 1232 has little to do with the enormous popularity of a visit here. ■ *T21014. June to August, tickets available from 0900, free admission to a video of the brewing process at 1500. And yes, there is a free drink.*

Essentials

Sleeping
■ *on map*
Price codes:
see inside front cover

AL *Hibernian*, 33 Patrick St, T71888, F71877, info@hibernian.iol.ie http://www.thehibernian.com Nineteenth-century bank building converted to a hotel but retaining original features, including the strong-room door. **AL** *Kilford Arms*, John St, T/F61018, phelanp@indigo.ie Guesthouse about 50m from the bus and rail stations. Traditional Irish restaurant, a night club and 3 bars. **AL** *Kilkenny River Court Hotel*, The Bridge, John St, T23388, F23389. Tucked away behind a small arched wall, in a private courtyard, with great views of the castle. Old world grandeur plus pool and gym.

L *Langton House Hotel*, 69 John St, T65133, F63693. Interesting if idiosyncratic rooms above a popular bar and restaurant. **L** *Newpark Hotel*, Castlecomer Rd, T22122, F61111, info@newparkhotel.com Choice of restaurants. Just outside of town and boasting an impressive leisure centre that includes a 52ft (16m) pool. **L** *Butler House*, Patrick St, T65707, F65626. Georgian house refurbished in a contemporary style with 12 bedrooms. Situated amidst secluded walled gardens.

A *Brannigans Glendine Inn*, Castlecomer Rd, T21069, F65897, branigan@iol.ie Guest-house with 7 bedrooms. Large pub on the main road. Close to the golf course (see page 220).

B *Brookfield*, Castlecomer Rd, T65629. B&B a little further out than others on this road.
B *Carriglea*, Archers Avenue, Castle Rd, T61629. Family home up past the castle in a residential cul-de-sac offers B&B. **B** *Chaplins*, Castlecomer Rd, T52236. B&B close to the Newpark Hotel. **B** *Glen View*, Castlecomer Rd, T/F51453. B&B, also close to the Newpark Hotel. **B** *Newlands Country House*, Seven Houses, Danesfort, T29111, F29171, newlands@indigo.ie B&B in a very modern house, 4 miles (7 km) outside of town just off the N10. Plush décor, canopied beds and room facilities to rival most hotels. A place to feel pampered in, and IR£18 multi-course dinners to boot.

D *Foulksrath Castle*, Jenkinstown, T67144, F67674. Inconvenient in that it is 8 miles (13 km) north of Kilkenny on the N77 road but *Buggy's Coaches*, T41264, run a daily bus that will stop nearby and the building itself is superb, a 15th-century tower house with medieval features, spiral staircase and stupendous dining room with fireplaces big enough for bunk beds. **D** *Kilkenny Tourist Hostel*, 35 Parliament St, T63541, F29242, kilkennyhostel@tinet.ie Open all year. Over 60 beds, including 6 private rooms for around IR£24. **D** *Ormonde Accommodation Centre*, Johns Green, T52733, F52737. Over 40 beds and about 12 private rooms at IR£22. Bikes for hire.

Camping *The Tree Grove Caravan & Camping Park*, Danville House, T70302, F21512. Good facilities, about a mile (2 km) from the city on the New Ross Road (R700). Open March to mid-November. Rates start at IR£5 for a one-person tent. There is another camp site at Bennettsbridge, 7 miles (11 km) away (see page 222).

Restaurants *Newpark Hotel Restaurant*, Castlecomer Rd, T22122, serves fresh food in a room that tries to evoke a Mediterranean feel with its hand-painted mural of classical ruins and colourful parrots. A set meal for around IR£20 has a choice from 5 starters and main courses of fish and meat; good wine list.

    On entering *Langton's*, 69 John St, T65133, you may be flummoxed by the dark cavernous interior and mullioned windows, all suitably medieval in mood, only to find fold-out laminated menus and marble tables with a chaise lounge or sofa. A convivial and popular restaurant where one can eat for under IR£10 or over IR£30, and a wine list that includes Dom Perignon champagne.

    Ristorante Rinuccini, The Parade, T61575, serves good lunches with main courses around IR£5 and specials such as home-made soup with salad for IR£4. The dinner menu starts from around IR£9 for pasta dishes to IR£16 for sole. Main dishes at the *Bengal Tandoori*, Pudding Lane (behind the Book Centre), T64722, range from IR£6 to IR£12 and on Sunday, 1300-1700, an eat-all-you-can meal is IR£9. Chinese food at *The Emerald Gardens*, High St, T61812, is very popular and at weekends reservations are often necessary. *Parliament House Restaurant*, Parliament St, T63666, offers lunches ranging from sandwiches with salad for IR£3.50 to enchilada for IR£5.50. The evening menu includes lamb for IR£12.50 and sole or duckling for IR£15.50. *Lautrec's Bistro & Wine Bar*, Kieran's St, T62720, has a range of fish, meat, Mexican and other dishes for around IR£5.

Cafés & pub food *The Pantry* is on Kieran's St, opposite Dunnes supermarket, and serves its own breads and cakes and quick lunches for hungry shoppers. Open until 1800 on Thursday and 2100 on Friday. The self-service café in the *Kilkenny Design Centre* in The Parade has good food but can become too full. The restaurant in *Kilkenny Castle* has a delightful setting and you don't have to have a ticket to visit the castle in order to eat there. Near the bridge at the town end of John St there is an old-fashioned, decidedly untouristy café, called simply *Bakery*, that cooks meals such as shepherd's pie for IR£4. On the other side of the road, down by the river, there are benches where you could have an enjoyable picnic on a fine day.

Eating
● *on map*
Price codes:
see inside front cover

County Kilkenny

Bollard's, where Kiernan St meets Parliament St, T21353, is a pub and restaurant serving snacks, lunches and evening meals. *Kyteler's Inn*, Kiernan St, is where Alice Kyteler (see page 218) lived and although the food is not bewitching the place is very popular with locals. *Anna Conda*, Parliament St, is an old pub with tables for diners and an above-average choice of bar food.

Pubs & music *Anna Conda*, Parliament St, T71657, has a beer garden and regular sessions of tradi-
Kilkenny's bustle can tional music. *John Cleere* is a couple of doors down, T62573, and has music as well as a
rush you off your feet tiny theatre bursting to the seams with a mixed crowd when something is on.
but Tynan's by the river *Langton's*, John St, T65133, is a very lively pub indeed with a disco and live music.
is the perfect place to *Matt the Millar*, at the bottom of John St, attracts a younger crowd. Other places
repose and recuperate worth checking out include *The Widow's* , Parliament St, T52520, which also has
music on Sunday mornings, and *The Pumphouse*, Parliament St, T63924. *The Bróg Maker* is out on Castlecomer Rd, T52900, and has an olde worlde atmosphere and a regular programme of music as well as a restaurant. The antiquarian and wonderfully civilized *Tynan's Bridge House* at St John's Bridge is a sheer delight, the kind of place that Irish theme pubs try so dismally to imitate.

Entertainment The *Kilkenny People* is a weekly local newspaper that carries details of what's on and where. **Theatre** *Watergate Theatre*, Parliament St, T61674. Regular programmes of theatre, dance and music.

Festivals **June** *The Cats Laugh Festival*, 50 John St, Kilkenny, T51254. Features comedy and theatre and is very popular. **August** *Kilkenny Arts Festival*, 92 High St, Kilkenny, T52175, F51704. The big event of the year, this is a multi-arts event with all kinds of music, sculpture, painting, literature, film and theatre. This is a very popular festival and tickets sell out quickly for many of the events. **October** *The Kilkenny Racing Festival*, T26225. Takes place at Gowran Park (see 'Sport', below).

Shopping *The Kilkenny Design Centre*, The Parade, is opposite the castle and has a comprehensive range of Irish craft goods for sale: ceramics, clothing, crystal, linens and assorted gifts. It is open every day from 0900 until 1800, except from January to March, when it closes on Sundays and national holidays. This area was Kilkenny Castle's stables and a number of studio showrooms under the aegis of the Crafts Council of Ireland occupy the grounds.

There is also a number of upmarket studio workshops in the Nore valley and the tourist board has a brochure with a map highlighting six of them, as well as small display cases exhibiting some of their products. One of these studios, *Rudolf Heltzel*, 10 Patrick St, T21497, specializes in jewellery with contemporary designs. *Liam Costigan*, Collier's Lane, T62408, creates jewellery using gold, silver and platinum. *Stoneware Jackson* (see page 222) have a shop near St John's Bridge. Another, more traditional, jewellery store is *Murphy*, 85 High St, www.gemnet.co.uk/ptmurphy *Blarney Woollen Mills* have an outlet in the Market Cross Shopping Centre, High St, with the usual range of quality pottery, crystal, jewellery and gifts. Next to the tourist office there is a *Kilkenny Crystal* shop, and *Katz*, selling craft items for the home. *The Book Centre* in High St has a good selection of books.

Sport **Birdwatching** T621390 (Pat Durkin). Local outings on 1st Sun of each month. Meet at Castle Park, 1000. **Golf** *Kilkenny Golf Club*, Castlecomer Rd, T22125. **Outdoor** *Countryside Leisure Activity Centre*, Bonnettsrath. One mile (2 km) outside of the city. Quad biking, archery and clay pigeon shooting. **Racing** Greyhounds: James Park, Freshford Rd, T21214. Wednesday and Friday, 2000. Reached from the R693 road out of town. **Horses:** *Gowran Park Racecourse*, Gowran, T26225. Admission IR£7. Just east of town.

Bicycle *JJ Walls*, 86 Maudlin St, T21236. Bike hire. **Car hire** *Barry Pender Motors*, **Transport**
Dublin Rd, T65777. **Bus** *Bus Éireann*, T64933, operates from the railway station
but also stops in Patrick St. Daily buses to Dublin, Cork and Waterford, and the
Waterford to Longford via Athlone bus stops in Kilkenny. On Thursday there is a
local bus to and from New Ross and Bennettsbridge. *JJ Kavanagh*, T31106, a private
bus company, has daily services between Kilkenny and Cashel via Kells and Fethard.
They stop in The Parade, opposite the castle. *Buggy's Coaches*, T41264, run buses
Monday-Saturday from The Parade to the An Óige hostel at Jenkinstown,
Ballyragget, Dunmore Cave and Castlecomer. **Taxis** *Kevin Barry*, T63017/088-
574343. *Mick Howe*, T65874/088-574141. *David Nagle*, T63300/088-586060. *Mike
O'Brien*, T61333/088-586085. **Train** Station: T22024, at the top end of John St.
Daily trains to Dublin and Waterford.

Banks Junction of High St and Friary St, and Parliament St. **Communications** Post office: High **Directory**
St. **Hospitals and medical services** Hospital: *St Luke's Hospital*, T51133. **Pharmacy**: *White's
Pharmacy*, 5 High St, T21328. **Language school** *Kilkenny Language Centre*, Office 6, Cashel
Crescent, Waterford Rd, Kilkenny, T51441, F51449, klc@iol.ie Summer courses. **Local
radio** *Radio Kilkenny* 96.6 FM. Daily 0700-0200. **Tourist office** Shee Alms House, Rose Inn St,
T51500, Apr-Jun and Sep, Mon-Sat 0900-1800; Jul-Aug, Mon-Sat 0900-2000, open Sun May-Sept
1100-1700. Oct-Mar Mon-Fri 0900-1700. **Tours** Coach: T4580054. Open-top coach tour of city,
Apr-Oct, daily 1000-1700, every half hour. Departs from Castle Gates area. **Walking**: *Tynan Tours*,
T65929. Mar-Oct, up to 6 tours a day; winter, Tue-Sat 3 a day. 45 mins long, covering all the main
sights except the castle, commencing from the tourist office. IR£3.

Around Kilkenny

Historically, the city and the county of Kilkenny prospered because of the gently- Phone code: 056
*flowing rivers and their pasture-rich valleys and today a rewarding day or two
could be enjoyed exploring the elegant countryside outside the city. The River
Nore, which flows through Kilkenny city, is particularly attractive as it winds its
tree-lined way through hill and vale in the south of the county, while further to the
east the lush valley of the River Barrow competes for the traveller's attention.*

A possible tour from Kilkenny by car or bicycle would be to travel south on the
R700 following the River Nore to Bennettsbridge and Thomastown, and then
picking up the N10 at Knocktopher after visiting Jerpoint Abbey. A short
detour to visit medieval Kells could be made on the return journey to Kilkenny, although it is close enough to the city to make a pleasant excursion in its
own right.

Kells

This little village nestles on the banks of a Nore tributary and is only eight miles *Colour map 4, grid C1*
(12 kilometres) south of Kilkenny. Not to be confused with its more famous
namesake in county Meath, Kells is a showcase for the beauty of the Nore valley. Its lovely stone bridge and ancient watermill are a treat to behold on a summer's day and close by are some of the most captivating monastic ruins you are
likely to come across in Ireland.

The priory was founded in 1193 by Augustinians brought over from Cornwall **Kells Priory**
but what you see today dates mostly from the 14th and 15th centuries. The survival of the church, and especially the complete wall with towers enclosing a
two-hectare site, creates a more tangible sense of what a medieval settlement
was like than most other ruins of this period in the country (including,

County Kilkenny

ironically, Kells in Meath). To the south of the church there are remains of what were the priory's domestic buildings. The entire site is freely open to the public and makes for a better investment of one's time than many a heritage centre that carries an admission charge.

Kilree Round Tower & High Cross The ruins of another monastic site lie just over a mile south of Kells and the way is signposted from Kells Priory. The church is in ruins and there is a well-preserved 17th-century tomb in the chancel, but what dominates the site is a 95-foot-high (29 metres) round tower, minus its top. In a field just to the west of the tower there stands a faded High Cross that is thought to date back to the ninth century. It is hard to make out any of the original pictorial representations, although various geometric patterns can be traced and on the east face a stag-hunting scene with a chariot has been discerned. The story that the cross commemorates Niall Caille, a king of Ireland who drowned while trying to save a squire, is apparently a piece of blarney.

Bennettsbridge

The main attraction in the village of Bennettsbridge is two of the country's finest pottery workshops. **Stoneware Jackson Pottery** is just north of the village and the workshop can be viewed from a relaxing garden setting before you are tempted to make a purchase in the showroom. There is also a modest selection of seconds on sale. ■ *T27175. Monday-Saturday, 0930-1800.*

Nicholas Mosse Pottery is based around an old mill by the river and water from the Nore is used to generate the electricity for firing the pots, which are brightly coloured earthenware with traditional motifs. There is also a small 'museum' of antique Irish spongeware and assorted artefacts. ■ *T27126, http://www.nicholasmosse.com September to June, Monday-Saturday 1000-1800; July-August, Monday-Saturday 1000-1800, Sunday 1330-1700.*

Sleeping & eating For snacks, light lunches or an evening meal there is the adjoining *Mosse's Mill Café*, T27644. Bennettsbridge is also home to the *Nore Valley Caravan & Camping Park*, T27229, F27748, open from March to October. Coming from Kilkenny turn right just before the bridge in Bennettsbridge.

Thomastown

Colour map 4, grid C1 Situated on the busy Dublin to Waterford N9 road, but worth considering as a place to rest for a drink or meal either before or after visiting Jerpoint Abbey and nearby Kilfane. In the town itself there are fragmentary ruins of the wall that enclosed this medieval settlement and the not-very-interesting ruins of a 13th-century church with only the north aisle and parts of the foundation still to be seen.

Ins & outs Dublin to Waterford buses, 5 a day, stop in Thomastown, outside O'Keefe's supermarket. As too do the twice daily Waterford to Longford buses, and this service also connects Thomastown with Kilkenny and Athlone. On Thursday only the local 374 New Ross to Kilkenny service travels via Inistioge, Thomastown and Bennettsbridge. The town is also serviced by the Dublin to Waterford railway line.

Jerpoint Abbey This impressive Cistercian abbey, one of the best monastic ruins in the country, was founded between 1163 and 1165. After the Dissolution of the Monasteries in 1540 it was leased to the earls of Ormond. The church retains Romanesque features, although the arches in the aisles are recognizably

Gothic, and there are a number of excellently preserved sculptured tombs. These include a bishop who died in 1202 and two knights from the late 13th century. The real highlight, however, is the restored cloister that dates from the 15th century and delights the eye with a very lively array of sculptured knights, saints and other figures. ■ *T24623. June to 13th September, daily 0930-1830; 14th September to 27th October, Wednesday-Monday 1000-1700; 14th March to May, Wednesday-Monday 1000-1700. IR£2. Dúchas site. Guided tours available. 1½ miles (2.5 kilometres) southwest of Thomastown on the N9.*

Kilfane

Kilfane, a small village just north of Thomastown on the N9 road, is noteworthy for its ruined 14th-century church. Inside you will be surprised by the imposing, bigger-than-life effigy of a medieval knight. With his legs crossed, wearing a fine suit of chain mail, spurs and accompanied by his trusty shield, this is Thomas de Cantwell, who died some time around 1320. History is suddenly brought to life by this animated Norman conqueror who displays in his figure and accoutrements the daunting new forces that came from across the water to subdue the native Irish. At one time the church was used as a school and the story goes that naughty scholars were chastised by being forced to kiss the forbidding lips of this conquering Norman.

Further along the road, less than two miles (three kilometres) from Thomastown, **Kilfane Glen and Waterfall** is a woodland garden dating from the late 18th century. There are paths to stroll along, a hermit's grotto, a waterfall and one of those little villas with an affectation of rusticity known as a *cottage ornée*. These diversions add to the charms of the planted woods and invite a leisurely picnic on a good day. ■ *T24558. May to mid-September, Tuesday-Sunday 1400-1800. IR£3. Teashop. Signposted on the N9.*

Sleeping

L *Mount Juliet Estate*, Thomastown, T73000, F73019, info@mountjuliet.ie Hotel and self-styled sporting estate beside the river, with rooms in the 18th-century house or adjoining lodges. Golfing, fishing, shooting, archery, tennis and an equestrian centre available. The Georgian, high-ceilinged Lady Helen dining room at the Mount Juliet

Cantwell Effigy

Estate is justly renowned for classic dishes using home-grown vegetables, herbs, and Nore salmon. Dinner daily, lunch only on Sunday. Around IR£30. **B** *Abbey House*, Jerpoint Abbey, T24166, F24192. Period house directly opposite the abbey offering B&B. Evening meal available for around IR£18. Closed at Christmas. **B** *Carrickmourne House*, New Ross Rd, T/F24124. B&B but no evening meals. Closed at Christmas.

Eating

In addition to the *Mount Juliet Estate* and *Abbey House*, you can eat at the pubs in Thomastown and *Carrolls*, Logan St, T24273, is worth a visit because as well as serving doorstep sandwiches and Irish stew there is a beer garden and sessions of traditional music. Outside of town, on the N9 Dublin road, the *Long Man of Kilfane*, T24774, has a bar serving food, a restaurant and music at weekends.

County Kilkenny

Inistioge

Colour map 4, grid C1

This quaint little village, pronounced 'Inisteeg', is situated on the west bank of the Nore and the agreeable 18th-century 10-arched bridge adds considerably to its charms. The photogenic quality is further enhanced by an ancient-looking church and neat lime trees in a village square from which spidery lanes radiate. Such an evocation of the past makes it not surprising that a number of films have used the location, including *Widow's Peak* in 1993. Inistioge derives its name from the Tighes, and their family seat was in a grand 18th century house that was burned down in 1922. The Tighes left for England when the War of Independence broke out and later the Black and Tans used it as a local headquarters. The empty house was burned down during the civil war. What was the Tighe demesne, Woodstock Park, is now state-owned and open to the public. There are various walking trails and picnic areas.

Mount Brandon stansds 1,693 feet (519 metres) high and lies to the northeast of Inistioge and a road leads through the mountain to the village of Graiguenamanagh.

Sleeping

AL *Berryhill*, Inistioge, T461532. Open April to mid-November, minimum booking 2 nights; breakfast a speciality and dinner available if booked in advance. Late 18th-century house on a hillside overlooking the Nore. **A** *Cullintra House*, The Rower, Inistioge, T051-423614. Minimum booking 2 nights; dinner, IR£16, at 2100. At the foot of Mount Brandon. **B** *Ashville*, Kilmacshane, Inistioge, T58460. B&B but no evening meals. Open March-October. Situated on the Kilkenny to Rosslare road. **B** *Nore Valley Villa*, Inistioge, T/F58418. Modern house, in the village.

Eating

In addition to the above, *The School House Café* is situated by the river and serves snacks and standard light meals during the summer. For a culinary adventure the menu at *The Motte*, Plas Newydd Lodge, Inistioge, T58655, has a reputation for literally and artistically spicing up old favourites and by all accounts doing so very successfully. Dinner only, closed Monday, around IR£20.

Graiguenamanagh

Phone code: 0503
Colour map 4, grid C1

The small town of Graiguenamanagh ('the granary of the monks'), very attractively situated on the banks of the River Barrow, has another of those pleasing 18th-century arched bridges and with your own transport the town is easily reached from Inistioge. The attraction of Graiguenamanagh, apart from the relaxing beauty of the location and pleasant walks along the riverside using the South Leinster waymarked route (see page 225), is the Cistercian abbey in the town.

Duiske Abbey

Founded in 1207 by William Marshall, Earl of Pembroke, and sufficiently well preserved after a restoration project in the 1970s for parts of it to be still in use today. Inside the church, in the baptistry near the organ, there is a fine doorway from the early 13th century that is considered to be one of the best examples of its type to have survived the Dissolution of the Monasteries. Equally eye-catching is an effigy of a knight from the same period and nearby a glass panel reveals some authentic fleur-de-lys tiling of the 13th century, the present floor of the church being over 6½ feet (two metres) above its original level. Outside the church there are two high crosses and the nearby **Abbey Centre** houses a modest exhibition on the abbey.

AL *Waterside*, The Quay, T24246, F24733, info@waterside.iol.ie All rooms overlook **Sleeping**
the river and midweek packages for 2 nights B&B and 1 dinner start at IR£75 per person. **B** *Woodside*, Ballynakill, south of Graiguenamanagh, T24765. B&B between
March and October. A modern house.

Waterside is a restaurant in a restored 19th-century corn store overlooking the river. **Eating**
An evening meal here is over IR£20. The *Café Duiske* opposite the abbey serves light
meals for around IR£5 and a couple of the town bars such as the *Anchor*, Main St,
T24207, serve pub food.

The South Leinster Way

The total length of this long-distance waymarked walk is 62 miles (100 kilometres), starting at Kildavin on the slopes of Mount Leinster in County Carlow
and finishing at Carrick-on-Suir in County Tipperary. It takes four to five days
to complete the journey and the first day's walk ends in the village of Borris on
the border between Carlow and Kilkenny. The second day is a very manageable eight miles (13 kilometres), which mostly follows a towpath alongside the
River Barrow as far as Graiguenamanagh. The distance on the third day is
about the same length and skirts Brandon Hill before reaching the lovely village of Inistioge. The fourth day, 12 miles (20 kilometres) in length, follows the
river and uses forest roads before ending in the village of Mullinavat in southern Kilkenny. The last day's walking crosses into Tipperary over farmland a lot
of the way but also using roads in places.

EastWest Mapping produce the *South Leinster Way Map Guide* and Ordnance Survey **Mapping**
maps Nos 68, 75 and 76 are needed to cover the whole walk. Maps and information **information**
are available from the tourist office in Carlow (see page 227) or Kilkenny (see page
221).

North of Kilkenny

This is the main town in the north of the county, but there are few places of **Castlecomer**
interest either in the town or the surrounding area and most visitors to the
county content themselves with a trip to Dunmore Cave, which is only a few
kilometres north of Kilkenny. Castlecomer rose to local prominence after the
discovery of anthracite in the 17th century and in the 1798 uprising (see page
676) the town was captured by insurgents led by Father John Murphy. All that
remains of the Anglo-Norman castle that gave the town its name is a mound,
so from a sightseeing point of view there is little point in making the journey
here from Kilkenny.

This site consists of limestone caverns and impressive calcite formations. **Dunmore Cave**
There is an exhibition centre and a compulsory guided tour that lasts about 45
minutes. Geology aside, there is a reference in Irish sources to a Viking massa-
cre at the cave in the year 928 and excavations in the 1970s did reveal the skele-
tons of nearly 50 women and children. ■ *Ballyfoyle. T67726. Mid-June to mid-
September, daily 1000-1900; mid-March to mid-June and mid-September to
October, daily 1000-1700. IR£2. Dúchas site. seven miles (10 kilometres) from
Kilkenny and signposted off the N78.*

County Kilkenny

County Carlow

Carlow and around

Phone code: 0503
Colour map 4,
grid B1 & 2

Carlow town is too easily dismissed as a one-street town, but the main drag, besides having plenty of affordable places to eat, boasts a buzzing nightlife with lots of pubs offering live music. There is also an absolutely superb restaurant – Danette's Feast (see next page) – just a couple of miles away. The town has a long history, being for centuries an Anglo-Norman base perched at the dangerous interface between Gaelic Ireland and the Pale, and it's regrettable there is so little to see beyond the crumbling remains of Carlow Castle in Castle St.

There might be a little more to see here had it not been for the crazy Dr Middleton who blew up most of the castle in 1814, in order to make space for a lunatic asylum. Far more interesting to look at, and well worth seeking out, is the courthouse at the top end of Dublin Street. Most of Ireland's most impressive courthouses were built just before and after the 1798 insurrection – hardly a coincidence – and the Greek style of architecture was highly popular (see page 169). Perhaps ancient Athens conjured up a suitable image of the rule of law because the Carlow courthouse, designed by William Morrison in 1830, is an unashamed copy of the Parthenon. There is a small **County Carlow Museum** in the town hall on Centaur Street. ■ *T40730. Year-round, Tuesday-Friday 1100-1700, Saturday and Sunday 1400-1700. IR£1.* One way to enjoy what Carlow has to offer is by joining the new **guided town tours**, starting from the tourist office (see page 227). ■ *T30411. Mid-April to mid-October, Tuesday, Thursday and Saturday 1430. IR£3.*

Browneshill dolmen   Weighing in at 100 tons as the heavyweight champion of Europe, the capstone of this dolmen is now stuck in the earth at one end while resting on three stones at the other. As the construction dates back to around 2500BCE, the individual who occasioned this feat of engineering and toil is now completely lost to time. The dolmen is beside a car-park, just two miles (three kilometres) from town on the R726 road to Hacketstown.

Sleeping   **AL** *Royal Hotel*, Dublin St, T31621, F31125, royal@iol.ie Maintains its original function as a Georgian coaching inn by providing comfortable rooms and stylish meals. **B** *T&G's*, 6 Oaklawns, Dublin Rd, T/F40557. B&B in a quiet part of town. **D** *Otterholt Riverside Lodge*, Kilkenny Rd, T30404/31170. Open all year. 39 beds including 9 private rooms around IR£22. **D** *Verona Hostel*, Pembroke St, T31700/31846. Open all year. 20 beds including 2 private rooms at IR£20. Camping is also possible, and meals can be arranged and bicycles hired.

Eating   The best place for a meal in town is the recently redesigned Bistro in the *Royal Hotel*, where some excellent Californian-style food is offered at around IR£16. You will quickly realise where *The Beams Restaurant*, 59 Dublin St, T31824, gets its name from once inside the door, and the menu of French-style Irish cuisine should not disappoint. Expect to pay around IR£27 for dinner, closed Sunday. Tullow St has a whole range of places to eat from good bar food at *Scragg's Alley* to a very exotic range of dishes upstairs in the same place at *Fitzoraldo's*, T42233, where dinner is around IR£18. In the arcade in Tullow St is *Brook's Café Bar* with a very modern themed interior and lots of Californian options. Near the SuperValu supermarket, the *Plough Bar* has its own restaurant and, across the road, *Reddy's*, 67 Tullow St, T42224, also provides meals. *Buzz's*, 7 Tullow St, T43307, serves food and alcohol on cast iron tables on wooden floors and lives up to its name. In Dublin St the very down to earth *Pepper Pot* does breakfasts and sensible lunches. For a memorable epicurean experience book a table at *Danette's Feast*, Urglin Glebe, T40817, where the quality of the food is matched by what must be the best background music to be heard in any restaurant in Ireland. The chef, who happens to be a musician, cooks imaginatively (especially Mexican food) with superb vegetarian options, organic vegetables and a margarita sorbet to die for. Dinner is IR£26.50, Wednesday to Saturday, and lunch on Sunday. Take the Hackettstown road from Carlow for two miles and turn left at the Burma garage.

Pubs & music

Carlow has a booming nightlife with lots of trendy places opening up and music everywhere. For traditional music you could try *Ewings*, Haymarket, T31138, next to the town hall or *The Quays* in the same street. *The Castle*, 24 Governey Sq, T41200, has music on Friday nights and *The Barge*, Castle Hill, also has music and bar food.

Sport

Bowling *Carlow Superbowl*, Lismard Centre, Barrack St, T41555.

Transport

Bicycle *Coleman Cycles* 19 Dublin St, T31273. Bike hire. **Bus** *Bus Éireann*, T31633, has daily services to Dublin, Kilkenny and Waterford. **Taxi** *Tierney's* T33339. **Train** Station at Railway Rd, T31633. A 20-minute walk from the town centre. Carlow is on the Dublin to Waterford line. Trains go to Dublin 9 times a day, 3 on Sunday, while trains leave for Waterford 6 times a day, 4 on Sundays.

Directory

Banks Green Lane, Tullow St, Court Place. **Communications** Post office: Bridewell Lane. **Tourist office** Bridewell Lane, T31554. May-Sep, Mon-Sat 1000-1730; Jan-Apr and Oct-Dec, Mon-Fri 1000-1700. **Travel agents** *LSA Travel*, Tullow St, T42244.

County Laois

Around Portlaoise

Travellers always used to pass through Portlaoise ('Portleash'), because it is on the major Dublin to south and southwest of Ireland route, and dutifully take note of the town's maximum security prison and its Ulster-style concrete observation posts at the east end of the main road. With a modern bypass, even that dubious claim to fame will pass unnoticed, but at least the town should benefit from the decline in heavy traffic.

Phone code: 0502
Colour map 2, grid C6
& colour map 4,
grid B1

Rock of Dunamase

The Rock of Dunamase, a few miles outside of town, is the best reason for lingering around Portlaoise for, although not much remains of the castle that once stood there, the site is extraordinarily well situated and on a fine day there are superb views of the surrounding countryside from atop the mound. An Iron Age fort predates the castle, which was built some time around the end of the 12th century and changed hands between Irish and English lords more than once before Cromwellian forces took it apart in 1650. It was briefly restored as a residence but little now remains of what must have been a spectacularly sited fortress. ■ *Open access. Three miles (five kilometres) east of Portlaoise on the N80 road to Stradbally.*

County Laois

Stradbally The town of Stradbally will interest steam train buffs, being home to a Guinness Brewery steam locomotive of 1895 that runs to Dublin half a dozen times each year. The town is on the N80 road west of the Rock of Dunamase. Its **Steam Museum** has a collection of traction engines. ■ *Easter to October, Monday-Friday 1100-1300 and 1400-1600. IR£1.50.*

Emo Court An impressive example of neo-classical architecture, Emo Court was designed in 1790 by James Gandon for the first earl of Portarlington but not completed until 1874. It was run as a novitiate by the Jesuits until the 1960s and is now open to the public. Combine a visit with a walk through the extensive grounds. ■ *T26573. Mid-June to mid-September, daily, 1000-1800. Guided tours. IR£2, free admission to Garden. Dúchas site. 1½ miles (2½ kilometres) from Emo, seven miles (13 kilometres) from Portlaoise, and signposted off the Kildare to Portlaoise N7 road.*

Mountmellick Six miles (10 km) north of Portlaoise, Mountmellick was founded by Quakers in the 17th century and a number of Georgian houses remain from its heyday in the late 18th century, when the famed Mountmellick linen was exported by canal to Dublin and beyond. There is a small heritage centre, T24525, on the Portlaoise road just outside of town.

About 8 miles (12 km) west of Portlaoise the picturesque little village of **Coolrain** is nestled in the foot of the Slieve Bloom mountains and bicycles can be hired from *The Thatched Village Inn*, T35277, which will also suggest routes and provide maps for trips in the local uncrowded roads. Accommodation is available in a restored thatched cottage next to and belonging to the inn, T35216, and the pub serves meals throughout the day. Sessions of set dancing and traditional music also take place here.

The Slieve Bloom Way This 2-day energetic walk covers 51 km (32 miles) offers sweeping views of the Slieve Bloom mountains as the Way makes its way through moors, valleys and forests. However, it is a Way that requires some planning because of the limited public transport in the area and the need to book accommodation in advance. Ordnance Survey map No 54 in the Discovery series covers the Way, and EastWest Mapping publish *The Slieve Bloom Way Map Guide* using the same 1:50,000 scale. There is also a booklet published by the local council, *Slieve Bloom Environment Park*, available from the tourist office in Portlaoise, and see page 64 for walking guides that cover the Way.

For a one-day excursion covering part of the Way consider parking on the R422 between Mountmellick and Clonaslee and heading off for a day's exhilarating walk with a picnic. On the south side of the mountains, **B** *Conlán House*, Killanure, Mountrath, on the R440 road, is a B&B with good information on the Way, and you can also enquire here about guided walks.

Sleeping **B** *Donoghues*, 1 Kellyville Park, Portlaoise, T21353. An evening meal for under IR£10 is also available at this B&B. **C** *Talltrees*, Cork Rd, Stradbally, T25412, epc@iol.ie   2 rooms for IR£14 per person. **D** *Traditional Farm Hostel*, Farren House, Ballacolla, Portlaoise, T34032, F34008. IHH. Open all year. 5 private rooms at IR£9 per person. Good amenities including bicycle hire and space for camping.

Eating Portlaoise town centre is littered with pubs serving food and at *O'Loughlin's Hotel*, Main St, T21305, food is served from 0800 until 2100, including à la carte in the restaurant. The Montague Hotel, Emo, T26154, serves a carvery lunch and evening meals in the Maple Room restaurant. The *Gandon Inn*, Emo, T26622, has 2 bars, a restaurant and accommodation.

Bus Buses from most parts of the country seem to pass through Portlaoise, T01-836611, especially the Dublin to the south and southwest of Ireland routes. **Trains** T21303. Services to and from Dublin and Cork, Limerick, Tralee and Tipperary stop in Portlaoise.

Tourist office Portlaoise, T21178. May-Sep, Mon-Sat 1000-1800. In the centre of the town.

Around Abbeyleix

Abbeyleix, about 10 miles (16 kilometres) south of Portlaoise, has an interesting story to tell. It grew up around a 12th century Cistercian abbey but 600 years later the local landlord, Viscount de Vesci, relocated the village to its present site and planned the layout that is so attractive a part of the modern town. The country house of de Vesci, Abbeyleix House outside of town on the Rathdowney road, was built by James Wyatt and remodelled in the Victorian age, but it remains closed to the public apart from the occasional opening of the gardens to the hoi polloi. Worth admiring is the architecture of the town's **Bank of Ireland**, replete with mullioned windows, classical columns, a corner oriel and a copper-domed tower, all built at the beginning of the 20th century. *Morrissey's*, half-pub and half-shop on Main St, Abbeyleix, T31233, is well known to discerning travellers on the Cork-Dublin run who value a place to rest and relax without being forced to listen to the blather of radio phone-ins or crass music. In the same family since 1775 and with ancient shelves packed with old biscuit tins and a pot belly stove there is little to suggest that much has changed since then. The perfect place for a quiet pint or a cup of Morrissey's own special brand tea.

Heritage House Off Main St, this was one of the two schools that de Vesci had built, and its interesting and well-presented displays are worth a look. With a coffee shop and a craft shop, it's worth considering as a place to stop when travelling between Dublin and Cork. ■ *T31653. March to October, Monday-Saturday 1000-1800, Sunday 1300-1800; November to February, shorter hours. IR£2.*

Heywood House Heywook House has a noted garden designed by Edwin Lutyens and thought to have been landscaped by Gertrude Jekyll, now well restored and open to the public. The actual house was destroyed by fire in 1960 and nothing of it remains. Picturesquely-framed views of inland Ireland can be seen through the *oeil-de-boeuf* windows in Lutyens' sunken terrace. ■ *Ballinakill, T33563/056-21450. Open during daylight hours. Tours can be arranged by telephoning in advance. Free. Four miles (seven kilometres) southeast of Abbeyleix off the R432 road to Ballinakill.*

Sleeping **AL** *Preston House*, Main St, Abbeyleix, T&F31432, has four large bedrooms handsomely furnished with antiques and makes canny use of the available space to incoporate modern facilities. **AL-A** *Hibernian Hotel*, Abbeyleix, T31252, F31888. Tudor-style, family-run hotel with good rooms. On the main N8 road. **AL-B** *Norefield House*, T31059. Rooms range from IR£17.50 to IR£35 per person. Secluded 18th-century residence. **A** *Castle Arms Hotel*, The Square, Durrow, T/F36117, has ten bedrooms and is one of the few places to stay in Durrow. **D** *Traditional Farm Hostel*, Farren House, Ballacolla, T34032, a couple of miles from Durrow on the R434, redeems the accommodation prospects with its 35 beds, which include five private rooms for IR£18 each, and camping space. Meals are available and bikes can be hired.

County Laois

William Conolly

William Conolly (1662-1729), regarded in his time as the richest commoner in Ireland, is said to have made his money by dealing in land exchanges in the tumultuous years following the Battle of the Boyne; hence the snobbish contempt of men like Sir John St Leger who wrote in 1717, 'our quality and old gentry are much offended at Mr Conolly's being one of them; this gentleman was lately an attorney, his father keeping an ale-house in the north of Ireland … but by making long wills and good bargains he is now reported to be worth eight thousand a year.'

Eating The comfortable *Hibernian Hotel* in Abbeyleix can be relied on for hearty meals, but it is first well worth checking out creeper-covered *Preston House* restaurant in Main St. Tasty scones and home-made preserves in the morning, while the lunch menu includes appetizing chowder with brown bread and delicious vegetarian dishes. Dinner, under IR£15, is especially good value. In Durrow the choice is disappointing: standard hotel food at the *Castle Arms* or more interesting choices at the modest *Copper Kettle* in The Square.

Transport **Bus** *Bus Éireann*'s Dublin to Cork service stops in Abbeyleix 3 times a day and twice on Sunday.

County Kildare

Castletown House, Maynooth and around

Phone code: 01
Colour map 4, grid B1

Head due west from Dublin's city centre for about 12 miles (19 kilometres) – though it will seem a lot longer if you get caught in rush-hour traffic – and a mixed landscape of rolling countryside and suburban dwellings awaits the traveller. This is modern Ireland, depressingly modern at times, and the key sights can be comfortably taken in on a day trip.

Castletown House Ease of access from Dublin, and its reopening in 1999 after a long period of closure, increases the appeal of a visit to Ireland's largest and architecturally most important country house. Castletown House was built around 1722 for William Conolly, the Speaker of the Irish House of Commons. He spared no expense in employing the Italian architect Alessandro Galilei, although the work was completed by Edward Lovett Pearce, an Irish Italophile architect, and others. It is the finest expression of the Palladian style to be found in the country and this can first be appreciated by simply standing outside and admiring the symmetry of the façade. The philosopher Bishop Berkeley was more aware of the type of stone that went into its building, 'fine wrought stone, harder and better coloured than the [English] Portland' stone, and like other Ascendancy figures rejoiced at what he saw as an expression of Irish culture.

Conolly died before the house was finished, but his wife lived for another 23 years and in 1740 she commissioned the building of a monumental **folly** in the grounds as a way of providing relief to the local poor. Before she died in 1752, she had a tent put up on the lawn so that she could admire her home for the last time. She died childless and the house ended up with Conolly's grand-nephew whose wife, the English Lady Louisa, daughter of the Duke of Richmond, was responsible for much of the interior decoration. Some of her ideas, like the Pompeii-style decorations on the walls, can be seen in the most distinctive room, the Long Gallery on the first floor. She also created the Print Room, the last surviving example of its kind in Ireland. ■ *Celbridge, T6288252. 23 April-September, Monday-Friday 1000-1800, Saturday-Sunday 1300-1800. Same times in October except the house closes at 1700. November, Sunday 1300-1700. Guided tours. IR£2.50. Dúchas site. 12 miles (20 kilometres) from the centre of Dublin on the R403; Bus No 67/67A from Middle Abbey St, and No 66X.*

Christopher Paris

Christopher Paris, the constable of Maynooth Castle in 1535, was bribed into betraying it with a promise of leniency but, nevertheless, executed afterwards. 'The pardon of Maynooth' became an ironic term for such breaches of trust.

Straffan

Only three miles (five kilometres) southwest of Celbridge, the village of Straffan has a **Steam Museum** with working steam engines and a small exhibition about the impact of steam power. The best time to visit is over the holiday weekend at the very beginning of August when an annual Steam Rally brings together a big display of steam engines and working models and an opportunity to ride on the longest established steam-powered narrow gauge railway in Ireland. ■ *Easter to August, Tuesday-Sunday 1400-1800. IR£3. Café. T25444, and best to telephone first.*

Close by is the **Straffan Butterfly Farm**, with its array of colourful butterflies and scary-looking insects and spiders. ■ *May to September, daily 1200-1800. IR£3.25.*

Maynooth

A famous place to the Irish, the town being home to the country's leading seminary for the training of priests. **Maynooth College** was founded in 1795, at a time when the government wanted the support of moderate Catholics, and Augustus Pugin was commissioned to design the college; building began in 1847. Architecturally, it is not a particularly interesting example of Victorian Gothic and there is little here to engage the visitor's attention. University colleges are now based here and they account for the majority of students seen about the place; young men actually studying for the priesthood are an endangered species. At the college entrance stand the ruins of Maynooth Castle, a stronghold of the Norman Fitzgerald family, the Earls of Kildare. It was treacherously taken in 1535 after a rebellion by its owner, 'Silken Thomas', the son of the ninth Earl of Kildare, against the English, and abandoned completely some time around 1656.

Larchill Arcadian Gardens

These are more interesting than Maynooth, and only four miles (6.5 kilometres) away. Here you will find what is claimed to be the only surviving example in Ireland or England of the mid-18th century style of a *ferme ornée*. A circular walk links 10 follies, with gazebos along the way and a tiny island with a Greek-style temple. ■ *Kilcock, T6287354. May to September, daily 1200-1800. IR£3.25. West of Maynooth on the N4. Bus No 66 from Middle Abbey St, Dublin.*

Essentials

Sleeping

AL-L *Glenroyal Hotel*, Straffan Rd, Maynooth, T6290909, F6290919. Attracts business trade but the modern 65ft (20m) swimming pool, gym, and aerobics studio has a wider appeal. **A** *Jassamine House*, Main St, Celbridge, T6272040. Typical of the more

County Kildare

expensive B&B places in this part of the world. **B** *Rosturk House*, Old Rail Park Lane, Maynooth, T6285310, F6290021. 1 mile (1.5 km) from the college and close to the train station.

Eating *Moyglare Manor Restaurant*, Maynooth, T6286351, is formal to the point of conformist, but the IR£22 lunch and IR£30 dinner menus offer carefully-prepared meals, especially seafood, and a wine list that is well above average. For more character and atmosphere *The Castle Restaurant*, T6288157, in the Barberstown Castle hotel in Straffan, wins hands down. Dining tables occupy whitewashed rooms in a basement setting with low lighting and the food includes sumptuous seafood and satisfying vegetarian dishes. Lunch is around IR£18 and dinner IR£33.

The Byerley Turk, T6017200, in the Kildare Hotel & Country Club in Straffan, specializes in French cuisine and does with classical panache: crisp white linen tablecloths and enough fine china, crystal and silver around your table to make you feel rich enough to afford one of the racehorses painted and framed on the walls.

Back in Maynooth, in addition to the *Glenroyal Restaurant*, the *Glenroyal Hotel* also has a carvery and a bar serving food. Pubs in Maynooth offer the usual pub food.

Transport **Bus** Bus No 67/67A from Middle Abbey St, and No 66X, connect Maynooth and Dublin. Many of the *Bus Éireann* services to Galway and Sligo also make a stop, T01-8366111. **Train** Suburban and main line trains stop at Maynooth station, T6285509.

Kildare Town and around

Phone code: 045
Colour map 4, grid B1

A valuable tip: try to avoid a drive between Kildare Town and Dublin during the morning or evening rush hours. There is a motorway, the M7, for a stretch of the way, but traffic snarls are still very common. Another tip is not to bother stopping at Naas (pronounced 'nace') unless there is a desperate need to do some shopping or grab a bite to eat in one of the pubs. The county town has little else to recommend it, unlike the pretty and prosperous little town of Kildare.

Kildare

The town is forever associated with the legendary St Brigid, who by the middle of the seventh century already had a church and shrine dedicated to her here. Very little is known about her life and there is reason to think that worship of St Brigid evolved from the cult of an earlier pagan goddess; by the ninth century she was the major saint in Ireland. She remains a very popular figure and St Brigid's Cross, easily crafted from reeds, is commonly found in souvenir shops.

The Protestant Cathedral of St Brigid The cathedral dates back to 1243. It was largely destroyed in the 17th century but rebuilt around 1875, following the original cruciform structure with a dose of Victorian romanticism thrown in for good measure. The adjoining **round tower** has an elaborate, Romanesque doorway and battlements added during the 19th-century rebuilding work on the cathedral. ■ *May to September, Monday-Saturday 1000-1300 and 1400-1700, Sunday 1400-1700. IR£2.*

The Curragh Some 2,000 hectacres of land, dedicated to dozens of studs and a famous racecourse, constitute the Curragh. The word itself means 'racecourse' though the origins of the area's association with horses is lost in time but may have something to do with its being flat and fertile or something to do with soil which builds strong bones in horses. Organized horseracing has been taking place uninterruptedly from at least the 18th century and in the 19th century the

Race meetings at the Curragh

Big flat races include the 2,000 and 1,000 Guineas towards the end of May, the Irish Derby and the Pretty Polly Stakes towards the end of June, the Irish Oaks in early July, the Moyglare Stud Stakes in early September, the Irish Leger and the Aga Khan Studs National Stakes in mid-September. Bord Fáilte issue more information and their annual Calendar of Events booklet includes a racing calendar. For big meetings at the Curragh, T441205, there are often special bus and train services running to and from Dublin; T01-8302222/8366111 for transport details.

British established a training camp here, which developed into a permanent military base. Visitors cannot just wander around the private studs – remember this is a multi-million pound business – but the government-owned **National Stud** is open to the public, includes a museum as well as tours of the stables and is within walking distance of Kildare town. ■ *T521617. Mid-February to mid-November, daily 0930-1800. South of Kildare town. IR£5 joint ticket with Japanese Gardens.*

Japanese Gardens

It seems an unlikely mix but the eccentric Colonel William Hall Walker, who established what is now the National Stud in 1900, also had an area of bog drained and brought in two Japanese gardeners to landscape the place. The resulting Japanese Gardens is an odd philosophical/garden tour based around various stages of male life from birth to the hereafter. ■ *See the Curragh.*

Sleeping

AL *Curragh Lodge Hotel*, Dublin Rd, T522144, F521247. Minimum IR£18 per person, excluding dinner. Best in town. On the N7 going south. **B** *Mount Ruadhan*, Old Rd, Southgreen, T521637. Typical modern bungalow signposted at the traffic lights in Kildare.

Eating

Restaurant and bar food is available in the *Curragh Lodge Hotel* and in the town square *Silken Thomas*, T521264, is a popular pub with decent food and a restaurant that opens for lunch and dinner every day.

Transport

Bus Numerous *Bus Éireann* services between Kildare and Dublin, T01-8366111, taking about 1hr 20mins. **Train** Kildare, T21224, is on the the main route from Dublin to the west and southwest, so there are good connections with Ballina, Westport, Galway, Ennis, Tralee, Cork and Waterford.

South Kildare

Ballitore and around

The Quaker origins of the village of Ballitore are remembered in the **Ballitore Quaker Museum**, located in the centre of Ballitore, and the walled Quaker cemetery in the village is also worth a visit. The most famous product of a Quaker education in Ireland is the political thinker Edmund Burke (1729-97), and he attended the village school, which was run by an ancestor of Ernest Shackleton of Antarctic fame. Just outside of Ballitore, within walking distance and signposted from the centre, is the functioning **Crookstown Mill**. ■ *Museum: Monday-Saturday 1100-1800. Mill: All year, daily 1000-1800. IR£2.50.*

Ballitore
Phone code: 0507
Colour map 4, grid B2

County Kildare

Canals – Royal and Grand

> Linking Dublin with the River Shannon through 44 locks, and with a branch that heads south to Waterford, the Grand Canal was built between 1756 and 1804 and stayed in operation until 1960. It is now managed by Dúchas whose Waterways Visitor Centre in Dublin provides information on its history and sells a guide to the canal. Cruises are available through Celtic Canal Cruises (see page 238). Dúchas manages the Royal Canal as well, which also links Dublin with the River Shannon and which is currently in the process of being cleaned up for boating. Its towpaths are being restored for walkers at the same time. Leisureways Holidays, T01-8225034, have boats for hire along some stretches.
>
> Now that the Shannon to Erne Waterway is up and running (see page 661) it is possible to travel from Belturbet in Fermanagh to Dublin.

Moone South of Ballitore, on the N9, this village would hardly merit attention were it not for the **Moone High Cross** on the site of an Early Christian monastery just to the west of the village. The highly attractive High Cross shows Daniel, the sacrifice of Isaac, Adam and Eve, and the Crucifixion on the east side, the Apostles on the west side, various miracles on the south and two saints breaking bread in the desert on the north side. A few miles south, **Irish Pewter Mill** has a casting room open to the public and a factory shop. ■ *Shop: T24164. Monday-Friday 1000-1630.*

Athy The town of Athy (pronounced 'a-thigh'), west of Ballitore, has the potential to make itself far more interesting to visitors and the **heritage centre** in the 18th-century town hall gives a good idea of why this is so. This local museum highlights the past history of Athy in relation to major events such as the 1798 uprising and the explorer Ernest Shackleton. ■ *March to October, Monday-Saturday 1000-1800, Sunday 1400-1800. Shorter hours in winter. IR£2.*

To find out more about the locality, including details of local walks along the Grand Canal (see box above) or visit the **Tourist Office** (see page 235).

Castledermot South of Ballitore, on the N9, is Castledermot, where there is a surprisingly
Phone code: 0503 large amount to see. As you come into town down Main Street there are reminders of an ecclesiastical past that goes back to a monastery founded by St Dermot and raided by the Vikings in 841. What stands today is a remarkable Romanesque doorway, a round tower and two fine granite crosses. Nearby Kilkea Castle (see 'Sleeping', page 234), though originally built in 1180, has been substantially modified and restored between the 17th and 20th centuries. At the southern end of town stand the remains of a Franciscan friary founded in the early 14th century and suppressed in 1541. ■ *A caretaker lives next door and will open the gates on request.*

Sleeping **LL** *Kilkea Castle*, Castledermot, T45156, F45187, kilkea@iol.ie The oldest inhabited castle in Ireland, this hotel has found the time to install an indoor pool and gym and to plan an 18-hole golf course around itself. **AL** *Tonlegee House & Restaurant*, Athy, T/F31473. 5mins outside of town and signposted off the Kilkenny Road. **B** *The Rath House*, Moone, T24133. L-shaped bungalow with 4 bedrooms, including a single. **B** *Woodcourte House*, Moone, T24167. Evening meal for IR£12.50. Rural setting.

Eating Dinner in Kilkea Castle's *d'Lacy's* restaurant is around IR£30. Pubs in Athy serve bar food, and for this you can enjoy splendid views from the atmospheric dining room and excellent food using local produce and fresh vegetables from the hotel's garden.

County Kildare

The roast of the day rarely disappoints and there is a delightful terrace for drinks before or after meals.

Transport

Bus *Bus Éireann* services on the Dublin – Kilkenny - Clonmel – Cork route stop in Athy, and Bus No 130 between Dublin and Kilkenny also stops daily in Athy as well as Moone and Castledermot, T01-8366111.

Directory

Tourist office Town Hall, T31859.

County Offaly

Clonmacnois

Phone code: 0905
Colour map 2, grid C5

Between the seventh and 12th centuries Clonmacnois was the largest and most important monastic centre in Ireland, developing around the nexus where the River Shannon meets the Eiscir Riada, a 'running ridge' formed at the end of the Ice Age and a legendary boundary dividing Ireland. Founded by St Ciarán in the mid-sixth century, the monastery attracted scholars from all over Europe as well as artists working with stone and metal, and such was its fame that high kings of Ireland were buried here. It also attracted marauders and between the ninth and 12th centuries was plundered some 35 times by Vikings and natives alike. The size and prosperity of Clonmacnois may be gathered from the fact that over 100 houses were destroyed when the Anglo-Normans attacked in 1179. When English forces from Athlone robbed the monastery of everything in 1552 the life of the centre was finally brought to an end.

Architectural sights

There are three impressive **High Crosses**, which have been moved inside the Visitors' Centre for safe-keeping, including one that is very unusual due to its probable representation of a non-biblical scene. The **cathedral**, which is not as impressive a building as the name might suggest, was originally built in the early 10th century but sections have been added over the centuries. The other buildings dotted around are the remains of eight churches from the 10th to the 13th centuries but again with additions, some as recent as the 17th century. One of them, the Nun's Church, is to the east of the main centre and well worth seeking out for its Romanesque doorway and chancel arch. Of the two **round towers**, one, O'Rourkes, is named after a high king of Connaught and the other, overlooking the river, is next to one of the eight churches, Teampall (church) Finghin.

Visitor's centre

The visitor's centre presents a not-very-engrossing audio-visual show and there is also a tourist information desk. ■ *Shannonbridge. T74195/74134. Mid-May to mid-September, daily 0900-1900; mid-March to mid-May and mid-September to October, daily 1000-1800; November to mid-March, daily 1000-1730. IR£3. Dúchas site. Coffee shop. 13 miles (21 kilometres) from Athlone and Ballinasloe, signposted from the N62 and the R357.*

Clonmacnois & West Offaly Railway

The Clonmacnois and West Offaly Railway runs on a narrow-gauge line, which trundles a five-mile (eight-kilometre) circular route around the Blackwater Bog. The journey is a surreal one with the forbidding towers of Bord na Móna's (Irish Peat Development Board) peat-fuelled power station reminding you that the bog is being exploited to extinction while it is Bord na Móna that runs the tour and shows a useful video on the flora and fauna that will one day disappear. ■ *Shannonbridge, T74114. April to October, daily 1000-1700. Trains leave every hour, on the hour, but try to view the video first. IR£3.95. Located on the R357 Tullamore Road.*

Sleeping **B** *Kajon House*, Creevagh, T74191. B&B with the option of an evening meal for IR£12.50. **B-C** *Glenderham House*, Cloghan Rd, Shannonbridge, T/F74205. IR£28 and IR£30 for double rooms. Modern bungalow.

Eating In Shannonbridge itself, pub food is available, and the *Shannonside Diner* serves light meals.

Transport **Bus** There is no *Bus Éireann* service but regular daily buses run from Athlone to Clonmacnois in the summer, run by *Paddy Kavanagh*, T0902-74839; details also available from Athlone tourist office, T0902-94630.

Banagher

Phone code: 0509
Colour map 2, grid C5

Banagher is the epicentre of Offaly's new-found identity as a leisure centre for the Midlands and the first place to visit is the tourist office (see below), which has information on various local places of interest. **Cloghan Castle**, a good half-hour's signposted walk south of town, is sure to be mentioned. It claims to have been continuously inhabited for over 800 years. From the castle there is a very pleasant, signposted, walk to **Victoria Lodge** where a picnic could be enjoyed on a fine day. ■ *Castle tours: May to September, Wednesday-Saturday 1400-1830. IR£4.*

Sleeping **A** *Brosna Lodge Hotel*, Main St, Banagher, T51350. Good restaurant and bar. Close to the river. **B** *Lakyle*, T51566. Open May to October. About ½ mile (1 km) outside of town. **D** *Crank House Hostel*, Main St, T/F51458. IHH. Open all year. 30 beds and 1 private room for IR£16. Not as zany as the name suggests but the beds, bathrooms and kitchen are all tip-top.

Eating There is a coffee shop in Crank House, Main St, and a couple of pubs in the town centre worth checking out for their pub fare. Close to the river, *The Vine House*, T51463, has seafood and meat dishes for around IR£9 while *The Snipes Restaurant* in the Brosna Lodge hotel is a tad more expensive and perhaps a little more interesting.

Transport **Bicycle** *K Donegan*, Main St, T51178. Bike hire. **Bus** *Bus Éireann*'s Dublin to Birr service stops daily in Banagher and also connects the town with Tullamore, T01-8366111. **Boat hire** *Carrick Craft*, T51189.

Directory **Tourist office** Crank House, Main St, T51458. Mar-Oct, Mon-Fri 0930-2000, Sat-Sun, 0930-1700.

Birr

Phone code: 0509
Colour map 2, grid C5

If you are thinking of basing yourself in Offaly for a day or two then the pretty, Georgian town of Birr competes favourably with Banagher as the place to stay overnight.

Heritage centre John's Mall, one of the most picturesquely elegant streets in Birr, is where a heritage centre tells the story of the town's creation by Sir Laurence Parsons in the 18th century. ■ *May to September, Monday-Saturday 1430-1730, Sunday 1500-1700. IR£1.*

County Offaly

The Parsons climbed the social ladder, became earls of Rosse and settled into Birr Castle on their estate, where they still live. The house is not open to the public but Birr Castle Demesne is, a superb 18th-century park with a lake, river, waterfalls, box hedges that have to be seen to be believed, and an astonishing collection of 2,000 species of rare trees and shrubs. Also to be found here is the **Great Telescope**, built in 1845 as the largest in the world (which it remained for 75 years), and now fully operational once again. The six-foot-diameter reflector is still in London's Science Museum, to where it was removed during the Troubles. The telescope, which in its time made many important astronomical observations, is just the most dramatic achievement of a remarkable family of Irish scientists and their story is told in the adjoining Science Centre. ■ *T20336. Demense and Telescope: all year, daily 0900-1800. IR£3.50. Science Centre: July-December. Ticket with Demense and Telescope IR£5. Guided tours, gift shop, tea rooms, plants and flowers for sale.*

Birr Castle Demesne

Outside of town, on the road between Kinnitty and Roscrea, a little way past Clareen, are the spooky remains of Leap Castle. It was widely believed to be the most haunted house in Ireland, if not the whole of Europe, with a renowned 'smelly ghost' manifesting itself to the senses. The house was destroyed by Republican ghostbusters in 1922 but some say the smell lingers....

Leap Castle

LL *Kinnitty Castle*, T37318, F37284. Gothic pile on a 8,000-hectare estate on the slopes of the Slieve Bloom hills, stuffed with antiques and the benefits of a recent multi-million-pound refurbishment. **AL** *Country Arms Hotel*, Railway Rd, T20791, F21234. Fine example of Georgian architecture in its own right and while interior features have been well cared for the rooms have been renovated and modernized. **A** *Dooley's Hotel*, Emmet Sq, T20032, F21332. Old coaching inn with a jolly atmosphere and modern bedrooms. **A** *Maltings Guesthouse*, Castle St, T21345, F22073. Sauna and gym. Riverside location close to Birr Castle. **B** *The Ring*, The Ring, T/F20976. Double rooms for IR£16 per person. Welcomes children.

Sleeping

Gourmet food, with dinner every evening in the IR£30 bracket and lunch also on a Sunday, may be enjoyed in *Kinnitty Castle*'s *The Slí Dála*. The restaurant in the *Country Arms Hotel* serves a good, traditional dinner for around IR£22 and has the benefit of fresh vegetables from its own gardens. An evening meal in *Emmet Restaurant* in Dooley's is around IR£17 and there is also a coffee shop providing lighter meals all day. *The Stables Townhouse Restaurant*, Oxmantown Mall, T20263, has bare brick walls and serves filling meals at lunchtime and at night. For a quick bite try the *Castle Kitchen*, which is opposite the entrance to Birr Castle in town.

Eating

Bus *Bus Éireann* have a daily service between Dublin and Portumna, via Maynooth and Tullamore, which stops in Birr. The Cork to Athlone service and the Athlone to Tralee services also make daily stops in the town square, T01-8366111.

Transport

Tullamore

The Victorian-style town of Tullamore on the Grand Canal has three worthy attractions, two in the town and one a few miles to the north.

Phone code: 0506
Colour map 2, grid C6

Tullamore is famous for its whiskey, and though it is no longer distilled here the Tullamore Dew Heritage Centre recounts its history and looks at the impact of the Grand Canal on the development of the town. The Centre is located in an 1897 warehouse on the banks of the Grand Canal and you can try on clothes from the 1850s and see bees making honey for the Irish Mist

Tullamore Dew Heritage Centre

County Offaly

liqueur. The customary courtesy tipple rounds off a visit to the Centre, in an old warehouse on the banks of the canal. ■ *Bury Quay, T25015. May to September, Monday-Saturday 0900-1800, Sunday 1200-1700; October to April, Monday-Saturday 1000-1700, Sunday 1200-1700. IR£3.50. Shop and café bar.*

Charleville Forest Castle The Bury family founded Tullamore in 1750 and their family home was Charleville Forest Castle, a superb Gothic-Georgian pile with everything you might expect: turrets, spires, ivy on the walls, dark trees. In 1875 William Morris was commissioned to decorate the interiors but his socialist sympathies led him to show more interest in the plight of the rural Irish and he never publicized this work of his for the super-rich. Most of his contributions, including wallpapers, have disappeared but there is some painted decoration and a frieze in the dining room. ■ *Charleville Road, T21279. June to September, Wednesday-Sunday 1100-1600; April to May, Saturday and Sunday 1400-1700. IR£3.50. South of town on the road to Limerick.*

Durrow Abbey Durrow Abbey, founded in the 6th century and birthplace of the famous illustrated gospel, the *Book of Durrow*, now in Trinity College Library, Dublin (see page 96), is long gone but a Georgian mansion and a deserted church stand near the site. The house was burnt down in 1922 but the owners rebuilt it, 'a rare example of a house improved as a result of its destruction in the Troubles' says Jeremy Williams in his excellent *Architecture in Ireland* (see page 61).

Sleeping **AL** *Moorhill Country House*, Clara Rd, T21395, F52424. Victorian retreat set amidst chestnut trees and manicured lawns. **A** *Sea Dew Guesthouse*, Clonminch Rd, T/F52054. Purpose-built edifice within walking distance of town centre. Benefits from a conservatory breakfast room. **B** *Ivy Lodge*, Daingean Rd, T41151. A mile (1.5 km) from the town centre. Really does justify its name. **B** *Littlewood*, Culleen, Durrow, T51364. One of those modern olde worlde houses that has to be seen to be believed.

Eating Elegant country-house style dining, complete with stone walls, exposed ceiling beams and polished floor, at the *Moorhill Restaurant* in *Moorhill Country House*, Tuesday to Saturday for dinner and Sunday lunch. *The Bridge House*, Bridge St, T21704, is a pub restaurant serving familiar dishes throughout the day. The *Tullamore Court Hotel* restaurant, O'Moore St, T46666, offers a happy medium between those two, as well as a bar serving pub food.

Transport **Bicycle** *Buckley Cycles*, Canal Pl, T52240. Bike hire. **Bus** The bus station is by the railway station and the Dublin to Portumna bus stops daily, as does the Waterford to Longford bus via Kilkenny and Athlone. **Train** The station, T21431, is south of town off Charleville Rd. Dublin to Galway trains stop at Tullamore throughout the day.

Directory **Banks** William St and Bridge St. **Tours** *Celtic Canal Cruises*, Tullamore, T21861, F51266. Boats for 2-9 people. **Tourist office**, Bury Quay, T52617. Jun-Aug, Mon-Fri 1000-1700.

County Offaly

The rain drove us into the church - our refuge, our strength, our only dry place. At Mass, Benediction, novenas, we huddled in great damp clumps, dozing through priest drone, while steam rose again from our clothes to mingle with the sweetness of incense, flowers and candles.

Limerick gained a reputation for piety, but we knew it was only the rain.

Frank McCourt grew up in Limerick city:
Angela's Ashes

7

Counties Waterford, Tipperary & Limerick

The coastline of county Waterford stretches for more than 50 miles (80 kilometres), but it is only 27 miles (44 kilometres) from the north of the county to the southern coastline. Despite these modest dimensions there is enormous variety in the cultural and physical landscape: wood-clad hills and sheltered inlets in the east, sandy beaches and resorts along the coast, a tiny Irish-speaking area around Ring to the west, and the Comeragh/ Monavullagh mountains in the north of the county, where historic river valleys frame castles and great houses which testify to the English invasions of the past.

Tipperary, on the other hand, is Ireland's largest inland county, with some of the best farming land in the country to be found in the aptly named Golden Vale that stretches westwards to Limerick.

County Limerick is more of a junction rather than a place to go in its own right, though Lough Gur, one of the most productive stone age sites in Europe, is well worth a visit. Limerick city booms with new money and is home to the amazing Hunt Collection and the beautiful old Church of Ireland cathedral; Adare has cute written all over it, but amongst the tour buses and gawking tour groups there are some fine old church buildings to visit.

★ *Try to find time for*

  The 18th- and 19th- century buildings in Waterford city

  An evening meal at Dwyer's in Waterford city

  Walking in the Knockmealdown Mountains

  Cormac's Chapel on the Rock of Cashel

  A visit to the Hunt Collection in Limerick city

  Ormond Castle

Counties Waterford, Tipperary & Limerick

County Waterford

Waterford

Phone code: 051
Colour map 4, grid C1

Waterford oozes a sense of the ancient, with modern shops squeezed into the narrow spaces of the medieval town centre, and no end of fine old buildings to admire. With good facilities, it invites a short stay before heading off to varied attractions to the south and west of the city.

Ins and outs

Getting there Waterford has an airport, train and bus links, and easy access to the ferry ports of Rosslare and Cork. A 7-min car ferry across Waterford harbour saves times travelling between Waterford and county Wexford. From Rosslare it takes about 45 mins driving time to Ballyhack, where the ferry hops over to Passage East in Waterford. Dublin is 2½ hrs away from Waterford, Cork about an hour.

Getting around The city centre is small and compact, and though the Waterford glass factory is on the outskirts of town there are bikes and taxis for hire (see 'Transport', page 247).

History

The town's history begins with the Vikings who established a settlement in the early 10th century close to where Reginald's Tower now stands. Vadrafjord, as they named it, prospered undisturbed until the king of Leinster, Dermot MacMurrough, called upon his Welsh Anglo-Norman allies to help him take the town. Led by Strongbow (see page 672), Waterford fell in 1170 and the significance of this Norman-Irish alliance was cemented by Strongbow's marriage to MacMurrough's daughter. Henry II arrived the following year to claim the town for himself and put his Welsh barons in their place, and this English power was further confirmed by King John, who turned up in 1210. Between them, John and Henry had firmly established the city of Waterford as a Norman town: it became the unofficial capital of Ireland and flourished as a European port into the 16th and 17th centuries.

Cromwell failed to take the city in 1649 but it fell to his son-in-law General Ireton the following year. Although this led to a Protestant elite, Catholic interests were not erased, and between 1750 and 1850 Catholic

Waterford

To Kilkenny & Dublin (N9)
To New Ross & Wexford (N25)

River Suir

Mary St
Bridge St
O'Connell St
Waterford Design Centre
Garter Lane Arts Centre
Lwr Yellow Rd
Patrick St
Morrisons Rd
Lwr Yellow Rd
Cannon St
College St
Manor St
Bath St
Johnstown
South Parade
William St
To Passage East (R683)
Cork Rd
John's River

To Waterford Crystal Factory, Cork
Rd Bed & Breakfasts & Cork (N25)

N

0 yards 200
0 metres 200

■ **Sleeping**
1 Brown's Town House
2 Dooley's Granary
3 Ivory Lodge
4 Portree Guesthouse
5 Travelodge
6 Waterford Hostel

● **Eating & drinking**
1 Dwyer's
2 Haricot's Wholefood
3 Hog's Head
4 Old Ground Pub

Related map:
A. Waterford city centre,
page 245

The Newfoundland Connection

It was around 1650 that fisherman from southeast Ireland first began crossing the Atlantic on a regular seasonal basis to take advantage of the lucrative fishing grounds off the coast of Newfoundland. This seasonal migration continued throughout the 18th century and from around 1800 people and families from Waterford and its hinterland began to settle on a permanent basis in that part of North America. By 1830 an estimated 30,000 people, the vast majority from the county of Waterford, had emigrated and begun to make their cultural presence felt. Linguistic studies have shown that, until very recently at least, echoes of this unique wave of Irish immigration could literally be heard in the language of the communities where they settled.

merchants rose to prominence as food exporters. Religious sectarianism seems not to have blighted the city and this helps explain why Waterford was one of the few places that did not register a victory for Sinn Féin in the 1918 general election. A recent resurgence in commercial life and trade with the continent has restored the port to the kind of importance it held in medieval times.

Sights

Waterford Treasures at The Granary
This is a fairly new heritage centre (though they don't call them by that name any more), bringing to life the 1,000-year history of the city with exhibits that include Viking jewellery and the 14th-century illustrated *Great Charter Roll*. There are also exhibits and information on T F Meager (see box on page 244). ■ *The Granary, The Quay. T304500; http://www.waterfordtreasures.com. June to August, daily, 0930-2100; May and September, daily 1000-1700. IR£3.*

Reginald's Tower
Possibly the oldest civic building in Ireland, this late 12th, early 13th-century pepper-pot tower built by the Normans stands on the site of a Viking tower that was built in the early 11th century. The upper floors date from the 15th century. Despite the busy flow of city traffic past it, the tower remains as solid and unyielding as it did in 1495 when it was subjected to the first artillery siege in Ireland. It now houses a collection of artefacts and material relating to the history of the city. ■ *Parade Quay. T873501. June-August, daily, 1000-2000; May and September, Monday-Friday 1000-1700, Saturday-Sunday 1400-1700. IR£1.*

County Waterford

Reginald's Tower

Meagher of the Sword

Thomas Francis Meagher (1823-67) was born in what is now the Granville Hotel in Waterford. He became a member of the Young Ireland movement, a romantic nationalist movement of the 1840s, and his disagreement with the more cautious approach of Daniel O'Connell earned him the epithet, 'Meagher of the Sword'. He was transported to Tasmania for his involvement in the abortive 1848 rebellion but managed to escape in 1852 to New York where he became a journalist. During the American Civil War he commanded the pro-Union Irish Brigade in Fort Sumter and Fredricksburg. He became a temporary governor of Montana territory in 1866 but died the following year after falling overboard on a Missouri paddle steamer.

City Heritage Museum Not perhaps the most riveting of museums, this centre focusses on the Viking and Norman settlement of Waterford and will mainly be of interest to visitors who want to find out more about the city's beginnings and very early history. ■ *Greyfriars. T871227. April-October, daily, 1000-1700; November-March, Monday-Friday, 1000-1700. IR£1.50.*

The Mall buildings The Mall, a broad street built in the 18th century, contains a number of fine buildings, and pride of place goes to the 1783 **City Hall**, built as a meeting hall for merchants and reflecting their self-confidence in its stately proportions. A municipal collection of art is on view, including works by Jack Yeats, Paul Henry, Seán Keating and others (tours are available by prior arrangement, T873510), while the council chamber is famed for its superbly wrought Waterford crystal chandelier. Next door, the **Theatre Royal** uniquely retains its original 19th-century features and the tiered horseshoe balconies add tremendously to the atmosphere of the annual opera festival held here. Also worth admiring is the nearby **Bishop's Palace**, built in the 1740s and designed by Richard Castle.

Continue into Parnell St, and a little way past the junction with John Street the road meets remnants of the **medieval city walls** and their towers. Turn right to follow a well-preserved section of the line of the wall that formed the western side of the old city.

Churches The Waterford designer John Roberts was responsible for both the Protestant and Catholic cathedrals here, but they are quite different in their style and mood. The Protestant **Christchurch Cathedral**, rebuilt in the 1770s, has the cool reticence of Georgian architecture and the removal of furnishings in the 19th century created a sense of space that allows one to appreciate its elegant proportions. Look for the fine stucco ceiling and the gory *memento mori*: a tomb of a 15th-century mayor. A 45-minute audio-visual show relates the cathedral's history. ■ *Bailey's New Street, T396270. Audio-visual show, June to September, Monday-Saturday 0930, 1130, 1430, 1600. Sunday 1430, 1600. April and May, September and October, Monday-Friday 1130, 1430, 1600. IR£2.*

The Catholic 1793 **Holy Trinity Cathedral**, modified in the 19th century, is by contrast a monument to ornateness, with a multitude of Corinthian columns, opulent Waterford glass chandeliers and a carved oak pulpit. Described in tourist literature as 'warm, luscious and Mediterranean', this may not be everyone's response to the place. ■ *Barronstrand Street. No admission charge.*

Greyfriars, dubbed the French Church, was founded for the Franciscans in 1240, and is now a substantial ruin with the nave, chancel and bell tower all intact. Converted into an alms house after the dissolution of monasteries in the 16th century, it acquired its French title after becoming a place of worship for

French Huguenot refugees throughout the 18th century. ■ *Greyfriars Street. Key available at City Heritage Museum.*

St Patrick's, a small but interesting Catholic church off Great George's Street, was built in the mid-18th century with funds from Irish merchants in Spain and remains substantially unaltered. Revisionist historians would pounce on the fact that it remained in use throughout Penal times.

The city's most famous export is its crystal, dating back to 1783 when George and William Penrose opened their first glassmaking factory. The mix of silica sand, potash and litharge (a form of lead) is transformed into a glowing ball of molten crystal before being fashioned by craftsmen and then cut and engraved into intricate patterns. Tours of the factory are popular and there is also an audio-visual presentation, a restaurant, and a gallery with a comprehensive display of items for sale. ■ *The Visitor Centre is over a mile out of town on the N25 road to Cork, T373311. Open April to October, daily 0830-1600; November to March, Monday-Friday 0900-1515. IR£3.60. Tickets available from the tourist office. Free admission to the shop.*

Waterford crystal

Essentials

LL *Waterford Castle*, The Island, Ballinakill, T878203, F879316, wdcastle@iol.ie. A short ferry ride brings guests to this idyllic retreat with fairytale bedrooms and heart-stirring views

Sleeping
■ *on maps*
Price codes:
see inside front cover

County Waterford

Waterford city centre

■ Sleeping
1 Granville
2 Tower
3 Viking House Hostel

● Eating & drinking
1 Café Luna
2 Olde Stand
3 Reginald's

4 T & H Doolans bar

L *Dooley's*, The Quay, T873531, F870262. Overlooking the river in the heart of the city and with over 100 rooms. **L** *Granville Hotel*, Meagher Quay, T855111, F870307. Former home to Thomas Meagher (see box above) a centrally located, waterfront hotel. It was originally an 18th century merchant's house and retains the original staircase of that period. No car park of its own but a public one directly opposite the hotel. **L** *Tower Hotel*, The Mall, T875801, F870129, tower@iol.ie The attraction here is the sauna, gym and 20m swimming pool.

A *Brown's Town House*, 29 South Parade, T870594, F871923. A centrally located Victorian house offering B&B with modern comforts. **A** *Ivory Lodge*, Tramore Rd, T358888, F358899, ivoryhotel@voyage.ie A relatively new hotel on the outskirts of the city that prides itself on not being a 'local hot spot'. Noisy entertainment. Room rates don't include breakfast, and various package deals are available.

B *Ashleigh*, Holy Cross, Cork Rd, T375171. B&B. Open all year. **B** *Portree Guesthouse*, Mary St, T874574. Another centrally located B&B, in a Georgian building close to the rail and bus stations. **B** *Travelodge*, on the N25 Cork road, T1800-709709 (0800-850950 from the UK). A motel with a set room price sleeping up to 3 adults and 1 child. **B** *Woodleigh*, Butlerstown, Cork Rd, T384601. B&B, opens March to October. Other B&Bs along the Cork Rd.

D *Viking House*, Coffee House Lane, The Quay, T853827, F871730. Large and modern hostel, with 100 beds and stylish touches that raise it above the average. Open all year and there are 8 private rooms from IR£27. **D** *Waterford Hostel*, 70 Manor St, T850163, F872064. Open between June and September, 20 beds but no private rooms.

Eating
● *on maps*
Price codes:
see inside front cover

Restaurants *Dwyer's*, 5 Mary St, T877478, has deservedly attracted the attention of food critics. Between 1800 and 1930 there is a set IR£14 dinner based around dishes such as salmon in filo pastry with cucumber sauce, or honey and mustard glazed bacon. Main courses from the à la carte menu cost around IR£14. *The Olde Stand*, 45 Michael St, T879488, is a Victorian-style pub specializing in steak and seafood dishes, around IR£11, in its upstairs restaurant and with a lunchtime carvery and salad bar downstairs in the bar. *T&H Doolans*, Great George St, T841504, is a pub that serves up Irish stew and oysters with Guinness as well as traditional music. The *Granville Hotel* has a comfortable dining area and a cafeteria-style arrangement for food, while in the hotel's *Bianconi* restaurant a conventional dinner is around IR£20. *Maxim House*, 8 O'Connell St, T875820, offers Cantonese and Szechuan food including affordable lunch specials and a takeaway service. *O'Grady's Restaurant*, Cork Road, T378851, opens for lunch and dinner Monday to Saturday and can be relied on for well-cooked food with imaginative touches. There is an early-bird menu before 2000 while the à la carte offers an enterprising mix of traditional lamb dishes and avant garde creations. Always good value lunches and dinner can be enjoyed for IR£20, more or less; closed Sunday.

Cafés *Haricots Wholefood Restaurant*, 11 O'Connell St, T841299, serves fish and meat as well as vegetarian meals for around IR£5. For a quick lunch combined with shopping opportunities, try the self-service restaurant at the *Waterford Design Centre*, 44 The Quay. Dinner, Monday-Saturday, from 1730. *Café Luna*, 53 John St, is a continental-style café serving good food, excellent coffee, and open until 0400. The *Voy@ger Internet Café*, Parnell Court, Parnell St, T843843, info@voyager.ie is open all year, Monday-Saturday 1000-2100, and 1500-2100 on Sunday.

Pubs & music *The Reginald*, 2/3 The Mall, T855087, has live music and/or the *Excalibur Knight Club* between Wednesday and Sunday. No cover charge at the nightclub before 2200. *T&H Doolans*, Great George St, T841504, is famous for its traditional Irish music sessions and proud of the fact that 'international megastar' Sinéad O'Connor begun her career here. *The Hog's Head Bar*, 15 The Quay, is an old-style pub with music ranging from traditional to rock. *The Old Ground*, 10 The Glen, is owned by a glass cutter, and crystal for sale is on display. *Henry Downes*, is worth squirrelling out at 10 Thomas St. It has been in the same family since the late 18th century, and the proprietors blend their own whiskey, Downes No 9.

Entertainment

The *Garter Lane Arts Centre*, 22a O'Connell St, T855038, opens Monday-Saturday, 1000-1800, with a rich programme of music, theatre, film, exhibitions, workshops and talks. The Waterford Show takes place in the City Hall every Tuesday, Thursday and Saturday, May to September, at 2100. It lasts 90 minutes and the cast in period costume bring to life the culture and history of the city. The IR£7 tickets, available from City Hall, T875788, the tourist office or from the Waterford Crystal Visitor Centre, include a pre-show drink and a glass of wine during the show.

Festivals

From around **19th September until early October** there is the *Waterford International Festival of Light Opera*. Contact Theatre Royal, The Mall, T874422. *Waterford Spraoi* is a street festival that takes place in **August**. See Tramore section on page 249 for details of Waterford and Tramore Racecourse Festival in mid-August. A couple of days in **late September** witness the *Waterford Estuary Mussel Festival* at Passage East. Tourist offices issue an annual Calendar of Events for Waterford, Wexford, South Tipperary, Kilkenny and Carlow.

Shopping

Camping equipment *Eugene Dunphy*, Arundel Square. **Clothing** *Faller's*, 17 Broad St, T854576, is an Irish knitwear shop. **Crystal** *Heritage Crystal*, 67 The Quay, T841787, http://www.heritagecrystal.com offers a less expensive alternative to Waterford crystal. *Joseph Knox*, 3 Barronstrand St, T875307, is centrally located and stocks Waterford crystal, Donegal china, Belleek pottery and the like. **General** The modern *City Square Shopping Centre* is packed with consumer outlets, 2 department stores and fast food places. *Waterford Design Centre*, 44 The Quay, T856666, is recommended for its range of clothes downstairs and pottery and glass upstairs, plus restaurant.

Sport

Golf *Waterford Castle Golf and Country Club*, an 18-hole course, T871633. *Waterford Golf Club*, T876748 is an 18-hole parkland course in Ferrybank.

Transport

Airport *Waterford airport*, Killowen, T875589. 7 km (4 miles) south of the city, with flights to Liverpool, Manchester, Luton and Cambridge in the UK (see page 33). **Bicycle hire** *Altitude*, 22 Ballybricken, T870356, rents bikes and sells hiking gear and clothing. *Wrights Cycles*, Henrietta St, T874411. **Bus** *Bus Éireann*, Plunkett Station, T879000, has express services to Dublin, Rosslare, Galway, Cork, Killarney, Tralee and Athlone. *Rapid Express Buses*, Parnell Court, Parnell St, Waterford, T872149, is a private bus company running several buses daily between Waterford and Cork via Lemybrien, Dungarvan, Youghal and Midleton. *Suirway*, T382209 (24-hr talking timetable T382422), is another private company operating from Waterford to Dunmore East and Passage East. **Ferry** *The Passage East Car Ferry*, T382480. Provides a useful shortcut between Waterford and Wexford by crossing the harbour between Passage East and Ballyhack in county Wexford. A continuous service, with first sailing at 0700 (0930 Sunday) all year and last sailing at 2000 October-March, 2200 April-September. IR£4 single, IR£6 return. **Road** The N25 road heading west to Cork offers fine views approaching Dungarvan but there is little of interest along the way. The road crosses a river at Kilmacthomas, birthplace of Tyrone Power's great-grandfather. An alternative route west is by the coastal R675, which can also be picked up from Dunmore East to the south of the city. **Taxi** Parnell Court, Parnell St, T877710. **Train** *Iarnród Éireann*,

T873401/873402 (24-hr talking timetable T876243), operates from Waterford's Plunkett Station, on the north side of the river, and serves Dublin via Kilkenny, Rosslare via Wexford and Limerick via Carrick-on-Suir.

Directory **Communications** Post Office: Keyser St, The Quay. **Internet**: *Voy@ger Internet Café* (see Cafés, page 246). **Hospitals & medical services** Doctor: *Dr Keogh & Partners*, 0900-1700, T855411, emergency T580935. **Hospital**: *Waterford Regional Hospital*, Dunmore Rd, T873321. **Pharmacy**: *Gallaghers Late Night Pharmacy*, Barronstrand St. **English language schools** *English Language Centre*, 31 Johns Hill, T877288, F854603, welc@iol.ie runs language courses for adult and young learners; individuals and groups. *Waterford Language Learning*, 9 Leoville, Dunmore Rd, T872227. **Launderette** *Boston Cleaners*, 6 Michael St. **Tour companies & travel agents** *Ray McGrath*, T382629, F382689, runs walking holidays in the county of Waterford. A 1-hour walking tour, covers the main sites, and meets in the Granville hotel at 1200 and 1400 between Mar and Oct, T873711, IR£3. **Cruises** operate Jun-Aug from Meagher Quay at 1500 for IR£6, T421723. **Tourist office** The Quay, T875823, Apr-Sep, Mon-Sat, 0900-1800, and on Sun in Jul and Aug, 1100-1700; Oct, Mon-Sat, 0900-1800; Nov-Mar, Mon-Sat, 0900-1700. There is also a tourist office at Waterford Crystal, T358397, Apr-Oct daily, 0830-1800; Nov-Mar daily, 0900-1700.

The Waterford coast

The Waterford coast offers a number of sandy beaches, water sports, and exhilarating coastal walks. There are good bus connections to Waterford city in the summer season but a bicycle is the best way to reach and explore lesser-known spots. Both Dunmore East and Tramore are possible day trips from Waterford.

Dunmore East

Phone code: 051
Colour map 4, grid C1

Dumore East is the kind of picturesque village that Bord Fáilte may have been tempted to create if it didn't already exist. Thatched cottages and a winding main street give the appearance of a quaint old-fashioned village, but this is a fairly affluent area and the big old houses that were built for British merchants are now owned by well-heeled Irish families and the herring boats of the 1960s have been replaced by ocean-going yachts. Dunmore East used to be the terminus for a mail-packet service between Waterford and Milford Haven in Wales and the erstwhile hotel servicing its passengers is now the town hostel.

There are two beaches: one is in the village itself while Counsellor's Strand, a Blue Flag beach, is near the golf course and has a car park above it. The large colony of seabirds nesting in the cliffs are kittiwakes. There is no tourist office but Discover East Waterford Co-Operative, T382677, run a tourist information point in Passage East, April to September.

Sleeping **AL** *Candlelight Inn*, Harbour Rd, T383215, T383289, has 11 rooms, a heated outdoor swimming pool June-August, and painting and activity weekends. **AL** *Haven Hotel*, Harbour Rd, T383150, F383488, has twice as many rooms, costs about IR£10 less than the *Candlelight* for a double room and is children-friendly. It was built as a family home for a shipping magnate. **A** *Ocean Hotel*, Harbour Rd, T383136, F383576, has 12 rooms. **B** *Ashgrove*, T383195, and **B** *Hillfield House*, Ballymabin, T383565, are both just outside the village and both close over the winter. **B** *Carraig Liath*, Harbour Rd, T383273, has 3 rooms open between April and October. **B** *Church Villa*, T383390, is a comfortable place with 6 rooms, close to the Protestant church, and open all year. **C** *Dunmore Harbour House*, T383218, F383728, gordon@harbourhse.iol.ie A former hotel, hence the 40 beds and 20 private rooms from IR£27 to IR£40. Bikes for hire.

The 3 hotels mentioned above all serve bar food and have restaurants serving dinner **Eating**
for under IR£20. *The Ship*, T383141, serves good seafood and attracts seafaring folk.
Overlooking the town beach, *The Strand Inn*, T383174, has a reputation for its seafood, around IR£20 for dinner in the restaurant, and the bar food is always worth
considering.

The Dunmore East Adventure Centre, T383783, F383786, offers water-based and **Sports**
land-based sports and summer camps for children aged 10-17 in June-August. **Golf**:
Dunmore Golf & Country Club, T383151. 18-hole course on the outskirts of the village.
Sea angling: this is very popular and daily or weekly charters can be arranged. Con-
tact *Sea Angling Charters*, Pelorus, Fairybush, Dunmore East, T&F383397; *South East
Charters*, Dunmore East, T&F389242.

Suirway, T382209 (24-hr talking timetable T382422). Private bus company operating **Transport**
from Waterford to Dunmore East via Passage East.

Tramore

Tramore deserves its name (*Trá Mhór* meaning 'big strand') and the three-   *Phone code: 051*
mile (five-kilometre) beach has turned the place into one of Ireland's most   *Colour map 4, grid C1*
popular holiday resorts. This inevitably means amusement arcades, fast-food
joints and family-oriented attractions, but there is also the signposted five-
mile (eight-kilometre) Doneraile Walk, which starts at the tourist office, as
well as opportunities for water sports.

AL *Grand Hotel*, T381414, F386428. Very plush hotel. **AL** *Majestic Hotel*, T381761, **Sleeping**
F381766. Best facilities in town. **AL** *O'Shea's*, T381246, F3900144. Smallest of the 3 **& eating**
hotels in town, with 18 rooms. **B** *Cliff House*, Cliff Rd, T&F381497. B&B with a seaview,
open mid-March to end of November. Other B&Bs line Cliff Rd.
   The hotels all serve bar food and have their own restaurants. Dinner at the *Grand*
or *Majestic* is around IR£16, a few pounds less at *O'Shea's*. *The Victoria* on Queen St
offers reasonable pub food.

Camping *Newtown Cove Caravan & Camping Park*, T381121, opens from early
April to 27 September. Take the R675 coast to Dungarvan and take the left turn opposite the golf course less than a mile from the town. There is also *Fitzmaurice's Caravan Park*, T381968, which has 10 pitches for tents.

Horseracing The *Waterford and Tramore Racecourse* at Tramore, T421861, has occa- **Sport &**
sional fixtures in January, March and November, but the main 4-day event is in mid- **Entertainment**
August. **Surfing** The *Tramore Surf Club*, T386022, located at the end of the promenade, has facilities for water sports and conducts surfing lessons at IR£10 an hour.
Another surf school is at 3 Riverstown, Tramore, T390944, oceanic@tinet.ie **Family
attractions** For water-based fun there is *Splashworld*, T390176, and wannabe time-
travelling warriors can indulge themselves at *Lazerworld*, T493968.

Bus *Bus Éireann*, T879000, has plenty of buses running daily to Waterford and on **Transport**
Wednesday and Friday a Dungarvan to Waterford service stops at Tramore. The No 4
Dublin to Dungarvan service also makes a stop.

Tourist offices The old railway station is now a seasonal tourist office, Railway Square, T381572. **Directory**

County Waterford

The Women of Dungarvan

Two stories about Dungarvan bear testimony to the seductiveness of its womenfolk. In 1649 Cromwell was about to wreak his usual bout of wanton violence on the place when his eye was drawn to a woman apparently drinking his good health at the town walls. Charmed and disarmed, he desisted. Given Cromwell's penchant for slaughtering the Irish this seems remarkable but there is another story that lends credence to the allure of the town's females. Before a bridge was built over the River Colligan there was a crossing point where the water was shallow and it was known as 'Dungarvan's Prospects' because men couldn't resist ogling when local women raised their skirts to negotiate the

Tramore to Dungarvan

Phone code: 051

The R675 stays inland west of Tramore before dropping down to the village of Annestown where the beach is popular with surfers and is safe for swimming. A short way before Bunmahon, **Waterford Woodcraft**, T396110, sells items sculptured from Irish timbers and stays open until 2100. Bunmahon has its own Blue Flag beach, which can be reached on foot from the village though it also has its own car park.

The beach at Stradbally is sandy and suitable for families. The village also has a Protestant church with an interesting old churchyard, which includes an early 17th-century tombstone with an incised skull and crossbones.

Clonea Strand is a Blue Flag beach that fits snugly into the coastline and further west there is another surfing beach at Ballinacourty. It is 25 miles (41 kilometres) between Tramore and Dungarvan.

Sleeping **L** *Gold Coast Golf Hotel*, Ballinacourty, T42249. 36 rooms and a swimming pool. **A** *Annestown House*, Annestown, T396160. **A** *Knockmahon Lodge*, Bunmahon, T384656. **B** *Park House*, Stradbally, T293185. Five rooms, some of which share bathroom facilities.

Dungarvan

Phone code: 058
Colour map 3, grid B6

The origins of the town go back to Anglo-Norman times but it was in the early 19th century that the Dukes of Devonshire established the grid design of streets around the generous space of Grattan Square. The town is a humdrum kind of place but it suggests itself as a possible base for trips to the Comeragh mountains, the Irish-speaking Ring Peninsula or the Ardmore beaches. The helpful tourist office makes the best of what is available and a **guided walking tour** of the town departs daily from their office between June and September at 1100 and 1500 for IR£3. They also dispense a useful little 75p booklet detailing 4 local walks, lasting from 45 minutes to three hours. There is a small museum of local history: **Dungarvan Museum.** ■ *Market House, Lower Main Street, T41231, Monday to Friday, all year, 1400-1700. Free.*

Sleeping **AL** *Lawlor's Hotel*, Bridge St, T41122, F41000, info@lawlors-hotel.ie Has 89 rooms. **AL** *Park Hotel*, T42899, F42969. Has 29 rooms and overlooks the River Colligan. It is situated at the Waterford end of town at the N25 roundabout. **B** *Abbey House*, Friars Walk, Abbeyside, T41669. A B&B in town and close to the sea. **B** *Hillcrest*, Waterford Rd, Tarr's Bridge, T42262. Next to the golf course on the N25. **B** *Rosebank House*, Coast Rd, T41561. Just over a mile outside town and found by following the signs for Clonea Strand. **D** *Dungarvan Holiday Hostel*, Youghal Rd, T44340, F36141. Open all year, has five private rooms for around IR£17, and bikes are for hire.

County Waterford

Ogham

Ogham is the earliest form of Irish writing, made up of an alphabet of eventually 25 letters. The letters were inscribed along the edge of a stone pillar, and over 300 examples have been found in Ireland, mostly in Munster and in parts of Wales colonised by the Irish, dating between the 4th and 7th centuries. The letters take the form of slashes in varying numbers and sizes and mostly spell out memorials to individuals.

Camping *Bayview Caravan & Camping Park*, Coast Rd, Ballinacourty, T45345. Open from Easter to September. *Casey's Caravan & Camping Park*, Clonea, T41919. Open from May to early September, and has direct access to the beach. No pre-booking between 9th July and 15th August.

Eating

The most interesting place to eat is undoubtedly *The Tannery*, 10 Quay St, T45420, with starters like roast red pepper soup with basil. There are fish and meat main courses with contemporary touches and suitably indulgent desserts. A full lunch costs between IR£12 and IR£15 and dinner, served 1830-2200, costs around IR£22. Closed Sunday and Monday. Dinner at *Lawlor's Hotel* or the *Park Hotel* is just a little less expensive.

Try *Ormond's Café* in Grattan Square, almost next door to the tourist office, for a decent coffee and a good range of cakes, sandwiches and IR£3-5 meals such as chicken, quiche, or shepherd's pie.

Festivals

The **Féile na nDéise** is a traditional music festival that enlivens the town over the bank holiday weekend, early in May. The sessions of live music are spread around the various pubs and for further information contact the tourist office or T42998.

Pubs & music

An Poc ar Buile, O'Connell St, has good sessions of music and so does the bar in *Lawlor's Hotel*. Other places worth checking out are *Bean a'Leanna* at the weekends, and the *Anchor* down by the quay. *Seanchaí Bar*, off the Cork road, T46285, is a lovely thatched pub far more spick and span than the traditional scene it evokes and when the music gets going, especially on the popular Saturday night session, there is a good atmosphere. There is a restaurant as well serving hearty, affordable fare.

Sport

Golf *Dungarvan Golf Club*, T43310. *West Waterford Club*, T41475. *Gold Coast Golf Hotel*, T42416. *Dungarvan Golf Range*, T44318. **Sea angling** *The Gone Fishin' Tackle Shop*, Parnell St, has boats for daily or weekly hire as well as tackle. *Brian Barton*, Ballinacourty, T44962/088-633242, also has a boat for hire. Tackle also available from *Baumann's*, Mary St, T41395.

Transport

Bicycle Bikes can be hired from the hostel and from Murphy Cycles, Main St, T41376. **Bus** *Bus Éireann* No 4 service connects Dungarvan with Lismore, Waterford and Dublin. The No 40 Rosslare Harbour to Tralee bus goes via Waterford, Dungarvan and Cork. No 362 Waterford – Ring – Ardmore bus stops as well and No 364 goes along the coast road between Dungarvan and Waterford. No 366 Waterford to Mallow stops at Dungarvan and Lismore and there is also the 386 service between Clonmel and Dungarvan.

Directory

Tourist office Grattan Square, T41741, May-Sep, 0930-1730, Mon-Sat; Oct-Apr, 0930-1730, Mon to Fri. **Tours** Local guided walks can be arranged by prior arrangement with Mr David O'Connor, T44957.

County Waterford

An Rinn (Ring)
Phone code: 058

An Rinn, eight miles (12 kilometres) south of Dungarvan, is a little oasis of Gaelic culture and famous for its language school. Follow the Cork road out of Dungarvan, and take the signposted left turning on to the R674. Shortly afterwards there is another left turning, signposted for An Cuinigear, that leads to a sand and shingle beach and a three-mile (five-kilometre) finger of land that stretches into Dungarvan Bay. It makes for a pleasant stroll and there are bird-spotting opportunities along the way. The Irish Language college, Coláiste na Rinne, T/F46128, is along this road and summer language courses are run for 10- to 18-year-olds. Back on the R674, the road leads to Ceann Heilbhic (Helvic Head) and along the way there is a sign for Criostal na Rinne, a workshop producing and selling crystal giftware, T46174, which is also on sale at 30 Parnell Street in Dungarvan.

Sleeping   **B** *Helvick View*, An Rinn, T46297, has 2 rooms overlooking the bay and Helvick harbour.

Transport   **Bus** *Bus Éireann's* 362 service links Ring with Waterford, Dungarvan and Ardmore. An inland road from Ring goes on to Ardmore, avoiding the N25 road.

Ardmore (Áird Mhór)

Phone code: 024
Colour map 3, grid B6

A popular seaside resort with four very lovely beaches to choose from, Ardmore is surprisingly picturesque and with a history to boot, which claims that St Declan established here the first Christian settlement in Ireland. The tourist information office has a free leaflet describing an undemanding 2½-mile (four-kilometre) circular **cliff walk** that begins just beyond the Cliff House Hotel and close by St Declan's Well. ■ *Tourist information office, sea-front car-park, T94444. May to September 1100-1600.*

St Declan's Cathedral & tower

Built on the site of the saint's original monastery, the church dates back to 1203, with parts of the walls and the east gable dating from the 14th century. The chancel, however, is formed from parts of an older church, probably from the ninth century. It is the west gable, however, that should not be missed because it carries Romanesque sculptures depicting biblical scenes that, though badly eroded in places, can still be discerned. Try to make out Michael the Archangel weighing souls, Adam and Eve, the Judgement of Solomon and the Adoration of the Magi.

Two Ogham stones have been placed inside the church, one of which carries the longest known Ogham inscription in Ireland. The 12th-century tower is in good condition and is just under 29 yards (29.5 metres) in height. There is a small oratory said to contain the grave of the saint.

Sleeping   **AL** *Cliff House Hotel*, T94106, F94496, cmv@indigo.ie All the rooms have seaviews over Ardmore Bay, there are weekend specials available, but closed between November and February. **A** *Newtown View*, Grange, T94143, F94054. A guesthouse on a working farm some 4 miles (6 km) from Ardmore, with seaviews and comfortable, well-provided rooms. **A** *Round Tower Hotel*, College Rd, T94494, F94254. Has 10 rooms and is within walking distance of the beach. **B** *Byron Lodge*, T94157. A fine Georgian house at the end of town, overlooking the beach. Opens from April to October. **D** *Ardmore Beach Hostel*, Main St, T94501. Has over 20 beds and some private rooms for IR£20.

There are a couple of tourist-friendly restaurants along Main St serving standard **Eating** meals around IR£5 and *Paddy Mac's* pub on the same street falls into the same category. For something more interesting the two hotels have their own restaurants and bars serving food. Local fish features prominently at the Cliff House, where dinner is around IR£20, while the Round Tower is less expensive.

There are daily buses to and from Cork, via Youghal and Midleton, and a Waterford to **Transport** Ardmore service, via Dungarvan and Ring, that does not operate on Sunday. They all stop outside O'Reilly's pub on Main St.

This is a 58-mile (94-km) walk that is based upon an ancient pilgrim's route that **St Declan's** connected the churches of Ardmore and Cashel. The tourist office in Ardmore **Way** have a IR£4.20 map guide covering the route in a series of strip maps, and while the Ordnance Survey 1:50,000 maps (the same scale as the strip map guide) would be a very useful addition you would need four of them – Nos 66, 74, 81 and 82 – to cover the whole Way. Generally speaking, the walk is not especially difficult and the only part that is critically dependent on good weather is the way through the Bearna Cloch an Bhuidéal pass in the Knockmealdown mountains. *Crystal Walks*, T048-44957/41741, http:// www.amireland.com/declan can arrange the walk based on daily journeys of 9-11 miles (16-18 km).

Lismore and around

Perhaps it was Lismore's charming location, situated on the River Blackwater Phone code: 058 *with the Knockmealdown Mountains as a backdrop, that appealed to St* Colour map 3, grid B6 *Carthage in 636 when he chose the place for a monastic school. It developed into a major European seat of learning and despite being attacked by Vikings on a number of occasions it retained its importance until falling into decline towards the end of the 12th century after the arrival of the English. The rest of the town was laid out in the early 19th century and the tourist office dispenses a **walking guide** for IR£1 that takes one on a tour of the main streets and places of interest, chief amongst which is **St Carthage's Cathedral**. The long-distance St Declan's Way (see page 253) passes close to Lismore.*

County Waterford

Henry II visited Lismore in 1171 to meet with the chiefs of Munster and chose a **Lismore Castle** site for a castle overlooking the river, but it was left to Prince John to start **& gardens** building it in 1185. At the end of the 16th century the castle passed to Walter Raleigh but he sold it to Richard Boyle, 1st Earl of Cork, who went on to become the richest man in Ireland. It was Richard Boyle who set about landscaping the countryside around Lismore in the style of an English estate. In 1753 the castle passed to the 4th Duke of Devonshire, though it was the 6th Duke in the 19th century who hired Joseph Paxton to fashion the imposing and dramatic edifice that now towers over the river, incorporating into the structure parts of the earlier castle and monastic remains. During this rebuilding work a 13th-century crozier was found hidden in the walls and this famous Lismore Crozier (as depicted on the 28p stamp) can be seen on display in the National Museum in Dublin. Also hidden, presumably during the Reformation years, was a 15th-century book recounting the lives of saints, along with an Irish translation of Marco Polo's travels.

Lismore Castle remains the private property of the Devonshires and as such is not open to the public. *Hoi polloi*, however, can enter the gardens and there are fine views of the castle from within these gardens as well as from the Ballyduff road.

The Book of Lismore

In the course of some home decoration on the castle in 1814, a box of 15th-century manuscripts secretly recessed behind a wall came to light. Known as the Book of Lismore, the texts contain both sacred and secular tales including one about three sinners who retreat into a vow of silence and after the first year one of them comments on the wisdom of their deed; after the second year another of them speaks his agreement; after the third year the last one complains that he is sick and tired of their chatter and contemplates a return to the world.

The lower level of the gardens, planted with peat from the Knockmealdown Mountains, is rich with rhododendrons, magnolias and the like, while the formal upper level retains an Elizabethan layout. ■ *T54424. 30th April to 28th September, daily 1345-1645. IR£2.50.*

Lismore Heritage Centre Located in the old courthouse, along with the tourist office, the centre offers an introduction to the history of the town through a multimedia presentation in the guise of Brother Declan, a follower of St Carthage. ■ *T54975. Open all year, daily 0930-1800, but closes on Sunday between November and the end of February.*

Cappoquin This small town, to the west of Lismore, is a renowned centre for both course and game angling and *Tight Lines Tackle Shop* (*Main Street, T54152*) is the place to visit for information and tackle. Fishing aside, the countryside around Cappoquin is delightful and at the town the River Blackwater makes an audacious 90-degree turn to the south for its descent into Youghal Bay. In the centre of town, an 18th-century Georgian mansion was built on the site of an old castle that commanded the river at this point and Cappoquin House and gardens offer a superb view of the Blackwater. The gardens are mostly informal and boast a magnificent rhododendron arboretum, if that's to your liking, with some interesting architectural plants dotted around the place. ■ *T54004. April to July, Monday-Saturday, 0900-1300. IR£2.*

Glenshelane Forest Tourist Park Close to Cappoquin is the Glenshelane Forest Tourist Park. There are some eight miles (12 kilometres) of riverside walks. Accommodation is possible in three-bedroomed self-catering log cabins, and camping is also possible (see 'Sleeping', page 255). The recommended walk is the one that brings you close to **Mount Melleray**, a Cistercian abbey about 6 kilometres (4 miles) north of Cappoquin. The Cistercian order was finished off in Ireland during the Reformation but was re-established in 1832 when a dozen or so monks came here and developed a community that numbered around 140 in the 1950s. Numbers are once again in serious decline but visitors who wish to visit the abbey for peaceful contemplation can stay in the guesthouse on the grounds. ■ *Glenshelane Forest Tourist Park T52132. Mount Melleray, T54404, F52140.*

Walking the Knockmealdowns Lismore is an excellent base for a one- or two-day walk across the wild and amazing scenery of the Knockmealdown mountains. The route is fairly simple since it forms part of the waymarked Blackwater Way, but getting to and from the walk can pose some problems. From Lismore you need transport for about 12 kilometres (8 miles) to the **Vee Gap**, there is no public transport but ask at your accommodation about a taxi there or consider hitching. The Vee Gap is a beauty spot on the R668 road to Clogheen and you could begin in Clogheen and follow the Blackwater Way from there to the Vee Gap. Once at the Vee Gap you are in the middle of the of the Knockmealdowns with the Blackwater Way

The sceptical chemist

Robert Boyle (1627-91), the son of Richard Boyle, the first Earl of Cork, was born in Lismore castle and educated at Eton. He returned to Ireland in 1652 for a couple of years but lived most of his life in Oxford and then London. He is famous for formulating the principle that the pressure of a gas varies with its volume at a constant temperature – Boyle's Law – and although a deeply religious man he played an important part in debunking the pseudo-scientific, scholastic explanations for the physical world. His best-known work in this respect is The Sceptical Chymist, published in 1661.

stretching off to the west over Knockolugga, through some very rugged territory and with glorious views of the surrounding countryside. To the east the waymarked route is less interesting, going through forestry at quite a low level.

At the Vee there is a Bianconi hut, used in the last century for changing horses on the big carriages that once travelled across the mountain road (see page 262). From here you will see paths and waymarkers threading the way uphill to the west. The route is quite challenging to begin with, as it makes its way over rocky tumbled stones, but it then meets a forestry road for a while before climbing above the young trees. As you climb Knockolugga the path is merely a series of markers and sheep tracks so choose a clear day or you could lose your way uphill. At the top spend a little time just taking in where you are and what you can see: on a windy sunny day it is truly exhilarating.

A wide tumbled road takes you west and downhill past some strange objects – an abandoned car nowhere near where it could possibly have driven to, pieces of corrugated iron roofing which must have been carried by the winds since there are no buildings for miles around. At the bottom of the hill you travel briefly along a tiny road and then head off west again up Crow Hill, with wide, worn footpaths that bring you down eventually to farmland and minor roads to Carran Hill. Araglin is a couple of miles to the south.

At Carran Hill or Araglin there are B&Bs that are very walker-friendly (see 'Sleeping', page 255), or you can walk on and make a day of it to Mountain Barracks, mostly along country lanes but pleasant enough. Staying overnight at Carran Hill keeps you on the Way but from Araglin you will need to walk a couple of miles to get back on the route. There is no accommodation at Mountain Barracks but there is a pub and from here you can ring for a taxi (T025-32816, 31718) to Fermoy.

Mapping & information From the Vee Gap to Araglin is about 9 miles (15 kilometres) while to Mountain Barracks is a much stiffer 21 miles (35 kilometres). Even though the walk is well provided with waymarkers, it would be useful to have the OS Discovery series map 74 or the Blackwater Way Map Guide published by EastWest Mapping. For organized walks contact Helen McGrath, T36359, or Verona Nugent, T36494, F36617. For organized walking trips in the **Comeragh Mountains** contact T36238, hiking@indigo.ie

Essentials

Sleeping **AL** *Ballyrafter House Hotel*, T54002, F53050. Built in the 1880s as part of the Devonshire estate, the hotel offers fine country-house accommodation, and game fishing enthusiasts are particularly well catered for. The atmosphere is genuinely laid-back, nothing pretentious in the air of this welcoming house. **AL** *Lismore Hotel*, T54555, F53068. Built as a lodge for the Devonshires, this lovely old house in the centre of town has big, old-fashioned rooms. **AL-L** *Richmond House*, Cappoquin,

County Waterford

T54278. An 18th-century country house offering accommodation and a fine restaurant open to non-residents. **B** *Beechcroft*, Deerpark Rd, Lismore, T/F54273. A modern house on the outskirts of town and also offers self-catering accommodation. **B** *Pine Tree House*, Ballyanchor, Lismore, T53282. At the edge of town and offers a similar standard of rooms. **D** *Barnahoun Farm Holiday Centre*, Carran Hill, T60077. A B&B that will provide packed lunches and has lots of advice on walks. **D** *Kilmona Farm Hostel*, T54315. Open all year, has 2 private rooms for IR£20, and being part of a functioning farm there is also space for camping. **D** *Mrs Norah Fennessy*, Creamery View, near Araglin, T60007. B&B.

Eating

A quiet place for a pint is the delightful traditional O'Brien's in Main St, T54816.

The restaurant at *Ballyrafter House Hotel*, T54002, has a menu that changes nightly, and fresh salmon from the Blackwater is one of the specialities. Sunday lunch is very popular. Expect to pay around IR£22 for dinner. Also recommended is dinner at the *Lismore Hotel* restaurant, T54555, where main courses are around IR£9. The bar in this hotel also does good food. *Richmond House* (see 'Sleeping', page 255) offers traditional country-house cooking with touches of more adventurous cuisines and interesting vegetarian options. A 4-course dinner is IR£27, from 1900-2130 but closed on Sunday and Monday to non-residents. *Madden's* pub, Main St, T54148, is worth considering for lunch but *Eamonn's Place* also in Main St, T54025, is better, serving generous portions of dishes like lamb's liver and bacon casserole and lovely puddings. Main courses in the restaurant at night are in the IR£5-11 range. *Buggy's Glencairn Inn*, Glencairn, T56232, is a couple of miles outside Lismore and has acquired a reputation for mighty good food. The bar itself is tiny and space is at a premium in the dining room too, so booking is essential. Starters are IR£2-5, main courses IR£12-16. Open from 1930 to 2100, but closed on Tuesday except for guests in the four bedrooms. Lunch is usually available in the summer, but phone to make sure.

Sport **Golf** *Lismore Golf Club*, T54026. A scenic 9-hole course signposted off the Ballyduff road.

Transport **Buses** *Bus Éireann* run a daily service between Dublin and Lismore via Waterford. On Friday and Sunday there is a service from Lismore to Waterford and Cork via Dungarvan and Cappoquin. There is also a daily local bus to Dungarvan.

Directory **Tourist office** In the *Lismore Heritage Centre*, T54975. Open all year, daily, 0930-1800, but closes on Sunday between November and the end of February. **Walking tours** Enquire at the tourist office about guided walks around town, which usually run twice daily during the summer months.

County Tipperary

Cashel

Phone code: 062
Colour map 3, grid A6

The ecclesiastical remains on the stupendous Rock of Cashel consist of a round tower, a 12th-century chapel, a 13th-century cathedral and 15th-century residential buildings. The rock is conveniently located just off the main Dublin to Cork road, making the market town of Cashel a major stopping-off point for travellers. The Rock of Cashel is Ireland's acropolis and should not be missed.

Rock of Cashel The Rock, a limestone outcrop that rises 61 metres (200 feet) above the plain, was the seat of Munster kings from the fourth to the early 12th century, and in 978 Brian Bóruma (Brian Boru) was crowned here. In 1101 the Rock was given to the Church, and Cormac's Chapel was consecrated in 1134 under the auspices of the king and bishop Cormac McCarthy. The cathedral was built in the following century, on the site of an earlier one, but in 1495 it was set alight by the Earl of Kildare because, as he later explained to the understandably irate Henry VII, he thought the archbishop was inside. The cathedral was plundered in 1647, and its lead roof was removed some time in the 18th century; a consequence of the fact that the archbishop of the time was said to be too lazy to climb the rock.

P J Kavanagh in *Voices in Ireland* (see page 60) describes how the Rock of Cashel 'jumps out of the Tipperary plains like an Edinburgh Castle in a sea of green'. He tells how when St Patrick baptized a king here in 450 he accidentally shoved his crozier through the king's foot, who kept mum in the belief it was all part of the ritual.

The Rock of Cashel is very popular with coach tours, and during summer months it is advisable to arrive early in the morning to avoid the crowds.

Hall of the Vicars Choral This 15th-century building is now the entrance to the Rock and home to the obligatory video that recounts the history of the site. There is a small museum, the chief exhibit of which is the famed **St Patrick's Cross**. It originally stood outside, where a replica now stands, and tradition states that the cross's plinth was the coronation stone for the inauguration of Irish kings, including Brian Ború.

Cormac's Chapel Found immediately to the south of the cathedral, this is the earliest and most beautiful Romanesque church in Ireland. Its remarkable steep stone roof, unusual twin square towers instead of transepts, and carved arcading are all noted features of its exterior. Above the north door, which was the main entrance before the cathedral got in the way, there is a lively sculpture of a lion being shot at with a bow and arrow by a helmeted figure that looks like a centaur.

The ribbed, barrel-vaulted nave is wonderfully small, and recent restoration work on the chancel roof has revealed some of the frescoes that once were probably a feature of the church ceiling as a whole, lending glorious colour to what is now a dark interior. There are many fine sculptures over the archway that leads to the east chancel, and there is also a superb **sarcophagus** that dates back to around the 12th century and is said to be the tomb of King Cormac. Its sophisticated decorative design of interlacing beasts is Ireland's best example of the Urnes style, chiefly recognizable by the intertwining of broad and narrower animals, which came to the country from Scandinavia at the end of the 11th century. Like the design of the square towers, which are thought to hail from Germany, this is another example of how remarkably open to European art Ireland was at this time.

Cathedral What you see today is the shell of a cathedral that was first built in the 13th century, but which was restored more than once over the centuries. The west side has the addition of a small castle built as a secure residence for the archbishop early in the 15th century, the main hall of which was spread over the top of the nave, the corbels being still visible. It was also in the 15th century that the central tower of the cathedral was raised to its present position of dominance. The tower reduces the length of the nave, so that the choir is actually longer, and the main attractions inside the church are the high-set lancet windows, classic examples of 13th-century style, and a multitude of memorial tombs. The adjoining round tower is the earliest surviving structure on the Rock and was part of the early Christian enclosure. ■ *The Rock of Cashel. T61437. Mid-March to mid-June, daily, 0930-1730; Mid-June to mid-September, daily 0900-1730; Mid-September mid-March, daily 0930-1630. IR£3. Dúchas site.*

County Tipperary

Heritage Centre **Brú Ború ('Palace of Brian Ború') Heritage Centre** This stands at the foot of the Rock adjoining the car-park. The centre is made up of a theatre, restaurant, genealogical centre, exhibition hall and craft shop. A theatrical show of music and dance takes place here each evening. ■ *T61122, http://www.mayo-ireland.ie/cce.htm Monday-Friday 0900-1700. Theatrical shows between June and September, nightly 2100.*

Cashel of the Kings Heritage Centre Next to the tourist office, the exhibition here includes a model of the 17th-century town. ■ *Town Hall, Main Street, T62511. January to March and September, Monday-Friday 0930-1730; April to June, daily 0930-1800; July and August, daily 0930-2000. IR£1.*

Cashel Folk Village A collection of house fronts, shops, farming implements, and memorabilia from the 18th, 19th and 20th centuries that together form a more interesting window into the past than one might be inclined to give it credit for. Ideal for a rainy day. ■ *T62525. Dominic Street. March to April, daily 1000-1800. Rest of year, daily 0930-1630. IR£2.*

Bolton library This is a specialist museum for connoisseurs of the printed word: a library of books, manuscripts and maps, some of which date back to the earliest days of printing. ■ *T61232. June-August, Monday-Friday 1100-1630. IR£2.50.*

Essentials

Sleeping **L-LL** *Cashel Palace Hotel*, Main St, T62707, F61521, reception@cashel-palace.ie Built in 1730 as an Archbishop's Palace and now a highly-rated and comfortable hotel with its own walled gardens and a private walk to the Rock. Ask for one of the rooms overlooking the Rock of Cashel.

A *Bailey's of Cashel*, Main St, T61937, F62038, a guesthouse with its own restaurant, is also a fondly restored period-piece house: a Georgian town house with its own parking area and some rooms with Rock views.

B *Georgesland*, T/F62788. B&B in a large modern bungalow less than a mile outside of town, on the Dualla Rd. Has a good reputation. **B** *Indaville*, T62075. Another Georgian house close to the town centre that provides accommodation. It is on the left after the N8 turn south to Cork after Main St. **B** *Maryville*, Bank Place, T61098. Guesthouse with its own parking area and views of the Rock. **B** *Ros-Guill House*, Dualla Rd, T62699, F61507. A guesthouse with a good reputation. **B** *Thornbrook House*, Dualla Rd, T62388, F61480, a ponderosa-style dwelling.

D *Cashel Holiday Hostel*, 6 John St, T62330, F62445, cashelho@iol.ie John St is a turning off Main St and the hostel has over 40 beds, and 3 private rooms for IR£20. **D** *O'Brien's Farmhouse Hostel*, St Patrick's Rock, Dundrum Rd, T61003, F62797. A short walk from the town centre and just far enough away to escape the traffic noise. A converted stone stable and excellent views of the Rock. There are 3 private rooms, charging from IR£20 to IR£25, and camping is also possible. Recommended.

Eating The best place for fine dining is *Ches Hans*, T61177, at the end of Dominick St, where you should expect to pay around IR£30. This ex-Wesleyan chapel has a catholic, French-inflected, menu with local Tipperary lamb always available. Over IR£25 per person, dinner only and closed Sunday. *The Spearman*, 97 Main St, T61143, is worth seeking out for a tasty lunch of pasta or whatever the daily specials have to offer. A good choice of starters, main courses are European with a faint touch of the orient, and prices are reasonable. For IR£50, two people could dine and wine the night away; but not on Sunday or Monday when it's closed. *The Bishop's Buttery* in the Cashel Palace Hotel is open all day for standard meals at affordable prices. *Legends*, The Kiln, T61292, is adjacent to the Brú Ború Heritage Centre and an evening meal could be enjoyed here for under IR£20.

Along Main St there are a couple of modest restaurants offering fairly predictable meals under IR£10 and there are a number of cafés at the foot of the Rock and near the tourist office. *Dowling's*, at the bottom of the main street heading towards Cork, T62130, is a pleasantly unreconstructed pub serving plain, homely food.

Larkspur Park, The Green, T61626. Provides golf, tennis, badminton and snooker. **Sport** **Angling** *Ryans Shop*, Friary St, T61106. Dispenses information and tackle.

Bicycle Both hostels in the town rent bikes (see 'Sleeping', page 258). **Buses** *Bus* **Transport** *Éireann* run 3 buses a day, 2 on Sunday, between Dublin and Cork via Cashel, Cahir and Fermoy. In the summer months 4 extra buses run daily between Cashel and Cahir, and there is also a daily service between Cork and Athlone that stops at Cashel. Contact *Rafferty's Travel*, 102 Main St, T62121, for schedules. *Bernard Kavanagh*, T056-31189, runs a Monday to Friday service between Dublin and Cashel and another private bus company called *Kavanaghs*, T51563, runs a Monday to Friday service between Clonmel and Thurles via Cashel.

Tour operators *Cashel Heritage Tram*, T62511. Runs a circular tour of the main sites and **Directory** includes entry to Cashel of the Kings Heritage Centre and Bolton Library. Hop on or off anywhere on the circuit. Jun-Sep, Tue-Sat, 1200-1800. IR£3. **Tourist Office** Town hall, Main St, T61333. Apr-Sep, Mon to Sat 0900-1800; Jul-Aug also on Sunday.

Tipperary town

Is it just nostalgia that makes Tipperary a name that still evokes something imag- *Phone code: 062* ined about a past Ireland? The town that actually carries the resonant name is a workaday kind of place that probably disappoints visitors who are seeking something more than the prosaic. A statue to Charles Kickham (1828-82), Fenian and author of *Knocknagow* (who came from the county, not the town) is proudly plonked in Main Street. The father of the American playwright Eugene O'Neill came from a farm just outside of town. There is a tourist office in James Street. ■ *T51457, May to September, Monday-Saturday, 0930-1730.*

For hearty meals drop in at *Kickham House* or *Kiely's Bar*, both on Main St, and for traditional Irish music check if anything is happening at *Kickham House*, T51716, or *Lowry's Bar*, T52774, also on Main St. For hotel accommodation there is **AL** *Royal Hotel*, Bridge St, T33244, F33596. **A** *Ballyglass Country House Hotel*, Glen of Aherlow Road, Ballyglass, T52104, F52229, 2 miles out of town. B&Bs include *Riverside House*, Galbally Rd, T51219, F33499, 5 mins walk from town by the River Arrow, on the R662.

Cahir

This massive castle was originally built in 1142 by Conor O'Brien and came **Cahir Castle** into the possession of the Anglo-Norman Butler family in 1375. It was the But- *Phone code: 052* lers who built most of what is seen today. After a ten-day siege in 1599, during the Elizabethan Wars, they lost it to the Earl of Essex but it stayed in the Butler family only to be again attacked by English artillery in 1647: the castle then surrendered to the Parliamentary commander, Lord Inchiquin. Three years later it surrendered again, this time without a shot being fired, after Cromwell had

County Tipperary

delivered a terse statement that grimly concluded: 'if I be necessitated to bend my cannon upon you, you must expect the extremity usual in such cases'; message understood.

The whole castle was restored first in the 19th century and again more recently but, notwithstanding the tremendous amount of space available, not very much has been done to the rooms, which contain lacklustre displays. However, a planned exhibition on the 1599 seige may improve matters. Tours lasting half an hour depart on the hour, and in addition there is a 17-minute video, a portcullis to admire and walls to walk along. ■ *Castle St, T41011. Mid-March to mid-June, daily 0930-1730; mid-June to mid-September, daily 0900-1930; mid-September to mid-March, daily 0930-1730 (1630 mid-October to mid-March). IR£2. Dúchas site.*

Swiss Cottage From the car-park at the side of Cahir Castle there is a path running alongside the river that leads to Swiss Cottage, a delightful *cottage orné* built in the early 19th century by Richard Butler to a design by the Regency architect John Nash. An Alpine look is discernible from the outside, hence the nickname it acquired some decades after it was built, but the interior is unique and quite beautiful. The elegant spiral staircase is worth admiring and the Dufour wallpaper in the salon that displays the Bosphorus was one of the first commercially produced Parisian wallpapers. ■ *Kilcommon, T41144. May to September, daily, 1000-1800; mid-March to April and October to November, Tuesday-Sunday, 1000-1300 and 1400-1700. IR£2. Dúchas site. Situated one mile south of Cahir off the R670, the road to Ardfinnan.*

Sleeping **AL-A** *Cahir House Hotel*, The Square, T/F42727. This fine Georgian building in the centre of town, home to Lord Cahir's family until 1961, has over 40 rooms. **A** *Castle Court Hotel*, Church St, T41210, F42333. A family-run hotel in the centre of town with a popular pub. **B** *Carrigeen Castle*, Cork Rd, T/F41370, less than a mile outside of town. Quite a remarkable sight and one of Ireland's more unusual B&Bs. **B** *The Homestead*, Mitchelstown Rd, T42043. B&B situated in a large bungalow near the town centre. **B** *Killaun*, Clonmel Rd, T41780. Standard B&B on the N24 and five minutes from town. **B** *Silver Acre*, Clonmel Rd, a bungalow in a cul-de-sac offering B&B that has been well-spoken of.

Eating The best place for a meal has to be the cosy *Butler's Pantry* in the *Cahir House Hotel*, offering steaks, fish and poultry for lunch and dinner. Set dinner is IR£19. The comfortable *O'Brien's Bar* in the same hotel serves food throughout the day. The tourist-orientated place opposite the castle looks forgettable, as does the *Italian Connection* a few doors up from the tourist office with pasta and pizza around IR£6, fish up to IR£14 and a couple of curries thrown in for good measure. For a light meal try the *Galtee Inn* in the main square or enjoy a picnic by crossing the wooden bridge in the car-park by the castle, a few doors up from the tourist office.

Sport **Angling** Contact Tom Butler, *Cahir Anglers Club*, Railway View, Cahir Abbey, T41167. **Horse-riding** Lissava House Stables, T41117.

Transport **Buses** Both of *Bus Éireann's* Dublin to Cork services stop in Cahir. The No 7 connects Cahir with both cities as well as Clonmel, Carrick-on-Suir and Kilkenny, while the No 8 travels via Kildare, Cashel and Fermoy. The Galway to Rosslare Harbour service also stops in Cahir and connects with Ennis, Limerick, Clonmel, Carrick-on-Suir, Waterford and Wexford. Once a day the Cork to Athlone bus also stops and there are local services to Clonmel and Carrick-on-Suir. **Train** T41578. A service between Cork and Rosslare Europort stops twice, Monday-Saturday, in Cahir, changing at Limerick.

Tourist office In the car-park next to Cahir Castle, T41453. Apr-Sep, Mon-Sat 0900-1800; Jul-Aug also Sun 1100-1700.

Directory

Clonmel

The lively town of Clonmel has at least two claims to fame: the birthplaces of Laurence Sterne (1713-1768), a novelist whose hilarious style predates post-modernism by a couple of centuries, author of freewheeling Tristram Shandy, and of the Bianconi system of public transport (see box on page 262). Other noted residents included the novelist Anthony Trollope, who left his homeland to set up house here in 1848, (the epitome of the style that Sterne so delightfully subverted), and the author George Borrow. The many fine old buildings dotted around Clonmel are a chief attraction of the town and the tourist office dispenses a Heritage Trail booklet with a location map that is very useful for nosing them out.

Phone code: 052
Colour map 3, grid B6

If nothing else, find time to stand before the **Main Guard** at the eastern end of O'Connell Street. It was built in the 1670s as a courthouse, one of the oldest public building in Ireland, and recently restored to give some idea of its imposing structure. It was not here, however, that the leaders of the Young Ireland movement were prosecuted for their part in the abject failure of the 1848 rising; by that time the County Courthouse in Nelson Street had been standing for nearly 50 years. To get there from the Main Guard continue eastwards along Mitchell Street and turn right into Neilson Street after passing Dowd's Lane (and a statue to the '98 rebellion, erected in 1904), also on the right. It was at the County Courthouse that Thomas Francis Meagher and others were sentenced to transportation to Australia (see box on page 244). Dramatic recreations of some trails form part of an evening entertainment's programme inside the courthouse (see below).

A buildings tour

Retrace your steps back up Neilson Street to Parnell Street and **Hearns Hotel**, where Bianconi started his cart transport system in 1815 (see box on page 262). Return to the Main Guard and walk down to the western end of O'Connell Street where, facing the Main Guard from this end of the street, is the **West Gate**. It was built in 1831 on the site of an original gate in the medieval walls that once enclosed the town. The Tudor style was being popularly imitated at the time and this shows in the inclusion of machicolated battlements; hardly a necessary feature of town planning in the 1830s, even in Ireland. On the other, west, side of West Gate lays **Irishtown**, a name commonly found in towns to designate the living area for the indigenous, non-Anglo-Normans who could work but not live inside the town walls. From the West Gate walk north up Wolf Tone Street, passing **White Memorial Theatre** that was built in the Greek Revival style in 1843 as a Weslyan Methodist chapel. Continue up to **St Mary's Church**, dating back to 1204 but largely rebuilt in the 19th century and boasting a superb, 84-foot ziggurat belltower that was built up on the foundations of an earlier tower. The only remaining section of the **town walls** can be seen nearby, restored and renovated 20 years ago.

County Tipperary

Song, dance and theatre come together at the County Courthouse when some of the county's more famous trials are recreated where they originally took place. Each show includes a presentation of Tipperary's history, and a light snack meal and local cider feature in the festivities. ■ *County Courthouse, Nelson Street, T22960. July to August, Friday-Saturday, 2100. IR£8.*

County Courthouse

Finn McCools & Massey Dawsons

Charles Bianconi (1786-1875) came to Ireland from Lombardy in 1802 at the age of 16 as a pedlar of prints. He was sent to Ireland to avoid a scandal over his friendship with a local girl who was betrothed to a nobleman. His travels across the country convinced him of the need for a low-cost system of public transport, and in 1815 he started the first service between Clonmel and Cahir using one horse to pull a two-wheeled car with passengers, mail and small freight. Success was instant and, taking advantage of low prices for horses and cars following the end of the long war against Napoleon, he was soon able to upgrade the quality of the service. Stage coaches continued to make long-haul trips out of Dublin and other large cities but Bianconi's open-topped cars were ideal for inexpensive and shorter journeys between small towns. By the 1840s Bians, as they came to be known, were operating across 3,000 miles of road every day and the largest coaches, called 'Finn McCools' and 'Massey Dawsons', could carry up to 20 passengers. For countless thousands of ordinary people, Bians opened up the Irish countryside and made travel affordable in a way that was undreamt of before the Italian began his first service from outside what is now Hearn's Hotel on Parnell Street in Clonmel.

Museums **County Museum** This delightfully unreconstructed museum has a miscellany of items relating mostly to the town's history in the 19th and early 20th centuries, and occasional temporary exhibitions of a more sophisticated nature. Check out the anti-DeValera election poster from 1932. ■ *Parnell Street, T25399. Tuesday-Saturday, 1000-1300, 1400-1700.*

Museum of Transport Situated opposite the town's large supermarket, this has exhibits dating from the earliest motorized vehicles. Jaguar, Mercedes and Rolls Royce are all represented and there is also a section on motorbikes, and memorabilia such as period petrol pumps. Unfortunately, the few items of Bianconi interest are not on show because of the space available, but visitors can request to see them. ■ *Richmond Mill, Market Place, T29727. June to September, Monday-Saturday 1000-1800, and Sunday 1430-1800.*

Essentials

Sleeping **LL** *Knocklofty Country House*, Knocklofty, 4 miles (6.5 km) from Clonmel, T38222, F38300. Dating back to the 16th century, suitably oak panelled and beautifully Georgian, and set in extensive private grounds by the River Suir (fishing rights for a mile of the river), this hotel has weekend deals that reduce the cost somewhat. **AL** *Hearns Hotel*, Parnell St, T21611, F21135. Has changed a lot since Bianconi's days in the 19th century but history clings on to the place. **AL-L** *Hotel Minella*, Coleville Rd, T22388, F24381. A little way out of town and offers comfortable accommodation, a leisure centre and a good restaurant with views of the River Suir flowing along. **L** *Clonmel Arms Hotel*, Sarsfield St, T21233, F21526. Ideal for anyone wanting to be in the heart of town with a lively bar and a popular restaurant. **A** *Brighton House*, Brighton Pl, T23665, F25210, brighton@iol.ie A Georgian guesthouse with hotel-standard facilities. **A** *Fennessy's Hotel*, Gladstone St, T23680. A fine Georgian building recently restored as a modern family-run hotel.

Eating *Mr Bumbles*, Richmond House, Kickham St, T29188, is a terrific all-purpose restaurant open daily in the centre of town. Everything from tea and cakes to slabs of steak and Tipperary lamb, and some interesting starters and desserts. Expect to pay around

Bicycle excursion from Clonmel or Cashel

*The small town of **Fethard** is 10 miles (15 kilometres) north of Clonmel and about the same distance east of Cashel and it suggests itself as an ideal destination for a cycle ride from either town. Fethard is not on the tourist trail but there are a surprising number of medieval remnants to be found in the town. Main Street has a **15th-century church** and the **town walls**, which were not strong enough to withstand Cromwell in 1650, have been reconstructed in a number of places and can be reached from the church. At the end of Watergate Street, to the south of the church, there are some **17th-century tower houses** and at the east end of town an **Augustinian abbey**, founded in 1306, is now a functioning church but retains an ancient atmopshere. On Sunday mornings a **Folk, Farm & Transport Museum**, T31516, opens in Cashel Road for IR£1, as does a popular car boot sale.*

IR£20 for a good dinner. In Abbey St, **Angela's** has specials posted on a blackboard, light lunches around IR£5 and some non-meat choices. Pubs are a good bet, especially **Tierney's** on O'Connell St with its truly vast menu; bar food and main courses in the restaurant from IR£6 to IR£13. Next door is **Barry's**, T29094, serving food such as chicken fajitas for IR£9 and Thai chicken and noodles for IR£8. Also on O'Connell St, **Emerald Garden** has a Chinese set lunch and a set dinner for 2 at IR£28.

Pubs & music There are a few pubs with music. Try **Lonergan's** on O'Connell St on a Monday night, and the **Sows Ears** or **Fennessy's Hotel** on a Tuesday. **Sean Tierney**, 13 O'Connell St, T24467, serves food upstairs but the bar area on the ground floor is worth looking into. It has more exhibits than many a small museum.

Sport **Swimming** Borstal Square, T21972. Swimming pool with 25m lanes, also a sauna and gym.

Directory **Tourist office** Sarsfield St, opposite the **Clonmel Arms Hotel**, T22960. Jul-Aug, Mon-Fri 0930-1900, Sat 0930-1400; Sep-Jun, Mon-Fri 0930-1300, 1400-1700.

Carrick-on-Suir

Phone code: 051
Colour map 4, grid C1

A superb Elizabethan mansion, the best example of its type in Ireland, is one very good reason for stopping off in Carrick-on-Suir, though there are also two High Crosses in the vicinity that might detain the visitor.

Heritage centre Housed in a former Protestant church off Main Street, this is part of the tourist office and contains a collection of photographs, artefacts and documents relating to local history. ■ *T640200. June to September, Monday-Saturday 1000-1700, Sunday 1400-1700; October to May, Monday to Friday, 1000-1700. IR£1.50.*

Ormond Castle The fact that Ireland was far from being a settled country in the 1560s, when this castle was built, makes this imposing Elizabethan mansion all the more remarkable. Its calm air of tranquillity, reflected in the steady repetition of mullioned windows, would not be out of place in Shakespeare's England, but this was a turbulent Ireland at a troubled time in her history. The first castle of sorts here was built at the beginning of the 14th century, and then in the mid-15th century a larger fortified enclosure was built on this side of the River Suir. A century later Thomas, Earl of Ormond, added a mansion, and further

County Tipperary

sophisticated improvements were to follow. The original motive for the Earl's substantial tarting up of the place was an expected visit by the queen, Elizabeth I, and portraits of her are decorated in stucco around the Long Gallery, part of a highly elaborate use of decorative plasterwork. This is the highlight of the castle's interior and the compulsory guided tour not unreasonably draws attention to it. ■ *Castle Park, off Castle Street, T640787. Mid-June to September, daily 0930-1830. IR£2. Dúchas site.*

Ahenny high crosses About three miles (five kilometres) north of Carrick-on-Suir, signposted off the road to Windgap, there are two highly decorated and unusual high crosses. Instead of the usual pictorial panels, the main body of each cross is covered with geometric, reticulated patterns of spirals. There are human figures found along the base: on their north sides there is a strange scene of travelling figures, but easier to interpret is the other side that shows Christ and the apostles. The Ahenny crosses make an interesting contrast with those at Monasterboice (see page 167), representing what is probably an earlier and abstract kind of Celtic aesthetic before a more didactic strain of Christianity was imposed on it. By this reasoning, the Ahenny crosses are dated a century earlier than the ninth-century crosses at Monasterboice.

Tipperary crystal Waterford crystal may have a more successful marketing history, but there are alternatives and one of them is Tipperary crystal, housed close to the River Suir at Ballynoran on the N24. ■ *Free guided tours are available Mid-March to September, Monday-Thursday 0900-1630, Friday 0900-1530. There is also a restaurant.*

Sleeping & eating **AL** *Carraig Hotel*, Main St, T641455, F641604. Has a garishly painted exterior. **A** *The Bell* and *Salmon Arms Hotel*, Main St, T645555, F641293. **B** *Orchard House*, Sean Kelly Sq, T645355. **B** *Fatima House*, John St, T640298.

The pubs along Main St are competitively priced for lunches though the *Carraig Hotel* offers a tad more comfort at mealtimes, especially in the evenings. Food is served in the bar from early morning until 2100, while its *Weavers Restaurant* is open for lunch and in the evening from 1830 to 2130 for set meals and à la carte.

Transport **Bike hire** *OK Sports*, New St, T640626. **Buses** 3 buses a day travelling between Dublin and Cork stop in town as well as in Kilkenny. 4 buses a day also stop on the Galway – Limerick – Waterford – Rosslare Harbour route. Local buses go to Waterford, Clonmel and Cahir. T79000. **Train** T40044. Once a day, Monday to Saturday, and twice daily in the summer, it is possible to travel by train from Carrick-On-Suir to Waterford and Rosslare Europort and to Limerick.

Directory **Tourist office** Just off Main St, T640200. Jun-Sep, daily 1000-1700; Oct-May, Mon-Fri

North Tipperary

Attractions in the north of the county are a scattered mix and it is very much a case of catching places of interest as one is travelling through to somewhere else, partly because there is no town or area that can be singled out and recommended as a base for a longer stay. Holy Cross Abbey is a good example because while the abbey is definitely worth seeing there is not much to detain the traveller in the nearby town of Thurles, six kilometres (four miles), to the north.

Benefitting from a new roof 25 years ago, the Cistercian abbey of Holy Cross **Holy Cross**
exhibits itself proudly as both one of the most accomplished 15th-century **Abbey**
churches in the country and a functioning place of parish worship. The foundations go back to the 12th century though most of what stands today was built
around 1440-70, almost certainly a reflection of the increasing popularity of
the place with pilgrims, based on the abbey's claim to hold a sacred relic from
Cavalry (hence the abbey's name). In medieval Ireland, Holy Cross surpassed
all other places of pilgrimage and the relic was still there when O'Donnell and
O'Neill stopped over on their way to Kinsale in 1601 – but it hardly brought
them much luck. Medieval pilgrims visiting the abbey would have donated
some alms for the upkeep of the shrine, and this accumulated wealth was used
to finance the costly 15th-century re-building programme that used the best
craftsmen available.

Aesthetically, the most successful part of this rebuilding programme is the
chancel with its delicate ribbed vaulting and an exquisite window on the east
side. Here you will also find a superb sedilia, stone seats for the priests, with
graceful arches, delicate foliage patterns, and finely sculpted with the royal
arms of England and the escutcheon of the Earls of Ormond. The transept
to the north, left of the nave, is of note because the west wall carries a rare example
of medieval wall painting in Ireland. The fresco shows a hunting scene, with
the helpless deer seeking refuge on its knees behind a tree, with the three original colours reasonably well preserved. The other walls of the church make no
such overt artistic impulse and plain whitewash is used instead.

There is a visitor information centre within the abbey complex, a shop selling crafts, and snacks are available as well as drink. Holy Cross Abbey, on the
R660, is signposted from Thurles and Cashel.

Roscrea

Roscrea is the most pleasant town in the north of the county, marred unfortu- *Phone code: 0505*
nately by having the Dublin to Limerick main road running not just through *Colour map 2, grid C6*
the town but also right by the side of the remains of the 12th-century **St
Crónán's Church**, with a truncated round tower on the other side of the busy
road. It is said that the British reduced the tower's height in 1798 after a gun
shot at the castle was thought to have been fired from it. **Roscrea Heritage**, a
Dúchas site, consists of a castle and the early 17th-century Damer House. The
castle – made up of a gate tower, curtain walls and two corner towers – dates
from the late 13th century while Damer House is a fair example of a prototype
Palladian architecture. Despite being used as a military barracks at one stage,
Damer House retains its original staircase gloriously intact and provides space
for temporary exhibitions. ■ *Centre of town, T21850. June-September, 0930-
1830, IR£2.50. Guided tours available.*

Sleeping & eating   For a meal or an overnight stay, **AL** *Grant's Hotel*, Castle St,
T23300, F23209, is centrally located and serves a carvery lunch and evening meals in
its bar. The hotel's restaurant, *The Lemon Tree*, is for a more formal meal.

County Tipperary

County Limerick

Limerick

Phone code: 061
Colour map 3, grid A3

If you ever wondered what Irish people do when they're not being engagingly disingenuous, playing traditional music or writing some major work of literature you should spend some time in Limerick city. It's a busy working town with bus queues, crowds of kids coming out of school and bickering and fighting for the bus, loud country music in naff theme pubs, steak houses, hideous out-of-town three-star hotels with highly priced restaurants full of wedding parties, and muzak-driven shopping malls. What is great about that is that you can disappear into this heaving mass of people getting on with their lives and enjoy the unrenovated Georgian buildings, sit in the park and be glad you're not at work, wander round the Custom House opening the drawers to find the small wonders inside, enjoy the dummies at King John's Castle and watch the renovations at the Cathedral. In a country that is becoming filled to the brim with heritage, Limerick has a down-to-earth quality to it which can be refreshing after a week or so in a more touristy spot.

Ins and outs

Getting there Shannon Airport is approximately a 35 minute drive from Limerick. It has both international and internal flights to Europe and the US, Dublin and Belfast. The bus and train stations are in Parnell St and have services to most cities and nearby towns. For further details, see **Transport**, page 272.

History

The very word 'Limerick' conjures up wars, treaties, betrayals, suffering, starvation. Even its most famous writer, Frank McCourt, wrote the most depressing account of the place in his novel *Angela's Ashes*. But it is worth noting that when they came to make the movie of the book, they didn't film in Limerick: there weren't any locations that looked poor enough, so they went to Dublin and Cork instead.

The very first Limerick men were Vikings, who built a settlement the middle of the river in 922. From here they raided far and wide until the Irish kings, King Mahon of Thomond and his brother Brian Boru, decided they'd had enough and took them on, in 967. The armies met at Solohead in County Tipperary and Mahon's troop went on to Limerick and sacked the place. The island became Inis Sibhton, the capital of the O'Briens for 200 years until the Anglo-Norman invasion, when the walled city came under Norman control and Gaelic families were moved out to the area now known as Irishtown. From the 12th to 17th centuries the town remained loyal to the English crown and flourished as a trading centre; there were 15 parish churches by the turn of the 17th century.

In 1642 the town was taken by Catholic forces but suffered little damage. Nine years later Cromwell's troops came through and took the town back again, but it was in 1691 that the real trouble started. As the Jacobite forces lost ground in the north they fell back to Limerick and a great 12-month siege began. A Williamite force of 22,000 attacked the town but a daring raid led by the Jacobite military commander, Patrick Sarsfield, behind the Orange lines and the brave defence of the breach in the walls drove William back. The following year a second attempt was made to take the city, and this time the Jacobites surrendered. The Treaty of Limerick allowed the Jacobite leaders, almost all the ruling native Irish families, to leave for France and promised to protect Catholic rights. Two months later, ironically, a huge French fleet sailed into the estuary, too late to defend the Jacobites.

The Treaty of Limerick led to enormous Protestant dismay – they wanted redress and punishment for the Catholic forces and within a few years they got it. Catholic rights were discounted, and by 1695 the Penal Laws gradually wore away at Catholic property, leading in turn to great resentment on the part of the Catholics.

The town recovered from the siege and kept on growing till it had outgrown the city walls and a new area was developed – Newtown Pery, named after the developer – where most of the town's Georgian buildings stand today. After the Act of Union and due to lack of investment, the 19th-century saw a period of decline for Limerick that continued well into the 20th-century.

County Limerick

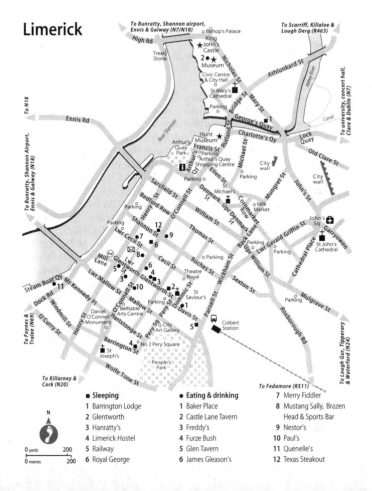

Limerick

■ Sleeping	● Eating & drinking	7 Merry Fiddler
1 Barrington Lodge	1 Baker Place	8 Mustang Sally, Brazen
2 Glentworth	2 Castle Lane Tavern	Head & Sports Bar
3 Hanratty's	3 Freddy's	9 Nestor's
4 Limerick Hostel	4 Furze Bush	10 Paul's
5 Railway	5 Glen Tavern	11 Quenelle's
6 Royal George	6 James Gleason's	12 Texas Steakout

0 yards 200
0 metres 200

English Town

This is the ancient part of the city whose early origins can be seen in the curve of the streets. Not actually in English Town but across the river opposite the cathedral is the treaty stone which Sarsfield is said to have actually rested the treaty on as he signed it in 1691.

King John's Castle

The castle, which dominates the town, was built in 1210, an Anglo-Norman bastion. Now called King John's Castle it is best viewed from across the river since a daft-looking conservatory has been built over where its east wall once stood. It is five sided, with one of its sides reaching down to the river. The original entrance is at the north side with two round towers either side and a portcullis between them. In the eighteenth century a military barracks was built inside the castle and in 1935 a block of council houses went up inside. Conversion to a tourist destination has recovered the basic structure as well as exposing some much-earlier buildings below the castle, which can be seen inside.

The castle is great to walk around and the views off the ramparts are frightening. The interpretive element isn't too bad – the audio-visual show is a bit high on pathos and the dummies inside the towers are suffering a little from the damp, but the information panels are good. The courtyard has a nice smell of peat and is full of little tents with people demonstrating ancient crafts. You can also watch the ongoing excavations although it's not immediately obvious what is happening. ■ *T361511. April to October, 0900-1800 (last admission 1700); November to December, Sundays 0930-1730 (last admission 1630). IR£3.80.*

St Mary's Cathedral

The cathedral is in a constant state of repair but even partly dismantled it's a wonderful old building. It is the oldest building in Limerick, built in the late 12th century, although only the west doorway, the nave and parts of the transepts and aisles are original. Most of the chapels are from the 15th century. The main attraction in the cathedral is the misericords, 15th-century carved oak seats that allowed their user to rest while appearing to be standing. They are carved with mythological figures and are labelled for the person who was to occupy them. In the Lady Chapel, (dating back to 1997!) the reredos (the ornamental screen behind the altar) was carved in 1907 by Michael Pearse, whose two sons took part in the Easter Rising. When the chapel was being constructed an ancient vault was found with three decapitated skeletons inside but there is no indication of how they arrived there in that state. In the Chapel of the Holy Spirit, the Leper's Squint (which was the original nave of the church) was where people suffering from leprosy could be given communion without infecting the righteous. ■ *June to September, Monday-Saturday 0900-1300, 1430-1700; October to May, Monday-Saturday 0900-1300. Visitors are asked to donate IR£1 to the upkeep of the cathedral.*

Limerick Museum

The museum has been recently housed in these purpose-built quarters in Nicholas Street, next to the cathedral. It is full of the usual bits and pieces that cities collect over the years, including a letter written during the Easter Rising from Padraig Pearse, one of the leaders of the 1916 Easter Rising and son of Michael who carved the reredos of the cathedral. There is a lot of information on the Lough Gur site, as well as some artefacts, so if you intend to visit the site this might be a good introduction. ■ *Tuesday-Saturday, 1000-1300, 1430-1700. Free.*

County Limerick

Irish Town

This is the place where the Normans sent the native Irish when they adopted the walled city for their own. It developed as an important trading centre and it was given its own set of walls, some of which remain near to **St John's Catholic Cathedral**, not so old as the Church of Ireland one but still quite beautiful and without that sense of not quite knowing what it should look like that other Catholic cathedrals in Ireland have. It was built in the style of Pugin by a London architect, Hardwick, who used light very effectively to create the sense of spirituality that so many modern cathedrals lack. Outside is a statue of Sarsfield.

Custom House

This has to be the main place of interest in Irish Town: its front is on the river side and is best viewed from the opposite bank. Built by a Sardinian, Davis Duckart, in 1765, it is Palladian with a three-bay pilaster frontispiece creating a sense of grandeur when approached from the river. Inside is the **Hunt Collection**, the most fascinating collection of artefacts in Ireland. It is only part of the private collection of the Hunts, antique dealers who ducked and dived around Europe until the Second World War, when they found themselves interned in England since Mrs Hunt was German. They offered, and were allowed, to leave for Ireland, which they made their home, first in Howth and then Limerick. They bought and sold antiques from all and sundry, and there were a lot of things going cheap in the 1930s, and out of the profits built up this amazing collection. In Ireland they took part in the Lough Gur excavations and eventually people just started to bring them things they had turned up while ploughing. In Howth they kept all their antiques lying about the place and there is a photo in the museum of the kitchen with the Picasso hanging next to the stove. It would be fruitless here to point out the most interesting items since the whole place is a wonder. Get on one of the guided tours or just wander about opening the drawers, but give yourself lots of time. ■ *Rutland Street, T312833. Tuesday-Saturday, 1000-1700, Sunday 1400-1700. IR£4. Shop, restaurant. Telephone in advance for tours.*

Newtown Pery

Built in beautiful Georgian straight lines, these old buildings, like many of those in Dublin, survived because there was no money to redevelop the area in the 1960s. The men who planned this part of the city had great expectations of Limerick's potential and this can be seen in Pery Square, which was to be 49 houses built as a tontine, the last of the original builders to survive to inherit the lot. Only six were built, Pery Square as you see it now, but they are an excellent example of Georgian architecture at its most confident, built in 1839 and symmetrically patterned, the two end houses having gable entrances. Number 2 is currently under restoration and will be open to the public with original Georgian furnishings. If it is not yet open when you visit, you are free to go inside and watch the renovation work, which is possibly more interesting than the finished article. As the house was stripped of its later partitioning and 1960s boxing-in, more and more of the original plasterwork and decorations appeared, including painted marbling on the walls. It gives a fascinating insight into the life of a family of the times with the servants' quarters downstairs (the housekeeper's room in sight of the pantry so she could keep an eye on it), and the children's rooms way up at the top where they could be out of earshot.

County Limerick

City Art Gallery Opposite the terrace in Pery Square is the People's Park, originally to have been the private park in the middle of the square and made into a public park in 1874. The gallery cum library is found at its corner: it was paid for by Andrew Carnegie and built in 1906 in an uneven mixture of Celtic Revival and Arts and Crafts styles. Inside there are paintings by Irish artists from the 18th century to the present, with Jack Yeats well represented as well as Sean Keating. It also hosts temporary exhibitions. ■ *Pery Square, T310633. Monday-Saturday, 1000-1300, 1400-1800. Free.*

Essentials

Sleeping Limerick is a busy commercial centre and *en route* to most tourist destinations in the
■ *on map* south which is reflected in its accommodation. There is a whole string of 3- and 4-star
Price codes: hotels on the Ennis Road, taking up great swathes of parking and garden space, but
see inside front cover the best hotels are right in town. In addition, there are a number of B&Bs, and an enormous number of holiday hostels, most of which are student accommodation let out in the holidays. The hostels listed below are open all year.

L *Jury's Hotel*, Ennis Rd, T327777, F326400, info@jurys.com All the comforts of a *Jury's* – 2 restaurants, bar, leisure facilities and closer to town than the others on Ennis Rd. **L** *Limerick Inn Hotel*, Ennis Rd, T326666, F326281, limerick.inn@limerick.inn.ie Vast 2-storey modern building with swimming pool and fitness centre. Very spacious comfortable rooms with all the technology you could hope for. 15-minutes drive from town but also on bus route. Close to Bunratty and on the road to Shannon Airport. **AL-L** *Limerick Ryan Hotel*, Ardhu House, Ennis Rd, T453922, F326333, ryan@indigo.ie Big out-of-town hotel built around an original Georgian house. Gym, restaurant, two bars.

A *Glentworth Hotel*, Glentworth St, T413822, F413073, modernized old hotel between the railway station and the centre of town. **A** *Hanratty's Hotel*, T410999, F411077. At the lower end of this grade, *Hanratty's* is close to centre of town with a nightclub, restaurant and bar. **A** *Railway Hotel*, Parnell St, T423653, F419762. Opposite the railway station, this is another busy city hotel with rates at the very bottom end of this range. Its location suffers a little from being in a busy part of town. **A** *Royal George Hotel*, O'Connell St, T414566, F317171. They don't come any more central than this busy hotel with a very popular lunchtime trade and a good restaurant, as well as live music in the traditional bar. The spacious rooms are well away from the noise, though, and this place has lots of history behind it.

B *Clifton House*, Ennis Rd, T451166. Not far from the city centre, this is a big B&B with 16 rooms and lots of facilities. **B** *Cloneen House*, Ennis Rd, T454461. Within walking distance of town, this B&B has quite expensive rooms but is set in a quiet garden. **B** *Mount Gerard*, O'Connell Avenue, T411886. A B&B that is a little further out of town but in an attractive Victorian house. Good value, radios in rooms. **B** *Rosmoy Town House*, O'Connell Avenue, T314556. Tastefully furnished, very central B&B with radios in rooms as well as the usual conveniences. Good value.

D *Barrington's Lodge and Hostel*, George's Quay, T4152222, F416611. Doubles are IR£9 per person sharing. Nice location, in old nurse's lodgings. **D** *Clyde House*, St Alphonsus St, T314357. Hostel with private rooms at IR£12.50. **D** *Limerick Youth Hostel*, 1 Pery Square, T/F314672. At the other end of the tontine block, An Oige rules, particularly closing between 1000-1700, apply. No private or family rooms. **D** *Summerville and Westbourne Holiday Hostel*, Courtbrack Ave, T302500, F302539. Purpose-built hostel accommodation. Double rooms IR£11 and above. Laundry, tennis, pool table.

The upmarket section of Limerick restaurants is a fairly traditional sort of place – steak, chicken and things served with accompanying vegetables and the occasional cheeky sauce. The most adventurous place is *Quenelles*, Unit 4, Steamboat Quay, Dock Rd, T411111, a long-established but recently moved place where bright Mediterranean colours are accompanied by some unusual menu items. Each course has a starting price with supplements for the more expensive items. Dinner could reach IR£25 or more. Monday-Saturday. Less rarefied is *Freddie's*, Theatre Lane, T418749, where the menu is Italian home cooking. Quiet, woody sort of place in a back lane. Main courses start at IR£13. Tuesday-Saturday.

Eating
● *on map*
Price codes:
see inside front cover

Moving down to single figures for each course there is *Paul's*, 59 O'Connell St, T316600, all beech wood and track lighting: a bright, spacious atmosphere inside a beautiful old exterior. The menu centres somewhere in the Mediterranean with a whole pasta menu that is shockingly reasonably priced. If pasta doesn't appeal, there is a fine, selective meat-based menu. Great starters. Still in O'Connell St is *Nestor's*, T317333, where someone has spent a great deal of money creating a theme restaurant with a long bar downstairs looked over by a huge gallery restaurant above. Food is fun, spicy, pasta stuff. The earlybird menu from 1700-1930 is IR£9.95 for 3 courses, or the à la carte operates from 1700 until late. This menu will come to around IR£15 for 3 courses although you might not want three. Right opposite on O'Connell St is the *Texas Steakout*, T410350, and there's no prize for guessing the theme or menu of this place: lots of steaks and burgers, fish, chicken and vegetarian options, children's menu, lots of waiters dressed as cowboys. You wouldn't want three courses, but steak dishes are around IR£12 and fish around IR£9. In between all the fajitas, enchiladas and and quesilladas are the rather out-of place mushroom vols-au-vent. Open 7 days.

Another very young, theme sort of place is the *Brazen Head/Sportsbar/Mustang Sally* complex at 102-3 O'Connell St, T417412. *Mustang Sally* is a Tex-Mex place, lunches only at weekends, with a vast menu of quesilladas, enchiladas, etc. The *Brazen Head* is basically a modern bar with a million miniature spirit bottles in glass cases, and quite a large bar menu at lunchtime ranging from filled baguettes to ragout of lamb. Main courses around IR£5. A great place to eat and to stock up on excellent delicatessen fare for a picnic lunch is *Mortell's*, 49 Roches St, T415547. It's a cheery fresh food shop with an upmarket fish restaurant at the back. It closes at 1830 but is open from breakfast onwards and is well worth a visit for both lunch and its deli counter. Another good place for lunch is the *Furze Bush*, 12 Glentworth St, T411733. It is small but quaintly decorated, and does sandwiches and desserts and lots of different teas.

Branching out from the success of Bunratty Castle's theme nights, a purpose built olde worlde pub is the *Castle Lane Tavern*, T360788, where for IR£25 you get dinner and a sort of Riverdance copy show. It's quite new, so ask around if it's any good.

Pub food is everywhere. The *Glen Tavern* in Lower Glentworth St does food from 1200-1500 in a cheery olde worlde sort of pub. *Baker Place* in Dominick St is a nicely renovated old pub with a good lunch menu and dinner options. *James Gleeson's*, on the corner of Glentworth and O'Connell St, is the most gloriously unreconstructed Victorian pub for many a mile and has a limited bar food menu but great atmosphere. The *Merry Fiddler* in Cecil St is vast, with old things everywhere and a menu of steaks, burgers and sandwiches.

An Sibin, in the Royal George Hotel, has music most nights, often traditional stuff in the summer in a quite authentic Shebeen atmosphere. Dolan's, 4 Dock Rd, has traditional music most nights all year round while *Hanratty's Hotel* bar and the *Glen Tavern* have traditional music at weekends. *Nestor's* often has various sorts of live music. Another place to check out is *Nancy Blake's* in Upper Denmark St. *Dolan's Warehouse*, T314483 for advance tickets, upstairs from the pub has seriously interesting modern Irish bands from Thursday to Saturday at varying prices for tickets depending on the fame or quality of the performer.

Pubs & music

County Limerick

Theatre & cinema The *Belltable Arts Centre*, 69 O'Connell St, T319866, often has performances by travelling theatre companies, traditional music performances, dance shows as well as a gallery and a film club. The Savoy Centre, T311900, is a cinema in Henry St with eight screens. At Castletroy, east of town, is the *University Concert Hall*, T331549, for details of events,where concerts of classical music take place regularly. The *Theatre Royal* is in Upper Cecil St, T414224, and hosts regular raves, jazz, dance, comedy and more.

Festivals In **February** is the *Kate O'Brien Literary Weekend*, T415799 for information, which involves readings, lectures, musical eveings all centred around the work of this important novelist. **March** (on the Sunday closest to St Patrick's Day) sees the *Limerick International Band Festival*, where there are competitions for drill and dance band recitals, T410777 for information. The *Limerick Film Festival* also takes place in **March**, focussing on Irish films and film-makers: T202986 (Fiona Fennell) for details. **May** sees the *Paddy Music Expo*, on the May bank holiday, with concerts, street music, and lots of events in the pubs. The *Food Festival* in **August** is a big event with food tastings, competitions between the restaurants and special offers all over the city: T302035 for details.

Shopping Limerick has all the usual gamut of department stores as well as Arthur's Quay shopping mall with lots of little boutique-type places to browse around. **Books** The *Celtic Bookshop*, Rutland St focusses on books of Irish interest and also has some nice maps and craft items. They will search for out-of-print books. **Clothes** *Irish Uniques*, Unit 13, sells designer clothes and lace things, and *Irish Handcrafts*, Patrick St and Arthur's Quay, sells expensive but lovely handknitted and handwoven jumpers, tweeds, linens and mohair while there is a branch of *Carraig Donn*, which does some fashionable things with Aran jumpers, in O'Connell Mall. **Gifts** *Decorum* sells Irish and foreign pottery, rugs, mirrors and lots of other goodies. *Pzzazz*, Foxes Bow, Thomas St, sells very nice silver, bronze and pewter jewellery as well as amber. **Markets** On Fridays there is an arts and crafts market from 1100 to 1600 at the Milk market on the corner of Ellen St and Wickham St. It is also good for a browse here on Fridays or Saturdays, when the regular market is open, or any weekday when the little shops around the market are full of unusual food, second-hand clothes, ethnic clothes and craft things.

Sport **Bowling** *Funworld*, Ennis Rd, T325088. *Savoy Bowling Centre*, Bedford Row, T419192. **Greyhound Racing** Market's Field, T417808. Meetings Monday, Thursday, Saturday 2000. **Golf** *Limerick County Golf & Country Club*, Ballyneety, T351881. 18 holes, driving range, Jacuzzi. *Limerick Golf Club*, Ballyclough, T414083. On N20, 18 holes, flat. **Karting** *Jetland Raceway*, Ennis Rd, T454700. **Snooker** *Victoria Club Leisure Centre*, Hartsong St, T418822.

Transport **Air** *Shannon Airport*, T061-471444, in County Clare is 24 km from Limerick and has international flights to Europe, the US and Britain as well as internal flights to Dublin, and Belfast (see box on page 389). **Bus** T313333. The bus station is in Parnell St, next to the train station. There are regular connections to Dublin, Cork, Galway, Tralee, Killarney, Sligo, Donegal, Shannon and towns in the north. **Train** Limerick station in Parnell St has services to Dublin, Rosslaire, Cahir, Tipperary, Cork. From Limerick Junction, southeast of Limerick, more connections are possible. T315555, Mon-Fri 0900-1800, Sat 0930-1730; T418369, Mon-Fri 1830-2045, Sat 1830-1945, Sun 0900-1800; 24-hour talking timetable (Dublin) T413355.

Directory **Banks** *AIB*, Arthur's Quay, 63, O'Connell St, 109 O'Connell St. *Bank of Ireland* 94 & 105 O'Connell St. **Bingo** *Stella Ballroom*, Shannon St, T411800. Wed, Fri Sun. **Car hire** *Dan Dooley*, Shannon Airport; *Budget Rent-a-Car*, T061-471361/471098. **Communications** Post office: Lower Cecil St. **Tourist office** Arthur's Quay, T317522. Jul-Aug, Mon-Fri 0900-1830, Sat-Sun 0930-1530; Sep-Jun, Mon-Fri 0930-1730. **Laundrette** *Speediwash*, 11 Gerard St, T319380.

County Limerick

Ringforts

Ringforts are the most numerous ancient monument found in Ireland. There are some 45,000 of them, dating from the early Christian period around 600-900CE, but their distribution is unevenly spread. Donegal, Kildare and Dublin have the lowest density; Roscommon, Sligo and Limerick the highest. One likely explanation is that they were built as a defence against cattle raids and where an area couldn't support many farming communities they were not necessary. Excavations reveal them to be the homesteads of single farming families, although where one ringfort is found there are usually more in the vicinity. Ringforts were first mapped in the mid-19th century but since then thousands – nearly 40 per cent, it has been estimated –

have been destroyed, especially in recent decades when EU financing encouraged the creation of large fields. Afforestation programmes in upland areas are contributing to this process.

Our knowledge of ringfort culture is supported by contemporary sources, which reveal a hierarchical society based around territorial units, known as tuath, each with a population of around 3,000. At the head of each tuath was a king and filling the next rank down were lords, aire, of varying status. The lowest grade of non-nobles were the bóaire, independent farmers who leased land and paid for it in the form of cattle. There is good reason to believe that the different sizes of ringforts reflected these social and economic ranks.

Lough Gur

One of the most productive and informative Neolithic sites in Europe, Lough Gur doesn't have the grandeur of Newgrange but it is an atmospheric place none the less, and anyone prepared to scramble about a bit and use their imagination can get a good sense of the life of this place 4,000 or more years ago. The lough is shaped like a large horseshoe, and scattered all around it are ring forts, burial chambers, houses, stone circles and middens. You can stop at the interpretive centre and have a look at Grange stone circle or spend the whole day with a map looking for sites. The best compromise is perhaps a walk around the lough, looking at the big sites.

The first site of importance as you approach the lough from Limerick is the huge **Grange Stone Circle**, the most impressive of the remains here. It consists of 113 contiguous orthostats, which basically means a lot of big stones. They are bedded into a perfect circle with other stones pegging them into the ground. In the centre, the post hole that men used thousands of years ago to draw the circle with a piece of string was found when the site was excavated. Soil is drawn up around the outside of the stones. An entrance passage way lined with more stones is at the northeast of the circle.

One kilometre further along the road after the stone circle take the left turn marked Lough Gur, then past a 15th century church ruin to find a wedge tomb. Another two kilometres brings you to the car park and interpretive centre which is, for once, a useful addition to the site. From the interpretive centre the next place to head for is **Knockadoon** where there are an enormous number of barely visible remains, including a circular dwelling, and a rectangular stone-age house. ■ *Lough Gur, T360788. May-September, daily 1000-1800 (last admission 1730). IR£2. Car parking. Sites 24 hour access and free. 17 miles (28 km) south of Limerick on N24. Look for sign to Lough Gur. Enquire in advance about walking tours.*

County Limerick

Adare

To the south of Limerick is Adare, created in the 19th century by the third Earl of Dunraven, to house his tenants prettily. Pretty is about the right word too – a row of quaint thatched cottages, only a couple of which are actually lived in by anyone. The rest are kitsch antique shops and restaurants catering to the busloads of tourists who are brought in here to be separated from their money. Add on a **heritage centre**, which explains the village and its ruins to anyone unable to understand what they are looking at, and a manor house converted into an extremely exclusive hotel that you have to pay to get into and you have a perfect recipe for a naff day out. What is good about the village is the **Augustinian Priory** at the edge of the village on the road to Limerick. It was built in 1325 and is Ireland's most unaltered intact church of that date. It still functions as the Church of Ireland parish church. There is also Ireland's only **Trinitarian Abbey** in the main street, founded in 1230, greatly enlarged in the 19th century, and now the Catholic parish church. Surrounded by the golf course is the 15th-century **Franciscan Friary** and an early 13th-century castle, which has been in ruins since the end of the 14th century. It's nice to look at but you can't explore because it's bricked up with warning notices around it. If you don't want to brave the flying golf balls you can just look from the bridge with the tour groups.

Sleeping **L-LL** *Adare Manor*, T396566. Its most expensive rooms are right off the scale at IR£355, while its least expensive are a snip at IR£120, but for that you get a 19th-century manor house in a neo-Gothic style, elaborate gardens, 900 acres to walk around, a pool, golf course, a river to fish, and horses. A clubhouse has just been added. **L** *Dunraven Arms Hotel*, Main St, T396633. In the middle of the village, this Georgian hotel has individually furnished rooms, lots of antiques and a leisure centre. **AL** *Fitzgerald's Woodlands House Hotel*, Knockanes, T396118, F396073. 1 mile (1.6 km) from Adare, this is a modern, busy place with a leisure centre and pool, big spacious modern rooms and a good bar with traditional music. **B** *Ivy House B&B*, Craigue, T/F396270. 1 mile (1.6 km) outside Adare this is a lovely old Georgian house full of antiques and set in a well-established garden. **B** *Riversdale B&B*, Station Rd, T396751. In the village itself, this is a modern, efficient, conveniently located place.

Eating Adare is not short of restaurants. The *Maigue* restaurant in the *Dunraven Arms* has a good reputation and serves local dishes with a Californian twist. Dinner IR£25 plus. The *Wild Geese*, T396451, is in one of the thatched cottages and also has a high reputation. French cuisine, each course at a set price with supplements for expensive items, classic desserts. IR£25 plus. The *Woodlands House Hotel* has a popular restaurant where dinner is an affordable IR£15 plus and still quite good and also serves food in the bar/bistro. In nearby Ballingarry is *The Mustard Seed*, T069-68508, which has an enormous reputation and very stylish food. The garden is the nicest part of the place. Book well in advance and order a table for later in the evening: if you book for 1900 you'll get hurried through dinner so they can seat the next sitting. Dinner is well over IR£25. If it's a light meal you're after try the café in the visitor centre, *Lena's Bar* or *O'Coleáin* in the main street.

Transport **Buses** There are 5 buses a day between Dublin, Limerick and Killarney, a summer only service from Limerick to Liskard via Adare, and 1 daily service connecting Limerick and Ballingarry via Adare. For times T061-313333.

Directory **Tourist information** In the heritage centre, Main St, T396255. June-Sept, daily 0900-1900, Oct-Dec and Feb-May, Mon-Sat 0900-1700..

County Cork

Oh, well I do remember the black December day,
The landlord and the sheriff came to drive us all away;
They set my roof on fire with their cursed English
spleen,
And that's another reason why I left old Skibbereen.

Anonymous (19th century):
'Old Skibbereen'

8

County Cork

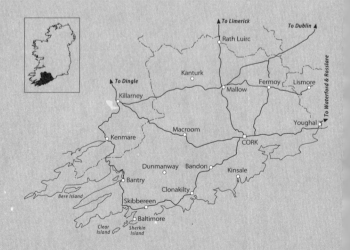

Cork city and the coastal route through West Cork remain highly popular with visitors, but the county's magic is that it rarely feels overcrowded. Easy accessibility by air and sea makes the city a contender with Dublin as a first point of arrival in Ireland, especially if you want to head off for a rural idyll in one of the most beautiful corners of the country. From Cork city it is a short hop to Kinsale, Ireland's self-proclaimed food capital, before meandering along the southwest coast, where the landscape plays second fiddle to the mesmerizing seascapes and where reminders of the Anglo-Irish legacy are dotted between the history-laden small towns that keep their dignity and character in spite of tourism.

None of this quite prepares the unsuspecting traveller for the three narrow peninsulas that jut out into the Atlantic, justifying the description by one addicted visitor as a 'geographic narcotic' where 'it is hopeless to resist the pressure of non-pressure'. The pleasures of West Cork are no longer a secret, but little has been spoilt by tourism.

★ **Try to find time for**

County Cork

Crawford Art Gallery, Cork city

The Queenstown Story, Cobh

The Viking boat in St Mary's Church, Youghal

A stay at Lettercollum House, Timoleague

The coast between Timoleague and Clonakilty

Dinner at the Sea View Hotel Restaurant, Bantry

A walk on Clear Island

A swim at Barley Cove, Mizen Peninsula

The Beara Way

The gardens at Timoleague, Clonakilty and Creagh

Cork City

Phone code: 021
Colour map 3, grid B5

Mildly cosmopolitan and yet engagingly Irish, Cork city is pleasantly spread out amongst the hills that rise up on both sides of the Lee Valley where the river meanders its way to the open water of Cork harbour. The city centre is actually a small island between two channels of the River Lee and the plethora of bridges can disorientate the visitor. Though Cork is a major port, there is little maritime activity in the city centre and the river is usually free of traffic. At night, the pubs fuel a mood of ebullience that never becomes rowdy, and while it is not a conventionally beautiful city its urban identity is worn lightly and the feel of the place is distinctively different from Dublin. Cork is an easy city to like and if the traffic could be taken out it would reclaim its homely beauty. It makes a good base for day trips to nearby sights including the famous Blarney Castle and the historical towns of Cobh and Youghal.

Ins and outs

Getting there From the airport a half-hourly bus service takes you into the city where the bus station is in Parnell Place near Merchant's Quay. Taxis from the airport cost about IR£8. Taxis are usually metered; otherwise ask for a price first. The rail station is a 20-minute walk away from the centre, east of the city, but a frequent bus service brings passengers into the bus station and St Patrick St, and taxis are about IR£2.50.

Getting around City buses radiate out from St Patrick St to all areas of the city. There is a taxi rank in the centre of St Patrick St and another beside the bus station. Most of the city's interesting sights are easily walkable, although the No 8 bus route is useful for the hostels and sights at the west of the city.

History

Early Irish literary and historical texts often reveal an obsession with topographical exactitude but this is not always the case with contemporary sources. Cork city's main street is St Patrick St but you may come across it as St Patrick's St. Similarly, Western Rd and Lancaster Quay often ellide into just Western Rd.

The Gaelic for Cork, *Corcaigh*, meaning marshy, evokes the city's origins in broad marshland formed by two channels of the River Lee. St Finbarr founded a monastic settlement here, some two centuries before marauding Vikings arrived in the ninth century. The Danes eventually established a permanent trading post and, after the Anglo-Norman invasion in the 1170s, this evolved into a walled city under Norman control. It wasn't until after a successful five-day siege by the armies of William of Orange at the end of the 17th century that the walls were torn down. By 1800 Cork was a prosperous city built upon trade, increasingly with the English who valued the city's harbour both for its imperial navy and for shipping home the county's agriculture, especially butter. Shandon, to the north of the city centre, was the centre of commercial life at this time and the city's harbour became the major transatlantic port in Europe, with ships calling in for provisions and butter being exported to Australia and South America. In the aftermath of Easter 1916, Cork began to develop a reputation for political opposition to Britain and in 1920 the mayor,

Cork

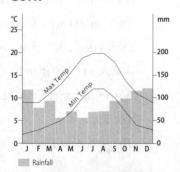

Rainfall

Thomas MacCurtain, was murdered by the British who also burnt down the city centre. Today, Cork is a thriving city with light industry providing much of the employment.

Sights

Not necessarily an essential place to visit, but this is the site traditionally associated with the birth of the city when St Finbarr in the seventh century came here from his hermitage in Gougane Barra and founded a monastery on the site of the present late 19th-century cathedral. The interior is as richly embellished as the splendour of the exterior suggests it will be, and no doubt the wealthy merchants who paid for its construction were pleased with the way the English architect, William Burges, combined his love of medievalism with a conspicuous display of Protestant affluence. Highlights include the statuary of the ornate west door, the 1930s roof of the sanctuary, and a memorial stone near the pulpit to Elizabeth Aldworthy, the only woman ever initiated into the Masons. ■ *Bishop Street. Monday-Saturday 1000-1700. IR£1 donation requested.* **St Finbarr's Cathedral**

As the salmon-inspired weathervane on the famous steeple might suggest, this church is an altogether different kettle of fish. Built in the early 18th century to replace a church destroyed by the Williamite besiegers, the curious-looking steeple has limestone sides looking down on the city and red sandstone on its other two faces. Climb up the steps for an opportunity to ring the bells that a Cork priest, Francis O'Mahony (1804-66, pen-name Father Prout; he later left **St Anne's Church, Shandon**

County Cork

Cork city centre

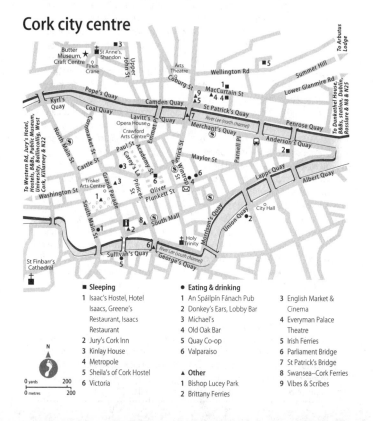

■ **Sleeping**
1 Isaac's Hostel, Hotel Isaacs, Greene's Restaurant, Isaacs Restaurant
2 Jury's Cork Inn
3 Kinlay House
4 Metropole
5 Sheila's of Cork Hostel
6 Victoria

● **Eating & drinking**
1 An Spáilpín Fánach Pub
2 Donkey's Ears, Lobby Bar
3 Michael's
4 Old Oak Bar
5 Quay Co-op
6 Valparaiso

▲ **Other**
1 Bishop Lucey Park
2 Brittany Ferries

3 English Market & Cinema
4 Everyman Palace Theatre
5 Irish Ferries
6 Parliament Bridge
7 St Patrick's Bridge
8 Swansea–Cork Ferries
9 Vibes & Scribes

0 yards 200
0 metres 200

A city tour

This lengthy stroll, starting outside the tourist office, goes across the city, past many of the places of interest described in this chapter. There is too much to see in one day so either curtail your walking and sightseeing drastically or consider it as two one-day walks.

Day 1 From outside the tourist office turn to the right and look for the first entrance to the English Market on the right, before the cinema but after the junction with Oliver Plunkett Street. Pass straight through this interesting arcade of shops, noting **On the Pig's Back**, a shop selling excellent breads and cheeses, and exit on the other side past the fountain on to the pedestrianized Princes Street. Turn left and walk up to the main thoroughfare of **St Patrick Street**. Cross to the other side and take the first left down Carey's Lane. This area around **Paul Street** has a number of restaurants and shops well worth checking out. Turn right into Emmet Place, passing the **Crawford Art Gallery** on the left; the gallery's café is an excellent place for mid-morning tea and cakes. Carry on to the river, cross the bridge and continue straight ahead to the junction with the **Cork Arts Theatre** on the right. Turn to the left here, crossing over Upper John Street and taking the left up John Redmond Street to the **Shandon sites**.

Retrace your steps to the Cork Arts Theatre and go down Coburg Street and straight across to MacCurtain Street. A formerly shabby thoroughfare leading to the railway station and roads to Dublin and the southeast, MacCurtain Street is gradually sprucing itself up. The ex-temperance Metropole Hotel has been refurbished, but the exterior still evokes a bygone age, while across the road Isaac's Hostel has a good restaurant and there are also some interesting small shops (see 'Shopping' on page 286).

Day 2 After passing the Metropole on MacCurtain Street, take the second turning on the right, Brian Boru Street, and cross the bridge of the same name that leads to the bus station. **Merchant's Quay** shopping centre is close by, but this route carries on down the street you are on, until you reach the south branch of the river and cross Clontarf Bridge to Albert Quay. Turn right and pass the stately City Hall, the last large-scale edifice to be built in Ireland in the classical style. The original building was burnt down by the British in 1920, but it was reopened in 1936 by De Valera, and in 1963 when President John F Kennedy spoke from its steps the largest crowd ever to be seen in Cork filled every space hereabouts. Continue along the riverside on Union Quay and when this turns into George's Quay notice the 18th-century houses and their very high roofs. On the other side of the river the distinctive exterior of the neo-Gothic Holy Trinity Church, designed by GR Pain in 1832, is difficult to miss. Cross over to this side by the next bridge, Parliament Bridge, which leads up to South Mall, characterized by solicitors' offices and other commercial premises. Turn to the left and walk to the end of the street where the baroque Maid of Erin monument commemorates nationalist heroes of the past. From the nearby footbridge there is a fine view of **St Finbarr's Cathedral**. Stay on the monument side, opposite the tourist office, and walk up Grand Parade. Before reaching the junction opposite the cinema look for the entrance gate to the Bishop Lucey park on the left; inside the gate there is a fragment of the medieval city walls. Walk through the park and exit in the right corner that comes out by the side of an old church, now the Cork Archive Centre; attached to it is the **Triskel Arts Centre**, which has a small café. Turn right and go up to join Washington Street, where a left turn will lead on to Western Road. After passing Jury's Hotel on the left it is a short way to the main entrance of **University College**, while across the street there is a short road that leads to Mardyke Walk, a mile-long (two-kilometre) avenue that was laid out in the early 18th century. Walk along here past a cricket ground and into Fitzgerald Park and the **Cork Public Museum**. Bus No 8 on Western Road brings you back to the city centre.

Ogham

Ogham, or ogam, is the earliest Irish form of writing, preserved on stone and dating from the period between the 4th and 7th centuries. Its alphabet has 20-25 letters and takes the form of a series of slashes of different lengths inscribed down the edges of stone pillars. Although the writing is thought to have its origins in a Celtic class of pagan priests, the examples that have been preserved on the 300 or so examples found mostly in Cork and Kerry translate into perfunctory statements of descent: x is the son of y and y is the son of z.

the priesthood and took up journalism in Paris) rendered famous in some forgettable doggerel. Further steep steps lead up to the very top for aerial views of the city. The Shandon clock, known as the 'four-faced liar' because the east and west faces tell slightly different time, has an inscription which wisely reads 'Passenger, measure your time, for time is the measure of your being.' The modest Georgian-style church interior could be skipped. ■ *Church Street and Eason Hill. Monday-Saturday 1000-1700. IR£2 (tower and bell ringing), IR£1 (interior).*

Other Shandon sites

St Anne's notwithstanding, the Shandon area is characterized by 19th-century vernacular architecture and two distinctive buildings that bear witness to Cork's butter market being the largest in the 19th-century world. Butter from all corners of the county found its way to Shandon, where it was weighed, traded and packed in casks (firkins) before being hauled down to the river for export to England. A self-important Doric façade fronts the **Cork Butter Market**, built in 1730 and now a craft centre (see page 287), while the pleasing rotunda of the **Firkin Crane Centre**, T5074817, is open to the public for cultural events such as plays and dance performances: check with the tourist office to see what is on. In O'Connell Square, the **Cork Butter Museum** tells the story of Shandon and the butter trade but there is not a lot to see for the IR£2.50 entrance charge. ■ *T300600. Monday-Saturday 1000-1700.*

University College & Honan Chapel

A pleasant stroll up through the grounds of University College leads to its Victorian quadrangle, opposite the late 20th-century Boole Library named after the radical mathematician who died in 1864 while a professor at the college. With your back to the library entrance walk directly across the square to enter the quadrangle building. Along both sides of the corridor stand a collection of Ogham stones with a plaque explaining this ancient form of writing. To the east of the library it is worth seeking out the resplendent, Celtic-inspired interior of the Honan Chapel. Built in 1916, the eye-catching mosaic floor is matched for beauty by the Harry Clarke stained glass windows. ■ *Bus No 8 from the city centre.*

Dunkathel House

This late 18th-century neo-classical residence was built for a wealthy Cork merchant and *aficionados* of interior design will appreciate the bifurcated staircase of Bath stone and the Adam fireplaces. There is also a collection of watercolours by one of the five Gubbins sisters who lived here in the early 20th century. ■ *Situated at the east side of Cork, just off the N25 road to Rosslare. May to mid-October, Wednesday-Sunday 1400-1800. IR£2 (guided tour).*

County Cork

Walking on water – St Patrick Street

The curving shape of Cork city's main thoroughfare is due to the fact that it was built over a tributary of the River Lee, and up until the beginning of the 19th century small boats made their way up and down the waterway. At the junction of Tuckey Street and Grand Parade one can still see a bollard where boats moored, and in St Patrick Street itself, outside the Château Bar not far up from Waterstone's bookshop, the tall steps bear witness to the days when boats moored beneath them. When the Black and Tans set the city aflame at the end of 1920 it was the north side of the street that was burnt down and if one walks along this side – between the two bookshops of Waterstone's and Eason's – you can look across to the other side and spot some of the original 18th-century bow windows.

Museums and art galleries

Cork Public Museum
The museum, situated in a Georgian building in Fitzgerald Park opposite University College, is good on Cork's eventful and significant role in the war for independence; the unstylish archaeological displays on the first floor are less appealing. The adjoining green is a quiet retreat for a picnic lunch and, unlike the Bishop Lucey Park on Grand Parade, is rarely crowded. ■ *Monday-Friday, 1100-1300, 1415-1700 (1800 in summer), Sunday 1500-1700. Free. Bus No 8 from city centre.*

Cork City Gaol
The city gaol, remarkably well preserved in its essentials, functioned from the 1820s for just under a century. A guided tour by tape comes with the admission charge, followed by a melodramatic audio-visual display. Also housed in the prison is a radio museum. From the city centre either take a taxi or bus No 8 as far as University College and then walk through Fitzgerald Park, over the delightful suspension footbridge bridge and up the hill to the right before turning left into Convent Avenue. From here a sign points the way to the gaol. ■ *Sunday's Well Road, T4305022. Monday-Saturday, 0930-1700. IR£3.50.*

Crawford Art Gallery
Even if time is short, spare some for a visit to Ireland's most important art gallery outside of Dublin. Jack B Yeats, Sean Keating, Harry Clarke, William Gerard Barry and Edith Somerville are some of those represented, as well as work by contemporary artists working in Cork. British artists include George Romney, Frank Bramley and Jacob Epstein, and there is usually a temporary exhibition of Irish or international art. New funds are preparing the way for important new galleries, making a visit to the Crawford even more compelling. ■ *Emmet Place, T4273377. Monday-Saturday 0930-1700. Free. Restaurant.*

Essentials

Sleeping
■ *on map*
Price codes:
see inside front cover

There is a reasonable spread of accommodation, covering most budgets, but in July and August it is advisable to have a room booked in advance or leave it to the tourist office to find somewhere for you. Along Glanmire Rd heading out east of town near the railway station there is a string of similarly-priced B&Bs (see **B** category, below), and the main cluster of hostels is at the bus station end of town.

L *Arbutus Lodge*, Montenotte, T4501237, F4502893. At the west side of the city, this Victorian townhouse offers country-house style in a city. Individually decorated rooms and original paintings by the likes of Anne Yeats and Patrick Scott around the place. Bar and restaurant. **L** *Jury's Hotel*, Lancaster Quay (though the address is often given as Western Rd), T4276622, F4274477, info@jurys.com is Cork's best known hotel. A pool, two restaurants and a popular bar serving food with a few tables in niches overlooking the river.

AL *The Metropole*, MacCurtain St, T4508122, F4506450. This was once the largest temperance hotel in Ireland. Refurbishment has retained some feel for the past and the rooms are comfortably large. Leisure centre includes a pool. Streetside rooms can be noisy at weekends so ask for a river view. Bar and Restaurant. **AL** *Ambassador Hotel*, Military Hill, T4551996, F4551997. A former military hospital, built in the 1870s, with views over the city. Bar and restaurant.

A *Forte Travelodge*, Kinsale Rd roundabout, south ring road, Blackash, T4310722, F4310707. Very reasonable value, especially for families. Room rate charged. Little Chef restaurant next door. **A** *Gabriel House* Summer Hill, St Lukes, T4500333, F4500178. Near the railway station with comfortable, smallish en-suite rooms and evening meals available. **A** *Hotel Isaac's*, 48 MacCurtain St, T4500011, F4506355. Free car parking nearby. City centre hotel with a courtyard garden. Good value. Restaurant. **A** *Jury's Cork Inn*, Anderson's Quay, T4276444, F4276144, info@jurys.com Excellent value for money with a room rate rather than price per person, this hotel offers modern comfortable accommodation. Restaurant. **A** *Lotamore House*, Tivoli, T4822344, F4822219, lotamore@iol.ie Just off the dual carriageway to the Dublin/Waterford roundabout. Georgian guesthouse set in very agreeable grounds and with a period feel but no bar or restaurant. **A** *Victoria Hotel*, St Patrick St, T4278788, F4278790, vicgeneral@tinet.ie Very central, but without a car-park the hotel is entered from Cook St. This was where Joyce once stayed, as recounted in *A Portrait of the Artist as a Young Man*.

The following guesthouses are all large three-storey Victorian houses alongside one another on Western Rd between Jury's Hotel and the entrance to University College Cork. They all have hotel-level room facilities and are within walking distance of the city centre. **AL-B** *Garnish House*, Western Rd, T4275111, F4273872, garnish@iol.ie has 24 hour reception and above-average breakfast menu. **A-B** *Redclyffe Guest House*, Western Rd, T4273220, F278382, chorgan@indigo.ie stands out with its red brick colour and there is car parking at the front and rear. **B** *Antoine House*, T4273494, F4273092, antoinehouse@tinet.ie Private car park at the rear and open all year. **B** *Killarney Guesthouse*, T4270290, F4271010, killarneyhouse@iol.ie Large and comfortable guesthouse situated opposite University College Cork, car park to the rear. Closed for two days over Christmas. **B** *Saint Kilda's Guesthouse*, T4273095, F4275015. Twenty rooms and closed between 22 December and 11 January.

County Cork

Less expensive accommodation tends to be clustered along Lower Glenmire Rd, heading east out of town and close to the railway station. They do not have car parks and to avoid having to pay for parking on the street, even where this is possible, cars need to be left up the hill behind Glenmire Rd. **B** *Kent House*, 48 Glanmire Rd, T4504260. B&B. **B** *Number Forty Eight*, 48 Glanmire Rd, T4505790. B&B. **B** *Oakland*, 51, Glenmire Rd, T4500578. B&B. **B** *Aaran House*, 49 Lower Glenmire Rd, T4551501.

Three B&Bs at the western end of Cork with singles for around IR£25 and doubles for IR£40 are **B** *Lisadell House*, Western Rd, T4546172, and **B** *55 Wilton Gardens*, off Wilton Rd, T4541705, and **B** *Larurnum House*, Dennehy's Cross, Model Farm Rd, T4541008. All three can be reached by bus No 8 from the city centre and the last two can also be reached by bus No 5. **B-C** *Árd Wilton*, 1 Wilton Rd, Wilton, T4342358, is beside the Wilton shopping centre, reached by bus No 8 and is open all year.

Other B&Bs in the same price range are found a little way outside Cork in the Douglas area and reached by bus No 7 from the city centre. Douglas has its own shops and restaurants and is convnient for the airport or ferry port. **B** *River View*, Douglas, T4893762, is in Douglas village near Barrys Pub. **B** *Coolfadda House*, Douglas Rd, T4363489, is near St Finbarrs Hospital.

D *Aaran House Tourist Hostel*, Lower Glenmire Rd, T4551566, is directly opposite the railway station and not to be confused with the B&B of the same name on the other side of the street. It belongs to the IHO group, includes three private rooms for IR£17, open all year and has bikes for hire. **D** An Óige *Cork International Youth Hostel*, 1&2 Redclyff, Western Rd, T4543289, F4343715. A smart establishment at the western side of town. **D** *Campus House*, 3 Woodland View, Western Rd, T4343531, F4343531. Has 20 beds and some family rooms. **D** *Cork City Independent Hostel*, 100 Lower Glanmire Rd. T4509089. A short way past the railway station, on the opposite side of the road. There are 25 beds and these include 7 private rooms for IR£7 per person. Bikes can be hired. **D** *Isaac's*, 48 MacCurtain St, T4500011, F4506355. Nearest to town and with good facilities. **D** *Island House*, Morrison's Quay, T4271716, F4271719, island@iol.ie Centrally located and has single and double rooms as well as dorm beds. **D** *Kelly's*, 25 Summerhill South, T4315612. A little way south of the city centre, and also worth considering. **D** *Kinlay House*, Shandon, T4508966, F4506927, kincork@usit.ie Bob and Joan Walk. Larger and friendlier. Private rooms and laundry facilities available and breakfast included. **D** *Sheila's of Cork*, Belgrave Place, Wellington St, T4505562, F4500940, sheilas@iol.ie Provides meals, laundry facilities, private and family rooms, sauna, money exchange and bicycle hire.

Camping *Bienvenue Ferry Caravan & Camping Park*, T4312711. Opposite the airport, this is handy if heading out to West Cork. *Cork City Caravan & Camping Park*, Togher Rd, T4961866. This is the nearest to the centre, reached by the No 14 bus.

County Cork

Self-catering *Castlewhite Apartments*, University College, T4902793, F4344099. Rents apartments between mid-June and mid-September. *Isaac's Apartments*, MacCurtain St, T4500011, F4506355. Has 2- and 3-bedroomed apartments for IR£325 a week.

The narrow lanes between St Patrick St and Paul St are home to quite a few reasonably priced restaurants, varying in quality but usually worth a visit for a mid-morning break, a quick lunch or a look at their dinner menus. Better restaurants are found at the Western Rd and MacCurtain St ends of town. The price ranges below refer to dinner only; lunch is usually around IR£5-7 wherever you go. 'Expensive' is around IR£30; 'Affordable' around IR£20; and 'Inexpensive' around IR£10.

Eating
● *on map*
Price codes:
see inside front cover

Expensive For seriously good food the *Arbutus Lodge* restaurant, T4501237, is hard to beat. Fresh seasonal produce, especially fish, and a very impressive wine list. The *Fastnet Restaurant*, T4276622, at the *Jury's* hotel on Lancaster Quay, opens Tuesday to Saturday at 1830. Lots of suits around but excellent French-style cuisine using local produce.

Affordable *Michael's*, 71 St Patrick St, T4277716. This restaurant, near Waterstone's, offers quality Irish cuisine for lunch or dinner (closed Sunday). There are interesting starters, such as haddock salad or Clonakilty black pudding gâteau, and a choice of six main dishes: fish, meat and game. Recommended. *Isaac's Restaurant*, 48 MacCurtain St, T4503805, remains very popular due to dependably good food at reasonable prices. It is not related to *Greene's Restaurant* in *Hotel Isaac's* at the same address. *Greene's* is a little more expensive but it is worth comparing their menus. *Haru Baru*, 5 Emmet Place, T4278006, is a small Japanese restaurant opposite the *Crawford Art Gallery*. A la carte and set meals, closed on Sunday. The *Eating Room*, T4272878, at Bodega in Cornmarket St, has a reputation for interesting dishes that blend Irish cuisine with international influences. *Paradiso*, T4277939, on Lancaster Quay opposite *Jury's* hotel, is Cork's quality vegetarian restaurant.

Michael's – run by a well-known and respected Cork restaurateur

Inexpensive *Gambieni's*, 6 Carey's Lane, T4272388, offers a menu fairly typical of the many small restaurants in this area. A choice of pasta, chicken, pizza and vegetarian dishes. *Fellini's*, 4 Carey's Lane, T4276083, is good for coffee, snacks and breakfast. *The Gingerbread House*, 10 Paul St, T4276411, at the other end of the lane, this is a large old brick building with a café downstairs and a restaurant upstairs. *Kethner's*, 9 Paul St, T270287, is a popular café for cheap eats like burgers, steaks and pasta. *Polo's*, 32 Washington St, T4277999, is a small café serving stir-fried meat and vegetable dishes and sinful desserts like Baileys chocolate chip cheesecake, until midnight during the week and 0400 at weekends. *Bica*, 7 Washington St, T4272999, does tasty sandwiches and light meals and also closes late. Cork's only Spanish restaurant, *Valparaiso*, T4275488, 115 Oliver Plunkett St, is reasonably priced. The *Quay Co-op* on Sullivan's Quay, T4317026, serves vegetarian dishes in a spartan setting quite unlike the stylish layout of the more expensive *Crawford Gallery Café*, Emmett Pl, T4274415.

For picnic provisions, visit the English Market (see page 280).

The *Lobby Bar*, T4311113, http://www.lobby.ie on Union Quay has free musical sessions downstairs on Monday to Wednesday and Friday at 2130. About IR£5 for regular appearances by Irish and international singers and groups. The neighbouring *Doc Holliday's*, T4964846, is also worth a look. *Mojo's* on George's Quay, T4311786, is home to the blues, with locals playing on a Thursday night. *Rosie O'Grady's*, T4278253, at 27 South Main St has traditional Irish music on Monday, Wednesday and Sunday nights. *An Spáilpín Fánach*, T4277949, is a wonderfully old-looking

Pubs & music

County Cork

Live events

To find out what's on at the moment and what is coming up within the week check out the flyers on the noticeboards, windows and doorways of the following places. For theatre, film, dance and other cultural events check the Triskel Arts Centre and the Granary Theatre. For live music, concerts and gigs in general the pubs in Washington St and Union Quay will have all the latest information.

establishment on South Main St with regular musical evenings (IR£5 cover charge). The *Old Oaks*, 113 Oliver Plunkett St, T4376265, has a nondescript exterior but plenty of *craic* inside.

The Comedy Club at *City Limits*, Coburg St, T4501206, has live comedy on Friday and Saturday nights. The pubs in Washington St have live music, mostly weekends, and attract students.

Entertainment **Theatre** *The Everyman Palace*, MacCurtain St, T4501673, has a summer season of classical Irish plays. Triskel Arts Centre, Tobin St, T4272022. Tucked behind Washington St, this is usually worth checking out for visiting theatre groups. The *Cork Opera House*, Emmet Place, T4270022, hosts plays and classical concerts, rarely operas, and tends to be conservative in its choice of productions. The *Granary Theatre*, Mardyke, T4904275, is on the one-way road coming into Cork from the west, parallel to Western Rd, and is run by University College Cork. *Cork Arts & Theatre Club*, 7 Knapps Sq, T4508398, is near the Shandon area and puts on work of varying quality. **Cinema** *Capital cineplex*, Grand Parade, T4278777. The main cinema in town. *Kino* Washington St, T4271571, is more of an art house cinema.

Festivals **16-19th March** *Celtic Flame Festival*, including a St Patrick's Day parade in the city centre. **Late April/early May** *Cork International Choral Festival*. Events taking place in the City Hall, cathedrals, churches and arts centres. T4308308. F4308309. **Late June/early July** *Sense of Cork Arts Festival*. Music, theatre, literature and visual arts. T4310597. F4314033. http://www.musweb.com/corkchoral.htm **July** The weekend around the 10th launches *Seisiún Cois Cuan* in Cobh, featuring sessions of traditional ballads, folk and celtic rock. **Mid October** *Cork International Film Festival*. World renowned film festival. T4271711. F4275945. **Late October** *Cork Jazz Festival*, with the *Metropole Hotel* hosting many events. T4278979. F4270463.

Shopping St Patrick St may be the main street but most of the shops are disappointingly familiar; more rewarding is the nearby pedestrianized area around Paul St and Emmet Pl. The tiny Paul Lane has *Anne McCarthy Antiques*, where most of the merchandise is small enough to be portable. Next door, *The Mills* specializes in paintings and prints and assorted *objets d'art*. There are also a couple of antique shops appropriately located on Fenn's Quay. This street was laid out in the 1720s and 2 antique shops occupy part of a row of the old houses, which were recently reconstructed, preserving the original internal panelling and staircases. *Marble and Lemon*, opposite the Opera House, is worth a browse for home decoration, ceramics and crafts. For straightforward purchases of consumer items and clothes there are two department stores on St Patrick St – *Roches* and *Cash's* – while the modern *Merchant's Quay* shopping centre near St Patrick's Bridge has a supermarket and decent clothes stores.

MacCurtain St has an appealingly eclectic range of shops, including *The Living Tradition* at No 40 that specializes in Irish music. The old *Cork Butter Market* in Shandon is now a craft centre with shops, most of which close on Saturday afternoon and Sunday, selling Irish crystal, Celtic-inspired jewellery and stained glass.

Cork has a good number of bookshops, all boasting a generous stock on subjects relating to Irish literature, history and the like. *Waterstone's* and *Eason's* are both on St Patrick St while *Connolly's* on Paul St deals in second-hand books, mostly 19th- and 20th-century literature. On the same street, *Mainly Murder* specializes in thrillers, while *Mercier Press* have a shop in nearby French Church St. *Vibes & Scribes*, just over St Patrick's Bridge before reaching MacCurtain St, has a large selection of discounted books on Ireland and most other subjects, and a café upstairs.

For camping and walking equipment try *Tent & Lesiure*, on York St but visible from the corner on McCurtain St, T500702, or *The Tent Shop*, 7 Parnell Place, T278833. For fishing gear and tackle *Murray & Co* are centrally located in St Patrick St, T272842.

Air Cork airport: T1800-626747/4313131. 5 miles (8 km) south of the city, reached **Transport** by the south city link road. Direct flights to Dublin, both London airports, Amsterdam, Paris and Rennes. Exeter, Jersey and Manchester are also directly served. *Aer Lingus*, Academy St, T4327155; Cork airport, T4327100.

Bicycles Bike hire: *A.A. Bike Shop*, 88 Shandon St, T4304154. *Cycle Scene*, 396 Blarney St, T4301183. *Irish Cycle Hire*, railway station T4551430. *Kilgrew's Cycles*, 6 Kyle St. *Rothar*, 2 Barrack St, T4313133.

Bus Bus station: Parnell Pl (opposite Merchant's Quay), T4508188. Regular services to all parts of Ireland including Bantry (2¼ hours IR£9), Dublin (4½ hours, IR£12), Killarney (2 hours, IR£8.80) and Wexford (3¾ hours, IR£12).

Car Driving around Cork is easy as the roads are good, petrol stations plentiful, and the nearest thing to a traffic jam is when a few cars wait for a farmer to guide his cows along a stretch of road. Out of the city, parking is not generally a problem although some of the towns have limited space at the height of summer. Cars can be hired at Cork airport or the Cork tourist office. Apart from the car park at *Merchant's Quay* shopping centre, hourly parking vouchers are needed for the limited street space. They're available from newsagents.

Car hire Familiar names have desks at the airport, including *Budget*, T4314000. *Avis*, T4281111. *National*, T4320755. Smaller companies, sometimes with better rates, include *Malone*, T4506744. *Grandons*, T4866217. *Top Car*, T4343366.

Sea Ferry terminal: Ringaskiddy, about 16 km southeast of the city. *Brittany Ferries*, 42 Grand Parade, at the terminal, T4277801. Provides a service to Roscoff between March and October. *Irish Ferries*, 9 Bridge St,T4551995. Handles routes to Le Havre, Cherbourg and Roscoff. *Swansea Cork Ferries*, 52 South Mall, T4271166; ferry terminal, T4378036. Services to the UK; closed between early January and early March.

Taxis Taxis are often parked in the middle of St Patrick St at the bridge end, while 24-hr companies are based in MacCurtain St (T4272222, T4505050).

Train Kent railway station: T/F4504888. Services to Dublin and other cities. A local service to Cobh also stops at Fota Wildlife Park.

Banks and bureaux de change Banks are located on South Mall and St Patrick St, and money **Directory** can also be changed at the tourist office. **Communications** Post office: Main post office in Oliver

County Cork

Plunkett St, smaller offices in Mac Curtain St and Washington St. *Cyber Café* Internet Centre, Thompson House, MacCurtain St, T4503511, adv1@tinet.ie **Hospitals and medical services** *Cork University Hospital*, Wilton Rd, T4546400. **Laundry** 14 Mac Curtain St, Mon-Sat 0900-2000. **Pharmacy** *Phelans*, 9 St Patrick St, T4272511, open daily until 2200. **Tour companies and travel agents** *USIT*, 10-11 Market Parade, T4270900. **Tourist office** Grand Parade, T4273251. Sep-May, Mon-Fri 0900-1730; Jun, Mon-Sat 0900-1800; Jul-Aug, Mon-Sat 0900-1900, Sun 1000-1300. *Usit Now* (student travel), 10 Market Parade, St Patrick St.

East and south of Cork

There are a number of places of interest that can be easily reached by bus, car or bicycle from Cork. An interesting day out could combine Blarney with the Royal Gunpowder Mills at Ballincollig, and along the way, it is difficult to miss the spectacular 330-metre-long Victorian façade of a former hospital on the other side of the river, while on the left side Cork's only high-rise building, County Hall, is notable for its tongue-in-cheek bronze statue, 'Men Watching' (1975) by Oisín Kelly.

Another day out, by car or train, could take in the Fota Wildlife Park and the historic town of Cobh to the east of the city. Either of these places could also be visited as part of a longer excursion taking in the distillery at Midleton and the historical sights at seaside Youghal, although there is a fair bit to see in both Cobh and Youghal and an overnight stay in either town is worth considering.

Blarney

Ins & outs Follow the N22 to Killarney (ignore the less interesting road signposted for Blarney
Phone code: 021 that keeps on the north side of the River Lee), signposted as a right turn off the West-
Colour map 3, grid B4 ern Road that heads out to West Cork. The road to Blarney (the R579) crosses the Lee after a long, straight stretch of road, and there is another right turn on to the R617 before the village and castle are reached. Buses 224 and 234 run to Blarney Monday-Friday, from the Parnell Place bus station in Cork.

Blarney Castle Tradition has it that the garrulous Cormac MacCarthy, the Gaelic lord of Blarney, was so successful at inventing excuses for not complying with the demands of the English that Queen Elizabeth I dismissed his blather as so much blarney. Kissing the stone of his 15th-century castle in order to gain the gift of the gab is itself a mighty piece of blarney played out on a daily basis to

Cork city and around

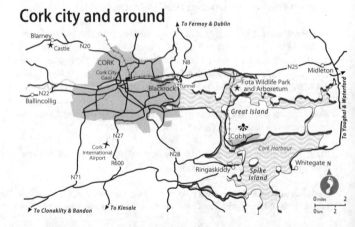

County Cork

countless visitors, but this is all part of the fun and as long as you turn up early enough to miss the queues an enjoyable time can be had. It does help to have a head for heights and care should be taken with children because, although only the one machicolated tower survives, the stairs are steep and accidents have occurred. ■ *T385252. Monday-Saturday 0900-1830, Sunday 0930-1730. IR£3.*

Next door to the castle, this is a turreted mansion from the late 19th century. Descendants of the original Jeffreys family are still in residence, while the rooms open to the public are handsomely furnished and decorated in period style. ■ *Monday-Saturday 1200-1800. IR£2.50.*

Blarney Castle House

The neat green that defines Blarney village (*An Bhlarna*) is very un-Irish, being laid out by General Sir James Jeffreys in the early 18th century: the MacCarthys' blarney had run dry and they had left in the Flight of the Earls after the defeat at the Battle of the Boyne. Everything is compactly together around the village green, including a small tourist information office, in the old woollen-mill buildings, the bus stop, a large Blarney Woollen Mills store that opens daily, pubs and restaurants. ■ *Tourist information office: T381624.*

Blarney village

Hotels like *Blarney Castle*, T385116, the Blarney Park, T385281, and *Christy's*, T385011, are all reliable sources for competitively-priced lunches in their bars and all have more expensive restaurants. However, like everywhere in Blarney at the height of summer, it only takes the disgourging of one mammoth coach to suddenly overwhelm a place. This can also happen at *Blair's Inn*, Cloghroe, T381470, about five minutes by car from Blarney on the R579. Food is served between 1230 and 1530 and from 1830 and there is also a beer garden. Between May and October traditional Irish music is featured every Monday evening.

Eating

Ballincollig

The **Royal Gunpower Mills**, established in the garrison village of Ballincollig, were, in the 18th century Britain's most important gunpowder manufacturing plant, and the largest of its kind in Europe. It closed in 1903 and reopened as a visitor attraction in the 1990s. Food is available every day until 2200 in the five bars that make up *Darbys Bar & Restaurant*, T870584, in the centre of the village. ■ *April to September, Monday-Saturday 1000-1800. IR£2.50. Situated on the N22 road west of Cork: there is also a bus service to the village from Cork, T4508188.*

Fota Wildlife Park

More than an open-air zoo, Fota was successfully established with the intention of breeding endangered animals. Situated 10 miles (16 kilometres) outside of the city, its 70 acres of open land will appeal primarily to families, given the roaming cheetahs, giraffes, kangaroos, monkeys, oryxes, ostriches and penguins. Children will enjoy a visit to the café where a troop of lemurs descend for freebies. Visitors walk around at will or take one of the small trains that regularly chug around the park. ■ *T812678. Monday to Saturday 1000-1700, Sunday 1100-1700. IR£3.70. IR£1 car park fee. Café. From Cork take the main road to Rosslare and take the signposted road to Cobh. The park is signposted off this road. Or take the Cork to Cobh train, T4504888, which stops at the park.*

County Cork

Cobh

Ins & outs
Colour map 3, grid B5

There is a regular train service between Cork City and Cobh. Car and passenger ferries cross Cork harbour from outside of Cobh, near the *Russbrook Hotel* on the road to Cork, but they only save time if heading for the main ferry terminal at Ringaskiddy or skipping Cork City and travelling west to Kinsale and beyond.

History

Pronounced 'cove', and named Queenstown between 1849 (when Queen Victoria dropped by) and 1922, the picturesque town houses rising up the slope of a hill was the last sight of Ireland for the millions of emigrants who left here for America in the 19th and 20th centuries. The scene is graphically described in an 1842 travel book: 'Mothers hung upon the necks of their athletic sons; young girls clung to elder sisters; fathers – old white-headed men – fell on their knees, with arms uplifted to heaven, imploring the protecting care of the Almighty on their departing children.'

The offshore Spike Island was a holding prison for political offenders prior to their enforced departure for Botany Bay. Cobh itself is on an island, Great Island, though it is easy to forget this when one looks out from the town's promenade. To add to the town's unfortunate associations, the *Titanic* paid its last call here in 1912, and three years later the *Lusitania* was torpedoed not far away by a German submarine, an event that brought the US into World War I. Hundreds of the drowned passengers are buried in an old graveyard to the north of town.

Today, Cobh is a bustling little place with a lively holiday air that attracts as many Irish tourists as overseas ones, due in no small measure to the justly acclaimed heritage centre. Back in 1720 the **Royal Cork Yacht Club**, possibly the oldest yacht club in the world, established a home here. The building they commissioned for their headquarters in 1854, in the very centre of the town, now houses temporary art exhibitions and a well-run **tourist office**.

Heritage centre

The town's heritage centre, **Cobh, The Queenstown Story**, located in the old railway station, is devoted to the town's poignant associations and there are interesting and touching displays covering the tragedy of mass emigration and the disasters at sea. Exceptionally well presented and genuinely informative. ■ *T813591. March to December, Monday-Saturday 1000-1800. IR£3.50.*

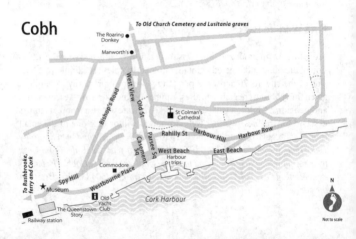

Cobh

To Old Church Cemetery and Lusitania graves

The Roaring Donkey

Manworth's

West View

Old St

Bishop's Road

St Colman's Cathedral

Rahilly St · Harbour Hill · Harbour Row

Casement Sq

Parsee Sq

West Beach · East Beach

Harbour trips

Commodore

Westbourne Place

To Rushbrooke, ferry and Cork

★ Spy Hill

Museum

Old Yacht Club

The Queenstown Story

Railway station

Cork Harbour

N

Not to scale

There is also a small museum, situated in a defunct Presbyterian church, on the right side as you walk into town from the railway station. The exhibits relate to local, especially maritime, history. ■ *T4814240. June to September, Monday-Saturday 1100-1300, 1400-1800, Sunday 1500-1800. 50p.*

Cobh Museum

From opposite the museum, walk up Spy Hill to enjoy a fine view of the harbour. The nearest island is Haulbowline Island, while Spike Island is closer to the mouth of the harbour. Carry on up Bishop's Rd as a right turn at the top provides a startling view of just how steeply the houses stand on the hillside. From here it is a short walk across to **St Colman's Cathedral**, designed by EW Pugin and GC Ashlin. Building began in the 1860s but wasn't completed until 1915. If arriving in Cork by ferry, the commanding presence of the church is hard to miss and the granite and limestone exterior is equally impressive when close up. The spire boasts the country's biggest carillon, with 47 bells covering a range of four octaves, the largest bell weighing in at 7,584 pounds (3,440 kilogrammes).

A town walk

Accommodation needs booking in advance during the *regatta* in the middle of August. **AL** *Rushbrooke Hotel*, T4811407, F4812042. A few miles outside of Cobh on the main Cork road, close to where the ferry crosses the Lee. Ask for one of the river-facing rooms, which have beds with tranquil and relaxing views. **B** *Ard Na Laoi*, 15 Westbourne Place, T4812742. B&B, with fine views of the harbour, at IR£18 per person. **B** *Bellavista*, Bishop's Rd, T/F4812450. This B&B is a good example of Cobh's Victorian houses. IR£40/25 for doubles/singles.

Sleeping

On the main street between the tourist office and the end of East Beach there are a number of cafés and small restaurants. The *River Room*, 15 West Beach, has wonky tables and closes at 1730 but offers tasty alternatives to the usual fare, such as ciabattas. The *Commodore Hotel*, T811277, overlooking the harbour between the tourist office and the heritage centre, serves conventional hot meals at lunch and evening time. Many of the pubs serve meals, and there is also a restaurant at the heritage centre, suitable for a quick meal.

Eating

The best 2 of the many pubs with music are close to one another: *Mansworth's*, T811965, on Midleton St, which dates back to the late 19th century, and the *Roaring Donkey*, T811739, on Oreleia Terrace.

Pubs

Ferry T811485. Daily service from 0715 to 2420. IR£3.50 return, IR£2.50 single, foot passenger IR£1. **Train** There is a regular train service between Cork City, T4504777/4504888, and Cobh, T811655.

Transport

County Cork

Directory **Banks and Bureaux de change** Banks: Westborne Pl and West Beach. **Bureaux de change**: money can be changed in a *Blarney Woollen Mills* shop at the entrance to the Cobh Heritage Centre. **Genealogy** For family research contact the *Cobh Heritage Centre*, T4813591; F4813595; cobhher@indigo.ie **Tourist Information** *Cobh Tourist Information Centre*, Old Yacht Club,T4813301. Publish a *Titanic Trail* guide, IR£3.50, and can provide details of cruise liners about to arrive in the harbour. Summer, Mon-Fri 0900-1800, Sat-Sun 1000-1800; winter, Mon-Sat 0930-1730. **Tours** Guided walks through the town 1100 and 1500, T4813878, IR£3.50. An hour-long harbour tour departs from the pier at 1215, T4811485, IR£3.50.

Midleton

Ireland's chief distillery is situated in Midleton, 15 miles (24 kilometres) east of Cork. When a new distillery was opened here the original 19th-century works were preserved and opened to the public as the **Jameson Heritage Centre**. The conducted tour starts with a film show, but the interesting part is the walkabout that takes you through the whole process, from the yard where local farmers arrived with their barley through to the massive machinery, including a powerful waterwheel and a steam engine, and the obligatory free taster in the bar. Further drinks can be purchased and there are some vintage whiskeys for sale. There is also a café serving light meals, but for something more substantial try the pub lunches at the Victorian-style *O'Donovans*, 58 Main Street, T631255. ■ *April to October, Monday-Sunday, guided tours, 1000-1600; November to March tours at 1200 and 1500. IR£3.50.*

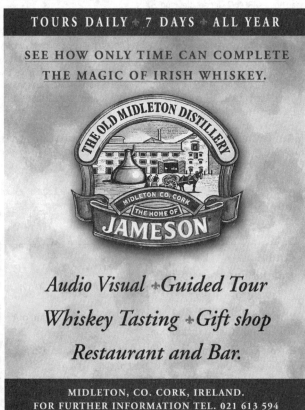
County Cork

Youghal

Pronounced 'yawl' (from *Eochaill* a 'yew wood'), the town is situated at the mouth of the Blackwater and was founded in the 13th century by Anglo-Normans, probably on the site of an earlier Danish settlement. It passed into the ownership of the Earls of Desmond and during the second Desmond rebellion (1579-83), a revolt by the dissident earldom of Desmond against Tudor centralisation, the rebel earl sacked and burned the town. The defeat of the rebellion paved the way for the plantation of Munster and during the Elizabethan age the town and surrounding land became the property of Sir Walter Raleigh and during his years as mayor in 1588 he is credited with having smoked the first pipe of tobacco in Ireland. In 1602 Raleigh sold out to Richard Boyle, later the Earl of Cork, and he spent far longer in residence here than Raleigh ever did. During the English civil war Youghall went over to the winning side and in 1649 Cromwell wintered his army in the town. Nowadays, it is the summer season that attracts most visitors and the Blue Flag beach makes Youghal popular with Irish families while the places of interest within the town justify at least a half day's visit.

Phone code: 024
Colour map 3, grid B6

Youghal is on the main road between Cork and Waterford (N25) and served by public transport from both cities.

Ins & outs

A good place to begin a walking tour is outside the **Clock Gate**, the quaint but striking structure that divides the town's long thoroughfare into South and North Main Streets. A gate of the original 13th-century town walls stood on this spot, but in the late 18th century the present structure was built as a gaol and the story goes that political prisoners were tortured here and publicly hanged from the windows. Make your way up North Main Street for about 500 yards (or metres), passing on your left the post office and then the **Red House** on the same side of the road. This Dutch-inspired house was built in the early 18th century and a few doors up there is a different and older type of architecture, a set of restored **Alms Houses** built in 1610 by Richard Boyle a few years after Raleigh sold his land to him. On the opposite side of the street stands **Tynte's Castle**, a 15th-century structure that is gradually crumbling away.

A walking tour

The real highlight, however, is the Protestant St Mary's Collegiate Church, reachetd by turning left a little way further up North Main Street. The church has had a chequered history; originally built in the early 13th century, on the site of an earlier church, it was restored by an earl of Desmond in the 15th century only to be partly destroyed by his namesake in 1579 when the town was occupied in the course of the Desmond rebellion. It wasn't until the 1850s that a thorough restoration took place; some of the Victorian excess, such as the plastering that covered the stone walls, has now been removed. One of the highlights is the flamboyant, though empty, tomb of Richard Boyle and his family. One of the best 17th-century tombs in Ireland, it was designed by a London sculptor and brought over to Youghal. Boyle's two wives are either side of him, the reclining figure at the top his mother-in-law, and his children are below. Catherine, a countess of Desmond, who danced with Henry VII after the battle of Bosworth Field and died after falling from a cherry tree at a very advanced age, also has her tomb in the church. The explanation of the 'leper's squint', at the entrance to the north transept is worth reading and the north-facing wall of this transept, which is thought o date from an original 11th-century church built by Christianized Vikings, carries an etching of a Viking boat inscribed on a lower stone. Interesting old

St Mary's Collegiate Church

County Cork

tombstones may also be found outside in the churchyard and there is a stepped path that leads up a handsome stretch of the medieval town wall. ■ *T91076. IR£1 donation requested.*

Myrtle Grove Next to the church gates is this rare example of a 16th-century unfortified house made more notable by local historians, who claim it as a home of Walter Raleigh. It is said that under a yew tree in the garden Edmund Spenser read parts of his *Faerie Queene* to him; far more probable than the old fallacy that Raleigh also planted the first potatoes from the New World here. It is not possible to visit the house, but by peeping over the church wall, on the right after passing through the church gate, the Elizabethan chimneys can be made out.

Fox's Lane Folk Museum At the other end of town, in North Cross Lane near the tourist office, Fox's Lane Folk Museum is filled with an miscellany of domestic artefacts from the late 19th century to the 1950s: moustache cups, hat irons, sausage makers and so on. ■ *Summer, Tuesday-Saturday 1000-1300 and 1400-1800. IR£2.*

Sleeping **AL** *Aherne's*, 162 North Main St, T92424, F93633. Offers upmarket accommodation and king-sized beds. **B** *Avonmore House*, South Abbey, T92617. A centrally located B&B just off Strand St. **B** *Hilltop Hotel*, Summerfield, T92911, F93503. 2 miles west of town on the N25 is this 1960s-style, gregarious hotel with large rooms and a lively bar. **B** *Stella Maris*, Strand St, T91820. An overpriced hostel with private en-suite rooms for IR£24 and dorm beds for IR£10.

Camping *Clonvilla*, Clonpriest, T98288. Only 10 pitches available for tents.

Eating The best place to eat is *Aherne's Seafood Restaurant*, T92424, on the main street at the Waterford end of town. Until 2200, the bar serves food such as seafood pizza, chowder and open chicken sandwiches in the IR£5-9 range. In the restaurant, lunch is around IR£15 and dinner IR£25. Steak, lamb and chicken dishes as well as locally caught fish are served. At the other end of town, on Main St near the clock tower, *The Perfect Blend*, T91127, serves tasty Italian-style dishes as well as home-made burgers. Lunch is around IR£5 and dinner IR£15.

Shopping At 14 Friar St, *Jack O'Patsy* is a pottery shop with 2 floors displaying a large selection of merchandise.

Pubs & music The *Walter Raleigh*, O'Brien's Place, T92011, has folk music on a Thursday, *The Nook*, Main St, has music on Wednesday nights (recommended) and the *Blackwater Inn*, Main St, also has music. The bar in the *Hilltop Hotel* has Irish-style country and western music nightly.

Directory **Tourist office** T92390, near Market Square at the harbour side of town. Apr-Sep, Mon-Sun 1000-1730; Jul-Aug longer hours; Oct-Mar, Mon-Fri 1000-1730. **Tours** *Walking tour*, Jun-Aug, Mon-Sat 1100 & 1430. IR£2.50. Depart from tourist office.

County Cork

Inland Cork

From Cork the N22 road can be taken direct to Killarney by car or bus, missing out West Cork entirely. Macroom would be the best place to stop for a meal and the town could also serve as a base for forays into West Cork or the Killarney area itself.

In **Macroom** the **AL** *Castle Hotel*, Main St, T026-41074, F026-41505, has a decent restaurant and a 16m pool and a gym. The **A** *Victoria Hotel*, Main St, T026-41082,
F42148, where William Penn once stayed, is a friendly place with affordable bar food
and a modest restaurant. *Café Musesli*, South Square, T42455, serves vegetarian and
Italian-style dishes for IR,4-IR,7.

Sleeping & eating

Bandon and Dunmanway

The above route will also take you from Cork to Bantry via Gougane Barra (see
page 321) but a more direct, though far less cenic, route to Bantry is by way of
the N71 to Bandon and then the R586 through Dunmanway. Bandon was once
a famous old Protestant town, ('even the pigs are Protestant' goes the old saying). Someone painted on the walls of 17th-century Brandon … 'Jew, Turk or
athiest may enter here, but not a papist'. A reply appears afterwards … 'whoever wrote this wrote it well, for the same is written in the gates of Hell'. It was
also a military barracks during the War of Independence that came under fire
from rebels and was the scene of an attempted assassination on Major Percival
(see page 304) as described in Tom Barry's *Guerilla Days in West Cork*. The
West Cork Heritage Centre, in an old church on North Main St, T023-44193,
explains just how important the potato once was to Irish life.

The best place to stay or stop for a meal is the **A** *Munster Arms Hotel*, Oliver Plunkett
St, T023-41562 (see page 304). Dunmanway has the highly recommended
D *Shiplake Mountain Hostel*, T&F023-45750, a converted 19th-century farmhouse
with woodburning stove, dorm beds and three private rooms for IR£16 to IR£25 each
depending on the time of year. There is space for camping, bikes can be hired and
meals can be arranged.

Sleeping & eating

North Cork

North Cork is heaven to fishing folk who flock here annually to cast on the
River Blackwater and Fermoy has a fishing shop, *Brian Toomey Sports*, 18
McCurtain St, T025-31101, who can advise and sell tackle. Finding an edible
meal in Fermoy is not easy apart from the creperie, *La Bigoudenne*, T025-
32832, 28 McCurtain St, which opens every evening except Monday.

The prosperous market town of Mallow has a far better choice of places to
stay and eat and is another major base for anglers.

To the west of Mallow at Kanturk, *Assolas Country House*, T029-50015, F50795, is a
gracious, 17th-century country house with elegant rooms and blazing log fires. The
IR£32 dinner in the high-ceilinged dining room provides a country house experience
and superb food using fresh local produce. 'We do not apply a service charge and gra-
tuities are not expected' – the admirable policy statement of Assolas Country House.
For less expensive fare *The Vintage* in O'Brien St, T029-50549, is a pleasing traditional
pub with food.

Sleeping & eating

County Cork

West Cork

West Cork begins in Kinsale with upmarket and stage-managed brouhaha of the culinary kind and ends with the desolate beauty of the remote Beara peninsula where restaurants of any kind are thin on the ground and picnic provisions are well worth planning for. In between there are towns, villages and places that will feed and nourish the soul for West Cork is rich with a natural and cultural diversity that takes in ancient stone circles and medieval castles, villages and houses still resonant with dwindling evocations of Anglo-Irish colonialism and seascapes and landscapes to die for, best appreciated by dipping into the long-distance walks that encircle two of the peninsulas. The latest and still devloping cultural layer comes in the form of a small but significant wave of emigrants from northern Europe ranging from impoverished New Age folk (still called 'blow-ins' after living here for twenty years) to well-heeled retirees who arrive in spring and only stay if they become reconciled to the quite different lifestyle imposed by West Cork winters.

Kinsale

Phone code: 021
Colour map 3, grid C5

A town haunted by history, Kinsale has an unusually generous choice of fine restaurants and, to boot, a growing number of small art galleries. It offers a hedonistic introduction to this corner of Ireland and the town may lure you back because, as an English captain who arrived here in a storm in the early 18th century observed, there is 'very good French claret in the taverns and we did not a little indulge ourselves'. The down side is that historical Kinsale has been marginalized, and the yuppie invasion of the town by non-locals, never mind tourists by the coachload, has helped dilute its West Irish identity.

West Cork

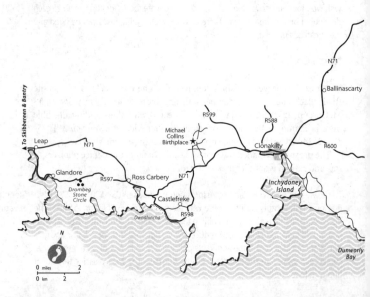

Buses in West Cork

All year Bus Éireann run daily services between Cork, Bantry and Glengarriff and between Cork, Clonakility, Rosscarberry, Skibbereen, Ballydehob, Schull and Goleen. There are also services between Cork, Cork airport and Kinsale and a Monday-Friday service between Skibbereen and Baltimore. A Saturday-only bus runs between Macroom and Kilcrohane via Bantry. For details contact Bus Éireann in Cork, T021-4508188.

24th May-19th September In addition, Bus Éireann run a daily service between Cork, Clonakility, Owenahincha, Rosscarberry, Leap, Skibbereen, Bantry and Glengarriff, with the bus continuing on to Kenmare, Killarney and Tralee. There is also a daily service between Schull, Ballydehob, Skibbereen, Bantry and Glengariff and a Monday-Saturday bus between Skibbereen and Baltimore. The all-year service between Cork and Glengariff continues in the summer to Castletownbere.

History

Kinsale was settled by the Anglo-Normans as early as the 12th century, but it was in 1601 that the town became the scene of what was probably the most decisive battle between Irish and English forces. Under O'Neill, the Earl of Tyrone, the Irish forces marched south and cut off the supply lines from Cork of the English army that was besieging some 4,000 Spanish soldiers inside Kinsale. The English had control of the sea, however, and supplies were brought in by ship. The Spanish were forced to surrender and O'Neill was forced back to Ulster and eventual exile in Europe. Kinsale's fate – it became an English town and Irish people were not allowed to live inside its walls – was the model for what happened to the rest of the country, because O'Neill's defeat precipitated the end of the old Gaelic civilization in Ireland.

County Cork

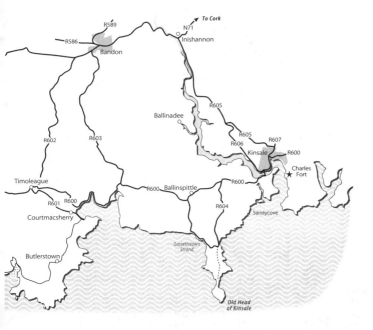

In 1689 James II of England landed in Kinsale in his doomed attempt to regain the throne. He was proclaimed king in the church of St Multose, and returned here finally to sail away after defeat at the Battle of the Boyne. In the 18th century the small winding streets that characterize contemporary Kinsale developed, and in the last 20 years or so they have gradually been converted to restaurants, galleries and gift shops.

Sights

Charles Fort The bare ruins of James Fort, built in the early 17th century, are hardly worth a visit, but on the opposite bank of the estuary stand the more extensive remains of Charles Fort built in 1670. Although substantial damage was incurred during the Civil War of 1922-23, the impressive size is still very apparent and the guided tour explains the significance of what was one of the largest military forts in the country. ■ *T4772263. Mid-April to October, daily 1000-1800. IR£2. Dúchas site.*

Desmond Castle Built as a customs house around 1500 by the Earl of Desmond, the Spanish used it as an arsenal during the 1601 siege. American sailors captured during the War of Independence were imprisoned here; their cells later being used to hold French sailors captured during the war against Napoleon. During the Famine it was used as a workhouse, but less deprived times have seen its rebirth as the International Museum of Wine. Unless you are particularly interested in the history of Ireland's wine link with Europe, there is not a lot to

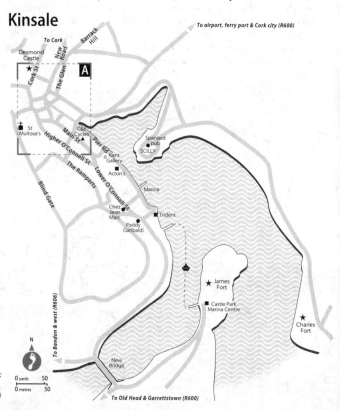

Kinsale

Related map:
A. Kinsale centre,
page 300

....

Kinsale's International Gourmet Festival

The four-day International Gourmet Festival usually takes place in the first or second week of October, and the year 2000 sees the 24th occasion of this very successful event. A membership fee costing over IR£100 covers the champagne opening and the cocktail-fuelled farewell plus the daily special events that take place during the day and at night. Accommodation and restaurant reservations need to be made independently. Details from The Good Food Circle, c/o Peter Barry, Sicily, Kinsale, Co Cork, T4774026, F4774438.

....

see. ■ Cork Street. T4774855. Mid-April to October, daily (closed Monday until mid-June) 1000-1715. IR£1.50. Dúchas site.

In the centre of town, the early 17th-century courthouse with an 18th-century façade is a local museum full of curios and memorabilia from the *Lusitania*. ■ Market Square. July and August, irregular hours. Enquire at tourist office. 50p.

Local museum

Essentials

L *Actons*, Pier Rd, Kinsale, T4772135, F4772231. Hotel with a lovely lawn for afternoon tea or evening cocktails. **L** *Blue Haven*, Pearse St, Kinsale, T4772209, F4774268. This hotel has tastefully decorated rooms named after French-Irish wine families. **L** *Old Bank House*, Pearse St, Kinsale, T774075, F4774296. A more upmarket guesthouse, with antiques in the rooms and above-average breakfasts. **L** *Trident*, World's End, Kinsale, T4772301, F4774268. More relaxing than the exterior suggests. A little less expensive than the other hotels in the **L** category. **L** *The Moorings*, T772376, F772675, is out at Scilly. The perfect place to escape the hustle and bustle of town, with sea-facing double rooms for £IR120; reductions for two nights and for rooms not facing the sea.

Sleeping
■ *on maps*
Price codes:
see inside front cover

AL *Atlantic Manor*, Garrettstown, T4778215, F4778103. 7½ miles (12 km) from Kinsale, this hotel is worth considering if arriving in your own transport. The rooms have spectacular views and the rates, IR£80-100 a double, are better value than those in town.

A *Old Presbytery*, Cork St, Kinsale, T/F772027. Has been recommended as one of the best B&Bs in town. **A** *Pier House*, Pier Rd, Kinsale, T/F4774475. A smart, centrally located and relatively quiet B&B.

B *The Gallery*, The Glen, Kinsale, T4774558. B&B close to the centre but not too noisy. **B** *Rock View*, The Glen, Kinsale, T4773162. B&B next door to *The Gallery* and charging a little less. **B** *Tierney's*, Main St, Kinsale, T772205, F774363. Guesthouse with doubles/singles for IR£28/37.

D *Castlepark Marina Centre*, Castlepark, T4774959, F4774958. Clean and modern hostel, about 2 miles (3 km) from town and reachable by ferry from outside the *Trident Hotel* during the summer. Has dormitory rooms, from IR£8 to IR£25, and sleeps from 2 to 8 people per room. Meals are available, and there are opportunities for deep-sea angling and scuba diving. **D** *Dempsey's*, Eastern Rd, Kinsale, T4772124. Next to a garage, this is a fairly basic hostel with IR£6 beds, but handy if coming from Cork as the bus will stop outside.

County Cork

Eating
● *on maps*
Price codes:
see inside front cover

The plethora of restaurants here is a distinguishing feature of the town that calls itself the gourmet capital of Ireland. Besides the self-selecting Kinsale Good Food Circle, made up of 11 reasonably expensive restaurants, there are many more establishments that aspire to the same standards. Cynics say that the whole gourmet scene in the town has more to do with successful promotions and advertising notions of Kinsale as a 'product' than with good food at competitive prices. But there is a certainly a generous choice of dishes to consider, from black pudding poached in pink champagne and Thai fish cakes to home-made burgers and chips.

Expensive The *Chez Jean Marc*, T4774625, Lower O'Connell St, has a local reputation as one of the consistently better Good Food Circle restaurants, serving continental cuisine with an imaginative flair. The *Blue Haven*, T4772209, on Pearse St has a nautical theme to the décor and it's worth trying to reserve a table by the waterfall. The wine list is based around Irish families who established vineyards around the world, especially in France, between the 17th and early 19th centuries. The *Vintage*, T4772502, on Main St is one of the most expensive restaurants in town, and perhaps one of the best, with main courses of meat and fish around IR£20.

Affordable The best deals for three-course meals under IR£20 come in the form of early bird menus and other set dinners. The *Cottage Loft*, T4772803, on Main St has a IR£14 menu for early evening dining and a set dinner for around IR£18. Almost next door, *Hoby's*, T4772200, remains outside the culinary magic circle but its IR£15 set dinner is reasonably priced and à la carte is also available. With *Max's Wine Bar*, T4772443, Main St, we are back inside the Good Food Circle and its bistro-style design is pleasantly informal. The *Little Skillet*, T4774202, is almost next door and main dishes here are around IR£12. A short journey away by car, the *Seasons*, T4778215, at the Atlantic Manor Hotel in Garrettstown (see page 299) has a set dinner for under IR£20 featuring a choice of chicken, duck, pork, steak and seafood. Live piano music and a decent wine list.

Kinsale centre

County Cork

■ Sleeping	● Eating & drinking
1 Blue Haven	1 1601 Pub
2 Gallery Bed & Breakfast	2 Café Palermo
3 Glen Bed & Breakfast	3 Cottage Loft
4 Old Bank House	4 Hoby's
5 Old Presbytery Bed & Breakfast	5 Kokopelli
6 Pier House Bed & Breakfast	6 Little Skillet
7 Tierney's Guesthouse	7 Mad Monk
	8 Max's Wine Bar
	9 Sam's Pub
	10 Shanakee
	11 Vintage

Inexpensive *Mad Monk*, Main St, T4774602, pub serves dishes like chilli bean burrito and chicken curry, for around IR£7, until around 2130 when music takes over. One of the reliably best places of all for a decent meal at lunch or dinnertime is the bar food at the *Blue Haven* on Pearse Street, T4772209. Recommended. Starters are IR£3-8, and main courses like Thai chicken curry or catch of the day are around IR£8. Tasty open sandwiches are about IR£6. *Mary Lane's Well & Tower Wine Bar*, T4774708 on Main St has fish and steak dishes and an evening special for IR£13.

Budget For a breakfast or a light lunch of home-made burgers, pasta or salad, *Kokopelli*, Guardwell St, T4773636, is worth seeking out. Good food. *Café Palermo*, Pearse St, T774143, is also good for an inexpensive meal, and hidden away in Lower O'Connell St, *Paddy Garibaldi's*, T774077, serves pasta and pizza dishes.

Throughout the summer, most of the pubs in Kinsale are packed with groups of revellers intent on having a good time, occasionally enlivened even more by weekend merrymakers from Cork. Old-time favourites include the *1601* Pearse St, and the nearby *Shanakee* can be relied on for live music every night of the week. *The Blue Haven* bar has music at weekends. Quiet pubs in town are difficult to find but *Sam's Pub*, The Glen, and the *Tap Tavern*, near St Multose Church, are both local pubs where conversation is more important than loud music. Out at Scilly *The Spaniard* is worth the journey for its civilized atmosphere, top drawer grub and traditional Irish music many nights of the week. **Pubs & music**

Apart from the two stores stocked with souvenirs and Irish crafts – *J Cronin* and *Bolands*, facing each other opposite the post office – the galleries along Main St are worth a browse. The *Giles Norman Photography Gallery* is a large place stacked with evocative black and white images of Irish life from IR£15 upwards. For antiques there is *Féinics Antiques* and *Linda's Antiques*. In Market St, *Kinsale Crystal* offers an alternative to Waterford glass and *Molly's* has antique and modern jewellery. The *Kent Gallery*, Quayside, has paintings, prints and sculptures by its resident artist. **Shopping**

Diving *Kinsale Dive Centre*, T4774959. **Fishing** Deep sea angling: *Collins Brothers*, T4774233. **Golf** *Old Head Golf Links*, T4778444. 18 holes. **Hillwalking** *Hike Those Heights*, 3 Short Quay, T4773669. Provides transport from and back to Kinsale. **Horse Riding** *Balinadee Stables*, T4778152. 10 min from town off the road to Bandon. Pony-trekking available. **Quad biking** T4776050. Minimum age of 16. **Sport**

Bicycles *C&B Cycles*, 18 Main St, T4774884. Bike hire. **Bus** See page 301. **Taxis** T4773600 or 4773000. **Transport**

Communications Post office: Pearse St. **Tourist office** Emmet Pl, T4772234. Mar-Nov, Mon-Sat 0900-1300, 1415-1800, Sun 1000-1300, 1415-1730. **Tours** Cruises: T4773188. 1-hr cruise of harbour and River Bandon, departing every hour on the hour from the quayside between *Acton's Hotel* and the *Trident Hotel*. 1100-1700. IR£5. **Directory**

Kinsale to Clonakilty

The quickest route west is to follow the road out of Kinsale past the *Trident Hotel* to Ballinspittle and Timoleague (R600) and then join up with the with the N71 road that continues west to Clonakilty and Skibbereen. A slower but more interesting route is to head south for Garrettstown, where there are two superb beaches, with a short excursion on to the Old Head of Kinsale. The entire headland has been shamelessly turned into a golf course and there is a IR£1.50 charge to pass through it to the ruins of an ancient lighthouse and a modern lighthouse at the extremity. The headland looks out to where the *Lusitania* was sunk in 1915 by a German submarine. **Garrettstown & Old Head of Kinsale**

Food and accommodation is available at the *Atlantic Manor Hotel* (see page 299) between the two beaches at Garrettstown, at the *Speckled Door* pub, T4778243, at the junction where the road from the hotel meets the direct road from Kinsale to the Old Head (R604), or at the bar of the *Blue Horizon* guesthouse, T4778217, at the top of the hill on the road from Garrettstown to Ballinspittle. **Sleeping & eating**

West Cork Gardens

The influence of the Gulf Stream and mild winters that rarely bring frost make West Cork a gardener's dream world and there are plenty of gardens to show what can be achieved. For two weeks in June every year the West Cork Garden Trail sees the opening of many small private gardens to the public and a brochure listing is available from Bord Fáilte. The best gardens that are open throughout the summer are Timoleague Castle Gardens (below), Lisselan Gardens (page 303), Creagh Gardens (page 309) and Ilnacullen on Garinish Island (page 321).

Timoleague
Phone code: 023
Colour map 3, grid C4

From here to Clonakilty the balmy scenery begins to intrude gently and the appeal of West Cork to north European emigrants seeking a new home starts to assert itself.

Approaching the small town of Timoleague the road hugs the coast and there are good opportunities to spot wading birds. **Timoleague Friary**, founded by Franciscans in the 14th century, is open to the public. The Spanish came here to trade wine and when English forces vandalized the abbey in the 17th century they discovered a thousand barrels of wine stored here. **Timoleague Castle Gardens**, T46116, is testimony to the benign West Cork climate that barely brings a frost (there is a superb bottle-brush plant to admire), and the little church near the entrance gate is worth a visit. ■ *June to end of August, Monday-Saturday 1100-1730, Sunday 1400-1730. IR£2.50*

Sleeping & eating
For accommodation and/or food **B** *Lettercollum House*, T46251, F46270, conmc@iol.ie is a real delight. A former convent, the chapel is now a restaurant serving multi-ethnic cuisine with a French inflection and a penchant for vegetarian dishes. Evening meals are IR£21 and lunch, Sunday only, is IR£12. The large bedrooms, mixing traditional forms with contemporary art, are good value at IR£20-26 and there is a hostel-style kitchen for use by guests.

Courtmacsherry to Clonakilty
Phone code: 023
West Cork at its purest opens up on the small coastal road to Clonakilty via Courtmacsherry. From the village of Courtmacsherry the road continues on to a superb beach at Donworly, only useable at low tide. After Donworly the coastal scenery is quietly stunning as the road unfolds its way alongside Clonakilty Bay.

Sleeping & eating
The **AL** *Courtmacsherry Hotel*, T46198, F46137, has a pleasing air of gentility and offers an escape from the modern world at IR£80 for a room. Main courses in the restaurant are around IR£13; or one could picnic instead at the wooden tables that look out across the estuary from the side of the road approaching the village. *Dunworly Cottage Restaurant*, T40314, near to the beach, offers Swedish-influenced cuisine with main courses in the IR£12-15 range.

Clonakilty

Phone code: 023
Colour map 3, grid C4

Etched into Irish folk memory as a synonym for deprivation – 'Clonakilty, God help us' was a familiar expression dating back to post-Famine times – the town of today has not reneged on its history as Kinsale has. In the 18th century it developed around a prosperous linen industry and reminders of the past have been preserved. The reconstructed shop fronts in a traditional style, and a sympathetic air of indifference to modernity, help give the place some character.

Sights

Dedicated to local social, economic and political history, this museum can prove fascinating. There is material on Michael Collins and the area's significant contribution to the War of Independence, a display cabinet on Castlefreke, and domestic artefacts from the past. ■ *May to October, Monday-Saturday 1030-1730,Sunday 1430-1730. IR£1.50.*

West Cork Regional Museum

Michael Collins (see page 681) was born on a farm outside Clonakilty at Sam's Cross in 1890, and although burnt down by the Black and Tans in 1921 the place has been partly and sensitively restored as a memory to the man who led the war against the British. To get here take the N71 west of Clonakilty and look for the sign pointing right after three miles (five kilometres). ■ *Open 24 hours, free.*

Birthplace of Michael Collins

The value of a visit to this restored ring fort, complete with a souterrain and thatched dwelling, partly depends on how knowledgeable the tour guide turns out to be; without a good guide the artefacts on show will seem scant reward for the entrance charge. To reach it, take the N71 road to Bandon and look for the sign-posting. ■ *Monday-Sunday 0900-1700. IR£2.50.*

Lisnagum Ring Fort

Inchydoney is a superb beach some three miles (five kilometres) south of town, but beware of the riptide and check with the lifeguard. The beach is sign-posted from the roundabout at the east end of Clonakilty.

Inchydoney Beach

Along with Creagh Garden this is the most satisfying Robinsonian garden in West Cork, not least because it has the Argideen River flowing through it. There is the usual horrible extravaganza of rhododendrons, but this can be forgiven as you stroll along the flagstone pathways to admire the rockery and the unusual plants flourishing here. ■ *IR£3, T33249. April-September, 0800-dusk. 3 km east of Clonakilty on the N71 road.*

Lisselan Gardens

County Cork

Essentials

A *O'Donovan's*, Pearse St, T/F33250. Hotel charging IR£50/25 for double/single rooms. **B** *Imperial Hotel*, Wolfe Tone St, T34185, F34722. Has doubles/singles from IR£32/17. **B** *Wytchwood*, off Emmet Sq, T/F33525. A pleasant townhouse with doubles/singles for IR£36/25. **D** *Old Brewery Hostel,* T/F33525, wytchost@iol.ie Directly opposite the Wytchwood, and run by the same owners, with beds for IR£8 and 2 double rooms available for IR£20. **Campsite** *Desert House*, Coast Rd, T33331, within walking distance of town, overlooks the muddy end of Clonakility Bay and is sign-posted from the roundabout at the eastern end of town. A small tent costs IR£5.

Sleeping

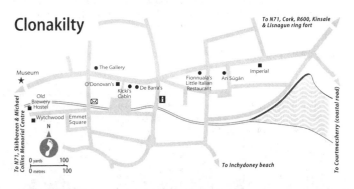

Clonakilty

The last day in the life of Michael Collins

At 0600 in a bedroom in the Imperial Hotel in Cork City, Michael Collins arose to unknowingly meet his last day. He had planned a tour around West Cork, dangerous to a degree because this was militant Republican territory and anti-Treaty men were active in the area. He arrived in Macroom at 0730 outside what is now the Castle Hotel and collected a local driver from the hotel before setting off for Bandon. The road to Bandon was blocked in places and taking side-roads led at one stage to uncertainty over what direction to take (still a hazard in this area). A local man outside a pub helped them but they were not to know he was a republican scout who recognized Collins and alerted anti-Treaty men, secretly meeting in the area. They guessed correctly that Collins would return along the same road because they knew the main Bandon to Cork road was impassable due to anti-Treaty sabotage.

Collins and his armed escort made a quick stop in Bandon before heading off for Clonakility, where they stopped at O'Donovans Hotel before leaving for Rosscarbery and then Skibbereen. They stopped here at the Eldon Hotel until about 1630.

The return journey to Bandon was taken via Sam's Cross in order to visit the ruins of Collins' family home burnt out by Major AE Percival (who years later would blunder into surrendering Singapore to the Japanese). He had a drink in the Five Alls pub before setting off for Bandon and what is now the Munster Arms Hotel. A final photograph (now hanging in the lobby of the hotel) was taken of Collins as he sat in his car for the journey back to Cork. On the way back, in the area of Béal na mBláth, Collins and his convoy were ambushed and the Commander-in-Chief of the Army of the Provisional Government was shot dead. Each year, on the anniversary of his death, a commemorative service takes place at the stone memorial at the site of the ambush.

To reach the site of the ambush from Bandon take the road to Macroom and follow the signs to Béal na mBláth. His family home at Sam's Cross may also be visited (see page 303).

Eating Nearly all the eating places are located on the long main street that changes its name a few times. The *An Súgán Pub*, 41 Wolfe Tone St, T33498, at the east end, serves local seafood though the specials advertised in the window may be better value. At the other end of town, *The Gallery*, 31 Pearse St, T35190, has lunch for around IR£5 and evening dishes such as blackened cajun chicken for IR£7. In the middle of town, *Kicki's Cabin* in Ashe St is a cosy little place, closed on Sunday, with affordable and tasty dishes for lunch or dinner. Equally appealing is the nearby *Fionnuala's Little Italian Restaurant*, 30 Ashe St, T34355, with bare stone walls and candles in bottles. The café-style restaurant in *O'Donovan's Hotel* is busy but OK for a quick meal.

Pubs & music Along the main thoroughfare, pubs like *An Súgán* and *De Barra's*, in Pearse St, as well as nearby *O'Donovan's Hotel*, can be relied on for lively and entertaining musical sessions most nights of the week.

Festivals The week-long *Clonakilty Festival*, at the end of August, is a musically rumbustious affair with bands playing in many of the bars.

Directory **Banks** On Pearse St and Ashe St. **Bicycle hire** *MTM Cycles*, Ashe St, T33584. **Tourist office** Rossa St, T33226, late Feb-12 Nov, daily 1000-1800, sometimes closed 1300-1400. **Tours** *Michael Collins coach tour*, T46107, departs from Emmet Square each Tuesday in the summer for IR£6. Enquire also at the tourist office.

West Cork's Anglo-Irish

West Cork has fascinating reminders of colonial days in the 19th and early 20th centuries when Anglo-Irish families lived in a grand style in their stately country houses, the Big Houses as they have become known. One of the best examples of the ambitious scale of some of these houses can be seen outside of Castletownbere on the Beara Peninsula, while in Castletownshend it is possible to stay a night in one, and though Castlefreake is one of the most delapidated remains it can prove remarkably evocative if Mary Carbery's recently published journals (see

page 64) are on on your holiday reading list. Mary was the mother of the last Lord Carbery, a flamboyant figure who showed off at local fairs by looping the loop in his airplane and later suddenly left his mansion for ever (giving rise to the story of how he shot out the eyes of the portrait of the first earl of Carbery before he left), and her account of living on her own in the house as a widow provides a tantalising glimpse of the Anglo-Irish fin de siècle as well as a tale of a remarkable woman who grew to to love West Cork and its people.

Clonakilty to Clear Island (coastal route)

It is a short run on the main N71 road from Clonakilty to Skibbereen but the coastal road from Rosscarbery via Castletownshend offers interesting diversions as well as outstanding coastal scenery, for this is where West Cork comes into its own. Small houses splashed with Mediterranean blue and burnt umber, quaint-looking pubs, yachts moored in small harbour and off-shore retreats like Sherkin and Clear Island. At times the picture is very continental but always with an unmistakeably Irish idiom that sets an ancient stone circle in a local farmer's field or has remnants of the old Anglo-Irish ascendancy happily co-existing in communities which, in the War of Independence, saw fit to burn down some of their big houses.

A right turn off the N71, at the end of the causeway across an inlet of the bay cut off by land, leads up to the town square of Rosscarbery. During the War of Independence the capture of the barracks here, under Tom Barry's Flying Column, led to the rebels controlling over 270 square miles in West Cork. There is little to see today apart from the Romanesque church off the town square, a craft shop, a bookshop, places to eat, and pubs of course. The town is named after the Carbery family, and an imposing statue of a Lord Carbery rests inside the church.

Rosscarbery
Phone code: 023
Colour map 3, grid C4

Walking tours of Rosscarbery take place every Tuesday at 1930 from the Celtic Ross Hotel for IR£3.50, T48726, and in July and August hill walking trips are available for IR£10 per person. For horse-riding in the area contact *Rosscarbery Pony Trekking and Riding Club*, T48232.

The startling *Celtic Ross Hotel*, T48722, F48723, on the N71 has another surprise inside in the form of an unusual bogwood sculpture. Rooms are IR£60 per person and there is a pool and gym. Its *Druid Restaurant* has a four-course dinner for IR£20; stick with the traditional dishes. Less expensive fare is on offer at *O'Callaghan Walshe's* seafood restaurant in the town square, T48125, or in the *Celtic Ross Hotel* bar that looks like an Irish theme pub. Nearby holiday homes draw the Irish to Rosscarbery, and the place is busier at night than one might imagine.

Sleeping & eating

The ruins of the Carbery home, Castlefreke, are buried in the remains of a nearby oakwood like some long-forgotten Mayan shrine. The last Lord

Castlefreke

West Cork Festivals

The dates below applied in 1999 but they will vary little in future years.

April
Rosscarbery Oyster Festival (3-4th)   T023-41271
Craic on the Coast (Kilcrohane, 3-5th)   T027-67068
Walking Festival   (Sheep's Head, 23-25th)   T027-61052

May
Bantry Mussel Fair (6-9th)   T027-50360
Glengarriff Walking Festival (17-20th)   T027-63445
Baltimore Seafood Festival (28-30th)   T028-20159

June
Michael Dwyer Festival (Ardgroom, Beara Peninsula, 4-7th)   T027-70054
Glandore at Home Sailing (6th)   T028-33446
West Cork Garden Trail (see page 302)
Glengariff Festival (1-3rd)   T027-63113
Union Hall Festival (18-26th)   T028-33768
Durrus Carnival   (27th)   T027-61022
West Cork Chamber Music Festival (Bantry, 27th-July 4th)   T027-61105
Union Hall Regatta (27th)   T028-33768

July
Black & White Festival (Clonakilty, 2-4th)   T023-33498
Match Racing - Sailing (Glandore, 3-4th)   T028-33446
Dinghy Week (Crosshaven, 8-11th)   T021-831023
Black & White Festival (Clonakilty, 8-11th)   T023-33498
Fastnet International Schools Regatta (Schull, 19-23rd)   T028-28315
Welcome Home Festival (Skibbereen, 23-28th)   T028-22070
Courtmacsherry Harbour Festival (24th-August 2nd)   T023-46170
Sherkin Island Regatta (25th)   T028-20336
Beara Community Arts Festival (26th-August 8th)   T027-70054
Kinsale Regatta & Homecoming Festival (30th-August 2nd)   T021-772640

August
Baltimore Regatta (1-2nd)   T028-20119
Calves Week, Sailing (Schull, 1-8th)   T028-28390
Castletownbere Festival of the Sea (1-8th)   T027-70054
Return to Ross Family Festival (Rosscarbery, 6-15th)   T023-48697
Schull Regatta (8th)   T028-28390
Ballydehob Festival (8-15th)   T028-37595
Glandore Regatta (15th)   T028-33446
Beatles and Beehive Festival (Clonakility, 26-29th)   T086-8245986
Liss Ard Festival (see page 308)

September
International Storytelling Festival (Cape Clear, 3-5th)   T028-39157
Courtmacsherry Storytelling Festival (10-12th)   T023-46170
Kinsale Arts Festival (16-26th)   T021-774959

October
International Gourmet Festival (see page 299)
Fringe Jazz Festival (Kinsale, 22-25th)   T021-772135
International Cartoon Festival (Skibbereen, 22-30th)   T028-22090
Storytelling Workshop (Cape Clear, 23-25th)   T028-39157

Carbery dramatically walked out of his castle in the early 20th century, never to return, leaving everything as it was, including tiger skins on the walls and valuable furniture. To get there, take the N71 east from Rosscarbery and follow the signs to Ownahincha beach; a left fork at the end of the caravan site leads up to a car-park in the woods and the crumbling ruins of the castle are tucked away in the trees. The house was occupied by the Irish army during the 'Emergency' (as the Second World War was called in Ireland), dances were held there from time to time in the 1950s before the leaded roof was taken off. Some of Castlefreke's stone carvings can still be seen and there is occasional talk of doing something with the ruined home.

Drombeg stone circle

A well-preserved circle of 17 stones dating back to around 150BCE and known today to pockets of discerning New Age folk, who come here to watch the sun's rays falling between the flat stone and the tall portal stones around the time of the winter solstice. Nearby there is a *fulacht fiadh*, an ancient cooking site that used hot stones to boil water in a pit before meat wrapped in straw was added. Take the coastal road for Glandore from Rosscarbery and look for the sign pointing left after a couple of miles.

Glandore & Leap
Phone code: 028

In 1830, Glandore, a highly picturesque fishing village, was the first to organize a regatta, part of its claim to be the oldest holiday resort in Cork, and it still attracts a yachting fraternity. The village of Leap (pronounced Lep), a little way north of Glandore, gets its name from a gorge that is now hardly noticed if whizzing past on the N71 which forms its Main St.

Sleeping & eating

In Glandore: **AL** *Marine Hotel*, T33366, is the place for a rest though bar food is also available at the *Glandore Inn*, T33468, coming into the village. In Leap: *Connolly's Bar*, T33215, has music of one sort or another most nights of the week and there are a couple of inexpensive places to eat of which *Kickshaw's*, T33210, is a few doors down from Connolly's. The *Bookshop Café*, T33031, has just opened, also on Main St, and sells secondhand books as well as hot drinks, open Tuesday to Saturday from 1100 to 1730.

Union Hall
Phone code: 028

The original name of this town, *Bréan Trá*, meant 'foul beach' but then it was changed – presumably in the spirit of improvement – to commemorate the Act of Union in 1801, which abolished the Irish parliament. Either way there is little to see in this odd little village, though there is the **Ceim Hill Museum** a short distance outside and signposted off the road to Castletownshend. The exhibits are a mixed collection relating to local history and the location is picturesque. ■ *Monday-Saturday, 1000-1900. IR£2.*

Sleeping & eating   Worth considering for an overnight stay is **D** *Maria's Schoolhouse*, T33002, a National School converted to a hostel with dorm beds for IR£8 and private en-suite rooms available. The *Banbery Restaurant* serves pasta, tofu, fish and meat dishes for IR£10-15 and there is an early evening menu for IR£15. Bar food is available in *Casey's* pub, T33590, which also does B&B for IR£36 double or IR£20 single.

Castletownshend

This unique village was developed by English settlers in the late 17th century, and in 1859 one of these families, the Somervilles, returned here from a military posting in Corfu. Edith Somerville was a young girl at the time and she spent the rest of her life here. She met her cousin from Galway, Violet Martin (whose pen-name was Martin Ross), and together they embarked on an unusual literary partnership (see page 62). The entrance to Drishane House,

Phone code: 028
Colour map 3, grid C3

Liss Ard Festival

The **LL Liss Ard Lodge**, T400000, F40001, is a luxury hotel outside Skibbereen presently closed and rumoured to be changing hands, but in the grounds of the adjoining Garden (page 309) the **Liss Ard Festival** takes place every year in early **September**. The event has attracted big stars like Lous Reed and Pati Smith in the recent past and the grapevine mentions Bob Dylan and the Divine Comedy as possible contenders for the 2000 show. A season ticket for all performances is IR£250, a day ticket IR£50, and IR£25 for a single event. Details from the **Lis Ard Foundation**, Liss Ard, Skibbereen, Co Cork. T22368, F22905, rosaleen@tinet.ie http://www.lissard.com.

---

where Edith lived, is on your right as you approach Castletownshend, just before the road takes a sharp left turn down into the village and immediately after signs point to the right to B&Bs and Tragumna. Both women were buried in the graveyard of St Barrahane's Church, reached by turning left at the bottom of the village, and while Violet's name is written on her tombstone Edith's is a simple slab of granite next to it. They are both behind the altar end of the church. The church interior is well worth a visit, littered with memorial stones to members of the Townshend and Somerville families, who all seemed to die in far-flung corners fighting for the Empire. The mosaic floor in the chancel was designed by Edith Somerville and she also commissioned the Harry Clarke stained glass window behind the main altar, though my favourite window is the one depicting the unlikely pairing of St Patrick with St George.

Sleeping & eating B&B is available in **A Castle Guesthouse**, T36100, F36166, the castellated seat of the Townshend family (it is said that George Bernard Shaw's mother-in-law changed her name from Townsend to Townshend hoping that society would assume she was related) at IR£50-70 a double. Self-catering apartments are also available from IR£230 a week. **Mary Ann's** is an olde-worlde pub serving bar food throughout the day in the IR£5-20 bracket, while dinner can be enjoyed in the upstairs restaurant or in the vine-covered room for around IR£23.

Skibbereen

Phone code: 028
Colour map 3, grid C3

In the not-too-distant past Skibbereen, like Clonakilty, was associated with some of the worst horrors of the Famine, and it is only during the last 20 years that the town has shrugged off its negative image. A traditional song speaks of 'the reasons why I left auld Skibbereen' but nowadays this lively market town suggests itself as a base for deeper excursions into West Cork. There are good transport links, supermarkets, places of interest in the vicinity and a refreshing sense that the town is going about its working life while accommodating visitors with a relaxed friendliness. If you are here on a Wednesday morning call in to the cattle mart in the centre of town and try to decipher the machine-gun patter of the auctioneer.

History The town's history is unique because it was founded when English families who survived the Algerian raid on Baltimore in 1631 (see page 311) moved inland for security. In the 17th century more English colonials moved in and they were still there when the Famine brought death and despair to the region. Three miles west of town, on the road to Ballydehob, the Abbeystrowery graveyard contains a mass grave that was kept open so that Famine victims could be added each day, and recently established memorial stones lend a grim grandeur to the tragedy of the Famine era. *Roycroft's* bicycle shop, on the road heading west to Ballydehob, was used as a soup house. The Maid of Erin statue at the tourist office end of town is a tribute to those who struggled for Irish independence. Tom Barry, leader of the famous Flying Column guerilla-force during the War of Independence, comments in his autobiography *Guerrilla Days* that Skibbereen was never a safe town for the rebels because of the fore-lock-tugging mentality of its townsfolk.

For a whacky homepage go to http://homepage.tinet.ie/mcommollyelectrical which has information on Skibbereen that includes a recording of the Columbia spacecraft passing over Ireland!

It is hard to quarrel with the philosophy behind Liss Ard Gardens but opinions are sharply divided as to whether theory ever becomes practice. A self-pro-claimed New Age regard for letting nature develop its horticultural identity with minimal manicuring is all well and good but all you get for IR£3 is a walk past a dull lake and woodland and some pretentious effects that could be enjoyed for free on any of West Cork's peninsulas or islands. To be fair the bro-chure does say that the garden will only reach maturity in 30 to 50 years time, so wait a few decades. ■ *T22368. May to September, daily 0930-1630. IR£3.* **Liss Ard Gardens**

Quite different in mood and character, these riverside Robinsonian gardens are romantic and idyllic, with a walled garden with greenhouses where datura, rhodochiton, lemon trees and globe artichokes co-exist in a happy unregimented fashion, inspired by the paintings of Douanier Rousseau. ■ *Take the road to Baltimore and the gardens are on the right after a few miles. T22121. April to September, daily 1000-1800. IR£3.* **Creagh Gardens**

In the middle of town on Bridge St the **A** *Eldon Hotel,* Bridge Street, T22000, F22191. A comfortable old hotel in the middle of town with small rooms and a confusing miscel-lany of prints, pictures and photographs that includes one of Michael Collins leaving the hotel on his last day (see page 304). **B** *Bridge House,*, Bridge St, T21273. A 19th-century house, across the road from the Eldon, which offers B&B in a superb shrine to Victoriana: the décor has to be seen to be believed. **B-C** *Ivanhoe*, 67 North St, T21749, is a traditional townhouse close to the pubs and restaurants and with rooms from IR£13 to IR£18 per person sharing. **C** *Riverview House*, Newbridge, T21516, is a farm-house dwelling outside of town but rooms have their own bathrooms and cost around IR£14/24 for singles/doubles. **D** *Russagh Mill Hostel & Adventure Centre*, T22451, F21256. On the Castletownshend road 1 mile (2 km) from town with private rooms for IR£24. The owner has climbed Everest, and various activities such as rock climbing may be available through the hostel. **Sleeping**

Ty Ar Mor, 48 Bridge St, T22100, is a fairly new seafood restaurant in town, with a minor nautical theme to the decor, that opens daily at 1830 for a IR£22.50 set dinner and a là carte that includes lobster as a speciality. The food at the *Eldon Hotel* might disappoint a gourmet but will satisfy a hungry stomach with curry, cajon chicken, vegetables with fajita, and mussels around IR£7, served in the bar area, a functional dining corridor or an attractive garden patio. Good value lunches, like Irish stew, for IR£5 and speciality coffees throughout the day. A few doors down from the hotel, *Annie May's* pub/restaurant, T22930, has a large menu, subtitled in Irish (though this is not a *Gaeltacht* area), of meat, fish and salad dishes around IR£8 as well as bar food around IR£5 and a special evening menu. A more gregarious place than either of these two places is *Bernard's*, T21772, close to the supermarket on Bridge St, serving inexpensive bar food, Monday to Saturday, and an evening menu with main courses from IR£6.50 for lasagne to IR£12.50 for a 10oz steak. On Friday and Saturday nights **Eating**

County Cork

there is an à la carte restaurant with dishes about twice the price. *Kalbo's Bistro*, at the other end of town at 48 North Rd, T21515, serves interesting lunches such as vegetarian tortillas and dinner courses of meat and fish for around IR£8. For picnic provisions and fresh Vienna-style bread baked on the premises *Fields* on Main St is the supermarket to visit. There is a small shed on the bridge between Bridge St and Main St selling fresh fish but Fields is better value and just as fresh.

Pubs & entertainment *Baby Hannah's*, 42 Bridge St, T22783, with sawdust on the floor of one bar, is the favourite venue for music in town. The *Corner Bar*, 37 Bridge St, T21522, has sessions of traditional music on Monday, Tuesday and Wednesday. The *Little Fox Tavern* in the Eldon Hotel has music at weekends but the quality varies. *Sean Óg's*, T21573, in Market St near the post office is the haunt of hippies and has some excellent music and *Annie May's*, T22930, in Bridge St is also worth checking out for its weekend sessions which attracts locals as well as visitors.

For a quiet drink without music try *Hourihane's* and its red interior in Ilen St or seek out the snug of *Bernard's* that is on the left before reaching the main bar area down the alleyway off the main street. The *Cellar Bar*, T21329, Main St, is the town's sports bar.

The *West Cork Arts Centre*, North St, T22090, has temporary art exhibitions and the noticeboard at the entrance is a good source of current information on current cultural events taking place in the area.

Directory **Banks** on Bridge St and on Main St. **Bicycle** *Roycroft's*, Ilen St, T21235. For bike hire. **Communications** E mail & Web service in the *Eldon Hotel*, IR£3 for 30 minutes. *J Connolly's*, jconn@tinet.ie on the corner opposite the post office charges IR£1.50 for 15 minutes, *Post office* on the corner of Main St and Market St. **Fishing** Gear and information on salmon and sea trout fishing on the River Ilen from *Fallons*, North St, T22246 **Hospital** T21677. **Sports** *Skibbereen Sports Centre*, Gortnaclohy, T22624 **Taxi** T21258 & 086-8346396. **Tourist office** North St, T21766. At the Cork end of town, the office sells a lot of tourist literature as well as dispensing information. *West Cork Arts Centre*, North St, T22090. Opposite the modern library, the arts centre has regular exhibitions, and the noticeboard carries details of any theatrical or other arts events in the vicinity.

Lough Hyne

Colour map 3, grid C3 Signposted off the road to Baltimore, Lough Hyne was once a freshwater lake that sank below sea level, became flooded with sea water and is now a tidal seawater lake with Mediterranean marine life.

This is a pretty walk through pleasant woodland to the top of Knockomagh, beside Lough Hyne. There are great views on the route up the hill, taking about half an hour, and an amazing panorama at the top.

From the car-park beside Lough Hyne go back to the Skibbereen road and turn left. Walk along about 500 yards (or metres) to where a boreen branches off to the left. Opposite is a track going up into the woods: follow this track until it comes to a ruin and bear sharp left in front of the ruin. From here your path to the top is quite clear.

The trees you are walking through are an interesting mixture. This is largely an oak wood, possibly even an aboriginal one; the ancestors of these oak trees may have stood here just after the ice sheets departed. In the 18th century, beech were planted and the children of those trees are still very much alive in the woods. Below the canopy of the oak and beech, holly, honeysuckle and ivy thrives. On the forest floor are great stands of wood rush while in spring more woodland plants make use of the period before the oak and beech leaves emerge to flower: bluebells, wood sorrel, and primroses. All summer long herb Robert, with its pungent perfume, flowers in the shade.

The forest is protected as a nature reserve and as you continue up the well-made stepped path look out for Irish yew trees, another aboriginal plant, and spindle trees, a low deciduous shrub rather than a tree, with inconspicuous flowers in May but glorious coral pink berries in autumn.

The panoramic view at the top of the hill is breathtaking. Before you lies a whole stretch of West Cork's coastline laid out like a section of an Ordnance Survey map. Immediately below is the lough and it is possible to see the nature of its unusual geography. It lies below the sea level beyond and is almost blocked at its seaward end by a wall of rock allowing only a small channel of water out of the lough. As fresh water feeds into the lough from feeder streams, the water flows out of the creek. But at high tide the sea level rises above the level of the water flowing out, and suddenly the water turns and starts to flow back into the lough raising its level considerably. As a result, it is a salt-water lough, and because it is only exposed to the open sea for part of the day its water is much warmer than the open ocean. Consequently, a very unusual eco-system has evolved here with plants and animals more like those of the Mediterranean than northern Europe. It is possible also to see how over the millennia the sea has risen and flooded the once-dry land valleys of this area. Out to sea is Cape Clear Island, once part of the mainland chains of mountains thrown up 300 million years ago by massive tectonic movements originating in southern Europe. Return to the road, going left past the ruin and down through modern conifer plantations.

Baltimore

Situated 13 km (8 miles) down the River Ilen from Skibbereen, Baltimore's resident population of around 200 souls swells to an almost unmanageable number of visitors in the summer as the harbour area overfills with people flocking to Cork's two most popular off-shore islands. But Baltimore is nothing if not laid-back and welcomes all and sundry, even in winter when the Mediterranean-style harbour, where the guesthouses, restaurants and pubs rub shoulders, is transformed into a wild and windy shelter from fierce Atlantic winds.

Phone code: 028
Colour map 3, grid C3

County Cork

In 1631 an Algerian raiding party sailed in to Baltimore and kidnapped 100 people for the white slave trade. Apparently some of their descendants can still be traced in Algeria through their family names. Before the 17th century, the land and islands around Baltimore were in the hands of the O'Driscoll family, who collected dues from Spanish and French boats fishing for mackerel and pilchards and using the safe harbour, and the ruined castle in the village harks back to that era. In the 18th century a profitable small industry developed along this part of the coast sending salted mackerel to the US, and as late as the early 20th century some 16 trains were leaving Baltimore packed with fish. Today, it is boats that are leaving on a daily basis, ferrying passengers to and from Cape Clear and Sherkin Island. The first lighthouse on the rock here was swept away by gales in 1865, but replaced in 1906.

AL *Casey's of Baltimore*, T20197, F20509. A family run hotel with lovely views over the bay. B&Bs in the town itself include **A** *Baltimore Bay Guest House*, T20600, F20495, has five of its eight rooms overlooking the harbour but all share a modern clean style with touches of old furniture alongside contemporary wall hangings. Breakfast, including smoked salmon, is downstairs in the *La Jolie Brise* restaurant, and **B** *Corner House*, T20143, a B&B with doubles/singles for IR£36/33 overlooking the harbour. **B** *Algiers Inn*, T/F20145. The rooms here are pleasant, but remember that the pub can get a little raucous at weekends. **D** *Rolf's Holiday Hostel*, T/F20289, has dorm beds for IR£7 and private doubles for IR£23. The place has a good reputation and bikes can be hired here. **Camping** It is pleasant at the spacious *Hideaway*, T22254, on the road to Castletownbere from Skibbereen.

Sleeping

Eating   *Chez Youen*, T20136, specialises in locally-caught fresh fish brought to your white-linen table in a cosy restaurant with art work by Dali, Sokolov and James Dixon around the walls. Duck and game also available on the menu with dinner prices starting at IR£18.50 and a *tarte tatin* that just might be the best in the world. *The Custom House*, T20200, has a plain but elegant style and fresh seafood is a choice on the two set meals of IR£14 and IR£19. *La Jolie Brise*, T20600, has great value pizzas, using fresh dough, from IR£6.50 for a delicious one using goat's cheese to IR£12.50 for a rich creamy smoked salmon version. Two people could share one for lunch, the house wine is superb, and food is available from 0830 to 2300. For affordable but catholic food try *Café Art*, T20289, next to Rolf's hostel, or any of the pubs.

Sport   **Diving** The *Baltimore Diving Centre*, T20300, serves beginners and experienced divers. **Fishing** Trips can be organized through the *Algiers Inn*, T20352. **Horse riding** *Limbo Riding Centre*, T21683. **Sailing** *Baltimore Sailing Club*, T20426. *Sailing schools*: T20141 and T20154. **Sea angling and shark fishing** through *Michael Walsh*, T20352.

Pubs &   *McCarthy's*, T20159, on one side the *La jolie Brise* restaurant, has music most nights of
entertainment   the week and attracts well-known bands; see the programme in the window. *Bushe's Bar*, on the other side, does not have music but is equally popular; at quiet times the display of nautical memorabilia can be appreciated. The *Algiers Inn*, T20145, with occasional sessions of music, has a beer garden and *Casey's*, T20197, by the road coming into the village, has music on Saturday all year, on Sunday between May and September, plus Wednesday in July and August.

Transport   **Sea** As well as buses (see page 297) there is a boat service between Baltimore and Schull, June to mid-September, T39153. Departures from Baltimore at 1000, 1345 and 1640, and from Schull at 1130, 1500 and 1740; bicycles are carried free.

Directory   **Boat hire** *Atlantic Boating Service*, T22145, absboat@indigo.ie **Lifeboat** T20101/20143. **Tourist information** The *Islands Crafts & Information Centre*, T20347, at the pier and open from May to Sep. Tours scheduled, day-long, guided cultural and archaeological tours of West Cork, including Sherkin, from *The White House*, Lough Hyne, Baltimore, T&F20566. IR£15-24.

Sherkin Island

Ins & outs   Boats leave from Baltimore, T20125, regu-
Phone code: 028   larly through the summer, IR£5 return. There is also a service from Schull, T28138.

Check out Sherkin on   Sherkin Island, 5 km by 2 km (3 miles
http://www.indigo.ie/   by 1) has safe sandy beaches by day
sherkin/   (with a tractor, T20218, waiting at the pier to tow you to them in the morning and back again in the evening) and opportunities for quiet walks spotting birds and flowers, while at night the island's two pubs are alive with sociable buzz and mercifully within staggering distance of the harbour for the last boat back to Baltimore. Bikes can be hired from Murphy's pub and wildlife tours can be arranged, T20615.

Sherkin Island

Bird-watching on Cape Clear Island

In the summer months thousands of manx shearwaters (a large bird, black on top and white underneath), kittiwakes and fulmars sweep past the southern end of the island on their way to fishing grounds south of Ireland from their rocky abodes off the Kerry coast to the north. In the evening they return along the same route and it is a spectacular sight at any time of the day. Ornithologists should write in advance to the Bird Observatory, Cape Clear Island, Co Cork, for information on organized trips and accommodation. However, all interested visitors arriving on the island are welcome to call in at the Observatory, the white two-storey building near the harbour, or just head off for Blananarragaun at the southwest tip of the island. To get to Blananarragaun follow the path from the harbour up to the café and uphill to the shop. Turn right here, signposted for the camping site, carry on to the end of the road and keep going to the end of the spur of land. Also look out for guillemots (black plumage with a large white area that makes them look like black and white ducks in the water), which breed on the island.

If you decide to stay overnight B&B and an evening meal for IR£8 is available at **B** *Cuina House*, T20384, five minutes from the pier and ocean views from the bedrooms. Other places offering B&B are B Island House, T20314, B Horseshoe Cottage, T20598, and **D** *Sherkin Island Hostel*, T20572.

    Murphy's Bar, T20116, does bar food all day as well as serving meals in its Islander restaurant. The other pub, the *Jolly Roger Tavern*, T20379, also does food and encourages musicians to play so there is often some live music. Cúisín, a snack bar at the Silver Strand, does teas, ice creams and snacks.

Sleeping & eating

Cape Clear Island

It takes 45 minutes to reach this, Ireland's southernmost island, from Baltimore with the boat weaving its way out of the harbour on the same route as the Algerian pirates of 1631. Unlike Sherkin, there are no sandy beaches but for exhilarating country walks, inspiring seascapes, bird-watching and heather-clad hillsides Cape Clear Island, three miles by one mile (five kilometres by two), is a very accessible and enjoyable destination. There is a small Heritage Centre focussing on the island's history and culture. Before your visit, try to collect the useful map brochure from the tourist office in Baltimore or from the small tourist information post, T39119, at the harbour when you arrive. About one-third of the 931 different plants in Ireland can be found on the island, so a flower identification book may be helpful.

Phone code: 028
Colour map 3, grid C3

Cape Clear International Storytelling Festival 1-15 September, T39157, http://www. indigo.ie/~ckstory

After disembarking, turn left at the end of the pier and head up the path to the café and pub and continue uphill to the shop. Turn left here and follow the road to the hostel, but just before reaching it turn left and follow the road that passes a lane to the post office. Continue past the windmills on your right and turn right at the T-junction to head out to the eastern edge of the island. Alternatively, turn left and head back to the pier, passing the Heritage Centre on the way.

A country walk

It is advisable to book accommodation before departing from Baltimore (see page 311). B&Bs include **B** *Ard Na Gaoithe*, T39160, **B** *Cluain Mara*, T39153, and **B** *Failte*, T39135, and the standard rate is IR£16 per person. There is an **D** *An Oigé* hostel, T39144, complete with a new adventure centre, as well as a basic campsite, T39119.

Sleeping

County Cork

Eating   There are a couple of pubs on the island, and one of them, *Ciarán Danny Mike's* has a café attached, T39172. There is also a chip van by the harbour serving food, but a stop-over in Skibbereen for picnic food is a good idea if you are staying for the whole day.

Transport   From Baltimore, T39135, boats, IR£4 single, depart at 1100 (1200 on Sunday), 1415 and 1900 in July and August, returning at 0900 (1100 on Sunday), 1200 (1300 Sunday) and 1800. There is a reduced service other times of the year. From Schull, T28278, boats depart daily in July and August at 1000, 1430 and 1630, returning at 1100, 1530 and 1730. Single fare is IR£6, return IR£9. In June there is one departure at 1430, returning at 1730, and in May and September it depends on the level of demand.

Ballydehob and the Mizen Peninsula

From Skibbereen the N71 main road continues west, turning northwards just before the small town of Ballydehob to head towards Bantry. The R592 road leads west from Ballydehob to Schull and out to Goleen near the end of the Mizen peninsula. From near Goleen you can take a smaller road back along the north side of the peninsula to the village of Durrus, from where the Sheep's Head peninsula or Bantry can be reached.

Ballydehob

Phone code: 028
Colour map 3, grid C3

Situated at the head of an inlet of Roaring Water Bay, Ballydehob was the mar-ket village for islanders from the Bay until it fell into decline after the islands gradually depopulated in the 1930s. Tourism has revived its spirits, and when in the 1980s a small number of well-known writers and the like bought up holi-day homes in the area Ballydehob became a small retreat for the London chat-tering classes. In the summer there is still a middle-class bohemian touch to the place, but in winter Ballydehob drifts back to being a sleepy Irish village. When entering the town from Skibbereen look out on the left for the picturesque, dis-used 12-arched tramway bridge. There is a café, a bookshop and a craft shop along the main street. Places to stay include

Sleeping   **C** *The Old Crossing*, Shanavagh, T37148, a former railway crossing cottage within walking distance of the village. **D** *Twelve Arch Hostel*, Palm grove, Church Rd, T&F37232, has over 20 beds and 3 private rooms for IR£22 each, bikes for hire and camping space.

Eating   *Annie's Restaurant*, T37292, on the main street, opens at 1900 for a pricey IR£20+ dinner (closed Sunday and Monday). The quaint little pub across the road, *Levis*, is popular with patrons of the restaurant while the otherwise-featureless *Irish Whip* bar at the Schull end of town has a faded display on the Ballydehob wrestling champion who invented the wrestling throw known as the Irish whip.

Schull

Phone code: 028
Colour map 3, grid C3

Lying beneath the slopes of Mount Gabriel, with aircraft tracking dishes on the summit, Schull bursts into life every summer with Irish and non-Irish visitors. Good restaurants, an excellent bookshop, pubs with music, and boats to Sherkin and Cape Clear Islands and Baltimore (see pages 312, 313 and 311) all draw in the crowds. The Republic's only **Planetarium** is also here. ■ *T28552. Star show March to September, 45 minutes. IR£3.*

Fastnet Lighthouse

Standing at the top of the Goat's Path on the Sheep's Head peninsula the blinking light that periodically sweeps the night sky emanates from the automated lighthouse on Fastnet Rock. The first cast-iron 1854 lighthouse, replaced by a granite one in 1906, was the last bit of Ireland that thousands of hapless emigrants glimpsed on their journey from Cobh to the New World. Trips to Fastnet, T028-28278, depart from Schull at 1900 on a Wednesday in July and a Tuesday and Wednesday in August, IR£10 return.

The busiest time of all is during Calves Week, at the beginning of August, when various sailing events take place. There is a summer boat service to Schull, T39153, and trips to the Fastnet Rock in July and August, T28138.

Sleeping A *East End Hotel*, Main St, T28101, F28012. Doubles/singles for IR£50/35 in this family-friendly small hotel. A *Corthna Lodge Country House*, Schull, T28517, F28032, a short distance west of the village, enjoys veiws of Roaring Water Bay from its hill-top position. B *Old Bank House*, at the west end of the village, T28101, is a friendly B&B. B *Hillside*, T28248. Has been recommended as a friendly B&B. D *Schull Backpackers Lodge*, Colla Rd, T/F28681. Offers dormitory beds and private rooms is at the Goleen end of town, and looks quite different inside from what the woody exterior might suggest.

Eating French-style cuisine at the chic *La Coquille*, Main St, T28642, is around IR£25 and excellent locally sourced ingredients at the similarly-priced *Restaurant in Blue*, Crookhaven Rd, T28305, a couple of kilometres outside the village but our favourite is *Adéle's*, Main St, T28459, with a deservedly popular coffee shop for light meals and a dinner menu for IR£17 with dishes like angelhair with artichokes and olives. The *Bunratty Inn* serves tasty mussels and bar food is also available at *The Waterside Inn* and the old-style *Hackett's Bar*. For fresh fish and take-away cooked fish, *The Fish Shop* at the pier is reliable and the *The Courtyard* pub in Main St sells a superb variety of local cheeses and fresh bread; ideal for a picnic.

Pubs & music Many of the pubs along Main St have musical evenings. Check to see what is on at *The Courtyard* pub or *Arundel's Bar*. *TJ Newman's* is a lovely old-fashioned pub for a quiet drink and a chat with locals.

Shopping **Books** *Fuschia Books* has a wide range of second-hand books on Irish subjects from paperbacks to first editions. **Clothes** *Irish Knitwear*, Main St. **Gifts** *Celtic Crafts*, Main St. Sells gifts such as jewellery and pottery. *The Courtyard* pub in Main St has a craft shop attached, selling pottery, jewellery and hand-knit garments. *Seagull Gallery, Main St*.

Mizen Head, Barley Cove and Crookhaven

Phone code: 027
Colour map 3, grid C2

After passing the brightly painted villages of Ballydehob and Schull, well-known retreats for well-heeled North Europeans, the social and physical landscape changes as you approach Goleen. The local TD once memorably described his constituency as in danger of becoming a land of 'briars, bullocks and bachelors' and indeed the land does become barren with small farms struggling to cope with the centralising farming policies of the EU and young people not always keen to grow up as farmers and farmers' wives. Outside of winter you will be struck by the flora and fauna with teeming birdlife off Mizen

County Cork

Head, wild thyme growing by the roadside and the hills turning yellow and purple with autumn gorse and heather.

The most unforgettable sight on this peninsula is the view of the crazy rock formations from the small bridge that takes one out to the **Mizen Vision**, the Mizen Head signal station, at the end of the peninsula. One has to pay the IR£2.50 entrance charge to reach the bridge, which is unfortunate because a visit to the signal station is a disappointing experience and hardly worth the money. To make matters worse, what used to be a spectacular clifftop walk from here to **Three Castles Head** has been closed off. However, what is recommended is a visit to the 13th-century O'Mahoney castle near the edge of sheer cliffs at Three Castles Head, with a lake in front. Do not be deterred by the sign at the farm entrance which gives access to the castle; the owners were dismayed at coaches disgorging groups who trooped across their land. Individual visitors are entitled to visit the castle: to get there from the car-park at the *Barleycove Beach Hotel* turn right, then left at the first T-junction and right at the next junction where a sign points left to the *Ocean View* B&B. Follow the road to the end where a gate leads up to a farmhouse; the castle is a 10-minute walk beyond. An exciting walk with astonishing views of the Atlantic can be enjoyed by following the road that leads to the *Ocean View* B&B and heading south along the clifftop to Mizen Head, when the road comes to an end.

The sandy expanse of surfable Barley Cove comes as a terrific surprise near the end of the Mizen Peninsula and, although there can be a dangerous undercurrent in places, lifeguards are on duty in the summer and flags indicate where it is safe to swim. If you leave Goleen by heading straight out of the village, instead of turning right for Mizen Head you will see Crookhaven on your left. Once an important harbour, Crookhaven is still patronised by sailing folk and there are a couple of undistinguished pubs serving food.

Sleeping The best place to stay is either the 1960s-style **AL** *Barleycove Beach Hotel*, T35234; F35100 – where the rooms are pleasantly retro sixties and look out over the bay – or the farmhouse **B** *Ocean View B&B*. **Camping** *Barleycove Holiday Park*, Crookhaven, T35302, accepts campers, if they like the look of you, but you could follow the example of others and camp for free at the Crookhaven end of the beach.

Eating There is one table at the restaurant in the *Barleycove Beach Hotel* that has a stunning view of the beach. A 3-course à la carte meal costs around IR£22; fish and meat dishes, including ostrich, are available and there is a bar menu with meals around IR£7. The bar does a roaring trade in reasonably priced bar food all evening. There are a couple of other restaurants in and around Goleen, but not everyone finds them good value.

Sheep's Head Way

Tourist office The nearby village of Goleen has a tourist office, T35255.

The Sheep's Head Peninsula

This is a modest peninsula of green beauty washed by the wide water of Bantry Bay to the north and the more placid Dunmanus Bay to the south. Returning from Goleen on the Mizen peninsula, take a left turn at the Toormore junction and enjoy the scenic coastal road along the north side of the Mizen peninsula to the village of **Durrus** at the head of Dunmanus Bay. A loop road runs west from here to the small village of **Kilcrohane** on the Sheep's Head and then north up the Goat's Path to head back to Bantry along the north side of this peninsula. The best reason for coming to the Sheep's Head peninsula is to walk the **Sheep's Head Way**, whole sections of which are truly spectacular. A shorter excursion takes one west beyond Kilcrohane to Toreen, where the road ends next to a mobile teashop, and from here it is a lovely walk out to the automated lighthouse at the peninsula's end.

Phone code: 027

Exposed, original beams and low-ceilinged, Fitzpatrick's pub at the start of the Goat's Path in Kilcrohane is one of the most authentic and sociable pubs in West Cork

B&Bs west of Durrus and signposted on the main road include **B** *Grove House*, T67060, and **B** *Reenmore Farmhouse*, T027-67051, both at Ahakista and both charging around IR£36/16 for doubles/singles.

Sleeping

Durrus has a number of pubs serving good bar food throughout the day, including the *Long Boat Bar* and *Ivo's*. In Kilcrohane *Fitzpatrick's* pub has real character and a friendly atmosphere and tea and cakes can be enjoyed in the olde-world post office. *Bay View Inn* has a new restaurant that is planned to open soon.

Eating

The Sheep's Head Way

The Sheep's Head Way is a four-day, 55-mile (88-kilometre) walk firstly along the mountain spine that dominates the centre of the peninsula and then out to the western extremity. The final day of the walk, from Durrus, is less exciting and can be skipped but the first three days are spectacular. Arrange accommodation in Bantry before setting off.

Phone code: 027

The Ordnance Survey map No 88 in the 1:50,000 series covers most of the Way, which is plotted on the map. To cover the whole Way you would also need map 85 for short stretches near Bantry, but it would be possible to get by just using the Way-marked signs along the route. There is also the locally produced *Guide to the Sheep's Head Way* (IR£5) , which has its own 1:50,000 map and a booklet that describes the route and gives some local history. These maps are available at the tourist office in Bantry (see page 320). The *Bantry Independent Hostel* (see 'Sleeping' on page 319) also has information on the Way.

Mapping & information

This is a 17-mile (28-km) walk along the central spine of the peninsula to Kilcrohane just below Seefin Mountain. The walk begins in Bantry but some time would be saved by staying west of town on the Way at **B** *Dromcloc House*, T027-50030, at Cappanaloha, which is open from March-October, with doubles at IR£34.

Day one

County Cork

From the car-park of Bantry House follow the waymarkers that direct you around the grounds and past the *West Lodge Hotel*. The way crosses the main road to Cork and heads off down a minor road lined with wild iris and meadowsweet. A little further on is a turn to the left and then the Way leaves the tarmac and starts to climb. After a time, the fields are left behind again and its route goes along some pleasant country roads for a time before striding out on to the central mountain ridge, where the views over Bantry Bay to the north and Dunmanus to the south are amazing. The ridge is followed until it descends just short of the mountain, but it is possible to walk on below Seefin and descend overland, although this is not part of the official Way. From here you should head down to Kilcrohane Village where there is some accommodation at the **B** *Bay View Inn*, T027-67068, or at the IHH **D** *Carbery View Hostel*, T027-67035, signposted from the village.

Day two
A new leg of the Way, starting at the top of the Goat's Path, has recently been signposted.

This is a circular 20-mile (33-kilometre) walk starting at Kilcrohane village and going to the western end of the peninsula. From the village, retrace your steps to the top of the Goat's Path and take the signposted boreen just beyond it off the road. This is an old road into the turf bog and was once used regularly by horse-drawn carts to draw the dried turf back to the farms to store for winter. Meeting a minor road, the route turns left and goes past a series of ruined cottages and the remains of a 19th-century copper mine. The route then follows the cliff edge closely before heading inland to Tooreen, where it meets the road back to Kilcrohane. But your route is uphill past the ruins of a signal tower before it descends to the shore and follows a lowland route through farms and then along a minor road back to Kilcrohane village.

Day three
The day's 12-mile (20-kilometre) walk follows first the seashore and then the hills through Ahakista to Durrus (see page 317). As you are heading east of the village on the road to Durrus, the markers send you down a boreen, past a few bungalows to the shore and a lake. There are usually swans on the lake, which breed here every year. The area is called Farranamanagh, 'the fields of the monks', and it is thought that one of the sets of ruins above the lake is an ancient bardic school where it said that a medieval king of Spain sent his son to study, only to have him drown on the journey there. From the lake the route follows an abandoned road to Ahakista, an apology for a village with two bars but a very pretty garden to peer into and some deciduous woodland. *En route*, the trail passes a tumbledown stone circle discovered only a few years ago. The old road heads across farmland and uses old roads and boreens. As it approaches Durrus an interesting detour leads to the grounds of the **B** *Durrus Court B&B*, T027-61169, where the ruins of a Jacobean mansion sit proudly in the garden with its Elizabethan chimneys intact. Ask permisssion to view the ruins from Durrus Court, which you might also want to make your stopping place for the night. There are B&Bs around the village of Durrus and one is **B** *Avoca House*, T027-61374, a friendly place that also serves meals.

Day four
This is a 12-mile (20-kilometre) walk through minor roads and forestry and doesn't come up to the standard of the first three days. A lift back to Bantry might be in order here. The Way leaves Durrus going east and where the road forks at the east end of the village takes the right fork, past a few shops and then some bungalows and finally along the minor road through fields. After a couple of miles it turns right on to another minor road through fields. It enters forestry and then joins another surfaced road, which meets the N71. The route then goes uphill and along a series of minor roads, descending through Vaughn's Pass to rejoin the outward leg of the route in Bantry.

Bantry

'God gave us Bantry Bay and we gave it to Gulf Oil'; so said the wise folk who objected to the oil company building a major oil depot on the island of Whiddy. In 1979, after a fire broke out at the depot and 51 people died, Gulf Oil departed and left behind the statue to St Brendan the Navigator as their gift. The sweeping entry into Bantry from the Cork road, with Whiddy visible across the harbour, suggests something rather special, but there is surprisingly little of interest in the town itself. What was a vast town square, Wolfe Tone Square, has been turned into a concrete garden and parking space is consequently at a premium. The town is at its best on the first Friday of each month when the traditional market fair still takes place. The main attraction is a visit to Bantry House while the town itself is a useful base for organizing visits to the peninsulas.

Phone code: 027
Colour map 3, grid C3

Bantry House

In the 1820s and 30s Viscount Berehaven, later the second Earl of Bantry, went on a European Grand Tour, periodically sending back art and artefacts to his family home in Bantry. Visitors walk over them – literally – when entering the porch tiled with panels taken from Pompeii. The rooms are an eclectic blend of the functional and the exotic: tapestries, fireplaces and Spanish chandeliers alongside items such as a 16th-century mosque lamp and a Tibetan water ewer.

The interior architecture is remarkably successful, especially the dramatic entrance to the library, and all part of a mastery of style that allows the building and the bow-fronted garden to complement their location. The backdrop is provided by Bantry Bay, with the Caha Mountains of the Beara Peninsula overlooking Whiddy Island. Inside the house there are tantalizing views from the drawing rooms while the baroque dining room cannot match the airy and graceful library. ■ *T50047, Mid-March to end of October, daily 0900-1800 (open to 2000 on summer evenings). IR£6 (combined ticket for the French Armada Exhibition available).*

Sleeping

L *Sea View House Hotel*, Ballylickey, T50462; F51555. A couple of miles out of Bantry on the road to Glengarriff, this 19th-century building has beautiful double/single rooms for IR£120/70 and deals for longer stays. **A** *Vickery's Inn*, T/F50006. The only hotel in town with a sense of history (and an internet service) and charges from IR£30/21 for doubles/singles.

■ *on map*
Price codes:
see inside front cover

County Cork

Bantry

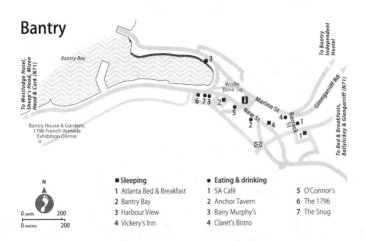

■ Sleeping	● Eating & drinking	
1 Atlanta Bed & Breakfast	1 5A Café	5 O'Connor's
2 Bantry Bay	2 Anchor Tavern	6 The 1796
3 Harbour View	3 Barry Murphy's	7 The Snug
4 Vickery's Inn	4 Claret's Bistro	

0 yards 200
0 metres 200

History is a funny old thing

In December 1796 Wolfe Tone (see page 676), arrived in Bantry Bay as part of a French invasion force of 50 ships, some 15,000 soldiers and a military band whose instructions were to teach the Irish the revolutionary 'Marseillaise'. The aim was to drive the British out of Ireland, but it was not to be. The weather was against them: fewer than a score of ships reached Bantry Bay and after six days struggling with winter gales they reluctantly returned to France. Richard White, the local English landlord, alerted the authorities when he heard the French had arrived and was later rewarded with a peerage. In 1801 he was made Viscount Bantry and became the first Earl of Bantry in 1816.

The irony is that part of Bantry House, still in the same family, now enjoys a tidy little earner from an exhibition devoted to the failed invasion that would have removed that family, as part of the English ruling class, from Ireland. The French Armada Exhibition Centre is in the grounds of Bantry House (see page 319). ■ Open daily, same hours as Bantry House. IR£3.

B *Atlanta House*, Main St, T50237. Has 6 rooms. **B** *Atlantic Shore*, T/F51310. One of the very best B&Bs on the road out to Glengarriff, which is plastered with them, and has been recommended for comfort and friendliness. Its IR£34/24 rate for doubles/singles is the standard rate along the Glengarriff road. **D** *Bantry Independent Hostel*, Bishop Lucey Pl, T51050. Dorm beds and doubles in this IHH hostel. There is the small and completely independent **D** *Harbour View Hostel*, T51140, tucked away on the road on the far side of the harbour.

Eating
● *on map*
Price codes:
see inside front cover

There are restaurants in Bantry but none are particularly attractive. *O'Connor's Seafood Restaurant*, The Square, T50221, makes a speciality out of mussels; dishes are around IR£14. Pubs like the *1796* and *The Snug*, and the *Bantry Bay Hotel*, serve reasonable bar food, while *Vickery's Inn*, opposite the supermarket, serves unexciting but filling and affordable meals in the attractive context of what was the lounge of this old hotel. The *5A café*, Barrack St, serves vegetarian food. *Larchwood House Restaurant*, Pearsons Bridge, Bantry, T66181. Take the road out of Bantry to Glengarriff and look for the sign pointing right after a couple of miles. Intelligently-cooked Irish dishes and very good value, around £IR20 per person, considering the quantity and quality. The *Sea View House Restaurant*, T50073, 3 miles (5 km) outside town on the road to Glengarriff, serves a IR£25 dinner and a IR£15 Sunday lunch that justifies the expense. A spacious dining room, first-rate, traditional Irish food and – dare we use the word – a classy ambiance.

Pubs & music
In the summer, finding a pub with music is not difficult. Try the *1796* or *Barry Murphy's* or the *Bantry Bay Hotel*, all facing the main square. The ugly-looking *Westlodge Hotel* on the Cork road has music nightly in its bar and the *Anchor Tavern*, New St, is always worth a visit for its crazy décor.

Entertainment
A *Mussel Fair* enlivens Bantry in early May and classical musical entertainment takes place in Bantry House in July.

Transport
Bicycle *Kramer's*, Glengarriff Rd, T50278. Bike hire.

Directory
Hospitals and medical services Hospital: T50133. **Tourist office** Wolfe Tone Square, T50229. Mar-Oct, Mon-Sat 0900-1800; Jul-Aug, Mon-Sat 0900-1900, Sun 1000-1800.

County Cork

Gougane Barra

Some time around the seventh century, St Finbarr established a hermitage on a tiny island in a beautiful lake, the source of the River Lee, in a glacial valley surrounded by hills and trees. The church that stands today on its ruin is of little interest but the scene retains its natural charm and on a fine day is worth a visit. Gougane Barra is signposted off the main Bantry to Macroom road.

Sean O'Faolain set a short story, 'The Silence of the Valley' in the *Gougane Barra* hotel, see below. The more infamous literary association comes from a local tailor and his wife whose memories of local folklore were recorded by an Irish writer and published as *The Tailor and Ansty* (short for Anastais, his wife) in 1942. The following year the book was banned by the Censorship Board as indecent but anyone reading it today will be hard put to find what offended them. The ban was revoked in 1964 but not before the poor tailor and his wife had suffered so much local hostility that police protection was necessary. (When the tailor was dying his police guard was cycling to his house with a bottle of whiskey for him.) The tailor and his wife are buried in the graveyard by the lake opposite Finbar's Island.

The solitary hotel, the comfortably old-fashioned **AL** *Gougane Barra*, T026-47069, has a useful IR£1 booklet detailing walks around the lake and recounting local history. Bar food is available as well as lunch, and evening dinner for IR£19. Ask for a table overlooking the lake.

Sleeping & eating

Glengarriff

Visit Glengarriff when the sun is out and it is easy to concur with Thackery's rhetorical conclusion after his 1842 visit that tourists need not bother travelling to the Rhine and Switzerland when places like this exist. (and this was after almost getting into a fight with locals at the Eccles hotel). But come here on a wet day and the place seems depressingly dank, the tourist shops seem tackier than ever.

Phone code: 027
Colour map 3, grid C3

County Cork

There are two attractions: an island and a hotel. **Garinish Island** has a beautiful Italian garden, Illnacullin, designed by Harold Peto, and complete with a Grecian temple and sub-tropical plants that only thrive in this corner of Ireland warmed by the Gulf Stream. ■ *T63040. March-October, daily 0930-1830 (shorter hours in winter). IR£2.50. Dúchas site. Boats depart regularly, T63116/63333/63167, from the village for IR£5 return, though it's a IR£1 cheaper from Ellen's Rock just outside the village on the road to Castletownbere.*

The **Eccles Hotel**, where Shaw wrote part of *St Joan*, exudes charm with its wrought iron balconies and period lobby. Enjoy a drink or meal, inside or out, but watch out for the coach parties that can destroy the atmosphere.

A *The Eccles*, T63003; F63319. Ancient lineage and the rooms have been modernized without losing all their old charm. Beware of disco nights. **AL** *Golf Links Hotel*, T63500, F63500. 4 km outside the village on the road to Bantry, offers some peace, a nice bar, good evening meals and comfortable rooms. **B** *Island View House*, T63081. Next to the *Eccles*, this B&B has only doubles for IR£35.

Sleeping

There are also three IHO places: the **D** *Cottage Bar Hostel*, T63226, in the village, and the **D** *Glengarriff Independent Hostel*, T63211, and **D** *Hummingbird Rest Hostel*, T63195, which are both on the road to Kenmare. All three are open all year and have private rooms, the two on Kenmare Rd have camping space and, except the Hummingbird, have bikes for hire. **D** *Murphy's Village Hostel*, in the village, T&F63555, is an IHH hostel and includes five private rooms for IR£21 each and also rents bikes. **D** *O'Mahoney's*, Bantry Rd, T63033, is completely independent and relatively basic. **Camping** is also available at *Dowlings Caravan & Camping Park*, Castletownbere Rd, T63154.

Eating Tourist places to eat dot the village and *Casey's Hotel* in the village, T63010, does bar food and fresh fish in the IR£10-15 range. The busy *Eccles* bar serves food from 1100 to 2100, while the hotel's *Garinish Restaurant*, T63003, has a superb old dining room serving dinner for either IR£12.50 or IR£18.50. Reserve a table by the window for views of the sea. If you want to escape the crowds, the restaurant at the *Golf Links*, on the road to Bantry, does bar food as well as a decent dinner for IR£18.

Pubs & music Music nightly at *Johnny Barry's*, and the *Blue Loo* has occasional blues or jazz sessions. *Harrington's* and *Casey's* also have music, though like the others they can get crowded. Consider a short trip out to the public bar at *Dowling's Camping Park* on the road to Castletownbere. Entertaining, nightly traditional Irish music sessions. At the *Eccles* on Wednesday nights there is an Irish dance night with audience participation.

Shopping Forget the shops with names like *Shamrock*. The large *Quills* store has a good range of woollen cardigans and Aran knitwear.

Directory **Tourist office** There is a shop and tourist information desk in the village, T63201, and an official information post, T63084, in the car-park of the *Eccles Hotel*.

Beara Peninsula

Without exaggeration, the Beara Peninsula can be described as one of the bleakest and stoniest corners of Ireland yet despite this – or because of it – the land possesses a haunting beauty that finds expression whatever the season. Stretching for 30 miles (48 kilometres) and accessible from Glengarriff or Kenmare, the peninsula is unspoiled and boasts a long-distance walk, **The Beara Way***, which is the ideal way to experience the beauty of the landscape.* **Hungry Hill** *is the highest point, at 2,247 feet (685 metres) – easily climbed hours until the last gruelling stage to the summit that helps make this a whole day's climbing – and four miles (seven kilometres) off Adrigole a sign points a route to the top.*

The **Healy Pass** *is a spectacular stretch of road that cuts across the backbone of the Caha Mountains and links the south side of the peninsula with the county of Kerry at its 360-foot (330-metre) summit. The stretch of the Beara peninsula that is part of the county of Kerry is covered in the Kenmare section of that chapter, see page 357.*

Castletownbere

Phone code: 027
Colour map 3, grid C2
The largest white-fishing port in the country is the largest town (officially named Castletown Bearhaven) on the peninsula and the departure point for a short ferry ride to Bere Island. There is a seasonal tourist information office in the square, a good supermarket that also rents bicycles, and a choice of restaurants and pubs. Between around the 25th July and 8th August some of the events in the Beara Arts and Allihies Theatre Festival take place in Castletownbere. ■ *Tourist office: T70054. Easter and June to September, Monday-Friday 1000-1700. Arts events information: T70765.*

The ruins of both these sites are close to one another though they have nothing in common. Puxley Mansion was the 19th-century home of the family whose wealth came from copper mines further west (see page 324). Commissioned in 1866, it was burnt down by the IRA in 1921 but the ghostly shell of this gothic extravaganza is still very impressive. It was built by Henry Puxley, supposedly as a gesture for his wife who was becoming ill through constant pregnancies, but she died giving birth before able to live here. Puxley then left for England and never returned. The interior ambitiously imitated a Gothic cathedral with vaulting arches and arcades, and the remains that can be seen are sufficient to give some idea of just how outlandish and colonial Puxley Mansion aspired to be.

Walk on to the end of the land belonging to Puxley Mansion and the very meagre but historically highly significant ruins of Dunboy Castle lie crumbling away. It was here in 1602 that O'Sullivan Beare mounted the last great act of tragic defiance at the English after the defeat of the mighty O'Neill at Kinsale. O'Sullivan refused to accept the authority of the Crown and dug in his forces at Dunboy under MacGeoghegan. The English came across from the Sheep's Head peninsula under George Carew and captured the castle before MacGeoghegan, knowing the end was nigh, tried to blow everything and everyone up. The Irish were slaughtered and O'Sullivan Beare set off for Ulster in winter time with 1,000 followers; only a handful survived and O'Sullivan fled to Spain.

Puxley Mansion & Dunboy Castle

Sleeping

AL *Ford Rí*, T70379, F70506. The only hotel in Castletownbere and not great value. **B** *Sea Breeze*, Derrymihan, T70508, is a couple of minutes on foot from the town centre, follow the Beara Way signs. **B** *Island View*, T70415, signposted off the main street has good views over the harbour. **D** *Beara Hostel*, Heathmount, T70184, is an IHO place with good facilities including camping space, bike hire, exemplary kitchen area and four private rooms for IR£19 each.

Eating

Seafood chowder, crab sandwiches and the like are served at Breen's Lobster Bar in the main square. *Niki's Restaurant*, T70625, on the main street occupies what was an old pharmacy; dinner is around IR£15 and lunch about IR£5. The nearby *Mariner*, T71111, is open for dinner and Sunday lunch, serving a Mediterranean-style cuisine of seafood, meat and pasta dishes. Main courses around IR£12. At the west end of town the *Old Bank Seafood Restaurant*, T778564, serves tourist fare.

Bere Island

The best reason for visiting Bere Island would be to walk around it as part of the Beara Way (see page 325). The ferries, T75009, run from Castletownbere's harbour. Monday to Saturday from 0900, 1130, 1330,1530,1730,1830 and 2030 and on Sunday at 1230,1500, 1700 and 2000. There is also a less frequent service, T75004, from The Pontoon, a couple of miles east of Castletownbere on the main road, departing at 1000, 1300, 1700 and 2030.

Sleeping & eating

C *Harbour View*, T75011, the only B&B on the island, is less than 1 km from the ferry on the main road. Singles are IR£16-IR£18, doubles IR£28-IR£32, and an evening meal is IR£7. B&B might become available at *Lawrence Cove House*, T75063. At Rerrin village there is a shop, post office and a pub and this is also where *Kitty's Café* serves lunch and evening meals. *Lawrence Cove House*, T75063, at Lawrence Cove is a seafood restaurant where you can be sure of eating fresh fish caught by the proprietor, Mike Sullivan, himself. He can also help you make arrangement to be ferried to and from the restaurant from Castletownbere.

County Cork

Allihies

Situated in the far west of the peninsula this small village of brightly painted houses overlooks Ballydonegan Bay and a white quartz strand, safe for swimming, that lends considerably to the astonishing beauty of the locality. There is a small, seasonal, tourist information post in the village and between around the 25th July to 8th August some of the events in the **Beara Arts and Allihies Theatre Festival** take place here.

Allihies copper mines

The unhappy story of the copper mines begins in the early 19th century, when the Anglo-Irish Puxley family opened the first mine. At one time well over a thousand people were employed here, including a whole community of Cornish miners brought in for their specialist skills. These English workers were boycotted by the locals who felt their chances of employment were threatened and the ships that carried away the ore to Swansea brought in essential supplies for the Cornish families. The mines finally closed in 1930, but only after producing tremendous wealth for the Puxleys, as the ruins of Puxley Mansion (see page 323) make clear.

To walk around the mines, leave Allihies at the top, northern end, go right at the first fork and look for an untidy dump area on the left of the road. This is the entrance to the mines, and a pathway leads up past the ruins and the chimney stack of one of the pumping stations. The mineshafts are fenced in, but be careful and stick to the pathway.

Sleeping

A *Sea View House*, T73004; F73211. In the village with en-suite doubles/singles for IR£40/23 but no evening meals. **B** *Veronica's*, T73072. Does B&B as well as food (see 'Eating', below). **D** *Village Hostel*, T73107, has four private rooms for IR£9 per person, as well as dormitory beds and camping space, open from April to October. **D** *An Óige's Allihies Hostel*, Cahermeelabo, T73014, is 2 km from the village and opens from June to September.

Eating

Touristy pub food and à la carte meals at the bright-red-painted O'Neill's, in the village, T73008. Both the *Lighthouse Bar* opposite the playground and the *Oak Bar*, next door to *O'Neill's*, have pub grub. *Veronica's* at the Dursey end of the village does soup and salads.

Pubs & music

The *Lighthouse Bar* has music (Wednesday and Sunday nights) and attracts a younger set than the *Oak Bar*, which has good sessions of traditional music on Sunday and Thursday nights. *O'Neill's* next door has music on Wednesday nights, while *O'Sullivan's* has a comfortably quiet atmosphere, which is sometimes enlivened by impromptu singing.

Dursey Island

Phone code: 027

At the end of the peninsula the apparatus of a cable car awaits to carry you over to Dursey Island. The cable car, which has operated since 1969, was designed to carry six people or one person and a cow across the 722-foot-wide (220-metre) Dursey Sound. Only a few people still live on the island and the only road ends in a pathway that continues out to a Martello tower on the highest point. Tracks also lead out to Dursey Head where the three rocks off the tip of the island – the Bull, the Cow and the Calf – can be admired for their stark beauty. Folk legend has it that the Bull was where one of the original invaders of Ireland, the so-called Milesians, wrecked a boat and was buried. The rock became one of the entrances to the isles of enchantment in the Gaelic afterlife. ■ *Cable car, Monday-Saturday 0900-1100, 1430-1700 and 1900-2000. IR£2.50 return. T73017 for Sunday service.*

The opportunity to spot bird life is one of the joys of a walk on Dursey. Gannets and choughs are often seen, as are skuas and terns in spring and autumn, and the island is home to a huge colony of fulmars. Windswept migrants, such as an albatross, are occasionally seen. Dolphins, harbour porpoises and minkie whales may also be spotted close to the shore.

The island's history is well told in *Discover Dursey* by Penelope Durrell, and the book is available in the supermarket in Castletownbere and a few other places. It tells the story of Dursey from the time of the Vikings, through the 1602 massacre by the English and up to modern times.

There is no accommodation on the island, but **B** *Windy Point House*, T73017, within walking distance of the cable car does B&B for IR£17, and evening meals are available for IR£8 (only for guests). During the day it functions as a café, closing at 1800. **C** *Skellig View*, T73129. This B&B is also close by and has rooms (not en suite) for IR£13, and evening meals for residents only.

Sleeping & eating

The Beara Way

This is a well established 122-mile (197-kilometre) walk around what is certainly the wildest countryside in Ireland with coastal views, two island walks, a cable-car ride, old mineworkings, and a sandy beach. It takes upwards of nine days, depending on how much you choose to do, and most of it is well worth the effort, with the last two days probably better completed on a bicycle. The way begins in Glengarriff in County Cork, travels westwards to Allihies at the end of the peninsula via Castletownbere and Bere Island and then returns along the northern shore, entering County Kerry but ending back in Glengarriff. If you have only one or two days the tour given for day five (a circular tour based on Allihies and taking in Dursey Island) has the best views.

Phone code: 027

The best maps to use are 84 and 85 in the Ordnance Survey (OS) 1:50,000 series. They have the Beara Way plotted accurately apart from the change noted below for day two. There is also a tourist board map of the Way, but it is not needed if you have the OS maps. The maps and information about accommodation should be available at the tourist offices in Glengarriff, T027-63201 and Castletownbere, T027-70054. See also the bibliography on page 64 for specialist walking guides to Ireland.

Mapping & information

This is a 10.1-mile (16.8-kilometre) walk through wild, open land. The walk begins in Glengarriff (see page 321) and heads west on the main road to Castletownbere. Beyond two caravan parks the route turns to the right along a narrow, easily missed boreen, signposted to the Magannagan Walk. At the end of the boreen the route crosses a gate and heads across sheep territory with the stark hillside of Shrone Hill to the right and open land to the left. It meets forestry and skirts its edge, heading uphill towards the next stage of the walk, a narrow valley between Sugarloaf Mountain and Gowlbeg Hill. If you look back at this stage you will see views over Bantry Bay. The walk passes the steep and forbidding sides of Sugarloaf Mountain to the sound of the nearby waterfall and climbs to meet an old road that runs parallel with the coast and the main road far below. The whole route to Adrigole is a series of panoramas over first Bantry Bay and then Adrigole Bay. The route follows the old road where occasional stone bridges testify to a period when this was the main road to Glengarriff. Descending through a sheep pen, the route joins a tarmac road through still more wild countryside, littered with standing stones, mass rocks and other signs of ancient habitation. The road gradually descends into Adrigole where there are several B&Bs, a hostel, pub and a grocery store where you can get

Day one
Glengarriff to Adrigole

County Cork

supplies for the next day. You could try **B** *Beachmount*, T60075, or **B** *Ocean View*, T60069, or **D** *The Adrigole Hostel*, T60228, which has no private rooms.

Day two
Adrigole to Castletownbere

This is 13.1 miles (21.7 kilometres) and is a challenging but manageable and very satisfying day's walk. From Adrigole head west along the main road before leaving it at Reen Bridge and heading uphill. It turns on to a green road but departs from the route marked out on the OS map at a point just west of Dereeny and goes south to avoid a very damp part of the walk. Rejoining the main road, it follows this for a few hundred yards (or metres) before heading very steeply uphill for about three-quarters of a mile (just over one kilometre) to meet an old turf road way up at 820 feet (250 metres) on a spur of Hungry Hill. From here the route curves around the flanks of Hungry Hill with its stark, blasted hillsides looming above. It continues along this line, joining and leaving old turf roads and climbing the flanks of Maulin Mountain at about 980 feet (300 metres) until it joins an old road down to Castletownbere where food and accommodation is available.

Day three
Bear Island

Boats from Castletownbere travel at regular intervals daily (see page 323) to the island where you will experience a scenic pretty walk, mostly around the island's roads but with one outstanding stretch over the island's highest point. The total distance is 13 miles (21 kilometres).

From the pier, follow the road until it meets a T-junction where you should turn left. This road has very little traffic on it and meanders around the northern shore of the island with pleasant views of Castletownbere and Hungry Hill. It climbs over the ridge at the centre of the island, passing a Martello tower on the left. At Rerrin, the island's main village, there are some shops and cafés. Here you take a left fork at Rerrin harbour and approach the eastern end of the island past an army training ground and increasingly rugged land where wild flowers fill the roadsides and the fields are full of iris and gorse. The road ends

Beara Peninsula and Beara Way

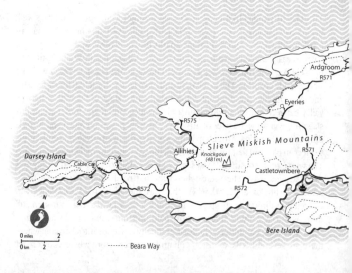

at a locked gate and the route returns to Rerrin by a gravelled road. At the southern shore of the island you have views of the Sheep's Head Peninsula and Bantry Bay. The coast is littered with the remains of the island's days as a British naval base. Returning to Rerrin you retrace your steps for a while over the saddle between the island's two hills and then your next route is clear as you can see a path snaking its way up to the island's highest point, Knockanallig. It is a glorious walk up a clear path through well-nibbled grass and amazing views behind. At the top you can rest for a time by a tumbled signal tower and take in the glory of the coastline and open sea. The route returns through sometimes boggy land along the southern cliffs to meet the lighthouse and then return to the pier via an excellent old military road.

Day four
Castletownbere to Allihies

This is 8 miles (13.6 kilometres) of hillwalking with views of both shores of the peninsula, numerous megalithic sites and a pretty walk through lanes into Allihies. Leaving Castletownbere and heading west on the main road, the route quickly heads right along a minor road, past a very well-preserved stone circle. Further on it heads uphill along an old turf road, and then heads west across the bog with fine views back to Castletownbere. It joins a tarmac road for a short distance and then climbs quite rapidly for fine views to the north of the peninsula. Descending through forestry it follows tarmac for a while and then climbs steeply through more forestry to find a long pleasant green road, which eventually meets a narrow boreen. This descends through ever prettier country lanes into Allihies where there is accommodation and a lovely beach (see page 324).

Day five
Allihies to Allihies via Dursey Island.

This is a lot of walking – over 20 miles (32 kilometres) – and an occasional bit of hitchhiking might suggest itself. The first few miles are on the main road to Castletownbere, which can be quite busy in summer. Then the route heads rapidly uphill, first over a boreen and then open, heather-covered moorland

County Cork

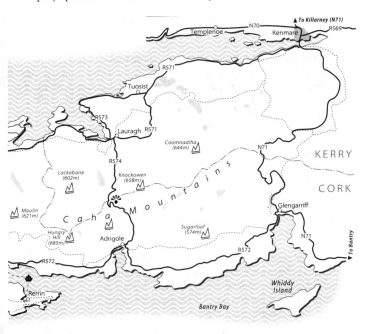

with the most glorious views of the whole of the southwest opening up behind you all the way to the Iveragh and beyond. The path crosses the northern coastline high up and descends to meet the road to Dursey Island (see page 324). It then heads out to Crow Head across more wild moors and descends to meet the cable car. You must be here before 1045 because the cable car stops operating at 1100, before working again in the afternoon. The cable car ride is good fun if you like swinging in a small box over a chasm, and the trip around Dursey Island is quite excellent, passing the island's village and heading out to the westernmost point where the sea views defy description. Back on the mainland you might want to ignore the rest of the Way around the northern shores of Garinish Bay, although it is quite pleasant, and head back to Allihies.

Day six
Allihies to Ardgroom

This is about 15 miles (24 kilometres) along old roads, open moor and the shores of Coulagh Bay.

The Way heads out of Allihies on the roads built when the copper mines were working. It passes the old office building, now converted to a home, several mineshafts surrounded by wired and a still-standing pumping station which kept the seawater out of the mines. Heading uphill on a wide track it crosses a little spur of Knockoura and follows a tarmac road along the flanks of the mountain. At Coulagh it meets the main road for a time and then arrives at Eyeries. From here the route follows the shores of Coulagh Bay before heading over moorland and then steeply downhill into Ardgroom. Here there are a few B&Bs. You could try **C** *Canfie House*, T74105, or **C** *Sea Villa*, T74369. At Eyeries the **D** *Ard Na Mara Hostel*, T74271, has nine beds with six of them in private rooms, from IR£18 each, and space for camping.

Day seven
Ardgroom to Tuosist

This is 12 miles (19 kilometres), chiefly along boreens but with two good hill walks. From Ardgroom, turn left at the *Holly Bar*, where the road starts to climb for a time and before it meets the main road again. After two miles (three kilometres) it leaves the road and heads over wild moorland to Lauragh. Another spell on a minor road brings you to Tuosist, where there is accommodation at **B** *The Lake House*, T84205.

Day eight
Tuosist to Kenmare

Rejoining the waymarked walk, the Way crosses the flanks of Knocknagarrane Mountain and meets a track passing between the two loughs Inchiquin and Cloonee. The track peters out and the Way continues eastwards overland through a high saddle between two unnamed hills. There are fine views of the loughs behind you as you descend to meet a minor road beside a stone circle near Lough Dromoghty. This road meets another minor road where the Way turns left to Kenmare (see page 357) following more minor roads. At this junction it is possible instead to go to the right and follow another minor road through wild rocky territory, where you might expect an ambush at any moment, back down to Glengarriff and end the walk there. The distance to Kenmare is 11 miles (18 kilometres).

Day nine
Kenmare to Glengarriff

There is a choice of walks here, both around 15 miles (24 km) along minor roads but through very wild and beautiful scenery. The first route retraces the steps of day eight to the shores of Lough Dromoghty. There it keeps on past the lough and heads towards Kenmare on the walk outlined in day eight's first route. The other route leaves Kenmare and turns left to follow a long minor road through the valley of the Sheen River. Its finest point is the crossing between the Esk and Barraboy Mountains at 369 metres (1,200 feet) before descending through a wood to join the N71 back to Glengarriff.

In the heart - fire,
Fire and clear air and cries of water-springs,
And large, pure winds; all April's quick desire,
All June's possession; a most fearless Earth
Drinking great ardours; and the rapturous birth
Of wingéd things.

Edward Dowden (1843-1913):
'Autumn Song'

County Kerry

Atlantic Ocean

Tarbert

To Limerick

Listowel

TRALEE

To Dublin

Dingle

Killarney

Cahersiveen

Macgillycuddy's Reeks

Kenmare

To Cork

To Bantry

Superlatives attach to Kerry: the highest mountain in Ireland, Carrauntoohill; the most spectacular island, Skellig Michael; two of the grandest long-distance walks; and the Gallarus Oratory, one of the country's most precious ancient buildings. Kerry is also home to Killarney, Ireland's premier tourist town, and the Ring of Kerry is the most travelled scenic route in Ireland. Kerry's enormous popularity with visitors, however, need not deter the traveller, because although masses of tourists crowd into the main towns and cars clog the coastal roads, it is very easy to escape the crowds.

There are four main towns, three of them on the coast: Kenmare in the south, Dingle on the famed Dingle Peninsula and Tralee at the northern head of it. Roughly halfway between Tralee and Kenmare lies Killarney, the bulky Iveragh Peninsula stretching out to its west.

★ Try to find time for

The monastic dwellings of Skellig Michael

Walking from Waterville to Cahersiveen on the Kerry Way

The views on Great Blasket Island

The Gallarus Oratory

The Dingle Way from Dingle to Cloghane

A meal and a bed at An Bóthar after walking from Dunquin on the Dingle Way

Shopping for pottery at Dunquin

Catching sight of a Manx shearwater at the western end of the Iveragh peninsula

The sub-tropical plants at Derreen Gardens or Glanleam House

The music in the Anchor Bar at Cahersiveen

Cycling through the Gap of Dunloe

County Kerry

County Kerry

Ins and outs

Getting there
See htttp://www. kerrygems.ie for a range of tourist-related information

Kerry Airport, T066-7134777/9764644, is about 10 miles (15 km) north of Killarney at Farranfore, off the N22. *Aer Lingus* flies to Dublin and Manx Airlines handles Luton and Manchester. Farranfore has a train link with both Killarney and Tralee. There are stations at Killarney, T064-31067, and Tralee T066-7123566, connecting with Dublin, Cork and other towns. All the main towns are served by *Bus Éireann* and details are given under the town entries.

Getting around
In the summer months both the Iveragh and Dingle peninsulas, unlike the Beara, are reasonably well serviced by buses. Cars can be hired at the airport, where companies like *Hertz* (T066-9764733) have outlets, or in Killarney. A host of companies are based in Killarney, Dingle and Kenmare: see those sections for details.

Killarney

Phone code: 064
Colour map 3, grid B3

Victorian tourists were the first to come to Killarney; they waxed lyrical over the natural beauty of its lakes and, with well over a century to build up and consolidate the hype, it should come as no surprise to learn that this is Ireland's premier tourist town. Indeed, considering the sheer multitude of visitors who come and go every summer, the ordinary citizens of the town deserve a prize for the way in which they go about their business seemingly oblivious to the tourist tumult around them. Ironically, the town itself is of very minor interest, and as all the attractions lie outside Killarney there is little good reason to stay here for long. But while you are here there are countless restaurants, shops and pubs with music dedicated to providing creature comforts.

Ins and outs

Getting there See the getting there section for Kerry, above.

Getting around Most of the sights in Killarney are accessible on foot, or, if you can take the embarrassment, there are horse-drawn jaunting cars willing to drive you around the place.

History

English landlords in the 18th century developed copper and iron mines in the area, smelting the iron using the rich supply of oakwoods, and when word spread of the natural beauty of the surrounding mountains and lakes early tourists arrived in Bianconi cars (stage coaches named after the Italian-born entrepreneur who introduced them to Ireland, see page 262). Later in the 19th century the introduction of a railway line transformed the tourist scene and Queen Victoria's visit in 1861 really put the place on the map. Before the English ever arrived there were two chief Gaelic clans, the McCarthys and the O'Donoghues, and while the O'Donoghues' territory was confiscated by Cromwell, the McCarthys managed to hold on to land, some of which passed by inheritance to the Herbert family, the people responsible for building Muckross House and creating the estate.

Some four miles (six kilometres) south on the N71 road and with a scheduled bus service from the town centre, the Muckross House complex is a major attraction (see page 341). The house itself is a fine Victorian mansion replete with the gentry's elegant rooms full of period furniture while the servants' working quarters in the basement now house various craft workshops. The gardens boast an attractive water garden, a rock garden and more rhododendrons than you may care to see. The traditional farms, brought to life with real animals, pay tourist homage to Eamon de Valera's idyll of rural life in the 1930s, though surely he would have disapproved of the splendid decadence of the 'vintage coach' that shuttles visitors around. Near the house there are maps showing a number of local scenic walks; the most popular route, also suitable for bicycles, heads around the north side of Middle Lake towards the Meeting of the Waters where the Upper Lake – the most beautiful of the three lakes – comes into view. ■ *T31440. House: July to August 0900-1900 (earlier closing outside of July and August). IR£3.80. Farms: June to September, 1000-1900 (shorter hours in other months). IR£3.80. Dúchas site: joint ticket for house and farms IR£5.50. Gardens: 24 hours. Free.*

Muckross House, gardens & traditional farms

The remarkably well-preserved Muckross Friary dates back to 1440, although General Ludlow arrived in 1652 and trashed the place after expelling the monks. The solid square tower is the most distinctive feature though the cloisters, surrounding an ancient yew tree, and a vaulted quadrangle are also in good condition. ■ *Mid-June to early September, 1000-1700. Free.*

Muckross Friary

The finest example of AWN Pugin's work in Ireland was begun in 1842 and restored in the 1970s through the drive of the now-disgraced Bishop Eamon Casey. Opinions of the exterior range from celebration of its mastery of Early English Gothic to denigration of its repressive factuality, but the interior is a minor masterpiece of Irish-inspired architecture. Despite some terrible gaffes in the restoration of the cathedral, Pugin's inspiring vision of an Irish medieval cathedral endures in the delicate use of lancet and rose-windows set against the solid interior buttresses. During the Famine, building work on the church was still in progress, and it was used as a shelter for the distressed; the large tree on the lawn marks a mass famine grave.

St Mary's Cathedral

County Kerry

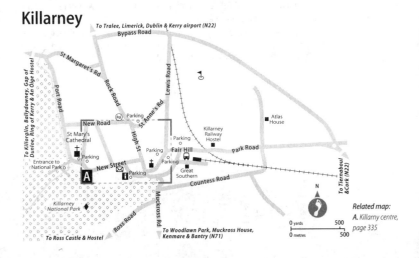

Killarney

Related map:
A. Killarny centre, page 335

To Tralee, Limerick, Dublin & Kerry airport (N22)
Bypass Road

St Margaret's Rd

Port Road

St Anne's Rd

Lewis Road

Rock Road

New Road

Parking

St Mary's Cathedral

High St

Atlas House

Killarney Railway Hostel

Park Road

Parking

Fair Hill

Parking

Parking

Entrance to National Park

New Street

Parking

Great Southern

Countess Road

Killarney National Park

Ross Road

Muckross Road

To Killorglin, Ballydowney, Gap of Dunloe, Ring of Kerry & An Óige Hostel

To Ross Castle & Hostel

To Woodlawn Park, Muckross House, Kenmare & Bantry (N71)

To Tiernaboul & Cork (N22)

N

0 yards   500
0 metres   500

Ross Castle The 15th-century Ross Castle, just outside of town off the N71 road to Kenmare, has gone down in popular history as one of the last strongholds in Ireland to hold out valiantly against Cromwellian forces. In 1652 General Ludlow received its surrender from Muskerry after bringing ships up to Killarney by land and river, thus fulfilling a prophecy that the castle "could not be taken until a ship should swim upon the lake". The truth is that Muskerry, knowing full well that defeat was imminent, had already decided to surrender and the appearance of the boats provided a suitable excuse. The castle has now been completely restored, perhaps a little too clinically, but the lakeside location has its charms – Shelley briefly lived nearby with Harriet in 1813 – and boats can be hired to row out to Inisfallen Island. ■ *T35851. June to August, 0900-1830 (shorter hours at other times). IR£2.50. Dúchas site.*

Inisfallen Island Nothing remains of the seventh century monastery founded by St Fenian the Leper, although the ruins of a 12th century oratory with a fine Romanesque doorway can be appreciated. You will have to travel on to the Bodleian Library in Oxford to see the famed *Annals of Inishfallen*, a chronicle of Irish history from the 11th to the 13th centuries, completed on Inisfallen by monks. Rowing boats can be hired from near Ross Castle, or boatmen ferry over passengers for IR£3. The 21-acre island is about a mile (1.6 kilometres) from the shore.

Museum of Irish Transport A worthwhile place to visit on a wet day, the museum has a varied display of veteran, vintage and classic vehicles of the road. My favourite is the 1910 Wolseley that belonged to the Gore Booth family in Sligo and carried Yeats around with Countess Markievicz at the wheel. ■ *T32638. April to October, 1000-1800; July to August, 1000-2000. IR£3.*

Model Railway Museum And on another wet day there is an excuse to come here and watch scores of trains running on over a mile of track across familiar European landmarks. ■ *T34000. Next to the tourist office. Mid-March to October, daily 1030-1800. IR£3.*

Essentials

Sleeping There is a good range of accommodation in and around Killarney. A vast number of
■ *on map* B&Bs, nearly all those registered with the Bord Fáilte, charge a standard rate of around
Price codes: IR£35 for a double and IR£25 for a single so you may as well take pot luck with the
see inside front cover tourist office. Very few are located within the town and without your own transport it is better to consider a private room in one of the hostels. A number of B&Bs close over the winter, so be sure to check. The less expensive B&Bs mostly belong to the Family Homes of Ireland group (see page 44)

Ross Castle in the 1770s, by Gabriel Beranger

LL *Aghadoe Heights Hotel*, T31766, F31345. Lakeside hotel a few miles out of town at Aghadoe, and one of the most expensive hotels in Ireland. The style is classical – all dark wood, chesterfields and antiques - plus a pool. **LL** *Great Southern*, T31262, F31642, res@killarney.gsh.ie Very centrally located hotel, which dates from 1852 and is the place to stay for old-fashioned style plus modern amenities such as a heated pool. The uninspiring neo-Georgian exterior hides a lush extravagance of style and a sumptuous foyer, which, along with the stately dining room and its Greek columns, makes a visit here worthwhile if only for a drink. **LL** *Hotel Europe*, T31900, F32118, khl@iol.ie http://www.iol.ie/khl Also out of town, at Fossa. Has one of the most scenic locations of Killarney's many hotels, the lakeside rooms have balconies to boot, and the 82-foot (25-metre) pool is complemented by a seaweed bath for the hyper health-conscious.

L *Cahernane*, T31895; F34340, cahernane@tinet.ie Hotel a short way out of town off Muckross Rd. Another grand period piece full of Victorian grandeur and no televisions in the rooms. **L** *Killarney Park*, T35555, F35266. In the town centre, next to the cinema complex, a modern 4-star hotel with bourgeois charm and a good restaurant. **L** *Killarney Ryan Hotel*, Cork Rd, T31555, F32438. Ideal for families with its crèche, a young teenagers' club and kids' menus. **L** *Randles Court Hotel*, Muckross Rd, T35333, F35206, randles@iol.ie Good-sized rooms built in 1894, with some period features retained and within walking distance of town.

AL *Arbutus*, College St, T31037, F34033. A friendly family-run hotel in the heart of town, but not the quietest location. **AL** *Fuschia House*, Muckross Rd, T33743, F36588. In this guesthouse, tea and cakes are served on arrival, breakfast transcends the usual fried food, and the firm beds are a treat in the large bedrooms. **AL** *Gleneagle Hotel*, Muckross Rd, T31870, F32646. A short way out of town, this hotel is geared up for fun-loving

County Kerry

Killarney centre

New Road
St Anne's Rd
Parking
6
Lewis Road
8
2
7
16
St Mary's Road
High St
15
1
11
8
Fair Hill
Bishop's Path
7
10
College Street
3
1
13
9
Old Town Hall
18
Bookshop
O'Neill's Fishing Shop & Bike Hire
Parking
6
5
2
3
12
New Street
Plunkett St
Museum of Irish Transport
Cathedral Place
14
4
17
4
Innisfallen Shopping Centre
Dero's Tours
East Avenue Road
5
Parking
Cinema
Jaunting cars pickup point

N
0 yards 100
0 metres 100

■ **Sleeping**
1 Arbutus
2 Eviston House
3 Fáilte
4 International Best Western
5 Killarney Park
6 Linden House
7 Neptune's Town Hostel
8 Súgán Hostel

● **Eating & drinking**
1 Allegro
2 Bricin
3 Carragh
4 Celtic Cauldron
5 Danny Man Inn
6 Dingles
7 Foley's
8 Gaby's
9 Laurels

10 O'Connor's
11 Robertino's
12 Scott's Gardens
13 Sheila's
14 Stella
15 Stone Chat
16 Swiss Barn
17 Taste of Eden
18 Teo's

families who want leisure facilities and late night musical entertainment. **AL** *International Best Western*, Kenmare Pl, T31816, F31837. Often busy with coach parties, a comfortable and conveniently located hotel opposite the cinema complex. **AL** *Killarney Lodge*, Countess Rd, T36499, F31070. Guesthouse set in walled gardens, with doubles/singles for IR£76/68. **AL** *Lake Hotel*, Muckross Rd, Lake Shore, T31035, F31902. Was an old mansion, which became a hotel in the 19th century (Queen Victoria stayed here in 1861 but don't let this put you off). Closed early December to mid-February.

A *Old Weir Lodge*, Muckross Rd, T35593, F35583. Doubles only, no singles, for IR£56, in this guesthouse. **A** *Victoria House*, Muckross Rd, T35430, F35439. Guesthouse with doubles/singles for IR£48/32.

B *Chelmsford House*, Muckross View, Dromhale, T36402, F33883. B&B open all year. **B** *Failte Hotel*, College St, T33404. Hotel with 12 rooms for IR£56/35 and is open all year. **B** *Linden House* New Rd, T31379, F31196. Hotel with singles/doubles for IR£40 and IR£60. **B** *Lynch's Farmhouse*, off Tralee Airport Rd, T31637. This B&B, open all year, is found 2½ miles (4 km) outside of town. **B** *Sika Lodge*, Ballydowney, T36304, T36746. B&B open all year.

C *Ashbury House*, Tieraboul, T36707. Within walking distance of town centre, B&B part of the Family Homes of Ireland group. **C** *Eagle View*, 21 Woodlawn Pk, T32779. B&B, part of Family Homes of Ireland group, and within walking distance of the town centre. **C** *Fallow Lodge*, Tralee Rd, T33891. This B&B is 5mins by car from the centre. **C** *Larkfield House*, Ballycasheen, T34438, ihk@tinet.ie B&B off the N22 Cork Rd. Has a very good reputation and charges a flat IR£15 per person. **C** *Tamara*, 9 Lewis Rd, T33357. B&B is in town with parking space.

Accommodation in Killarney

Throughout July and August there is a long queue every morning at the accommodation desk in the Killarney tourist office. Hotels and guesthouses, and especially B&Bs and hostels, can all be oversubscribed and without an advance booking you may end up being forced into a higher accommodation bracket than you anticipated. Hotels are uniformly expensive and rooms under IR£60 are as rare as leprechauns. Guesthouses usually offer the comfort of a small hotel, but for good value consider also the private rooms in the hostels. Some of the hostels have their transport waiting outside the bus and train station and if you don't have a bed booked it may be worth arranging something on the spot.

D *Aghadoe House*, T31240, F34300. This An Óige hostel is a superb 17th century mansion, 3 miles (5 km) west of town on the road to Killorglin. **D** *Atlas House*, off Park Rd, T36144, F36533. New hostel with lots of facilities, including parking spaces, and a variety of rooms; the rates, from IR£8.50 for dorm beds to IR£27 for a private double, include continental breakfast. **D** *Bunrower House Hostel*, Ross Rd, T33914, eoshea@tinet.ie On the road that heads down to Ross Castle: is a 20-minute walk from town but hostel transport is available and its location makes it a peaceful place at night. Of the 10 hostels in and around Killarney, Bunrower House wins hands down for its relaxed atmosphere and garden setting. **D** *Fossa Holiday Hostel*, Fossa, T31497. Worth considering if everywhere else is full. **D** *Four Winds*, New St, T33094. Well-equipped and centrally located hostel. **D** *Killarney Railway Hostel*, T35299. Opposite the railway station, is very well equipped and includes a laundry facility. **D** *Neptune's*, off New St, T35255, F36399, neptune@tinet.ie Has been recommended by travellers as the best organized hostel in town. **D** *Park*, Park Rd, T32119. Hostel with 1 private room. **D** *Peacock Farm Hostel*, Gortdromakiery, Muckross, T33557. Although there is a pick-up service it helps to have your own transport. **D** *Súgan*, Lewis Rd, T33104. Was a friendly hostel but a recent change of management may have changed the atmosphere; no private rooms.

Self-Catering *Accommodation Killarney*, 52 High St, T31787, F35238. Handles quality town houses and plush 3-bedroomed suites.

Camping There are a few 4-star sites near town: the *Flesk Muckross Caravan & Camping Park*, Muckross Rd, T31704, F34681, killarneylakes@tinet.ie *Fossa Caravan & Camping Park*, Fossa, T31497, F34459, on the road to Killorglin; and *Fleming's White Bridge Caravan & Camping Park*, T31590, F37474, just off the N22 Cork road. Camping is possible at the following hostels: the *Four Winds*, *Killarney Railway*, *Bunrower* and *Park*.

Expensive *Foley's Restaurant*, High St, T31217, is fairly typical of the town's expensive places, as is *Dingles Restaurant*, New St, T31079, with a mixture of meat and fish dishes, including lobster at IR£18 a pound. Dingles closes on Sunday and between November and March and serves only dinner, while Foley's is open all year around for lunch and dinner. *Gaby's*, High St, T32519, has a reputation, not accepted by everyone, as the best seafood restaurant in town and prices to match; it is open only for dinner and closed on Sunday. Apart from the fresh seafood like lobster, Gaby's also serves steaks and Kerry lamb, and the salmon pâté is a house speciality when it comes to starters. The *Celtic Cauldron*, Plunkett St, T36821, specializing in traditional dishes from Scotland and Wales as well as Ireland, serves a tasty Irish stew flavoured with Guinness for lunch, and starters in the evening such as cockles and mussels. From Wales comes a vegetarian sausage dish and Scotland produces pheasant on the

Eating
● *on map*
Price codes:
see inside front cover

County Kerry

menu. The décor is a bit of a hoot, perhaps a tad too close to an Irish theme pub for comfort, but the food is grand. Expect to pay around IR£20 a head at night. Also worth considering is the Italian-style *Chequers* restaurant in the Randles Court Hotel.

Affordable *Bricín*, High St, has been around for a while and is still a reliable place for a decent meal. St *Teo's*, New St, T36344, has a range of Mediterranean-style dishes served in a modern setting. *Swiss Barn* 17 High St, T36044, specializes in dishes such as fondue and veal Zurichoise, but standard meat and fish dishes are available. Open from 1730 and there is an early bird menu before 1900 for under IR£10 as well as set dinners. *Robertino's*, High St, T34966, has arty Italian décor and serves lunches of pizza, pasta and open sandwiches for around IR£5 and a set dinner between 1600 and 1830 for IR£13. Opposite the *Killarney Park Hotel*, in St Anthony's Place, *Taste of India*, T37770, offers an Asian alternative for lunch or dinner and stays open until midnight or later. Alternatively, *A Taste of Eden*, Bridewell Lane, T33083, offers authentic vegetarian food from 1800, closed Monday, and the restaurant has been recommended by travellers.

Cheap The *Allegro* in High St and *Stella's* on Main St are two well-established restaurants serving quick meals of fish and chips, pizzas and burgers. The *Stone Chat*, down Flemings Lane off High St, is an excellent little joint for café meals (recommended). Also on High St both the *Caragh Restaurant* and *Sheila's* are equally adept at catering to a busy crowd of hungry diners at lunch and dinnertime. Opposite the tourist office in the Innisfallen Centre there are inexpensive cafés suitable for a quick meal. Also here is a large supermarket, ideal for stocking up on picnic meals and other provisions.

Pubs & music At the height of the season it seems as if every pub in the town has music of one sort or another. The hugely popular and undeniably touristy *Laurels*, Main St, T31149, and *Scott's Gardens*, College St, T31060, are both in the centre of town and while not to everyone's taste or musical ear, they can be good fun, especially Laurels. *Charlie Foley's* on New St, T33920, might seem sophisticated by comparison and *O'Connor's* on High St has regular sessions of traditional music. So too does *Tatler Jack* on Plunkett St, T32361, while *McSorley's Pub*, in College St, T37278, has a late night bar until 0100 but no cover charge. The *Danny Man Inn* in the *Eviston House Hotel* on New St, T31640, has music every night from 2100 but coach parties can take over the place. The quaint little *Strawberry Tree* in Plunkett St doesn't have the space for musicians but it has some character when not bursting at the seams with thirsty visitors.

The best pub for young people is *Yer Man's* in Plunkett St and the *Fáilte* hotel has a disco on Friday, Saturday and Sunday nights. The *Gleneagle Hotel* on Muckross Rd has discos for all ages every night of the week.

Many of the hotels within town and out along the road to Kenmare have musical entertainment. The *Gleneagle Hotel*, T36000, has live musicians or singers every night of the week. The *Killarney Manor*, T31551, offers an Irish theme night conjured out of an imaginary social gathering in a 19th-century stately manor, and *Kate Kearney's Cottage* at the Gap of Dunloe has traditional music on Wednesday, Friday and Sunday nights.

In town, the *Arbutus* hotel in College St has traditional music every night, and in the same street the bar in the Fáilte hotel has traditional music on Tuesday, Wednesday and Thursday. The posh *Great Southern Hotel* has suitably restrained nightly cabaret sessions. The *Lake Hotel* has traditional music on Monday, Wednesday and Saturday while *Hotel Europe* goes for Wednesday and Friday nights and confines itself to piano music on Saturday and Sunday.

Shopping **Art** *Fred's Art Studio* is devoted to miniature art and is open from April to October on the Mangerton Rd. Head towards Muckross, turn left immediately after Molly D'Arcy's pub, T34478, and it is 1 mile (1.6 km) up the road. **Books** *Frameworks*, 37 New St,

T35791. Has antique prints and books and a good selection of Irish maps. Shipping arranged. *The Killarney Bookshop*, 32 Main St. **Gifts** *Blarney Woollen Mills*, 10 Main St, have two floors devoted to Irish crafts – especially pottery and crystal - and Aran knitwear, open daily until 2300. *House of Names* in Kenmare Place retails quality heraldic products for Irish and other European names.

Sport

Fishing Tackle, permits and information at *O'Neill's*, 6 Plunkett St, T31970. River Flesk gets spring salmon and peel (grilse), River Laune has salmon and trout while Barfinnihy Lake is stocked with trout. Permits required for rivers and Barfinnihy Lake but not for Killarney lakes. **Horse Riding** *Killarney Riding Stables*, Ballydowney, T31686. 1 mile (1.6 km) west of Killarney off the R562 road to Killorglin. Trips from 1hr to 6 days. **Leisure centre & gym** Indoor heated pool, sauna, gym and outdoor tennis courts at *Club Columba*, T36949, in the *Great Southern Hotel* and open to non-residents.

Transport

Bus There is a regular bus service from Killarney to Cahirsiveen, and in addition during the summer months numerous coaches ply the Ring in an anticlockwise direction. Most of them leave from opposite the tourist office in Killarney, and by arrangement will drop you off along the way; enquire at the tourist office. **Bicycle** *O'Neill Cycle Store*, 6 Plunkett St, T31970. Bike hire: can be delivered to your accommodation place complete with pannier and lock. *Killarney Rent-A-Bike*, T32578. Bike hire with outlets at Market Cross in the town centre, Súgán Hostel and the Flesk Shop opposite the National Park. Have daily and weekly rates and children's bikes. Most of the other hostels also rent bikes. **Car** Car parking can be a problem in July and August. Use one of the designated pay and display car parks or park for free in the parking area next to St Mary's Cathedral. **Car hire**: *Budget Rent a Car*, International Hotel, Kenmare Place, T/F34341 *Hertz*, Plunkett St, T34126. Also have an office at the airport. *Randle's Car Hire*, Muckcross Rd, T31237, F37635. A local firm; better rates. **Taxi** *Vincent Counihan*, 15a High St, T35025. *Sexton Hackney Service*, Mangerton View, T087-221913.

Directory

Banks All the main banks are centrally located and there is also a money exchange office in the tourist office. **Communications** Post office: New St. *Café Internet*, 49 Lower New St, T36741, cafeinternet@tinet.ie **Hospitals and medical services** Hospital: Killarney District Hospital, T31076. Pharmacy: Donie Sheehan, 34 Main St, T31113. Jul-Aug, Mon-Sat 0900-2200, Sun 1100-1300. **Launderette** *James Gleeson*, Brewery Lane, T33877. Mon-Sat 0900-1800, Thu-Fri, 0900-2000. There is also a launderette adjacent to *Atlas House* hostel off Park Rd. **Local radio** *Radio Kerry*, 97FM. **Tourist office** off High St, T31633. Open all year, daily at the height of the season. This is the place to gather information for the whole Kerry region and there is also a bureau de change as well as an extensive range of gifts and literature. **Tours** Boat: Lake cruises on Lough Leane with a commentary on the local ecology and history. The boat departs from Ross Castle and there is a shuttle service from the Destination Killarney Information Kiosk, Scott's Garden, T32638. Sailings at 1100, 1230, 1430, 1600 and 1715, subject to the weather. *Killarney Watercoach Cruises*, T31068 (also bookable through *Dero's*, see coach tours). Sail from Ross Castle on the *MV Lily of Killarney* at 1030, 1200, 1345, 1515 and 1630 and with a commentary covering the folklore and history of the lakes. **Coach**: *Dero's*, Main St, T31251. Offer the standard Ring of Kerry coach tour and a Gap of Dunloe tour, both departing at 1030. *O'Donoghue Brothers*, Old Weir Lodge Guesthouse, Muckross Rd, T31068. Trips through the Gap of Dunloe. **Jaunting cars**: gather on East Avenue Rd opposite the cineplex, opposite the entrance to Muckross House and around Kate Kearney's Cottage at the Gap of Dunloe. The price of a trip, including the services of the jarvey, depends on a variety of factors – time of year, number of passengers, and the weather especially – but expect to pay at least IR£15 and possibly a fair bit more. **Walking**: *Walking Tours*, T7133911/7144339. Daily from Shell Petrol Station in Lower New St, opposite the cathedral, 1100 for a stroll around the National Park. IR£4. *Wilderness Tours*, T066-9760101, F066-9760104, climbers@iol.ie Have various trips, starting at IR£15 for a guided boat and walking tour around the lakes of Killarney or a guided climb of Carrauntoohill. **Useful addresses and telephone numbers** Garda (Police): New Rd, T31222.

County Kerry

Around Killarney

Gap of Dunloe

Ins & outs Take the road out of town towards Killorglin and a short way after the village of Fossa the Gap is signposted on the left. No public transport.

The novelist Charlotte Bronte came to Killarney on her honeymoon in 1854 and while riding through the Gap of Dunloe was suddenly thrown off her horse who took a start and started kicking and trampling around her. Luckily, she emerged unscathed.

Arrive at the head of this glaciated valley mid-morning in July or August and the scene resembles rush hour in a city as coaches, buses and cars jostle for space, never mind the importuning jarveys and camera-toting crowds around Kate Kearney's Cottage. The Gap of Dunloe, however, is some eight miles (12 kilometres) in length and as many visitors walk or pony ride only a couple of miles it is not difficult to leave the crowds behind, either on foot or on a bicycle. A whole-day tour – bookable from any tour company in Killarney (see 'Directory' on page 339) or on the spot outside Kate Kearney's Cottage – is to ride through the Gap on a pony trap and lunch at Lord Brandon's Cottage before returning to Killarney by boat.

The name of *Kate Kearney's Cottage*, T44146, may conjure up an image of a cute, stone-washed, thatched dwelling with a big black kettle on a turf fire, and it probably was when Charlotte Brontë passed this way, but it is now a hectically busy bar, restaurant, souvenir and gift store where the staff deserve a medal for their patience. Nearby, *Moriarty's*, T44144, is a clothing and craft shop with a range of Aran handknits, sports jackets, cashmeres, linens, jewellery, Waterford crystal and Belleek china.

Walks and cycling around Killarney

Killarney may be a busy town but it is very easy to find beautiful and quite empty countryside in the immediate area. *Mac Publications* in Killarney produces a small pamphlet, available from the tourist office, showing maps of several walks and cycles in the area. It includes two excellent expeditions to the east of the lakes, one at Tomies Wood and one along the Gap of Dunloe.

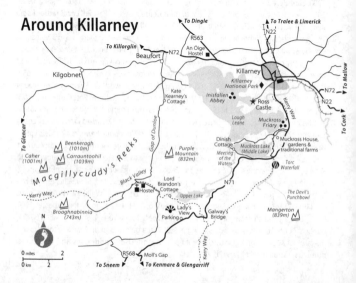

Around Killarney

County Kery

History of the Muckross Demesne

The Muckross Estate belonged to the McCarthy clan, whose leader was known as McCarthy Mór, until the 18th century, despite various attempts at confiscation. It finally passed to a family called Herbert in 1770 and they had Muckross House built between 1840 and 1843. In the process they overspent on their budget and in 1899 the house and estate were sold to Lord Ardilaun, a member of the famous Guinness family. In 1910 the whole property was bought by an American, WB Bourne, as a wedding gift for his daughter, whose family later donated all 11,000 acres of it to the Irish nation.

Tomies Wood

The Tomies Wood walk can be reached by taking the first signposted road to the Gap of Dunloe, just after passing Fossa, a few miles out of town, on the N72. Go down here to a bridge over the road at the River Laune: a left turn here brings you to a wooden gate where it is possible to park a vehicle or leave a bicycle. From here a circular walk of about four miles (6.4 kilometres) is possible. Through the gate the walk passes through a farm and enters forestry. The path forks and makes a circuit of the hillside far up above Lough Leane with wonderful views over the water. Red deer are very common in these woods. The forestry is not overbearing, with a great deal of larch and spruce, and much of the walk is over bare rock with the underlying old red sandstone very conspicuous. The walk passes O'Sullivan's Cascade, down by the lakeside and a short detour off the path.

Gap of Dunloe

The Gap of Dunloe is a much more strenuous walk and makes a much better cycle. The journey through the gap is six miles (9.5 kilometres) and, although a steady climb, it is full of reasons to stop and admire the view. At the top of the gap you are in the Black Valley and a left turn brings you to the *Black Valley Hostel* (see page 363). From here the route takes you to Lord Brandon's Cottage and a spell over quite rough ground, cycling along the shores of the Upper Lake, following the route of the Kerry Way.

The path finally meets the main N71 road at Derricunnihy and where a left turn takes you back into Killarney (but this is not suitable for walkers). The first part of the route also makes a pleasant walk but both cyclists and walkers should be prepared for a very busy scene at the start of the gap where tour buses, tourist and jarveys jostle for places. The crowds soon fall away once you begin the journey into the gap.

Muckross

There are a number of walks around Muckross demesne, following the shores of Muckross Lake and around the house and gardens. One walk begins at the first entrance to the park where the jaunting car drivers wait. The walk goes along the main drive and then cuts over to the lake following its shores. This is a particularly interesting walk since it crosses intercut sections of limestone and sandstone rock where the flora change radically from one section to another. The walk goes around the shores of the lake finishing back at the gate you entered by.

Other walks that have been laid out in the demesne with markers and a description of the sights are **Arthur Young's Nature Trail**, which makes a loop around the little Doo Lough, and the **Mossy Woods Nature Trail** which is close by Muckross House. The house has leaflets describing both walks. Cyclists are welcome in the demesne and there are any number of possible cycle routes around the grounds.

County Kerry

The **Blue Pool** is another short, circular walk, taking about an hour. Its entrance is on the left a few hundred yards/metres beyond the entrance to Muckross along the road to Kenmare. A left turn at the sign for Mangerton brings you to a signposted nature trail, complete with guide ropes for the visually impaired. The walk follows the shores of the Blue Pool, an old mill pond with a strange blue colour due to the large amounts of limestone dissolved in the water. The area around the pool has been planted at various times with beech, alder, and pine but the oak, holly and willow are naturally occurring. This is a good place to notice the devastating effects of the rhododendron that grows invasively here and has to be culled regularly. Its evergreen nature prevents seedlings of native trees from germinating and threatens the life of all the woods around Killarney (see box above).

Ross Castle To the southwest of Killarney is Ross Castle, and a pleasant five-mile (eight-kilometre) walk around the castle and the shores of the lower lake starts in town at the Cathedral. From the cathedral the walk goes into Ross Road, then goes to Ross Island and passes Ross Castle. A circuit can be made of the island, taking in the viewing point at Governor's Rock. Another path goes north along the shores of the lake making a loop back to Ross Road. The walk is through woodland with views of the lake and Innisfallen Island. There are several possible routes for this walk, another taking you over the Deenagh River and back to your starting point via Knockreer House. This route is also suitable for cycling.

Crohane Mountain Travelling on the Kenmare Road out of Killarney (N71) a quite strenuous walk is possible to the summit of Crohane Mountain (2,152 feet/656 metres). About two miles out of the town centre a left turn is signposted to Lough Guitane. Just after this a right turn sets off up the mountain, at first a wide tarmac road but gradually giving way to green road and then open hillside. The goal of the walk is the hilltop and, while there is no path, a route to the top is quite clear. The return journey is about four miles (6½ kilometres) and takes about four hours to complete. A clear day is essential for this walk.

Ring of Kerry

The Ring of Kerry is a 112-mile (180-kilometre) road route around the Iveragh peninsula and throughout the summer months it becomes periodically clogged with traffic as a line of vehicles follows in the wake of a slow-moving coach, caravan or car. The mornings are particularly gruesome because this is when massive tour coaches trundle around, in an anti-clockwise direction, but at any time of the day it is difficult to understand the point of setting out to complete the circuit in one or even two days. At times though, the Ring of Kerry is unavoidable simply because it reaches the far west of the peninsula, where some of the most interesting sites in Kerry are to be found.

The best way to see and enjoy the Iveragh peninsula is by walking part or all of the Kerry Way, a long-distance walk that is described in its relevant sections, beginning on page 360. It takes well over a week to complete the entire Way but with the help of the summer-only *Bus Éireann* service it is quite feasible to walk parts of the Way and return by bus to one's base. Another alternative to driving is to cycle and, while the Ring of Kerry itself is best avoided whenever possible – the roads are narrow and impatient drivers pose a threat to life and limb – there is a little-used route across the middle of the peninsula from Killorglin to Waterville via the Ballaghbeama Pass that is worth taking (see page 353). And

Rhododendrons: the death of the woodlands

As you drive around the peninsulas of the southwest, especially in May, you will notice the beauty of the deep purple flowering rhododendron with its dark evergreen leaves. The plants make an excellent windbreak and, being evergreen, keep the gardens looking alive in winter. There are many different species of rhododendron but the only one to have naturalized here is the purple variety, Rhododendron ponticum. It can grow to over 19½ feet (six metres) in height, loves the acid soil of Kerry and West Cork and produces about 5,000 seeds for each flower head. It was introduced some time in the 18th century from its native habitat around the Black Sea, and it became very popular with the local landlords who planted it as cover for game birds to give their winter sporting activities an extra edge.

What they did not plan for was the ferocity with which the plant colonized the area. Its evergreen leaves, so good for pheasants and windbreaks, are wide and permanent and quickly cover all the ground available. Where they grow in open land this is no problem to other wildlife, except that after several years they will have formed a dense thicket, which will need cutting back, but in Kerry's native woodlands the tree is a disaster. It takes the niche of holly in the oak and beech woods, resulting in a loss of all the wildlife that depends on those trees. Worse still, it provides a permanent shade on the forest floor, wiping out the woodland flowers such as wood sorrel, bluebells, rush, primroses and the many other ground layer plants as well as the insects that depend on them. Worst of all, it prevents the germination of seedling deciduous trees, such as beech and oak, which make the woodlands of Killarney so special. Unchecked it would wipe out the oak forests in a few generations, leaving great tracts of purple flowering woodland with little animal or plant diversity within it. Around Muckross, Torc Mountain, Tomies Woods and Glengarriff eradication programmes take place with people wandering the forests looking for the plants with herbicidal sprays. The pest is hardly likely to be eradicated around these important woodlands, but for the moment it is under control.

County Kerry

to the west of Waterville and Cahersiveen there is a looped route along minor roads, called the Skellig Ring, that accesses Valentia and the Skelligs.

Killorglin

The inland 13-mile (21-kilometre) stretch west of Killarney along the R582 is fairly unremarkable until reaching the small messy-looking market town of Killorglin above the River Laune. During the time of the annual Puck Fair a visit is highly recommended (see box on page 346), but at other times of the year, apart from the angling, there is little to detain the visitor. A short distance north of the town, at Ballykissane Pier, a monument commemorating the death of revolutionary nationalists whose car plunged into the sea in 1916 on their way to meet Roger Casement near Tralee (see box on page 369).

Phone code: 066
Colour map 3, grid B2

L *Caragh Lodge*, Caragh, T9769115, F9769316, caragh@iol.ie A laid-back atmosphere prevails in this elegant Victorian country house on the shores of Lake Caragh a few miles outside Killorglin. **A** *Bianconi*, Lower Bridge Rd, Killorglin, T9761146. B&B with doubles/singles from IR£48/27. **B** *Riverside House*, Killorglin, T9761184. B&B overlooking the River Laune. **B** *Laune Bridge House*, Killarney Rd, Killorglin, T9761161. B&B within walking distance of the town. **D** *Laune Valley Farm Hostel*, T9761488. Just over a mile from town and has 4 private rooms.

Sleeping

Eating At *Caragh Lodge*, fresh seafood, Kerry lamb, home-grown vegetables and home-baking make up an excellent menu in the graceful restaurant overlooking the lake. A reservation for a dinner table (IR£30) is welcome, though essential for non-residents. In Killorglin itself, 2 well-established restaurants are next to each other on Lower Bridge St. The *Bianconi*, T9761146, has bar food all day and in the restaurant, from 1830-2030, seafood and pasta dishes from IR£8 to IR£12. The neighbouring *Nick's Restaurant*, T9761219, is a little more upmarket with starters such as smoked salmon mousse for IR£6, lobster for IR£20 and other meat and fish dishes in the IR£15 range.

Pubs & music *The Fishery*, The Bridge, Killorglin, T9761670, has traditional music on Monday and Saturday nights and mixed cabaret sessions of ballads and traditional the rest of the week.

Directory **Bicycle hire** *O'Shea's*, T9761919. Near the bridge at the Killarney end of town. **Tourist office**, T9761451. 50p-shaped building, close to the roundabout where the road heads out to Glenbeigh. Apr-Oct, daily 0930-1900.

Glenbeigh

Phone code: 066
Colour map 3, grid B2

In Smith's 1786 *History of Kerry* the author recalls how he 'accidentally arrived at a little house in a very obscure part of the parish [of Glenbeigh] where I saw poor lads reading Homer, their master having been a mendicant scholar at an English Grammar School at Tralee.' Modern visitors are unlikely to hear any

Ring of Kerry & Kerry Way

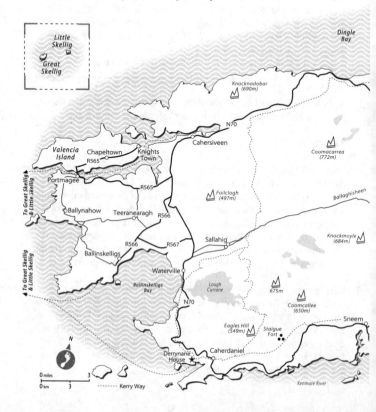

ancient Greek but the small seaside resort of Glenbeigh, six miles (10 kilometres) west of Killorglin, is still a surprisingly pleasant place to stay. Before entering the town from the direction of Killorglin it is difficult to miss the large *Red Fox* pub and adjacent **Kerry Bog Village Museum** by the side of the main road. The pub, T9769288, serves reasonable food and hosts regular musical evenings on Friday, Saturday and Sunday nights, but coach groups make regular stops here and the museum is hardly worth the IR£2.50 admission charge. ■ *T9769184. Daily 0800-1830.*

Glenbeigh itself has a lively pub scene; but on a fine day the real attraction lies outside the village where three miles of uninterrupted beach make up Rossbeigh Strand, a spit of land pointing out into Dingle Bay with sand on either side and no shelving. The area is safe for swimming, challenging for surfers, ideal for horse-riding, and there is a pub nearby. To reach the beach area bear right at the Y-junction at the Cahersiveen end of town. ■ *Horse riding: T9768143. From IR£5 for half an hour, to IR£50 for a full day.* **Rossbeigh Strand**

The Kerry Way passes through Glenbeigh and a recommended local walk can be enjoyed by following the Way west up through Glenbeigh Woods, at the Cahersiveen end of town. The Way makes it way up to high ground from where there is a dramatic view of Rossbeigh Strand and the Dingle peninsula to the north. With a bicycle or car an excursion can be made to the southwest and **Local walk**

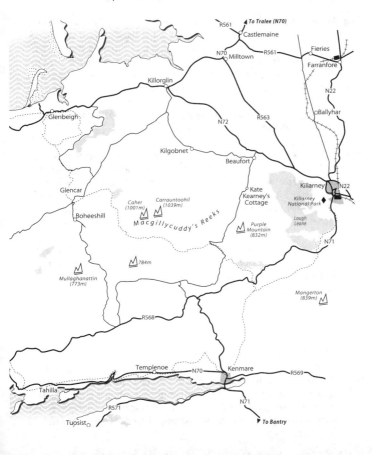

County Kerry

Puck Fair

The oldest festival still being celebrated in Ireland, Puck Fair has an unmistakable pagan heritage that dates back to the Celtic celebration of the god Lug and the beginning of the harvest. The Gaelic word for August is Lughnasa, the festival of Lug, and Puck Fair takes place around the middle of the month, from the 10th to the 12th August in Killorglin. The bacchanalian celebrations begin on Gathering Day when a white male goat is escorted into the market square, lifted on to a makeshift three-tiered platform and crowned with garlands as the King of the Fair. The goat remains perched there, 40 feet above the street, to preside over the alcohol-fuelled revelry that occupies the next couple of days. All the pubs have a special licence to extend their opening hours and the influx of visitors, musicians and assorted entertainers ensures a heady atmosphere. On the evening of 12th August, Scattering Day, the goat is ceremoniously brought down from its perch and led away. Further details available on the internet at http://www.puckfair.ie

the glen of the River Behy along any of the minor roads that branch off south of the N70 west of Glenbeigh. These minor roads peter out in a glorious Kerry landscape where three loughs are surrounded by an amphitheatre of forbidding mountains. If you spend time in the Glenbeigh area it is worth having a copy of map 78 in the Ordnance Survey Discovery Series.

Sleeping **AL** *Towers Hotel*, T9768212, F9768260. Comfortable, old hotel with doubles/singles at IR£94/65. A leisure centre with pool and gym is about to open. **A** *Falcon Inn*, T9768215; F9768411. Hotel at the Killorglin end of town. Charges IR£50/30 for doubles/singles. **A** *Sleeper's Nest*, T9769666, F9769667. just outside Glenbeigh on the N70 at the Killorglin end, does B&B for IR£23 per person and also has a self-catering kitchen where guests can prepare their own meals, plus a laundry.

Camping *Glenross Caravan & Camping Park*, T9768451, F9737474, is next to the *Glenbeigh Hotel* at the Killarney end of town.

Eating If you do not plan to picnic for the day the pubs offer the best bet at lunchtime. At night the *Towers Hotel Restaurant*, T9768212, offers good food and an elegant setting. There is a separate bar for cocktails and the warm dark colours of the décor provide a suitable backdrop for a lazy meal to the accompaniment of live classical piano music. Starters include oysters in a Guinness sauce, while lamb, veal, duck and steaks make up the main courses alongside fish freshly caught in Dingle Bay. Expect to pay about IR£25.

Pubs & music Glenbeigh has the usual quota of pubs: Sweeney's only opens in the summer and is usually as packed as the bar in the *Towers Hotel*, which attracts a younger crowd. The *Glenbeigh Hotel*, at the other end of the village, has music some nights and is popular with locals. The *Village Pub* has music every night.

Directory **Tourist office** There is no tourist office but local information is available at *Brennans* craft shop, T9768252, or the post office, T9768201, both on Main St.

Cahersiveen

Phone code: 066
Colour map 3, grid B1

Both the location and the easy-going character of the place make Cahersiveen (also spelt Caherciveen or Cahirciveen) worth considering as a base for a short stay on the Iveragh peninsula. The town itself is agreeably unprepossessing, accommodating visitors with a sufficient number of amenities – and with 52 pubs, more than sufficient in one respect while conveniently accessing destinations like Valencia Island and the Skelligs, as well as providing some enjoyable local walks. Cahersiveen is also on the Kerry Way, with Glenbeigh easily reached in a day and Waterville an invigorating eight hours walk away. From either town, public transport could return you to Cahersiveen.

The Barracks

An unexpected sight is the fearsome white-painted building that now houses a heritage centre and tourist office. It was built by the British in the 1870s as a Royal Irish Constabulary barracks in response to the Fenian uprising of 1867, which it was feared might lead to a future attack on the new telegraph cable station on Valentia. Is it just pure local blarney or did the British really mix up two sets of building plans and construct in Kerry an edifice intended for the northwest frontier of India? When you see the Barracks you may well wonder.

The **Heritage Centre** occupies three floors of the Barracks, costs IR£3 and includes, on the half hour, the obligatory 15-minute audio/visual show on local history. ■ *T9472777. May to September, Monday-Saturday 1000-1300, 1415-1800, Sun 1300-1800; October to April, Monday-Friday 1000-1300 1415-1700.*

Local walks

The Kerry countryside around Cahersiveen offers opportunities to enjoy a lazy day's walk to a beach and a hill-top picnic and take in along the way excellent examples of stone forts. A useful walking booklet is available for IR£1.50 from the tourist office, but if you are planning to spend more than a day or two in the area then Ordnance Survey Map 83 is ideal. A popular walk takes one across the River Valentia and then the first turn to the left that leads past the Cahergal stone fort. Just before the fort there is a road on the left that leads south to the remains of Ballycarberry Castle. To continue the walk return to the road that leads to the fort and just after it turn to the right along a road that passes Leacanabuaile, another stone fort, before leading to Kimego Wood via a small beach at Cooncrome harbour.

Heading out along the main road in the direction of Glenbeigh brings one to the birthplace of Daniel O'Connell. Today it is just an ivy-clad ruin, but just opposite it there is a landscaped **O'Connell Memorial Park** and a bust of the man who led the highly successful campaign for the right of Catholics to sit in the British parliament.

County Kerry

Sleeping

AL *Cahersiveen Park*, T9472543, F9472893. The only hotel in town, a 2-star establishment, at the Valentia end. Pleasant bar and decent restaurant. **B** *Castleview*, T9472252. At the Valentia end of town. Charges the same as O'Shea's but the rooms don't have their own bathrooms. **B** *Fransal House*, Foilmore, T/F9472997. Very convenient for walkers, being four miles (six kilometres) out of town on the Kerry Way. **B** *Iveragh Heights*, Carhan Rd, T9472545. Handy if walking into town on the Kerry Way. **B** *O'Shea's*, Church St, T9472402. A very central B&B in a large town house next to the post office. **D** *Mortimer's Hostel*, T9472338. Very central. 2 private rooms for IR£15, as well as bikes for hire. **D** *Sive Hostel*, T9472717. Sociable place in the centre of town. Includes 2 private rooms for IR£19.

Camping The *Mannix Point Camping and Caravan Park*, T9472806, F9472988. A good 10-minute walk from town. Has a good reputation.

Eating

Modish *Brennan's Restaurant*, 12 Main St, T9472021, serves lunch Monday to Saturday and daily evening meals with the option of an early bird menu between 1800 and 1900. Expect to pay around IR£20 for an à la carte dinner of locally caught seafood or Kerry lamb. A good place for an evening meal is the *Cahersiveen Park Hotel*, T9472543, where a set dinner is IR£16 or à la carte starters like fried camembert with cranberry sauce for IR£5 and meat and fish dishes around IR£15. Good-value children's meals attract families so perhaps book around 2000 if you'd prefer a quiet meal.

The *Old Oratory* (see 'Shopping' on page 348) has a little coffee shop. Opposite the post office *Frank's Corner* has meals of the 'with chips' variety for under IR£10 while opposite the massive cathedral-like church the Italian-style *Grudles* has pizza and pasta dishes in the same price range. There are a couple of other cafés along the street and some of the pubs, like the *Fertha Bar*, serve food at lunch and dinner time.

Pubs & music There is a good choice of pubs and some of the best serve more than drinks. The ancient-looking *Anchor Bar*, Main St, T9472049, with fishing tackle sold alongside pints, is always worth a visit and especially on a Thursday night when the Kerry orchestra plays here. The *Shebeen Bar*, T9472361, at the Glenbeigh end has Irish dancing some nights while close by *Mike Murt's* is a real old farmer's pub with some character and a hardware section. *O'Donaghue's* also pulls a pint or two for customers not interested in its range of shoes, thermal underwear and assorted items.

Shopping On Main St at the Valentia end of town *Nautical Antiques*, T9473279, has an interesting collection of lamps, portholes, nameplates, bulkhead lamps and the like. *Biggs*, Old Rd, T9472580, is a more conventional antique shop on while *The Old Oratory* is an art gallery and craft shop set up in a disused Protestant church at the Valentia end and selling batik, ceramics, glass, jewellery and knitwear.

Sport **Fishing** *E Casey*, T9472474. Can arrange fishing off a boat. 1800-2130. IR£15 including the tackle.

Transport **Bicycles** Bike hire. At the Valentia end of town.

Directory **Tourist office** the Barracks, T9472589. May-Sep, Mon-Sat 1000-1300, 1415-1800, Sun 1300-1800; Oct-Apr, Mon-Fri 1000-1300 1415-1700. **Tours** Every Wednesday morning a Culture Bus provides transport and a guide for visits to the local fort, castle and turf briquette-making machine. The IR£7 seats can be booked at the tourist office.

Valentia Island

Ins & outs There is a land bridge from Portmagee and a passenger and car ferry that operates a shuttle service throughout the day, T9476141, from Reenard just west of Cahersiveen. IR£4/3 return/single.

Phone code: 066
Colour map 3, grid B1

In a mad rush simply to 'do' the Ring of Kerry travellers often skip Valentia Island and thereby pass up an ideal chance to slow down the pace and explore at leisure one of the modest gems of the area. The island is easily reached by land or ferry and even though the land bridge was only completed in 1971 Valentia had a distinguished role in the history of communication. Late-night listeners of the BBC will be familiar with the name of Valentia, the island being the former site of an important meteorological station (now moved to Cahersiveen). It was also the site for the first transatlantic cable station (see box on page 349), and a railway line was built so that

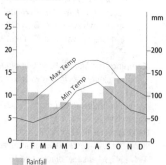

Valentia

Rainfall

Subterranean blues

The first attempt to lay a cable under the Atlantic Ocean took place in 1857 but ended in failure. A small fleet of ships set off slowly from Valentia lowering cables as they went, but after only 280 miles the cable snapped and the enterprise was put on hold. The following year, a second attempt was made, this time using an American ship leaving Halifax and laying cable on its route east while a British ship did the same in its route west from Valentia. The two boats met successfully in the middle and the first transatlantic radio link between the new and old worlds was made. The underwater cable was to snap more than once in those pioneering days but a permanent station was established on the island and Morse code was transmitted at the rate of 17 words a minute.

The cable operators on Valentia were a highly paid, non-Irish elite with their own cricket pitch and tennis courts, but one or two locals were also employed and one cable message did slip out to the US in 1916 with news of the Easter Rising. New technology, ironically developed on Valentia, saw the demise of the cable station and it finally closed down in 1965. Today the wind blows across the crumbling asphalt of the tennis courts and the empty houses of the operators are

travellers from Europe could make their way here for the shortest possible transatlantic sea crossing. This never happened and the railway closed down in the 1950s. Go back a hundred years, though, to when the first transatlantic cable was being laid, and Valentia was the Silicon Valley and Cape Canaveral of Victorian Britain. Today the appeal of a visit to Valentia is simply its off-the-beaten-track location, the remains and reminders of its past history and the opportunity to linger aimlessly around a sub-tropical corner of Kerry. The Irish poet Aubrey de Vere (1814-1902) advised his friend Tennyson to visit Valentia (which he did) and listen to the sound of the waves, assuring him that those at Beachy Head in England would pale into insignificance.

The Skellig Experience

This interpretative centre is on the left side immediately after reaching Valentia from Portmagee. Exhibits deal with the lives of the monks and the story of the lighthouse that was built on Skelligs in 1826 and operated until 1986, manned by a team of three who were relieved by helicopter from Castletownbere. A 15-minute audiovisual show focuses on the Skellig Michael monastery and there is also a section on the wildlife, very useful for brushing up on bird identification before actually visiting the Skelligs. Also useful is the retail area with books on local history and wildlife and a café serving snacks and light meals. ■ T9476306. Daily 1100-1700. IR£3.

County Kerry

Slate quarry   Another ambitious Victorian enterprise that focused on Valentia was a slate quarry that opened in 1816 and operated until 1911, employing up to 400 men at its height. Huge sheets of slate 14 feet (four metres) long were lifted out of the mine and cut to size on site by a steam-powered saw, the remains of which can be seen at the mouth of the quarry. Valentia slate, possessing what experts call a good cleavage, could be easily split into thin slabs of exceptional length; it was highly valued and used to grace the roofs of noted London buildings (like the Houses of Parliament) as well as being exported to South America (San Salvador railway station). Although there is little to see nowadays, apart from a tasteless shrine constructed in one of the tunnels, the location and the vast piles of broken slate lying about help create a strong sense of place. ■ *24 hours. Signposted at the T-junction when approaching Knightstown from the west.*

Heritage centre   The ex-National School setting for this little museum suits the educational content of what was the schoolroom, now devoted to the history of the cable station. There are also sections on local craft industries. Interesting any time and a godsend on a wet afternoon. ■ *T9476353. April to September, Monday-Saturday 1100-1700. IR£1. Situated on the right-hand side of the road just outside Knightstown on the road to the slate quarry.*

Glanleam   The house was the seat of the local 19th-century bigwigs, the Knights of Kerry,
House   but it is the collection of exotic plants in the gardens that make a visit so
subtropical   intriguing for interested visitors. Despite strong winter winds, which occa-
gardens   sionally wreak havoc on the gardens, the balmy influence of the Gulf Stream makes Valentia a subtropical greenhouse when it comes to cultivating plants that would not survive outside the southwest of the country. ■ *T9476176. May to October, daily 1100-1700. IR£2.*

Sleeping   **B** *Glenreen Heights*, T9476241. About one mile west on the way to Chapeltown, charges around IR£34 for doubles or IR£22 for singles. **B** *Moorings Guesthouse*, Portmagee, T9477108. Doubles/singles for IR£42/25. **B** *Spring Acre*, Knightstown, T9476141. One of the few B&Bs in the area, charges around IR£34/22 for doubles/singles. **C** *The Islander*, Knightstown, T9476171. Has doubles for IR£29, singles for IR£17.50 if a room is available after 2100, and an evening meal is only IR£7.50. **D** *Coombe Bank House*, Knightstown, T9476111. This Victorian house is a combined B&B and hostel, stays open all year and includes private rooms for IR£10 per person. **D** *The Ring Lyne Hostel*, Chapeltown, T9476103. Has lots of facilities, including private rooms, B&B and bike hire. There are also some B&Bs in Portmagee, including the superior **D** *Royal Pier Bar & Hostel*, T9476144. Overlooking the harbour. Includes private rooms for IR£17 and despite its very faded elegance there is still some character to the place. **D** *Valentia Island Hostel*, Kingston, T9476141. An Óige hostel that uses the old coastguard cottages. While here too there is plenty of character the creature comforts are at a premium.

Eating   In Knightstown *The Gallery*, T9476105, is an interesting place to visit and not just for a meal; it combines its dashing restaurant with a gallery of ethnic art and opens daily for lunch and dinner. *Boston's* bar also has a restaurant, T9476140, serving tasty and affordable meals. The *Ring Lyne Bar*, T9476103, in Chapeltown serves food all day along the lines of seafood specials, steaks and Irish stew. The tea room at *Glanleam House* does lovely home baked goodies between 1100 and 1900 and the *Fisherman's Bar*, T9477103, has outside tables when the weather is not inclement: the bar menu includes a tasty chowder and appetizing crab claws for starters or snacks, and meals of seafood and an Irish stew. Pubs in Portmagee also do food and the *Moorings Guesthouse* has a small restaurant for evening meals and a set menu for around IR£15

Hermits and hedonists on the Skelligs

The desert sands of Egypt provide the unlikely backdrop to the Skelligs, because it was here that the Coptic Church based itself as a splinter Christian group in the sixth century, practising a strict monastic tradition. In the seventh century a group of eremetical Irish monks first established a settlement on Skellig Michael and their anchorite community remained there until the 12th century. They survived a Viking raid in 823 but eventually moved to Ballinskelligs on the mainland.

Although Pope Gregory decreed a 10-day change in the calendar in 1582 it was never applied to the Skelligs and out of this developed the scurrilous Skellig Lists. They arose from the tradition of marrying just before the onset of Lent, during which no marriage could take place, and the riling of those who remained eligible but unwed. The Skellig Lists paired off in comic and unkind verse suitable bachelors and spinsters. In fact the Skelligs, where Lent had still not started, did become popular for late marriages and occasionally they became infamous for all-night drinking binges, so much so that one occasion the police were called and they had to row out to Skellig Michael.

before 1900. *The Islander*, T9476171, has an agreeably affordable restaurant below its B&B and though the style of the place may be a little plain the speciality is fresh fish brought in at the local harbour. At Reenard Point, the ferry runs continuously, so linger as long as you like at *Point Bar*, Reenard Point, T9472165, nearby. It's been here since the middle of the 19th century and now serves delicious seafood, salads and brown bread sandwiches as well as hot meals for under IR£ 10.

Sport **Diving** *Des Lavelle*, T9476124. Well established. *Dive Centre*, T9476204. *Valentia Hyperbaric Diving Centre*, T9476225. **Fishing** Deep-sea fishing: *Michael O'Sullivan*, Royal Pier, T9476144.

The Skelligs

"Whoever has not stood in the graveyard on the summit of that cliff among the beehive dwellings and their beehive oratory does not know Ireland through and through." Hyperbole indeed from George Bernard Shaw, but it is difficult not to agree with him. When a sea mist swirls above the Skelligs they seem to float on the ocean like eerie volcanoes in an imaginary scene from Celtic mythology. The only problem with this magic is that so many people are now heeding Shaw's advice that attempts are being made to limit the number of visitors who can stand on the 44 acres of Skellig Michael, the largest of a group of three rocky islets that make up the Skelligs.

Skellig Michael (also called Great Skellig) with its twin peaks 715 feet (217 metres) and 650 feet (198 metres) rising above the Atlantic, is the only one of the rocks that can be landed on and, while a visit here is justifiably the main point of the boat trip, the journey there and back also affords a priceless opportunity to view and admire the sea birds that inhabit these rocky outposts of Europe.

'Moving about the coasts of Kerry afterwards, I understood what a symbol Skellig Michael must have been to those who were neither monks nor clergy, seeing it on the horizon, a single or a double peak, but always blue, always or often, with its nimbus of white cloud, its trailing coif of holiness.'

Geoffrey Grigson (1905-85), Country Writings

The monastery Skellig Michael is home to some of the few surviving examples of domestic monastic buildings in the early Christian era. After disembarking, visitors follow a path, created in the days when a lighthouse was operating on Skellig Michael, along the southeast cliffs to a series of enclosures perched on steep terraces. The monastic settlement, dedicated to St Michael, the saint of high places, is made up of six beehive cells, the largest of which is 15 feet by 12 feet

(4.5 metres by 3.6 metres), and two oratories, one of which seems designed for solitary meditation. The guides will explain their characteristic features, but the sense of wonder comes from being here and wondering why – and in the winter months how – anyone even thought of living here. The dry masonry structures are truly remarkable, and not least because they have survived for so long in such an exposed location.

Bird life During the course of the boat trip, and especially around the landing area on Skellig Michael, itself there are exceptional opportunities to admire the sea-birds at close quarters. It helps to have some basic ornithological knowledge, and a visit to the Skellig Heritage Centre on Valentia will help in this respect (see page 349), but it is usually easy to recognzie the yellow-headed gannet because of its size – a wing span of around six feet (1.8 metres) – the elegant angle of its wings in flight and its dramatic vertical dive into the water. Some 20,000 pairs inhabit Little Skellig and these may be seen at close quarters if your boat goes in close to the rock for a view of basking seals, which are also a common sight. The guillemot, seen and heard particularly around the landing stage area, is a seagull with a black tip to its wings. They spend the winter out at sea but come to Skellig Michael to breed between March and August. The razorbill is similar to but smaller than the guillemot and is sometimes recognized by its habit of flying in line in small flocks. Both these birds nest in crevices and ledges of the cliff face. Up until around the first week of August it is difficult to avoid seeing the puffin, unmistakable due to its multicoloured beak, dutifully standing at the head of its burrowed nest and occasionally waddling away with as much dignity as it can muster.

Sleeping & eating If you want to spend a night on Skellig Michael you will have to become a tour guide for the summer months. Otherwise it is strictly a day trip, bring your own picnic and sensible footwear and be extremely careful with children or elderly folk when disembarking and making your way to the monastic buildings.

Directory **Tours** There is a bewildering number of operators running boat trips to the Skelligs but their prices are constant and it is more a matter of choosing one that departs from somewhere you find convenient. **From Ballinskelligs**: *Sean Feehan*, 9479182; *Joe Roddy*; T9474268; or *Brendan Walsh*, T9479147. **From Portmagee**: *Casey's*, T9477125; *Murphy's*, T9477156; *Brendan O'Keefe*, T9477103; or *Michael O'Sullivan*, T9474255. **From Valentia**: *Dan McCrohan*, T9476142. **From Caherdaniel**: *Sean O'Shea*, T9475129. **From Cahersiveen**: *Casey's*, T9472437/9472069; *Seanie Murphy*, T9476214. *Eoin Walsh*, T9476327, operate from Valentia, Renard and Portmagee.

Waterville

Phone code: 066
Colour map 3, grid B1

Another landmark town on the Ring of Kerry, Waterville is pleasantly low-key and consists of the usual range of pubs, hotels and restaurants: like Cahersiveen to the north it suggests itself as a base for exploring the western end of the peninsula. From Waterville there is also the very useful cross-peninsula road to Killarney via the Ballaghisheen Pass, which accesses the frequently ignored interior and also allows one to escape the traffic on the main N70 road. There is little of note in the town itself but all the attractions of the Iveragh peninsula are conveniently accessible. In addition, Waterville does have an attractive beach, which is safe for swimming, and at times it is possible to spot a porpoise or dolphin close to shore and terns may often be seen doing their acrobatic searches for a meal in the water.

AL *Bay View*, T9474122, F9474504. Dates back to the late 19th century and has comfortable rooms with some nice sea views for IR£80/45. In the very centre of town. **AL** *Butler Arms Hotel*, T9474144, F9474520. Facing the sea, this hotel has a wonderful air of faded elegance as if reluctant to forget the era when star guests like Charlie Chaplin and Virginia Woolf came here to stay. There are various deals available when staying more than 1 night. **A** *The Strand*, T9474436, F9474635. A 1-star hotel charging IR£50/25. **A-C** *The Old Cable House*, Cable Station, T/F9474233. Just what the name indicates and dates back to 1856 when the cable to North America was being laid (see box on page 349). Double rooms rates vary from IR£27 to IR£60 depending on the season and supply and demand so bear this in mind. **D** *Peter's Place*, Main St. An IHH independent hostel. As well as dorm beds there is 1 private room but there is no telephone.

Camping *Waterville Caravan & Camping Park*, T9474191, F9474538. An award-winning place just outside of town off the main N70 road to Cahersiveen.

Sleeping

The *Beachcove Café* is at the *Butler Arms* end of town and serves inexpensive chicken/lasagne/scampi 'with chips' meals. Close by, the bistro-style *Shéilin Seafood Restaurant*, T9474231, is recommended for its affordable and well-prepared meals. Specials are on the blackboard outside and between 1800 and 1930 there is a set dinner for IR£14. Also open for lunch. Just past the *Butler Arms* hotel at the *Huntsman*, T9472124, Kerry lamb and veal are available but this expensive restaurant focuses on fish, especially shellfish, and specials such as shark or black bream may be available depending on local catches.

Eating

Perhaps it is a legacy from the Victorian and Edwardian times when genteel folk came to Waterville, but the music scene here is comparatively subdued. The bar in the Bay View Hotel is always worth a look as traditional music sessions take place most nights in July and August and at weekends during the rest of the year. The *Villa Marie* and the *Lobster Bar* have music some evenings during the week, and the *Jolly Swagman* comes alive with a tune or two on Saturday nights. The *Fisherman's Bar* in the *Butler Arms* hotel has no music but it is a comfortable place to relax and have a chat.

Pubs & music

Fishing Waterville has long been famous as an angling centre. *Tadhg O'Sullivan's* T9474433. Shop dispensing information and retailing tackle.

Sport

County Kerry

Ballinskelligs & the Skellig Ring

The Skellig Ring is the name given to a scenic route that links Waterville and Cahersiveen via Ballinskelligs and Portmagee. Characterized by narrow roads and unmarked junctions it is ideal for cycling, and with map No 83 in the Ordnance Survey Discovery series one could explore the landscape as well as fitting in a trip to the Skelligs from Ballinskelligs.

From Waterville take the main road to Cahersiveen and after three miles (five kilometres) take the left turn signposted the Skellig Ring (R567). After 1.8 miles (2.8 kilometres) from the beginning of this Skellig Ring road there is an unmarked road going south down to a lovely little inlet of Ballinskelligs Bay; a perfect spot for anyone wishing to enjoy Kerry in complete isolation. Back on the R567 road carry on for another two miles (3.2 kilometres) and turn left at the T-junction. This road leads to Ballinskelligs, passing the *Sigerson Arms* pub and reaching an unmarked crossroads. The left turn goes down to a lovely expanse of sandy beach overlooking Ballinskelligs Bay and the sea-worn ruins of Ballinskelligs Abbey, where the monks from Skellig Michael are said to have moved to when they left their rocky sea-girt abode. The ruins at the western end of the beach are those of a McCarthy castle. Straight ahead at the

Phone code: 066
Colour map 3, grid B1

crossroads leads to the departure point for boats to the Skelligs while a right turn passes the *An Óige* hostel before weaving its way to Portmagee and a route back (on the R565) to the main N70 road south of Cahersiveen. After passing the *An Óige* hostel the first left turn takes one along a bumpy road out to Bolus Head, passing the pre-Famine village of Kildreelig.

Cycle ride An exhilarating cycle, or a drive if you must, from Caherciveen to Killarney via Ballaghasheen is a journey of 40 miles (64 kilometres), with the option of an overnight stay at Glencar. Leave Cahersiveen on the road to Kells and after almost two miles (three kilometres) turn right on the 11-mile (17-kilometre) road to Lissatinnig Bridge. At the bridge the spectacular route through the Pass rises to about 1,000 feet (300 metres). Turn left at the Bealalaw Bridge junction, where the route meets the Kerry Way, which shortly bends to the right for Glencar and the *Climbers' Inn* (see page 363).

From Glencar travel for 3½ miles (six kilometres), passing Lake Acoose, ignoring the turn-offs for Glenbeigh and then Killorglin. Follow the signs for Killarney and Beaufort.

Sleeping **B** *Sigerson Arms*, T9479104. Pub that does B&B. **B** *Island View*, T9479128. The only place registered with Bord Fáilte, with 2 double rooms that cost either IR£34 en suite or IR£30 sharing a bathroom; singles are IR£23.50 or IR£21.50, and a IR£12 evening meal is also available. **D** *Ballinskelligs Hostel*, T9479229. An Óige hostel. Bring your own food for lunch.

Entertainment Set dancing takes place every Wednesday and Saturday night at the *Sigerson Arms*. The *Ballinskelligs Inn*, T9479106, has live music most nights but telephone to make sure.

Directory **Tours** Sea cruises around Puffin Island, the Skelligs and St Finian's Bay are offered by *Glen Pier Boats*, T9479272.

Caherdaniel to Sneem

Phone code: 066 Along the southwest coast of the Iveragh peninsula, sandwiched between the small towns of Caherdaniel and Sneem, there are two major attractions - Derrynane House and the Staigue Fort – as well as a fine stretch of beach. Two diving schools in the vicinity complement the cultural attractions, while the very touristy town of Sneem only serves to highlight the relative worth of towns like Cahersiveen that manage to avoid selling out completely to the summer tourist trade.

Derrynane Derrynane House is the ancestral home of **Daniel O'Connell**, who earns his **House & park** place on the IR£20 note as one of the most important figures in 19th-century Irish history. It was built in 1702 and Daniel O'Connell, the adopted heir of a childless uncle who had inherited the house, took up residence in 1825 and made substantial alterations. The O'Connell family lived in Derrynane until 1958, but the house had begun to decay long before that and what you see today are largely the restored parts that O'Connell himself built. Some of his original furniture is still in place and there are various portraits of him, the most outlandish being an allegorical painting of the hero as Hercules breaking the chains of slavery. His library contains various gifts presented to him as well as personal items such as his duelling pistols, and many of the knick-knacks around the House are highly ornate and artistic but typically Victorian in their ugliness. ■ *T9475113. May to September, Monday-Saturday 0900-1800, Sunday 1100-1900; April and October, Tuesday-Sunday 1300-1700; November*

The Great Liberator

Daniel O'Connell (1775-1847) was born just outside Cahersiveen, the nephew and future heir of a Catholic landowner. As a barrister he rose to fame for his opposition to legislation that prevented Catholics from sitting in parliament and from holding senior positions such as that of a judge. The demand for Catholic Emancipation became a highly successful mass-movement across the country and O'Connell's skill as an organizer and an orator played no small part in the eventual success of the campaign, with O'Connell himself becoming the first Irish Catholic to sit in the British House of Commons. He went on to campaign for the repeal of the Act of Union, although he was not a separatist and envisaged Ireland as a self-governing unit within the British state. The repeal movement reached a crisis in 1843 when a series of huge open-air demonstrations led to the British government banning such a 'monster meeting' due to be held at Clontarf in 1843. O'Connell backed down and a week later he was arrested and imprisoned. Although released soon after, the whole experience seems to have weakened his resolve and he died in 1847 worn out by a lifetime of struggle. He remained a potent figurehead for moderate nationalists and when the foundation stone for his statue was laid in what is now O'Connell Street in Dublin some half a million people gathered to pay tribute; it was the largest single political event in the history of Ireland in the 19th century.

to March, Saturday and Sunday 1300-1700. IR£2.50. Dúchas site; guided tours available, café. Signposted on the N70 at Caherdaniel.

The 300-acre grounds are now part of the Derrynane National Park and contain pleasant gardens exhibiting many of the delicate sub-tropical plants that flourish in this corner of Ireland. The monstrous-looking palms that grow near the water as you approach the house are gunnera. From the house a path leads south to an excellent beach with an ogham stone and sand dunes; at low tide it is possible to walk out to Abbey Island, which has a footpath around it offering splendid views of the coastline and the Skelligs.

Staigue Fort is a superb stone ringfort, one of the finest to be seen anywhere in **Staigue Fort** Ireland, complete with a finely constructed system of stairways that lead up to the 13-foot-thick (four metres) ramparts. Its walls stand up to 18 feet (5.5 metres) high and while its age is uncertain it is likely to have been constructed in the Iron Age, roughly contemporary with the fortress of Dún Aengus on the Aran Island of Inishmore. Considering that Staigue Fort is around 2,000 years old, the intact state of its dry-stone walls is literally a monumental testimony to the skill of its builders and designers. In the *Staigue Fort Hotel*, where the road up to the site begins, the **Staigue Fort Exhibition Centre** has the obligatory video. ■ *Easter to end September, daily, 24 hours. Honesty box requesting 50p. Situated west of Caherdaniel, before Castlecove, and signposted up a narrow road off the N70.*

AL *Derrynane Hotel*, T9475136; F9475160. Facilities include an outdoor pool, steam **Sleeping** room, sauna, gym and tennis courts. Walking weekends are organized regularly and doubles/singles are IR£70/45. Best accommodation in the area. Recommended. B&Bs in Caherdaniel include **B** *Angela O'Sullivan*, Caherdaniel, T9475124. B&B charging IR£34 for a double and IR£23.50 for a single. **B** *The Olde Forge*, Caherdaniel, T9475140. B&B at IR£34/23.50 for doubles/singles. **D** *Caherdaniel Village Hostel*, T/F9475277, skelliga@aol.ie Has a dozen beds but no private rooms. **D** *Carrigbeg Country Hostel*, T9475229. A short distance to the west of town, this hostel includes 1 private room for

IR£15 and laundry facilities. **D** *Traveller's Rest*, T9475175. IHH hostel open all year, includes 2 private rooms for IR£17.

Camping *Wave Crest Caravan Park*, T/F9475188. Overlooking Kenmare Bay, accepts tents and is a mile (1.6 km) from town in the direction of Sneem.

Eating There are a couple of places to eat in Caherdaniel but nowhere to write home about. The restaurant in the *Derrynane Hotel* serves a remarkably good and very popular dinner for IR£22 and you are well advised to book, while there is always the *Scarriff Inn*, T9475132, out on the main road but this place is overrun with coach parties. *The Stepping Stone*, T9475444, a short walk from the harbour and open nightly for dinner only, is a tiny place serving modern-style dishes like duck with roast pear. Prices are reasonable: expect to pay around IR5 for a meal. *The Blind Piper*, T9475126, opens between May and September, for IR£5-10 lunches and dinners around IR£25 in a traditional-style restaurant with exposed beams and stone walls. Seafood and local lamb are the specialities; closed Monday. The café in Derrynane House is not bad and the adjoining beach suggests itself for a picnic.

Sport **Diving** *Skellig Aquatics Dive Centre*, T9475277, skelliga@iol.ie Handles scuba diving for experienced divers as well as complete beginners and also organizes sea angling and boat trips. **Walking** *Derrynane Walks*, T9475136. Based at the *Derrynane Hotel*, organizes walking weekends that cover the history and ecology of the area. Average price for a package IR£90 per person. **Water sports** *Derrynane Harbour Water Sports Centre*, T9475266. Open daily for windsurfing, sailing, canoeing and water skiing.

Sneem

Phone code: 064
Colour map 3, grid B2

This figure-of-eight town, joined in its centre by a picturesque little bridge, is pronounced 'shneem' (Gaelic *snaidhm*, meaning 'knot', describing the twisting course of the river that bisects the village). Tourist literature describes it as "a cornucopia of colour" and the small houses painted brightly and cheerfully suggest an organized and determined effort to woo the visitors who might think this is what a quaint Irish village should look like. An unusual attraction is the **Sculpture Park**, which consists of a strange series of sculptures from assorted exotic locations in Asia and elsewhere. The park includes a 1983 monument to an Irish president, Cearbhaill Ó Dálaigh (1974-6), who has been completely forgotten about by most people, but whom Sneem remembers because he retired here. In the old courthouse in the centre of the village the tiny **Sneem Museum** has a motley collection of items of local interest, best reserved for a wet afternoon, but no mention of the poet Alfred Percival Graves (1846-1931), father of the writer Robert Graves, who grew up in the area.

Sleeping **LL** *Parknasilla*, T7145122, F7145323. Top of the range in town. A massive Victorian mansion set in acres of semitropical gardens and boasting an indoor swimming pool, sauna, tennis courts and its own 9-hole golf course. If you need to ask what the room rates are then you probably can't afford to stay here: IR£166 for a double and IR£96 a single, and children under 10 are not welcome. **AL** *Tahilla Cove Guesthouse*, T7145204, F7145104. Another upmarket establishment situated by the sea shore, 5 miles (8 km) east of Sneem. Set in a beautiful shoreline garden with original pre-war décor; a 3-day package including dinners is IR£150 or IR£135. Not terribly child friendly. **B** *Arch House*, North Square, Sneem, T7145127. B&B. **B** *Bank House*, North Square, Sneem, T7145226. B&B. **B** *Derry East Farmhouse*, T7145193. B&B outside of town at the Waterville end but within walking distance. **D** *Fáilte Hostel*, Shelborne St,

T7142333. Has two private rooms and offers bike hire. **D** *Harbour View Hostel*, T7145276. IHH hostel with a laundry and 2 private rooms for IR£20. Rents bicycles.

The *Blue Bull*, T7145382, is a pub in South Square that serves food for lunch, dinner in the IR£10 to IR£20 range, and seafood a speciality as well as traditional Irish fare like bacan and cabbage and Irish Stew. The *Sacre Coeur*, T7145186, is a well-established restaurant at the other end of town, also open for lunch and dinner and in a similar price bracket as the Blue Bull. The *Riverain Restaurant*, T7145245, in North Square does light snacks as well as lunch and candle-lit dinner and the nearby *Village Kitchen* serves inexpensive, decent home-cooked food. The *Pygmalion*, T7145122, in the Great Southern Hotel is the place to go for a special night out, dinner being around IR£23 in this elegant restaurant, and it is worth arriving early enough to enjoy a stroll around the gardens and woods.

Eating

The *Blue Bull* usually has music Wednesday to Friday and Saturday nights, the *Fisherman's Knot* has sessions on a Sunday night and *O'Shea's* bar in North Square has traditional music every Wednesday and Sunday nights in August and September.

Pubs & music

Kenmare

This market town, along with Killarney and Sneem, completes the Iveragh's tourist triumvirate. It used to offer itself as a sedate alternative to Killarney's summer mayhem but in terms of restaurants and hullabaloo Kenmare is fast catching up. Given its location, however, it is difficult to avoid Kenmare and the amenities are useful, especially if *en route* to or from the Beara or the Kerry Way. The town was founded by Sir William Petty in 1670 and laid out in the late 18th century by the first Marquess of Lansdowne. The English influence is apparent in the X-shaped design of the town, which is not at all typical of Irish settlements.

Phone code: 064
Colour map 3, grid B3

Fair day of the year is 15 August, when farmers trade cattle and horses in hard cash and a slap of the palm, and a general air of roguery enlivens the atmosphere.

County Kerry

The Heritage Centre displays a great deal of information on the history of the town and has separate sections on the town's association with lacemaking through the Kenmare Poor Clare Convent and with the radical nun, Margaret Anna Cusack (1829-99) who was forced to leave Kenmare because of her politics. ■ *T41491. Mid-June to late September, Monday-Saturday 0915-1900. Rest of the year Monday-Saturday 0915 to 1730.*

There is also a **Kenmare Lace and Design Centre**, where one can see lace being made in the traditional manner and purchase finished lace as well as a DIY beginner's kit. Pick up a free copy of the *Kenmare Heritage Trail*, which guides one around the local sites of historical interest.

Kenmare Heritage Centre

The official full title for this park is the Glen Inchaquin Waterfall Amenity Area and there is a free leaflet available from the tourist office that includes a map. There is a set walk that takes one past the waterfall, streams, a bathing spot, lakes and woodland and the whole place is very suitable for families or anyone wanting a gentle stroll. Bring a picnic or make do with the shop selling hot drinks and home-baked snacks. For a more serious day's walking consider completing a day or two of the Kerry Way. ■ *Daily. IR£2. Situated eight miles (12 kilometres) from Kenmare on the road to Castletownbere and then signposted on the left.*

Glen Inchaquin Park

Kenmare's stone circle, easily reached from the tourist office along Market Street and across the bridge over the River Finnehy, is one of the largest in Ireland. There are 15 stones making up the circle and in the centre is a fine dolmen.

Stone circle

Derreen garden	Derreen is a woodland garden planted by the fifth Marquess of Lansdowne in the 1870s. Visitors can collect a useful little map that describes and identifies some of the numbered plants, and there is plenty to see. The 140-foot (42-metre) giant conifers seen here today were introduced from North America, and the exotic tree ferns came from New Zealand. One tree, the 60-foot-high (18 metres) *Cryptomeria Japonica Elegans* with a girth of 10 feet (three metres), grows directly across the path in the rock garden and requires an artificial support. The Caha Mountains and Kilakilloge Harbour, which afford such stunning views from Derreen Garden, help shelter and protect the grounds and facilitate the healthy array of plants and trees that are rarely found outside of the southwest. ■ *April to September 1100-1800. IR£2. Tea room and picnic area. Situated at Lauragh, 15 miles (24 kilometres) west of Kenmare on the R571 road.*

Sleeping   Two of the country's most exclusive 5-star hotels are in Kenmare, along with a number of regular 3-star places, but there are also countless B&Bs, all charging around IR£35/IR£24 for doubles/singles.

LL *Park Hotel*, T41200, F41402, phkenmare@iol.ie http://parkkenmare.com For sheer aristocratic class it is hard to beat this place, where each room is furnished with wonderful antique furniture, a giveaway at IR£316 for a night in the high season. The Great Southern and Western Railway Company built the Park Hotel in 1897 for the idle rich from England who spent a night here, after reaching Kenmare by train, before being taken by horse and carriage to the sister hotel at Parknasilla (see page 356). **LL** *Sheen Falls Lodge*, T41600, F41386, sheenfalls@iol.ie http://www.iol.ie/sheenfalls A snip at IR£270, this is a modern luxury hotel with all the amenities one would expect. **L** *Riversdale House Hotel*, T41299, F41075. Just over the double-arched bridge on the road to Killarney. Ask for a room with a view of the estuary and hills to take full advantage of the hotel's riverside location.

AL *Lansdowne Arms*, William St, T41368, F41114. Charges IR£80/50 for doubles/singles. **A** *Brass Lantern*, Old Railway Rd, T42600, F42601, thebrasslantern@tinet.ie This newish place is an upmarket guesthouse that offers comfort and good service. **A** *The Rose Garden*, Gortamullen, T42288, F42305, rosegard@iol.ie http://www.euroka.com/rosegarden A smart, meticulously run guesthouse just outside of town on the Ring of Kerry road. The Dutch owners provide hotel-standard service, including in-house movies, and a good-value evening meal for around IR£12. **A** *Wander Inn*, T41038, F41408. Small hotel with rooms for IR£50/20.

B *Ard na Mara*, Pier Rd, T/F41399. B&B with a riverside location. **B** *Rose Cottage*, The Square, T41330. Open all year and as central as you can get.

Camping   *Ring of Kerry Caravan & Camping Park*, Reen, T41648, F41631. 3 miles (5 km) west of town on the road to Sneem.

Eating   **Expensive**   The *Park Hotel Restaurant*, T41200, offers the best of Irish modern cuisine under the relatively new, non-Irish, head chef Bruno Schmidt. Style is everything and at the *Park* it comes in the form of a grand high-ceilinged dining room with huge bay windows looking across water, well-spaced tables with crisp white linen serviced by a bevy of attendants, and a wine list of 600 wines. Paltry house wine is around IR£18, expect to pay around IR£40 for a superb meal, and if you are a non-smoker expect some trouble because smokers have the run of the place. *La Cascade*, T41600, at the *Sheen Falls Lodge*, is similarly priced and revels in French-inflected cuisine. Both restaurants open for dinner only.

Affordable If you prefer a more conventional style of décor and food then *The Lime Tree*, Shelburne St, T41225, fits the bill. Tables are a little squashed together inside this handsome stone building, the atmosphere is convivial and good steaks and local lamb accompany attractive starters and desserts. Popular with locals as well as visitors, always make a reservation in the summer; open for dinner only. Facing the town square, above the *Square Pint* bar, the à la mode *Café Indigo*, T42357, really is very blue but at least it is a bit different. Dinner, in the IR£20 plus bracket, is served from 1900 but there is also a late night menu that starts at 2230, with last orders taken at midnight. Open for lunch too.

Henry St is fairly littered with food places but some of the pubs serving food may prove disappointing and it might be better trying a smaller place like the *Old Dutch Restaurant*, T41449, where the chef is Dutch and, while the menu is not that different to others along the road, the IR£11 set dinner is good value. Henry St also boasts one of Ireland's very few vegetarian restaurants, the *New Delight*, T42350: organic, vegetarian, and with an Asia touch to the lunch (IR£5) and dinner (IR£8-12) menus, it lives up to its name. On the other hand, *Packie's*, T41508, in Henry St has been around for some time and earned a reputation for good seafood and Mediterranean-style dishes. Dinner only, around IR£20, and closed Monday. For economically priced daytime meals try nearby *The Purple Heather*, T41016, for soups, seafood salads, omelettes and the like.

Main St has its own sprinkling of restaurants like *D'Arcy's*, T41589, which opens only for dinner at 1800 and the Italian-style *An Leath Phingin*, T41559, at No 35 which has been recommended for its pasta dishes. Afternoon tea at the *Sheen Falls Lodge*, T41600, is worth considering on a wet day. At 3 Main St, *The Horseshoe*, T41553, is a relaxed pub with a restaurant to the rear that serves nourishing chowders and burgers and evening meals (around IR£15) of steaks and other standard but well-cooked dishes. At the top of Main St, *Giuliano's*, T41952, specializes in Italian pasta and pizza, good for vegetarians, with lunch from IR£4 to IR£10 and dinner from IR£6 to IR£15; every day between March and November.

Pubs & music One of the oldest buildings in town is now *Moerans Pub*, which as well serving food has some lively evenings of music and song. The *Square Pint* near the tourist office, with traditional music nightly, is usually packed out with revellers, but for a plain pint in a plain bar so small that customers have little choice but to converse together, drop in to the *Courthouse Bar* adjacent to the tourist office.

Shopping For its size, Kenmare is reasonably well-endowed with shops catering to visitors' credit cards. There is a largish Quills store in the very centre of town, open daily until 2200, that sells designer handknits, woollen and cashmere garments and assorted merchandise. On Henry St there are a couple of antique shops and other stores dedicated to arts, crafts and souvenirs, including *Sue-D-Knits* at No 29 with a good selection of Irish cashmere and hand-knitted items and *Soundz of Muzic* at No 36 with a range of bodhrans, tin whistles, flutes, Irish music and dance videos. On Main St *De Barra* is a small but enticing Irish jewellery shop. *Crúiscín Craftworks* is tucked away down Old Bridge St, not far from the tourist office, and embraces a pottery studio as well as selling candlesticks, clocks, oil paintings and assorted bric-à-brac.

Directory **Tourist office** T41233. On the right as one enters the town from the Sneem direction. Mid-Jun-late Sep, Mon-Sat 0915-1900. Rest of the year Mon-Sat 0915-1730. **Tours** Boat: *Seafari*, T83171. Departs regularly from the Pier for a 2-hour, 10-mile (15 km) cruise of Kenmare Bay with an ecological emphasis. Colonies of grey seals and sea otters are usually spotted and occasionally minke and killer whales are seen chasing shoals of mackerel. There is also a sunset cruise featuring a barbecue and live Irish music. To reach the pier walk out of town towards Killarney and turn right just before the double-arched bridge. This is a pleasant destination in its own right, especially when the tide is in and the Kerry mountains look down on the graceful flow of the river.

County Kerry

⟩ The Kerry Way

This is nine or ten days of glorious walking around some of the most beautiful scenery in Ireland. The walk is well established and several organizations will be glad to plan your entire trip, including luggage transfer and pickups where the route meets roads into towns. It is perfectly possible to do the trip without this and at your leisure, taking days off to enjoy the villages and make side trips to places such as Valentia and the Skelligs along the way. Car drivers can plan the walks in sections, basing themselves at Glenbeigh, Killarney or Waterville, doing one or two days and then moving on. The walk is about 135 miles (215 kilometres) and consists of the following:

Day 1	Killarney to the Black Valley	14 miles (22 kilometres)
Day 2	Black Valley to Glencar	12 miles (20 kilometres)
Day 3	Glencar to Glenbeigh	8 miles (13 kilometres)
Day 4	Glenbeigh to Cahersiveen	17 miles (28 kilometres)
Day 5	Cahirsiveen to Waterville	19 miles (30 kilometres)
Day 6a	Waterville to Caherdaniel	17 miles (28 kilometres)
Day 6b	Waterville to Caherdaniel	8 miles (12 kilometres)
Day 7	Caherdaniel to Tahilla	18 miles (29 kilometres)
Day 8	Tahilla to Kenmare	13 miles (20 kilometres)
Day 9	Kenmare to Killarney	16 miles (25 kilometres)

Mapping and information The first six days are the best for views and terrain while Day 8, Tahilla to Kenmare, is seriously not worth doing as it involves walking about four miles on the main Ring of Kerry Road, a very dangerous activity. The Kerry Way is generally well signposted but the Ordnance Survey (OS) Discovery Series maps sheets 78, 83 and 84 are essential. *Cork-Kerry Tourism* produces a strip map of the walk, which is less useful and not essential if using the OS map.

Day 1: Killarney to the Black Valley

14 miles (22 km); 7 hrs; total ascent 1,230 ft (375m) The walk starts just outside the town centre of Killarney at the River Flesk. The first section is along the pavement and then the walk enters Muckross Park with views of Killarney's lakes. It passes by Muckross Friary and Muckross House (see page 333)and emerges from the park at the foot of the Torc waterfall. Above the waterfall the route heads off along the Old Kenmare Road, quite boggy in places, across deer country with Mangerton Mountain looming ahead and McGillycuddy's Reeks in the distance. Passing a deserted church, the route crosses the Killarney to Kenmare road and heads downhill, following the course of the Derricunnihy River and then the Upper Lake. At a little landing stage and café the route meets a minor road and follows it to the *Black Valley Hostel*, which is quite small and should be booked well in advance if you intend to stay there. Close by is *Hillcrest Farmhouse* B&B. This is simply the only accommodation at this stage (for details see 'Sleeping' on page 363).

Day 2: Black Valley to Glencar

12 miles (20 km); 8 hrs; total ascent 1,640 ft (500m) This is the most stunning day's walk between Killarney and Glenbeigh. It passes through the Black Valley and even on a sunny day you can see why the place has earned the name. The walk climbs gradually up through rugged jagged peaks, leaving all idea of roads and civilization behind. It meets an old butter road and descends into a farmyard and valley and then climbs again over a pass on a spur of Curraghmore Mountain, finally meeting Lough Acoose and a road to Glencar. There are several B&Bs and guest houses around Glencar, such as Blackstones House and Rocklands Country Home. There is also *The Climbers' Inn*, offering hostel accommodation (for details, see 'Sleeping' on page 363).

Day 3: Glencar to Glenbeigh

This day's walk goes through the Caragh River valley, along some road and forestry roads and culminates in a scenic climb up Seefin Mountain. From here there is a choice of routes skirting Seefin to the east and west, both equally beautiful and both descending into Glenbeigh. For accommodation in Glenbeigh see the Glenbeigh section on page 346.

11 miles (17½ km); 6 hrs; total ascent 984 ft (300m)

The first three days of the Kerry Way are worth considering as a walking excursion from Killarney with a return by bus after spending the third night in Glenbeigh. With your own transport, the beginning of the first day could be shortened by leaving your car at the Torc Waterfall carpark.

Day 4: Glenbeigh to Cahersiveen

This day and the next day's walk could be shortened by four miles by staying at Foilmore rather than going on into Cahersiveen. The first section of the route heads southwest out of Glenbeigh and follows the coast, first ascending Glenbeigh Hill with spectacular views of the coastline. There is a short spell along roads and then another climb up Drung Hill and more wonderful views. There follows a turn inland along the flanks of Been Hill to Foilmore where there is *Fransal House* B&B. Staying here means you can avoid the long trek into Cahersiveen and back out again if you intend to continue the walk another day. On the other hand, going on means you have a greater choice of where to stay, and if you intend to break your walk for a few days you are better placed for trips to Valentia or the Skelligs. For accommodation and food see the Cahersiveen section on page 347.

17 miles (28 km); 9 hrs; total ascent 2,100 ft (650m)

Day 5: Cahersiveen to Waterville

This distance includes the spur from Cahersiveen back to the main route at Foilmore and another at the end of the day into Waterville. Foilmore to Waterville is 15 miles (24 km). The day's walk climbs on to high ground and for much of the first half of the day you are climbing and descending hills with 360° scenery. The walk eventually descends into Mastergeehy, a small village with a tiny post office selling very basic supplies, and then follows an old mass path up Coomaduff Hill and along another series of ridges with fine views into Waterville. On Coomaduff Hill the Way divides, one route going on to Caherdaniel and the other into Waterville. You should take the Waterville route as the final ridge walk to Waterville is well worth the effort. For accommodation see the Waterville section on page 353.

19 miles (30 km); 8 hrs minimum; total ascent 2,400 ft (730m)

Day 6: Waterville to Caherdaniel

This distance includes walking back to Coomaduff Hill from Waterville and then, at the end of the day's walk, walking away from the main route towards Caherdaniel. It is an excellent walk despite the length and detour, and if you wanted to make the route shorter you might try hitching from Waterville to Dromod, making the walk to Caherdaniel about 13 miles (21 kilometres).

17 miles (28 km); total ascent 1,750ft (535m)

County Kerry

The Way begins by retraces the ridge walk back from Waterville to Coomaduff Hill and then halfway down it meets the fork in the route to Caherdaniel. It skirts around the north side of Lough Currane, crosses some rough land where markers are not clear and meets a boreen, which it follows for a while close to the eastern shore of Lough Currane. The Way then turns east along another minor road past Lough Isnagahiny. Just beyond an old school, now a heritage centre, the route leaves the minor road and sets off southwards climbing Mount Eagle, crossing to the right of the summit at Windy Gap. The route down is a wide green road, easy to walk until it meets another branch of the Kerry Way travelling from Caherdaniel to Sneem. Your route is westwards to Caherdaniel and a signpost points the way along quite marshy ground but with some excellent views down into Derrynane Bay and the Kenmare River. For accommodation see the Caherdaniel section on page 355.

Day 6: Waterville to Caherdaniel (alternative route)

8 miles (12 km); 6 hrs;
total ascent 984 ft
(300m)

This route is shown on the OS Discovery series sheet 83 and even without the markers is quite easy to follow. It heads east out of Waterville and takes the first minor road right, beside a mini golf course. It follows the minor road for about 1½ miles and then sets off across a field at a place called the Pound. This is an obvious looking, fenced-off area for collecting sheep on the left of the road. It climbs a little to find the Old Kenmare Road, just below the main Ring of Kerry Road, and runs along parallel to it for some miles, eventually crossing it to climb a small spur and then heading downhill at the Scarriff Inn. It follows the coast for some miles, giving very pleasant views of the coastline, passes through the outskirts of Derrynane National Park and emerges at Caherdaniel. For accommodation see the Caherdaniel section on page 355.

Day 7: Caherdaniel to Tahilla

16 miles (26 km); 7 hrs;
total ascent 1,300 ft
(400m)

The route sets off backtracking yesterday's walk to the junction at the bottom of Eagle Mountain, takes the right fork and for most of the day follows the Old Kenmare Road in its modern incarnations of green road, boggy pasture and minor tarmac road. The walk is pleasant enough but has no spectacular sections like the previous day's walk. There are views south over the Kenmare River for most of the day and a pleasant stop can be had at Sneem. You might want to break your walk at that point and move on to Kenmare via one of the daily buses, cutting out the next day's section which really isn't worth the trouble of the long walk along the Ring of Kerry road with absolutely no footpaths and completely mad drivers travelling way too fast for such a narrow road. Accommodation at Tahilla is at *Hillside Haven* (for details see 'Sleeping' on page 363).

Day 8: Tahilla to Kenmare

13 miles (21 km); 7 hrs;
total ascent 1,150 ft
(350m)

This is a fairly pleasant walk as far as Templenoe, where a long stretch on the Ring of Kerry road is not worth walking. From Tahilla the route rejoins the Old Kenmare Road as far as Blackwater Bridge where it enters woodland beside the Kenmare River, emerging west of Templenoe. From here a bus will take you into Kenmare or you can follow the rest of the route along the main road to Reen where the route leaves the main Ring of Kerry road and heads uphill over Gortamullin Hill and then down into Kenmare.

Day 9: Kenmare to Killarney

A thoroughly pleasant walk still following old roads, firstly along minor roads and then through a saddle high up between Knockanaguish and Peakeen mountains with fine views over Killarney's lakes. Descending, the route follows the Derrycunnihy River, finally meeting up with the Kerry Way out of Killarney.

15 miles (24 km); 8 hrs; total ascent 1,970 ft (600m)

Essentials

D *Black Valley Hostel*, Black Valley, T064-34712. An Óige hostel, which is quite small and should be booked well in advance if you intend to stay there. It opens at 5pm, has a small shop next door and good cooking facilities, but gets crowded and noisy. **B** *Blackstones House*, Glencar, T066-9760164. B&B open February to December. Packed lunches, evening meals, laundry facilities and luggage transfer. **D** *The Climbers' Inn*, Glencar, T066-9760101, F066-9760104, climbers@iol.ie http://www .iol.ie/~climbers Hostel accommodation. Kitchen, drying rooms, pub food, information about other walks in the area, luggage transfer to your next stop and packed lunches. Open all year. In the same area are several B&Bs and guest houses. **B** *Fransal House*, Glencar, T066-9472997. B&B open all year with a laundry, drying room, evening meals and packed lunches, and luggage transfer. **B** *Hillcrest Farmhouse*, Black Valley, T064-34702. B&B, close to the **B** *Black Valley* hostel, which does evening meals and luggage transfer and has a drying room – essential if you hit bad weather. **B** *Hillside Haven*, Tahilla, T064-82065. **B** *Rocklands Country Home*, Glencar, T066-9768215. B&B, evening meals, packed lunches, laundry facilities and luggage transfer. Open all year except at Christmas.

Sleeping

Dingle Peninsula

County Kerry

Stretching for 30 glorious miles (48 kilometres) from the town of Tralee, the Dingle peninsula is characterized geographically by high central ridges running up to Mount Brandon at 3,127 feet (952 metres) and the scenery as a whole, etched by the glaciers of the last Ice Age, reveals itself in an epiphany of natural beauty that is stunningly unique and unforgettable. Less rugged and wild than the Beara or the Iveragh, there is a distinct quality to the light and the colours that on a fine day transforms the Dingle into Ireland's most wonderful and magical peninsula. Nowadays more and more visitors are being drawn to the Dingle peninsula and in July and August it is advisable to have accommodation booked in advance; come here outside of the high season and you will feel especially privileged to be here.

There are two approaches to the peninsula: coming from the south on the N22 or the N70 it is possible to branch off at Farranfore or Castlemaine and head directly west to the town of Dingle along the road that skirts the south coast. Coming from the east or the north one first reaches Tralee at the head of the peninsula's north coast before heading west to the village of Camp. From here one road continues along the north coast before descending to Dingle via the phenomenal Connor Pass, while another road heads southwest across the peninsula to Annascaul where the south coast road is picked up.

Getting there

Anyone spending much time on the Dingle peninsula, especially if planning to cycle or walk, should consider purchasing the Ordnance Survey Map No 70 in the Discovery series. There are so many minor roads and so few main ones – and, on top of that, the practice of signposting places in Irish (see box on page 375) – that it is easy to get confused.

Getting around

Insectivores of Kerry and Cork

Bog land is nutritionally poor but the plant world responds with species that trap and digest insects. The most conspicuous is the large-flowered butterwort, often encountered in wet patches along the Beara, Iveragh or Dingle Way. Commonly growing in clumps, the butterwort is a low-lying perennial with violet flowers in a starfish-like rosette and fleshy sticky leaves, which attract and trap their victims before they are consumed by digestive enzymes.

The leaves of the small reddish sundew family also trap insects, an estimated 2,000 annually, with their long, sticky, inward-curving hairs. Look closely and you will see the fine hairs tipped with a sticky globule.

The rootless bladderworts live underwater but their yellow flowers may be seen above the surface of pools. Their leaves have tiny bladders with supersensitive bristles and when a water flea unwittingly brushes past the bladder opens, expelling water and sucking in the victim aided by the vacuum effect.

In a bog near Listowel a species of pitcher plant from North America has been successfully introduced.

History Surely this is partly what attracted the island's earliest inhabitants for the ancient constructs that litter the peninsula – megalithic tombs, cup and circle stones, oratories, beehive huts, high crosses – seem like testimony to the sense of awe that the landscape inspired in them. Later groups of visitors – Norsemen in the 10th century, Anglo-Normans in the 13th century followed by traders from Spain – may have felt the same, but the Dingle peninsula also bears the scars of England's colonialism. People around Ballyferriter still recount the story of the Dún an Óir massacre (near Smerwick, see page 378) and how workmen collecting stones at a nearby beach once refused to go on working when they discovered that this was the infamous 'beach of the heads'; the heads of those massacred, cut off by English troops, washed up on shore and buried by local people.

County Kerry

Dingle Peninsula & Dingle Way

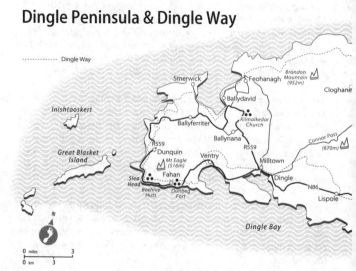

Tralee

Not the cutest of Irish towns, the county capital is metamorphosing into a thriving centre of local employment that seasonally tunes into the tourist market whilst otherwise busying itself with new-found wealth and security emanating from Ireland's tiger economy. Tralee makes a useful base for a day or two before heading west and there are a few attractions to while away the time while planning an itinerary or plotting a route along the Dingle Way, a superb long-distance walk around the peninsula that provides an ideal introduction to Dingle's charms (see page 381).

Phone code: 066
Colour map 3, grid B2

Kerry the Kingdom

The history of Kerry is told through an audio-visual display, a museum and a 'time car' that ferries visitors through a reconstructed set of medieval Tralee. Families will appreciate the trolley ride and the museum is dense with information, though the admission charge is a bit steep. ■ *March to October, daily 1000-1800 (1900 in August); November and December 1400-1700. IR£5.50.*

Blennerville windmill & Jeanie Johnson shipyard

The largest working mill in the British Isles is the centrepiece of this visitor attraction just outside of town on the N86 road to Dingle. The exhibition focuses on the history of 19th-century Blennerville, an emigrant port from where thousands departed for the long and painful journey to North America.

The rebuilding of the *Jeannie Johnson*, one of the 'coffin ships' that made the transatlantic journey many times without losing any passengers to disease, is well under way and when it is ready the journey will be made once more. The shipyard adjoins the windmill. ■ *T7129999. April to October, daily 1000-1800. IR£3.*

Steam railway

The first 1.8 miles (three kilometres) of the narrow-gauge Tralee and Dingle Steam Railway, which ran from 1891 to 1953, has been restored and every hour a train chugs from Ballyard Station in town to the Blennerville Windmill. The journey lasts 20 minutes and makes for a pleasant journey to the windmill (plus a 10 per cent discount on the windmill admission) and railway memorabilia is sold on the train. ■ *T7121064. May to 4th October, daily 1100-1700; closed on certain days in June and July. IR£2.75.*

County Kerry

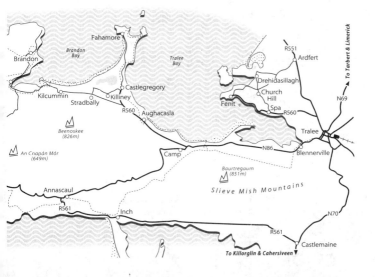

Sleeping
■ *on map*
Price codes:
see inside front cover

AL *Meadowlands*, Oakpark, T7180444, F7180964. Recently opened hotel, out on the road to Listowel. **AL** *Tralee Court*, Castle St, T7121877, F7122273. Well situated for comfort and convenience, being in the very centre of town, this is a new hotel. **B** *Tralee Townhouse*, High St, T7181111, F7181122, michaeloshea@tinet.ie http://www.traleetownhouse.com A hotel-like building with an elevator to the floors where rooms with their own bathrooms are located. **B-C** *Denton*, Listowel Rd, Oakpark, T7127637. Close to town on the N69 and has private parking. Room rates range from IR£15 to IR£18 per person. No en suite rooms. **C** *Upton House*, 7 Clash Rd, T7125219. Near the bus and train station and charges from IR£20 to IR£16 for doubles. Bathroom facilities are shared. **C** *Kay Rael*, Oakview, T7121903. B&B in a quiet location within walking distance of town centre. Some rooms have private bathroom facilities. **C-D** *Westward Court*, Mary St, T7180081, F7180082. Offers 'superior budget accommodation', meaning a private double/single room with a continental breakfast for IR£30/17, or a bed in a 4-bed/6-bed room for IR£10/8. There is also the use of a kitchen, launderette, security lockers and TV lounge. **D** *Atlas House*, Castle St, T7136144, F7136533. Similar in style to *Westward Court*. **D** *Collis-Sandes House*, Oakpark, T7128658. Has 9 private rooms for IR£18. **D** *Finnegans Holiday Hostel*, Denny St, T7127610. A regular hostel with good facilities including private rooms for IR£20 and an atmospheric restaurant in the basement. **D** *Lisnagree Hostel*, Ballinorig Rd, T7127133. Has private rooms but otherwise is fairly basic. **D** *O'Casey's*, 5 Church St, T7127199. An IHH hostel with 3 private rooms for IR£20. **D** *Tralee Townhouse Hostel*, High St, T7181111. IHH place with 20 private rooms at IR£15 per person but no dormitory accommodation.

Camping *The Bayview Caravan & Camping Park*, Kileen, T7126140. A mile (1.6 km) out of Tralee on the R558 road to Ballybunion. *Woodlands Park*, South Circular Rd, Tralee, T7121235. A modern camping and caravan park. *The Seaside Camping & Caravan Park*, Camp, T7130116, F7130331. Has only 10 pitches for tents.

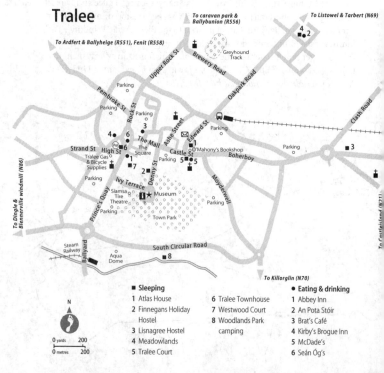

Tralee

■ **Sleeping**
1 Atlas House
2 Finnegans Holiday Hostel
3 Lisnagree Hostel
4 Meadowlands
5 Tralee Court
6 Tralee Townhouse
7 Westwood Court
8 Woodlands Park camping

● **Eating & drinking**
1 Abbey Inn
2 An Pota Stóir
3 Brat's Café
4 Kirby's Brogue Inn
5 McDade's
6 Seán Óg's

The secret of the rose

The annual week-long Rose of Tralee festival at the end of August begins with street bands welcoming the would-be Roses – woman of Irish descent from every corner of the world – for a revival of the traditional welcome, in which they were led through the streets with an escort of riders bearing burning sods of turf. While tickets to the contest are sold out well in advance there is still plenty of entertainment around town – street theatre, pub extensions, concerts, fireworks – and big names like Van Morrison appear on the stage. The actual contest to choose the Rose takes up two nights, and not a bikini in sight, for the women compete by way of interviews on stage followed by a display of some expertise, anything from an Irish jig to a belly dance. The stage event is laudably low-octane but goes on for a couple of hours too long and while the winner is not hurled into an international limelight all the contestants enjoy a week-long freebie and publicans laugh all the way to the bank. The secret of the festival's success is hard to fathom, but it is growing increasingly popular.

Eating
● on map
Price codes:
see inside front cover

At the *An Pota Stóir*, T7180444, at the *Meadowlands Hotel*, a cheerfully informal restaurant with a Mediterranean-style character, go for the locally caught seafood: oysters, lobster, turbot, John Dory and sole feature regularly. While an à la carte dinner is around IR£30 there is also a set dinner around IR£23. A good wine list and the usual wicked desserts. *McDades*, a pub and restaurant on Castle St, is recommended for anyone wishing to get away from the usual fish and meat dishes. The interesting menu includes delicious potato skins for a starter while fajitas are around IR£10 and pasta dishes under IR£8. *Kirby's Brogue Inn*, T7123221, in Rock St, might look like a contrived tourist trap but the food is surprisingly good. *Brat's* in Milk Market Lane opens at 1230 for vegetarian lunches with a small but authentic menu of tasty ideas.

Pubs & music

There is no shortage of pubs and many of them have live music during the summer. Kirby's *Brogue Inn* can usually be relied on for an entertaining night out and the cavernous *Seán Óg's* in Bridge St has music every night except Wednesday and Saturday. *The Abbey Inn*, also in Bridge St, has music every night of the week until late.

Entertainment

Festivals *Samhlaíocht Chiarraí*, Main St, T7129934, F7120934. Contact for details of the Tralee Easter Arts Festival. **Theatre** *Síamsa Tíre*, T7123055. The National Folk Theatre of Ireland, founded in 1974 to present theatrical entertainment based around Irish folklore music and dance. Shows usually start at 2030, and advance booking is recommended in July and August.

Shopping

Books *O'Mahony's*, Castle St, T7122266.

Sport

Racing *Greyhound Stadium*, Oakview, T7180008. There is a grandstand restaurant and a bar and the first race starts at 2000 every Tuesday, Friday and Saturday. Admission and dinner is IR£13 and pre-booking is required. **Swimming** *Aqua Dome*, T7128899. A fun waterworld with slides and raging rapids open daily from 1000 to 2200.

Transport

Air *Kerry airport*, Farranfore, T9764644. 10 miles (16 km) southeast of Tralee. **Bicycle** *Dunworth Cycles*, 97 Rock St, T7120666. Bike hire. *Tralee Gas & Bicycle Supplies*, Strand St, T7122018. Bike hire. **Bus** *Bus Éireann*, T7123566. Buses to Dublin, Rosslare and other towns as well as scenic tours of the peninsula, Cliffs of Moher and West Cork in the summer months. Depart from Tralee bus station. **Car** *Duggan's Garage*, Ashe St, T7121124. Car hire; will also deliver to the airport. **Taxis** Taxi rank in Denny St,

County Kerry

T7123159. **Train** Train station: T7123522/7126555. Daily service to Dublin and connections to other towns around the country like Cork and Ennis from Limerick Junction and the west of Ireland from Portarlington.

Directory **Communications** Email: Internet access at *Cyberpost*, 26 Upper Castle St, T7181284, cyberpost@tinet.ie Emails can be sent and the net surfed. **Post office**: Edward St. **Tours** *Jackie Power Tours*, 2 Lower Rock St, T7129444. Coach tours of the Ring of Kerry and Dingle peninsula for IR£10 and Killarney for IR£8. **Tourist office** Ashe Memorial Hall, Denny St, T7121288. Sep-Jun Mon-Sat 0900-1800; Jul-Aug, Mon-Sun 0900-1900. Rose of Tralee festival office also here, T7121322. Café and craft shop on the premises. *WALK-IN-formation Centre*, T7128733, stocks OS maps and walking guide books: useful if planning or considering the Dingle Way or other walks in the region.

North of Tralee

Apart from the sights mentioned below, the flat rolling farmland of North Kerry has little to detain the traveller and if you're heading on to Clare, stay on the N69 and cross the Shannon by way of the very regular car ferry from Tarbert.

Listowel On the way to Tarbert, the small town of Listowel is worth noting because of its literary fame as the home of the playwright, John B Keane, who also runs a pub in the town. There is a seasonal tourist office, T068-22590, in St John's Church and if you plan a visit to the annual Listowel Writer's Week in May it is advisable to have accommodation booked in advance. Details of the festival are available from PO Box 147, Listowel, Kerry. Throughout the year, something is usually on at St John's Theatre and Arts Centre, The Square, T068-22566.

Ardfert Cathedral Depending on your interests and time, it could well be worth skipping the attractions in Tralee and journeying five miles (eight kilometres) to the northwest to visit the cathedral in Ardfert. St Brendan founded a monastery here in the sixth century, but what you see today is a medieval cathedral with a superb Romanesque doorway on the west side, and a dramatic triple-lancet window typical of the Gothic style that had been introduced to Ireland by the Cistercians. The 13th-century east window, framed by two ecclesiastical effigies, is also worthy of attention. On the site there are also two other smaller 15th-century churches. ■ *May to late September, daily 0930-1830. IR£1.50. Dúchas site; guided tour available. Situated on the R551 Tralee to Ballyheigue road at Ardfert.*

Banna Strand The five-mile (eight-kilometre) stretch of safe and sandy beach at Banna is popular with Irish families, and camping and caravan sites are dotted along the coast up to and including Ballyheigue. On the beach there are panoramic views over Tralee Bay and Banna Strand has a particular significance in Irish history because it was here that Roger Casement landed and was arrested in 1916 (see box on page 369). To reach the memorial look for a sign pointing to the left as you approach the beach; from here it is a ten-minute walk past the caravans.

Crag Cave A limestone cave discovered by accident in 1983 and now open to the public by way of a guided tour. As caves go this one is quite impressive and the lighting system underground is used to good effect to highlight some of the more dramatic formations. Above ground there is a restaurant and a minimarket of souvenirs. ■ *T7141244. March to November, daily 1000-1800 (1900 in July and August). IR£3. Situated on the N21 road at the Limerick end of Castleisland.*

Sir Roger Casement

Casement was a British diplomat, born in 1864 in Sandycove (County Dublin), who first became famous for his denunciations of the exploitation of native workers in the Congo and South America. He was knighted in 1911, but ill-health caused his early retirement, and he settled in Ireland in 1912. His commitment to the cause of Irish nationalism led him to Germany in 1914. The government there agreed to send a shipload of arms, but this was far less than he had anticipated and he returned to Ireland in 1916 in order to try and postpone the planned rising. A German submarine brought him into Tralee Bay, but he was arrested after landing on Banna Strand. Put on trial for treason and sentenced to death, he attracted a lot of support and there were many appeals on his behalf. To discredit him, the government released extracts from his 'Black Diaries' that revealed his homosexuality. He was hanged in London in August 1916. In 1965 his body was returned to Ireland for a state funeral.

Inch and Annascaul

Coming from Killarney and the south the route west from Castlemaine follows the coast to Dingle, and the two main villages along the way are Inch and Annascaul. They are places to stay, but finding somewhere for a meal is not so straightforward, and this should be borne in mind. See page 380 for the other route out to Dingle via Camp and Castlegregory.

Phone code: 066
Colour map 3, grid B2

The main attraction at Inch is the gorgeous four-mile (six-kilometre) beach that provided a location for the filming of *The Playboy of the Western World*. The strand and the two opposite on the Iveragh peninsula – Rossbeigh and Cromane – are gradually building up and one day Castlemaine Bay will be enclosed. The beach is vast and even on a fine summer's day it is easy to find a private spot. Ringed plovers and turnstones, distinctively small black and white birds with white legs, are non-breeding visitors to the beach where they are seen turning stones and weeds with their bills searching for food.

Inch

Sleeping There are no restaurants in the area so staying in a hostel makes a lot of sense. The nearest is the IHH **D** *Inch Farm Hostel*, T9158181/088-593596, at Ballinagrown and there are 2 private rooms at IR£7 per person. More amenities, including meals, laundry, bike hire and private rooms, are to be found in **D** *Bog View Hostel*, T9158125, at Lougher, half way between Inch and Annascaul.

In the one-street village of Annascaul visitors often wonder why a pub should be named the South Pole Inn. A villager, Tom Crean, accompanied Scott and Shackleton to the South Pole and he set up this pub afterwards. There is a small tourist office in the main street, T9157419. When facing **Annascaul Lake**, you are standing at the bottom of a glacier-carved valley, the lough itself having been carved out by the base of the glacier. The scree slopes on the other side have been broken off the top of the sandstone mountain by centuries of weathering. The green road leading away from the lough leads up to the valley following the course of the River Garrivagh, and it is a pleasant stroll in dry weather.

Annascaul

Even though the lake is signposted, it is not much visited, and you can usually have the place to yourself. About four miles (six kilometres) from Inch

County Kerry

on the road to Dingle you will reach a T-junction: take the right turn for Annascaul and after just under a mile (1.2 kilometres) the road for Annascaul turns to the right, while the left turn is signposted for Annascaul Lake.

Sleeping The hostel, *Fuchsia Lodge*, T9157150, has all the amenities, including bike hire, and it is a friendly and comfortable place to stay for a night or two. Half way between Annascaul and Dingle there is the *Seacrest Hostel*, T9151390, at Kinard West, Lispole, with one private room for IR£15.

Dingle

Phone code: 066
Colour map 3, grid B1

The small town of Dingle, with barely half a dozen streets, has changed almost beyond recognition in the last few years, tourism being the catalyst. Such is the growing popularity of a visit to the peninsula, by Irish holiday-makers and foreign visitors, that Dingle has been forced to build car-parks and introduce one-way systems to cope with the traffic. Out of season the town reclaims its identity as a market town and fishing port but in July and August it becomes the main base for visits to the sights and sites west of Dingle. There are places to stay west of town but they are in limited in number and, because this end of the peninsula is small enough to make most places accessible as day excursions, Dingle heaves with people and vehicles in the summer months.

History

The Irish form of Dingle, *An Daingean* (fortress), suggests its early involvement in defensive wars, although it has a long history of friendly trade with Spain, and Spanish blood is said to still be noticeable in the dark hair and eyes of the inhabitants. In Green Street just past the library there are plaques, still visible, which were set above some of the doors to indicate that Spanish families lived within and, walking up this street from the pier, part of the original town wall can be seen in the old wall on the left.

Sights

Fungie the dolphin When a bottlenose dolphin first appeared in the harbour in 1984 the chirpy little chap flirted and frolicked and made a lot of friends with the humans who doggie-paddled in the water hoping for a meaningful relationship. Over 15 years later and he is still there – or have the locals replaced him with an

County Kerry

Nuala Ní Dhomhnaill

So many figures from the famed Irish literary tradition, or at least the version marketed by Bord Fáilte, are dead white males that it comes as a refreshing change to know that the Dingle area nurtured the poet Nuala Ní Dhomhnaill. She was born in England in 1952 but her Irish parents sent her back to the Gaeltacht Dingle peninsula at the age of five. Her first collection of poetry arrived in 1981, announcing a new voice able to blend Irish mythology and folklore with an acute political and social awareness. Marrying feminism with the Gaelic tradition, her work has been translated by Seamus Heaney and other contemporary poets (see page 63).

inflatable version? – and he surely deserves an award from Bord Fáilte for promoting tourism. Weather permitting, boats depart regularly from the pier, and the IR£6 charge is returned in the unlikely event of his non-appearance. There is also an early morning boat for people who want to swim with him and a wet suit can be hired. (See 'Directory' on page 374 for details.)

It is also possible to get reasonably close to where he usually appears without leaving dry land. Take the road out of town towards Tralee and take the right turn about a mile (1.6 kilometres) after the Esso garage. It is a narrow lane with gateposts but no gate and there is a small parking area at the bottom: from here it is a short walk in the direction of the old tower.

Dingle Oceanworld This Fungie-inspired aquarium is a cut above the average and presents a good opportunity to view at close quarters the local sealife, from cuttlefish to small sharks, including examples of most of the fish that appear on restaurant menus in Ireland. Children will enjoy the touch pool and there is also a café and a shop. ■ T9152111, marabeo@aol.ie All year. July to August, daily 0900-2030; May, June and September, daily 0930-1800; October to April, daily 0930-1700. IR£4.50.

Essentials

Sleeping
■ on map
Price codes:
see inside front cover

There are quite a few B&Bs in and around Dingle but most have only a few beds and fill up quickly. Join the queue at the tourist office or try to book up before arriving.

L *Dingle Skellig Hotel*, T9151144, F9151501. Panoramic views, pool, gym and children-friendly hotel with kids' entertainment and creche available. **AL** *Hillgrove Hotel*, Spa Rd, T9151131, F9151277. A comfortable hotel a short way out of town at the foot of the Conor Pass Rd. Doubles/singles are IR£80/50. **AL** *Milltown House*, T9151372, F9151095, milltown@indigo.ie A decidedly superior guest house serving an above-average breakfast and providing some fine views of the harbour; reached by crossing the bridge heading for Ventry and turning left immediately.

A *Greenmount House*, Gortonora, T9151414, F9151914. Includes some rooms with their own fridge and balcony, and the conservatory overlooks the harbour. **A** *Pax House*, Upper St John St, T9151518, F9152461, paxhouse@iol.ie This really friendly and relaxing guesthouse is good value, with views of the water from the balcony where guests can linger over a drink as the sun goes down. A superb breakfast menu with homemade breads, jam and maramalade and lots of healthy alternatives to the heart-stopping Irish fry.

B *Barr na Graide*, Upper Main St, T9151331. Rooms above a pub, from IR£32 to IR£50 for a double and IR£20 to IR£30 a single. **B** *Captain's House*, The Mall, T9151079. Has a

County Kerry

picturesque setting by a running stream and charges IR£44 for a double. *Mall House*, The Mall, T9151692. Charge around IR£38 for B&B. **B** *Quayside*, The Tracks, T9151068. Overlooks the harbour above a row of shops and charges IR£17 per person for B&B. **B** *Russell's*, The Mall, T9151747, F9152331. B&B charging around IR£38.

D *An Caladh Spáinneach*, Strand St, T9152160. An IHH hostel opposite the pier, with 2 private rooms for IR£10 per person and bikes for hire. **D** *Ballintaggart House*, T9151454, F9151385, btaggart@iol.ie One of the better hostels in Ireland, a 20-minute walk out of town on the Tralee road, with private rooms, a restaurant and shop, laundry, bike and wet-suit hire, pony trekking, riding lessons, and lovely cobbled courtyard adjoining the self-catering kitchen. **D** *Grapevine Hostel*, Dykegate, T9151434. 24 beds in a smallish house and no private rooms but the atmosphere is convivial. **D** *Lovett's Hostel*, An Cuilin (Cooleen Rd), T9151903. On the road opposite the Esso garage.12 beds in a friendly family house. **D** *Marina Hostel*, Strand St, T9151065. Camping space also available at this independent hostel. **D** *Rainbow Hostel*, Milltown, T9151044. Hip place a short way out of town, with private rooms and camping space. **D** *Westlodge*, Strand St, T9151476. Independent hostel with camping space.

Camping *Ballintaggart House Caravan & Camping Site*, T9151454, F9152207. Has a 2-star rating and is next to the hostel outside of town on the Tralee road.

Eating
● on map
Price codes:
see inside front cover

Expensive Under new management but keeping the old name, *Doyle's*, John St, T9151174, continues to attract American tourists who have heard of the original legendary seafood restaurant. Traditional Irish-inn decor, with tables too close together, the food might be considered expensive for the crowded milieu though the IR£18 early bird 3-course dinner between 1800 and 1900 is worth considering; dinner only, closed Sunday. *The Beginish*, on the other hand, Green St, T9151588, has a relaxed formality that comes from years of satisfying customers wanting carefully prepared seafood and local lamb. Lobster a speciality. Lovers of seafood should also consider

County Kerry

Dingle

■ **Sleeping**
1 Captain's House
   Bed & Breakfast
2 Grapevine Hostel
3 Hillgrove
4 Lovett's Hostel
5 Mall House Bed & Breakfast
6 Marina Hostel
7 Marina Inn
8 Milltown House Bed &
   Breakfast
9 Quayside Bed & Breakfast
10 Rainbow Hostel

11 Russell's Bed &
   Breakfast

● **Eating & drinking**
1 An Droichead Beag
2 An Literátha
3 Armada
4 Beginish
5 Bun Appetit
6 Doyle's Seafood Restaurant
7 El Toro
8 Global Village

9 Greany's
10 Half Door
11 Lord Baker's
12 McCarthy's Bar
13 O'Flaherty's Bar

▲ **Other**
1 Foxy John's Bike Hire
2 Lisbeth Mulcahy's Shop
3 Mountain Man Shop
4 Dingle Web

The Half Door, Mail Rd, T9151600, and its seafood platter as either a starter or main course; lunch, and dinner around IR£20, Monday-Saturday. *Lord Baker's*, Main St, T9151277, is an old pub and restaurant that only comes into the expensive bracket when dining at night. Seafood is always the main draw, of course, but plenty of meat-based alternatives; Sunday lunch always requires a reservation.

Affordable Some of the more pleasant places are along Main St away from the hustle and bustle of the harbour area. *The Global Village*, T9152325, deserves its name with a menu featuring Thai curries, stir-fried Chinese, German bratwurst sausage, Indian tikka masala, Italian pasta, and UK fish and chips. Open for breakfast, lunch and dinner; expect to pay around IR£10 for main courses. *The Armada*, T9151505, opens 1800-2100, closed Monday, and has a 4-course dinner menu for IR£15 consisting of traditional Irish meat dishes and local seafood. *Bun Appetit*, The Mall, T9152323, is also in one of the quieter streets and offers a reasonably priced set meal for IR£12 as well as à la carte dishes such as lemon sole for IR£9. Given Dingle's historical links with Spain a Spanish restaurant is not out of place and at *El Toro*, Green St, T9151820, Spanish and Mediterranean cuisine make a change from the usual fare.

Cheap *Greany's*, Holyground, T9152244, is deservedly busy because of the location, the prices and the quality of the food. Main dishes from IR£7.25 for lamb cutlets to IR£12 for the fish of the evening. Go late in the evening for a quieter atmosphere. The pubs opposite the pier, like *Tigh Maire De Barras* and the *Marina Inn*, are the best bet for cheap eats and *Paudie's Bar* along here has bar food and its own *Longs Restaurant*, T9151231, serving food all day.

On The Mall *O'Flaherty*, T9151983, is the kind of authentic pub that Irish theme pubs (and you will find one or two of them even in Ireland) use as a model: flagstoned floor, high ceiling, music sessions. The harbourside *Tigh Maire De Barras* has music every night in the summer and nearby *Paudie's Bar* has traditional music from Thursday to Sunday, starting at 2130. *An Droichead Beag*, T9151723, on Main St has nightly sessions of traditional music and is popular with tourists, while *McCarthys Bar*, T9151205, is further east on Upper Main St and also has regular sessions of music.

> **Pubs & music**

There is a popular night club at the *Hillgrove Hotel* on Monday, Wednesday and Friday nights that attracts young revellers. Nothing happens until at least 2230 and there is a cover charge. On Thursday nights there is a traditional Irish dancing session that attracts people of all ages. At the *Skellig Hotel*, T9151144, on a Tuesday night there is a IR£5 cover charge for an evening of musical entertainment and a chance to learn some Irish dancing.

County Kerry

Dingle centre

A blues, jazz and folk festival takes off in early September and in the past has attracted names like Mary Black, Albie Donnelly and Don Baker, T/F9152427, T087-2286533, dingmus@aol.ie http://www.iol.ie/~dingmus/

> **Festivals**

Antiques *Antique Corner* in Main St has lace, jewellery as well as small antique pieces. *Fadó Antiques*, Main St, has a selection of curios, prints, clocks, and jewellery. **Books** *An Liteártha* on Dykegate St has a terrific selection of books on most aspects of Irish history and culture. *Léigh Linn*, the Dingle

> **Shopping**

Bookshop, situated in Green St is also worth a browse. **Fashion** *Banshee* in Strand St has designer knitwear and handmade Irish lace as well as jewellery. *Lisbeth Mulcahy*, Green St. Perhaps the classiest shop in Dingle, specializing in quality fashion accessories, like scarves, made from Irish linen, cotton, wool, alpaca and silk. **Gifts** *Celtic Fragments* is at Kilvicadomhnasigh, Ventry, and sells stone carvings and related items. *The Craft Village*, on The Wood a short way west of the pier, has a cluster of arts and crafts shops. *Dick Mack's Yard* is a small shop selling celtic-inspired jewellery, off Green St. *Brian de Staic*, across the road, has a good selection of handmade Celtic-inspired jewellery on which names can be engraved in the Ogham script. **Music** *The Dingle Record Store* in the Green St Arcade stocks cassettes, CDs and bodhrans.

Sport **Diving** *Dingle Marina Diving Centre*, The Marina, T9152422, divedingle@tinet.ie **Fishing** *Nicholas O'Connor*, Anglers Rest, Ventry, T9159947. **Golf** *Ceann Sibéal Golf Club*, Ballyoughterach, Ballyferriter ,T9156255, F9156409, http://www.dingleskellig.com. **Horse riding** *Ballintaggart House*, T9151454. *Dingle Horse Riding*, Ballinaboula, T9152018, dinglehorseriding@tinet.ie *Horseriding and Trekking Centre*, Mountain View, Ventry, T9159723. *The Mountain Man* Strand St, T9151868. **Sailing** *Dingle Sailing Club*, The Marina, T9151984. *Dingle Sea Ventures*, Holyground, T9152244, jgreany@iol.ie *The Kimberly Laura*, a 41-ft (12.5m) sailing yacht, departs from the marina at 1030 for a day's sailing around Dingle Bay and trips ashore. IR£40 per person, including food. T9159882. **Windsurfing** *Focus Windsurfing*, T7139411, jamieknox@tinet.ie based at Ventry beach, hires gear and conduct training sessions for children and adults.

Transport **Bicycle** *Fios Feasta*, Holy Ground, T9151937. Rents bikes. *Foxy John's*, Main St, T9151316. Offers the Raleigh Rent-a-Bike scheme. *The Mountain Man* Strand St, T9151868. Bike hire. Next to the tourist office. *Tadgh Ó Coileáin*, Holyground, T9151606. Bike hire **Bus** There is a regular bus service between Tralee and Dingle; enquire at the tourist office.

Directory **Communications** Email: *Dingleweb*, Lower Main St, T9152477, info@dingleweb.com Emails can be sent or received and the web surfed. IR£1.50 for 15mins, IR£5 for 1hr. **Post office**: Main St, T9151661. **Tourist office** *Tourist office*, Strand St, T9151188. Close to the pier and bus stop. Apr-Oct, Mon-Sat 0900-1800. **Tours** **Boat**: *Bá Draíochta*, The Pier, T87-2461591. *Dingle Boatmen's Association*, The Pier, T9151163. *Dingle Marine Eco Tours*, The Pier, T087-2858802. Two-hour trips cover archaeology,geology, history, birdlife, sealife, and local folklore. Tours go either east or west along the southern part of the peninsula. **Coach** *Moran's Tours*, T9151155. 2-hour trip departing from the Pier daily at 1015, 1230, 1430 and 1630 and taking in most of the major sites on the peninsula. IR£8. **Walking** *Sciuird Archaeological Adventures*, T9151937. Daily 2½-hr tours departing at 1030 and 1400 from the pier. Tour numbers are kept below 10 so booking is

··

Gaelic place names on the Dingle Peninsula

Annascaul	*Abhainn an Scáil*	Cloghane	*An Clochán*
Ballydavid	*Baile na nGall*	Dingle	*An Daingean*
Ballyferriter	*Baile an Fheirtéaraigh*	Dunquin	*Dún Chaoin*
Blasket Islands	*Na Blascaodaí*	Inch	*Inse*
Brandon	*Bréanainn*	Lispole	*Lios Póil*
Brandon Creek	*Cuas a Bhodaigh*	Ventry	*Paróiste Fionn Trá*

··

advisable. IR£8. **The Mountain Man**, Strand St, T9151868, F9151980. Handles tours of Slea Head and other scenic destinations and daily guided walks. **Dolphin-spotting**: *Dingle Boatmen's Association*, T9151163/9151967. Weather permitting, boats depart regularly from the pier, 0800-1000. IR£6. Early morning trip to swim with the dolphin also available. **Ballintaggart House**, T9151454, **Dingle Marina Diving Centre**, T9152422, and **Flannery's**, T9151163, also hire out wet gear and can arrange swimming trips.

Dingle to Dunquin

Along the coast between Dingle and Dunquin (Dún Chaoin) there are a number of ancient beehive huts and forts and these are signposted along the road. Following the Dingle Way to Dunquin is a fascinating and enjoyable walk (see page 381) and one could skip the first few miles by taking a bus to Ventry and then begin the walk on Ventry beach. There would be time to visit the Blasket Heritage Centre at Dunquin before catching the bus back to Dingle or one could walk back by taking the inland road across Coumaleagua Hill. With fine weather, there is no better way of enjoying this corner of the Dingle peninsula.

Phone code: 066

Ins and outs

The R559 road is the route most visitors take when heading west from Dingle, passing through Ventry (*Fionn Trá*) and following the coast around the majestically scenic Slea Head before turning north for Dunquin, the departure point for Great Blasket Island. An alternative and swifter route to Dunquin is by way of Coumaleagua Hill; take the signposted turning on the right, less than a mile (1.6 kilometres) after the Ventry post office. Walkers will need a copy of Map 70 in the Ordnance Survey Discovery series. Bus 1555 runs a service between Dingle and Dunquin.

Getting there & around

Sights

This is a particularly well-preserved promontory fort with two souterrains, underground tunnels used for storing food or perhaps as an escape route in times of trouble. The clifftop location is the most impressive aspect of the eighth- or ninth-century fort, although the remains of a dwelling can be discerned inside four earthen defensive rings. ■ *T9159070. IR£1. Signposted, about four miles (6.4 kilometres) west of Ventry.*

Dunbeg Fort

Above the road and stretching for some distance is a group of ancient stone huts, known as the **Fahan group**. Very little is known about them for sure, though a plausible explanation is that they represent a late pagan or early Christian settlement that stretched out along some long-lost highway, with Eagle Mountain rearing up behind as a natural form of defence. The fact that they have survived for so long is eloquent testimony to the masonry skills of whoever built them. ■ *IR£1. Signposted, between Dún Beg Fort and Slea Head.*

Beehive huts

County Kerry

Slea Head Slea Head, where the coastal road turns north towards Dunquin, offers spectacular views, and vehicles accumulate here. The Iveragh peninsula and the Skelligs can be seen to the south, while to the west the Blasket Islands impose themselves on the view. To escape the crowds carry on for a short distance and descend to Coumeenoole Strand, a tiny beach with fine white sand. On a fine day it is tempting to go for a swim, but bear in mind that Robert Mitchum almost drowned in the strong undertow here while filming a scene from *Ryan's Daughter*.

The Enchanted Forest This folklore museum, above the *Bearfoot Café*, is organized around the four seasons and each section is composed of a miniature landscape dense with tiny models relating to customs and folklore from around the world. Painstakingly put together by the proprietor as a labour of love, the place is magnetically attractive to young children who will find it far more engrossing than stone ruins. ■ *T9156234. Easter to May, and September, daily 1200-1700; June to August, daily 1100-1800. IR£2.50.*.

Kruger's The fame of this pub derives from the eponymous Kruger Kavanagh (Kruger was his nickname). Amongst other achievements, he served in the US army in First World War, became a bodyguard to Eamon de Valera and a Hollywood agent. The pub itself – "the most westerly pub in Europe" – is remarkably unprepossessing, but anywhere that Robert Mitchum drank regularly has got to be worth a visit. The black and white photographs adorning the walls are fascinating and the pub also hosts sessions of Irish set dancing. Film buffs should enquire here for directions to the remains of the partly fibreglass schoolhouse that was built for *Ryan's Daughter*. ■ *T9156127. Just off the R559 at Dunquin on a road that leads down to the departure point for the Great Blasket Island.*

The Blasket Hertiage Centre The exterior of this heritage centre at Dunquin makes some people feel the architect and planning authority should be sacked from their jobs – it is unquestionably a blot on the landscape – but the interior is a masterpiece, and a visit here should not be missed, preferably before making a trip out to the island itself. The 20-minute audio-visual presentation, with archive material of interviews with Blasket islanders, is excellent, and there is also a wealth of material and photographs, including an amusing photograph that accompanies an islander's quote: "I looked west at the edge of the sky where America should be…" from Maurice O'Suillivan's *Twenty Years a Growing*. Scholars came to the Great Blasket and encouraged the islanders, to whom storytelling and poetry was a part of everyday life, to write down their stories and record their memories. Their books are all on sale in the Centre and the Dingle bookshops and there is some consensus that O'Sullivan's book is one of the more enjoyable texts. ■ *T9156444. Easter to June, and September, daily 1000-1800; July and August, daily 1000-1900. IR£2.50. Dúchas site. Self-service restaurant.*

Essentials

Sleeping **B** *An Portán*, T9156212. At the junction on the main road where one turns off for *Kruger's*. B&B. **B** *Caitlín Firtéar*, Coumeenoole, T9156120. Farmhouse charging around IR£36/24.50 for en-suite rooms and IR£32/22.50 sharing a bathroom. **B** *Kruger's*, Dunquin, T9156127. This famous pub has 7 beds charging IR£16 per person but they are not worth writing home about and bathroom facilities are shared. **D** *Dún Chaoin*, T9156145/9156121, F9156355. An Óige hostel, situated on the main road near *Kruger's* and enjoying a wonderful view of the sea.

Just beyond Slea Head, on the right side of the road, the *Bearfoot Café* does salads **Eating**
and sandwiches; lunch, from IR£5 to IR£13, extends from 1230 to 1700. Bar food is
available at *Kruger's* and just up the road *An Portán*, T9156212, has a menu of fish and
meat dishes in Gaelic, subtitled in English, but only opens for dinner between 1900
and 2200; expect to pay around IR£20 for a meal. They also provide the lunches that
are available at the self-service restaurant in the *Great Blasket Centre*. The *Dunquin
Pottery and Café* serves soups, savouries and home-baked goodies.

On the main road just past *Dunquin Louis Mulcahy Pottery*, T9156229, has 2 floors **Shopping**
devoted to ceramic items for the home, ranging from egg cups to huge lamps. The
designs are very attractive and distinctive and overs`eas delivery is regularly arranged
for the larger items.

Great Blasket Island

This whale-shaped and marooned-looking island is the largest of a group of *Colour map 3, grid B1*
islands off the coast near Dunquin, and a trip across Blasket Sounds to view the
remains of the island's village and to walk to its western end is a highlight of any
visit to Kerry. It also has one of the best beaches anywhere in the county, *An
Trágh Bhán*, outstanding for its
cleanliness and the sheltered location, which helps make it safe for
swimming.

The island is now uninhabited,
though in summer there is a small
café and a craft shop, and boats,
departing from Dunquin every half-
hour, can only make the crossing in
fine weather. Visitors are free to camp
anywhere on the island; but choose a
sheltered spot. ■ *Boats to Great
Blasket Island: T9156455/ 9156422/
9152400. From 1000 onwards, IR£10
return.*

Inishvickillane and Tearaght Islands

These two islands also belong to the Blasket group and, though neither can be
visited by the public, they still have a remarkable presence for anyone walking
west on the Great Blasket. Inishvickillane is the one furthest to the southwest; it
is partly visible from the mainland but a clear view of it opens up from the western end of Great Blasket. The whole island was purchased by Charles Haughey,
a one-time taoiseach of Ireland who 'forgot' being given a huge sum of money
by a businessman, for IR£22,000 in 1972, and he still occasionally visits his
island by helicopter. The smaller island to the north of Inishvickillane is
Inishnabro.

Tearaght Island is the small westernmost craggy island to the northwest of
Great Blasket, distinguished from Inishtooskert, which is closer to Great
Blasket, by its lighthouse on the southern side. Tearaght supports large colo-
nies of storm petrels and Manx shearwaters.

County Kerry

An anarchist society – with a king!

Life on the Blasket Islands consisted of a self-sufficient community of farming families who lived peacefully without a government, a priesthood or a police force, but at some time or other the notion of a monarchy crept in and the islanders took up the practice of electing a notional king from amongst themselves.

The earliest records document families living on the island around 1700, and they were very healthy indeed, only falling sick if they left to go to the mainland. In 1821 there were 128 islanders, rising to 153 before the Famine, which seems not to have been as catastrophic as elsewhere, probably because their diet was not so dependent on the potato. Fishing had

always been an important source of food, supplemented by rabbits, seabirds and their eggs.

The difficulty of landing on the island – readily apparent even today – helped preserve their independent way of life, and stories have been told of how the women of the island bombarded landing bailiffs with rocks from the cliffs above as they tried to get ashore. In the early 20th century a school was established, and a post office in the 1930s but by 1953 there were only 22 inhabitants. The death in 1952 of a young man simply because the weather prevented him reaching hospital in time, helped the government decide the following year to offer mainland homes to the remaining islanders.

Ballyferriter

Phone code: 066
Colour map 3, grid B1

The road from Dunquin continues on to Ballyferriter (*Baile an Fheirtearaigh*), a small village that would be well worth considering as an alternative accommodation base to Dingle if only there were more choice of places to stay. The serene beauty of the surrounding landscape, the closeness of the Gallarus Oratory and other sites, plus the nearby lovely Wine Strand beach are all good reasons to linger in the area. The beach, a few hundred yards/metres north of Ballyferriter, is safe for swimming and is usually well sheltered from the wind. The village is named after Pierce Ferriter (c.1600-53), a love poet and soldier whose Norman ancestors had settled the Dingle peninsula, and whose participation in the 1641 rebellion led to his hanging in Killarney. JM Synge, the playwright, came to Ballyferriter in 1905 to polish up his Irish.

Ballyferriter Museum A modest little museum devoted to local history and culture and covering topics like the Ogham alphabet, cross slabs and promontory forts. *T9156333. Easter and June to September, daily 1000-1700. IR£1.50.*

Dún An Óir Fort In 1580, in support of the Desmond rebellion, a party of Italians and Spaniards landed in the bay just north of Ballyferriter and established themselves in a fort that had been built earlier by Irish rebels. While waiting for reinforcements they were besieged by the English under Lord Grey. After three days the fort surrendered and some 700 soldiers and a score or so of Irish were cold-bloodedly and systematically butchered by groups of executioners. Edmund Spenser, the English poet who wrote *The Faerie Queene*, was secretary to Grey at the time and was almost certainly present at the massacre. Grey was later recalled to England but Spenser, who stayed to live on in Ireland, remained a hearty supporter of the methods used to suppress the rebellion. The stone sculpture near the remains of the fort commemorates those who died. The beauty of the location is rendered melancholy by the haunting memory of what occurred here. ■ *Going west from Ballyferriter, after less than a mile turn right at the brown sign pointing to Smerwick harbour. At the Y-junction bear*

County Kerry

right and right again at the T-junction; after 300 yards/metres the fort is signposted left on a poorly surfaced road.

B *Carraig An Fhiona*, Wine Strand, T9156470, F9156399. A guest house with doubles/singles for IR£44/30. **D** *Black Cat Hostel*, in the village, T9156286. Has camping space with use of hostel facilities but no private rooms. **D** *Tigh An Phoist Hostel*, T9155109. IHH hostel outside of Ballyferriter, on the road to Ballydavid. Has 4 private rooms at IR£8.50 per person and has bicycles for hire.

Self-catering *Wine Strand Holiday Cottages*, T061-325125, F061-326450. Consists of modern self-catering cottages. Ideal for a long stay on the peninsula.

The museum café, open daily from 1000 to 1700, serves hot meals like pork and chicken pie for IR£5. Next to the post office, the *Tigh Pheig* pub (which under previous management astonished everyone by hosting topless dancers) serves food all day – lunch specials are posted on a blackboard – and at night main dishes are in the IR£10-13 range. The pub opposite, *Tigh Uí Mhurchú*, is a quieter place, also serving lunch and dinner meals, and with turbot for under IR£11, the prices are very reasonable. Next door, *Tis an Tobair*, T9156404, is a restaurant with dishes like courgette and coriander fritters with a red pepper tapenade in the IR£8-13 range.

Ancient and Medieval sites

The first of these sites, Riasc, is just east of Ballyferriter on the road to Ballydavid and it is also the least engrossing so if time is limited this is the one to skip. Excavations of the Riasc monastic site in the 1950s revealed that the ruins were built over an earlier site dating back to 400CE. The main attraction for visitors is a pillar stone inscribed with a cross and curling patterns typical of La Tène art; though this is an early Christian site, and La Tène decoration is mainly pre-Christian Celtic. ■ *24 hours. Free admission.*

Of all the sites on the Dingle peninsula, the Gallarus Oratory is the one you must not miss. Probably built between the ninth and 12th centuries as a place of prayer for monks, this beautifully crafted little hut, similar in style to the beehive huts but boat shaped, has stood intact without the aid of mortar for what could be twelve centuries. The seamless dry stone wall turns into a roof, and it is impossible to tell where the wall ends or the roof begins. The building method, known as corbelling, has each stone supporting another above it, which juts in beyond the perpendicular of the wall. As each stone also slopes slightly downwards, rain is kept out of the building by just running off, as if on a tiled roof. There is no admission charge to this Dúchas site, so feel free to ignore the parasitic little heritage centre that has materialized not far away and which charges IR£1 for the predictable 15-minute audio-visual presentation. ■ *Signposted on the R599 road going east from Ballyferriter. Coming from Dingle, cross the bridge for the road west to Ventry and Dunquin and take the first right for three miles (five kilometres) before bearing left at the Y-junction for the Oratory and Ballyferriter.*

This Romanesque church is thought to date from the 12th century and seems to represent a transitional stage in architecture between the corbelling of the Gallarus Oratory and a tiled roof, as part of the roof remains is similar in style to the oratory. An interesting feature of the church is the design over the doorway: the tympanum has a head on one side and an imaginary animal on the other. The remains of other monastic buildings are in the vicinity including

St Brendan and Brandon Creek

Legend has it that St Brendan set out from here on the first transatlantic crossing in the sixth century. Brendan was born in 484, and as a young man travelled around Ireland, founding a monastery at Ardfert and building an oratory on Mount Brandon. His wanderlust went into a higher gear when he heard about a wonderful island far to the west of Ireland, and taking 14 monks with him, he set out in a curragh to find the place. An early port of call was an island that turned out to be the back of a whale but after seven years – with stops at what might have been Greenland, Iceland and Newfoundland – he finally reached America. He returned safely to Ireland and died in 578. Improbable as this voyage sounds, Tim Severin showed in 1976 that it could be done. With a group of friends he built a similar boat and reached Newfoundland after a 13-month, 3,000-mile journey.

Coming from Dingle, cross the bridge for the road west to Ventry and Dunquin and take the first right that heads north to Murreagh (An Mhuiríoch). Just before Murreagh turn right for the village of An Bóthar Bui, carry on north to Dooneen Pier and follow the road until it ends at Brandon Creek (Cuas an Bhodaigh).

Brendan's House, a two-storey medieval building, and there is an Ogham stone in the church graveyard. The road between the church and Brendan's House is the beginning of the Pilgrim's Way, the traditional route to the summit of Mount Brandon. ■ *From Ballyferriter: take the R559 road eastward at Murreagh (heading south back to Dingle); the church is on the left side of the road about a mile (1.6 kilometres) east of Murreagh. Coming from Dingle: cross the bridge for the road west to Ventry and Dunquin and take the first right for three miles (five kilometres) before bearing right at the Y-junction for Kilmalkedar Church.*

Cloghane and Mount Brandon

Phone code: 066
Colour map 3,
grid B1 & B2

Cloghane might make a pleasant alternative to staying at *An Bóthar* in Brandon Creek. It is a good base for the many walks around Mount Brandon and Brandon Ridge.

Sleeping & eating

O'Connor's, T7138113, is a pub and B&B, open March to October. Pub food and evening meals for guests are available. Further along the street is *Mount Brandon House*, T7138299, a recently opened hostel with en-suite dormitory rooms and some family rooms. Next door is *Tigh Tomsi*, a pub owned by the same people with pub food and live music in summer. A local B&B that caters for walkers is *Abhain Mhor*, T7138211. Both O'Connor's and Abhain Mhor have details of walks in the area. There is a small shop opposite Tigh Tomsi's.

Camp, Castlegregory and the Connor Pass

Phone code: 066
Colour map 3, grid B3

As you travel to the Dingle peninsula from Tralee, the road heads west to the village of Camp – which is strung out along the road and characterized only by a couple of pubs – where a fork in the road leads either southwest to Annascaul or straight on along the northern coast of the peninsula to Cloghane and the Connor Pass. Before reaching Cloghane, a right turn off the road leads to the Castlegregory peninsula and the village of Castlegregory (Caisleán Ghriare) itself. The village is of little interest other than as a place in which to stay and eat but the peninsula and its beaches attract holiday-makers and there are a

County Kerry

number of caravan and camping sites. Far better to stay on the road to Cloghane where Fermoyle Beach is a lovely stretch of sand, safe for swimming and safe for cars, which can be driven onto it.

The Connor Pass connects Cloghane with Dingle and at 1,496 feet (456 metres) the pass offers spectacular views of both Mount Brandon and Dingle to the south. The car-park at the summit is clogged with cars during the summer months.

AL *Crutch's Country House*, T7138116, F7138159. Tucked away off the main road and conveniently close to Fermoyle Beach. **A** *Barnagh Bridge*, Camp, T7130145, F30299. A guesthouse, which avoids looking like the standard bungalow B&B. Floral-patterned bedrooms, a breakfast room with glorious views of Tralee Bay and a morning menu of smoked salmon, home-baked breads and other alternatives to fried food. **B** *Bedrock House*, Stradbally, T7139401. Double rooms around IR£36 in this B&B. **B** *The Fuschia House*, West Main St, Castlegregory, T7139508. B&B charging around IR£36 for a double. **B** *Strand View House*, Connor Pass Rd, Kilcummin, T7138131, F7139434. B&B. **D** *Connor Pass Hostel*, Stradbally, T7139179. On the main road but there are no private rooms.

Sleeping

Camping At Castlegregory both *Green Acres Caravan Park*, T7139158, and *Sandybay Caravan Park*, T7139338, accept campers.

At Camp *The Junction Bar* serves light snacks throughout the day and there is a pool room and dart board for rainy afternoons while *The Railway Tavern*, T7130188, has traditional music sessions on Sundays from 1730.

Eating, pubs & music

In Castlegregory, *O'Riordan's Cafe*, T7139379, has more to offer than the name suggests. As well as tasty home-cooked snacks and light meals there is an enlightened menu that offers non-meat eaters something over than a revolting lasagne made from frozen vegetables, as well as local seafood, Kerry lamb and beef in Guinness. Open daily, June to September, from 1200 to 2100; around IR£6 for lunch and IR£10-15 for dinner. *Ned Natterjack's*, T7139491,West End, Castlegregory, is a family-friendly pub with garden seating that serves good food throughout the day and livens up on a Saturday night with live music. *Ferriter's Loft*, T7139494, is a pub serving steaks, seafood and burgers and evening sessions of traditional music.

County Kerry

The Dingle Way

The Kerry Way is scenically stunning and the Beara Way is wild and empty, but the Dingle Way has touches of both and the largest variety of walks and the most fun things to do when not walking. From miles of empty sandy beaches to fossil-clad cliffs to long mountainside paths and a stiff climb up Mount Brandon this Way has so much to offer it seems a waste that anyone should leave the area not having walked for at least a couple of days.

To complete the Dingle Way requires about seven or eight days:

Day 1	Tralee to Camp	11 miles (17½ km)
Day 2	Camp to Annascaul	10½ miles (17 km)
Day 3	Annascaul to Dingle	12 miles (19 km)
Day 4	Dingle to Dunquin	14 miles (22 km)
Day 5	Dunquin to Ballydavid	13 miles (21 km)
Day 6	Ballydavid to Cloghane	17½ miles (28 km)
Day 7	Cloghane to Castlegregory	18 miles (29 km)
Day 8	Castlegregory to Tralee	16 miles (25 km)

Mapping The Dingle Way is covered by the Ordnance Survey (OS) Discovery series sheets 70 and 71 and these are essential for the walks. Cork-Kerry Tourism produces a strip map for the Dingle Way, which is not essential but could be used in conjunction with the OS maps.

Day 1: Tralee to Camp

12 miles (19 km); 6 hrs; total ascent 410 ft (125m)

The walk begins with a long spell on tarmac amongst traffic but does have the advantage of bringing you along the canal to Blennerville Windmill. Otherwise, hop on a bus or catch a lift about two miles out of town to where the route leaves the main road and heads uphill. Be careful here, as the waymarker is skilfully disguised. The left turn off the main road is followed by a sharp right almost immediately. The route quickly finds the open hillside and rolls gaily along past boulder fields, over streams, by ancient waterworks, with the beauty of the hills to the left and the panoramic scene of the coastline below you. An added bonus is looking down at the vehicular traffic that looks like little dinky toys scuttling about. The route follows the ditch between the fields and the upland pasture. Camp, the day's destination, is strung out along two or three miles of road, so if you are booking accommodation in advance – for example at *Daly's Bar* or the *Railway Tavern* (see 'Sleeping' on page 384) – enquire where exactly it is, since there are several places where you can leave the route.

Day 2: Camp to Annascaul

10½ miles (17 km); 6 hrs; total ascent 1,475 ft (450m)

The walk is largely along tarmac but the scenery more than makes up for the sore feet. The route crosses the peninsula, travelling through a low central valley inhabited only by sheep. Emerging on the southern coast it brings stunning views of the beach and sand dunes at Inch. Turning back inland, the route goes uphill and crosses Ardroe and Maum, a saddle between two mountains. From here there are excellent views down into Annascaul Glen. At Annascaul, besides the two hostels mentioned in the Annascaul section below, there are some B&Bs, which include *Four Winds* and *Anchor House* (see 'Sleeping' on page 384 for details).

Day 3: Annascaul to Dingle

14 miles (22 km); 7 hrs; total ascent 1,312 ft (400m)

Another day largely on tarmac but with some good views, lots of antiquities to poke around in and a brilliant storm beach with huge boulders. Leaving Annascaul, the route travels via a minor road to the coast. For most of the day the route keeps close to, and high above, the southern coast, passing by the ruins of Minard castle, destroyed by Cromwell's armies, and an interesting old graveyard at Aglish where bodies are interred in stone mausoleums rather than buried in the ground. Lispole, a few miles east of Dingle, has the IHH *Seacrest Hostel* (see 'Sleeping on page 384). See also the Dingle section for accommodation in the town itself (page 371).

Day 4: Dingle to Dunquin

14 miles (22 km); 7 hrs; total ascent 1,150 ft (350m)

After a long, rather dull section of the walk on tarmac to Ventry the route takes off with a glorious walk around Ventry Harbour and then a cliff walk around the coast, with Mount Eagle looming to the landward across a landscape littered with clocháns and other ancient remains. The views are amazing along the last section and more than make up for the little bit of walking that is necessary along the main road. For accommodation and restaurants, see the Dunquin section on page 376.

Natterjack toads

Visitors flock daily to Dingle to catch sight of one socially maladjusted dolphin (naturally gregarious creatures living in large communities) when Kerry's real zoological treat lies croaking very loudly on the north side of the peninsula near Castlegregory. The natterjack is Ireland's only toad, looking like a frog but darker and with a yellow stripe along its spine, and if you lurk around Lough Gill at night with a torchlight you should be able to spot one during the mating season between April and June. Their blaring croaks attract females but the male will launch itself on the first fellow natterjack spotted until a female catch has been confirmed and mating can proceed. The male is a possessive creature, determined to prevent anyone else from mating with his betrothed, and the poor female remains encumbered by the male clutching her around the abdomen until she is ready to spawn. This encourages her to spawn as soon as possible, up to 4,000 eggs at a time.

This day's walk could be accomplished as a day trip from Dingle by catching the afternoon bus (1555, July and August only; 1825 Monday and Thursday only, all year) from Dunquin back to Dingle. Alternatively, with your own transport you could park at Ventry and have time to reach Dunquin and then walk back to Ventry by taking the short inland road across Coumaleagua Hill.

Day 5: Dunquin to Ballydavid

A long wonderful day's walk around Slea Head, first climbing the lower slopes of Croaghmartin and then dropping down to Clogher Beach where there are huge (and dangerous) waves, and ancient fossils of ferns and shelled creatures in the rocks at the northern end of the beach. Beyond Clogher the route travels for a time along tarmac roads to Smerwick Harbour, where it follows the line of the shore as far as Ballydavid. From there, another spell on tarmac along a desolate windswept road brings you to Brandon Creek where there are some B&Bs. The best place to stay, the *An Bóthar* pub and restaurant, is very comfortable and has live music most nights in summer (for details, see 'Sleeping' on page 384). *15 miles (24 km); 8 hrs; total ascent 656 ft (200m)*

Day 6: Ballydavid to Cloghane

Of the many amazing walks that this peninsula has to offer, this has to be the best. The walk starts with a long, challenging walk up to a saddle of Mount Brandon with the most amazing views behind, growing more panoramic the higher you climb. Over the saddle the descent is rapid and the path runs past more stunning views, but to the north this time. On a fine day the coastline around Sauce Creek looks as if it has been painted on. The Way carries on through a country park area on wide stony tracks and then through Brandon village before following the coast around to Cloghane. For accommodation, see the Cloghane section on page 380. *14 miles (22 km); 8 hrs; total ascent 2,640 ft (750m)*

Day 7: Cloghane to Castlegregory

After a few miles of tarmac the route meets the beach and spends the rest of the day following the coastline around Fahamore and into the village of Castlegregory. Even on the hottest summer's day the beach is quite empty with occasional anglers fishing for plaice in the surf. The beach is wide and firm and makes a great walk, even at high tide when there is always some sand still exposed. It passes Stradbally where the church ruins and the wildlife sanctuary *14 miles (22 km); 6 hrs*

County Kerry

at Lough Gill can be explored. There are more ruins at Kilshannig at the end of the peninsula. Castlegregory has B&Bs as well as the hostel listed in the Castlegregory section on page 381.

Day 8: Castlegregory to Tralee

14 miles (22 km), 6 hrs; total ascent 900 ft (275m)

After a spell of walking along the shoreline the route meets first of all the main road and then the outward leg of Day 1, which you follow in reverse back to Tralee. The first part of the walk is well worth the effort and the hillwalk back to Tralee is just as pretty as it was on the way out but, if you don't like backtracking, the Annascaul to Tralee bus can be hailed as it passes. There is a daily bus from Dingle, and two buses from Castlegregory to Tralee on Fridays only. Check in Castlegregory for times. For accommodation, see the Tralee section on page 366.

Sleeping *Daly's Bar*, Camp, T7130125. In the village, with en-suite rooms at IR£15 per person sharing. *The Railway Tavern*, Camp, T7130188. On the main road to Tralee a little out of the village, and has en-suite rooms. **B** *Four Winds*, Annascaul, T9157168. B&B at IR£17. Also does evening meals. **B** *Anchor House*, Annascaul, T/F9157382. Does evening meals and charges IR£17 per person for B&B. **D** *Seacrest Hostel*, Lispole, T/F9151390. IHH hostel a few miles east of Dingle, which includes 1 private room and camping space. **D** *An Bóthar*, Brandon Creek, T9155342. Pub and restaurant, also offering accommodation. About half a mile inland, this pub caters to walkers and can organize packed lunches and walks in the area.

You picture them dotted over with flocks of sheep, which nibble the short sweet grass ... But these Burren hills are literally not clothed at all. They are startlingly, I may say scandalously, naked ...

Emily Lawless (1845-1913):
Hurrish

10

County Clare

From the sublime to the ridiculous, Clare has much to offer the visitor. Sublime describes the majestic, almost frightening beauty of the Burren, with its sulky grey limestone hills and abundance of wild flowers; the ridiculous is the tourist ghetto of Bunratty Castle with students dressed up in daft clothes to pay for next year's college and coachloads of the gullible disgorging at a rate that almost comes close to Killarney in August. In between are ancient tower houses lurking in fields, mighty dolmens and ring forts, medieval church ruins, the terrifying Cliffs of Moher, a hippy musical centre at Doolin, the seasoned tourist villages of Lisdoonvarna and Ballyvaughan, and the long caravan-dotted western coast from Lahinch, where the Atlantic surf crashes ashore to Loop Head.

★ Try to find time for

Studying the amazing wild flowers in the Burren

Taking a guided tour of Ailwee Cave to see the giant bear prints

Admiring Maire Rua's house on the road from Ennis to Ballyvaughan

Wondering what the purpose of sheela-na-gigs is at the ruins of Killinaboy Church

Enjoying the music at Doolin and Ennis

Taking part in the matchmaking festival in Lisdoonvarna

Relaxing in a hot sulphur bath at the Spa Wells in Lisdoonvarna

Doing some communing with the Dolphins at Carrigaholt

Walking in the karst scenery of the Burren

Eating the chocolate dessert and wondering at the skyscapes at Ballinalacken Castle Hotel

County Clare

Ins and outs

Shannon Airport (see box opposite) is in eastern Clare, and is a major entry point for many travellers. There are buses to Ennis several times a day from Galway, Dublin, Cork and Limerick. Trains link Ennis with Limerick from where there are connections to Cork, Waterford and Dublin. If you are arriving in Clare from Kerry there is the Killimer-Tarbert ferry, an excellent way of saving a long drive round the coast to Limerick. The ferry crosses at half-hourly intervals, takes about 20 minutes, and costs IR£8 per vehicle (for fuller details see page 416).

Ennis

Phone code: 065
Colour map 3, grid A4

Bursting at the seams, this 11th-century market town is the major shopping area for the villages around it as well as a major summer tourist destination. Its narrow streets groan under the weight of modern traffic and O'Connell, towering over the lot of it in the centre of town, must be wondering whatever happened. But it's a pleasant little town with an amazing amount of really good traditional music in the summer months and a few places to keep you busy. Better still, use Ennis as a base for visiting east Clare before moving on to the real highlight of the county – The Burren.

Ins & outs Ennis is easily walkable. Bikes are available for hire and are the nicest way of getting to sights outside the town, and there are several taxi companies. ***Bus Éireann*** runs limited summer services to towns in west and north Clare. From Lisdoonvarna a connection can be made with the Galway to Tralee bus which goes via the Killimer-Tarbert ferry.

Sights

The Friary Ennis is a compact little town bisected by the river Fergus. It has expanded south of the original heart of the city, which is around the Friary in Abbey Street. Established in the 13th century by the O'Briens, kings of Thomond, the Friary now stands in a state of beautiful ruin. What you see is largely 14th century, with the beautiful east window dating back to the original with its fine thin mullions between the lancet windows. In the 14th century there was a large school here with 600 pupils and about 350 friars. The west end of the church is probably 15th century. On the southwest face of the tower is a carving of St Francis showing the stigmata. Inside the tower is a carving of the Virgin and child and at the east end of the south wall is the ornately carved McMahon tomb, which depicts a bishop giving benediction, and scenes of the arrest and crucifixion of Christ, all dating to around 1475. On the east side is the figure of a woman, thought to be More Ni Brien, the woman who founded the tomb.

The Friary was the last school of catholic study to survive the Reformation. Franciscans came and went through the 17th century, as the buildings gradually decayed and the school dissolved. It was deserted by the end of the 17th century. ■ *Abbey Street, T29100. Late May to late September, daily 0930-1830. Possibly open at Easter weekend. IR£1. Guided tours available on request.*

De Valera Museum The other place to see in Ennis is the De Valera Museum. De Valera was MP for Ennis for 42 continuous years, and the museum holds a collection of memorabilia of the man himself and other momentous occasions in Ennis' past. ■ *Harmony Row, T6821616. Monday and Thursday 1100-1730, Tuesday, Wednesday and Friday 1100-2000. Free.*

Shannon Airport

Once a vital stopover for transatlantic flights, Shannon is now little more than another regional airport in Ireland. Most transatlantic flights to Dublin stop over at Shannon, and it may be the first sight of Ireland for many American visitors. Most visitors will move on to Limerick, 15 miles away, from where there are connections by bus and rail to other parts of Ireland but Ennis and the rest of County Clare are an equally good route to take from Shannon. Flights to other parts of Ireland are run by Ryanair, T061-471444, Aer Lingus, T061-471666 and some smaller companies. There are frequent buses from the airport to Ennis, Bunratty and Limerick, T061-474311 for times. A single fare to Limerick or Ennis is around IR£5. Bus Eireann also has services from Shannon to Galway and Dublin. A taxi from the airport to Ennis or Limerick costs IR£15. Car hire is available at the airport.

There is a cafe and a restaurant at the airport as well as a tourist information desk, T061-471664, which will make bookings. Opening hours to match arrivals. A Bank of Ireland counter operates similar times.

Car hire at Shannon Airport

Avis, T061-471094; **Budget**, T061-471361; **Dooley**, T061-471098; **Hertz**, T061-471369; **Johnson & Perrot**, T061-471094; **Murrays**, T061-701200; **National**, T061-472633.

For those who have missed the big tours of Waterford Crystal or Tyrone Crystal there is the Shannon Crystal Factory Shop, where there are daily demonstrations of crystal cutting. ■ *Sandfield Centre, T6821250. Monday-Friday 0900-1800, Saturday 0900-1200, Sunday 0930-1700.*

Shannon Crystal

Essentials

L *Woodstock Hotel & Golf Club*, Shanaway Road, T6844777, F6844888. Golf-orientated hotel, 1 mile (2 km) out of town on the Lahinch Road. All amenities. **AL** *Auburn Lodge Hotel*, Galway Rd, T6821247, F6821202. Another big, golf-orientated, conference type of place. 1 mile (1.6 km) out of town on the Galway Road. Live traditional music nightly in the bar. **AL** *Old Ground Hotel*, O'Connell St, T6828127, F6828112. In the centre of Ennis and very popular with lunchtime eaters: lots of bars. **A** *Magowna House Hotel*, Inch, T6839009, F6839258. A small hotel set in large grounds, 4 miles (6.4 km) west of Ennis but good value. Bar, restaurant, drying facilities for walkers, golfers, etc. **B** *Aisling Gheal*, St Flannan's Cross, Limerick Rd, T6823810. Slightly more expansive B&B, with 6 rooms. or the smaller **B** *Clonrush*, Lahinch Road, T6829692. B&B with 4 en-suite rooms. **B** *Moyville*, Lahinch Road, T6828278. B&B with 4 rooms

Sleeping
■ *on map*
Price codes:
see inside front cover

County Clare

and the option of dinner. **B** *St Anne's* T6828501. Smaller B&B, open from March to December. **D** *Clare Lodge*, Summerhill/Carmody Rd, T6829370. Has private rooms as well as dormitories. **D** *Abbey Tourist Hostel*, Harmony Row, T6822620. Has a great location overlooking the river and single and double rooms.

Eating
● *on map*
Price codes:
see inside front cover

There are a few restaurants in town with an attitude so your nights here should be filled with good things to eat. In Abbey St, beside the **Queen's Hotel** is the old style **Cruises**, T6828963, which serves interestingly cooked fish and meat in a traditional Irish style. It has won lots of awards, none of them recent. Dinner around IR£15 plus. *Brannagan's* at Mill Rd, T6820211, serves modern Irish steak and seafood at around IR£15 for dinner. At the *Auburn Lodge Hotel* is *The Oyster Room* serving traditional Irish steaks and fish. IR£15 plus for dinner. The *O'Brien Room* at the *Old Ground Hotel* serves a mixture of traditional and innovative dishes, served largely to lunchtime eaters but doing dinner also.

In Parnell St is *Sicilian*, T6843873, serving pizzas and pasta dishes from 1700 to 2300. On the opposite side of the road is *Punjab*, T6844655, serving Indian food.

Several of the pubs do good lunchtime food at very reasonable prices, mostly IR£5 or less. *Alexander's Restaurant* in Knox's Bar in Abbey St, T6829264, is a theme pub with a nostalgic window display and does self-service hot lunches. Further along

Ennis

To Dysert O'Dea Castle, Corofin, Ennistymon,
Lahinch, Cliffs of Moher & The Burren (N85)

To Auburn Lodge Hotel,
Gort & Galway (N18)

People's Park

New Road

River Fergus

To golf course, Kilmaley &
Milltown Malbay (R474)

Cusack Rd

Sanfield Park

College Road

Mill Road

Harmony Row

Bindon St

Pound Ln

St Columba's

Bank Place

Considine Tce

Cornmarket St

De Valera Museum & Library

Ennis Friary

Parking

Abbey St

Francis St

Tierney's Bike Hire

MacCool's Internet Café

Franciscan Friary

O'Connell Square

Wood Qy

Parking

Parnell St

Simms Lane

Parking

Cabey's Ln

Fahy's Ln

Summerhill

Lwr Market St

Cook's Ln

Market Place

Shopping centre

Parking

Camboy St

Lwr Dumbiggle

Old Barrack St

O'Connell St

Parking

St Peter & Paul's Pro Cathedral

Parking

Henry St

To Scariff, Mountshannon
& Lough Derg (R352)

To Feakle, Quin, Quin Abbey, Knappogue
Castle & Craggaunowen (R469)

Clon Road

Station Rd

To Kilrush Creek Marina,
Loop Head, Carrigaholt
& Killimer car ferry (N68)

Clare Rd

To West County Inn, Clare Abbey, Shannon airport,
Bunratty Castle, Dromoland Castle & Limerick (N18)

N

0 yards   100
0 metres   100

■ **Sleeping**
1 Abbey Tourist Hostel
2 Clare Hostel
3 Old Ground
4 Queens & Outer Limits
5 Temple Gate

● **Eating & drinking**
1 Alexander's & Knox's Bar
2 Brandon's Bar
3 Brannagan's Bar
4 Brogan's Pub
5 Ciaran's Bar

6 Cloister's Pub & Restaurant
7 Cruise's Pub & Restaurant
8 Henry J's

County Clare

Abbey St is *Cloisters* bar and restaurant, T6840011, where there is bar food till late, but the restaurant needs a reservation and can set you back IR£25 plus. Along O'Connell St are 2 pubs doing very good bar food, Brogan's at number 24, T6829859, has an inexpensive set lunch while just along the road at number 70 is *Brandon's Bar*, T6828133, with a similar menu of chips and things.

This is where Ennis shines as a place to visit. Most pubs and the hotels have some kind of live music, usually traditional Irish. *Cruises* has live traditional music every night all year round, *Ciarans*, 1 Francis St, T6840180, has live traditional music Thursday to Sunday from June to October, while *May Kearney's Bar*, 1 Newbridge Rd, Lifford, T6824888, has music Wednesday to Sunday in summer. Other pubs with at least 1 night of Irish music are *Tailor Quigley's*, Galway Rd, T6821247 (Tuesday and Wednesday), *Preacher's* in the Temple Gate Hotel, T6823300 (Saturday), *O'Halloran's Bar*, 8 High St, T6823090 (Wednesday-Monday). Sessions start late so if you can't find any music on take a cruise around town and listen, or just wait where you are. At *Cois na hAhna* in Galway Rd, T6822347, on Wednesdays throughout the year at 2030 there are ceili dancing sessions. *Maoin Cheoil an Chláir*, T6841774, is a school of traditional music, which often puts on concerts. Other pubs have country and western music or tribute bands. For these you could try *Brannagan's*, *Darcy's Corner* in Upper O'Connell St, the *Porter Stall* in Market St or *Henry J's Cocktail Bar* in Upper Market St. Ennis also has nightclubs for those who like late nights and loud music. *The Sanctuary* and the *Outer Limits* are in the *Queen's Hotel*, *Central Park* in Brannagan's and *The Boardwalk* is at *Brandon's* in O'Connell St.

Pubs, clubs & music

Among the many festivals and events that take place in Ennis each year, two are worth looking out for – the *Fleadh Nua*, a traditional music festival usually held around the last week in **May** (T6828366 for details) and the *Ennis Arts Festival*, held in **October** (T6820166 for information). There is another, less well known traditional music festival around the middle of **November** (T6828366 for information).

Festivals

Fishing *ME Tierney Cycles and Fishing*, 17 Abbey St, T6829433. Also rents bicycles.

Sport

Bicycle *ME Tierney Cycles and Fishing*, 17 Abbey St, T6829433. Bike hire; also hires out fishing gear. **Car** Car hire: *TMT Rentals*, 70 O'Connell St, T6824211. **Car parks**: in Abbey St, Parnell St, Temple gate and The Friary. **Ferry** For details of the Killimer-Tarbert ferry see page 412. **Taxi** *Abbey Taxis*, T6822646. *Banner Taxis*, T6821021.

Transport

Banks and bureaux de change Most of the banks are around O'Connell Square. The tourist office and post office can also change money. **Communications** Post office: Bank Pl, T6821054. Mon-Fri 0900-1730, Sat 0930-1300. Internet: *MacCools Internet Café*, Brewery Lane, T6821988. **Places of worship** The Friary, Francis St. St Columba's Church of Ireland, Bindon St. St Peter and Paul's Catholic Cathedral, O'Connell St. **Tourist office** Arthur's Row, T6828366. Jul-Aug, Mon-Sat 0900-1800; Sep-Jun, Mon-Sat 0930-1730.

Directory

County Clare

Around Ennis

Using Ennis as a base there are several sites of interest to the north and south of the town. The N18 south to Limerick is well worth avoiding if you are cycling and the suggested route east to Quin and Craggaunowen and Knappogue avoids the worst of it, although if you want to see Bunratty part of it is unavoidable. Dysert O'Dea to the north can be done as a day trip from Ennis or taken in *en route* to the Burren.

Quin Abbey A building of some kind has stood on this site since the 13th century when a church here was burned and replaced with a De Clare castle, part of the towers of which still survive here. In 1236 the castle was sacked by warring Irish clans and the castle replaced by another church the restored version of which you see before you. If you think about it, quite a lot of murdering must have taken place on this site over the centuries. Hopefully, the Franciscans brought a bit of peace to the place. The ruins are very beautiful and well preserved and you can climb the tower and look down over the cloisters, which are some of the best preserved in Ireland. Inside the church are some 15th and 16th century tombstones. The little church on the other side of the river is 13th century. The nearby village of Quin is famous for the discovery of a huge hoard of gold, some of which found its way to the National Museum in Dublin. ■ *June to September, daily. Free.*

Knappogue Castle From Quin Abbey travel two miles south on the L31 and you come to Knappogue Castle, a medieval castle built by Sean McNamara in 1467, which somehow never fell into ruin. It has a long history and probably owes its intactness to the fact that Cromwell used it as a headquarters rather than blow it up, which is what he did to any other place that could be fortified. The ground floor additions are 19th century. If you like that sort of thing you can attend a medieval banquet there and listen to stories about women in Irish myth and history. ■ *Banquets: May to October, daily 1730 and 2045. T061-360788 to book. Castle: April to October, daily 0930-1730. Last admission 1630. IR£2.75.*

Craggaunowen This, another medieval tower house built by the family that built Bunratty Castle (see page 392), is the basis for another heritage project. The castle itself is home to a series of 16th-century European woodcarvings, part of the Hunt Collection, most of which is in Limerick. The grounds of the castle hold reproductions of a *crannog* (a house built on to an artificial island in a lake), a ring fort and an outdoor cooking place. Young people, dressed in Celtic outfits practise making objects using ancient tools. There is also a genuine Iron Age roadway brought from a bog in County Longford. The most interesting exhibit there, in a glasshouse designed by Liam McCormack who has had a hand in so many Irish cathedrals, is the *Brendan*, a boat built and sailed across the Atlantic by Tim Severin in 1976. The boat is based on descriptions of the kind used by St Brendan to cross the Atlantic and was built and successfully sailed in an effort to prove that St Brendan's journey was possible (see box on page 380). Its hull is made from tanned oxhides stretched over an ash frame. ■ *April to October, daily 1000-1800. Last admission 1700. IR£4. Teashop, guided tours, picnic area.*

Cratloe Woods House From Quin you can continue on along the L31 to Cratloe, where there is the Cratloe Woods House, a 17th-century Irish longhouse open to the public but still lived in. Pets corner, old farm machinery and curios. ■ *June to mid-September, Monday-Saturday 1400-1800, T 061-327028. IR£2.50. Café, parking.*

Bunratty Castle From Cratloe you can head back towards Ennis on the N18 to come to Bunratty Castle. This is the leprechaun and shillelagh version of the Ulster American Folk Park in Northern Ireland, which is surprising since the castle is quite genuine and so are several of the buildings in the Folk Park. The castle was built in 1460 (1425 in some versions of the story) by MacNamaras and later came into the possession of the O'Briens who held it until 1712. During the English civil war and Cromwell's invasion of Ireland it was held by the republican forces. What you see is the keep, the main building of the castle,

*Bunratty Castle in 1830,
by RO'C Newenham*

which would have been well inside a curtain wall. Some time after 1712 the keep fell into ruins, which were then bought by Lord Gort in 1954 and restored. Very little of the renovations are invention or guesswork and the furnishing inside are quite genuine. The same for the village street and different styles of houses and their contents in the park, yet somehow it all has that air of Disneyland about it. Perhaps it's the gift shop, or the girls in period dress. Anyway, ignore the tour bus groups, dodge the group photos, squeeze through the crowd buying totally unrelated tea towels in the gift shop and have a good look round the old houses. They are a fascinating insight into a bygone but still almost tangible age. ■ *September to May, daily 0930-1730, last entry 1645; June to August, daily 0900-1830, last entry 1745. Last entry to castle 1600 all year. Closed Good Friday, Christmas Eve, Christmas Day and St Stephen's Day. Banquets daily 1730 and 2045. Reservations T061-36078.*

North to the Burren

Dysert O'Dea

Travelling north of Ennis on the R476 brings you to Dysert O'Dea, on the way to Corofin. This is a whole collection of ancient remains, the chief interest being the 1487 O'Dea Castle, which is now a museum. Cromwell's forces ruined the castle in 1651, but it was renovated in 1986 and has won a number of awards for its exhibitions on archaeology. The actual dysert or anchorite church was founded some time in the eighth century by St Tola, after whom it was first named. What you see is a Romanesque ruin that has been reassembled, incorrectly in places. Particularly beautiful is the Romanesque doorway with carved geometric patterns and series of carved heads, human and animal. In the northwest of the site are the remains of a round tower built as a defence for the church property some time around the turn of the last millennium. The church and tower suffered the same fate as the castle in 1651. There is also a 12th-century high cross depicting the crucifixion and a bishop, and with geometric patterns and human and animal figures decorating the sides. The museum has a suggested walk around these sights and several other historic places in the area. ■ *Castle: 1st May to 30th September, daily 1000-1800. T065-6837401. Café, shop. IR£2.50.*

Clare Heritage Centre

This heritage centre is to be found in the village of **Corofin**, in a converted church. Inside are exhibitions on the Famine, emigration and living conditions in the 19th century as well as a room focusing on the 1798 uprising. It's a pleasant little place: no high-tech audio-visuals but lots of source materials. In the same building is a genealogical research centre where people with roots in Clare can search out their ancestors. ■ *Heritage centre: April to October, daily 0930-1730. IR£2. Research centre: T065-6837955. Monday to Friday, 0900-1730; May to September, daily 0900-1730. http://clare.irishroots.net/*

County Clare

Sheela-na-gigs

These very unusual figures, 'the hag with the breasts' or 'the hag squatting', appear all over Ireland and England, usually associated with medieval churches. They are crudely drawn, grimacing female figures pointing to their genitalia, which figure prominently in the carving. Most of them were made between the 13th and 16th centuries. The origin of the word is the same as the Australian slang for woman, from the Irish for 'old woman'. Possibly they are intended as the symbolic representation of lust, the evil thats can beset devout men on their way into church! A more positive interpretation of them is that they are protective figures, representing Irish women warriors who frightened their enemies by exposing their genitalia to them, just as the ancient Scottish soldiers showed their genitals before charging into battle. There were probably far more of them at one stage but their removal was ordered in the 17th century. Another figure is on White Island in County Fermanagh, there is one in the National Museum in Dublin and opening one of the many drawers in the Hunt Collection in Limerick reveals another.

Sleeping, eating, pubs & music

Corofin has a good hostel, the **D** *Corofin Village Hostel*, Main St, T065-68537683. There are some family rooms as well as doubles. Camping in the grounds. B&Bs line the road to Kilfenora and Lisdoonvarna. The *Inchiquin Kitchen* serves bar food all day and has a beer garden, while the *Corofin Arms*, Main St serves food until 1900. You can hear traditional music there on Tuesdays, Fridays, Saturdays and Sundays from around 2130. *Bofey Quins*, Main St, has one huge menu served in the bar and in the seafood restaurant. Main courses around IR£6. The really posh place to eat here is the *Gairdín Restaurant*, Market St, T065-6837425. Seafood and meat dishes are on the menu and dinner will cost around IR£15. Open Tuesday-Saturday 1900-2130, Sunday 1230-1430.

The Burren

Leaving Corofin and heading north you enter the Burren (Boireann – a rocky place), a strange, at times unearthly looking place where it is difficult to imagine anyone could ever have eked out a living in the bare limestone rock. But eke they did, since earliest times as the hundreds of prehistoric sites in the area demonstrate. The 100 square miles of it is a little paradise for geologists, archaeologists, botanists and people with flashy cameras. It's also a great place for the inexpert with miles and miles of walking, brilliant views and some cute little villages where there is music, good food and good company.

Ins and outs

Getting there & around

From Ennis the best route into the Burren is the one suggested above (on page 393): via Corofin. From there a good way to proceed is towards Lisdoonvarna: it's a good place for a base and the journey is shockingly beautiful.

If you are using public transport, Bus Nos 337 or 15, summer only, travel from Limerick to Ennis and then through Inagh, Ennistymon, Lahinch, Liscannor, the cliffs of Moher to Lisdoonvarna and then on to Doolin, so this might make a better route around the Burren. There are 2 or 3 buses a day.

If you are heading straight to the Burren from outside Clare there are buses from Galway into various villages in the Burren, one of which connects with Tralee via the Killimer Tarbert ferry.

Máire Rua

Some women just get a bad press and
Máire Rua is one of them. Máire O'Brien,
neé Neylan from Ballynagowan was the
wife of Conor O'Brien, the owner of
Leamanagh Castle. Legend has it that she
often accompanied her husband in his
attacks on English settlers in the area. In
1651 Conor met Cromwell's forces in
battle and was mortally wounded. Seeing
his prostrate form being carried home
Maire is said to have called out, rather
callously, 'We need no dead men here!' She
nursed him all night until he died than
promptly rode into Limerick and offered
herself to any one of General Ireton's
Cromwellian forces who would marry her.
Her offer was taken up by a man called
John Cooper, who lived to regret it because

she bumped him off along with 24 other
unfortunate husbands. Her offer to Ireton
was intended to secure her son's
inheritance because she would have been
driven out of her house otherwise. Other
legends of her unladylike ways include
hanging her servants out of the windows.
She died the death she deserved, being
entombed alive in a hollow tree.

In reality the house was occupied by
Cromwell's troops until 1660, whether
Máire was married to one of them or not.
Her son, Donal, reclaimed the house in
that year and found it ruined. He became
the MP for Clare and served in that
position for 20 years, to be followed
centuries later by de Valera and Daniel
O'Connell, who also held the job.

History

Since limestone is very high in nutrients plants flourished here, and after the last Ice Age these hills would have been covered in hazel scrub, pine and yew trees. Later, oak ash, and elm replaced them. It wasn't erosion that removed the trees but humans, arriving around 5,000 years ago and clearing the tops of the hills for farms, defence and places of worship. The earliest signs of humans are the huge dolmens dating back to 3000BCE. Later graves are smaller, the wedge tombs of around 1500BCE. By the iron age ring forts had started to be built, still on the tops of the hills, lived in by important men and surrounded by defensive stone walls. There are around 500 of these on the Burren. The 12th century gave us the church ruins and high crosses such as the one at Dysert O'Dea (see page 393). The 15th century saw the building of the fortified houses such as Lemenagh Castle, where Maire Rua lived (see box on page 395). Towns such as Lisdoonvarna or Doolin arrived much later some time in the 18th century. At that time the Burren was crowded with wood cabins thatched with mud, later replaced by stone buildings. Most of these are on the lower slopes of the hills, near to old butter roads or routes into the villages. The 19th century saw a vast reduction in the numbers of people living on the Burren. Death and emigration saw many people off and the trend has continued into the present day when finally as you walk around the hillsides, which are now bare of grazing animals, you can see, in the cracks in the limestone, blackthorn and hazel scrub building up again, creating a new forest until farming here becomes viable again.

Geology

350 million years ago this was the bed of a great sea, its warm waters filled with tiny, shelled creatures and coral which, as they died, sank to the bottom. Aeons later mud and shale was dumped on top of the thick layer of shell, crushing it and forming limestone rock. Then the great upheaval that made the Swiss Alps and shook Ireland like a great rug into the huge folds of west Cork and Kerry threw up these lower, rounder hills. The erosion that rounded the tops of the

Kerry mountains and removed the limestone from their tops just removed the shale from the Burren, leaving the great sheets of almost horizontal limestone bare to the elements. But limestone is highly soluble and the rain and ice filled cracks in the stone wearing them away and widening them so that what you see today looks like huge pieces of crazy paving with deep fissures. The Ice Ages further rounded and eroded the hills and left great lumps of granite rock abandoned as the meltwaters departed. You can see these huge incongruous boulders as you walk around the hills. Below the surface, underground cave systems were created by the water, which formed underground streams where it met harder, less soluble rock. In places caves collapsed, forming deep depressions in the rock above, called turloughs, which can fill with water very quickly when it rains and the land below becomes soaked.

Corofin to Lisdoonvarna

Continuing on the road to Lisdoonvarna brings you first to **Killinaboy Church**, a ruined 16th-century church up on the left-hand side of the road in a field. Not much to look at but worth the stop for the **Sheela-na-gig** over the south doorway (see box on page 394). Next stop is **Leamanagh Castle**, rudely bursting out of a field beside the road to Ballyvaughan. The eastern side is a 14th-century fortified tower with a stone vault on the roof with gun emplacements. The rest of the building was a house added in the 1640s and lived in by various people, among them **Máire Rua**, one of Ireland's very wicked women. The castle is not accessible, being in a privately owned field whose owner has had to deal with visitors knocking his walls down, but there is a good view from the road.

The Burren

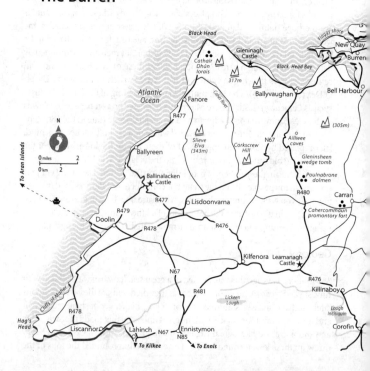

County Clare

Kilfenora

This is a major part of the tour bus route around Clare. The **Cathedral** is probably one of the smallest you'll ever see and it is still used for worship. The church was founded by St Fachtnan in the sixth century, replaced by a stone building, which was burned down in 1055 by an unfriendly O'Brien, rebuilt, destroyed in an accidental fire in 1100, rebuilt again and made into a bishopric in 1152, an event that you can see pictured on the Doorty high cross (west of the church; the 12th-century equivalent of the Polaroid snap). It was never a popular place with bishops; Dr Richard Betts, offered the job by Charles I, said he had no wish to become bishop of the poorest see in Ireland.

The current building is a 13th-century site restructured in the 19th century. The chancel (the east end of the church where the altar was sited) has 13th- and 14th-century badly carved bishops on it and the north wall has a quite beautiful sedilia (a seat set into the wall) with delicate stone traceries on the three-arched design. Around the church and in a field to the west are the famous stone crosses.

Beside the church is the **Burren Centre**. It has information about the Burren, audio-visual displays and lots of people milling about. You'd be better off taking a walk around the Burren. ■ *March to May and October, daily 1000-1700; June to September, daily 0930-1800. IR£2.50. Café, shop.*

Sleeping, eating Not much in the way of accommodation here. **B** *Carraig Liath*, T065-7088075. On the R476 just outside of town, this is a pleasant place that does an evening meal on request. *Mrs Murphy*, Main St, T065-7088040. B&B in the village itself. **D** *Kilfenora Boghill Centre Hostel*, T065-7074644. A must for traditional-music-loving vegans who don't mind dormitory accommodation. Nice big drawing room.

Entertainment Musical entertainment is supplied by *Linane's*, which has traditional music every night in summer and *Nagle's*, which has music at weekends all year. *Vaughan's* T7088004, has traditional music, set dancing in the barn on Thursdays and Sundays and pub food.

Lisdoonvarna

Colour map 2, grid C3

From Kilfenora a fairly uneventful road leads to Lisdoonvarna, home of the famous song and the even more famous matchmakers. Until quite recently families would bring their daughters here in September, after the hay was in, to meet gentlemen, or so they hoped, farmers. Nowadays the matchmaking festival is a good excuse for a party, with the various pubs in town and around each putting on events such as ballroom dancing, ceilidhs and live music. The month-long festival has a host of regular visitors, mostly middle-aged Irish people

County Clare

A typical day at the matchmaking

1200-1400
A dance at the Spa Wells *or the dance hall*

1500-1800
Ballroom dancing at the Ballinalacken
Castle Hotel

1800-2000
Crowds gather at O'Donoghue's *bar.
Dances at the* Ritz *and several other big
hotels, ending at around 0200.*

who come every year to see friends and
enjoy the ballroom dancing. Midweek
the party is good fun but it can get
somewhat inebriated and loud at
weekends.

The town is a quiet and pleasant
holiday destination for the rest of the
year, another good place to consider
as a base for your walks around the
Burren, especially since the *Carrigan
Hotel* organizes walking holidays and
also has self-guided walks all over the
Burren for its guests.

Spa Wells Lisdoonvarna's chief place of interest is the Spa Wells, Ireland's oldest and
only working spa where the waters are drunk and bathed in. The water contains sulphur, iron, magnesium and iodine. The spa offers a sulphur bath,
massage, wax treatments aromatherapy and reflexology: rates range from
IR£10 for a massage or sulphur bath to IR£25 for an aromatherapy treatment.
■ *T7074023. Sulphur Hill, Lisdoonvarna.*

Burren Also in town is the Burren Smokehouse, on the Doolin Road where you can
Smokehouse learn all about the traditional way of smoking salmon, try a bit and perhaps buy
some. There is a shop and a pub, the *Roadside Tavern* where you can try locally
smoked trout, salmon, mackerel and eel. ■ *T7074303. Daily 0900-1900.*

Sleeping Lisdoonvarna has an inordinate number of hotels, most of which close down in the
winter reducing the town to an empty shell. In summer they compete for custom and
evening meals are competitively priced and really quite good. For all of the places
listed here it is a good idea to book in advance if you intend to come in September.

AL *Ballinalacken Castle Hotel*, Ballyvaughan Rd (R477), T7074025. If you can afford it,
stay here. The views are stupendous and the rooms quaintly old fashioned and huge.
Lovely big library, Victorian lobby with an amazingly ugly Connemara marble fireplace, stunning views from the dining room of the cliffs of Moher and the vast skies
beyond. **A** *Carrigan Hotel*, Doolin Rd, T7074036. A modern, busy hotel, which caters
to an interesting crowd of sporty types and walkers as well as the passing trade. The
hotel organizes walking weekends and can arrange individual excursions as well as
offering self-guided walks. Lots of information on walking in the area. Drying rooms
are a godsend in this rainy country. **A** *Kincora House*, T7074300, is a guesthouse in the
centre of town. Small, with popular pub and hostel attached. **A** *Sheedy's Restaurant
and Country Inn*, T7074026. Small but very popular place, very stylish with a lobby
that wouldn't be out of place in a London warehouse conversion. Nice minimalist
décor downstairs while the rooms are more traditionally furnished. Great service.
B *Déise*, Bog Rd, T7043660. Picturesque stone cottage offering B&B, all rooms en
suite. **B** *Hilltop*, Doolin Rd, T7074134. B&B withing walking distance of village, 1 family
room, 3 en-suite doubles. **B** *Lynch's Hotel*, T7074010. Nicely small place in the centre
of the village. **B** *St Judes*, Coast Rd, T7074108. B&B on N67 Doolin Rd, 4 en-suite
rooms, 1 3-bed room. **D** *The Burren Hostel*, T7074300. On road to Ennistymon. Dormitory rooms and doubles. Bike hire, and music at the pub next door.

The most fun eating in Lisdoonvarna is at Sheedy's *Orchid Restaurant* where there is **Eating**
an excellent balance between stylish cooking and adequate portions. Menu is nouvelle Irish and the chef has lots of awards. Nice wine list and lots of attention for the
guests. Dinner at around IR£20. The restaurant at the *Ballinalacken Castle Hotel* has
just expanded to take bookings as well as guests and is another rare treat of a place.
More nouvelle Irish in admirable portions and without the pretentious vocabulary of
more well-known places. The best dark and white chocolate mousse cake on the
planet, eaten while studying the stunning skyscapes of the cliffs of Moher and the
Atlantic Ocean. Ask for a window table when making a reservation, or get there early.
Dinner around IR£20.

Back in the less rarefied atmosphere of town there is the *Dolmen Inn*, open till
2130, in the centre of the village where there are quick meals with main courses
around IR£7.50. The *Royal Spa* and the *Rathbaun* are opposite each other in the main
street. Both with a fairly wide and conventional menu of fish and meat dishes for
around IR£6-8 for a main course.

This is tourist country and any pub that doesn't put on traditional music in July and **Pubs & music**
August is on to a loser. Most of the pubs will have some music some nights so look
around town for notices. The Roadside Tavern is a good bet with music every night
except Sunday in summer, or the bar in the *Royal Spa* has a good reputation locally.
The *Kincora Bar* on the Doolin Road has music at weekends in summer, and *Meg
Maguire's* in Main St has music nightly in summer.

Bicycle *Burke's*, The Square, T7074022. Bike hire. **Transport**

Banks and bureaux de change *Bank of Ireland*, the Square. *Mace's Minimarket*, Church St, will **Directory**
also change money. **Communications** **Post office**: Main St.

West of Lisdoonvarna

*To the southwest of Lisdoonvarna is the little village of Doolin, famous for its tra-
ditional music; the frighteningly high Cliffs of Moher with, beyond them,
Liscannor, quieter but with nice pubs and a good hostel; Lahinch, on the very outskirts of the Burren, a popular family resort; and Ennistymon, quietly mouldering
inland but with some good music pubs and a stunning waterfall. Part of the Burren Way follows the coast a little way inland, coming close to the cliffs at Doolin
and following them closely round to Hag's Head.*

Doolin

This is a long, drawn-out strip of a village, one that you couldn't imagine could *Colour map 2, grid C3*
be a mecca for anyone. But every summer it heaves with budget travellers and
musicians from as far away as Canada, Australia, Sweden, Germany and
you're more likely to hear a foreign language here than English. The draw is its
reputation as a centre for traditional music and if you spend a night listening to
some of the excellent music there you're just as likely to be listening to a German or Swiss playing as an Irish person.

The north end of the village is called Doolin while the next block of houses,
pubs and the post office is called Roadford and the southern end of the village
is known as Fisherstreet. Here are a couple of the hostels and *O'Connor's Pub*.

Doolin gets very crowded in the summer, especially at the budget end of the range. It **Sleeping**
is a good idea to book your accommodation well in advance of a visit here.

AL *Aran View House Hotel and Restaurant*, Coast Rd, T7074061, F7074540. Comfortable small hotel in a Georgian house at the north end of the village. **B** *Churchfield*, Fisherstreet, T707429. B&B with 6 rooms, close to pubs. **B** *Cullinan's Restaurant and Guesthouse*, T7074183. In the centre of the village this is a small comfortable and reasonably priced place with a good restaurant. **B** *Doonmacfelim House*, T7074503. In the middle of the village is this farmhouse/guesthouse, which is very popular. **B** *Sancta Maria*, Fisherstreet, T7074124. B&B with 4 rooms and very central for the music. **C** *Garden Vale*, Fisherstreet, T7074307. Small bungalow B&B. Good value, close to the pubs. **C** *Westwinds*, Roadford, T704227. In the centre of the village, this B&B caters to vegetarians. Good value. **D** *Aille River Hostel*, Roadford, T7074260. Nicely converted old farmhouse between Roadford and Fisherstreet. Scenic location beside old stone bridge. Some double rooms. Open March to mid-November. **D** *Doolin Holiday Hostel (Paddy's)*, Fisherstreet, T7074006, F7074421. Very modern, lots of facilities good rate for double rooms. Book in advance. **D** *Fisherstreet House*. Hostel owned by same people as Paddy's, but this one is usually reserved for group bookings. **D** *Flanagan's Village Hostel*, Roadford, T7074564. Dormitory rooms only. Camping available. **D** *Rainbow Hostel*, Roadford, T7074415. Small hostel in a typical cottage of the area. Very laid back, some double rooms, turf fires.

Camping *Nagle's Doolin Caravan & Camping Park*, T7074458. By the harbour, IR£4 per tent plus IR£1.50 per person. May to September. *O'Connor's Riverside Camping & Caravan Park*, T7074314. IR£4 small tent, IR£6 large tent, IR£1.50 per person. April to September.

Eating   *Bruach na hAille*, Roadford, T065-7074120, is the big name in the village, serves seafood and vegetarian dishes in an elegant old house. Open 7 days in summer, closed November to mid-March. Dinner at around IR£18 plus for the set dinner and IR£20 plus for the à la carte. It has an early bird menu at IR£10 served 1800-1930. *Cullinan's* specializes in Irish and continental-style seafood using locally caught fish, but also has meat dishes. The set dinner is quite reasonable at IR£15 between 1800 and 1900, and the à la carte is IR£20 plus served from 1800-2130. *The Lazy Lobster*, Roadford, T065-7074390, is a seafood restaurant, serves dinner between 1800-2130 at slightly lower prices than those above.

Pub food abounds. *McGann's*, Roadford, does typical pub food at good prices – Irish stew, garlic mussels, baked salmon, at around IR£6 for a main course. Food is served till 2130 in a dark, candle-lit interior. *Doolin Café* Roadford, has vegetarian food, and O'Connor's, Fisherstreet, T065-7074168, is also good for pub food.

More good food is available at the excellent *Doolin Crafts Gallery*, Ballyvoe, T065-7074511. Open for morning coffee, lunch and tea, it has home cooked and baked delights. More importantly it has an excellent collection of art and craft work, particularly batik.

Pubs &   Considering the number of people in town in the summer it is surprising that they all
music   fit into the three pubs. *O'Connor's* in Fisherstreet is the most renowned of them, with music every night from June to October. *McGann's* at the Roadford end also provides music every night in summer while *McDermott's* is the place where the locals go to get away from the tourists, but there is often music there too. If you want a rest from the noise, try the bar in *Aranview House Hotel*.

Transport   **Bicycle**   *Burren Bike Tours* Roadford, T065-7074429. Bike hire. *Doolin Holiday Hostel* (see 'Sleeping', page 399). Bike hire. **Bus**   Doolin connects with the Galway to Tralee bus, 3 times a day, once on Sundays, summer only. The Lisdoonvarna to Limerick bus passes through Doolin and Ennis 3 times a day in summer, while a Doolin to Galway service operates once a day in winter. The Limerick bus connects with Dublin. T065-

Cornelius O'Brien

One of Ireland's many eccentric landlords, Cornelius O'Brien, a lesser scion of the O'Brien clan, was MP for Clare from the 1830s until he died in 1857. He helped select Daniel O'Connell for the job before he took it over and supported the repeal of the Act of Union. In the 1847 election he came close to a duel with the agent of his opponent. Lord Palmerston said about him: "He was the best Irish MP we ever had. He didn't open his mouth in 20 years." He was never an absentee landlord and history tells that he improved the conditions of his tenants, a rare enough activity. There were no evictions on his land during the Famine or at any other time. A sour note is that the contributions towards the column erected to his memory after his death by grateful tenants were actually written into their tenancy agreements. Besides his efforts at building cottages for the tenants he restored and improved St Brigid's Well and built O'Brien's tower. His house, Birchfield, is now a ruin in Liscannor. His mausoleum is difficult to miss in the cemetery above St Brigid's Well in Liscannor.

6824177 for local bus details **Boat** From Doolin it is possible to get ferries to each of the Aran islands, T065-7074455. Ferries run 7 times a day to Inisheer (IR£15 return; April to October only) and once a day to Inishmór (IR£20 return). To Inishman the ferry operates between May and August only, IR£18. It is possible to get singles and travel on to Galway from the islands. Journey times are between 30 and 50 minutes; see the Galway chapter for details about the islands.

The Cliffs of Moher

From Lisdoonvarna the cliffs are signposted on the R478. They're impossible to miss –a gigantic car and coach park, free to enter, IR£1 to leave, marks the spot. Pass beyond the visitor centre, which explains that these are cliffs, leave behind the tour groups who walk to the edge and take a photo and follow the path a little way to the south. The cliffs face due west and the best time to go is at sunset on a clear day. In front of you are the Aran islands, and beyond to the north are the hills of Connemara. A little to the north of the visitors' centre is the O'Brien Tower built by Cornelius O'Brien (see box above), from where you can still see the Atlantic and the Aran Islands and pay 75p to do so.

The cliffs soar five miles (eight kilometres) all the way south to Hag's Head, and the Burren Way footpath follows them. The wall along the edge of the cliff was erected by Cornelius O'Brien. You can join the waymarked route, which isn't signposted from the car-park, at the O'Brien tower. Hop over the wall and head southwest. From Hag's Head the best way back is to retrace your steps.

Liscannor

Prettier and quieter than Doolin and not so towny as Lahinch further down the coast, Liscannor might make a good place to stop over in the area. It has two sights to visit, one very old and the other very new and should have a catamaran up and running to the Aran islands by the time you read this: T065-7081424 for details. Nice pubs, a good hostel some B&Bs and a hotel – what more could you ask for?

Colour map 2, grid C3

On the road into Liscannor from the Cliffs of Moher is St Brigid's Well, noticeable by the enormous great pillar erected by grateful tenants to Cornelius O'Brien at his suggestion (see box above). O'Brien improved the well, which is

St Brigid's Well

County Clare

one of the most revered holy wells in Ireland, dedicated to the sixth-century Kildare nun. The grotto is filled with pictures and discarded crutches of the sick who have found healing here. The Aran Islanders traditionally came her to worship in October, but in modern times it is July when the crowds arrive to seek healing and attend services here. It is almost certain that the site is pre-Christian in origin, adapted by the Christian missionaries to suit their own needs and adopted into the Christian religion.

Liscannor Stone Continuing on into Liscannor you pass the ruins of Birchwood House, O'Brien's pile on the left and then arrive at Liscannor's newest contribution to the culture of Ireland – Liscannor Stone, a heritage centre-cum-shop with displays about the area's wavy patterned slate, which you can see all over Ireland as street paving, stone cladding on houses and even roof tiles. At the western end of the village is a sandy beach. ■ *Liscannor Stone: summer only, daily.*

Sleeping L *Liscannor Bay Hotel*, T065-7081186. Excellent views across the bay from some of its rooms and is a very comfortable place. **C** *Seahaven* T065-7081385. B&B just out of the village on the way to Lahinch. It's a big house with 6 rooms, open January to November with good sea views. **D** *Village Hostel*, T065-7081385. Open from March to November, has private rooms at a very good IR£16 per room, and is well run.

Camping *Liscannor Caravan & Camping Park*, Clahane Beach, T065-7081714. A vast trailer park, which takes tents.

Eating & entertainment At the west end of town, up the boreen beside O'Brien's monument is the *Cottage Restaurant*, a single-storey, low white building with tables outside, again serving mostly seafood, with lots of paupiettes and daunes in the menu. Main courses IR£9-15. Open for lunch and dinner.

The village's pubs all do good pub food with extensive menus, dominated by seafood. *Vaughan's Anchor Inn* has an attached restaurant serving lots of seafood at around IR£8 for a main course and does pub food and B&B as well, although since it also has music during the summer this might be a noisy experience. Next door is *Joseph McHugh* a totally unreconstructed Irish pub with grocery section and all. It serves some food and has music on Tuesday nights. The *Captain's Deck*, T7081666, is at the west end of the village next to the hostel and serves food 1000-2200. It offers a set dinner at around IR£12 and à la carte main courses for about the same. At the east end of town is the glaringly painted *Mermaid Café*.

Lahinch

Colour map 2, grid C3 A typical seaside town, Lahinch is full of places to eat and lots of places to stay, some good music pubs, a huge beach with crashing breakers, a golf club and **Seaworld**, T7081900, a leisure centre and aquarium with a swimming pool, Jacuzzi and dolphins, among other sea creatures. ■ *Aquarium: IR£3.95. Pool and Jacuzzi: IR£6.25.*

Sleeping AL *Aberdeen Arms Hotel*, Main St/Station Rd, T701100, F7081228. Modernized traditional Irish country town hotel with lots of lunchtime visitors, comfortable big rooms. **A** *Atlantic Hotel*, Main St, T7081049, F7081029. Family-run small refurbished traditional hotel. **A** *Sancta Maria*, T7081041. Guesthouse close to the golf course and overlooking the beach. Good restaurant. **D** *Lahinch Hostel*, Church St, T7081040, F81704. Nice modern hostel with family and double rooms. Downstairs is a very popular restaurant.

Flora of the Burren

Nobody can fail to be moved by walking through one of the Burren's many pastures and seeing the embarrassment of riches they are stepping over. What botanists exclaim over is the strange combination of mountain flora, used to cold thin climates, and Lusitanian or southern flora, dependent on a warm southern climate. Their explanation is that in the period before the last glaciation the Burren enjoyed a warm, Mediterranean climate, which supported the Lusitanian flora. The ice sheets brought with them plant seed from a colder climate and, when they withdrew, seeds from both types of flora survived and germinated, creating this unique environment. They survive because of the fertile limestone base, its capacity to store heat and protect the plants against the wind and chill of winter, and the moderating effect of the gulf stream. The lack of tall competitive plants that would shade out the light is another important factor in the abundance of meadow plants. Yet another factor is in the way in which cattle are kept in the Burren. Because of the heat in the limestone uplands the hills are warmer than the lowlands so in winter the cattle are moved up into the hills and not brought down into the valleys as in other areas. The grazing cattle keep the taller grasses down in winter leaving the wild flowers room to compete in spring.

The real glory, though, is not in the unusual combination of plants, which only a botanist would spot anyway, but in the amazing diversity. Even along the roadsides the bright purple flowers of bloody cranesbill (geranium sanguineum) are profuse. Its name comes not from the purple flower but from the bright red seed head visible in August. In early summer there are many different species of orchids in the hedgerows and fields. The early purple orchid (orchis mascula) is everywhere in several different forms. Outstanding in July and August is the bee orchid (ophrys apifera) whose flowers could easily be confused with the bumble bee. Also common are the fly orchid, the Irish orchid, Kelly's orchid (a pure white flower), the lesser butterfly orchid with its pale yellow flowers, and if you are lucky in August or September you might spot ladies tresses (spiranthes spiralis) with its delicate white spiralling flowers.

The plant that everyone comes to look for in the Burren is the spring gentian (gentiana verna), which would be difficult to miss in May with its deep blue flowers. The same month sees the flowering of Mountain avens (dryas octopetala) so that the hillsides seem carpeted in blue and yellow flowers. The burnet rose (rosa spinosissima) covers the ditches and fields in June with its fragrant yellow flowers. These are just the flashier of the flowers that burst out of every rock and crevice in the Burren. If you're really keen on spotting, take a flower identification book and walk on to any slope in the Burren. You won't have to go far.

County Clare

Lots of cafés and pub food here. Top of the posh list is *Mr Eamon's* in Kettle St, **Eating** T7081050, serving modern Irish seafood. Open mid-March to mid-January, 1900-2200. Just outside Lahinch on the way to Milltown Malbay is *Barrtrá*, T7081280, set in a pleasant garden overlooking Liscannor Bay. It is a modern seafood restaurant, focusing on locally available sources but including oddities such as rollmops, duck, and several good vegetarian options. It has an early evening set menu 1700-1900, at IR£15. Later than that dinner will work out at IR£23 plus. Non-smoking area. Closed Mondays except in July and August. Back in town the hotels all have restaurants doing good potato-based set lunches. The *Aberdeen Arms* has an earlybird menu at IR£11.50. Below the *Lahinch Hostel* is the *Bay View Restaurant*, serving basic dishes with main courses at lunch time around IR£7. The pubs also focus on seafood menus, *Kenny's* in Main St is a very touristy place, which closes for the winter but has music as well as a good seafood menu in summer. The *Village Inn* Main St, has a similar menu and does music.

Pubs & music All the pubs in town offer some nights of music in summer. The best of them are *The 19th*, Main St, with music every night in summer and Saturdays in winter, *Galvin's*, at the top of Main St with music Monday, Wednesday, Friday and Saturdays in summer, and the aptly named *O'Looney's* with pub food and music Monday, Wednesday and Friday.

Shopping **Clothes** *Celtic T-shirt shop*, T7081564. 7 days, 0930-1800. **Sport** *Lahinch Surf Shop*, Old Promenade, T7081543.

Transport **Bus** The Limerick to Lisdoonvarna bus passes through Lahinch 3 times a day in summer, and once on Sundays and the rest of the year. T061-313333 or enquire at Lahinch Faílte.

Directory **Tourist office** *Lahinch Faílte*, The Dell, T7082082. Summer, daily 0900-2200; winter, daily 0900-1700.

Ennistymon

To complete this circuit of the area west of Lisdoonvarna head east out of Lahinch to Ennistymon, a backwater on the tourist trail, which probably looks very much like it did in 1950 or thereabouts. The chief point of interest here is waterfall known as the Cascades, especially if it has been raining. They are signposted in the village through a laneway beside the *Archway Bar*. The town has a couple of interesting old shops whose window displays can't have been changed in years, and an interesting antique shop, *Hasset's*, T71964.

North of Lisdoonvarna

The area around Ballyvaughan is really the most beautiful part of the Burren, with its wild coastline and cornucopia of wild flowers. To the west the coast road skirts around to Fanore, a little strip of a village, and to the east is Carron where there are a couple of interesting places to visit. There are lots of good walks in the area, including a section of the Burren Way. The route from Lisdoonvarna to Ballyvaughan passes through Corkscrew Hill, a famine relief road which twists its way down to the village through some outstanding views of Galway Bay.

Ballyvaughan

Colour map 2, grid C3 Ballyvaughan is a tourist-centred village where one of the first holiday villages in Ireland was built. Basically a group of houses, post office, mobile bank and hotel built around a T-junction it isn't as busy as Lisdoonvarna or Doolin but might make a pleasant night's stay with its quiet pubs and a couple of good places to eat.

Burren Exposure This centre is east of the village on the coast road, and is a good idea for a rainy day or as an introduction to the Burren early on in your visit. It uses giant screens with videos and slide shows to explain the history and mythology and flora of the Burren as well as the nature of the rocks themselves. There is a good restaurant with amazing sea views and a shop selling knitwear and crafts. ■ T707727. IR£3.50. On N67 ¼ mile outside Ballyvaughan on route to Galway.

Other sights A little way beyond the Burren Exposure is **Bishop's Quarter Beach**, excellent for swimming, with a sandy beach and dunes. At Belharbour are the ruins of

Corcomroe Abbey, founded by the O'Briens in the late 12th century. Cistercians ran this place, probably well into the 17th century. In a county where Romanesque carvings are ten a penny, these are well worth the visit with carved heads, opium poppies, and lilies of the valley. ■ *Half a mile (one kilometre) inland from Bellharbour.*

The little peninsula along this stretch of coast is called Finnvarra. Here is **Mount Vernon Lodge**, one-time home to Lady Gregory and temporary home to such luminaries as Yeats. West of the little village of New Quay is the **Flaggy Shore**, a place where the Burren limestone flags go right down to the sea.

Beyond Belharbour is a fascinating and undemanding walk around Abbey Hill, especially if you are interested in wild flowers. At Belharbour, instead of turning left for Burrin take the right turn, which brings you out to the road from Corofin to Galway. Around 2½ miles along this road look for a green road on the left as you pass Abbey Hill (also on your left). Park the car or bikes here and head along the green road to a gate into a field. The green road continues around Abbey Hill but your walk takes you higher and around the brow of the hill to the south. The glory of this walk are the wild flowers in this field though it is difficult to walk without crushing orchids or burnett roses underfoot. At the top of the hill there are excellent views of Corcomroe Abbey and the green valley that gave it its original name Sancta Maria de Petra Fertili – Saint Mary of the Fertile Rock. Following the contour of the hill round to the west there are stunning views over the long inlet from Ballyvaughan Bay and Bell Harbour, with a Martello tower visible way over to the west at Finavarra Point. Due west at the other side of Poulnaclough Bay is the site of a battle fought in 1267 where Conor O'Brien, whose tomb can be seen in the abbey, died. Follow the contour of the hill around until you can see the green road again below you and return to your vehicle.

Abbey Hill walk

Ballyvaughan to Fanore

Heading west out of Ballyvaughan begins a scenic drive through Gleninagh and Fanore around the Gleninagh Mountains. About four miles (six kilometres) west of the village is **Gleninagh Castle**, a 16th-century edifice built by the O'Loughlans and inhabited by them until the 1840s. Continuing on, the road hugs close to the coast. Just before pier a green road sets off around the mountain and makes a pleasant walk above the road. You can climb anywhere here to the stone ring fort at the top of the hill and on a clear day see what an excellent defensive position it made for a fortified farmhouse. The hillside will be covered in a botanist's daydream of wild flowers depending on what month you are walking. Continuing round Black Head to Fanore brings you to a strung out-little village of a few houses, a shop and a pub. There is a good sandy beach with sand dunes and it is fairly safe for swimming with a lifeguard there for part of the year. The Atlantic breakers are often good for surfing.

County Clare

South of Ballyvaughan

On the road to Lisdoonvarna is the Aillwee Cave, another good rainy-day activity. The cave system is typical of the caves that run throughout the Burren, usually where the limestone rock meets the shale or sandstone at the border between the two areas. The huge cave was discovered in 1944 and is about 600 yards/metres long with side caves, a waterfall, and stalactite and stalagmite formations. There are also the remains of bear pits where the claw marks of giant brown bears which once inhabited the caves can still be seen. Outside the caves

Aillwee Cave

is a nature walk and you can also scramble up the hill above the cave to look at the views over Galway Bay. In the entrance are shops making cheese, extracting honey, and so on. ■ *T7077036. March to June and September to November, daily, 1000-1800; July and August, daily 1000-1900. Admission by tour only. Last tour 1830 July and August, 1730 March to June and September to November. IR£3.95. Café, shops. Best time to visit is early morning before the tour groups build up.*

Gleninsheen wedge tombs A little way south of the cave on the N480 are the Gleninsheen wedge tombs, a series of tombs constructed of slabs in a box formation, facing west and tapering to the east. They are Bronze Age burial places and nearby, indicated on the *Rambler's Guide & Map, Ballyvaughan*, is the spot where in the 1930s a small boy found a gold gorget, or neck collar, one of the most beautiful and undamaged in existence and now in the National Museum.

Poulnabrone Portal Dolmen Continuing along the N480 brings you to Poulnabrone Portal Dolmen, swathed in summer in tour buses but beautiful none the less. It rears up out of the bare limestone as if Liam McCormack just designed it, but has been there for the last 5,000 years. When excavated it revealed urns containing the cremated remains of 16 Late Stone Age people, and some polished flint implements.

Burren Perfumery East of the N480, just beyond the dolmen along a minor road, is Carron, a tiny village worth visiting for the Burren Perfumery, which has audio-visual displays on the making of perfume and you can walk around the still and extracting machinery to watch the process in action. Another good rainy-day activity. ■ *T7089102. March to May, October to November, daily 0900-1700; June to September, daily 0900-1900; December to February, phone in advance. Free. Shop. From Ballyvaughan take the first left after the Poulnabrone Dolmen, and at Carron turn right at the church and then left to find the perfumery.*

Essentials

Sleeping There are lots of B&Bs all around the coast east of Ballyvaughan and all of them get very booked up in summer so book your trip in advance.

L *Gregan's Castle Hotel*, Corkscrew Hill, T707705, F7077111. Lovely old country house with lots of room to relax and imagine you are the landed gentry. Big library, lounge, bar. Country house style bedrooms, no TV, excellent restaurant. **AL** *Hyland's Hotel*, Ballyvaughan, T7077037, F7077131. Attractive, old-fashioned hotel run by the same family for generations. **A** *Rusheen Lodge*, Corkscrew Hill Rd, T7077092, F7077152. Pleasant guest house on road to Corkscrew Hill. Closed November to February. **B** *Stonepark House*, Bishop's Quarter, T7077056. Close to a good swimming area, ½ mile (1 km) from village on Galway Rd. **C** *Micko's Place*, Ballyvaughan, T7077060. Small B&B in village, pleasant atmosphere. **D** *The Bridge Hostel*, Fanore, T7076134, F7076134. Small 200-yr-old house in beautiful location between the hills and the sea. One private room, camping possible in the garden, bike hire. **D** *Clare's Rock Hostel*, Carron, T7089129. Dormitory and family rooms, laundry, kennels. Open May to October.

Eating The grandest place to eat is *Gregan's Castle Hotel* but you should book well in advance since they expect guests to eat there, and book tables for them. Lovely views out the windows, especially at dusk as the Burren hills turn a dull Mars red. Food is well cooked, and comes stacked in little mountains. The service is excellent; these people know their trade. Dressing for dinner is both expected and good fun. In Ballyvaughan

Hylands Hotel has a restaurant serving traditional fare at around IR£18 for dinner. The *Whitethorn Restaurant* at the Burren Exposure serves self-service lunches at around IR£6 and snacks during the day and is open for dinner on Fridays and Saturdays in July and August. Beautiful views from the huge windows, main courses around IR£12, good wine list.

In the village *Monk's*, T7077059, a pub just beside the pier on the Fanore Rd has a big seafood menu and is very popular. The *Tea Junction*, in the centre of Ballyvaughan, has interesting snacks including vegetarian choices. On the Fanore Rd, *O'Donoghue's* pub does barfood while ½ mile (1 km) beyond it is *Admiral's Restaurant*, T7076105, again focusing on seafood.

Pubs & music

Monk's and *O'Brien's*, T7077003, have traditional music in the summer, *Monk's* on Wednesdays and *O'Brien's* at weekends. *O'Brien's* often gets Country and Western bands on Sundays if you like that kind of thing. *Greene's*, also in the village, has traditional music on Wednesdays while O'Lochlain's also has occasional music sessions but is more a pub for the locals.

Transport

Bicycle *Monk's Bar*, T7077059. Bike hire.

Sport

Horseriding *Burren Riding Centre*, Fanore, T7076140. Daily 5hr trails at 0930; beach trails 0930 and 1100; 3hr Burren trails 1100,1500. **Watersports** *River Ocean Kayak*, 2, Muckinish West, T7077043. Sea kayaking trips in Galway Bay.

Directory

Banks and bureaux de change A bank comes to Ballyvaughan on Mon, Wed and Fri. *Burren Exposure* (see page 404) will also change money.

Lough Derg and around

The area around Lough Derg is green pastureland set in a landscape of mountain and lake. The major town is Killaloe with its ancient cathedral, said to be the home of Brian Boru, the ancient Irish king. The East Clare Way, a signposted walking route, crosses the area, boats can be hired and there are lots of riding centres and golf courses. This is an area for activity holidays rather than a touring holiday.

Killaloe

Killaloe and Ballina in County Tipperary are joined by a beautiful old arched bridge over the river Shannon. The main point of interest in Killaloe is **St Flannan's Cathedral**, named after an abbot who led the monastery that stood here before the cathedral. The building you now see is late 12th century, built by an O'Brien, and it encloses the doorway of an earlier church in its southwest corner. Inside is one of the only stones in existence to have both Ogham and runic writing on it – probably erected by the man whose name it bears: Thorgrim – asking for prayer. The cross once stood at Kilfenora but was moved here in 1821. Beside the cathedral is **St Flannan's Oratory**, 12th century also and with a stone roof. Also in Killaloe, in the grounds of the Catholic church is **St Molua's church**, which is older than both of these buildings. It stood originally on Friar's Island in the Shannon estuary but was moved here in 1929 when the island was flooded in the Shannon hydroelectric scheme. Also in town is the **Heritage Centre**, with material on local history and the history of the abbey. ■ *June to September, IR£1.50.*

County Clare

Long-distance walks

Starting off in Killaloe the **East Clare Way** covers 112 miles (180 kilometres) of very untouristy east Clare, travelling through Broadford, O'Callaghan's Mills, Tulla, Feakle, Flagmount, Whitegate, Mountshannon, and Ogonnelloe. Half of the journey is along tarmac road, albeit very quiet tarmac. The best of it is the section between Tulla and Mountshannon: three days walking through open land, forestry and some road walking. There is accommodation at Mountshannon, Feakle and Tulla.

The **Lough Derg Way** passes through Killaloe on its route from Limerick and follows the eastern shore of Lough Derg to Dromineer in County Tipperary. This is a finer walk than the other, keeping close to the shores of the lake for most of its route but accommodation is a little harder to come by. For more information about the walk you can pick up the *Lough Derg Way Information Sheet* at Ennis Tourist office or the Clare section of the walk is mapped out on the Ordnance Survey Discovery series sheets 65 and 58.

North to Mountshannon & Holy Island

Heading northwards along the shores of Lough Derg brings you to Tuamgraney where the **10th century church** is now another heritage centre. It is the oldest Irish church still used for services and is said to have been repaired in 1000 by Brian Boru himself. Continuing north you come to Mountshannon, a quiet little town popular with fishing enthusiasts but where you can get a ferry to **Holy Island** (*Inis Cealtra*). A monastery was founded here by St Caiman in the seventh century, but was burned down by Vikings in 836 and again in 922. The Abbot of the monastery around 1000 was the brother of Brian Boru, who is said to have built one of the churches on the island. A church remained here into the 16th century but by the 17th this had become a place of pilgrimage rather than a working church. There are around 10 sites of interest on the island, including three churches, all predating the 13th century: a round tower, a tiny tomb known as the 'anchorite's cell', and the holy well that makes this place the centre for pilgrims. ■ *T061-921351 to arrange trips. May to September. IR£4.*

Essentials

Sleeping

In Killaloe there is a variety of accommodation, which can be supplemented by walking over the bridge into Ballina, and accommodation is also available along the lough at Mountshannon.

AL *Kincora Hall Hotel*, Killaloe, T376665, F376665. Just outside Killaloe, with its own marina, grand old fireplaces, small enough to make the guest feel welcome. **AL** *Lakeside Hotel and Leisure Centre*, Killaloe, T376122, F376431. Slightly more expensive than *Kincora Hall*, but bigger, with lots of facilities including a pool, water slide, Jacuzzi and snooker room. Overlooks Lough Derg. **A** *Mountshannon Hotel*, Mountshannon, T927162, F927272. A small traditional 2-star hotel with lots of old-fashioned atmosphere. **B** *Carranmore Lodge*, Killaloe, T376704. B&B in the village itself with big gardens and pleasant views over the river. **B** *Derg Lodge*, Mountshannon, T927180. This B&B is good if you like fishing since they can arrange a ghillie and boat hire. **B** *Rathmore House*, T379296. B&B, just over a mile (2 km) outside Killaloe. **C** *Ballyheefy Lodge*, Ballyheefy, T376016. B&B 2½ miles (4 km) outside Killaloe. **C** *Oak House*, Mountshannon, T/F927185. B&B with great views over the lough, a private beach and boats: useful if you are after fishing. There are no en-suite rooms.

Camping *Lakeside Caravan & Camping Park*, Mountshannon, T927225, F927336. On the shores of the lough with lots of facilities, mobile homes to hire, boat hire, café, bike hire, pony riding and much more. Two adults in a small tent works out at around

IR£7 while a 2-berth motor home for a week is around IR£200. *Lough Derg Holiday Park*, Scarrif Rd, Killaloe, 13786329. A big place with lots of facilities – including takeaway and shop, games room, laundry – but with prices to match. IR£7.50 for the tent/camper/ caravan, IR£2 for a car, and then IR£2.50 per person. There are mobile homes to hire.

Eating In Killaloe the two hotels both have restaurants, while the *Piper's Inn*, T376885, has a good restaurant and traditional music every day in summer and at weekends in winter. There is also the *Anchor Inn*, which does pub food and has music on Wednesdays in summer, and on the Ballina side of the river *Molly's Bar and Restaurant*, T376632, has food and music (Thursdays, all year). In Mountshannon the hotel does good basic food with set dinner at around IR£15, while the *Bridge* does pub food and *Cois na Abhna* in the main street has music.

Sport **Fishing** *TJ O'Brien*, Main St, Ballina/Killaloe, T376009. Tackle for game, sea, sport and coarse fishing. **Golf** *East Clare Golf Club*, Bodyke, T921322. 18 holes. *Liam O'Flannery*, Woodpark, Scarriff Rd, T921460. 18-hole pitch and putt, 9-hole golf. **Horseriding** *Carrowbaun Farm Trekking Centre*, Killaloe, T376754. *East Clare Equestrian Centre*, Tuamgraney, T921157. **Walking** *East Clare Walking Club*, ECDA, Feakle, T924303. Organize regular walks every other Sunday. *Green Boreen Holidays*, ECDA, Feakle, T924303, F924289. Packaged walking and cycling holidays. **Watersports** *Thomas Bottcher*, Mountshannon, T927225. Sailing, canoeing, windsurfing.

Directory **Banks** *AIB*, Main St, Killaloe, T376115. *Bank of Ireland*, Scarriff, T921015. **Boats** *PJ Mason*, Broadford, T473194. Boat hire on Doon Lake. *Whelan's*, Church St, Killaloe, T376159. 19ft (5.7m) lake boats with outboard motors.

West Clare

The west coast of Clare from Lahinch down through the seaside towns of Miltown Malbay, Quilty, Kilkee and Loop Head is a pleasant day's drive. Kilkee is a serious Irish family holiday destination while Kilrush offers a heritage centre, trips to Scattery Island, and dolphins in the estuary of the Shannon.

Lahinch to Kilkee

Miltown Malbay Through fairly uneventful countryside, the road south from Lahinch finds its way along the coast down to Miltown Malbay, a Victorian resort close to Spanish Point: an excellent sandy beach with good surfing when the waves are high. Legend tells that in 1588 sailors from the shipwrecked Spanish Armada swam ashore here to be arrested on the orders of Richard Bingham, the governor of Connaught, and later executed.

From Miltown Malbay the road continues past occasional caravan sites to **Quilty** where there is a sandy beach. The next town along the route is **Doonbeg**, a tiny village with a white sandy beach and dunes beyond. Another Armada ship ran aground here in 1588, and its survivors were also carted away to execution.

Kilkee, Loop Head and Carrigaholt

Kilkee
Phone code: 065
Colour map 3, grid A2

A seaside resort since Victorian times, Kilkee is bucket-and-spade and amusement-arcade territory. The beach here explains the popularity of the place –

long, golden and sheltered, with beautiful cliffs at its western end. At the same end of the beach are 'pollock holes', so called because pollock lurk about in them, as do lots of other interesting varieties of marine life. There is also a golf club, some excellent walks along the cliffs, and **Waterworld**, a leisure centre with water slides, a wave machine and kiddies' pools ■ *June 1200-2000; July, August 1100-2100; Sept-end May 2100-2200 (adults only), T065-9056855.*

Loop Head   Loop Head makes an interesting drive or an exciting cycle or walk. The coastline is full of sea stacks and bird life and a coastal path follows the cliffs all 15 miles (24 kilometres) down to Loop Head. At **Intrinsic Bay**, named for the emigrant ship that sank here in 1836, is a sea stack with a medieval oratory on it. In Kilbaha in the church at Moneen is the **Little Ark** dating back to penal times when Catholics were prohibited from saying mass on land: this moveable altar was carried down to the shore and mass said there. The church stained glass window holds a portrayal of such a mass.

Carrigaholt   Carrigaholt has some nice pubs, a tiny beach and **Dolphinwatch**, which does trips out into the estuary to see one of only five known groups of bottlenose dolphins in the waters of Europe. There are about 80 of them and trippers are rarely disappointed, often spotting nursery groups of young dolphins. There is an information centre and booking office in the village with audio visual displays about the dolphins, and of course t-shirts. ■ *The Square, Carrigaholt, T9058156. April to October, weather permitting. Bookings begin at 0800 on day of trip. Two-hour trips. IR£10. Look for information about individual trips/weather on the pier.*

Carrigaholt also has a 15th-century, five-storey tower house very strategically placed overlooking the Shannon. Over the doorway is a murder hole, placed there so that heavy objects could be dropped on to unsuspecting invading heads. The trick didn't work, though, in 1598, when Daniel O'Brien took the castle from the MacMahons. The O'Briens held it till Cromwell turned up in 1651 but got it back for a while at the Restoration in 1666. William of Orange reallocated it in 1691 to the Earl of Albemarle, who sold it to a family called the Burtons. They managed to hold on to it until the late 19th century.

Sleeping   Kilkee makes a down-to-earth alternative if you've got tired of the ethnic rusticity of the rest of Clare, while Miltown Malbay and Carrigaholt are quieter and might make a good base if you want to do some walking in the area. Unless you book in advance the chances are you'll get whatever is still available when you turn up at the tourist office. Most of the B&Bs in Miltown Malbay charge the standard rate of IR£18 per person sharing, but a few out of the village itself are a little cheaper.

AL *Halpin's Hotel*, Erin St, Kilkee, T9056032, F9056317. Very central, small renovated townhouse hotel and restaurant. Open fires, old-fashioned bar. **A** *Armada Hotel*, Spanish Point, Miltown Malbay, T7084110, F7084632. Big, yellow, new place with huge restaurant and banqueting facilities. Definitely a family place. **A** *Bellbridge House Hotel*, Spanish Point, Miltown Malbay, T0650-7084038, F0650-7084830. Smaller new place, close to the golf course and beach. Open from March to May. **A** *Kilkee Bay Hotel*, Kilkee, T9060060. On the road to Kilrush, this huge complex of hotel and apartments is geared to the longer-stay family groups. Restaurant, nightclub pub. **A** *Marine Hotel and Apartment Complex*, Kilkee, T9056722. Not so big as the *Kilkee Bay*, and right on the seafront, but still family holiday accommodation. **A** *Stella Maris Hotel*, Kilkee, T9056455. Small, better value than the bigger hotels, in the centre of town, open fires, nice views over the bay. **A** *Strand Guest House*, The Strand Line, Kilkee, T/F9056177. On the seafront. **B** *Bayview*, O'Connell St, Miltown

Malbay, T9056058. Big B&B, good views of the bay. **B** *Hillview*, Kilrush Rd, Miltown Malbay, T9056213. B&B a little way out of town, nice gardens. **B** *Purtill's*, O'Curry St, Kilkee, T/F9056771. B&B in nicely restored townhouse in the main street in town. Bar and restaurant, traditional music in summer. **C** *Barkers*, Spanish Point, Miltown Malbay, T7084408. Small home run by musical family close to the beach. Good value B&B. **C** *San Antone*, Drummin, Miltown Malbay, T7084511. B&B 2 miles (3 km) out of town, quiet location, good views. **C** *Summerville*, Kilrush Rd, Miltown Malbay, T9056527. Pleasantly located B&B, good-value bungalow accommodation. **C** *The Sycamores*, Lisdeen, Miltown Malbay, T9056517. B&B just over a mile (2 km) out of town in quiet rural area. **D** *Kilkee Hostel*, O'Curry St, Miltown Malbay, T9056209. Well run but no double rooms, just dormitory or family rooms. Café. Bike hire.

Camping *Cunningham's Holiday Park*, Miltown Malbay, T9056430. Camping site and mobile homes to hire. Small tent and two people IR£9. Caravan, car, 2 people IR£11. 6-berth mobile home IR£330 per week. *Green Acres*, Doonaha, Kilkee, T9057011. Smaller place, 2 people plus small tent IR£8. Six-berth mobile home IR£150 per week. Signposted off the N67 Kilkee to Kilrush road.

Eating

Kilkee abounds with fast food of one sort or another. The big hotels all have reliable restaurants with set dinner at around IR£15, while *Halpins* and *Purtill's* are both well worth trying out. In Carrigaholt the *Long Dock*, T9058106, is a pub/restaurant where you might want to eat and listen to some good music.

Pubs & music

In Kilkee is *Myles Creek* in O'Curry Street, which has cover bands and traditional music on Mondays. In the same street is *O'Mara's*, which has traditional music 3 days a week, while *Normoyle's* in Grattan Street and the *Stella Maris* hotel also have traditional sessions several nights. Carrigaholt has *The Long Dock*, where there is music most nights in summer, and the *Village Pub*, where there is occasional set dancing. Miltown Malbay is home to the Willy Clancy Summer School in the first week or so of July, when everyone in traditional music turns up there. Outside of the festival, Clancy's is the place to find good music. In Doonbeg, between Miltown Malbay and Kilkee, is the *Igoe Inn* with music on Mondays and *Morrisseys* with occasional music sessions. Both pubs do good food.

Sport

Watersports *Kilkee Diving & Watersports Centre*, Harbour, T065-9056707.

Directory

Banks *AIB* and *Bank of Ireland*, O'Curry St. **Tourist office** O'Connell St. Jun-Sep, Mon-Sat 1000-1800.

Kilrush and Scattery Island

Kilrush
Colour map 3, grid A3

Unless you are a boating aficionado there's not much reason to spend any time in Kilrush. The old gaol is now a Supervalu supermarket and the new self-flushing toilets are a treat, but that's about it. At the mouth of the creek is the marina. Due to open in 2000 are the renovated walled gardens of the local landlord family the Vandeleurs. The town has a **Heritage Centre** telling the story of Kilrush in landlord times ■ *The Square, T9051596. June to August, Monday-Saturday 1000-1300, 1400-1600. IR£2.*

Scattery Island

The best reason to come to Kilrush is to make the trip to Scattery Island, inhabited until quite recently and worth visiting for the remains of the monastic settlement that was established there in the sixth century by St Senan, who first fought a monster called Cata on the island. There is a 120ft (36.5m) high tower, and the remains of the cathedral and several other churches. The settlements

County Clare

were attacked by Vikings, who settled there for a time before Brian Boru took it back. Then the churches were desecrated by an Englishman called William Hoel in 1179. The site became a place of pilgrimage and sailors sailed new boats sunwards round it and collected pebbles from the beach for luck. On the mainland, in Merchant's Quay, is an interpretive centre that tells the story of the island. ■ *Interpretive centre: Merchant's Quay, T9052114. mid-June to mid-September, daily 0930-1830. Last admission 30 minutes before closing. Free. Ferry to island: Scattery Island Ferries, Kilrush Marina Building, T9051327. Phone for times. IR£5. Journey time 20 minutes.*

Sleeping & eating There are no hotels or guesthouses in Kilrush. Accommodation is either in B&Bs (around IR£18 per person sharing) or hostels.

B *Bruach na Coille*, Killimer Rd, T9052250. B&B ½ mile (1 km) out of town set in pretty gardens, nice breakfast menu. **B** *Central*, 46 Henry St, T9051332. A big townhouse in Kilrush itself, offering B&B. **B** *Crotty's*, Market Square, T9052470. Very central B&B and above the pub/restaurant with live music every night in summer. **B** *Fortfield Farm*, Donail, T9051457. B&B about 2½ miles (4 km) outside town on the road to Killimer, where there is an agricultural zoo to visit with llamas, deer and lots of other creatures. Children might enjoy staying here. **D** *Bels House Hostel*, Moanmore South, T9052801. Private doubles for IR£9. **D** *Katie O'Connor's*, Frances St, T9051133. Hostel with private and family rooms. **D** *Kilrush Creek Lodge*, Kilrush marina, T065-9052595. Hostel with single and family rooms.

Food is mostly found in cafés or pubs. *Crotty's* has a good reputation, while the *Haven Arms*, *Kelly's*, and the *Island House*, all close together in Henry St, all do good bar food. In the square are the *Central Restaurant*, T9052477, and *Coffey's Café Pizzeria*, T9051170 both doing inexpensive café-type food.

Pubs & music *Crotty's* is the place to go for good music sessions every night in summer, but you could also check out several other pubs in town – The Colleen Bawn, Moore St, which has music every Thursday all year, the *Island House*, Kelly's, Henry St, and *O'Brien's*, also in Henry St. In early August is a festival celebrating Mrs Crotty, the one time owner of Crotty's bar who was a renowned concertina player. In June, based in Kilbaha, Cross and Carrigaholt is the annual West Clare Jazz School, with classes in Kilbaha and free performances in the bars in those three villages. T9058229 for details.

Sport **Watersports** *Kilrush Creek Lodge & Adventure Centre*, Kilrush marina, T9052855.

Transport **Bicycle** *Gleeson Wholesale*, Henry St, T9051127. Bike hire. **Ferry** A car ferry operates between Killimer, 5 miles from Kilrush, and Tarbert in County Kerry. The ferry, T065-53124, operates on the hour from Killimer April-September 0700-2100; October-March 0700-1900. IR£8 per car, IR£3 for bikes and foot passengers. Journey time is 20 minutes.

Directory **Banks and bureaux de change** *Tourist office*, Market Sq, will change money. **Communications** Post office: Frances St. **Tourist office** Town Hall, Market Sq, T9051577. Jul-Aug only, Mon-Sat 1000-1300, 1400-1800; Sun 1200-1600.

County Clare

Some time ago, before the introduction of police, all the people of the islands were as innonent as the people here remain to this day. I have heard that at that time the ruling proprietor and magistrate of the north island used to give any man who had wrong a letter to a jailer in Galway, and send him off by himself to serve a term of imprisonment.

J M Synge (1871-1909):
The Aran Islands

11

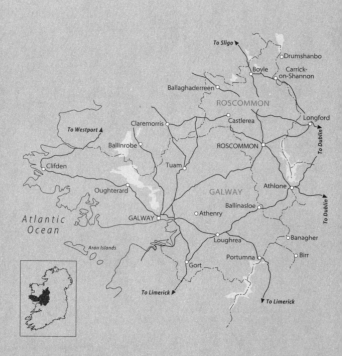

Galway is a large county, but Lough Corrib splits it into two quite different regions. For the majority of travellers it is the land to the west, Connemara, that stirs the imagination. Here, a wilderness of bog and mountains rivals Cork and Kerry for splendid scenery and the wild beauty of nature. East Galway is dull by comparison, and it may be hard to find the time to include anywhere in east Galway when the famed Aran Islands and the exuberantly lively city of Galway are added to an itinerary that includes Connemara.

The inland county of Roscommon is Irish country life without the tourist trimmings: no spectacular sights but a relaxed pace of life and, as ever, history lurking in unexpected places. Few visitors make it their holiday destination, but anyone passing through should definitely take some time to visit Strokestown, Roscommon town and Boyle.

★ *Try to find time for*

Walking on Inis Meáin (Inishmaan) and taking in the views from Dún Chonchúir

Cocktails and dinner at Currareveagh House, Oughterard

Choosing a bodhrán in Roundstone

A night in Day's Bar on Inishbofin

Identifying flowers in the Connemara National Park

Visiting Killary Harbour and travelling the road to Louisburgh from Leenane

Absorbing the Yeats associations at Coole Park and Thoor Ballylee

A Wednesday night's traditional music at Kate Lavin's in Boyle

County Galway

Galway

Phone code: 091
Colour map 2, grid C3

If any one place in Ireland can sum up what the country is all about it has to be this ancient, prosperous and culturally dynamic little city. Easily walked from one end to another in half an hour it is a tourist paradise of culture, shopping, friendliness, good accommodation, and even better eating. In summer the whole city centre teems with people out having fun, bars and restaurants spill out on to the streets, and with major festivals in July, August and September there is rarely no excuse for some craic.

Ins and outs

Getting there
See Transport, page 428, for further details

Air Galway airport is 7 miles (10 km) east of the city at Carnmore and there are 2 daily *Aer Lingus* flights to and from Dublin as well as services to Manchester and Teeside in Britain.

Bus Galway city's station services main towns throughout Ireland and there are some private companies also running useful routes: Dublin and Dublin Airport to Galway; Belmullet, Newport and Westport to Galway city; see the Inishbofin Island section on page 448 for services between Galway city and Cleggan.

Train From the railway station in Galway city, T091-564222, daily trains service Dublin, stopping at Athlone for connections elsewhere in the country.

Getting around Galway's city centre is tiny. The bulk of the city is on the northwest side of the river Corrib, the main route across town being made up of Eyre Square, a kind of hotch potch of statuary, grass, bus queues, phone boxes, and then Williamsgate, William's Street, Shop Street, High Street and Quay Street, all busy shopping streets, although you would hardly notice that you are passing from one of these streets to the next. On the southwest side of the river is the ancient settlement of the Claddagh, which is mostly rebuilt but worth a wander around. Most travellers without their own transport arrive in the very centre of Galway either by bus or train. From the airport there is a daily bus service or taxi. From your arrival point in the city most places are easily walkable. Taxi ranks are in Eyre Square and by the railway station. Buses leave Eyre Square for Salthill every 20 minutes, but the distance is easily walked. For bicycle hire see page 429.

Tourist Information The main tourist office for the county is in Galway city (see page 429) but the Aran Islands, Aughrim, Ballinasloe, Clifden, Oughterard and Salthill also have offices.

History

The *Annals of the Four Masters*, a 17th-century compilation history of Ireland (see box on page 513) records a fort at the mouth of the River Corrib in 1124. This would have been the crossing place for traders and travellers moving from Dublin to the west, the route to the north being blocked by Lough Corrib. In 1232 history records that the Richard de Burgh, a powerful Anglo-Norman baron, took the area from the dominant Gaelic clan, the O'Flahertys. By 1247 there was a walled town of about 35 acres here. In the 15th century the town was given a royal charter and control of the parish church of St Nicholas built in 1320, enhancing the power of Galway. For 150 years the townsmen of

Lynch law

The Lynches were an important Galway family, 84 of whom became mayors of the city between the 15th and 17th centuries. One of them is said to have given the English language the word lynch.

In 1493, James Lynch Fitz Stephens' son Walter and his girlfriend, Ann, were at a dance with their Spanish friend Gomez who, being a polite sort of chap, was very attentive to Ann. Walter became fiercely jealous and secretly followed Gomez home and murdered him. When the body was found Walter's hat and knife were beside it. Walter, an otherwise saintly young man, was accused of the murder and confessed, whereupon his father James Lynch Fitz Stephens dragged him to the town jail. Walter was such a nice young man that the whole town begged James for mercy on his son and even the hangman refused to do the dirty deed. James, in a fury of righteousness and finding his way to the scaffold blocked by angry townspeople, threw his son out of the window, first tying him by the neck to a stake inside the room.

Galway grew wealthy on trade with Spain and France, and even with the Caribbean: animal pelts and fish in exchange for wine and fine cloth. The evidence of the wealth is still there in the fine old stone buildings in the town and the many tower houses of the surrounding countryside.

The 17th-century English wars brought an end to Galway's prosperity. The cityfolk supported the losing side in both the English civil war – suffering the attacks of Cromwell's troops as a result – and the war between James II and William of Orange, surrendering to William's forces in 1691. After that things declined for about 200 years. There was a brief economic boom in Victorian times and then things began to look up again around the 1960s due to deliberate state policies and the inevitable move from the country to the cities. Now Galway booms with hotels and new developments and the outskirts have roundabouts popping up like mushrooms.

Sights

Eyre Square, with Kennedy Park in the middle, has become a kind of dumping ground for memorabilia that doesn't fit in too well anywhere else. The **Browne Doorway** was in the way of some redevelopment and got moved here – it's a piece of a 17th-century building consisting of a bay window and the eponymous doorway with the date and coat of arms carved into it. Two statues adorn the park: one of **Padraic O'Conaire** (1882-1928), local author of *M'asal Beag Dubh* (My little Black Donkey), and another of **Liam Mellows** (1892-1922), a republican and socialist who fought in the 1916 Easter Rising and later in the civil war on the side of the anti-treaty party. He was executed in 1922 as a reprisal against the murder of two Daíl deputies. When this area of the square was being excavated in 1955 human remains were found and this spot is thought to have been the town's place of execution where the bodies of those hung would have been thrown down and buried beneath the gallows.

Eyre Square

There is also a **plaque** in the square dedicated to JF Kennedy who addressed the people of Galway from this spot in 1963, after which the park was renamed in his honour. Two ancient iron canons, formerly the property of the Connaught Rangers (see page 420), are also in the square while the fountain erected in 1984 to commemorate Galway's 500 years as a town is in the shape of a Galway Hooker, the traditional sailing ship of the area.

In summer the square is often a venue for concerts and other events. At the southwest corner of the square is the **Eyre Square Centre** in whose basement

County Galway

Galway city

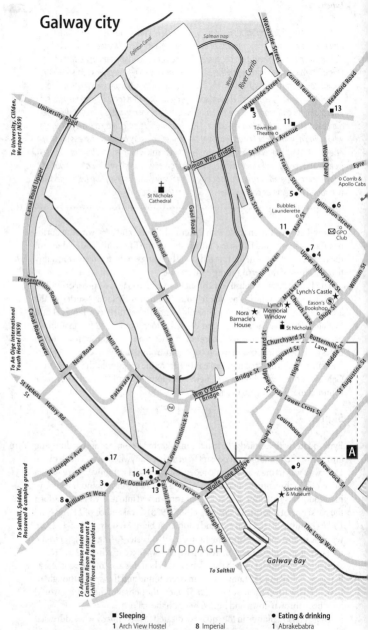

Related map:
A. Galway city centre,
page 421

| 0 yards | 200 |
| 0 metres | 200 |

■ Sleeping

1 Arch View Hostel
2 Celtic Tourist
3 Corrib Villa
4 Eyre Square
5 Galway Hostel
6 Great Southern
7 Great Western House

8 Imperial
9 Kinlay House Hostel
10 Park House
11 Salmon Weir Hostel
12 Skeffington Arms
13 Woodquay Hostel

● Eating & drinking

1 Abrakebabra
2 An Púcan Pub
3 Blue Note
4 Brannagan's
5 Cactus Jack's Café Bar
6 Conlon's Takeaway
7 Couch Potatoes

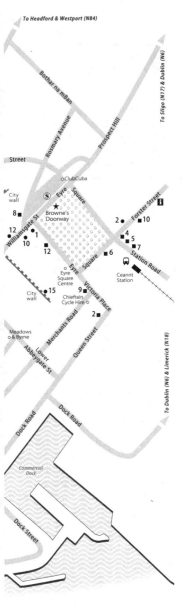

To Headford & Westport (N84)

Bothar na mBan

Rosmary Avenue

Prospect Hill

To Sligo (N17) & Dublin (N6)

Street

ClubCuba

City wall

Eyre Square

Forster Street

Browne's Doorway

Williamsgate St

Eyre Square

Station Road

Eyre Square Centre

Ceannt Station

Victoria Place

Chieftain Cycle Hire

City wall

Meadows o & Byrne

Merchants Road

Queen Street

Lower Abbeygate St

To Dublin (N6) & Limerick (N18)

Dock Road

Dock Road

Commercial Dock

Dock Street

can be seen part of the original medieval walls of the city, although it's difficult to distinguish ancient remains from modern reconstruction. The square is a busy sort of place, what with the statuary, parked cars, phone boxes, bus queues, traffic. The recent pedestrianization of the roads leading down to the harbour have shifted the balance of the town a little away from here to the cafés and shops of Quay Street.

On the corner of Abbeygate Street and Shop Street the Allied Irish Bank occupies what was once Lynch's Castle, a building thought to date back to 1320 and occupying the centre of the medieval city. It is a single, four-storey block decorated on the outside with gargoyle water spouts. The original building would probably have been thatched but much of it burned down in 1473 and was rebuilt by 1503. Cromwell's troops did considerable damage and it sank into mediocrity for a few hundred years. Before 1820, when the street to the west was rebuilt, the building was much larger, extending westwards. Inside the lobby of the bank are a number of panels telling the story of the building and its owners, as well as a 17th-century bridal fireplace, common to this area, celebrating the marriage of members of two important local families, the Blakes and the ffrenches. It does not belong in this building but was brought here in 1927 from another nearby building which was being remodelled. The entrance doors to the bank were constructed in 1933.

Lynch's Castle

Further south, along Shop Street, is the church of St Nicholas of Myra, which has been the city's church since the 14th century. St Nicholas is the man we all revere as Santa Claus, the fourth-century bishop of Myra in Lycia and the patron saint of sailors. The nave, chancel and transepts were built at this time and it is the largest medieval parish church in Ireland. In

St Nicholas of Myra

County Galway

The Claddagh

When the Anglo-Normans took the settlement and began the development of Galway City, the native population settled to the south in the area known as Claddagh or beach. Like other Gaelic settlements all over Ireland it had its own laws and a ruler who functioned as law maker and judge. Long after other Gaelic settlements assimilated and learned English the Claddagh survived, a little pocket of Gaelic Ireland right up to the early 20th century, with its own customs, dress, and economy based on fishing using the Galway Hookers. The little township of thatched cottages was demolished in 1937 when the area was needed for modern housing and the Gaelic-speaking residents dispersed. The only thing that remains now is the name, which has been given to a style of ring common to Connaught: the Claddagh ring. This shows a pair of hands, the symbol of friendship, holding a heart, the symbol of love, with a crown, a symbol, to some at least, of loyalty.

the 16th century the north and south aisles were added, as well as the chapel of the Blessed Sacrament and the belfry. In 1652, the church was desecrated by Cromwell's forces who used the building as stables. Legend has it that Christopher Columbus worshipped here in 1477. It is a pretty little church and well worth a wander around for its ornaments.

From the entrance the room above you in the porchway was once the living quarters of the sexton: legend has it that the last sexton who lived here in this tiny room had a family of eight children. In front of you is the **baptismal font**, perhaps 16th century in origin, carved with a figure of a dog, a fleur-de-lys and a three-leaved clover. In front of the Chapel of the Blessed sacrament are **banners of the Connaught Rangers**, whose cannon decorates Eyre Square and who mutinied in India in support of the Irish War of Independence in 1920. In the north aisle are some ancient gravestones, some of which carry the trade symbols of the men buried beneath them including a goldsmith's, stonemason's and a wool merchant's. In this area is a mass grave with several hundred skeletons.

In the Chapel of Christ is a 13th-century tomb of a crusader, the oldest tomb in the church. Under the Lynch window is the tomb of Stephen Lynch with the figures of two angels, damaged by Cromwell's forces. Some of the original paintwork of the tomb can still be made out. Further along the south transept is another Lynch tomb, with the figure of Christ displaying the five wounds, also damaged by 17th-century soldiers. Here too is the tomb of the infamous James Lynch who hung his own son, Walter (see page 417). Of particular interest is the apprentice's column in the southeast nave of the church, bearing particularly fancy carvings and thought to be the apprentice's master piece, the work he had to do to pass his apprenticeship. All around the church are stone fragments found during various renovations and set into the walls of the church to preserve them.

Outside the church in the wall of the churchyard is the Lynch Memorial, a completely modern collection of fragments all said to be connected with James Lynch. ■ *Shop Street. April to September, daily 0900-1745; October to March, daily 0930-1430. Free.*

Other sights   At No 8 Bowling Green is the erstwhile **home of Nora Barnacle**, now dedicated to the memory of the woman who captured James Joyce's heart. Joyce visited the house in 1909 and 1912 and wrote the powerful short story *The Dead*, based on the story of the young man, Michael Bodkin, who died after making his way in the rain to sing to Nora. ■ *April to September, Monday-Saturday irregularly. On request during winter months. Variable phone number in the window of the house. IR£1.*

In Flood Street is the **Spanish Arch**, one of the remaining sections of the city walls of Galway. It is thought that this was a place where ships could unload their goods in the town's harbour. Its age or function is not really known nor is the origin of its name. Behind the arch, the walls of the city and the ditch that lay outside it can be seen.

Close by is the **town's museum**, a collection of trivia and flotsam representing the hundreds of years of the city's existence, all cluttered together anyhow, including straw rattles, feeding bottles, an assortment of broken yokes, neolithic axe heads and bits of masonry with little tags suggesting their origins. ■ *Flood Street. Monday-Sunday 1000-1715. IR£1.50.*

Beyond the Wolfe Tone Bridge is the **Claddagh**, once an independent little state with its own king, laws, language and dress code and later a fishing village where the Galway Hookers were built and used. It once had a population of about 8,000 Irish speakers living in tiny thatched cottages.

Over to the northwest of town is **St Nicholas' Cathedral**, seat of the disgraced Bishop Eamon O'Casey, perhaps still resident somewhere in South America along with British great train robbers and ex-Nazis. The church, dedicated in 1965, is an epiphany of '60s bad taste: built of limestone blocks with

Galway city centre

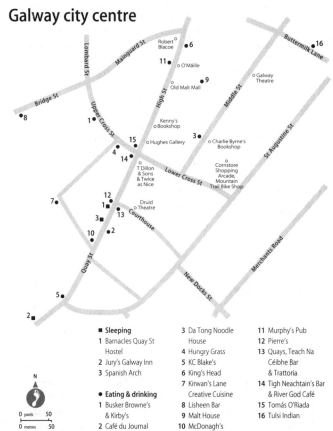

■ **Sleeping**
1 Barnacles Quay St Hostel
2 Jury's Galway Inn
3 Spanish Arch

● **Eating & drinking**
1 Busker Browne's & Kirby's
2 Café du Journal
3 Da Tong Noodle House
4 Hungry Grass
5 KC Blake's
6 King's Head
7 Kirwan's Lane Creative Cuisine
8 Lisheen Bar
9 Malt House
10 McDonagh's
11 Murphy's Pub
12 Pierre's
13 Quays, Teach Na Céibhe Bar & Trattoria
14 Tigh Neachtain's Bar & River God Café
15 Tomás O'Riada
16 Tulsi Indian

N

0 yards 50
0 metres 50

County Galway

copper streaks from the roof cutting crazy patterns down its walls and an excess of Connemara marble inside.

West of the city is **Salthill**, a seaside resort and still rapidly developing. It has a leisurore centre, some interesting night life and a beach that is a bit pebbly. After September, when the schools reopen, Salthill is a perfect place for lovers of deserted seaside towns. In summer there's not much to keep you there except lots of family entertainment such as **Leisureland**, with lots of pools, and rides, and **Seapoint**, with a casino, video games snooker and daily bingo. The promenade is the longest in Ireland and at the western end is Blackrock diving area, once a men-only swimming spot. When you get to the end of the promenade, kick the wall – it's a tradition. ■ *Leisureland: The Promenade, T521455. Mon-Fri 0930-1400, 2000-2200; Sat 1400-1715; Sun 1100-1800. IR£3.50. Seapoint: Seapoint Pmenade, T521716. Daily 1000-0100. Variable rates.*

Essentials

Sleeping
■ *on map*
Price codes:
see inside front cover

During festival time, in July, August and September, accommodation becomes very scarce indeed and should be booked well in advance.

The city abounds with hotels, both in the city and on the feeder roads into town, good inexpensive hostels, and lots of B&Bs. There are very few B&Bs or guesthouses within the city centre: most are in suburbs along Newcastle Rd or Salthill. B&Bs tend to cost around IR£18-20 per person sharing a double room. Most do 25-50% reductions for children. If you turn up in the city with no accommodation try the Ireland West Tourism Office (see 'Directory' on page 429), but there can be long delays queuing for attention there at the peak of the season. A possibility worth considering is Salthill, which is a brisk but stimulating walk from town, has lots of accommodation at all price ranges and another Tourism West office where the queues may be shorter (see 'Directory' on page 429). Galway is crowded with hostels, most of which offer single and double rooms as well as the usual kitchens, lounge area and laundry. The dormitory accommodation attracts a very young crowd whose habits tend to be late and noisy: do not expect a quiet, restful time in any of the Galway hostels during the summer months. Room rates in the bigger hotels expand during festival times but by the same token can be negotiated downwards in the off season.

Galway City   **LL-L** *Ardilaun House Hotel*, Taylor's Hill, T521433, F521546. Including leisure centre with pool, extensive facilities. Very smart, individually furnished rooms with fine views. Privately owned, friendly hotel sitting in its own grounds; originally a mansion owned by one of the Galway tribes, the Pearses. Well out of the noise of the city.

County Galway

L *Great Southern Hotel*, Eyre Square, T564041, F566704, res@galway.gsh.ie Rates vary according to season, and whether weekends or weekdays; some good special offers. Spacious rooms, award-winning restaurant, roof-top pool. **L** *Park House Hotel*, Forster St, T564924, F569219. Lots of comfort and a pleasant welcome. Spacious rooms in this quiet hotel, just off Eyre Square. Good value for the price range. **L** *Skeffington Arms Hotel*, Eyre Square, T563173, F561679. Newly refurbished rooms, lively bar, carvery restaurant. This small place has been here for a hundred years so it must be doing something right. **L** *Victoria Hotel*, Victoria Place, T567433, F565880. In a quiet part of the city centre, big spacious rooms individually furnished, pleasant guest areas. **LL-AL** *Galway Ryan Hotel & Leisure Centre*, Dublin Rd, T753181, F753187. Very modern out-of-town hotel with swimming pool and leisure facilities, restaurant, bar; no need to go into town, it's all here. **LL-AL** *Hotel Spanish Arch*, Quay St, T569600, F569191. Boutique hotel with individually decorated rooms, nice Victorian bar, bits of 16th-century walls.

AL-A *Atlanta Hotel*, Dominick St, T562241, F563895. Out of the main city centre, small family run hotel, guests' car-park. **L-A** *Imperial Hotel*, Eyre Square, T563033, F568410. Very centrally located, popular restaurant with locals.

B *Abbey View*, Bushy Park, T524488. Around £18 per person sharing an en-suite room in this B&B in the Dangan area. **B** *Achill House*, 9 Winestrand Rd, T589149. Guesthouse 5 minutes walk from the city centre and close to beaches. Has a private car-park. **B** *Bredagh House*, Ballybane Rd, T770936. Very new, quite large guesthouse over a mile from city centre. **B** *Cois Na Tine*, Barr Aille, Glenanail, T758787. Guesthouse just over a mile from the city centre on a main bus route. **B** *Coolavalla*, 22, Newcastle Rd, T522415. Guesthouse close to the city centre and university. Private car-park. **B** *De Sota*, 54 Newcastle Rd, T585064. B&B close to the city centre. **B** *Jury's Galway Inn*, Quay St, T566444, F568415, info@jurys.com Charging per room, not per person, this has to be the best value hotel in town for more than 2 people sharing. Pleasant, close to river. **B** *Kilbree House*, Circular Rd, Dangan Upper, T527177. B&B about 2 miles from city centre, en-suite rooms, around IR£18 per person sharing. **B** *Lakeland House*, Bushy Park, T524964. B&B in the Dangan area, around IR£18 per person sharing. **B** *Petra*, 201 Laurel Park, Newcastle, T521844. B&B over a mile from city centre. **B** *Santa Maria*, 5, Glenina Heights, Dublin Rd, T755363. Guesthouse on a bus route but less than a mile from the city centre, close to the *Galway Ryan Hotel*. **B** *Villa Nova*, 40 Newcastle Rd, T524849. Guesthouse close to the city centre. **B** *Winacre Lodge*, Bushy Park, T524964. B&B on the road to Connemara, at around IR£18 per person.

D *Arch View Hostel*, 1 Upper Dominick St, T586661. No private rooms. **D** *Barnacles Quay Street House*, 10 Quay St,

County Galway

T/F568644, qshostel@barnaclesiol.ie 7 private rooms at IR£14.50 per person sharing, family rooms, a laundry. Near the harbour. **D** *Celtic Tourist Hostel*, Queen St, Victoria Pl, T/F566606. Private rooms at IR£11.50 per person. **D** *Corrib Villa*, 4 Waterside, T562892. In the northwest of the city, has no private doubles but has 4-bed family rooms at IR£8.50 per person sharing. Rates include breakfast. **D** *The Galway Hostel*, Eyre Square, T566959. In an elegant old stone building, has several private double rooms for IR£9.50 per person. Open 24 hours with no curfew. **D** *Galway International Youth Hostel*, St Mary's College, St Mary's Rd, T527411, F528710. An Óige hostel, half-way between Salthill and the city centre; has a cafeteria, laundry, cycles for hire and family rooms at IR£9 per person including breakfast. Open summer only. **D** *Great Western House*, Frenchville Lane, T561150, F561196, shaungwh@iol.ie The 22 private en-suite rooms are IR£15 per person sharing, there is a bike hire service as well as secure storage for bikes, a laundry service and dormitory and family rooms. **D** *Kinlay House*, Merchant's Rd, T565244, F565245. Just off Eyre Sq, with private rooms for IR£13 per person. Washrooms and toilets not gender specific. Price includes continental breakfast. **D** *Mary Ryan Apartments*, 4 Beechmount Ave, Highfield Park, T523303. Open from June to September inclusive. No dormitory accommodation, only twin and family rooms, at IR£7.50 per person sharing. Price includes breakfast, evening meals are available. **D** *The Salmon Weir Hostel*, St Vincent's Ave, T561133. Has private doubles at IR£10 per person sharing, a laundry, bike hire and does evening meals. In the northwest of the city.

Sleeping out of the city

Furbo **L** *Connemara Coast Hotel*, Furbo, T592108, F592065. This smart new hotel is ten minutes by car from Galway on the coast road west of Salthill. Stirring views over Galway Bay and a small library to help pass the time on a rainy day.

Salthill **L** *Eyre Square Hotel*, Forster St, T569633, F569641. All the facilities, centrally located, lively pub. **L** *Galway Bay Hotel*, The Promenade, T520520, F520530. Vast, yellow, spacious but fairly bland, very new hotel with leisure centre, pool, library, sea views. **AL** *Hotel Salthill*, T522711, F521855, infosh@indigo.ie Previously known as *Murrays*, a friendly hotel with refurbished, pleasant rooms; family owned and run. The bar has live music every night in summer, very popular restaurant; sea views.

A *Anno Santo Hotel*, Threadneedle Rd, T523011, F522110. Small, family run, on main bus route into city. Away from the sea front. **A** *Eglinton Hotel*, The Promenade, T526400, F526495. Pleasant hotel on sea front, close to new leisure complex. **A** *Holiday Hotel*, 181 Upper Salthill, T523934, F527083. Away from the sea front, small hotel, family owned. **A** *Rockbarton Park Hotel*, T522286, F527692. Family-run hotel in residential area.

B *Atlantic View House*, 4 Ocean Wave, Seapoint, T582109, F528566. Guesthouse close to the city, sea views. **B** *Knockrea Guest House*, 55 Lower Salthill, T520145, F529985, knockrea@tinet.ie On bus route, 300yds/m from seafront, walkable distance from city. Friendly atmosphere, car-park. **B** *Osterly Lodge*, 42 Lower Salthill, T523794, F523565. Guesthouse away from the seafront, lots of facilities, private car-park.

Camping There are several campsites to the east and west of Galway along the coast. The best of them is *Ballyloughane Caravan and Camping Park*, Ballyloughane Beach, Renmore, T755338, F752029. About 5 minutes drive outside the city centre along the Dublin road. Shop, laundry, TV room. Tent, 2 people and a car around IR£6. At Barna, west of Salthill on the R337 to Spiddal is *Hunters Silver Strand Caravan Park*, Barna, T592040. Small shop and laundry. 2 people, tent and car IR£7. Both open Easter to 30th September.

**Eating:
Restaurants**
● on map
Price codes:
see inside front cover

Expensive Best of the restaurants in Galway is the *Camilaun Room*, in *Ardilaun House Hotel* (see 'Sleeping' on page 422). Its line-up of awards is quite stunning and its style is modern Irish with the emphasis on fresh local produce. Dinner will cost IR£20 plus. Reservations necessary. A city-centre, family-run place with a relaxed atmosphere and fine menu is *The Malt House*, T563993, in the Old Malt Shopping Mall. Its stone walls are ancient and it is the right size for comfort – not too many tables but not so small that everything you say is heard by the other customers. A small, traditional Irish menu, extensive wine list and reasonable prices ensure a great meal. Dinner will cost up to IR£20 and there is an early evening menu. At the bottom of Quay Street is *K.C. Blakes*, T561826, a very fashionable-looking place with lots of beech and steel. The menu is extensive and runs to pizzas, pasta and fajitas. No lunch menu but open 1700-2230, 7 days a week in summer. Attached to Busker Browne's in Cross St is *Kirby's*, T569404, a place that is visually very pleasing, with Munch-like oil paintings on the walls and a nice extensive menu including boxtys (Irish potato pan-cakes) parsnip soup, lots of fish and vegetarian choices. Dinner can be up to IR£20. Nearby in Kirwan Lane is *Kirwan Lane Creative Cuisine*, T568266, a classy looking place with prices to match. In Long Walk, Spanish Arch, is *Nimmo's*, T563565, a tiny place with a very good reputation. Minimalist menu but the dishes are a surprise when they reach you. Dinner IR£20 plus. Nouvelle Irish.

Affordable Along Quay St are a series of restaurants worth browsing through if you're after some good food. The *River God Café*, T565811, at No 2 above the *Tigh Neachtain* pub serves snacks and pastries as well as lunchtime and evening meals. Delights on the menu include fish in coral sauce and Creole turkey stir fry. The off-season evening menu at IR£10 for 3 courses and a glass of wine is excellent value. You can also bring your own wine. Reservations necessary at weekends. Further along is *Pierre's*, T566066, open 7 days till 2300 in summer, with a similar winter offer of 3 courses for IR£10 and French cuisine. The *Quays* restaurant at the back of the *Teach Na Céibhe* pub, T568347, is another themed place but nicely done. The restaurant has an extensive menu both for lunch and dinner. Main courses in the evening are around IR£10 and a 2-course meal and wine will work out at about IR£20. The *Trattoria*, still in Quay St at No 12, T563910, a pasta and pizza place is open 7 days. The setting is very Italian dimly lit with lots of chianti bottles. Dinner could work out at around IR£20.

In Abbeygate St is *Brannagan's* , T565974, a very young, stylish place with lots of brick walls and a very trendy menu including Mexican, Cajun, and oriental dishes. Open daily from 1700. In the same street is *Conlon's Fish Restaurant*, a very popular place with an enormous menu and great fish and chips. In nearby St Francis St is *Cactus Jack's* with everything on a Mexican theme – burgers, steaks, fajitas, Cajun dishes – all at reasonable prices, a cocktail happy hour 1700-2000 and very brightly decorated. Close by in Main St, T501475, is *The Home Plate*, selling more Mexican stuff and some Thai dishes too. Midday-2130 daily.

If you have a sudden hankering after Asian cuisine there are a few good places to try. *Da Tong Noodle House*, Middle St, T561443, has authentic noodle based Chinese cuisine with lots of vegetarian options. At 3, Buttermarket Walk, Middle St, T564831, is *Tulsi*, and Indian restaurant with lots of vegetable dishes, enough for a vegetarian to have a banquet. For more meaty kind of Indian food try *Eastern Tandoori*, 21, Spanish Parade, T564819, with lots of naan and nut-based sauces.

Galway has the full range of fast-food joints and an emporium of fast-food options all under one roof in the southwest corner of Eyre Square, but there is little need to use these kind of places with so many good places for a sandwich, pub lunch, or lunch-time specials.

Fast food, cafés & pub food

In the Eyre Square Shopping Centre are several places to consider. There is a *Kylemore* bakery on the ground floor, where you can get filled rolls and pastries while

County Galway

upstairs is their restaurant serving hot meals at reasonable prices. Upstairs there is also an open-plan eating area called *Sails*, which does soup and sandwiches and more substantial dishes for lunch if you don't mind the taped muzak of the shopping centre. Next door to it is *La Croissanterie*, which serves soup and all kinds of filled croissants. The Eyre Square Centre links up with Corbett Ct where there is an excellent sandwich bar, one of a chain in Ireland, *O'Brien's*. Both these shopping centres close at 1800.

Along the main Eyre Square to Shop Street route are lots of snackeries and very recently renovated theme pubs. In Williamsgate St is the homely *GBC Coffeeshop*, which does lunchtime food and has a restaurant upstairs for more substantial dishes, while opposite is the big and busy *Maxwell McNamaras* doing snacks and sandwiches, with a menu full of fish, steak and chicken options as well as a tiny box describing what vegetarians can have. Still in Shop St, at No 12 *Elle's* café serves soups and sandwiches, filled potatoes and pittas and a nice array of desserts, open until 1830, Monday-Saturday, 1800 Sunday. The *King's Head* at the junction of Shop St and High St is a vast, recently themed old pub, which seems to go on for ever, with some good pub food that ceases by early evening. *Tomas O Riada* in Quay Street is another genuinely old pub that has been themed and now forms a warren of little bars and a connected café called *The Front Door*. You can order the food in any part of the bars or eat in the café itself. Slightly more choices than the typical bar food menu with good vegetarian options and sandwiches. Food finishes about 1600.

In Abbeygate St Lower is *Couch Potatoes*, a very busy place nicely decorated with potatoes dominating the menu from filled baked potatoes to potato pizza. A good, value-for-money place, with lots of vegetarian choices.

On Cross St, the *Hungry Grass* café has lots of vegetarian dishes such as hummous and basil pittas, salads, as well as a breakfast menu and some meat options; open 7 days till 2200 in summer. Further along is *Busker Browne's* pub, serving soups and more substantial choices till 2000, daily in summer. At the bottom of Quay St *Donagh's Seafood* is more of a restaurant than a snack place but does excellent fish and chips with a wide range of fish on the menu at café prices. On the other side of the river in Henry St, the *Pumphouse*, a vegetarian pub, has an extensive menu of vegetarian meals, open for food till 2000, daily in summer. Rather more than a coffee shop *Café du Journal*, The Halls, Quay St, T568426, is a bookish sort of place where many different coffees are served with newspapers to read; it also offers stylish soups and main courses with lots of seafood dishes and delicious sauces. Open till 2230.

Pubs & music **Town centre** In summer there is music all around – in the street and in almost every pub – just wander down the street and follow the noise. *List Galway* is a free fortnightly publication listing what's on in town available from the tourist office, newsagents, pubs and the station. There is live music most nights in *Busker Browne's* in Upper Cross St with jazz on Sunday mornings. *The King's Head* in High St has music ranging from jazz to traditional Irish every night and a good atmosphere to match, while *Taafe's*, next door is a more traditional bar also with live music as well as sports on TV.

Similar in style and probability of live music to the King's Head is the *Quays* in Quay St. Probably the most authentic, and the least brought-in-for-the-tourists, music is to be found in the *Lisheen Bar*, in Bridge St. Other places to check out are the *Drum Bar*, in Eglinton St, with disco music rather than live bands; *Red Square* in Eyre Square with live music every night ranging from jazz to traditional music as well as rock, and *An Púcán* in Forster St, just off Eyre Sq.

West of the river On the other side of the river are *The Pumphouse* in Henry St *The Róisín Dubh* in Upper Dominick St where the music is definitely not traditional, *Monroe's* also in Dominick St where there is a wide variety of activities each night including set dancing 1 or 2 nights a week, *Taylor's* Bar, again in Dominick St with traditional Irish music most afternoons and evenings, and the *Blue Note*, in West William St, which features largely DJ-driven sounds with live music in between.

A quiet drink Bars to look out for if you enjoy genuine unreconstructed spit and sawdust or just quiet in the eye of the Galway hurricane are *Murphy's*, in the High St, run by the same family for 3 generations and with special reductions on beer for pensioners, and *The Bal*, in Salthill, offering a quiet pint in the midst of bingo, karaoke, drum and bass and British stag parties.

Nightclubs When the bars close the nightclubs open. *ClubCuba* in Eyre Square is open 7 nights a week till the early hours with chart music and special events in the *CubaLive* section. *Central Park* is in Abbeygate St and is the very trendiest place to be. Opens at 2300 and gets very crowded. The *GPO* nightclub in Eglinton St has a wide range of events starting at 2300. All have entry charges that vary according to what's on. Check the listings for details.

Entertainment

Theatre & cultural centres *Druid Theatre*, Courthouse Ln, T568617, is an interesting and experimental theatre committed to new works, often by young Irish writers, while *Town Hall Theatre* in Courthouse Sq, T569777, puts on more established material and travelling theatre groups. There is also an Irish-language theatre in Middle St called *An Taibhdhearc na Gaillimhe*, T562024. Look out for notices of events, especially in *List Galway* and on the noticeboards in the *Galway Arts Centre*.

Galleries There are several art galleries, including the *Bridge Mills Gallery* at O'Brien's Bridge and the *Kenny Gallery* in Middle St, selling local artists' work. The *Galway Arts Centre* is on Lower Dominick St with changing exhibitions of local and national artists' work. It is sometimes also used as a performance space.

Salthill has a festival in early **July** with aeronautical displays and live music, but there are 3 big festivals that are special to Galway City.

Festivals

The *Galway races* are in the last week in **August** and the racing takes place in Ballybrit track, just over a mile outside the city on the road to the airport. The race track can accommodate 20,000 people, and usually does, and restaurants, bars and hotels stay open 24 hrs a day for the duration. Book early.

The 22-year-old *Arts Festival*, T583800, in the 2nd and 3rd week of **July** is, if anything, even bigger with theatre companies from all over the world and the customary 24hr opening for everything. Music, art exhibitions, and lots more. Book even earlier, especially for the events. Part of the Arts Festival is a week-long film festival.

The last week in **September** sees the *Oyster Festival*, T522066 (see page 454); lots of free oysters and Guinness, free street concerts, lots of music and craic and of course lots of licence extensions.

Galway heaves with places where tourists can part with their money, often for quite pretty things totally unconnected with Galway except that they have found their way to one of its shops.

Shopping

Antiques For connoisseurs of old clothes there is *Twice as Nice*, at 5 Quay St, which sells vintage clothing and jewellery, while antique afficionados could have a look in *Tempo Antiques* in Cross St, is full of lovely things.

Art At *Hughes Gallery*, the owner sells his own works and will do commissions from photographs, frame your own works of art and offers painting lessons. The tiny gallery is in the High St, T25963.

Books Galway has a huge number of bookshops as you would expect in a university city. *Easons*, 33 Shop St, has lots of local interest stuff including maps and guides as well as international newspapers. In the High St is *Kenny's*, which seems to go on forever, with the largest stock of second-hand books in Ireland and lots of rare and wonderful tomes such as first editions of Seamus Heaney, Beckett, Yeats and many others. The same company have a bookstore on Merchant's Rd, with out-of-print books where you can spend many hours looking for just the right book. In Eglinton St is *Keohanes*, which has a wide range of subject areas but is particularly good on books of Irish interest. It has a children's bookstore in the next building. In Eyre Sq Shopping Centre is *Needful Things* a specialist comic and graphic novel bookstore with movie-associated cards, games and toys. At 23 Abbeygate St Lower is *Book Exchange* with lots of 2nd-hand paperbacks and comics, while in Middle St in the Cornstore Shopping Centre is *Charlie Byrne's*, with lots of remaindered, 2nd-hand and discounted books.

Clothes Jumper and woollens shops abound. Try *Ó'Máille* in the High St, which has the full range of chunky sweaters, tweeds, and jackets. It is open daily in summer. *Tribes* in William St is another gorgeous place but there are so many of them it is impossible to list them all. Just start at the top of Eyre Sq and work your way down to Quay St.

Crafts As well as the locally made clothes, there are a number of places selling little wooden and ceramic things around Eyre Sq and Quay St. Other good craft shops are *Kelly's* in High St, and *Meadows and Byrne* in Castle St, which is more of a designer furniture and household goods place but has some attractive and functional pottery.

Jewellery A good local purchase is, of course, a claddagh design in a piece of jewellery. Start off in *T Dillon and Sons*, on the corner of Quay St and Cross St. They have a little museum (1000-1700) at the back of the shop dedicated to the history of the claddagh design (see page 420), lots of rings, brooches and necklaces to choose from, and a very famous clientele. Using their prices as a starting point, you could compare prices with any of the other jewellers in town who also sell the Claddagh designs, notably *Robert Blacoe* in Shop St who has other interesting Irish/Galway designs.

Sport **Fishing** Information from the *Western Region Fisheries Board*, T563118. The Corrib System allows trout and salmon fishing, and the season opens on Lough Corrib in February. A boatman can be hired for about IR£45 per day: contact Sonny Martyn, Galway Road, Tuam, County Galway, T093-24151. *Feeney's Sports*, 19-23 High St, T568794, can arrange guides on Lough Corrib, and sea angling trips from July onwards.

Golf *Galway Bay Golf and Country Club*, Salthill T790500, to the southwest of the city was designed by Christy O'Connor. Surrounded on three sides by the sea, 18 holes. *Don Wallace Pro Shop*, T523038, is in the club.

Horse-riding *Feeney's Equestrian Centre*, Toonabrockey, Bushypark, T526553. Organizes trekking and hacking around Galway, beach rides, hourly rates, unaccompanied children welcome. *Rusheen Riding Centre*, Salthill, T521285. Beach riding, trekking, lessons. *Rockmount Riding Centre*, Claregalway, T798147. 5 miles (8 km) from the city on main Galway to Sligo road. Indoor arena, trekking and hacking, lessons.

Transport **Air** Galway airport, T755569, is 7 miles (10 km) east of the city at Carnmore. Taxis cost around IR£12. A once-daily bus service goes to the airport from the bus station, price IR£2.50. The airport has two *Aer Lingus* flights a day to Dublin, which are costly and time-consuming considering the journeys to and from the 2 airports. There are also flights to and from Manchester and Teeside (see page 33).

Bicycle Not really necessary for getting about Galway City, but bikes can be hired for longer journeys. Most of the hostels do bike hire as do *Chieftain Cycle Hire* in Merchants Rd, next to the tourist office, and *Flaherty's Cycles* in West William St. Mountain bikes can be hired from *Mountain Trail Bike Shop*, Cornstore, Middle St, T569888, IR£3 per day.

Bus Ceannt Bus Station, T563555/562000, is next to the railway station at the north end of Eyre Sq behind the *Great Southern Hotel*. There are hourly buses to Dublin as well as frequent buses to other cities in the Republic and the North. Several private companies also operate out of Galway. *Citylink*, T564163, do 8 buses a day to Dublin and Dublin Airport, departing from Forster St coach park. Other companies do regular services to some of the smaller towns in the area. *Edward Walsh Coaches*, T098-35165, does a Sunday service to Westport, departing from Eyre Sq at 1700. *McNulty Coaches*, T097-81016, do a service on Fridays to Belmullet via Westport and Newport, leaving Eyre Sq at 1600, 1730 and 1800. *Nestor Travel*, T091-797144, run a service from Dublin and Dublin Airport to Galway.

Car *Windsor Rent-A-Car*, Monivea Rd, Ballybrit, T770707. On the way to the airport.**Taxis** There are several taxi companies operating in the city. *Galway Taxi* T561111 is on Mainguard St while *Corrib and Apollo*, T564444, is on Eyre St, to the north of Eyre Sq. There is a taxi rank by the railway station.

Train T563555/562000. Trains for Athlone, Tullamore, Portarlington, Kildare, Newbridge and Dublin leave Galway 6 times a day (4 on Sundays). Connections can be made at Kildare for towns in the south.

Directory

Banks & bureaux de change There are two *Bank of Ireland* branches in Eyre Sq, an *Allied Irish Bank* in Lynch's Castle in Shop St. There are ATM machines outside all the branches. There is a bureau de change in the tourist office in Forster St. **Communications Post office:** The main post office is in Eglinton St, open Mon-Sat 0900-1800. There are card and coin call boxes in the post office and at key points around the city. **Hospitals & medical services Hospital:** *University College Hospital*, Newcastle Rd, T563081. **Pharmacy** *The Crescent Pharmacy*, 18 Fr Griffin Rd, T583956, Mon-Sat 0900-1800, Sun 1100-1300. **Language schools** *Atlantic Language School*, Abbeygate St, T566051; *English in Galway*, Spanish Arch, T569896; *Galway Language Centre*, The Bridge Mills, T566468; *Westlingua*, Cathedral Buildings, Middle St, T568188. **Laundry** *Bubbles Laundrette*, Mary St, T563434.**Library** *Galway County Library* Hynes Building, St Augustine St, T561666.**Tour companies & travel agents** Several tour companies have offices in the tourist office in Galway. *Lally Tours*, T553555, do tours of Connemara, Westport and the Burren daily as well as a sightseeing tour of Galway. *O'Neachtain Day Tours*, T553188, do tours of Connemara, the Burren and the Cliffs of Moher as well as a daily coach service to the Aran islands. **Boat trips** *Corrib Tours*, Furbo Hill, Furbo, T592447. Daily cruises on Lough Corrib from Woodquay, Galway. 1½hr cruises. **Tourist offices** *Ireland West Tourism* Forster St, T563081. Main office. Jul-Aug, daily 0830-1945; Jun, daily 0900-1845; May, Mon-Sat 0900-1745; Sep-Apr, Mon-Fri 0900-1745, Sat 0900-1200. There is another office in Salthill, at the junction of Seapoint Promenade and Upper Salthill Rd. *Usit Now* (student travel) Victoria Pl, Eyre Sq.

Aran Islands

Three small islands lying 28 miles (45 kilometres) southwest of Galway across the   Phone code: 099
*mouth of Galway Bay – Inishmore, Inishmaan, and Inisheer – plus three very
small uninhabited islands make up the famous Aran Islands that continue to act
as a magnet for travellers in search of the 'real' Ireland. The course of history
helped preserve the islands' traditional way of life, but beginning in the early
decades of the 20th century writers and filmakers celebrated and broadcast the
pre-industrial culture of the Aran Islands, which turned the spotlight on them.*

County Galway

The rest is history of another kind and in 1998 the authorities even talked of a 'tourist tax' to help cover the cost incurred by the annual invasion of visitors arriving by boats and planes from the mainland. The tax has not materialized but it gives you some idea of the numbers arriving on the islands.

The good news is that two of the Aran Islands have not been destroyed by fame; the bad news is that Inishmore, at least in July and August, is best avoided. The two smaller islands, especially Inish, are rarely inundated with visitors and in many respects they retain much of the charm that first drew artists to Inishmore. However, the largest island is home to major archaeological sites and the tourist infrastructure has its advantages in terms of creature comforts.

Ins and outs

Getting there **Air** *Aer Árann*, T091-593034, F593238, aerarann@iol.ie fly to all 3 islands, using 8-seater Islander aircraft, from Connemara Regional Airport at Inverin, off the main coastal road 17 miles (28 km) west of Galway. With flights every hour in peak months, the single/return fare is IR£29/35 and the connecting bus from the tourist office in Galway and Salthill costs IR£4 but takes longer to reach the airport from the city than the 10-minute actual flying time. A package deal with 1 night's B&B and return fare is IR£47, and 1 way by air and 1 way by boat is IR£29.

The perfect book to bring with you on the boat is J.M. Synge's The Aran Islands (1907) though you're unlikely to encounter the fellow passengers he shared passage with (see overleaf).

Boat *Island Ferries*, T091-568903/561767, travels to all 3 islands from Rossaveal, 26 miles (37 km) west of Galway. The journey takes about 40 minutes and in July and August there are up to 6 boats a day to Inishmore. The boat to the other 2 islands departs at 1030 daily; return fare is IR£15 and, if travelling from Galway, another IR£4 for the bus to Rossaveal that leaves from theoffice at Victoria Pl opposite the tourist office, 90 minutes before departure. Tickets may also be purchased from the *Island Ferries* office at Rossaveal, T091-561767. Between June and September *Island Ferries* have a ferry direct from Galway to Inishmore; IR£18 return for the 90-minute journey.

"...a couple of men going out with young pigs tied loosely in sacking, three or four young girls who sat in the cabin with their heads completely twisted in their shawls, and a builder, on his way to repair the pier at Kilronan." J.M. Synge, The Aran Islands

O'Brien Shipping, T091-567283/567676, with a desk in the Galway tourist office, run a ferry from Galway to all 3 islands daily between June and September, and Tuesday, Thursday and Saturday the rest of the year. The boat departs from Galway Dock at 1030, returning at 1700, taking 95 minutes and IR£15 return.

Doolin Ferries, T065-74455, run a service from Doolin to Inishere and Inishmore between Easter and September. The return fare is IR£15 and the journey takes about half an hour.

Boat services between the islands are operated by *Sunda Teo*, T091-561767, a branch of *Island Ferries*, and in the summer there are daily links between the three islands. Outside of the summer the service is much reduced.

Getting around Only Inishmore is large enough to justify an alternative to walking and upon disembarkation a fleet of bicycles are waiting to be hired. Tour vans are now increasingly common on the island for set tours of the main sites of interest, and pony traps with a driver may also be hired for around IR£20.

Background

Ecology Geologically, the islands are a continuation of the limestone karsts that are so prominent a feature of the nearby Burren in County Clare. Countless generations of Aran Islanders spent winter months collecting sea sand and seaweed with which to layer the thin surfaces of bare limestone rock. Although no longer practised, this method produced a soil capable of being planted by farmers and many of the small fields one sees today with their rows of potatoes and vegetables were built up from bare rock in this way. It is difficult not to notice the

County Galway

characteristic arrangement of 'lazy-beds' in the fields, which is the term that describes the practice of using the soil dug for a trench as a bed to build up the adjoining ridge in which to plant potatoes. In this way the risk of a waterlogged field is minimized. Equally characteristic are the numberless, small, dry-stone walls that fence off one small field from another and create a maze-like filligree around the islands.

Well over 400 varieties of wildflower testify to the rich flora, and seals are not too difficult to spot when they swim into shallow coves – Port Chorrúch is one of their favourite haunts (see page 433) – and the occasional dolphin may be seen off shore. A bird book will be just as useful as a guide to wild flowers, with the increasingly uncommon chough seen around the coast and cuckoos galore heard in May.

History

The pre-historic stone forts found on the islands are testimony to an occupation by Iron Age and possibly late Bronze-Age people, though next to nothing is known about their history. The first records of island life relate to the lives of early Christian saints like St Enda who around the sixth century founded a monastery that attracted like-minded ascetics from across Europe. In the Middle Ages the islands were fought over by the rival clans of the O'Flahertys and the O'Briens but the squabbling of Gaelic chiefs was eclipsed by the English, who first took control in 1587. In the following century Cromwell established a garrison on the islands but, as the west of Ireland gradually lost its importance to the colonial power, the Aran islanders were left to themselves.

The outside world rediscovered the islands when their archaeological sites and the remarkable preservation of Gaelic culture by the islanders attracted notice. The playwright JM Synge made visits to listen to the Irish language and collect stories, and in 1932 the documentary film-maker Robert Flaherty made his now famously contrived film *Man of Aran*. In the last two decades of the twentieth century, tourism has played a pivotal role not only in regenerating the islands' economy but also in their mythologization as the heartbeat of Celtic culture.

Local culture

WB Yeats urged Synge to head for the Aran Islands, and one result of Synge's sojourn was *The Aran Islands* (1907), a book that proved influential in highlighting the traditional culture of the islanders. Synge preferred Inishmaan because of the Irish spoken there but nowadays you will hear Gaelic spoken on all three islands and students of Irish arrive annually to practise their language. Flaherty's documentary made famous the islanders' involvement in fishing, and the traditional canvas-covered curragh is still used as a boat. Gone are the heel-less rawhide shoes that were so well adapted to clambering over rock but there is no shortage of the hand-knitted white sweaters with various patterns that the islands have given their name to. The novelist Liam O'Flaherty (1896-1984), who in 1921 ran up the red flag over the Rotunda in Dublin and occupied it for three days as "Chairman of the Council of the Unemployed", was born on Inishmore. A contemporary writer, Tim Robinson, has found inspiration on the Aran Islands and, while his *The Aran Islands: A Map & Guide* can be recommended, readers some may find his *Stones of Aran* books a bit heavy. Two anthologies of essays are worth dipping into: *The Book of Aran*, brought out by Tír Eolas, a local publisher, and available in Galway bookshops, and *An Aran Reader*, edited by Breandán & Ruairí Ó hEithir (Lilliput Press, Dublin).

'Some one, whose name I forgot, told me there was a poor Irishman at the top of the house, and presently introduced us ... He told me that he learned Irish at Trinity College, so I urged him to go to the Aran Islands and find a life that had never been expressed in literature, instead of a life where all had been expressed. I did not divine his genius, but I felt he needed something to take him out of his morbidity and melancholy.' WB Yeats, Autobiographies

County Galway

Inishmore (Inis Mór)

Colour map 2, grid C2

*The largest of the three islands, Inishmore is about nine miles (14 kilometres) long and over two miles (four kilometres) at its widest. Boats arrive at **Kilronan** (Cill Rónáin), the main village, and from there the island's chief road travels west to Kilmurvey, close to the major archaeological site and an alternative base for accommodation, and east to Killeany where St Enda's monastery once stood.*

Heritage centre

Ionad Árann (Aran Heritage Centre), in Kilronan, introduces the history, geology and lifestyle of the islanders. The *Man of Aran* film is shown at 1200, 1345 and 1500, and there is a small café, gift shop and a bureau de change. ■ *T61355. April to October, 1000-1900. IR£2.50.*

Stone forts

Tours of the island in a van will get you around the main sites quickly but they have little else to recommend them. Hiring a bike and cycling the Inis Mór Way is a lot more fun.

Dún Aengus (or Dún Aonghasa) is the most spectacular site on Inishmore, not least because of its location on the edge of a 300-foot (91-metre) cliff. This stone fort, one of the finest examples of Iron Age building in Europe and approximately 2,000 years old, is made up of three concentric enclosures, each with walls of dry masonry. The middle wall is defended by a remarkable *chevaux-de-frise* – vertical, jagged, sharp stones set at various angles to entrap an enemy force – while the main, innermost fort is 148 feet (45 metres) in diameter, with walls nearly 13 feet (four metres) thick. The parapet and stairways of the inner walls were put in place when restoration work of questionable authority was carried out in 1881, but supporting evidence for this feature comes from the stone fort at Staigue in Cork. Be careful – extremely so with children – when approaching the edge because it is a sheer drop and the erosion that cut off the missing wall of the fort continues to eat away the land.

There are a number of other stone forts and ancient sites dotted around, and a copy of Tim Robinson's map is essential for anyone wishing to locate and really explore these pre-historic sites. One of the more important is **Dún Eoghanachta**, an impressive circular fort northwest of Kilronan and best reached by taking the main road west of Kilronan looking for the sign pointing south. There is also **Dún Eochla** inland less than halfway between Kilronan and Dún Aengus. However, for another dramatically situated fort it is worth seeking out **Dún Dúchathair**, situated to the south of Kilronan and surrounded by cliffs on three sides.

Monastic sights

Continuing along the road west of Kilronan brings one to **Clochán na Carraige** on the north side of the road. This 19-foot-long (eight-metre), dry

Inishmore

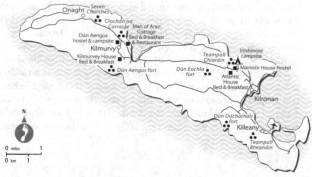

County Galway

stone *clochán*, with the corbelled roof characteristic of early Christian buildings, is very well-preserved. Travelling a little further west along the road accesses the **Seven Churches**, though you will only find two actual churches plus the ruins of monastic houses, assorted portions of cross-slabs and fragments of high crosses. One stone is inscribed with *VII Romans*, a fact that has given rise to various interpretations, including the unlikely one that Christian Romans are buried here. It is more probable that the graves are of pilgrims who made a journey to Rome.

An interesting ecclesiastical site is **Teampall Chiaráin** (Church of St Kieran), reached by taking the road south that is opposite *Joe Watty's* pub at Mainistir, complete with a high cross in the churchyard and an ancient holy well that probably marks a pagan site that early Christians expropriated. Just to the south of Killeany, **Teampall Bheanáin** (Church of St Benignus) is built on the rock oriented north to south and dates back to around the sixth century.

The Inis Mór Way

To enjoy walking or cycling on the island it is essential to get off the main road, and the 21-mile (34-kilometre) Inis Mór Way is fairly well signposted. The drawback is that too much of the Way uses surfaced roads that are hard on your feet, but compensation comes in the form of the sweeping views with the sea nearly always in view, enough stone-walled fields to last a lifetime and numerous opportunities to wander off and poke around archaeological and historical sites. The least expensive guide is the *Inis Mór Way* leaflet (IR£1.50), which includes a map and some brief descriptions. Ordnance Survey map No 51 in the Discovery series covers the island, and there is also Tim Robinson's map (see page 431) as well as specialist walking guides that cover the Way (see page 64).

The Way begins at Kilronan and heads north past the shingle and sand Trá na bhFrancach (Beach of the French) before turning west and staying fairly close to the coastline, passing Port Chorrúch and meeting the white, sandy beach at Port Mhuirbhigh where the width of the islands shrinks to only ½ mile (one kilometre). On the other side of the beach the Way heads uphill and inland, close by Clochán na Carraige, Dún Eoghanachta and the Seven Churches. It descends to the coast once more and then inland to a T-junction near the western end of the island. From here the Way returns inland and eventually rejoins the outward route as far as Port Mhuirbhigh, where there is a spur to Dún Aengus, before heading southwards to the village of Gort na bPéist, where Liam O'Flaherty (see page 431) was born. It continues eastwards to Dún Dúchathair before heading north back to Kilronan.

Kilronan

Aharla Hostel

Joe Watty's Bar

Ionad Árann (Aran o Heritage Centre)

St Kevin's Hostel

Aran Islands Hostel

American Bar

Aran Fisherman

Bayview Guesthouse

Dún Aonghasa Seafood Restaurant & Bar

0 yards   100
0 metres   100

N

Essentials

Sleeping

There are no hotels to choose from on the island, although there is a range of other accommodation. The average B&B rate is IR£17 per person and while there is a lot to choose from it is advisable to have somewhere booked before arrival. The Kilronan, Dún Aengus, Mainistir and Aharla hostels are open all year.

B *Ard Einne*, T61126, F61388. To the west of the village, this B&B enjoys sweeping views of the mainland coast and Galway Bay. **B** *Atlantic House*, Mainistir, T61185. Has cheaper rooms sharing bathroom facilities as well as en-suite rooms. **B** *Bayview Guesthouse*, Kilronan, T61260. Overlooks the harbour. **B** *Man of Aran Cottage*, Kilmurvey Bay, T61301. This B&B, where part of the famous film was shot, charges a little above the average. **B** *Pier House*, Kilronan, T61416, F61122. Smartish guesthouse charges IR£20 in the high season. **B** *Ti Eithne*, Kilronan, T61303. A short walk away from the harbour.

At the eastern end of the island, **C** *Ard Aoibhinn*, Killeany, T/F61130. At the eastern end of the island, this B&B has doubles/singles from IR£28/14 with shared bathroom facilities and is within walking distance of Kilronan. Open May to September.

D *Aharla Hostel*, Kilronan, T61305. Near the pier, no private rooms. **D** *Dún Aengus Hostel*, T61318. Has a scenic location near Kilmurvey Bay and allows for a late evening, atmospheric visit to the nearby fort. Private rooms are IR£7 per person. Come here to get away from the crowds. **D** *Killeany Lodge Hostel*, T61393. IHH hostel to the southeast of Kilronan, lacking private rooms and charging 50p for a shower but a relatively quiet place. **D** *Kilronan Hostel*, Kilronan, T61255. Being in Kilronan, near to the pier and above a pub combine to make it both convenient and noisy. no private rooms. **D** *Mainistir House Hostel*, Kilronan, T61169, F61351. Within walking distance of the pier but a pick-up service is usually waiting. It has a family room, doubles, twin and small dormitories and package deals with *Island Ferries* use this accommodation. **D** *St Kevin's Hostel*, Kilronan, T61125. Between the *Tí Joe Mac's* pub and the supermarket. No private rooms.

Camping Near the beach at Mainistir, the *Inishmór Camp Site*, T61185, is very basic, while the one attached to the *Killeany Lodge Hostel* has the use of its kitchen and showers.

Eating In Kilronan the pubs serve food and *Joe Watty's Bar* comes recommended. The *Aran Fisherman* is fine for a casual meal and there is a choice of meat, pasta, pizza, seafood and vegetarian dishes under IR£12. The *Dún Aonghasa Seafood Restaurant and Bar*, T61104, is open May to September from 1800 and offers fixed priced dinners for around IR£13 and à la carte. Dinner for IR£8 at *Mainistir House Hostel* is self-described as a 'vaguely vegetarian buffet' and diners are welcome to bring their own drinks. On the road up to Dun Aengus the *An Sunda Caoch* café opens daily 1100-1700 for sandwiches and cakes.

Pubs & music Every weekend at the *Dún Aonghasa Seafood Restaurant and Bar* there are sessions of traditional Irish music and nearly all the pubs on the islands have some form of entertainment at night during the summer months. *Tigh Fitz* at Killeany involves a journey if not staying at the east side of the island but the musical sessions are very good. The *American Bar* in Kilronan itself is a popular place that caters to every type of visitor: it isn't the plushest pub in Ireland but you'll rub shoulders with an amazing mix of people – from salty fisherman to clueless tourists – enlivened by occasional outbursts of song.

Shopping Inishmore would be the place to purchase a genuine hand-knitted Aran sweater and there are a few places selling them. *Carraig Donn* in Kilronan has a selection as well as factory knitwear, tweed and wax jackets. A nearby shop, *An Teach Ceoil*, is crammed with CDs and cassettes of traditional Irish music.

Directory **Banks & bureaux de change** Banks: *Bank of Ireland* in Kilronan. Jun-Aug, Wed-Thu; Sep-May, Wed. **Bureaux de change**: money can be changed at the post office, or the *Carraig Donn* shop.

Inishmaan (Inis Meáin)

Inishmaan is the second largest of the Aran Islands, with a population of less than 200 as compared to the 800 or so who live in Inis Mór. Figures like Synge and Pearse came here because of its reputation as the least culturally spoilt of the three islands and even today, probably because it attracts fewer visitors, this still holds true.

Colour map 2, grid C2

Ins and outs

Boats land at An Córa on the east side of the island and the main route leads across the island with boreens leading off to the north and south. The airstrip is in the northeast of the island.

Getting there

Inishmaan is only about three miles (five kilometres) long by about two miles (three kilometres) wide, and with little high ground it is not difficult to explore on foot.

Getting around

The Inis Meáin Way

By walking the undemanding five-miles (eight-kilometre) Inis Meáin Way from An Córa, mostly along surfaced roads and quiet boreens, it is still possible to experience the appeal of an island that drew Synge back for five summers in succession at the turn of the 19th century.

From the pier keep the rocky shore on your left and head inland to the remains of **Cill Cheannanach**, a small oratory that dates from the eighth or ninth century, and what was the island graveyard until 1940. Follow the boreen uphill to **Dún na Fearbhaí**, a stone fort from around the same time, which provides good views of Connemara and Clare on a clear day. The Way continues westwards to the village of Baile an Mhothair and the island's only pub before passing the island's church, with its startling stained-glass windows by Harry Clarke. On the other side of the boreen, the ruined **Synge's Cottage** comes into view; the playwright spent his summers here between 1898 and 1902 and his *Riders to the Sea* is set on the island.

nishmaan

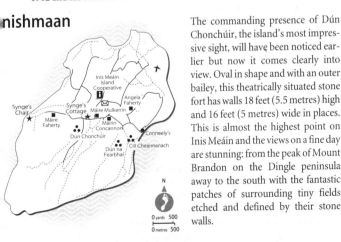

The commanding presence of Dún Chonchúir, the island's most impressive sight, will have been noticed earlier but now it comes clearly into view. Oval in shape and with an outer bailey, this theatrically situated stone fort has walls 18 feet (5.5 metres) high and 16 feet (5 metres) wide in places. This is almost the highest point on Inis Meáin and the views on a fine day are stunning: from the peak of Mount Brandon on the Dingle peninsula away to the south with the fantastic patches of surrounding tiny fields etched and defined by their stone walls.

Dún Chonchúir
Dún Chonchúir, the most eye-catching hill fort anywhere in Ireland, can be enjoyed in relative peace while hordes of visitors are tramping across Inishmore.

County Galway

Synge's Chair The Way continues, uphill along a road for a while and then across bare rock, to the western coastline and Synge's Chair. This dry-stone shelter was built by Synge because he liked to come here on a daily basis to contemplate the view and compose his thoughts.

The Way then returns eastwards, a little to the north and at a lower level. It gradually turns into a tarmacked road and turns to the left along a road, before the Way then turns right for the route back to the pier. Just before the Way turns to the right, a boreen on the left leads down to the beach, Trácht Each.

Essentials

Sleeping **C** *Creig Mór*, T73012, F73111. This B&B, about 500yds/m from the pier, has been recommended as a place for a comfortable night's stay on the island and an evening meal can be arranged for IR£10. **C** *Máirin Concannon*, T73019. Welcoming B&B near the pub in the middle of the island. **C** *Máire Faherty*, Ard Alainn, T73027. B&B at the end of the road that leads to Dún Chonchúir, open from the end of April to September and doubles/singles with shared facilities are IR£26/20. **C** Máire Mulkerrin, T73016. In the middle of the island, near the pub. Welcoming.

Self-catering For the 'get away from it all' self-catering option contact Pádraig o Fatharta at the pub, T73047, or *Nora Concannon*, T55893.

Eating There are limited opportunities for eating out on Inishmaan, especially outside the summer months, and you might want to bring a picnic for lunch. The island's only pub, T73003, serves light meals in the summer until around 1900 but most of the B&Bs will provide an evening meal if you arrange this in advance. There is a restaurant, *An Dun*, T73068, near the junction where you turn left for Dún Chonchúir, which opens in the summer for lunch and dinner. Closer to the pier, *Connely's*, T73085, is the only other restaurant.

Directory **Bank** *Bank of Ireland* operates on the second Tuesday of each month. **Tourist Information** The *Inis Meáin Island Co-operative*, T73010, in the middle of the island just north of the post office, is the place to make enquiries.

Inisheer (Inis Óirr)

Colour map 2, grid C2 *The smallest of the Aran Islands, with a population of around 300, is six miles (nine kilometres) off the coast of Clare and receives a steady flow of travellers from Doolin as well as from Galway. The absence of any major archaeological attractions or other sights, however, helps ensure that the place is rarely overcrowded.*

Ins and outs

Getting there & around The pier where boats arrive is on the north side of the island and the airstrip is a short distance away to the east. The best way to explore this small island is on foot.

Sights

O'Brien's Castle Dominating the harbour side of the island, O'Brien's Castle (Caisleán Uí Bhriain) was built by the O'Briens at the very end of the 14th century in the centre of an ancient stone ringfort, Dún Formna, and on a clear day there are panoramic views from the walls. Close by stand the ruins of a signal tower from the days when the British feared an invasion by Napoleonic forces.

On the beach stands – or rather, sinks – **Teampall Chaoimháin** (Church of St Keevaun), a little 11th-century church with a graveyard that was still being used even when sand had begun to submerge the church. To the west of the pier **Cill Ghobnait** is a small church from around the ninth century dedicated to the female St Gobnait.

Churches

At the West Village, Heritage House, T75021, is a stone-built thatched cottage with a collection of old photographs relating to life on the island, a craft shop and a tearoom. ■ *July and August, daily 1400-1600. 50p*

Heritage House

As on Inishmaan, the best way to visit these sights and at the same time enjoy the strange and desolate beauty of the landscape is to follow the waymarked Inis Óirr Way. The 6½ miles (10.5 km) that make up the Inis Óirr Way is well marked with Way signs but contents itself with tracing a route around the northern part of the island and sticking to surfaced roads, when there you are just itching to break out across the tiny fields and explore parts of the limestone landscape for yourself. With a copy of map No 51 in the Ordnance Survey Discovery series this is very feasible indeed. The Way starts from the pier where you disembark and heads east along the road, with the beach, An Trá, on your left. It then turns inland, passing Teampall Chaoimháin and the airstrip, before heading southwards to circle its way around An Loch Mór (the Big Lake). The wrecked ship that you see was the *Plassy*, driven aground and tossed onto the rocks in 1960. The Way makes its way north up the west side of the lake, with high walls (10 feet/three metres) to either side, to the tiny village of Formna. The Way turns south for a brief while before heading west, with O'Brien's Castle close by to the north. The Way then turns south again, passing the signal tower, and makes its delightful way alongside stone walls that stretch maze-like in every direction.

The Inis Óirr Way

When the Way meets the shore on the western side of the islands it turns northwards and follows the coast. You meet the remains of Cill Ghobnait before the Way moves inland a little, passing one of the island's pubs and returning to the pier.

The road that leads to O'Brien's Castle continues on in the direction of a lighthouse at a southern tip of the island. It makes for an enjoyable walk and along the way there are superb views across to the Cliffs of Moher on the Clare coastline to the east. The road peters out at the shore a little way to the west of the lighthouse but it is easy to make your way across the slabs of limestone to the black-and-white strips of the 19th-century lighthouse. It was built in 1857 and though abandoned after being automated in 1978 the sturdily built and photogenic stone cottages built for the lighthousemen remain alongside the cylindrical tower. Either return via the same road or scramble past the lighthouse a little way to the east and find the road that heads north, parallel to the one you travelled south along. With a good map it is more enjoyable to leave the road, shortly after passing through a gate, and head down to the eastern shore to

A walk to the lighthouse

County Galway

Inisheer

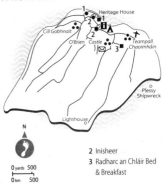

N

0 yards 500
0 km 500

■ **Sleeping**
1 Brú Radharc na Mara Hostel

2 Inisheer
3 Radharc an Chláir Bed & Breakfast

● **Eating & drinking**
1 Fisherman's Cottage
2 Tigh Ned Pub

find a grassy path that heads inland for a little while to a junction where a right turn touches the shoreline again – the *Plessy* shipwreck is clearly visible – before heading northwards past the lake to meet the road near the airstrip.

Essentials

Sleeping A *Inisheer Hotel*, T75020. A 1-star hotel near the pier, but with doubles/singles at IR£46/25 the B&Bs might seem better value. **C** *Radharc An Chláir*, T/F75019. Within walking distance of the pier, near O'Brien's Castle, and opens from February to October. There are rooms with and without their own bathrooms and doubles/singles are from IR£26/IR£15 to IR£32/18. An evening meal is IR£11. These rates are more or less the same for the other B&Bs but not all do an evening meal. **C** *Strand House*, T75002. B&B. **C** *Suzanne O'Donnell*, T75064. B&B. **C** *Mairead O'Reilly*, T75094. B&B. **C** *Maura Sharry*, T/F75024. B&B. **D** *Bru Radharc Na Mara Hostel*, T75024/75087, F75024. IHH hostel, close to the pier, has nearly 40 beds for IR£7 per person and 2 private rooms at IR£18. **D** *Rory's Hostel*, T75077. A small private house behind the post office, has eight beds for IR£6 each.

Camping The Inisheer Camp Site, T75008, functions from May to September and is situated by the beach.

Eating Local seafood, organic vegetables, more than just the token vegetarian dish, outdoor tables and terrific views combine to make the *Fisherman's Cottage Restaurant*, T75073, just west of the pier and open from May to September, the best place for a meal. Expect to pay around IR£6 for lunch and IR£12 for a main course in the evening. The *Rory Conneely* pub is less than a 5-minute walk from the pier and pub food is served daily. Another possibility is the restaurant at the *Inisheer Hotel*, open for lunch and dinner.

Pubs The *Tigh Ned* pub in the hotel, a mere 200 yds/m from the pier, has sessions of traditional music, but the lively *Rory Conneely* pub is also worth a visit.

Directory **Banks and bureaux de change** Bank: *Bank of Ireland* operates on the 4th Tuesday of each month. **Bureau de change**: at the *Inisheer Hotel*. **Tourist office** Tourist information available from a small post near where the boats arrive: Jun-Sep, 1000-1900. Also available from the *Inis Óirr Island Co-operative*, T75008.

Lough Corrib

Lough Corrib is the largest lake in the Republic and stretches for some 30 miles (48 kilometres) from Galway city to the border with Mayo. Inchagoill, the largest of the 300 or so islands studded across its surface, is worth visiting for its unique Latin inscription on an obelisk and the photogenic remains of early Christian places of worship.

Ask an angler about Lough Corrib, however, and Pavlovian glee accompanies thought of the mayfly dapping season in early summer; it brings in anglers from all over Europe and beyond, lured in by the chance of catching sea trout, brown trout and salmon. Thomas Tuck, T552335, at the Clifden end of Main Street in Oughterard (see page 440), sells tackle and licences and some of the hotels are able to advise and facilitate angling guests.

Cruise boats Cruise boats operate between Oughterard and Cong, and a cruise is also available from Galway with Corrib Tours, T592447. Daily sailings from Woodquay in Galway city at 1430 and 1630 in May, June and September, and with an extra sailing at 1230 in July and August.

Connemara

Connemara is the land to the northwest of Galway – a geographical region and a mythologized one – framed by the sea on three sides. It is famous for its desolate landscape of bogs and mountains and extensive veins of green marble, which were traded in Neolithic times certainly as far away as Lough Gur in Limerick and possibly as far as the Boyne Valley as well. In Connemara geology, landscape and shifting weather patterns (one way of saying it rains a lot) translate into a singular natural beauty that sets the imagination going: mist-covered mountains, transitory gradations of light and colour, craggy glens and poetic contours of land and sea.

Ins and outs

Bus There is a daily non-stop service between Galway and Clifden and, between the end of June and the end of August, a daily service that also stops at Oughterard, Cashel, Roundstone and other smaller towns. The early morning bus on this route continues on from Clifden to Letterfrack, Kylemore, Leenane and Westport. Check with the bus station in Galway, T562000, for the schedule. — **Getting there**

Road Travelling by car or bike, there is a choice of routes west from Galway: the N59 road through the middle of Connemara via Oughterard and straight on to Clifden, or the R336 road that follows the coast via Spiddal, Rossaveel (departure point for the Aran Islands) and north to Maam Cross where it meets the N59. A mountain road cuts a scenic route through a hill pass and a beautifully brooding landscape to link Oughterard with Rossaveal.

Organized coach tours from Galway City are available. *Lally Coaches*, T091-562905, has a IR£10 tour that departs from the city at 0945 and takes in most of the main sights before returning at 1645. *O'Neachtain*, T091-553188, run a similar tour that departs from the Galway tourist office at 0945 and the Salthill tourist office at 0955 (see page 429). — **Getting around**

Background

Central Connemara is dominated by the Twelve Bens (see page 444) and the Maumturk mountain ranges, with their peaks composed of quartzite, while the lowland to the west is more schist and gneiss. — **Geology**

The southern part of Connemara, covered by the Spiddal to Clifden section (see page 444), has a different geographic complexion. The land is equally boggy but low-lying and characterized by small lakes of assorted shapes, a heavily indented coastline with tiny islands, and granite rock that imparts a geology different from the central and northern areas. This is also where the traveller is most likely to hear Gaelic being spoken.

At one time Connemara was a byword for cultural backwardness, and even prehistoric communities were thought to have shunned its terrain. In the last 20 years a wealth of Neolithic and Bronze Age sites have been discovered, complementing the rediscovery of Connemara as a place of escape from the metropolitan world. — **Prehistory**

County Galway

Oughterard

Phone code: 091
Colour map 2, grid B3

The village of Oughterard, where the main Galway to Clifden road crosses the little Owenriff river, is renowned as an angling centre but it also serves as a comfortable introduction to the wilder Connemara that lies just west of here. There is a good choice of accommodation and places to eat, a castle and a mine worth visiting and the chance of an excursion to an island on Ireland's second largest lake.

Aughanure Castle

A trip to Aughanure Castle, an exceptionally well-preserved tower house built on an island of rock, is well worth the short detour off the N59 road

This is one of the best examples of how Gaelic chiefs lived in the pre-Plantation era. There is little to see inside but the opportunity to view the elemental architecture of a fortified home justifies a visit. Aughanure Castle is basically a tower house, built in the 16th century as a stronghold for the O'Flaherty clan, and its excellent state of preservation is what singles it out. The approach along a footpath by the River Drimneen and across a natural bridge is picturesque but this sturdy tower house was not built for the fine view. Bartizans are still in place half-way up the walls and on all sides there are superb examples of machicolated galleries (galleries with openings between the corbels for dropping stones on to attackers).

Connemara

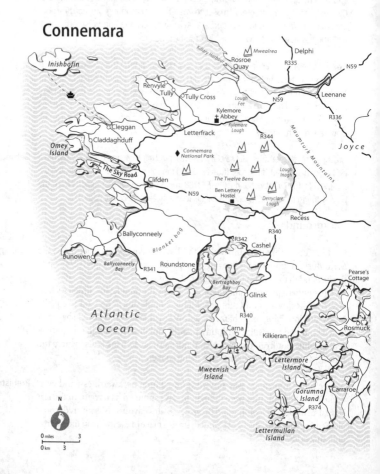

To the south stand the remains of the east wall of a banqueting hall, which is said to have contained a trap door for dropping unwanted guests into the subterranean river that flows under the hall. The elaborately carved decorations on the windows of the remaining wall are worthy of appreciation, although the watch tower in the southeast corner is more eye-catching. ■ *T552214. Mid-June to September, daily 0930-1830. IR£2. Dúchas site. Under 2 miles (3 km) east of Oughterard, off the main N59 road.*

Glengowla Mines

The mines dates back to the 19th century and have now being opened by the family who live on the land above them. A 25-minute guided tour takes you through the mineral-studded chambers with their lead, pyrite and veins of calcite and quartz, and there is a small exhibition area above ground which includes some minerals for sale. ■ *T552360. March to November, daily 0930-1830. IR£3.Outside of Oughterard and signposted off the main N59 road to Maam Cross.*

Inchagoill Island

Inchagoill is the largest of the islands in Lough Corrib (see page 438) and the most intriguing of its ancient remains is the Lia Luguaedon Mac Menueh ('stone of Luguaedon, son of Menueh') burial stone. Less than three feet (75 centimetres) high, it is possibly the oldest Latin inscription of Christian origin in Europe (apart from the catacombs). It stands near the Church of the Saints (Teampall na Naoimh), a worthy example of Irish Romanesque from the ninth or 10th century, while the Church of St Patrick (Teampall Phádraig) is another small oratory of lesser architectural interest on the island. ■ Corrib Cruises, T552644, has a daily sailing between Oughterard and Cong, which stops off at Inchagoill for half an hour. Tickets are IR£10, obtainable from the tourist office, and departures are at 1100, 1445 and 1700 between May and October.

The Owenriff Way

To enjoy a gentle 45-minute riverside stroll walk westwards out of Oughterard as far as the bridge next to the Catholic church. Cross the bridge and turn immediately to the right to walk along the footpath that follows the river downstream. Continue for about 400 yards/metres to a green metal bridge and walk out along the road – the Glan road – taking the first right turn signposted to the Camillaun & Corrib Country B&Bs. After about 200 yards/metres cross the river at the footbridge and after another 100 yards/metres you walk onto Camp Street and take the first turning on the left (the Owenriff

County Galway

Way is signposted on the corner behind greenery) to return to the riverside. Carry on downstream, past the sheds and across a stile. The path leads onto the Pier Road where a right turn returns you to the village.

Essentials

Sleeping **L** *Currarevagh House*, T552312, F552731. Built as a wedding present in 1840, this hotel has a tranquil location on the shore of Lough Corrib and a 2-night stay here should prove terribly relaxing. Old-fashioned in the best sense of the word, and with an air of dignity: Irish hospitality with comforting rituals. No televisions, afternoon tea at 1600, a tiger skin over the stairway and dinner announced promptly at 2000 to the ring of a gong. Doubles/singles are IR£102/66 and evening dinner is IR£20.

Fishing folk are taken in hand and well taken care of at Corrib Wave guesthouse

AL *The Lake Hotel*, T552275, F552794. in the centre of the village, with doubles only for IR£70. **A** *Boat Inn* guesthouse, T552196, F552694. Doubles/singles for IR£50/30, in the very centre of the village. **A** *Corrib Wave*, Portacarron, T552147, F552736. A guesthouse with warm hospitality and a pleasing waterside location that guarantees serenity, plus reliable home-cooked evening meals.

B *Westerway*, Camp St, T552475. B&B within walking distance of the village. **B** *River Run Lodge*, Glan Rd, T552697, F552669, rivrun@indigo.ie Higher-quality B&B within walking distance of town. It has its own restaurant and the rooms are spacious and well-equipped.

D *Canrawer House*, Station Rd, T552388, F552388. While it only has 1 private room, at IR£18, the overall standard is very high in this new purpose-built, spacious IHH hostel with stone tile floors and smart bedrooms. Just before the Catholic church at the Clifden end of town. **D** *Lough Corrib Hostel*, Camp St, T552866, F550279, hickey@bigfoot.com IHH hostel a few hundred yards/metres from the village centre and has private rooms and bikes for hire.

Eating Both the *Boat Inn* and the *Lake Hotel* in the centre of the village do bar food throughout the day and have restaurants for more formal meals. *O Fatharta's*, on Main St, T552692, has a pretty exterior while the quiet, plain inside is still a pleasant place for a casual meal. Irish stew is IR£8 while the price of main courses in the evening is IR£10. The *Corrib Hotel*, on Bridge St, T552329, does a reasonable evening meal for IR£15.

Shopping *Fuschia Craft*, in the centre of the village and open daily until 2200 in the summer, has Galway crystal, porcelain from Donegal, claddagh rings, tweeds, designer knitwear, prints, bodhrans, jewellery … and a bureau de change. At the Clifden end of the village *Galway Woollen Market* has the usual range of garments, souvenirs and gifts.

Sport **Canoe hire** from Lough Corrib hostel. **Fishing** *Keogh's*, The Square, T552583. Tackle and information. *Tuck's*, Main St, T552335. Tackle and information. **Horse-riding** *Oughterard Pony Trekking Centre*, Canrower, T552120.

Transport **Bicycle** *Lough Corrib hostel* (see 'Sleeping' on page 442). Bicycle hire. **Taxi** *Sean Conneely*, Main St, T552299.

Directory **Banks & bureaux de change** Banks: Main St. **Bureau de change**: available at the 2 craft shops. **Communications** Post office: Main St. **Local radio** *Raidió na Gaeltachta*, 556m MW, 0800-1930, in Gaelic but music also broadcast. **Tourist information** Non-Bord Fáilte tourist office, Main St, T552808, in the centre of village, also acts as agents for *Corrib Cruises*, air or boat passage to the Aran Islands and the boat to Inishboffin.

🦶 Walking in the West

Oughterard, the self-proclaimed "gateway to Connemara", is indeed a good place to plan and organize a walking trip in the 'real' Connemara that lies just a short distance to the west. The tourist office (see page 442) has a good selection of maps, guides and general information: for local walks and cycle rides there is a IR£2 booklet that outlines a number of undemanding routes. another useful publication is the IR£1.50 Walking in the West booklet that outlines the main long-distance walks such as the Aran Way and the Western Way and gives details of companies that specialize in organizing walks in Connemara.

Maps The tourist office sells a map and guide to the Western Way by McDermott and **Mapping &**
Chapman for IR£6, but many walkers prefer the similarly priced Mountains of **information**
Connemara booklet by Joss Lynam that comes complete with a 1:50,000 map.

Length and Access The Western Way, which begins outside of Oughterard and amounts to over 135 miles (217 km) on its journey across Connemara and Mayo, is the main long-distance walk, and while the whole Way could take not far short of two weeks to complete most people choose a one-, two- or three-day section. With the help of the Bus Éireann timetable it would be possible, for example, to leave one's transport at Oughterard and walk for three days to Leenane before catching a bus back to base. Public transport will help with a two-day walk to Kylemore or even a one-day walk to Maam Cross.

Oughterard to Clifden

Shortly after leaving Oughterard on the N59 the landscape opens up and the appeal of Connemara begins to make itself felt. Lakes and mountains majestically proclaim themselves, and as the bogland spreads out on either side of the road mounds of turf set out to dry become a common site. The junction at Maam Cross is overshadowed by a huge craft and souvenir shop by the side of the road, and while the adjoining bar and teashop serve a purpose the place as a whole is a bit of an eyesore.

From Oughterard the N59 road carries on due west all the way to Clifden but there are several al0ternative routes you might consider. At the **Maam Cross** junction, the R336 road heads north to Leenane, skipping out west Connemara altogether and accessing Mayo. The R336 road also heads south to Screeb where a turning westwards takes the R340 through south Connemara hugging the coast nearly all the way to Clifden (and briefly rejoining the N59 west of Recess).

Then again, you could to stay on the N59 until shortly after Recess and before heading north on the very scenic R344 road through the Lough Inagh Valley. This could be travelled as a roundabout route to Clifden via Letterfrack.

Recess is just a couple of houses, a bar and a shop on the N59 between Maam **Recess**
Cross and Clifden but the area around here is interesting and a couple of diver- *Phone code: 095*
sions suggest themselves. Ballynahinch Castle is now a hotel (see 'Sleeping' on *Colour map 2, grid B2*
page 444), but it was once the home of Humanity Dick (1754-1834), a member of the Martin family who acquired a fearsome reputation for his defence of animal rights. He is reputed to have fought duels on behalf of animals and imprisoned miscreants on his estate in the old tower by the lake for mistreating animals. Humanity Dick also played a pivotal role in establishing the RSPCA. Expensive to stay here but a passing visit to the public bar at *Ballynahinch*

Castle Hotel is a great way to savour the mood of a fine Victorian mansion that was once reputed to have the longest drive of any country house in the land.

West of Recess the scenery becomes breathtaking as the **Twelve Bens** mountain range comes into view. Legend has it that St Patrick came to the Twelve Bens but turned back on the assumption that no sane Christian would want to live there. Look for the turning for the R344 road north to Letterfrack and consider this route around to Clifden through the **Inagh Valley**. This wide valley has stirring views of the forbidding Twelve Bens to the west/left and the Maumturks to the east/right. After just over a mile (2.2 kilometres) on the road there is the Lough Inagh Lodge (see 'Sleeping' on page 444), and a few hundreds yards/metres past the hotel there is a forestry track that leads to a bridge over the strait dividing Lough Inagh from Lough Derryclare. This is the starting point for a demanding climb to the summits of Derryclare and Bencorr, which should not be undertaken without the OS map No 37 and a specialist walking guide (see page 64).

Sleeping **LL** *Ballynahinch Castle Hotel*, T31006, F31085, bhinch@iol.ie Doubles/singles for IR£160/100. **LL** *Lough Inagh Lodge*, T34706, F34708. Rates similar to *Ballynahinch Castle*. Makes a suitable place to stop for a rest while admiring the natural spectacle all around you. Lots of period details, some 4-poster beds, and a down-to-earth bar where anglers compare catches.

Spiddal to Clifden

The alternative route through Connemara from Galway is by way of the R336 coastal road that follows the northern coastline of Galway Bay through Spiddal to Ballynahown. Then it turns north for Maam Cross but takes the R340 off to the west at Screeb that branches beforehand. The R340 stays close to the coast for most of the way around Kilkieran Bay and then Bertraghboy Bay before finally approaching Clifden from the south.

The Screeb to Clifden route is definitely for travellers who find journeying at least as interesting as the actual destination. Conventional places of interest are few and far between but there are numerous small roads that weave their way into coastal crevices, and interesting opportunities to encounter a delightful spot while in the process of getting lost. Sommerville and Ross travelled through here in the 1890s, equipped with a spirit-lamp, Bovril and a revolver, and noted how "every road we have seen in Connemara makes for water like an otter and finds it with seeming ease, sometimes even succeeding in getting into it." (*Through Connemara in a Governers-cart* (1893)) At Costello, the headquarters of Radio na Gaeltachta, a road heads south to **Carraroe** where there are splendid coral and shell beaches, which are rarely crowded, while at **Carna** there is an easy walk out to Mweenish Island and sandy beaches.

Pearse's Cottage, where Padraig Pearse (1879-1916) spent summers and used the cottage as a summer school for the students of his bilingual St Enda's School in Dublin, may prove disappointing because there is precious little inside. But a path runs past the front door and down to a bench by a lake where one imagines Pearse enjoyed the view. ■ *T091-574292. IR£1. Mid-June to mid-September, daily 0930-1830. Dúchas site.*

Roundstone

Phone code: 095 The village of Roundstone, quaint and quietly popular, is worth considering as a place to stop over for a night or two. One of the attractions is a climb to the summit of **Mount Errisbeg** (298m/977ft), because it only takes a couple of hours and the going is not difficult. Take the path that goes along the side of O'Dowd's pub and turns into a track up the mountain. From the top there are remarkable views of bog land, mountain peaks and coastline: the essence of Connemara.

Workshops

Another attraction is the cluster of art and craft workshops that are open to the purchasing public, including the much-visited *Roundstone Musical Instruments*, Tin whistles, harps and flutes are all here, though pride of place goes to the *bodhrán*, the goatskin hand-held drum without which no group of traditional Irish musicians is complete. There is also a branch, the *Music Shop*, in the centre of Clifden. ■ *T35808, F35980, bodhran@iol.ie http://www. bodhran.com Workshop: daily 0900-1900.*

Beaches

Some of the most wonderful beaches in Ireland are to be found around Roundstone and if the climate were more friendly to the tourist industry it would not be difficult to imagine the odd Club Med-type development mushrooming here. To reach them stay on the road west to Ballyconneely and turn south for **Gurteen Bay** and **Dog's Bay**; the incredible whiteness of the sand is produced by millions of microscopic foraminiferous seashells. It is only another eight miles (12 kilometres) to **Ballyconneely** where there is another splendid beach and the ruins of Bunowen Castle.

Sleeping

AL Eldons, T35933, F35722. Hotel charging IR£80/60 for doubles/singles. **AL** *Roundstone House*, T35864, F35944. IR£80/60 for doubles/singles in this hotel. **B** *Seals Rock*, T35860. A 1-star hotel with rooms at IR£18 per person. **B** *St Joseph's*, T35865, F35930. A friendly B&B charging IR£34/25 for doubles/singles and IR£12 for an evening meal.

Camping The *Gurteen Beach Caravan & Camping Park*, T35882, is just west of town near the beach.

Eating

O'Dowd's, Main St, T35809, has bar food and a seafood restaurant that is very good and open for lunch and dinner. There is also the *Beola Restaurant*, T35871, not far away that serves lunch for around IR£6 and main courses for dinner around IR£12. If shopping at the art and craft workshops, there is a pleasant little teashop.

Clifden

Phone code: 095
Colour map 2, grid B2

Its size and location – the largest town west of Galway, 48 miles (78 kilometres) away – makes Clifden the capital of Connemara. The town, laid out by a 19th-century English landlord, is characterized by its geometry, broad streets and the twin spires of 19th-century churches, with the Twelve Bens providing a dramatic backdrop. Travellers' attitudes to Clifden vary and some feel that its forced birth into tourism – the shops and restaurants have all sprung up comparatively recently – has left it strangely bereft of an identity; others revel in its creature comforts, especially welcome after a day or two spent walking in the surrounding countryside.

Museum

There is little to see in the town itself and the **Station House Museum**, sited in what was the engine shed of the Clifden railway station, is of limited interest. There is an exhibition on the Connemara pony alongside assorted memorabilia. ■ *Free.*

County Galway

♪ Walks and cycle rides around Clifden

Maps Map No 31 in the Ordnance Survey Discovery Series covers these walks and makes the journeying a lot more interesting.

Sky Road The views are magnificent on the Sky Road, heading directly west out of town and around a small peninsula. It is fine for cycling and could be enjoyable as an easy walk depending on the amount of cars – do everyone a favour and avoid driving along this road. The total distance is about eight miles (13 kilometres); take a picnic because there are no pubs or restaurants until the Sky Road meets up with the main N59.

Old Bog Road You can enjoy an undemanding 1½-hour walk along an old bog road if you leave your car at the *Ardagh Hotel* on the Ballyconneely road and walk south for a short distance, until the road crosses Ballinaboy Bridge. Take the left fork there, signposted for Cashel and Recess, and keep the Ballinaboy River on your left after crossing it by another bridge. Turn round after reaching the next small bridge, Beaghcauneen Bridge, and on the way back turn left about 500 yards/metres before Ballinaboy Bridge, signposted for Lough Fadda. Walking south to Lough Fadda, passing the much smaller Lough Enask on the way, adds less than an hour to the walk.

The Alcock & Brown monument & beyond In 1919 the first aeroplane to cross the Atlantic, a Vickers Vimy, landed to the south of Clifden and John Alcock and Arthur Whitten Brown stepped on to land for the first time in over 16 hours. To reach the Alcock and Brown monument, walk or cycle to the Ballinaboy Bridge on the Ballyconneely road, as for the old bog road walk (see page 446), but then bear to the right, staying on the R341 for 500 yards/metres until you reach a crossroads. Take the left turn, signposted for the landing site, and walk south, passing a small lake and heading for the white monument when it comes into view. This stretch of road follows the line of a narrow-gauge railway and it also passes the place where Marconi operated the first transatlantic wireless, now marked by a plaque.

Retrace your steps from the monument or continue westwards on the green road, passing a lake and then a quarry on your left, until you get to a small road. You will then pass the larger Lake Emlanabehy before rejoining the R341; after that you will have to walk back to Clifden along the main road. The entire walk takes about 1½ hours.

Omey Island This walk starts from the village of Claddaghduff, which is eight miles (13 kilometres) northwest of Clifden near Cleggan, and easily reached by car or bicycle by heading out on the N59 to Letterfrack and then taking the signposted road to the left. You get to the island by following the markers across the sand from the beach at Claddaghduff but you should avoid high tide, you can check the times either at the Walking Centre in Clifden (see page 448) or the pub in Claddaghduff.

Essentials

Sleeping There are a number of hotels in Clifden but for what you pay a more satisfying level of personal service can be enjoyed in some of the town's guesthouses. There is also a range of B&Bs –while most are hideous bungalows some at least have locations that provide superb views – and hostels. The average price for doubles/singles in B&Bs is IR£36/20.

AL *Abbeyglen Castle*, Sky Rd, T21201, F21797, info@abbetglen.ie http://www.abbeyglen.ie Built in 1832 and looking just like you might imagine a castle hotel to look, this is a wonderfully laid-back place with an elegant drawing room and views over Clifden and the sea. **L** *Ardagh Hotel & Restaurant*, T21384, F21314, ardaghhotel@tinet.ie Nearly two miles (three kilometres) outside of town on the road to Ballyconneely and a more relaxing hotel than those in the town. Some of the rooms have enchanting views of Ardbear Bay, and the hotel has an excellent restaurant. **AL** *The Quay House*, Beach Rd, T21360, F21608. Prettily located by the harbour, this guesthouse, the oldest building in Clifden, dates back to 1820 when it was a harbourmaster's residence, and breakfast is a leisurely affair in the conservatory. There are also self-catering studio rooms for rent. **AL** *Station House Hotel*, T21699, F21667. In town, on the left when approaching on the Galway road, a modern 4-star hotel with a leisure centre and pool and contemporary-styled bedrooms.

A *Sunnybank House*, T21437, F21976. This guesthouse enjoys fine views from a garden setting and has a heated pool, sauna and tennis court.

B Ardmore House, Sky Rd, T21221, F21100. B&B 3 miles (5 km) out from town, in a location that provides superb views. **B** *Ben View House*, Bridge St, T21256, F21226. A guesthouse in a smart town house with an air of antique grace about the place. **B** *Dun Aengus House*, T/F21069. B&B. **B** *Sky Cottage*, T/F21706. B&B. **B** *Dan O'Hara's Farmhouse*, T/F21246. B&B 5 miles (8 km) from town on the N59 Galway Rd. It is a working farm but the IR£38/25 rooms are smart and well equipped.

D *Ard Ri Bayview Hostel*, T21886. Tucked away on a pier behind King's Garage off Main St, has over 30 beds, which include some private rooms, bicycles can be rented, and has a warm and welcoming atmosphere. **D** *Blue Hostel*, Sea View, T21380. Independent hostel. Opposite *Leo's*. **D** *Brookside Hostel*, Hulk St, T21812. IHH hostel. Includes 2 private rooms for IR£16. **D** *Clifden Town Hostel*, Market St, T21076. Has 2 private rooms for IR£20, rents bikes, and has a hotel-style sitting room area and good facilities. **D** *Leo's Hostel*, Sea View, T21429. IHH hostel. No private rooms. Has superb camping space, rents bikes and is famous for its 'loo with a view'.

There is no shortage of restaurants around the town but the quality varies at the height of the tourist season. Dinner at the *Ardagh Hotel and Restaurant*, Ballyconneely Rd, T21384, is around IR£26 but worth splashing out for the quality cuisine and therapeutic view of Ardbear Bay. Signposted off the same road, the *High Moors Restaurant*, Dooneen, T21342, opens for dinner Wednesday-Sunday and should cost below IR£20.

Eating

In summer, book ahead for one of the window tables at the excellent Ardagh Restaurant away from the bustle of Clifden town

On Main St the *Marconi Restaurant* opens in the evening with a IR£12 menu but a limited choice of dishes. *Destrys*, Main St, T21722, is a chic, little restaurant that stresses its informality and concocts slightly off-beat dishes for around IR£10-15 with delicious home-baked breads. Open for lunch and dinner. *O'Grady's Seafood Restaurant*, Market St, T21450, charges around IR£15 for a main dish but there are surprisingly few seafood choices. A better bet might be *Fogerty's*, T21427, on the other side of the road where lobster is around IR£19 and a set dinner IR£18. *Vaughan's*, at the tourist office end of Market St, has lunch specials and evening dishes like Irish stew for IR£7.

Most of the pubs serve bar food and both *Mitchell's*, Market St, T21867, specializing in seafood, and *EJ Kings*, T21085, have their own restaurants.

The bar at the back of *Foyle's Hotel* on Main St, T21801, has authentic sessions of local music and singing on a Thursday night and a visit is recommended. *Mannian's Pub*, Market St, provides enjoyable evenings of traditional music while *EJ Kings* is more pop and rock.

Pubs & music

County Galway

Festival Towards the end of **September** the *Clifden Community Arts Week*, T21164/21295, planet@iol.ie http://www.connemara.net/artsweek/ takes off with a packed week of musical and theatrical events, lectures, walks, book events, story-telling and more.

The *Connemara Walking Festival*, T21379, F21845, walkwest@indigo.ie http://indigo.ie/~walkwest/ is usually a 4-day event, organized by the Connemara Walking Centre, with walks varying in difficulty. The cost including B&B is around IR£130 and there is usually one towards the end of **May** and another one towards the end of **September** so as to overlap with the Arts Week.

Shopping The site of the old Clifden railway station is now a modern little complex with shops like the House of Mag Aoide that sells prints and pictures of nostalgic bygone times. *Clifden Bookshop* is on Main St and next door is a small jewellery shop and then the *Music Shop*, the place to go for a *bodhrán* and other musical gear if unable to visit Roundstone. On the other side of the bookshop *Wooden Treasures* sells expensive wooden crafts. *Millar's Connemara Tweeds*, T21038, sells products from its own mill using wool from local mountain sheep.

Transport **Bicycle** Bicycles may be hired from some of the hostels and from *Mannions* at Railway View, T21155.

Directory **Banks** There are banks near the Square. **Communications** Post office: Main St. **Tourist office** Market St, T21163. Mid-Apr-Sep. The Clifden Walking Centre (see 'Tours', below) is also a good source of local information. **Tours** *Clifden Walking Centre*, T21379. Walks from the Centre are regularly organized May-Aug, IR£10-25 per person.

Cleggan

Phone code: 095 This small fishing village, 12 miles (16 kilometres) northwest of Clifden, is primarily of interest for visitors heading for the island of Inishbofin. Boats also depart from here for the island of Inishturk in County Mayo (see page 474). The Cleggan Riding Centre, T/F44746, provides riding lessons and treks along the beach, to Omey Island. The Sky Road will take you to the tiny village of Claddaghaduff and when the tide is out it is easy to walk over to Omey Island where there are good beaches.

Sleeping Food is available from *Oliver's Bar* or in the pink-coloured *Pier Bar* at the harbour.
& eating At night there is music in *Joyce's Bar* and B&B is available from *Harbour House*, T44702.

Inishbofin Island

Phone code: 095 *Inishbofin can be as whimsical as its name suggests: a magical silence during the*
Colour map 2, grid B1 *day and gregarious pub life at night. This little island – only four miles (six kilometres) long by less than two miles (three kilometres) wide – is easily reached from Cleggan either as a day's excursion or with the option of staying a night. Inishbofin has not been spoiled by tourism – yet – because the majority of the few hundred inhabitants do not depend on the highly seasonal flow of visitors to sustain their way of life. Come here for fresh-air walks and a sense of calm, although the islanders are not immune to tragedy after a terrible fire in 1999, and enjoy the feeling that not everywhere in the west of Ireland is being packaged and marketed by Bord Fáilte.*

Ins and outs

Getting there

Inishbofin is six miles (10 kilometres) west of Cleggan from where it takes 45 minutes to reach the island. *Kings Ferries*, T44642/21520, F44327, conamara@indigo.ie www.faite.con/cleggan/ have departures from Cleggan more or less on demand in July and August (scheduled for 1000, 1130, 1400, 1745 and 1915) and at 1130 and 1845, April to June and September to October. Departures from Inishbofin at 0900, 1045, 1300, 1700 and 1815 in July and August, and at 0900 and 1700 the other months. Tickets, IR£12 return, from the signposted shop on the main street in Cleggan and there is also a ticket office in Clifden. Bikes are carried free.

Michael Nee Coaches, T51082, runs buses from the Square in Clifden and from Forster St in Galway to Cleggan between June and mid-September for IR£7/5 return/single. The 0915 and 1200 buses from Clifden connect with the ferry and buses from Clifden depart at 1100, 1335 and 1745.

History

St Colman came to Inishbofin from Iona in the seventh century to found a monastery after quarrelling with Rome over a new calendar that changed the date of Easter. Nothing remains of his original settlement, but the ruins of a 13th-century church are supposedly standing on the original site. Grace O'Malley, the pirate queen (see page 472), used Inishbofin, and the ruins of the castle that can be seen when approaching the harbour date from the 16th-century when she was active. Cromwell captured the castle in 1652 and fortified it for the purpose of incarcerating prisoners. A variation on the haunting theme of Cromwell's perfidy, the story goes that he chained a bishop to a large rock in the harbour and left him there until the tide came in and drowned him.

Island walk/cycle

Head west (left) after disembarking at the harbour and follow the road as it turns into a green road and passes, after about 20 minutes of walking, a sparkling little sandy beach. Carry on westwards until the green road fades away and then head for the most westerly point, clearly visible and quite safe to reach on foot or cycling because the ground is flat and there are no cliffs. Sheep, rabbits, seabirds and the occasional seal may be your only company on a quiet day. On reaching the western extremity walk over to the northern side of the island and pick up the path near the metal cross and head back as far as the lake and then south to rejoin the road you started on.

The road going eastwards from the harbour passes the church ruins and accesses a second beach. By following the round around to the north side a third beach is encountered.

There is a small **heritage centre** near *Day's Hotel*, ■ *Summer, daily 1200-1700. IR£2*.

Essentials

Sleeping & eating

A *Day's Hotel*, T45809, F45803. Open from April to September, a convivial place at the east side of the island: walk to the right after disembarking. Rooms with/without bathrooms for IR£25/20 per person (plus 10% service charge). **A** *Doonmore Hotel*, T/F45804. Also a 10-minute eastwards walk from the harbour, has similar rates and seasonal opening as *Day's*, but no service charge. **C** *Hy Brazil*, T45817, F45804. Open from Easter to end of October, has doubles for IR£30-34 and singles for IR£20. Named after an enchanted island (Tír na nÓg) that appears every 7 years and supposedly visible from islands off the west coast, this much more down-to-earth non-smoking B&B is reached by walking west/left from the pier until the sign points inland. **D** *Inishbofin*

County Galway

Flowers of the bogland

It is worth taking a flower guide with you on a walk through the boglands of Connemara, for the reward is being able to identify so many wild flowers. In springtime, look for primrose, silverweed, cowslip, milkwort, celandine and violet. In July, there is an abundance of colourful flowers: wild thyme, lady's bedstraw, harebell, yarrow, kidney vetch, ox-eye daisy, cuckoo flower, foxglove, tufted vetch and fuchsia. In autumn, the landscape seems covered in a floral carpet of heathers and gorse but look out too for devil's bit scabious. In the wetter bogland there is butterwort and sundew, and the range of orchids to be found includes the heath: spotted, early purple, butterfly and pyramidal.

Island Hostel, T45855, F45803. Open from April to October. Has nearly 40 beds, including 4 private rooms at IR£9 per person. Camping is also possible.

Both hotels have small restaurants serving lunch, and evening meals for around IR£16, and *Day's Bar* has good pub food.

Pubs & music *Day's Bar* has music on Wednesday to Sunday nights and the bar in the *Doonmore Hotel* has traditional music on Wednesday and Saturday nights.

Directory **Bicycle** Bikes for hire are usually waiting at the harbour. **Tourist office** Ask at either of the hotels for general tourist information. **Trekking** *Trekking Centre*, T45853. Behind *Day's Hotel*. Treks on horseback for beginners or experienced riders.

From Clifden to Linane

Letterfrack
Phone code: 095
Not so much a town as a roadside collection made up of shops, pubs and assorted houses on the N59 between Clifden and Leenane. It is a possible base for a day or two because Connemara National Park and Kylemore Abbey are close by, Cleggan lies to the west and there is an interesting coastal region to the north.

Connemara National Park
Managed by Dúchas, much of the Park area once formed part of the Kylemore Abbey estate but the expanses of bog, heath and mountains are now open to the public. At the Visitors' Centre there is a 15-minute audio-visual presentation every half-hour and guide books and maps are for sale. The one-mile (1.4-kilometre) **Sruffaunboy Nature Trail** is an undemanding self-guided stroll, and a useful 50p booklet is available that points out ecological features along the way, including Connemara ponies, 'lazy bed' cultivation ridges, bogland flora and fauna and types of Connemara rock. A more vigorous walk may be enjoyed by walking to the summit of **Diamond Hill** (1,460 feet/445 metres), the unmistakable knob of rock overlooking the Centre. For serious walkers, some of the Twelve Bens are situated within the Park. ■ *T41054. Easter to May and September, daily 1000-1730; June, daily 1000-1830; July and August, daily 1930-1830. Closed October to Easter. Guided nature walks (two to three hours) in July and August on Monday, Wednesday and Friday mornings. Evening talks every Wednesday at 2030. IR£2. Outdoor and indoor picnic tables, café.*

Built as a gift for his wife in the 1860s by Mitchell Henry, an English industrial magnate and MP who was charmed by Connemara, the appeal of Kylemore Abbey is inseparable from its location. The buildings are stepped on terraces overlooking the lake and there are two buildings to admire: the neo-Gothic castle built as a family home and a small chapel a short distance away. Benedictine nuns acquired Kylemore in 1920 and is now run as a private boarding schools for girls. This means that many of the rooms are off-limits to visitors and, combined with the fact that a fire destroyed many of the interiors anyway, the result is that there is not much really that much to see inside. The chapel, designed by James Fuller in 1868, is an imitation of an English 14th-century church and the stone vaulting has recently been restored to its former glory.

Kylemore Abbey gardens have recently opened to the public, restoring the late Victorian walled garden that was an integral part of Henry's plan to transform the wilderness of Connemara into a country estate. Alas, it was not to be. His wife's health was seriously impaired by the winter climate, Henry himself became bankrupt trying to maintain Kylemore and he died a few years after being forced to sell the property. ■ *T41146. March to October, daily 0900-1800. IR£3. Self-service restaurant.*

Kylemore Abbey & gardens
Some of the best self-service food in Ireland, including black-eye bean casserole for vegetarians, is available at Kylemore Abbey. Look out too for the wholesome home-made jams.

Sleeping

L *Rosleague Manor*, Letterfrack, T41101, F41168. A Georgian country house overlooking Ballinakill Bay set in 30 acres of landscaped gardens and complete with a billiard table and tennis court. B *Diamond Lodge*, T41380, F41205. Standard B&B. B *Gearbi House*, T41023. B&B at the post office. D *Old Monastery Hostel*, T41132, F41680, oldmon@indigo.ie A solid 19th-century house with some character, this is one of Ireland's best hostels. It has been a favourite with travellers for some years now and with good reason. The room rates, whether sharing (IR£7-9) or in a private room (IR£9 per person), include a tasty, non-fried breakfast and an evening meal is available at a very reasonable rate. **Camping** is also possible and bikes can be hired.

Eating

Rosleague Manor, Letterfrack, T41101, F41168, welcomes non-residents if a booking is made in advance for its IR£30 dinner. The seafood is locally caught and always fresh and Connemara lamb is another speciality that can be relied on, along with fresh vegetables and herbs straight from their garden. The best place for a good and economically priced meal is the self-service restaurant in *Kylemore Abbey*, where meals are under IR£5; the café at the visitor's centre in *Connemara National Park* with its picnic tables (indoors and out) is also worth considering if entering the Park. There is a good food shop in Letterfrack near the main junction.

Shopping

Outside of Letterfrack on the road to Clifden, *Avoca Handweavers*, T41058, is one of the better craft shops in Connemara with a large collection of clothes and crafts plus a bookshop and a café. The *Kylemore Craft Shop*, at Kylemore Abbey, is run by the Benedictine nuns and has a selection of Irish knitwear and accessories as well as pottery, which is thrown and glazed on the premises, china, crystal and jewellery. The shop can be freely visited, as can its above-average self-service restaurant.

Renvyle Peninsula and around

Another literary corner of Ireland (though not one of the better-known ones). Its fame is thanks to Oliver St John Gogarty (1878-1957) having a home here and inviting Yeats, Shaw and others to share his "faery land of Connemara at the extreme end of Europe, [where] the incongruous flowed together at last, and the sweet and bitter blended. Behind me, islands and mountainous

*Phone code: 095
Colour map 2, grid 2B*

County Galway

mainland shore in a final reconciliation, at this, the world's end." The good news is that life is not quite so terminal around Renvyle and there are a number of modest diversions.

At **Lettergesh**, a mile east from Tully Cross, there is a lovely little beach and another one, the spectacular white-sand **Glassillaun Beach**, is just past Lettergesh. From the small golfing green at Renvyle House, you can go for a pleasant walk past the lake and along the pebbly beach to the ruins of an old O'Flaherty Castle.

Ocean's Alive This aquarium and maritime museum, scenically located on Derryinver Bay, is devoted to Connemara's marine life. It offers a useful introduction to the ecological richness of the local area. ■ *T43473. May to September, daily 0930-1900; October to April, daily 1000-1630. IR£3. Signposted on the road from Letterfrack to Tully. Picnic area and café.*

Coastal cruises Under the management of *Ocean's Alive*, four sailings a day cruise around Ballinakill Harbour, Letter, Derryinver and Fahy bays and there is a good chance of seeing a few sociable dolphins and porpoises, perhaps a basking seal or two and certainly seabirds. ■ *T43473. IR£10 (cruise), IR£15 (fishing). Sailings at 1000, 1200, 1600 and 1800. Sunset cruises at 2030 (see 'Pubs & music' on page 452).*

Sleeping **LL** *Renvyle House*, T43511, F43515, renvyle@iol.ie www.renvyle.com/ This is Gogarty's original house, where Yeats sat for his first portrait by Augustus John, which was burned down in the Civil War but rebuilt. Doubles/singles are a hefty IR£200/120 and the hotel organizes a variety of special interest weekends; contact Renvyle House for details. **B** *Fuschia House*, Renvyle, T43502. Near to the castle ruins, and charges IR£34/23.50. Evening meal at IR£12. **C** *Diamond's Bar*, Tully, T43431, F43914. B&B at IR£28-32 for a double. Bicycles may also be hired from here. **C** *The Little Killary Adventure Centre*, T43411, B&B for IR£12-15 per person and dinner is IR£9.50. **C** *The Olde Castle House*, Renvyle, T43461/43460. This B&B justifies its name when their washing line is stretched out between the house and the ruins of Renvyle Castle. Doubles/singles are IR£28-32/IR£19-21. Provides an evening meal for IR£12.

Camping The Connemara Caravan & Camping Park, T43406, open May to September, is at Gowlaun near Lettergesh. The *Renvyle Beach Caravan & Camping Park*, T43462, just west of Tully, is smaller and has fewer facilities but enjoys a glorious view of Mweelrea, the highest peak in Mayo.

Eating Dinner at *Renvyle House*, T43511, is IR£23 but book ahead in summer. For less expensive meals the best bet is Tully, where *Diamond's Bar* has pub food throughout the day, as does the *Renvyle Inn*, T43954, which also has a restaurant with fairly unexciting main courses, average around IR£8.

Pubs & music From June to August, *Ocean's Alive*'s evening cruise at 1800 often includes a session of traditional music and on particularly fine summer evenings there is a Sunset Cruise at 2030. On Sunday afternoons in the café at the *Ocean's Alive* visitor centre there is a session of traditional Irish music from 1515 to 1700. Non-residents are welcome at Renvyle House and the music evenings in the bar often continue late into the night.

Sport **Cycling** Bicycles may be hired at *Diamond's Bar*, T43431, in Tully. **Diving** *Scubadive West*, Renvyle, T43922, F43923, scuba@anu.ie Conduct half-day sessions every day at 1000 and 1400 for IR£30 and this covers tuition and a supervised dive in sheltered water. **Horse-riding** At *Diamond's Bar*, T43431, in Tully enquires may be made regarding horse-riding. **Outdoor pursuits** *Little Killary Adventure Centre*, Salruck, T43411, F43591. Runs a variety of outdoor activities: rock climbing, sailing, canoeing and the like.

Leenane and Killary Harbour

Whether coming from Clifden to the southwest or from Mayo in the north the approach into Leenane along Killary Harbour is unforgettably beautiful. Regarded as Ireland's only fjord, it is sublime or sinister, depending on the play of light. The philosopher Wittgenstein (1889-1951) found it inspiring, living for six months in 1948 near the mouth of the harbour at Rosroe while working on *Philosophical Investigations*. The house where he lived is now the Killary Harbour Hostel, and facing the hostel on the north side of the harbour is Mount Mweelrea (2,687 feet/819 metres).

Phone code: 095
Colour map 2, grid B2

Ins & outs If travelling north into Mayo from Leenane be sure to take the R335 road via Delphi and not the main N59, especially if travelling by bicycle. The R335 route offers up a landscape of such serenity and melancholy that is hard to find anything to compare with it in the whole of Ireland. Praise indeed.

Leenane is picturesquely situated at the head of the harbour and such is the grandeur of the scene that many travellers feel compelled to make a stop. The village makes the most of the fact that scenes from John B Keane's *The Field* were filmed here, and an enjoyable walk leads to the **Asaleagh Waterfall** where the church scene was filmed.

At **Leenane Cultural Centre**, the focus of interest is on the local wool industry and several breeds of sheep are, as it were, open to the public. Visitors can mingle with the flock and its collie dog in order to identify the different breeds. The Wool Museum demonstrates the arts of carding, spinning and weaving and a 13-minute video covers the woollen industry and local places of interest. ■ *T42323. April to October, daily 1000-1900. IR£2. Café on the premises.*

Sleeping **B** *Portfinn Lodge*, Leenane, T42265, F42315. B&B in the village, with rooms with bathrooms for IR£39. **C** *Ben Gorm Farmhouse*, T42205. A few miles outside of Leenane on the road to Louisburgh, with stunningly beautiful views of Killary Harbour from the north side. Doubles/singles are IR£30-35/21.50. **C** *Sancta Maria*, Leenane, T42250. B&B, with rooms sharing a bathroom for IR£30.

Eating *Portfinn Lodge Restaurant*, T42265, hits the jackpot twice with magnificent views over Killary harbour and superb fresh seafood on the menu. Meat dishes, like local lamb, are also available, but the lobster, prawn and turbot are hard to beat. Expect to pay around IR£25 per person. For a causal meal that doesn't involve visiting a pub, the *Leenane Cultural Centre* has a café with a decent range of meals and snacks and wines. In the village itself there is a healthy smattering of cafés and pubs offering food, including the affordable *Field Restaurant* with seafood, stews, chowder and the like and *Gaynor's Bar*, which also milks the *Field* theme.

South Galway

In 'Coole Park, 1929' Yeats imagined a time:

Coole Park
Phone code: 091

> *When all those rooms and passages are gone,*
> *When nettles wave upon a shapeless mound*
> *And saplings root among the broken stone.*

County Galway

County Galway

Clarinbridge and the Oyster Festival

Clarinbridge is passed on the main N18 road, 10 miles (16 kilometres) south of Galway City, and apart from the second weekend in September there is little reason to make a stop other than for a shopping trip to Clarenbridge Antiques, T796522, or Clarenbridge Crystal & Fashion Shop, T796178. When the Oyster Festival arrives, however, the place is bursting with visitors and Paddy Burkes Inn, T796226, in the village and Moran's pub and restaurant, T796113, a little further south near Kilcolgan, are two of the most popular venues associated with the festival. Paddy Burkes is a pub of character and while most famous for its seafood, its bar food menu includes steaks and curries. Check out its visitors' book to get an idea of how the Oyster Festival attracts celebrities from all over the world. For Festival information, T796342, F796016, for ticket enquiries T796766.

The rooms have indeed gone but saplings have a problem because the house where Lady Gregory lived and where Yeats spent summers writing poetry was demolished for no good reason in 1941 and the site cemented over. Frank O'Connor sardonically commented, "sold by Mr de Valera's Government to a Galway builder for £500 and torn down for scrap. Merely as a literary museum its value to the nation was almost incalculable; one feels they should have held out for at least £600." Coole Park is now a nature reserve with an audio-visual show and while the trails, from half an hour to 90 minutes, are self-guided the IR£1 guide booklet is still good value. The booklet also explains the signatures on the **Autograph Tree**, a beech tree on which Lady Gregory invited her literary guests (Shaw, Synge, Yeats, O'Casey and others) to carve their initials. ■ *T631804. Mid-June to September, daily 0930-1630. IR£2. Dúchas site. three miles (five kilometres) north of Gort.*

Thoor Ballylee   Thoor Ballylee, a Norman tower purchased by the poet in 1916 for £35, is the other Yeats attraction in the area. The poet called his tower "a powerful emblem" and some of his best poems were written with the place in mind. An audio-visual presentation tells the story and there is a bookshop of Anglo-Irish literature, a pleasant tearoom, bureau de change and riverside walks. ■ *T563081. May to September, daily 1000-1800. IR£3. Dúchas site. Less than a mile off the N18 Galway to Limerick road.*

Kilmacduagh   In the vicinity of Gort, Kilmacduagh has an almost embarrassing richness of ecclesiastical ruins that owe their existence to a monastery founded here in the seventh century. The best-preserved building is a slightly leaning but very elegant 115-foot (35-metre) round tower, while the roofless cathedral dates mostly from the 15th century though its blocked-up doorway on its west side is possibly 10th century. The ruins of two small churches, St John's and O'Heyne's, lay to the north and O'Heyne's is worth a visit for its decorated chancel pillars and carved windows. The ruins of St Mary's Church are on the east side of the cathedral but are not as interesting.

Eating   In Gort there is the usual run of pubs serving food and *The Blackthorn*, T632127, on the left coming in from Coole Park, is a comfortable bar with tables for eating and a more formal restaurant area upstairs. Lunch is around IR£5, evening dinner IR£13, and there is live music on a Saturday night.

Lady Gregory

Lady Gregory (1852-1932) first met Yeats in 1893 and he first stayed at Coole four years later, at the time they conceived the idea of a national theatre. They remained friends for the rest of her life and shared an interest in Irish folklore. Lady Gregory wrote her own plays as well as editing and publishing various books on Gaelic culture. Her collections of Irish legends and myth were praised by Yeats as "the chief part of Ireland's gift to the imagination of the world." There is an Annual Autumn Gathering at Coole Park with lectures,

plays and local excursions to places associated with Lady Gregory. Contact Shelia O'Donnellan, Kingston Rd, Taylor's Hill, Galway, T091-521836, F091-567421. At Kilartan Cross, 2 miles (3 km) north of Gort on the N128, Kiltartan Gregory Museum contains memorabilia and manuscripts associated with Lady Gregory and the Irish Literary Revival.

■ *T632346. June to September, daily 1000-1830 and October to May on Sunday 1330-1700. IR£1.50.*

"No animals were permitted in Coole ... [but] Yeats was fond of his cat. So Pangur was deposited in the stables until, everyone having gone to bed, Yeats crept out in his slippers and brought him up to the bedroom."

Frank O'Connor, Leinster, Munster and Connaught.

Kinvara

The natural prettiness of this coastal village on the main route between Galway and the Burren invites a stop, not least because of the surprising number of good places to eat. So far, the charm of the place has not been diluted by its popularity and as a village that has the potential to become another Kinsale, it is well worth visiting before it does so.

Phone code: 091
Colour map 2, grid C4

Kinvara hosts two festivals each year, which bring in musicians and other entertainers: the *Fleadh na gCuach* (Cuckoo Festival) in **May** and the *Cruinniú na mBad* (Meeting of the Boats Festival), 7th-9th **August**.

Festivals

This 16th-century castle, perched on a promontory, has been well restored and the contents of each floor are devoted to a different period in its history. It was once owned by Oliver St John Gogarty but the last proprietor has also left her mark and one of the rooms is decorated in the style that the owner employed when living here in the 1960s. ■ *Mid-April to September, daily 0930-1730. IR£2.50.*

Dunguaire Castle

A medieval-style banquet at Dunguaire Castle kicks off nightly with harp music, salted bread and mead, and chicken eaten with a dagger, followed by just under an hour of singing and story-telling from assorted sources in Irish culture. Coach parties can make up the bulk of the audience but it is all good fun and individuals are welcomed. ■ *Freephone 1800 269811, T061-360788. May to September, daily 1730 and 2045. IR£29.*

AL *Merriman Inn*, Main St, T638222, F637686. A comfortable, modern and relaxed hotel with a huge thatched roof and doubles/singles rooms for IR£70/55. **C** *Burren View Farm*, Doorus, T637142, F6381381. B&B with a pleasant location and rooms from IR£30/21.50. **D** *An Óige Doorus House*, T637512. A hostel with literary associations, being the house where Yeats and Lady Gregory first discussed setting up a national theatre. "On the sea-coast at Duras, a few miles from Coole, an old French Count, Florimond de Basterot, lived for certain months in every year. Lady Gregory and I talked over my project of an Irish Theatre, looking out upon the lawn of his house, watching a large flock of ducks." WB Yeats. Some four miles (six kilometres) away to the northwest and signposted off the road to Ballyvaughan. **D** *Johnston's Independent Hostel*, T637164. Next door to the *Merriman Inn*, this hostel has 24 beds but no private rooms.

Sleeping

County Galway

Eating The smart *Quilty Room* restaurant in the *Merriman* hotel has appetizing starters, such as local clams with grilled courgettes, and a decent wine list. The hotel bar serves pub grub from 1200 until 2200. The *Pier Head* bar and restaurant, off the road at the harbourside, has good pub food as well as steaks, and seafood like a crab salad for IR£9.

The brightly painted *Café on the Quay*, T637654, where it is worth getting the single window table overlooking the harbour, opens from 0900 for breakfast and the IR£5 lunches are posted on a blackboard outside. At night, main dishes are around IR£6 and there is a good selection of salads. Or, on a fine day, enjoy a picnic on the grass near the castle.

Pubs & music The *Winkles* pub has nightly traditional music between Thursday and Sunday and *Conoles*, popular with locals, has music on a Sunday night. The bar in the *Merriman* hotel has music on Saturday and Sunday nights, but for somewhere genuinely old and flavoursome you can't beat *Tully's*, T637146, with its stone-floor, attached grocery store and traditional music on assorted days of the week.

East Galway

Ballinasloe

Phone code: 0905
Colour map 2, grid C5

On the main N6 Dublin to Galway road, Ballinasloe and its surrounding places of interest may not be worth a special journey from Galway or Connemara for those that are not historically minded. For those with a fascination for Irish history, however, the area is important as the site of the Battle of Aughrim.

The Battle of Aughrim Interpretative Centre In 1691 Aughrim was the site of the final battle, of momentous significance for European history, between the Protestant William of Orange and the Catholic James II. The Jacobite army was under General St Ruth and his reluctance to work with Sarsfield, his second-in-command, was one factor in their defeat by the numerically inferior Williamite army. The Centre has models and displays, and explains the European dimension to the battle. ■ *T73939. IR£3. Easter to October, 1000-1800. Tearoom. Tourist Information Centre. 4 miles (6 km) southwest of Ballinsloe on the N6.*

Clonfert Cathedral Also in the vicinity, this 12th-century Cathedral, remarkable for its exemplary Irish Romanesque doorway, is baroquely Celtic in its love of ornamentation. Well worth viewing, the cathedral is 10 miles (15 kilometres) southeast of Ballinasloe at Clonfert.

Sleeping **A** *Haydens*, Ballinasloe, T42347, F42895. Hotel with doubles/singles for IR£64/34. **D** *Hynes Hostel*, T73704. Very close to the *Aughrim Interpretative Centre*, and has 2 private rooms for IR£9 per person.

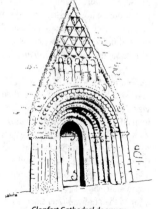

Clonfert Cathedral doorway

Richard Castle

Richard Castle (c.1695-1751), also called Cassells, was of German origin and designed many of Ireland's most famous country houses and other noted buildings. His achievements include Leinster House, Dublin (page 101); Newbridge House, Dublin (page 151); Powerscourt House, Enniskerry, County Wicklow (page 184); Russborough House, Blessington, County Wicklow (page 190); Westport House, Westport, County Mayo (page 467); and 80 St Stephen's Green, Dublin (page 104).

Portumna

The attraction of a visit to this small market town is **Portumna Castle and Gardens**, a semi-fortifed house built in the early 17th century and the best example of Irish Jacobean architecture in the country. Restoration work is ongoing but the ground floor and the highly formal garden is now open and there is an exhibition giving the background story. ■ *T41658. Mid-June to mid-September, daily 0930-1830. IR£1.50.*

Phone code: 0509
Colour map 2, grid C5
There is a seasonal tourist office, T42131, in town.

L-AL *Shannon Oaks Hotel & Country Club*, T41777. This very modern hotel, located by the shore of Lough Derg, with a gym and a comfortable bar serving food as well as a restaurant, makes for a comfortable stopover for accommodation and/or food.

Sleeping

County Roscommon

Strokestown

Of all the big houses of the Anglo-Irish open to the public, Strokestown Park House must rate as one of the most enjoyable and educational to visit anywhere in the country. Its history goes back to the 17th century, when an Englishman named Nicholas Mahon was granted a vast estate of nearly 30,000 acres (12,141 hectares) in the county as a reward for being on the winning side in his country's civil war. The house you see today is largely an early 18th-century creation, designed by the prolific Richard Castle (see box on page 457), while many of the contents are 19th century. The house stayed in the same family until 1981, when it was sold to a local business family, and its interior was never denuded like so many of these houses, so there is a wealth of well-preserved furnishings to admire. The most infamous owner was Denis Mahon who, at the time of the Famine, shipped off his evicted tenants to America in the overcrowded and unsafe ships, which were suitably dubbed 'coffin ships', until he got his come-uppance in 1847 from an assassin's bullet.

Strokestown Park House
Phone code: 078
Colour map 2, grid B5

Tours of the house are well worth it, because there is so much to see, and take in the dining and living rooms, library and schoolroom. The kitchen also is a must-see, opening up some sociology with its out-of-reach gallery designed for the mistress to drop down messages without having to converse with the servants. Along the same lines, and like many Anglo-Irish houses, there was a brick tunnel running between the kitchen and the yard so that the beastly menials were not encountered in person.

The four-acre (9.9-hectare) **walled garden** is another attraction of the place, having been carefully restored to some of its original beauty. The highlight for many visitors is the herbaceous border (listed in the *Guinness Book of Records* as the longest in the Britain and Ireland).

County Roscommon

The Great Famine

After the introduction of the potato to Irish agriculture in the late 16th century it became the staple crop of the mass of Irish peasantry who lived almost entirely off potatoes and buttermilk, a diet just capable of sustaining life. Only the larger farmers or the better off included bread, grain or meat in their diet. Over the centuries there were periodic spells of crop failure caused by the fungal disease phytophthora infestans. Before the 1840s these crop failures had caused deaths and emigration, but on a local scale. Starting in 1845 the crop failure was national and lasted until 1849 in varying degrees. In 1846 only one-quarter of the national yield was produced, and while in 1847 there was no blight, there were few seed potatoes planted. In 1848 the blight came again and the yield was around two-thirds of normal.

To the Irish peasantry this was disaster on a national scale. More people died during this period from disease than starvation. Potatoes had provided iron and vitamins and suddenly the loss of these made thousands of people susceptible to disease. People flocked to the cities and towns in desperation hoping for relief from the Poor Houses, which became impossibly overcrowded. Typhus and cholera spread like wildfire and the young and the old were particularly vulnerable. Recent research suggests that over one million people died, while untold hundreds of thousands escaped to the coffin ships, many of whom, already weakened by starvation and disease, died on the journey. The country's population declined by one-fifth and the trauma of the famine was so haunting and searing that a collective act of denial set in, which is only now in the process of being acknowledged.

A widespread fungal disease that attacks a staple crop is often thought of as a purely natural disaster, so it is difficult for many English people to understand why a term like 'genocide' is sometimes levelled against their country, or why Tony Blair felt he had to apologize on behalf of Britain in 1997. The famine was not genocide in the way that the Holocaust was, and historians disagree about the level of responsibility that can be laid at Britain's door, but there are certain facts about Britain's handling of the disaster which must be recognized. At the time there was general approval of the concept of laissez-faire, which dictated that any tampering with market forces, such as supporting the starving Irish, would destroy the economy and not solve the problem. In the first year of the famine Peel's Tory government imported Indian meal to Ireland to be sold as replacement for the lost crop, but no one could afford to buy it. While this and the following Whig government introduced public work schemes in exchange for food (which generally made the situation worse because the work was so hard and the food so poor), neither interfered with the export of grain from Ireland, which might have been used to feed people. In 1847, two years into the famine, soup kitchens were finally introduced without the imposition of public work in payment. This lasted only six months and then the workhouses were expected to support the starving, which they were hopelessly unable to do.

The same belief in laissez-faire saw the potato failure as an opportunity to reorganize the Irish economy, removing thousands of tiny smallholders and creating larger, more economic farms. Absentee landlords took the opportunity to evict tenants who could not pay their rents, and knock down their houses to prevent reoccupation. Some landlords bankrupted themselves keeping their tenants alive, but others paid their tenants' fares on the emigrant ships to get rid of them: the majority of English landlords saw the opportunity to rid themselves of unwanted people.

Ultimately, responsibility for the deaths of so many people surely rests on the shoulders of the colonial power that created the subsistence economy in the first place.

County Roscommon

A visit to the adjoining **Famine Museum** complements the glimpse into the Anglo-Irish lifestyle afforded by Strokestown Park House. While the lady of the manor was dropping down her menus from the gallery of the kitchen the peasants were dying of starvation in their homes and in the fields. Much of the fascinating material in the museum consists of primary source material from the House but the portrayal of famine extends to the contemporary world and the exhibition as a whole, an exemplary showcase of how history could be presented, puts to shame many of the lacklustre heritage centres around Ireland that claim to offer an insight into past and present times. ■ *Strokestown Park House, Garden, and Famine Museum, Strokestown. T33013. April to October, daily 1100-1730. House, IR£3.25; Garden, IR£3.25; Famine Museum IR£3.25; joint admission for any two, IR£6; joint admission to all three IR£8-50.*

The best place for B&B is **B** *Church View House*, 4 miles (6 km) east of Strokestown, a Georgian house set on a working farm. *Strokestown Park House* has a restaurant, keeping the same hours as the House, and serving light meals like tuna salad for IR£2.50, tandoori chicken for IR£5, home-made jam tarts for 50p and sherry trifle for IR£1.30. **Sleeping & eating**

Strokestown can be reached by bus on the Dublin to Ballina service, which runs 3 times a day (2½ hrs from Strokestown). The Ballina to Athlone bus also stops once a day and there is also a daily service between Sligo and Athlone that makes a stop in Strokestown. The bus stop is outside Corcoran's on Main St. **Transport**

West of Strokestown

About six miles (10 kilometres) northwest of Strokestown, the neat little village of Elphin can claim Oliver Goldsmith and William Wilde, the father of Oscar, as famous products of its school and there is a thatched working windmill nearby on the road to Carrick-on-Shannon; but that's about it. **Elphin**

On the N5 road at Frenchpark is this centre, commemorating the academic who was hugely influential in the cultural revival at the turn of the nineteenth century as well as being a collaborator with Yeats and Lady Gregory on various theatrical productions. The Centre is in an old church, where Hyde is buried. ■ *T0907-70016. May to September, Tuesday-Friday 1400-1700, Saturday and Sunday 1400-1800. Free; donation requested.* **Douglas Hyde Interpretive Centre**

Just west of Castlereagh, reached from Strokestown via Tulsk though the usual route by the N60 Castlebar to Roscommon road, is Clonalis House. The house is the ancestral home of the O'Conor clan, the only chiefdom to be recognized by the Anglo-Normans as Celtic kings, and the present building is an Italianate mansion built in 1878. It was the first of its kind to be built of concrete in Ireland. The archives contain documents, some written on calf skin, that go back over 60 generations, including a copy of the last Brehon Law judgment and a 16th-century prayerbook. Also here is the harp of Turlough O'Carolan (see page 701), Sheraton and Louis Quinze furniture, portraits and assorted jumble. ■ *T0907-20014. June to mid-September, Tuesday-Sunday 1100-1700. IR£3.50.* **Clonalis House**

Roscommon Town

Harrison Hall, in Market Square, is in the centre of town is a good place to start. Here you will find the County Museum, one of those wonderful unreconstructed museums where you while away some time and find something unexpectedly absorbing (our favourite here is the sheela-na-gig). The same **County Museum**
Phone code: 0903
Colour map 2, grid B5

County Roscommon

building houses the tourist office (see 'Directory' on page 460 for details). ■ *Mid-June to mid-August, daily 1000-1730. Free.*

Roscommon Castle The substantial remains of Roscommon Castle, on the road out to Boyle, are worth admiring. Built as a Norman castle in 1269, it passed through many hands and was captured by the O'Conors more than once. The mullioned windows that look so out of place were added in the late 16th century. ■ *Open access. Free.*

Dominican Priory At the other end of town, off Circular Road, are the ruins of a Dominican Priory founded in 1253 and deserving a visit for the effigy of its founder, Felim O'Conor. The effigy stands upon a later 15th-century tomb in the north wall and surrounding the figure are eight mail-clad gallowglasses (see box on page 520) with angels above them. ■ *Open access. Free.*

Sleeping **L-AL** *Abbey Hotel*, Galway Rd, T26240, F26021, cmv@indigo.ie Ask for a room in the old wing to savour the feeling of staying in this 18th-century manor house. **A** *O'Garas Royal Hotel*, Castle St, T26317, F26225. In the centre of town and buzzing with local social life. **A-B** *Gleesons*, Market Square, T26954, F27425. A fine 19th-century manse with excellent guesthouse accommodation. **B** *Cav Ros*, Racecourse Rd, T25881. A B&B within walking distance of town and charges IR£16 per person for a double or single. **B** *Regans*, Market Square, T/F25339. B&B that also has 2 self-catering apartments. **B-C** *Mullach Lodge*, Galway Rd, T/F25364. Has rooms at IR£14-IR£18 per person.

Eating The best place for a meal, light or substantial, indoors or outdoors, is *Glessons*, Market Sq, next to the tourist office. Its coffee shop opens from 0800. *Regans* is next door and offers economically priced meals. *O'Garas Royal Hotel*, Castle St, has reliable hotel fare, including a carvery lunch and a filling set dinner for around IR£16.

Transport **Buses** T071-60066, arrive and depart outside Regans in Market Sq. The Dublin to Westport bus passes through 3 times a day, Monday-Saturday, and once on Sunday. The Belfast to Galway bus stops daily and the Athlone to Sligo bus stops twice daily and once on Sunday. **Train** The Dublin to Westport train service, T26201, stops 3 times a day, T26201, and takes 2 hrs to reach the capital and 1½ hours to reach Westport.

Directory **Banks** Castle St, Church St. **Communications** Post office: Market Square. **Hospital** *Roscommon County Hospital*, T26200. **Taxi** *Kilduff Thos Taxi Service*, 5 Circular Rd, T25299. **Tourist office** Harrison Hall, Market Sq, T26342. May-Sep, daily 1000-1800.

Boyle

Phone code: 079
Colour map 1, grid C1 &
colour map 2, grid A5

A tranquil little country town, quite at peace with its slow pace of life, Boyle is worth a visit for its beautiful ruined abbey, interesting interpretive centre and a giant dolmen just outside the town.

Ins and outs *Bus Éireann*'s Sligo to Dublin service, T071-60066, stops in Boyle 3 times a day and Sligo to Athlone buses also make daily trips through the town. The bus stop is opposite Daly's pub on Bridge St. Trains on the Sligo to Dublin line stop in Boyle, T62027, 3 times a day in each direction. Journey time to Dublin is 3 hours and to Sligo is 40 minutes. The railway station is just south of town.

Woodbrook

One of the best books about the Anglo-Irish is Woodbrook, written by David Thomson (see page 64) who, as an 18-year-old Oxford student in the 1930s, took a summer school post as tutor to Phoebe Kirkwood of Woodbrook House. The lyrical style of the prose lures the reader into thinking it will be just a doomed love story and a nostalgic evocation of the past, but there is a sting in the tail that brings one back to social and political realities. Woodbrook, set in the countryside around Lough Key, has a strong sense of place and the house still stands on the N4 road, a little way past Lough Key Forest Park, on the way to Carrick-on-Shannon.

Boyle Abbey

The abbey was founded in the 12th century by Cistercian monks settling here from the great abbey at Mellifont in County Louth, itself a scion of the abbey at Clairvaux in France. The ruins are well kept and it is possible to get some idea of the details of the monks' lives as you wander round the remains. During the period in which the monastery was built, the then-dominant Romanesque style of architecture was giving way to a Gothic style, and the church has gothic arches on one side and Romanesque arches on the other. If the ruins are closed you can ask at *Abbey House*, the B&B next door to the ruins, for the key. ■*T62604. June to September, daily 0930-1830. IR£1. Guided tours. Dúchas site. In Boyle, off the N4 Dublin to Sligo Road.*

King House

This building, which now houses the tourist office, was lived in by the local landed gentry, the Kings, who built it around 1730 and then moved on 45 years later to the even bigger Rockingham estate, now the Lough Key Forest Park. Serious social climbers, the Kings did everything they could to force their way into the ruling classes, including putting down any local opposition to English rule, for which they were given the land that King's House now stands on. By 1768 the head of the family had obtained an earlship. By the time of the Famine they were absentee landlords, having crawled their way up the social ladder by forcing the Irish off the land and into coffin ships to America. After their complete departure from Boyle in 1775, the house became a garrison for the Connaught (or Connacht) Rangers (see page 420). The interpretive centre is a very hands-on place with lots of activities to try, including a set of building blocks that, when correctly assembled, make a vaulted ceiling of the type that can be admired for real in the house. There are displays on the Rangers, the construction and renovation of the house, the King family and early Connacht as well as some local art. ■ *T63242. May to September, daily 1000-1800; April and October, Saturday and Sunday 1000-1800. IR£3.*

Frybrook House

Back in the middle of town beside the river is Frybrook House, built in 1750 and more modest in conception than King House. It was built by Henry Fry, an English Quaker, brought over by the Kings, the local landlords, who wanted

County Roscommon

to establish a weaving community in the town. It changed hands in 1986 and has been massively renovated although it retains its original Georgian plasterwork and an Adam fireplace. It is furnished with items from the same period and has some good paintings. ■ *T63513. June to September, Tuesday-Sunday 1400-1800. IR£3.*

Lough Key Forest Park Less than two miles (three kilometres) east of Boyle, a part of the Kings' Rockingham Estate is now a picturesque forest park with nature walks, boat hire, a camping park, and the ruins of an old castle on a small island. Rockingham House is gone but the tunnels that the servants used, so as not to disturb the equanimity of their masters, can be seen near the lake. If you hire a boat go to Trinity Island where WB Yeats had plans to set up a mystical-political cult. ■ *T62363. Open all year, 24 hours. IR£2 car parking. Access via the N4, east of Boyle.*

Sleeping

For a special country house near Boyle see page 503.

AL *Royal Hotel*, Bridge St, T62016, F62505. In the centre of town and next to the river, this small, 250-year-old, owner-run hotel has a very popular restaurant. **A** *Forest Park Hotel*, Dublin Rd, T62229. A small, modern family-run place with a good reputation for its food. **B** *Abbey House*, T62385. Next door to the ruins of the abbey, a Victorian house with 6 rooms offering B&B; most rooms have their own bathroom. **B** *Avonlea*, Dublin Rd, T62538. Opposite the *Forest Park Hotel* is this modern house B&B within walking distance of the *Lough Key Forest Park*.

Camping Camping is possible at the *Lough Key Caravan & Camping Park*, T62212. Open May to 29th August.

Eating Near the clocktower is *An Craoibhín*, which does good pub food, while next door is *The Blue Moon*, T64586, serving dishes like Mexican chicken for IR£4.60. The *Royal* is very popular with locals at lunchtime, with meat and gravy dinners, while a few doors further down is *Chung's*, serving Chinese food, 1730-2300. The *Forest Park Hotel* is also popular with locals at lunchtime and does a set dinner at around IR£20. In St Patrick St, *Feighans* does pub food. *King House* also has a very pleasant coffee shop/restaurant.

Pubs & music In St Patrick St, *Kate Lavin's* has traditional music on Wednesdays while the *Abbey Bar* entertains on Thursday and Saturday. Kate Lavin's first opened its door to customers in 1889 and shut them for 20 years before reopening around its centenary. Mercifully, very little has changed and the pub exudes authenticity. Back in the Crescent by the clocktower, *Moylburg Inn* has live music while further out of town, *O'Dowd's Railway Bar* is a lively place for a drink and some good music.

Festivals For a small town Boyle has a surprising number of festivals. In mid-July there is a *country and western carnival* with live music, line dancing, a beanfeast and late bars. The following week there is the *Gala Festival* with talent competitions, buskers, a firework display and lots of other activities. The *Arts Festival* takes place in late July and includes art exhibitions, theatre, poetry readings, and traditional music and jazz. There is also a *walking festival*, T62083/62624, in September and a *pike-angling festival*, T63659, at Easter.

Transport **Bicycle** *Brendan Sheerin*, Main St, T62010. Bike hire. **Taxis** *McKenna's Taxis*, Cootehall St, T63344.

Directory **Banks** Corner of Bridge St and St Patrick St, and Main St. Money can also be exchanged at the tourist office. **Tourist office** King House, T62145. May-mid-Sep, Mon-Fri, 1000-1700.

*The train was over half an hour behind its time
and the traveller complained to the guard of the
train, and the guard spoke to him bitterly. He said,
'You must have a very narrow heart that wouldn't
go down to the town and stand your friends a few
drinks instead of bothering me to get away.'*

Jack B. Yeats (1871-1957):
Sligo

Counties Mayo, Sligo & Leitrim

12

Counties Mayo, Sligo & Leitrim

There may regretfully come a time when Mayo is as successfully marketed as places like Killarney, but until then the county remains a connoisseur's corner of Ireland. The bustling town of Westport plays the tourist tune but retains its dignity, while to the west the easily accessible islands of Achill and Clare offer superb scenery in an unspoilt setting. North and northwest Mayo is a rarely visited, desolate paradise of lonely bogland, calm mountains and haunting beauty, in utter contrast to the village of Cong in the south where the John Wayne connection has been milked for all it is worth. But Cong is easily forgiven in a county that offers more in the way of isolation and remote beauty than anywhere else in Ireland. County Mayo is also one of Europe's top angling destinations with four great lakes – Conn, Cullins, Carra and Mask – all famous for their wild brown trout.

It is hard to travel very far around Sligo and Leitrim without noticing the name Yeats cropping up here and there. But even if you aren't a lover of WB Yeats' poetry or Jack Yeats' art there is much to admire in the countryside of Sligo and Leitrim, from the surreal protrusion of Benbulbin to the long scenic coastline and the quiet tranquillity of Lough Gill. In the south of Leitrim are gentler, rolling hills, and the new tourist route of the Shannon to Erne waterway. There are some fine ancient sites to visit, one of which holds the only known evidence of a settled Paleolithic culture anywhere in Europe, and the more modern settlement of Sligo with its pubs, fast food chains, malls and cybercafés.

★ **Try to find time for**

Achill Island on a fine day

The utterly remote beach at Portacloy

Climbing Croagh Patrick for views of Clew Bay

Walking across Clare Island

Visiting Céide Fields

Visiting the Jack Yeats collection at The Niland
Gallery in Sligo

Having a wander around Sligo Abbey to admire the
Romanesque architecture

Making a day trip to the seaside towns of Strandhill
or Rosses Point

Paying a visit to the faded elegance of Lissadell House,
home of the Gore Booth family

Cruising on a river boat across Lough Gill to Parke's
Castle

Walking up to Carrowmore – one of the most
extensive Stone Age sites in Europe

Enjoying a boat trip out to Inishmurray and its
monastic ruins

Having a butchers in Michael Quirke's in Wine St – a
butcher turned sculptor's

Taking a canal boat journey up the Shannon all the
way to Enniskillen

Reading a bit of Yeats looking out over the Lake Isle of
Innisfree

County Mayo

Westport

Westport may be the tourist capital of Mayo but it remains a town of some elegance. It acts as a magnet for young folk who fill the many pubs from early evening onwards, while also attracting a well-heeled set of travellers drawn by the location, the good hotels and restaurants and the air of Georgian refinement that comes from a town designed by James Wyatt in 1780. Beware the Reek Weekend at the end of July when pilgrims climb Croagh Patrick (see box on page 471) and unbooked accommodation is hard to find.

Phone code: 098
Colour map 2,
grid B2 & B3

Ins and outs

Knock Airport is about 25 miles (40 kilometres) away and has scheduled flights to England and charter flights to parts of Europe. *Iarnrod Éireann* operates several trains daily between Dublin and Westport. *Bus Éireann* connects Westport with most other large towns in Ireland and a number of the smaller towns in Mayo.

Getting there

Westport is a fairly compact town and has no bus service of its own. Places of interest are on the outskirts of town but within walkable distance of the town centre. Bicycles can be hired in town.

Getting around

Sights

Built in 1730 and superbly designed by the master of Irish country-house building, Richard Castle (see page 457), Westport House is still in the hands of the Browne family. Highlights include Chinese hand-painted wallpaper in one

Westport House

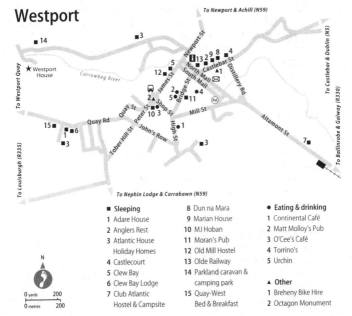

Westport

To Newport & Achill (N59)

To Castlebar & Dublin (N5)

★ Westport House

Carrowbeg River

To Westport Quay

To Ballinrobe & Galway (R330)

To Louisburgh (R335)

Quay Rd

Altamont St

To Nephin Lodge & Carrabawn (N59)

0 yards 200
0 metres 200

County Mayo

■ **Sleeping**
1 Adare House
2 Anglers Rest
3 Atlantic House
  Holiday Homes
4 Castlecourt
5 Clew Bay
6 Clew Bay Lodge
7 Club Atlantic
  Hostel & Campsite

8 Dun na Mara
9 Marian House
10 MJ Hoban
11 Moran's Pub
12 Old Mill Hostel
13 Olde Railway
14 Parkland caravan &
  camping park
15 Quay-West
  Bed & Breakfast

● **Eating & drinking**
1 Continental Café
2 Matt Molloy's Pub
3 O'Cee's Café
4 Torrino's
5 Urchin

▲ **Other**
1 Breheny Bike Hire
2 Octagon Monument

☞ Grand Tour rip-offs

Not a few of the treasures that adorn the interiors of Irish country-houses were 'collected' by their 19th-century big-wig owners while doing the Grand Tour around Europe. Classical antiquities of Greece and Rome were sometimes blatantly robbed by fobbing off the local officials with bribes, and loot ranged from Pompeii tile panels to entire architectural pieces of masonry. The owner of Westport House in the early 19th century, Howe Peter Browne, was particularly struck by a pair of columns from Mycenae dating back to the era of Agamemnon and the Trojan War and fancied they would look good back in Mayo. Until early in the 20th century they adorned an entrance to Westport House, where replicas now stand; the originals are in the British Museum.

of the bedrooms, a painting attributed to Rubens and doors of Caribbean mahogany (from the family's estates in the West Indies), but whether a visit is worth the hefty admission price is very dubious. However, there is a host of other activities designed to attract families, from a model railway and hill slide to a children's zoo, antique shop, craft shop and boating. ■ *T25430. Easter weekend, 1400-1700; May, Saturday and Sunday 1400-1700; June, Monday-Saturday 1330-1730, Sunday 1330-1730; July-20th August, Monday-Friday 1130-1730, Saturday and Sunday 1330-1730; 21st-31st August, Daily 1300-1730; 1st-24th September, Daily 1400-1700. IR£6 (IR£12 including the children's zoo). By bicycle or car take Quay Road out of town towards Louisburg and the entry is on the right.*

Westport Heritage Centre Crammed with local historical documents and artefacts and with none of the gimmicky presentations that pass for substance in heritage centres, this collection is most interesting when showing the role of Westport in the land and nationalist struggles of the 19th and early 20th centuries. **John MacBride** (1865-1916), a revolutionary who was executed for his part in the 1916 rebellion and who was married to **Maud Gonne** (see box on page 469), came from Westport (a bust of him is opposite St Mary's church on the South Mall), and the museum has the gift of a spinning wheel that Mayo people gave Maud Gonne in recognition of her leadership. ■ *T26852. May to October, Monday-Friday 1000-1700, Sunday 1430-1700. IR£2. The Centre is on Westport Quay, reached by turning right off Quay Road after passing the turn-off for Westport House.*

Essentials

Sleeping
■ *on maps*
Price codes:
see inside front cover

L *Castlecourt Hotel*, Castlebar St, T25444, F28622. Comfortable rooms and modern facilities in this centrally located hotel. **AL** *Clew Bay Hotel*, James St, T28088, F25783, clewbay@anu.ie www.clewbay.anu.ie A compact hotel with a lively bar and restaurant. **AL** *The Olde Railway Hotel*, The Mall, T25166, F25090, railway@anu.ie Thackeray stayed at this hotel, built in 1780 as a coaching inn for guests of Lord Sligo. Recommended. **B** *Adare House* Quay Rd, T26102. B&B. **B** *Angler's Rest*, Castlebar St, T25461. The least expensive guesthouse listed here, with doubles/singles for IR£34/18. **B** *Clew Bay*

County Mayo

Westport Quay

Heritage Centre

Sheebeen pub

Ardmore House

Towers Seafood Restaurant

Asgard Tavern & Restaurant

Harbour Mill self-catering

Carrowbeg River

Quay Cottage

To Westport House

Quay Road

Granary Hostel

N   Not to scale

Maud Gonne

Maud Gonne was born in Surrey in 1866 into an army family which moved to Ireland the following year. She never went to school, so avoiding its gender indoctrination, and gave up an upper-class life of hunt balls and dinner parties for revolutionary politics. She went to Paris to campaign for Irish nationalism, where she had two children by a lover, returning to Ireland where she married John McBride, a disastrous marriage in view of his alcoholism, but divorced him after the birth of their son.

William Butler Yeats and Gonne formed a deep friendship, but the poet was driven mad with unreciprocated love, though whether they ever had sex (and even then only once) remains uncertain. Some of Yeats' greatest poetry had its inspiration in their relationship, and when he complained she comforted him with the fact that 'you are making beautiful poetry out of what you call your unhappiness and you are happy in that.' Their friendship haunted Yeats throughout his life, and twenty years after meeting her he could still feel blessed for having known her, even though 'While up from my heart's root/So great a sweetness flows/I shake from head to foot.'

Lodge, Quay Rd, T28699. B&B. **B** *Dun Na Mara*, Castlebar St, T25205. This B&B has rooms with and without their own bathrooms at IR£30-36 for doubles and IR£22-25 for singles. **B** *Marian House*, Castlebar St, T25636. One of half a dozen B&Bs in this road. **B** *Nephin Lodge*, Leenane Rd, Carrabawn, T27146. B&B. **B** *Quay-West*, Quay Rd, T27863. **D** *Club Atlantic*, Altamount St, T26644, F26241. Near the railway station, an IHH hostel with a variety of rooms including private ones and the best place in town for budget accommodation. Breakfast, packed lunches available. **D** *Country School Hostel*, Kilmeena, T41099, F28800. A couple of miles (5 km) northwest of town, this IHH hostel has 2 private rooms for IR£16 and bike hire. **D** *The Granary Hostel*, The Quay, T/F25903. An IHO hostel with no private rooms but with meals available. **D** *Old Mill Holiday Hostel*, Barrack Yard, off James St, T27045, F28640, oldmill@iol.ie Open all year and with one private room for IR£14. Bicycle hire is also available at this well-run hostel.

Camping The best facilities are available at the *Club Atlantic Hostel*, Altamount Rd, T27045. The *Parkland Caravan & Camping Park* is in the grounds of Westport House, T27766. But this place is relatively expensive and makes the *Old Head Forest Caravan & Camping Park*, Louisburgh, T66021, worth considering.

Self-Catering Westport is a convenient base for exploring the whole of Mayo, so a longer stay might be appropriate. *The Harbour Mill*, T28555, F28636,

County Mayo

info@activeireland.ie This has apartments, sleeping 3, from IR£290 per week in July and August. Other places include *Atlantic Coast Holiday Homes*, T27711, F26121, Each@iol.ie There are detached houses here for IR£475 a week and apartments for 4/6 people for IR£350.

Eating

● *on maps*
Price codes:
see inside front cover

Quay Road Out near the entrance to Westport House there are a number of quality pubs and restaurants specializing in local seafood. *Quay Cottage Restaurant*, Quay Rd, T26412. Opens only for dinner at 1800. *The Asgard Tavern & Restaurant*, Quay Rd, T25319. Serves barfood 1200-1500 and 1800-2100 for around IR£5, while the restaurant opens at 1830 for oysters, lobster and the like. On the other side of the road is *The Towers Seafood Restaurant*, Quay Rd, T26534. Opens only for dinner at 1730. The *Ardmore House Restaurant*, on Ardmore Rd, which meets Quay Rd a little further down, T25994. Opens in the summer months at 1800. Reservations are usually necessary for all these restaurants, and expect to pay over IR£20 for a meal. The *Sheebeen Pub*, also on Quay Rd and past the Ardmore Rd turning, serves a more informal and less expensive lunch or dinner.

In town *The Olde Railway Hotel Restaurant*, The Mall, T25166. Back in the town centre, this restaurant serves a good dinner for IR£20, and the Victorian-style bar area is also worth considering for a more informal meal in comfortable surroundings. *The Urchin*, Bridge St, T27532. Opens from 1000 to 2200 and has an interesting menu with main dishes around IR£10. *Torrino's*, Market Lane off Bridge St, T28338. Has been recommended for its Italian-style offerings of pizza and pasta dishes around IR£8. *O'Cees*, Shop St. Worth considering for a quick meal while waiting for a bus at the Octagon. Near to the High St is the *Continental Café*, which serves wholefood and vegetarian dishes, and is probably a better bet.

Pubs & music The town's most famous pub is *Matt Molloy's* in Bridge St, owned by the Chieftains' musician who hails from Westport. It is also one of the most frequented, however, and finding the elbow space to lift a pint can be difficult. Across the road, *Moran's* has a small grocery store at the front and a tiny bar to the rear, and is patronized by locals seeking to escape the better-known pubs. At the Octagon, *M.J. Hoban* is a popular bar with regular musical entertainment, and the bars out along Quay St have musical entertainment, especially at weekends. Other pubs that have been recommended include *P McCarthy's* on Quay St and *Tommie Nolan's* on Mill St.

Festivals *The Westport Arts Festival*, T26787/28575. Theatrical and musical events dominate this festival, which takes place in the second half of **September**. Tickets from the Festival Caravan parked on Shop St. *The Westport International Sea Angling Festival* takes place around the end of **June** and includes a 3-day boat competition. For further information, T27297/27344.

Shopping Along Quay St near the harbour, the dilapidated warehouses are being restored and developed into a tourist-orientated complex. *The Waterfront Gallery* offers the usual ceramics, glass and jewellery, and *Westport Crystal Glass*, a short way before the Asgard restaurant, has a range of stemware and gifts. *Carraig Donn*, Bridge St, opposite Matt Molloy's pub, has wide range of crafts and their own knitwear.

Sport **Horse-riding** *Drummindoo Stud*, T25616.

Transport **Air** Knock International Airport T094-67222. Has connections with Birmingham, Jersey, London's Stansted and Manchester. In the summer there are chartered flights from Dusseldorf, Frankfurt and Munich with *Lufthansa*, and from Zurich with *Crossair*. **Bicycles** Bike hire: *Breheny's*, Castlebar St, T25020. *Sean Sammon*, James

The Pagan Way

The aninual Reek Sunday, the last Sunday in July, sees more than 30,000 devout Catholics setting off to climb Croagh Patrick, many of them unaware they are following in the footsteps of pagan pilgrims. As far back as 3000BCE, people climbed to the summit to mark Lughnasa (the festival of Lug, a god whose name occurs throughout the Celtic world), a pagan celebration of autumn; St Patrick's association with the mountain probably reflects his victory over paganism. The night before they ascend Croagh Patrick, the most devout of modern pilgrims begin their journey by walking 22 miles (35 kilometres) from Ballintubber Abbey along an ancient pilgrim trail, then they attend one of the 15 masses celebrated on the mountain's summit from 0800. Archaeological research shows that a massive rampart enclosed the summit long before the foundations of an oratory were laid some time between 430 and 890CE. Glass beads excavated near part of the rampart date to the thrd century BCE.

St, T25471. **Bus** *Bus Éireann* buses depart from the Octagon. Scheduled daily services run to Achill, Ballina, Belfast, Cork, Galway, Limerick and Sligo. *Walsh Coaches*, T35165, run a weekend service to Galway. **Taxis** *Dever*, T27220/087-413722. *Hoban*, T25247/087-423107. *Road Runner*, T27050/087-428338. *Valley Cabs*, T26015/098-428338. **Train** The train station is on Altamount Rd, T25253, and within walking distance of town.

Banks Branches of the main banks may be found in Shop St and on the North Mall. **Communications** Post office: North Mall. **Tour companies** *Adventure Centre*, T64806. Covers canoeing, windsurfing, sailing, rock climbing, abseiling and hill walking. *Geotreks*, T/F28702, geotracks@anu.ie www.anu.ie/geotreks/ Conducts tours into gold-panning areas of south Mayo. *Gerry Greensmyth*, T26090. Offers guided walking tours, including Croagh Patrick. *Island Otterwatch*, T41048. Walking trips to spot otters. **Taxis** *Christy Cawley*, T28282; *Conor Dever*, T27220; *Brenda McGing*, T26319. **Tourist Office** The Mall, T25711. Apr-Sep, Mon-Sat 0900-1800; Jul-Aug, daily 0900-1800. **Directory**

Around Westport

The pyramidal Croagh Patrick (2,500 feet/762 metres), home to St Patrick in 441CE for a period of 40 days and the site for his miraculous banishment of snakes (there are no snakes in Ireland), is Ireland's most popular mountain. It is not particularly difficult to climb and there is a well-trod path to the top but the scree-laden slope that leads to the summit is steep and when there is a wind about some climbers are reduced to crawling up on their hands in order to avoid the risk of a tumble. Forget the tradition of climbing Croagh Patrick on bare feet, use suitable footwear and consider bringing a staff-like stick for the final ascent. Allow two hours to reach the top and one for the descent. **Croagh Patrick** *Phone code: 098*

The trail begins at the side of Campbell's pub in Murrisk to the west of Westport on the road to Louisburgh. There is a car-park alongside the **National Famine Monument**, a sculptured coffin-ship with skeleton bodies by John Behan, that was unveiled in 1997 on the 150th anniversary of the Famine.

Possibly the most laid-back town in Ireland owes its name to Louisburgh in Nova Scotia, Canada, where an uncle of the first Marquess of Sligo was part of a besieging force in 1758. Despite its proximity to Westport, Louisburgh is contentedly indifferent to tourism although there is the interesting **Granuaile** **Louisburgh**

County Mayo

Granuaile – pirate queen and feminist icon

Grace O'Malley (c.1530-c.1603), 'Granuaile' being a corruption of her Gaelic name Gráinne Ni Mháille, was the daughter of a Connacht chief who achieved fame in her own lifetime as a fiercely independent woman. In 1577 her piratical activities led the Lord Deputy of Ireland to mark her down as 'a notorious woman in all the coasts of Ireland'. She married twice, first Donal O'Flaherty and then Richard 'Iron Dick' Burke, with whom she had an agreement that either party could dissolve the relationship after one year (which she duly did, see page 475).

She maintained her own maritime power base from Clare Island and cunningly appeased the English without sacrificing her own independence. At one stage she was attacked by the English but never decisively beaten and in 1593 she came to London with other Connacht chiefs to complain about the heavy-handedness of English rule. Insisting upon regal status as an Irish queen, she petitioned Queen Elizabeth (in Latin, as she had little English and Elizabeth no Irish) for her own lands, because under Gaelic law a widow had no right to her husband's property.

Visitor Centre, dedicated to the 'pirate queen' Grace O'Malley (see box on page 472) and the Famine. ■ *Church Street, T66341. IR£2.50. June to mid-September, Monday to Saturday 1000-1800. Coming from Westport, turn right at the main junction in town and the Centre is a short way down on the left.*

There are two local beaches, Silver Strand and Old Head, which are gloriously sandy, safe for swimming and suitable for surfing. Bicycles may be hired from Stauntons, the chemist shop on the corner of the crossroads in the centre of town.

Sleeping Accommodation can be arranged through the Westport tourist office. **D** *Durkan's Hotel*, T66140, charges a flat IR£20 per person in rooms with shared bathrooms, and virtually every B&B in town charges the same rate of IR£34 for a double and IR£23.50 for a single. Possibilities include *Springfield House*, Westport House, T66289, and *Ponderosa*, Tooreen Rd, T66440.

Self-catering houses in the area are available through *Old Head Holiday Villages*, Esplanade Properties, 36 Lower Clanbrassil St, Dublin 8, T01-4731315, F4731321. The *Old Head Forest Caravan & Camping Park*, T66021, opens from 22nd May to 13th September, and is near the beach to the east of Louisburgh.

Eating Food is available at the *River Café* or the *Derrylahan* pub, both at the west end of town, and *Durkan's* hotel serves both bar food (the mussels and brown bread are delicious) and meals.

Doo Lough Valley The recommended route for travel between Connemara and Mayo is via the Doo Lough valley on the R335 road, because this part of Mayo is stunningly beautiful and rarely explored. The road skirts the shore of Doo Lough itself, which is sandwiched between the Mweelrea Mountains that overlook Killary harbour to the south, and the wild Sheeffry Hills to the east. The long-distance walk, the Western Way, works its way up from Leenaun in Galway to the south side of Croagh Patrick before turning eastwards towards Westport.

Along the R335 by Doo Lough there is a monument by the side of the road to the hundreds of victims who, during the Famine, set out from Louisburgh in winter to walk through the valley to their landlord to beg for assistance. It was a wasted journey and on the return leg of the journey some 400 died from hypothermia and lack of food. Each May a Famine Walk commemorates the event (T01-4785100).

Sleeping
& eating

The best base for accommodation in the area is at **Killadoon**, a village on the coast with a small beach, about halfway between Louisburgh and Killary harbour. The **B** *Killadoon Beach Hotel*, T/F68605, is a modest little hotel with doubles at IR£36-44 and a restaurant that serves an evening meal for IR£18.

Clare Island

Situated at the mouth of Clew Bay, Clare Island has a population nowadays of about 150, but in pre-Famine days it was over 1,500. The remains of a 15th-century castle, from where Grace O'Malley set off on her piratical excursions (see box on page 472), are close to the harbour and further to the west is a 13th-century Cistercian abbey where legend has it she is buried. On a fine day, a visit to Clare Island is highly recommended because the place is blessed with an absence of heritage centres, there are superb walks to be enjoyed in all directions, bicycles may be hired from the harbour, T26250, and the beach is safe for swimming.

Ins & outs

Clare Island Ferries handle the 96-seater *Pirate Queen* ferry service, T28288/087-414653, and the *Ocean Star Ferry*, T25045/087-2321785, runs services from Roonagh Quay, 5 miles (8 km) west of Louisburgh; IR£10 return. Check their schedule, but the first boat from Roonagh usually departs at 1015 and the last one back from the island is at 1900.

Walking

The highest point, **Mount Knockmore**, is a manageable 1512 feet (461 metres), and for a longer day's exploration of the island map No 30 in the Ordnance Survey Discovery series would be useful but not essential. If you are staying overnight, a whole day's walk could begin by walking from your accommodation to the lighthouse at the most northerly point of the island and then setting off across hillocks along the north side *en route* to Knockmore. Several small hills are crossed and, although there are high cliffs with sheer drops, by keeping on the safe side of the sheep fencing there is no danger. There is a trigonometry point at the summit and from here it is simply a matter of heading down to the signal tower near the sea at the western end of the island, zig-zagging at times to avoid an inlet. From the tower at the western end a path leads across to the road on the south side of the island, which returns to the harbour. To complete this circuit of Clare Island takes about six hours.

On a day trip there would be plenty of time for a walk out to the west end of the island by following the road along the southern side of the island from the pier. This road (which one comes back along if completing a circuit of the island) passes the abbey where Grace O'Malley is buried, and the O'Malley plaque is clearly visible on the left side after entering the church.

The *Bay View* hotel has a simple but useful little walking guide with sketches that outlines five walks on the island, lasting from one to over five hours.

*Clare Island
Lighthouse*

County Mayo

Sleeping & eating

It is best to bring a picnic but food is available at the Bay View Hotel.

AL *Clare Island Lighthouse*, T/F45120, clareislandlighthouse@tinet.ie http:// homepage.tinet.ie/~clareislandlighthous At the eastern end of the island, this was originally two lighthouses built between 1804 and 1812, which operated until 1965. It has been restored and renovated and offers the unique opportunity of spending a night or two in one of its five rooms. Open all year, doubles/singles are IR£80/50 and an evening meal is IR£17.50. **A** *Bay View Hotel* T/F26307. The only hotel on the island, charges IR£40-60 for a double and IR£23 a single. It also operates a simple hostel with beds for IR£7. **B** *Sea Breeze*, T26746; F25649. This B&B is only 300yds/m from the harbour and is signposted. Doubles are IR£30-34 and singles IR£17-18. **B** *O'Malley B&B*, T26216. A couple of miles (5 km) from the harbour.

Inishturk Island

Ins & outs The Caher Star ferry, T45541, departs from Roonagh at weekends and daily from Cleggan in County Galway, but telephone to confirm their schedule.

Inishturk is smaller than Clare Island and lies to the south, seven miles (11 kilometres) off the coast. It is one of Ireland's least visited destinations, which is a little surprising because it makes a delightful getaway, offering modest accommodation, a pub, two sandy beaches, and undemanding walks with terrific seascapes. To the east of Inishturk the tiny **Caher Island** has some strange pre-Christian stones and while there is no scheduled boat service it might be possible to arrange something from Inishturk.

Sleeping & eating

B *Tranaun House* T45641, F45655. Has double rooms with shared facilities for IR£30, singles IR£17, and also has hostel beds for IR£12. **B** *Ocean View House*, T45520, F45655. Has rooms with bathrooms for IR£32/17. Both these B&Bs provide an evening meal for IR£10.

Newport and around

Colour map 2, grid B2

Near the northeast corner of Clew Bay, and eight miles (12 kilometres) north of Westport, the small town of Newport is often just hurried through on the way to Achill Island. There is a **tourist information office** at the western end of Main Street, and they sell 10p sheets detailing walks around Rockfleet Castle and Lough Furnace, which are useful if used with the OS Discovery Series map. ■ *Main Street, T41895. May to August.*

Town walk This walk begins by turning left after leaving the tourist office and heading up to the corner to view the colourful **mural** depicting the trial and public execution of a rebel priest, Father Manus Sweeney, for his part in the 1798 rebellion. Facing the mural, turn left and walk up the hill to **St Patrick's church** where the stained glass east window of the Last Judgement was designed by Harry Clarke and painted under his supervision in 1900, the year he died. From the church, go down the steps and turn right for access to the **Old Viaduct**. Walk across the red sandstone viaduct, built as a railway bridge in 1892 and functioning up until 1937, and down the embankment on the other side. Cross back over the River Black Oak by the road bridge and up Main Street to the tourist office.

Burrishoole Abbey The ruins still standing of this late 15th-century Dominican abbey include the central tower, the vault supported by Romanesque arches and some of the windows. It is hardly worth a special trip, but if travelling on the N59 Newport to Achill road it is signposted on the left less than two miles (1.5 kilometres) outside of Newport.

The Western Way long-distance walk starts in County Galway (see page 440) **The Western** and crosses into Mayo just north of Leenane. Skirting the shoulder of Croagh **Way** Patrick, it continues north through Westport and Newport and up to the north coast before swinging eastwards to reach Ballina via Ballycastle and Killala. The ideal way to experience North Mayo would be to take four days and walk the Western Way from Newport to Ballina. A problem with the first day's 21-mile (33-kilometre) walk, from Newport to Bellacorick, is a lack of accommodation in the village of Bellacorick. Unless a pick-up could be arranged there, the only alternatives are either an extra five-mile (eight-kilometre) walk to Bangor, or catching the Bus Éireann 446 service from Ballina to Bangor that passes through Bellacorick at 1855. The day's journey could be reduced by starting from the *An Óige Traenlaur Lodge hostel*, T098-41358, which is five miles (eight kilometres) north of Newport. The second day's walk, from Bellacorick to Ballycastle, is another 21 miles (33 kilometres) but the next day's journey, from Ballycastle to Killala, is a more manageable 14 miles (23 kilometres). The last day's walk is a mere nine miles (15 kilometres) to Ballina, and while it is interesting, the surface is tarmac nearly all the way.

Also known as Carrigahowley Castle, Rockfleet has an undisputed association **Rockfleet** with Grace O'Malley because it was a Burke stronghold before her second **Castle** marriage to Richard Burke. The story goes that she dissolved this marriage (see box on page 472) by having the castle gates shut in his face and in 1553, after he died, this became her main residence. Situated in a sheltered inlet of Clew Bay that gave safe anchorage to ships, the castle was an ideal base for a sea-faring character such as O'Malley, and she beat off an English attack here in 1574. The Newport tourist office has a sheet describing a two-hour walk of 31 miles (six kilometres) from the castle.

The castle is signposted on the N59, after passing the turn-off for Burrishoole Abbey.

L *Newport House*, T41222; F41613. The most expensive place to stay, and patronized **Sleeping &** by well-heeled anglers, this charges IR£146 for a double, but there are affordable **eating** alternatives. **B** *Black Oak Inn*, T41249, F41984. On the Westport side of the river. **B** *Debille House*, in the centre of Main St, T41145, F41777. Has four rooms.

Meals are available at both the Black Oak Inn and *Debille House* while dinner at *Newport House* is a cool IR£30. See page 489 for an An Óige hostel north of Newport.

Mullaranny and the Curraun Peninsula

This village is on the N59 road west of Newport, where the R319 heads west to Achill and the main road continues north to Bangor. There is a garage, and a good-sized supermarket if stocking up on provisions for Achill. *Cowley's Restaurant*, T36287, a thatched cottage next to the supermarket, serves lobster for IR£15 and other seafood meals.

From Mullaranny the R319 follows the route of a disused railway line to Achill Sound, where a bridge connects the Curraun Peninsula with Achill Island. A more leisurely route, signposted the **Atlantic Drive**, goes around the southern end of the peninsula and on fine days offers tremendous views. Food is available *en route* at the *George Pub*, where B&B is also available, T45228.

County Mayo

Achill Island

Phone code: 098
Colour map 2,
grid A1, A2 & B2

Ireland's largest island has a population of 3,000 people, and its five Blue Flag beaches give some indication of just how singularly unspoilt it remains. 'The naturalist, the antiquary, the artist, the poet, will find much in Achill that harmonizes with their tastes'; as true today as when a visitor made this remark in 1884. When first-time visitors to Achill hit a spell of bad weather they leave wondering what was so special about the place, but when there is blue in the sky and the light weaves its magic on the landscape a stay on Achill is a memorable experience. The German writer, Heinrich Böll (1917-85), certainly found it so while living at Doogort in the 1950s. His house is now used as a retreat for writers, as specified in his will, and his Irish Journal *(1957) would make suitable reading for visitors while on Achill.*

Ins and outs

Getting there Achill is separated from the mainland by a channel of sea, Achill Sound, but the Michael Davitt Bridge spans the water at a narrow point, so there is no need for a ferry service. The nearest large town on the mainland is Westport, and from here and Ballina buses run to the island.

Getting around A bicycle is the ideal way to get around the island, and if based near Dooagh or Doogort many places can be reached on foot. The main road crosses the island from Achill Sound to Keem Bay. Also starting at Achill Sound a loop road runs south through Dooega, and at Bunacurry a northern loop accesses Doogort and Slievemore and returns to the main road at Keel.

Achill Island

■ **Sleeping**
1 Achill Head
2 Alice's Harbour Inn & Tourist Office
3 Atlantic
4 Grogin Mór Bed & Breakfast
5 Keel Sandybanks Caravan & Camping Park
6 McDowell's
7 Ostán Ghoib a' Choire
8 Railway Hostel
9 Seal Caves Caravan & Camping Park
10 Slievemore
11 Strand
12 Valley House
13 Wave Crest
14 Wayfarer Hostel
15 Wild Haven Hostel

● **Eating & drinking**
1 Atoka
2 Boley House
3 Calbey's
4 Chalet
5 Village Inn

▲ **Other**
1 Esso Garage (tourist information)
2 O'Malley's Supermarket

The Colony

In 1831 Edward Nangle, a young Church of Ireland minister, came to Achill and established the Achill Mission soon after. Learning and using the Irish language, they leased 130 acres of land and established a school and a church on the southeast slopes of Slievemore. The Colony, as the Achill Mission became known, proved highly successful, and a printing press turned out regular publications, to the chagrin of the local Catholic authorities whose previous indifference to the islanders now proved an embarrassment. In the 1840s the Mission had its own hotel and various enterprises, which were able to survive the years of the Famine. By the 1850s, by which time the Mission owned about two-thirds of the island, the Catholic hierarchy fought back by strengthening its presence on Achill and taking an interest in the welfare of its parishioners. A National School was established in 1852 and its success saw the eventual closure of the Mission schools. Emigration in the 1880s, combined with financial difficulties for the Mission, saw a gradual decline in its influence, and the Mission was wound up in 1886.

The Slievemore Hotel, the original Mission hotel, stands in the middle of the Mission complex of buildings, and old photographs in the lobby show that the basic layout has remained largely unchanged. The Mission church, a stone's throw from the hotel, has a photograph of the remarkable Edward Nangle. He died in 1883 and his recorded last words were, 'Achill may well be called the Happy Valley. In spite of all our trials, I know of no place like it.'

Geography

At 14 miles (22 kilometres) long and 12 miles (19 kilometres) wide but with an indented coastline of some 80 miles (129 kilometres), Achill is Ireland's largest island. The western side is dominated by Mount Slievemore (2,201 feet/671 metres) and Mount Croaghaun (2,182 feet/665 metres), and the northwest face of Croaghaun has been eroded to form some of the highest seacliffs anywhere in Europe. Much of the island is heathland and bog, and the scarcity of good farming land goes some way to explaining the poignant history of emigration from Achill. But there is land, and archaeological evidence shows that people have been living here since about 4000BCE.

History

A period in the 19th century when proselytizing Protestants chose Achill for a mission is an interesting and well-documented piece of recent history (see box on page 477) that shares some intriguing similarities with a much more recent controversy. From the mid-1990s onwards coaches were bringing 15,000 pilgrims a year to visit the House of Prayer, a disused convent bought by Christina Gallagher following a vision she had received telling her to open a place of worship surrounded by water. Many people claimed to have experienced or witnessed miracles here, and Christina Gallagher was being invested with too saintly and supernatural an aura to suit the church hierarchy. There are different interpretations as to why it happened but in 1998 the closure of the House of Prayer was tearfully announced by Gallagher.

County Mayo

Captain Boycott

Charles Cunningham Boycott (1832-97) came to Achill in 1857 after selling his army commission. He became a tenant farmer for a landlord who leased Keel West from the Achill Mission, and lived in Corrymore Lodge, which may still be seen west of Keel. He acquired a reputation for brutality, running down geese on his horse if they strayed on to his roadway. He left after 20 years to become the land agent for Lord Erne's estates in Ballinrobe, County

Mayo and came into conflict with Michael Davitt's Land Leaguers. When Boycott refused to reduce tenants' rents he was ostracized: labourers on the estate refused to work for him; local suppliers refused to sell him food. Orangemen were recruited from Ulster to replace the farmhands but it took 1,000 troops to protect them. The word 'boycott' quickly entered English and other European languages as a synonym for social ostracism.

Sights

Beaches
Even on a fine day it is possible to have one of Achill's beaches all to yourself. The largest, stretching for over 21 miles (four kilometres) is at Keel and it is safe for swimming apart from one part, indicated by a notice, where a riptide occurs. On the north side there are two sandy beaches, Silver Strand and Golden Strand, at Doogort with fine views over Blacksod Bay to north Mayo; both beaches are safe but Golden Strand has one section marked as dangerous. The most spectacular-looking beach is at Keem Bay, when it is first seen from the road above at a height of 600 feet (182 metres).

Slievemore Deserted Village
The deserted village of Slievemore consists of about 75 houses, built of unmortared stone and mostly parallel to one another with south-facing gables, east-facing doorways and a window to the northeast. Recent research suggests that the origins of the village lay in the early medieval period, 500-1200CE. In the 19th century, cattle were tethered to the southern end of the houses and tethering rings can still be seen in the walls. Poor management by the landlords, who later sold their land to the Mission, and the effects of the Famine saw villagers move south to Dooagh. It is possible that the Mission ownership of the land in 1851 accelerated the process of abandonment. Up until the 1940s the houses were used as 'booley' dwellings, summer residences cattle grazers, but they are now in ruins.

Mount Slievemore
This is one of the most easily managed and enjoyable climbs on the island; it takes about 1½ hours to reach the summit from the Deserted Village car-park. Head first for the white stone that is clearly visible on the slope up behind the ruins and from there head for the ridge and along it eastwards to the summit. There are magnificent views of Blacksod Bay and the Mullet. Descend by the same route.

Mount Croaghaun
Almost as high as Slievemore but a decidedly more difficult climb and best undertaken with the help of Ordnance Survey map No. 30. From Keem Bay take the turning on the main road that heads north to Corrymore Lough and begin the climb from there. Precipitous cliffs drop down to the sea from close to the summit, so only climb when the sky is clear and likely to remain so for the rest of the day. Allow five hours for the return journey.

Essentials

The main accommodation centres are Keel and Dooagh in the south and Doogort in the north of the island.

A *Achill Head*, Keel, T/F43108. Close to the beach, this hotel also has pub food in the bar. **A** *Gray's Guesthouse*, Doogort, T43244. Comparable in facilities to the island's hotels and with a croquet lawn to boot. Dinner, IR£17.50, served at 1900. **A** *McDowells*, Slievemore Rd, Doogort, T43148, F94801. A pretty, cottage-like exterior to a small 10-room hotel at the foot of Slievemore. **A** *Slievemore Hotel*, Dugort, T43224, F43236, is a hotel with a history (see box on page 477), and is a comfortable and friendly place to stay. Architectural features, such as the fine staircase and balcony, have been retained and the proprietor has a keen regard for the hotel's history. Open all year. Bike hire for residents. Recommended. **A** *Strand Hotel*, Doogort, T43241. Close to a Blue Flag beach.

B *Atlantic Hotel*, Dooagh, T43113. Like many of the Achill hotels, the *Atlantic* has weekend, 3-day and weekly rates. A Friday and Saturday night with 1 dinner, for example, is IR£55 per person. **B** *Groigin Mor*, Pollagh, Keel, T43385. B&B in a small house, not a bungalow, on the main road between Keel and Dooagh. No evening meals available. **B** *Joyces Maian Villa*, Keel, T43134. B&B overlooking the beach, open Easter to November. **B** *Óstán Gob A'Choire* (Achill Sound Hotel), Achill Sound, T45245, F45621. The largest hotel with 36 rooms, but perhaps too close to the mainland to give a sense of being on an island. **B** *Wave Crest*, Dooagh, T43115. Rooms with and without their own bathrooms.

D *Railway Hostel*, Achill Sound, T45187. Situated on the mainland just before the Michael Davitt Bridge and looking rather drab, this is nevertheless a roomy hostel with 2 kitchens, 1 private room, and open all year. **D** *Valley House Hostel*, The Valley, Doogort, T47204. A fine, spacious old residence converted into a hostel and with its own bar. **D** *The Wayfarer Hostel*, Keel, T43266. Open from early March to early October and with 3 private rooms. **D** *Wild Haven Hostel*, Achill Sound, T45392. The first hostel on the island itself, just over the bridge. Enhanced by a comfortable old-fashioned living room and a conservatory for meals; also open all year and with private rooms.

Camping Camping is possible at the *Railway Hostel*, the *Wayfarer Hostel* and the *Valley House Hostel*. The *Seal Caves Caravan Park*, Doogort, T43262, is open from April to September and accepts tents. The *Keel Sandybanks Caravan & Camping Park*, Keel, T094-32054, F094-32351, is on the beach.

Self-catering *Achill Island Luxury Self-Catering Homes*, Keel, T43259, F43210, jrachill@tinet.ie There are various individual houses and cottages for rent: *Minaun Cliff Cottages*, T43341; *Teach Cruachan*, T43301; *The Green*, Keel, T43246; *Riverside Cottage*, at Dooagh, T43181; and *Links Cottages*, also at Keel, T094-58152, F094-58377. Fully serviced mobile homes and 2- and 3-bedroomed cottages can be rented through the company that runs the *Keel Sandybanks Caravan & Camping Park*, Belcarra, Castlebar, Co Mayo, T094-32054, F094-32351.

Keel has a few places to eat and one of the easiest to find is Calbey's, T43158, next to the police station on the main road by a junction. A lunch menu runs from 1200 to 1730 with dishes such as salmon and chips for IR£7, as well as salads and sandwiches. A candlelight dinner features starters such as crab claws or oysters and main dishes such as lamb or baked cod with pernod for just under IR£10. A seafood platter of local fish is IR£14. The *Boley House Restaurant*, T43147, is nearby and expect to pay around

Sleeping
■ *on map*
Price codes:
see inside front cover

Eating
● *on map*
Price codes:
see inside front cover

County Mayo

IR£20 for a meal here. The *Chalet Seafood Restaurant*, T43157, also at Keel, opens from April to October, and has an attached gift shop selling knitwear and pottery. The *Village Inn* pub at Keel does bar food, and the *Beehive* is a self-service coffee shop.

At Doogort the Atoka, Valley Cross Rd, T47229, is a small but popular little restaurant with unsurprising main courses around IR£10 and also open for lunch. The *Slievemore Hotel* does a pleasant dinner for around IR£15.

Pubs & music Hotels are always a good bet (see 'Sleeping' on page 479). The Slievemore, for example, has music every night in the summer and occasional Irish dancing. At nearby Golden Strand, *Mastersons* pub is worth checking out for live music. At Keel the *Achill Head* hotel has live entertainment and nearly all the pubs in the vicinity will have some form of musical entertainment. The bar at the Valley House hostel is a good place to meet fellow hostellers. At Achill Sound, *Patten's Lounge Bar* has music during the holiday season and there are regular sessions of Irish music at the *Óstán Gob A'Choire*.

Sport **Diving** *Achill Island Scuba Dive Centre*, T087-2349884. Based at Purteen Harbour at Keel. *Dol-Fin Divers*, Achill Sound, T45473. Supplies gear and runs PADI courses. **Golf** *Achill Golf Club*, T43456. Has a 9-hole golf links at Keel. Holds an Open Golf festival in August. *Valley House*, T47204. Pitch and putt. **Outdoor activities** Achill Outdoor Education Centre, T47253; *McDowell's Hotel*, T43148. Adventure and leisure centres, which offer activities, canoeing, coastal walks, sailing, surfing and windsurfing. **Sea angling** *John Johnston*, Dooega East, T45743. Conducts fishing trips to Clare Island from Kildavnait Pier, Cloughmore. *Tony Burke*, Cashel, T47257.

Festivals The *Achill Archaeological Summer Field School* takes places between **late June and mid-August** at the Folklife Centre, Dooagh. Details available from Irish Archaeological Services, St O'Hara's Hill, Tullamore, County Offaly, T0506-21627/098-43343, F0506-22975, theresa@iol.ie www.iol.ie/theresa/index.html The cultural programme of *Scoil Acla* (Summer/Winter School) is available from William Creane, T47248, F47346. The summer school, which claims to be the oldest in the EU, takes place in the first half of August.

Shopping At Keel, the *Beehive Craft & Coffee Shop* has pottery, knitwear, jewellery and the like and the *Shell Craft Shop* has a selection of semi-precious stones such as amethyst, agate and onyx, as well as shell jewellery and other shell crafts. *Achill Island Pottery* shop is also at Keel, as is the *Western Light Art Gallery*, T43325, and the *Chalet Craft Shop*. At Dooega there is the *Yawl Art Gallery & Painting School*, T36137.

Transport **Bicycles** Bicycles can be hired from some of the hostels and hotels and from *O'Malley's Supermarket*, T43125, at Keel. **Bus** A *Bus Éireann* service runs Monday to Saturday between Dooagh and Ballina, via Keel and Doogort on the island and Newport and Westport on the mainland. **Taxis** *M.T. Taxi*, T45491.

Directory **Banks** No bank on the island; travelling banks visit. *Bank of Ireland*, T087-2375138. Visits on Mon, Tue and Wed. *AIB Bank*, T098-25466, aibmayo@iol.ie Visits twice weekly. **Communications** Post office: The main post office is in Keel at *O'Malley's Supermarket*, T43125, and money can also be changed here. There is also a post office at Dooagh, T43107. **Bureaux de change**: Beehive Craft & Coffee Shop at Keel (see 'Shopping' on page 480). **Hospitals and medical services** Doctors: Dr King, Achill Sound, T43105. Dr Lineen, Achill Sound, T45284. Dr O'Leary, Pollagh, T43476. **Pharmacies**: *Achill Pharmacy*, Achill Sound, T45248. **Tourist office** There is no Bord Fáilte tourist office as such but tourist information is available from *Alice's Harbour Inn*, T45138, at Achill Sound on the mainland or at the Esso garage, T47242, on the road to Keel. Information available on the web: http://www.achill-island.com **Useful addresses** Car repairs at *Sweeny's Garage*, T45243/45102.

Northwest Mayo

The desolate northwest of Mayo is as far off the tourist trail as one can get in Ire- Phone code: 097
land. There are only two towns of any size – Bangor Erris (usually just called
Bangor) and Belmullet – and everything in between is bogland, heather, bare
hills and the occasional farmhouse or weather-beaten bungalow. Travel here for
wildlife, walking, fishing, angling – you won't feel crowded whatever you do.

Belmullet and the Mullet Peninsula

One of the least populated corners of Europe, the Mullet peninsula has its own Colour map 2, grid A2
charms, although you won't be thinking this if you arrive on a wet day. At its
best it offers splendid wild beauty of an unconventional kind, and in mythology it was the final resting place of the four Children of Lir. Under a spell, they
spent their last 300 years here as swans until they heard the bell of a monk, a
disciple of St Patrick, who was searching for them. The monk cared for them
but when a local chief wanted the swans as a present for his wife they were
turned back into humans. But Irish mythology has a hard edge, for when the
swans returned to human form they were 900 years old and quickly withered
away and died.

Belmullet was founded in the early 19th century by an English landlord, and
little has happened since to change the basic layout of the place. There is precious little to see but travellers pass through on their way south to the Mullet
peninsula on the R313. The road goes to Blacksod Point at the southern tip of
the peninsula and passes two good beaches at Elly Bay and then Mullaghroe.
Blacksod Point looks out to where, in 1588, the *La Rata Santa Maria*
Encoronada, the flagship of the Spanish Armada, was stranded. The Spanish
commander, Don Alfonso de Leyva, was rescued but later lost his life off
County Antrim.

There are a number of promontory forts in the area and the one worth seeing is at Doonamo, reached by taking a road northwest from Belmullet. Dating

Mullet Peninsula

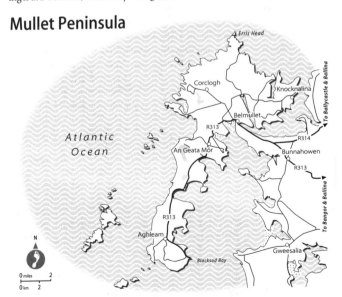

County Mayo

back to the Iron Age, it is strategically positioned for defensive purposes and inside it stands a ring fort. Off the west coast of the peninsula lie the islands of Inishglora, Inishkea North and Inishkea South. The Inishkea islands, where inscribed pillar-stones of uncertain provenance stand, can be visited by boat (see 'Directory' on page 483).

Portacloy & Benwee Head If you like to have a beach all to yourself then take the turning for Portacloy off the R314 road between Belmullet and Ballycastle. After a journey of eight miles (13 kilometres) across an incredibly flat landscape populated mostly by sheep, a delightful beach is reached, hemmed in by cliffs, at the northwest extremity of Ireland. There are no shops or pubs so bring everything you need. To the west of Portacloy, at Benwee Head, towering cliffs look out to a group of rock-stacks standing some 100 yards (90 metres) high.

Bangor Erris & the Bangor Trail The Bangor Trail is a long-distance walk between Newport and Bangor, but for the first few miles north of Newport it shares a route with the Western Way (see pages 440 and 485). A short way beyond the An Óige Traenlaur Lodge hostel, T098-41358, which is 5 miles (8 km) north of Newport, it turns northwestwards towards Bangor and leaves the Western Way behind. Maps and a guidebook, *County Mayo: The Bangor Trail* by McDermott and Chapman, are available in Westport or Ballina.

Sleeping **B** *Channel Dale*, Ballina Rd, Belmullet, T81377. B&B within walking distance of town, has 3 doubles and 1 single. **B** *Coe na Mara*, Clogher, Blacksod, T/F85685. On the Belmullet peninsula and the proprietor is happy to cook what you bring her from the natural mussel beds in nearby Cartron Bay. **B** *Hillcrest House*, Main St, Bangor, T83494. Has 1 twin and 3 triple rooms. **B** *Western Strand*, Main St, Belmullet, T/F81096. The only hotel in Belmullet, this has 10 rooms. **C** *Mill House*, American St, Belmullet, T81181. The rooms in this B&B share bathroom facilities.

Self-catering possibilities include *The Old School House*, Bangor, T83583, and cottage apartments at Barnagh, Clogher, on the Belmullet peninsula, which can be booked through Mary Edwards, T81187.

Eating In Belmullet, the restaurant in the Western Strand hotel does an evening meal for IR£15. There is also *Paddy's Family Fare Restaurant* at the top of Main St, serving fairly predictable meals, and pub grub at the *Anchor Bar*. On Main St, *Lavelles Bar* has a coffee shop and serves seafood, plus a large-screen TV and a pool table for those inevitable wet days. In Bangor the food scene is even more dismal but there is a pub next to the *Hillcrest House* B&B on Main St that serves pub food throughout the day. There is also *Sizzlers* coffee shop and a supermarket.

Sport **Fishing** Possible on Cross Lake, stocked by the fishery board and suitable for boat and shore angling. Boat hire and permits available from George Geraghty in Belmullet, T81492. In Bangor, day permits for local fishing are available in the *West End Bar*. **Boat hire** for angling is available through Vincent Sweeney, T85774.

Transport **Bicycle** Walsh's garage, Chapel St, T82260. Bike hire. **Bus** A daily bus service operates between Ballina and Belmullet, via Bangor, and continues south to Blacksod Point. Check times with the Belmullet tourist office or the Ballina bus station. *McNulty Coaches*, Chapel St, Belmullet, T81016, run a daily service to Castlebar and a Sunday service to Galway and Ennis via Westport.

Banks The Bank of Ireland and the Ulster Bank have branches in Belmullet. **Directory**
Communications Post Office: at the western end of Main St in Belmullet. **Tour**
companies Boat trips to the small island of Inishkea North through Josephine Geraghty, T85741.
Tourist Information *Iorras Domhnann Rural Tourism Co-operative*, have a seasonal office on
the left side of the R313 as one enters Belmullet.

Ballina and around

For many visitors the major attractions in Ballina is the River Moy itself, rich in *Phone code: 096*
salmon and trout, which passes through the town, and the river's bridges are *Colour map 2, grid A3*
regularly used by anglers for their sport. The town originally developed on the
east side of the river, close to where the Victorian cathedral of St Muredach
now stands, but from the 18th century onwards it was the west side that developed into the modest commercial centre one sees today. The tourist office has
a good range of information, including free maps of local walks and full details
of where to fish and obtain permits. A popular walk is nearby Belleek Forest,
just over a mile (two kilometres) from the town centre, and about a mile (1.6
kilometres) southwest of town, past the railway station, there is the neolithic
Dolmen of the Four Maols, associated with a legend of four foster-brothers of
the early Christian era who murdered their master and were buried here after
being executed.

There are two abbeys in the vicinity of Ballina, both reached by taking the
R314 north to Killala, and while not especially spectacular they are worth a visit
if travelling in that direction.

The 15th century was a good time for ecclesiastical architecture, not least **Rosserk Abbey**
because of the Franciscans who proceeded to build some of their finest monasteries around Ireland: Rosserk Abbey is a particularly good example of what
they achieved. Highlights include a double piscina, which is rare due to the
inscribed relief of a round tower, and very well-preserved windows and substantial remains of the domestic wing. ■ *24 hours. Free. After four miles (six
kilometres) on the R314 north of Ballina take the signposted road to the right, left
at the next junction and then a right at the next signpost.*

This is also a Franciscan abbey, contemporary with Rosserk, though apart **Moyne Abbey**
from the cloisters it is not as well preserved. An adjoining tower with stairs still
stands; however, it is none too easy for the untrained eye to make out the various domestic buildings that surround the church. The English governor of
Connaught burned the abbey down in 1590 but the friars remained living there
until the end of the 18th century. ■ *Open 24 hours. Free Admission. Continue
for over a mile (3 km) on the R314 after the turn-off for Rosserk until the abbey
comes into view on the right near a farm.*

L *Enniscoe House*, Castlehill, near Crossmolina, Balina, T31112, F31773. Handsome **Sleeping**
Georgian house, in the same family since the 1660s, with good food, great atmosphere and reasonable rates. If not staying, consider making a reservation for the
£IR26 dinner. **A** *Downhill Hotel*, Sligo Rd, T21033, F21338, thedownhillhotel@
tinet.ie Its leisure centre, with pool, saunas, squash court, gym, all-weather tennis
courts, and snooker table, is an inducement to stay here. Situated a short way outside
of town on the N59. **B** *Deanwood Hotel*, Bury St, T21655, F21028, deanhotel@
tinet.ie http://web.idirect.com/~amazing/deanwood.htm A small but pleasant
establishment in the centre of town with 12 rooms and a Chinese restaurant in the
hotel grounds. **B** *Downhill Inn*, Sligo Rd, T73444, F73144, thedownhillinn@
tinet.ie Sister-hotel to the *Downhill Hotel*. **B** *Errigal*, Killala Rd, T22563, F70968. This

County Mayo

Humbert's March and the Castlebar Races

Humbert marched from Killala to Ballina and took the town with ease. On 26th August his army, swelled in size by a growing numbers of Irishmen, marched on Castlebar. The next day, 800 French soldiers and 1,500 Irish rebels confronted General Lake's army outside Castlebar. Opening gambits saw the rebels advance behind a cover of requisitioned cows, but the English stampeded them back to the French ranks. However, when Humbert ordered his whole army forward the *enemy lost their nerve and the English fled to Athlone in an ignominious rout that was christened the Castlebar Races. Humbert occupied the town and declared the Republic of Connaught! Early in September, however, Humbert was defeated at Ballinamuck in County Longford and Irish insurgents, who fled into bogland, were cut down by cavalry charges. Over 500 were massacred, and any survivors were hanged the following day.*

B&B is handy if heading north on the R314. **B** *Greenhill*, Cathedral Close, T22767. B&B in the centre of the town, near the cathedral. **B** *Salmon Weir Hostel*, Barrett St, T71903, F45502, salmonweir@mayo-ireland.ie Utilizing the generous space of an old warehouse by the riverside, this hostel has a deserved reputation for offering quality accommodation and there are 8 private rooms at IR£22. **B** *San Remo*, Sligo Rd, T70162, F71155. B&B on the N59.

Camping *Belleek Caravan & Camping Park*, north of town off the R314 road to Killala, T71533, lenahan@iol.ie http://www.iol.ie/belleekpark/camping Nearly 60 pitches of which 20 are for tents. Open from mid-March to mid-October.

Eating There are some hotel and guesthouse restaurants worth checking out, the most expensive of which is at Mount Falcon Castle Guesthouse, Foxford Rd, T70811. An evening meal is around IR£25. In town the *Lantern Chinese Restaurant*, Bury St, T70236, serves Chinese food with an Irish inflection and a takeaway service is available. *The Broken Jug*, Bury St, T72379, is a pub that serves a carvery lunch for around IR£5 and restaurant meals in the evening. Closed Sunday evenings. More pubs serving meals are to be found along Pearse St and in O'Rahilly St, the continuation of this street; *Gaughan's* has received plaudits for its crab salads at IR£6 and home cooked ham salads at a pound less. *Cafolla's Restaurant*, Tolan St, is a straightforward café serving quick and inexpensive meals.

Pubs & music There is the usual plethora of pubs in Ballina, and during the summer months many of them are alive with the sound of traditional Irish music. *Murphy Brothers* on Clare St and *Brogan's* on Green St have both been recommended, and *The Broken Jug* has its own nightclub, which attracts a fairly young crowd.

Festivals The *Ballina Street Festival* takes place through **mid-July** and lasts for a week. The highlight of the festival is National Heritage Day when shop fronts take on a Victorian character, proprietors dress accordingly, and music and theatre enliven the atmosphere. T70905.

Shopping **Bookshop** *Keohane's* bookshop in Tone St complements the tourist office in its stock of maps and local guides.

Transport **Bus** Bus station: on Kevin Barry St in the southwest of town, close to the train station. *Bus Éireann*, T71800, manage to connect Ballina with most parts of the country and this includes Northern Ireland. There are a couple of private companies: *Barton*

County Mayo

Transport, T01-6286026. Runs a daily service between Dublin and Ballina; *Treacy's*, T70968. Runs to Sligo. **Trains** **Train station:** on Kevin Barry St, near to the bus station. The Dublin to Westport train service stops at Ballina two to three times a day, and connections to most other parts of the rail network are made at Athlone.

Directory

Banks The banks are located along Pearse St. **Communications** **Post Office:** at the top of O'Rahilly St. **Tourist office** Cathedral Rd, on the east side of the river, T70848. Coming from Sligo it is on the left before crossing the river into the centre; coming from Killala or Crossmolina, it is necessary to cross Ham Bridge or West Bridge. Mon-Sat 1000-1300, 1400-1745.

Killala and the north coast

On 22nd August 1798, three French frigates dropped anchor at Kilcummin Strand in Killala Bay and put this quiet corner of North Mayo on the map. General Humbert had over 1,000 men and when they charged the 80 yeomanry outside of Killala with fixed bayonets the English forces quickly surrendered. Killala became the first place in Ireland to be occupied by French revolutionary soldiers, and peasants armed with pikes soon joined them (see box on page 484).

Phone code: 096
Colour map 2, grid A3

Although Killala also boasts a Church of Ireland cathedral with a fine steeple, and a wonky round tower, it is the merging of the insurrectionary United Irishmen movement with Napoleon's revolutionary army that gives this area its powerful sense of history. To reach the beach at Kilcummin, four miles (six kilometres) west of town, take the R314 road north and take the signposted turning on the right. Along the road there is a stirring monument depicting a French soldier in solidarity with an Irish peasant.

Accommodation is limited to B&Bs. **B** *Beach View House*, T32023, and **B** *Chez Nous*, T32056. Both at Ross, which is reached by taking the road out to Ballycastle and turning right at the sign pointing to Ross Strand. **B** *Rathoma House*, Rathoma, T32035. A couple of miles outside of town. **C** *Avondale House*, Pier Rd, Killala, T32229. Has 4 rooms with shared facilities.

Sleeping

There is no restaurant in Killala, though the B&Bs mentioned in 'Sleeping' above all do an evening meal for around IR£12. The *Golden Acres* pub serves home-cooked food at the bar and the food at the unprepossessing-looking *Anchor Bar* includes tasty open sandwiches of crab and scampi. The *Golden Acres* is also a good bet for live music between Wednesday and Sunday nights.

Eating

Bus *Bus Éireann* service 445 runs Monday to Saturday between Ballina and Ballycastle via Killala.

Transport

Tourist office Seasonal tourist information office, on Ballina Rd just before entering town, T32166.

Directory

County Mayo

Ballycastle and Céide Fields

On a fine day, if coming from Killala, take the R314 to Ballycastle but after a short while take the signposted turning to the right for Kilcummin and Lackan Bay. The beach at Lackan is sandy and safe, and further along the coastal road there are superb views at Downpatrick Head.

Phone code: 096
Colour map 1, grid A5

The small town of Ballycastle on the north coast would be a fairly forgettable place on the road between Killala and Belmullet were it not for the nearby

Céide Fields

Wanted – dead or alive?

Castlebar is the birthplace of notable characters such as Louis Brennan, inventor of the mono-rail and the torpedo; Margaret Burke Sheridan, the soprano; and Charles Haughey, the former Taoiseach infamous for his financial shenanigans. But the most notorious individual associated with Castlebar is Richard John Bingham Lucan (1934-?), the alleged murderer of his nanny in London in 1974, and Ireland's best-known absentee landlord. A coroner's jury charged him with the murder, the nanny being apparently mistaken for his estranged wife. Some tenants around Castlebar still pay rents to the Lucan estate, which is now officially in the hands of his son, and around the corner from the tourist office there is a Lucan Street. The town park, known as the Mall, was once the cricket pitch of the Lucan family and it now contains a monument to the 1798 rising. In 1999 Lord Lucan was officially pronounced dead, but a body has never been found.

phenomenon of Céide (pronounced 'cage-a') Fields, the largest known neolithic farm settlement in the world. A schoolteacher in the area had long suspected there was something worth exploring under the blanket bog but it was not until his son became an archaeologist that a proper examination became possible. The result was astonishing, for sealed under the layers of bog was a sophisticated 5,000-year old network of stone-walled fields. Picks and shovels and resinous pine chips have been found, suggesting the existence of early copper mining, but no signs of defensive walls: the pioneering farmers who worked these fields had little to fear from their neighbours because they didn't have any.

The story of Céide Fields is told at the Visitor Centre by way of an excellent 20-minute audio-visual show, one of the best to be seen anywhere in Ireland, that sets the geological and historical context. Guided tours take visitors around the site and, because the place is not immediately dramatic, a lot depends on getting a knowledgeable and helpful guide who can interpret the scene for you. The centre has a self-service restaurant, or a picnic can be enjoyed outside overlooking a spectacular vista of sea and land. ■ *T43325. Mid-March to May, Tuesday-Saturday 1000-1700; June to September, daily 0930-1830; October, daily 1000-1700. IR£2.50. Five miles (eight kilometres) west of Ballycastle on the R314. Look for a pyramidal roof innocuously situated on the bare bog.*

Sleeping **B** *Céide House*, Main St, Ballycastle, T43105. This pub does B&B but it might not be the quietest place to stay. **B** *The Hawthorns*, Belderrig, T43148. Open all year and an evening meal is IR£12. **B** *Suantrai*, T43040. Outside of Ballycastle, on the road to Downpatrick Head, Mr & Mrs Chambers do B&B here from mid-June to mid-August, but no meals are available. **C** *The Yellow Rose*, Belderrig, T43125. Some four miles (six kilometres) west of Céide Fields and is open all year. The house overlooks the sea, serves an evening meal for IR£8, and the excavated remains of a smaller Stone Age farm site are nearby. Recommended.

Eating In Ballycastle, *Céide House* has a restaurant serving café-style meals from 0900 to 2100. *Mary's Bakery*, a stone-built house at the other end of the street, does scones, salads and soups and more tempting dishes like wild Atlantic salmon with mayonnaise and soda bread. More substantial meals are served at *Doonferry House*, an odd red-coloured pub outside of town on the road to Céide Fields. The *Céide Fields Visitor Centre* has a good self-service café and restaurant.

Céide House has sessions of traditional music at weekends and just next door at *Katie Macs* pub there is more of the same. *Polke's* is a traditional grocery and pub combined, a place to sit and while away some time. **Pubs & music**

Bus *Bus Éireann*'s 445 service runs Monday to Saturday between Ballina and Ballycastle. **Transport**

Castlebar and around

With a population approaching 8,000, Castlebar is a thriving and commercially successfully town, and while there is a distinct lack of charm about the place there are places of interest in the vicinity. Castlebar makes a suitable base for excursions north to Pontoon and Lough Conn, primarily of interest to fishing folk; east to Turlough, Strade and Foxford where there is a round tower, museums and shopping opportunities; or south to Ballintober Abbey, one of the most evocative old churches in Ireland. To the southeast there is also Knock, putative site of visions, apparitions and miracles but also home to an interesting folk museum. *Phone code: 094 Colour map 2, grid B3*

A monastery was founded here in 1216, though parts of the church were rebuilt after a fire in the late 13th century. Sensitive restoration work has done wonders for this church, which, notwithstanding the aesthetically doubtful Stations of the Cross outside, manages to evoke a sense of ancient spirituality unique for Irish churches. The Early Gothic details in the transepts and nave are interesting and the west door, ascribed by experts to both the 13th and 15th centuries, was removed from the church in the 19th century and only returned in 1964. ■ *T30934. Daily, 0900-2000. Free. Tours sometimes available from 1000. Take the N84 south from Castlebar: signposted on the left after eight miles (13 kilometres).* **Ballintober Abbey**

Knock's claim to fame goes back to 1879, when two local women claimed to have seen Mary, Joseph and St John appear at the south end of the church, and 13 other people confirmed the apparition. The place quickly became a place of pilgrimage, fuelled by alleged miraculous cures and the blessing of official Church investigations. Thousands turn up every day, and in the summer there is an amazing number of stalls selling religious bric-à-brac. The Knock Folk Museum is surprisingly interesting, with graphic details of the apparition (and photographs of the crutches donated by cured pilgrims) and well-presented displays on local farming life. ■ *Museum: South of the church in the centre of the village, T88100. May to October, daily 1000-1800. IR£2. From Castlebar take the N60 south to Claremorris and turn left on to the N17 for Knock.* **Knock**

This is a well-preserved round tower, perhaps a little stouter and shorter (70 feet/21 metres) than most, built between the 10th and 12th centuries next to a church founded by St Patrick. The ruined church that stands here today is 18th century, though it incorporates a 16th-century mullioned window. ■ *24 hours. Free. About four miles (six kilometres) northeast of Castlebar on the N5 road to Ballina.* **Turlough round tower**

Michael Davitt (1846-1906) was a founding member of the Irish National Land League in 1879 (in Daly's hotel in Castlebar) but his socialist ideas for land reform later brought him into conflict with Parnell. Davitt, himself the son of an evicted tenant farmer from Strade, was jailed for his Fenian activities in the 1870s and his *Leaves from a Prison Diary* (1885) is still worth reading. This small **Michael Davitt Memorial Museum**

County Mayo

museum in Strade, 10 miles (16 kilometres) northeast of Castlebar, has material relating to his life and times. ■ *Strade, T56488. April to October, daily 0900-1700. Take the N5 road to Dublin and turn left on to the N58 to Strade.*

Foxford If visiting the Michael Davitt Museum in Strade it is only a few miles further along the N58 to Foxford and the **Foxford Woollen Mills Visitor Centre**. The original woollen mill was founded in 1892 by a nun, and today Foxford is a big producer of quality tweed, rugs and blankets. Tours last 35 minutes and as well as the Centre's excellent shop, which sells a wide range of woollen products, there is a jewellery workshop and a woodcraft shop. There is also a self-service restaurant. ■ *Swinford Road, Foxford, T56756. Monday-Saturday 1000-1800, Sunday 1400-1800. IR£3.50.*

While in shopping mode, *Open Sun Pottery*, Swinford Road, sells functional pottery made on the premises as well as small craft objects. To get there from the Mill, turn left as you leave, pass the post office and take a left turn on to Swinford Rd.

The Foxford Way is a long distance walk that extends the Western Way south through the Ox Mountains, from Foxford to Strade and around Lough Cullin. The total distance is 53 miles (86 kilometres) and it starts on the road outside the Woollen Mills Visitor Centre. For a short 45-minute walk follow the signs as they lead you away from the River Moy until meeting a surfaced road where the Foxford Way sign points left but a right turn returns to Foxford along the road. Mayo County Council publish a guide, *The Foxford Way (Bealach Béal Easa)*, available from the Castlebar tourist office, and Ordnance Survey Maps Nos 24 and 31 are required in the 1:50,000 Discovery series.

Pontoon & Lough Conn Life in Pontoon, a premier angling centre not only for Mayo but the whole of Ireland, revolves around two hotels on the narrow strip that divides Lough Conn and Lough Cullin. Pontoon's reputation has taken some flack in recent years because of a decline in the quality of the water due to pollution, and the effects this has had on the fish. But Lough Conn stretches for some nine miles (14 kilometres), has an estimated stock of half a million brown trout and also enjoys runs of spring salmon and grilse, so all is not lost. One of the hotels runs a School of Fly Fishing (see 'Directory' on page 489).

Sleeping **L** *Breaffy House*, Breaffy Rd, Castlebar, T22033, F22276. An imposing and spacious hotel on the N60 road to Claremorris. **AL** *Pontoon Bridge Hotel*, T56120, F56688, pontoonb@mayo-ireland.ie www.pontoon.mayo-ireland.ie. Situated on the narrow peninsula between Lough Conn and Lough Cullin and geared up for the angler, cooking enthusiast or budding landscape painter (see 'Directory' on page 489). Open April to November. Recommended. **AL** *Welcome Inn*, New Antrim St, Castlebar, T22288, F21766. A well-established hotel, close to town centre on the road to Pontoon and Ballina. A *Knock House Hotel*, Ballyhaunis Rd, T88088, F88044. Lage modern hotel. A *Healys*, Pontoon, T56443, F56572. Hotel that, like the *Pontoon Bridge Hotel*, opens between April and November. **B** *Heneghans Guesthouse*, Newtown St, Castlebar, T21883, F25125, 101352.246@compuserve.com Situated in the centre of town and the best non-hotel accommodation in town. **B** *Ivy House*, Castle St, Castlebar, T21527. B&B in the centre of town near the Mall. **C** *Gannon's*, Providence Rd, Foxford, T56101. Hostel open all year, with 4 private rooms at IR£14. **D** *Hughes House Holiday Hostel*, Thomas St, Castlebar, T/F23877. Conveniently located in the centre of town near the tourist office, has 1 private room for IR£22. Open May to September. **D** *Lonely Planet Hostel*, Moneen Roundabout, Castlebar, T21030/24822. Some way outside the town centre, but has 3 private rooms for IR£17; bike hire and open all year.

Camping *Camp Carrowkeel*, Ballyvary, Castlebar, T31264. Open from Easter to the end of September. *Carra Caravan & Camping Park*, Belcarra, Castlebar, T32054, F32351. Open from early June to 26th September. *Knock Caravan & Camping Park*, Claremorris Rd, Knock, T88100, F88295. Open from March to the end of October. Camping is also possible at the *Lonely Planet* hostel (see above).

Eating

The best places for a meal are at the *Pontoon Bridge Hotel*, Pontoon, T56688, for IR£25 or *Breaffy House*, Breaffy Rd, Castlebar, T22033, for IR£20. Also in Castlebar, *Daly's Hotel*, The Mall, T21961, has a comfortable Victorian atmosphere and serves brasserie-style food in the restaurant, lunch specials, and a good bar food menu between 1500 and 2100. A plaque to the left of the main door notes the founding of the National Land League here in 1879. *McGoldricks*, Rush St, Castlebar, is near the tourist office and serves bar lunch daily and bar food until 1900. If visiting Foxford or Strade the *Foxford Woollen Mills Visitor Centre* has a pleasant restaurant serving affordable meals until closing time at 1800.

Sport

Angling *Game Angling Ireland West*, Spencer St, Castlebar, T25006, F27279, mayo_nat@anu.ie Dispenses a free brochure on game angling in the west of Ireland as well as stocking all the necessary gear. *North Western Regional Fisheries Board*, Ardnaree House, Abbey St, Ballina, T096-22788, F70543, nwrfb@iol.ie General information, guides and maps available. *School of Fly Fishing*, Pontoon Bridge Hotel, T56120, F56688, pontoonb@mayo-ireland.ie www.pontoon.mayo-ireland.ie Runs 1- and 2-day courses for complete novices or those with some experience. **Horseriding** *Turlough Equitation Centre*, T26646.

Transport

Bus *Bus Éireann*, T096-71800, have an express service between Castlebar and Dublin as well as services to Ballina, Cork, Derry, Shannon and Sligo. Buses arrive and depart from *Flannelly's* pub in Market St, Castlebar. **Car** Car hire: *Casey Auto Rental*, Castlebar, T21411, F23823. **Train** The Dublin to Westport train stops at Castlebar, T094-21222; the station is outside of town on the N84 Ballinrobe road.

Directory

Banks are located in the town centre on Market St and around. **Communications** Post office: the central post office is at the west end of the main street running through town, in the direction of the N5 road to Westport. **Courses** *Pontoon Bridge Hotel* (see 'Sleeping' on page 488) runs 4-day courses for the *School of Cooking*, and 2- and 4-day non-residential courses between April and October for the *School of Landscape Painting*. **Tourist office** Linehall St, Castlebar, T26727. Mid-Apr-early Sep, Mon-Sat 0930-1300, 1400-1730.

County Mayo

The John Wayne Connection

Wayne devotees who flock to Cong will tell you that The Quiet Man *is better than* Gone with the Wind *(true), and that there is talk of reshooting a scene in 2001 on the 50th anniversary of the making of the film. There is an annual John Wayne lookalike contest and plans are apace to find a Maureen O'Hara double. The irony is that the film was always expected to flop and was only bankrolled on the understanding that the entire cast shot a western afterwards to recoup the anticipated losses. The film now seems to finance half the village and the story goes that the five-star Ashford Castle hotel had to stop playing the video in the evenings because no one came to dinner un til it had finished. Apart from the eponymous hostel and the coffee shop there is the Quiet Man heritage cottage and The Quiet Man Festival in June, with a midsummer ball. Dress code for men is cap, breeches and waistcoat and for women it's bonnets and pretty pinafores. T46155. IR£6.

Cong

Phone code: 092
Colour map 2, grid B3

The Cong phenomenon, a tourist extravaganza that is a bit of an anomaly in Mayo, shares with Knock a doggedly fixed identity, this time in the form of John Wayne, who came here in 1951 to star with Maureen O'Hara in John Ford's *The Quiet Man*. The event has not been forgotten, as visitors quickly realize, and movie fans should buy the excellent *Complete Tour Guide to The Quiet Man Locations* (IR£2) from the tourist office before heading off for the day hunting down all the links to the film that the area still has to offer. My favourite is the sweet shop, used in the film as The Pat Cohan Bar (the one that the horse automatically pulls up outside), owned by a man who was an extra in the movie.

Hollywood apart, Cong would still be worth visiting for Cong Abbey and the archaeological remains in the vicinity, and the tourist office sells a useful archaeological guide (IR£2). There is a series of nearby caves but more interesting is the **Ballymacgibbon Cairn** at Cross and the nearby stone circles at **Moytura**.

Ashford Castle is a noted nearby Victorian edifice, built for the Guinness family and now such an exclusive hotel that it costs IR£3 just to enter the grounds between June and September.

Quiet Man Heritage Cottage

An exercise in post-modernism: a replica of a Hollywood set of an Irish cottage interior but located in a real Irish cottage interior, with items such as a replica of Wayne's jacket made by the person who made the original, and an infinite number of video copies of the film for sale; a video about the film is shown upstairs. The blurred line between film and reality is thankfully brought into focus with the cottage's modest exhibition on local archaeology and history. ■ *Circular Rd, Cong, T46089. Daily 1000-1800. IR£2.*

Cong Abbey

Situated in the ultra-secular grounds of Ashford Castle, this Augustinian abbey was rebuilt in the very early 13th century, though the site has

Cong

To Clonbur & Leenane (R345)

O'Connor's Bike Hire & Craft Shop

Bus stop

Heritage Centre

Toilets

Cong Abbey

Cong River

Dry canal

To Neale, Cross & Galway (R345)

To Ashford Castle & Hotel

N

0 yards 200
0 metres 200

■ **Sleeping**
1 Cong Travel Inn
2 Danagher's
3 Quiet Man Hostel
4 River Lodge Bed & Breakfast
5 Ryan

● **Eating & drinking**
1 Echoes
2 Quiet Man Coffee Shop
3 Rising of the Waters Pub

County Mayo

religious associations going back another 500 years and, like the neighbouring island monastery of Inchagoill (see page 441), probably usurped a place of Celtic worship. Not too much of the church itself remains but the most outstanding feature – the Romanesque doorway on the north wall, which was actually inserted later – is notable for its sculptured capitals, which represent the last flowering of Romanesque architecture in Ireland. The adjoining Chapter House also boasts fine examples of windows and decorated stonework. ■ *24 hours. Free. In the centre of Cong village, opposite the tourist office.*

Sleeping
■ *on map*
Price codes:
see inside front cover

LL *Ashford Castle*, T46003, F46260. With a rack rate approaching IR£500 for a double it seems only proportionate charging IR£3 to enter the grounds. It is situated about a mile south of the village. **AL** *Ryan Hotel*, T46243, F466634. In the centre of the village. **A** *Danaghers*, T46028, F46495. A hotel with a *Quiet Man* connection (Maureen O'Hara played the headstrong Mary Kate Danagher in the film) in the centre of Cong. **B** *Dolmen House*, Drumsheel, T/F46466. B&B in a large modern bungalow just north of Cong. **B** *Inishfree Farmhouse*, Ashford, T46082. B&B. **B** *Lydons Lodge*, T46053. B&B typical of the area. Can fill up in summer. **B** *River Lodge*, T/F46057. Another B&B that is often booked up in summer. **C** *Cong Travel Inn*, Circular Rd, Cong, T/F46310. Next to the heritage cottage and equipped with a self-catering kitchen and a flat rate per person like a hostel, but with no shared rooms. New and family-run. **C** *Rocklawn House*, Drumshiel, T46616. B&B. **D** *Cong Hostel*, Lisloughrey, Quay Rd, T46098, F46448. Next to the camping site, off the R346 road to Galway and about a mile (1.6 km) out of Cong. There are 11 private rooms at IR£17 and the place has been recommended for its homely atmosphere. **D** *Courtyard Hostel*, Garracloon Lodge, Dowagh Estate, Cross, T/F46203, http://www.galway-guide.com/pages/courtyard/ Out beyond Cong hostel and belongs to an interesting organic farm, which oddly includes its own golf course. Private rooms for IR£16. **D** *Quiet Man Hostel*, Abbey St, Cong, T46089, F46448. In the village itself, and has 4 private rooms for IR£17.

Camping *Cong Caravan & Camping Park*, Lisloughrey, Quay Rd, Cong, T46089, F46448. Only 40 pitches for tents and caravans. Camping is also possible at the *Courtyard Hostel*, Cross, T/F46203.

Eating
● *on map*
Price codes:
see inside front cover

The hotels offer the most comfortable setting for a leisurely meal, ranging from IR£37 at *Ashford Castle* to under IR£20 at the other 2 hotels. *Echoes*, Main St, T46059, has a reputation for above-average food, costing over IR£20 per head. For a more straightforward repast, the *Rising of the Waters* pub, the bars in the village hotels, and the *Quiet Man Coffee Shop* all serve a reasonable range of meals.

County Mayo

Around Cong

Sport

Fishing Contact the *Courtyard Hostel*, T46203, for boat hire.

Transport

Bicycle A day's cycling in the Cong area, with the local archaeological guide, is recommended and bikes can be hired from some of the hostels and from *O'Connor's*, Main St, Cong, T46008. **Bus** *Bus Éireann*'s daily 420 Galway to Clifden service stops at Cong in the morning for Galway and in the evening for Clifden.

Directory **Banks** No banks in Cong but money can be changed at the hostels or *O'Connors* craft shop on Main St. **Communications** Post office: on Main St. **Tour operators** *Lough Corrib Cruises*: there is a daily sailing between Ashford Castle and Oughterard with a stop-off and guided tour of the 5th-century ruins on the island of Inchagoill (see page 441). Apr-Oct, 1000, 1100, 1445 and 1700; Nov-Mar at 1100 and 1445. Tickets from the tourist office, T46029/46542. **Tourist office** Abbey St, T46542, opposite Cong Abbey. May-Sep, daily 1000-1800.

County Sligo

Sligo

Phone code: 071
Colour map 1, grid B1

A rewarding mixture of Irish boom town and rural market town, Sligo is growing by the minute but still has that laid-back Irish charm that you came here looking for. It's just small enough to make walking to sights and places to eat comfortable, but still has the amenities of the county town – leisure centres, a cinema, loads of good places to eat, internet cafés, three festivals and lots of good lively music and other entertainment. Stop here for a few days before moving on into the north and experience your last taste of so-laid-back-it's-horizontal life.

Ins and outs

Getting there
See Transport, page 496, for further details.

Sligo airport is at Strandhill, 5 miles (8 km) west of town. It has daily flights to Dublin from where connections can be made to other airports. Car hire is available at the airport, or there are taxis. Trains connect Sligo with Boyle, Carrick-on-Shannon, Dublin and Mullingar 3 times a day, but your best bet is *Bus Éireann*, which connects the town with Derry, Donegal, Dublin and Galway. The bus and train stations are in Lord Edward St.

Getting around

Car hire and taxis are available in town, as are bikes for hire. The easiest and most pleasant way around town is on foot.

Walking tour

The sights of Sligo might be nicely taken in by a walk around the town. The walk should begin at the biggest building in town, the **Cathedral of the Immaculate Conception**, designed by George Goldie and consecrated in 1874. Built to hold the masses, it can seat 4,000 people, despite its relatively small size. It is built in a Germanic Romanesque style and has huge stained glass windows by the French stained glass artist Lobin. No sign of the Celtic revival here. From the Cathedral continue along John Street to the other cathedral, St John's, designed in 1730 by Richard Castle, the man who created so much of Georgian Dublin, and seriously altered in the early 19th century. The church contains a memorial to Susan Yeats (née Pollixfen) the mother of the famous Yeatses, as well as the tomb of Sir Roger Jones (d. 1637), the first governor of Sligo.

Opposite the court are the now defunct offices of the wonderfully-named solicitors Argue & Phibbs.

Continuing on along John Street to Market Street and the High Street, you come to the **Friary**. This is a 1973 building, which partly replaces a Victorian Gothic creation, retaining the apse of the older building. Turn left at Old Market Street and head towards the river. You pass the Gormenghast-like **Courthouse**, still in use and untouched inside since it was built in 1878. It is built in sections, the octagonal tower with dormer windows and a chimney stack popping up through it. The entranceway is a great gabled arcade with twin towers at either side. On a working day it is possible to go into the public gallery and view the courtrooms themselves, as well as the top-lit entrance hall.

The Yeats family

Sligo is forever associated with the Yeats family; not only the really famous ones, Jack and tWilliam, but also the sisters, Susan and Elizabeth, the father, portrait artist John, and the mother Susan Pollexfen. The connection with Sligo is through the Pollexfen family who owned a small shipping company in the town. John, a trained lawyer turned portrait painter, spent little time in Sligo, but he family lived in a kind of genteel poverty for most of their lives and the children often spent months at a time in Sligo with their grandparents. Jack grew up to become a writer and painter, and many of his best paintings are based around the life that he knew in Sligo as a child. William wrote a great deal and many of his poems are also about the Sligo of his childhood; he and Jack also spent periods of their adult lives there. The sisters became leading members of the Arts and Crafts movement in Ireland. John ended his years in New York, Jack lived to a ripe old age in Dublin, a successful painter, while William became an occultist and admirer of fascism.

Past the courthouse, turn right into Abbey Street, where you can view the remains of **Sligo Abbey**, a 13th-century Dominican Friary, established by Maurice Fitzgerald, the Baron of Offaly. In 1416 it was rebuilt after an accidental fire two years earlier. In the 1641 rebellion the whole town came under attack and the Friary was burned again, deliberately this time. The ruins are elegant with an intact 15th-century east window and carvings of various figures in the iconography of Christianity on a tomb of 1506: you can see St Katherine's wheel, St Peter's keys and the shield and sword of St Michael. ■ *Abbey Street, T46406. Mid-June to mid-September, daily 0930-1830. IR£1.50.*

From the abbey go along Kennedy Parade, named after the President, and cross the river Garavogue at Bridge Street to Stephen Street, where a right turn brings you to the **Model Arts Centre**, now an art gallery and housed in the 1855 Model School, designed by James Owen for the Board of Works. It was a non-denominational school and was the best chance of an education anyone in Sligo had during the 19th century.

Back along Stephen Street towards the river you come to the **County Museum and Art Gallery** in an old Congregational Chapel of 1851. The art gallery is housed in the old schoolroom and is home to some interesting material including work by Jack Yeats, George Russell, Sean Keating, Patrick Collins, Estella Solomons and Evie Hone. The museum has lots of old pictures of Sligo, objects belonging to WB Yeats, including his Nobel medal, and other artefacts discovered in and around the town over the years.

From the museum cross Douglas Hyde Bridge – pausing as you do to reflect on the fact that Jack Yeats once claimed to have learned his craft of painting by looking over this bridge into the waters of the Garavoge River – to find the **Yeats Memorial Building**. Another version of the story has it that he learned his craft by spitting over the bridge into the Garavoge – doesn't sound quite so arty though. Yeats Memorial Building has a summer-only exhibition relating the lives of all the Yeatses to Sligo and hosts the annual Yeats Summer School. Its art gallery hosts travelling art exhibitions. It was originally built by the Belfast Banking Company, became the Royal Bank of Ireland in 1899 and was designed by Vincent Craig, the brother of Lord Craigavon, Prime Minister of Northern Ireland. The building was donated to the Yeats society in 1973.

Essentials

Sleeping
■ *on map*
Price codes:
see inside front cover

There are a number of hotels in town, and most of the B&Bs seem to be strung out along Pearse Rd, easily accessible by car and even walkable. There are several hostels in town, all of them getting very full at the peak of summer and around the Yeats festival so booking in advance is advisable.

AL *Ballincar House Hotel*, Rosses Point Rd, T45361, F44198. In a pleasant country location with brilliant views from the back bedrooms over Benbulbin. Soon to add a pool and more leisure facilities to its rose gardens, tennis, snooker and fitness room. Good restaurant. **AL** *Sligo Park Hotel*, Pearse Rd, T60291, F69556. Big, busy hotel, 1 mile (1.6 km) outside town with all the facilities you could want – pool, jacuzzi, fitness centre, nice big restaurant, music, open fires, big sofas, pub food. Rooms are spacious and those on the ground floor open into a little courtyard. Checking-in time is 1500. At the very top end of this price range. **AL** *Tower Hotel*, Quay St, T44000, F46888. Built

Sligo

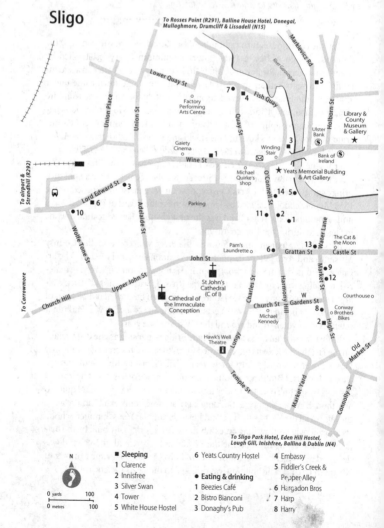

To Rosses Point (R291), Ballina House Hotel, Donegal,
Mullaghmore, Drumcliff & Lissadell (N15)

Markievicz Rd

River Garavogue

Lower Quay St

7

Fish Quay

5

Holborn St

Union Place

Union St

Quay St

Factory
Performing
Arts Centre

Library &
County
Museum
& Gallery

Ulster
Bank

Gaiety
Cinema

1

Wine St

Winding
Stair

3

Bank of
Ireland

To airport &
Strandhill (R292)

Michael
Quirke's
shop

Yeats Memorial Building
& Art Gallery

Lord Edward St

3

O'Connell St

14

5

6

10

Parking

11

2

1

Adelaide St

Water Lane

Wolfe Tone St

Pam's
Launderette

6

Grattan St

13

The Cat &
the Moon

Castle St

John St

9

Market St

12

Upper John St

Charles St

Harmony Hill

Courthouse

St John's
Cathedral
(C of I)

W
Gardens St

Conway
Brothers
Bikes

To Carrowmore

Church Hill

Cathedral of
the Immaculate
Conception

Church St

8

High St

Michael
Kennedy

2

Hawk's Well
Theatre

Lungy

Old
Market St

Temple St

Market Yard

Connolly St

To Sligo Park Hotel, Eden Hill Hostel,
Lough Gill, Inishfree, Ballina & Dublin (N4)

N

0 yards   100
0 metres   100

■ **Sleeping**
1 Clarence
2 Innisfree
3 Silver Swan
4 Tower
5 White House Hostel

6 Yeats Country Hostel

● **Eating & drinking**
1 Beezies Café
2 Bistro Bianconi
3 Donaghy's Pub

4 Embassy
5 Fiddler's Creek &
  Pepper Alley
6 Hargadon Bros
7 Harp
8 Harry

County Sligo

beside the town hall and mirroring it architecturally, this is a small, quiet hotel, with modern, well-laid-out rooms, and lots of comfort. **A** *Clarence Hotel*, Wine St, T42211, F45823. A small hotel in a beautiful old stone building. Music 4 nights a week and busy lunchtime bar trade. **A** *Innisfree Hotel*, High St, T42014, F45745. Busy small hotel catering to both commercial and tourist trades. Nightclub and music in the bar at weekends. **B** *Avila*, Pearse Rd, T60562. A B&B with 4 rooms, opposite *St Theresa's* and *St Anne's*. **B** *Renate House*, Upper John St, T62014. A little more expensive than the other B&Bs further out of town, but very central. **B** *St Anne's*, Pearse Rd, T43188. This B&B is next door to *St Theresa's*, but slightly larger with an outdoor pool. **B** *St Theresa's*, Pearse Rd, T62230. Small B&B with 3 en-suite rooms. **D** *Eden Hill Hostel*, Marymount, Pearse Rd, T/F43204. About a mile (1.6 km) out of town but well sign-posted. It is open all year, has family and double rooms and has bikes for hire. **D** *Harbour House*, Finisklin Rd, T71547. Has double rooms and also hires bikes. It's a good walk out of town but very new and well run. **D** *The Ivy Hostel*, 26-8 Lord Edward St, T45165, F60441.

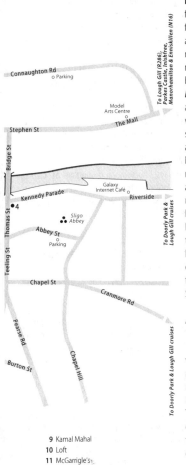

9 Kamal Mahal
10 Loft
11 McGarrigle's
12 McLaughlin's Pub
13 Shoot the Crows
14 The Loft

Eating

● *on map*
Price codes:
see inside front cover

Expensive Nouvelle Irish hasn't really found its way to Sligo yet, although fajitas and tacos and thalis have arrived, and vol-au-vents and prawn cocktails never left. The big hotels all have sound restaurants with traditional potato-based evening meals. The classiest is at *Ballincar House Hotel*. The mood here is a kind of late seventies quiet, with big windows opening on to the gardens. The set menu is 4 courses and lots of it, with accompanying vegetables in side dishes, but well cooked, and nice desserts. Dinner around IR£18. Lunch is also good at around IR£12 for 4 courses. The restaurant at the *Sligo Park Hotel* is very popular, set in a conservatory area. The set lunch is IR£11.50 and there is pub food in the bars. Similarly in the *Tower*, which has a darker atmosphere with lots of deep brown panelled wood. Set dinner is fairly traditional and works out at IR£18. Some interesting sauces.

Affordable In town the nicest place is *The Loft*, in Lord Edward St. T46770, open 1800-2300. It has an interesting menu, which includes Mexican dishes, and a pleasant atmosphere. You might want to make a reservation here. Dinner around IR£15. In O'Connell St is *Bistro Bianconi*, T47350, open 7 days from 1730 till the customers stop, a cheery tiled place with the chefs making the pizzas in the window. Lots of vegetarian options and other Italian dishes. *The Embassy*, Kennedy Parade, T61250, looks like a big old hotel, which is what it used to be, but

County Sligo

now it's a restaurant and snooker hall. Traditional potato-oriented food, set lunch IR£9, dinner around IR£15. A pizza and dessert will cost around IR£13. In Market St is *Kamal Mahal*, T47700, a nicely decorated Indian place, quite authentic, offering a large menu with set thalis at IR£11.95 for a regular and IR£9 for a vegetarian. In Rockwood Parade, the little pedestrianized alley beside the river, there are a whole range of places about to open up. Up and running is *Pepper Alley*, serving Mexican food till late, closed Monday evenings. At lunchtime it's a sandwich bar. Also along here is another pub, *Fiddler's Creek*, T41866, which serves lunch till 1600 and evening meals till 2200. It has live music on special occasions.

Cheap For lunch there are too many places to choose from. The entire fast-food world is represented around O'Connell St, while a very trendy place to eat is *Beezie's*, T45030, in Tobergal Lane, the alley leading from O'Connell St to Rockwood Parade, which serves pub food. For internet freaks there is the *Galaxy Internet Café*, Riverside, T40441, open 0800-midnight, serving food all day, chiefly filled jacket potatoes, salads, breakfast, all at less than IR£3. The *Winding Stair*, Hyde Bridge House, T41244, might appeal to all those of us who still get pleasure from handling our printed material. It's a bookshop café, doing coffee, sandwiches and cakes. Its windows are a great place to find notices of upcoming events. For basic chip and potato meals you might try *The Tea House*, O'Connell St, or the *Roof Top Restaurant*, Wine St Car Park, T44421, which closes at 1800.

Pubs that do reasonable food include the *Ark*, High St; *The Harp Tavern*, Lower Quay St; *McGarrigles*, O'Connell St; *Donaghy's*, Lord Edward St; and *Murray's*, Connolly St.

Pubs & music Places to look out for music in are manifold. *The Ark* bar and, above it, *Schooner's Nightclub*, T42014, have karaoke and nightclub music, while the Embassy *Toffs Nite Club* has disco music most nights of the week. *The Harp*, Quay St has traditional sessions on Mondays and jazz at lunchtime on Sundays, while there are traditional sessions at *Foleys*, Castle St, on Saturdays, *McGarrigles* on Wednesdays and Sundays, and *Fureys* in Bridge St on Mondays, Tuesdays, Thursdays and Sundays. *MJ Carr's*, downstairs from the Loft, has traditional sessions on Saturdays and other forms of live music on Mondays. *Shoot the Crows* in Market St is a very trendy scruffy sort of place with unusual ladies' toilets and music most nights. *Donaghy's* has traditional sessions on Sunday nights.

Entertainment **Cinema** The *Gaiety* cinema complex, Wine St, T74004, has 7 screens. **Theatre** The *Hawk's Well Theatre*, Temple St, T61526, hosts travelling theatre groups as well as local efforts. *The Factory Theatre*, Lower Quay St, T70431, is home to the Blue Raincoat Theatre company, who perform there and at the *Hawk's Well*.

Festivals The *Sligo Arts Festival* is in **May** (T69802 for details) while the *WB Yeats Summer School* takes place in **late July to early August** and is worth attending, even if you don't approve of Yeats, for the music and dancing sessions (T42693 for details).

Shopping Sligo has the usual slew of outlets, but there are 3 places worth seeking out. *The Cat & the Moon*, 4 Castle St, Monday-Saturday 0930-1800. Sells exclusive designer jewellery by Martina Gillan as well as lots of other really nice, functional stuff by other Irish designers. *Michael Kennedy Ceramics*, Church St. Sells pottery by the eponymous potter, and very attractive and useful it is too. *Michael Quirke's*, Wine St. A butcher-turned-sculptor who carves figures from pieces of wood that he finds.

Transport **Air** *Sligo Airport* (68280) is 5 miles (8 km) west of town at Strandhill. There are daily flights to Dublin with connections to Europe. Taxis can be hired at the airport and there is a car hire service at the terminal, *Avis*, T68396. A bus service connects the airport with Sligo town. **Bus** There are four *Bus Eireann* buses a day connecting Sligo with Derry via Bundoran, Donegal, Ballybofey and Letterkenny. Sligo to Dublin buses leave Sligo three times a day calling at Ballysadare, Boyle, Carrick-on Shannon and Longford. To Belfast buses leave three times a day calling at Enniskillen. For Athlone there are two buses a day. Five buses a day connect Sligo with Galway. To Rosses Point there are four buses a day (none on Sunday), and for Strandhill there are four buses a day (none on Sunday). A bus to Ballina leaves five times a day (once on Sunday), connecting from Ballina with Castlebar, Westport and Newport. The bus station is in Lord Edward St, T60066. A private bus company, *Feda O'Donnell Coaches*, T 075-48114, 091-761656, runs a twice-daily service between Donegal and Galway calling at Sligo and lots of smaller towns en route. There are three buses on Friday and Sunday. At Sligo the bus stops outside Matt Lyon's shop in Wine Street. **Train** There are four trains a day to Dublin calling at Collooney, Ballymote, Boyle, Carrick-on Shannon, Dromod, Longford, Edgeworthstown, Mullingar, Enfield and Maynooth, T69888. **Car hire** Cars can be hired from *Hertz*, T44068 and from *Murrays Europcar*, Sligo Airport, T42091. **Taxi** *Joe's Cabs*, T68900. **Bike** *Conway Bros*, T61370, High St, Sligo; *Gary's Cycles*, T45418, Lower Quay St; *Flanagan's Cycles*, T44477, Market Yard, Sligo.

Banks *Ulster Bank*, Stephen St; *Bank of Ireland*, Stephen St. **Laundrette** *Pam's* Johnstone Court, Mon-Sat 0930-1900. **Communications** Post office: Wine St. **Tourist office** Temple St, T61201. Jul-Aug, Mon-Sat 0900-2000, Sun 1000-1400; Sep-June, Mon-Fri 0900-1700. | **Directory**

North County Sligo

Drumcliff, Grange and Cliffony, all the places along the N15, are well served by public transport since they are on the Sligo to Donegal route, with about 10 buses a day in summer in either direction. A day trip by public transport is feasible, with the last bus back to Sligo passing through Cliffony some time after 1800. Inishmurray is accessible by boat from Murraghmore (Rodney Lomax, T66124) or Rosses Point (Tommy McCallion, T42391). There is no landing stage on the island and any poor weather will prevent boats going out. | **Ins & outs**

Immediately north of Sligo town is Rosses Point, where the north shore of Sligo Bay juts out into the sea. It's a seriously quaint little seaside resort with a long sandy beach. Jack Yeats painted it, his brother wrote about it, and in 1257 Maurice Fitzgerald, the man who gave us Sligo Friary, was cut down here in hand-to-hand battle with Godfrey O'Donnell, the chieftain of another local clan. The reason for the battle no longer matters to the golfers, who now carry irons rather than swords around the ancient battlefield. A bus from Sligo travels out to Rosses Point six times a day. | **Rosses Point**

This might make a quiet weekend alternative to Sligo, where the population tends to stagger a little after 2300. **AL** *Ballincar House Hotel* has already been mentioned (see 'Sleeping on page 494), but in Rosses Point itself the place to stay is the **A** *Yeats Country House Hotel*, T77211, F77203. It has everything you could want from swimming pool to concessions at the nearby golf club and is a cheery, family-orientated sort of place. There are B&Bs strung out all along the road to Rosses Point and there is a camp site, *Greenlands Caravan and Camping Park*, T77113, at Hughes Bridge. Two people and a small tent costs IR£9.50. For food there is the *Ballincar House Hotel*, the *Yeats* or the *Moorings*, T77112, serving mainly seafood. | **Sleeping & eating**

From Rosses Point you can follow the northern coast road back towards the N15 and on to Drumcliff, where WB Yeats is buried. The main road cuts across | **Drumcliff**

County Sligo

The death of Diarmid

Benbulben is the mountain where, according to legend, the mythical warrior Diarmid died. He had been chased all over Ireland by his best friend Fionn MacCumhaill – angry at Diarmid for, having run off with his woman, Grainne – but the two heroes had reconciled and were out hunting boar. Diarmid was invulnerable except for his ankle, but a boar's bristle caught Diarmid in the foot and he lay dying. Fionn had the power of healing and could have saved Diarmid, but every time he brought water to his dying friend he imagined Diarmid and Grainne together and let the water fall, until eventually Diarmid died. There's a moral there somewhere.

the site of a sixth century monastic settlement founded by St Colmcille, the left-hand side of the road revealing the remains of a round tower, struck by lightning in1396, and the right-hand side a 10th-century high cross bearing the figures of Adam and Eve, David and Goliath, Daniel and the lions' den, and the Crucifixion, as well as mythical animals. Beside the high cross is the Protestant graveyard with the grave of William Butler Yeats and his wife George, with his famous epitaph 'Cast a cold eye/On life, on death/Horseman, pass by'. Yeats died in 1939 and was buried in France, but in 1948, in accordance with his wishes, his remains were dug up and brought here.

To the east rears **Benbulbin**, a massive dollop of carboniferous limestone that popped up in relatively recent times, geologically speaking. It appeared during the last ice age as a nunatak: an inland, cliffed, flat-topped peak

Around Sligo

standing out above the ice. David Marshall in *Best Walks in Ireland* describes an excellent, strenuous five-mile (8.5-kilometre) walk from close by Drumcliff. Wild plant spotters will be pleased to know that the mountain is a niche for some arctic alpine plants rare in Ireland – mountain avens, mountain sorrel, and purple saxifrage.

Three miles (five kilometres) east of Drumcliff is Glencar Lake, good for fishing and a walk to the waterfall that feeds the lough.

Lissadell

Famous for being rhymed with 'gazelle' by Yeats and as the home of the Gore Booth women (see box on page 500), Lissadell House is open to the public for part of the summer. The house is an essay in early Victorian austerity, its straight lines undecorated as if to strengthen it in its exposure to Atlantic gales. It is a single block, the usual outhouses being all shoved down into the basement and a tunnel leading to the stable blocks. Inside is a family house, full of paraphernalia from over the years. It still belongs to the Gore Booth family, to whose ancestors the people of Sligo owe much: the house was mortgaged to feed the tenants during the Famine and the next generation gladly entered into selling the land to the tenants. Visit is by guided tour and it's well worth the detour. ■ *T63150. June to September, Monday-Saturday 1030-1215, 1400-1615. IR£2.50. Tour lasts 40 minutes. Teashop and craft shop. N15 to Drumcliff. Turn west following signs to Carney and Lissadell.*

It's worth driving on to the end of the peninsula to Raghly, where there are views of the bay and coastline.

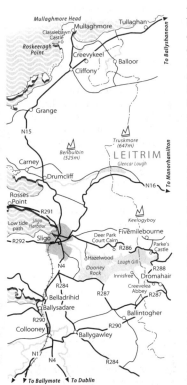

North to Mullaghmore

From Drumcliff the N15 heads on towards Cliffony where a left turn brings you to **Streedagh Point**: an excellent stretch of sandy beach, with caves at the far end. North of Cliffony is the **Creevykeel Court Cairn**, probably dating back to 2500BCE, standing on high ground overlooking the sea. It is called a court tomb because of the open courtyard made from stones at its entrance, perhaps used for worship or for mourners. Inside, the tomb itself tapers down and narrows towards the rear and is divided into two chambers; other chambers have been added at a later stage. Four cremation burials were discovered when the tomb was opened in 1935, as well as neolithic pottery. These types of tomb are largely centred around Sligo and Mayo and this one is considered the best and most intact of them all.

As the road approaches Mullaghmore, **Classiebawn Castle** appears, built in 1875 for the Hon. Cowper Temple, son of Lord Palmerston, whose family owned a large estate here. The castle is in the baronial style, austere in local

County Sligo

Constance Markievicz

Eva Gore-Booth, Constance's less well known sister, was a poet, feminist, lifelong socialist and pacifist. Besides her poetry she wrote on women's issues and used Celtic mythology in her work to illustrate women's right isssues

Lissadell's most famous scion is of course Constance Gore Booth, later Countess Markievicz, who was a revolutionary, condemned to death after the Easter Rising and the first woman elected to the British Parliament (while she was in gaol in Reading). She never took her seat, although she went to the House of Commons after her release to have a look at her name on her coat hook. She was nominated the Minister for Labour in the first, illegal, Irish Dáil and became the first woman cabinet minister in Europe, albeit one constantly on the run from the British. In the civil war she found herself on the antitreaty side, taking part in some of the fighting in Dublin. She was elected to the Dáil again in 1927, but would not take her seat. She was a staunch socialist and spent her large fortune on helping the poor of Dublin, bringing turf into the city

in her car for her constituents' fires. She died of appendicitis aged 59, having lost most of her possessions in various government searches of her Dublin house, and her body lay in the Rotunda Hospital, mourned by thousands, having been refused a state funeral by the Free State government.

In 1913, in the great lockout strike she had manned soup kitchens, in the Easter Rising she commanded the rebels at St Stephen's Green, she fought in the civil war, worked in St Ultan's children's hospital in the great TB epidemics of the 1920s, and spent all her money training young men and women in the republican cause. Yet she is remembered chiefly as the friend of a man whose ideals came dangerously close to fascism towards the end of his life, and as the subject of one of his lesser poems.

sandstone with a square tower and conical turret. The estate eventually passed into the hands of Countess Mountbatten, whose husband was murdered by the IRA in 1979 while boating from Mullaghmore harbour.

Mullaghmore is a quiet little fishing village, with another long sandy beach, and good for fishing enthusiasts. The area has lots of stables and both this beach and Streedagh are good for riding.

Difficult to get to, but well worth the effort, is **Inishmurray**, an uninhabited island four miles off the coast. Its last inhabitants sailed away in 1948, leaving behind a monastic site that had been in continuous use since its foundation by St Molaise in the sixth century, despite being sacked by Vikings in the eighth century. The monastic settlement is enclosed by thick dry-stone walls: much of this was reconstructed in the late 19th century, but the rooms built into the wall are probably original. Inside, the enclosure is divided into three areas, one containing what has come to be known as the men's church, where the later islanders buried their male dead, and a much older, smaller church known as Teach Molaise. In this enclosure are the famous 'cursing stones', *'bullauns'*, with smooth stones fitting into their depressions. Originally prayer stones, they came to be used for cursing one's enemies by turning them anticlockwise. In another section of the enclosure is a corbelled, roofed *clochain* used by the islanders as a schoolroom, but probably originally an oratory. The island contains many more remains, including inscribed stones around the island marking the Stations of the Cross, as well as another church known as the women's church, where the women were laid to rest. North of the enclosure is a sweathouse.

Sleeping Mullaghmore is a good place to stop if you intend to spend more than a day travelling around here. **A** *Beach Hotel and Leisure Club*, The Harbour, Mullaghmore, T66171, F66448. Very well-endowed hotel looking out over the harbour, with a swimming-pool, sauna and gym. Definitely a family holiday sort of place with a crèche in the summer. Restaurant. Nightly entertainment in the summer. **A** *Pier Head House*,

County Sligo

Mullaghmore, T66171, F66473. Smaller hotel, but with equally panoramic views. Restaurant. Nightly entertainment in the summer. **B** *Armada Lodge*, Donegal Rd, Grange, T/F63250. B&B off the N15 looking out over the beach. Around IR£36 for a double room. **B** *Mount Edward Lodge*, Ballinfull, T63263. B&B in lovely setting, with Benbulbin looming up behind. Around IR£36 for a double room. **C** *Dervogilla House*, T/F66300. Good, comfortable bungalow B&B with a couple of rooms to let. Between Cliffony and Mullaghmore. **C** *Truskmore House*, Donegal Rd, T66346. Good, comfortable bungalow B&B with a couple of rooms to let. Between Cliffony and Mullaghmore. **D** *Karuna Flame Hostel*, Celtic Farm, near Grange, T63337. Includes 1 double room for IR£16, bikes for hire, and meals available.

Both the *Beach Hotel* and *Pier Head House* have good restaurants serving seafood, and bars with bar food. At Drumcliff is *Yeats Tavern Restaurant*, and also *Davis's Pub*, T63117: near to the cemetery, does pub food, has music at weekends and traditional sessions in summer.   **Eating**

Horse riding *Horse Holiday Farm*, Grange, T66152, F66400. Easter-November.   **Sport**

West of Sligo

The little chink of land to the south and west of Sligo is home to the seaside town of **Strandhill**, with 21 miles (four kilometres) of sand dunes, and waves good enough to bring surfers from all over Ireland. Behind the village, **Mount Knocknaree** dominates the skyline with the cairn of Queen Maeve at its summit and the Carrowmore megalithic complex on its western slopes. **Coney Island** can be reached on foot at low tide, there is a golf course, riding centre and good fishing.

Miosgán Meadbha sits on the summit of Mount Knocknaree, a steep 1-hour walk from the car-park. At 33 feet (10 metres) high and 180 feet (55 metres) in diameter, it is visible from the surrounding countryside. The cairn has never been opened but is thought to cover a passage tomb built perhaps 5000 years ago. There are lots of other sites around the cairn, with huge north and south markers, and little huts that may have been lived in by the men who built the cairn during construction: when these were excavated, lots of building implements were found. The connection with Maeve, the Iron Age queen of Connaught, is traditional, rather than based on fact. ■ *24 hours. Free. From Strandhill follow the R292, southern coastal road, till you see the car-park opposite the Sligo Riding Centre.*   **Maeve's tomb**

Continuing on towards Sligo on the R292 brings you to this enormous site full of standing stones, stone circles, and dolmens. It was in use for a vast period in time, its oldest constructions dating back to the fifth century BCE, making it older than Newgrange (see page 692), and all the tombs were reused many times. There were once 84 monuments here, but quarrying and land use cleared a great number of them. Thirty monuments are now contained here in a preserved Dúchas site, excavated each summer by a Swedish team of archaeologists. There is an interpretive centre and you can watch the archaeologists at work. ■ *May to September, daily 0930-1830. IR£1.50. Audio-visual presentation, guided tours, toilets.*   **Carrowmore megalithic cemetery** *In 1999 the Swedes identified the oldest tomb in Western Europe here, 7,400 years old.*

AL *Ocean View*, Strandhill, T68641. The only hotel in town, small and comfortable, with a respected restaurant. **B** *Knocknaree House*, Shore Rd, Strandhill, T68313. A B&B close to the beach. **B** *Mardell*, Seafront, Strandhill, T68295. Small B&B with nice views,   **Sleeping**

very central. **C** *Rossford House*, Seafront, Strandhill, T68152. An attractive modern B&B beside the sea, open April to October. **D** *Knocknaree Hostel*, Strandhill, T68777. Hostel with family rooms, but no doubles, and camping possibilities in the garden.

Eating　　The *Strand*, T68461, serves bar food in the pub and more substantial food in the restaurant. *Rollers* in the *Ocean View* and the *Galley*, T68167, are also good options.

Pubs & music　　The *Venue* has folk and traditional music several nights a week and the *Strand* has music of some sort every night.

South and southwest of Sligo

Aughris　　Aughris is a tiny fishing village, almost but not quite unspoiled by tourism and worth a visit for its sandy beach, nice bar and, if you're into that type of thing, the promontory fort at Aughris Head. Just before Aughris, the road passes a tiny place called Skreen, where the 14th-century church has a much longer history, dating back to its foundation by St Adaman in 704CE. The graveyard contains box tombs, including one beautifully carved 19th-century tomb, and east of the church is a holy well. ■ *North of the N59, west of Sligo.*

Dromore West　　Heritage centre lovers will enjoy Dromore West for **Culkin's Emigration Museum**, where the original shipping agent's shop is preserved inside a larger building dealing with the Famine and emigration. ■ *Cannaghanally, Dromore West, T096-47152. May to September, Monday-Saturday 1100-1700, Sunday 1300-1700. IR£2.*

The coast　　Surfers will want to go to **Easky**, five miles (eight kilometres) northwest of Dromore, where assorted surfing championships are held. There is also a 15th-century castle. A little further along the coast is **Inishcrone**, with an excellent blue flag beach three miles (4.8 kilometres) long, caravan parks in the sand dunes, a golf course, and **Kilcullen's Seaweed Baths**, a beautiful Edwardian bath house where you can experience a steam bath followed by a high iodine salt water, seaweed bath in the original 1912 equipment. ■ *T096-36238. May to June and September to October, daily 1000-2100; July and August, daily 1000-2200; November to May, Saturday, Sunday, bank holidays 1000-2000. Tearoom.*

Collooney　　If instead of taking the N59 west you head south, your first port of call is Collooney, nondescript except for the **Teeling Monument**, which commemorates the Battle of Carricknaget in 1798 and Bartholemew Teeling's part in it. He was in the French invading force that had landed at Killala and was marching on its way to join the United Irishmen in Ballinamuck in County Longford. They had already met English forces that day at Tobercurry and defeated them, and were met in battle again by 600 English troops strategically holding a hill on their route: Teeling single-handedly shot the gunner in the English force. The French then moved on to Ballinamuck, where they were defeated and Teeling, being an Irishman, executed. The other claim to fame of Collooney is Markree Castle, at which you can stay if you can afford it: a 17th century pile with Victorian additions.

Tobercurry　　Pressing on southwards on the N17 brings you to Tobercurry, a working market town, which, as its advertising says, is probably as close as you'll come to the real Ireland. Its traditional Irish music scene is strong and in summer there is the South Sligo Summer School in the second week in July, when traditional

Irish music students come from all over Ireland and America to study under the masters. ■ *Contact Rita Flannery T071-85010.*

L *Cromleach Lodge*, Castlebaldwin, T071-65155, F65455. On the banks of Lough Arrow, accessed via Riverstown after Collooney. Very modern with panoramic views over the surrounding countryside, for those who really like to get away from it all. It draws more people to its nouvelle Irish restaurant (see 'Eating', on page 503) than to its accommodation. **L** *Markree Castle*, Collooney, T071-67800, F67840. A seriously grand, oak-panelled, 17th-century castle with a 3-star rating from the tourist board and lots of family heirlooms lying about the place. Horse riding on the estate, lots of walks and a good restaurant where a reservation is a good idea and dinner in very grand surroundings will cost around IR£20. **L** *Coopershill House*, T071-65108, signposted off the N4 halfway between Sligo and Boyle, is an utterly authentic and very graceful Georgian house where a couple of days will comfortably slide by in understated luxury. **AL** *Glebe House*, Collooney, T071-67787, F30438. More a restaurant with accommodation than a guesthouse (see also 'Eating', on page 503). It is set in an old rectory and has only six rooms so it has a homely atmosphere. **A** *Castle Arms Hotel*, Inishcrone, T/F096-36516. A reasonably priced 2-star hotel with a family atmosphere. **A** *Cawley's*, Emmet St, Tobercurry, T071-85025, F85963. Ten rooms in a restaurant-cum-guesthouse in the centre of the village. Mundane but comfortable. **D** *Barr Na Dtonn*, Easky, T096-49376. The village's only hostel.

Camping The *Atlantic 'n' Riverside Caravan and Camping Park*, Easky, T096-490001. Lots of facilities including TV room, laundry and shop. *Atlantic Caravan Park*, Inishcrone, T096-36980. Despite its name, takes tents also, but is very small with few facilities.

Nouvelle Irish cuisine can be found at *Cromleach Lodge*, Castlebaldwin (see 'Sleeping' on page 503), where seating is in a series of small rooms, best suited to small groups than couples, with a 5-course gourmet tasting menu at IR£25 plus, as well as à la carte and others. There is also *Glebe House*, Collooney, with good vegetarian options and fresh local produce. Easky's pubs are good for music in summer and there is food in several of them, and at Inishcrone your best bet for food is the *Castle Arms Hotel*. In Tobercurry, there is the restaurant at *Cawley's* (see 'Sleeping' on page 503), but there is also *Killoran's*, T071-85111, a pub with a great reputation for both traditional music and dancing and traditional Irish cooking and where you can try boxty, colcannon, and stampy. They also do a good line in tourist information about the area.

Lough Gill

There are lots of good things to do around Lough Gill, the laziest of them being to take the 50-minute cruise on the Wild Rose Waterbus (T64266) from beside the sports complex at Doorly Park. The tour goes to Parke's Castle in County Leitrim, passing the **Isle of Innisfree** – immortalized, or at least included, in a poem by Yeats – pauses at Parke's Castle for an hour, and then makes its way back along the northern shore of the lough.

Cycling or driving, the best thing to do is go clockwise round the lough, following its northern shore. Take the N16 out of town until you meet the R286. Turn right and right again following the signs for Hazlewood. It's a 30-mile (48-kilometre drive), the first stop on the drive being **Hazlewood Forest Park Sculpture Trail**, which is a park set on the shores of the lake full of carved wooden figures. Continuing on round the lough the next stop is the **Deerpark Court Tomb**, on a limestone ridge overlooking the lough. It is signposted

Colour map 1, grid C1

I will arise now, and go to Innisfree,
And a small cabin build there, of clay and wattles made;
Nine bean rows will I have there, a hive for the honeybee,
And live alone in the bee-loud glade

County Sligo

from the R286, just after the road divides and you take the Lough Gill Loop sign. The site is a 10-minute walk to the top of the ridge.

Parke's Castle, County Leitrim, is the next stop on the trip round the lough, back on the R286. It is almost entirely a reconstruction of the original 17th century building, which in turn was a reconstruction from the stones of an earlier castle. The original owner was hanged at Tyburn for sheltering a survivor from a wrecked Spanish armada vessel. It is now home to a heritage centre. ■ *Fivemile Bourne, T64149. April to May, Tuesday-Sunday 1000-1700; June to September, daily 0930-1700; October, daily 1000-1700. IR£2. Guided tours available, audio-visual show, exhibition. Coffee shop.*

Creevelea Abbey is well worth a stop on the circuit of the lough, on the R288 now. It has to be unluckiest of all the early friaries in Ireland, since it was the last to be built in 1508, was accidentally burned in 1536, and before it could be fully repaired was sacked by 1590, when Bingham, the Governor of Connaught, turned it into a stables. After his departure the friars were allowed back in, but then, at the end of his Irish campaign in 1650, Cromwell turned up and it was ruined once more. It's a very picturesque ruin with two well-preserved windows and some good carvings. There are lots of outbuildings and it is possible to get a sense of the life that went on here with refectories, dormitories, a kitchen and other less easily identified buildings. ■ *Dromahair village. 24 hours. Free.*

Re-entering County Sligo the road (the R287) rises and stays some distance from the lough until you see a sign for the Isle of Innisfree. The road then takes you down to the shore where you can gaze at the island and wonder that one person with a few words can change a place so much. There's a second opportunity to look at the lake in more touristy surroundings from Dooney's Rock, where the tour buses tend to congregate, just to make the place as much like Yeats' poem *The Lake Isle of Inisfree* as possible. From Dooney's Rock it is a short stretch back to Sligo.

County Leitrim

Leitrim, like Cavan, is a watery country, but Cavan collects the water into a thousand little lakes and Leitrim, being hilly, indeed a maze of mountains and hills, pours it all over the place. It is a boggy, soggy rushy land, full of burrowing streams, tiniest crevices of water everywhere and this I found very affecting like a tearful woman.

Sean O'Faolain, *An Irish Journey*

Here you are definitely off the main tourist circuit, and probably for quite good reasons. Leitrim is tiny, 50 miles wide with only two miles of coastline, but it has some mountain scenery to nod at and the large Lough Allen with its water sports and fishing. It shares its biggest attractions with County Sligo around Lough Gill and these have been covered as part of the scenic tour of Lough Gill on page 503.

Carrick-on-Shannon

Phone code: 078
Colour map 1, grid C1

A good place to base yourself for any length of time in Leitrim, Carrick-on-Shannon sits scenically on the shores of the Shannon, with lots of very expensive motor launches bobbing about as they do the long trip from Belleek in County Fermanagh to the Shannon, or even travel further on to Dublin. Carrick's one sight is **Costello Chapel**, an 1877 tomb to the wife of one Edward

Costello, a local shopkeeper. He bought a Methodist chapel and knocked it down to build this place, where he joined her in 1891. This wacky little oratory is stuck incongruously between two high-street shops. Their coffins lie either side of the tiny aisle, right in the middle of town, a little essay in self-importance.

Getting there

Carrick's main entrance route is by road, with buses from Sligo, Dublin and other towns stopping outside Coffey's Pastry Case close to the tourist office. There is also a rail link to Dublin and Sligo.

Getting around

The town itself is easily walked from one end to the other. If you want to visit places around the town there is bike hire available (see 'Transport' on page 505).

Sleeping

A *Bush Hotel*, T078-200014, F21180, bushhotel@tinet.ie Recently renovated, an old-town hotel where some of the old-world charm has survived the construction of theme bars, cafés, etc. **A** *Hollywell*, Liberty Hill, T21124. Guesthouse beyond the bridge in town, with river frontage and fishing in the garden. Nice rooms, comfortable lounge area with open fire. No evening meals. **B** *Aisleigh Guest House*, Dublin Rd, T/F20313. Small, amenable guesthouse with games room, sauna, nice big rooms. **B** *Meadow Vale*, Dublin Rd, T20521. Modern farmhouse situated about 1 mile (1.6 km) out of town, evening meals an option. **D** *The Town Clock Hostel*, Main St, T/F20068. Small hostel built around a courtyard in the centre of town. IR£18 for a double room but book it in advance. Open early June to late September.

Eating & pubs

Nothing to over-excite the palate here, but there is good food on offer at the *Oarsman* pub in the evenings with the mostly seafood menu making dinner around IR£13 plus. The *Mariner's Reach* also has food in the evening till about 2130, and very delicious and good value it is too. *Cryan's* is another pub where the food fills the stomach. The oriental flavour in town may be found in *Chung's* restaurant and takeaway. Carrick-on-Shannon is awash with pubs, the best of which do good music sessions – try *Cryan's* or the *Oarsman*. Young people might want to try the *Anchorage*.

Sport

Fishing *Geraghty's*, T21316; *Carrick-on-Shannon Angling Association*, T20489. **Horseriding** *Lisnagat Riding Centre*, T20598. Hacking and trekking.

Transport

Bicycle *Geraghty's*, Main St, T21316. Bike hire. **Boat** There are several companies that hire out cabin cruisers in town: *Emerald Star Line*, T20234. *Tara Cruises*, Rosebank Marina, Dublin Rd, T20736. River trips set off daily from the Marina, organized by *Moon River*, T21777. **Bus** The *Bus Éireann* bus stop is outside *Coffey's Pastry Case* near the bridge. The Dublin to Sligo bus passes through 3 times a day in both directions. 2 buses a day connect with Athlone and Sligo in both directions, T071-60066 for information. **Train** The train station, T20036, is on the Roscommon side of the river. Trains link the town with Dublin and Sligo 3 times a day in both directions.

Directory

Banks *AIB*, Main St. **Communications** Post office: Bridge St. **Tourist office** West Quay, T20170. May-Sep, Mon-Fri 0900-1300.

South of Carrick

Jamestown

If you are travelling through this part of Leitrim, Jamestown is a good place to pause for a while. It was named after James I by Sir Charles Coote, who organized the plantation of the area in 1625 (see page 674). The old town gate is all that remains of the original planter town. You will go through it as you pass by on the Dublin to Sligo road. The arch of the gate was removed in the 1970s. It is a peaceful Georgian village full of people swapping fish stories and a couple of good pubs, especially the *Arch Bar*.

Mohill   Mohill is serious fisherman territory, with five loughs in the immediate area, and its chief claim to fame is its association with Turlough O'Carolan, the last of the travelling bards. He was born in 1670, the son of a blacksmith who worked in an iron foundry in County Roscommon. The wife of the foundry-owner took a fancy to the child, had him educated, and when he went blind at age 18 had him taught the harp. He travelled the countryside playing at the big houses, with a guide and horse supplied by his benefactress Mrs MacDermott Roe. He met and married May Maguire and settled in Mohill. After her death he took to the road again. He was welcome in the wealthiest of houses, and played to Jonathan Swift, and his music has been revived in modern times by the Chieftains. His portrait hangs in the National Gallery. Close by Mohill is another literary association: Anthony Trollope worked for the post office in Ireland for some years, and on a walk in Drumsna discovered the ruin of a house that inspired him to plan the novel *The Macdermots of Ballycloran*. If you stop in Mohill, look out for the art nouveau Bank of Ireland building.

Other sites   Close to Mohill is the **Lough Rynn Estate**, owned by the Clements family, better known as the Earls of Leitrim. The third earl, a notoriously bad landlord, erected most of the 19th-century buildings on the estate, before he was assassinated in Donegal in 1878. The house and grounds are open to the public and there is a craft shop and restaurant. ■ *T078-31427. Mid-May to mid-September, daily 1000-1900. IR£3.50 per car, plus IR£1.50 per person.*

At the southeastern and southwestern extremes of the county are two small places good for fishermen: **Carrigallen** and **Roosky**.

North of Carrick

Travelling north from Carrick, you come to the place that gave the county its name, but drive slowly or you'll miss it. Beyond it is **Drumshanbo**, another fishing centre on the southern shore of Lough Allen. For many years this was a small-scale coal-mining area, and the **Sliabh an Iarrain Visitor Centre** gives lots of information about the traditions of the area, from the methods of coal and iron extraction to the unusual tradition in this area of the sweat house: a kind of Celtic sauna. ■ *April to September, Monday-Saturday 1000-1800, Sunday 1400-1800. IR£1.50.*

Another good reason to come to Drumshanbo is the **Joe Mooney Summer School**, held in one week in July, where there are classes in traditional music for serious learners but also lots of sessions in the bars at night and lots of set dancing to join in.

Oh, then, fare ye well sweet Donegal, the Rosses and Gweedore
I'm crossing the main ocean, where the foaming billows roar.
It breaks my heart from you to part, where I spent many happy days
Farewell to kind relations, for I'm bound for Amerikay.

Anonymous (19th century):
'Mary from Dungloe'

13

County Donegal

© Crown Copyright

All the superlatives that Bord Fáilte spreads out like jam for Ireland would still apply if the rest of the country floated off and sank in the Atlantic and all that was left was the county of Donegal. It's big country: a place for hiking boots and binoculars during the day and cosy corners in pubs at night. It stretches further north than anywhere in Northern Ireland and by any reasoning other than those of sectarian politics it belongs historically and culturally with neighbouring Tyrone, Fermanagh and Derry. Even in July and August the county is never crowded, unless you are stuck in Donegal town or Buncrana, and out of season you will have the place to yourself.

★ *Try to find time for*

  Climbing Mt Errigal

  Walking Horn Head

  Seeing Glebe House and Gallery

  Chowder and home-baked bread at Smugglers Creek Inn at Rossnowlagh

  Wandering round Donegal Castle

  Visiting the craft village in Donegal town

  Visiting the workhouse in Dunfanaghy (ideal on a rainy day)

County Donegal

Ins and outs

Getting there There are daily flights between Dublin and Donegal airport, T075-48284, F075-48483. The airport is situated not near Donegal town but in the Rosses between Dungloe and Crolly. Most travellers in cars arrive via Sligo on the N15 from on Enniskillen in County Fermanagh, but if your heart is set on wild Donegal then pass quickly through the diversions of Bundoran, Ballyshannon and Donegal town; only when Killybegs or Glenties is reached does the adventure really begin. Alternatively, hit the Inishowen peninsula directly by entering the county from Derry.

Getting around *Bus Éireann* does not provide comprehensive travel to all corners of Donegal but there are private bus companies that fill most of the gaps as well as competing with *Bus Éireann* in places. *McGeehan's*, T075-46150, is one of the biggest companies: their daily Dublin to Glencolmcille bus serving Donegal, Ardara, Killybegs, Kilcar and Carrick is very useful. Other companies worth using are *Feda O'Donnell Coaches*, T075-48114, 091-761656, *O'Donnell Buses*, T075-48356, *John McGinley*, T074-35201, and *Busways*, T077-82619. As an example of fares, *O'Donnell Bus* charges IR£7/IR£13 for a single/return between Dunfanaghy and Belfast while *McGinley* charges IR£9/IR£12 for a single/return between Dublin and Letterkenny.

Southern Donegal

Bundoran

Phone code: 072 Bundoran has a superb stretch of beach, but this has helped turn the place into a fairly conventional seaside resort packed with families in the months of July and August. It is a favourite destination for Catholic families from across the border seeking a respite from the marching season and there are some lively pubs at night, like the *Allingham Arms* on Main St. A big draw is **Waterworld**, an indoor complex with exciting-sounding gimmicks like a tidal wave, aqua volcano and tornado slide. ■ *T41172*.

A few miles further along the N15, before reaching Ballyshannon, the **Donegal Parian China Centre** is easy to spot on the right side of the road. There are free guided tours of the factory, purchases can be mailed home from the shop and there is an adjoining tearoom. ■ *T51826. Monday-Saturday 0900-1800, Sunday 1000-1800*.

Ballyshannon

The scruffy town of Ballyshannon bursts into life over the holiday weekend at the beginning of August. This is the time of the **Folk and Traditional Music Festival**, which has been going for over 20 years, with a programme of street entertainment, workshops and a busking competition through the day, and pubs and a marquee overflowing with revellers at night. Big names like Christy Moore, Mary Black, Dervish and Sean Keane have appeared in past years so expect a full line-up of talented performers and have accommodation booked in advance. ■ *For advance information, T51088, F52832*.

Tony Blair, the British prime minister, has a family connection with Ballyshannon, and the poet William Allingham (1824-89) was born and educated in the town. Known to the Brownings and pre-Raphaelites, he became a good friend of Tennyson (see box above) and worked in London before

County Donegal

Tennyson ...

Tennyson: Couldn't they blow up that horrible island with dynamite and carry it off in pieces – a long way off?
Allingham: Why did the English go there?
Tennyson: Why did the Normans come to England? The Normans came over here and seized the country, and in a hundred years the English had forgotten all about

it, and they were living together on good terms ... The Irish with damned unreasonableness are raging and foaming to this hour.

From a conversation between Tennyson and William Allingham, as recorded by Allingham

moving to Surrey near where Tennyson was living. His ashes are buried in the Church of Ireland, easily reached by walking up Main St and taking the left turning after passing *Dorrian's Imperial Hotel* on the other side of the road. Go to the left after entering the churchyard and look for the word 'poet' on a tombstone.

Continue walking further up Main Street and take the left on to Bridge Street, which leads to the R231 road signposted for Rossnowlagh. A short way along and a sign points left for **Abbey Assaroe Mills and Waterwheels**. Only one wall by the graveyard stands as testimony to a Cistercian abbey founded here in the 12th century, but their water-powered mill inspired the interpretive centre and its displays on the legacy of the medieval monks in Ireland. There is a small coffee shop, and a signpost near by points the way to St Patrick's Well overlooking the bay, where the saint himself is said to have once trod. ■ *T51580*.

Rossnowlagh

If time allows, the R231 road is a more attractive way of reaching Donegal town than the main N15, not least because it accesses the splendid 2½-mile (four-kilometre) sweep of sandy beach at Rossnowlagh. This is Robinson Crusoe land compared to the beach at Bundoran, surfers often have it all to themselves, and walks can be enjoyed across the hinterland of dunes and fields. Overlooking the beach from the road is a Franciscan Friary, open to the public for walking in the garden or taking tea in the tearoom, and housing a small museum run by the Donegal Historical Society. ■ *T51342. Daily 1000-1800.*

Essentials

Sleeping **L** *Sand House Hotel*, Rossnowlagh, T51777, F52100. This has transformed itself from a 19th-century fishing lodge into a superb hotel perched on the edge of a beach. Great views from the conservatory. **AL-A** *Dorrians Imperial Hotel*, Main St, Ballyshannon, T51147, F51001. Dates back to the pre-Allingham era and there is a small leisure centre with a gym and steam room. **B** *Creevy Pier*, Creevy, T/F51236. Like the *Sand House Hotel*, has a wonderful location overlooking Donegal Bay but a lot less expensive. Take the road out to Rossnowlagh from Ballyshannon and turn left at the signpost for Creevy after a couple of miles. **B** *Rockville House*, Belleek Rd, Ballyshannon, T51106. Overlooks the river. **C** *Col na Mara*, Creevy, T52715. Overlooks the sea outside of town. **C** *Hillcrest House*, Tirconail St, T52203. Back in the centre of town. **D** *Duffy's*, Donegal Rd, T51535. A useful hostel with camping space, bikes for hire, and 1 private room. **D** *Homefield House*, Bayview Ave, Bundoran, T41288, F41049. Hostel.

Camping *Lakeside Centre Caravan and Camping Park*, Belleek Rd, Ballyshannon, T52822. Overlooks Assaroe Lake and charges IR£9 for a tent.

County Donegal

Hiking and biking tours in Donegal

If you prefer an organized walking or cycling trip with food and accommodation sorted out for you in advance, the following companies all cover Donegal:

SOS Walking, An Bhealtaine, Gortahork, Co Donegal. T074-35374, F074-24797, info@sosdonegal.com http://www.sosdonegal.com

Countryside Tours Ltd, Glencar House, *Glencar, Co Kerry. T066-9760211, F066-9760217, country@iol.ie http://www.iol.ie/~country*

Go Ireland, Old Orchard House, Killorglin, Co Kerry. T066-9762094, F066-9762098, goireland@fexco.ie http://www.goireland.ie

Irish Cycling Safaris, Belfield House, Dublin 1. T01-2600749, F01-7061168, ics@kerna.ie htttp://www.krena.ie/ics/

Eating **The Sand House Hotel Restaurant** at Rossnowlagh, T51777, has a 5-course dinner menu that changes nightly, but stick with the more traditional dishes. The pub food at **Smugglers Creek**, Rossnowlagh, T52366, is excellent and the clifftop location is hard to beat. Stone-flagged floors and open fires characterize the place but extension work was in progress at the time of writing (due to be finished in early 2000). For quick lunches or coffee and cakes there are a couple of decent places in Ballyshannon, such as **Cúchulainn's**, Castle St, and **Grimes Kitchen Bake**, on Main St, not forgetting the coffee shop at **Abbey Assaroe Mills and Waterwheels** just outside of town.

Pubs & music Live music, traditional and modern, can be enjoyed in some of Ballyshannon's pubs throughout the summer and one of the best is **Sean Ógs**, Market St, T51585, with something happening every Wednesday and perhaps at weekends as well. On the other side of the road, **Dicey Reilly's** is worth checking out and on Bishop St the tiny **Thatch Pub** has character as well as live music most nights. Out at Rossnowlagh **The Smugglers Creek**, with timber beams everywhere, has traditional music every Friday and Saturday and has been recommended by travellers.

Sport **Golf** *Bundoran*, T41302. **Horse-riding** *Stracomer Riding Centre*, T41787.

Transport **Bus** *Bus Éireann* run daily buses connecting Bundoran and Ballyshannon with Donegal, Derry, Sligo, Galway and Dublin, T074-21309. *Feda O'Donnell*, T075-48114, runs its private buses connecting Ballyshannon with Crolly, Donegal, Dunfanaghy, Gweedore and Letterkenny as well as another service heading west for Galway and Sligo.

Directory **Banks** Main St, Ballyshannon. **Communications** Post office: Market St, Ballyshannon. **English Language Summer School** *Homefield House* (and hostel), T41288.

Donegal Town

Phone code: 073
Colour map 1, grid B2

A harmless little place, Donegal attracts far more visitors each year than the town warrants, possibly attracting them with its name, which makes it seem like the hub of the county. It's good for a couple of days stay – with its lively bars, one or two places to visit, and a lovely walk along the river – but longer than that and the traffic will start to irritate.

The name, Donegal (*Dún na nGall*) means 'fort of the foreigners', and it was probably originally established by Vikings. Later, the O'Donnell clan built a tower here overlooking the river Eske. They held it for a hundred years or more

The Annals of the Four Masters

Annála Ríoghacta Eireann, *The Annals of the Kingdom of Ireland, are a compilation of all the ancient histories of Ireland put together by Mícheál Ó Cléirigh, and three colleagues in the years following the English conquest of the area in 1607. These four friars left the church in Donegal town after it was granted to Sir Basil Brooke: as Franciscans they were not considered Catholic priests and were not able to move freely. They travelled post-Reformation Ireland gathering older manuscripts and making copies, in an attempt to collect all the history and culture of Ireland in the face* of the encroaching Anglicization. There are two memorials to the Four Masters in Donegal town – the obelisk in the Diamond and the new Catholic Church – but in fact the annals weren't written in the Friary here, but in Drowes, County Donegal between 1632 and 1636. They cover Irish history from the years before the flood to 1616 and several of their sources, older manuscripts held in other monasteries, are now lost, making the Annals an important source for early Irish history. Early copies of the Annals are in the National Library in Dublin.

before burning it to prevent it falling into English hands, when the town itself fell to Sir Basil Brooke after the flight of the Earls in 1607. Brooke planted the town with English settlers and laid out the modern streets, including the Diamond. The town passed into modern times little changed from the days when Brooke planned it.

O'Donnell's Castle

O'Donnell's Castle, in the centre of town is a largely Jacobean building, erected by Brooke with the 15th-century tower rebuilt and extended and a 17th-century three storey house added. It was abandoned in the 18th century and adopted by the Office of Public works in the late 19th century. The tower has been restored and holds displays about the history of the castle and the O'Donnell's, one of whom was St Colmcille (see page 523). The grand fireplace in the main room in the tower shows Brooke's coat of arms and that of his wife's family. It's a grand place to visit, at once a cosy house and a defensive tower, and the exhibitions inside are well worth studying. Visit before this place gets turned over to banquets as Bunratty has. ■ *May to October and St Patrick's Day, daily 0930-1830. Possibly open at weekends November to January from 2000. IR£2.*

Franciscan friary

Another O'Donnell construction is the very ruined but picturesque Franciscan friary, on the town side of the river Eske. It was built in1474 by Red Hugh O'Donnell and his wife Nuala O'Brien and, like most other defensible buildings in Ireland, was taken and taken again in the assorted wars between the clans and the English. At one stage there were gunpowder stores in the friary, which exploded and destroyed most of the buildings. In 1607 under Sir Basil Brooke the building became the Protestant church, and it serves as a graveyard now. On the opposite bank a quiet pathway leads behind bungalows along the river bank in a 1½-hour walk to Revlin Point, a route that has been popular since the turn of the century. There is an accompanying leaflet that tells you about the plant life you can see, which can be picked up at the tourist office.

Donegal Railway Heritage Centre

Donegal town has a collection of steam-train fanatics who are renovating old carriages, and hopefully will eventually resurrect a bit of the line and run trains. For now, however, you can visit the Donegal Railway Heritage Centre with lots of information, old posters and restored carriages and engines. Good for a wet afternoon. ■ *Old Station House, Tirconaill St, T22655. June to September,*

County Donegal

Monday-Saturday 1000-1730; October to May, Monday-Friday 1000-1600. IR£1.

Donegal Craft Village
Part shopping centre, part tourist attraction this is a purpose-built village where craftworkers have their workshops and sell their produce. You can watch uilleann pipes being made, observe a jeweller making traditional designs, or see potters hand-throwing their work, and of course you can buy what you like best. A good activity for a rainy day. ■ *Ballyshannon to Sligo Road. All year, Monday-Saturday 0900-1800; Summer Monday-Saturday 0900-1800, Sunday 1100-1800. Coffee shop, picnic area. Half a mile (800 metres) south of the tourist office.*

Essentials

Sleeping
■ *on map*
Price codes:
see inside front cover

L *Harvey's Point Country Hotel*, Lough Eske, T22208, F22352. Only 3½ miles (6 km) from town but its alpine location on the lonely shores of Lough Eske takes you a million miles away from the bustle of Donegal. Famous restaurant and inspiring opportunities for country walking (see box on page 517). **AL** *Abbey Hotel*, The Diamond, T21014, F23660. A very busy place with lots of night-time entertainment. Restaurant and bar food. **AL** *Hyland Central Hotel*, The Diamond, T21027, F22295. Very busy but comfortable hotel in the heart of the town. Big rooms, nice views of the river from the back, leisure centre with a big swimming pool available to guests, 2 restaurants. **B** *The Coach House*, Main St, T22855, F23229. Pleasant rooms in a lively pub with traditional music. En-suite and regular rooms. IR£15 single. **B** *Fisherman's Catch*, Waterloo Place, T22507. IR£31 for standard room, in quiet street. **B** *Railway Lodge B&B*, Tirconaill St, T23656. Right beside the railway museum, this is in a quiet area of town, away from

Donegal

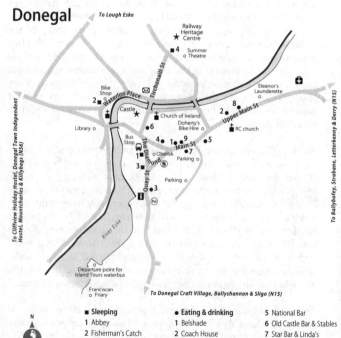

■ Sleeping	● Eating & drinking	5 National Bar
1 Abbey	1 Belshade	6 Old Castle Bar & Stables
2 Fisherman's Catch	2 Coach House	7 Star Bar & Linda's
3 Hyland Central	3 Four Lanterns & Harbour	Crusty Kitchen
4 Railway Lodge	4 McGroarty's Bar &	8 Talk of the Town
Bed & Breakfast	Stella's Salad Bar	9 Zack's

the fuss of a Saturday night. **C** *The National Bar*, T21035. Good value rooms in a fairly quiet pub. **D** *Cliff View Holiday Hostel*, Killybegs Rd, T21684, F22667. This is budget motel accommodation rather than a hosteller's hostel. Very comfortable with 6-8 beds per room, which have their own keys, and access to kitchen and lounge area. **D** *Donegal Town Independent Hostel*, Killybegs Rd, T22805. IR£15 for a double room in this regular hostel with attractive murals on the walls and garden space for tents.

Harvey's Point Country Hotel Restaurant, Lough Eske, T22208, is noted for its French and Swiss gourmet cooking and opens daily for lunch and dinner. Evening set dinner starts at under IR£25 and the calming views are thrown in for free. The poshest place in the town itself is the *Old Castle Bar and Stables Restaurant*, the Diamond, T21262, which is very popular and has all kinds of interesting sauces, including elderberry wine, garlic and rosemary and Grand Marnier. Lots of pine furniture and comfortably spaced. 1200-1600 for lunch, 1800-2200 dinner. IR£20 plus. Opposite the tourist office in Quay St is the *Harbour Restaurant*, T21702, with stone walls, pine beams and bric à brac. Nice food too – seafood and steaks. Very popular, not much standing room, open all day till 2230. Next door is the *Four Lanterns*, one of a fast-food chain doing burgers and fish things. The two hotels have busy lunchtime and evening restaurants. The set dinner at the *Hyland* is IR£17 and has a wide range of choices in a three-course menu. It's an old-fashioned kind of setting with lots of food. If it's less formal eating you are after there's *Just William's*, downstairs in the hotel, where you serve yourself from the counter and lunch costs around IR£5.50. Lots of space. Next door at the *Abbey Restaurant* there are basic potato dinners for around IR£11 for a main course. Around IR£13 for two courses.

For lunch or a very early evening meal the *Belshade Restaurant*, T22660, in the Diamond, serving inexpensive soups and fish-and-chip type meals is quiet and pre-sentable, while *McGroarty's Bar* in the Diamond not only does good pub food, but caters for vegetarians.

Eating
● *on map*
Price codes:
see inside front cover

The *National* bar has Irish music at weekends all year round in an unreconstructed fif-ties sort of place while the *Star Bar* has live music but a younger, Irish crowd and trendier music. Inside is *Linda's Crusty Kitchen* which does good cheap breakfasts and sandwiches and some hot meals. In the Diamond is the *Talk of the Town* with music of some kind most nights – check out the windows for details. The *Abbey Hotel* has a disco on Sundays aimed at the over-21s, and at weekends and when a tour bus calls in, as they regularly do, there is an organized Irish session, featuring the Londonderry Air and suchlike. In Main St is *Zack's*, a very trendy young spot where there is some interesting music.

Pubs & music

Fishing permits and licences for salmon and trout from *Doherty's*, Main St, T21119. **Golf** *The Park Golf Centre*, Ballyshannon Rd, T22779.

Sport

Bicycle Bike hire: *Doherty's*, Main St, T21119, Monday-Saturday 0900-1800. IR£6 per day, IR£30 per week. IR£40 deposit. *The Bike Shop*, Waterloo Place, T22515. IR£6/day; IR£30/week; IR£40 deposit. **Boat** *Island Tours Waterbus*, T23666. Orga-nize twice daily tours of Donegal Bay during the summer months. Departure times are determined by the tide. The guided tour includes a sighting of Seal Island, where 200 harbour and Atlantic seals breed. **Bus** *Bus Éireann* has services to Dublin, Cork and Limerick in the south, Galway and Sligo to the west and Belfast, Derry and Enniskillen in Northern Ireland. *McGeehan Coaches*, T075-46150, have a daily service between Dungloe and Dublin, which calls at Donegal, and a Glencolmcille to Dublin service, calling at Donegal twice daily. Another private company is *Busana Feda*, T075-48114 for a timetable and list of towns served, which has a twice-daily service between Donegal and Galway and less regular services between Donegal and Glasgow and

Transport

☛ *A pilgrim's progress*

In 1397 a courtier of King John of Aragon set off from France for Lough Derg in the hope that he could redeem the soul of his master, who had died too suddenly to confess his sins. When he reached Dublin from England he was warned of the dangers of 'savage, ungoverned people' but an armed escort took him as far as Ulster from where he continued alone. The courtier met King O'Neill who took him to Lough Derg where monks rowed him across to the island where he meditated and suffered visions of lost souls. On his return he spent Christmas with the O'Neills where "his table was of rushes spread out on the ground while nearby they placed delicate grass for him to wipe his mouth".

Donegal and Belfast airport. *O'Donnell Buses*, T075-48356, has a daily Donegal to Belfast via Derry service leaving Donegal at 0715. **Taxi** Taxi rank opposite the *Abbey Hotel*. Most taxis in town are individually operated, and their mobile number is lit up on the top of the cab.

Directory **Banks** *AIB*, The Diamond, T21016. *Bank of Ireland*, The Diamond, T21079. **Communications** Post office: Tirconaill St. **Launderette** *Eleanor's*, Upper Main St. Mon-Sat 0900-1600. **Tourist office** The Quay, T21148. Mon-Fri 0900-1600.

Lough Derg

Ins and outs Special buses run to Lough Derg during the pilgrim season, and bookings and transport information are available from *The Prior*, T61518 or T61550. The shore of Lough Derg can be reached on the remote R233 road from Pettigo.

Phone code: 072
Colour map 1, grid B2

Ireland's most historic penitential pilgrimage site lies to the west of Donegal town, and its lineage is indeed impressive. An 1184 text, the *Tractatus de Purgatorio Sancti Patricii*, referred to an island where St Patrick fasted to expel demons, and the earliest maps of Europe marked Lough Derg as the destination for medieval pilgrims in search of Patrick's island. A pope tried to forbid the practice in 1497, and Cromwell vandalized the place, but all to no effect, and an increasing popularity in the 19th century established the practice that is still followed every year between June and August, when thousands visit the small Station Island in the lough. They pay IR£20 for a retreat lasting three days, or IR£12 for one day, walking barefoot and living off black tea and toast (plus smuggled supplies of chocolate bars) without proper sleep.

The **Lough Derg Centre** in **Pettigo** has background information on the history of the pilgrimage site, and some of Seamus Heaney's poems in his Station Island collection may inspire you to visit and experience the place. ■ *Main Street, Pettigo, T61546. April to September, Monday-Saturday 1000-1800, Sunday 1200-1700. IR£2.*

Lough Eske and the **Blue Stack Mountains** that lie to the north make for a superb day trip by bicycle or car from Donegal town. Take the N56 heading north out of Donegal town, and look for the sign pointing to a road on the right for the Lough Eske Drive. A small road loops around the lough and it is possible to join up with the N15 road on the east side of the lough and return to Donegal that way. Walks in the Blue Stack Mountains begin at the northern end of the lough but a map is essential, and David Herman's book usefully covers this area (see box on page 517).

....

Walking books

Walking books for Donegal don't come   *Alan Warner's* Walking the Ulster Way
any better than Hill Walkers' Donegal *by*   *and Patrick Campbell's* Rambles around
David Herman (IR£3.50): over 30 walks   Donegal, *both available in paperback for*
with maps and directions and usually   *under IR£7. The Ordnance Survey*
available in bookshops around Donegal.   *Discovery series maps are essential for any*
Other books worth considering include   *long walks in the county.*

....

For luxury accommodation and food, **Harvey's Point Country Hotel** (see page 515) is   **Sleeping**
tucked away on the water's edge of Lough Eske. Food is served all day at the **Pettigo**   **& eating**
Inn & Milers Restaurant, Main St, Pettigo, T61720.

Southwest Donegal

Donegal to Killybegs

The N56 road leaves Donegal for the route west to Killybegs and Glencolmcille   *Phone code: 073*
and it is not long before Donegal Bay comes into view with Benbulben and the   *Colour map 1, grid B2*
mountains of Sligo providing an impressive backdrop. The first village,
Mountcharles, is strung out along the road and the attractive water pump that
might catch your eye is dedicated to Seamus MacManus, a local storyteller and
author. A sign points left down to the sea where a boat can be hired for sea fishing trips. ■ *T35257*.

The N56 speeds on through the village of **Inver**, where there is a small beach
and the *Rising Tide* pub. At the next village, **Dunkineely**, a detour can be
worth taking to **St John's Point** if a quiet picnic spot or scenic views seem in
order. The signposted road goes south for five miles (eight kilometres) and
ends in a surprising limestone enclave, where there is a splendid, little-visited
sandy beach and a lighthouse.

Back on the main road at Dunkineely the **Killaghtee Heritage Centre**
charges IR£2 for a fairly superfluous set of models of local archaeological sites,
but ask about a proposed Heritage Trail that may allow you to see the sites for
real. The neighbouring gallery has paintings of Donegal scenes for sale, and a
framed watercolour of your own place can be commissioned for between
IR£250 and IR£650. ■ *T37453. Daily 1000-1800.*

The last village before Killybegs is **Bruckless**, home to a holy well that has
some early Christian cross-slabs near by. There is a good B&B and a hostel
here, so the village makes a possible stopping point if somewhere quieter than
Killybegs beckons.

A *Bruckless House*, Bruckless, T37071, F37070, bruc@iol.ie An 18th-century house   **Sleeping**
overlooking the bay, furnished with artefacts and art from the orient. You can practise
your French or Chinese here. There are 4 rooms, 1 of which has its own bathroom.
B *Grove House*, Brenter, Dunkineely, T37297. A large house in a rural setting with sea
and mountain views. **C** *Cloverhill*, Cranny, Inver, T36165. A neat little house with a
lovely garden, and the small beach is 5 minutes away. **D** *Blue Moon Hostel*, Main St,
Dunkineely, T37264. Pleasant hostel with private rooms and camping space.
D *Gallagher's Farm Hostel & Camping Park*, Darney, Bruckless, T37057. An attractively converted stone-built barn with two kitchens, bikes for hire, maps for walking,
but no private rooms. Campers have their own facilities in a converted hay barn.

☞ *Gaelic place names*

The Irish language is alive and well in parts of southwest Donegal and place names on signs often appear in Irish as well as, or instead of, English.

		Cill Chartha	Kilcar
		Dún Chionn Fhaola	Dunkineely
		Gleann Cholm Cille	Glencolmcille
		Gleann Locha	Glenlough
		Málainn Mhóir	Malinmore
An Charraig	Carrick	*Málainn Bhig*	Malinbeg
An Caiseal	Cashel	*Na Gleanntaí*	Glenties
An Port	Port	*Na Cealla Beaga*	Killybegs
Ard a'Ratha	Ardara	*Tamhnach an Salainn*	Mountcharles
An Bhroclais	Bruckless	*Port Nua*	Portnoo
An Tráigh Bhán	Silver Strand	*Ros Beag*	Rosbeg

Eating Not a lot of choice, and it is better to bring a picnic or eat in either Donegal or Killybegs. At night, though, the *Castle Murray House Hotel Restaurant*, Saint John's Point, Dunkineely, T37022, is noted for its French-style cuisine, with dinner at around IR£25. On the main road at Dunkineely the *Killaghtee Tearoom*, part of the gallery and heritage centre, does simple snacks and cake, and fairly basic pub grub may be available in the summer from a couple of pubs in Mountcharles and Dunkineely. Nothing to write home about.

Transport *Bus Éireann*, T21101, runs a Monday-Saturday service between Killybegs and Donegal, stopping at Mountcharles, Inver and Dunkineely.

Killybegs

Phone code: 073
Colour map 1, grid B1

Killybegs, as your nostrils will soon inform you, is a major fishing port, and the large fish processing plant is what blocks the view of the bay when arriving from the east. The piscine theme is hard to escape in Killybegs; it accounts for the best dishes on restaurant menus, and there are various sea-angling events during the summer that culminate in a major festival in late July. Fresh fish can be purchased from the quayside each evening after the boats come in and it is easy to arrange angling trips. ■ *For example, the* Pinalia, *T31569, or the* Galilee Shore, *T31401. Enquire at the large Harbour Store, T31569, down by the quayside, or look for the flyers in the window for details of other boat operators.*

The Harbour Store has a good selection of fishing and nautical gear as well as wet gear, camping equipment and a selection of gifts. There is no tourist office but there is a town map and noticeboard in front of the Harbour Store and there are a couple of banks and a post office along the main street formed by the N56 running through the town.

For something non-fishy in nature, take a stroll up the hill from the main road to St Catherine's church to admire the Celtic-inspired carvings of gallowglasses on the tomb of Niall Mór MacSweeney (see box on page 520).

Without being facetious, you get the best of Killybegs when you leave the place, for as the road swings west out of town the seascape begins to take on some of the characteristics that make Donegal so special. Fintragh Bay comes into view, with the expanse of sea beyond it, while the mountains of Crownarad and Mulnanaff loom up inland. Look for the sign pointing left for a spectacularly scenic coastal route to Kilcar, and consider following the signs that appear along the route to White Strand or Muckros Head for a picnic spot and viewing point.

County Donegal

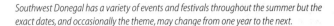

Festivals and events in southwest Donegal

Southwest Donegal has a variety of events and festivals throughout the summer but the exact dates, and occasionally the theme, may change from one year to the next.

Mid-March	Hillwalking Festival, Ardara	075-41518
April	Hillwalking, Glencolmcille	073-30248
May	Killybegs Sea Angling, Killybegs	073-31137
June	Seafood Festival: Narin & Portnoo	075-45302
	Sea Angling, Killybegs	073-31137
	Weavers Fair, Ardara	073-41103
July	International Sea Angling Festival, Killybegs	073-31137
	Painting Summer School, Glencolmcille	073-30248
	Irish Language & Culture School, Glencolmcille	073-30248
August	Sailing Regatta, Killybegs	073-31950
	Mardi Gras Festival, Killybegs	073-31950
	Sea Angling Festival, Kilcar	073-38185
	Street Festival, Kilcar	073-38185
	Donegal Dances Summer School, Glencolmcille	073-30248
	Archaeology Summer School, Glencolmcille	073-30248
	Fiddle Music Summer School, Glencolmcille	073-30248
	Patrick McGill Summer School, Glenties	075-51103
	Agricultural Show, Ardara	073-41103
September	Fiddlers' Weekend, Glenties	075-51333
October	Traditional Music Festival, Carrick	073-39333

Sleeping There is only 1 hotel, but B&Bs line the roads going in and out of Killybegs, especially the road to Kilcar, and it is difficult to differentiate them, for they are all variations on the bungalow theme, and most charge a fixed rate of IR£18 per person.

AL *Bay View Hotel*, Main St, T31950, F31856. Benefits from a smart leisure centre and indoor pool. **B** *Bannagh House*, Fintra Rd, T31108. The archetypal bungalow, but with an elevated site overlooking the harbour. **B** *Oilean Roe House*, Fintra Rd, T31192. This B&B differentiates itself by having 2 storeys. **C** *Ashville*, Donegal Rd, T31073. Within walking distance of town and charges IR£32 for a double and IR£19 for a single.

Eating *The Fleet Inn*, Main St, T31518, has a restaurant with a small menu featuring dishes like steamed brill for IR£14, as well as shellfish and steaks. Closed Sunday and Monday. *Cope House*, Main St, T31834, has a nautical theme pub serving bar food and a restaurant serving Chinese-style dishes. *The Sail Inn*, Main St, T31130, serves toasties, open sandwiches and burgers and has a seafood restaurant upstairs with an early bird menu. A little way outside Killybegs on the road to Kilcar, *Kitty Kelly's*, Largy, T31925, has a mixed menu of seafood, pizzas and pastas and last orders at 2130.

Pubs & music In the summer there will usually be musical entertainment in at least one of the pubs at night. In Main St the *Harbour Bar* is a good place to try and the Fleet Inn usually has music at weekends and midweek. *The Sail Inn* is always worth checking out for informal sessions of Irish music at weekends, and the *Bay View Hotel* has nightly entertainment.

Transport *Bus Éireann*, T21101, runs Monday-Saturday services between Killybegs and Glencolmcille, between Killybegs and Portnoo via Ardara and Glenties, and between Killybegs and Donegal. McGeehan's private buses, T075-46150, also stops in the

County Donegal

The Gallóglaigh

Gallóglaigh (a gall-óglach *is a 'foreign warrior'), anglicized to gallowglasses, came from the Hebrides in Scotland and were a mixture of Norse and Gaelic. When the Norwegian connection with Scotland had been severed in the late 13th century they were happy to hire themselves out as quality mercenaries to feuding Ulster chieftains. A gallowglass had two men of his own to look after his coat of mail, battle-axes, spears and swords. His prowess was vital to the task of holding*

back a cavalry charge, supporting and supplementing the native kern who had no fancy weapons but fought "bare nakyd, saving their shurtes to hyde their prevyties, and those have dartes and shortes bowes."

In time, leading gallowglasses were given land as a reward and eventually became part of the medieval aristocratic nobility of Ireland. The MacSweeneys were one such clan and another were the even more successful MacDonnells.

village on its daily services between Glencolmcille and Dublin, and between Letterkenny and Glencolmcille.

Kilcar to Glencolmcille

As the road from Killybegs approaches Kilcar the N56 bears to the right and goes over the mountains to Carrick, while a smaller road bears left into Kilcar and continues to Carrick along the coast. **Kilcar**, a small village and a centre for the Donegal handwoven tweed industry, is pleasantly low-key compared to Killybegs, or at least it is ouside of the sea-angling festival and then the street festival that raise the jollity level in the five pubs. Good food, pubs with music and accommodation are all available and *Studio Donegal* is one of the community's small spinning and handweaving factory shops that can be visited. ■ *The Glebe Mill, T38194.*

There are also opportunities to arrange guided walks and fishing trips or attendance at a weekend writing workshop. The new tourist office can supply a map and brochure of the local **Kilcar Way** walk. They are also planning a computerized display on local history and the tweed industry that may be of interest.

Further along the main road at **Carrick**, a road is signposted to the left for Bunglas and Slieve League and walking along this stretch of coast is one of the highlights of a trip to Donegal. From the main road it is a few miles to the tiny Irish-speaking village of **Teelin** and its pub, and just beyond it the road divides: left for Bunglas and right for a signposted Slieve League walking trail.

Walking trails Going left, vehicles can be taken up the steep and winding road around the southern slopes of Slieve League to a rough car-parking area and from here, Bunglas, there are awesome views of the cliffs and their shifting colours, while hundreds of feet below the silent sea churns up foam against coloured rocks (bunglas means 'green bottom').

Walkers have a choice of routes. From the first signpost for the Slieve League Walk the lengthier but less precipitous route leads on to One Man's Pass and the summit of Slieve League (1,952 feet/595 metres). Alternatively, walking can start at the parking area up a well-trodden route to Scregeighter (1,010 feet/308 metres) and Eagle's Nest (1,060 feet/323 metres; see box on page 521) and then a very precipitous five-foot-wide (1.5 metres) path to One Man's Path (this section is not as scary as the five-foot-wide steep stretch). While due warning needs to be given about proper footwear and avoiding

Eagle's Nest

David Marshall in his excellent Best Walks in Ireland *retells a story first recorded in 1867 about the point on the walk from Bunglas known as Eagle's Nest. An 80-year-old woman, Nanny O'Byrne of Malinbeg, remembered her great-grandmother who, when only nine months old, was carried off by an eagle from the nest on the cliff. The bird was pursued and the child was dropped near Carrigan Head; although seriously injured she survived to a ripe old age bearing the scars from her abduction. The nest was apparently destroyed in the early 19th century after human limbs (probably sheep bones) were discovered inside it. Eagles from Scotland have been spotted between Slieve League and Glencolmcille, and there is a chance they will nest here again.*

windy or misty days (there have been fatal accidents), reaching the summit of Slieve League is more than ample reward. On a clear day it should be possible to make out the distinctive shapes of Croagh Patrick in County Mayo and Ben Bulbin in County Sligo.

From the summit the walk can be continued to Malinbeg along the edge of the cliff, and from Teelin this amount of walking takes about six hours. It will take another hour or more to reach accommodation at Malinmore, or on a little further still to Glencolmcille and a choice of places to stay and eat.

Sleeping **C** *Cairnsmore*, Glen Rd, Carrick, T39137. B&B in a quiet little bungalow with Slieve League in the background. Single and double rooms sharing bathroom for IR£14 per person, evening meal available for IR£8. **C** *Don-Ross*, Shalvy, Kilcar, T38125. B&B a 5-minute drive from Kilcar with 3 doubles for IR£28 each. **D** *Derrylahan Independent Hostel*, Derrylahan, Kilcar, T38079, F38447. Popular IHH hostel with terrific views of the bay and good facilities. Includes 3 private rooms at IR£16 each, and camping space is also available. Telephone for pick-up from Kilcar or Carrick. Closer to the village, **D** *Dun Ulun Hostel*, Kilbeg, Kilcar, T38137, is more of a guesthouse with hostel accommodation and camping space included. The 8-room **D** *Cara's Hostel*, Kilbeg, Kilcar, T38368, is a thatched cottage with lovely traditional features. **D** *Slieve League Hostel*, Carrick, T39041. Has rooms above the *Slieve League* pub.

Eating Two of Kilcar's pubs, *John Joe Byrne* (known to everyone as *John Joe's*) and *Kilcar House*, serve basic pub grub while a third one, *The Piper's Rest*, T38205, has a well-deserved reputation for its seafood chowder, and a plate of oysters with a Guinness is a favourite combination here. On the other side of the road *Restaurant Teach Barnaí*, T38160, specializes in seafood and international dishes; main courses range from IR£8 to IR£12.

A mile from Carrick on the road to Glencolmcille, the stone-built *Gate House* tea-room, T39366, has indoor and outdoor seating for home-baked goodies, open 1000-1800, May to September. There is an attached craft shop selling handloomed knitwear. The *An Sliabh a'Liag*, T39041, does pub food.

Before reaching Kilcar on the road from Killybegs, the *Blue Haven*, T38090, is open for lunch and dinner and the food is reasonably priced.

Pubs & music Kilcar's 5 pubs are all within staggering distance of each other on the same side of the street and between them there will be music most nights of the week in the summer. In Carrick, between *Enright's*, T39070, the *An Sliabh a'Liag*, T39041, *Tigh Mhic Fhionnlaoich*, T39120, and the *Cellar Bar (Doc's)*, T39067, there should be a session of traditional music on most nights of the week.

County Donegal

Sport **Fishing** *Mc Breaty's*, Main St, Kilcar, T38492. Supplies tackle and information on where to fish. *SWD Angling Service*, T38211. **Horse riding** *Little Acorn Farm*, Carrick, T39386.

Transport **Bus** *Bus Éireann's* Killybeg to Glencolmcille service, Monday-Saturday, stops in Kilcar and Carrick, T21101. *McGeehan's* private buses, T075-46150, also stop in both villages on their daily services between Glencolmcille and Dublin, and between Letterkenny and Glencolmcille. **Bicycle** Bike hire: *Boyle's*, Main St, Carrick, T39195. *Derrylahan* hostel (see 'Sleeping' on page 521). **Taxis** *Curran*, Bogagh Rd, Carrick, T39141.

Directory **Tours** Walking: *Walkabout*, T38211. Walking through Donegal. **Tourist office** Should now be open in the Aislann Building in Kilcar on the road out to Carrick. **Writing workshops/literary weekends** T38448.

Glencolmcille

Phone code: 073
Colour map 1, grid B1

After leaving Carrick, instead of staying on the main road all the way, a more leisurely approach to Glencolmcille can be enjoyed by taking the signposted road to the left for Malinbeg. Along the way you will see a signpost for **portal tombs**, a line of six that make up the largest group of portal stones in Ireland. After passing them take another signposted left turn which ends in Malinbeg and its secluded, little-visited sandy beach of Silver Strand. The island you can see from here, **Rathlin O'Birne Island**, marks the northern entrance to Donegal Bay, and ruins of an early Christian hermitage are crumbling away on the island. Retrace your route to the junction, where a left turn leads to the *Glencolmcille Hotel*, and carry on to Glencolmcille this way. There is another sandy beach at Glencolmcille, but unlike Silver Strand it is not safe for swimming.

Folk Village Museum

Glencolmcille is a culturally vibrant, Irish-speaking area – the village itself is called Cashel and is basically one main street – well-tuned to tourism but thankfully on its own terms. There is a spirit of independence here that was nurtured by that most rare breed in Ireland, a priest with a socialist conscience, who came here in 1951 to a community impoverished by emigration and government indifference. Father James McDyer spent 30 years encouraging community-based industries and a video about him can be seen in the Folk Village Museum that he established in the village. Informative displays on history and geology make this a useful first call when visiting the area and there are guided tours around a series of cottages devoted to aspects of local cultural life, including a shebeen and a schoolhouse. A shop sells local wines and some crafts, and there is a tearoom. Local guidebooks and brochures are available from the

County Donegal

Portal Tomb

The Valley of Colm Cille

Glencolmcille is the anglicized form of Gleann Cholm Cille, the 'valley of Colm Cille', an important Irish saint (see page 537) up there with St Patrick and St Brigid. Colmcille (521-597), St Columba, achieved most fame after he left Ireland in 565 and established a church at Iona, but the ruins of more than one early church associated with him are to be found in southwest Donegal. Every 9th June there is a three-mile (five-kilometre) pilgrimage walk, known as a turas, around a set of inscribed stones in Glencolmcille that is undertaken in bare feet and lasts up to four hours. On the 23rd June there is another turas in Teelin.

museum shop and from the combined tourist office and craft shop in the main street; look for the lovely *Gleann Cholm Cille* guide (IR£5.95), illustrated in colour and including some of Rockwell Kent's paintings inspired by his stay here. ■ *T30017. Easter to September, Monday-Saturday 1000-1800, Sunday 1200-1800. IR£2.50.*

Local walk

An enjoyable walk, which is highly recommended, leads out of the village, past the Church of Ireland church and across a bridge, to the cliff top at **Glen Head** (769 feet/234 metres) and an old watch tower built in the early 19th century when a French invasion was expected (another one can be seen at Malinbeg). There are superb views from here of the jagged Sturral promontory, and the walk can be continued by following the coastline to Port and then over Port Hill to the deserted and hauntingly lonely valley of Glenlough. This is where the American landscape painter Rockwell Kent (1882-1971) stayed, and where he was prevented from returning to live in the early 1950s because his government refused him a passport, on account of his left-wing sympathies and a visit to the Soviet Union. Some years later Dylan Thomas stayed in the same house in Glenlough, but he was not enamoured of the place and took off, leaving unpaid bills for food and accommodation. The walk from Glencolmcille to Glenlough will take about four hours, but you could also cycle or drive to Port and walk from there to Glenlough. Ordnance Survey Map No 10 in the Discovery series covers the walk.

Sleeping

A *Glencolmcille Hotel*, Malinmore, T30003. The only hotel in the area. **B** *Corner House*, Cashel, T30021. On the road to Ardara, 5 minutes from the Folk Museum. **B** *Ros Mór*, Malinmore, T30083. A short way from Cashel, and overlooks Rathlin O'Birne Island. **C** *Atlantic Scene*, Dooey, T30186. Outside the village. Close to the hostel and shares with it breathtaking views of the Atlantic. **D** *Dooey Hostel*, T30130, F30339. This honourable establishment was a founding member of the IHO, and is a mile (less than 2 km) from the village. Superb location overlooking the bay and with part of the building built on to the rockface. Includes 6 private rooms for IR£14 each and camping space for IR£3.50.

Eating

The *An Chistin Restaurant*, T30213, above *Foras Cultúir Uladh* (Ulster Cultural Institute) on the same road as the Folk Museum, is appropriately devoted to traditional Irish cooking and has fresh seafood on a daily basis, open 0930-2130. *Teach an Lása*, T30116/30363, is a restaurant and teashop above the Lace House in the main street, and seafood is also the speciality here at night. The Folk Museum has a tearoom serving home-made scones and light meals between 1000 and 1800, and the *Óstán Ghleann Cholm Cille* pub in the main street, T30003, has bar food and a small restaurant. Out at Malinbeg overlooking Donegal Bay, *Silver Strand House*, T30220, is a seafood restaurant in the IR£15 to IR£20 range.

County Donegal

Irish language and culture courses

Between April and October a rich variety of courses are held around Glencolmcille and Glenfin. Irish language courses cater for complete novices as well as those wishing to improve their fluency, and the bilingual cultural activity programmes are open to all. For details of all the courses – Irish, hill-walking, archaeology, landscape & culture, marine painting, Donegal dances, celtic pottery, flute playing, bodhrán playing, and tapestry weaving – contact Oideas Gael, Gleann Cholm Cille, Co. Dhún na nGall, Éire (Oideas Gael, Glencolmcille, Co. Donegal, Ireland), T30248, F30348, oidsgael@iol.ie http://oideas-gael.com A weekly Irish course is IR£110, cultural activity courses, from three days to a week, cost IR£70-IR£90. Accommodation can be arranged from IR£60 a week sharing a self-catering house to IR£125 a week for B&B and

Pubs & music Glencolmcille is not Killarney, which means traditional music is not on tap, but when it is played in the pubs or at the fiddle festival in early August you can be sure you are hearing the real thing. *Roarty's Bar*, T30273, and *Glen Head Tavern*, T30008, both in Cashel, have fairly regular sessions.

Shopping A little south of the village on the R263 in Malin More Valley there is the *Glencolmcille Woollen Mill* shop, T30069, open daily during the summer, Monday to Friday 0930-2100, and at weekends 1000-1900. Quality knitwear is produced here in a small factory open to the public for demonstrations of knitting, hand-loomed spinning and hand-weaving of Donegal tweeds. As well as clothes, the shop stocks Donegal china, ceramics and jewellery. Handmade garments are also on sale at *Lace House*, and the craft shop in the Folk Museum has a range of knitwear, pottery and other handicrafts. Original paintings by Kenneth Ring are on sale in the *Marine Art Gallery*, Straide, T30126.

Sport **Outdoor activities** *Malinmore Outdoor Pursuits Centre*, T30123. Diving, canoeing, hill walking, boat trips and archaeological trails, among other activities.

Transport **Bicycle** *An Phríomhrsráid*, T39195. Bike hire. **Boat hire** T39117. **Bus** *McGeehan's* private buses, T075-46150/46101, connect Glencolmcille with Dublin, daily, via Carrick, Kilca, Killybegs, Ardara, Donegal and Cavan on one route and with Killybegs, Fintown and Letterkenny on their second route.

Directory **Hospitals and medical services** Doctor: T30234. **Tourist office** *Lace House*, T30116, craft shop in the main street, Jun-Aug, daily 1000-1800.

Northern Donegal

North to Gweebara Bay

Phone code: 075

If you have a bike then cycle the minor road from Maghera to Port (11 miles/17 km) through lonely, unspoilt scenery.

The road to Ardara from Glencolmcille travels through the Glengash Pass with its intoxicating views of Loughros Beg Bay, framed by mountains and luring one to take the road that is signposted on the left for Maghera and its caves. This road cuts its way through the rock, as does the magnificent Assarancagh Waterfall, passed on the route. A signposted way takes you to the beach in 15 minutes but don't explore the caves without checking the state of the tide. From Ardara there is an equally scenic five-mile (eight-kilometre) route

County Donegal

leading out along the north side of the bay to the sparkling white stones at Loughros Point.

Ardara

Ardara is a centre for the manufacture of handwoven tweed and handknit garments, and the **Heritage Centre** in the centre of town has an interesting exhibition on the history of the industry, with a weaver busy at work on the premises. ■ *T41262. Easter to September, Monday-Saturday 1000-1800, Sunday 1400-1800. Free.*

The Romanesque-style Catholic church in town has a startling wheel window at the west end: *Christ Among the Doctors*, designed by the Irish artist Evie Hone in 1953.

Dawros Head

Dawros Head to the north of Ardara might look suitably remote on a map, but a vast sandy and safe beach at Narin and Portnoo and nearby camp and caravan sites combine to make this corner of Donegal very popular with families on holiday from other parts of Ulster. Come here outside of summer, however, and it's another proposition altogether. A picnic spot worth seeking out whatever the season is **Doon Fort**, situated on a tiny island in the middle of Lough Doon. To reach it, take the road signposted to Rosbeg on the road for Ardara outside of Narin, and then a right turn just past a school on to a narrow lane. Look for a sign advertising boats for hire on Doon Lake, and here a rowing boat can be rented for IR£3 to reach the fort.

Sleeping

A *Woodhill House*, T41112, F41516, yates@iol.ie   Under 2 miles (3 km) from town taking Woodhill Rd from the Diamond. Offers the best accommodation, and restaurant, in the area. **B** *Greenhaven*, Portnoo Rd, Ardara, T/F41129. Named after a shipwreck the ship's wheel and mast-head lamp of which now decorate the breakfast room. A comfortable place within walking distance of town. **C** *Brae House*, Front St, Ardara, T/F41296. In the centre of town, but with its own parking area. **C** *Whinecrest*, Loughros Point, T41254. Well and truly away from it all with miles of beach, a turf fire, and a piano in the guest room. Open June to September. **D** *Drumbaron Hostel*, the Diamond, Ardara, T41200. IHO hostel with over a dozen beds, flagstone floors, and 1 private room for IR£12.

Camping *Dunmore Caravan and Camping Park*, Dawros Head, T45121. and *Tramore Beach Caravan & Camping Park*, Dawros Head, T51491.

Eating

Woodhill House Restaurant, T41112, with a licensed bar and occasional music, has a well-deserved reputation for good food; expect to pay around IR£25. There is a tea-room in the Heritage Centre serving sandwiches and cakes. There are 13 pubs in Ardara and some of them serve food in between their efforts at slaking the mighty thirst of the town. From the Diamond, cross the bridge for the road to Glenties and *Nancy's Bar*, T41187, serving toasties and meals, is on the right. *Charlie's West End Bar*, Main St, serves standard pub grub.

Shopping

There are a number of factory shops in Ardara and they are all worth sampling for their share of shirts, hats, caps, ties, socks, grandfather shirts, table linen, scarves, rugs and throws. Their tweeds and knitwear, which find their way into Bloomingdales and Liberty's, include items that are sold only in their own stores. In Front St you will find *Bonner*, T41196, and *Kennedy*, T41106, while *McGills*, T41262, is at the west end of Main St. Outside of town on the Killybegs Rd you can buy tweeds and knitwear from *John Molloy*, T41133, and in the summer there are free tours of the factory.

County Donegal

The Navvy Poet

Patrick MacGill (1889-1963) was 12 when he became a bonded servant at Strabane's hiring fair, a slave market by any other name, and two years later he was in Scotland as a 'tatie-hoker' (potato digger). Later a labourer on the railways, hence the 'navvy poet', MacGill wrote two novels – Children of the Dead End and The Rat-Pit – that shock the reader with their desolate tales of poverty and emigration.

However, they only came back into print in the 1980s. Perhaps no other writer has so successfully captured the Third-World lifestyle of Ulster's poor and their stoical resistance, but his Glenmornan is also worth reading for its anti-clerical blast. Glenties, where the writer grew up as the eldest of eleven children, is home to an annual MacGill summer school, run by his niece Mary Clare O'Donnell. T51103.

Sport **Horse-riding** *Castle View Ranch*, T41212. Rides on the beach at Loughros Point.

Transport **Bicycle** Bike hire: *Don Byrne Bikes*, West End, Ardara, T41658. *Drumbaron Hostel* (see 'Sleeping' on page 525). **Bus** *Bus Éireann*'s Dublin to Donegal service is extended to Ardara on a Friday. A local, Monday-Saturday, service also runs between Killybegs and Portnoo via Ardara in July and August, and the rest of the year between Killybegs and Glenties via Ardara on Tuesday and Thursday only, T074-21309. *McGeehan's Coaches*, T075-46150, also run through Ardara on routes to Dublin, Glencolmcille and Letterkenny.

Directory **Bank** *Diamond*, Ardara. **Communications** Post office: opposite the Ulster bank on the Diamond, Ardara. **Tourist office** Tourist information available at the entrance to the *Heritage Centre*, T41262 (see page 525).

Glenties and around

Phone code: 075

Brian Friel's play, Dancing at Lughnasa, is set in a house in Glenties.

Glenties is every bit as neat and pristine as you would expect for a four-times winner of the national Tidy Towns Award, and the town is a comfortable place to stop off for refreshments or even a night's stay to enjoy a night of traditional music in the many pubs. For quiet walks or cycle trips away from tourist attractions, there are scenic diversions to Dooey Point to the north and Fintown inland to the east, and the latter also provides an interesting route to Letterkenny and Derry, if there is not enough time to take in the northern coastline.

St Conal's Museum & Heritage Centre

There is no tourist office in Glenties but information is available from the hostel or St Conal's Museum & Heritage Centre, at the Ardara end of town, which houses a miscellany of local memorabilia relating to the Famine era, a railway line which once serviced the town and assorted bits and pieces. ■ *June to September, Monday-Friday 1100-1300 and 1430-1700, Saturday and Sunday 1430-1800. IR£1.*

Dooey Point

From Glenties the N56 goes north to Maas before crossing a bridge on the River Gweebarra and then, at Lettermacaward, a coast road is signposted to the left for Dooey Point at the end of the peninsula. The scenic road, with picnic tables along the way, ends in a cul-de-sac, but walking over the dunes from here leads to a long beach with fine views of the two bays.

Inland to Ballybofey

The R250 from Glenties heads inland through bleak moorland and valley to Fintown, with poetic glimpses of the River Finn rushing into a lake surrounded by heather-coloured hills. A little way past the lake the R252 can be picked up for Ballybofey, where there is a very interesting hostel with horse-riding facilities and information on local walks in the hills (see 'Sleeping' below). Bikes can also be hired here, and if you want a couple of days away from Bord Fáilte land this is the place to stay.

Sleeping

A *Highlands Hotel*, Main St, Glenties, T51111, F51564. The only hotel in the area. B *Avalon*, Glen Rd, Glenties, T/F51292. B&B in a bungalow. B *Marguerite's*, Lower Main St, Glenties, T51699. Town house B&B. C *Aileach*, Station Rd, Glenties, T51326. Bungalow B&B. D *Campbell's Holiday Hostel*, Glenties, T51491, F51492. A welcoming place, on the left side of the road as you enter Glenties from Ardara. D *Finn Farm Hostel*, Cappry, Ballybofey, T074-32261. No need to book in advance at this hostel, where there is also camping space. D *Fintown Hostel*, Fintown, T46244. Has a dozen beds and 3 private rooms for IR£20 each, but you need to phone in advance and make a booking.

Eating

Not a great deal of choice, but the *Highlands Hotel* in the middle of Glenties is a comfortable hostelry with a comfortable and spacious eating area for bar food and meals, as well as a separate restaurant. A pasta dish or a vegetarian salad with brown bread and tea is IR£4.70 in the bar and in the hotel's *Owenea Restaurant*, T51111, grills, chicken, duck and fish dishes are between IR£7 and IR£10.

Pubs & music

Glenties has some good pubs and *John Joe's Bar*, Main St, T51333, is always worth a visit when sessions of traditional music are on. *Paddy's Bar*, Main St, T51158, usually has sessions on a Wednesday. *The Limelight & Molloy's Bar*, Main St, T51118, has a popular disco at weekends. *The Glen Tavern*, halfway between Glenties and Fintown, is famous for its musical entertainment on a Saturday night.

Transport

Bus *McGeehan's* buses, T46150, stop in Glenties and Fintown and so do *Bus Éireann's* Dublin – Donegal – Killybegs bus and the local Killybegs to Glenties service.

The Rosses

Phone code: 075
Colour map 1, grid A1

The Rosses is a rocky stretch of land, a stalwart Gaeltacht area, that takes in Dungloe in the south, Burtonport on the coast from where boats leave for Arranmore Island, and Crolly in the north.

Ins & outs

McGeehan's Coaches, T46150, have a daily service in the summer between Dublin and Burtonport via Dungloe, Donegal and Enniskillen. *Feda O'Donnell* buses, T48114, run a limited service between Annagry to Killybegs, which stops in Dungloe, but check which days the bus operates. *O'Donnell Buses*, T48356, run a daily service that leaves Donegal early in the morning to reach Belfast at noon via Derry and stopping at Dungloe, Burtonport, Dunfanaghy, Cresslough and Letterkenny. *Bus Éireann* does not serve the Rosses.

Dungloe and Burtonport

Dungloe (An Clochán Liath) is not a particularly attractive place and, apart from having a quick meal here, there is little reason to linger. There is a small tourist office in Main Street. ■ *T21297. June to September, Monday-Saturday 1000-1300 and 1400-1800.*

At the end of July and beginning of August the annual Mary from Dungloe Festival livens up the town, but the festival itself is an utterly synthetic event dating from the 1960s, which serves mainly as an excuse for late-night drinking.

County Donegal

The Gaeltacht

The Gaeltacht means areas where Irish is still spoken: despite sustained government encouragement and vigorous support from concerned groups, some people claim that the term is becoming more and more notional because spoken Irish is in terminal decline. Supporters, however, can point to the burgeoning applications for places on language summer schools, the Irish-language television and radio stations, and places such as Glencolmcille and the Rosses where spoken Irish seems alive and well. Donegal has the largest Gaeltacht areas in the country but pockets can also be found in Connemara, Dingle, the Ring area west of Waterford, Ballingeary in Cork, west Mayo near Belmullet and a vigorous community in county Meath where Gaeltacht families were resettled in the 1930s.

Burtonport (Ailt an Chorráin) is the departure point for Arranmore Island, which is the main attraction of the Rosses. The small town is also a centre for sea angling and fishing trips can be organized with the Burtonport Sea Angling and Boating Centre on their 36-foot (11-metre) boat. ■ *T/F42077.*

Sleeping **A** *Delaney's Hotel*, Main St, Dungloe, T21033. **B** *Campbells Pier House*, Burtonport, T42017. Close to the pier and convenient for trips to and from Arranmore. **B** *Park House*, Burtonport, T21351. Caters especially for fishing folk. **B** *Sea View*, Mill Rd, Dungloe, T21353. B&B, which overlooks Dungloe Bay and is walkable from the town. **D** *Greene's Hostel*, Cornmare Rd, Dungloe, T21943. Has over 20 beds, including 7 private rooms for IR£19 each, and has bikes for hire.

Eating The *Courthouse Restaurant*, opposite the hotel on Main St in Dungloe, T21459, does lamb and steaks for IR£7-IR£10, and a few doors down the *Riverside Bistro*, T21062, has a slightly more interesting menu with 'surf and turf' for IR£12 and seafood, such as sea bass for IR£10.50. In Burtonport, the affordable *Lobster Pot Restaurant* in the main street, T42012, serves seafood and meat and has *Kelly's Bar* alongside.

Arranmore Island

Getting there *Arranmore Island Ferries Service*, T20532, runs an all-year service from Burtonport. In July and August there are 8 boats departing daily (7 on Sunday) from 0830 to 2000 and returning between 0900 and 2130. Between April and June, and in September, there are 6 to 7 journeys a day, and around 5 a day the rest of the year. IR£6 return for passengers, IR£18 for cars.

Colour map 1, grid A1 The boat trip to Arranmore, 5½ miles by 3 miles (nine kilometres by five kilometres), only takes 25 minutes; while there are places to stay overnight, a day trip with picnic provisions is feasible because the island can easily be walked around in a day if you catch the first and last ferries. Most of the 900 inhabitants live on the eastern side of the island, around where the ferry lands at **Leabgarrow**, and to the south around **Aphort**, but to enjoy the fresh air, a spot of ornithology and views from high ground

Arranmore Island

County Donegal

head inland from Leabgarrow on the road that terminates at the lighthouse in the northwest. Another enjoyable walk goes to **Torries** in the southwest, looking across to uninhabited **Green Island**. It is also to possible to follow the little-known **Arranmore Way**, which is signposted on the island with colour-coded routes, but unfortunately the Way is not regularly waymarked and is not indicated on the relevant Ordnance Survey map, No 1. Call in at the shop next to *Phil Bans Bar* for an island map that does show the route.

B *Glen Hotel*, T20505. One-star establishment to the west of the ferry, with 10 rooms. **C** *Bonners Bed and Breakfast*, T20532. Conveniently situated close to where the ferry lands. By the pier, *Bonners* also manage the *Ferryboat Restaurant*, T20532, which serves standard meals, or there is the small restaurant at the hotel. Some of the 6 pubs on the island serve light meals, including *Phil Bans Bar* near the pier in Leabgarrow and *O'Donnell's* at Aphort.

Sleeping & eating

Upper Rosses

If not visiting Arranmore, the chances are you will skip the Upper Rosses by travelling directly between Dungloe and Crolly, but the road via Burtonport and Annagry has mixed diversions along the way, including a signposted road that leads to **Cruit Island** across a small bridge. There are beaches and scenic views of the bay that on a sunny day make a quiet destination for a picnic.

Back on the road to Annagry the village of Kincasslagh has local fame for its hotel, the *Viking House* owned by the inordinately popular Irish singer, Daniel O'Donnell, who hails from here. Beyond the village are the reedy waters of **Mullaghderg Lough**, near where a sign points to tiny **Donegal airport**. The road continues on to a T-junction, where it meets the N56 just outside the village of Crolly (Croithlí), which marks the boundary with the Gweedore area. Just before the village a sign points the way to *Leo's Tavern*, Menalck, home to both the group Clannad and the singer Enya, with gold and platinum discs lining the pub's walls and regular singsongs in the evening

A *Viking House*, T43295. Hostel owned by Daniel O'Donnell. A couple of miles outside of Crolly the (**D**) *Screag An Iolair Mountain Centre*, Tor, T48593, is a hostel that receives rave reviews from travellers who enjoy the physical and metaphysical comfort of a laid-back retreat some 800 feet (250 metres) up in the mountains. Open from March to late October, with 15 beds, three private rooms at IR£17 each, and a free pick-up from Crolly or Gweedore if you arrange this in advance. This is the place to stay if you desire rural bliss with sociable evenings thrown in as a bonus.

Sleeping & eating

Gweedore to Dunfanaghy

There are two routes between Gweedore and Gortahork: the coastal R257 road that runs west of Gweedore to Bunbeg, Derrybeg and Magheroarty before rejoining the N56 just before Gortahork, and the main N56 itself that travels inland.

Phone code: 075 (Tory Island and Gortahork to Dunfanaghy: 074)

This accesses the departure point for ferries to Tory Island from Bunbeg and Magheroarty, but as it passes on through Bunbeg and neighbouring Derrybeg there is little reason to stop until reaching a viewing point off the road at **Bloody Foreland**. The name suggests the site of another ungodly massacre from a chapter of Ireland's relations with the English, so it comes as a pleasant surprise to discover that the term refers to the startling red hue that the setting

Coastal route

County Donegal

sun casts on the rocks. As the R257 continues eastwards the unmistakable outline of Tory Island stays in view and Horn Head rears up in the east.

Inland route The N56 has its own unforgettable charisma as it takes you through empty countryside so shockingly beautiful that you will wonder what everyone is doing in Killarney when places like this exist. About nine miles (15 kilometres) south of Falcarragh look for a sign pointing down a road off the N56, the R251, to the Errigal youth hostel and the **Dunlewy Lakeside Centre** (*Ionad Cois Locha*) two miles (three kilometres) away by the side of Lough Dunlewy (also spelt Dunlewey). Here, in the shadow of the distinctively shaped Errigal, there is a tiny village where a famed weaver, Manus Ferry, lived and worked until his death in the mid-1970s. His home is now the centre for weaving and spinning displays and a craft shop selling Donegal tweeds, paintings, pottery and other crafts. There are story-telling trips on a 50-seater boat on the lough, activities for children, a reasonably priced restaurant and tearoom, and traditional music on a Tuesday night in July and August. ■ *T31699. Easter to October, Monday-Saturday 1030-1800, Sunday 1100-1900. IR£2.20 for house and grounds. IR£2.50 boat trips. IR£4 combined ticket.*

From Dunlewy signs point the way to the Poisoned Glen, which most probably got its name from local spurges with a distinctive milky sap (*Euphorbia peplus* and *Euphorbia amygdaloides*), a perfectly benign and beautiful place that is wonderful for walking.

Mt Errigal A climb up the quartzite cone of Mt Errigal (2,467 feet/752 metres) is highly recommended because there are unsurpassed views of the county from the summit and, as long as you choose a suitable day when winds or visibility are not a problem, it is a reasonably manageable hike that takes less than four hours. There are various well-trod paths up the mountain, and a good place to start is from the R251, a little way past the Errigal youth hostel: it may be worth calling in here or at the Lakeside Centre (see page 530) for suggested routes. Whatever route is taken, the walk begins by walking across boggy grass and up the slope to the ridge of the summit, where a series of cairns mark the way. From here you should be able to see from Malin Head on the Inishowen peninsula to Slieve League in the south. Map No 1 in the Ordnance Survey Discovery series covers the walk.

Sleeping **AL** *Ostán Gweedore Hotel*, Bunbeg, T31177, F31726. Good views and its own pool and leisure centre, which attracts families during school holidays. **AL** *Ostán Radharc Na Mara* (Sea View Hotel), Bunbeg, T31159, F32238. Has rooms just a little less costly than the Gweedore. **B** *Bunbeg House*, T31305. By the harbour in Bunbeg. **C** *Ocean Lodge*, Bloody Foreland, Brinlack, T32084. A quieter place where you can sleep with views of Bloody Foreland from the window. Double rooms for IR£15 per person and a IR£2 supplement for a single. **D** *An Óige Errigal Hostel*, Dunlewy, T31180. In a perfect position if you're going to climb Mt Errigal: 3 km to the northwest of the village and stays open all year. **D** *Backpacker's Ireland Lakeside Hostel*, Dunlewy, T32133. IHO hostel, ideally placed for climbing Donegal's highest mountain, Errigal. Opens from 17th March to end of October, has 30 beds including 8 private rooms at IR£14 each, and bikes for hire. **D** *Backpacker's Ireland Seaside Hostel*, Magheragallon, Bunbeg, T32244. Open 17th March to end October, with private rooms costing IR£25 each, and also bikes for hire.

Eating There is a good restaurant at the *Ostán Gweedore Hotel*, overlooking the Atlantic from where the seafood on the menu has been caught, with an evening meal around IR£25. The restaurant at the *Ostán Radharc Na Mara* (Sea View Hotel) is less expensive, and bar food is available at both hotels. The *Lakeside Centre Restaurant* is good value for lunch, but closes early in the evening (see page 530). There are a few pubs, cafés and fast-food-type places scattered along the road between Dunbeg and Derrybeg and while none are worth singling out, they will suffice for a quick bite.

Tory Island

Getting there

Donegal Coastal Cruises, T31991/31340, from Bunbeg, June to September at 0900, returning at 1800, or from Magheraroarty at 1130, 1330 and 1700, returning at 1030, 1230 and 1600. There is usually 1 sailing a day from Bunbeg between October and May. Always check departure times as the schedule varies according to the season, the tides and the weather. IR£12 return.

Wind-swept Tory Island, under four miles long and only a mile wide (6 kilometres by two), was infamously difficult to reach or leave, until a new 40-minute ferry-boat service was introduced a few years back. It lies seven miles (11 kilometres) off the mainland and the boat ride there is an excursion in itself as it churns its way along the rocky northwest coast and then out to sea to the island. St Colmcille founded a monastery on Tory in the sixth century, and there are scanty monastic remains and the ruins of a round tower made, uniquely, from rounded beach stones. A day trip allows time for invigorating walks around the island and some bird-watching, but there are a couple of places to stay and two pubs to while away an evening. The island's hotel has one of these pubs, *The People's Bar*, and any entertainment, like evening sessions of music, will be advertised here. What might inspire a longer stay is a visit beforehand to *Glebe Gallery* (see page 539), where there are some excellent examples of paintings by Tory Island painters who were inspired to paint by Derek Hill when he visited Tory.

Tales of life on Tory, from childbirth to wakes and a bit of poitín-making along the way, are collected in Stories from Tory Island (see page 61).

Sleeping & eating

AL *Ostán Thóraigh*, Oileán Thóraigh, T/F35920. A fairly new hotel with 14 beds, but it closes between January and March. **B** *Ms Grace Duffy*, East Town, T35136. Opens all year for B&B. **D** *Radharc Na Mara Hostel*, Seaview, T65145. Open from April to October, and camping is also possible, though there are no private rooms. The *Ostán Thóraigh* is the best place for a meal; expect to pay around IR£20 for a seafood dinner. *Ms Grace Duffy*'s B&B can do an evening meal for around IR£10.

Gortahork to Dunfanaghy

Gortahork and Falcarragh are two small villages strung out along the coastal N56 road that leads to Dunfanaghy. During the day nothing much happens but at night the pubs are lively enough and sessions of traditional music occur on an irregular and impromptu basis. From Falcarragh there are small roads at both ends of the long main street that lead down to a stupendous stretch of wild and lonely beach; beware of swimming here, an unpredictable undercurrent has caused accidents.

Sleeping

B *Ferndale*, Main St, Falcarragh, T65506. At the Gortahork end of the village, a large bungalow with 4 bedrooms, open April-September for B&B. **D** *Baile Conaill*, Falcarragh, T35363. Huge hostel with beds for 140 guests and private rooms for IR£18. Take the coast road from the village and the entrance is signposted on the right. **D** *Shamrock Lodge Hostel*, Main St, Falcarragh, T35859. Above a busy pub and, depending on your tastes, this will be either a bonus or a blight.

County Donegal

Eating   In Falcarragh, *Mighty Mac's Café* is right in the centre of the village with a menu of chicken, lasagne, curry, baguettes. The nearby *Gweedore* pub has a restaurant upstairs serving standard meals in the evening. Inexpensive meat and vegetarian meals are available at *Baile Conaill*.

Dunfanaghy

Colour map 1, grid A2   Dunfanaghy, tucked on the edge of a long inlet of Sheephaven Bay with majestic Horn Head to the north and flat-topped Muckish Mountain to the south, has a more rounded appeal than Falcarragh. There are better amenities and Horn Head offers irresistible clifftop walks or a scenic tour by bicycle or car, *tour de force* scenery, and a safe beach for swimming. In the village itself there is an interesting museum devoted to local history.

The workhouse   The workhouse was built in 1844 for 300 'paupers', but that figure swelled to over 5,000 during the Famine; it evolved into a hospital and home, which closed in 1922. The place reopened recently as a museum and study centre with sensitively presented material. A nine-minute audio-visual show sets the scene for the exhibition area that tells its tale through the true story of a workhouse resident who died in 1926. A study room has books on the Famine to consult and an audio-visual on the local ecology; a craft shop and a coffee shop complete an admirable centre for visitors. On your visit, ask about the occasional sessions of traditional music and storytelling that take place in the evening. ■ *Main Street, T36540. Easter to October, Monday-Friday 1000-1700, Saturday and Sunday 1200-1700. IR£2.50. No charge for art exhibition, shop, café or study room.*

Sleeping   **L** *Shandon Hotel & Leisure Centre*, Marble Hill Strand, T36137, F36430. Enhanced by a seaside location, with its own grounds sliding down to the beach, a leisure centre, bar and restaurant and bedrooms that mostly face south for the unbeatable views. **AL** *Arnold's Hotel*, T36208, F36352. Has been in the same family for three generations and travellers have recommended it for comfort and friendliness. **AL** *Carrig-Rua Hotel*, T36133, F36277. Formerly the Stewart Arms Hotel, named after the Scottish landlord who created the village. Very accommodating. **B** *Carrigan House*, Kill, T/F36276. B&B 5 minutes from the village on foot. **B** *Rosman House*, T/F36273. B&B in a large bungalow with above-average room amenities and evening meals for around IR£15. **C** *Rockhaven*, Kill, T36159. A good-value B&B with doubles for IR£33. **D** *Corcreggan Mill*, T36507/36409. Hostel on the N56 2 miles (3 km) west of Dunfanaghy, has some character with beds in the main house and adjoining wheelless railway carriage, and a small camping space outside for IR£4.

Eating   Both hotels do good pub food and the *Carrig-Rua Hotel* has the *Copper Grill* for informal meals and the more elegant *Sheephaven Restaurant* with fresh seafood the highlight of the menu. The restaurant in *Arnold's Hotel* benefits from seaviews. In the main street a seafood restaurant serving lobster, *Danann's*, T36150, is currently up for sale but may reopen in a similar form, and *Danny Collins*, T36205, is a pub and affordable restaurant in the centre of the village. The Workhouse's modern, airy café with flagged floor, open fire and art-work for sale, is fine for scones and cakes.

On the main road to the southeast of Dunfanaghy, at Port Na Blagh, *The Cove Restaurant*, T074-36300, open daily 1000-2200, has a local reputation for quality seafood and meat dishes.

Shopping   Next door to the workhouse, *The Gallery*, T36224, has a vast collection of pottery, clothes, handbags, prints and jewellery, besides its main gallery of paintings for sale.

In the coffee shop at the Workhouse, shifting art exhibitions of work are also for sale, from IR£50 to IR£500. In the village centre is also *McAuliffe's* craft shop, T36135, with knitwear and handcrafts and a overseas mailing service.

Golf *Dunfanaghy*, T36335. 18-hole. **Horse-riding** *Dunfanaghy Stables, Arnold's Hotel*, Dunfanaghy, T36208. **Sea angling** *Dunfanaghy Angling Association*, T36208. *Pat Robinson*, Kill, Dunfanaghy, T36290, F36505. **Sport**

Bus *O'Donnell Buses*, T48356, run a daily service that leaves Donegal early in the morning to reach Belfast at noon via Derry, stopping at Dungloe, Burtonport, Dunfanaghy, Cresslough and Letterkenny. **Transport**

Around Dunfanaghy

In his book *The Way That I Went* (see page 64) RL Preger was not exaggerating when he labelled Horn Head the "finest headland on the Irish coastline". The signposted Horn Head Drive circles its eastern side and, if only cars were banned from driving around it, a trip around the headland on a bicycle would be a highlight of any visit to Ireland. Modern farming methods have destroyed the haunts of the now-endangered corncrake, but the area around Dunganaghy is one of the few places where it can still, occasionally, be heard. Horn Head is alive with birds: gannets dive-bombing vertically into the ocean, puffed-up puffins, the not-so-common chough (like a blackbird but with red legs), guillemots, storm petrels. It takes a good six hours to walk the 11 miles (18 kilometres) around the perimeter of Horn Head, and in places there are mildly scary stretches along the clifftop. A lot of walkers prefer to stick to the west and north sides by walking across the Horn Head bridge for an easy-going jaunt across the dunes and along Tramore Strand and, further north, Pollaguill Bay and its smaller beach. From here follow a ruined stone wall to **Marble Arch**, a tremendous arch in the rock formed by nature over the millennia. If you are driving, go clockwise; the road is very narrow. **Horn Head** *Phone code: 074*

The N56 road passes through the village of Cresslough, and here what will surely catch your eye is the flowing white curvature of St Michael's Church, designed to reflect the formidably solid outline of Muckish (*An Mhucais* being 'the pig's back'). The church, built in 1970 and influenced by Le Corbusier's ecclesiastical work at Ronchamp, adds a delightful touch of modernism perfectly at ease with rugged north Donegal. Inside, etched in glass, are the names of the architects, builders and artists who brought this elegant building into existence. **Cresslough & beaches**

For a scenic detour follow the signposted road on the left, coming into the village from Port Na Blagh, for a Capuchin friary established here in the 1960s. A half-mile walk (800 metres) from the friary leads down to tiny **Monk's Beach**, usually only visited by locals, while another half-hour walk leads on to the lovely **Silver Strand**. One quarter of all Ireland's beaches are in Donegal, and these are two of the lesser-known ones. **Marble Hill Strand**, a more populous beach safe for swimming and windsurfing, is reached by turning off at Port Na Blagh, and there are canoes and boogie boats for hire. The beach you can see on the other side of Sheephaven Bay is Rosapenna. **Ards Forest Park**, signposted off the N56 and free to enter, offers a quieter and more rural destination, with nature trails winding their way through the former estate of the Scottish landlord who once owned this land and Horn Head.

County Donegal

Doe Castle The sturdy, romantically sited fortress of Doe – built in the early 16th century by the MacSweeneys, and said to have provided refuge to some shipwrecked Spanish Armada sailors in 1588 – was constantly fought over throughout the 17th century. An English assault on the castle early in the century, headed by Sir Oliver Lambert, led him to exclaim that it was "the strongest hold in all the province which endured 100 blows of the demi-cannon before it yielded". A Captain George Vaughan Hart, his initials are over the door, converted the castle into a home in the early 1800s and the last occupant by one account was a Victorian rector from Cresslough who had nowhere else to live. ■ *Three miles (five kilometres) from Cresslough, signposted off the road, N56, to Carrigart. Free.*

Carrigart and the Rosguill peninsula

Phone code: 074
Colour map 1, grid A2

Carrigart is a neat little village on an isthmus between Sheephaven Bay and the Fanad peninsula: it opens the door for the gratifying Rosguill peninsula with its signposted seven-mile (12-kilometre) **Atlantic Drive** that takes you past the modest resort of **Downings**, known for its popular caravan ground. During summer weekends, and particularly the August bank holiday period, the Atlantic Drive has its share of vehicles but at other times the road provides an enjoyable route for a cycle or even a stimulating walk, with photogenic views of Horn Head and Tory Island. A recommended destination is the extremity at **Melmore Head** (Meall Mor), passing a hostel occupying a hunting lodge designed by Lutyens and a signpost pointing the way to the ruined Meagh Church with its ancient Latin cross and an Ogham stone.

Sleeping **A** *Hotel Carrigart*, Carrigart, T55114, F55250. Built in 1882, with its mansard-style façade, plus one of Ireland's first hotel swimming pools and a challenging links golf course, this hotel is in the middle of the village and the friendly owner is a mine of local information. **B** *Beach Hotel*, Downings, T55303. Can get busy, but it's the only hotel on the Rosguill peninsula. **B** *Shorewinds*, T55790. B&B with 4 bedrooms at IR£15 to IR£17 per person in doubles and IR£5 extra for a single, unless the room is unbooked by 2100. **C** *Baymount*, Downings Post Office, T55395. Has terrific views of the hills and Marble Hill across the water, and opens between April and September. **D** *Trá na Rosann*, Downings, T55374. An Óige's most northerly hostel in Ireland, open Easter to September, is 3½ miles (6 km) from Downings.

Self-catering *Coastguard Holiday Cottages*, Downings, T38032, F24788. Modern 3-bedroomed, self-catering cottages that cost from IR£200 to IR£350 a week between mid-March and September (negotiable rates over winter).

Doe Castle

County Donegal

The old-fashioned and spacious dining room of the *Hotel Carrigart* has dinner for **Eating**
under IR£25. The *Weavers Restaurant* across the road serves inexpensive meals
for under IR£10 and the bars do pub grub. *McNutts*, Downings, T53314, is a coffee
shop where a good seafood lunch and homebaked goodies are always available.
McNutts run a tweed shop next door, which also sells pottery and mails worldwide.

In Downings, the *Fleet Inn* attracts youngsters off the caravan site, and they set the **Pubs & music**
tone at the discos that take place here during the summer. The *Harbour Bar* is quiet
during the day but a younger crowd livens it up at night.

If the Downings pubs don't appeal to you then take the road from Carrigart to the
minuscule village of Glen and the *Old Glen Bar*, where locals and knowledgeable visitors escape for a quiet drink. The television over the bar comes only on for a sports fix-
ture (though Manchester United fans will find no comrades here) and there is the
occasional burst of live music. Another heartwarming, traditional bar is *The Singing
Pub* on the Atlantic Drive road, which has good music and good food.

Angling 3-hour trips for mackerel off a boat, T55386, depart from Downings at 1300 **Sport**
and 1800, Monday to Friday, gear provided and cost depends on number of people.
Horse-riding *Carrigart Riding Course*, T53583.

Banks 1 bank in the centre of Carrigart. **Directory**

The Fanad Peninsula

Travelling south from Carrigart and reaching nondescript Milford, the R246 can Phone code: 074
be taken for an approach up the west side of the Fanad peninsula but it's hard to Colour map 1, grid A2
*think of a good reason for making this journey because the scenery is unspectacu-
lar and there is nothing that compels a stop. The west coast has far more to recommend it, but if time is limited and a choice has to be made, the Inishowen
peninsula further east wins hands down in terms of stirring scenery.*

Rathmelton

Rathmelton is the first town on the west coast and though its slightly rickety
appearance is not instantly endearing, the place can grow on you and a picnic
could be enjoyed on the quayside overlooking the River Leannan (also spelled
Lennon), as it flows past towards Lough Swilly. Behind you stand some ram-
shackle but attractively gaunt warehouses that date back to the second half of
the 19th century when Ramelton prospered from corn mills, linen works and a
brewery. The Meeting House in the village, now restored as a genealogical centre, dates back to the 17th century when Rathmelton was laid out by William
Stewart, a Scottish planter. ■ *T51266.*

You'll see signs to **Killydonnell Friary**, four miles (six kilometres) away,
and though only the ruins remain, the tranquil setting is another inviting picnic spot. The river Leannan is a favourite cast for salmon and, though the nearest place for gear and tackle is Letterkenny (see page 537), fishing packages can
be arranged through the *Bridge Bar*, T51119.

B *Crammond House*, Market Square, T51055. B&B in an 18th-century house near the **Sleeping**
old grain miller's building. **C** *Lough View House*, Glenleary, T51550. A comfortable 2-
storey house overlooking the lough and village, which stays open all year. **C-
D** *Lennon Lodge*, T51227/8. New hostel round the corner from Crammond House,

which has opened charging IR£10 per person sharing facilities and IR£12 per person in a private room with bathroom. A good modern kitchen with and a lounge for guests.

Eating The *Mirabeau Restaurant*, The Mall, T51138, does steaks and seafood, with a set dinner at IR£17. *The Bridge Bar*, signposted after crossing the bridge coming into town from the south, T51119, has a fish restaurant upstairs with reasonably priced chowder for IR£2.60 and baked seabass for IR£11. The new *Lennon Lodge Cultural Centre*, T51055, is basically a pub that has bar food all day, with traditional music on a Thursday night from 2130 and live music of some kind at weekends. (Around the time of opening a passing wag quipped that 'Agri'(cultural) was missing from the large sign above the place.)

Rathmullan

Colour map 1, grid A3 There are satisfying views of Lough Swilly from Rathmelton to Rathmullan, and as you approach the village the ruins of **Rathmullan Priory** are on your right. From just outside this Carmelite friary, founded in the 15th century, a momentous event took place in September 1607, when "leaving their horses on the shore with no one to hold their bridles, they went aboard a ship". The "they" in question included the earls of Tyrone and Tyrconnell, and their departure, with other members of the cream of Irish aristocracy, signalled the end of a millennium of Gaelic rule in Ireland, and the *Annals of the Four Masters* (see box on page 513) recorded the significance of the event known to history as the Flight of the Earls: "Woe to the heart that meditated, woe to the mind that conceived, woe to the council that decided on, the project of their setting out on this voyage."

In the centre of Rathmullan village the **Heritage Centre** unfolds the historical background and consequences of the event through a series of text-based displays. If the lovely safe beach at Rathmullan tempts you to stay in the area the Heritage Centre also doubles as an unofficial tourist information office. ■ *T58178, Easter to mid-September, Monday-Saturday 1000-1800, Sunday 1200-1800. IR£1.*

Sleeping **L** *Fort Royal Hotel*, T58100, F58103. Good reputation for comfort and for food, set in private grounds with its own beach and tennis courts. **L** *Rathmullan House*, Lough Swilly, T58188, F58200. 19th-century hotel with award-winning gardens, indoor pool and top-notch breakfasts. **B** *Pier Hotel*, T58178. Gregarious place in the centre of the village. **C** *Eileen Gallagher*, Pier Rd, T58177. Modern town house 100m from the beach offering B&B. **D** *Bunnaton Hostel*, Glenvar, T50122. 6 miles (10 km) northwest of Rathmullan. Made up of a row of coastguards' cottages above the coast including 3 private rooms for IR£18 each.

Eating For good food in the IR£30 bracket, the *Fort Royal Hotel* and *Rathmullan House* are contenders, and our vote goes to the country-house style of Rathmullan House. More affordable meals can be enjoyed at the *Ferrygate Restaurant*, T58131, just around the corner from the *Pier Hotel* as you head north. This is a new, small restaurant with main dishes of fish and meat around IR£10 and attractive starters like goat's cheese with spinach, or mushroom with spices and yoghurt for IR£4.

The pleasantly shabby *Beachcomber Bar*, the first pub you see when coming into the village from Ramelton, does not do food, but a quiet drink can be enjoyed here with views of the water and outdoor tables by the beach.

The journey to the northern tip of the peninsula is signposted as the Fanad **Fanad Head**
Drive and includes, a little way before the village of Portsalon, a viewing point
that looks down on Ballymastocker Bay and its triple array of beaches. A left
turn in the village of Portsalon, where there really is nothing to detain you,
leads on along the coast to Fanad Head and a lighthouse. The nearby *Lighthouse Tavern*, T59212, serves light meals like garlic mussels with brown bread
and chicken sandwiches until around 2100.

Letterkenny

Letterkenny is County Donegal's largest town, a thriving commercial centre *Colour map 1, grid A2*
with good transport links and supermarkets but with little of intrinsic interest.
A number of main roads converge on the town, from Donegal in the west and
Derry in the east, while the N56 heads up to the northern coast accessing
Glenveagh National Park and the must-see Glebe House (see pages 539 and
539) along the way. Letterkenny is a good place to stop over for a meal and collect provisions if planning a picnic on the Fanad or Inishowen Peninsula and
the town has some indoor activities for rainy days, including the local history
Donegal County Museum. ■ *High St, T24613. Tuesday-Friday 1100-1230
and 1300-1630, Saturday 1300-1630. Free.*

On the R250 Churchill Rd the **Newmills Corn and Flax Mills** is a complex
of machinery powered by one of the largest watermills in Ireland, using the
power of the River Swilly. ■ *T25115. Mid-June to mid-September, daily 1000-
1830. Dúchas site. Three miles (five kilometres) from Letterkenny. IR£2.*

There are a few B&Bs strung out along the R245 road to Ramelton, and a few hostels in **Sleeping**
town, but no hotels.

B *Glencairn*, T24393. A large house with television and tea in the bedrooms, fairly typical of the B&Bs in town. **B** *Hill Crest House*, Lurgyback, Sligo Rd, T22300. On the N13
road to Ballybofey, just over a mile (2 km) from town, has good beds and facilities in
the rooms. **C** *Killerein House*, Ballaghderg, T24563. On the N56 road to Glenveagh
National Park and there is a pub a few minutes away serving meals. **D** *The Manse Hostel*, High Rd, T25238. A well-organized Victorian detached house open all year and
includes 8 private rooms for IR£16 each. Bikes for hire. **D** *Rosemount Hostel*, 3
Rosemount Terrace, T26284. A small terraced house off Upper Main St offering dormitory beds, but enquire here about private rooms in a separate house 2 miles (3 km)
away. **D** *Port Hostel*, 24 Port Rd, T26288. This hostel, near the cinema, which doesn't
belong to any of the hostel organizations, is the least satisfying of the three. If no one
answers the door, enquire at the small shop next door.

Eating places are competitively priced, and while there is nowhere really special, *The* **Eating**
Mews, 25 Lower Main St, T26867, is one of the better places to eat inexpensively in the
town centre. On Saturday, IR£25 buys a set dinner for 2 diners, with a half bottle of
wine thrown in, while the rest of the week an evening meal is around IR£17 for 1 person. A carvery is available Monday to Saturday between 1200 and 1500 for IR£4. The
Yellow Pepper, 36 Lower Main St, T24133, is a bistro-style café with a wine bar open
for breakfast, lunch and dinner 1030-2200 Monday to Saturday, and 1600-2000 on
Sunday. A catholic menu of chicken, fish, pasta and vegetarian meals, priced between
IR£6 and IR£12.

The *Beanery*, Market Sq, T28883, at the entrance to the pedestrianized Market
Centre shopping area in the middle of Main St, is justly popular for its range of decent
coffees and light meals; it is on 2 floors, open daily. Student specials, for IR£3, are highlighted in the front window. *The Quiet Moment* is a new teashop and sandwich bar

County Donegal

that has opened on Upper Main St next to Gallagher's hotel. Across the road, *Galfee*'s advertises itself as a gourmet takeaway, and light meals are available inside.

Pubs & music Quite a few pubs in the town centre have music, but the nights vary, and it is not always of the traditional kind. *McGinleys*, 25 Lower Main St, T21106, can be relied for traditional sessions on Monday nights and other places worth checking out include *Downtown*, 19 Lower Main St, T25291, and *Brewery Bar*, Market St, T27330.

Sport **Bowling** *Letterkenny Bowling Centre*, Ballyraine, T26000; Cinema Port Rd, T21976. **Fishing** *McCormick's*, 56 Upper Main St, T27833. Fishing gear. **Squash** *Squash Club*, Lower Main St, T26706.

Transport **Bus** From *Bus Éireann*'s large bus station, T21309, daily buses run to and from Dublin, Galway, Westport, Sligo, Derry, Enniskillen and Belfast. Private bus companies also stop near here, including *John McGinley*'s daily service, T35201, between Cresslough and Dublin via Letterkenny, *McGeehan*'s, T075-46150, daily route between Glencolmcille and Letterkenny. *Busway*'s, T077-82619, daily services to Inishowen, Derry and Dublin leave from opposite *Bus Éireann*'s station and from *Charlie's Café* on Pearse St. **Taxis** *Letterkenny Cabs*, T1800-272000. *Swilly Cabs*, T1800-216666.

Directory **Banks** On Main St and Port Rd. **Bookshop** *Browse-A-While*, Upper Main St. **Communications** Post office: Upper Main St. **Hospitals and medical services** Hospital: *St Conals*, T21022. **Supermarket** *Dunnes Stores* at the end of Main St. **Tourist office** A couple of kilometres out of town on the Derry road, T21160. Jul-Aug, Mon-Fri 0900-2000, Sat 1000-1400, Sun 0900-1700.

Around Letterkenny

Colmcille Heritage Centre The life story of St Colmcille (see box on page 523) is told through illustrated panels and a wax model and there are other displays on the era that gave rise to Ireland's epithet as the 'land of saints and scholars'. Perhaps the most engrossing displays are those that cover the craft of ancient manuscript-making.

Around Letterkenny

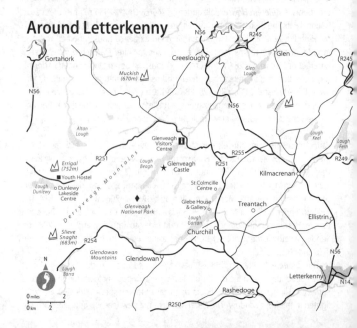

Gartan, Churchill, T37306. Easter week and from first Sunday in May to last Sunday in September, Monday-Saturday 1030-1830, Sunday 1300-1830. IR£1.50.

Everything about this house is a wonderful surprise. Inside you will find paintings by Picasso, Kokoschka, Jack Yeats, Passmore and Bonnard, not to mention some work by the Tory Island painters that Derek Hill, the man who made Glebe House so special, inspired to take up a brush and easel. Hill decorated his Regency house with William Morris textiles alongside superb touches of Islamic and other oriental art. To cap it all there are beautiful gardens that sweep down to the lake shore. ■ *T37071. Easter week and mid-May to 27th September, Saturday-Thursday 1100-1830. IR£2. Coffee shop. Situated 11 miles (18 kilometres) from Letterkenny on R251.*

Glebe House & Gallery
The best value IR£2 spent anywhere in Ireland is the cost of admission to Glebe House & Gallery

John George Adair was a 19th-century landlord who lorded it over 25,000 acres of land and was regarded as a tyrant even by his own class. When his steward was murdered in 1860 he felt sure that his tenants were behind the deed and so, over a period of three days in winter, he had all 244 of them evicted and their homes unroofed, so that "the police officers themselves could not refrain from weeping" it was said. A fund raised money for the former tenants to emigrate to Australia and many of the families left as a group to start a new life. Adair went on to build Glenveagh Castle in 1870. The property passed into the hands of the American Henry McIlhenny, who later donated the house and gardens to the state and it is now part of Glenveagh National Park. Self-guided walking trails meander through the Park.

Glenveagh Castle

A visit to the Park begins at the Visitors' Centre, where there are informative displays on the local ecology and the perfidious Adair. Glenveagh Castle is well worth a visit, for it is a particularly successful example of a mock castle, partly due to its setting on a promontory with the battlements set against a backdrop of mountains, and partly because this is a castle really built to defend its occupants against attack. Glenveagh Castle was built, as Williams in his definitive *Architecture in Ireland* puts it, "to ensure a sybaritic existence to inmates holding out against the vagaries of Irish politics or climate". Everything worth admiring inside, the fireplace and the wall-hangings for example, was put there by McIlhenny, while the lovely garden outside was a combined effort of McIlhenny and his wife Cornelia. ■ *Churchill, T37088. 14th-17th March and early April to November, daily 1000-1830. Closed Fridays in October. IR£2.50. Tearoom and restaurant. 14½ miles (24 km) north of Letterkenny.*

The Inishowen Peninsula

The terminal attraction to the Inishowen peninsula is Malin Head, Ireland's most northerly point, and even though north Donegal has scenically more exciting headlands, there is something enticing and irresistible about simply reaching this extremity of land. The bonus along the way comes in the form of unheralded scenic delights and, once you are away from Buncrana, the exhilarating absence of mass tourism. The area is often visited on speedy four-wheeled trips but as a place where people linger it is probably one of Ireland's least-known peninsulas and to do it justice a stay of a few nights is necessary.

*Phone code: 077
Colour map 1, grid A3*

County Donegal

Ins and outs

Getting there   The route that follows works its way up the Lough Swilly west side, through Fahan and Buncrana and along to Cardonagh before heading north to Malin Head. The route then returns down the east side to Inishowen Head before moving down the coast along Lough Foyle and into Derry. Much of the way is signposted as the Inishowen 100 (*Inis Eoghain 100*), from the approximate distance in miles it takes to complete a circuit of the peninsula.

Getting around   *Busways*, T077-82619, run a daily service between Letterkenny and Moville stopping at Burt, Fahan, Buncrana, Clonmany, Ballyliffin, Carndonagh (with a connection to Malin Head) and Culdaff. There is also a Monday-Saturday service between Carndonagh and Derry via Buncrana and a daily service between Carndonagh and Dublin via Buncrana, Derry and Monaghan. *John McGinley*, T074-35201, has a daily Inishowen to Dublin service.

Inishowen Peninsula

Self-catering on Inishowen

Ballyliffin: Ballyliffen Self-Catering, T76498. Sleeps 6-8 from IR£345 to IR£450 per week in modern houses with good facilities.

Carpenters, T76457. Sleeps up to 6, from IR£145 to IR£335 in cottage on private site.

Carndonagh: Gruckrooskey Cottage, T74780. Sleeps 6 from IR£205 to IR£275 in restored 18th-century cottage.

Clonmany: Mamore Cottages, T76710.

Sleeps 2 to 5 from IR£150 to IR£400 in 1- and 2-bedroomed cottages with open fire and turf supplied.

Greencastle: The School House, T/F70612. Sleeps 8 from IR£120 to IR£250 in purpose-built self-catering house.

Malin: Clochadonn, T79121. Sleeps 4 from IR£150 to IR£225 in 2-storey apartment.

Moville: The Gables, T82012, F82189. Sleeps from 2 to 7 from IR£100 to IR£300 in 3 town-centre apartments.

Grianán of Aileach

Colour map 1, grid A3

Grianán of Aileach is a stone fort strategically placed overlooking the flat land that separates the Inishowen peninsula from the rest of the county. Built during the early Christian period, it was the headquarters of the O'Neill clan who ruled from here for centuries until a revengeful king of Munster attacked in 1101 and, so the story goes, ordered his men each to take away a stone from the walls. What you see today is largely a 19th-century reconstruction, but managed more sensitively than what you might imagine a contemporary focus group from Dublin might come up with if given a free rein on the site.

Visitor Centre

There is no charge to visit the stone fort, unlike the nearby Grianán of Aileach Visitor Centre, on the main road where you turn off for the fort, which is basically a restaurant with a fairly uninspiring exhibition on the top floor devoted to the fort's history. The *Grianán of Aileach Restaurant* is below the Visitor Centre and occupys the main space of a 19th-century church. Notwithstanding the rather crass advertising (a 'holy different experience' proclaims a sign), the menu is imaginative, with starters like turbot and apricot salsa or lobster and prawn bisque for IR£3-4 and main courses for around IR£10, and a wine list. A carvery lunch starts at IR£4 during the week, and on Sunday a grander lunch is IR£11. ■ *T68000. Monday-Sunday 1100-2200. IR£1.*

Burt Church

Burt Church, the modern functioning church that stands on the corner before turning uphill for the stone fort, was designed in the mid-1960s by the same team of architects that produced the church at Cresslough (see page 533). The same philosophy applies, and this time the church is designed to harmonize with the fort.

Fahan and Buncrana

Colour map 1, grid A3

There are three reasons to stop in the village of Fahan: a modest but good beach, superb food for an evening meal that outclasses anything Buncrana can offer, and a cross slab near the modern church that dates from around the eighth century, decorated with elegant Latin crosses and carrying a barely decipherable but unique Greek inscription from early Christian Ireland.

There is very little reason to stop in Buncrana, even though this is the main town and resort on the peninsula. The beach (three miles/five kilometres long) attracts crowds of Irish holidaymakers during the summer, but you can escape

County Donegal

the hustle and bustle by seeking out the small beach that is reached by a path from the pier at the north end of the long main street. There is a seasonal tourist office on the seafront, and a **Vintage Car and Carriage Museum** at the north end of town that will help occupy a wet afternoon. ■ *Tourist office: T62600/20020. April to September. Museum: T61130.*

Eating *St John's Country House Restaurant*, T60289, at the Buncrana end of Fahan, has an established reputation for Donegal lamb and seafood served in a restored Georgian house with a lough-side setting. Expect to pay around IR£25 for an evening meal but make a reservation. In Fahan itself, the *Railway Tavern* bar and restaurant, T60137, cooks food on an open wood-burning firebox and opens for dinner Tuesday-Sunday 1800-2200 and for lunch on Sunday. *The Ubiquitous Chip*, 47 Main St, Buncrana, T62530, serves vegetarian balti or spicy vegetables with fajita, both at IR£7, chicken enchiladas or trout for around IR£9. *The Town Clock Restaurant*, 6 Main St, Buncrana, T63279, is more of a café and opens for breakfast, lunch and dinner.

Buncrana to Ballyliffin

An alternative to the direct inland route to Cardonagh from Buncrana involves taking the R238 road north and following signs for **Dunree Fort** where there is a small military museum with displays on the fort's history, assorted weaponry, and a tearoom. It is not very interesting, but the small sheltered beach has its charm and there are fabulous views of Lough Swilly across to Fanad Head. ■ *T61817. June to September, Monday-Saturday 1000-1800, Sunday 1300-1800. IR£2.*

Back on the main road the journey continues north up through the dramatic Mamore Gap before descending 800 feet (243 metres) and bringing **Dunaff Head** and the bay into view. *The Rusty Nail*, T76116, is a fine old country pub passed on the road that serves food in the evenings during the summer and a popular Sunday lunch. Shortly after the pub a signposted turning off to the left leads to sandy Tullagh Bay, while the R238 continues on to the village of Clonmany where an angling festival takes place annually in August. A little way before entering the next village of Ballyliffin, on the main road, bicycles can be hired from *McEleney's Cycles*, T76541, and day trips to nearby **Pollan Bay**, sandy but not safe for swimming, could take in a picnic near the ruins of Carrickabraghy Castle at the beach.

For self-catering accommodation in Ballyliffin and Clonmany, see box on page 541.

Carndonagh

Colour map 1, grid A3 Carndonagh is an undistinguished small town but a useful watering hole and home to the last supermarket south before Malin Head. There is a helpful **tourist office**. ■ *Chapel St, T74933, F74935, info@inishowen.com http://www.inishowen.com June to August, Monday-Friday 0930-1900, Saturday 1000-1800, Sunday 1200-1800.*

Local sites If you are staying hereabouts for a night or two the tourist office can provide details of a surprising number of early Christian sites in the vicinity. Entering the village from Ballyliffin you will have already have passed **Donagh Church**, where there is a group of early Christian monuments made up of a cross and two carved stones from around the ninth century, while to the east of town there are the **Carrowmore high crosses** and the **Clonca Church cross**. They are not visually arresting and will prove disappointing if you are expecting

Éire

something along the lines of Clonmacnoise; some archaeologists think they may be the result of some independent missionary movement from Scotland.

Local entertainment In the middle of July each year the Inishowen Agricultural Show has competitions with judging of sheep, cattle and horse in the morning and family activities during the afternoon. A street festival that takes place later in the month is not as much fun.

Sleeping **B-C** *Ashdale Farmhouse*, Malin Rd, T74017. A homely 2-storey house on the road to Malin and charges from IR£16 to IR£18 per person sharing. **C** *Radharc na Coille*, Tiernaleague, T74471. A dormer house a few miles from town via Church St and charging around IR£15 per person.

For self-catering accommodation, see the box on page 541.

Eating The best place for a good meal is the *Corncrake Restaurant*, Malin St, T74534, on your right leaving the village for Malin. The speciality is Donegal lamb and wild salmon for around IR£12 with starters like mussels in cream sauce for IR£3, but seafood addicts might be attracted to the seafood thermidor, a rich combination of monkfish, scallops, prawns, cod and mussels in a mustard and cream sauce! Open nightly June to September, but only weekends at other times. *Tul Na Rí* (Simpson's Bar), outside town on the Culdaff road, T74499, is an olde-worlde pub serving good food 1230-2200, booking ahead is often necessary to secure an evening table. For pub food try the *Sportsman Inn*, T74817, or *Trawbreaga Bay House*, T74352, both in The Diamond, T74352, or the nearby *Quiet Lady* on Malin Rd, T74777. For picnic provisions the *Centra* supermarket in Malin St opens daily from 0900 (1130 on Sunday) until 2330.

For pub music try *The Persian Bar*, T74823, or the *Sportsman Inn*, T74817, both on the Diamond, or *Bradly's* on Bridge St, T74526.

Transport **Bicycles** Bikes can be rented from *McCallions Bikes & Toys*, T74084, 3 miles (5 km) from Carndonagh on the Ballyliffin Road, with delivery and collection anywhere on the peninsula.

Malin and Malin Head

Colour map 1, grid A3 The R238 presses on to the village of Malin, situated where a charming 10-arch stone bridge crosses Trawbreaga Bay. The neat triangular village green bears testimony to its origins as a 17th-century planter's creation and the sparse tidiness of the place evokes a suitable sense of the terminal. North of the village a signposted detour leads to **Five Fingers Strand** and the oldest church (1784) still functioning on the peninsula. The beach is exhilarating to walk along but swimming is dangerous here.

County Donegal

Malin Head, marked by the remains of a 19th-century signal tower, lacks visual drama, so your imagination must get to work on the flat vista of surrounding grass that faces out to uninhabited Inishtrahull Island. You are standing on the most northerly piece of Irish mainland and the next stop north is Greenland. Weather reports, first recorded here in 1870, still feature in radio broadcasts and the buildings of the meteorological station can be seen at the head. Just east of the head, *The Cottage* has some photographs of historical interest and a path leads east past the *Seaview Tavern* to the Wee House of Malin, a hermit's rock cell in the cliff. Bird-watchers can listen for the elusive corncrake and in autumn time migrating gannets, shearwater and skuas pass overhead.

Sleeping **A** *Malin Hotel*, Malin Village, T70645, F70770, faces the green and has a pleasant old-fashioned appeal. Singles/doubles are IR£35/60 June to September (IR£30/50 the rest of the year) but there are weekend rates of IR£70 for 2 nights bed and breakfast and 1 dinner. **C** *Barraicín*, Malin Head, T70184, overlooks the Atlantic and charges IR£16 per person. **C** *McLaughlin's*, T74491, is a hostel-style place that charges IR£28 for a couple in a small room with bathroom facilities and a self-catering kitchen. From Malin village cross the bridge on the R238 towards Cardonagh, turn left at the B&B sign and *McLaughlin's* is just up this road. **D** *Malin Head Hostel*, Malin Head, T70309. In the home of a local teacher 2 miles (3 km) from the headland, beside the post office, and open from mid-March to October. A private room and camping space available. **D** *Sandrock Holiday Hostel*, Port Ronan Pier, Malin Head, T70289. Open all year, has a laundry, bikes for hire and suggested walking routes. No private rooms.

For self-catering accommodation, see box on page 541.

Eating The *Malin Hotel* does bar food until 2115 and there is a comfortable restaurant in the evening that has a IR£15 set dinner as well as a choice of fish, chicken and grills around IR£7. At Malin Head *The Cottage*, T70257, does soup and sandwiches and light meals and opens June to September 1100-1830 (from 1330 on Sunday), and March to May Sundays only. The *Seaview Tavern*, Malin Head, T70117, is Ireland's most northerly pub and is open daily 0900-2100 for meals. *Bree Inn*, T70161, opens all year with a welcoming turf fire in winter. Meals available daily and their Sunday lunch a speciality. Live music can be heard every Saturday night, but if you prefer a quiet pint try *Farren's Bar*, near the weather station and Portmore Pier.

Culdaff

Colour map 1, grid A3 The route south that avoids going back through Malin takes you through the small village of Culdaff before carrying on through fairly deserted countryside as far as Moville or by way of a narrow winding road to Stroove. There is more to Culdaff than meets the eye. In late June every year the **Culdaff Sea Angling Festival** attracts anglers from all over the country and overseas for cash prizes, cups and trophies. ■ *T79141*.

In early October the **Charles Macklin Autumn School** is a festival of the arts based around the life of the actor and playwright Charles Macklin (1697-1797). ■ *T79019, F79235*.

While both these occasions bring seasonal life and laughter to Culdaff, there is entertainment most of the time at the remarkable *McGrory's pub*: it is worth checking to see what is lined up, for some big time entertainers appear here on a regular basis. ■ *T79104, F79235, mcgr@tinet.ie http://www.mcgrorys.ie*

Bocan stone circle lies to the south of Culdaff near Bocan church, but many of the stones have collapsed. The Carrowmore high crosses and the Clonca Church cross (see page 542) could also be visited from here but, as with the stone circle, there is not a lot to see.

McGrory's was undergoing refurbishment at the time of writing, but you can expect **Sleeping** to find new accommodation available in 10 bedrooms with their own bathroom facil- **& eating** ities. A new restaurant is also about to open, under the same management. **C** *Ceecliff House*, T79159, does B&B in a modern house for around IR£17 per person. **C** *Culdaff House*, T79103, is an established B&B in a 300-year-old Georgian farmhouse with views over a beach.

Stroove to Muff

The lough-facing east side of the Inishowen peninsula stretches from Stroove and Inishowen Head to the blink-and-it's-gone village of Muff barely inside the border with Northern Ireland. At Stroove there is a signposted walk, with fine views of Inishowen Head along the way, to picnic tables near a lighthouse, and you could walk from here to Kinnagoe Bay and return by the same route.

Greencastle is a fishing port at the mouth of Lough Foyle with the ruins of an **Greencastle** ancient castle; an early 19th-century fort, which is now a bar and restaurant; and the ruins of an ancient castle that are crumbling away on the coast. There is a fair choice of places to enjoy a meal, and infinitely better than what is available further down the coast in listless Moville.

The R238 hugs the coast all the way from Moville to the tiny village of Muff, **Muff** where there is more going on than meets the eye. The place comes alive when the annual festival is unleashed over the holiday weekend at the end of July. ■ *T84024*.

The Flough is a traditional Irish cottage with sessions of song and dance but telephone ahead to check what might be on. ■ *T84024*.

Lenamore Stables is between Muff and Bridgend, offering horse-riding over quiet country roads or on a beach, and catering for novices as well as experienced riders. ■ *T84022*.

A *Castle Inn*, Greencastle, T81426. A sociable place running a public bar as well as **Sleeping** doing B&B for IR£25 per person, situated next to the fort and the ruins of the castle. **B** *Brooklyn Cottage*, Greencastle, T81087. By the water's edge at the harbour and views of Lough Foyle can be enjoyed over breakfast in a conservatory. Free fishing trips if staying three nights. IR£17.50 per person. **B** *Tardrum Country House*, Greencastle, T81051. An early Victorian house and a 5-minute walk from the village. IR£22 per person. **D** *Moville Holiday Hostel*, Moville, T82378. A refurbished stone building 5 minutes by foot from the village and including private rooms for IR£11 per person.

For self-catering accommodation, see the box on page 541

Greencastle has a few places close to each other along the seafront. *Kealy's Seafood* **Eating** *Bar*, T81010, is a trendy-looking place doing dinner for about IR£20, lobster thermidor IR£26, and bar food includes chowder, salads and meals around IR£7. Closed Monday. A little further on, *Greencastle Fort*, T81044, has an atmospheric interior in the old fort and does seafood from IR£3 to IR£15 as well as steaks and duck, and the menu is chalked up on blackboards in the spacious bar area. Next door, *Castle Inn*, T81426, specializes in steaks.

County Donegal

Northern Ireland

The names of a land show the heart of the race;
They move on the tongue like the lilt of a song.
You say the name and I see the place -
Drumbo, Dungannon, or Annalong.
Barony, townland, we cannot go wrong.

John Hewitt (1907-87):
'Ulster Names'

14

Counties Derry & Antrim

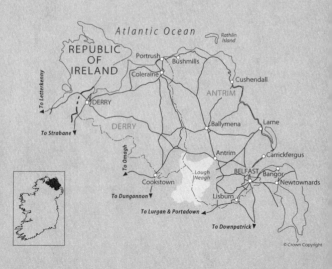

© Crown Copyright

Derry – energetic, creative and confident – is one of Ireland's most lovely cities and a visit here should be a highlight of any trip to Ulster. Travel to Derry from Belfast through the Sperrin mountains that dominate the south of the county or, by way of contrast, along the spectacular coastline of County Antrim. Traditional resort towns like Portrush dot the northern coast while the famed glens of Antrim make their way gracefully from inland moorland to charming villages clustered on the shore, communities connected by the stunning Antrim Coast road that hugs the sea from just north of Belfast all the way to elegant Portstewart, a short way east of Derry.

★ *Try to find time for*

Visiting the excellent Tower Museum in Derry where you'll learn more about the Troubles than you will anywhere else in Ireland

Walking the city walls of Derry

Admiring the stained glass in the Guildhall in Derry

Treading in the steps of Finn McCool at the Giant's Causeway

Enjoying fine food at Ramore in Portrush

Walking the North Antrim Coast Path between Portballintrae and Ballintoy

Scaring the life out of yourself on the Carrick-a-rede ropebridge

Musical nights of traditional music in the pubs of Ballycastle

Bird-watching at the west end of Rathlin Island

County Derry

Derry

Colour map 1, grid A3 *With the most fun to be had anywhere in Northern Ireland, Derry is a lovely, compact, vibrant little city, full of business and bustle, where life has moved on so far from the Troubles that it is hard to recognize the old ruins, and except for the red, white and blue in-your-face kerbstones of the Fountains area there is little sign of sectarian divisions.*

Ins and outs

Getting there Derry is a very accessible city. The airport is 11 km (7 miles) northeast of the city on the A2, and access to the city is by Ulsterbus service 143 or cab. The railway station is in Duke Street, and there is a free bus service to the Ulsterbus Depot in Foyle Street. Express Ulsterbus buses, T71262261, connect Derry with Belfast and all major towns in Northern Ireland, while Bus Éireann has services to most major towns in the Republic.

Getting around Local buses begin their journeys at the Ulsterbus depot: they are indicated by the letter D in front of the service number. Black taxis wait at Foyle Street and collect a full load of passengers before setting off. Regular cabs (see page 562) operate around the city in the usual manner; ask the price before you set off, since few have meters.

History

Early history The earliest settlement here was in an oak grove on an island in the river Foyle. Archaeological sites in the area tell us that people lived in the region and revered the wooded hill long before St Colmcille (Columba) built a monastery on it in the sixth century. During mediaeval times it expanded from an Augustinian settlement to a flourishing town with prestigious buildings, a school and the patronage of the Mac Lochlains, a local clan who had claims to the kingship of all Ireland.

English settlement In 1566 an unsuccessful English garrison was established in the town. At the turn of the 17th century a more concerted attempt was made when another garrison was established and the town was given the status of city, but the settlement lasted only until 1608, when the O'Dohertys attacked it and erased the English presence.

Under James I a new settlement was established in 1613 using Protestant settlers from Scotland and England who were more likely to be loyal to the crown, financed by the wealthy London guilds, which is why the city spent the next 380 years under the name Londonderry. Great walls were erected around the city, while within the walls great buildings were constructed, including St Columb's Cathedral. Despite this, the population grew slowly in numbers, perhaps deterred by the continuing unrest in the province. In 1649 England's internal divisions came to Derry when the city fathers declared themselves in support of the English Republic, while the Catholic Irish and the Scottish Presbyterian settlers, all of whom were condemned to live outside the city walls, besieged the town in support of King Charles I. Strangely, this is one act of loyalty to the crown that the Apprenticeboys don't celebrate each year!

County Derry

The big event in Derry's history is the shutting of the gates by some apprentices **The seige of** against Catholic troops loyal to James II in 1688, as the town had declared its **Derry** allegiance to William of Orange. When James' forces rode up to the city, the gates were slammed shut. Protestants fled to the city, increasing its population from around 2,000 to 30,000. A siege began later that same year and lasted 105 days. After a third of the people inside had died, of mortar attack or starvation, the siege was finally broken by a fleet of ships that broke through the barriers across the river. The siege held up the Catholic forces long enough for William of Orange to gather strength and win the Battle of the Boyne (see page 674). The event is celebrated every 12th of August with bonfires and the ritual burning of an effigy of Protestant Governor Robert Lundy, who escaped from the siege, went to London, and was forever known in the city as a traitor.

A few centuries of relative peace brought Derry to the Partition and made it a **The twentieth** key location, sitting as it does on the border of Northern Ireland and the **century** Republic. Returning First World War veterans inured to the most terrible conditions found themselves being recruited into the UVF or the IRA as the Black and Tans, ex-British soldiers recruited into the RIC, carried out British policy in the War of Independence in the southern counties. In 1920 streetfighting broke out between Catholics and Protestants, and the Royal Ulster Constabulary made a bayonet charge against a Catholic crowd in the Bogside; Protestants with guns held the city walls, shooting into Catholic areas; the army intervened on the side of the Protestants; and Protestant militias were set up as the RUC withdrew from rural areas. The Anglo-Irish Treaty, signed in 1921, created Northern Ireland and put Derry in a key location, sitting on the border of Northern Ireland and the Republic.

The Second World War brought prosperity and activity to Derry, as it became a base for refuelling and rearming destroyers and other escort ships for the transatlantic convoys. In early 1941 technicians from the US arrived in Derry and began building a new quay, a ship repair base, a radio station and personnel camps. By May 1942 there were 149 vessels and 20,000 American sailors based in Derry. A massive underground bunker and the most important radio station in the Western Approaches made Derry a vital link in the war in the Atlantic.

After the war Derry found itself a manufacturing city on the extreme west of the United Kingdom. It attracted few big businesses, and unemployment rose to about 10 times that of the rest of Northern Ireland. Housing became a big issue, as the Unionist-run city council was afraid to extend the city's boundaries with housing estates since it might affect their electoral chances. Moderate organizations such as the Derry Housing Associations raised money to build houses while the protests against Unionist policy grew ever more vocal and physical.

The 1970s and 80s saw IRA atrocities all over the north and in Great Britain. **To the present** Over the years new housing developments went up on the east bank and were **day** allocated to Protestants, while Catholics moved into the untenanted houses they left behind. The river became a peace line with only the Fountains area left on the west bank as a Protestant area. Gradually, the old slums of the Bogside were cleared and wide boulevards were created. In the early 1990s a major programme of investment began, clearing bombed-out buildings within the city walls, rebuilding the courthouse, creating the craft village, the museum and the genealogy centre. Since 1973 the Derry Council has been dominated by SDLP majorities, but they have regularly elected Unionist mayors as a gesture of goodwill. For many years there has been genuine power-sharing in this city, which could teach some of the big names in Belfast quite a lot about compromise.

County Derry

Derry's part in the Troubles

In October 1968 civil rights marchers in Derry including John Hume, Gerry Fitt (both leaders of the moderate SDLP) and three Westminster Labour MPs were trapped by police and bludgeoned till they fled. Fitt was taken to hospital with head injuries. The event was filmed by an Irish film crew and broadcast worldwide – Ulster policemen were seen randomly hitting out at demonstrators and bystanders alike. This event was the trigger that sent Northern Ireland spiralling into the Troubles. Prior to this, the RUC had commanded the respect of the minority communities in Northern Ireland; after this they lost it.

In 1969 the civil rights movement had grown, become largely Catholic and contained socialist and republican elements, who had their own goals – a socialist Republic of Ireland. A march planned from Belfast to Derry turned into utter chaos as Loyalists attacked the participants, who got no protection from the police, seen and filmed joining in the attacks on the marchers. In Derry, policemen smashed their way into a supermarket and attacked shoppers; in the Bogside policemen rioted in the streets smashing windows and attacking anyone foolish enough to be out. All of this fuelled the Free Derry movement: its slogan appeared on the gable end of a block of houses; moderates left the movement and it became dominated by Republicans. Support for the IRA, which was practically defunct, rose.

In August 1969 began the Battle of the Bogside, when fighting broke out between the Loyalist Apprenticeboy marchers and Catholics from the Bogside. The battle raged for two days, and CS gas was fired into the Bogside. The Taoiseach, Jack Lynch, called for the UN to enter what was effectively an anarchic situation. Finally British troops entered the city, replacing the RUC. Three years later worse was to come: in January 1972 a civil rights march was fired on by paratroopers, killing 13, mostly by wounds to the back. Another person died later of his wounds. The event came to be known as Bloody Sunday.

During this time areas of the city had become no-go areas for the army. After a series of horrific IRA bombs in Belfast and Derry the British Prime Minister, James Callaghan, gave the order to clear the no-go areas, and operation Motorman began. Tanks and armoured cars were brought into the city as the biggest British military operation since Suez began in the Bogside and in Protestant no-go areas.

Sights

The city walls The city centre of Derry can easily be experienced in a day's wander around the walls, dropping down into the city to visit the various sights. Considering Derry's history, it is amazing the walls are intact: two-storey ramparts of earth and stone a mile long with a wide protected walkway along their top. Starting the walk at Shipquay Gate, one can imagine the 17th century walled town. The gate had a drawbridge that could be closed against attackers and the river lapped against the walls themselves.

Inside the gate there are steps up on to the wall, which you can follow in a clockwise direction. At regular intervals bastions project out beyond the walls; they were used as defensive positions when the city was under attack. Beyond the third gate, New Gate, the Church of Ireland cathedral comes into view with its tower projecting above the walls. During the siege of Derry the tower was given wooden platforms for the defenders to use. The walls around the church are built higher than usual, again as a defensive measure during the siege. Beyond the church and outside the walls is the Fountains area, distinguished by its red, white and blue decorations.

County Derry

Approaching Bishop's Gate you can see the one remaining tower of the old Derry jail which has a long list of famous inmates including Wolf Tone, the leader of the United Irishmen, and Eamon de Valera, later to be President of Ireland. Descending by the Bishop's Gate, notice the carved ornamentation on the gate, which is built like a triumphal arch, rebuilt in 1789 to honour William of Orange. After its construction a united procession of church leaders passed through the gate: in those days William of Orange represented order, not sectarianism. Passing along Bishop's Gate Within you pass the pink, columned Bishop's Palace on the left where the wife of a later bishop, Cecil Francis Alexander, lived, famous for writing a collection of hymns for children including

'The rich man in his castle, The poor man at his gate, God made them high or lowly And ordered their estate.'
Cecil Francis Alexander (1818-1895), from his hymn 'All things bright and beautiful'.

Derry city

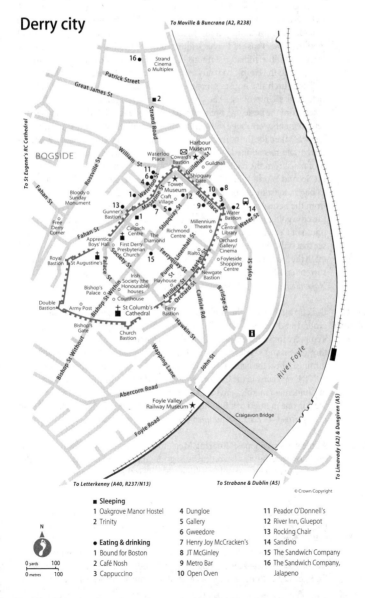

To Moville & Buncrana (A2, R238)

© Crown Copyright

■ **Sleeping**
1 Oakgrove Manor Hostel
2 Trinity

● **Eating & drinking**
1 Bound for Boston
2 Café Nosh
3 Cappuccino

4 Dungloe
5 Gallery
6 Gweedore
7 Henry Joy McCracken's
8 JT McGinley
9 Metro Bar
10 Open Oven

11 Peador O'Donnell's
12 River Inn, Gluepot
13 Rocking Chair
14 Sandino
15 The Sandwich Company
16 The Sandwich Company, Jalapeno

those old favourites 'There is a Green Hill' and 'All things Bright and Beautiful'. On the right is the courthouse, which suffered three major car bomb
attacks and was restored in 1994. Turning to the right brings you past the Irish
Society (The Honourable) houses where the clergy live, and into the grounds
of the Cathedral.

St Columb's This is the first post-Reformation church to have been built in the British Isles.
Cathedral It was built by the Irish Society between 1628 and 1633 and is one of the few
churches in Ireland that is in a single style – late Gothic. The spire is the
church's third – the first was wooden and was pulled down in preparation for
the siege, the lead being used to make bullets; another spire went up in 1778
but was taken down again in 1801 since it was about to fall down, and the spire
you see before you was put in its place. The interior is impressive, with great
wooden pews, those at the back illustrating the need to rest one's head while
listening to interminable sermons. The regular pew ends are all individually
carved, and the Gothic roof arches rest on the carved heads of past bishops.

The church also houses some crumbling flags, one of which is a pre-St Patrick's cross Union Jack. The yellow flags are replacements for Bastille flags
taken from the besieging French troops; they ought to be white, but when the
replacements were made the originals had turned yellow with age and that yellow was taken for the correct colour. The other flags were donated by American battalions stationed in Derry during the war. There is a silver cross made of
roof nails from the ruins of Coventry cathedral, which was destroyed during
the Second World War. The Chapter House is a treasure of junk – a chair said
to be made from the pear tree that Robert Lundy climbed when he escaped
from the besieged city (see page 553), huge padlocks used to lock the gates of
the city, gold pieces given by William to his loyal supporters, and a doctored
photo of Cecil Francis Alexander (see page 555) – if you look closely you will
see that only the face and shoulders are a photo and the body has been painted
in. In the lobby is the cannonball that carried the message telling those inside to
surrender. ■ *T71267313. £1. March to October, Monday-Saturday 0900-1700;
November-February, Monday-Saturday 0900-1300, 1400-1600.*

St Columba's Back up on the walls, the double-bastioned west side looks out over some waste
Church ground and beyond to St Columba's Church, which stands on the site of
Tempull Mor (the medieval cathedral). It is possible to walk down to the church
through Bishop's Gate, passing the barricaded Fountains Estate on the left, and
turning right at the lights at Barrack Street. The church now standing dates back
to 1784, very early in the Catholic church-building era. Inside are vast quantities
of Connemara marble, and banks upon banks of fluorescent lights and candles,
putting one in mind of a Buddhist temple rather than a Catholic church. ■ *Off
Bishop Street, T71262301. Summer 0900-2100; winter 0900-2030.*

Bogside As the walls go on, past **'Roaring Meg'**, the cannon dedicated by the London
Fishmongers, the view becomes the Bogside, and beyond it the Creggan estate.
Below, out of sight, tucked in behind the wall, is the monument to those who
died on Bloody Sunday. To the right is the **Free Derry mural** and beyond all
the newly erected and already crumbling council houses is **St Eugene's
Roman Catholic Cathedral**, designed by several hands, the last of which was
Liam McCormack, author of the pagan sacrificial altar in Armagh.
■ *T71262894. 0700-2100.*

Behind you, inside the city walls, is the **Apprenticeboys Hall**, built in 1937.
On the walls overlooking the Bogside once stood a 27-metre-tall monument to
George Walker, the governor of Derry at the time of the siege. It was blown up

in 1973, and the head changed hands several times and is now reputed to be in someone's back garden. It was beside this statue that the effigy of Lundy was traditionally burned in December, but in recent times, out of respect for their Bogside neighbours, the Apprentice boys burn it elsewhere (see page 553).

Continuing along the city wall, you pass the First Derry Presbyterian Church, originally built in 1690, rebuilt during the Georgian period and added to in 1863. What you see is almost entirely of Victorian construction with sandstone Corinthian pillars. This was one of the first places of worship not affiliated to the Church of Ireland that was allowed within the city walls.

Calgach Centre

Next you pass over Butcher's gate and, looking inside the walls, can see much of the new investment in the city. At the corner of Butcher Street and Magazine Street is the Calgach Centre, where you can watch *The Fifth Province*, an audio-visual experience about Celtic life based around the ancient warrior Calgach, one of the Tuatha de Danaan – the legendary warrior-kings of Ireland: interesting information; good fun for kids. In the same building is the genealogy centre where experts will look into your family history using a vast database of old records. ■ *Butcher Street, T71373177. Monday-Friday, 1000 and 1430. Check times before arriving as these may change with the seasons. £3. Café. Genealogy Centre T71261967. Monday-Friday 0900-1500. Free.*

Tower Museum

At Magazine Gate in the north corner of the walled city, this is a modern recreation of an ancient tower house that once stood here. The museum has won many awards, and deservedly so: it's the only museum in Ireland that makes any effort at all to confront the events of the last 30 years with anything near objectivity. What's more, it's interesting, relaxing and provides an excellent balance between information and artefacts. Towards the end of the trip around the museum you enter a mocked-up street with orange, white and green kerbstones on one side, and red, white and blue stripes on the other. Above the kerbstones display cases give two versions of the events of the last century. In the lobby of the museum is a wonderful photograph of Loyalist leader Ian Paisley smiling as he stands in this section of the museum beneath the roadsign pointing to Independence for Ireland. One exhibit you won't see is the AK47 machine gun contributed by the IRA, which was confiscated by the police. ■ *Union Hall Place, T71372411. September to June, Tuesday-Saturday and Bank Holiday Mondays 1000-1700, last admission 1630; July to August, Monday-Saturday 1000-1700, last admission 1630. £3.65. Shop.*

Craft Village

The exit from the museum fetches you into the Craft Village. Out of the summer months this really doesn't shine as a place to visit, but in summer the cafés, shops and open areas, where there is often live music, are well worth a visit.

Guildhall

Leaving the walled city by Magazine Gate brings you to this Gothic extravaganza built in 1887 and burned down three times, once in 1908 by accident when only the main outer walls were left standing and the second and third times in 1972 by design, when the entire interior was wrecked. One of those convicted of the bombings in 1972 later sat as a councilman in the same building. Inside is Victorian bombast, with vast stained glass windows representing the London liveries and the stories associated with Derry. Upstairs in the little kitchen alongside the great hall, look at the feet of George V in the stained-glass window portraying his coronation: he has his shoes on the wrong feet. In the Great Hall most of Brian Friel's plays were premiered. In the lobby is a stained-glass panel representing those who lost their lives on Bloody Sunday with, for some unaccountable reason, a sled with 'Rosebud' written on it. The statue of

The Irish workhouse

In 1838 the Irish Poor Law Act allowed for poor relief to take place within the confines of poor houses, which were to be built at the taxpayer's expense. In Derry, land was bought from a Major Bond and the poor house opened its doors in 1840, just in time for the Famine. Those who walked up to the house had to be truly desperate, because conditions inside were deliberately harsh so as to deter everyone but those at death's door from starvation from going inside. Once inside, the family was separated into women, girls, boys and men, who were not permitted to have any contact. Their clothes were taken and they were given a workhouse uniform. Daily life was organized around slave labour – women cleaned and sewed, men kept animals and broke rocks – and in this way the workhouse met some of its own costs. Rations were just enough to keep people alive, and punishment for indiscipline was harsh – usually deprivation of food.

Ironically, it was the Famine eight years later that temporarily did away with the poor houses since the buildings couldn't cope with the vast numbers of destitute and dying people who turned up there, and outdoor relief was allowed. The Poor Laws and the workhouses did not finally go out of operation until the creation of the Welfare State in 1948.

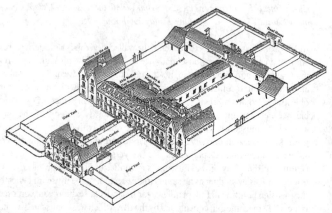

Queen Victoria has several fingers missing from when she was toppled over in one of the 1972 blasts. ■ *T377577 for tours, July and August only.*

Harbour Museum Close to the Guildhall this museum contains a great deal of historically interesting items from when the harbour was an active commercial port, shipping linen and people to America. Vaguely interesting for a wet afternoon. ■ *Guildhall St/Harbour Square, T71377331. Monday-Friday 1000-1300, 1400-1600. Free.*

Foyle Valley Railway Centre Beside Craigavon Bridge is this museum representing Derry's years as a rail destination: old rolling stock, exhibitions about the railway and a 20-minute diesel ride. Good for children. ■ *Foyle Road, T71265234. Tuesday-Saturday, 1000-1630. Free. Train ride £2.50.*

Amelia Earhart Centre Five kilometres north west of Derry is the Amelia Earhart Centre, commemorating the spot where she accidentally landed in 1932 having just made the first female solo crossing of the Atlantic. She mistook the village of Ballyarnett for Paris and landed there instead. Includes photos and memorabilia.

■ *Ballyarnett, T354040. Monday-Thursday, 0900-1700, Friday 0900-1300. Free. Bus number D17 from the bus station.*

This museum is on the other side of the river from the walled city and represents an excellent piece of reconstruction and renovation. Downstairs in the old workhouse building is a public library, while the upper floors are the unaltered sleeping quarters of the women's section of the poor house. Not much to look at here, but a fascinating insight into the conditions that these poor women must have lived in. There is also a permanent exhibition about Derry's part in the Battle of the Atlantic during the Second World War. There are often other temporary exhibitions and performances here. Those who died in the Workhouse during the Famine were buried in the yard, now a housing estate. When the estate was built hundreds of remains were exhumed and reburied in local graveyards. ■ *23 Glendermott Road, Waterside, T71318328. October to June, Monday-Thursday 1000-1630, Saturday 1000-1630; July to September, Monday-Saturday 1000-1630, Sunday 1400-1600. Free.*

Workhouse Museum & Library

County Derry

Essentials

While hotels are not burgeoning here at the same rate as in Belfast, there is a good range of accommodation, but in the cases of hotels and hostels it would be well to book in advance. The tourist office will book accommodation for you if you arrive in town with none organized.

Sleeping
■ *on map*
Price codes:
see inside front cover

AL *Beech Hill Country House Hotel*, 32 Ardmore Rd, T71349279, F71345366. Well away from the city, a pleasant place if you have transport. Reputable restaurant. **AL** *Everglades Hotel*, 41-53 Prehen Rd, T71346722, F71349200. Set in a pleasant location on the route into Derry on the banks of the river Foyle, this is Derry's only 4-star hotel. Big luxurious rooms, lots of lounge area, good restaurant. **AL** *Trinity Hotel*, 22 Strand Rd, T71271271, F71271277. City hotel, very new, pleasantly appointed rooms, very popular bar and bistro. Ask for a room on the top floor and at the back because of the unholy noise coming from the many discos held here and in the pub opposite. **AL** *Waterfoot Hotel and Country Club*, 14 Clooney Rd, T71345500, F71311006. Big, anonymous place well out of the centre of town. Breakfast is continental. **A** *Beechwood House*, 45 Letterkenny Rd, T71271444, F71264900. Small guesthouse, close to town with lots of facilities including gym, sauna, games room. Same place also does self-catering chalets. **A** *The Inn at the Cross*, 171 Glenshane Rd, T71301480, F71301394. Out-of-town guest house with popular restaurant and bar, more of a hotel in style.

B *An Mointean*, 245 Lone Moor Rd, T71287128. Comfortable, out of town, off-street parking. 15 mins walk to city. **B** *Arkle House*, 2, Coshquin Rd, T71271156. A Victorian house offering B&B, 1½ miles northwest of the centre of Derry. **B** *Number 10*, 10 Crawford Square, T71265000. A B&B 5 minutes from the city centre near the technical college. **C** *Aberfoyle*, 33 Aberfoyle Terrace, Strand Rd, T71283333. A B&B 5 minutes from the city centre. **C** *Acorn B&B*,17 Aberfoyle Terrace, Strand Rd, T71271156. 5 minutes from the city centre in the student area of town. **D** *Oakgrove Manor*, 6 Magazine St, T71284100, F71284101. Purpose-built hostel. Dorm beds are £7.50 with special offers in the off-season, while beds in a room sleeping 4 are £9.50. Doubles at £30. Right in the heart of the city, bike hire £7, games room, restaurant, self-catering.

Eating
● *on map*
Price codes:
see inside front cover

While Derry isn't overrun with exciting restaurants, there are enough places to keep you out of McDonald's during your stay. The *Trinity Hotel* has *Nolan's Bistro*, whose menu has the usual range of meats and fish with nods to modernism in the form of ciabatta bread, olives, wild mushrooms and apricot and rosemary chutney. Also has two vegetarian options, one of which is the unmentionable vegetable lasagne. Dinner at around £16 plus, set menu around £14. The hotel bar also does bar food 7 days a week and there is a restaurant that serves lunch as well as dinner. The *Ardmore* is at *Beech Hill Country House* (see 'Sleeping', page 559) and serves haute cuisine. Reservations in order at weekends. The restaurant at the *Everglades* is the *Satchmo*, where the food is very traditional – little moon-shaped dishes of vegetables, with two kinds of potato – but it's nicely cooked and reasonably priced. Dinner at under £20. A way out of town at the *Inn at the Cross* (see 'Sleeping', page 559) is *Companion's*, where there is a set menu as well as à la carte. The bar also does bar food.

At lunchtime the range of options is much wider with most of the pubs in town doing food of some kind. Along Waterloo St the *Rocking Chair*, T71265200, *Bound for Boston*, Henry Joy McCracken's, T71360177, the *Dungloe*, T71267716, the *Gweedore* T71263513, and *Peadar O'Donnell's*, T71372318, all do pub food and in summer you might catch some live traditional music. The *Metro*, T71267401, in Bank Place does food from 1200 to 1500 weekdays, longer at weekends, is seriously touristified but has decent meals at around £4. The *Gluepot*, T71367463, in the *River Inn* in Shipquay St has a long menu of filled potatoes, things with chips and lots more, which it serves 7 days till 1430; it also has evening food 1900-2100 Wednesday-Saturday. At 61 Strand Rd is *The Sandwich Company*, T71266771, very popular with lunchtime eaters, and which becomes a Mexican restaurant called *Jalapeno's* in the evenings. There is another branch of this popular shop, which closes early, between 1630 and 1730, 6 days, at the Diamond, T71372500.

Around the bus station are a whole rash of places. *Open Oven*, *Cappucino's*, T71370059, and *Café Nosh*, T71308273, all in Foyle St, do things and chips, filled rolls, jacket potatoes and have a high turnover of fresh food. *Café Nosh* actually opens Sunday evenings till 2100. *J T McGinley*, T71360066, next door to *Café Nosh* is a theme pub with lots of old stuff in the window and a fake old bar but has cooked lunches for around £4 including vegetarian choices. Round the corner in Water St is *Sandino's*, T71309297, hideously yellow outside with lots of items on the menu for lunch all at around £4 plus.

Pubs & music
For traditional Irish music the bars in Waterloo St are the best bet. *Peadar O'Donnell's* often has set dancing and the *Gweedore*, close by, has music and dancing upstairs. The other pubs along Waterloo St will have notices up advertising their music nights. Inside the walls the *Gluepot*, the *Townsman* and *Metro* have live music. In Foyle St *McGinleys* has live music six nights a week, while *Sandino's* is home to the Derry Folk Club and has a jazz night too. For the young and studenty there is *Café Roc*, T71309372, on the corner of Rock Rd and Strand Rd. The café does pub food and caters largely to a student clientele, while upstairs *Earth* nightclub has disco music on

Tuesdays, Fridays and Saturdays. At the *Delacroix*, on Buncrana Rd, T71262990, there is a comedy club while *Da Vinci's*, T71372074, in Conmore Rd has a disco at weekends and ballroom dancing in the restaurant late on Saturday evenings. In Waterside, *The Gallery*, 14 Dungiven Rd, is a popular pub and restaurant.

Art galleries In addition to the *Rialto*, the *Playhouse* and the *Foyle Arts Centre* (see **Entertainment** 'Theatre' below), there are several other art galleries. *The Orchard Gallery* in Orchard St is very innovative, while the *Context Gallery*, at 5-7 Artillery St, T71373538, has changing exhibitions of contemporary art, is open 1000-1530, charges no entry fee. The *Mc Gilloway Gallery*, 6, Shipquay St, T71360011, sells modern Irish paintings, which one can view free from 1000 until 1730. Evening viewing is available by appointment.

Cinema *The Orchard Cinema*, T71262845, is the town's film club and is housed in *St Columb's Theatre* (see below). The *Strand Multiplex* , Strand Rd, T71373939, has 7 screens and, when it opens, the Millennium complex will house a cinema.

Theatre The vast Millennium Complex, when it opens, will house a theatre, but in the mean time there is the Rialto, 5 Market St, T71260516, which holds art and photographic exhibitions, concerts and plays. Box office Monday-Saturday, 0930-1700. The *Playhouse*, 5-7 Artillery St, T71268027 is another multimedia venue, where at various times you can catch art exhibitions, theatre, dance and concerts. The *Foyle Arts Centre*, Lawrence Hill, T71266657, is home to a studio theatre and larger auditorium and holds lots of amateur productions as well as art exhibitions. *St Columb's Theatre*, Orchard St, T71267789, was Derry's major theatre and hosts *árd fheis* and visiting theatre companies.

There is a *Celtic Spring Festival* in Derry celebrated at varying dates in **March** and **Festivals** involving theatre, music and Gaelic events. The *Foyle Film Festival* takes place in **late April** and the *Southern Comfort Jazz and Blues festival* is in **late May**. The largest and noisiest festivals in Derry take place in **October** with the two Cathedrals festival followed by a week or so of fireworks and fun at Halloween.

Bowling *Brunswick Superbowl*, Brunswick Lane, T71371999. 0900-late. 10-pin bowl- **Sport** ing. **Fishing** *Enagh Trout Lake*, 12, Judges Rd, T71860916. *The Foyle Fisheries Commission*, 8 Victoria Rd, T71342100. Information and licences. *Glenowen Fisheries Cooperative*, Creggan reservoir, T71371544. Licences, accommodation, equipment. **Gaelic** *Gaelic Athletic Association*, Gaelic football, hurling, camogie, T71342561. **Golf** *Foyle International Golf Centre*, 12, Alder Rd, T71352222, 18 holes. £9 weekdays, £11 weekends. Discounts for accompanying member. *The City of Derry Golf Club*, Victoria Rd, Waterside, T71311610. 18 holes. Monday-Saturday 0800-2330. Weekdays £20, weekends £25. Discounts with member. **Greyhound racing** *Brandywell Greyhound Racing Co*, Brandywell Football ground T71265461. **Karting** *Daytona Karting*, 20B Drumahoe Industrial estate, Drumahoe, T71313718. 1100-2300. Book in advance. **Leisure centres** *Brandywell Sports Centre*, Lone Moor Rd, T71263902. Indoor football arena and handball arena. *Brooke Park Leisure Centre*, Rosemont Ave, T71262637. Squash, fitness training, sauna, tennis, bowls. *Lisnagelvin Leisure Centre*, Richill Park, T71347695. Pool, wave-making machine. *Templemore Sports Complex*, Buncrana Rd, T71265521. Pools, sauna, squash, major sporting events in the main sports hall. **Riding** *Culmore Riding School*, 130 Culmore Rd, T71359248.

Air From Derry Airport, Longfield Rd, Eglinton, T71810784, there are flights to **Transport** Aberdeen, Amsterdam, Belfast, Birmingham, Blackpool, Bristol, Brussels, Exeter, Frankfurt, Glasgow, Guernsey, the Isle of Man, Jersey, Leeds, Liverpool, Gatwick,

Manchester, Newcastle and Paris. The airport is 11 km from the city centre on the A2. At the airport, facilities include a free car-park, information desk, bar and café. **Bike hire** *An Móintean Rent-a-bike and Cycle Tours*, 245 Lone Moor Rd, T71287128: Raleigh Rent-a-bike scheme, £7 per day. **Bus** All buses depart from the Ulsterbus Depot in Foyle St, T71262261. Express services go to Belfast via Dungiven, Coleraine, Dublin, Belfast via Omagh. Local buses connect with most of the towns in the north. A private bus company, the Lough Swilly Company T71262017, connects with Buncrana, Moville, Carndonagh, Letterkenny, Dungloe and Fanad. North West Busways, T0035377-82619 offers similar services operating out of the Republic. An Airporter bus, T71269996, operates between Clarendon St and the two Belfast airports. **Car** *Ford Rent-a-car*, Desmond Motors Ltd, 173 Strand Rd, T71360420. City of Derry Airport, T71812220. **Taxis** *A1 Taxis*, 7 Chapel Rd, T71342626. *Auto Cabs*, 85 Spencer Rd, T71343030. *Black Taxis*, Foyle St, T71260247. **Train** From the rail station in Waterside, T71342228, trains go to Belfast via Coleraine, Portrush, Ballymena, Antrim and Lisburn. There are around 7 trains a day. From Belfast there are connections to Dublin and other towns in the Republic.

Directory **Banks** *Bank of Ireland*, Strand Rd, T71264141, Shipquay St, T71264992. *First Trust*, Shipquay St, T71363921. Racecourse Rd, T71267722. Spencer Rd, T71348442. Waterloo Pl, T71262446. *Northern Bank*, Guildhall Sq, T71265333. **Bureaux de Change** *NW Money Exchange*, Foyleside, 68 Strand Rd, Richmond Centre, Wed-Fri, 0900-2100. **Communications** Post Office: Custom House St, T71223344. Mon 0830-1730, Tue-Fri 0900-1730, Sat 0900-1230. **Laundry** *Duds 'n' Suds*, 141 Strand Rd, T71312297, 0800-2000. **Library** Foyle St, T71266888, Mon, Thu 0915-2000, Tue, Wed, Fri 0915-1730, Sat 0915-1700. **Places of worship** Baptist: Fountain St, services Sun 1130, 1830. Church of Ireland: St Columb's Cathedral, services Sun 0800, 1600 (Evensong). Methodist: Clooney Hall, services Sun 1145, 1830. Quaker, 23 Bishop St, Sun 1100. **Roman Catholic**: St Eugene's Cathedral, Gt James St, services weekdays 0800, 0900, 1000, 1930; Sat 0900, 1000, 1815, 1930; Sun 0700, 0830, 1000, 1100, 1215. **Tourist office** 44 Foyle St, T71267284. Jul-Sep, Mon-Fri 0900-1900, Sat 1000-1800, Sun 1000-1700; Oct-Jun, Mon-Thu 0900-1715, Fri 0900-1700 (Easter-Jun also Sat 1000-1700).

Derry to Coleraine

To Downhill The A2 follows the south side of Lough Foyle, moves inland a wee bit to Limavady, then heads north to Magilligan where the B202 is a spur off to **Magilligan Point** and the incredible 7-mile (11-kilometre) stretch of sandy **Benone Strand**. The A2 continues to Downhill where, on top of a 180-foot (55-metre) cliff, a Bishop of Derry in the 1780s commissioned the building of an extravagant palace and a Greek-style temple. The whole project was manifestly absurd, cost a small fortune to build and decorate with paintings by

Rubens, Dürer and Tintoretto, and the whole lot burnt to the ground in 1851. The bishop had taken off in the 1790s for a tour of the continent where, thought to be a spy, he was arrested by Napoleon and found in possession of more valuable works of art. 'Oh, what a lovely thing it is to be an Anglican bishop or minister,' exclaimed a French visitor to Ireland at the time. The ruins of **Downhill Palace** and the intact **Mussenden Temple** are National Trust properties and can be visited. ■ *Mussenden Rd, Castlerock, on the A2, T70848728. Grounds always open. Temple: July and August, daily 1200-1800; April to June and September, Saturday and Sunday 1200-1800. Free.*

Hezlett House Also on the A2, four miles (6.5 kilometres) northwest of Coleraine, Hezlett House is another National Trust property, a thatched 17th-century former rectory noted for its cruck truss roof. ■ *T70848567. June to August, Wednesday-Monday 1200-1700; April to May and September, weekends only. £4.50.*

Portstewart The A2 takes one through **Coleraine** but there is little good reason to stop in this depressing urban centre when the seaside towns of the north coast are so close at hand. The main town on the coast is Portstewart, a bustling seaside town popular with families and surfers, and a good place to stop between Derry and Portrush for a meal and a fresh-air walk along the seafront. Start at the Crescent area in the west end of town where the Dominican convent, now a school, is perched on the hilltop and follow the surfaced path along the cliff until the glorious vista of the **Portstewart Strand** opens up. Descend to the beach here: access by car costs £2.50. In places, signs warn of dangerous currents but this is a prime surfing beach.

Sleeping B *Craigmore House*, 26 The Promenade, Portstewart, T70832120. Facing the ocean and in the thick of the seaside scene. B *Strandeen*, 63 Strand Rd, Portstewart, T70833159. A corner-house in a quieter location for a B&B with the beach only five minutes away. D *Causeway Coast Hostel*, 4 Victoria Terrace, Atlantic Circle, T70833789. Open all year, its 30 beds include 3 private rooms at £15 each and it has bikes for hire.

Eating *Skippers*, in the *Anchorage Inn* at 87 The Promenade, Portstewart, T70834401, is open for lunch with the same menu of meat and chicken dishes for £4 available in the bar. From 1700 there is a fair choice of pasta, half of which are vegetarian dishes as well as meat and fish dishes and all for £6-£8. Time is of the essence in the dark and cavernous interior of the *Montague Arms*, 68 The Promenade, Portstewart, T70832150, where a 10oz steak is £5 at 1700 but increases in price by 25p every 15 minutes to £9.50 at 2130! *Morelli's*, 57 The Promenade, Portstewart, opens daily until 2300 in summer for pasta, pizza, ice cream and cappuccino. Fast pub food can be found at *Shenanigans*, 78 The Promenade, Portstewart.

Sport **Diving** Scuba-diving and PADI courses through *Aquaholics*, T70836909. **Surfing** gear and information in Portstewart from *Ocean Warriors*, opposite the *Anchorage Inn*, on The Promenade.

Directory **Tourist office** Town Hall, The Crescent, Portstewart, T70832286.

Inland Derry

The appeal of inland Derry is limited but there are some interesting alternatives if seaside resorts such as Portstewart and Portrush are not to one's liking.

Roe Valley Country Park The Roe Valley Country Park stretches for three miles (five kilometres) along both sides of the Roe River near Limavady, the best of the walks pass industrial relics from the time when clattering water wheels powered machinery here for the manufacture of linen (see page 584). Head south, upstream, to see the bleaching greens where the cloth was spread out and guarded from the watch towers that still stand (stealing linen was a capital offence), cross by the first or second footbridge and return on the other side for a hour's walk. A second walk, downstream, passes a greater variety of industrial buildings, and returning via the second footbridge this way is also an hour's return walk. The Centre provides an slide-show on the linen industry and there is a separate Weaving Shed Museum. If industrial machinery really hooks you, request a visit to the Power House, Ulster's first domestic hydro-electric power station that opened in 1896. ■ *Monday-Friday. Once in the park, a sheet outlining short walks is available. The park is located off the B192, 1 mile (1.5 km) south of Limavady, from where the Bus No 146 runs.*

There is a café serving chips and burgers, but picnic tables near the Centre make a more attractive proposition. Come dusk on a summer's day otters can be spotted in the river and buzzards occasionally fly overhead, while in springtime the woodland floor is dotted with wood anemones and lesser celandine. ■ *T77722074. June to August, daily, 1000-2000. Shorter hours the rest of the year. Free.*

Plantation towns South Derry detains few travellers but a pit stop at one of the Plantation towns may be made whilst journeying between Derry and Belfast on the A6. **Draperstown** is a short detour off the A6 but has the benefit of the **Plantation of Ulster Visitor Centre** and museum technology to bring alive the story of the plantations by London companies starting in 1595. There is a café and small shop. ■ *50 High Street T79627800. Daily, 1100-1700. £3.*

The town of **Moneymore**, further south and close to the border with Cookstown and county Tyrone, is a veritable museum in itself, so well preserved and decorous are the Georgian houses. Close by, **Springhill**, on the B18 one mile (1.5 kilometres) southeast of Moneymore, is a 17th-century manor house characteristic of the type built by the planters and, true to its spirit, saw the UVF training in the grounds in 1913 in preparation for armed resistance to Home Rule. ■ *T86748210. Easter and July to August, Friday-Wednesday 1400-1800; April to June and September, weekends only. £2.50.*

Sleeping **L** *Radisson Roe Park Hotel*, Roe Park, Limavady. T77722222, F77722313. Has big bedrooms, indoor pool and gym and its own 18-hole parkland golf course. **B** *Alexander Arms*, 34 Main St, Limavady, T77763443, F77722327, is a town-centre pub with rooms and serves inexpensive food. **C** *Keady View Farm*, 47 Seacoast Rd, Limavady, T77764518, has only 2 rooms, but there are quite a few more B&Bs along this road.

Eating The Brasserie at the *Radisson Roe Park Hotel* has dishes such as Singapore chicken, lamb kebab for £7, and more-expensive steaks. The hotel's octagonal *Courtyard Restaurant* has a £20 set dinner plus à la carte, serving imaginatively presented food. In Limavady town *Gentry's*, 18 Main St, T77722017, is open until 2230 most nights and midnight over the weekend for balti chicken and lamb as well as pizza and pasta dishes for around £6.

County Antrim

Travelling the coastline of county Antrim is a memorable experience, and coming up the coast from Belfast the departure from cityscapes to sudden vistas of rock and sea is an instant therapy for any lingering urban blues. This chapter's route starts from the other end, in seaside Portrush just across the Derry border, and works its way along the northern coast to the Giant's Causeway and delightful Ballycastle before heading south past the Glens of Antrim and a string of settlements that dot the highly scenic journey down to Belfast.

County Antrim

Portrush

Portrush is a busy seaside resort packed with activities for families, a place to head for on wet days, and while the downside may be the usual tackiness and the excess of buckets and spades dangling from shop doorways there are upbeat surprises in store as well. Portrush is a superb centre for surfing and in town you will also discover one of the best restaurants in Ireland.   Colour map 1, grid A4

Sights

Curran Strand is the sandy beach, that stretches eastwards for over a mile, past the famous golf course, to the **White Rocks**, perfect for picnics, where erosion has weathered and sculptured arches and caves into weird shapes. Surfing is good here: try the East Strand, which can be reached by car, although the West Strand is just as good. For gear and advice see 'Sport' on page 567.   **Curran Strand**

The Ulster Way path, rising up to clifftop level, follows the coast from Portrush to Portstewart. From Portrush Harbour, **boat trips** head out to tour The Skerries, a chain of small islands off the coast. Horseriding is also available: see 'Sport', page 567   **Ulster Way**

Dunluce Centre This boasts three sensations: *Turbo Tours*, a film theatre with thrill rides, *Earth Quest*, with hands-on exhibitions of local wildlife, and *Myths & Legends*, a top-of-the-bill multimedia show based on local folklore. ■ *Sandhill Drive, T70824444. Separate admission charges or all three for £5, and family tickets as well.*

Waterworld By the harbour, a water playground with all the works and extending to evening shows. ■ *T70822001. Admission £4.25 but a variety of family tickets is available.*

Barry's Behind the seafront, Barry's is the largest amusement park in Ireland, with indoor and outdoor entertainment. *Fantasy Island*, on the promenade, is an indoor adventure playground with a café and supervisory staff. ■ *Fantasy Island: T70823595.*

Portrush Countryside Centre This is an exhibition centre covering local natural history. Raining or not, go hunting for fossil impressions on the seashore next to the Centre beside the car park. ■ *Lansdowne Crescent, T70823600. June to September, Wednesday-Monday, 1200-2000. Free.*

Public transport along the North Antrim coast

Between 25th May and 27th September (between 5th July and 26th September for Sunday services) the Ulsterbus 252 Antrim Coaster service runs twice daily between Belfast and Coleraine and stops at all the main towns of interest around the coast. Buses leave Coleraine at 0950 and 1610, (departing from Belfast at 0910 and 1400) and stop at Portrush, Portballintrae, Bushmills, Giant's Causeway, Ballintoy, Ballycastle, Cushendon, Cushendall, Carnlough, Glenarm, Larne, Carrickfergus (morning service only), and Belfast.

In July and August there is an open-topped bus running five times a day between Coleraine and the Causeway, via Portstewart, Portrush, Portballintrae and Bushmills, but flaggable anywhere along its route. For details of public transport, T20731337.

The Ulsterbus 152 service runs throughout the year between Ballycastle and Portrush on the B146, via Carrick-a-rede, Ballintoy and the Giant's Causeway.

Essentials

Sleeping B&B rates peak in July and August to £18-£25 per person, dropping to around £15 at other times for rooms sharing bathroom facilities. Most of the caravan parks will take only a token number of tents, but a couple are listed that will take more.

L *Magherabuoy House Hotel*, 41 Magherabuoy Rd, T70823507, F70824687. Outside of town with unrivalled views over the Atlantic Ocean. **A** *Maddybenny Farm*, 18 Maddybenny Park, T70823394. This may be out of town, but a more gregarious guest-house would be hard to find and your enjoyment of a visit will be proportional to your appetite for a gargantuan breakfast (porridge with Drambuie and cream as an appetizer) that makes the usual B&B offering seems like child's play. **A** *Peninsula Hotel*, 15 Eglinton St, T70822293, F70824315. A new hotel in the town centre with 25 double rooms. **B-C** *Atlantis*, 10 Ramore Avenue, T70824583. A B&B not in a quiet part of town, but with the advantage of a kitchen available for snacks. **B-C** *Casa-A-La-Mar*, 21 Kerr St, T/F70822617. B&B with six well-provided rooms that overlook the West Strand. **B-C** *Windsor Guest House*, 67 Main St, T70823793. A family-run period town house in the heart of town. **D** *Macools*, 5 Causeway View Terrace, T70824845. An independent hostel with a good name and 18 beds, including a private room at £16, for £7 per person.

Hilltop Holiday Park, 60 Loguestown Rd, T70823537, off the A29. Caravan park, will take up to 50 tents at £7 each. *Skerries Holiday Park*, 126 Dunluce Rd, T70822531. This caravan park will take up to 50 tents at £10 each.

Too many stodgy meat-and-potato meals? *Ramore*, overlooking the harbour, T70824313, provides an antidote. In the main restaurant, look for the specials: fish of the day might be grilled monkfish on puff pastry with bits of lobster tucked away inside, plus shiitake mushrooms and truffle cream. There is an impressive, predominantly French, wine list starting at around £9 a bottle. All of this for around £25 for a three-course meal. As well as the main restaurant there is a wine bar downstairs (closed Sunday and main restaurant closed Monday), which serves less expensive food. Interior décor in both outlets is based around sharp, jazzy themes and the food is exceptionally satisfying. The *Snapper Restaurant*, Ballyreagh Rd, on the road between Portrush and Portstewart, T70824945, is the next best, with main dishes like chicken kebabs and seafood paella around £10 and pizzas for £6. Consider a trip to nearby Coleraine where the *Water Margin*, Hanover Place, T70342222, overlooking the river, has been recommended for its Chinese food. A set meal for two is £18.

There are some truly dreadful places in the centre of town serving fish-and-chips-type meals, don't be misled by nautical themes and reasonable prices. *Donovan's*, 92 Main St, T70822063, is one of the better pubs, serving food daily at lunchtime for around £5, and in the evening offering a variety of grills, salads and the like. *Don Giovanni's*, 9 Causeway St, T70825516, is fine for pizzas and pasta and also does some veal and fish dishes.

Entertainment

On summer nights pubs and hotels are blasting out music, but not of the traditional Irish kind. *Lush!*, Bushmills Rd, T70823539, is a disco of local renown and the *Magherabuoy House Hotel*, T70823507, has better musical entertainment than most of the hotels. For a pub with some character try the *Harbour Inn*, behind *Ramore's* wine bar at the harbour.

Sport

Golf *Royal Portrush*, T70382231. Less expensive 18-hole courses are *Moyola Park*, T79668468, and *Masserene*, T94428096. **Horseriding** *Maddybenny Riding Centre*, 18 Maddybenny Park, T70823394. **Microflights and flying school** *Microflight Ireland*, 67 Main St, T70823793, F70824625. **Surfing** *Rock Bottom Surf Shack*, 18 Main St, T70825665.

Transport

Bus See page 566 for details of the Antrim Coaster service. Ulsterbus services also connect Portrush with Antrim, Armagh, Ballymena, and Cookstown. **Train** From Portrush station, T70822395, there are 7 trains a day to Coleraine from where connections to Derry, Belfast and Dublin can be made.

Directory

Tourist office Dunluce Centre, Sandhill Rd, T70823333. Apr-mid-Jun, Mon-Fri 0900-1700, Sat and Sun 1200-1700; Mid-Jun-Sep, daily, 0900-2000; Mar and Oct, Sat and Sun, 1200-1700. **Tour companies** *Lynchpin (Ireland) Ltd* creates customized tours for individuals, T70823232, www.lynchpin-ireland.co.uk

Portrush to the Giant's Causeway

Between Portrush and the Giant's Causeway there are two points of interest. Dunluce Castle, beside the A2 and not to be missed on a fine day, is just west of the small harbour at Portballintrae, while Bushmills and its famous distillery are just off the A2 a little further to the east. Bushmills makes a convenient watering hole for lunch, before or after a visit to the Causeway.

Dunluce Castle

The castle at Dunluce, one of the most enjoyable to visit anywhere in Ireland, is not one of those brutal Norman impositions, for there is something whimsical as well as dramatic about its spectacular location on a rock-stack. A fortification of some kind here goes back two millennia perhaps, but the earliest of the castle walls were built for the MacQuillans, Scottish mercenaries originally, in the 14th century and completed later by the MacDonnells. The English under Sir John Perrott, determined to clear the Scots from Antrim, took the castle with artillery in 1584, but the following year Sorley Boy MacDonnell (see box on page 578) and his men scaled the cliffs on ropes and hung the constable (his Scots mistress is said to have played an invaluable part in this). Perrott was philosophical: 'I do not weigh the loss but can hardly endure the discredit'. The MacDonnells made a deal and remained the residents and their subsequent repair work lasted 60 years until the kitchen and servants' quarters collapsed into the sea and ruined a perfectly good night's dinner. There is plenty of the castle left standing and a visit is recommended. ■ *T20731938. April to May and September, Monday-Saturday 1000-1800, Sunday 1400-1800; June to August, Monday-Saturday 1000-1800, Sunday 1200-1800; October-March, Monday-Saturday 1000-1600. £1.50. Visitor Centre, guided tours.*

Bushmills Bushmills developed with the rise of water-powered industry in the early 17th century – the first hydro-electric tramway in the world came through here on its way from Portrush to the Causeway – and whiskey was first legitimately distilled here in 1608. A guided tour of **The Old Bushmills Distillery** covers history and technology and finishes with the customary taster of the famous single malt, triple distilled, whiskey. ■ *T20731521. April to October, Monday-Saturday 0930-1730, Sunday 1200-1730, last tour at 1600; November to March, Monday-Friday, tours on the hour between 1030 and 1530 (but not 1230). http://irish-whiskey-trail.com £3.*

---

*You are welcome
to visit*

The Old Bushmills Distillery Co. Ltd

Tour and Whiskey Tasting at
The World's Oldest Licensed Whiskey Distillery

APRIL - OCTOBER
Monday-Saturday 9.30am - 5.30pm
Sunday 12 noon - 5.30pm
(Last tour 4pm each day)

 Enjoy our Audio-Visual Presentation followed by a guided tour of the Distillery when you can learn about the age-old art of whiskey making.

 Relax in the 1608 Bar where you are invited to enjoy a complimentary glass of one of our famous Bushmills Whiskeys.

 Explore our shops where you will find an exciting range of gifts. Treat yourself to a bottle of exclusive 12 year old "Distillery Reserve" Single Malt Whiskey.

 The cemtre also has an elegant coffee shop "The Distillery Kitchen" serving delicious home made food and refreshments.

**For any other information and Winter Tour times please
Phone 012657 31521 or fax 012657 31339**

AL *Bayview Hotel*, 2 Bayhead Rd, Portballintrae, T20731453. Hotel with an indoor **Sleeping** pool. **AL** *Beach House Hotel*, Beach Rd, Portballintrae, T20731214. Has a reputation for good food and it's hard to beat the view that stretches from Donegal to Scotland from the restaurant window. Bedrooms are plain, but the views…! **AL** *Bushmills Inn*, 25 Main St, Bushmills, T20732339. A hotel as well as a restaurant. **C** *Ahimsa*, 243 Whitepark Rd, T20731383, a traditional cottage specializing in vegetarian meals and using produce from its organic garden. **C** *Keeve-Na*, 62 Ballaghmore Rd, Portballintrae, T20732184. At £32 for a double room, a good-value B&B.

Portballintrae Caravan Park, Portballintrae, on the B145 towards Bushmills, T20731478. Has 16 tent pitches for £6.

Bushmills Inn, 25 Main St, Bushmills, T20732339, has a comfortable and very inviting **Eating** bar, an inexpensive brasserie open at weekends, and a restaurant open daily and serving the best food in the area at around £22 for a meal. A few doors up the *New Mill Restaurant* is a new place doing bar snacks and meals like chicken and bacon for £5.50 and 10oz steak for £10. In the summer *Sallie's* craft shop in Portballintrae, Beach Rd, T20731328, serves up pizzas and light meals until 1800. *Sweeney's*, Seaport Ave, Portballintrae, T20732405, is a pleasant stone built pub with a conservatory, and popular sessions of live and loud music; decent food is served daily.

If Bushmills Distillery has whetted your appetite, Bushmills Inn serves beef fillet strips in a sauce of cream mixed with more of the hard stuff

Banks *Northern Bank*, 62 Main St, Bushmills. Money can also be changed at the Visitor's Centre **Directory** at Giant's Causeway. **Communications Post office:** 67 Main St, Bushmills, by the roundabout in the centre of town. Will also change money. **Tourist information** Visitor's Centre, Giant's Causeway, T20731855.

Giant's Causeway

Formed by the cooking and cooling of vast quantities of basalt, the giant crystals of the Giant's Causeway have been attracting countless visitors since first 'discovered' by the Victorians. The novelist Walter Scott selected four of the basalt columns to take home with him but changed his mind, the poet Keats set out to walk here from Donaghadee but found it too long a journey, while Thackeray in his 1842 tour was led to exclaim that when God fashioned the world out of chaos 'this must have been *the bit over* – a remnant of chaos'.

One version has it that the polygonal columns were spewed forth as the result of a cataclysmic convulsion in the crust of oceanic tectonic plates, but the Causeway Centre is not bound by modern dogma and the exhibition allows visitors to choose between this fanciful account and the more prosaic account that lusty Finn McCool (Fionn Mac Cumhaill) wanted a passageway across the water to reach a giantess on the island of Staffa, off the coast of Scotland. This is backed up by science, for similar rock formations are indeed to be found there as well.

From the Causeway Centre it is a short walk to the shore and Finn's stepping stones but in summer you will have to dodge minibuses and hordes of visitors. Follow instead the path up behind the Centre and take the **North Antrim Cliff Path** from where further along a few hundred steps bring you down to the shore.

There is no charge to visit the Giant's Causeway unless arriving by car or wishing to hop in the minibus, £1 return, from the Causeway Centre to the shore. ■ *Giant's Causeway Centre. T20731159. July to August, daily 1000-1900. Shorter hours rest of the year. Audio-visual show £1. Car park £3. Tea room open March to November.*

The *Causeway School Museum*, an original 1920s classroom and situated next to the Centre, is worth a visit with children or on a wet day. ■ *T20731777. July to August, daily 1100-1700. 75p.*

County Antrim

Walking the Having ticked off the Giant's Causeway on the 'been there, done that' list, it
Causeway coast seems a pity to leave the majestic North Antrim coast too quickly, and luckily
the **North Antrim Cliff Path** provides an exhilarating way of extending one's
stay. It takes about five hours to walk the 17 kilometres (10 miles) between
Portballintrae and Ballintoy, and with the aid of a bus timetable it should be
possible to catch a bus (see page 566) back to your vehicle or accommodation.
While it the path (marked on the Ordnance Survey sheet 5 in the Discovery
series) be walked in either direction there is a high in both senses if you start
from Ballintoy and cross White Park Beach to the little harbour of
Portbraddan, where St Gobhan's claims to be the smallest church in Ireland,
and on to Dunserverick and up to the clifftop for a spectacular couple of miles
to the Giant's Causeway. Walking in Northern Ireland doesn't come much
better than this.

The tourist office in Portrush has a leaflet describing a walk following the
tracks of the Causeway Tram that ran between Portrush and the Causeway
between 1883 and 1949. There is talk of relaying part of the line.

For sleeping and eating at the Portballintrae end see the Portrush to Giant's
Causeway section on page 569 and for the other end of the walk see the Giant's
Causeway to Ballycastle section on page 571. For organized walks contact *Dal
Riada*, 68 Station Road, Portstewart, T70832832, info@dal-riada.com
http://www.dal-riada.com For organized cycling trips: *Ardclinis Outdoor
Adventure*, T/F00-44-12667-71340, ardclinis@aol.com

Sleeping   A stay at the **A** *Causeway Hotel*, Causeway Rd, T20731226, F20732552, should prove
more satisfying than it did to Thackeray in 1842: 'It was impossible to feel comfortable
in the place, and when the car wheels were heard, I jumped up with joy to take my
departure and forget this awful shore, that wild, dismal, genteel inn.' **B** *Whitepark
House*, Whitepark Rd, T20731482, with three rooms sharing bathroom facilities, has
been warmly recommended. B&B is £45 for a double and the odd-looking place is
hard to miss on the road between the Causeway and Ballintoy.

Giant's Causeway to Ballycastle

Dunserverick   As well as the main A2 coast road there is also the B146 road, running parallel
to it but closer to the coast, and this leads past the fragmentary ruins of
Dunserverick Castle, and by the harbour, the small **Dunserverick Museum**.
There is a meagre collection related to disasters at sea – parts from the doomed
Spanish Armada and coal from the *Titanic* – but the location makes an attractive spot for a picnic. Emigrants used to be rowed out from here to hitch a ride
on a passing schooner for Derry or Glasgow, thence to America or Australia
and never to return. ■ *June to August, Monday-Saturday 1000-1600.*

Causeway coast

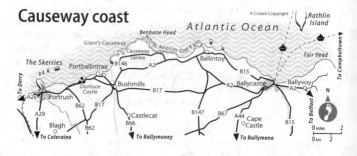

From the village of Ballintoy a winding road leads down to the shore, passing **Ballintoy**
the white-towered Ballintoy church: if you're thinking the tower looks a little
incongruous you're quite right, for there used to be a steeple before a hurricane
demolished it in 1894. The rocky but quaint limestone harbour, sheltered by
basalt rocks like Sheep Island, was built to ship out sett stones from a nearby
quarry that employed over 100 men in the 19th century. Now there are a few
fishing boats, in summer a £1 boat service to Carrick-a-rede, and a satisfying
teashop. From here from it takes half an hour to walk around the headland
leads to the mile-long sandy **White Park Bay**, and if you want to continue
walking follow the North Antrim Cliff Path signs (see page 570) for a most dramatic approach to the Giant's Causeway. Plans to open a clifftop walk
eastwards to Carrick-a-rede may have been completed.

Every year some 100,000 visitors cross the rope bridge at Carrick-a-rede but **Carrick-a-rede**
that may prove scant comfort when you are half-way across and you realize
that turning back means going as far as carrying on to the other side. It's only
80 feet (24 metres) above the sea, but when the rope bridge starts to sway and
your nerves wither try to remember you're really just having holiday fun. The
bridge is erected annually by fishermen throwing a string across with a lead
weight, to access a salmon fishery on the small island. The Centre by the
carpark has information panels on the geology and the quarrying in the 1930s
to 50s that removed the entirety of Larrybane Head and the remains of a promontory fort. ■ *T20731159. May to mid-September, daily. Car park £2. Centre
and tearoom: June to August and weekends in May, daily 1200-1800.*

A couple of miles before Ballycastle the remaining walls and main tower of the **Kinbane Castle**
16th century Kinbane Castle are worth visiting just for the location, perched
on a limestone headland amidst basalt cliffs with Rathlin Island directly across
the water and the towering majesty of Fair Head in the distance. Primroses and
orchids in Spring and perfect for a picnic any time.

B-C *Ballintoy House*, Main St, Ballintoy, T20762317. The house carries the 1737 date **Sleeping**
of its building on its front wall and the B&B rate ranges from £13 outside of summer
and sharing bathroom facilities to £17 for en suite in July and August. **D** *Sheep Island
View*, Main St, Ballintoy, T20769391. Has a terrific kitchen, includes one double at £16,
rents bikes, can organize guided walks and has camping space. **D** *Whitepark Bay
Hostel*, 6 miles west of Ballycastle on the A2, T20731745, F20732034. A top-notch
YHANI hostel overlooking White Park Bay with 6-bed and 4-bed rooms, and 4 superb
double rooms with TV and coffee-making facility. Bicycle hire, foreign exchange and a
restaurant. Beds start at £8.50.

In Ballintoy village the *Carrick-a-Rede* pub, T20762241, has pub food and a restaurant **Eating**
upstairs in the summer. Across the road the *Fullerton Arms*, T20769613, has a similar
set-up, but the restaurant opens only between Wednesday and Sunday.

Perched on the rocks at Ballintoy, *Roark's Kitchen*, T20762225, is open daily
between June and August from 1100 to 1900, and at weekends in May and September, for lovely light meals such as buttered mackerel or baked potato with filling for
around £2.75 and lunches listed on a blackboard outside. The *National Trust tearoom*
at Carrick-a-rede serves dismal fried food redeemed by some local breads.

County Antrim

Ballycastle

Colour map 2, grid A3

Ballycastle is a modestly vivacious little place with some history, and a character reminiscent of the Republic. There are pubs with traditional music, fair restaurants, and an infrastructure that recommends it both as a base for exploring the North Antrim coast and as a place to pause before or after seeing the Glens of Antrim on the east coast. Northern Ireland's only inhabited island lies off the coast, Scotland is a short ferry ride away, and every year three festivals light up the place with song and dance and live music on a stage in the Diamond. The tourist office hands out the useful **Ballycastle Heritage Trail** leaflet that covers a variety of places of historical interest around town, including the little **Ballycastle Museum**, ■ *59 Castle Street, T20762942, July to August, daily, noon-1800. Free.*

Sleeping
■ *on map*
Price codes:
see inside front cover

AL *Marine Hotel*, North St, T20762222. Has a swimming pool and self-catering options sleeping 2-6 people. **B** *Beechwood*, 9 Beechwood Ave, T20763631. Can be recommended for its quiet location and friendly welcome. The house has 2 double rooms at £25 and sharing a bathroom, but best value has to be the two chalet-type rooms at the back with their own facilities including a fridge and sink, £35 for each chalet. No avoiding the Ulster fry-up though. **B-C** *Ammiroy House*, 24 Quay Rd, T20762621, two rooms in a family house, is typical of the B&Bs along this road. **B-C** *Silversprings House*, 20 Silversprings, T20762080, is a distinguished-looking, 7-chimneyed house in a quiet cul-de-sac. **D** *Ballycastle Backpackers*, 4 North St, T20763612. A small hostel, but with four private rooms from £15. **D** *Castle Hostel*, 62 Quay Rd, T20769391. Has 30 beds including 2 private rooms for £15. Is the preferred hostel for some travellers.

Maguire's Strand Caravan Park, 32 Carrickmore Rd, off the A2 south of town, T20763294. A tent pitch costs £9. *Silvercliffs Holiday Village*, 21 Clare Rd, T20762550. Popular campsite that charges £10 for a tent pitch, but there is an indoor pool, sauna and bar. *Watertop Open Farm*, 188 Cushendall Rd, is 6 miles southeast of town on the A2, T20762576. Charges £8.50 for each of its 5 pitches around a working farm.

Ballycastle

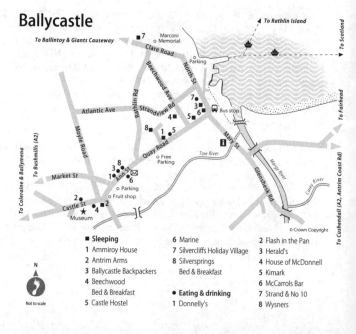

© Crown Copyright

■ **Sleeping**
1 Ammiroy House
2 Antrim Arms
3 Ballycastle Backpackers
4 Beechwood
  Bed & Breakfast
5 Castle Hostel

6 Marine
7 Silvercliffs Holiday Village
8 Silversprings
  Bed & Breakfast

● **Eating & drinking**
1 Donnelly's

2 Flash in the Pan
3 Herald's
4 House of McDonnell
5 Kimark
6 McCarrols Bar
7 Strand & No 10
8 Wysners

Not to scale

County Antrim

'And her hands were bound behind her back'

When Deirdre was born, a druid named her as a source of misfortune but Conchobar had her brought up in secret with the intention of marrying her. It was not to be, for Deirdre knew in her heart that her lover would have black hair, a white body and red cheeks. She met such a man at Emain Macha (Navan Fort) and together with his two brothers they fled, pursued by the revengeful Conchobar, until they found refuge in Scotland and then on a remote island. Lured back with a false message they landed at Ballycastle, but the brothers were murdered and Deirdre brought to Conchobar – 'and her hands were bound behind her back' and later forced to marry one of his accomplices. At Emain Macha, on the day of her wedding, Deirdre commited suicide.

So runs a tale, first written down in the eighth century, that inspired Lady Gregory and through her Yeats and Synge and 20th-century writers a plenty.

No 10, facing the marina on North St, T20768110, serves modern Irish cuisine in generous proportions and with colourful presentation: about £25 for an meal featuring local seafood and occasional rarities such as char from Arctic waters off Iceland, plus lamb, duck and chicken. Reserve a window table for views looking across to the Mull of Kintyre (a mere 20 miles away), Fair Head and Rathlin Island. **Wysner's**, 16 Ann St, T20762372, has won awards for its meat-based dishes, though fish is also available. Steaks and surf & turf are around £12 and a separate day menu features bangers and champs (pork sausages and potato and shallots), pasta, and chicken dishes for around £5. Opinions differ about **Kimark**, 52 Quay Rd, T20762888, a smartly arranged restaurant in the front room of a house looking out on the street. Early evening meals such as steak, roast and baked salmon are inexpensive while main courses on the menu, duck, beef stroganoff, chicken, are £8-£13 and starters include spare ribs and fried brie.

The Strand, 9 North St, T20762349, is the best place for inexpensive dishes of chicken, grills, pizza and pasta at around £6 and a choice of tempting ice-creams at £3.50. **Flash in the Pan**, Castle St, is an excellent, sit-in or take-out, traditional fish and chip outlet. There are two places next to Wysner's on Ann St competing for quick meals and coffee breaks: **Herald's Restaurant** at No 22 comes up with beef, potato and vegetables for £3.50 while **Donnelly's** at No 28 is a bread shop and an OK café. The **Antrim Arms**, 75 Castle St, serves pub food including lamb cutlets, steak, and trout.

The Central Bar, Ann St, has a regular Wednesday night session of traditional music that goes al fresco in the summer with the occasional barbecue thrown in for good measure. For traditional Irish music, on a Thursday night head for **McCarrolls Bar** on Ann St and save Friday for **The House of McDonnell**. In the same family for over two hundred years, the House of McDonnell pub is grand for a quiet chat and a drink, and on a Saturday night musicians are welcomed. The **Marine Hotel** has tame live music most nights in the summer.

Towards the end of May there is the 3-day **Northern Lights Festival** and in mid-June another three days are devoted to the Fleadh Amhrán Agus Rince. At the end of **August** the Oul' Lammas Fair, with a good claim to be Ireland's oldest traditional fair, is a very lively event. All the festivals see an explosion of live music in the pubs.

Bus UlsterBus station, T20762365, Station Rd. Buses run to and from Belfast and Coleraine, Monday-Saturday. See also page 566. McGinn T20763451. A private company running a Ballycastle to Belfast return bus. It departs from the Diamond at 1600 on Friday, 2000 on Sunday, and from outside the Europa Hotel in Belfast at 1815 on

---

Eating
● on map
Price codes:
see inside front cover

If seeking out a local edible seaweed, dulse, go to the Fruit Shop in the Diamond. The shop also stocks yellowman, a chewy toffee eaten hereabouts.

Entertainment

Festivals

Transport

Friday, 2145 on Sunday. Single £3.50, return £6. **Ferry** *The Argyll & Antrim Steam Packet Company* operates between Ballycastle and Campbeltown in Argyll, Scotland. **Taxis** *Connors*, T20763611; *Delargys*, T20762822; *Ronnies*, T20763221. £6 to Ballintoy, £10 to the Causeway or Bushmills, £13 to Portrush, £28 to Belfast airport.

Directory **Banks** *First Trust, Northern Bank* and *Ulster Bank* are all in Ann St. Money can also be changed at the tourist office and the Marine Hotel. **Communications** Post office: 3 Ann St. **Tourist office** 7 Mary St. T20762024. Mon-Fri 0930-1700 (Jul-Aug until 1900), Sat 1000-1800 and Sun 1400-1800.

Walking around Ballycastle The Ulster Way passes through Ballycastle but the route west of town is not recommended until Ballintoy is reached (see Walking the Causeway coast on page 570). While the route east is a tough hike of 20 miles (32 kilometres) to Cushendall, a more manageable trek could end in Cushenden and would take in a glorious clifftop walk around Fair Head and the ascent of Caranmore (1,243 feet). You need Ordnance Survey maps 5 and 9 in the Discovery series.

For gentle strolls collect the *Forest Walks* leaflet from the tourist office which maps out the circular 2-mile Glentaisie Trail and the 3-mile Glenshank Trail, both waymarked.

Rathlin Island

Colour map 1, grid A5 Just six miles (9.6 kilometres) from Ballycastle and 14 (22.5 kilometres) from the Mull of Kintyre in Scotland, Rathlin has an inverted L-shape, four miles by three (6.5 by 4.8 kilometres), and is never wider than a mile (1.6 kilometres). Collect a map from the tourist office in Ballycastle and jump on the ferry for a day out in the fresh air.

Famous people come to Rathlin. The Vikings started their tour of Ireland here in 795CE. Half a century later, Robert the Bruce, in hiding after a whipping by the English at Perth, was inspired by a spider to never give in, and left to fight the English again at Bannockburn. Sir Francis Drake commanded a ship sent here in 1575 to hunt down the family and friends of Sorley Boy MacDonnell (see box on page 578) and massacre them. Marconi, or at least his assistant, sent the world's first wireless message here from Ballycastle in 1891, and around a century later the entrepreneur Richard Branson came down in a balloon near here.

Activities on Rathlin **Walking** and **bird-watching** are the main attractions of a visit, and there is a viewing platform at the West Lighthouse. In late spring and early summer the rocks are crowded with fulmars, guillemots, kittiwakes, Manx shearwaters, razorbills and puffins. ■ *April to August, T20763948.*

Diving trips can be arranged, **fishing** off the rocks is possible and boats can also be hired. Colonies of grey and common seals can be seen at Mill Bay, just south of the harbour and near the hostel and camping ground, and at Rue Point near the South Lighthouse. ■ *Diving: Tommy Cecil, T20763915. Boat hire: T20763922.*

Rathlin Island
© Crown Copyright

Sleeping **C** *The Manor House*, T20763964. A large Georgian house by the harbour, open all year and run by the National Trust as a B&B establishment. Good-value doubles for £30 but a single is £26. **C** *Rathlin Guest House*, The Quay, T20763917. Open April-

Roger Casement (1864-1916)

A British diplomat and Irish nationalist, he negotiated with Germany for a shipment of arms for the planned rising in 1916. He was returning to Ireland, to postpone the rising due to lack of German arms, when he was arrested on landing in Tralee.

September, four rooms at £16 a single and £30 a double. **D** *The Richard Branson Centre*, T20763915. Hostel with 26 beds, opens all year and charges £10 per person. Camping is free near the hostel. **D** *Soerneog View Hostel*, T20763954. Overlooks Mill Bay and is a short walk from the harbour. Open all year but only 6 beds, so book ahead in the summer.

Eating Dinner at the *Rathlin Guest House*, last orders at 1900, is £9.50, but needs booking in advance. *Chip-a-Hoy Restaurant*, at the harbour, opens in the summer between 1100 and 1800 for quick fish meals. *McCuaig's Bar* is nearby and serves breakfast, fish and chips, and champ and opens daily for food from 0900 until 2100. For a picnic on the island stock up with provisions at *Brady's* supermarket in Castle St or the *Co-Op* at the Diamond, Ballycastle.

Transport **Ferry** *Caledonian MacBrayne*, T20769299, run the M.V. *Canna* on its 45-minute journey to Rathlin 4 times a day between June and September (0830, 1030, 1500 and 1700 and returning one hour later) and twice a day the rest of the year. Day return £7.80, bicycles £2, and best booked ahead in the summer.

Ballycastle to Cushendun

Unless you're in a hurry to be somewhere else, the inland route between Ballycastle and Cushendun on the A2 is best passed over for the sake of the coastal road via **Torr Head** and **Murlough Bay**. Other than walking parts of the Ulster Way, this route offers the best coastal scenery in Northern Ireland. At Murlough Bay there is a series of three car-parks with noticeboards detailing short walks in the area, and near the middle car-park a commemorative stone to Roger Casement (see box above). After being hanged in London in 1916 for treason, his remains were finally returned in 1965 to this corner of Ireland where his family roots were.

Cushendun

The distinctive buildings of Cushendun were designed by the architect Clough Williams Ellis, who also designed Portmeirion in north Wales, where the cult 1960s television series *The Prisoner* was filmed. In 1912 Ronald and Maud MacNeil, later Lord and Lady Cushendun, commissioned William Ellis to design the highly formal Square with its quaint dormer windows and slate roofs, and so pleased were they that more building followed in the same style. Most of Cushendun, the nearest port in Ireland to Britain, is now owned by the National Trust and it is a strange place, which manages to be attractive and alienating at the same time. There is a small **information office** in Main St, T21761506, and a leaflet describing three local walks of two, four and six miles in length should be available.

Colour map 1, grid A5

Sleeping **B** *Cushendun Guesthouse*, Strandview Park, T21761266. Overlooking the harbour, only opens in July and August. B&B is £20 per person, sharing bathroom facilities, credit cards not accepted and 'room reservations at weekends for overseas visitors only'. Meals are served in the evening for around £10 and its *Ropeworks Bar* opens at 1700 each day. **B** *Villa Farmhouse*, 185 Torr Rd, T21761252. A more orthodox guest-house with a reputation for good breakfasts and evening meals available if booked in advance. **C** *The Burns*, 116 Torr Rd. T21761285. Charges a flat £15 for person in each of its two rooms.

The *Cushendun Caravan Park*, Glendun Rd, T21761254. Next to the safe beach, with 10 pitches for tents at £5 a night.

Eating The *Cushendun Village Tea Room*, Main St, T21761281, looks the ideal place for a homely cup of tea and apple pie, but fails to live up to expectations. Sandwiches and toasties and grilled food with chips from £4-£8 are served and on Saturday evenings an à la carte menu beckons. Just across the road, *McBride's* is a tiny pub that needs squeezing into, with hardly the elbow space needed to lift a pint to your mouth. Pub food is served daily in the summer.

Transport For transport to and from Cushendun, see Cushendall below.

Cushendall

Colour map 1, grid A5   Cushendall is an engaging village, the name of which had been changed to Newtown Glens until a certain Francis Turnley turned up in the early 19th century, having made his fortune trading in China, bought the whole village, restored its original name and generally injected life and commerce into what was a very sleepy backwater. A predominantly Catholic village, Cushendall was frequently visited by the Belfast poet John Hewitt (an annual summer school on Hewitt is held further down the coast at Garron Point) who was led to reflect on the religious divisions of Ulster:

> *This is our fate: eight hundred years' disaster*
> *crazily tangled as the Book of Kells;*
> *the dream's distortions and the land's division,*
> *the midnight raiders and the prison cells.*
> *Yet like Lir's children banished to the waters*
> *our hearts still listen for the landward bells.*

The village is gratifyingly free of tourists and there is not a great deal to see other than the Curfew Tower that Turnley had built in 1817 to house those who failed to share his ultra-industrious attitude to life. *McCollam's Bar* on Mill Street is definitely worth calling into, because the sessions of traditional music will give a fillip to any Friday night, and often a Saturday and a Tuesday in the summer as well. The second week in August, when the Heart of the Glens Festival arrives in Cushendall, sees all the pubs full to overflowing.

Take either Layde Road from the village past the hostel and a campsite or a cliff-top path from the north end of the beach to reach **Layde Old Church**, its miscellany of MacDonnells tombs and a church with a Michael Healy window *The Light of the World*.

Sleeping **A** *Thornlea* Hotel, 6 Coast Rd, T21771223, F21771362. The only hotel in town, has 13 rooms and charges £48 for a double. **B** *The Meadows*, 81 Coast Rd, T21772020. An award-winning B&B establishment on the main A2 road. **B** *Riverside*, 14 Mill St, T21771655. As central as you can get, next to the tourist office. **C** *The Burn*, 63 Ballymean Rd, T21771733. A mile outside of town on the B14 road. **D** *Cushendall Hostel*, Layde Rd, T21771344. YHANI hostel, one mile north of the village, with over 50 beds.

There are two caravan parks, which accept a small number of tent pitches: *Cushendall*, 62 Coast Rd, T21771699, £5; *Glenville*, 22 Layde Rd, T21771520, £3.

Harry's Restaurant, 10 Mill St, T21772022, with a bar menu from 1230 to 2130 of dishes such as chicken curry and prawn sandwich, and a more formal menu from 1800 featuring steak and fish dishes around £11. Sunday lunch is £8.25. *The Half-Door*, 6 Bridge St, T21771300, opens in the evening for French-style cooking with similar prices to Harry's. For coffee breaks, salads and sandwiches, *Gillian's*, 6 Mill St, is a congenial place that opens daily until 1800. See page 577 for other establishments in the area, at the Glenariff Forest Park. | **Eating**

Celtic Crafts, 3 Shore St, T21772019. Sells Celtic jewellery, Aran knitwear, Irish music CDs, instruments and even the odd hurling stick. | **Shopping**

Boat hire *Red Bay Boats*, Coast Rd, T21771331. **Fishing** licences and information from *O'Neills* shop next to the tourist office in Mill St. **Walking** Sundays in summer at 1100 and 1400: enquire at the tourist office. | **Sport**

Bicycle Hire from *Ardclinis Activity Centre*, High St, T21771340 and the *Cushendall Hostel* (see page 576). **Buses** Buses serve Cushendall and Cushendun from Belfast and Ballymena, Monday to Saturday. No 162 travels daily between Cushendun and Larne via Cushendall and the 162A travels Monday-Friday between Cushendall and Ballycastle via Cushendun. See also the Antrim Coaster service on page 566. | **Transport**

Tourist office Mill St, T21771180. Jul-Aug, Mon-Sat 1000-1300 and 1500-1930. Shorter hours rest of the year. | **Directory**

The Glenariff River flows down to Waterfoot, just south of Cushendall, and its attractive glen is the most accessible of the famed Glens of Antrim, due mainly to the Forest Park and its waymarked trails. The Park's visitor centre is fairly useless, but consult the map on the board near the car-park for a brief explanation of the four available walks. The longest is a 5-mile Scenic Trail through forest and across the Inver river for views down the glen, and the most popular is a three-mile Waterfall Trail. These walks can also be reached from a separate entrance at the back of the Manor Lodge restaurant and its free car-park, though someone will still be there to collect the £1.50 between June and August. The timber catwalk from the restaurant was originally built by the railway company in the late 19th century to encourage day-trippers to use their Ballymena train to Parkmore station at the top of the glen. | **Glenariff Forest Park**

The trails are rich in flowers: liverworts, mosses and ferns abound; in spring, bluebells and wild garlic and in summer woodruff, pink herb Robert and bugle. ■ *On the A43 Ballymena/Waterfoot road, T21758232. Daily from 1000. Car park £3, pedestrian £1.50.*

Eating There is a *Tea House*, T21758769, in the Forest Park serving quiche and salads, and the *Manor Lodge*, Glen Rd, T21758221, reached before the Park if travelling up from Cushendall, serves burgers, cod and chips, and salads for £6-£7 as well as grills and fish dishes from £11 to £16. There is also a bar and picnic tables.

Apart from walks in the Glenariff Forest Park (see page 577), the tourist office has a *Heart of the Glens Guide* that describes a variety of short walks from Cushendall and Cushendun into the glens. A section of the Ulster Way, from Cushendall or Waterfoot (also called Glenariff) to Carnlough is an exciting day's walk of around 11 miles (18 kilometres). Although the Way signs peter | **Walking from Cushendall**

County Antrim

Sorley Boy and the MacDonnells

The MacDonnells were a branch of the Scottish MacDonalds who took over most of Antrim in the 16th century, a process completed by Sorley Boy MacDonnell who then had to deal with an early English attempt to colonize Ulster. His family were massacred on Rathlin Island by the English in 1575 but Sorely Boy fought back (see page 567)

with grit. His son, Randy MacDonnell, accepted the English Crown in return for a grant of 300,000 acres and the earldom of Antrim. His great-great-grandson was the grandfather of Francis Anne Vane Tempest, Marchioness of Londonderry, who built a coaching inn that is now the Londonderry Arms *at Carnlough.*

out as you near Carnlough this will not present a problem if you have Ordnance Survey maps 9 and 5.

The *Moyle Way* is a 20-mile (32-kilometre) route between Glenariff Forest Park (the starting point is opposite the Park entrance on the A43) and Ballycastle. The entire walk needs completing on one day and it no longer goes over Knocklayd, which was one of the highlights, but the tourist office in Cushendall sells a £2 leaflet covering the walk.

Carnlough and Glenarm

Colour map 1, grid A5 The splendid coast road that continues south to Carnlough was being completed when Thackeray reached this part of the country on his grand tour of 1842, and he was quick to perceive its importance: 'one of the most noble and gallant works of art that is to be seen in any country … torn sheer through the rock here and there; and immense work of levelling, shovelling, picking, blasting, filling, is going on along the whole line.' The local limestone, which gives Carnlough its characteristic colour, had already been blasted and picked for the coffers of the Marquis and Marchioness of Londonderry, and the fine stone bridge can still be seen that carried a rail line down to the harbour for export of the stone.

Carnlough In Carnlough there is a tourist office of sorts in *McKillop's* shop on Harbour Road, and you could ask here about the planned completion of a walk utilizing part of the track followed by the old railway line. Or just see for yourself by walking up Waterfall Street from the *Waterfall Inn* and along Private Road (which is not private in any sense), signposted to the waterfall, and then back to town following the route of the disused railway line.

Glenarm There are also some walking possibilities around Glenarm, a couple of miles south of Carnlough on the other side of the bay, including a historical trail through the village itself, and the Layde Walk, which leads to a scenic viewing point and places for a picnic. Leaflets with maps are available from the irregularly opened local tourist office in the Community Hall, or the Larne tourist office. If coming up from Belfast the picturesque village of Glenarm, with its attractive patterning in sections of pavement, lies at the foot of the first of the nine glens of Antrim and may be the first place that tempts you to linger. You might even like to find the time to do a little window-shopping (see 'Shopping', page 579

Sleeping **AL** *Londonderry Arms Hotel*, Carnlough, T28885255, F28885263, ida@glensofan trim.com This ivy-clad building is the most comfortable and historic (see page 578) place for a night's lodging, but ask for one of the older-style bedrooms. The establishment has a real period feel and the package rate of around £88 per person for two nights' B&B and a dinner represents value for money. Packed lunches can be provided and suggested walk sheets are available. **B** *Bethany House*, Bay Rd, Carnlough, T28885667. Outside the village on the coast road overlooking the bay. **B** *Bridge Inn*, 2 Bridge St, Carnlough, T28885096. Has rooms sharing bathroom facilities for £17.50 per person and there is a popular pub below the bedrooms. **B** *Riverside House*, 13 Toberwine St, Glenarm, T28841474. In the centre of the village with its rear overlooking the river. **C** *Nine Glens*, 16 Toberwine St, Glenarm, T28841590. Is 200 yards from the harbour, private parking, open all year. **C** *Town Brae House*, Town Brae Rd, Glenarm, T28841043. A country house overlooking the village and with views of the Ayrshire coast, for those who want to get away from street pavements.

The lunch menu at the *Londonderry Arms* in Carnlough has excellent choices such as **Eating** Caesar-style salads or mussels for £3.50, pasta dishes for £5 or salmon for £7.50. High tea from 1700 to 1830 and formal dinner from 1900. There are two bars in Carnlough serving reliable pub food: the *Glencloy Inn* and the *Bridge Inn*, near each other on Bridge St and High St respectively. *The Gallery Coffee Shop*, 7 Toberwine St, Glenarm, is a small place with pine tables serving salads under £5 and roast beef and chips for £6. *The Schooner* bar on Castle St, Glenarm, serves pub grub from 1100 until 2300.

Glenarm Pottery, 26 Altmore St, T28841013. The workshop here uses traditional **Shopping** designs in sponge and sgraffito. O'Kane's antique shop, Toberwine T28841470. Opposite the Gallery Coffee Shop.

Tourist offices *McKillop's Shop*, Carnlough, T28885236. *Community Hall*, Glenarm, T28841087. **Directory** Opening hours irregular.

Glenarm to Larne

Travelling south, the sharply defined topography of the Antrim coast is coming to an end as one leaves Glenarm for the final stretch of road that continues to command the sea until Larne is reached. If you've just arrived off the ferry at Larne or travelled up from Belfast this is where the coastal scenery makes an immediate impact but in either direction a place that might suggest a quick stop is **Ballygally**, mainly due to the eye-catching **AL** *Ballygally Castle Hotel*, T28583212. Sweeping sea views can be enjoyed from the lacklustre 1960s-style bar while a remnant of the original 17th-century castle has bedrooms with modern pine furniture and a ghost-room, which can be visited by non-residents. Bar food is around £6, a three-course dinner in the restaurant is £17 and a pot of poorly-made coffee in the bar is a pricey £2.60.

Larne

Chances are you will only spend time in Larne if delayed by the ferry, but there *Colour map 1, grid B6* are ways to while away time: the well-organized tourist office has local information, including an Ulster American Heritage Trail, with maps describing plaques and graveyards associated with emigration and American forces stationed here in the Second World War.

The **Carnegie Arts Centre** has old photographs and artefacts, and tells the story of the building of the Antrim coast road. ■ *2 Victoria Road, T28279482. Tuesday-Saturday 1400-1700. Free.*

The more recent history of Larne has little to boast of: in 1974, to destroy the Sunningdale Agreement, masked UDA men closed the ferry, built a barricade of vehicles around the town and forced shops to close down.

Sunningdale

A power-sharing executive of Protestants and Catholics and cross-border cooperation through a Council of Ireland. Sound familiar? Not the Good Friday agreement, but the Sunningdale agreement of December 1973. The Unionist leadership had trouble carrying their own members (sound familiar again?) and the agreement was destroyed before it got off the ground by concerted strikes and intimidation, organised by the Ulster Workers Council.

Sleeping **AL** *Highways Hotel*, Ballyloran, T28272272, F28275015. Just off the A8 road a mile outside Larne on the road to Belfast. **A** *Curran Court Hotel*, 84 Curran Rd, T28275505, F28260096. On the continuation of Main St and close to the ferry. **B** *Cairnview*, 13 Croft Heights, Ballygarry, T/F28583269. A B&B 4 miles north of Larne on the Antrim Coast Rd. 3 rooms at £18 per person. **B** *Manor*, 23 Olderfleet Rd, T28273305. B&B virtually next door to the ferry. **C** *Killyneedan*, 52 Bay Rd, T28274943. This B&B is close to the ferry. **C** *Bellevue*, 35 Olderfleet Rd, T28270233. On the right, at the bottom of the road directly ahead when disembarking. No en-suite rooms.

Eating The two hotels serve bar food and have restaurants and Kiln, out of town on the Old Glenarm Rd that runs north parallel to the coast road, T28260924, is a pub restaurant with a good local reputation. *Rumbles*, 116 Main St, T28274445, is plain, but white table linen imparts a clean and looked-after appearance. Pasta and steaks around £6, non-smoking in the evening and bring your own wine. Closed Monday but otherwise open from 1000 to 2200 (1300-1800 on Sunday). Café-style food is available at the ferry terminal but *The Bailie*, 111 Main St, is a cheerful-looking pub serving inexpensive meals daily at lunchtime and from 1700 until 2000. There are a few other inexpensive places in Main St including *Carriages*, 105 Main St, and the *Golden Inn*, 117 Main St.

Sport **Diving** *North Irish Lodge*, Islandmagee, T93382246. **Horse-riding** *Rainbow Equestrian Centre*, 24 Hollow Rd, Islandmagee. T93382929. *Islandmagee Riding Centre*, T28382108. **Leisure Centre** Tower Rd, T28260478, closes 2200 Monday-Friday and 1700 at weekend.

Transport **Bicycle** Hire from *Tourist Centre*, Narrow Gauge Rd, T28260088. **Buses** Bus station on Circular Rd, T28272345. **Car hire** *Avis*, Terminal Building, Larne Harbour, T28260799. *Hertz*, Ferry Terminal, Larne Harbour, T28278111. **Ferry** *P&O*, T0990-980777, operate two routes out of Larne: to Cairnryan in Scotland, with a 1-hour service on the *Jetliner* and 2¼ hours on the *Pride of Rathlin*; and to Fleetwood in England. Larne Harbour, T28279221, is at the end of Olderfleet Rd. **Taxis** *AA*, T28277888. *Cas Cabs*, T28274983. **Train** Station, Circular Rd, T28260604.

Directory **Banks** *Bank of Ireland* and *Northern Bank* in Main St along with building societies; *First Trust Bank*, Upper Main St; *Ulster Bank*, Upper Cross St. Exchange facility also at the tourist office. **Bird watching and boat trips** Mr Galbarith, Islandmagee, T93382539. **Communications** Post office: Main St. **Tourist office** Narrow Gauge Rd. T28260088. July and August, Mon-Fri 0900-1800, Saturday 0900-1700. Easter to June and September, Mon-Sat 0900-1700. Oct to Easter, Mon-Fri 0900-1700.

The good old days

'The inhabitants of all sexes and classes [of Islandmagee] are perhaps a more immoral race than is to be found in any other rural district in Antrim ... What makes their immorality the more disgusting is the openness and want of shame with which it is exhibited. The women whenever from home, or indeed whenever they can procure the means, drink raw spirits in such quantities as would astonish any but a native ... several have lost their reason, and many still remain as examples and warnings, in their paralysed bodies and shattered intellects, to those who are treading in their footsteps."

After Lord Dungannon broke up all 14 pubs on Islandmagee in the early 19th century a born-again temperance set in, the legacy of which can be seen today when you look for somewhere to have a drink on the peninsula. The same report also noted that Islandmagee had not "the slightest tinge of party or sectarian feeling."

Islandmagee

Islandmagee can be reached on the B90 from Whitehead or by foot on a passenger ferry, T28273785/T28274085, between Larne and Ballylumford, that departs at 0730 and on the hour between 0800 and 1500 and then on the half hour until 1730. **Getting there & around**

Little known outside the North of Ireland, Islandmagee is an island-like peninsula pointing north between Whitehead and Larne, with basalt cliffs facing Scotland but a more welcoming west side and a sandy and safe beach, Brown's Bay, on the north end, which receives a smattering of families on sunny summer days. Islandmagee, a teetotalling, conservative retreat where few foreign travellers venture, has its own little surprises. On the road between Mill Bay and Ballylumford, for instance, look out for the astonishing location of the **Ballylumford Dolmen**. **Sights**

Talk of repairing **The Gobbins**, a clifftop walk on the east side, is still just talk and only a short part of it can be safely traversed. For information on walks and birdwatching call in to **Ford Farm Museum**, where the main attraction is butter-making and spinning demonstrations. ■ *Low Rd, T93353264. March to October, daily 1400-1800. £2.*

Halfway along on the west side, at Mill Bay facing Larne Lough, there is an oyster and mussel farm at the harbour, T93382246, where produce can be purchased, including lobster and crab.

See 'Sport' on page 580 for details of diving and other activities in the area.

The **A** *Millbay Inn*, 77 Millbay Rd, T93382436, has 4 rooms and is also the best place for food and the only place for a drink. It opens daily for lunch and, except on Sunday, from 1900 for dinner. Traditional dishes such as champ and sausages, plus à la carte, under £15 for a meal. **Sleeping & eating**

C *The Farm*, 69 Portmuck Rd, T93382252. Enjoys sea views and also has a self-catering cottage for rent, from £175 to £300 a week depending on the season. *Brown's Bay Caravan Park*, Brown's Bay, T70382497. Camping site run by the council, where a tent pitch is around £5.

County Antrim

Carrickfergus and around

Passing the town on the A2 heading on along the north side of the Belfast Lough, it is impossible to miss Carrickfergus Castle, but don't be misled by its dramatic posture into thinking that the town itself is an exciting place. It is an unastonishing place that need hardly detain the visitor, especially if travelling north where more interesting destinations await. But if the weather is inclement there are sufficient diversions in and around Carrickfergus to pass a day.

Carrickfergus Castle The castle is a formidable-looking Anglo-Norman edifice with a long history. A famous siege by Edward Bruce in 1315 was resisted for longer than it could otherwise have been with the help of the capture of some Scots, eight of whom provided an edible repast for the beleaguered forces. Sorley Boy MacDonnell ran amuck here in revenge for the massacre on Rathlin (see box on page 578), and there is plenty more to learn either in the castle or on the **Knight Ride**, a monorail journey through history, situated in the tourist office complex ■ *Castle: T93351273. April to May and September, Monday-Saturday 1000-1800, Sunday 1400-1800; June to August, Monday-Saturday 1000-1800, Sunday 1200-1800; October-March, Monday-Saturday 1000-1600, Sunday 1400-1600. £2.70. Knight Ride: T93366455. April to September, Monday-Saturday 1000-1800; Sunday 1200-1800. Closes an hour earlier the rest of the year. Joint ticket saves 10%.*

Carrickfergus Gasworks The industrial history here will make a welcome relief for anyone suffering from castle fatigue. The only Victorian coal-fired gasworks in Ireland, built in 1855 to light street lamps, they were still producing gas here in the early 1960s. ■ *T93351438. June-August, Sunday 1400-1700. £1.50.*

The poet Louis MacNeice (1907-63) grew up in Carrickfergus, for his father was the rector of St Nicholas' church in the Market Place. The interior is not dull, there is a fine memorial to the Chichester family, and the adjoining cemetery is where the poet could 'hear the voice of the minister tucking people into the ground'. ■ *T93360061, mornings only.*

Andrew Jackson Centre The parents of the 7th US President emigrated from Carrickfergus in 1765, and a recreated dwelling of that period makes up the Andrew Jackson Centre and houses exhibitions on the president and the USA connection. Quite a dull place, which is enlivened a little by the adjoining **US Rangers' Centre** devoted to the First Battalion US Rangers who trained in Carrickfergus before leaving for Europe. ■ *Boneybefore. 2 miles north of Carrickfergus on the Larne Rd, T93366455. April to October, Monday-Friday, 1000-1300 and 1400-1800, Saturday and Sunday 1400-1800. £1.20.*

Sleeping & eating **AL** *Dobbins Inn Hotel*, High St, T/F93351905. Ancient lineage but modern facilities in town-centre hotel. **C** *Langsgarden*, 72 Scotch Quarter, T/F93366369, overlooks Belfast Lough. Most rooms, at £16.50 per person, share bathroom facilities.

Meals throughout the day in comfortable, olde-worlde setting of *Dobbins Inn Hotel* or try trendy *Chandlers*, 13 High St, T93369729. *The Courtyard Coffee House*, 38 Scotch Quarter, is fine for lunch or afternoon tea, plus a take-away menu until closing time at 1645, Monday to Saturday. Large portions for lunch at the *Northgate*, 59 North St, T93364136, and the *Tamarind*, 32 West St, T93355579, is OK for Indian food.

Directory **Tourist office** Heritage Plaza, Antrim St, T93366455. Apr-Sep, Mon-Sat 1000-1800, Sun 1200-1800. Closes an hour earlier the rest of the year.

Inland Antrim

Inland Antrim is pleasant countryside but of limited appeal to the traveller, especially when the scenic coast road beckons, but if travelling between Belfast and the north coast on the A26 the town of Ballymena makes for a far more diverting stop than nondescript Antrim town itself.

Ballymena and around

Presbyterian and ultra-loyal Ballymena was founded in the 17th century, for *Colour map 1, grid A5* Lowland Scottish settlers, by William Adair from Kinhilt and developed into a thriving commercial town on the back of the linen industry from the middle of the 18th century onwards. Ballymena is where Loyalist leader the Revd Ian Paisley comes from, and the actor Liam Neeson also grew up here. While there is not a lot to see in the town itself, Ballymena is a classic Protestant town and an essential part of the complex whole that makes up Northern Ireland. Adjoining the tourist office in Bridge Street (which will be moving into new premises), there is a tiny **museum** filled with old photographs, radios and shaving mugs and every Wednesday between June and August a **town tour** takes place from the town hall. Contact the tourist office for confirmation of time and place. Try to find time for a short trip west of town to the Moravian church at Gracehill (see box on page 584).

Arthur Cottage The area's American connection is kept alive at Arthur Cottage, the ancestral home of long-forgotten 21st US president, Chester Alan Arthur. Worth a visit for the occasional summer evenings of song and storytelling or the afternoon craft demonstrations. ■ *Dreen, Cullybackey: from Cullybackey, northwest of Ballymena, take the B96 to Portglenone and it is signposted on the right, T25660300. May to September, Monday-Saturday 1030-1700 (1600 on Saturday). £1.75. Craft demonstrations June to August, Tuesday, Friday and Saturday at 1330.*

Slemish Mountain To the east of town the A42 goes to the floral village of Broughshane, best visited in early summer or at the end of August when bulbs from the stock of the famous daffodil breeder, Guy L Wilson, can be purchased. From Broughshane the B94 to the distinctively contoured Slemish Mountain is signposted, and the way up the mountain is clearly marked from the car-park. People flock here on St Patrick's Day because of the mountain's association with the saint, he tended pigs here for six years as a young slave, but it is a quiet enough spot the rest of the year and outside of weekends the climb to the top and its views can be enjoyed in splendid isolation. The mountain is 1,437 feet (438 metres) high but it is only a 700-foot (213-metre) climb from the carpark.

Sleeping **L** *Galgorm Manor*, Fenaghy Rd, Ballymena, T25881001, F25688080. This 19th-century house was previously the home of a textile magnate, and can deliver comfort and recreation by way of river views, fishing rights, riding stables and clay pigeon shooting. **A** *Tullymore House*, 2 Carnlough Rd, Broughshane, T256861233, F256862238. Has a good reputation and a lovely setting. **B** *Ben Vista*, 79 Galgorm Rd, Ballymena, T25646091. A large Victorian house conveniently close to the bus and train stations, charging £18 per person for B&B.

Eating Good food in a classical-style restaurant at the *Galgorm Manor*, Fenaghy Rd, Ballymena, T25881001. Halibut with a vermouth sauce or duck with coriander pesto might appear for lunch at £9, while dinner for £25 includes familiar dishes with a

County Antrim

County Antrim

Moravians in Antrim

The Moravian church made a dramatic impact in Antrim with the arrival of the evangelist John Cennick in 1746. Of the 200 religious societies he established in Ireland most of them were in County Antrim, and Cennick has left a dramatic record of his encounters with traditional Protestantism and the numerous personality clashes he seemed to engender both within and outside of his church. The extent to which the establishment of a model church community at Gracehill furthered the

Moravian cause is debatable but there is no mistaking the evangelical zeal with which they pursued and applied their religious beliefs. Their dignified and unaffected village square, with the church open for services on a Sunday morning, and their gender-based cemetery with its flat tombstones are endearing and idiomatic expressions of their cult.

To reach Gracehill from Ballymena take the A2 west for less than two miles and look for a brown sign indicating the church down a road to the left.

touch of class and an impressive wine list and, at weekends, live piano music. In Ballymena the **Fern Room**, 80 Church St, is a self-service restaurant inside **McKillens** department store and closes at 1700, but it is the best place for a quick meal and value for money: peppered meat balls with rice or chicken goulash are under £5. The **Thatch Inn**, 57 Main St, is the best place for pub food at lunchtime during the week while the **Pantry**, Jubilee Mews off Main St, opens until 1700 Monday to Saturday and serves soup, stews and home-baked goodies.

Pubs & music For traditional music head out west along the A42 to Ahoghill and follow the signs to New Ferry for the **Cross Keys** pub where, during the summer, sessions take place each Saturday, Sunday and Wednesday night in a quaint, whitewashed, thatched cottage.

Transport **Car hire** Ballymena Car Hire, 205 Cullybackey Rd, T25630077. **Taxis** Regent Taxis, 1 Hill St, T25644777.

Directory **Tourist office** Presently located at 80 Galgorm Rd, T25653663, but there are plans to move to Church St near McKillens department store and open 7 days a week in summer.

Lisburn

Colour map 1, grid B5

Situated to the southwest of Belfast, and easily visited from the city by bus from the Europa Buscentre, the best reason for coming to Lisburn is the **Irish Linen Centre & Lisburn Museum**. The growing of flax and making of linen was a part of Irish farm life from earliest times but the plantations brought artisans from Britain, and before the end of the 17th century Ulster linen had acquired a particular renown. This did not conflict with any commercial interests in England and was allowed to develop unhindered. In 1698 a group of Huguenot weavers were paid to settle in Lisburn and their special skills were rapidly assimilated. By the end of the following century mechanization had been introduced into the bleaching process, and this set the stage for the development of Ireland's only major industry in the 19th century, with Belfast the world centre for linen manufacturing. Not until the 1920s and 30s did demand begin to drop and a terminal decline set in. The Centre and Museum tell the story and weaving workshops bring the craft to life. See page 564 for another linen-related place of interest. ■ *Market Square, T92663377. Monday-Saturday 0930-1700. Free admission to Museum; £2.75 for the Centre. Restaurant and linen and craft shop.*

I'll tell my ma when I go home,
The boys won't leave the girls alone,
They pull my hair, they stole my comb.
But that's all right till I go home.
She is handsome, she is pretty,
She is the belle of Belfast city,
She is courtin' one, two, three,
Please won't you tell me who is she?

Anonymous (20th century):
'I'll Tell my Ma'

15

Belfast

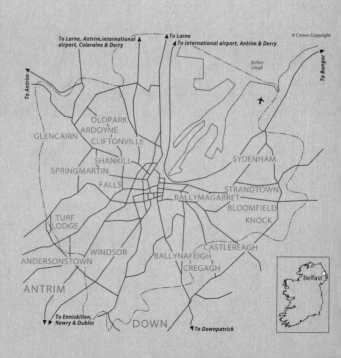

© Crown Copyright

A name long synonymous with bombs and sectarianism, Belfast is today undergoing a miraculous renaissance. Big money is pouring in from governments and corporations, and restaurants and housing are mushrooming where derelict factories and burned-out buildings reigned. Only time will tell whether Belfast's people's will to live a normal life outweighs the minority's need to cling to the hatreds of the past. The Falls Road, the Divis Flats, The Shankill, Andersonstown – these names still resound with visions of horror and mayhem. A first-time visitor to Belfast sees the armoured cars, the gates that were once used to close down the city at night, the RUC posts and the grim murals, and their instinct is to move on, find somewhere nice to go. But this would be a mistake. This city has a life: its tourist infrastructure is sorted, hotels are bursting out of the pavement, restaurants have Michelin listings, and its pompous nineteenth-century architecture is still a worthy monument to the men who built this city.

★ *Try to find time for*

Admiring the nineteenth century architecture

Taking a tour of City Hall and trying on the
councillors' robes

Going to Stormont where peace is happening

Visiting the Ulster Folk Park and transport museum

Having a drink in the Crown Liquor Saloon

Walking through the tropical ravine in the
Botanic Gardens

Eating dinner at Deane's in fin-de-siècle splendour

Taking a taxi tour of West Belfast

Wandering around the footpaths of Cave Hill

Ins and outs

Getting there Belfast is served by two airports (both T90457745): the Belfast International, which handles most international flights, including flights from Heathrow, and Belfast City Airport, which handles a smaller number of flights, largely from regional airports in Britain. The international airport, at Aldergrove, is 19 miles (30 km) north of the city on the M2. From outside the airport, buses run to the Europa and Laganside bus stations every 30 mins, hourly on Sundays. Taxis go from beside the bus stop and cost around £20. The city airport is 3 miles (5 km) northeast of the city. Citybus 21 runs from the airport to City Hall, or Sydenham Halt rail station is nearby and will connect with Central Station.

Ferries arrive at several locations along the river. The Seacat ferry from Stranraer and the regular Isle of Man ferry arrive at Donegall Quay, from where it is a 15-min walk to the city centre, unless you prefer to take a cab. From Ballast Quay, where the Stena ferry docks, the chief option is again a cab, while an Ulsterbus connects Larne, 20 miles (30 km) north and where the P&O from Cairnryan docks, with the Laganside bus station.

Trains arrive at Central Station and a free bus service goes into the centre of town. Alternatively, it is possible get another train into Botanic Station for the university area.

Long-distance buses from the Republic or within Northern Ireland arrive at either Laganside bus station or the Europa bus station, both of which are very central.

Getting around A series of buses radiate out from the city centre in Donegall Square, Upper Queen Street, Wellington Place and Castle Street. Taxi stands are outside the Europa Bus Station and in Donegall Square, Smithfield market, and Bridge Street. The Smithfield market cabs travel into Catholic west Belfast, taking several passengers at a time for about £1 per passenger, while the Bridge Street cabs travel to Protestant west Belfast. Both groups of taxis do tourist tours of their territories for about £10 an hour and offer what may reliably be called partisan versions of Belfast's recent history. The Donegall Square and Europa bus station taxis have a starting price of £1.50 and do not wait to load up with passengers first.

Car owners should note that while the severe parking restrictions of yore are more relaxed there are still no parking areas around sensitive buildings such as RUC posts and the courthouse. There is no shortage of secure car parks and most streets have pay and display systems.

Tourist information The Northern Ireland Tourist Board office is in St Anne's Court, 59 North Street, T90246609, Sep-Jun Mon 0930-1715, Tue-Sat 0900-1715; Jul and Aug Mon 0930-1900, Tue-Sat 0900-1715, Sun 1200-1600, has lots of useful, free information and will book accommodation and travel for you. Borde Faílte is at 53 Castle St, T90327888, Mon-Fri 0900-1700, Sat 0900-1230, Mar to end-Sep only, and provides information for your onward journey to the Republic. There is a Usit Now office at the Foontain Centre, College Street, BT1 6ET, T90324073, and at Queen's University Student Union Building, University Road, BT7 1PE.

History

The city of Belfast sits in a valley created by two rivers, the Lagan and the Farsett, now piped below the streets but once necessitating a series of forts to guard its crossings. If you had wandered this way in the 12th century you would have seen little more than a Norman castle, built in 1177. The land was under the control of the Gaelic lords, the O'Neills, until the Plantation (see page 674) began under James I following the settlement of Sir Arthur

Chichester with a royal charter that gave him the right to create a borough. By the middle of the century a small town had blossomed. Carrickfergus, in Antrim, dominated trade in the area until Belfast's population rose to a critical mass with the immigration in the late 17th century of Huguenots fleeing persecution in France. With them they brought their traditional industry, linen production, and the burgeoning city now had a reason to expand. The Plantation continued with rope making, shipping, and export of beef, corn and butter to Britain and France, making the city the fourth largest town in Ireland by the end of the century.

The 18th century saw a fourfold increase in population, and the further development of the shipbuilding and linen industries. Unlike other areas of Ulster, Belfast was inhabited by both Catholics and Protestants who lived harmoniously throughout the century, culminating in the formation in Belfast in 1791 of the United Irishmen, a cross-denominational nationalist organization. It was, of course, stamped out and many Protestant and Catholic men, who would be national heroes in other circumstances today, lost their lives.

The 18th century

The next half-century saw the development of sectarian differences in Belfast. From an initial apathy following the eradication of the United Irishmen, northern Protestants began to see the increasing militancy of the Catholics throughout Ireland as a threat. In the 1820s Protestant clubs were set up all over Ulster; their members made great parades, bore arms and formed bands to play anti-Catholic songs. After Catholic Emancipation in 1829 an Orange Order parade on the 12th July was banned, which led to riots all over the city.

Beginnings of sectarianism

As agricultural prices declined and the Industrial Revolution came to Belfast thousands of the rural poor of both denominations flocked to the city to compete for scarce work. Catholic and Protestant no longer had a common interest; Catholic emancipation was restricted. Protestants now held all the power in the city, owned most of the industry and were increasingly reluctant to give up any power in the light of the increasing Irish Catholic militancy that threatened their power base. The Famine (see page 678) drove ever more people into the city where the inevitable fight for work and housing drove the two groups ever further apart.

In 1857 more riots hit the streets of Belfast as huge Catholic and Protestant mobs met in open battle in the streets. This happened again in 1864, forcing the closure of factories. The Catholic minority suffered the worst of the attacks, the Catholic Pound district being sandwiched between Sandy Row and the Shankill Road. Reform of parliament and changes in the property qualification to vote in 1867 gave Catholics more rights, but every move in favour of equality was met with an Orange, unionist reaction, with ever-increasing displays of affection for William of Orange each year on the 12th July. Further reforms, the disestablishment of the Church of Ireland and the introduction of the secret ballot, disturbed the control of the Protestants, but were met with the repeal of the act banning sectarian marches. Home Rule gained power in the rest of Ireland, but in Belfast it became the bogey that kept the riots coming each year on the glorious twelfth. The Home Rule Bill of 1886 polarized even liberal Protestants' feelings with Monster Meetings of Conservatives and Orangemen in Belfast opposed to the bill. Its eventual defeat was accompanied by the worst riots so far. Catholics drove Protestants out of their workplaces and were in their turn driven out of work and beaten by Protestant mobs; Catholic pubs were attacked and burned out. The police became a third party in the fighting, battling both Protestant and Catholic crowds: the police force was largely Catholic, commanded by Protestant officers. The riots continued out of the housing estates and factories and into the city centre, lasting from June to the end of September; between 31 and 50 people died. In the rest of Ulster the fighting was about landlords and land ownership but in Belfast it was purely sectarian – working people fighting among themselves for scarce resources and work.

Into the 20th century In 1891 Belfast officially outstripped Dublin in terms of population. Around 26% of its population was Catholic. It had an opera house and many grand commercial buildings. Besides shipbuilding and linen there was a flourishing engineering industry and Ireland's centre for building steam engines. In the early 20th century the Gaelic Revival came to Belfast, and committed intellectuals on both sides of the sectarian divide found a common interest in Irish culture and tradition. In 1911 the issue of Home Rule reared its head yet again, bringing to an end the period of relative peace. Unionists began to talk of taking power in Ulster, rather than accepting Home Rule for Ireland. The Ulster Volunteer Force was established in order to fight for independence and by 1912 there were 90,000 volunteers, with the old town hall in Belfast as their headquarters.

The First World War brought a certain amount of prosperity to the region. In 1914 Harland and Wolff, the Belfast-based shipbuilders, were producing 8% of the world output of ships. At first orders declined as workers were called up and materials became scarce but then the war orders came flooding in, and in 1918 Harland and Wolff launched 201,070 tons of merchant ships. Farmers knew a wealth previously unimagined as imports died away under U-boat attacks. The linen industry also boomed with orders for uniforms, tents and aeroplane fabric.

After 1918 hundreds of men inured to the horror of war returned to Belfast ready to take up the old quarrels. In the south the Black and Tan war was a particularly bloody interlude, while in Belfast sectarian violence reached new heights. In 1920 Loyalist mobs drove all Catholics and socialists out of Harland and Wolff, Sirocco, Mackie's, McLaughlin and Harveys: all the big employers in Belfast. About 11,000 Catholic people lost their jobs in this way while Catholic houses and businesses were attacked and the convent of St Matthew's Church in Belfast was burned down. Belfast Catholics, now a quarter of the population, fought back just as violently but were greatly outnumbered. The violence continued unabated for two years, the Catholics never regaining their jobs, which were given to Protestants. Because of the fear of the increasingly powerful IRA the Ulster Special Forces were created, made up entirely of Protestants: the B Specials in Belfast were part-time, uniformed and armed. Ironically, in 1921 the Protestants, who had fought for so long against it, got Home Rule while the 32 southern counties received dominion status.

In 1922 more riots and deaths occurred, 61 people were killed in March in Belfast alone. Outside the city the IRA was burning and looting, while inside the Catholic population suffered reprisals from Loyalists and B Specials alike: the Special Powers Act allowed suspects to be detained indefinitely without charge or trial. After the murder of an MP internment was introduced, as well as a curfew. In May 1922, 66 people died, two-thirds of them Catholic.

After the assassination of Michael Collins (see page 681) in that year things calmed down a little, with the southern government encouraging the IRA to join the mainstream Irish army. While the civil war and its aftermath raged in the south, those who might have caused disruption in the north were occupied and so peace broke out for a time in Belfast.

By the 1930s Belfast had settled to become an anti-Catholic, sectarian city with annual displays of Orange power attended by cabinet ministers who abused their southern Catholic neighbours, who in retaliation abused them. The economic war between Dublin and London polarized attitudes even more, and employers were encouraged by the Belfast government to employ Protestants who would be loyal to the state. In 1935 there were more riots as the Orange parades were first banned and then allowed. In 1937 the new constitution for the south set out a claim on the sovereignty of the north, as well as establishing the special position of the Catholic church in the south; these claims made matters considerably worse.

The Second World War

During this period Belfast suffered during the Great Depression, but things began to boom again as war began to seem likely. An airport was built, and the industries that had benefited from the First World War came into their own again; Harland and Wolff received commissions to convert passenger ships for war use and two huge warships were built. In 1941, however, Belfast became a target for the Luftwaffe. The first waves of bombers missed the industrial targets, and hit instead the impoverished housing estates of the north city centre. 140 fires raged throughout the city, and fire engines from the south were sent up to help deal with them. Hundreds of people died and their corpses were laid out in the swimming baths and St George's Market. After this first night of bombing tens of thousands of people left the city. The second wave of attacks in May the same year saw Belfast become one huge conflagration across the harbour, with small firestorms breaking out in the industrial sites: half of the houses and most of the industry in the city were destroyed. The glow was visible 50 miles away. Middle-class ladies living outside the city took in refugees, and were appalled at the condition of the slum children, whereas wealthier Belfast citizens retired to the hotels of Donegal for the duration of the war. Catholic churches opened their crypts to one and all as air raid shelters, and Protestant and Catholic stood shoulder to shoulder putting out the flames, uniting the two sides of the religious divide. That, fortunately, was the last of the air raids over Belfast.

In 1942 American soldiers came to the city, completing a circle that began during the Famine years when thousands of Belfast Protestants left for the US. The arrival of foreign troops on Irish soil sparked a protest from De Valera, and increased activity on the part of the IRA. After a gunfight in west Belfast six men were arrested and sentenced to death for the murder of an RUC man. Only one was executed but it brought back all the old antagonisms in the city. In 1943 an IRA man held up the audience of the Broadway cinema in the Falls Road and insisted that they take part in a commemoration for the dead of the Easter Rising. But suppression and arrest in both north and south ensured that by the end of the war the IRA was defunct.

To the present

From 1945 to the mid-1960s the city experienced not so much sectarian harmony but at least a degree of peace. The modern trouble in the North began in the civil rights demonstrations in Derry but Belfast communities enthusiastically joined in (see page 686).

The present situation is one where an entire generation of people in their 20s want nothing to do with the old disputes; Belfast clubs resound to the enjoyment of young people who don't know or care what sect their dancing partners belong to, restaurant owners are glad of the custom from whomever walks into their place, the murals are fading away and only the desperately sad parts of the city still paint their kerbstones red, white and blue.

Belfast city centre

SHANKILL

FALLS

Crumlin Road

Antrim Road

Shankill Road

Leisure Centre

North Street

Linen House Youth Hostel

The Kremlin

St Anne's Cathedral

Parliament bar

Nick's

Maddens

Royal Ave

Donegall St

Ulster Bank

AIB

Northern Ireland Tourist Board

Duke of York

Albert Memorial Clocktower

Castle Court Shopping Centre

Bewley's Oriental Café

Delaney's

McCausland

Divis Street

Waterstone's Bookshop

White's Tavern

High St

Waring St

Cornmarket

Morning Star pub

Falls Road

Kelly's Cellars

Castle St

Bord Fáilte

Eason's Bookshop

St Peter's Cathedral

USIT/ Belfast Student Travel

Anne St

Kitchen Bar

Old Museum Arts Centre

College St

Dillons Bookshop

Victoria Centre

A12 Westlink

Linen Hall Library

Donegall Pl

Donegall Sq N

Café Society

Familia Bookshop

City Hall

Donegall Sq E

Shenanigan's

Donegall Sq W

Grosvenor Road

Grand Opera House

Travelodge Belfast City

Donegall Sq S

Deanes

Bedford St

Robinson's, Fibber Magee

Crown Liquor Saloon

Ulster Hall

Blue Cat Antiques

Great Victoria St Station & Europa Bus Centre

Europa

Morrison's

Aero

Beaten Docket

Larry's

Fatty Arbuckle's

Strike Four

Limelight Nightclub

Factory Square

Virgin cinema Complex

Ormeau Ave

Ormeau Baths Gallery

Great Victoria St

Ventry St

Dublin Rd

Dempsey's International Archana Balti House, Little India vegetarian

Graffiti Italiano

Keating

La Belle Epoque

Revelations Internet Café

Jenny's Coffee Shop

Donegall Pass

To Dunmurry, Lurgan, Dungannon & Enniskillen (M1, A4), Newry & Dublin (M1, A1)

Donegall Road

Botanic Station

City Hospital Station

City Hospital

Botanic Ave

Claremont St

Holiday Inn Express

Arnie's Backpackers

Bookfinders Café

Fitzwilliam St

A

University Rd

Queen's College

Lisburn Road

Palm House

Avenue House Bed & Breakfast

Liserin Guesthouse

Pearl Court House

Botanic Gardens

Ulster Museum

Eglantine Ave

Eglantine Guesthouse

Wellington Park

Stranmillis Rd

Malone Grove Suites

Botanic Inn

Eglantine Inn

The Strand

Malone Rd

Related map:
A. Around Botanic Station, page 597

N

0 yards   200

0 metres   200

Belfast

Sights

The chief tourist attraction in Belfast may strike you as a little tasteless: both the tourist association and local taxi drivers do tours of West Belfast, covering the major streets of the Troubles and their associated deaths. Tours of the city hall also tend to focus on the difficult times, while the city museum takes the opposite approach and denies that any trouble ever happened. Added to these, the zoo, the Botanic gardens, a 19th-century castle and a new weir over the river take up no more than a couple of days' sightseeing, while there are nights and nights of good places to eat, and lots of places to go to if you are a clubber.

City centre

Dominating the centre of town in Donegall Square is the massive **City Hall**, a great slab of pompous Victoriana and a testament to what money can buy. Completed in 1906, the Portland stone monstrosity, designed by Brumwell Thomas and covering 11 acres, is topped by a copper dome 173 feet high. You can't wander around it at will but there are guided tours Monday to Saturday during the summer. Inside is an extravaganza of imported marble, stained glass dedicated to assorted moneymen and soldiers, and paintings of assorted mayors in their regalia. Very few women feature in this place at all, except those who lead the guided tours. The tour takes in the council chamber, laid out in adversarial mode with tables in the middle for the press; the Great Hall, whose stained-glass windows were one of the few items to be protected from the German air raids during the Second World War; the banqueting hall; and robing rooms, where those interested enough can try on the gown of some unsuspecting council member.

City Hall

The grounds contain some more testimony to the doings of men. Statues of Edward Harland, James Haslett, the Rt Hon Daniel Dixon, Lord Dufferin and RJ McMordie, assorted movers and shakers of the 19th century, all pay court to the quite lissom figure of Queen Victoria, flanked by figures representing spinning and shipbuilding and, as an afterthought, education. A cenotaph also stands in the grounds, as does a memorial to one of Belfast's biggest mistakes, the *Titanic*, which was built here.

The pediment over the main door depicts Hibernia, Minerva, Mercury, Industry, Labour, Liberty and Industry and some small boys.

For many years the city council was dominated by unionist politicians who were partly responsible for the failure of the 1985 Anglo-Irish agreement, in large part the same agreement that was made on Good Friday 1998. They refused to take part in council business while the Agreement was in place, effectively making the city unrunnable. A huge banner hung along the front of the building expressing their opposition to any dealings with the republic.

In 1988 an IRA bomb did what German air raids had failed to do, and destroyed the stained glass windows of the Great Hall. Currently the city council is split between Sinn Féin and Unionist members, which must make work there noisy. ■ *Tours of City Hall: July to September, daily, 1030 and 1430; October to June, Wednesday only, 1430. Free.*

Donegall Square

There are a few other buildings around Donegall Square of some interest. At number 17 is the **Linen Hall Library**, which has been a lending library for over 200 years. Not much to look at from the outside (or inside, come to that), it has a vast collection of early Irish material and is used by research students studying the recent history of the Troubles. It is not a public library, although you can wander in and use the reading room and café on the first floor. Sporadic tours of the building take place: enquire within. The library was established in 1788 and originally occupied the Linen Hall building, which was demolished to make way for the City Hall. Its first librarian, Thomas Russell, was hanged in 1803 after an abortive Republican uprising. ■ *17 Donegall Square. Monday to Wednesday and Friday, 0930-1730, Thursday 0930-2030, Saturday 0930-1600. Free.*

A wander around the square reveals some more late Victorian bulwarks of respectability. The 1884-5 Robinson and Cleaver building stands out among the Victorian solidity: six storeys high with rounded corners rising to ornate turrets, its exterior is highly carved with cherubs, fruit and contemporary figures such as Victoria, Albert and, for some reason, George Washington. At the east side of the square is the Pearl Assurance building, originally called the Ocean building, erected between 1899 and 1902 in a Gothic revival style, with oddly shaped pinnacle towers creating a startling skyline. At the west of the Square is the Scottish Provident building (1897-9) covered in wild carvings of dolphins, sphinxes and lions as well as figures representing Belfast's industry.

Around the Albert Clocktower

Northwest of City Hall and close to the river is another cluster of late 19th-century constructions. The **Albert Clocktower** leans rather more with every year that passes, and has had several bits chopped off that looked as if they might bring the whole thing down. Plans are afoot to pin the tower in its present position rather than bring it back to the perpendicular. Beside it the newly renovated AIB bank was formerly the Northern Bank head office. Built in 1852 in Portland stone and granite, it makes a grandiose statement about the permanence of Protestant values, with giant Doric columns and a great carved frieze above the entrance. Along Waring Street, a block to the north of the clock tower, is the **Ulster Bank**, another magnificent temple to the god Mammon. Its architect won the commission in a competition where 67 other architects proposed designs. It is based on St Mark's Library in Venice, and has just about every architectural idiosyncrasy known at the time: Doric and Corinthian columns, allegorical sculptures, ornate railings and Victorian lamps. The inside is even more elaborate, so visit during banking hours and watch commerce at work in its finest environment.

Back down Victoria Street a little way, take time out to admire the façade of the **McCausland Hotel**, once two great warehouses whose fronts were preserved with their marble relief figures of the five continents and animals, and arcaded windows. Back at the Albert Tower the road sweeps round through some ugly modern road building, past the **Custom House** where once the commercial life of the city bustled around. Built in 1854-7, it still functions as the city's customs building. Its two fronts, one facing the river and the other the city, are highlighted by ornate Corinthian columns, but the river side is the more elaborate with the traditional riverine heads as the keystones of arches, and figures of angels, Britannia and Roman gods decorating the pediment.

Further north along Victoria Street the name of the road changes to Clifton Road past the still intact poorhouse, **Clifton House**, built in 1774. Also on the waterfront is the **Harbour Office**, its exhibition of maritime history occasionally open to the public. Enquire at the tourist office.

Belfast

Lagan Lookout

Slightly more hands-on is the modern **Lagan Lookout**, a little exhibition centre built on the weir. Part of a huge scheme to renovate the rundown waterfront, the weir holds back the tidal flow of the river, which in the past made the area very unsavoury as great banks of fetid mud were exposed twice a day. With the water held back regeneration of the area beyond it was possible and now the place resembles London's Barbican, with a state-of-the-art concert hall, bijou apartments whose prices are rising at a rate of knots, and the jewel in the crown that is the Hilton Hotel – big, foreign money that puts the seal of respectability on the largely government-sponsored developments. The whole area around Laganside and St Anne's Cathedral, at the moment very run down, is about to have money poured into it making, the planners hope, a new Temple Bar of cheap accommodation, trendy shops and pubs and offices.

The Lookout sits right on the weir and has the usual displays of history and audio-visual material. You can watch the water rising and falling over the bollards, which are designed to hold back high tides and prevent the city from flooding. A walk across the weir reveals the massive cranes of the shipyards reflected in the glass-walled buildings on the other bank. The river is about to be developed as a highway for water boats, and it is possible to take a boat ride upstream. Occasionally a tunnel under the river is opened up to the public, but usually only on special occasions or for private parties. You could enquire at the visitor centre. ■ *1, Donegall Quay, T01232-315444. April to September, Monday to Friday, 1000-1700, Saturday 1200-1700, Sunday 1400-1700; October to March, closed Monday, Tuesday to Friday 1100-1530, Saturday 1300-1630, Sunday 1400-1630. £1.50.*

Grand Opera House & Crown Liquor Saloon

Great Victoria Street is dominated by the much-bombed Europa Hotel, an ugly place that looks like some brutalist piece of architecture from behind the Iron Curtain. Also in this street are two Belfast institutions. The Grand Opera House was opened in 1895 and is mostly restoration work nowadays after two IRA bombs reduced it to rubble in 1991 and 1993. The best way to see it is in operation – it is in constant use with concerts, operas and plays. Inside is lurid red velvet, elephant head brackets and a fake renaissance painted ceiling circa 1991.

On the other side of the road is the the Crown Liquor saloon, which looks like some over-the-top 90s theme pub but is in fact the genuine Victorian article. It was built for a man called Patrick Flanagan, the publican, in 1839 and later encased in the glorious exterior tiles you see today. Inside are carved wooden snugs, each with its own motto and brass match striker, gas lamps, the original carved wooden bar and beautiful lighting through the stained glass windows. It was damaged by the bomb in the opera house in 1993. Upstairs is fake Victoriana, but the bar itself is well worth a visit. If you are in Belfast on one of its deadly Sundays go in around lunchtime when it's quite empty; otherwise you'll have to fight your way in.

West Belfast

West Belfast was a working-class area which developed around the linen industry, an area where sectarian violence created two entirely separate communities as far back as the late 19th century: the Catholic Falls and the Protestant Shankill. When the Troubles started in 1969, the West Belfast, separated from the city centre by the Westlink motorway, became a battleground. The Falls Road, Crumlin Road, Divis Street, the Shankill are names that ring of riot, burning, assassination and mayhem. However, walk down any one of them today, and it is ludicrously safe to do so, and you see streets that could be any suburb of Manchester or London – dull, suburban maisonettes, corner shops, kids on bikes, Victorian terraces. True, there are intermittent RUC posts looking like something from the Berlin Wall, the occasional armoured car with flaps at the sides to stop anyone rolling a petrol bomb underneath, and most places have rather more security devices than one would normally expect, but you have to look carefully to spot that there has been a sectarian war going on here for 25 years or more. The gable ends of houses tell the story in a series of badly drawn symbols – red hands, shamrock leaves, silhouettes of gunmen – a few which identify this struggle with those in other parts of the world. While a mural on the Falls Road pictures David Trimble, with a list of things he has wasted while the Good Friday agreement stagnated, murals on the Shankill Road look backwards to past supremacies and depict any change as bad.

The Falls A pleasant, if that is an appropriate word, walk is along the **Falls Road** to the **Milltown cemetery**, where the Republican graves commemorate some of the many lives lost. The walk begins at the Smithfield market where, if you choose, you can negotiate with one of the cab-drivers for a personal tour of the area. Alternatively, head westwards along Divis Street towards Divis Tower, the last remaining building of the notorious **Divis Flats**. The roof was occupied for a time by a republican group, but is now part of an army post, along with the top two storeys; access by helicopter only. As you walk away from the city centre you can see the 'peace line' between the houses on your right, the iron wall built to keep apart the residents of the Falls and Shankill roads. What strikes home as you walk is the small size of the war zone – a few blocks east and west and only one block between the two warring groups. As you pass the former Sinn Féin offices, notice the boulders along the kerb, put there to deter car-bombers. You will also pass on the right the **Royal Victoria Hospital**, which dealt with many of the victims of the Troubles.

The **cemetery** itself is a quiet place, watched over by an army post opposite. In 1988 the war invaded the cemetery when a grenade was thrown at mourners at the funeral of Séan Savage, one of the IRA members killed in Gibraltar by the SAS. To find the Republican graves head south until the graves run out and then turn right along a tarmac path. Bobby Sands is buried here.

Beyond the cemetery the Falls Road continues into **Andersonstown**, another Republican estate where there are more murals. Beyond that is **Twinbrook**, where Bobby Sands lived, and where a gable end has been turned into a permanent memorial.

A walk along the Shankill begins further north from the city centre. The murals are more in evidence here and are slightly more threatening: silhouettes of gunmen and slogans such as 'We know who you are' adorn the walls. Typical symbols are the red hand of Ulster, maps of the six counties detached from the rest of the island, William of Orange on horseback, flags (usually the Union Jack and St George's cross but also the Scottish flag), and generally lots of red, white and blue posts, kerbstones, fences, and so on.

The Shankill Road

Other less famous streets include Sandy Row, strangely incongruous now right beside the heart of Belfast's nightlife, with its Rangers Supporters club, painted kerbs and general air of a place left behind.

Trips along the Shankill can be arranged with the cab-drivers who park at North Street. They should ask for about £10 for an hour, and will give a unionist viewpoint on what you see. One possibility is to negotiate a trip out to **Fernhill House**, a museum that explores the history of the Shankill area. ■ *Glencairn Park. April to September Monday to Saturday 1000-2200, Sunday 100-1800; October to March Monday to Saturday 1000-1600, Sunday 1300-1600. £2. No public transport.*

South of the City Centre

Around Botanic Station

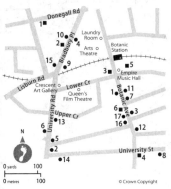

Donegall Rd

1
10 Laundry
2 Room
4 Arts
Theatre Botanic
Station
15
9
3 Empire
Music Hall
Crescent
Art Gallery Lower Cr
Queen's
Film Theatre
Lisburn Rd University Rd
Upper Cr
13
6
5
2
14
University St
4 8
11
1
7
6 3
17
16
12

N

0 yards   100
0 metres   100
© Crown Copyright

■ **Sleeping**
1 Belfast City Hostel
2 Benedicts & Restaurant
3 Crescent Townhouse
4 Dukes & Glassroom Restaurant
5 Macpacker's Hostel
6 Madison's

5 Elms
6 Fitzy's & La Salsa
7 Julie's Kitchen
8 Kaos Nightclub
9 Lavery's
10 M Club
11 Maggie May's
12 Maharajah & Dragon City

● **Eating & drinking**
1 Antica Roma
2 Beatrice Kennedy's
3 Café Vincent & Moghul
4 Chez Delbert & Bishop's

13 Mange Tous
14 Opus One
15 Spuds
16 The Other Place
17 Ventnor's & Acapulco

This is probably the least stressful place to visit in Belfast. Here you will find no mention of the Troubles; it is as if they never happened. The museum is laid out in a kind of walk around the interesting features of Ulster with some dinosaurs, an art collection and geology thrown in. The ground floor is occupied by some massive machinery connected with linen production and steam power. The size of it all is admirable, but there is no proper explanation of what any of it does. Huge boards set apart from the machines give a description of the process of linen manufacture, but it is difficult to connect the two. Heading onwards on this floor, you find a children's dinosaur exhibition. On the second floor are some interesting exhibits on early Ireland, this time much more hands-on, with video clips, reconstructed huts and other bits and pieces. There is an interesting video regarding the making of flint tools, which accompanies the Ballyclare hoard, a collection of used and blank flints that must once have been the stock in trade of a

Ulster Museum & the Botanic Gardens

Neolithic flint maker. A display of Spanish artefacts, taken from the Girona, a sunken armada vessel excavated near the Giant's Causeway in 1968, gives a nice insight into life on the boats, and some odds and ends of Ancient Egyptian and Native American artefacts complete this level.

Level three is taken up with a jewellery, glassware and a wildlife exhibition, while the top floor displays some of the museum's collection of art. Displays change regularly. ■ *Monday to Friday 1000-1700, Sunday 1400-1700. Free.*

Around Belfast

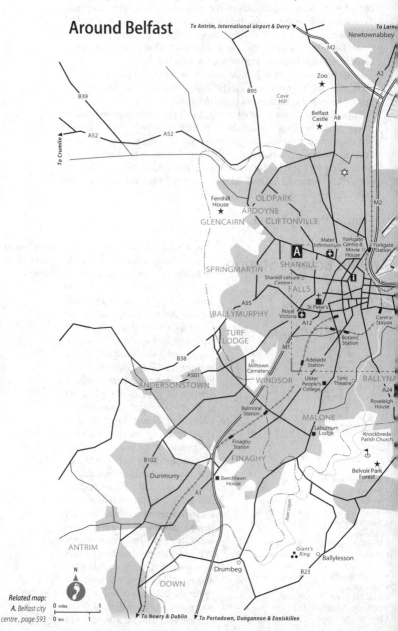

Related map:
A. Belfast city
centre, page 593

The museum is in the grounds of the Botanic Gardens, rather a dull park, except for the two beautiful glasshouses it contains. The gardens were begun in 1827, during the 19th-century craze for plant hunting. The 14 acres were open to the public for a fee, but those who bought shares in the enterprise were allowed in free. After 1841 the working classes were allowed in free on Saturdays. The gardens never really became self-supporting financially and were eventually sold to the Belfast City Corporation, which made them a public park in 1895.

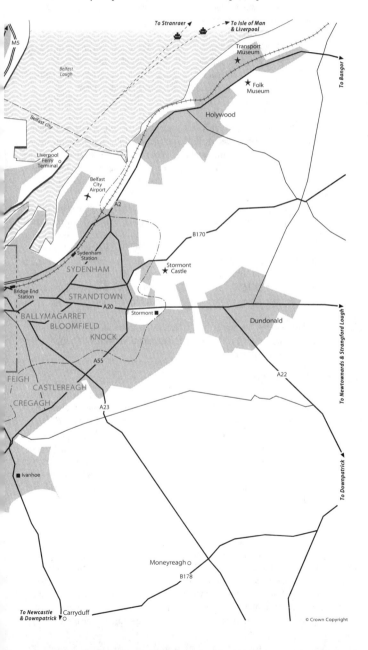

Belfast

© Crown Copyright

Stormont

Stormont, the site of the parliament of Northern Ireland, has become a shorthand for the parliament itself. It was established as a result of the Government of Ireland Act of 1920 which devolved all domestic government except taxation to the Northern Ireland parliament at Stormont. When the civil rights campaign developed into open conflict with the Unionist-dominated government, and especially after the British army was called out in 1969, there was pressure on the government to cede its control over internal security. The refusal of Unionism to do this led to the dissolution of Stormont in March 1972. It remained in limbo until 29 November, 1999 when the impasse over the implementation of the Good Friday Agreement was overcome and a new power-sharing executive was formed ending direct rule from London (see page 689). However the spectre of decommissioning still hovers over the new Assembly as we go to press.

The best section of the gardens is the reconstruction of a tropical ravine, begun in 1889 and extended in 1900 and again in 1902 to include the heated pond where you can see giant water lilies growing. It was renovated once more in 1980. Look out for pitcher plants, tree ferns, bananas, cinnamon trees, papyrus at the water's edge and a great mass of water hyacinth, an invasive weed all over the Far East.

The Palm House, completed in 1852, is more beautiful, but less interesting inside being filled with the kind of plants you can buy in department stores. The designer, Lanyon made use of the new invention of curved glass to create the central elliptical dome with two wings. The building was renovated in 1975 when whole sections of glazing were replaced and a new heating system installed. ■ *April to September Monday-Friday 1000-1700, Saturday, Sunday, bank holidays 1400-1600; October to March Monday-Friday 1000-1600, closed 1300-1400. Free. Buses 69, 70, 71 from Donegall Square east.*

Ormeau Road Southeast of the city centre is the Ormeau Road, more recently famous for its tenants associations, which have entered negotiations with the Orange orders who like to march past their houses.

North of the City

Cave Hill The north of the city is defined by the high backdrop of mountains, which make up the country park of Cave Hill. Bought up by the city at various times from 1911, the park consists of about 750 acres of parkland, escarpments and woodland. It is grand wandering territory, criss-crossed with numerous footpaths, and is dotted with Bronze Age sites, including the caves themselves (which are man-made Iron Age mines). The best walk of all is to the top of the hill from where there are wonderful views of the city and lough, and even beyond them to the Scottish coast.

Belfast Castle Set in the grounds of the country park is Belfast Castle, a Scottish baronial pile built in 1870 for the Marquis of Donegall. From a distance it looks imposing enough set against the mountains but close up it is twee, with too many turrets and curlicues, rather in the style of Balmoral. It almost bankrupted the family, who fortunately married well and were able to complete it. It was given to the city in 1934 and refurbished in the 1970s at a cost of a couple of million pounds. It is run now as a series of businesses – a classy restaurant, a bistro, shop and pub all done up in Victorian street style – and is available for hire for weddings and functions. Inside is a small heritage centre with information about Cave Hill. ■ *Belfast Castle, Antrim Road. T90776925. Daily, 0900-1800. Free. If the heritage centre is closed ask for the key at reception. Citybus 45, 46, 47, 48, 49, 50, 51 from Donegall Square west.*

The zoo affords a nice day out for children of all ages, as long as you enjoy looking at captive animals. It is a vibrant place, and so it should be. It has had around £10 million invested into the creation of new enclosures and general renovation, meaning the animals are well kept and there are some unusual creatures. Some Falklands penguins live here, as do tapirs, spectacled bears and assorted monkeys.■ *April to September, 1000-1800 daily; October to March 1000-1530. £4.80.*

Belfast Zoo

East of Belfast

There are two routes east out of Belfast: the A20 goes past Stormont to Newtownards while the A2 passes the Ulster Folk & Transport Museum on its way to Bangor. Buses and train travel to Bangor and there is the 15-mile (24 km) **North Down Coastal Path**, from Holywood to Groomsport, east of Bangor.

Ins & outs

When Stormont was opened in 1932 it was accompanied by a triumphalist Protestant pageant, but now that the new, post-Good Friday, Assembly has finally been inaugurated here (see page 689), the political balance is a wee bit more level. Presumably, a public gallery will open in due course but the grounds are always open and the shining neoclassical parliament building stands at the end of a mile-long drive before a statue of Edward Carson. Bus 16 or 17 from Donegall Square in Belfast. Edward Carson (1854-1935) was a Unionist leader who brought Ulster perilously close to civil war by using the threat of military action to scupper attempts at Irish independence in the years leading up to the establishment of Northern Ireland.

Stormont

This is justly praised as one of Ireland's best museums. Dozens of buildings have been transplanted here to form a vibrant recreation of life in Ulster around 1900, complete with staff in period costume. Both entertaining and educational, a visit to this outdoor folk park is recommended. A bridge leads across the road to the transport museum where the largest locomotive built in Ireland is just one of the myriad forms of transport represented. The Titantic exhibition pulls in the crowds but there is a lot more to see. ■ *Cultra, T90428428. July and August, Monday-Saturday 1030-1800, Sunday 1200-1800; April to June and September, Monday-Friday 0930-1700, Saturday 1030-1800, Sunday 1200-1800; October to March, Monday-Friday 0930-1600, Saturday and Sunday 1230-1600. Last admission one hour before closing time. £4. Tea room. Trains and buses to Bangor stop at Cultra, 7 miles (11 kilometres) east of Belfast.*

Ulster Folk & Transport Museum

Essentials

Sleeping

In Dublin hotel prices go up in summer and at weekends; here the opposite happens. During the summer places close down for the marching season, and at weekends the city centre empties, a throwback to the old days of car bombs and assassinations. Hotels are popping up all over but none has that genteel, laid-back quality of the best

Belfast

Belfast

southern hotels; the Protestant work ethic pervades everything in Northern Ireland. There are no great bargains in the city centre, but the hotels are classy enough. There are more modest places to the south of the city around the university, while B&Bs and hostels provide cheaper accommodation: the 3 or 4 regular hostels in the city are supplemented during the long summer holiday and at some other times by the various halls of residence, which let their student accommodation. The guesthouses and B&Bs tend to cost around £34-45 for a double room, the higher end having en-suite rooms in slightly bigger houses, the lower end being 1 or 2 rooms in someone's house with a shared bathroom. The most convenient of these are situated in the university area in the side streets between Malone and Lisburn Rd. In Eglantine Avenue are several good-value places.

Hotels
■ on maps
Price codes:
see inside front cover

LL *Belfast Hilton*, 4, Lanyon Place, BT1 3LP, T90277000, F90277277. Don't be put off by the dull reception and uniformed staff: if you can possibly afford it stay here. It is a masterpiece of modernity in a sea of pompous Victoriana. Great views over the river, wonderful Hilton rooms, fluffy bathtowels, fitness centre and tiny pool, lovely Sonoma Restaurant with glass walls overlooking a hundred years of industry. Amazing discounts at weekends. Nice breakfast. **LL** *Europa Hotel*, Great Victoria Street, BT2 7AP, T90327000, F90327800, restaurant. The most bombed hotel in the world, this rather ugly eastern-European looking building is nevertheless both safe and comfortable. **LL** *McCausland Hotel*, 34-8 Victoria Street, T90220200, F90220220, info@mccauslandhotel.com Made from gorgeously restored 19th-century warehouses, the best feature about this hotel is its façade and lobby. Rooms are relatively cramped, and a little disconcertingly unsoundproofed. Nice, popular café bar and dining room. Good breakfasts.

L *Duke's Hotel*, 65-67 University St, BT7 1HL, T90236666, F90237177. Nicely located at the end of the Golden Mile, interesting restaurant, big rooms, gym, good weekend rates. **L** *Stormont Hotel*, 587 Upper Newtownards Rd, BT4 3LP, T90658621, F90480240, two restaurants. Three miles out of the city, a business hotel with lots of facilities to make the holidaymaker happy too. Some self-catering apartments. **L** *Wellington Park Hotel*, 21 Malone Rd, BT9 6RU, T90381111, F90665410, restaurant. Very new, geared to business clientele, near to the Golden Mile.

AL *Beechlawn House Hotel*, 4 Dunmurry Lane, Dunmurry, BT17 9RR, T90612974, F90623601. Outside the city on the road to Dublin, a family-run hotel. **AL** *Benedicts of Belfast*, 7-21 Bradbury Pl, Shaftesbury Sq, BT7 1RQ. T90591999, F90591990. Restaurant. Very new theme hotel with vaguely Gothic décor using reclaimed features from older buildings. Very central, lovely big rooms, excellent value for money. Breakfast to the

A word of warning

Any writer presenting a handbook of information to the city of Belfast would be irresponsible to ignore a dire warning concerning the health and wellbeing of visitors, which must be made about this city: it shuts on Sundays. Before about 1300 hours it genuinely resembles a scene from a horror movie where all the citizens of a town have been eaten by carnivore cabbages from the planet Nerd. Only the homeless and unsuspecting tourists walk the streets. Empty McDonald's cartons roll around the deserted streets like latterday tumbleweed and the debris of Saturday night congeals in the gutters. The only place to get a cup of coffee is Burger King or Dunkin Donuts. If you must be here on Sunday, stay in bed. Do not check out of your hotel. At lunchtime some of the pubs open and in the afternoons some of the big shops open too but all is deadly quiet. The evenings are the worst – I have spent hours wandering looking for somewhere to eat, and all the good places are battened down. All the little grocery stores are shut up tight; the only places to open their doors are the fast food chains. Sadly, this hazard extends to all of the North, in places like Armagh extending to weeknight evenings too. A state of siege seems to come over the place with stuff pulled inside, shutters brought down just like they are expecting the bad guys to ride into town and shoot the place up. Well, perhaps they are.

Belfast

sound of local music stations. Checking-in time 1400. **AL** *Crescent Townhouse*, 13 Lower Crescent, BT7 1NR, T90323349, F90320646. At the top of this price bracket, this is a small hotel with large, attractively appointed rooms. Set in the centre of the Golden Mile its restaurant and bar are popular with office workers on their way home from work. The hotel itself is quiet, with the lobby upstairs, away from the activity of the bar and restaurant. **AL** *Ivanhoe Hotel*, 556 Saintfield Rd, BT8 8EU, T90812240, F90815516. Restaurant and bistro. Small, family-run hotel, nicely appointed big rooms, comfortable bar that doubles as a bistro in the evenings, more formal restaurant for dinner. Bus or cab ride back into the city, in pleasant rural surroundings. Open for Sunday lunch, a rare treat in Belfast. **AL** *Madison's*, 59-63 Botanic Ave, BT7 1JL, T90330040, F90328007. Restaurant. Very trendy, modern hotel, popular with local swingers. **A** *Holiday Inn Express*, 106 University St, BT7 1HP, T90311909, F90311910, express@holidayinn-ireland.com Restaurant. Excellent value, rate includes breakfast, close to the Golden Mile. **A** *Travelodge Belfast City*, 15, Brunswick St, T90333555, F90232999, restaurant. The best value for the city centre, at £59.95 per room without breakfast. Newly renovated but slightly cramped rooms, this would suit non-breakfast-eaters.

A *Avenue House*, 23 Eglantine Ave, T90665904, F90291810, a B&B with en-suite rooms. **A** *Laburnum Lodge*, 16 Deramore Park, T90665183, F90681460, Guesthouse with 6 en-suite rooms. **A** *Old Rectory*, 148 Malone Rd, T90667882, F90683759. Slightly more expensive guesthouse in this price bracket. **A** *Pearl Court*, 11 Malone Rd, T90666145, F90200212, a guesthouse with 10 rooms and an evening meal option.

Guesthouses & B&Bs

B *Eglantine Guest House*, 21 Eglantine Ave, T90667585, is inexpensive for a guest-house, but has no en-suite rooms or evening meal – not a problem in this restaurant-saturated area. The same rates and facilities are available at **B** *Liserin Guest House*, 17 Eglantine Ave, T90660769.

B *Ulster People's College*, 30 Adelaide Pk, BT9 6FY, T90665161, F90668111. A community education centre that has rooms available all year, mostly twins and family rooms. Breakfast included in the price. **C** *Europe House*, 19 Rugby Parade, BT7 1PY, T90234550, F90434639. Near to the Botanic Gardens and golden mile, this hostel has

Halls of residence/ Hostels

family, twin and double rooms as well as dorm beds. Secure parking. **C** *Stranmillis College Halls of Residence*, Stranmillis Rd, BT9 5DY, T90381271. Another college opening its halls to the public. Single rooms only, set in pleasant grounds.

D *The Ark*, 18 University St, T90329626. Hostel comprising 2 Georgian town houses, 2 kitchens, double and single rooms. **D** *Arnie's Backpackers*, 63 Fitzwilliam St, BT9 6AX, T90242867. Dorm beds only, self-catering hostel in a small Victorian house just off the golden mile. **D** *Belfast City Hostel*, 22 Donegall Rd, BT8 4AE, T90324733, F90439699. If you don't mind stepping outside to the sight of painted kerbstones and Union Jacks this is a very central hostel, right beside the heart of the best nightlife in the city. No self-catering, some double and family rooms. **D** *Linen House Youth Hostel*, 18-29 Kent St, BT1 2JA. Close to the main bus and train terminals, the main shopping area and City Hall, this is the largest and newest of Belfast's hostels. Lots of room, big, well-equipped kitchen, good security. Mixed and single-sex dormitories. Left luggage room, bike storage. Book in advance in the high season. **D** *Macpackers Independent Hostel*, T90220485, 1 Cameron St, very new hostel beside the Empire in Botanic Ave. **D** *Queen's Elms Halls of Residence*, 78 Malone Rd, Belfast, BT9 5BW, T90381608, F90666680. Single and twin rooms available during vacation periods, March to April, June to September.

Self-catering Most self-catering accommodation in the city is centred around the university area. Units can be hired for a week or a weekend and accommodate between 2 and 6 people. All work out at the range of a budget hotel for 6 people and much less for larger parties. **A** *L'Academie Apartments*, 14 College Gardens, T/F90666046. 1-bedroom flats in renovated Victorian house close to university. **A** *Malone Grove Suites*, 70 Eglantine Ave, BT9 6DY, T90382409, F90382706. 1- to 2-bedroom luxurious apartments near university. Price includes housekeeping and breakfast. **B** *Belfast Town Homes*, Ardenlee Green, Ravenhill Rd, BT6 0DL, T/F90806116. 2- to 3-bedroom apartments in south Belfast. Sleep 2-6. **B** *Gleneagles*, 25a Knockbreda Park, BT6 0HB, T90693646, F90330713. Bungalow, sleeps 5. **B** *Malone View*, 52 Malone Ave, BT9 6ER, T90776889. Close to university and golden mile. 3-bedroom house. Dogs welcome.

Eating

Ten years ago this section of the book would have been much shorter. People just didn't go into town after dark; the roads were closed and it was downright dangerous. Some time during the last 10 years people decided that it was time to reclaim the city, and now, apart from the odd silly drunk and a few notices warning about incendiary devices, you wouldn't know you were in Belfast. The obvious place to look for food is the Golden Mile, along Botanic Ave and the parallel University Rd, but the city centre has some good options, especially for lunch. The area around St Anne's is all set to turn into Temple Bar in the next few years so it's worth enquiring about any new places in that area.

The Golden Mile
● *on maps*
Price codes:
see inside front cover

The golden mile really gets going in Dublin Rd, extends a little into Donegal Pass and takes off along University Rd and Botanic Ave as far as University St, extending a little into the side roads. At night the area is full of punters discussing where to go and the doorways to pubs and clubs are blocked by the incongruously black-tied, largely good-natured bouncers. Restaurants vary with regard to price and style of food, and there is certainly something along this stretch of road to suit everyone's budget and tastes.

Affordable Starting at the haute (culinary as well as financial) end of the market La Belle Epoque, at 61 Dublin Rd, T90323244, comes very well recommended. Very traditional in style with authentic French food. Dinner may set you back £20 a head. Closed on Sundays. At number 103 Great Victoria St is the newly fashionable **Keating**, T90594949, where lunches are very good, popular and affordable with modern cuisine featuring all the trendy stuff – rocket, truffle oil, bubble and squeak. Dinner would be £18 plus. Open 5 days for lunch, 6 for dinner. Further out of town, but in the same price range and offering a choice of early evening and dinner menus is **Beatrice Kennedy's**, 44 University Rd, T90202290, serving modern Irish cuisine. Early evening menu is around £13 for 2 courses, while dinner works out around £18 plus. For classy Italian food, try **Antica Roma**, at 67 Botanic Ave, T90311121, where dinner is £20 plus. Closed Sundays. Very popular with lunchers is **The Strand**, 12 Stranmillis Rd, T90682266, a good way out of town past the Ulster Museum. It serves fairly rich, meat-dominated dishes and has 2 menus, one aimed at the lunch market at around £10 for 2 courses but which is served until 1900, and the other served all day at around £18 for dinner. Lastly, **Opus One**, 1 University St, T90590101 replaces the old **Saints and Scholars** in a very fashionable, beautifully designed place all wood and steel, goat's cheese and sun-dried things, dinner at £18 plus. Open Sundays till late. Very reasonable business lunches.

Affordable-Inexpensive   At around £15 or less for an evening meal there are lots of good choices to make all along the golden mile. At 50 Dublin Rd is **Graffiti Italiano**, T90249269, very popular indeed if the queues outside are anything to go by. Several vegetarian choices. Open Sunday evenings. Directly opposite, at number 53 is **Archana**, T90323713, winner of lots of awards for its Indian food and holder of the distinction of the most bombed restaurant in Ulster (not because of the food but because of its location next to an Orange Lodge). Downstairs for all those vegetarians fed up with choosing from the 2 options of most regular restaurants is a vegetarian restaurant called **Little India**. Very respectable vegetarian lunch thalis for around £3. Dinner upstairs at around £15. Open Sunday evenings. At 89 Dublin Rd is **The Square**, where a set menu offers 3 courses at £11.50. Very fashionable place. Upstairs the à la carte is more expensive at around £20 plus. The style is modern Irish.

At 60 Great Victoria St is **Fatty Arbuckle's**, an American diner with an extensive menu of burgers, steaks, and chicken, all with a swipe at Californian cuisine, and best of all it's open Sundays. One menu all day will set you back about £15 for three courses and coffee. Full wine list. If you can eat all of three designated courses they'll give you a T-shirt. Kid's menu, vegetarian options.

Along Botanic Ave are some more pleasant places to eat. At 75 is **Acapulco** where you can eat inexpensive Mexican food daily. Just opposite are **Dragon City** at 82 and **The Maharajah** at 62, both serving western versions of their respective cuisines, but good places. Heading back into town, **Café Vincent** at 78 is open 7 days, does pasta dishes and is good for lunch. Next door is another reliable Indian, **The Moghul**, while across the road at **Madison's** is an inexpensive and quite popular restaurant, open 7 days, serving modern Irish cuisine. On the corner of Botanic and Lower Crescent is **Metro**, a very stylish place with an early evening menu (1800-1900) of 3 courses for £12.50, modern with Californian overtones.

Running parallel with Botanic Ave are Bradbury Pl and University Rd with more middle-range places to eat. In Bradbury Pl at number 10 is **Chez Delbert**, very popular, inexpensive, open Tuesday to early evening Sunday, serving crêpe-oriented French food. Opposite is **Benedicts**, a new hotel and restaurant in town with a heavily designed restaurant and a dizzying range of menus. Dinner in this Californian influenced but fairly traditional restaurant will be around £15. If you haven't tried wild boar, now's your chance. Several vegetarian options. Lunch around £8. Open Sunday evenings. At number 32 is **Bishop's**, where you can get posh fish and chips.

Further out of town the road becomes University Rd, where at number 23 is **La Salsa**, for inexpensive Mexican and close by is **Fitzy's**, open Sundays, with a large menu of sandwiches and more substantial pasta and steak choices. Vegetarian possibilities. *Mange Tous* at number 30 is popular and inexpensive and has a vaguely French menu. At number 65, in *Duke's Hotel* is the *Glassroom*, small and intimate with a huge window out on to University Rd where you can people-watch. It has an interesting menu, including an early evening menu at £10.95 for three courses. Try the black pasta, made with squid ink. Vegetarians can luxuriate in an entire vegetarian menu.

Fast food If you are after fast food or a snack the area abounds in them. Bradbury Pl probably has the largest range of big names but in addition there are local places worth a look. *Spuds*, in Bradbury Pl, looks awful but has a nice menu of filled potatoes, and other fast things. *Jenny's* in Dublin Rd is country kitchenish and has a range of sandwiches, quiche and lasagne till 1700, 6 days a week. *Revelations Internet Café* in Shaftesbury Sq has, besides the World Wide Web, sandwiches and soup. In Botanic Ave are *The Other Place*, *Ventnor's*, *Julie's Kitchen* and *Maggie May's*, all within sight of each other and offering sandwiches, and more substantial choices. *The Other Place* caters to the student population and has loud music.

Pub lunches In the same area there are any number of pubs that do quite large lunch menus but which tend to focus on music and drink at night. In Bradbury Pl is *Lavery's*, which does pub food till about 1400, Monday to Saturday. The *Botanic Inn* and the *Eglantine*, both in Malone Rd are student pubs but do pub food, the Botanic having the slightly better menu. *Elms* in University Rd does hearty dishes from 1100-1800 except Sunday, while the *Empire* in Botanic Ave does pizzas and pasta from 1200-1400.

The city centre **Affordable-inexpensive** The place to be seen in the city centre is *Deane's*, 38 Howard St, T90560000, which has a brasserie with quite interesting, very much in demand food, focussing on modern Irish cooking where dinner will cost £15 plus. Upstairs is a restaurant where reservations well in advance are necessary as well as a well-endowed charge card. Interestingly decorated with a kind of *fin de siècle* mood to the dining room, big silver lids on the dishes and little brushes for the crumbs between courses. Nice for a special occasion. At 3 Donegal Sq East is *Café Society* with a rather dull-looking café downstairs but an excellent reputation upstairs for modern Irish/Californian cuisine. Way over in Hill St is an excellent place, *Nick's Warehouse*, T90439690, serving thoughtful modern Irish cuisine in a vast old warehouse. Avoid weekends when it gets very busy and noisy. Lunch is very popular too. *Aero*, at 44 Bedford St, open for lunch and dinner Monday to Saturday serves more modern Irish food in a stark but pleasant environment. *Flannigan's*, above the Crown Liquor Saloon at 19 Amelia St serves basic food till 2100, 7 days a week. Not much for the vegetarian to get excited about but children accompanying an adult eat free on Sundays. *Larry's Piano Bar*, 36, Bedford St, T90325061, has a set dinner menu at £17 7 days a week, live piano music till 0130 and lots of pictures around the walls. The menu is substantial with the occasional nod toward California. Best of all for the food and the views is the restaurant in the *Hilton Hotel*, which will set you back £20 plus, but has a glorious curtain window out on to the river and the industry beyond.

Inexpensive-cheap At lunchtime the city centre abounds with reasonably priced places for a designer sandwich or something more substantial. Several of them open late on Thursdays till about 2100 for the late-night shopping. In Donegall Arcade is a branch of *Bewleys*, which isn't quite as trendy as the one in Grafton St in Dublin but can still offer a little more than the traditional scones and tea. Nearby is *Delaney's*, attractively designed with a wide, inexpensive menu, open six days a week 0900-1700.

Pub lunches City centre pubs also do a roaring lunchtime trade. In Commercial Court, the *Duke of York* is very popular, serving slightly more than the usual pub grub. The *Morning Star* in Pottinger's Entry is very adventurous about its food, and has gourmet evenings once a month. Expect crocodile and ostrich among the more regular menu items. Serves lunch from 1130-2100. In another of the little entries of the city centre is *White's Tavern* with a more traditional menu, but the food has an excellent reputation. Get there early. In *Dempsey's* there are a variety of food options, the best for lunch being the bar food, which is quite exotic, leaning towards unusual breads, with lots of vegetarian options. The bistro offers a more extensive and expensive menu, with a sit-down lunch with tablecloths. It also does an early evening dinner but shuts down when the music in the pub starts at about 2100. *Strike Four* in Bedford Pl is a theme pub with vast TV screens broadcasting sporting events and a good lunch menu. *Fibber Magee's* in Keylan's Place also does good food. In Victoria Square is the *Kitchen Bar*, which does good authentic Ulster food till 1500 most days and later on Thursdays. Nothing Sunday. Lastly, worth visiting for its views alone is the restaurant in the Waterfront Hall, which does breakfasts and lunches, and dinner when there is a show on.

Entertainment

There are very few pubs in the city that don't have music of some kind or a late-night club attached somewhere. For up to date listings of events consult the free *The Big List* newspaper, available from the tourist office and most public places. If it's just a drink you're after the most atmospheric is of course *The Crown* in Great Victoria St with its authentic decorations and cosy snugs but you must get there early if you want a seat. In the same area is *The Beaten Docket* with very loud disco music and a young crowd, and *Robinsons'* with 4 floors of assorted ways of drinking and listening to music. A board outside announces what is on.

Pubs &music

Moving out of town along the golden mile is another cluster of places. *Morrison's* in Bedford St has music at weekends and a nice atmosphere at other times. In Bradbury Pl is *Lavery's*, a regular pub with a disco upstairs but the odd habit of charging an entry fee to the pub on busy nights. *The Elms* on University Rd is very studenty with either live music or a disco from Thursday to Saturday. The 'Bot' and the 'Egg', as the *Botanic Inn* and *Eglantine Inn* in Malone Rd are affectionately known, are also very popular with a young crowd and have either live music or a disco at weekends.

Back in town there are several pubs in the entries that are well established with good music nights. The *Morning Star* in Pottinger's Entry is quiet at night but has a beautiful interior, *White's Tavern* is in Winecellar Entry and has jazz on Thursdays, and traditional Irish music on Friday and Saturday. The *Globe*, Joy's Entry, has also been recommended.

For good Irish music *Kelly's Cellars* at 30 Bank St is worth a look in as is The *Liverpool Bar* opposite the Seacat terminal where traditional music is often played on Saturdays and Sundays. *Maddens*, in Smithfield, has music on Monday, Wednesday and Saturday afternoons and evenings. *The Kitchen* in Victoria Square has live music sessions at weekends.

For other types of live music there is *McHughes* in Queen's Sq with jazz on Thursdays and something going on most other nights, *The Front Page* in Donegall St with live music from Wednesday to Sunday, *The Duke of York* in Commercial Court with live music at weekends, and *Shenanigan's* in Howard St with live music from Thursday to Sunday. Way out on Saintfield Rd is the *Ivanhoe Hotel* where there is a good bar for bar food and regular live jazz.

Night clubs Clubbers might like to try out the *Trilogy* night club in Frames Complex, Little Donegall St, *The Factory* in Dublin Rd where there is an entrance fee on Fridays and Saturdays and Tuesdays (this last date includes free cocktails). *Thompson's Garage*, 3 Patterson's Pl, Arthur St, is the big draw in town on Saturday night. *The Limelight*, in Ormeau Ave is another seriously dedicated club. Others are clubs above the trendy pubs in town, *Madison's*, *Kaos*, in Renshaw's Hotel, *The M Club* in Manhattan's, 23 Bradbury Pl.

Art galleries There are a burgeoning number of galleries in the city exhibiting contemporary work by local artists. *The Crescent Arts Centre* at 2-4 University Rd has a changing exhibition of significant local painters such as Barrie Hall and Felim Egan while the *Ormeau Baths Gallery* in Ormeau Ave presents work of visiting artists from all over Europe. The *Old Museum Arts Centre* in College Sq North also has varying exhibitions of local artists in a converted Georgian house with a drama space upstairs. Smaller galleries can be visited at *Arches Art Gallery* in Holywood Rd, *Cavehill Gallery* in Cavehill Rd, *Catalyst Arts* at 5 Exchange Pl and the *Eakin Gallery* in Lisburn Rd.

Cinemas *The Virgin Cinemas*, T90243200 are at the end of Dublin Rd, at Shaftesbury Square, *The Movie House*, T90755000, is in the Yorkgate Centre on York St and *The Curzon*, T90641373, is on Ormeau Rd. The city's arty cinema is *Queen's Film Theatre*, 7 University Sq Mews, T90244857. Good value.

Music venues The *Ulster Hall*, T90323900, in Bedford St, hosts classical performances by the Ulster Orchestra as well as some rock concerts. The *Waterfront Hall*, T90334455, Lanyan Place, Laganside, hosts a whole range of performances from classical music to school parents evenings, stand-up gigs by ageing comics, ballet, jazz, big name pop stars. *King's Hall*, T90665225, at Balmoral stages the really big rock shows.

Theatres The *Arts Theatre*, T90316900, is in Botanic Ave and has fairly run-of-the-mill productions, while the *Empire*, T90328110, also in Botanic Ave puts on various activities, its chief draw being the Comedy Club on Tuesday nights: this gets very full, so get there early. It starts at 2100 and entrance is £4. The *Grand Opera House*, Great Victoria St, T90241919, is worth a visit just for the decorations, but it regularly has big-name shows transferred from Dublin or the West End. The *Lyric Theatre*, T90381081, is the city's serious theatre, situated off Ridgeway St, which is off Stranmillis Rd south of the city. It regularly has important modern productions. There is a student standby scheme where remaining tickets will be sold off at reduced prices to students after 1930 on the night of the production, and has a deal with *Dukes Hotel* where ticketholders can get a pre-show dinner for £9. The *Old Museum Arts Centre*, T90233332, in College Sq North, has a small theatre where the avant garde can be found.

Festivals

Ardoyne Fleadh T90751056, is 3 days of open-air concerts and community events in north Belfast. Early August. *Belfast Carnival Parade*, T90460863, in late June is a procession of strangely dressed entertainers. *Belfast City Summer Festival*, T90320202, late May to June includes all kinds of events from local stuff to major concerts, including the Lord Mayor's Show. *Belfast Festival at Queens*, T90667687 for information, T90665577 for bookings. An arts festival with 400-plus shows during 3 weeks around November, based around Queen's University. Belfast's answer to the Edinburgh Festival. *Féile an Phobail* T90313440, takes place during the first 2 weeks in August and includes street parties, concerts, Irish-language events and a carnival parade. Originally a Republican inspired event, it is now huge and includes contributions from

Unionists. *Orange Marches*, basically the city shuts down for 2 weeks around the height of the marching season, the first 2 weeks in July. Restaurants close, people take their holidays, nightlife draws to a halt. If you want to watch the last stand of triumphalist Loyalism, this is your chance.

Gay and lesbian

Belfast being the intolerant place it has been this last quarter-century, the gay scene is a fairly low-key affair, with the nearness of Dublin and its laid-back acceptance sending lots of pink pounds there at the weekends. *The Crow's Nest*, T90325491, on the corner of High St and Skipper St has entertainment most nights while the *Parliament* on the corner of Dunbar Link and Gordon St does good lunches and has entertainment at night. *Kremlin*, T809700, 96 Donegall St, is a recently-opened bar and nightclub (see listings in *The List*). **Cara-friend**, PO Box 44, Belfast BT1 1SH, T90322023 men, evenings only; T90238668 women, Thurs only. Advice on gay and lesbian matters.

Organized tours

Bailey's Historical Pub Tour of Ireland, T90683665. June and August, Tuesday 1900, Friday 1730, Saturday 1600; July and September, Friday 1530, Saturday 1600 from Flanagan's (above the Crown). *Belfast Castle* free tour. One hour. Advance booking necessary, T90776925. *Belfast City Hall* (see page 593) has free tours of the building, T90270456. *Belfast Walking Tour* T90246609, April to October, 1400 Sundays only. From TIC North Street. Covers the old town; 1½ hours from 1600-1835. *Citybus Tours* T90458484, http://www.citybus.co.uk Offers 2 tours of the city, one that takes in much of the city's recent history around the Falls and Shankill Roads and another that takes a tour of the more regular tourist attractions of the city. Check for details of tours. £8. Tickets can be booked in advance or bought on the bus.

Shopping

Belfast is a little depressingly similar to every other United Kingdom shopping centre with its pedestrianized streets, lookalike malls and big chains, but at least it is in the city centre and not out in some disused quarry or beside a motorway. The main shopping area is around Donegall Pl, Royal Ave and the Fountain area. Parking is simple enough in the centre, with lots of well-marked car parks, and many of the big stores open on Sunday afternoons, which is amazing for this sect-ridden town. Thursday is late-night shopping in many stores. All shops are closed on Easter Day and on Sunday and Monday when 12th July falls on a Sunday. The Castlecourt Shopping Centre is right in the middle of the pedestrianized area and bursts with British names, including *Debenhams*. North of the centre is the Yorkgate Centre with more shops, and smaller, less prosperous malls lurk around town.

Antiques *Donegall Pass* is the best place for looking for curios and more expensive items. Shops include *Alexander the Grate* which has an antiques market on Saturdays, *Past and Present* and *Oakland Antiques*. Nearby, in Bedford St, is *Blue Cat Antiques*. Particular mementos of the area might be the many pottery representations of King Billy on his white horse.

Books *Bookfinder's Café*, 47 University Rd, is good for browsing through their vast selection of second-hand books and reading for a while in the café upstairs. *Familia Bookshop* is at 64 Wellington Place and has books on Irish issues while *An Leathrá Póilí*, 513 Falls Rd, has books on Irish issues from a Republican perspective. It also has a café. *Ex Libris*, Unit 28, Victoria Centre has a large stock of second-hand material and sells graphic novels while antique books can be found at *Roma Ryan's*, 73 Dublin Rd, which has prints and rare books. Two private dealers are *Emerald Isle Books* T90370798, F90777288, 539 Antrim Rd, and *P&B Rowan* T90666448, Carleton House, 92 Malone Rd. Appointments are necessary at both. The regular bookshops can be found in the city centre. *Waterstones* is at 8 Royal Ave, *Dillons* at 42 Fountain St, *Eason's* at 16 Ann St.

Markets *St George's Market* in May St has existed for many years and has undergone major renovations recently. It is still a fruit and vegetable market, but also has stalls selling bric-à-brac, second-hand and new clothes, and on Fridays and Tuesdays has more than 200 stallholders. Behind Castlecourt Shopping Centre the *Smithfield Retail Market* sells new and second-hand furniture and clothes.

Sporting goods *Surf Mountain* at 12 Brunswick St specializes in surfing gear but also has an excellent collection of camping gear. There is a branch of *Millets* in Cornmarket with its usual collection of sportswear and camping equipment, and a shop called *Beaten Track* in Arthur St.

Sports

Football There are regular matches at Seaview, off Shore Rd, home ground of the Crusaders; the Oval, Redcliffe Parade, in the Newtownards Rd, home ground of Glentoran; and Solitude, Cliftonville, the home ground of Cliftonville. For details of matches check the weekend papers or ring the Irish Football League on T90242888. **Gaelic Football** Matches at weekends at Roger Casement Park, Andersonstown Rd. **Hurling** Weekends, Roger Casement Park. The hurling final is in early July. **Ice skating** *Ice Bowl*, 111 Old Dundonald Rd, T90482611. Olympic sized rink. **Leisure centres** *Shankill Leisure Centre*, 100 Shankill Rd, T90241434, includes 'Water Wonderland' a leisure pool. *Maysfield Leisure Centre*, East Bridge St, T90241633. *Olympia Leisure Centre*, Boucher Rd, T90233369. **Motor racing** Kirkistown, T9171325, and Bishopscourt, T44842202. The Ulster Grand Prix takes place at Dunrod to the west of the city each August. **Rugby** *Malone Rugby Club*, Malone Park, off Woodstock Rd. *Collegians*, Deramore Park, Malone Rd. For details try the Irish Rugby Football Union at T90649141. **Tennis** Belfast Tennis Arena, Ormeau Embankment, T90458024. **Ten-pin bowling** *Superbowl*, Bedford St. *Ice Bowl*, 11 Old Dundonald Rd, 30 lanes, 5 miles out of city centre.

Transport

Car hire There are Avis, Budget, EuropcarRental, Hertz and McCausland desks in the arrivals hall at Belfast International Airport and Budget and Avis desks at the City Airport. Desks are manned as incoming flights arrive. Rental is per day or per week. *Avis*, 69 Great Victoria St, T90240404, Belfast International Airport T01849-422333, City Airport, T90452017. *Budget*, 96-102 Gt Victoria St, T90230700, Belfast International Airport T01849-422333, City Airport T90451111. *Dan Dooley*, 175 Airport Rd, Crumlin, Co Antrim. *Europcar*, Belfast City Airport T01849-423444, City Airport T90450904. *Hertz*, International Airport T01849-422533. McCausland Car Hire, 21-31 Grosvenor Rd, T90333777, International Airport T01849-422022, City Airport T90454141.

Bike hire *McConvey Cycles*, 467 Ormeau Rd, T90491163, hires bikes for £7 per day with a deposit of £30. A second branch at 10 Pottinger's Entry, T90330322, can arrange hire but the bikes are kept at the other shop. *Recycle* T90313113, 1-5 Albert Square also has bikes for hire. The tourist office has details of some possible cycle tours of the region.

See the Getting there section of the Essentials chapter (page 32) for flight connections **Air** to Britain, Europe and the US. For most flights the exit point will be Belfast International Airport. An airport bus goes to the airport at half-hourly intervals from the Europa Buscentre, passing through Laganside Buscentre on its route. You can pick up the bus at either stop. Cost is around £4 for a single. A taxi to the airport will cost around £20. Some private minicabs are not metered, so you should agree a price before setting off.

Belfast City Airport, T90457745, is more conveniently located, but as yet has limited flights to provincial British destinations. It is accessible by train from Botanic station to Sydenham Halt, or Citybus 21 goes there from City Hall. A taxi will be about £5. The airport has a shop, buffet, cashpoint and postbox in the departure area, and a café in the arrivals hall. There are no left luggage facilities.

From Belfast *Norse Irish Ferries*, T90779090, travel to Liverpool from the Victoria ter- **Ferries** minal on West Bank Rd. *Stena Line*, T90747747, goes to Stranraer from Ballast Quay, while the Seacat catamaran, T905235, leaves from Donegall Quay for Stranraaer. Belfast-Isle of Man is served by the Isle of Man Steam Packet Co, T90351009, summer only from Donegall Quay. From Larne *P&O European Ferries*, T9098 0777, travels to Cairnryan in Scotland.

Except for the excellent Belfast to Dublin route, trains are a slow and expensive option **Trains** when moving on from Belfast. There are three train routes out of Belfast: one travels north and then west along the coastline to Derry, another west and then south through Portadown towards Dublin, and a third, smaller line, travels east to Bangor. Trains leave from two stations, Gt Victoria St, T90230671, and Belfast Central, T90899411. From Belfast Central trains go to Larne, Derry, Bangor, Portadown, Newry and Dublin, while Gt Victoria St serves Portadown, Lisburn, Bangor, Larne Harbour and Derry. A free citylink bus serves Belfast Central from Donegall Square. The Belfast to Dublin route is very fast and comfortable and costs £15 one way, stopping at Portadown, Newry, Lisburn and Dundalk. There are no left luggage facilities at the stations.

The Europa Buscentre, T90333000 for enquiries, in Glengall St, has services to **Buses** Enniskillen, Tyrone, Derry, Armagh, Downpatrick, Kilkeel, Newcastle, Newry, Limavady, Portadown via Lurgan, Dungannon, Bundoran, Ballycastle, the ferry termi-nals, and destinations in the Republic, including Achill, Sligo, Ballina, Westport, Galway, Athlone, Cork, Dublin. The Laganside bus station has services to Cookstown, Portrush, Ballymena, Antrim, Larne, Coleraine, Portstewart, Ballycastle and Carrickfergus. There are no left luggage facilities at either bus station. A private com-pany, O'Donnell Buses, T075-48356, operates a daily service between Donegal, Derry and Belfast. A pre-bookable express bus service operates between the City Airport and Derry and Coleraine, T40328500.

Directory

Airlines *Aer Lingus* T0645-737747, 46 Castle St in same building as Borde Faílte. *British Airways* T0345-222111, *British Midland* Suite, 2, Fountain Centre. *Jersey European* T01392-360777.

Banks *Bank of Ireland* T90234334, 54 Donegall Pl (linked with Barclays). *Northern Bank* T90245277, Donegall Sq West. *Ulster Bank* T90244112, 47 Donegall Pl (linked with Natwest). **Bureau de change:** *Northern Ireland Tourist Board* T90246609, St Anne's Court. *GPO* Castle Pl and Shaftesbury Sq. *Thomas Cooke* T90550232, 11 Donegall Pl and at *Belfast International Airport*, T01849-422536, open till 2000.

Communications *GPO*, Castle Pl and Shaftesbury Sq Mon-Fri 0900-1730, Sat 0900-2100. **Internet**: *Revelations Café* Bradbury Pl, T90320337, info@revelations.co.uk

Embassies and consulates Denmark and Sweden: *G Heyn & Sons Ltd*, Head Line Buildings, 10 Victoria St, BT1 3GP, T90230581. **Greece, Norway, Portugal**: *M F Ewings, (Shipping) Ltd*, Hurst House, 15-19 Corporation Square, BT1 3AJ, T90242242. **Italy**: 7 Richmond Park, BT9 5EP, T90668854. **USA**: Consulate General, Queen's House, 14 Queen St, BT1 6EQ.

Hospitals and medical services Accident and Emergency services are at *Belfast City Hospital*, Lisburn Rd, T90329241, *Mater Hospital*, Crumlin Rd, T90741211, *Royal Victoria Hospital*, Grosvenor Rd, T90240503, and *Ulster Hospital*, Dundonald, T90484511.

Laundry *The Laundry Room*, 37 Botanic Ave, 0800-2100 Mon-Fri, 0800-1800 Sat, 1200-1800 Sun.

Libraries *Belfast Central Library*, Royal Ave, Mon and Thu 0930-2000, Tue, Wed, Fri 0930-1730, Sat 0930-1300.

Places of worship *St Peter's Roman Catholic Cathedral*, Derby St. *St Anne's Church of Ireland Cathedral*, Donegall St. *Ballynafeigh Methodist Church*, Ormeau Rd. *The Belfast Hebrew Congregation*, 5 Fortwilliam Gdns, Belfast, T90775013.

Tour companies and travel agents *Thomas Cooke* 11 Donegall Pl, T90550030, *USIT* 13B Fountain Centre, College St, T90324073. Tourist offices *Northern Ireland Tourist Board*, St Anne's Court, 59 North St, Sep-Jun Mon 0930-1715, Tue-Sat 0900-1715; Jul and Aug Mon 0930-1900, Tue-Sat 0900-1715, Sun 1200-1600. *Borde Failte*, 53 Castle St, T90327888, Mon-Fri 0900-1700, Sat 0900-1230, Mar to end Sep only.

Useful addresses *AA*, 108-110 Gt Victoria St, T0990-989989, breakdowns T0800-887766. *RAC*, T0345-3311133, breakdowns T0800-828282.

McCausland Hotel, Belfast

Ceo draíochta I gcoim oíche do sheol mé
tré thíorthaibh mar óinmhid ar strae,
gan prómhcharaid díograis im chóngar,
is mé I gcríochaibh tar m'eolas I gcéin.

Through the deep night a magic mist led me
like a simpleton roaming the land,
no friends of my bosom beside me,
an outcast in places unknown.

Eoghan Rua Ó Súilleabháin (1748-84):
'Ceo Draíochta' ('Magical Mist')

Counties Down & Armagh

16

Counties Down & Armagh

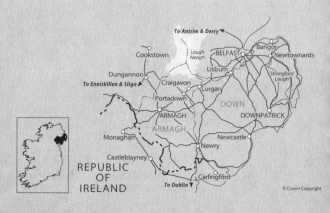

© Crown Copyright

Counties Down and Armagh are like neighbours that haven't spoken to each other for years: they share a fence but don't acknowledge one another. It is a generalization but Down likes to think of itself as British, whereas Armagh displays its Irish identity, and while Armagh has suffered disproportionately through the troubles of the last 30 years, Down has cocooned itself within a certain degree of smugness. Travelling through the county is a series of surprises: reminders of ugly sectarianism in towns like Kilkeel or Newtownards in the morning and yet by afternoon standing in awe of the shifting shades of green and purple where, in the words of the familiar song, 'the Mountains of Mourne sweep down to the sea'.

★ *Try to find time for*

Walking in Tollymore Forest Park

A drink and a chat in M C Larkin in south Armagh

Bird-watching around Strangford Lough

Looking out for eighteenth century graffiti in the old gaol in Down County Museum

A steam train ride and a look around the repair shed at Downpatrick railway museum

Watching Gulliver tell his story at St Patrick's Trian in Armagh

A visit to Armagh Gaol, beautiful on the outside, but frightening inside

Admiring the unusual mixture of architectural styles in Armagh Catholic Cathedral

Watching the universe go by and admiring the beautiful old observatory buildings in Armagh city

Visiting Navan Fort and imagining what it must have been like thousands of years ago

Finding out how the rich and famous lived in the eighteenth century at the Palace Stables

County Down

Bangor

The railway link from Belfast put Bangor on the map as a late-Victorian seaside resort. However, these days the marina has put paid to the beach, and while a lingering seaside feel is still faintly in the air the town is basically a commuter-fuelled, overwhelmingly Protestant, suburb of Belfast. Places of interest in the area mean that travellers find themselves here looking for a meal or even an overnight stay. There are some free parking spaces on The Marina opposite the Marine Court Hotel.

For the town's only point of interest, cross the road from the train and bus station and walk down to the rear of the town hall and the **North Down Heritage Centre** with its mixed collection that ranges from a fifth-century BCE set of swords, a ninth-century handbell, the Jordan Room with an engrossing set of Far Eastern *objets d'art* and an observation beehive in the summer. ■ *Castle Park Avenue, T91271200. July and August, Monday-Saturday 1030-1730, Sunday 1400-1730; September to June, Tuesday-Saturday 1030-1630 and Sunday 1400-1630. Free. Café.*

Sleeping   **AL** *Marine Court Hotel*, 18-20 Quay St, T91451100, F91451200, has a gym, comfortable rooms, deserves an award for having a place where you can eat on a Sunday morning. Weekend rate includes dinner. **AL** *Bangor Bay Inn*, 10 Seacliff Rd, T91270696, F91271678, a pleasingly small hotel in a former doctor's residence where American officers were billeted in the 1940s and with large rooms overlooking the sea. Less expensive at weekends. **A** *Cairn Bay Lodge*, 278 Seacliff Rd, T91467636, F91457728, a detached house that is a B&B a cut above the rest. **B** *Glenallen House*, 16 Seacliff Rd, T91473864, is more typical of the other B&Bs also found lined up in Seacliff Rd and facing the sea. **C** *Leaside*, 22 Southwell Rd, a B&B just behind the rail and bus station.

Eating   *Shanks*, 150 Crawfordsburn Rd, Bangor, T853313, is one of Ireland's best restaurants and don't be put off by knowing it's designed by Conran . The food is broadly European, using local produce with imaginative, contemporary touches and venison off the Clandeboye Estate, where the restaurant is situated, is a winter speciality. In summer, lobster salad niçoise is a typical creation from the kitchen of Robbie Millar. Open Tuesday to Friday for lunch, around IR£15, and Tuesday to Saturday for dinner for around twice that amount. House wine starts at below IR£13. The dining room at the *Bangor Bay Inn* on Seacliff Rd is a cosy little restaurant offering a relaxing evening meal for £15 and a good-value bistro menu. The *Marine Court Hotel* has a restaurant, and a popular bistro open until 2200 (closed Sunday). The *Castle Garden Room* restaurant at the North Down Heritage Centre, T91270371, is a peaceful place for a coffee or lunch (closed Monday). *Bokhara*, 2A King St, T91452439, just off Main St, is an Indian restaurant with specials for around £8, good, if you don't mind the lurid food colouring in some dishes – it's a friendly and welcoming place. *Brazilia*, facing the clock tower on The Marina, T91272763, has outdoor tables and is *the* place to enjoy a decent cup of coffee and one of their dozen toasties, potato bakes or sandwiches, all around £3. *Wolsey's Pub*, in the High St, T91460495, next to a useful second-hand bookshop, does a two-course lunch for £5.50, while for fast-food joints, carry up the road and round the corner into the *Flagstaff Centre*. Up the hill of High St, *McElhill's*, T91463928, is an old-style Irish pub and restaurant with a two-course lunch for £5.25 and main dishes on the menu around £8. *Jenny Watts*, T91270401, next door, does food and has folk music on a Tuesday and jazz on Sunday from 1300-1500.

Scuba diving: contact *David Vincent*, T91464671, or *Norsemaid Sea Enterprises* **Sport**
T91812081. **Sailing**: *Bangor Sea School*, T9142788214.

Bus, T91271143, and **rail**, T91899400/91270141, stations are next to each other on **Transport**
Abbey St and there are frequent services between Bangor and Belfast.

Car hire 34a Central Ave, T91464447. **Tourist office** Located in one of Bangor's few surviving **Directory**
buildings of historical note, the *Old Custom House and Tower*, in Quay St between the *Marine
Court* and *Bangor Bay Inn* hotels. T91270069. Jun-Sep, Mon-Fri 0900-1700 (1900 in Jul and Aug),
Sat 1030-1630, Sun 1300-1700 (1200-1800 in Jul and Aug); Oct-May, Mon-Fri 0900-1600, Sat
1000-1600.

Around Bangor

This is on the coast and makes a pleasant change from museums and the like. **Crawfordsburn**
Grey Point Fort, with its restored gun site, is a popular destination and the Park **Country Park**
Centre provides an excellent introduction to the park's flora and ecology, the
chief delight of coming here. ■ *Helen's Bay, off the B20, T91853621. Park open
to dusk. Gun site 1400-1700, April-September, closed Tuesday. October-March,
Sunday only. Free.*

When the First World War broke out the parliamentary leaders of nationalists **Somme**
and unionists, John Redmond and Edward Carson, urged their supporters to **Heritage**
enlist and many thousands did so. The 16th and the 10th Divisions were Cath- **Centre**
olic and nationalist respectively, while the 36th Ulster was a new division, created by 30,000 UVF men volunteering virtually as one body. In total some
200,000 Irishmen saw active service, and around 30,000 paid with their lives.
The Ulster 36th Division were at the battle of the Somme from the beginning,
in July 1916, suffering 5,000 casualties in the first 48 hours; they were joined by
the 16th Division in September of that year. The Centre also has a static wall
display reflecting the 10th Division's participation in the Gallipoli campaign.

Guided tours through the various displays and a reconstructed trench take
from 45 minutes to an hour and, while interesting, rarely manage to convey the
visceral horror of the war. A static exhibition on the role of Irish women during
the war is just as enlightening. A good selection of books, posters and educational material is available. ■ *233 Bangor Road, Newtownlands. T91823202.
July and August, Monday-Friday 1000-1700, Saturday and Sunday 1200-1700;
April to June and September, Monday-Thursday 1000-1600, Saturday and
Sunday, 1200-1600. October to March, Monday-Thursday, 1000-1600. £3.50.
Situated north of Newtownlands on the A21.*

On the other side of the A21 from the Somme Heritage Centre, the Ark Open **Ark Open Farm**
Farm has over 80 rare species of pigs, goats and poultry. There is also a tea
room and picnic sites. ■ *T92820445. Monday-Saturday 1000-1800, Sunday
1400-1800. £2.30, children £1.70.*

The park itself is dominated by Scrabo Tower (122 steps to the top) built in **Scrabo**
1857 as a memorial to the 3rd Marquis of Londonderry. However, come here **Country Park**
not for the tower, but instead for the panoramic views of Strangford Lough
(see box on page 618) and walks in the surrounding country park.
■ *T91811491. Tower open Easter and June-September, 1100-1830, closed Friday. Free. Just over a mile south-west of Newtownlands and signposted from
there.*

County Down

Strangford Lough

Strangford Lough would be a lake but for a narrow five-mile (eight-kilometre) gap at the southern end between Portaferry and Strangford that closes to 500 metres, whipping up some treacherous tides that probably explain the Viking appellation Strangfjörthr *(the strong fjiord)*. The lough is rich in wildlife: be in the northern half in winter to watch wildfowl, waders, gulls and auks feeding off the soft muds and sands; in autumn up to 15,000 pale-bellied brent geese fly in from Arctic Canada for rest and recreation on their way south; common and grey seals cling to rocks close to the shore and the occasional killer whale slips through the narrows.

Now managed by the National Trust, based at Castle Ward near Strangford, *T44881411*, a Wildlife Centre has a wealth of ecological and wildlife information and displays and opens July and August, 1400-1800, daily except Thursday; April, May to June and September, Saturday and Sunday 1400-1800.

County Down

Newtownards An ugly place with union jacks in your face but there is a **tourist office** with useful information on the Ards peninsula. ■ *31 Regent St, T91826846. July and August, Monday-Saturday 0900-1730; September to June, Monday-Saturday 0930-1700.*

Ards Peninsula The Ards Peninsula is the narrow slot of land between Strangford Lough and the Irish Sea. Of the two roads that run down either side of it, the windier A2, trailing its way through legions of caravan parks, takes a lot longer than the A20, which also passes Grey Abbey and Mount Stewart along the way. Without your own transport, relying on scheduled bus services (see Portaferry below) could prove time-consuming, but Ulsterbus conduct half-a-dozen day tours – general, historic homes, gardens, heritage, and wildlife – starting in Newtownlands. Contact *Ulsterbus*, T91812391, or the tourist office in Newtownlands, T91826846 (see page 618). For a literary flavour of Presbyterian life on the peninsula in the early 20th century there is no better novel than *December Bride*, written by Sam Hanna Bell in 1951 and later made into a film.

Coastal Route, A2

As you head east from Bangor on the A2 you will come to the village of **Donaghadee** where ferries plied to and from Scotland until Larne took over the service in 1849. Daniel O'Connell left from here six years earlier, after a failed attempt to gain the support of Ulster for the repeal of sectarian laws barring Catholics from sitting in parliament. After having a cup of tea thrown at him by a woman he remarked to a fisherman, 'You have very pretty girls here.' 'Yes,' the man replied, 'but none of them are Repealers.' The only boat journey now possible is a day trip to the uninhabited **Copeland Islands** off the coast for bird watching. The RSPB, T90491547, handle trips to one of the islands; the two others can be reached with *Nelson's Boats*, Donaghadee, T91883403.

Continuing south, near caravan-infested Millisle, **Ballycopeland Windmill** is a late 18th-century tower mill in use until 1915 and still in working order. ■ *April to September, Tuesday to Saturday, 1000-1900. £1. On B172, one mile west of Millisle*. **Portavogie**, further down the coast, is a fishport of local renown and fresh catches can be purchased here. At **Cloughey** there is a sandy beach safe for swimming, and at Kearney a fine beach walk before the main road heads inland for Portaferry.

B *Anathoth*, 9 Edgewater, T91884004, is typical of the many B&Bs around **Sleeping** Donaghadee. *Ballyvester Caravan Park*, Millisle Rd, Donaghadee, T91472118, includes 5 tent sites at £4 each, while *Donaghadee Caravan Park*, Edgewater, T91882369, has 10 sites at £6 each.

In Donaghadee, *Grace Neills Inn*, 33 High St, T91882553, is a good bet for food or try the **Eating** Copelands Hotel, 50 Warren Rd, T91888189. In Millisle the *Woburn Arms*, Main St, T91861461, and other inexpensive places to grab a bite. Save your appetite for Portaferry.

Strangford Lough Route, A20

The chief attractions of travelling the A20 route, apart from access to the east side of Strangford Lough where there are parking spaces and points to observe bird life, are Mount Stewart House and Greyabbey.

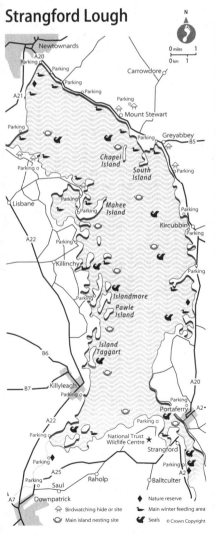

Strangford Lough

County Down

The English class structure was nothing if not precise and at Mount Stewart even the visiting ladies' maids could pull some clout, having meals with the housekeeper in a special room and waited on by a lowly footman. One large bedroom was divided into cubicles for their sleeping arrangements, supervised by the head housekeeper who 'wore grey alpaca in the morning and black silk in the evening' according to a maid who went home to her own lady to boast of the lavish wealth. Mount Stewart was home to the powerful Marquess of Londonderry, who also owned large tracts of County Durham in England from where coal from family mines was shipped in by the boatload to Strangford Lough. Unfortunately, very little of the social history of this grand country house is conveyed during the sometimes oleaginous tour, that becomes like an animated page from a Sotheby's catalogue as it relates the date of this, the value of that, where Castlereagh penned a letter, and whether the eyes in one portrait show a family resemblance to some other aristocratic has-been.

Mount Stewart House & Gardens

The **gardens** are also hugely disappointing, but best in the early morning when peacocks stroll, hares and rabbits sport and serene swans glide by on the lake. There are some fine specimens of mature trees, and a leaflet map guides you through the various set pieces laid out by Lady Londonderry in the 1920s. It is enlivened by the occasional jazz band on Sundays between April and September.■ *T42788387. House: May to September, 1300-1800, daily except Tuesday; daily over Easter; April and October, Saturday and Sunday 1300-1800. Last tour 1700. Garden: April to September, daily 1100-1800; March, Sunday only 1400-1700; October, Saturday and Sunday 1100-1800. House and gardens, £3.50. Garden only £3. Tearoom.*

Greyabbey If you've ever endured a ferry journey to Ireland in a winter storm you will believe the story that Affreca, wife-to-be of John de Courcy, made a vow on her voyage to build an abbey if she arrived safely. The result in 1193 was one of the earliest Gothic churches in Ireland, peopled by Cistercian monks from Cumberland in England. The Gothic style has survived best in the superb west door, while inside there are stone figures, a Norman knight and a female figure taken to represent Affreca. Very pleasing is the **herb garden** containing examples of medicinal plants that medieval monks nurtured. ■ *East side of Greyabbey village, less than two miles south of Mount Stewart House on the A20, T90543033. April to September, Tuesday-Saturday 1000-1900; Sunday 1400-1900. £2.*

Portaferry

Colour map 1, grid B6 Portaferry, the visitor-friendly village from where ferries ply their way across the lough to Strangford, is the most interesting place on the Ards peninsula for an overnight rest. Once an important little port with a herring industry, the village saw some action in the 1798 uprising and might have been captured by the rebels but for the timely presence of a government ship that fired on them from the quay. A more peaceful pursuit is offered nowadays at *Exploris*, an aquarium that attracts families of interest to all. There is a seal sanctuary, and sting rays, starfish and sea urchins to stroke in the touch tank. ■ *Castle St, T42728062. 1000-1800, Saturday 1100-1800, Sunday 1300-1800. September to Februrary, closes one hour earlier. £3.85.*

Collect a map of the village from the tourist office and walk up Windmill Hill for fine views of the vicinity or shop in *The Harlequin* with two floors of familiar crafts and gifts. The *Fiddler's Green* pub facing The Square has music at night.

Sleeping **AL** *The Narrows*, Shore Rd, T42728148, F42728105, reservations@narrows.co.uk Not cheap at £39 per person sharing but packages with dinner for 1 to 3 nights stay are worth considering, for this is Portaferry's smartest accommodation, with a sauna and views of the ferry drifting by through the windows from uncluttered bedrooms (no alternative to the fried breakfast in the morning, however). **B** *Adairs*, 22 The Square, T42728412, is in the centre of the village or, for a few pounds more, try **B** *Lough Cowey Lodge*, 9 Lough Cowey Rd, T27728263, just outside the village. **C** *Barholm*, 11 The Strand, T42729598, is a detached house overlooking the lough with hostel beds from £11. B&B also available.

Eating *The Narrows* restaurant in Shore Rd serves fresh fish and meat dishes with all the telltale touches of the modern and trendy – Puy lentils, shiitake mushrooms, Parmesan shavings – in a plain, pine-furnished room looking out at the lough. Expect to pay about £25 for an evening meal, £7 for lunch. The best alternative for a meal is *The Cornstore*, Castle St, T42729779, with chowder for £4.50, open prawn sandwiches for £8.50 and main dishes a little less.

Greyabbey

Greyabbey Antiques, Main Sreet, Greyabbey village is home to over a dozen antique shops; opening hours vary, with Wednesday, Friday and Saturday being good days to visit. The Irvine Gallery, T42788744, has oils and watercolours as well as paintings on silk. Rara Avis, T42788300, stocks textiles, painted furniture, ethnic jewellery. The Antique Shop, T42738333, sells ... antiques.

Transport The Ulsterbus 205/6 Goldline service runs Monday to Friday from Belfast at 0900, via Newtownlands and Greyabbey, arriving in Portaferry at 1014. For local services check with the tourist office. Ferries depart from Strangford, T44881637, on the hour and half-hour 0730-2230 weekdays, 0800-2300 Saturday, and 0930-2230 Sunday. From Portaferry, departures are at quarter past and quarter to the hour 0745-2245 weekdays, 0815-2315 Saturday, and 0945-2245 Sunday. Single/same-day return fare for passengers is 80p/£1.30, for cars £4/£6.40.

Directory **Banks**: the **Northern Bank** has a branch in The Square, and the Post Office is next door. **Tourist office**: The Stables, Castle St, T42729882. Easter and June to September, 1000-1700, Saturday 1100-1800, Sunday 1300-1800.

Western shore of Strangford Lough

An alternative route to the Ards Peninsula for travel between Belfast and south Down is the A22 road by the western shore of Strangford Lough, and there are a couple of diversions along the way. **Castle Espie**, run by the Wildfowl and Wetlands Trust, is home to a large collection of ducks, geese and swans, and provides access to bird-watching hides over the lough. ■ *Ballydrain Rd, Comber. T9187414. March to October, Monday-Saturday 1030-1700, Sunday 1130-1800. Shorter hours in winter. £3. Signposted, three miles south of Comber.*

A little further south the **Nendrum Monastic Site** makes up for its scattered and scant remains by an informative visitor centre and a pacific setting appropriate to the site of a monastic settlement. Founded in 445 by St Mochaoi, a pupil of St Patrick, it was rediscovered in 1844. ■ *Mahee Island. Museum April to September, Tuesday-Saturday 1000-1900, Sunday 1400-1900. Shorter hours in winter. 75p. Free access to site.*

Comber has a few places to eat including pub food at the *Castle Inn* in Castle St, but the *Old Schoolhouse Restaurant*, T91870870, next to Castle Espie, maintains its reputation for serving the best dishes, especially seafood, in the area.

Near the bottom of the lough, **Killyleagh Castle** looks like a film set but is actually one of Ireland's oldest inhabited castles, going back to the 12th century but given its schmaltzy appearance by Victorians. In 1913, when Unionists resolved to use 'all means which may be found necessary' to scupper Home Rule, the newly founded Ulster Volunteer Force trained in the grounds here. Open-air concerts in the summer, tickets available from the **A** *Dufferin Arms*, T44828229, in the village.

Downpatrick

This is a thriving, tolerant little town. It has several cracking sites to visit, and it is well worth an overnight stay to do so. If you can make your visit on St Patrick's Day, all the better: you will see genuine cross-cultural celebrations. *Colour map 1, grid B6*

County Down

History

In the 12th century, Down was the capital of Dál Fiatach; the real trouble started when the Norman John de Courcy turned up here in 1177 from Dublin with 22 horsemen and 300 foot soldiers. Down's Gaelic ruler, Rory MacDonleavy, was routed from the town; several major battles followed, with hand-to-hand fighting along the banks of the Quoile River, but the small Norman force held fast.

So Down became the first Norman foothold in Ulster. De Courcy gave the ancient site of Dún-da-lethglas which had been an Augustinian Priory before the Norman takeover to the Church, and renamed it Downpatrick. By the 13th century it was the second most important Norman settlement in Ulster, after Armagh, with defensive walls, and a Benedictine monastery.

Downpatrick gaol saw its share of executions during the 1798 rebellion, whne the area was second only to Wexford in the strength of the rebels and the ferocity with which they fought. After this the town went into a decline, which in a way is lucky for visitors, who can see the 18th-century structure of the town almost unencumbered by modernity.

Sights

Down Cathedral A church stood here long before de Courcy generously gave back a little of what he had taken in the 12th century. The site is associated with Patrick, who built his first church, and is reputed to have died, at Saul, a few miles to the north. Before de Courcy, there was an Augustinian settlement on the hill. Nothing remains of it, or of the building that replaced it, which was destroyed in the 14th century. In 1609 James I made Down a cathedral, despite the fact that it was a set of ruins and the bishop was enthroned here beneath a gaping roof. Rebuilding got underway in the 18th century. Inside, it's a cosy little place with 18th-century box pews labelled with the names of their owners on little brass plaques. The organ is built on to a pulpitum, which you walk through to enter the church. The two thrones that face each other aross the nave are the bishop's throne and the judge's seat, dating back to a time when trials were held in the church. In the graveyard the remains of St Patrick, St Colmcille and St Brigid are said to be buried. The stone that supposedly marks the site was put there in 1900. In the grounds are several other antiquites, which have largely been removed here from other places. ■ *The Mall, T614922. Monday-*

Downpatrick Cathedral in 1840, by JH Burgess

Saturday 1000-1700, Sunday 1400-1700. Free. Services at 1130 Sunday, 0930 daily. Choral evensong third Sunday of the month at 1530.

Situated in the town's gaol, this really is an excellent little museum. There are exhibitions on St Patrick, the history of County Down with lots of fascinating material on the 1798 rebellion, a changing series of exhibitions of art and artefacts, and the barely changed prison cells complete with 18th century graffiti and some unrealistic models. Sensors along the passages set off recorded prison noises, which can be quite startling if you are not expecting them. ■ *The Mall, T615218. July to mid-September, Monday-Friday 1100-1700, Saturday and Sunday 1400-1700; mid-September to June, Tuesday-Friday 1100-1700, also St Patrick's Day, Easter Monday. 1100-1700.Free. Shop.*

Down County Museum

If nothing else convinces you that you are in the United Kingdom and not the Republic of Ireland, this wacky little museum will: only the British are this barmy. This museum is run entirely by volunteers and is populated by every crumbling railway carriage that farmers could take off their fields and dump here. One of the trains actually works, and you can take a short train ride to King Magnus Halt on a restored but creaky steam engine whose provenance will be lovingly described by the volunteer guides. You can also visit the worksheds where skeleton carriages are being worked on, the signal box (carried brick by brick from Ballyclare), and the station house itself (actually the old gasworks building, also shifted block by block). The volunteers have great plans for expanding the line and adding more carriages, and their enthusiasm alone is worth the visit. ■ *Market Street, T615779. Trains run from July to mid-September, 1400-1700, Sundays only. Also St Patrick's Day, Easter Sunday and Monday, Hallowe'en weekend, December weekends 1400-1700. Workshop and Station House: June to September, Monday-Saturday 1100-1400.*

Downpatrick Railway Museum

County Down

There are a good few other things to peer at in this city. The **Roman Catholic church**, 'St Patrick's', is quite an impressive building: much more modern than the cathedral, Gothic-looking, and set on another hill. It was built in the late 19th century and replaces an earlier church of around 1787. Most of what you see, though, is a modern extension added to hold the increasing congregations in this predominantly Catholic town. Stained glass and mosaic panels detail the life of St Patrick. ■ *Daily. Services Tuesday, Wednesday, Friday 1930; Sunday 0800, 1000, 1200, 1700.*

Other sights

In Mount Crescent is a pathway leading to the **Mound of Down**, the remains of de Courcy's fortifications. It is a motte and bailey fortification, said to be the finest example of such in Ulster, probably built around 1200. Within sight of the Mound, and reached from the Belfast road, is **Inch Abbey**, another de Courcy job. Built around 1180, it was a Cistercian monastery, and is on the site of a much older place, called Inis Cumhscraigh, which dates back to at least 800. In its 12th-century state, this was a church, with a cloister and several community buildings, including a bakehouse, of which the oven has been found nearby. There are a good few walls remaining, even though the abbey was burned in 1404, and completely suppressed by 1541. ■ *April to September, Tuesday-Saturday 1000-1300, 1330-1900, Sunday 1400-1900; October to April closes at 1600. 75p. Turn left off the Belfast Road at the Abbey Lodge Hotel.*

Around Downpatrick

At **Saul** (Sabhal Pádraic), two miles (three kilometres) northeast of town, is the reputed site of Patrick's first church in Ireland, which was said to be in a barn given to him by the local lord. An Augustinian monastery was built here some time after 1130, but today the site is occupied by a Church of Ireland building, erected in the 1930s in the style of a medieval church. There are a few ancient relics to be seen in the graveyard, including two mortuary houses of unknown date, cross pillars and a medieval gravestone. Inside the church, the font is 13th century. If you are feeling a bit under the weather, there is **Struel Wells**, 1½ miles (two kilometres) east of Downpatrick: four ancient wells reputed to have the power to heal internal organs, eyes, and body and limbs. ■ *Ardglass Road. Free.*

Essentials

Sleeping **AL** *Tyrella House*, 100 Clanmaghery Rd, T851422. A good choice of an out-of-town, country-house sort of stay, has its own beechwoods, private beach and stables. Also has a self-catering cottage. **A** *Abbey Lodge*, 38 Belfast Rd, T614511. Outside of town. **A** *Denvir's Hotel*, 14-16 English St, T612012. An ancient building recently renovated to a Spartan prettiness. The dining room has the most enormous fireplace with the old hooks that were used for smoking meat still in place. Huge rooms, very central but quiet. The best place to stay in Downpatrick. **B** *Arolsen*, 47 Roughal Park, T612656. Fairly central B&B. **B** *Dunnleath House*, 33 St Patrick's Dv, T613221. B&B with 2 big triple rooms. **B** *Hillside*, 62 Scotch St, T613134. A B&B in a listed Georgian house with 3 double rooms.

Eating At the risk of sounding partisan, your best bet is *Denvir's*, which is enormously popular with locals and visitors alike; nothing special, but good hearty food and very reasonable prices. *Harry Afrika's* is the gaily painted place opposite the bus station in Ballyduggan Rd that does grills and the like, and opens on Sunday too, while *The Pepper Pot* is a conventional meat-centred caff in St Patrick's Ave (closed Sunday). *The China Garden*, 16 English St, T613364, offers a touch of the Orient and 2 courses for £7.50.

Pubs & music *Denvir's* has music at weekends, ususally country-style folk music or something louder. Downpatrick has a folk music club in Pillarwell Lane, T614842 for enquiries. The other pubs have music, occasionally live, but, judging from the security fencing around them, you might want to think carefully about visiting, bearing in mind the state of the the peace talks at the time you're there.

Festivals The big event of the year is St Patrick's Day, which is extended into a week of cross-cultural activities that attracts large crowds.

Sport **Bowling** *Ownebeg Bowling Club*, St Patrick's Drive, T613287. **Cricket** *Downpatrick Cricket Club*, Strangford Rd, T612829. **Golf** *Downpatrick Golf Course*, Saul Rd, T615497. **Horseriding** *Tullymurry Equestrian Centre*, 145 Ballyduggan Road, T811880. **Sailing** *Quoile Yacht Club*, 21 Castle Island Rd, T612266.

Directory **Banks** *First Trust*, 15 Market St, Mon-Fri 0930-1630, cashpoint. *Northern Bank*, 58 Market St, Mon 0930-1700, Tue-Fri 1000-1530, Sat 0930-1230, cashpoint. **Communications** Post Office: 65 Lower Market St, Mon-Fri 0900-1530, Sat 0900-1230. **Cultural centres** *Down Arts Centre*, Irish St, T615283. **Hospitals and medical services** *Down Hospital*, T613311. **Library** 79 Market St, T612895, Mon Tue Thu 1000-2000, Fri 1000-1700, Sat 1000-1300, 1400-1700. **Places of worship** *Down Cathedral*, English St (see page 622 for services). **Tourist office** 74 Market St, T612233, Sep-Jul Mon-Fri 0900-1700, Sat 1000-1300, 1400-1700; Jul Aug Mon-Sat 0900-1800. **Useful addresses and telephone numbers** RUC: 8 Irish St, T615011.

Local maps

A useful series of free leaflets with maps outlining short walks in the Kilclief/ Killyleagh/Downpatrick/Castlewellan and districts is available from most tourist offices. Ordnance Survey Map No 21 in the Discovery series is also very useful if staying in the Strangford Lough area.

Strangford to Newcastle

Strangford

If it wasn't for the ferry crossing to Portaferry, Strangford would be a place to miss. **Strangford Castle**, one of the many tower houses you'll see dotted around Strangford Lough, dates from the late 16th century (key keeper lives opposite at 39 Castle Street) but that's all there is to see. The *Cuan Bar & Restaurant*, serving meals like mussels with pasta for £8.20, has a good local reputation but nowhere else is recommended. Two local campsites are *Castle Ward Caravan Park*, just over a mile west of the village on the A25, T44881680, with tent pitches for £7.50, and *Strangford Caravan Park*, Shore Rd, T44881888, at £5 a night for tents.

Castle Ward

Outside the village of Strangford, on the Downpatrick Road, Castle Ward is a distinctly odd 18th-century manor house now managed by the National Trust, but formerly the property of Bernard and Ann Ward. The couple eventually parted, but before they did, the divorce of their minds had been reflected permanently in the design of their house. The front of Castle Ward is in the classical style (his taste) while the rear is Gothic (her preference) and the dichotomy is also apparent in the interior. The extensive grounds include a tower house and landscaped gardens. ■ *T44881204. House: June to mid-September, 1300-1800 daily except Thursday; April, May and mid-September to October, Saturday and Sundays 1300-1800; Easter daily 1300-1800. £2.60. Last guided tour 1700. Grounds, £3.50 for car. On A25, under two miles west of Strangford.*

Kilclief Castle

Another quick stop could be made here, a couple of miles south of Strangford on the A2, where another fortified tower house stands in good condition and the interior gives some idea of just how well-provided they could be. ■ *July and August, Tuesday-Saturday 1000-1900. Sunday 1400-1900. 75p.*

Ardglass

If you've taken a fancy to comparing tower houses, there are no less than seven of them at Ardglass, eight miles (13 kilometres) south of Strangford, one of which is now in the grounds of a golf club. In its late 19th-century heyday Ardglass was a profitable little fishing port cashing in on seasonal shoals of herring and mackerel, which were salted and exported to the West Indies. It is still a good place to purchase fresh fish and there are a couple of restaurants worth visiting. *Aldo's*, T44841315, in Castle Place, next to the post office, opens Thursday to Sunday at 1700 for high tea and à la carte dishes, while **B** *Burford Lodge*, Quay Street, T44841141, happily serves tea and snacks as well as evening meals to non-residents. **B** *The Cottage*, Castle Place, T44841080, has rooms but no evening meals .For pub food try *The Moorings*, opposite the only visitable tower house, **Jordan's Castle** ■ *July and August, Tuesday-Saturday 1000-1900, and Sunday 1400-1900. 75p.*

Killough

The A2 follows the coast around an inlet, through the village of Killough, and from the coastguard station just south of the village there is an enjoyable 4-mile (6.4-kilometre) circular **coastal path** that follows the shore across stiles until reaching Point Road near St John's Point Lighthouse. Turn right on to Point Road to head back to the village.

Tyrella beach The A2 between Killough and Clough passes this beach, ideal for families due to a shallow sands, warden service and amenities, but consequently busy on a fine summer's day. When it is quieter, enjoy the dune walks or a beach walk to the east for up to an hour. £2 to park a car.

Clough Before reaching Newcastle the road passes Clough, at the junction with the A25 from Downpatrick, and its eponymous **motte castle** with free access and fine views from the top of the mound. The original occupant of the castle living in his fortification on top of this artifical mound needed a good view to espy hostile movements, and the Clough motte also had defensive wooden palisades around the perimeter.

Dundrum This village is the last stop, with a particularly fine castle: 'one of the strongyst holtes that ever I sawe in Ireland' reported a henchman for the Tudor monarchy in 1538. The Norman de Courcy first established a castle here known as Rath. When he fell out of favour with King John and the land passed to Hugh de Lacy, de Courcy found himself unsuccessfully besieging his own Dundrum Castle in 1205. Hugh de Lacy added a sturdy keep and later a gatehouse to the castle and what you see today is still a very impressive sight. There are picnic tables in the car park, but more appealing is one of the many grassy areas under the shade of trees inside the castle grounds. ■ *April to September, Tuesday-Saturday 1000-1900; Sunday 1400-1900. 75p.*

Newcastle to Newry and the Mourne Mountains

South Down, between Newcastle and Newry, has a schizophrenic quality. On the one hand there are the majestic Mourne Mountains imposing their granite beauty on the surrounding wilderness, while down on the coast there are unimpressive towns that range from tasteless Newcastle to the downright sectarian Kilkeel. Seen in terms of nature and nurture there is no question about who wins out in this part of the world.

Newcastle

Colour map 1, grid C5 The excellent tourist office here is a good place to collect information and pick up a colour town map that lists useful amenities such as banks and chemists. Once your business is done, however, there is little reason to linger in Newcastle. When it comes to enjoying a decent meal the choice is poor, and for a favourite holiday resort (mainly because of its expansive sandy beach) the atmosphere is woefully soulless. To enjoy a touch of real popular culture head out to 94 Dundrum Road where you'll find Route 66, a museum dedicated to American automobiles from the 1930s onwards, with jukeboxes and other memorabilia thrown in. ■ *T43725223. Easter to September, daily 1030-1800; October to Easter, Saturday and Sunday 1400-1800. £2.50.*

The Mountains of Mourne

1. Oh, Mary this London's a wonderful sight, Wid the people here workin' by day and by night; They don't sow potatoes, nor barley, nor wheat, But there's gangs o' them diggin' for gold in the street; At least when I axed them that's what I was told. So I just took a hand at this diggin' for gold, But for all that I found there I might as well be, Where the Mountains of Mourne sweep down to the sea.

You remember young Peter O'Loughlin, of course –
Well, here he is now at the head o' the Force,
I met him today, I was crossin' the Strand,
And he stopped the whole street wid wan wave of his hand:
And there we stood talking of days that are gone,
While the whole population of London looked on;
But for all these great powers, he's wishful like me
To be back where dark Mourne sweeps down to the sea.

There's beautiful girls here – oh, never mind!
With beautiful shapes Nature never designed,
And lovely complexions, all roses and crame,
But O'Loughlin remarked wid regard to them same;
'That if at those roses you venture to sip,
The colour might all come away on your lip,'
So I'll wait for the wild rose that's waitin' for me
Where the Mountains o' Mourne sweep down to the sea.

Percy French

County Down

suggested walks. Experienced walkers will want to ascend to Slieve Donard, using Ordnance Survey Map No 29 in the Discovery series, while a gentler introduction to the mountain is provided by Donard Park to the south of Newcastle. From here the mountain can be climbed, or a shorter walk can by just following the path up the slopes for a hour or so.

For even shorter walks, take Bryansford Road out of Newcastle to Tollymore Forest Park, covering some 500 acres at the foot of the Mourne mountains and with four way-marked trails. Once a private estate, the mansion house fell into disrepair after the Second World War and was demolished in the early 1950s. What does remain is a stupendous avenue of cedar trees leading up to where the house stood, which form a magnificent entrance to the park. The most interesting short walk is the Rivers Trail that follows the Shimna River through swathes of violets in early summer before crossing by Parnell's Bridge and returning through forest on the other side. A longer eight-mile (13-kilometre) trail heads into the forest and offers excellent views of the surrounding countryside the Mourne mountains. ■ *T43722428. Daily, 1000-dusk. Car £3.50, pedestrian £2. Tea room.*

Further inland, the Castlewellan Forest Park is famous for its arboretum surrounding countryside the Mourne mountains. ■ *T43722428. Daily, 1000-dusk. Car £3.50, pedestrian £2. Tea room.*

Further inland, the Castlewellan Forest Park is famous for its arboretum that dates back to 1740, but walking is restricted to a three-mile trail around a lake with sculptures created from local materials. Enjoy tea in the Queen Anne-style courtyard or bring food to eat in the picnic and barbecue areas. ■ *Castlewellan. T43778664. Daily 1000-dusk. Car £3.50, pedestrian £2.*

Sleeping **AL** *Enniskeen House Hotel*, 98 Bryansford Rd, T43722392, has bedrooms with views and the benefit of being a mile out of town, giving it the edge on the other available **AL** hotels. **B** *Arundel Guest House*, 23 Bryansford Rd, T43722232, is nearer town, and offers a reasonably priced but very early evening meal for £7 at 1730. **C** *Golf Links House*, 109 Dundrum Rd, T43722054, is also good value for rooms and meals. The YHANI **D** *Newcastle Hostel*, 30 Downs Rd, T43722133, is 50 yards from the bus station and has over 40 beds and serves meals; open all year. There are loads of caravan parks around town but the only one accepting campers is *Tollymore Forest Park*, Tullybrannigan Rd, T43722428, on the B180 3 miles from town and charging between £6.50-£10 a night.

Eating The oak-panelled restaurant at *Enniskeen House* has a £15.50 dinner with home style dishes like stuffed pork and apple sauce, steak, and scampi. The *Buck's Head* Restaurant further out of town at 77 Main St, Dundrum, T43751868, is regarded as the most upmarket place in the area, and serves oysters and ostrich, though thankfully not in the same dish. Expect to pay £20-£25. Back in Newcastle, *Mario's*, 65 South Promenade, T43723912, has a large à la carte menu featuring Italian-style dishes, a set dinner for £16.50, and a £9 carvery Sunday lunch. Closed Monday and open for evening meals from 1830. For pub food in comfortable and congenial surroundings, try the olde-Irish *Quinns* down from the tourist office in the direction of town.

Transport **Bus** **Bus station**: Railway St, T43722296. Ulsterbus Goldline 237 runs Monday-Saturday between Kilkeel and Belfast via Newcastle. The 240 is a daily service between Downpatrick and Newry, also via Newcastle, and connecting with the daily 200 Newry to Dublin service.

Directory **Banks** and their cashpoint machines are situated along Main St. Money can also be changed at the tourist office. **Bicycle hire** from *Wiki Wiki Wheels*, 10b Donard St, T43723973, £6.50 a day or £30 a week. **Golf** *Royal County Down Golf Club*, T43723314. **Tourist office** on Central Promenade on the way out of town on the A2 to Kilkeel, T43722222, Monday-Saturday 1000-1700, Sunday 1400-1800.

Annalong

Colour map 1, grid C5 Annalong is a small fishing village, eight miles (12 kilometres) south of Newcastle, and worth considering for an overnight stay. The beach is too shingly to attract hordes of visitors, and near the harbour the 1830 **Annalong Corn Mill** makes for a mildly interesting visit when a flour-making demonstration is taking place. There is an adjoining herb garden. ■ *T43768736. February to November, Tuesday-Saturday, 1100-1700. £1.30. Guided tours. Café.*

Sleeping **LL** *Glassdrumman Lodge*, 85 Mill Rd, T43768451, signposted off the main road at the Newcastle end of the village. Luxury accommodation. **B** *The Sycamores*, 52 Majors Hill, T43768279, old-farmhouse building with parts dating back to the 18th century and views out to sea. A couple of miles out of the village **C** *Oldtown Lodge*, 46 Oldtown Rd, T43768350, a non-smoking B&B house which would make a useful base for local hillwalking, but no meals available.

A five-course dinner at *Glassdrumman Lodge* is £30. Pub food is available at *The Half-* **Eating**
way House at the Newcastle end of the village and there is also *The Lighthouse Bar* in
Bath St.

Kilkeel

The small fishing town of Kilkeel seems an unlikely setting for the ugly face of *Colour map 1, grid C5*
sectarianism but there is no mistaking the in-your-face triumphalism of the
wall murals and the intimidating fluttering of a Ulster Volunteer Force flag in
the town centre. Come the marching season, the minority of Catholics living
here are virtual prisoners in their own homes and it is definitely a place to avoid
at weekends in the summer when there is often a march or parade of one kind
or another and roads are blocked off to traffic.

The **Mourne Grange Craft Shop**, 169 Newry Rd, T41760103, is worth a
visit with heaps of craft goods and a tea room. Kilkeel also has a **diving school**,
San Miguel, T41765885, F41764760, at the harbour, running fishing trips as
well as diving courses for novices. For a general introduction to the role of fishing in Kilkeel's history, the **Nautilus Centre** by the harbour has displays and
exhibits and a shop selling fresh fish. ■ *Rooney Rd. T41765555. Easter to September, Monday-Saturday 1000-2100, Sunday 1200-1800. Same hours the rest
of the year but closing at 1800.*

B *Heath Hall*, 160 Moyadd Rd, T41762612, a friendly B&B, about a mile out of town in **Sleeping**
the countryside. **B** *Mourne Abbey*, 16 Greencastle Rd, T41762426, half a mile south of
town, opens from Easter to September and an evening meal is £10.

Self-catering *Mountain View House*, 20 Head Rd, Moyadd, T41723120, rural self-
catering from £25-£35 per night or £170-£250 a week. *Mourne Park*, Mourne Park,
T41762533, similar prices to *Mountain View House*, a traditional Irish cottage in a private demense.

For one of the most substantial pub lunches anywhere in Ireland, try *Jacob Halls* in **Eating**
Greencastle St in the middle of town. There is also *Food for Thought*, at the Nautilus
Centre.

Tourist office Newcastle St, T41762525, Apr-Sep, Mon-Sat, 0900-1730 (shorter hours in winter), **Directory**
an excellent source of local information.

The Silent Valley

A huge reservoir supplying Belfast from the valley of the River Kilkeel was *Colour map 1, grid C5*
completed in 1933 and its story is told in the Information Centre near the car
park in the reservoir grounds. The most incredible aspect of the whole project
was the building of the **Mourne Wall** around the catchment area – Ireland's
Great Wall – up to eight feet high, 22 miles long and connecting the summits of
15 mountains. Why it was built, apart from being a massive job creation
scheme, is not entirely clear but it took from 1904 to 1923 to complete. A three-
mile **walk** by the side of the reservoir is recommended for the fine views
afforded. ■ *Easter to September, 1000-1830; October to April, 1000-1600. £3
per car. In May, June and September at weekends, and daily in July and August, a
bus service operates between the car park and the top of Ben Crom. £1.20 return.
Coffee shop and craft shop.*

County Down

Kilkeel to Newry

A detour southwest from Kilkeel leads to the tip of a promontory where **Greencastle Fort** is situated. It was built by the rapacious Hugh de Lacy to stand sentinel over Carlingford Lough and the views from the castle are a better reason for making the journey here than the remains themselves. ■ *July to August, Tuesday-Saturday 1000-1900, Sunday 1400-1900. 75p.*

The A2 road gradually creeps closer the north coast of the lough, looking across to the Cooley peninsula in Louth, and passing a signpost to the **Kilfeagham dolmen** with its 35-tonne capstone, a few miles out from Kilkeel.

Rostrevor

Colour map 1, grid C5 The village of Rostrevor has more charm than most of the coastal towns in south Down and nearby **Kilbroney Park** has plenty of open space, riverside walks and an energetic path up to the 40-tonne, pink granite, Cloughmore boulder stone from where there are scenic views across to the Republic, as well as tennis courts and picnic areas. ■ *T41738134. June to August, daily, 0900-2220. Shorter hours the rest of the year.*

The last week in July is the setting for Rostrevor's **Fiddler's Green Festival**, a lively celebration of Irish culture with a ceilí band on an open-air stage in the village, nightly folk sessions in the pubs and classes for traditional instruments such as the fiddle, flute and pipes. Enquiries to 5 Cherry Hill, Rostrevor, Co. Down, BT34 3BD. T/F41739819, f.d.green@fnmail.com

Sleeping **B** *Fir Trees*, 16 Killowen Old Rd, T41738602, a bungalow B&B overlooking the lough. **B** *Forestbrook House*, 11 Forestbrook Rd, Rostrevor, T41738105, a B&B in a quietly situated 18th-century detached house where an evening meal for £8 can be arranged in advance.

Self-catering *Lecale Cottages*, 125 Kilbroney Rd, Rostrevor, T41738727, 3 self-catering, traditional-style cottages, overlooking the lough and costing £200-£350 a week. The park is also home to *Kilbroney Caravan Park*, T41738134, with 40 tent pitches for around £6 per night.

Eating Rostrevor has a few decent places to eat, better than any in Warrenpoint. They include the *Southfork Restaurant* in Church St, T41738276, *Top of the Town* in Bridge St, T41738236, and pub food at the *Cloughmor Inn*.

Warrenpoint

Colour map 1, grid C5 On the road between Rostrevor and Warrenpoint is the **Narrow Water Castle** where de Lacy built a fortress in the 13th century to guard access to the river up to Newry. Narrow Water Castle was where, in 1979, the Provisionals hid a bomb in a haystack and detonated it from the shore of the Cooley peninsula when a platoon of the 2nd Parachute Regiment passed by. Survivors took refuge in the gateway to the castle where another bomb had been planted. A total of 18 soldiers died and an Englishman on holiday was accidently shot dead by an army helicopter returning fire on the Cooley peninsula. ■ *Castle: guided tours normally available in July and August, Tuesday-Friday 1100-1630, but check with the tourist office in Warrenpoint T41752256.*

Warrenpoint is not as interesting a town as its picturesque appearance and location might suggest. The pubs cater to Irish holidaymakers in the summer and at the *Marine Tavern* opposite the marina all spirits cost £1, pints £1.50, and at night the place is heaving with intoxicated revellers. Many of the pubs have live music, but more likely to be in the Country and Western vein than traditional Irish.

The **Burren Heritage Centre** is a couple of miles west of town, but with nothing to show except some fading models of archaelogical sites, it is hardly worth a visit except on a very wet afternoon. ■ *T41773378. April to September, Tuesday-Friday 1100-1700, Sunday 1400-1700. Shorter hours in winter and closed on Sunday. £1.*

A **ferry**, T41777370, to Omeath in the Cooley peninsula operates 1100-1800, June to September, for £2 return and is usually peopled by locals crossing into the Republic to play the lottery and take advantage of pub opening hours.

The **Maiden of the Mournes Festival** is a week-long festival at the beginning of August, established in 1990 along the lines of the Rose of Tralee festival.

Sleeping

Not a lot of choice, but not a problem either, for Newry and Rostrevor are nearby. **B** *Fern Hill House*, 90 Clonallon Rd, T41772677, opens all year and does an evening meal for £10. **B** *Lough View*, 10 Osborne Promenade, T41773067, is on the sea front overlooking the lough, but may not be the quietest place at the height of summer.

Eating

The food scene is also rather dismal, with standard fare available at *Bennett's*, Church St, T41752053, which stays open until 2200 at weekends in the summer. *The Whistledown Inn*, facing the sea in aptly named Seaview, T41752697, has a large menu of snacks and salads plus fish, meat and grills from £5 to £10.

Sport

Adventure centre: *The East Coast Adventure Centre*,T41774006, covers windsurfing, canoeing, archery and other activities.

Directory

Banks Located in The Square, Queen St and Charlotte St. **Taxis** *Ace Taxis*, T41752256; *Classic*, T41752888. **Tourist office** T41752256, should be moving to the town hall in Church St, though at the time of writing it is a few doors down in the same street.

County Down

Newry

Newry has suffered from a bad press for years and guide books have tended to write the place off; don't believe a word of it. It's not postcard pretty, but it has history and attitude, and in the coming years could see quite a few changes as the importance of the border further diminishes.

Colour map 1, grid C5

The flourishing activity of the 18th century associated with the Newry canal petered out with the coming of the railways, and economic decline set in. At the time of partition in 1922 it was so widely accepted that the Boundary Commission would allocate the town to the Republic that two businessmen, one Catholic and one Protestant and living respectively in Newry and Warrenpoint, exchanged their houses so they could live in the state of their choice. It was not to be, but the legacy surfaced in 1969, with the Civil Rights Association calling for pressure to be taken off the Bogside, when Newry was quick to rise in revolt. Finally, 30 years later, the appearance of two new hotels and the expansive Buttercrane Shopping Centre point to a new and more equitable future for the town.

Nowadays Newry is at peace, and while there are no special attractions it is an interesting place to wander around because the lack of developments over the last 30 years has helped preserve examples of industrial architecture that will soon no doubt succumb to the bulldozer.

Newry Canal

The River Clanrye and the Newry Canal make an unusual sight, running cheek by jowl through the centre of town. When restoration work is completed, the canal may well come into its own once more. Surveying work for it started in 1703, prompted by the notion of transporting newly discovered coal in east Tyrone from Lough Neagh and out to sea through Newry and the Carlingford Lough. The canal's completion in 1741 was a remarkable achievement. It pre-dated the first canals in Lancashire, England, was built without machinery, and remained in operation for almost 200 years. The whole canal is now in public ownership.

Architectural attractions Right next to the tourist office, where a town map can be collected or a town walking guide purchased, stands the magisterial **town hall**. It dates from 1893, built on a bridge near where the the road from Armagh becomes Canal Street and meets Merchants Quay by the side of the canal. Tucked away behind it is a more interesting example of late-Victorian building, a five-storey brick-built structure with three arched doorways built in 1879. An even better example of Victorian industrial architecture can be admired by leaving the town hall and walking away from the town centre and across the junction with Canal Street to **Sand's Mill** in New Street: seven floors of red and yellow bricks, arcaded, and still in use since it first opened to business in 1873.

Newry Museum The Newry Museum, next to the town hall, is a history-based museum with assorted exhibits and a restored early 18th-century room, using original panelling taken from a local house of that period. Not rivetingly interesting but OK for a rainy afternoon. ■ *Arts Centre, Bank Parade. T30266232. Monday-Friday 1030-1630. Free.*

Essentials

Sleeping **AL** *Canal Court Hotel*, Merchants Quay, T30251234, F30251177. Alex Ferguson stayed here and, while that might deter the anti-Man-U league, he knew, as usual, what he was doing and chose the best on offer. A new hotel with smart new rooms and weekend packages. **AL-A** *Francis Court Hotel*, Francis St, T30266926, F30252706, is another new kid on the block with 16 rooms and a gritty exterior that blends well with the town's character. **AL-A** *Mourne Country Hotel*, 52 Belfast Rd, T30267922, F30260896 is a little way out of town at the roundabout on the Belfast Rd, with weekend and midweek deals. **B** *Millvale House*, 8 Millvale Rd, T30263789, B&B with four rooms, serves high tea for £5, dinner for £7 and stays open all year. **C** *Carrow House*, 22 Newtown Rd, Belleeks, T30878182. This B&B is not in town, but a bed there is only £12.50. Numerous other B&Bs in and around town: enquire at the Tourist Office.

Eating First choice should be *Brass Monkey*, 1 Sandy St, T30263176, serving seafood, steaks and salads daily till 2130. Expect to pay between £12 and £20 for a meal. The *Old Mill Restaurant* at the Canal Court has a set dinner for £24 plus à la carte offering a wide choice of starters, meat and fish dishes; stay with the tried and tested dishes. Bar food is served all day and the carvery lunch is £6. There are a couple of inexpensive cafés on Hill St, as you walk into the town centre from the tourist office and *Delilites*, 12 Monaghan St, serves up better-than-average sandwiches.

Bus Bus station: T30263531, Edward St (off Monaghan St). The 238 express service runs daily between Belfast and Newry and from Newry the bus goes on to Warrenpoint, Rostrevor and Kilkeel. The 240 service runs between Downpatrick and Newry, also daily. The daily Belfast to Dublin express bus also stops in Newry.

Train Train station: T30269271, a local bus ride out of town. The Belfast to Dublin trains stop every day.

Banks On Hill St. **Tourist office** Town hall, T3068877. Open Jun-Sep, Mon-Fri, 0900-1700, Sat 1000-1600; Oct-May, Mon-Fri, same hours but closed 1300-1400.

The Brontë Homeland

The tourist board has made the best out the least interesting part of Down by dubbing an area to the south of Banbridge, about halfway between Newry and Belfast, the Brontë Homeland, as it was here that Patrick Brontë, father of the famous literary family, lived and worked before moving to Haworth in Yorkshire. If travelling south to Banbridge from Belfast the Georgian-style town of **Hillsborough** offers a touch of genteel elegance: break here for tea and cakes. Alternatively, push on for Banbridge and stop outside of town at the **Banbridge Gateway Tourist Information Centre**. There is a café serving lunches and light meals and the Centre sells a useful little collection of eight route cards with directions and maps for suggested local walks (including a Brontë walk) averaging five miles each and using public paths. ■ *200 Newry Rd, T40623322. July and August, Monday-Saturday 0900-1900, Sunday 1400-1800; September to June, Monday-Saturday 1000-1700; Easter to October, Sunday 1400-1800*

The first stop on a Brontë tour should be the **Brontë Homeland Interpretative Centre** at Drumballyroney Church and School House near Rathfriland, eight miles from Banbridge off the B10. Patrick Brontë and the novelist sisters' brother, Bramwell, taught and preached here. The importance of Ireland in gaining an understanding of Emily and her brother is not a tenuous one, as Terry Eagleton shows clearly in his book *Heathcliff and the Great Hunger*. A free leaflet with a map outlines a tour that takes in four other sites associated with the Brontë's father and provides a good a reason as any for threading one's way through a little-visited part of Down. ■ *Church Hill Rd, T40631152. March to September, Tuesday-Friday 1100-1700, Saturday and Sunday 1400-1800. £1.*

County Armagh

Armagh has always been border country, forming with Monaghan and Louth the southern edge of the drumlin belt that formed Ulster as a place apart when the Ice Age retreated, leaving massive boulders in its wake. St Patrick still found his way here and Cromwell confiscated over a third of the county. Armagh is a beautiful place, both the city and the countryside, and even a fleeting visit will whet the appetite for a longer stay. The historic city of Armagh should not be missed while the secret delights in the south of the county are waiting to be discovered by a new generation of visitors.

Armagh City

At first sight a closed-up, defensive-looking place, Armagh has seen its share of the Troubles and very obviously hasn't achieved the level of tolerance that Derry, Downpatrick or even Belfast have managed. Dominated at one end of the town by the Court House and at the other by the now closed-up gaol, and with the two cathedrals glaring at each other from the hilltops, this place doesn't seem to want to let go of its sectarian past: however, its history, along with several interesting sights, is a good reason to stay for a day or so.

Everything in this little city is packed into three parallel streets and their side roads with a couple of sights outside the town yet easily accessible by bus or car.

History

In the ninth century Armagh was the largest and most important settlement in all Ireland, but the place was settled long before that. A Neolithic circular enclosure, filled with pot shards, was revealed by a bomb in Scotch Street in 1979, and, outside of town, the Navan hill fort was the capital of the kings of Ulster from around 600BCE. St Patrick established a church here in the fifth century and a large monastic community developed, supporting schools, poor houses, and a lay community. Armagh became a beacon of learning while the rest of Europe fell into the Dark Ages.

At the height of its power Armagh bore the brunt of the Viking raids of Ulster. The Annals of Ulster record three raids; in 832 and again in 840 and 852, this time by Vikings who had settled in Dublin and came overland. After 866 there was a respite from the attacks as the Viking threat in Ulster passed on to the southern provinces, until 921 when a fresh series of plunderings began. The next to set his sights on Armagh was Brian Boru, the 10-11th century High King of Munster, who came relatively peacefully, paid a tribute to the church of Armagh and declared it the primacy of Ireland.

For the next 300 years the city remained an important centre of learning, while all around the Irish clans fought first one another and then the Normans for supremacy in Ulster. In the middle of the 16th century the Reformation came to Armagh, more powerfully than in other parts of Ireland because of the city's position within the Roman Catholic church. The monasteries were disbanded, church property confiscated and all forms of religion except Anglicanism were banned from the churches. Armagh ceased to be a city.

Armagh entered a new golden age in the 18th century with a massive wave of building projects that created most of the modern city. Archbishop Richard Robinson and his friend the architect Thomas Cooley built the Bishop's Palace, The Public Library, the Gaol and the Royal School. A second wave by Francis Johnson built the Courthouse, the Bank of Ireland (now part of St Patrick's Trian) and the Observatory.

In the late 19th century the efforts of the Land Leaguers to get a fairer deal for small tenant farmers were met with Protestant riots in the city, the first real example of sectarian differences in Armagh, and in the 20th century the Depression brought more of the same. Never the flashpoint for disturbance that Derry or Belfast were during the Troubles, Armagh nevertheless saw some unpleasant scenes, notably the night in November 1968 when a convoy of Protestant cars led by Ian Paisley was stopped and 220 weapons, including two revolvers, were seized. The Loyalists held Armagh city refusing to leave while a civil rights march approached the city. Fortunately the civil rights marchers were persuaded to divert, thus avoiding serious bloodshed. Riots followed the introduction of internment in August 1971 and as the IRA gathered strength and support Armagh saw its share of bombs.

These days an uneasy peace reigns in the city – the gates that shut up the centre remain open at night, the courthouse is rebuilt after its destruction and the Arts Centre is trying to encourage a nightlife back to the city.

Sights

This is really a day out for the kiddies, or something to do on a very wet afternoon when you've done all the other things you can do on wet afternoons. Trading on the association of Swift with the town the best thing here is the story of Gulliver, told in one room by an extremely realistic giant, in others by a series of models in glass cases. There is also the story of Armagh, which is vaguely interesting but a bit too dependent on gadgetry, and the story of St Patrick. ■ *40, English Street, T521801. September to July Monday-Saturday 1000-1730; July and August, additional opening Sundays 1300-1800. £3.75. Café, shop.*

St Patrick's Trian

Set in an old 1833 schoolhouse this is a pleasant hour's meander through the detritus of Armagh's past. Collected here are assorted bits and pieces – bog butter, leather shoes, an ox yoke discovered in the bogs, assorted carved stone heads found while renovations were taking place, old clothes, examples of the city's past as a lacemaking centre, Orange memorabilia, and an interesting display about the railway and its great disaster of 1889 when a day trip went horribly wrong and 89 people died. There is also a little display of stuffed animals and an art gallery, and downstairs an exhibition on the museum itself and its

Armagh County Museum

County Armagh

Armagh City

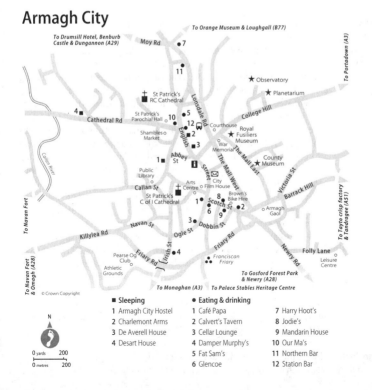

© Crown Copyright

■ Sleeping	● Eating & drinking	
1 Armagh City Hostel	1 Café Papa	7 Harry Hoot's
2 Charlemont Arms	2 Calvert's Tavern	8 Jodie's
3 De Averell House	3 Cellar Lounge	9 Mandarin House
4 Desart House	4 Damper Murphy's	10 Our Ma's
	5 Fat Sam's	11 Northern Bar
	6 Glencoe	12 Station Bar

County Armagh

work. ■ *The Mall, T523070. Monday-Friday 1000-1700, Saturday 1000-1300, 1400-1700. Closed bank holidays. Free.*

Royal Irish Fusiliers Museum Vast collections of First World War medals, a dugout, uniforms, silver cups, banners, and more interestingly an exhibit on the terrible damage done by the IRA bomb in 1993 aimed at the nearby courthouse. The whole building more or less folded in on itself but the museum was closed at the time and so there were no injuries. Most of the material on display was picked out of the rubble. ■ *The Mall, T522911. Monday-Friday, 1000-1230, 1330-1600; Easter to September, also Saturdays. £1.50.*

The Armagh Planetarium & Observatory While the Observatory (1791, Francis Johnston) is not open to the public it is possible to walk through the park and observe the classically styled building and its telescopes. At the rear of the building the dome, which is still visible, is one of the earliest surviving rotating domes and was used to house an Equatorial, which measured the movements of the stars. For those less interested in architecture, the Planetarium is on College Hill beside the observatory and has lots of hands-on exhibitions as well as the star shows. The grounds of the buildings hold an astropark, which you wouldn't notice unless you looked. ■ *College Hill, T523689. Planetarium January to June, September, December, Monday-Friday, 1000-1600, shows daily at 1500, Saturday and Sunday, 1315-1645, shows at 1400, 1500 and 1600; July and August, Monday-Friday 1000-1600, shows at 1200, 1300, 1400, 1500, 1600, Saturday and Sunday 1315-1645, shows at 1400, 1500, 1600. Entrance to exhibition £1, shows £3.75. Observatory grounds Monday-Friday, 0930-1630. Free. Observatory dome April-September 0930-1430. Free.*

St Patrick's Church of Ireland Cathedral This building has been knocked down 17 times in eight centuries – anyone else might think it was time to find somewhere else, but not here. A church has stood on this site since Patrick's time, and from the eighth century the hill was covered in monastic buildings. The present design is an enlarged version of a church of 1268, restored in 1834. Thackeray visited the renovated building and said it had as much religious feeling to it as a drawing room. It certainly lacks the awesomeness of Dublin's cathedrals or even Belfast's but it has a cosy sort of parochial austerity to it.

Just as the Victorians' efforts to Gothicize Christ Church Cathedral in Dublin (see page 111) didn't go down too well, so the efforts here lack power. There are lots of accumulated bits and pieces around the church, the most fascinating of which is the brutal-looking Tandragee Man, an ancient granite idol: thus named because of the theory that he came from Tandragee in County Down. This and several other human figures in the church are thought to have been discovered when the church was renovated in the 19th century. Another of the figures shows a crudely carved man with rays radiating from his head, perhaps a sun god from pagan times or a representation of an early Irish man, who wore their hair in stiffened dreadlocks pulled back from their heads. There is also an amalgam of two high crosses, possibly 11th century, thought to have been brought to the cathedral in 1441. Brian Boru is supposedly buried here; a slab on the exterior wall claims to be his burying place. ■ *Cathedral Close, T523142. April to October, daily 1000-1700; November to March 1000-1600. Conducted tours July and August, Monday-Saturday, 1130 and 1430. Services Sunday 1000, 1100, and 1430. Photographic permit £1 from verger or at the shop.*

Armagh Public Library Close to the church in Cathedral Close is the public library (1771, Cooley), still very much in its original condition. You must ring to be let in. In the lobby is a series of displays about the Book of Armagh, currently in Dublin, while upstairs in the library itself is a pretty impressive collection of old books including an annotated copy of *Gulliver's Travels*, a 1611 Breeches Bible, a case of tiny books, a Roman missal from 1587 and a 13th century Dutch missal. ■ *Cathedral Close, T523142. 0900-1700. Free.*

Begun in 1840 in a Neolithic style the design and building of this Cathedral were abandoned during the famine. When work began again it was in a different style altogether. A third architect designed the interior of mosaic, fresco and stained glass while the last person to have a hand in the design of this place was Liam McCormack in 1977-82. The result is, as many have pointed out, a little schizophrenic but it certainly grips the imagination. The altar, like many other efforts of the 70s, looks like it's used for pagan sacrifices rather than Catholic worship. ■ *Cathedral Road, T37522802, services daily at 0900, 1030, 1200.*

St Patrick's Roman Catholic Cathedral

It's worth enquiring at the tourist office about Armagh Gaol, which, though it is not regularly open to the public, is well worth having a look at if you are lucky enough to be in town on one of the occasions when it is opened up. Destined to be a major tourist attraction in the next decade or so it is presently crumbling badly but still stands as it was when it became notorious for its strip-searches of women political prisoners during the 1980s. Thomas Cooley is responsible for its design, and its façade is certainly beautiful enough. Inside are still the nets put up to catch suicides, the execution area (a nasty little corner of the building), and the burial places where the bodies of the truly bad were buried in quicklime. When this place was built there were no distinctions between types of criminal: debtors were incarcerated with murderers. Inside the yard was the treadwheel (no longer in existence) where, as a punishment for bad behaviour, prisoners were set to turn the wheel, stepping on to eight-inch-high steps and making 48 steps per minute. ■ *The Mall. For opening and entrance fee, enquire at the tourist office.*

Armagh Gaol

County Armagh

When Archbishop Robinson decided to make Armagh his headquarters in the 1760s he couldn't be expected to live in any old shack and so this complex of buildings, restored in the late 1980s, is his personal statement of authority. The palace itself is now council offices, but a tour can be arranged to see the rooms and paintings. The chief tourist attraction here are the stables, which have been converted into an exhibition about life in the late 18th century. Full of video clips, talking dummies and period bits and pieces, it's vaguely interesting, if it's a wet day. The other exhibits are more interesting: period rooms including a kitchen full of lovely old pots.

The Palace Stables Heritage Centre

It's when you can see the mechanics of the big nob's house that this place really gets fascinating. In the ground is the ice house – filled in winter with packed snow and used to keep food fresh through the summer. Also there is the obligatory servants' tunnel, so that the good archbishop wouldn't have to watch the minions at work; a restored Victorian curvilinear conservatory; and the primate's chapel, an elegant personal church built in 1781 to a design by Francis Johnston. By the entrance gates are the remains of a 13th-century Franciscan friary founded in 1264. The grounds are full of things too, such as a sensory garden, walking trails, and an ornamental garden. Extra marks to this place for being open on Sunday afternoons. ■ *Palace Demesne, Friary Road, T529629. September to March, Monday-Saturday, 1000-1700, Sunday 1400-1700; April to August, Monday-Saturday, 1000-1730, Sunday 1000-1800. £3.50. Courtesy bus.*

Navan Fort An unremarkable-looking mound on a hilltop two miles out of Armagh, this is Ireland's most significant ancient site. There is evidence of habitation here going back 7000 years, but the most significant activity took place during the Bronze Age when the place was built and rebuilt about seven times, and finally, inexplicably, a huge wooden building was created, filled with limestone blocks and burned to the ground. In 1993 it acquired the obligatory heritage centre, which is quite attractively designed and does a pretty good job of explaining what is basically a big grassy mound at the moment. Excavations are planned for the future, which may open up the site a little more. The centre is open on Sundays. ■ *Killylea Road, T525550. July, August daily 1000-1900. Last entry at 1745; October to March, Monday-Friday 1000-1700, Saturday 1100-1700, Sunday 1200-1700, last entry at 1545; April to June and September, Monday-Saturday, 1000-1800, Sunday 1100-1800, last entry 1645. £3.95. Access to the fort 24 hours and free. Courtesy bus in summer, or No 93 from the Mall.*

Essentials

Sleeping
■ *on map*
Price codes:
see inside front cover

You're not exactly spoilt for choice here – no major hotel chains but there's a hostel and several B&Bs to choose from. **A** *Charlemont Hotel*, 63-5 English St, T522028. Very central, a little caged-up looking with window grilles and CCTV, but comfortable. **A** *Dean's Hill*, College Hill, T524923. A little out of town, and hard to find up a long, unsignposted drive, this is a Georgian residence. It is a little crumbling in places but the rooms are beautifully appointed with wonderful views, and the breakfast room and hallway put the displays at the Bishop's Palace to shame. Check out the allegorical painting that dominates the dining room. **A** *Drumshill House*, 35 Moy Rd, T522009. Out of town and slightly more expensive is this quite small, family-run establishment. It can get noisy at weekends when the nightclub operates, however. **A** *De Averell Guest House*, 3 Seven Houses, English St, T511213. Has a respected restaurant and comfortable rooms. **C** *Desart Guest House*, The Desart, Desart Lane, off Cathedral Rd, T37522387. Actually classed as a B&B by the tourist board, this is small, with no en-suite rooms but good value. **C** *Ni Eoghain Lodge*, 32 Ennislare Rd, T525633. B&B with self-catering chalets. All rooms en suite, breakfast choices, cheap evening meals (a godsend on Armagh Sunday nights), vegetarians catered for. Remarkably reasonably priced. **D** *Armagh City Hostel*, 39 Abbey St, T511800, F511801. YHANI hostel with dormitory accommodation and twin rooms, all en suite, cooking facilities and a restaurant. The place closes between 1100 and 1700 between October and March, which could be very inconvenient in miserable weather, but this is the best value for 2 people or a group of 4 sharing in town. Book well in advance.

Eating
● *on map*
Price codes:
see inside front cover

Eating out in Armagh needs considerable planning beforehand. Most places shut by 1730 and those that don't require a booking. *De Averell Guest House* (see above) has a good reputation, serves a mixture of ethnic stuff and more conventional dishes and dinner, 7 days until 2200: will cost around £18 per person. The *Drumshill Hotel*, on Moy Rd, serves fairly conventional steaks, salmon and a lunchtime carvery as does the *Charlemont Arms*, see page 638, where last orders are 2130. *Jodie's*, 37 Scotch St, T527577 is open for lunch; dinner Saturday and Sunday when it shuts at 2000, offers fairly standard dishes – cod, chicken, etc – has a vegetarian option and several salads. Closed Wednesday. The *Pub With No Beer*, 30 Thomas St, T37523586, opens Monday-Saturday till 2130 and serves pub food – champ, salads, chicken pie etc. *Calvert's Tavern*, 3 Scotch St, serves lunch and evening pub food till 2200 and *Harry Hoot's*, 143 Railway St, T522374, has pub grub 7 days till 2130. Your last chance for evening food is *Mandarin House*, 30 Scotch St, T37522228, which serves Chinese and western food till 2300. Closed Mondays. You might also check out *Our Ma's Café*, 2 Lower English

St, T511289, which has an extensive menu of caff-type food, does a 3-course lunch for £3.50 and has plans to open in the evenings.

If it's just lunch you're after there are a few more options. The best place in town is probably the *Pilgrim's Table*, 38, English St, T37521801, inside the St Patrick's Trian complex. It does homely kinds of dishes, filled potatoes, soups, hotpot and in pleasant surroundings. Nice for a snack is *Café Papa*, 15 Thomas St, T37511205, which does filled rolls and sandwiches and pastries. *Fat Sam's*, 7 English St, T37525559, is good for filled potato, sandwich or pastry, Monday-Friday only.

Most of the pubs do lunchtime pub grub. The best of them is a little out of town: the *Northern Bar*, 100 Railway St, T37527315, has a large menu ranging from sandwiches to a 3-course meal from 1200 to 1500. The 3-course option will set you back around £7.50. Also open for Sunday lunch. Other pubs to try for food are The *Station Bar*, T37523731, the *Strawberry Bar*, the *Diamond Bar*, T37523865, all in English St, the *Cellar Lounge* and *Glencoe* in Thomas St, and *Damper Murphy's* in Lower Irish St.

There is quite a lively nightlife among the pubs in Armagh. For traditional Irish music **Pubs & music** you could try the *Station Bar*, which has bands on Tuesdays and Thursdays, or the *Railway Bar*, Mondays. Other pubs have music at weekends but it's likely to be tribute bands or a disco. *Harry Hoot's* is the liveliest place in town, with a disco Thursday and Friday and live bands Saturday and Sunday. The *Strawberry Bar* and the *Shambles Bar* have live music of some sort or another at weekends and *Wolly Tom's*, in Nursery Road has live music from Friday to Sunday. Armagh City Folk Club meets in the *Charlemont Arms* on one variable Thursday a month (T37522928, Mr John Butler), or there are ceilidh dancing classes at St Patrick's Parochial Hall in Cathedral Rd every Thursday from 2100 to 2230, where tea is served (T37526088, Seamus Mc Donagh). Set-dancing classes are held on Mondays at the *Pearse Og* club in Dalton Rd and visitors are welcome: £2, (T37511004, Pat Prunty). There are no classes during the summer months. The *Armagh Pipers Club* meets at the Palace Stables Heritage Centre on a monthly basis and visitors are welcome (T37511248, Eithne Vallely).

Due to open in December 1999 the £3.67 million Arts Centre built thanks to lottery **Entertainment** funding will be a major venue for theatre and concert performances. Other centres used for theatre and other performance are St Patrick's Parochial Hall, The Orchard Leisure Centre in Folly Lane, T515920, and St Patrick's Trian (see page 635). In Market St, at the bottom of the Arts Centre is *Armagh City Film House*, T511033. The Arts Centre has a display area for artwork and there are three galleries in town: *Adam Gallery*, 28 Linenhall St; *Browser Gallery*, English St; *Orchard Gallery* in Barrack St.

In early **June** is the Armagh County *Fleadh Ceol*, a traditional music festival, including **Festivals** ceilidhs, street music and traditional music sessions in the pubs. *St Patrick's Day*, **17th March**, is celebrated with pub music, set dancing at the Palace Stables, a huge parade and a concert at St Patrick's Hall in Cathedral Road.

Books *Armagh Books*, 16 Thomas St, T511988, Monday-Saturday 0930-1730. **Shopping**

Bike *Brown's Bikes*, 21 Scotch St, T522782. **Bus** The bus station is at 14 Londsale **Transport** Rd, T37522266. There are direct express buses to Belfast (14 or more a day, last bus leaves Armagh at 1815, fewer at weekends), Dublin (1 a day, 2 on Fridays), Cork (1 a day, no Sunday service), Galway (2 a day, 1 on Sunday) and Enniskillen (1 a day, no Sunday service), stopping at major towns along the route. Local buses connect with smaller towns in the area and a change at Dungannon brings connections to the northern coast and Derry. **Taxi** *Central Taxis*, T37526999; *City Taxis*, T37528852; *Shambles Taxis*, T37511170. **Train** The nearest train station is at Portadown, T38351422, which connects with the Dublin to Belfast line.

County Armagh

County Armagh

Directory **Banks** Around the junction of English St and College St. **Communications** Post Office: English St. **Genealogy** *Armagh Ancestry*, 42 English St, T521802, F510033. **Hospitals** *Craigavon Area Hospital*, T01762-334444 **Tour companies & travel agents** *Hill Travel*, Scotch St, T522161. *Lunn Poly*, Scotch St, T510786. *UlsterTravel*, English St, 522919. **Tourist Offices** 40 English St, T521800. Bureau de Change, faxing service, B&B booking. Sep-Jun, Mon-Sat, 0900-1700, Sun 1400-1700; Jul, Aug, Mon-Sat 0900-1730, Sun 1300-1730.

South Armagh – a tour

*Steeped in ancient culture, this is the most beautiful part of the county despite the assorted remnants of military paraphernalia that blight the green and grey hills. Even on a wet and doleful day the allure of Slieve Gullion is palpable and this tour starts in **Newtownhamilton**: reached to the south of Armagh city or the north-west of Dundalk on the A29, or from Newry by going due west on the A25. The tour finishes in Crossmaglen.*

Camlough From Newtownhamilton, take the A25 road east to Newry, and consider stopping in tricoloured Camlough for a drink or bar food in *Finnegan's* or the *Village Inn*, both in Main St, before passing on to Bessbrook, a purpose-built, time capsule of a mill town laid out in the 1840s by the Quaker Richardsons. This gem of a place, characterized by the generous use of local granite stone in its buildings, was known as 'the village without three Ps' because there were no pubs and thus no pawnshop nor need for a police station. Five soldiers were killed by a landmine near here at the height of the violence unleashed by the deaths of hunger strikers in May 1981.

Derrymore House On the Newry side of the A25, Derrymore House is a National Trust thatched 18th century cottage where the Act of Union was drafted, and the picturesque

South Armagh

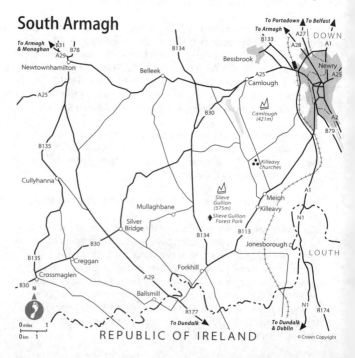

© Crown Copyright

Newtownhamilton

The genesis of the very literal Newtownhamilton can be traced back to an advertisement that appeared in the Belfast Newsletter in 1747. A landlord, Alexander Hamilton, advertised some of his estate for leasing:

'On each of the said farms there is plenty of good meadows and turf; a large river runs through the middle of said lands that never wants water sufficient to turn many mills … and a fall of 180 feet in less than two miles, and places where mill ponds may easily be made. By the great plenty of turf, water, bog, timber for building and meadows, the linen manufacture may be carried on, as cheap as in any part of Ireland.'

park and woodlands that surround the cottage are always freely open. ■ *T30838361. May to August, Thursday-Saturday, 1400-1730; daily over Easter. £1.80.*

Hop back to Camlough and turn left to take the road south passing a lake setting that can match Killarney's for sheer breathtaking beauty. Continue south to the Killeavy churches on the gentle slopes of Slieve Gullion, where St Monenna's nunnery lasted for a millennium after her death in the early sixth century. The western, 12th-century church is joined by a shared wall to a later 15th-century place of worship. St Monenna's likely burial place is marked by a large slab near the churchyard wall to the north and a holy well associated with her is a little way up the mountain to the west.

Killeavy churches

County Armagh

Kilnasaggart Pillar Stone, 1854

South Armagh Festivals

Crossmaglen Horsefair, first Saturday in **September,** enlivened by traditional music and dancing. On the Sunday 'The Big Race' takes place.

Singing Weekend in Forkill and Mullach Bán on the first weekend of **October.**

South Armagh Community Festival is a family event that takes place in **July.**

Lislea Drama Festival in **February** and **March** sees plays and scripted folklore.

Forest Park On the other side of Killeavy village, on the B113, you will find the entrance to the Slieve Gullion Forest Park where an eight-mile (13-kilometre) drive and a walking trail lead up to the summit. Weather permitting, there are unrivalled views of the random set of volcanic hills known as the Ring of Gullion. ■ *T30738284. Easter to August, 1000-dusk. £2.50 for a car. Visitor Centre and coffee shop.*

A short detour to the east goes to **Jonesborough**, famous for its Sunday market which draws in a fair crowd. A couple of miles south of the village a path to the handsome **Kilnasaggart Stone** (*Cill na Sagart*, church of the priests) is signposted across fields. This eighth-century pillar is clearly and elegantly inscribed and marks an early Christian burial place. Jonesborough is also a good place to stop for a meal.

Local entertainment Travel back to the B113 and continue south to tiny **Forkhill** where a perfect Guinness is served at *M C Larkin*, a lovely old-style pub on the right-hand side of the road. North of the village at Mullaghbawn (*An Mullach Ban*), the **Tí Chulainn Cultural Centre** has exhibitions and occasional live performances of traditional music, song and dance. Contact in advance to see what might be on. ■ *Mullach Ban. T30888828. tculainn@dial.pipex.com July and August, Monday-Saturday, 1000-1730, Sunday 1300-1800. Rest of year, slightly shorter hours. Free.*

Crossmaglen & around From Mullach Ban continue north to the junction with the B30 and turn left for Crossmaglen. In the 1880s over a 150 young women were employed here in lace schools. Less than a century later the town's proximity to the border had made it infamous as the epicentre of militant republicanism; by the beginning of 1976 over 30 soldiers had been killed here, over half in the town square where a tourist office now stands as a refreshing sign of changing times. Every second Friday a fair is held in the square.

In the village of **Creggan**, four kilometres northeast of Crossmaglen, the parish churchyard has interesting tombstones of local 18th-century Gaelic poets and other curiosities. Between Easter and September guided tours of the churchyard are available on Sunday afternoon; contact the rectory in Dundalk for details, T00353-4271921, or pick up the the useful leaflet on the churchyard from the tourist office in Crossmaglen.

Essentials

Sleeping **B** *Murtaghs*, 13 North St, Crossmaglen, T30861378. A family-run bar and B&B place in the centre of town. Two double rooms, one with its own bathroom, and a single. **B** *Slieve Gullion House*, 1 Dromintee Rd, Meigh, T30848225. Close to Killeavy and within walking distance of the bus stop, shops and a pub. **C** *Greenvale*, 141 Longfield Rd, Forkhill, T30888314. A farmhouse with views of Slieve Gullion. One double and one single, and horse-riding available on the farm.

Self-catering Self-catering in south Armagh would enable you really to get to know the area as well as making a useful base for visiting Dundalk and the Cooley peninsula. *Benbree Self-Catering Cottage*, 67 Carrive Rd, Forkhill, T30888394. £175 a week for three bedrooms and good facilities. *Country Farm Cottage*, 139 Longfield Rd, Forkhill, T30888314. £110 a week and sleeps five. *Mountain View*, 11 Cranny View, Mullach Ban, T30888410. £150 for the week, two bedrooms sleeping five.

In Jonesborough the *Flurrybridge Inn*, T30848181, serves the best choice of food – **Eating** European, Chinese and Indian – for miles around and opens in the evening Thursday to Sunday and at lunchtime on Sunday, 1230-1530, for the open-air market. *Lima Country House*, 16 Drumalt Rd, Silverbridge, T30861944, serves evening meals between Monday and Saturday, but telephone first.

The *Slieve Gullion Courtyard Restaurant*, 89 Dromintee Rd, Killeavey, T30848084, at the Slieve Gullion Forest Park, does meals on Saturday and Sunday from 1400 to 2200 with dishes from £5 to £15 and if you telephone ahead it is possible to book a meal during the week.

Crossmaglen has a few places to eat, including pub food in The Square at *Cartwheel*, Monday-Saturday, in the evening. *Chums*, 46 The Square, does pub lunches while a couple of miles down the road the *Ashfield Golf Club*, Freeduff, Cullyhanna, T30868180, serves standard fare from 1200 to 2100 (from 1400 on Monday).

Hearty's Folk Cottage, Glassdrummon, T30868188, is a delightful whitewashed cottage in the countryside that only opens on Sunday afternoons for tea and delicious home-baked scones with jam and cream, accompanied by live traditional music. Crafts and antique jewellery are on sale as well.

The *Ti Chulainn Cultural Centre*, Mullaghbawn, T30888828, has traditional music **Pubs & music** every second Saturday, and on every second Tuesday there is a likeminded musical session at *The Welcome Inn*, 35 Main St, Forkhill, T30888273. Also in Mullaghbawn, *O'Hanlon's Pub*, T30888759, is a favourite place for improvised eruptions of music whatever the day. Hearty's Folk Cottage in Glassdrummon near Crossmaglen, T30868188, offers traditional music on Sundays (see page 643).

Bicycle hire: *McCumiskey Cycles*, Dromintee, T30888593 **Horse-riding**: *Crossmag-* **Sport** *len Equestrian Centre*, T30861661. *Greenvale Trekking Centre*, Forkhill, T30888314. *Ring of Gullion Trekking Centre*, Mullaghbawn,T30889311.

Buses There is a bus service Monday to Saturday between Newry and Crossmaglen **Transport** via Camlough, T30263531. Other services run Monday to Saturday between Forkhill and Newry and between Bessbrook and Newry. **Taxis** *Cross Cabs*, Crossmaglen, T30868550. *M.T. Taxis*, Crossmaglen, T30868300.

Banks The Square, Crossmaglen. **Communications** Post office: Newry St, Crossmaglen. 29 **Directory** Main St, Forkhill. 2 Dromintee Rd, Killeavy. **Tourist offices** Community Centre, The Square, Crossmaglen, T30868900. Mon-Fri, 0900-1700.

North Armagh

A greater contrast with south Armagh is hard to find for in place of attractive countryside and progressive culture there is an unsightly industrial landscape and the backward sectarianism of Portadown.

The town of Portadown, where loyalist mobs rioted against the Anglo-Irish **Portadown** Agreement in 1985, is probably the least attractive place to visit in the whole of Ireland. At the time of writing, the Drumcree issue is still unresolved but if a settlement is found it may well involve a substantial injection of cash and

County Armagh

☞ *Drumcree and Garvaghy Road*

The issue of whether the Orange Order has the right to march from Drumcree church down Catholic Garvaghy Road on its route back to Portadown each July has become a major issue in the evolving politics of Ulster. David Trimble's rise to the leadership of the Unionist Party received vital support from diehard loyalists after he joined the march and championed their cause. In 1998, after the Parades Commission banned the march, the resulting violence resulted in the death of three children in a Catholic house firebombed by loyalist extremists. The Orange Order is adamant about its right to march down the road, and the residents of Garvaghy Road are equally adamant that the days of triumphalist and provocative marches through Catholic areas are over. In 1999 the stand-off was peaceful, but loyalists insist that they will maintain a presence outside Drumcree church until their 'constitutional rights' are respected.

resources into the beleagured Garvaghy Road area and, who knows, perhaps it will begin to lose its fatigued and battle-torn appearance.

To visit **Garvaghy Road** leave your vehicle in the Dunnes store car park or, closer still, the Wilson Street car park opposite the *Laser* electronics store. Garvaghy Road begins where the Haldane Fisher & Ulster Carpet Mills Factory sign can be seen and the Union Jacks soon give way to the tricolours of the Catholic enclave. To reach **Drumcree church**, walk up the road for one mile and take the second turning on the right after the Mayfair Centre. Continue along this road for about a mile and it is on the left by the Y-junction.

There are also two National Trust houses in the area. The 17th-century **Ardress House** has a renowned neoclassical interior and a working farmyard outside. Close by on Derrycaw Rd in Moy, is **The Argory** with what was a state-of-the-art gas lighting system in the early 19th century still illuminating some of the original furniture. ■ *Ardress House: on B26, 7 miles west of Portadown, T38851236. Easter and June to August, Wednesday-Monday, 1400-1800; April to May and September, Saturday and Sunday same hours. Guided tour. £2.40. The Argory: T38784753. Same hours as Ardress House. £2.60.*

Loughall A sectarian conflict at a crossroads near Loughall, the Battle of the Diamond, cost the lives of 30 men and a Protestant victory. An immediate result was the founding of the Orange Order in 1795 to celebrate the more momentous victory of Protestant William of Orange at the Battle of the Boyne in 1690. The inn where the Order was inaugurated is now the **Dan Winter Ancestral Home** and contains memorabilia from the Battle of the Diamond. ■ *9 The Diamond, Derryloughan Road, Loughall, T38851344. Monday-Saurday, 1030-2030, Sunday 1400-2030. Voluntary donation. Call at the house next door for the key.*

In 1986 the Provisionals mounted an attack on the RUC station at Loughall but a tip-off led to an ambush by SAS soldiers, who fired 1,200 rounds killing eight of the Provisionals as well as an innocent civilian driving past in his car.

Loughall has some quality antique shops along its main street, including *Heritage Antiques*, T38891314, and *Meredith Antiques*, T38528739, and a noted restaurant, *The Famous Grouse*, T38891778, a couple of miles out on Ballyhagan Road.

They proceeded to strike, mangle, slaughter, and cut down one another for a long time, so that men were soon laid low, heroes wounded, youths slain, and robust heroes mangled in the slaughter.

Annals of the Four Masters
[Shane O'Neill's battle with the O'Donnells, 1567]

Counties Tyrone & Fermanagh

17

Counties Tyrone & Fermanagh

© Crown Copyright

While the small county of Fermanagh has a modest and developing tourist infrastructure based around Lough Erne and the town of Enniskillen, Tyrone, which shares with Fermanagh a central role in defining Ulster both geographically and historically, tends not to feature highly in most travellers' itineraries. County Tyrone generally lacks the Bord Fáilte factor – the readily identifiable pre-packaged image – but of course this is precisely what makes the county so appealing. Public transport is adequate in both Tyrone and Fermanagh, and Enniskillen is well served by bus routes, but visitors without private transport are handicapped to some extent when visiting places around Enniskillen, organizing walking trips in the Sperrins or exploring the recesses of south and north Tyrone.

★ *Try to find time for*

> *The Ulster American Folk Park near Omagh*
>
> *Walking in the Sperrins*
>
> *Boa Island, Devenish Island and Killedeas Churchyard north of Enniskillen*
>
> *The Ulster History Museum and museums in and around Castlederg (for a wet day)*

County Tyrone

For anyone contemplating a few days in an unhyped part of Ireland, taking in country walks and quiet villages where nothing much happens and where the local population is thin on the ground, County Tyrone fits the bill. Private transport, car or bicycle, makes a big difference, and planning ahead for meals and accommodation is fairly vital outside of Omagh and Cookstown, but when that is done the region is all yours.

History

History lies at the heart of Tyrone for the Elizabethan conquest of this county, the most intractable part of an intractable province, sealed the fate of Gaelic Ireland. Surrounded by wood, bog and the Sperrin mountains to the south, the O'Neills held out in their Tyrone homelands against the English in the second half of the 16th century. In 1562 Shane O'Neill came to London to parley with Elizabeth's government and the clash of cultures was evident to all: the doublets and hose and fancy ruffs of the English confronted the Gaelic entourage with their shoulder-length hair, cloaks, and shirts of linen dyed yellow with urine. Shane only managed to buy some time and it was left to his nephew, Hugh O'Neill, to witness the final subjugation of Gaelic Ireland and the door left open for the plantations of the early 17th century.

In 1641 a rebellion started in Tyrone and spread across the country, and the same year the massacres of settlers by hungry and dispossessed Catholics – an event that still haunts the loyalist subconscious – was Cromwell's justification for his own massacres, 'the righteous judgement of God', which reasserted foreign rule over Ireland. The killing and counter-killing continued intermittently over the following centuries, the most recent outrage being the horrific bombing that killed 29 people out shopping on a sunny Saturday afternoon in Omagh in August 1998.

Omagh

Colour map 1, grid B3 Church and State are represented in Omagh by the two overbearing monuments to the claims in this part of the world on people's lives: the Catholic church and the courthouse – an example of monstrous Victorian architecture, built in 1863 some 30 thirty years before the church – loom over the top half of the town, calling everyone to obedience to the crown or to God. The dissident Republican group responsible for the 1998 slaughter were probably intending to destroy the courthouse at the western end of the town's main street, . The 1998 bomb went off at the east end of the street, where sad bouquets still mark the spot and empty ground bears mute testimony to the force of the 500 pounds of explosives. By the time of your visit, a memorial garden for those who tragically lost their lives should be open to the public.

The Ulster American Folk Park Emigration from Ireland has become so entwined with the Famine and with post-Famine history that it often comes as a surprise to learn that an exodus of impoverished Protestants began in the early 18th century from Ulster, which alarmed the government, for 'the humour has spread like a contagious distemper, and the people will hardly hear any body that tries to cure them of their madness'. By the 1770s some 10,000 were leaving annually and Benjamin Franklin estimated that one-third of Pennsylvania's population were Ulster

Scots-Irish emigrants. The Ulster American Folk Park, which can claim that half of all US presidents to date are of Ulster descent, celebrates and records emigration to North America with a wealth of reconstructed buildings and entire streets that make up one of Ireland's most successful museums. ■ *On A5, 3 miles north of Omagh, T82243292, http://www.folkpark.com Easter to September, Monday-Saturday 1100-1830, Sunday 1130-1900; October to Easter, Monday-Friday 1030-1700. Last admission 90 minutes before closing. £4. Café and shop.*

AL *Silverbirch*, 5 Gortin Rod, T82242520. Omagh's only hotel: one of those large modern places where the corridors are interchangeable and there are always big wedding parties at weekends. The rooms are comfortable and there is a popular but dodgily decorated restaurant. **A** *Hawthorn House*, 72 Old Mountfield Rd, T82252005. A way out of town off the Gortin Road, but a comfortable guest house with an excellent restaurant. **C** *Ardmore*, 12 Tamlaght Rd, T82243381. Closest to town of the B&Bs, which are all around the outskirts. **C** *Bankhead*, 9 Lissan Rd, T82245592. Very reasonably priced, with 3 rooms, open all year. **D** *Omagh Independent Hostel*, Glenhordial, 9a Waterworks Rd, T82241973. Has rooms ranging in size from singles to dormitory and lots of room to relax. | **Sleeping**

Not being overly dependent on tourism, restaurants in Omagh tend to cater to shoppers or people out for a treat. The restaurant in the *Silverbirch* has an extensive menu, with dinner costing £15 or less, and lunchtime specials. *Hawthorn House* is the classiest place to eat – fresh local food, traditional Irish dishes, mixed with a welcome Californian touch – and usually needs booking in advance. Dinner £20 plus. In town, opposite the Catholic Church at 29 George's St, T82250900 is *Grants*, a bistro-cum-pub open for lunch and dinner till 2200. It has lively dishes, which include chilli prawns, as well as more conventional food. Along the High St/Market St are lots of lunch time places like *Bogan's Bar*, at 26 Market St, T82242183, and the *Shopper's Restaurant*, 38 High St, T82243545, which does things with chips and filled potatoes. The comfortable *Coach Inn*, Railway Terrace, T82243330, is on the right just after the railway bridge on the road out to Enniskillen from the town centre. Bar food, including an excellent vegetarian salad, is served until 1800 when a separate dining area opens up with a menu of standard main courses between £8 and £12 and a small wine list. | **Eating**

The trendiest place is town is *Sally O'Brien's*, just behind the Town Hall on John St, with its wonderful window display. Open till past midnight, on the nights it has live music you can catch country and western, blues and the occasional traditional session here. *The Inn at the Bridge*, which displays it allegiances in its Manchester United colours, has live music at weekends, mostly Irish country and western. On Castle Street is *McElroy's* with lots of big copy bands. The *Silverbirch* has occasional live music but your best bet for traditional music is *Bogan's* on Market St. Check out also the *Dún Uladh Cultural Heritage Centre*, on the Carrickmore Rd, T82242777, which often has concerts, ballroom and Irish dancing sessions and traditional music. | **Pubs & music**

Bicycle *Conway Cycles*, 1 Old Market Place, T82246195. Bike hire. **Car rental** *Tattyreagh Car Hire*, 110a Tattyreagh Rd, T82841731. **Taxi** *Glen Taxis*, T82246058. *P&I Taxis*, T82757200. | **Transport**

Tourist Office 1 Market St, T82247831. Jul-Aug, Mon-Fri 0900-1730; Sep-Jun, Mon-Fri 0900-1700; Easter-Sep additional Sat 0900-1300, 1330-1730. | **Directory**

County Tyrone

The Sperrins

The Sperrin Mountains, rolling areas of blanket bog with summits over 1,640 feet (500 metres), stretch across north Tyrone from the border with Derry for some 35 miles (56 kilometres) and encapsulate the appeal of the county: fresh air, uncluttered space, country and hill walks from the casual to the demanding, archaeological sites, and a cultural history that is only now emerging from a long period of censorship. Omagh is the nearest town of any size and with a fair choice of accommodation; though Gortin is a more convenient base for the area, accommodation and places to eat are scarce.

The Sperrin Heritage Centre This Heritage Centre provides introductory information on the ecology and culture of the Sperrins, including the history of gold mining in the area and the chance to pan for some in a stream nearby. There is also a decent café. ■ *Glenelly Road, Cranagh, Gortin, on B47, nine miles east of Plumbridge, T81648142. Easter to October, Monday-Saturday 1100-1800 (1130 on Saturday), Sunday 1400-1900. £2, and 65p for pan hire.*

The Ulster History Park Recreating the history of human settlement in Ireland from the Stone Age to the plantations of the 17th century, this is quite a sophisticated display. The guided tours are highly informative, and there is a restaurant and picnic area. ■ *Cullion, on B48, seven miles north of Omagh, T81648188. April to September, Monday-Saturday 1030-1830, Sunday 1130-1900; October to March, Monday-Friday 1030-1700. Last admission 90 minutes before closing. £3.25.*

An Creagán Visitor Centre This is another information centre, but with more activities, in the foothills of the Sperrins. The Centre is spearheading an attempt to resuscitate the culture of the area, and details of local festivals dedicated to this purpose are available here. There is a restaurant, a bar with live music at weekends, sessions of storytelling and song throughout the year, self-catering cottages (see 'Sleeping' on page 651), and an 'interpretative exhibition' with an overview of the cultural, archaeological and environmental landscape of the area. Bicycles can also be hired and there are walking possibilities from the Centre. ■ *Creggan, on the A505 half way between Omagh and Cookstown, T80761112. April to September, daily 1100-1830; October to March, daily 1100-1630. £2.*

Walking in the Sperrins Little is gleaned by just travelling through the Sperrins, but there are some waymarked trails and walking routes and one of the easiest to organize is a six-mile (10-kilometre) section of the Ulster Way between Gortin and Glengawna. Both places are on the B48 road along which Bus No 92 (Monday-Saturday) travels between Omagh and Gortin, so with the help of a bus timetable it is possible to catch a bus to the start and/or from the end of the walk. The Way is marked on Ordnance Survey map 13, although there is a small change from the map just south of Gortin where it crosses the B48. Along the Way the route passes the Ulster History Park (see page 650) and the **Gortin Glen Forest Park**, which has its own waymarked trails and from here one could also walk 10 miles (16 kilometres) of the Ulster Way as far as the Ulster-American Folk Park (see page 648, from where Bus No 97 travels to Omagh. Gortin Glen Forest Park also has a vehicular drive through the forest and there is a café. ■ *On B48, seven miles north of Omagh, T81648217. Daily 1000-dusk. £3 for car.*

Short walks of between six and ten miles are also possible from the An Creagán Visitor Centre, which provides walk sheets, and most of these take in archaeological sites along the way.

Walking festivals

Many of these festivals combine walking with evening entertainment and music. **Sperrin Walking Weekend** mid-June. T71382204/883735

Cookstown Walking Festival late June. T86762205/66727

Carntogher Festival mid-July. T796300050

Sperrins Hillwalking Festival early August. T796300050

Feeny Folk Festival early October. T77781876/796300050

The two highest points in the Sperrins, **Sawel Mountain** and **Dart Mountain**, can be climbed in one day and a good starting point is just to the east of Sperrin village on the B47 in the Glenelly valley. However, there have been problems with some landowners in the area and walking west of Dart mountain is definitely not on. Ordnance Survey map No 13 is essential for this walk, and it might be worthwhile calling in at the Sperrin Heritage Centre (see page 650) and check your proposed route with them.

Essentials

Sleeping **B** *Lenamore Lodge*, 19 Crickanboy Rd, Gortin, T/F8248460. Has 2 rooms, 1 with its own bathroom, for £30. **D** *Gortin Outdoor Centre*, Glenpark Rd, T82648083. A hostel with nearly 20 beds for £6 each, but only opens July to September.

Self-catering *An Clachan* self-catering cottages at Creggan are managed by the An Creagán Visitor Centre, T80761112, F80761116, sleep from 2 to 6 people and cost from £60 for a 1-bedroom cottage over a weekend in the low season to £330 for a week in a 3-bedroomed cottage at high season. *Craignamaddy Barn*, 45 Gorticashel Rd, Gortin, T/F82647949, sutherland@btinternet.com has similar prices for a 2-bedroomed refurbished barn.

Gortin Glen Caravan and Camping Park, Lisnaharney Rd, Lislap, T/F81648108, has plenty of tent pitches for £6 a night and is situated opposite the Gortin Glen Forest Park.

Eating The *An Creagán Restaurant*, at Creggan on the A505, T80761112, at the Visitor Centre is open daily for inexpensive lunches, and evening meals from £7 Thursday to Sunday. In Gortin the *Badoney Tavern*, 16 Main St, T81648157, serves pub meals in the evening from 1800 to 2100. The *Sperrin Heritage Centre*, east of Plumbridge on the B47, T81648142, serves very light meals until 1800 Monday to Saturday and from 1400 to 1900 on a Sunday. In Plumbridge *Pinkertons Café*, 25 Main St, T81648327, is open daily for steaks, curry and chicken meals.

Transport **Bicycle** *An Creagán Visitor Centre*, T80761112. Bicycle hire, also cycling route information for 10- to 14-mile trips. *Gortin Glen Caravan and Camping Park*, Lisnaharney Rd, Lislap, T81648108. Bicycle hire. *Sperrins Cycling Festival* at the end of May. Contact 1 Lisnaharney Rd, Lislap, Omagh, BT79 7UE. T81647998/81247831.

Directory **Tour companies & travel agents** *Sperrin Hillwalking*, 2 Churchwell Lane, Magherafelt, County Tyrone, BT45 6AL, T79300050, F79300009, activities@sperrins.iol.ie Organizes walking packages: charges £130 for 2 days walking plus accommodation, food and guide, £300 for a week.

Castlederg and around

This is one of the least visited parts of Ireland and the Castlederg Visitor Centre is worth calling in at to learn something about the area and receive instructions

Colour map 1, grid B3

on how to reach local archaeological sites. Such were the sectarian divisions of Castlederg that the town used to have separate Protestant and Catholic Christmas trees erected annually, and one can wonder what the frontiersman Davy Crockett, whose family came from here, would have made of that. ■ *Visitor Centre: 26 Lower Strabane Road, T81670795. April to October, Tuesday-Friday 1100-1600, Saturday 1130-1600, Sunday 1400-1700. £1.20.*

Newtownstewart There is a more idiosyncratic museum here in the **Gateway Centre and Museum** on the outskirts of town, an eccentric but diverting collection of the vernacular sort that major repositories of cultural relics never think are worth bothering about. It was all collected by one person: there is a lot relating to the two world wars but my favourite is the yoke specially designed for lifting hedgehogs. ■ *21 Moyle Road, T81662414. April to October, Tuesday-Friday 1100-1600, Saturday 1130-1600, Sunday 1400-1700. £1.20.*

If travelling the road between Newtownstewart and Strabane, Sion Mills is worth a look if only to peer in at the still-functioning linen factory that gave rise to this purpose-built mill village created by the Herdmans in 1835. It was praised by the myopic Halls in their 1843 tour of the country for giving work to 700 workers, mostly women, conveniently forgetting the 15-hour days and the horrific accidents that led Dickens to call the linen employers' union the Association for the Mangling of Operatives.

Strabane A beleaguered Catholic enclave that has seen its share of rioting during the last 30 years, Strabane has the rather sad distinction of being noted for the people that left the place. The novelist, Flann O'Brien, deserted at the age of 12 in 1923, and two centuries earlier John Dunlap, having learnt his trade as a printer, went off to America and printed the American Declaration of Independence. This, and other stories, can be found at the fairly uninspiring **Gray's Printer's Museum**. ■ *49 Main Street, Strabane, T71884094. Tuesday-Friday 1100-1700, Saturday 1130-1700. Guided tours of the printing press April to September, 1400-1700. £1.80.*

Less significant was the emigration of one James Wilson in 1807, even though his grandson managed to end up in the White House. Hence the **Wilson Ancestral Home**. ■ *Dergalt, 2 miles from Strabane off the Plumbridge Road, T71883735 for hours of opening. £1.*

Sleeping **A** *Hunting Lodge Hotel*, Letterbin, Newtownsend, T81661679, F81661900. A 19th-century converted schoolhouse with weekend breaks including a dinner for £70 per person. Activities such as clay-pigeon shooting and fishing can be arranged. **B** *Bide-A-Wee*, 181 Melmount Rd, Sion Mills, T81659571. Has an outdoor pool and tennis courts and a weekend package with meals is around £90 per person. **B-C** *Derg Arms*, 43 Main St, Castlederg, T81671644, F81670202. A pub in the centre of town. **C** *Ardmourne House*, 36 Congary Rd, Castlederg, T81670291. A modern house with kitchen facilities for guests, and pony trekking available.

Eating There are a few pubs in Castlederg serving pub grub, including *Castle Inn*, 48 Main St, T81671501, *Market Bar*, 59 Main St, T81671247, and the *Crescent Inn*, 1 Ferguson Crescent, T81671161, which also has live music in the evening. In Newtownstewart, pubs with food include the *County Inn*, 43 Main St, T81662105, and the *Harry Avery Lounge*, 19 Dublin Rd, T81661431. If just passing through, the town is bypassed by the main road and inexpensive meals are available at *Aunt Jane's*, 21 Moyle Rd, right next to the Gateway Centre and Museum. The best place for a meal, though, is the *Hunting Lodge Inn*, Lettbin, T81661679.

In Strabane food is available every lunchtime except Sunday at Flann O'Brien, 3 Derry Rd, T71884427, and the *Fir Trees Hotel*, Dublin Rd, T71382382, which serves meals such as duck in sweet and sour sauce, and grills.

Car hire *McGillion*, 132 Melmount Rd, Sion Mills, T81658275.

Transport

Tourist office *Pagoda Tourist Information Centre*, Abercorn Square, Strabane, T71883735. Apr-Oct, Mon-Thu 0900-1730, Fri and Sat 0900-1600.

Directory

Cookstown and around

The east of Tyrone is home to a scattered set of archaeological sites with Cookstown being the main town in the area.

Cookstown

Cookstown has had a troubled past since a Scottish landlord established a small town and market here in the 1620s. In the 1641 uprising the town was taken by the native Irish and burnt to the ground after its recapture by the army, and it lay derelict for a century until 1736. In that year the grandson of the original settler, inspired by the streets of Dublin and Edinburgh, laid out a new town with a main street stretching for well over a mile. During the Troubles in the 1970s, '80s and early '90s, a major army camp was established in the centre and driving into the town involved having a rifle pointed at your head until clearance was given.

Colour map 1, grid B4

County Tyrone

Beetling was a stage of linen production, consisting of pounding the fabric with wooden hammers, the 'beetles', until the weave was tightened and a smooth sheen gave the cloth its characteristic texture. Beetling started at this mill in the 1760s, and Wellbrook was the last mill still in operation when it finally closed down two centuries later. Working demonstrations are given in this National Trust property and exhibits explain the process. ■ *T86751735. July and August, Wednesday-Monday 1400-1800. April, May-June & September, Saturday and Sunday 1400-1800. £1.80. 4 miles west of Cookstown off A505.*

Wellbrook Beetling Mill

Beaghmore Stone Circle is the most interesting of the ancient sites in the area and a more worthwhile journey than the flat and boring B73 road that leads to the largely illegible **Ardboe High Cross** on the shore of Lough Neagh. At Beaghmore, on the southern foothills of the Sperrins, archaeologists in 1945 discovered under the peat a strange series of stone circles and stone alignments as well as cairns. The run-of-the-mill stone circle is relatively easy to explain but the complex arrangement of stones at Beaghmore has so far eluded interpretation, especially the presence of many hundreds of small stones inside one of the seven circles. ■ *Free access. Between Cookstown and Gortin, signposted off A505.*

Beaghmore Stone Circle & Tullaghoge Fort

The enjoyment of a visit to Tullaghoge Fort will be in proportion to the degree of historical imagination brought to bear on the place, because all that remains today is a hillock, albeit with fine views. Between the 11th and 16th centuries the chieftain of the O'Neills was inaugurated here as ruler of Tyrone, an area which then extended beyond the present county confines, until Mountjoy arrived here in the wake of Kinsale and symbolically destroyed the ancient coronation stone seat. More to the point, he also burnt the corn in the fields, which led to cannibalism in the ensuing famine that brought O'Neill to his knees. ■ *Off B162 2½ miles (four kilometres) southeast of Cookstown.*

Dungannon and the Clogher Valley

County Tyrone

Dungannon   Dungannon is a dreadfully dreary town, which sparked into life in 1968 when it became a focus of demonstration for the early civil rights movement in Northern Ireland. It was well know that Dungannon, like Derry, was gerrymandered to produce a permanent Unionist council even though the population was split evenly between Catholics and Protestants, and the first civil rights march in August '68 planned to end in Dungannon but was stopped by the RUC on the outskirts with dogs and 400 men. The only reason to pause here today is for a visit to the cross-community-inspired **Tyrone Crystal**, where guided tours of the factory workshop make it hard to resist to purchasing something afterwards from the shop. ■ *T87725335. Monday-Friday 0930-1530, and also Saturday between April and October. £2.*

Benburb   To the south of Dungannon, the graceful village of Benburb, with a population under 300, has a quiet charm of its own, and a scenic riverside walk along the Blackwater in **Benburb Valley Park** has a rich and surprising bonus when the ruins of **Benburb Castle** are seen towering over the river. Shane O'Neill fortified the cliff-top location in the 16th century but it was a planter, Sir Richard Wingfield, who built the castle at the beginning of the following century and it was another hundred years before a house was actually built inside its walls. In 1646 an overwhelming victory by the Irish under Owen Roe O'Neill took place near here by the river Blackwater and resulted in the death of over 3,000 Scottish soldiers, an event which did a great deal to convince Cromwell of the need thoroughly to subdue the Irish once and for all. The Ulster historian Jonathan Barden (see page 60) has described this Battle of Benburb as 'the greatest and most annihilating victory in arms the Irish ever won over the British'. A model layout of the battle can be seen, just south of the village, in the **Benburb Valley Heritage Centre**. The centre is set in a 19th-century weaving factory and if you have missed the other places in Tyrone devoted to the history of the Ulster linen industry then this is a place to catch up on the subject, and enjoy a cup of tea in the tea room. ■ *Valley Park: 10 Main St, T37548170, 1000-dusk. Heritage Centre: Milltown Rd. T37548170. Easter-September, 0900-1800. £2.*

Clogher Valley   The Blackwater River forms the Clogher Valley to the west of Benburb and the A4 travels west to Enniskillen. Along the way the **Grant Ancestral House** is yet another reminder of Ulster's connection with the US, this time through John Simpson, who was born here in 1738 and whose great-grandson distinguished himself in the American Civil War and became the 18th President, Ulysses Simpson Grant. The two rooms of Grant's small cottage have been restored in the style of the 19th century and there is also an outdoor display of Victorian farm equipment. ■ *Off A4, 13 miles (21 kilometres) west of Dungannon, T85557133. April to September, Monday-Saturday 1200-1800, Sunday 1400-1800. £1.50.*

The Carleton Trail   The novelist William Carleton (1794-1869) was born into a family of Irish-speaking peasants near Clogher, and his connection gives its name to this series of three walking and cycling routes, from 6 miles to 30 miles (10 kilometres to 48 kilometres), that all start and finish in Clogher and follow minor roads and forest paths. Details and a map are available from the tourist office in Dungannon and the cottage where Carleton lived for a while before leaving for Dublin can be seen in **Clogher**, a village on the A4 halfway between Dungannon and Enniskillen. Food and accommodation is available here or a little further west at **Fivemiletown** (five miles from Clogher) on the border with Fermanagh.

Essentials

AL *Glenavon House Hotel*, 52 Drum Rd, Cookstown, T86764949, F86764396. Has a **Sleeping** pool and gym, and a double room is £80. **A** *Corick House*, 20 Corrick Rd, Clogher, T85548216, F85549531. Offers the most comfortable accommodation in south Tyrone but there are also a couple of friendly B&Bs around Clogher. **A** *Four Ways Hotel*, Main St, Fivemiletown, T89521260. This friendly place has 10 rooms, and weekend and 3-day packages. **A** *Tullylagan Country House*, Tullylagan Rd, Cookstown, T86765100, F68761715. Quite good value and a decent restaurant. **B** *Killycolp House*, 21 Killycolp Rd, Cookstown, T86763577. Does B&B for £20 per person in a Georgian house with original features that help make this friendly place a terrific night's lodging. **C** *River Furey House*, 24 Monaghan Rd, Clogher, T82548843. B&B at around £32 for a double room. Can also provide an inexpensive dinner. **C** *Sperrin View*, 37 Ballynagilly Rd, Cookstown, T86763990. Inexpensive, but the two rooms share bathroom facilities. **C** *Timpany Manor*, 53 Ballagh Rd, Clogher, T/F85521285. B&B charges around £32 for a double room. **D** *Benburb Valley Hostel*, 89 Milltown Rd, Benburb, T37549752. Beside the Heritage Centre and can be reached by bus from Dungannon.

Dungannon Park, Moy Rd, T87727327. A caravan and camping park off the A29 less than two kilometres from Dungannon, with 12 tent pitches at £6 each. *Killymaddy Tourist Amenity Centre*, 190 Ballygawley Rd, west of Dungannon on the A4, T87767259. Has a dozen tent pitches for £6 each. *Clogher Valley County Caravan Park*, Fardross Forest, T85548932. Signposted a couple of kilometres west of Clogher on the A4 and accepts tents.

Benburb The *Cornmill Tea Room*, 89 Milltown Rd, T37549752, is in the Benburb Val- **Eating** ley Heritage Centre and opens from 1000 to 1700, Tuesday to Sunday, in the summer and Monday to Friday between October and Easter.

Clogher Pub food is available in *McSorley's Tavern*, 39 Main St, T85548673, and *Trident Inn*, 97 Main St, T85548924, while *Corrick House*, 20 Corrick Rd, T85548216, opens in the evening from 1730, Tuesday to Sunday, for dinner under £20.

Cookstown *Otter Lodge*, 26 Dungannon Rd, T86765427, has a riverbank setting and, while the restaurant only opens Friday and Saturday nights and Sunday for lunch, the wine bar opens daily for lighter meals from 1200 to around 2200. The *Tullylagan Country House Restaurant* is a few miles south of town and serves an evening meal in a pleasant dining room for under £20 every night and lunch every day except Saturday. Good value and tasty set lunches can be enjoyed in town at the *Courtyard*, 56 William St, T86765070, which closes at 1730 Monday to Saturday and a couple of hours earlier on Wednesday.

Fivemiletown Pub food and meals available at the *Four Ways Hotel*.

Bicycle *Clogher Valley County Caravan Park*, Fardross Forest, T85548932. Bike hire. **Transport** **Buses** Bus station: Molesworth St, Cookstown, T86766440. Handles *Ulsterbus* services to Belfast and Dungannon. Scotch St, Dungannon, T87722251. Buses connect Dungannon with Cookstown every 30 mins or so during the day and there are also services between Dungannon and Armagh, Monaghan and Dublin.

Banks Situated in James St and William St in Cookstown. **Communications** Post office: 49 **Directory** James St, Cookstown. 20 Market Square, Dungannon. **Tourist offices** 48 Molesworth St, Cookstown, T86766727, Apr-Sep, Mon-Fri 0900-1700, Sat 0900-1300. (T86762205 rest of the year.) Killymaddy Tourist Information, Ballygawley Rd, Dungannon, 7 miles (10 km) southwest of town on the A4, T87767259. Open all year.

County Tyrone

County Fermanagh

County Fermanagh

The county of Fermanagh is defined by its central lake, Lough Erne, which is 50 miles long (80 kilometres). The lake is now joined to the River Shannon by the Shannon to Erne Waterway, making it the longest navigable inland waterway in Europe. The lakeland setting invites water-based activities and this undoubtedly is Fermanagh's main attraction, but the county also has a small number of cultural sites that rank as some of the most significant and intriguing to be found anywhere in Ireland.

History

Fermanagh's natural isolation is part and parcel of the county's stubborn resistance to early Norman intrusions in the 13th century, so imagine how prolonged and complex must have been the process of transition from the pagan world of the Celts to Christianity. This may help explain the exceptional nature of the ancient stone monuments found north of Enniskillen. The Maguires came to rule Fermanagh from the early 14th century and before their land passed after two centuries to the O'Donnells one of their bards praised the family to high heaven:

> *Towards Ulster he [Brian Maguire] is the ocean's surface; towards*
> *Connacht a rampart of stone ...*
> *Fermanagh of the fortunate ramparts is the Adam's paradise of Inisfáil.*

After the defeat of Gaelic Ireland at Kinsale and the Flight of the Earls, Fermanagh eventually went the way of the rest of the island: planters took over Adam's paradise and built the castles still standing around Lough Erne. Enniskillen became a major military fortress and in the early 1920s the town and county were embroiled in conflict over Partition. The nationalist voice in this part of Ireland reached a climax in 1981 when the democratically elected Member of Parliament for Fermanagh and South Tyrone died in prison on a hunger strike.

Enniskillen

Colour map 1, grid B2 & 3 Another predominantly Catholic border town, Enniskillen doesn't have the old-world charm of Derry but it's a lively enough place, with lots of development going on and a blossoming nightlife. The main reason to spend any time here is as a base for exploring the area or taking off on a boat trip around Lough Erne.

Enniskillen Castle This is the chief tourist attraction of the town: a beautiful old building not used particularly effectively but worth a wander around. The castle has certainly seen some bloodshed over the years; the 16th century was probably its worst time: it changed hands from its original builders, the Maguires, to the O'Neill's (*not* by a negotiated sale), then later the same century the English took it off the O'Neills – poetic justice you might say. The only original 15th century part of the building is the lower storey of the keep – now the regimental museum full of polished brass and pride. On the river side of the complex is the Watergate, a 17th-century addition with no gate in it. The heritage centre is housed in buildings from around the 18th century and holds assorted rural paraphernalia, two pretty naff videos about the area and changing

The Hunger Strike

The origins of the hunger strike in Ireland are not clear and, while the suffragettes certainly offered an example to follow, the tactic has also been traced back to an early Irish tradition of fasting before an enemy in order to shame him for his misdeeds. Thomas Ashe was the first hunger strike to die, in 1917, protesting at conditions in Dublin's Mountjoy jail and in 1920 Terence MacSwiney, the mayor of Cork, and two others died in London prisons. In Northern Ireland the tactic developed out of the withdrawal of 'special category' status in 1976 which denied political status to republican prisoners. A 'dirty protest' campaign began, with prisoners refusing to clean out their cells, and in May 1981 a hunger strike began. The first hunger striker was Bobby Sands, a Member of Parliament for Tyrone and Fermanagh, but that cut little ice with Thatcher's government and he died in due course followed by ten more men before the strike was called off in

exhibitions. ■ *Castle Barracks, T66325000. Monday 1400-1700, Tuesday-Friday 1000-1700, Saturday and Sunday 1400-1700. October to April closed Saturday and Sunday; May and June closed Sunday. IR£2.*

Buttermarket The other place for a good wander around, this is now a craft village full of nice things to buy, especially the hand-painted furniture and copies of the White Island stone figures, although you'd need a big rucksack to carry one of those away. ■ *Monday-Saturday 0930-1730. Coffee shop, craft workshops, gallery, craft shop, yoga studio.*

Sleeping
■ *on map*
Price codes:
see inside front cover

AL *Fort Lodge Hotel*, 72 Forthill St, T66323275, F66320275. A little way out of town this hotel is beside Forthill park, and done out in a kind of Baronial Hall style. It's a traditional pub with lunchtime carvery, comfortable bar and lots of travelling salesmen. **AL** *Killyhevlin Hotel*, Dublin Rd, T66323481, F66324726. At the very highest end of

County Fermanagh

Enniskillen Castle

this price bracket, this is definitely the nicest place to stay in Enniskillen. Beside Lough Erne with truly stunning views (ask for a room at the back but be aware there's a £10 supplement for the view), lovely gardens to walk in and spacious rooms it's a little holiday all on its own. You can tie your boat up at the jetty or rent one of the self-catering bungalows for a week for £395 (less in the off-peak season). **B** *Belmore Court Motel*, Tempo Rd, T66326633, F66326326. Self-catering rooms, prices based on room size, not.the number of people staying, so this could work out at the very lowest end of this price bracket. Modern, nice rooms. **B** *Dromard House B&B*, Tamlaght, T66387250. 2 miles out of town in converted stable loft in farmhouse. Close to scenic walks. Good value. **B** *Mountview*, 61 Irvinestown Rd, T66323147, pretty house and gardens close to town, snooker room, evening meal option. **B** *Railway Hotel*, 34 Forthill St, T66322084, F66327480. Busy, small hotel, which has been here for 150 years. Music at weekends. **D** *Lakeland Canoe Centre*, Castle Island, T66324250. Very basic dormitory accommodation. Camping available. Free ferry service to island 0800-2400.

Eating
● *on map*
Price codes:
see inside front cover

While there are any number of places open for lunch in town, breakfast and dinner can be a little more tricky. The *Killyhevlin* has a set evening meal, which is really quite good: three courses £15, two for £12. Ask for a window seat. The *Fort Lodge* has an à la carte menu 7 days. Last orders at both hotels are 2130. The *Railway Hotel* does bar food till 2130 in a fairly lively atmosphere. If you want classy food, there is *Oscar's* Belmore St, T66327037, open 7 days till 2300 with lots of recommendations to its name, some interesting items on the menu and attractive surroundings. Dinner will cost around £15 plus and there are vegetarian choices. *Saddlers* at 66 Belmore St, T66327432 does pub food and has an à la carte menu till 2245, 7 days, mostly seafood with several vegetarian choices. Beyond these your evening options are to eat early, try pub food or eat Chinese or Indian food. *Kamal Mahal's*, 1 Water St, T66325045, is open till midnight Wednesday-Monday and serves good Indian food in attractive surroundings. *Franco's Pizzeria*, Queen Elizabeth Rd, T66324424, is very popular, opens 7 days till 2200 and serves much more than pizza – shark and veal is also on the extensive menu. If you eat earlier the *Crow's Nest*, High St, T66325252, is a pub that has

Enniskillen

To airport, Castle Archdale & Kesh (B82)
To Irvinestown, Omagh & Londonderry (A32)

River Erne
Kestrel Waterbus
Cherry Island
Erne Hospital
Brook Park
Queen St
The Brook
Library
St Macartin's Cathedral
Head St
Ann St
Darling St
Methodist Church
St Michael's RC
Castle & Museums
Buttermarket
Coles Monumento
FORTHILL
Town Hall
War Memorial
Paget Lane
E Bridge St
Belmore St
Dunnes Stores
Castle Island
Wellington Rd
Fermanagh Lakeland Forum
River Erne
Erneside Shopping Centre
Irvinestown Rd
Hollyhill Link Rd
Forthill St
Tempo Rd
Dublin Rd

To Portora Royal School, Belleek, Ballyshannon & Donegal (A46)
To Florence Court, Marble Arch Caves & Sligo (A4)
To Killyhevlin Hotel, Castle Coole (NT), Ardhowen Theatre, Armagh, Belfast & Dublin (A4)
To Tempo (B80)
To golf club

N

0 yards   200
0 metres   200

■ **Sleeping**
1 Belmore Court Motel
2 Fortlodge
3 Lakeland Canoe Centre
4 Railway

● **Eating & drinking**
1 Barbizon Café
2 Blake's of the Hollow
3 Crow's Nest
4 Franco's Pizzeria
5 Kamal Mahal
6 Melvin House & Pat's Bar
7 Mulligan's
8 Oscar's
9 Rebecca's
10 Saddler's
11 Vintage

© Crown Copyright

seriously gone into pub food with a huge menu of snacks and much more substantial dishes and serves food 6 days till 2100, 1430 Sundays. *Mulligan's*, 33 Darling St, T66322059 is a very renovated sort of old pub with stained glass, tiled floors, cosy nooks and a bar-food menu, with one room dedicated to pub-style dining. It serves moderately interesting food 7 days till 2130. You might want to try the Irish stew with Bushmills. Lastly there's *Melvin House Restaurant*, over *Pat's Bar* in Townhall St, T66322040 doing grills and things with chips with main courses around £5-£7. Set lunch on Sunday is £8.

At lunchtime there are so many places to choose from that it's difficult to know where to start. All the pubs already mentioned do pub food and in addition there is a string of good lunchtime stops along Townhall and East Bridge St all doing filled potatoes, chips and things, sandwiches and more substantial fare. You could also try *Rebecca's* in the Buttermarket, the *Bistro* in the shopping centre, or *Barbizon* on the corner of East Bridge St, which, incidentally, is the only place in town to open for breakfast before 0900. Quite new is Vintage, Townhall St, which is a trendy theme pub with open fires and tiled floors but nicely done and a very good lunchtime menu where three courses will set you back £8.

There are some good pubs in Enniskillen. *Blake's of the Hollow* in Church St is very old and is divided up into little private rooms. At the back is a pool table and there is music on Thursdays. The *Crow's Nest* (see 'Eating', page 658) is a very trendy place at night and has a nightclub, *Thatch*, Wednesday, Friday, Saturday and Sunday as well as live music in the bars every night and weekend afternoons in summer. The *Vintage* (see 'Eating', page 658) has a nightclub – *Merlin's* – open Wednesday, Saturday and Sunday. Other pubs have occasional music sessions – check for notices. In addition to pubs and music there is the *Ardhowen Theatre*, Dublin Rd, T66325440, where there are performances of music and theatre and a good daytime café.
Pubs & music

Boat hire *Erne Tours*, Round 'O' Jetty, Brook Park, Belleek Rd: hire the Kestrel to Devenish Island (1hr 45 mins), or self-drive boats with outboard per day. T66322882. **Bowling** *Outdoor bowls*, Celtic Park Dublin Rd, May to September, 1200-1700. £2. *Castle Entertainment Centre*, T66324172. **Fishing** *Erincurragh Cruising*, Blaney, T66641507. *Fermanagh Tourist Information Centre*, Wellington Rd, T66323110. *Home, Field and Stream*, 18 Church St, T66322114. **Leisure centre** *Lakeland Forum*, T66324121.
Sport

Air St Angelo Airport, Trory, T66325050. 4 miles north of Enniskillen and handles charter flights in and out of Zurich (*Brymon Airways*) and Jersey (*Crossair*). It also offers pleasure flights of the area and a flight training school. **Bicycle** *Lakeland Canoe Centre*, Castle Island, T66324250. Bike hire. **Bus** Bus station: Wellington Rd, T66322633, opposite the tourist office. It handles local buses to small villages in the area as well as regular services to Belfast, Derry, Omagh, Dungannon, Cork, Sligo, and the *Bus Éireann* Dublin to Donegal bus stops here. For the cross-border buses you can pay in either currency. **Car hire** *Lochside Garages*, Tempo Rd, T66324366. *Cyril Treacy*, 115 Sligo Rd, T66323610. **Taxis** *Belcoo Taxis*, T66386597. *Call-a-Cab*, T66324848. *Diamond Taxis*, T0800-123444.
Transport

Banks *Bank of Ireland*, Townhall St. *First Trust*, East Bridge St. *Northern Bank*, Townhall St. *Ulster Bank*, Darling St. **Library** Halls Lane, T66322886. **Communications** Post office: East Bridge St. **Tourist office** Wellington Rd, T66323110. Oct-Apr 0900-1700; May-Jun and Sep 0900-1730; Jul-Aug 0900-1900.
Directory

County Fermanagh

Around Enniskillen

Castle Coole Built in the late 18th century at massive expense by the 1st Earl of Belmore, who ruined himself in the process, this is said to be the finest neoclassical mansion in Ireland. It certainly cost enough and created lots of employment in the area for the many stonemasons, plasterers, carpenters and other craftsmen brought to the place to build it over two decades from 1789. Levelling the site took 18 months, while shipping the Portland stone for its exterior involved building a quay at Ballyshannon, chartering the brig *Martha*, and 10 miles of bullock carting. By 1791 there were 25 stone cutters, 26 masons, 10 stone sawyers, 17 carpenters and 83 labourers on the site, costing a total of £159.13s in wages for that year.

The house is a great day out, especially on a rainy day when its chilly interior matches its name perfectly. It is difficult to imagine the Belmore children having a good romp round this place. It was designed by James Wyatt, a contemporary of Gandon who designed many of the big houses of the Irish countryside. The main rooms are all pomp and austerity, the later 19th-century furniture adding a lumpiness to the fine lines of the 18th-century building, but that's what happens when dad blows everything he has on the building and you have to wait a generation to put the furniture in. ■ *On A4, one mile east of Enniskillen, T66322690. May-August, daily except Thursdays 1300-1800; April and September, Saturday and Sunday 1300-1800; Easter, daily 1300-1800. £2.80. Guided tour only.*

Florence Court What would the landed gentry of Northern Ireland do without the National Trust? They bought this pile in 1950 from the Coles, Earls of Enniskillen. The original building predates Castle Coole by 30 years; the wings are later additions by later generations of Coles. The place was damaged by fire in 1955 but has been partly restored. It is smaller and homelier, if such a word can be applied to these huge places, than Castle Coole. There is a walled garden and walks around the 200-year-old oakwoods. ■ *Southwest of Enniskillen on A4, then A32, eight miles (13 kilometres), T66348249. House: May to August, daily 1300-1800, except Tuesdays; April and September, Saturday, Sunday, bank holidays 1300-1800; October to March, closed. Last admission 1715. £2.80. Gardens: April to September 1000-1900; October to March, 1000-1600. Car £2. Tearoom.*

Marble Arch Caves This is a very busy commercial enterprise and is best booked well in advance; you should be prepared for the 1-hour guided tour to be spent in a large company. The tour starts off with a boat trip underground and then on foot past stalactites and stalagmites and underground waterfalls. A good rainy day activity and great fun for children. ■ *Off A4, then A32, 12 miles southwest of Enniskillen, T66348963. Mid-March to September, 1000-1600 (last tour). £5. Café, exhibition, shop.*

Around Lower Lough Erne

Colour map 1, grid B2

A tour around Lower Lough Erne is a journey through cultural history from the prehistoric, Celtic, Iron Age, which began roughly around 500BCE, through the transition to Christianity a millennium later and down the ensuing centuries to the Plantation of Ulster and the 1641 uprising. The journey is recorded through a series of remarkable stone monuments – pagan and semi-pagan deities, early Christian images, round towers, and castles – relieved by a healthy small dose of 21st-century consumerism at the Belleek pottery works.

Cruising through Ireland

With the restoration of the Ballinamore-Ballyconnell Canal in Leitrim, a 19th-century disaster which operated for nine years and was used in all that time by eight boats, a waterway route has opened up from Belleek at the far end of Lough Erne to the mouth of the River Shannon in County Kerry/ Clare in the south, and to Dublin via the Grand Canal in the east. The route can encompass weeks of pottering about Lough Erne and the islands, side routes and jetties along its banks, or it can steam straight through to the Woodford River which is the start of the Shannon-Erne waterway. The river is navigable to Ballyconnell, where it joins the 62.5 km canal and lough stretches with their 34 stone bridges and 16 smart card-operated locks. From there the route passes by river, canal and lough to Leitrim, where it joins the Shannon. At Shannon Harbour the river links up with the Grand Canal, and it is possible to motor all the way to Dublin along the canal.

There are cruiser and canal boat hire companies all along the waterways. Many of them will arrange one-way hires, so that you do not have to return to your starting point, and all of them have fairly luxurious bases with restaurants, pools and other facilities. The following list covers the Shannon-Erne, section but boats from some of these operators can be taken on to the Grand Canal. Prices vary according to status and number of berths, but on average a 4-6 berth cabin cruiser costs around £900 per week in the high season, around £700 in spring or autumn.

Carrick Craft, The Marina, Carrick-on-Shannon, Co. Leitrim, T078-20236. F068-21336. One way hires.
Celtic Canal Cruisers, Tullamore, Co. Offaly, T0506-2186, F0506-51266.
Emerald Star Line, 47, Dawson St, Dublin 2, T01-679-8166. One way hire.
Erne-Shannon Link Hire, Drumetta, Derrylin, Co. Fermanagh, T03657-48712, F03657-48493. Hire out barges from lock no. 1 on the Shannon-Erne waterway.
Manor House Marine, Lough Erne, Killadeas, Co. Fermanagh, T03656-28100, F03656-28000. Huge marina with lots of resort facilities and up to 8-berth boats for hire.
Riversdale Barge Holidays, Ballinamore, Co. Leitrim, T078-44122, F078-44813. Luxury canal barges with wood burning stoves, lots of facilities at the site.
Shannon Castle Line, Dolphin Works, Ringsend, Dublin 4, T01-6600964, F01-6689091.
Tara Cruisers Ltd, Carrick-on-Shannon, Co. Leitrim, T078-21369, F078-21542. One way hire in off season.
Shannon-Erne Waterway Holidays, Blaney, Enniskillen, Co. Fermanagh, T01365-641507. One way hire.

County Fermanagh

The following circular route follows the A32 north of Enniskillen and proceeds along the east shore of Lower Lough Erne on the B82 to the village of Kesh and Boa Island. The A47 then goes along the northern shore to Belleek, where the A46 can be picked up for the return to Enniskillen back down the west side of the lough.

Sometimes it seems that round towers are two a penny in Ireland, but the one on Devenish Island (a 10-minute ferry ride from the mainland) is a particularly fine example and can be climbed right to the top. The doorway is the customary 10 feet (three metres) above ground level, and this common feature led to the conjecture that round towers were built as defensive structures. The old Irish name for the towers (*cloig theach*) means simply 'bell house' and the height of the doorway may have had more to do with preserving the physical integrity of the building, research having shown the foundations to be often quite shallow for a structure typically five storeys high. The mystery of the round towers is why builders chose to erect such tall structures beside typically

Devenish Island

small churches. Whatever the reason, they were built across Ireland between the late 10th and 13th centuries, and the example on Devenish can be partly dated to the 12th century because of the Romanesque sculptural decorations near its top.

Other sites and sights on the island are the ruins of the church and abbey, a High Cross, old gravestones, and a small museum. ■ *April to September, Tuesday to Saturday 1000-1800, Sunday 1400-1900. £2.25. Admission to round tower is 75p. Ferry departs from Trory Point, four miles (seven kilometres) from Enniskillen and signposted off the A32.*

Killadeas Churchyard The establishment of Christianity in the northwest of Ireland is marked with a series of carved crosses and slabs thought by some to be associated with a particular outside impetus, perhaps from Scotland. Whatever the explanation, one of the most curious is the stone carving that lies in the graveyard of a church a few miles outside Enniskillen. One side of the rectangular slab bears the traditional image of a bishop with a bell and crozier, but the other side bears a startling image of a face that is anything but conventional and its positively pagan appearance contrasts dramatically with the ecclesiastical form. It looks as though the face was carved before the bishop, but both are impossible to date with any certainty. Showing clear signs of having been trimmed at probably a later date, the stone is thought to have been carved some time between 800 and 1000CE, a time when Christianity was still having to come to terms with pagan Ireland. ■ *To reach the churchyard take the B82 road along the eastern side of the lough and the church is on the left a short way after the turn-off for the Manor House Country Hotel.*

Castle Archdale Country Park This park, containing a marina from which ferries depart, was a military base during the Second World War. There is a Centre with a tea room, nature trail, activities and an exhibition on the Battle of the Atlantic. ■ *10 miles (16 kilometres) from Enniskillen on the B82 Kesh Rd, T68621588. July and August, Tuesday-Sunday 1100-1900; Easter-June, Sunday 1200-1600.*

White Island The earliest references to a stone church in Ireland dates from CE788, and while the remains of the church on White Island are from the 12th century there is archaeological evidence of an earlier wooden structure, which may well be contemporaneous with the curious stone figures built into the interior north wall. They are thought to date from the 9th or 8th century, compelling evidence of White Island as one of Ireland's earliest Christian sites and lending support to one theory that the sculptured figures represent pilgrims and/or

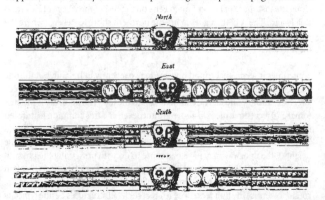

Devenish Tower carvings, by George Petrie

Belleek picnic site

The views over the lough are tremendous, and a car is needed to complete the 11-kilometre (seven-mile) route through **Lough Navar Forest** to the viewpoint, but bring provisions for a picnic with a panorama. ■ Daily 1000-dusk. Car £2.50. Signposted off A46 between Belleek and Tully Castle.

clerics. When you see the figures you may feel this is too prosaic an explanation, for there is something mysterious and even haunting about these large, grimacing faces, and presumably there was some iconographic significance to their belongings: bell, a staff, sword, shield, pouch, and small griffin-like animals. One of the figures is also a *sheela-na-gig* (see page 394). ■ *The 15-minute ferry journey to White Island departs from Castle Archdale marina (in the Castle Archdale Country Park, see page 662) departing every hour on the hour for £3. T68621333. July and August, daily, 1100-1800; April, May and June, Sunday 1400-1800; Easter weekend, 1100-1800.*

Boa Island Quite extraordinary is one of the two stone figures found on Boa Island at the northern tip of the lough. It is a Janus idol comprising two figures joined by their backs, with interwoven hair and sharing a belt; they have a stiff posture with arms crossed, bearded triangular faces and strange penetrating eyes that evoke Celtic magic in a startling manner. It has been compared with the Tandragee Idol, now resting in Armagh Cathedral (see page 636), because of a supposedly shared sense of pagan inhumanity, but this could be disputed. The Tandragee figure is undoubtedly menacing, and if you come to Boa thinking of pagan gods as fearsome and a little barbaric then this Janus figure may seem similar in spirit; shake off these associations, however, and the face of the Boa idol can be read as genial and even a little mischievous. The mystery of interpretation is deepened when the context is taken into account: the idol is situated in an early Christian burial ground, as is the other two-sided figure in Killadeas Church, which also shows sign of being trimmed from a larger piece of stone. Virtually nothing is known about how the transition from paganism to Christianity was experienced in Ireland but these stone figures provide a fascinating and tantalizing glimpse of the interface between the two belief systems.

The other figure on Boa is known as the Lustymore or Lusty Man idol since it was brought here from nearby Lusty Beg Island. It is not as intriguing, and while the squatting posture has been likened to *sheila-na-gig* figures this is mostly conjecture. ■ *Caldragh cemetery at the west end of Boa Island connected by a bridge and signposted off the A47.*

Castle Caldwell Forest Park Within two decades of the defeat of the Irish at Kinsale even wild Fermanagh was ripe for plantations, and Castle Caldwell was one of the early castles built on the shores of the lough. The crumbling ruins that stand today give little indication of how impressive it once looked and when Arthur Young toured Ireland in 1776 the castle was already over 150 years old and enhanced by the natural beauty of the setting: 'the promontories of thick wood, which shoot into Lough Earne, under the shade of a great ridge of mountains' led him to exclaim that 'nothing can be more beautiful than the approach to Castle Caldwell'. The grounds are now a wildlife reserve with shore walks and leaflets on trails can be picked up at the small centre during the summer. ■ *On A47 four miles (seven kilometres) east of Belleek, T68631253. Free access 24 hours.*

County Fermanagh

Belleek A quiet little village on the shores of Lough Erne – looking a little bit like it has just emerged from the twilight zone, with burnt-out buildings, abandoned border crossings and huge observation posts badly disguised on the hillsides above – Belleek is home to the **Belleek Pottery Works**, T68658501. There is a good tour of the factory where you can see the parian china being made, a video about the history of the place and lots of display cabinets showing the evolution of the style of the china. The pottery is highly burnished, hand-made and delicate: not much use for anything except admiring but it sells well, particularly the clover leaf design. This is the best place to buy some if you want a piece. All seconds are smashed rather than allowed to lower the standard of the work. ■ *T68659300. April, June and September, Monday-Saturday 0900-1800, Sunday 1400-1800; October, Monday-Saturday 0900-1730, Sunday 1400-1800; November to March, Monday-Friday 0900-1730; July and August, Monday-Friday 0900-2000, Saturday 1000-1800, Sunday 1100-2000.*

Also in Belleek is the **Explore Erne** exhibition in the little tourist office, just outside the village. It has information on the waterway and its history. ■ *T68658866. March to October daily.*

Tully Castle Built in the early 17th century for Sir John Hume, a Scottish planter, Tully Castle had a short life as a residence: in the 1641 uprising the Maguires laid siege to it. Hume surrendered upon a promise of being spared, but this proved of little worth to all the others who had fled here for safekeeping for they were slaughtered and the castle set alight. The castle and its formal garden have now been restored and there is a small visitor's centre, but if you only have time for one castle visit then consider instead a visit to the ruins of Monea Castle (see below). ■ *April to September, Tuesday-Saturday 1000-1900, Sunday 1400-1900. £1.*

Monea Castle This castle was built around the same time as Tully and for another Scottish planter, Malcolm Hamilton, and although it has not been restored the ruins and the setting are more successful in evoking the past, and a Scottish past at that, than Tully. Four storeys high and with imposing towers there is little doubt that this castle was built with defence in mind. In 1641 it did fall for a short while to the insurgents but remained a home until well into the 18th century. The ruins slumber on. ■ *On B81 seven miles (11 kilometres) northwest of Enniskillen. Free access 24 hours.*

Essentials

Sleeping **AL** *Hotel Carlton*, 2 Main St, Belleek, T68658282. Modern hotel situated beside the lough with pleasant big rooms and friendly attention from staff. Nice grounds, good breakfasts but don't expect an early start. **A** *The Courtyard*, Lusty Beg Island, T68632032, F68632033. Has its own car ferry from the pier on Boa island, for transport to this private island with B&B single/doubles for £45/£65, restaurant and bar, indoor pool, sauna, tennis, cycling and canoeing. **B** *The Cedars*, 301 Killadeas Rd, Castle Archdale, T/F68621493. A smart country house guesthouse with a bar and small restaurant area serving high tea and evening meals. **B** *The Fiddlestone*, 15-17 Main St, Belleek, T68658008. Traditional Irish pub with nice atmosphere and a bar close at hand. **B** *Tudor Farm Country House*, 619 Boa Island Rd, T/F68631943, has a scenic location on the shores of the lough and its own watersports available. **C** *Willowdale*, Drumbarna, T68631596. A B&B on the road between Kesh and Lisnarick and with views of the lough from the bedrooms. **D** *Castle Archdale Youth Hostel*, Castle Archdale Country Park, T/F68628118. Occupies a wing of an old courtyard complex with 2 main dormitories and 2 family rooms.

Camping *Blaney Caravan & Camping Park*, on the A46 at Blaney and adjacent to the service station, T68641634. Open all year but has only 10 pitches for tents, all at £6. *Castle Archdale Caravan Park*, T68621333. Charges £10 for one of its 50 tent pitches. *Clareview House Caravan Park*, 89 Crevenish Rd, T68631588. 12 tent pitches, £3.50 each. *Lakeland Caravan Park*, Boa Island Rd, Drumrush, T68631578. Tent pitch £10. *Tir Navar Holiday Village*, Creamery St, Derrygonnelly, T68641673, has 10 pitches at £4, and for an extra charge it is possible to use the kitchen facilities that are on site. *Lough Melvin Holiday Centre*, Main St, Garrison, T68658142. Run by Fermanagh District Council and has plenty of tent pitches for £6.

Self-catering *Carlton Cottages*, right on the shores of the lough, Belleek, T68658947. A cottage with 3 double bedrooms costs £380 per week in the high season and includes a rowing boat. *Rathmore Cottages*, Belleek, T68658947. Lets cottages by the week for £495 for a cottage sleeping 5. Weekend lettings in the off season.

Eating

Belleek The *Hotel Carlton* has a restaurant and does pub food with lots of spicy options and a couple of vegetarian choices. The set menu is £18.95 and fairly traditional and the à la carte works out around £20 for 3 courses. The *Fiddlestone* and *McMorrow's* do bar food aimed at the passing tourists and there is a fast-food joint and the *Thatch Coffee Shop* doing cakes and soup. Vegetarians could try the *Black Cat*, which has several good vegetarian choices.

Kesh *Lusty Beg Island Restaurant*, Lusty Beg Island, T68631342. Opens daily in the evening from 1830 to 2130 and there is also a tea room open from 0900 in the summer. *Drumrush Lodge*, Boa Island Rd, Kesh, T68631578, opens daily in the summer for affordable lunches and dinners and *Willow Pattern Pantry*, Clareview House, Crevenish Rd, Kesh, T68631012, opens daily except Sunday for soups, stews and homebakes. There are other eating possibilities along Main St in Kesh including pub food at the *May Fly* at No 14.

Sport

Bicycle hire, Canoeing and Ponytrekking *Castle Archdale Country Park*, T68621588. **Watersports** *Boa Island Activity Centre*, Tudor Farm, Boa Island Rd, T68631943. *Drumrush Watersports Centre*, Lakeland Caravan Park, Boa Island Rd, T68631943.

Transport

Buses *Ulsterbus* No 194 Enniskillen to Pettigo via Irvinestown and Kesh, daily. Nos 59 and 59A Enniskillen to Derrygonnelly via Monea and Blaney, Monday to Saturday. No 64 Enniskillen to Belleek via Garrison, Monday to Friday and Sunday; on Thursday travels on to Bundoran. No 261 Belfast to Bundoran via Enniskillen and Belleek, daily. No 99 Enniskillen to Bundoran via Blaney and Belleek, daily. T66322633.

Directory

Craft courses in painting, crafts, sculpture, pottery, cooking, spinning and weaving: *Ardress Craft Centre*, Ardress House, Kesh, T68631267. £25 a day including lunch or £60 full board.

County Fermanagh

Background

18

Background

History

Ten thousand years ago, after the ice caps had melted and Ireland was becoming an island, nomadic people from Europe came to the northwest fringes of the continent bearing flint instruments and very little else. Before these early people arrived the land was populated by the giant Irish deer with ten-foot antlers, hairy mammoths and hyenas. The physical landscape was shaped millions of years earlier when mountains formed in the wake of cooling lava, and a mere 200,000 years ago the famous valleys of Killarney were created by shifting blocks of ice.

Prehistory

Around 4000BCE people arrived with farming skills, and the first settled communities arose, as revealed in north Mayo at Céide Fields, giving rise, in the due course of centuries, to megalithic stone tombs which survive to this day. Court-tombs are probably the earliest, dating as far back as 3500BCE and characterised by an open space or court in front of the tomb, flanked by standing stones.

Passage-tombs are similar in that they are also covered by a stone mound but are more interesting to visit, not least because of the geometrical motifs inscribed on the stones, and the best places to see them are at Carrowkeel, Newgrange and Knowth. Equally dramatic are the portal-tombs or dolmens (from a Breton word meaning a 'stone table'), popularly known as Druids' altars, composed of three, or more, massive standing stones supporting one large capstone which can weigh up to 100 tons. They were built somewhere around 3000-2000BCE.

Newgrange, dating from around 2500BCE, stands as testimony to the astonishing engineering skills possessed by these people, and the National Museum in Dublin has dazzling displays of their achievements working with gold and silver and later, bronze.

The Bronze Age, 2000-500BCE, gets its name from the main material used during a period which also made use of copper and gold, and a major site from this period is the stone circle at Lough Gur. Other stone circles belong to the ensuing Iron Age, built by a people who never developed an alphabet beyond the characters known as Ogham.

The Celts

The Iron Age Celts are best viewed as a linguistic group, an offshoot of the Indo-European family, which emerged around 2000BCE and spread from Turkey in the east to Ireland in the west. By 100BCE they were established in Ireland and, though finally absorbed by the Roman empire, remnants of Celtic culture survive in the language and lore of the Scots, Welsh, Bretons and Irish.

In the late 1990s Simon James, a scholar at the British Museum (see page 63), attacked the notion that the Celts as a uniform people ever existed, and he claimed that the idea they were somehow the first nation to emerge north of the Alps is a myth born of Celtomania. His debunking thesis is a useful corrective to the excessive claims of born-again Celtomaniacs, who would have us believe they are part of a long-repressed culture. Nevertheless, 'Celtic Ireland' remains a useful shorthand term for the pre-Christian period, and there are intriguing cultural overlaps between the Celts and those who followed them.

The Celtic calendar was premised on the duality of dark and light – they counted nights rather than days – and great significance was attached to those pivotal moments when the two came together. Sunrise and sunset were such moments,

---

Ice caps melted, sea levels rose, and Ireland detached itself from Britain, but it took a longer time for the land joining Britain with Europe to be submerged. This is why snakes that had reached Britain on land could not travel further west to the island of Ireland, though the idea that St Patrick banished them is part of the Irish ABC.

Background

'A land of fog and gloom ... Beyond it lies the Sea of Death, where Hell begins.'

Homer's Iliad describes the far northwest of Europe

while the two annual equinoxes – when day and night were momentarily balanced by the sun crossing the celestial equator – were profoundly magical in their import. The supernatural was most alive at these critical times and paganism was in awe of this cosmic balancing act. Julius Ceasar wrote of the celts in his History of the Gallic Wars '...they commit to memory immense (etc.).'

The summer and winter solstices, when the sun is furthest away from the equator, were also powerful and dangerous moments in time. There were four great pagan festivals when Celts celebrated the turning points between the seasons. Most is known about Lughnasa, celebrated at the beginning of August and dedicated to the god Lug. Much of what we know about pagan Celtic society in Ireland is due – ironically – to the earnest chronicalling efforts of early Christian monks.

Monasticism

The Romans never settled in Ireland, but men from Ireland served with Roman legions, and it was through the Romans that Christianity arrived on the island. The first bishop was appointed in 431 (the first *bona fide* date in Irish history) but it was the missionary, Patrick who is now best associated with early Christian Ireland. Notwithstanding his iconic Irishness, Patrick first arrived as a captured slave from Britain and returned years later as a proselytising missionary, establishing his main church in Armagh.

Christianity brought with it a world of learning and literacy as well as technological innovations like the mouldboard plough and the horizontal mill. Monastic organizations also allowed for organized farming, and the overall effect of these influences from 'across the water' was an increase in population which is associated with the 45,000 ring-forts that were built across Ireland during this era.

From the sixth to eighth centuries, when the rest of Europe was in the doldrums after the collapse of the Roman empire, Ireland's monasteries continued to burn the light of culture and learning. Irish monks travelled throughout Europe, rekindling some of the intellectual embers endangered by barbarism, and the survival of wonderful illuminated manuscripts provides eloquent testimony to their achievement.

Irish monasticism, associated above all with the great figure of Colum Cille, gave the Irish church a unique idiom through its ability to fuse the sacred with the profane, recording pagan myths and soothing the revolutionary transition from a pagan world of magic and mysticism with a degree of sympathy that seems difficult to comprehend today. What explanation, other than a sensibility capable of being excited by paganism, accounts for Irish monks recording and preserving the pagan vernacular literature of their island? The stories and chronicles that they recorded are the primary source materials for the contemporary study of early Irish history, and it is thanks to them that we know the tales of Cuchulainn and the other Irish heroes and heroines.

Irish monasticism was also enriched by an ascetic Coptic strain, more akin to the eastern church than Rome, which incorporated a tradition of holy people seeking out secluded and remote hermitages – a *fuga mundi* or 'flight from the world' – which often became the seedbeds of monastic communities. This is the origin of Glendalough and the fastness of Skellig Michael – an 800-ft rock eight miles off the remote Kerry coast – two holy sites which now attract tourist pilgrims in greater numbers than they ever did in their own austere times.

The Vikings

Norse Viking invaders first raided the monasteries of Ireland in the late eighth century, and in the following century Irish annals report sightings of vast fleets of ships appearing on the Boyne and the Liffey. The Danes came in their wake, and fierce fighting developed between the invaders and between them and the Irish. Settlements and intermarriage with the Irish gave rise to coastal communities that would evolve into the towns of Dublin, Wexford, Waterford, Cork and Limerick. In 917 the king of Leinster was defeated by the Norse, commanded by Sitric, who went on to establish a strong kingdom in Dublin. Raiding parties by the Norse into the Irish interior is one plausible explanation for the building of defensive round towers near monasteries, for this is when many of them were built.

The Vikings kept paganism alive and healthy in Ireland until around the 11th century, a period which saw their defeat by the Irish under Brian Bóruma (Brian Boru) at the momentous battle of Clontarf in 1014. Brian Bóruma was killed at Clontarf and his body carried in state to Armagh, then the ecclesiastical capital of Ireland, the significance of this epic battle being recorded in both Irish annals and Icelandic sagas.

The coming of the Normans

After the death of Brian Bóruma, Ireland was torn apart by internecine dynastic wars that petered out when Rory O'Connor was accepted as king of all Ireland in the middle of the 12th century. Then in August 1167 one of his erstwhile rivals, Dermot MacMurrough, arrived home from exile, and with the help of Welsh soldiers set about reclaiming his kingdom. MacMurrough had earlier sought out the Norman King Henry II of England, and with promises of land had procured his support for an invasion of Ireland. The event proved to be traumatically momentous, for MacMurrough's support included the Earl of Pembroke, better known as Strongbow; when the Earl arrived in 1170 the stage was set for 800 years of foreign rule and conflict which still bedevils politics and peace in Northern Ireland. With the arrival of these French-speaking Normans, mostly from South Wales, Irish history would never be the same again.

Strongbow brought a professional army of 1000 men and their menacing longbows, and he first captured Waterford and then Dublin. Henry II, alarmed that this rich new conquest might slip from his personal grasp, began assembling his own fleet for an invasion. He landed in 1171 near Waterford with a fleet of 400 ships and as many as 4000 men. In the course of the 13th century the Normans began to build their great stone castles, and those at Kilkenny, Carrickfergus and Trim give some idea of the awe they must have instilled in the minds of the wood-building Gaels.

Conquered, not colonised

Henry II secured Waterford, Wexford and Dublin, and the Irish nobility submitted to his rule. Ireland had been conquered, and after a visit to Lismore the acquiescence of the Irish bishops was obtained, but the country was not yet colonised in any systematic kind of way. Before leaving Ireland, Henry gave the central swathe of the country from the Shannon to the Boyne to the English family of Hugh de Lacy who, together with Strongbow, established a permanent English presence in Ireland. They soon intermarried with the Irish, and by the time Henry's son, who became King John in 1199, strengthened royal rule over Ireland, the first Anglo-Irish families had become established. A trickle of new English settlers came, lured by the promise of good land, and families like the Desmonds and the Butlers began to emerge as powerful Anglo-Irish political forces.

The mass of Irish peasants struggled and toiled as before, while their Irish lords brooded in the background ever ready to take advantage of internal power squabbles amongst the Anglo-Normans. English rule was confined to an area around Dublin known as the Pale (hence the expression 'beyond the pale') while Gaelic custom and Brehon law – with communal property, secular marriage and divorce – operated for the majority of the population. The most powerful Norman-Irish families, known as the 'Old English', were the loyal Butlers and their earldom of Ormond, and the Fitzgeralds, whose earldoms of Kildare and Desmond became a thorn in the side of the English crown. Kilkenny became the political and cultural centre of medieval Anglo-Norman Ireland, and in 1366 a set of 36 clauses, the Statutes of Kilkenny, were passed as law in an attempt to preserve the English culture from the encroachments of Gaelic life. 'Now many English of the said land, forsaking the English language, fashion, mode of riding, laws and usages, live and govern themselves according to the manners, fashion and language of the Irish enemies, and also have made divers marriages and alliances between themselves and the Irish.' From the Statutes of Kilkenny.

During the 16th century Henry VIII of England had trouble keeping some of these Anglo-Irish magnates under his control, and after his breach with Rome over his marriage to Anne Boleyn in 1533 this became a serious problem, because of the danger of European Catholic plots being hatched in Ireland. England became more serious about combatting dissent in Ireland and suppressing Brehon law, but there were still five Anglo-Irish rebellions between 1568 and 1574. In 1580 Spanish and Italian Catholics landed at Smerwick in Kerry where, trapped by Lord Grey, 500 were slaughtered after they had surrendered. It was a sign of the times to come.

After the failure of rebellions by the Desmonds in 1569-73 and 1579-83, and consequent confiscations of land, the first plantations, planned in London, began in Munster. By 1592 there were over 3000 settlers, but some were killed after the Nine Years War broke out and their land was taken over by former owners. The colonists who were still around in 1598 fled to Irish towns and to England for safety. The colony was successfully re-established after 1601, spreading around Youghal, Kinsale and Baltimore and exporting wool and cattle. By 1641 there were over 20,000 settlers – England's most affluent colony to date – and the remnants of these families can still be traced in parts of West Cork.

'They looked like anatomies of death; they spake like ghosts crying out of their graves ... And if they found a plot of watercress or shamrocks, they flocked there as if to a feast.'

Edmund Spenser, poet of The Faerie Queen, described the aftermath of the Desmond rebellion in Munster where he was stationed

The end of Gaelic Ireland

The ruthless conquest of Ireland under Elizabeth I extended English control far beyond Dublin, but it met with strong resistance in Ulster, where the queen thought she had a willing ally in Hugh O'Neill. Instead, joining forces with Red Hugh O'Donnell, he rose in rebellion in what became known as the Nine Years War (1593-1603). Lacking artillery but employing successful guerrilla tactics, the rebels spread across Ireland, attempting unsuccessfully to enlist the support of the Anglo-Irish. Support came from the Spanish who landed a storm-weakened army at Kinsale in 1601, but they were trapped there. The English forces, who by now had been strengthened by the new military leadership of Lord Mountjoy, pursued a scorched earth policy as they pursued the rebels. At the same time the rebellion which had broken out in Munster was effectively met by Sir George Carew. The rebel leaders, O'Neill and O'Donnell, had no choice but to move their armies south in an attempt to join forces with the beleaguered Spanish. A tactical blunder by O'Neill handed victory to Mountjoy, the Spanish secured terms and sailed home, and the greatest challenge yet to English rule – one that would not be repeated until the War of Independence in the early 20th century – was over. It cost the English a massive £2 million, eight times more than any previous attempt to subdue the Irish, but English control over Ireland was now complete.

An emotive and emblematic postscript to the end of Gaelic Ireland came in 1607 when the pardoned and humbled O'Neill left Ireland for ever, in the company of other chieftains. Known as the 'flight of the earls' it concluded with the death of

Background

Oliver Cromwell

Oliver Cromwell, with God on his side, meted out divine revenge for the 1641 rising to the 'barbarous and bloodthirsty Irish'. The massacre at Drogheda , where possibly 1,000 citizens were slaughtered, has ensured Cromwell's infamy as Ireland's most ruthless public enemy, though a remarkable book by Tom Reilly, published in 1999, paints a different picture (see page 164).

Cromwell went on to capture Cork, Kinsale and Bandon from the rebels, Catholicism was driven underground and his soldiers, as well as fresh waves of settlers, were rewarded with extensive grants of confiscated land.

Hugh O'Neill in Rome in 1616. It was the legacy of the flight of the earls and its aftermath that erupted on the streets of Derry and Belfast in 1968.

Plantation and rebellion

The seeds of the present discord in Northern Ireland were laid within two weeks of Hugh O'Neill's departure, for this is how long it took to submit proposals for the plantation of the lands left behind in the flight of the earls. Ulster was surveyed, mapped and divided as thousands of Protestants took root, especially Scots in Down and Antrim, as both landlords and tenants. Such was the influx that by 1636 the government prohibited further emigration without licence from Scotland.

Settlers, known officially as undertakers, also moved into other parts of Ireland, and a radical and far-reaching change in the ownership of land took place. Nearly all of Gaelic Ireland was owned by about 2,000 Catholic gentry, but by 1660 they held only a little over 20%, and by the beginning of the 18th century the figure was below 15%.

Old English families grew alarmed at anti-Catholic measures and the threats to their property rights, and rebellion broke out in Ulster in 1641. Many of the leaders considered themselves loyal to the Crown, while others like Sir Phelim O'Neill were probably more keen to recover their lost land. The real revolutionaries were the native dispossessed Irish who rebelled against the injustice of plantation and the consequent shortage of land. The 1641 rising has gone down in loyalist mythology as a savage sectarian bloodletting, and violent outrages were indeed inflicted on Protestant settlers. Many were stripped naked in cruel mockery of having arrived in Ireland with nothing, and driven from their homes to perish in the winter cold. As many as 8,000 may have died, but propaganda multiplied this number out of all proportion and fuelled anti-Catholic hatred with lurid and exaggerated tales of torture and rape, and a premeditated plot to ethnically cleanse Ireland of Protestants. The rising was used as justification for the confiscation of two million acres of Irish land, while in England the rebellion became entwined with the emerging civil war as Charles I was accused of supporting the rebels. In 1649, after the execution of Charles, an army of 12,000 men landed in Ireland under Oliver Cromwell. When he left nine months later the ground was prepared for the final chapter in the colonisation of Ireland, and the only refuge left for Catholics was across the Shannon in land-poor Connacht – thus the saying 'to hell or to Connacht'.

'You, unprovoked, put the English to the most unheard of and most barbarous massacre (without respect of sex or age) that ever the sun beheld.'

From a broadsheet published by Cromwell in Cork in 1650, referring to events at Drogheda.

The Siege of Derry and the Battle of the Boyne

An estimated 150,000 emigrants arrived in Ireland in the 20 years after 1652, and it was the 17th century that saw large-scale deforestation as a direct result of the felling of trees for charcoal to sustain English industry. The second half of the century also witnessed a European power struggle that was to involve Ireland in a

Background

highly momentous manner. James II, who had been deposed from the English throne, landed in Kinsale in 1689 with French troops. The new king of England, William of Orange, was allied with Spain, the Dutch and the Pope, and together they were determined to oppose any increase in French power. 'If Ireland should be lost, England will follow' was the fear in the English Houses of Parliament when they voted funds of over £1 million for another army to land in Ireland and oppose James. European politics became entwined with the Catholic and Protestant struggle in Ireland, and the stage was set for another dramatic confrontation.

The defeat of James was played out in two events that were to shape Ireland in fact and in myth: the resistance of Derry to James' army, and the Battle of the Boyne, north of Dublin. The military commander in Derry, Robert Lundy, with the support of the Protestant bishop, was prepared to recognise James as the legitimate king before he arrived in Ireland, but many townspeople, alarmed at the thought of another 1641 massacre, thought otherwise. In December 1688 thirteen apprentice boys slammed the gates of Derry shut and Lundy, whose name and image is still reviled in loyalist wall art in Northern Ireland, was forced to flee the city in disguise. In April 1689 James laid siege to a defiant Derry – 'No surrender' was the clarion call – until, in July, a Williamite fleet managed to break through with supplies and save the city from starvation.

In May 1689 the last Irish parliament to include Catholics until 1922 took place in Dublin, and in July William's army defeated James at the Battle of the Boyne, with cathedrals across Catholic Europe offering prayers in thanksgiving. King James fled the battlefield, earning for himself the epitaph Séamus a chaca (James the Shit), though Irish resistance lasted another year. The end truly came with Sarsfield surrendering at Limerick in October 1691 after securing an honourable peace and exile to France, where he died two years later fighting William of Orange: 'Oh, that this were for Ireland' were his reported last words. Pockets of Irish soldiers fighting in Europe became known as the 'Wild Geese'; one became a general in the Russian army, another a governor of Spanish Louisiana.

The 18th Century

The treaty negotiated at Limerick in 1691 promised religious tolerance, but this was reneged on with the passing of laws like one in 1695 that made it illegal for a Catholic to own a horse worth more than £5. By this time only about 5% of useful land in Ireland was owned by Catholics. The Protestant ruling class ruled the roost, Dublin flourished as their commercial and cultural capital, and the Protestant Ascendancy seemed too secure to ever feel threatened again. It was not to be.

The decade which began in 1790 is one of the most important in Irish history, not just for the tumultuous events of the 1798 uprising but also for the fact that it saw the birth of republicanism, unionism and Orangeism.

The Irish parliament can be traced back to medieval times, but it met very irregularly and even in the 18th century only once a year. Like its parent British institution, it was riddled with patronage and, quite apart from bizarre franchises that led to the election of MPs for 'rotten boroughs' where no one actually voted, only Protestants and Presbyterians were allowed to vote in elections. There were few Presbyterian MPs, mainly due to the property criteria for those eligible to vote, and in Ulster this led to Presbyterian interest in parliamentary reform. For most of the 18th century the parliament sitting in Dublin was completely subordinate to Westminster, but with the emergence of the Volunteers and the pressure they were able to apply there were constitutional changes in 1792 that came to be known under the term 'legislative independence'.

The Volunteers were a part-time military force originally created in 1778-9 for the purpose of protecting Ireland against a French invasion and generally maintaining

'Landlords of consequence have assured me that many of their cottiers would think themselves honoured by having their wives or daughters sent for to the bed of their masters, a mark of slavery that proves the oppression under which they live.'

From Arthur Young's account of his travels around Ireland in 1776-1778

Background

Theobold Wolfe Tone

Wolfe Tone was born in 1763 into a Protestant middle-class family in Dublin. His father was a coachmaker and his mother the daughter of a sea captain. He more or less drifted into Dublin politics, and the height of his early political ambitions was a hoped-for seat in the Irish parliament. The French Revolution and Thomas Paine's Rights of Man helped radicalise his thinking and in 1791 he published An Argument on Behalf of the Catholics of Ireland. Calling for a united front of Catholics and Protestants, Tone's pamphlet was enormously popular and influential. In 1792 a further 10,000 copies were printed and Dublin Castle sent a copy to London to warn of this dangerous new polemic. By 1796 Tone was in France promoting a French invasion of Ireland, and before the year was out he was sailing into Bantry Bay with over 14,000 French troops, only to be defeated by adverse weather that saw the remnants of the fleet returning to France in January 1797. In 1798 Tone was once again on board a French ship as part of a third invasion force (the second invasion had landed earlier in north Mayo). Bad weather again thwarted the expedition, but it was anyway too late to effect the outcome of the general uprising of 1798. Even the few ships that made it to Donegal were intercepted by the British. The ship Tone was on decided to make a fight of it, and Tone himself refused the offer of escaping on a French frigate. Tone was captured and sentenced to death, but took his own life before he could be hanged.

law and order at a time when regular troops were needed to deal with the American Revolution. Predominantly based in Ulster and rising to 60,000 in number, the force consisted of urban, middle-class men, and as such emerged as a powerful expression of that class's aspirations for a greater say in the running of their country.

The 1792 reforms did not actually make the Irish parliament autonomous, but they did help create a political climate which nurtured the idea that further constitutional change was both desirable and possible. There were demands for more regular sittings of parliament, an extension of the Protestant electorate and other reforms, but they all came to nothing. English aristocratic rule, operating through Dublin Castle, remained firmly entrenched. The major reason for the failure of the post-1792 movement, led by Dublin radicals like James Napper Tandy (c.1737-1803) and the Belfast Presbyterian William Drennan (1754-1820), was the Catholic question. This revolved around the repeal of the Penal Laws, an issue that aroused deep-rooted fears amongst Protestants whose worst nightmares imagined a return to sectarian massacres and Catholic supremacy. They therefore argued for further political reforms, but these were clearly not to include equal rights for Catholics. Yet without the involvement of Catholics it was impossible for any reform movement to move up a gear and mount an effective challenge to British hegemony. As Wolfe Tone put it, it was foolish to plan 'an edifice of freedom on a foundation of monopoly'.

Wolfe Tone and 1798

Wolfe Tone changed everything by confronting the Catholic question and successfully arguing that Catholics be brought into the political equation. Tone was by no means the first to propound the idea that Irish people should unite behind a non-denominational front, but he did crystallise the notion and made it common currency. Towards the end of 1791 he was invited to Belfast to help establish a new political association being formed there by Presbyterian radicals. It was Tone who suggested the name United Irishmen for this new political club, and on his return to

Dublin he quickly set up a branch there consisting of both Protestants and Catholics. Events moved quickly within the next couple of years: the Volunteers were outlawed, and in 1794 the Dublin society of United Irishmen was also outlawed. This pushed the movement underground, closer to outright republicanism and the contemplation of armed insurrection. When war broke out between Britain and France, Tone saw the opportunity to recruit some foreign help.

The first French invasion force was defeated by winter storms in 1796, but it gave the British a jolt – 'England has not had such an escape since the Spanish Armada', declared Tone at the time – and the Irish such a fillip that within the next 18 months the United Irishmen claimed to have well over a quarter of a million members. The British authorities too were not idle, and developed counter-insurgency policies that would seriously weaken the effectiveness of the general insurrection that came in 1798. Many of the leaders were arrested, and the revolutionary movement suffered from a lack of co-ordination and the prevarications of the French in mounting another invasion fleet. Napoleon became more interested in a campaign in Egypt than in Europe's northern fringes, and his ships were in the Mediterranean when the uprising broke out.

The 1798 insurrection broke out across the country, starting in counties Dublin, Kildare and Meath in May, when mail coaches leaving the capital were stopped and set on fire. Government forces subdued the rebels, as they also did in eastern Ulster, but the uprising in county Wexford was not so easily quashed. The insurrection cost around 30,000 lives, and was easily the most bloody event in Irish history since the 17th century.

Union and Daniel O'Connell

The events of 1798 convinced Britain that only the abolition of the Irish parliament and a union of the English and Irish kingdoms could guarantee security. 'Ireland is like a ship on fire, it must be extinguished or cut adrift' observed the British prime minister, Pitt, who set about securing the Act of Union which came into effect in 1801. The Catholic clergy was won over by a promise of Catholic emancipation that would allow Catholics to sit in the new parliament and hold other important positions, and existing members of the Irish parliament were bought off with pensions and bribes.

The year 1803 marked the short-lived and abortive rebellion planned by 25-year-old Robert Emmet, who paid for his daring by being sentenced to be hanged, drawn and quartered. 'Let no man write my epitaph … When my country takes her place among the nations of the earth, then, and not till then, let my epitaph be written. I have done.' Emmet's last words from the dock in 1803.

The promised Catholic emancipation did not arrive until a new leader arrived on the scene, Daniel O'Connell (1775-1847). The man who has given his name to countless streets in Irish towns was a prosperous middle-class radical of liberal instincts who captured the minds and hearts of ordinary Irish people. He created a political mass movement for Catholic emancipation through a Catholic Association with a membership of one penny a month. It was a revolutionary act and one that would reverberate through Europe, for never before had a popular reform movement been organised in this manner. Membership climbed to half a million, and with 100,000 Catholic 40-shilling freeholders with a vote the time was ripe for change. Public rallies were held throughout the country, and O'Connell stood for election in a Clare by-election. He gained nearly 70% of the vote, and the British knew that a concession had to be made. Catholic emancipation became a reality in 1829, and a new mood of confidence spread like wildfire across Ireland.

Buoyed by success, O'Connell set about securing home rule – a repeal of the Act of Union and the return of an Irish parliament. It was a far cry from Wolfe Tone's republicanism, and although it was meant to be achieved without physical force it had a very physical dimension. Giant public meetings, dubbed 'monster meetings' by *The Times*, attracted hundreds of thousands of people and, although he tried to keep within the law, legal grounds were found for him to be tried for sedition and he was sentenced to jail. Now aged 70, he was released after 6 months. A younger wing of the movement was now calling for more radical opposition to British rule.

Nationalism and famine

Thomas Davis (1814-45) split with O'Connell and articulated a new and more exciting idea by calling for a brake on Anglicisation, a revival of the Irish language, and a 'nationalism which may embrace Protestant, Catholic and Dissenter ... the Irishman of a hundred generations and the stranger who is within our gate.' Davis died suddenly of scarlet fever, but an Ulster Presbyterian, John Mitchel (1815-75), took the movement further forward by agitating for an independent Irish republic. He was sentenced to transportation for 14 years in 1848, and a small rebellion broke out the same year but achieved little.

The failure of the 1848 rebellion was due not least to the awful famine that was traumatising Ireland. A potato blight was first noticed in 1845 when the population of Ireland was over 8 million, and by 1851 when the famine was over the population had dropped to six and a half million; by 1901 the figure was four and a half million. Death through starvation and disease accounted for a million deaths, and accelerated the process of emigration from Ireland as peasants desperately sought a new and better life in North America and Australia. The famine has been seen by some historians as an act of genocide, with ships leaving some of the worse-affected areas carrying profitable grain for export to Europe while peasants died for want of a meal. Others point out that the prevailing philosophy of free trade made it impossible for people to think otherwise, and indeed for some the haemorrhaging of people was seen as a positive economic gain.

Fenians and home rule

Irish tenants had no security of tenure on the land they rented, and if they could not afford the rent most landlords had them evicted so that the land could be rented to someone else. In 1850 a Tenant League was formed for land reform, but in 1858 an organization of more consequence was formed, the Irish Republican Brotherhood (IRB), more popularly known as the Fenians. In 1867 they mounted an abortive uprising: some of the participants were hanged, and a failed Fenian rescue of prisoners in London led to an explosion which killed 30. For his part in this botched rescue a Fenian was executed in the last public hanging in England.

Fenianism focused the minds of English liberal politicians like Gladstone on the problem of Ireland. In 1870 he introduced the first in what would become a series of land reforms that the Tenant League had called for. At the same time a new home rule movement arose in Ireland, its leader, Charles Stewart Parnell, taking up where Daniel O'Connell had foundered. Parnell, a Protestant landlord with an American mother, was quite prepared to use the threat of direct action alongside conventional political action, and joined forces with the newly-formed Land League. The Land League was founded by the Fenian Michael Davitt in 1879 with Parnell as president, and together they led a formidable campaign. Davitt used official statistics to show that fewer than 20,000 men owned the whole of Ireland; in fact fewer than 2,000 owned 70% of the land, while 3 million tenants and labourers owned nothing. Radical mass action, which became known as the Land War, demanded redistribution of land with compensation to landlords, and backed it up with a vigorous campaign that became famous for ostracising anyone who dared take

Parnell's Downfall

After the 1885 general election Parnell's Home Rule party wiped the board in southern Ireland and the following year Gladstone announced his conversion to the need for a dissolution of the union. Aged 76, he introduced the first Home Rule Bill to parliament and then a bombshell came out of the sky in the form of one Captain O'Shea filing for divorce on the grounds of his wife's adultery and naming Parnell as the third party. It gave opponents of home rule a moral excuse for denouncing Parnell and when the Irish Catholic church jumped up on the moral bandwagon the Irish parliamentary party was split. Parnell married Katherine O'Shea in 1891 but died the following year, a broken and tired man.

over the land of an evicted tenant. One of the first to suffer was a Captain Boycott – hence the new synonym for ostracism – and when Parnell was imprisoned in 1881 he became even more of a hero, and a policy of withholding rents altogether was put into action. He was released with a promise by Gladstone to introduce further, more far-reaching land reforms.

Even before the divorce issue destroyed Parnell (see box above) he had started to lose some of his political clout in Ireland when he failed to back campaigns for more vigorous action for land reform. His sister Anna never lost her drive in organizing the Ladies Land League, and struggled tirelessly across America for the cause, suffering disillusionment only when she realised that the Land League tended to benefit larger tenants and was not prepared to see through the need for a radical redistribution of land.

Gladstone's land reforms were carried even further by later Liberal and Conservative administrations which sought quite consciously to 'kill home rule by kindness'. The Ashbourne Act in 1885 allowed landlords to sell land to their tenants at fixed prices, and this was encouraged by the Wyndham Act of 1903 which saw landlords gaining a 12% payment, the Bonus, on top of the sale price. George Wyndham is said to have encountered an Irish peer in Monte Carlo brandishing his stack of chips and exclaiming to the Chief Secretary, 'George! George! The Bonus'. These reforms saw the end of the Protestant Ascendancy, because without the regular income from rents their economic base was terminally fractured. Leaking roofs went unrepaired, and as many of the 'big houses' entered the final chapters of their existence so too did the memorable lifestyle of those who lived in them. To many observers, like Louis MacNeice, the end was long overdue: 'In most cases these houses maintain no culture worth speaking of – nothing but absolute bravado, an insidious bonhomie, and a way with horses'.

The land reforms introduced a whole new class of peasant proprietors, but the problem of Ireland – or rather, Ireland's problem with England – did not go away. A new struggle for national independence was under way.

Cultural revolution

'Damn Home Rule! What we're out for is the land. The land matters. All the rest is talk.' This remark by a nationalist was recorded during the Land War, but the speaker was wrong, for all the rest was not just talk. In the closing decades of the 19th century an emerging sense of national consciousness gave rise to a cultural revolution that allied itself with and radicalised the political movement in preparation for a break with Britain. The cultural renaissance started with events like the 1884 founding of the Gaelic Athletic Association (GAA) and its call for Irish sports to replace English ones.

In 1893 the Gaelic League was established in the wake of a seminal lecture by the Protestant Douglas Hyde on 'The necessity of de-anglicising the Irish people'. 'We are daily importing from England ... her music, her dances and her manifold mannerisms, her games and her pastimes, to the utter discredit of our own grand national sports...as though we were ashamed of them', Hyde declared. In response there followed – in all senses of the word – a dramatic literary revolution that began with Anglo-Irish writers. Lady Gregory, W.B. Yeats and others founded the Irish Literary Theatre, later the Abbey Theatre, in 1898, and the following year Arthur Griffith started the *United Irishmen* newspaper. Griffith knew Yeats, but he also knew the socialist James Connolly, and out of such a matrix evolved the movement for complete separation from Britain and not just home rule. Sinn Féin ('Ourselves') was formed in 1907, and the idea of withdrawing elected Irish MPs from the British parliament at Westminster began to take shape.

At this stage Irish MPs were still committed to Home Rule rather than complete independence, and when elections in 1910 left the nationalists holding the balance of power it seemed certain that the Liberal party would have no choice but to push through a Home Rule Bill. The ability of the House of Lords to veto legislation was limited by the Liberals to two years, and when Home Rule legislation was blocked by the House of Lords in 1912 it was only a matter of waiting. In September 1914 the bill became an Act. By that time, however, events outside parliament's control were shaping Ireland's future.

Easter 1916

Armed opposition by Protestants to home rule in Ulster and the obvious willingness of groups in Ulster and Britain to subvert Home Rule quickly led to the formation of parallel nationalist forces. The Irish Volunteers were founded in 1913, and in March of the following year the Irish Citizen Army was re-formed from a nucleus force that had emerged in response to the lockout in a great Dublin strike of the year before. Militants like Hanna Sheehy Skeffington formed Cumann na mBan ('Association of Women') to make sure women were not left out of the struggle. Erskine Childers, with his wife Molly and Mary Spring Rice, imported guns on his yacht *Asgard*, and soon Volunteers were marching openly on the streets of Dublin.

The outbreak of the First World War in August 1914 led to the suspension of the Home Rule Act, and when Redmond, the leader of the Irish MPs, declared support for the war and a willingness for nationalists to volunteer, this led to a decisive break with Sinn Féin. Redmond and the bulk of the Volunteers formed their own group and the radicals who were left, members of the IRB, began planning for an armed uprising in conjunction with James Connolly and the Irish Citizen Army.

On Easter Monday, 24 April, 1916 strategic areas around Dublin were occupied, and an Irish Republic was declared from outside the occupied General Post Office on O'Connell St.

While middle-class Dubliners were quick to condemn the rising as British troops moved in and the city centre became a war zone, the rebels gained some support in working-class areas. The insurgents surrendered on the 29 April with the loss of around 64 republicans, 132 British troops and 250 civilians. Military trials and the shooting dead of 15 rebels, the first execution of rebels since Robert Emmet in 1803, led to a dramatic shift in public opinion and a surge in support for Sinn Féin. In July 1917 Eamon de Valera, the only commander of the rising to survive, won a by-election in Clare and became president of Sinn Féin. By the following year, after the death of Redmond, the Irish parliamentary party withdrew from Westminster and in the 1918 general election Sinn Féin swept the board. At the beginning of 1919 an alternative Irish government was formed in Dublin, with the minutes recorded in Irish and French, and the republic first declared in 1916 was ratified. In the same

Background

Outside the GPO Patrick Pearse declared 'the right of the people of Ireland to the ownership of Ireland and the unfettered control of Irish destinies to be sovereign and indefeasible' and called for the 'allegiance of every Irishman and Irishwoman'.

month the first shots were fired in what became known as the War of Independence.

War of Independence

By January 1919 the Volunteers, who had shot dead two Royal Irish Constabulary men in Tipperary that month, were becoming known as the Irish Republican Army (IRA). Britain faced the problem that, much as they wanted to ignore the illegally constituted Irish government, it was fast becoming the *de facto* ruling body for the people of Ireland. Homeowners were paying tax, in the form of rates, to the new Dáil Éireann (Irish Parliament) and alternative Sinn Féin courts were operating across the country.

The ranks of the IRA were being filled by professional soldiers returning from the First World War, and Michael Collins emerged as the charismatic and intelligent director of organisation for the new rebel army. Collins had taken part in the 1916 rising and was subsequently elected to the first Dáil for South Cork, becoming minister for finance, but he achieved popular and lasting fame as a guerrilla republican fighting the British. There were by now around 3,000 IRA men on active duty, and they forced the British into recruiting thousands of ex-servicemen to help the RIC defeat them. Known as the Black and Tans (a famous pack of hounds in Limerick) because they wore khaki and police caps and belts (there was no immediate supply of police uniforms available), they were responsible for retaliating against Collins' most daringly planned deed in 1920 when 10 government intelligence officers were assassinated one Sunday morning. The Black and Tans retaliated by executing three prisoners in jail, and driving lorries into Croke Park where a GAA game was taking place. They fired into the crowd, killing 14 and shooting a Tipperary player. The next month, December 1920, a large part of Cork City was burned in retaliation for a guerrilla attack that killed 18 Black and Tans at Kilmichael in County Cork.

Attempts by British intelligence to infiltrate the guerrilla republican movement failed because its officers could not understand the Irish accent; surveillance equipment, according to a secret report written in 1921 by the head of Dublin Castle (the headquarters of Britain's counter-insurgency group), failed because 'microphones of English manufacture seem ill-adapted to the Irish brogue'. The report went on to make an observation that could just as easily have been made in Belfast in the 1970s or 80s: 'It has been said that no European can fathom the mind of an Oriental, and it might equally be said that no Englishman can fully grasp the inner psychology of the Irish rebel character'.

Partition and civil war

By May 1920, when the IRA were able to launch an attack on the Custom House in the heart of the capital, the British were ready to start talking. A truce was signed in July and peace talks scheduled in London. The perceived difficulty for the British in recognising an Irish republic was the impact it might have in other parts of the Empire, especially India, so they bargained for an independent Ireland owing allegiance to King and Commonwealth. The Ulster problem was dealt with by the partition of Ireland, and the notion of a boundary commission that, the Irish delegates were told, would later recommend the transfer to Ireland of counties with a nationalist majority and thus render impractical the continued partition of Northern Ireland.

The sticking point was not partition but the required oath to the King and the British Commonwealth, the latter term being used here for the first time by Britain, and the denial of republican status to an independent Ireland. The delegates should have consulted with de Valera and others who were back in Dublin before signing

Ulster Says No

Background

The British Conservative Party's attitude to Ireland and the nature of present-day opposition to the Good Friday Agreement can be directly traced back to events in the early decades of the 20th century. Opposition to home rule in Ulster led to calls for retaining the union with Britain and Edward Carson, the lawyer who destroyed Oscar Wilde in court, emerged as the unionist leader. The Ulster Volunteer Force was formed in 1913, arms were imported from Germany, and calls for violent opposition to home rule became strident. There was no doubting the willingness of the 'law and order' Conservative Party led by Bonar Law to support such extra-parliamentary measures, and the facade of parliamentary politics was further weakened in 1914 when 58 British army officers stationed at the Curragh made it clear that they would refuse to take action against an armed uprising in Ulster. The Orange Order, resurrecting the 1641 rising and the Siege of Derry, was able to point to the Catholic church's ruling that mixed marriages between Catholics and Protestants take place only in Catholic churches and that children of such marriages be brought up as Catholics. The fear that Home Rule meant Rome Rule was not paranoia, it was a fear fully justified in the light of the later Catholic-inspired legislation that characterised post-independence Ireland, but unionists acted as if the whole of Ulster was Protestant when they only constituted 56% of the population and held a majority in only four counties. This did not prevent Bonar Law from pledging active support for resistance to home rule: 'We intend, with the help of the Almighty, to keep the pledge, and the keeping of it involves more than the making of speeches.'

any treaty, but Michael Collins, who was in London, knew that his guerrilla army was running out of ammunition; so, on the morning of 10 December, the treaty was signed in London pending ratification in the Dáil in Dublin.

The treaty was ratified but it was a close call – a majority of only 7 secured its passage – and de Valera and his anti-treaty supporters walked out of the Dáil in protest.

The split vote in the Treaty debate in the Dáil also led to a split in the IRA, and those opposed to the deal signed in London became known as the Irregulars. In April 1922 the Four Courts in Dublin were occupied by Irregulars, and following the assassination of a British army officer in London demands were made by Britain for action against the rebels. In June the Four Courts were shelled under orders from Collins, and a civil war began that divided families, occasioned terrible atrocities on both sides, and led to a trauma in Irish politics that was felt well into the 1970s. It also killed far more people – over 800 government soldiers and around 5,000 anti-treaty men – than the War of Independence, even though it lasted only a year.

Anti-revolution, 1920s-1950s

When the Irish finally took charge of their own country – or at least most of it – they inherited a sorry state of affairs. The British had confined industrial activity to the North, and the rural economy of the new state was stagnant after years of neglect. The political and social conservatism of the Church helped institutionalise a national malaise that was to last nearly half a century. In 1927 de Valera left Sinn Féin and founded a new party, Fianna Fáil ('Soldiers of Destiny'), which became the main opposition in the Dáil.

Disagreement with Britain over the payment of land annuities – de Valera refused to pay – led to Britain imposing high tariffs on Irish imports. Ireland retaliated in like manner, and life was hard for many. After the turmoil of

Ireland remained officially neutral during the Second World War. Conscription was never extended to Northern Ireland. Yet 68,000 men enlisted from Southern Ireland, 52,900 from Northern Ireland. Southern Irishmen won 8 Victoria Crosses, one went to a Belfast sailor

revolutionary struggle and a bitter civil war, Ireland's leaders embarked on a social and political programme decidedly un-revolutionary in nature. In 1926 a Committee of Inquiry into Evil Literature led to the creation of a censorship board that kept most twentieth-century classics out of the country. Freud, Sartre, Steinbeck, Salinger, Orwell, Gide, Mailer, Tennessee Williams, Dylan Thomas were all banned, not to mention every Irish writer then winning recognition elsewhere: Shaw, O'Casey, Joyce (for *Stephen Hero*, not *Ulysses*), Beckett, Behan, Kate O'Brien. Under successive de Valera governments the country went into a near-terminal state of moribund conservatism: Sean O'Casey summed up the malaise by declaring 'We're standing on our knees now'. The country closed in on itself, and the legacy of resentment at England saw Ireland refuse to take sides in World War II, withdraw from the Commonwealth, and decline to join NATO.

In 1937 de Valera produced a new constitution that enshrined church ideology: blasphemy was made a crime, divorce made impossible and, until the 1998 referendum allowed for their change, Articles 2 and 3 claimed the right to unite the whole of Ireland and oppose partition. In a radio broadcast in 1943 de Valera evoked a vision of Ireland as a rural paradise filled 'with the contests of athletic youths and the laughter of comely maidens'.

1960s – the awakening

Background

In 1959 de Valera finally moved aside to become President of Ireland, a non-executive and largely ceremonial role, and his successor, Sean Lemass, started to breath new life into the country. The emigration rate halved as new jobs were created, and the ebullience of this era was enshrined in John F Kennedy's presidential visit in 1963. The great-grandson of an Irish emigrant, Kennedy's visit gave a much-needed boost to the national psyche. Three years later saw the fiftieth anniversary of the Easter Rising, and the event was marked by the blowing up of the 36m-high Nelson's Pillar in O'Connell St in Dublin by unknown nationalists. The event, causing no injuries or damage to property, was received with glee, much humour being directed at the military experts who managed to damage surrounding properties while demolishing what remained of the statue's column. In 1962 the republic's own television channel was established.

The Haughey era

Charles Haughey attracted a few nicknames during his long reign as Taoiseach between 1987 and 1992; while respected by many, his political machinations and dubious accumulation of wealth and privilege led to him also being labelled 'The Great National Bastard'. An acronym, GUBU ('Grotesque, Unprecedented, Bizarre and Unbelievable') was coined to define the era, based on Haughey's response to events surrounding a suspected serial killer staying in the apartment of the Attorney General and the latter's decision to go on holiday before discussing it with him.

GUBU sums up fairly well the life of a politician who in 1970 was on trial for gun running to the besieged nationalists in the north, before going on to successfully manage the economy by winning the confidence of both business and trade unions. He bought Inishvickillane, a small island off the Dingle Peninsula, and a mansion set in 200 acres of land, at the same time as owing a bank nearly IR£1 million. Largesse from important businessmen, most spectacularly IR£1 million from Ben Dunne (of Dunne's stores) which had not been declared to the income tax authorities, have been the subject of government tribunals, and there is no shortage of other scandals associated with Haughey's reign as Taoiseach. He finally came to political grief in 1992 over the phone tapping of journalists, but the Houdini of his age has still somehow managed to survive imprisonment over his financial shenanigans.

Fianna Fáil and Fine Gael – Spot the Difference?

Sometimes, it seems, the historical difference between the two main political parties in Ireland is the only one worth mentioning. Fine Gael (pronounced 'Feen Gale') was formed in 1933 from an older pro-Treaty party whereas Fianna Fáil (pronounced 'Feena Foil') was founded by de Valera from the anti-Treaty faction of nationalists. Fianna Fáil still carries the mantle of republicanism, and because they were in power at the time of the 1998 negotiations over the North they were able to sell the Agreement to nationalists in the Republic in a way that Fine Gael could never have done. Apart from this ideological difference it is difficult to tell the two parties apart. Fine Gael portrays itself as more middle class, gaining more support from farmers, professionals and business people than Fianna Fáil, which likes to present itself as the party of ordinary working people and small farmers. Their economic policies are basically the same, and what makes contemporary politics in Ireland so boring is the fact that the other main parties, the Progressive Democrats and Labour, offer few alternatives to the electorate. Coalition governments come and go, and the electorate seems not to care who really runs the country. What matters is that the economy is booming, unemployment is at a record low, and it's cool to be green.

Contemporary Ireland

Background

After Haughey's resignation in 1992 Albert Reynolds was elected Taoiseach of a Fianna Fáil-Progressive Democrat (PD) government, but this fell apart when Reynolds accused a PD of dishonest testimony to an inquiry into fraud in beef exports. It was a deliberate attempt to force an election and gain an outright majority for Fianna Fáil, but it failed miserably, and this a time a coalition government with Labour was formed. Another election followed in 1994 and a Fine Gael-Labour government took its turn until June 1997, when it was the turn of Fianna Fáil and the Progressive Democrats to rule under Bertie Ahern. This remains the ruling coalition of government, although in Ireland general elections and new governments are formed with what seems startling frequency.

Travelling through the countryside in the west of Ireland one is struck by what appears to be a cow-based economy. Indeed, over 70% of farm output comes from cattle and milk. In the eastern counties the land supports more cereals and giant fields of barley and beet thrive alongside the ubiquitous herd of black and white Fresian cows. What is surprising, however, is that less than 15% of the working population is engaged with the land. The prosperity that is so evident in contemporary Ireland is based on new light industries like electronics and computer components. Ireland's economic growth rate of 8.5% is three times the European average, her GDP has outstripped Britain's, and Eurokids flock to the capital for work and language learning. The 1916 rising is no longer celebrated, problems in the North are being argued over in constitutional non-violent terms, and Irish people at long last feel confident about themselves because, as more than one commentator has noted, Ireland may have lost the leprechaun but has most definitely found the pot of gold.

Northern Ireland

The origins of the Province

Northern Ireland came into existence with the Government of Ireland Act of 1920 and remained within the United Kingdom after the rest of the island achieved dominion status following the treaty of 1921. The story starts with the plantation of Ulster in the seventeenth century (see page 673), but the more pressing background to the partition of Ireland lay with the successful resistance of Ulster unionists in the 1911-14 period to the increasing likelihood of home rule for Ireland (see page 677). They originally wanted to be ruled directly from London, but grew to cherish their devolved parliament, where they enjoyed an overall majority of seats, once it became clear the British would let them get on with what was in effect a one-party state. In 1925 the boundary commission recommended no significant changes in the border between the Free State and Northern Ireland, and an issue that was not paramount in the causes or course of the civil war was left to fester.

From inequality to direct rule

From its inception in 1920 until the Good Friday Agreement of 1998, Northern Ireland was an artificial construct designed to secure unionist control. Three counties of Ulster – Cavan, Donegal and Monaghan – were excluded from its creation because their majority Catholic populations would have weakened the ability of unionists to control the state and form every government, until direct rule from Westminster was established in 1972. The Northern Ireland parliament began life in Belfast City Hall in June 1921, moving to the grandiloquent, purpose-built building at Stormont, in the eastern suburbs of Belfast, in 1932. By this time, gerrymandering of the constituencies ensured unionist majorities and the Special Powers Act of 1922 gave the government the right to prohibit meetings or processions without cause. The 12 July, marking the defeat of Catholics at the Battle of the Boyne (see page 673), became a national holiday and Easter processions by Catholics were attacked. The Royal Ulster Constabulary (RUC) was formed in 1922 and its Catholic element rapidly declined from a peak of around 20% in 1923 to half that.

The civil and political strife that erupted in 1968, and which led four years later to direct rule, was the result of decades of misrule which saw Catholics became second-class citizens, discriminated against in housing and employment and their cultural identity as Irish people vigorously suppressed.

The Northern Ireland Civil Rights Movement, modelling itself on the movement for racial equality in the USA, was formed in 1967. The following year saw their marches attacked by loyalist gangs. In 1969 an Apprentice Boys' march notched up the level of violence. The event was an annual march, triumphantly celebrating the siege of 1689 (see page 673) that paraded through Catholic residential areas in Derry, but this time the march provoked rioting. The Protestant backlash saw Catholics fleeing as refugees across the border in trains that were stoned by mobs as they passed through Protestant areas. British troops were called in to restore order, the IRA re-emerged, direct rule was introduced and thirty years of bombing and bloodshed followed. Unionist control of the Stormont government between 1920 and 1972 allowed its permanent majority to vote down every nationalist proposal, bar one solitary measure – the 1930 Wild Birds Act.

It is easy to blame sectarian unionism for the inequalities and iniquities that led to the explosive events of the late 1960s and their aftermath, but it is equally clear that the sectarian Catholicism of the southern Ireland state gave Protestants in the North good reason to fear for their cultural survival in a united Ireland.

The British Army arrived in Northern Ireland in August 1969, intended as a short-term measure to deal with the escalating violence that was developing between Catholic street action and the loyalist backlash. At first, beleaguered Catholic residents welcomed the presence of troops but this soon changed as the army was seen to be not acting impartially. At this stage, the IRA was virtually non-existent but it quickly re-emerged as Catholic communities looked for support. The violence began to spiral upwards, with events like Bloody Sunday (see page 554) and the Provisional IRA soon eclipsing the less militant official wing of the movement. The Provisionals launched a campaign of terrorist warfare against the security forces and commercial targets, and the introduction of internment, imprisonment without trial, caused the violence to escalate even more. In 1970, 25 people died and by 1972 this number had reached 467 and all but 30 of these fatalities occurred after internment.

In March 1972, the British government suspended the Northern Ireland government at Stormont and direct rule was introduced. A new government post was created at Westminster, a secretary of state for Northern Ireland.

The collapse of politics

In 1973, the Sunningdale agreement (see box page 580) was an attempt to find a political settlement. Although its power-sharing executive was established for a brief while it was destroyed by the Ulster Workers Council, a loyalist grouping with paramilitary support. The inability or unwillingness - it depends on your point of view - of the British government to stand up to the Council heralded a new and bloodier chapter in the province's history.

What followed was an intense period of open warfare between the IRA and the security forces. The IRA campaign was extended to the British mainland, hoping to force the hand of the government into making a political deal. In 1974, a bomb in a pub in Birmingham killed 21 people and more pub bombings followed in Woolwich and Guildford. The Prevention of Terrorism Act was introduced to allow lengthy detention without trial and although people were found guilty and imprisoned for the Birmingham and Guildford bombings they were released after 15 years behind bars and admitted to be innocent (one died in prison).

Up until 1976, prisoners in Northern Ireland jails who were there by dint of their involvement in the ongoing conflict had a special status that gave them the right not to wear prison uniforms. Republican protests led to hunger strikes and in 1981 this led to the death of Bobby Sands (see box page 657), who by the time of his death had been elected Member of Parliament for Fermanagh and South Tyrone. Nine more hunger strikers died over the following months.

The road to peace

The mid-1980s saw a fresh start with the signing at Hillsborough in county Down of the Anglo-Irish Agreement. A chief architect was John Hume, leader of the moderate Catholic Social and Democratic and Labour Party, and the signatories were the British and Irish prime ministers. It was a significant step forward, recognising the failure of attempts to bring peace to Northern Ireland by a purely internal settlement, and was motivated to some extent by alarm at the growing electoral success of Sinn Féin, the political wing of the IRA.

Even more significant was the Downing St Declaration in 1993 which pointedly invited dialogue with Sinn Féin and the IRA. In August 1994 the IRA dramatically announced 'a complete cessation of military operations', and loyalist paramilitary groups followed likewise. It seemed that everyone, including the gunmen, was tired

Background

of the endless violence, and Sinn Féin under Gerry Adams emerged with a new voice that recognised continual violence was not going to solve the problems. Unionism, also aware that some kind of compromise was necessary, would later elect David Trimble as a leader willing to negotiate with the traditional enemy.

Enter President Clinton, stage right, who now brought a powerful American influence to bear on the various talks and discussions that were going on in every camp. US Senator George Mitchell headed an international commission that pushed matters forward with the enunciation of six ground rules for future discussions between the various parties. These included a commitment to peaceful means, but the astonishing progress that seemed to be in the making was shattered by a bomb at Canary Wharf in London, in 1996, announcing the end of the IRA ceasefire. The fragile alliance between moderate and diehard members of the IRA had come to an end over the perceived willingness of the British government to bow to Unionist intransigence by insisting on the decommissioning of IRA weapons before talks could get under way.

The electoral defeat of Britain's Tory government in mid-1997, and its replacement by a Labour government not dependent on the Unionist votes at Westminster, heralded another fresh start. The IRA declared a restoration of their ceasefire and new talks got under way. Despite some outbreaks of violence at the end of 1997, including the assassination of Billy Wright, the leader of a loyalist paramilitary group, by a republican paramilitary group known as the Irish National Liberation Army (INLA), a breakthrough emerged and the Good Friday Agreement was signed in April 1998.

The Good Friday Agreement

The Good Friday Agreement provided for a new Assembly of 108 members and an executive of twelve from the various communities. The new Assembly would bring direct rule from Westminster to an end and return to a devolved government responsible for the affairs of Northern Ireland. The essential difference is that the new Assembly cannot be gerrymandered to ensure unionist control.

The Good Friday Agreement in 1998 reached as fine a political balance as could ever be achieved in Ireland and the terms of the agreement were resoundingly endorsed by referendums held both sides of the border: 71% in the North and 94% in the Republic voted yes to peace and a political settlement that accepted the need for compromise. Elections for the new assembly that would govern the six counties gave the Social and Democratic Party (SDLP), representing the moderate middle-class nationalist vote, 24 seats and 21.99% of the vote, the Ulster Unionist Party (UUP) 28 seats with 21.28% of the vote, the Democratic Unionist Party (DUP), hardline unionists opposed to the Good Friday Agreement, 18% and 20 seats, and Sinn Féin 18 seats with 17.65% of the vote.

Opposition to the Good Friday Agreement continued to threaten the chances of a lasting peace. The summer of 1998 saw the continuation of conflict over the Orange Order's traditional march through the Catholic Garvaghy Rd area of Portadown (see box page 644). On the morning of July 12, a loyalist firebombing of a Catholic house in a mainly Protestant estate resulted in the death of three young children. Breakaway IRA dissidents formed the Real IRA and in August 1998 their bombing campaign led to horrific atrocity in Omagh, the worst in 30 years, a bomb which saw the slaughter of 29 people. Sinn Féin came off the fence with an unequivocal statement, followed by IRA visits to the homes of 60 members of the Real IRA within a 90-minute period making them an offer they could not refuse: on 7 September the Real IRA declared a total ceasefire.

Opposition to the Good Friday Agreement from hardline unionists continued to bedevil progress. As much as Trimble and his supporters wanted to move forward

Glossary of political terms

Black and Tans *British recruits, so-called from the colours of their uniform, recruited to combat republicans fighting for independence after 1918; infamous for their brutality*
Civil War *war that broke out in Ireland, after the signing of the 1921 Treaty, between those who accepted the Treaty and those who opposed it*
Dáil Eireann *the Irish parliament, often referred to as simply the Dáil (pronounced doil)*
DUP *The Democratic Unionist Party, led by Ian Paisley, vehemently anti- Republican and opposed to the Good Friday Agreement*
Fenian *a member of the 19th-century Irish Republican Brotherhood*
Fianna Fáil *a political party ('Soldiers of destiny'), founded in 1927 by de Valera in terms of opposition to partition and while still perceived as some to be more republican than Fine Gael it is every bit as right wing*
Fine Gael *a right-wing political party, with origins in the pro-Treaty group after 1922, barely distinguishable from Fianna Fáil*
Gallowglass *mercenaries from Scotland hired from the 13th century by chiefs in Ulster and north Connacht and used to oppose the spread of English colonialism.*
IRA *Irish Republican Army Between 1916 and 1921 the IRA was the army of the Provisional Government fighting the British and relatively dormant until trouble erupted in Northern Ireland at the end of the 1960s. Between 1970 and the still-existing ceasefire called in 1998 the IRA was actively engaged in a guerilla war against the British*
Loyalist *people in Northern Ireland, staunch Protestants mostly, who are strongly in favour of remaining part of Britain*
LVF *Loyalist Volunteer Force; Sectarian, paramilitary banned group*
Nationalists *people who wish to see an united Ireland*
Orange Order *Protestant society dedicated to preserving the memory of William's victory at the Battle of the Boyne. Founded in 1795 and formerly represented within the Ulster Unionist Party*
Progressive Democrats *a political party founded in 1985 by a group of Fianna Fáil politicians opposed to the rule of the then leader, Charles Haughey*
PUP *Progressive Unionist Party, seen by many as the political wing of the UVF, and crucial to the success of the Good Friday Agreement*
Republicans *people committed to a united Ireland as a republic; sometimes used interchangeably with the term nationalist*
RUC *Royal Ulster Constabulary, Northern Ireland's armed police force, predominantly Protestant. Regarded by the Catholic community as sectarian; currently being reformed as a result of the post-Good Friday Agreement Patten report*
Sinn Fein ('Ourselves Alone'): *Nationalist organization founded in 1903 and nowadays a political party in Ireland, particularly strong in the North, where it represents the political wing of the IRA.*
SDLP *Social Democratic and Labour Party, led by John Hume for many years, nationalist but not as republican as Sinn Fein*
Treaty *the Treaty of 1921 that divided Ireland into the Republic and Northern Ireland*
Taoiseach *the Prime Minister of the Republic*
UDA *Ulster Defence Association; Protestant military organisation*
UDF *Ulster Defence Force, an illegal paramilitary Protestant organisation*
UDP *Ulster Defence Regiment, political wing of the LVF*
UFF *Ulster Freedom Fighters, an illegal Protestant paramilitary force*
UUP *Ulster Unionist Party, the largest and most important party opposed to republicanism, led by David Trimble.*
UVF *Ulster Volunteer Force, an illegal Protestant paramilitary force*

Background

there was sufficient unwillingness within his own party to bite the bullet of compromise, never mind the pressure from Ian Paisley to insist on IRA decommissioning as a pre-condition for any further movement.

A totally new government

The impasse over the implementation of the Good Friday Agreement was finally overcome in November 1999 when, after 300 hours of face-to-face talks between David Trimble and Gerry Adams, agreement was reached. In a remarkable switch of the language codes that characterise political talk in the six counties, Trimble spoke of the need to recognise different cultural traditions (acknowledging that both nationalists and republicans have rights) while Adams spoke of the need for de-commissioning (a possible end to the IRA).

On 29 November 1999 a new date entered the annals of Irish history when a coalition government was formed in Northern Ireland and direct rule from London was finally ended. The local government that had been dissolved in 1972 was replaced by one with David Trimble as First Minister but which for the first time included three Sinn Féin ministers, including a minister for education, Martin McGuinness, who could easily have been shot dead by security forces when he was the most wanted republican in Derry in the 1970s.

The future looks promising, though many hurdles still lie ahead. Diehard loyalists from Paisley's Democratic Unionist Party have taken their seats in the new Assembly with the sole purpose of trying to destroy it by whittling away at Protestant support for the present leader of the Ulster Unionist Party, David Trimble. The British government's decision in January 2000 to reform the overwhelmingly Protestant RUC, including a change of its name to the Police Service of Northern Ireland, has annoyed Unionists. Trimble has to play a fine balancing act, trying to keep the new Assembly in existence while knowing that he won the support of just 58% of his party to form the executive in advance of IRA decommissioning. At the time of writing, the thorny issue of decommissioning remains balanced on a knife's edge: it seems to hold the key to further progress. The future will still be acrimonious, but at least there is a better chance of peace now that at any time in the past thirty years. Watch this space.

Land and environment

Geography

Ireland is an old country. Its oldest rock, near Rosslare in County Wexford, is 2,400 million years old. Geologists suggest that four thousand million years ago Ireland was two separate halves, one attached to early America and one to early Europe. When the two continents collided Ireland was squashed together and raised above sea level; huge rivers appeared which dumped red sand into the south, making the old red sandstone of the Cork and Kerry peninsulas. Three hundred and seventy five million years ago, Ireland found itself under a shallow warm sea where millions of tiny sea creatures lived and died, their remains forming great limestone swathes filled with fossil remains. On top of the limestone, shale and clay collected and supported primaeval trees which in their turn decayed to form coal. Then, three hundred million years ago, the European and African tectonic plates collided, and the old red sandstone with its covering of limestone and shale burst upwards and sideways to make the mountains of West Cork and Kerry, the Ballyhouras, the Galtees, the mountains of Limerick, and finally the Clare hills. If you compare these today you will see how the Kerry mountains took the worst of the upheaval, folding alarmingly into almost vertical sandstone sheets, while the Clare hills are almost flat, demonstrating how the power of the movement declined.

The next big burst of activity occurred 65 million years ago as the American and European continents drifted apart, creating the Atlantic Ocean. The west of Ireland sank as its support fell away, while to the north and east great lava flows and molten rock poured upwards creating the Giant's Causeway, the Mourne Mountains, and Doon Hill in Connemara. About 35 million years ago a depression formed in the middle of Ireland, creating a central low lying plain drained by the Shannon and surrounded by mountains. The basic structure of the country was now in place, only requiring erosion by rivers, glaciers and icesheets, and a few late tectonic shifts. These relatively recent landforms include the Wicklow hills, Lough Hyne in West Cork, thousands of drumlins, and many U-shaped glacier-carved valleys.

A thousand years ago Ireland was covered in dense broadleaved forests with **Forests** cleared patches on the tops of hills. Its main arteries were the rivers and coasts. As various waves of invaders encroached on the land, roads were built for their armies and the forests were cleared for settlements, to fuel mineworkings or to build English ships, so that today almost none of the aboriginal forests of Ireland remain. The best examples are in the southwest, at Muckross in Killarney, Glengarriff and Knockomagh Woods near Skibbereen, West Cork, and Shillelagh in south Wicklow. Visiting these places, especially in autumn, is one of the delights of the southwest of Ireland. Despite Ireland's limited range of plants the woods are pollution-free, and you can see this in the enormous range of lichens that cover the trees. Holly, ferns, honeysuckle, wood sorrel, anemones, bluebells and celandines flourish in the spring before the trees grow leaves to shade out the light. By contrast, if you look into the understorey of the fast-profit conifer plantations which now seem to cover so much of the upland areas of Ireland, very little thrives at all.

Thanks to hundreds of years of decline and neglect, much of rural Ireland is today a **Raised bogs** paradise of undamaged environments, worked on in the past only by farmers using small-scale technology. As a result, ecological niches such as raised peat bogs which were lost years ago in other countries are still thriving here. When the ice retreated from Ireland nine thousand years ago it left great dammed lakes which gradually filled with water plants. As they decayed and formed a subsoil, a habitat was created for plants such as reeds and sedges which could tolerate partly wet conditions. The decay process continued until the debris rose above the water level and became fenland. Meanwhile, in the middle of the bog, oxygen depletion was taking place and plants which could tolerate low levels of oxygen moved in, notably sphagnum moss. This plant can capture and store rainwater, and needs very little else as nutrient. It quickly builds great domes which stand above the water level and hold large quantities of water, raising the water table as they do so. Other plants are starved out and the sphagnum takes over the area. Over thousands of years these plants flourished, creating ever higher mounds as the plants underneath died and formed a new base.

The bogs of Ireland are most abundant along the west coast and almost non-existent in the east. They are an important habitat for thousands of plant and animal species, and in addition have covered and protected thousands of years of human habitation, so that any little museum in Ireland will contain artefacts found in the bogs, ranging from fossilised bog butter to jewellery, from weapons to whole bodies which have hardly deteriorated at all. Roadways, villages, field systems have all emerged from the bogs as they have been excavated. But there lies the problem. The bog is an intact entity, its structure holding the water which keeps it growing and surviving. If the bog is cut, even by a hand tool, the water drains away and the bog dies, becoming dry enough to support first heathers and then other moorland plants and trees. With the wholesale peat cutting taking place in modern times in the biggest bogs in Ireland, the entire bog habitat, even those parts protected by the government, is ultimately doomed.

The fields The Irish landscape, even nowadays, is a network of small fields bounded by stone ditches or hedgerows of whitethorn and blackthorn. The east of the country is largely fertile arable land, growing vegetables and sugar beet, while the north has small orchards and the west is given over to bog, cattle, sheep and grass. Most farms once had both pasture land and cultivated fields for oats and rye, but in modern times this is rare. Animal feed is bought in, there are few horses to grow oats for, and barley is produced on a large scale or not at all. Many of the fields systems you see are ancient, having been marked out long before any recorded history took place. Traditionally field boundaries were made of earth and stone ditches, each year's cleared sods of grass being added to the ditch along with anything else the plough turned up. The ditches were planted with hawthorn slips, and over the years the seeds of oak, ash, elder, wild rose and honeysuckle were brought by birds and small creatures. The hedgerows have become highways for animal life, providing home and food for hundreds of species of animals. In the west of Ireland fuchsia, an introduced plant, has become the dominant hedgerow plant – not a good choice for the native bees which cannot feed on the narrow flowers. Rhododendron has become another useful plant, providing windbreak all year round, though its invasive nature threatens the few remaining oakwoods.

The seashore

A planned golf course at Doonbeg, Co Clare, was put on hold in December 1999 after it was found to be the habitat of the rare narrow-mouth whorl snail (Vertigo angustior)

Ireland has more than 2000 miles of coastline, the eastern coasts being more heavily populated and sheltered. The major ports of Waterford, Wexford, Dublin and Belfast, being heavily industrialised, have taken over much of the coastal habitat, but the west and southern coasts are exposed and have high cliffs and so provide an unspoiled habitat for plant and animal life. From the cliffs all over the west coast seals, dolphins and migrant birds can be spotted, while in the mouth of the Shannon colonies of dolphins thrive. Although golf courses are breeding like rabbits all over the west, there are still some undamaged sand dunes which make up a complex ecosystem of their own. The marram grasses bind the dunes together and provide a solid base for other plants such as sea holly, heartsease, sea sandwort, burnet rose and the rare ladies tresses orchid to find a niche. These plants are a food source and shelter for snails, sand hoppers, and butterflies, which in their turn provide a food source for birds such as skylarks and meadow pipits. Many of Ireland's dune systems have revealed evidence of Neolithic culture, shell middens and cooking places, and even traces of iron smelting. In the shallow seas in front of the dunes systems wading birds feed, and the summer sees migrants from northern climates which come to the west of Ireland to breed. High cliffs and the offshore islands provide a breeding ground for other sea birds. Here too there is evidence of early cultures in the many promontory forts and other antiquities.

Flora & fauna

After the end of the last Ice Age both Ireland and Britain were connected to Europe by land bridges, and plants and animals from the mainland quickly recolonised both soon-to-be islands. But Ireland was cut off sooner by the rising sea levels and consequently has a much smaller range of both plants (around 70% of Britain's species) and animals (65% of Britain's insect species, for example), even in today's polluted times. There are no snakes in Ireland, only two amphibians as compared with Britain's six, 354 bird species compared with Britain's 456, and so on. Not that you'd notice when walking around the countryside in Ireland where plants that survive in tiny niches in Britain peek out of every hedgerow. The plants and animals that Ireland is home to are less endangered here than in most of the rest of Europe. Interestingly, Ireland has fifteen native species that are missing in the British flora and fauna. If you imagine a post-ice-age land link from Europe to Britain and then to Ireland you have to ask how the plants could have hopped over Britain, missing it completely and landing in Ireland The theory is that at some point a land link existed between Ireland and southern Europe, and that these plant and animal species travelled to Ireland this way, bypassing Britain. Three heathers, St Daboc 's heath, Mediterranean heath and Mackay's heath, are found in tiny colonies in Connemara and Donegal and southern France, while the greater butterwort, an insectivorous plant, is found only in the southwest of Ireland. The strawberry tree is found only in the southwest of Ireland, Brittany and the Mediterranean, and the spotted slug is again restricted to the southwest of Ireland.

Fauna are a little less easy to spot – you're more likely to see a dolphin than a stoat for example. Neither are they as safe in the Irish environment as you would think. Woodpeckers disappeared when the last of the primaeval forests were cut down, the very common corncrake almost disappeared because improved artificial fertilisers have made two harvests of grass possible each year. The birds, which nested in the long grass, had no time to rear their young before the first grass was cut – consequently very few young Irish people have heard the call which was so familiar to their parents. With the commercial cutting of the peat bogs, hundreds of species could disappear. In contrast minks, not a native species, are a common roadkill. They were introduced in farms, from which they of course escaped, and have found a niche in the woodlands and hedgerows. In 1999 the varroa mite, which infests bee colonies and eventually destroys them, was found in County Sligo, so it is merely a matter of time before the wild bee population in Ireland is wiped out. That would change the entire face of the Irish countryside, since so many of its wild flowers depend on pollination by bees.

Culture

Art and architecture

At Carrowmore in County Sligo, Swedish archaeologists have recently discovered the world's oldest building. The site (see page 501) has always been considered a Neolithic graveyard, built by people who had acquired the skills of farming and led fairly settled lives; then in summer 1999 a new site was discovered containing the cremated bones of about 50 people which carbon-dated to about 7,400 years ago, making its construction 700 years earlier than the oldest previously known free-standing building, a Neolithic tomb near Poitiers in France. This indicates that in Ireland a Mesolithic culture, a hunter-gatherer society, had all the skills required to erect substantial buildings.

Pre-Christian art & architecture

Most of our knowledge of the architecture of early Ireland comes from funeral buildings. The earliest are the dolmens, tripod-like structures with upright megaliths supporting one or two massive capstones and covered by a cairn. Newgrange (see box on next page) represents the next stage of Irish art and architecture, adding the sophistication of corbelling for the roof and several chambers, many of them decorated with our earliest examples of Irish art – triple spirals, double spirals and lozenge patterns. The Bronze Age in Ireland has left us a legacy of quite stunning complex designs in gold torques, collars and pins, decorated bronze shields where the design is both functional and decorative. Like the weaponry, the architecture of

Newgrange

The monuments at Newgrange were constructed around 2500BCE, following a sweeping bend of the River Boyne and utilising an area of some 12 square kilometres. There are three huge similarly-sized hilltop mounds, Newgrange, Knowth and Dowth, with one tomb in the Newgrange cairn and two in each of the other two. A score of smaller passage tombs, known as satellite tombs, have been found and excavated in the area around the main monuments. Fragments of bones belonging to a few people, some cremated, were found by archaeologists working at Newgrange in the 1960s, but the site has been open for three hundred years so this find is not conclusive.

Excavations at other passage tombs in Ireland have revealed evidence of mass burials, up to 24 people being buried together. The nearest equivalent grouping of megalithic tombs outside of Ireland are in Brittany and Orkney, and one theory is that the people who build these tombs at Newgrange came from Brittany, and before that the Iberian peninsula. However, the art work of Newgrange has few parallels outside of Ireland, and it has been argued that the Boyne valley represents a unique Irish development.

The artwork inscribed on the stones at Newgrange are geometrical in design, and their non-representational nature suggests symbolic meanings. Whether they were conceived as ornamental in nature or whether they signify spiritual or magical ideas remains a mystery. In the case of some of the stones, like the huge entrance boulder, it is clear that the artist or artists regarded the whole stone as a canvas which was to be filled with an intricate and integrated pattern of spirals, concentric arcs and other designs that strove to utilise even the curving surface of the material. Tools – flint stones and wooden hammers – would have been fairly basic, and the carved motifs may be divided into curvilinear ones, like triple spirals, circles, arcs and serpent shapes, and rectilinear chevron zigzags, parallel lines, lozenge and triangular shapes. What is odd is that other types of megalithic tombs in Ireland show little evidence of any wish to inscribe patterns on stone in this way. Considering the unwieldy nature and the sheer size of these giant stones, the artwork that has survived represents one of the finest achievements of prehistoric art in western Europe.

this time reflected the need for defence with hill forts and promontory forts being simple stone boundaries which possibly had wooden structures inside.

The Iron age/early Christian period still saw defensive buildings in the raths and stone cashels, but usually no longer on high ground, and often with a souterrain for escape or hiding. Stonework had become decorative as well as functional, and we have several items in Armagh cathedral and county museum reflecting this primitive but distinctly creative form, particularly the stone heads like the Tandragee Man with his brutalist appearance, and the figure with what seems rays emanating from its head. Other decorative effects are consistent with the La Tène style of decoration – swirling loops and whorls both on stonework and weapons.

The early Christian period This was a peaceful and productive time for Irish art and architecture before the Normans arrived, bringing their European sensibilities with them. Many people still lived in raths and crannógs, essentially settlements with an eye to defence, while church architecture was largely in the medium of wood, only a few stone buildings – such as the beehive huts of Skellig Michael or the ruins on Inismurray in County Sligo – still surviving. Where church buildings are of stone and have survived they are simple in design with arched doors, a simple nave added to the basic cell structure, and perhaps sculpture around the doors and windows. Some round towers such as the one at the monastery at Kells, County Meath, were built in the latter part of this period. The arts on the other hand were flourishing in the monasteries around the coast, demonstrated by the production of illuminated manuscripts such as the Book of Kells, the gold and metalwork of the beautiful Ardagh chalice in the National Museum, and the work of the stonemasons building the high crosses and tombs.

High crosses

Many of Ireland's Celtic crosses date back to this period before the Norman invasion. Sometimes as tall as 5m/15ft, they are carved from whatever stone was available, often sandstone or limestone which has not subsequently worn well. Their east side is often decorated in scenes from the Old Testament while the west side conveys stories from the New. Usually in the centre of the west face is the crucifixion surrounded by the typical carved and decorated ring of stone which may have stood for the cosmos, with Christ and his sacrifice at its centre. The stories chosen often illustrate a theme, and their purpose was practical – to teach and inspire the congregation. The base and side panels are covered in complex geometric designs like those in the illuminated manuscripts of the period, and when first erected they were probably painted so that the designs and stories stood out much more clearly. The best examples of high crosses from this period are at Glendalough, County Wicklow, Durrow and Clonmacnoise in County Offaly, and Monasterboice in County Louth, a particularly beautiful example.

Round towers

The earliest of the Irish round towers are pre-Norman, although they continued to be built into the twelfth century. They are the mediaeval equivalent of the muezzin's minaret, and once held a bell to call the monks in from the fields. Usually five storeys high, they have one window at each level, and their defensive nature is seen in the fact that the doorway is about ten feet off the ground so that the steps could be drawn up to protect the church property in time of attack. Inside would have been a series of wooden storeys and steps.

County Carlow

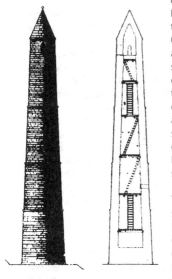

Round Tower at Ardmore, County Waterford

Irish Romanesque

The Irish Romanesque style is most clearly seen in Cormac's Chapel at the Rock of Cashel in County Tipperary, and the twelfth century doorway to Clonfert Cathedral in County Galway. A typical arched doorway at Clonfert is surrounded by highly decorated columns which shelve inward in a style typical of this period, with ever more complicated swirls and patterns on the arches above the doorspace. The steeply-arched pediment is again ornately carved with primitive human heads set in triangular recesses and surrounded by more ornate carvings.

Norman Gothic

The Normans brought European sophistication to the architecture of Ireland with complex gothic-style church buildings such as Christ Church cathedral in Dublin and many monasteries, such as Sligo Abbey, which included a quadrangle with the church on the north side, the sacristy and meeting rooms on the east, refectory and dormitories on the south and storerooms on the west. Buildings were bigger and arches pointed, not for aesthetic reasons but because they were more efficient at loadbearing. Churches became larger with ornate triple-arched windows where the main characteristic of the Romanesque church had been a bulk of stone wall. Stained glass made an appearance, and later in the period the lancets between the windows become narrowed to thin stone pillars or mullions.

Secular architecture has been preserved in the form of castles, reflecting the period of warfare which filled the power vacuum after the death of Brian Boru. The first Normans built motte and bailey castles consisting of a huge mound of earth with a wooden tower on top and a semicircular fenced area at the bottom where the cattle were kept. Later, more settled Normans built square stone castles such as King John's Castle in Limerick, with towers at the corners.

Artistic expression in Norman times found its outlet in religious paraphernalia such as the shrines built to hold holy relics. Examples of these are in the Hunt Collection in Limerick and the National Gallery in Dublin.

The 15th & 16th centuries This period was marked by the struggle between the Norman lords and the Gaelic chieftains, and as you might expect art and architecture was dominated by the need to build fortified houses and towns with protective walls around them. This is the age of the tower houses, a high square building capable of being defended but essentially a home. Artwork of the time is very practical – the misericords of St Mary's Cathedral in Limerick date back to this period, for example, and while they are beautifully carved with the figures of mythical animals they are also eminently useful pieces of church furniture.

The 17th & 18th centuries The end of the 17th century saw the first completely domestic and non-defensive Irish architecture. The castles and fortified houses of the Plantation years began to give way to grand mansions without any fortifications. An example of seventeenth century architecture at its most creative is the 1680 Royal Hospital at Kilmainham, Dublin's oldest existing public building. Here style is as important as the purpose of the building, and great attention to detail has gone into both the exterior and interior of the building. The Georgian period saw a flowering of architecture in both public buildings and private houses in all of Ireland's cities, and in the countryside in the grand houses; a proud statement of ownership of the land on the part of the Protestant Ascendancy. Georgian architecture is modelled on the work of the sixteenth century architect Palladio, who left books of his designs for later architects to admire. Buildings are highly symmetrical with fake doors mirroring real doors so as to keep the symmetry. There is very little exterior ornamentation and much emphasis on proportion. The most famous and prolific of the Irish Georgian architects was Richard Castle (see page 457), who designed much of Georgian Dublin as well as Powerscourt in County Wicklow.

The enormous creativity of the time was also expressing itself in the paintings of Nathaniel Hone and George Barret, and in the craft skills of the men such as Michael Stapleton, who created the plasterwork and woodcarvings of public buildings. In many cases the names of these artists are lost, but the men who made the intricate plasterwork of Newman House which still survives were called the Francini brothers. Georgian silverware is also very distinctive, as is cut glass.

Victorian Ireland With the Act of Union the great Georgian building spree came to an end, and apart from some public buildings architecture went into a decline. The Gothic Revival style emerged, characterised by architectural decoration such as flying buttresses, pointed arches and ribbed vaults. The middle years of the century saw a massive number of churches being built as Catholic emancipation gained momentum, but the Famine brought most building to a full stop. Railway station buildings in particular provided an outlet for the eclectic style of the time. Portrait painting was popular and sentimental, as were allegorical historical and biblical paintings such as those of Francis Danby. James Arthur O'Connor was another important painter of the time, concentrating on landscapes.

After a brief Arts-and-Crafts-influenced Celtic Revival (Limerick Art Gallery contains some excellent examples) the modernist movement was the next big influence on Irish architecture, characterised by Busáras in Dublin and Dublin airport. Big blocks of concrete and glass followed, many of them borrowing ideas from ancient Irish structures – the public library in Bantry, for example, looks a little like a concrete dolmen if you squint sideways at it. In church architecture this pre-Celtic look has influenced the work of Liam McCormick in his additions to cathedrals such as the Catholic Cathedral in Armagh or the Church of St Aonghas at Burt, County Donegal. In the field of pure art Jack Yeats and Paul Henry are well-known figures, focusing on ordinary events in the lives of their Irish subjects. In more modern times the most visually obvious aspect of art is in the many sculptures which decorate the cities and towns. With typical irreverence Dubliners have given these sometimes peculiar objects their own names, so Dublin now has 'the floozy in the jacuzzi', 'the hags with the bags' and 'the tart with the cart' among others.

The twentieth century

Literature

When it comes to Irish literature it is hard to know where to start. Take Irish playwrights, poets and novelists out of university English Literature syllabuses and there wouldn't be a lot left to teach. The Irish took the language that the English imposed on them and made their own inspired use of it, superimposing their own patterns and making it a musical language rather than one of shopkeepers and factory owners. But Irish literature flourished long before English ever drove out the native language, and is the oldest written literature in Europe.

Just as in ancient Greece, an oral tradition existed in pre-Christian Ireland for centuries before the monks arrived around the fifth century CE with their writing skills. It wasn't long before the monks began to write these epic stories down, and many of them have survived. The earliest of these is the Mythological Cycle which tells stories in prose of the Tuatha Dé Danaan, the deities of the pagan Irish. When the monks came to write down these stories the characters changed from deities (not allowed in Christianity with its single omnipotent god) to the heroes of the earlier culture. The main characters are Lug, the leader of the gods, the sea god Manannán and their families, and the chief story is that of their battle with the Formori, giants who firstly oppress them and then are defeated by them, calling up parallels with the Greek stories of the Olympians and Titans, and perhaps also reflecting an earlier struggle between belief systems.

The best-known of the early Irish stories is the Ulster Cycle, a group of tales which features people called the Ulaid and the Connachta, the children of the gods, and the conflicts between them. The stories involve gods and heroes, magic and lots of fighting, death and blood, and feature Cú Chulain (or Cúchulainn) , the son of the god Lug, and Medb, a queen with magical powers associated with the goddess of sovereignty, often called Macha. The *Taín Bó Cuailnge*, (The Book of the Dun Cow), so called because part of it was written on vellum made from cowhide, contains many of these stories.

A third cycle of stories concerns the early rulers of Ireland, people such as Cormac McAirt, Conaire King of Tara, and others. They were composed between the ninth and twelfth centuries and deal with real figures from the sixth to eighth centuries. These stories would have been memorised by the *ollam*, professional story tellers and poets who would have brought them out on public occasions to recite.

Background

The last cycle of stories is known as the Ossianic Cycle and deals with the exploits of Fionn mac Cumhaill and his sons and grandsons. The source of the stories is a twelfth century text, featuring St Patrick, who meets Oisín, Fionn's son, and hears his stories and orders that they be written down. The cycle is seen as a reaction of the Gaels to the dominance of Cistercian monasticism in Ireland. Fionn and his band or Fianna are outlaws in the stories. Although the first written versions are mediaeval in origin, they are probably as old in oral tradition as the Ulster Cycle.

In the Middle Ages a tradition of bardic poets developed. These were a combination of praise-singers and *fili*, professional poets who memorised and told the stories of Celtic warriors and gods. Their function was to legitimise the chieftain who showed them patronage. As the centuries progressed the bards took up the political and social changes of the time, writing songs about the history of Ireland, the many battles fought, and the gradual decline of Gaelic Ireland in the face of Anglo-Irish control. By the 19th century the bardic tradition was almost extinct; some of the poems had been translated and printed but many were lost. Gaelic as a language was fast disappearing from Ireland. The Gaelic Revival in the late nineteenth century stirred things up a little, but the old style of epic writing had finished and the Irish-language poets of the twentieth century wrote in a modern vernacular idiom about things that were real to them. In modern times there is a large output of writing in Irish, but a very small reading public.

As Gaelic went into terminal decline Anglo-Irish writing, as if to rub salt in the wounds of the conquered, flourished. The 17th century saw the terrible wit of Jonathan Swift (1667-1745), the son of an Englishman, born in Dublin and educated in Ireland. Deeply committed to Anglicanism, opposed to religious toleration or equality, he nonetheless used his writing to accuse the government in England of misgovernment and short-sightedness in relation to Ireland. A contemporary of Swift was William Congreve, genetically English but educated in Kilkenny and Dublin, and a lawyer at the Middle Temple in Dublin. He wrote comedies of manners and is considered one of the English Restoration dramatists. George Farquhar (1677-1707), another contemporary of Swift's, was the son of an Anglican clergyman from Derry, and may well have lived through some of the siege of that city. His stage comedies featured some of the first sympathetic stage Irishmen who, unlike those of previous writers, had a higher moral sense than the Englishmen they dealt with, and often, like Roebuck in *Love and a Bottle*, were the hero of the play. From Clonmel, County Tipperary, the son of an Englishman and Irishwoman, Laurence Sterne (1713-68) is famous for his novel *Tristram Shandy*. The novel is innovative and stands in the Anglo-Irish tradition despite his only half-Irishness. It self-consciously refers to Swift, and its influence can be seen in the work of James Joyce. Sheridan (1751-1816), Wilde (1854-1900) and Shaw (1856-1950) are more widely-read authors, all in the Anglo-Irish tradition but all living their adult lives in London.

An innovative novelist of the early nineteenth century is Maria Edgeworth (1767-1849) whose novels are among the earliest to be set in a specific region of the country; she inspired Sir Walter Scott in his writings. Much of the work of her middle years is heavy and moralistic, influenced by her father who actually wrote the worst of the sermonising contained within them, but *Castle Rackrent*, *Belinda* and *Ormonde* are good reads and provide great insight into the Irish landlord classes of the nineteenth century. In her later years she spent much time trying to alleviate the sufferings of the people on her estate during the Famine.

Later writers from the same class are Edith Somerville (1858-1949) and Violet Martin (1862-1915), who wrote as Somerville and Ross. They examine the foolishness and pathos of the declining years of the big houses and their occupants. After Martin's death Somerville wrote several more successful novels, which she continued to publish under the joint names in the belief that she had an understanding with her partner which went beyond death.

At the end of the 19th century the Irish literary revival began with writing both in Irish and English. William Butler Yeats (1856-1939) was a member of the movement. The son of Irish Church of Ireland parents, he grew up in England and Ireland. He read translations of the Irish myths and became determined to revive the cultural heritage of Ireland, and his early poetry reflects that determination. In 1894 he met and made close friends with Lady Gregory, and the two planned the Irish Literary Theatre, to be realised as the Abbey Theatre in Dublin. His poetry is full of a sense of the mystical nature of the Irish countryside and sadness for the loss of the Celtic culture. In his last years he became disillusioned with Irish politics and took to spiritualism.

James Joyce died just two years after Yeats, but was a very different kettle of fish. He scoffed at the mysticism of the Gaelic Revival, but his work is in many ways more recognisably Irish than anything Yeats wrote. He was the son of a Catholic chancer, who put his money into this and that and lost all of it. Extremely intelligent, Joyce was educated free of charge by the Jesuits, but then turned his back on his religion and Ireland and never lived there again. His works – *Dubliners*, a series of short stories; *Portrait of the Artist as a young Man*; *Ulysses*; and *Finnegan's Wake* – make great reading for anyone interested in the workings of the Irish mind, and since the Irish state started to acknowledged his existence – some time after his death – he has gained the recognition in his own country that he deserves. You can see him artificially smiling at you from a ten pound note, or join the hundreds of people who celebrate his novel *Ulysses* on June 16th every year in Dublin.

A good friend of Joyce was Samuel Beckett (1909-1989), Nobel Prize winner and author of the play *Waiting for Godot*. Beckett's biography reads like an adventure story – stalked by Joyce's daughter Lucia, stabbed by a pimp in the backstreets of Paris, a member of the Resistance during the war, betrayed but escaped to Free France, holder of the Croix de Guerre. His works are painfully funny though full of suffering, and he was notorious for refusing permission for his material to be produced for fear that it wouldn't be done exactly right. His shortest play is *Breath*, which lasts about a minute. He too despised the Celtic Revival, and in his novel *Murphy* the protagonist attempts to kill himself by repeatedly headbutting the buttocks of the statue of Cú Chulain in the GPO in O'Connell St, which was erected in memory of those who died in the Easter Rising.

Kate O'Brien (1897-1974) was born in Limerick, the daughter of a horse dealer who made lots of money and then lost it. Her novels are about the complexities of being female and living up to the demands of the church. Several of them were, as you might expect, banned in Ireland. Her most famous novel is *The Ante-Room*. Although she lived most of her adult life in England, her novels are centred very much in the Irish middle classes.

Brendan Behan (1923-64) is another writer whose life story would fit neatly into one of his plays. Born into a working class Dublin family, he was arrested and imprisoned in Britain at the age of sixteen for taking part in an IRA bombing campaign. He spent three years in English borstals, where he began to practise his craft of writing. Back in Ireland he was arrested again for the attempted murder of a detective, and spent five more years in prison in Ireland. While in prison he wrote poetry in Irish and his autobiographical novel *Borstal Boy*. He died from the drink at the height of his popularity. His best works are *The Quare Fellow* and *The Hostage*, both plays.

Like Behan, Sean O'Casey (1880-1964) was working class, but this time born into a Protestant family. Like Behan he did manual work to make ends meet and in his early years was a great joiner, joining both the fledgling IRA and the Orange Order, but it was James Larkin's trade union which finally claimed his allegiance. His first play, *Shadow of a Gunman*, was produced by the Abbey Theatre in 1923, and was followed by *Juno and the Paycock*, *The Plough and the Stars*. His plays are written in

Field Day

At a time when no-one wanted to know about Ireland and its culture, a relatively unknown writer, Brian Friel, and a very unknown actor, Stephen Rea, formed a theatre group called the Field Day Theatre company in Derry. They attracted the cooperation of other writers and people in the arts – Tom Paulin, Seamus Deane (a poet who later became the director of Field Day), David Hammond the film maker, and Seamus Heaney. Situated on the border of the two states, with the benefit of two cultural traditions, Catholic and Protestant, Field Day offered writers and audiences a 'Fifth Province', a place where it was safe to look at what Ireland was without breaking cultural taboos. One of its first successes was Friel's Translations, which was performed in the Guildhall in Derry and then went on tour around Ireland with Stephen Rea and Liam Neeson in its cast, playing in school halls to audiences of farmers who recognised its cultural significance. Throughout the eighties Field Day grew in reputation, putting on productions by Friel, Tom Kilroy, Stewart Parker and Terry Eagleton, and producing pamphlets on all aspects of Irish culture, culminating in 1991 in the Field Day Anthology of Irish Writing, which sadly left out most women writers. Coming under a barrage of revisionist and feminist criticism, Field Day closed down in 1992 but reformed in 1994.

the Dublin vernacular, and shocked and horrified middle class Irish audiences with their language and honesty. Like other writers of his generation he was disgusted by the new Irish government and moved permanently to England.

In modern times the names come thick and fast. Christy Brown, Roddy Doyle, J P Donleavy, Liam O'Flaherty, John McGahern, John Banville, Mary Lavin, Edna O'Brien, Frank McCourt, Iris Murdoch, Clare Boylan, Molly Keane, Maeve Binchy, are all highly successful and revered novelists.

Playwrights include Brian Friel, whose brilliant play *Translations* changed the way that people looked at Irish history, John B Keane whose play *The Field* is an essential read for anyone who wants to understand the Irish attitude to the land, Hugh Leonard, Tom Mackintyre and Martin Mc Donagh. Sebastian Barry, a novelist, short story writer and playwright, has had considerable critical success in London and New York with his plays *The Steward of Christendom* and *Our Lady of Sligo*, which are concerned with the sense of Irish identity and fitting in.

In poetry there is the Nobel Prize winner Seamus Heaney (1939-) from County Derry, Louis MacNeice (1907-1963) whose poetry, like Heaney's, is influenced by his Northern Ireland childhood, Patrick Kavanagh whose poetry reflects the harsh lives of a farming community in the north, and Tom Paulin (1949-) from Belfast, whose poetry is full of the state of mind created by the political situation in the North. Other poets who write about Ireland include Thomas Kinsella, John Montague, Eavan Boland and Brendan Kennelly.

Cinema

Ireland has always provided an excellent source of actors and locations for movies, although it hasn't always had the cash to play around with that it has attracted in the last decade. In recent years both Dublin and Belfast have rarely had a day without a film crew blocking the streets, and in little pubs all over Ireland you can see black and white stills of the locals dressed up as mariners, Scottish warriors, 19th century peasants and whatever else. In the 1950s the village of Cong came to the screens of the world in the movie *The Quiet Man* directed by John Ford, and has never really recovered. Then *Ryan's Daughter* was filmed on the Dingle Peninsula in

1970, and you can now take guided tours of the spots where Robert Mitchum nearly drowned and the set was built for the village, although most of it blew down in 1997. The next big star movie made with chiefly American actors was *Far and Away* in1991, a Cruse and Kidman vehicle which left everyone wincing at the Irish accents and actually used some of the backstreets of Dublin to represent Boston. These were all movies with an Irish theme, but Ireland has provided some other strange locations. *Moby Dick* was filmed around Youghal in County Cork in 1956, while *Educating Rita*, a movie about an English Open University student and her tutor, was filmed in Trinity College. In 1994 a piece of Irish mountainside became Scotland for a few weeks while Mel Gibson filmed *Braveheart*, and lots of Irish students as well as the territorial army filled in the crowd scenes. If you look very carefully you might see some of the same faces in *Saving Private Ryan* directed by Stephen Spielberg. The biggest surprise hit movie made in Ireland has to be *The Commitments*, directed by Alan Parker in 1990, filmed with an entirely Irish cast around north Dublin and displaying the grim reality of north Dublin life as opposed to the quaint beauty of the Irish countryside in the earlier big movies. It, and the previous year's *My Left Foot*, the story of a paralysed young boy's life directed by Jim Sheridan, set a high standard and created interest in the real Ireland which has spawned several good films since. In 1990 Jim Sheridan made *The Field*, from the play by John B Keane, about the desperate fight for one small field in western Ireland. Filmed around Leenane in County Galway, it is harsh and unsentimental in its portrayal of rural Ireland. In 1992 the movie *The Crying Game* directed by Neil Jordan tells the bleak story of an IRA man who strikes up a relationship with the lover of the man he helped to kill. Jim Sheridan took up the theme of the Troubles in 1993 to make *In the Name of the Father* with Daniel Day Lewis and Emma Thompson about the injustice meted out to the Conolly family, better known as the Guildford Four, in the early 1970s. In 1995 *Nothing Personal* took up the theme of the North again, this time looking at the chaos created in the lives of bystanders caught up in the Troubles and the terrible waste of young lives which the last twenty-five years has brought about. 1996 saw the big blockbuster *Michael Collins*, which set the whole of Ireland arguing about the treatment of de Valera and displayed Julia Roberts' feeble efforts at an Irish accent. By this time the Troubles had become a moneyspinner, and 1996 also saw the release of *Some Mother's Son*, another innocent person caught up in the troubles as her son takes part in the hunger strike which killed Bobby Sands. Helen Mirren does an excellent job as the respectable mother. By this time the North and the IRA were almost a cliché as Harrison Ford inadvertently twice got caught up in the Troubles, once with Brad Pitt doing the worst Irish accent ever recorded in *The Devil's Own* (1996).

Back to intelligent movie-making, the best movie to come out of Ireland in 1998 was *The General*, directed by John Boorman, about a comical Dublin thug who gets caught up with the UVF and suffers the consequences. In the same year the first Irish road movie was released, *I Went Down* directed by Paddy Breathnach, a funny story about innocents mixed up with gangsters and refreshingly free of hooded gunmen.

Neil Jordan stands out in particular as an excellent Irish film-maker. Before he got big money and made *Michael Collins* his films included *Angel* (1982), set in Northern Ireland long before it became chic, *Mona Lisa*, *The Crying Game*, *The Company of Wolves*,and his most recent movie, set in small town Ireland, *The Butcher Boy*.

Music

The earliest form that Irish music is known to have taken is in the songs sung by the bards to the music of the metal-stringed harp. None of it was written down until the 17th century, and the earliest music to survive is the work of the harpist Turlough O'Carolan. Later collections date back to the Belfast harp festival of 1792. These were

Background

The bent note and the twisted word

Our understanding of pre-Christian attitudes to music depends on surviving Gaelic myths which suggest that the songs and music of the bards were much more than a bit of light entertainment while they feasted. Rhyme and music formed a powerful magical weapon in the war against one's enemies as a story from Lébor Gabadla, the Book of Invasions tells. Daghda, one of the three leaders of the Tuatha de Danaan, the triumvirate of deities of pagan Ireland, has the power of music and one day slips into his enemies' camp to rescue a friend. He uses music to put three spells on the enemies, making them weep with sad music, dance with happy music and finally fall asleep to soothing music, allowing the captive to escape. Another story, of Oengus son of Daghda, tells how he and his lover Caer Iborméith, in the form of swans, make such beautiful music as they fly together that all who hear it fall asleep.

Much later, in early Christian Ireland the bards were highly valued intellectuals who could make or break a reputation with their poetry and the idea of the power of rhyme and music lingered a long time in Irish culture. In the 1959 play by John B Keane, Sive, a travelling tinker poses real threats to the local people with his chanted curses.

Gaelic and Scottish jigs and reels which took on an Irish character. In the eighteenth century the Irish traditional music that we recognise emerged. The harp, the instrument of the bards, was in decline, and the playing of reels and hornpipes on fiddle, flute and uillean pipes emerged. Each county had its own style of music, and some of the distinctions can still be heard. Early in the century the flute was introduced via Dublin.

The most commonly available printed source of music was the ballad sheets which emerged after every national event, telling the story in song; these sheets were bought and copied, thus making their way around the country. Murders, rebellions, hangings – the news travelled via the songsheets. Some of these songs outlived their immediate interest and survived; other disappeared. Dance masters travelled around the country, staying in each village for a few weeks and teaching the latest dances and tunes to the locals. They were eagerly awaited and received a royal welcome when they arrived. If two masters met on their journey the village would have a contest between the masters. This powerful social custom attracted even the Ascendancy class, busy listening to Handel in Dublin, and traditional music concerts took place in the houses of the rich.

In the nineteenth century traditional music continued as an unschooled family event, celebrated at wakes and weddings and at the crossroads at holiday periods. Songs were traditional ones or made up for the moment, about friends and relatives or events in history. Instruments were the tin whistle, the fiddle and the bodhrán, a quite modern instrument made a goatskin stretched over a frame and played with the hand or both ends of a wooden stick. Less common but much older are the uilleann pipes, a complicated version of the bagpipes with a much more complex range of sounds. You'll be lucky to see anyone play this instrument in Ireland – it takes a good few years to master.

The Famine almost destroyed Irish music altogether as those who practised it died or emigrated. The music that survived did so because the emigrants in America, Australia, London, Liverpool and Glasgow kept their culture alive and, thankfully, had the sense to record the tunes, far away from the music's origins. In the USA piping clubs emerged and Irish performers joined the Variety Club circuits, adapting their music to American tastes. The Taylor Brothers, an emigrant family from Drogheda, developed the uillean pipes, bringing them to concert pitch and making them more suitable for performance. Then in 1890 the Gaelic League

Francis O'Neill

Born near Bantry, County Cork, in1849, the youngest of seven children, Francis O'Neill was a typical child of his time, speaking both Irish and English, attending the school in Bantry, and learning by ear to play the wooden flute. He was good at remembering the tunes – an advantage since no-one he knew was literate in musical notation. He spent his first adult years on board ships and was shipwrecked on Baker Island, a little atoll 1,650 miles south west of Honolulu, for some time before a passing American ship rescued him. Landing in San Francisco he settled in America and eventually became chief of police in

Chicago, arresting the anarchist Emma Goldman in 1901. His hobby remained traditional Irish music, and with the help of a musically literate fellow officer he began collecting and transcribing Irish tunes from the many Irish immigrants he encountered. Between 1903 and 1924 he published nine volumes of Irish tunes which would otherwise have been lost. While the collections became essential material for traditional musicians his work as a collector and biographer of American Irish musicians was never recognised in Ireland, until in 1999 he got a hotel named after him in Smithfield, Dublin.

regenerated interest in music in Ireland itself, inventing the *ceili*, a showcase for Irish music and dancing. Traditional music went into a bit of a decline in the middle years of this century with the advent of radio, but it emerged again in the 1960s, first with Seán O Riada and traditional band Ceoltórirí Chualann, but it was The Chieftains who took the combination of traditional instruments and orchestral arrangements of Irish music all over the world.

There are several branches of the traditional music scene. One is the rebel song, sung late at night in bars in Donegal and made almost respectable by bands such as the Wolfe Tones. Another is the Dublin-based bawdy strain, epitomised by the Dubliners and their song *Seven Drunken Nights*, the last two of which were too bawdy to record. The most inward-looking and sentimental is the ballad, often involving dead wives and abandoned homes, sung by Daniel O'Donnell and a host of clones and closely linked to the American country music scene. In pubs all around the country what you are most likely to hear is a mixture of Irish dance tunes, Fonn Mall or slow airs, and rebel songs. If you are lucky you might come across *sean nós*, a strange nasal unaccompanied singing in Irish which takes a great deal of effort both to sing and to listen to. To the untrained ear it sounds like a monotone but the trick is to listen for the subtle nuances of the song.

As traditional music has lost its sweater-and-corduroys image it has changed and fused with other musical traditions as new generations of talented players have taken it up. Christy Moore is probably Ireland's favourite traditional musician. He has been in the business since the early days of the 1960s and early on formed the band Planxty with Liam O'Flynn, Donal Lunny and Andy Irvine. Planxty mixed traditional music with acoustic guitar folk music and ballads, but above all it was their skill with instruments which marked them out. All of them have moved on to other careers, Moore forming the band Moving Hearts which fused his traditional style with his own compositions, jazz and rock music. Many of Moore's songs have political overtones and comment on the Troubles and Irish politics. Since 1998 he has retired to West Cork. Other musicians who have influenced the traditional music scene are Moore's brother, Luka Bloom, and Paul Brady, both of whom have played with Moore in different bands.

Most dynamic of all were the band Pogue Mahone (Kiss my Arse), Londoners led by the musical icon Shane McGowan. They were a wild mix of punk, rebel song, traditional ballad and just plain rock music. McGowan and the Pogues split over

Dancing

'During the intervals the devil is busy; yes, very busy, as sad experience proves, and on the way home in the small hours of the morning, he is busier still.'

A statement on all-night dances by the Irish bishops, The Irish Catholic, 23 Dec 1993

Dancing has always been a tricky thing in Ireland. Traditionally Irish people have always loved to dance, and in the days before the radio and TV a good night out would have been spent at the crossroads where there was enough space and where people knew to meet each other, dancing set dances – a little bit like a hoedown with someone calling out the moves as partners moved about in fixed patterns of jigs and reels to the tune of a tin whistle, violin or accordion. In the 40s and 50s, when dance halls opened up, it offered the possibility of all kinds of shenanigans between unmarried men and women, and the church frowned heavily on it with the parish priest often turning up late at night to check on the souls of the young.

Then there is Irish dancing, the name given to the peculiar rigid dancing performed mostly by young girls in heavily embroidered dresses. All over Ireland – and England too – there are competitions for these dances with little girls competing for medals which they collect and sew on to a harp-shaped frame. Rooted in the dancing of sailors on shipboard (hornpipe) and probably a hangover from the military past, this quite frigid kind of dancing with the arms held firmly at the sides somehow produced Riverdance, the modern version with very short skirts and bare-chested leading men stamping about the stage. Unlike traditional music which is green and cool, Riverdance, which was a breath of fresh air when it first hit the stage, must surely now have a limited lifespan.

McGowan's chaotic lifestyle, and he now plays with a new band The Popes. If you listen to nothing else in Ireland, listen to some of McGowan 's songs, some of the finest music to emerge from the rock music scene in the last decade.

Another icon of the Irish music scene is Van Morrison, who came to the fore via a very different route. In the 1960s he led the band Them with pop hits in Britain. He spent many years in the USA and made his mark with albums such as *Astral Weeks* and *Moondance*. As a solo singer he has recorded with the Chieftains and has figured prominently in the efforts to reach peace in the North, where his home town is Belfast.

There are many other names to mention in a description of the vibrant Irish music scene. You can't go far in Dublin without tripping over U2, who own the Clarence Hotel and the Kitchen nightclub, two of the coolest places to be seen in. Clannad belong to the traditional music scene and have been around for what seems like a very long time. Rory Gallagher, who died in 1996, achieved world fame with his music in the 60s and 70s, selling 30 million records and touring all over the world first with his band Taste and then pursuing a solo career. There are also the Boomtown Rats and Bob Geldof, who have produced some good pop music. The early 90s witnessed Sinead O'Connor's tempestuous appearance on the world music scene, while other women such as Mary Black, Dolores Keane and Maura O'Connell have had quieter but equally successful careers. Sharon Shannon is based firmly in the traditional music scene and plays vigorous accordion and fiddle music. A big name in the pre-teen market is Irish boy band Boyzone. Also very successful in the pop charts in 1998 were the four sister of The Corrs, who have broken all kinds of sales records with their albums *Talk on Corners* and *Forgiven, not Forgotten*.

Irish sports

In Ireland you will encounter all the regular sports, and Irish people tune in to the Sky Sports stations just like the rest of Europe, but Ireland also has some sports which are purely Irish in origin, even if that origin wasn't too long ago. The Gaelic Athletic Association was established in 1884, around the time of the Gaelic Revival, and established rules for games which had more or less existed before but had never been organised. Gaelic football is the Irish version of the game played in America and is a cross between English rugby and English football. There are fifteen players and the round ball is played with both the hands and feet. Goals, as in football, and scores, as in rugby, are possible, with one goal equal to three scores. It is a very physical, fast game with few rules about physical contact.

More popular is hurling, a kind of hockey which is played on the same pitch as Gaelic. It is a very old game. Brehon Law, the law which operated in pre-Christian Ireland, allowed for compensation for the families of those injured in hurling matches, and tradition says that the battle of Moytura, fought in 200BCE, began as a hurling match. Between the fourteenth and seventeenth centuries hurling was banned three times. Nowadays it's a little less rough than the days when whole clans became professional hurling players and fought for the various clan chiefs. As in Gaelic there are 15 players to a team, and the object is to get the soft ball between the opponent's goal posts. The stick is wide at one end, and good players can carry the ball for several paces balanced on the stick. It is recognised as one of the fastest team sports in the world. Both games are just as popular as regular football, and each year the whole country bedecks itself with its county's colours as the two sets of teams play towards the All Ireland finals at Croke Park in September.

Lifestyle

The last ten years have seen such changes that make it almost difficult to believe that the Ireland of the past ever existed. Ireland was an amazing little country, stuck out on the very western edge of Europe, poor, underdeveloped, underpopulated, and with a history that just wouldn't go away and let it move on. Dominated by the Church physically, politically and emotionally, it was seriously in danger of becoming a banana republic, taking handouts from the EU, sending its brightest and best off to other countries to find work, forever in the shadow of its bullying big brother, Britain. It seemed unable to move decisively into the future.

Take women for example. Half the population, well-educated, women have contributed to every aspect of Irish life from politics and war to science, medicine, art and literature. But try naming ten famous Irish women. At the turn of the century Irish women were pretty much the social equals of their sisters in Britain – no vote, none in parliament, none at universities, no doctors. Irish suffragettes fought and suffered for their demands just as British ones did. Under the Free State Irish women got the vote, stood for the Dáil, attended universities, practised medicine, did very nearly everything that Irish men did. But within twenty years most of that had disappeared – under the Irish constitution and the laws passed in the 1930s women had no access to contraception, no right to terminate a pregnancy under any circumstances whatsoever, no right to divorce, no right to own the family home or take authority over the children, no senior civil service jobs, no place in industrial management, and certainly no equality of pay. It was as if Irish women voluntarily gave up all the rights and freedoms they had won in the early years of the century. And, weirdly, this continued more or less well into the 1980s. The first women sat on juries in the 1970s, the first condoms became available outside a prescription from a chemist shop in 1993, it was EU laws that forced equal pay and opportunities into Irish law (if not into practice). Finally, in the late nineties, contraception and abortion advice became available in Ireland, and a referendum narrowly put divorce in a very limited number of cases on to the statute books.

In the last decade Ireland has undergone seismic changes that no one would have believed possible. The church has lost its place in politics forever, with terrible stories emerging about child abuse by priests and nuns (and covered up by the church), the treatment of unmarried mothers in the Magdalen laundries (laundry

Background

When the city authorities tried to prevent an Ann Summers sex shop opening in O'Connell Street in Dublin, a 10,000-strong petition was part of the campaign directed against the attempted ban

workshops run by nuns), the scandal – hilarious though it was – of Bishop Eamon Casey and his teenage son. There have been corruption charges against once invulnerable men; the Good Friday Agreement saw the end to Ireland 's claim to sovereignty over the North; the 1995 divorce laws brought about after a very narrow referendum finally liberated thousands of people from dead marriages; and most amazingly of all the emergence of high-wattage economic growth which has led to Ireland becoming dubbed 'The Celtic Tiger'.

For two centuries Irish people have had to leave their homes in order to prosper or even survive. There are millions of Irish-descended people living in Britain, something like 43 million Americans claim Irish descent, and the diaspora spreads to Australia and beyond. When American visas became hard to get in the 80s the Irish government set up emigration agencies to arrange for young people to go to Europe for work. Suddenly the reverse is true, and not only are Irish people returning home to take up work but for the first time since the Plantation English people are emigrating to Ireland in large numbers. Europeans have been settling in Ireland for the past thirty years, but it was always the oddballs who discovered the real Ireland and gave up money, possessions and city life to live as blow-ins and hippies in little cottages in the west of Ireland, setting up hostels, potteries, small engineering businesses or cafés, or just signing on for unemployment benefit each week. But in the last few years companies like Microsoft and Dell, Fruit of the Loom and others have taken advantage of government subsidies and moved into the cities, providing employment and spending power that never existed before on such a scale. A few miles west of Dublin, in Leixlip, Co Kildare, Intel has set up a $2.5billion plant employing 4,000 people, the biggest building project in the history of Ireland. FÁS, the employment agency, had 10,000 unfilled skilled vacancies in 1999. Forty-four thousand people moved to Ireland in 1998 to take up work, 21,000 of them from Britain. Dublin, Limerick, Galway, Belfast even, have become young vibrant, cosmopolitan places where there are opportunities, a great social life, lots of beautiful countryside, and lots to spend your euros on, whether it be an extremely expensive apartment (Dublin prices now match London's), beautifully designed Irish clothes, or a theme café bar serving post-modern bacon and cabbage.

If Dublin belongs to the young and mobile, the west still belongs to the culchies (see Glossary). In the villages of the west of Ireland scant attention is paid to Microsoft or Intel, although mobile phones have their uses when you're bringing the cows in. In Dublin not locking your front door is asking for trouble – in the west anyone with a door locked too often has something to hide. In Dublin the man walking towards you is a potential danger – in the west he's someone to chat to for a few minutes. No one locks up their car or even bothers parking it properly, pub closing time depends on how close the police are, while shops, banks and any other useful place you could visit in your lunch hour are firmly closed so that everyone can enjoy their lunch.

The Ireland that you visit in the 21st century is not the Ireland of the eighties. It has undergone changes that the leaders of the 1916 Rebellion, de Valera, Michael Collins or even Gay Byrne, the radical TV chat show host of the 60s, could not have imagined or even wanted. It has moved into the 21st century with skill and panache, and in doing so has managed to preserve, or at least not yet lose, much of what was good about the old Ireland.

Footnotes

19

706

Footnotes

Place-names, townlands and translations

A townland, a division of land which defies its name by very often being non-urban, can vary in size from 1 acre to 7,000 acres. Their origins can sometimes be traced back to plantation divisions and old clan divisions while the etymologies of many of the 60,000 townlands in Ireland suggest ancient Gaelic origins rooted in a reverence for natural features. In Brian Friel's seminal play Translations (1980) the compulsory translation of Gaelic place-names into English by soldiers working on the Ordnance Survey becomes a powerful cultural metaphor for the invasion and expropriation of Ireland by the English.

The following glossary offers some help in recovering the original meaning behind the evocative names of places and townlands across Ireland. They are nearly all Gaelic in origin, although some reveal the impact of Christianity, like kill/cill from the Latin cella.

agh, augh, achadh	field	*fóin*	small cove
aglish	church	*géar*	sharp
ah, atha, áth	ford, crossing	*glas, gleann*	valley, green
aill, anna, canna	cliff	*inbhear (inver)*	river mouth
árd, ar	marshland	*inis*	island
as, ess, eas	high ground	*kill, cill*	church
aw, ow, atha	waterfall	*kin*	headland
bal, bel, béal	river	*knock, cnoc*	hill
bal, bally, baile	town	*leac*	flat rock
bán	white	*léith*	grey
beann (ben)	peak	*lis, lios*	fort
bearna	gap	*lough, loch*	lake
beg, beag	small	*mainistir*	monastery
binn	peak	*moy, magh*	lake
buí	yellow	*maol*	bare hilllock
bun	bottom, base	*mona, móna*	bog, turf
caher, cahir	rock	*mór*	big
caol	narrow	*oileán*	island
carraig	rock	*owen*	river
cashel, caisel, caisleán	castle	*poll*	hole, hollow
céibh	quay	*rath*	ring-fort
cloich, cloch	stone	*rinn, reen*	headland, point
cnoc	rocky hill	*rón*	seal
cuainín	small harbour	*ross*	wood
derg, dearg	red	*sceilig (skellig)*	rock
doire	oakwood	*sidh*	a hill of the fairies
doo, dubh	black	*slieve, sliabh*	mountain
dumhaig	of the sandy shore	*staca*	pinnacle/stack (of rock)
dúna	of the fort	*tir*	country
dun, dún	fort	*tubber, tobar*	well
dysert	hermitage	*trá, tráigh*	beach
fada	long		

Map index

Footnotes

Index

Complete listing

Latin America

Argentina Handbook 1st
1 900949 10 5 £11.99

Bolivia Handbook 1st
1 900949 09 1 £11.99

Bolivia Handbook 2nd
1 900949 49 0 £12.99

Brazil Handbook 1st
0 900751 84 3 £12.99

Brazil Handbook 2nd
1 900949 50 4 £13.99

Caribbean Islands Handbook 2000
1 900949 40 7 £14.99

Chile Handbook 2nd
1 900949 28 8 £11.99

Colombia Handbook 1st
1 900949 11 3 £10.99

Cuba Handbook 1st
1 900949 12 1 £10.99

Cuba Handbook 2nd
1 900949 54 7 £10.99

Ecuador & Galápagos Handbook 2nd
1 900949 29 6 £11.99

Mexico Handbook 1st
1 900949 53 9 £13.99

**Mexico & Central America
Handbook 2000**
1 900949 39 3 £15.99

Peru Handbook 2nd
1 900949 31 8 £11.99

South American Handbook 2000
1 900949 38 5 £19.99

Venezuela Handbook 1st
1 900949 13 X £10.99

Venezuela Handbook 2nd
1 900949 58 X £11.99

Africa

East Africa Handbook 2000
1 900949 42 3 £14.99

Morocco Handbook 2nd
1 900949 35 0 £11.99

Namibia Handbook 2nd
1 900949 30 X £10.99

South Africa Handbook 2000
1 900949 43 1 £14.99

Tunisia Handbook 2nd
1 900949 34 2 £10.99

Zimbabwe Handbook 1st
0 900751 93 2 £11.99

Wexas

Traveller's Handbook
0 905802 08 X £14.99

Traveller's Healthbook
0 905802 09 8 £9.99

Asia

Cambodia Handbook 2nd
1 900949 47 4 £9.99

Goa Handbook 1st
1 900949 17 2 £9.99

Goa Handbook 2nd
1 900949 45 8 £9.99

India Handbook 2000
1 900949 41 5 £15.99

Indonesia Handbook 2nd
1 900949 15 6 £14.99

Indonesia Handbook 3rd
1 900949 51 2 £15.99

Laos Handbook 2nd
1 900949 46 6 £9.99

Malaysia & Singapore Handbook 2nd
1 900949 16 4 £12.99

Malaysia Handbook 3rd
1 900949 52 0 £12.99

Myanmar (Burma) Handbook 1st
0 900751 87 8 £9.99

Nepal Handbook 2nd
1 900949 44 X £11.99

Pakistan Handbook 2nd
1 900949 37 7 £12.99

Singapore Handbook 1st
1 900949 19 9 £9.99

Sri Lanka Handbook 2nd
1 900949 18 0 £11.99

Sumatra Handbook 1st
1 900949 59 8 £9.99

Thailand Handbook 2nd
1 900949 32 6 £12.99

Tibet Handbook 2nd
1 900949 33 4 £12.99

Vietnam Handbook 2nd
1 900949 36 9 £10.99

Europe

Andalucía Handbook 2nd
1 900949 27 X £9.99

Ireland Handbook 1st
1 900949 55 5 £11.99

Scotland Handbook 1st
1 900949 56 3 £10.99

Middle East

Egypt Handbook 2nd
1 900949 20 2 £12.99

Israel Handbook 2nd
1 900949 48 2 £12.99

Jordan, Syria & Lebanon Handbook 1st
1 900949 14 8 £12.99

Will you help us?

We try as hard as we can to make each Footprint Handbook as up-to-date and accurate as possible but, of course, things always change. Many people write to us - with corrections, new information, or simply comments.

If you want to let us know about an experience or adventure - hair-raising or mundane, good or bad, exciting or boring or simply something rather special - we would be delighted to hear from you. Please give us as precise information as possible, quoting the edition number (you'll find it on the front cover) and page number of the Handbook you are using.

Your help will be greatly appreciated, especially by other travellers. In return we will send you details about our special guidebook offer.

Write to Elizabeth Taylor
Footprint Handbooks
6 Riverside Court
Lower Bristol Road
Bath
BA2 3DZ
England
or email info@footprintbooks.com

Dublin's Viking Adventure

Malahide Castle

Fry Model Railway

Something to write home about

James Joyce Museum

Shaw Birthplace

Dublin Writers Museum

Dear Sarah

We're having an amazing time, Dublin is even more than we expected. Our first stop was **Malahide Castle** - a magnificent place with splendid rooms and antique furnishings. In the grounds we found the **Fry Model Railway**, it's like a small boy's wildest dream and your Father couldn't get enough of it. Back in town we went to **Dublin's Viking Adventure**. We didn't just meet live vikings, we smelt them as well ! It was just like being in Dublin a thousand years ago.

The history here is something else, it's certainly the land of scholars (though we're not sure about the saints yet). We started our literary round-up at the **Shaw Birthplace** (where 'GBS' was born) - a real Victorian experience. Our next stop was the **Dublin Writers Museum**, in a gorgeous old Georgian house all gilt and plasterwork, full of literary memorabilia. It's astonishing how many great writers were Irish, and all with such fascinating lives ! Of course the best of the lot has the **James Joyce Museum** all to himself in a great spot by the sea in Sandycove. I was so thrilled to be there where Ulysses begins that I made your Father promise to read it - tonight ! We had planned to come home at the weekend but we're having such a great time we might just stay another week.

Bye for now,
Lots of love -
Mum & Dad

**For further information
please contact:**
Tel:+353 1 846 2184 Fax:+353 1 846 2537
enterprises@dublintourism.ie
www.visitdublin.com

Dublin
Tourism
Enterprises

Here's an invitation to visit some of Ireland's finest gardens.

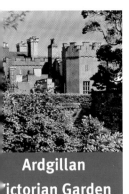

Ardgillan Victorian Garden

Talbot Botanic Gardens

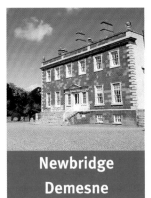

Newbridge Demesne

RDGILLAN DEMESNE,
ALBRIGGAN, Co. DUBLIN
EL: + 353 1 849 2324 (Gardens)
EL: + 353 1 849 2212 (House)

MALAHIDE CASTLE DEMESNE,
MALAHIDE, Co. DUBLIN
TEL: + 353 1 872 7777 (Gardens)
TEL: + 353 1 846 2184 (Castle)

DONABATE, Co. DUBLIN
TEL: + 353 1 843 6064 (Demesne)
TEL: + 353 1 843 6534 (House)

agrant Rose Gardens.
estored Walled Garden
f herbs and vegetables
eaturing an unusual fruit
cove wall.
eriod House furnished
n Victorian style.
ea Rooms and Walks.

22 acre Botanic Gardens
including a walled garden and
a fine collection of southern
hemisphere plants.
Magnificent Medieval Castle -
beautiful furniture & paintings,
Restaurant and Playground.
Fry Model Railway.

Walled Orchard Garden.
Delightful Georgian Manor -
fine interiors, original
furniture and Museum.
Traditional Farm with
farmyard animals.
Tea Rooms, Picnic area,
Walks & extensive Playground.

arden open all year 10:00 - 17:00
uided tour each Thursday at
5:00 during June, July & August.

Garden open 1st May - 30th
September 14:00 - 17:00 daily.
Guided tour each Wednesday at
14:00 or by appointment.

Demesne open all year.

For further information contact:
Dublin Tourism Enterprises on + 353 1 605 7754
Gardens managed & operated by Fingal County Council

Skellig Group Hotels

Dingle Skellig Hotel
Conference & Leisure Centre
Dingle, Co. Kerry
Tel: 353 66 91 51144
Fax: 353 66 91 51501
e-mail: dsk@iol.ie
www.dingleskellig.com

Kilkenny River Court Hotel
Conference & Leisure Centre
The Bridge John St Kilkenny
Tel: 353 56 23388
Fax: 353 56 23389
e-mail: krch@iol.ie
www.kilrivercourt.com

Barrow House
West Barrow Tralee Co. Kerry
Tel: 353 66 71 36437
Fax: 353 66 71 36402

our **views** make the
difference...

WATERFORD CASTLE

Waterford Castle is uniquely situated on a private 310-acre island, enjoying a picturesque and enchanting location of the surrounding River Suir and countryside. Access to the Island by our private car ferry, operating throughout the day.

The Hotel combines the gracious living standards of an elegant past with every modern comfort, service and convenience. The antiques, stylish décor and delicate period details will captivate the most discerning guest. Traditional fabrics and exquisite furnishings are featured in the 5 suites and 14 guestrooms all individually decorated.

Dining at Waterford Castle provides an opportunity to sample the best of traditional and contemporary cuisine. The Munster Dining room with its original oak panelled walls and ornate ceilings sets the tone for a wonderful evening. The restaurant's seasonal menus place emphasis on both Irish specialities as well as the finest international cuisine. Also an enjoyable feature of the restaurant is our resident pianist who plays nightly (peak season) during dinner.

On the Island activities include an 18 Hole Golf Course, tennis, croquet, garden walks and an indoor heated 16 metre pool. We are also happy to arrange off site, horse trekking, fishing, hill walking, water sports and beauty treatments for our guests.

So, if you want to relax, enjoy good food and friendly atmosphere with the occasional round of golf, Waterford Castle Hotel is the place to be.

The Island, Waterford, Ireland. Telephone: 353 51 878203 Fax: 353 51 878342
Email: info@waterfordcastle.com Web Site: www.waterfordcastle.com

Advertisers

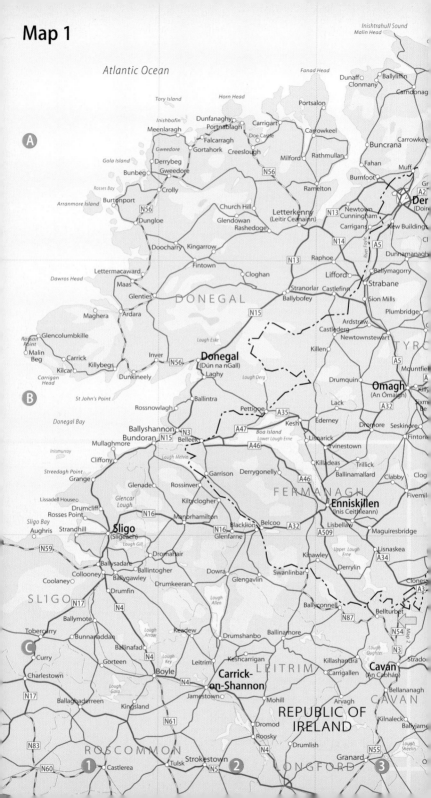

Map 1

Map 2

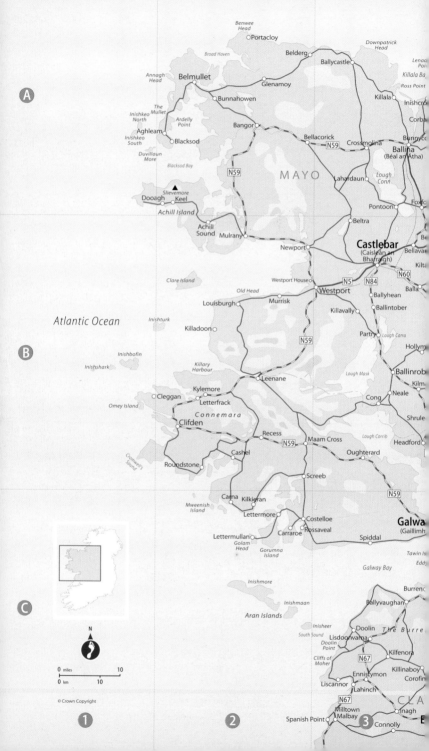

Benwee Head
Portacloy
Broad Haven
Belderg
Ballycastle
Downpatrick Head
Lenaun Point
Killala Bay
Glenamoy
Killala
Ross Point
Inishcrone
Annagh Head
Belmullet
Bunnahowen
Corbally
The Mullet
Bangor
Bellacorick
Crossmolina
Bunnycc
N59
Ballina
(Béal an Átha)
Inishkeo North
Ardelly Point
Aghleam
Blacksod
Inishkeo South
MAYO
Lahardaun
Lough Conn
Duvillaun More
Blacksod Bay
N59
Foxfc
Slievemore
Pontoon
Dooagh
Keel
Beltra
Achill Island
Bellava
Achill Sound
Mulrany
Castlebar
(Caislean an Bharraigh)
Kilta
Newport
N60
Clare Island
N5
Balla
Westport House
N84
Old Head
Westport
Ballyhean
Louisburgh
Murrisk
Ballintober
Killavally
Inishturk
Killadoon
Partry
Lough Carra
Hollym
Atlantic Ocean
N59
Ballinrob
Inishbofin
Killary Harbour
Lough Mask
Inishshark
Leenane
Kilm
Kylemore
Cong
Cleggan
Letterfrack
Neale
Omey Island
Clifden
Connemara
Shrule
Recess
Maam Cross
Headford
Cashel
N59
Laugh Corrib
Oughterard
Roundstone
Screeb
Cromwell's Sound
Carna
Kilkieran
N59
Mweenish Island
Lettermore
Costelloe
Galway
(Gaillimh)
Lettermullan
Carraroe
Rossaveal
Golam Head
Gorumna Island
Spiddal
Tawin Is
Eddy
Galway Bay
Inishmore
Burren
Ballyvaughan
Inishmaan
Aran Islands
Inisheer
Doolin
The Burre
South Sound
Lisdoonvarna
Doolin Point
Kilfenora
Cliffs of Moher
Ennistymon
Killinaboy
Corofin
Liscannor
Lahinch
CLA
N67
Milltown Malbay
Inagh
Spanish Point
Connolly

© Crown Copyright

N

0 miles 10
0 km 10

1 2 3 E

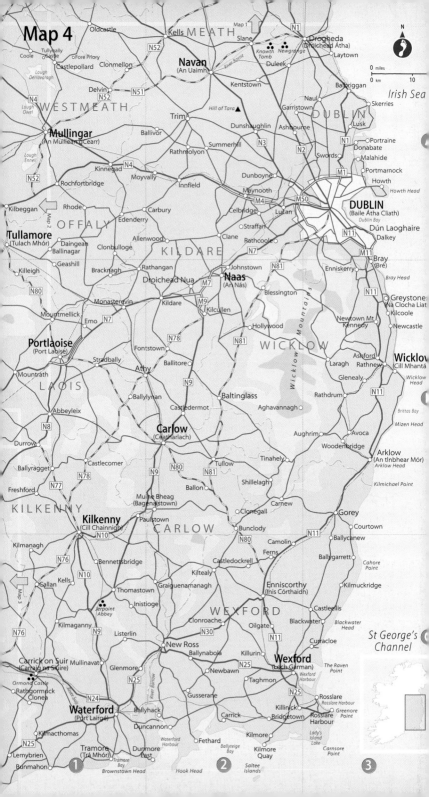